THE Java™ Developers ALMANAC 1999

The Java™ Series

Lisa Friendly, Series Editor

Tim Lindholm, Technical Editor

Please see our web site (http://www.awl.com /cseng/javaseries) for more information on these titles.

Ken Arnold and James Gosling, *The Java™ Programming Language, Second Edition*
ISBN 0-201-31006-6

Mary Campione and Kathy Walrath, *The Java™ Tutorial, Second Edition: Object-Oriented Programming for the Internet* (Book/CD)
ISBN 0-201-31007-4

Mary Campione, Kathy Walrath, Alison Huml, and the Tutorial Team, *The Java™ Tutorial Continued: The Rest of the JDK™* (Book/CD)
ISBN 0-201-48558-3

Patrick Chan, *The Java™ Developers Almanac 1999*
ISBN 0-201-43298-6

Patrick Chan and Rosanna Lee, *The Java™ Class Libraries, Second Edition, Volume 2: java.applet, java.awt, java.beans*
ISBN 0-201-31003-1

Patrick Chan, Rosanna Lee, and Doug Kramer, *The Java™ Class Libraries, Second Edition, Volume 1: java.io, java.lang, java.math, java.net, java.text, java.util*
ISBN 0-201-31002-3

Patrick Chan, Rosanna Lee, and Doug Kramer, *The Java™ Class Libraries, Second Edition, Volume 1: 1.2 Supplement*
ISBN 0-201-48552-4

James Gosling, Bill Joy, and Guy Steele, *The Java™ Language Specification*
ISBN 0-201-63451-1

James Gosling, Frank Yellin, and The Java Team, *The Java™ Application Programming Interface, Volume 1: Core Packages*
ISBN 0-201-63453-8

James Gosling, Frank Yellin, and The Java Team, *The Java™ Application Programming Interface, Volume 2: Window Toolkit and Applets*
ISBN 0-201-63459-7

Graham Hamilton, Rick Cattell, and Maydene Fisher, *JDBC™ Database Access with Java™: A Tutorial and Annotated Reference*
ISBN 0-201-30995-5

Jonni Kanerva, *The Java™ FAQ*
ISBN 0-201-63456-2

Doug Lea, *Concurrent Programming in Java™: Design Principles and Patterns*
ISBN 0-201-69581-2

Tim Lindholm and Frank Yellin, *The Java™ Virtual Machine Specification*
ISBN 0-201-63452-X

Henry Sowizral, Kevin Rushforth, and Michael Deering, *The Java™ 3D API Specification*
ISBN 0-201-32576-4

THE Java™ Developers ALMANAC 1999

Patrick Chan

ADDISON-WESLEY

An imprint of Addison Wesley Longman, Inc.

Reading, Massachusetts • Harlow, England • Menlo Park, California
Berkeley, California • Don Mills, Ontario • Sydney
Bonn • Amsterdam • Tokyo • Mexico City

The publisher offers discounts on this book when ordered in quantity for special sales. For more information, please contact:

Corporate, Government, and Special Sales Group
Addison Wesley Longman
One Jacob Way
Reading, Massachusetts 01867

Library of Congress Cataloging-in-Publication Data
Chan, Patrick
    The Java developers almanac 1999 / Patrick Chan.
        p.   cm. -- (The Java series)
    Includes index.
    ISBN 0-201-43298-6
    1. Java (Computer program language) I. Title. II. Series.
    QA76.73.J38C474 1999
    005. 13'3--dc21   98-43581
                                                        CIP

ISBN 0-201-43298-6
1 2 3 4 5 6 7 8 9-CRS-0201009998
First Printing, December 1998

To Kevin and Melissa
For the things that really matter.

Contents

Preface

Welcome to the second edition of *The Java™ Developers Almanac*.

There was a time, not long ago, when I intimately knew *all* of the Java class libraries. I knew how it all worked and exactly how everything fit together. I knew what subclassed what, what overrode what, and so on (of course, it helped that I was one of the original developers :-). But aside from the occasional inability to remember which argument of `Vector.insertElementAt()` is the index, I rarely had to refer to any reference documentation.

With version 1.1, my mastery of the Java class libraries was reduced to half. This left me feeling a little disoriented since I no longer knew my way around, and the increased size of the libraries exceeded my ability to recall the details of the signatures. When I took a peek at version 1.2, I was initially thrilled by all the new functionality I would now have at my fingertips. But as I browsed the new classes, I began to realize that my expertise was being reduced further to just a tiny fraction. I felt lost in this wonderful but vast sea of classes.

Since I make my living writing Java code, it was important that I find an efficient way of "navigating" the new libraries. What I wanted was a quick overview of all of the libraries; something that covered every class and briefly showed their relationships; something that would allow me to explore and quickly learn about new packages. This need led to this book.

The *The Java™ Developers Almanac* is like a map of the Java class libraries. It's a compact and portable tool that covers almost all[1] of the libraries, if only from a bird's-eye view. It's great for reminding you of things like method names and parameters. It's great for discovering the relationships between the classes, such as determining all methods that return an image. It's also great for quickly exploring a new package.

While this book is comprehensive, the libraries are so vast that there simply isn't enough room to provide equally comprehensive documentation. So if you're working with a package that is new to you, you'll probably also need a tutorial book such as *The Java Tutorial, Second Edition* (Campione and Walrath, Addison-Wesley, 1998), a detailed reference such as *The Java Class Libraries, Volumes 1 and 2* (Chan, Lee, and Kramer, Addison-Wesley, 1998), and/or the on-line documentation at *http://java.sun.com/docs*.

---

1. Due to size constraints, the `javax.swing.plaf.*` packages are left out.

The book is divided into four parts, briefly described next.

Part 1: Packages

This part covers each package in alphabetical order: a brief description of the package, a description of each class and interface in the package, and a hierarchy diagram showing the relationship between the classes and interfaces in the package. This part is useful when you need an overview of a package or want to see what other related classes are available in a package.

Most packages provide a number of "examplets" demonstrating common usage of classes in the package. The examplets are designed to demonstrate a particular task using the smallest amount of code possible. Their main purpose is to show you which classes are involved in the described task and generally how they interact with each other.

Part 2: Classes

This part contains 500 pages of class tables, one for each class in all the covered packages. Each class table includes a class tree that shows the ancestry of the class and a list of every member in the class. Also included in the member lists are inherited members from superclasses. Thus you have a complete view of all members made available by a class. This part is useful when you're already working with a particular class and want a quick reference to all of the members in the class.

Part 3: Topics

This part is a set of quick-reference tables on miscellaneous topics. For example, the topic title "Java 1.2" contains a detailed analysis of the API differences between Java 1.1 and Java 1.2. Other useful tables cover documentation comment tags and available system properties, among other topics.

Part 4: Cross-Reference

This part is a cross-reference of all of the Java classes and interfaces covered in this book. It includes classes from both core and extension packages. This part is useful when you have questions such as What methods return an `Image` object? or What are all the descendents of `java.io.InputStream`?

Updates

As the title suggests, this book is intended to be updated whenever a new major version of the Java class libraries is released. Since it is designed for you to use in your everyday programming-related work, I would love to hear how I could improve it for the next version or simply what you thought about it. For example, are there any more useful tables you'd like to see in Part 3? Although I'm afraid I probably won't be able to reply, I promise to read and consider each suggestion I receive. You can reach me at the following e-mail address:

almanac@xeo.com

Acknowledgments

First and foremost, I thank Mike Hendrickson, who spent a great deal of time collaborating with me on this project. He helped me hone the ideas in this book and then supported me all of the way. It's been tremendous fun working with him.

Arthur Ogawa (*ogawa@teleport.com*), TeX master extraordinaire, provided me with TeX macros without which this book would have been impossible. Thanks for working with me in the wee hours of the morning trying to get everything just right.

I want to thank Lisa Friendly, the series editor, for all sorts of help getting this book off the ground and for getting me all of the support I needed.

Special thanks to Rosanna, my wife, who helped me with writing examplets and many other parts of the book.

Many people gave me feedback or provided some other assistance in the making of this book. Thanks to Jens Alfke, Ken Arnold, Josh Bloch, Paul Bommarito, David Brownell, Michael Bundschuh, Bartley Calder, Casey Cameron, Norman Chin, Mark Drumm, Robert Field, Janice Heiss, Jeff Jackson, Doug Kramer, Sheng Liang, Tim Lindholm, Hans Muller, John Pampuch, Rob Posadas, Mark Reinhold, Dan Rudman, Georges Saab, Bill Shannon, Ann Sunhachawee, Joanne Stewart-Taylor, Laurence Vanhelsuwe, Bruce Wallace, Kathy Walrath, and Tony Welch.

Finally, I want to thank the wonderful people at Addison-Wesley who made this project a lot of fun: Sarah Weaver, Tracy Russ, Deborah King, Marina Lang, and Katherine Kwack.

Patrick Chan
November 1998

Part 1

PACKAGES

This part contains information about each package covered in this book. For each there is a description of the package, a description of each class and interface in that package, and a hierarchy diagram showing the relationships between the classes and interfaces in the packages. The following legend describes each of these pieces.

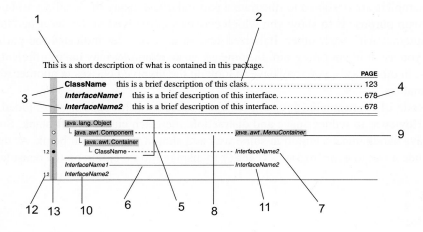

1. A brief description of the package
2. A brief description of the class or interface
3. The class or interface name (interface names are italicized)
4. The number of the page on which you will find more information about the class or interface
5. The classes in the current package, arranged so that all subclasses of a class appear as children of that class
6. Solid line signifying "extends"
7. Interfaces that are implemented by the classes on the left
8. Dashed line signifying "implements"
9. The gray background behind a class or interface signifying that the class or interface is not part of the current package
10. The interfaces in the current package
11. Interfaces that are extended by the interfaces on the left

12. The version of Java in which this class or interface was introduced
    You need the specified version of Java or higher in order to use the class. If the field is blank, the class or interface was introduced in Java 1.0. If the field contains an X, the class or interface belongs to an extension package. If the field contains a D, the class is deprecated.
13. A symbolic representation of a class's modifier set:

    ○ An abstract class
    ● A final class

Note: The class and interface descriptions were derived from Java Software's online documentation and so some of them may be missing since they have not yet been updated.

Examplets

Most packages provide a number of "examplets" demonstrating common usage of classes in the package. The examplets are designed to illustrate a particular task using the smallest amount of code possible. Their main purpose is to show you which classes are involved in the described task and generally how they interact with each other. Italicized text in an examplet indicates the parts that should be replaced if you use it in your program. In some cases, an examplet may have sufficient detail for you to use directly; in other cases, you may have to look up the involved classes in another reference book for more information.

If the code of an examplet throws a checked exception, the code is surrounded by a `try/catch` statement. However, to reduce space and distraction, the catch clause is left blank. Such catch clauses should always handle the exception in some way and should never be left blank. At the very least, you should include a call to `e.printStackTrace()` to display the exception on the console.

Contents

Packages

3

Examples

java.applet

This package contains the classes necessary to create an applet and the classes an applet uses to communicate with its applet context. An applet is an embeddable window with a few additional methods that the applet context uses to initialize, start, and stop the applet. The applet context is an application that is responsible for loading and running applets (e.g., a Web browser or applet development environment).

```
java.lang.Object
  └ java.awt.Component ------------------------------- java.awt.MenuContainer,
                                                       java.awt.image.ImageObserver,
                                                       java.io.Serializable
        └ java.awt.Container
              └ java.awt.Panel
                    └ Applet

AppletContext
AppletStub
AudioClip
```

The Quintessential Applet
Every applet must subclass Applet.

```
import java.applet.*;
import java.awt.*;

public class BasicApplet extends Applet {
    public void init() {
        // Called once by the browser when it starts the applet.
    }
    public void start() {
        // Called whenever the page containing this applet is made visible.
    }
    public void stop() {
        // Called whenever the page containing this applet is not visible.
    }
    public void destroyed() {
        // Called once when the browser destroys this applet.
    }
    public void paint(Graphics g) {
        // Called whenever this applet needs to repaint itself.
    }
}
```

This is the applet's accompanying HTML file.

```
<applet code=BasicApplet width=100 height=100>
</applet>
```

Getting an Applet Parameter

```
String s = getParameter("p");
```

Here is a sample HTML file containing a value for the parameter *p*.

```
<applet code=AppletClassName width=100 height=100>
<param name=p value="some text">
</applet>
```

Making the Browser Visit a URL

```
try {
    getAppletContext().showDocument(new URL(getDocumentBase(), "http://hostname/page.html"));
} catch (MalformedURLException e) {
}
```

Showing a Message in the Browser's Status Bar

```
showStatus("Your Message Here");
```

Loading and Playing Audio in an Applet

```
AudioClip ac = getAudioClip(getDocumentBase(), "http://hostname/audio.au");
ac.play();
```

Loading and Playing Audio in an Application

```
try {
    URL url = new URL("http://hostname/audio.au");
    AudioClip ac = Applet.newAudioClip(url);
    ac.play();
} catch (MalformedURLException e) {
}
```

Loading and Painting an Image in an Applet

```
Image image;
public void init() {
    image = getImage(getDocumentBase(), "http://hostname/image.gif");
}
public void paint(Graphics g) {
    g.drawImage(image, 0, 0, this);
}
```

Animating an Array of Images in an Applet

This is the simplest applet to animate an array of images. In practice, you should use double-buffering (which this example does not use) to eliminate "flickering."

```
import java.applet.*;
import java.awt.*;

public class AnimApplet extends Applet implements Runnable {
    Image[] images = new Image[2];
    int frame = 0;
    Thread thread;

    public void init() {
        images[0] = getImage(getDocumentBase(), "http://hostname/image0.gif");
        images[1] = getImage(getDocumentBase(), "http://hostname/image1.gif");
    }
    public void start() {
        (thread = new Thread(this)).start();
    }
    public void stop() {
        thread = null;
```

```
        }
        public void paint(Graphics g) {
            g.drawImage(images[frame], 0, 0, this);
        }
        public void run() {
            int delay = 1000;        // 1 second
            try {
                while (thread == Thread.currentThread()) {
                    frame = (frame+1)%images.length;
                    repaint();
                    Thread.sleep(delay);
                }
            } catch (Exception e) {
            }
        }
    }
```

java.awt

This package is for creating user interfaces and for painting graphics and images. A user interface object such as a button or a scrollbar is called an Abstract Window Toolkit (AWT) component. The AWT package contains classes for various components such as button, scrollbar, and window. Components can be contained in other components called containers. A container can also have a layout manager that controls the visual placement of components in the container. The AWT package contains several layout manager classes.

java.lang.Object

1.1 AWTEventMulticaster - *java.awt.event.ActionListener*,
java.awt.event.AdjustmentListener,
java.awt.event.ComponentListener,
java.awt.event.ContainerListener,
java.awt.event.FocusListener,
java.awt.event.InputMethodListener,
java.awt.event.ItemListener,
java.awt.event.KeyListener,
java.awt.event.MouseListener,
java.awt.event.MouseMotionListener,
java.awt.event.TextListener,
java.awt.event.WindowListener

1.2 ● AlphaComposite - *Composite*
1.2 BasicStroke - *Stroke*
BorderLayout - *LayoutManager2*, *java.io.Serializable*
CardLayout -
CheckboxGroup - *java.io.Serializable*
Color - *Paint*, *java.io.Serializable*
1.1 ● SystemColor - *java.io.Serializable*
○ Component - *MenuContainer*, *java.awt.image.ImageObserver*,
java.io.Serializable
Button
Canvas
Checkbox - *ItemSelectable*
Choice -
Container
Panel
1.1 ScrollPane
Window
Dialog
FileDialog
Frame - *MenuContainer*
Label
List - *ItemSelectable*
Scrollbar - *Adjustable*

Packages

13

java.awt

java.lang.Object

○ ├ Component - *MenuContainer*, `java.awt.image.ImageObserver`,
`java.io.Serializable`

│ └ TextComponent
│ ├ TextArea
│ └ TextField

1.2 ● ├ ComponentOrientation - `java.io.Serializable`
1.1 ├ Cursor -
├ Event -
1.1 ├ EventQueue
├ FlowLayout - *LayoutManager*, `java.io.Serializable`
├ Font - `java.io.Serializable`
○ ├ FontMetrics -
1.2 ├ GradientPaint - *Paint*
○ ├ Graphics
1.2 ○ │ └ Graphics2D
1.2 ○ ├ GraphicsConfigTemplate - `java.io.Serializable`
1.2 ○ ├ GraphicsConfiguration
1.2 ○ ├ GraphicsDevice
1.2 ○ ├ GraphicsEnvironment
├ GridBagConstraints - `java.io.Serializable`, `java.lang.Cloneable`
├ GridBagLayout - *LayoutManager2*, `java.io.Serializable`
├ GridLayout - *LayoutManager*, `java.io.Serializable`
○ ├ Image
├ Insets - `java.io.Serializable`, `java.lang.Cloneable`
├ MediaTracker - `java.io.Serializable`
○ ├ MenuComponent -
│ ├ MenuBar - *MenuContainer*
│ └ MenuItem
│   ├ CheckboxMenuItem - *ItemSelectable*
│   └ Menu - *MenuContainer*
1.1 │   └ PopupMenu
1.1 ├ MenuShortcut - `java.io.Serializable`
├ Polygon - *Shape*, `java.io.Serializable`
1.1 ○ ├ PrintJob
1.2 ├ RenderingHints - `java.lang.Cloneable`, `java.util.Map`
1.2 ○ ├ RenderingHints.Key
1.2 ├ TexturePaint - *Paint*
○ ├ Toolkit
1.2 ○ ├ java.awt.geom.Dimension2D - - - - - - - - - - - - - - - - - - `java.lang.Cloneable`
│ └ Dimension - `java.io.Serializable`
1.2 ○ ├ java.awt.geom.Point2D - `java.lang.Cloneable`
│ └ Point - `java.io.Serializable`
1.2 ○ ├ java.awt.geom.RectangularShape - - - - - - - - - - - - - - - - *Shape*, `java.lang.Cloneable`
1.2 ○ │ └ java.awt.geom.Rectangle2D
│   └ Rectangle - *Shape*, `java.io.Serializable`
1.2 ○ ├ java.security.Permission - - - - - - - - - - - - - - - - - - - `java.io.Serializable`, `java.security.Guard`
1.2 ○ │ └ java.security.BasicPermission - - - - - - - - - - - - - - - - `java.io.Serializable`
1.2 ● │   └ AWTPermission

14

```
        java.lang.Object                                      -  java.io.Serializable
1.1       ├ java.util.EventObject - - - - - - - - - - - - - - - - - - ┐
1.1 ○     │   └ AWTEvent                                                │
          └ java.lang.Throwable - - - - - - - - - - - - - - - - - - - - ┘
              ├ java.lang.Error
              │   └ AWTError
              └ java.lang.Exception
                  ├ AWTException
                  └ java.lang.RuntimeException
1.1                   └ java.lang.IllegalStateException
1.1                       └ IllegalComponentStateException

1.2   ActiveEvent
1.1   Adjustable
1.2   Composite
1.2   CompositeContext
1.1   ItemSelectable
      LayoutManager
1.1   LayoutManager2 ──────────────────────────────── LayoutManager
      MenuContainer
1.2   Paint ───────────────────────────────────────── Transparency
1.2   PaintContext
1.1   PrintGraphics
1.1   Shape
1.2   Stroke
1.2   Transparency
```

The Quintessential Drawing Program

This example creates a frame and draws an oval within the frame.

```java
import java.awt.*;
import javax.swing.*;

class BasicDraw extends JComponent {
    public void paint(Graphics g) {
        Graphics2D g2d = (Graphics2D)g;

        g2d.drawOval(0, 0, getSize().width-1, getSize().height-1);
    }
    public static void main(String[] args) {
        JFrame frame = new JFrame();
        frame.getContentPane().add(new BasicDraw());
        int frameWidth = 300;
        int frameHeight = 300;
        frame.setSize(frameWidth, frameHeight);
        frame.setVisible(true);
    }
}
```

Drawing Basic Shapes

There are two ways to draw basic shapes like lines and rectangles. The first is to use specific drawing methods like Graphics.drawOval(). This example uses these methods. The second is to construct a shape and then use Graphics2D.draw() to draw the shape. See the java.awt.geom package for examples that create shapes.

```java
g2d.drawLine(x1, y1, x2, y2);
g2d.drawArc(x, y, w, h, startAngle, arcAngle);
```

15

```
g2d.drawOval(x, y, w, h);
g2d.drawRect(x, y, w, h);
g2d.drawRoundRect(x, y, w, h, arcWidth, arcHeight);

Polygon polygon = new Polygon();
polygon.addPoint(x, y);
// ...continue adding points
g2d.drawPolygon(polygon);
```

Filling Basic Shapes

There are two ways to fill basic shapes like lines and rectangles. The first is to use specific drawing methods like Graphics.fillOval(). This example uses these methods. The second is to construct a shape and then use Graphics2D.fill() to fill the shape. See the java.awt.geom package for examples that create shapes.

```
g2d.fillArc(x, y, w, h, startAngle, arcAngle);
g2d.fillOval(x, y, w, h);
g2d.fillRect(x, y, w, h);
g2d.fillRoundRect(x, y, w, h, arcWidth, arcHeight);

Polygon polygon = new Polygon();
polygon.addPoint(x, y);
// ...continue adding points
g2d.fillPolygon(polygon);
```

Loading an Image

```
// This call returns immediately and pixels are loaded in background.
image = Toolkit.getDefaultToolkit().getImage("image.gif");

// This method ensures that all pixels have been loaded before returning.
Image image = new ImageIcon("image.gif").getImage();
```

Drawing an Image

```
public void paint(Graphics g) {
    // Drawing an Image object.
    g.drawImage(image, x, y, this);

    // Drawing an ImageIcon object.
    imageIcon.paintIcon(this, g, x, y);
}
```

Drawing an Image Transformed

The available operations are shearing, scaling, translation, and rotation.

```
AffineTransform tx = new AffineTransform();
tx.translate(x, y);
tx.shear(shiftx, shifty);
tx.rotate(radians);
tx.scale(scalex, scaley);

g2d.drawImage(image, tx, this);
```

Drawing Simple Text

```
// Set the desired font if different from default font.
Font font = new Font("Serif", Font.PLAIN, 12);
g2d.setFont(font);

// Draw the string such that its base line is at x, y.
g2d.drawString("aString", x, y);

// Draw the string such that the top-left corner is at x, y.
FontMetrics fontMetrics = g2d.getFontMetrics();
g2d.drawString("aString", x, y+fontMetrics.getAscent());
```

Drawing Rotated Text

```
// Draw string rotated clockwise 90 degrees.
AffineTransform at = new AffineTransform();
at.setToRotation(Math.PI/2.0);
g2d.setTransform(at);
g2d.drawString("aString", x, y);

// Draw string rotated counter-clockwise 90 degrees.
at = new AffineTransform();
at.setToRotation(-Math.PI/2.0);
g2d.setTransform(at);
g2d.drawString("aString", x, y);
```

Getting the Dimensions of Text

```
// From within the paint() method.
public void paint(Graphics g) {
    Graphics2D g2d = (Graphics2D)g;
    Font font = new Font("Serif", Font.PLAIN, 12);
    FontMetrics fontMetrics = g2d.getFontMetrics();

    int width = fontMetrics.stringWidth("aString");
    int height = fontMetrics.getHeight();
}

// From within a component.
class MyComponent extends JComponent {
    MyComponent() {
        Font font = new Font("Serif", Font.PLAIN, 12);
        FontMetrics fontMetrics = getFontMetrics(font);

        int width = fontMetrics.stringWidth("aString");
        int height = fontMetrics.getHeight();
    }
}
```

Drawing Anti-Aliased Text and Graphics

```
// Text only
g2d.setRenderingHint(RenderingHints.KEY_TEXT_ANTIALIASING, RenderingHints.VALUE_TEXT_ANTIALIAS_ON);

// Text and graphics
g2d.setRenderingHint(RenderingHints.KEY_ANTIALIASING, RenderingHints.VALUE_ANTIALIAS_ON);

drawGraphics(g2d);
```

Drawing with Alpha

```
drawGraphic1(g2d);

// Set alpha. 0.0f is 100% transparent and 1.0f is 100% opaque.
float alpha = .7f;
g2d.setComposite(AlphaComposite.getInstance(AlphaComposite.SRC_OVER, alpha));

drawGraphic2(g2d);
```

Setting the Clipping Area with a Shape

```
g2d.setClip(shape);
drawGraphics(g2d);
```

Changing the Thickness of the Stroking Pen

dashPhase is the offset to start the dashing pattern.

```
float strokeThickness = 5.0f;
```

```
// A solid stroke
BasicStroke stroke = new BasicStroke(strokeThickness);
g2d.setStroke(stroke);
drawShape(g2d);

// A dashed stroke
float miterLimit = 10f;
float[] dashPattern = {10f};
float dashPhase = 5f;
stroke = new BasicStroke(strokeThickness, BasicStroke.CAP_BUTT,
    BasicStroke.JOIN_MITER, miterLimit, dashPattern, dashPhase);
g2d.setStroke(stroke);
drawShape(g2d);
```

Creating a Shape from a Stroked Shape

```
float strokeThickness = 5.0f;
BasicStroke stroke = new BasicStroke(strokeThickness);
Shape newShape = stroke.createStrokedShape(shape);
```

Stroking or Filling a Shape

```
// Stroke the shape.
g2d.draw(shape);

// Fill the shape.
g2d.fill(shape);
```

Stroking or Filling with a Color

```
// Use a predefined color.
g2d.setColor(Color.red);
drawShape(g2d);

// Use a custom color.
int red = 230;
int green = 45;
int blue = 67;
g2d.setColor(new Color(red, green, blue));
drawShape(g2d);
```

Stroking or Filling with a Gradient Color

```
Color startColor = Color.red;
Color endColor = Color.blue;

// A non-cyclic gradient
GradientPaint gradient = new GradientPaint(startX, startY, startColor, endX, endY, endColor);
g2d.setPaint(gradient);
drawShape(g2d);

// A cyclic gradient
gradient = new GradientPaint(startX, startY, startColor, endX, endY, endColor, true);
g2d.setPaint(gradient);
drawShape(g2d);
```

Stroking or Filling with a Texture

The buffered image used to create the TexturePaint object is scaled down/up to width w and height h. Conceptually, the scaled down/up buffered image is first painted at (x, y) in user space, and then replicated around it.

```
TexturePaint texture = new TexturePaint(bufferedImage, new Rectangle(x, y, 50/*w*/, 25/*h*/));
g2d.setPaint(texture);
drawShape(g2d);
```

Animating an Array of Images in an Application

This is the simplest application to animate a an array of images.

```java
import java.awt.*;
import javax.swing.*;

public class AnimApp extends JComponent implements Runnable {
    Image[] images = new Image[2];
    int frame = 0;

    public void paint(Graphics g) {
        Image image = images[frame];
        if (image != null) {
            g.drawImage(image, 0, 0, this);
        }
    }

    public void run() {
        images[0] = new ImageIcon("image1.gif").getImage();
        images[1] = new ImageIcon("image2.gif").getImage();
        int delay = 1000;      // 1 second

        try {
            while (true) {
                frame = (frame+1)%images.length;
                repaint();
                Thread.sleep(delay);
            }
        } catch (Exception e) {
        }
    }

    public static void main(String[] args) {
        AnimApp app = new AnimApp();
        JFrame frame = new JFrame();
        frame.getContentPane().add(app);
        frame.setSize(300, 300);
        frame.setVisible(true);

        (new Thread(app)).start();
    }
}
```

Setting a Component's Cursor

See the Cursor class for available cursors.

```java
component.setCursor(Cursor.getPredefinedCursor(Cursor.HAND_CURSOR));
```

java.awt.color

This package contains classes for color spaces. It contains an implementation of a color space based on the International Color Consortium (ICC) Profile Format Specification, Version 3.4, August 15, 1997. It also contains color profiles based on the ICC Profile Format Specification.

```
      java.lang.Object
1.2 ○  ├ ColorSpace
1.2    │  └ ICC_ColorSpace
1.2    ├ ICC_Profile
1.2    │  ├ ICC_ProfileGray
1.2    │  └ ICC_ProfileRGB
       └ java.lang.Throwable ------------------------------- java.io.Serializable
          └ java.lang.Exception
             └ java.lang.RuntimeException
1.2             ├ CMMException
1.2             └ ProfileDataException
```

java.awt.datatransfer

This package contains interfaces and classes for transferring data between and within applications. It defines the notion of a clipboard, which is an object that temporarily holds data as it is being transferred between or within an application. It is typically used in copy and paste operations. Although it is possible to create a clipboard to use within an applications, most applications will use the system clipboard.

```
      java.lang.Object
1.1    ├ Clipboard
1.1    ├ DataFlavor --------------------------- java.io.Externalizable, java.lang.Cloneable
```

```
java.lang.Object
1.1        StringSelection - - - - - - - - - - - - - - - - - - - - - - - - - - - - - - - ClipboardOwner, Transferable
1.2 ●      SystemFlavorMap - - - - - - - - - - - - - - - - - - - - - - - - - - - - - FlavorMap
1.1        java.lang.Throwable - - - - - - - - - - - - - - - - - - - - - - - - - - - java.io.Serializable
              java.lang.Exception
1.1              UnsupportedFlavorException

1.1    ClipboardOwner
1.2    FlavorMap
1.1    Transferable
```

Retrieving Text from the System Clipboard

```
Transferable t = Toolkit.getDefaultToolkit().getSystemClipboard().getContents(null);

try {
    if (t != null && t.isDataFlavorSupported(DataFlavor.stringFlavor)) {
        String s = (String)t.getTransferData(DataFlavor.stringFlavor);
        process(s);
    }
} catch (UnsupportedFlavorException e) {
} catch (IOException e) {
}
```

Placing Text on the System Clipboard

```
StringSelection ss = new StringSelection("aString");
Toolkit.getDefaultToolkit().getSystemClipboard().setContents(ss, null);
```

java.awt.dnd

This package contains interfaces and classes for supporting drag-and-drop operations. It defines classes for the drag-source and the drop-target, as well as events for transferring the data being dragged, and giving visual feedback to the user performing the operation.

PAGE

Packages

java.awt.dnd

java.lang.Object

1.2 ●   ├ DnDConstants

1.2 ○   ├ DragGestureRecognizer

1.2 ○   └ MouseDragGestureRecognizer - *java.awt.event.MouseListener,*
                                                            java.awt.event.MouseMotionListener

1.2   ├ DragSource

1.2   ├ DragSourceContext - *DragSourceListener*

1.2   ├ DropTarget - *DropTargetListener, java.io.Serializable*

1.2   ├ DropTarget.DropTargetAutoScroller - - - - - - - - - - - - - - - - - - *java.awt.event.ActionListener*

1.2   ├ DropTargetContext

1.2   ├ DropTargetContext.TransferableProxy - - - - - - - - - - - - - - - - *java.awt.datatransfer.Transferable*

1.1   ├ java.util.EventObject - *java.io.Serializable*

1.2   ├ DragGestureEvent

1.2   ├ DragSourceEvent

1.2   ├ DragSourceDragEvent

1.2   └ DragSourceDropEvent

1.2   └ DropTargetEvent

1.2   ├ DropTargetDragEvent

1.2   └ DropTargetDropEvent

  └ java.lang.Throwable -

    └ java.lang.Exception

      └ java.lang.RuntimeException

1.1   └ java.lang.IllegalStateException

1.2   └ InvalidDnDOperationException

1.2   *Autoscroll*

1.2   *DragGestureListener* ——————————————————— *java.util.EventListener*

1.2   *DragSourceListener* ———————————————————

Making a Component Draggable

This example demonstrates the code needed to make a component draggable. The object being transferred in this example is a string.

```java
public class DraggableComponent extends JComponent implements DragGestureListener, DragSourceListener {
    DragSource dragSource;

    public DraggableComponent() {
        dragSource = new DragSource();
        dragSource.createDefaultDragGestureRecognizer(this, DnDConstants.ACTION_COPY_OR_MOVE, this);
    }
    public void dragGestureRecognized(DragGestureEvent evt) {
        Transferable t = new StringSelection("aString");
        dragSource.startDrag (evt, DragSource.DefaultCopyDrop, t, this);
    }
    public void dragEnter(DragSourceDragEvent evt) {
        // Called when the user is dragging this drag source and enters
        // the drop target.
    }
    public void dragOver(DragSourceDragEvent evt) {
        // Called when the user is dragging this drag source and moves
        // over the drop target.
    }
    public void dragExit(DragSourceEvent evt) {
        // Called when the user is dragging this drag source and leaves
        // the drop target.
    }
    public void dropActionChanged(DragSourceDragEvent evt) {
        // Called when the user changes the drag action between copy or move.
    }
    public void dragDropEnd(DragSourceDropEvent evt) {
        // Called when the user finishes or cancels the drag operation.
    }
}
```

Making a Component a Drop Target

```java
public class DropTargetComponent extends JComponent implements DropTargetListener {
    public DropTargetComponent() {
        new DropTarget(this, this);
    }
    public void dragEnter(DropTargetDragEvent evt) {
        // Called when the user is dragging and enters this drop target.
    }
    public void dragOver(DropTargetDragEvent evt) {
        // Called when the user is dragging and moves over this drop target.
    }
    public void dragExit(DropTargetEvent evt) {
        // Called when the user is dragging and leaves this drop target.
    }
    public void dropActionChanged(DropTargetDragEvent evt) {
        // Called when the user changes the drag action between copy or move.
    }
    public void drop(DropTargetDropEvent evt) {
        // Called when the user finishes or cancels the drag operation.
    }
}
```

Packages

23

Handling a Drop Event

The drop target in this example only accepts dropped String objects. A drop target must implement DropTargetListener and supply an implementation for drop().

```
public void drop(DropTargetDropEvent evt) {
    try {
        Transferable t = evt.getTransferable();

        if (t.isDataFlavorSupported(DataFlavor.stringFlavor)) {
            evt.acceptDrop(DnDConstants.ACTION_COPY_OR_MOVE);
            String s = (String)t.getTransferData(DataFlavor.stringFlavor);
            evt.getDropTargetContext().dropComplete(true);
            process(s);
        } else {
            evt.rejectDrop();
        }
    } catch (IOException e) {
        evt.rejectDrop();
    } catch (UnsupportedFlavorException e) {
        evt.rejectDrop();
    }
}
```

java.awt.event

This package contains interfaces and classes for dealing with different types of events fired by AWT components. See the java.awt.AWTEvent class for details on the AWT event model. Events are fired by event sources. An event listener registers with an event source to receive notifications about the events of a particular type. This package defines events and event listeners, as well as event listener adapters, which are convenience classes to make easier the process of writing event listeners.

```
    java.lang.Object
1.1 ○   ├ ComponentAdapter - - - - - - - - - - - - - - - - - - - - - - - - - ComponentListener
1.1 ○   ├ ContainerAdapter - - - - - - - - - - - - - - - - - - - - - - - - - ContainerListener
1.1 ○   ├ FocusAdapter - - - - - - - - - - - - - - - - - - - - - - - - - - - FocusListener
1.1 ○   ├ KeyAdapter - - - - - - - - - - - - - - - - - - - - - - - - - - - - KeyListener
1.1 ○   ├ MouseAdapter - - - - - - - - - - - - - - - - - - - - - - - - - - - MouseListener
1.1 ○   ├ MouseMotionAdapter - - - - - - - - - - - - - - - - - - - - - - - - MouseMotionListener
1.1 ○   ├ WindowAdapter - - - - - - - - - - - - - - - - - - - - - - - - - - - WindowListener
1.1     └ java.util.EventObject - - - - - - - - - - - - - - - - - - - - - - - java.io.Serializable
1.1 ○      └ java.awt.AWTEvent
1.1            ├ ActionEvent
1.1            ├ AdjustmentEvent
1.1            ├ ComponentEvent
1.1            │   ├ ContainerEvent
1.1            │   ├ FocusEvent
1.1 ○          │   ├ InputEvent
1.1            │   │   ├ KeyEvent
1.1            │   │   └ MouseEvent
1.1            │   ├ PaintEvent
1.1            │   └ WindowEvent
1.2            ├ InputMethodEvent
1.2            ├ InvocationEvent - - - - - - - - - - - - - - - - - - - - - - - java.awt.ActiveEvent
```

Packages

25

java.awt.event

```
         java.lang.Object
1.1        └ java.util.EventObject - - - - - - - - - - - - - - - - - - - - - - - - - - - - - - - -   java.io.Serializable
1.1  O          └ java.awt.AWTEvent
1.1                 ┤ ItemEvent
1.1                 └ TextEvent
          ─────────────────────
1.2      AWTEventListener ───────────────────────────────────────    java.util.EventListener
1.1      ActionListener ──────────────────────────────────────
1.1      AdjustmentListener ──────────────────────────────────
1.1      ComponentListener ───────────────────────────────────
1.1      ContainerListener ───────────────────────────────────
1.1      FocusListener ───────────────────────────────────────
1.2      InputMethodListener ─────────────────────────────────
1.1      ItemListener ────────────────────────────────────────
1.1      KeyListener ─────────────────────────────────────────
1.1      MouseListener ───────────────────────────────────────
1.1      MouseMotionListener ─────────────────────────────────
1.1      TextListener ────────────────────────────────────────
1.1      WindowListener ──────────────────────────────────────
```

Handling Events with an Anonymous Class

If an event handler is specific to a component (that is, not shared by other components), there is no need to create a class to handle the event. The event handler can be implemented using an anonymous inner class. This example demonstrates an anonymous inner class to handle key events for a component.

```
component.addKeyListener(new KeyAdapter() {
    public void keyPressed(KeyEvent evt) {
    }
});
```

Handling Action Events

Action events are fired by subclasses of AbstractButton and includes buttons, checkboxes, and menus.

```
AbstractButton button = new JButton("OK");
button.addActionListener(new MyActionListener());

public class MyActionListener implements ActionListener {
    public void actionPerformed(ActionEvent evt) {
        // Determine which abstract button fired the event.
        AbstractButton button = (AbstractButton)evt.getSource();
    }
}
```

Handling Key Presses

You can get the key that was pressed either as a key character (which is a Unicode character) or as a key code (a special value representing a particular key on the keyboard).

```
component.addKeyListener(new MyKeyListener());

public class MyKeyListener extends KeyAdapter {
    public void keyPressed(KeyEvent evt) {
        // Check for key characters.
        if (evt.getKeyChar() == 'a') {
            process(evt.getKeyChar());
        }

        // Check for key codes.
        if (evt.getKeyCode() == KeyEvent.VK_HOME) {
            process(evt.getKeyCode());
```

```
            }
        }
    }
```

Handling Mouse Clicks

```
    component.addMouseListener(new MyMouseListener());

    public class MyMouseListener extends MouseAdapter {
        public void mouseClicked(MouseEvent evt) {
            if ((evt.getModifiers() & InputEvent.BUTTON1_MASK) != 0) {
                processLeft(evt.getPoint());
            }
            if ((evt.getModifiers() & InputEvent.BUTTON2_MASK) != 0) {
                processMiddle(evt.getPoint());
            }
            if ((evt.getModifiers() & InputEvent.BUTTON3_MASK) != 0) {
                processRight(evt.getPoint());
            }
        }
    }
```

Handling Mouse Motion

```
    component.addMouseMotionListener(new MyMouseMotionListener());

    public class MyMouseMotionListener extends MouseMotionAdapter {
        public void mouseMoved(MouseEvent evt) {
            // Process current position of cursor while all mouse buttons are up.
            process(evt.getPoint());
        }
        public void mouseDragged(MouseEvent evt) {
            // Process current position of cursor while mouse button is pressed.
            process(evt.getPoint());
        }
    }
```

Detecting Double and Triple Clicks

```
    component.addMouseListener(new MyMouseListener());

    public class MyMouseListener extends MouseAdapter {
        public void mouseClicked(MouseEvent evt) {
            if (evt.getClickCount() == 3) {
                // triple-click
            } else if (evt.getClickCount() == 2) {
                // double-click
            }
        }
    }
```

Handling Focus Changes

```
    component.addFocusListener(new MyFocusListener());

    public class MyFocusListener extends FocusAdapter {
        public void focusGained(FocusEvent evt) {
            // The component gained the focus.
        }
        public void focusLost(FocusEvent evt) {
            // The component lost the focus.
        }
    }
```

java.awt.font

This package contains classes and interfaces relating to fonts. It contains support for representing Type 1, Type 1 Multiple Master fonts, OpenType fonts, and TrueType fonts.

java.lang.Object

1.2	FontRenderContext
1.2 ●	GlyphJustificationInfo
1.2 ●	GlyphMetrics
1.2 ○	GlyphVector - *java.lang.Cloneable*
1.2 ○	GraphicAttribute
1.2 ●	ImageGraphicAttribute
1.2 ●	ShapeGraphicAttribute
1.2 ●	LineBreakMeasurer
1.2 ○	LineMetrics
1.2 ●	TextHitInfo
1.2 ●	TextLayout - - - - - - - - -
1.2	TextLayout.CaretPolicy
1.2 ●	TransformAttribute - *java.io.Serializable*

```
      java.lang.Object                                              ┌ - java.io.Serializable
1.2     └ java.text.AttributedCharacterIterator.Attribute - - - - - - - - - - - ┘
1.2 ●      └ TextAttribute
      ─────────────────────────────────
1.2   MultipleMaster
1.2   OpenType
```

Listing All Available Fonts

```
GraphicsEnvironment ge = GraphicsEnvironment.getLocalGraphicsEnvironment();
String fontNames[] = ge.getAvailableFontFamilyNames();
for (int i=0; i<fontNames.length; i++) {
    process(fontNames[i]);
}
```

Drawing a Paragraph of Text

In order to change the font of the text, you need to supply an attributed string to the LineBreakMeasurer. See "Drawing Text with Mixed Styles" for an example.

```
public void drawParagraph(Graphics2D g, String paragraph, float width) {
    LineBreakMeasurer linebreaker = new LineBreakMeasurer(
        new AttributedString(paragraph).getIterator(), g.getFontRenderContext());

    float y = 0.0f;
    while (linebreaker.getPosition() < paragraph.length()) {
        TextLayout tl = linebreaker.nextLayout(width);

        y += tl.getAscent();
        tl.draw(g, 0, y);
        y += tl.getDescent() + tl.getLeading();
    }
}
```

Getting the Shape from the Outline of Text

```
Shape getTextShape(Graphics2D g2d, String str, Font font) {
    TextLayout tl = new TextLayout(str, font, g2d.getFontRenderContext());
    return tl.getOutline(null);
}
```

Drawing Text with Mixed Styles

This example applies a new font and background color to a part of the text. You can apply styles to as many parts of the text as you need. See TextAttributes for available styles.

```
// Apply styles to text.
AttributedString astr = new AttributedString("aString");
astr.addAttribute(TextAttribute.FONT, font, start, end);
astr.addAttribute(TextAttribute.BACKGROUND, color, start, end);

// Draw mixed-style text.
TextLayout tl = new TextLayout(astr.getIterator(), g2d.getFontRenderContext());
tl.draw(g2d, x, y);
```

java.awt.geom

This package contains classes for creating and representing various shapes such as points, lines, arcs, curves, ellipses, and rectangles. Also included are transformation classes used to transform shapes and drawing coordinates (see java.awt.Graphics2D).

Packages

java.awt.geom

```
      java.lang.Object
1.2     ├ AffineTransform ----------------------------------  java.io.Serializable, java.lang.Cloneable
1.2     ├ Area----------------------------------------------  java.awt.Shape, java.lang.Cloneable
1.2 ○   ├ CubicCurve2D-------------------------------------┐
1.2     │  ├ CubicCurve2D.Double                            │
1.2     │  └ CubicCurve2D.Float                             │
1.2 ○   ├ Dimension2D --------------------------------------  java.lang.Cloneable
1.2     ├ FlatteningPathIterator ---------------------------  PathIterator
1.2 ●   ├ GeneralPath -------------------------------------┐  java.awt.Shape, java.lang.Cloneable
1.2 ○   ├ Line2D-------------------------------------------┘
1.2     │  ├ Line2D.Double
1.2     │  └ Line2D.Float
1.2 ○   ├ Point2D ------------------------------------------  java.lang.Cloneable
1.2     │  ├ Point2D.Double
1.2     │  └ Point2D.Float
1.2 ○   ├ QuadCurve2D-------------------------------------┐  java.awt.Shape, java.lang.Cloneable
1.2     │  ├ QuadCurve2D.Double                            │
1.2     │  └ QuadCurve2D.Float                             │
1.2 ○   ├ RectangularShape -------------------------------┘
1.2 ○   │  ├ Arc2D
1.2     │  │  ├ Arc2D.Double
1.2     │  │  └ Arc2D.Float
1.2 ○   │  ├ Ellipse2D
1.2     │  │  ├ Ellipse2D.Double
1.2     │  │  └ Ellipse2D.Float
1.2 ○   │  ├ Rectangle2D
1.2     │  │  ├ Rectangle2D.Double
1.2     │  │  └ Rectangle2D.Float
1.2 ○   │  └ RoundRectangle2D
1.2     │     ├ RoundRectangle2D.Double
1.2     │     └ RoundRectangle2D.Float
        └ java.lang.Throwable -----------------------------  java.io.Serializable
           └ java.lang.Exception
              ├ NoninvertibleTransformException
              └ java.lang.RuntimeException
1.2              └ IllegalPathStateException
1.2  PathIterator
```

Creating a Shape with Lines and Curves

```java
GeneralPath shape = new GeneralPath();
shape.moveTo(x, y);
shape.lineTo(x, y);
shape.quadTo(controlPointX, controlPointY, x, y);
```

Packages

```
shape.curveTo(controlPointX1, controlPointY1, controlPointX2, controlPointY2, x, y);
shape.closePath();
```

Creating Basic Shapes

```
Shape line = new Line2D.Float(x1, y1, x2, y2);
Shape arc = new Arc2D.Float(x, y, w, h, start, extent, type);
Shape oval = new Ellipse2D.Float(x, y, w, h);
Shape rectangle = new Rectangle2D.Float(x, y, w, h);
Shape roundRectangle = new RoundRectangle2D.Float(x, y, w, h, arcWidth, arcHeight);
```

Combining Shapes

```
Area shape = new Area(shape1);
shape.add(new Area(shape2));
shape.subtract(new Area(shape3));
shape.intersect(new Area(shape4));
shape.exclusiveOr(new Area(shape5));
```

Transforming a Shape

The available operations are shearing, scaling, translation, and rotation.

```
AffineTransform tx = new AffineTransform();
tx.translate(x, y);
tx.shear(shiftx, shifty);
tx.rotate(radians);
tx.scale(scalex, scaley);
Shape newShape = tx.createTransformedShape(shape);
```

java.awt.im

This package contains classes and interfaces for the input method framework. This framework enables users to enter thousands of different characters using keyboards with far fewer keys. Characters (in many Asian languages such as Japanese and Chinese) are entered using a sequence of several key strokes to text-editing components.

```
java.lang.Object
1.2      ├ InputContext
1.2      ├ InputMethodHighlight
1.2      └ java.lang.Character.Subset
1.2 ●         └ InputSubset

1.2      InputMethodRequests
```

java.awt.image

This package contains classes for creating and modifying images. Images are processed using a streaming framework that involves an image producer, optional image filters, and an image consumer. This framework makes it possible to progressively render an image while it is being fetched and generated. Moreover, the framework allows an application to discard the storage used by an image and to regenerate it at any time. This package provides a number of image producers, consumers, and filters that you can configure for your image processing needs.

Packages

```
java.lang.Object
1.2      ├ AffineTransformOp - - - - - - - - - - - - - - - - - - - - - - - -  BufferedImageOp, RasterOp
1.2      ├ BandCombineOp - - - - - - - - - - - - - - - - - - - - - - - - - -  RasterOp
1.2      ├ ColorConvertOp - - - - - - - - - - - - - - - - - - - - - - - - - - BufferedImageOp, RasterOp
  ○      ├ ColorModel - - - - - - - - - - - - - - - - - - - - - - - - - - - - java.awt.Transparency
1.2      │   ├ ComponentColorModel
         │   ├ IndexColorModel
1.2 ○    │   └ PackedColorModel
         │       └ DirectColorModel
1.2      ├ ConvolveOp - - - - - - - - - - - - - - - - - - - - - - - - - - -  BufferedImageOp, RasterOp
1.2 ○    ├ DataBuffer
1.2 ●    │   ├ DataBufferByte
1.2 ●    │   ├ DataBufferInt
1.2 ●    │   ├ DataBufferShort
1.2 ●    │   └ DataBufferUShort
         ├ FilteredImageSource - - - - - - - - - - - - - - - - - - - - - -  ImageProducer
         ├ ImageFilter - - - - - - - - - - - - - - - - - - - - - - - - - -  ImageConsumer, java.lang.Cloneable
1.2      │   ├ BufferedImageFilter - - - - - - - - - - - - - - - - - - - -  java.lang.Cloneable
         │   ├ CropImageFilter
  ○      │   ├ RGBImageFilter
1.1      │   └ ReplicateScaleFilter
1.1      │       └ AreaAveragingScaleFilter
1.2      ├ Kernel - - - - - - - - - - - - - - - - - - - - - - - - - - - -
1.2      ├ LookupOp - - - - - - - - - - - - - - - - - - - - - - - - - - -  BufferedImageOp, RasterOp
1.2 ○    ├ LookupTable
1.2      │   ├ ByteLookupTable
1.2      │   └ ShortLookupTable
         ├ MemoryImageSource - - - - - - - - - - - - - - - - - - - - - - -  ImageProducer
         ├ PixelGrabber - - - - - - - - - - - - - - - - - - - - - - - - - - ImageConsumer
1.2      ├ Raster
1.2      │   └ WritableRaster
1.2      ├ RescaleOp - - - - - - - - - - - - - - - - - - - - - - - - - - -  BufferedImageOp, RasterOp
1.2 ○    ├ SampleModel
1.2      │   ├ ComponentSampleModel
1.2 ●    │   │   ├ BandedSampleModel
1.2      │   │   └ PixelInterleavedSampleModel
1.2      │   ├ MultiPixelPackedSampleModel
1.2      │   └ SinglePixelPackedSampleModel
  ○      └ java.awt.Image
1.2          └ BufferedImage - - - - - - - - - - - - - - - - - - - - - - -  WritableRenderedImage
```

```
       java.lang.Object
          └ java.lang.Throwable ------------------------------- java.io.Serializable
             └ java.lang.Exception
                └ java.lang.RuntimeException
1.2                ├ ImagingOpException
1.2                └ RasterFormatException

1.2    BufferedImageOp
       ImageConsumer
       ImageObserver
       ImageProducer
1.2    RasterOp
1.2    RenderedImage
1.2    TileObserver
1.2    WritableRenderedImage ─────────────────────────── RenderedImage
```

Converting an Image to a Buffered Image

```java
BufferedImage toBufferedImage(Image image) {
    // This code ensures that all the pixels in the image are loaded.
    image = new ImageIcon(image).getImage();

    // Create the buffered image.
    BufferedImage bufferedImage = new BufferedImage(
        image.getWidth(null), image.getHeight(null), BufferedImage.TYPE_INT_RGB);

    // Copy image to buffered image.
    Graphics g = bufferedImage.createGraphics();

    // Clear background and paint the image.
    g.setColor(Color.white);
    g.fillRect(0, 0, image.getWidth(null), image.getHeight(null));
    g.drawImage(image, 0, 0, null);
    g.dispose();

    return bufferedImage;
}
```

Getting Pixels from a Buffered Image

```java
// Get one pixel.
int rgb = bufferedImage.getRGB(x, y);

// Get all the pixels.
int w = bufferedImage.getWidth(null);
int h = bufferedImage.getHeight(null);
int[] rgbs = new int[w*h];
bufferedImage.getRGB(0, 0, w, h, rgbs, 0, w);

// Set a pixel.
rgb = 0xFF00FF00; // green
bufferedImage.setRGB(x, y, rgb);
```

Blurring an Image with Image Convolution

This example demonstrates a 3x3 kernel that blurs an image.

```java
float[] kernelArray = {
    1f/9f, 1f/9f, 1f/9f,
    1f/9f, 1f/9f, 1f/9f,
    1f/9f, 1f/9f, 1f/9f
};
Kernel kernel = new Kernel(3, 3, kernelArray);
```

```
BufferedImageOp op = new ConvolveOp(kernel);
bufferedImage = op.filter(bufferedImage, null);
```

Getting a Sub-Image of an Image

```
// From an Image.
image = createImage(new FilteredImageSource(image.getSource(), new CropImageFilter(x, y, w, h)));
```

```
// From a BufferedImage.
bufferedImage = bufferedImage.getSubimage(x, y, w, h);
```

Creating and Drawing on a Buffered Image

```
// Creating a BufferedImage with a component.
bufferedImage = (BufferedImage)component.createImage(w, h);
```

```
// Creating a BufferedImage without a component.
bufferedImage = new BufferedImage(w, h, BufferedImage.TYPE_INT_RGB);
```

```
// Draw on the image.
Graphics2D g2d = bufferedImage.createGraphics();
drawGraphics(g2d);
g2d.dispose();
```

Transforming a Buffered Image

In order to transform (such as rotate) a buffered image, you need to essentially clone the buffered image and then draw a transformed version of the original image into the new buffered image. The available transformation operations are shearing, scaling, translation, and rotation.

```
AffineTransform tx = new AffineTransform();
double radians = -Math.PI/4;
tx.rotate(radians, bufferedImage.getWidth()/2, bufferedImage.getHeight()/2);
BufferedImage newImage = new BufferedImage(bufferedImage.getWidth(), bufferedImage.getHeight(),
    bufferedImage.getType());
Graphics2D g2d = newImage.createGraphics();
g2d.drawImage(bufferedImage, tx, null);
g2d.dispose();
```

Converting a Color Image to Gray

```
ColorSpace cs = ColorSpace.getInstance(ColorSpace.CS_GRAY);
ColorConvertOp op = new ColorConvertOp(cs, null);
bufferedImage = op.filter(bufferedImage, null);
```

Packages

java.awt.image.renderable

This package contains classes and interfaces for producing rendering-independent images.

java.lang.Object

1.2	├ ParameterBlock - *java.io.Serializable*, *java.lang.Cloneable*
1.2	├ RenderContext - *java.lang.Cloneable*
1.2	├ RenderableImageOp - *RenderableImage*
1.2	└ RenderableImageProducer - *java.awt.image.ImageProducer*,
	java.lang.Runnable

1.2	*ContextualRenderedImageFactory* ————————— *RenderedImageFactory*
1.2	*RenderableImage*
1.2	*RenderedImageFactory*

java.awt.peer

This package is for interfacing with the underlying window system. It is for accessing the platform-specific facilities in order to build AWT toolkits. It is only used by AWT toolkit developers.

ButtonPeer	————————————	ComponentPeer
CanvasPeer	————————————	
CheckboxMenuItemPeer	————————————	MenuItemPeer
CheckboxPeer	————————————	ComponentPeer
ChoicePeer		
ComponentPeer		
ContainerPeer	————————————	
DialogPeer	————————————	WindowPeer
FileDialogPeer	————————————	DialogPeer
1.1 FontPeer		
FramePeer	————————————	WindowPeer
LabelPeer	————————————	ComponentPeer
1.1 LightweightPeer	————————————	
ListPeer	————————————	
MenuBarPeer	————————————	MenuComponentPeer
MenuComponentPeer		
MenuItemPeer	————————————	
MenuPeer	————————————	MenuItemPeer
PanelPeer	————————————	ContainerPeer
1.1 PopupMenuPeer	————————————	MenuPeer
1.1 ScrollPanePeer	————————————	ContainerPeer
ScrollbarPeer	————————————	ComponentPeer
TextAreaPeer	————————————	TextComponentPeer
TextComponentPeer	————————————	ComponentPeer
TextFieldPeer	————————————	TextComponentPeer
WindowPeer	————————————	ContainerPeer

java.awt.print

This package contains classes and interfaces for printing AWT components. It defines the notion of a book, which consists of a list of pages to be printed. Each page is described using its page format and a printable object.

```
java.lang.Object
1.2    ├ Book ------------------------------------------- Pageable
1.2    ├ PageFormat ----------------------------------┬- java.lang.Cloneable
1.2    ├ Paper ---------------------------------------┘
1.2 ○  ├ PrinterJob
       └ java.lang.Throwable -------------------------- java.io.Serializable
          └ java.lang.Exception
1.2          └ PrinterException
1.2             ├ PrinterAbortException
1.2             └ PrinterIOException

1.2    Pageable
1.2    Printable
1.2    PrinterGraphics
```

The Quintessential Printing Program

Note that (0, 0) of the Graphics object is at the top-left of the actual page, outside the printable area. In this example, the Graphics object is translated so that (0, 0) becomes the top-left corner of the printable area.

```java
import java.awt.*;
import java.awt.print.*;

public class BasicPrint extends JComponent implements Printable {
    public int print(Graphics g, PageFormat pf, int pageIndex) {
        if (pageIndex > 0) {
            return Printable.NO_SUCH_PAGE;
        }
        Graphics2D g2d = (Graphics2D)g;
        g2d.translate(pf.getImageableX(), pf.getImageableY());
        drawGraphics(g2d, pf);
        return Printable.PAGE_EXISTS;
    }

    public static void main(String[] args) {
        PrinterJob pjob = PrinterJob.getPrinterJob();
        PageFormat pf = pjob.defaultPage();
        pjob.setPrintable(new BasicPrint(), pf);
        try {
            pjob.print();
        } catch (PrinterException e) {
        }
    }
}
```

Getting the Dimensions of the Page

Note that (0, 0) of the Graphics object is at the top-left of the actual page, which is outside the printable area.

```java
public int print(Graphics g, PageFormat pf, int pageIndex) {
    // The area of the printable area.
```

```
        double ix = pf.getImageableX();
        double iy = pf.getImageableY();
        double iw = pf.getImageableWidth();
        double ih = pf.getImageableHeight();

        // The area of the actual page.
        double x = 0;
        double y = 0;
        double w = pf.getWidth();
        double h = pf.getHeight();
        return Printable.NO_SUCH_PAGE;
    }
```

Setting the Orientation

```
    PrinterJob pjob = PrinterJob.getPrinterJob();
    PageFormat pf = pjob.defaultPage();

    if (portrait) {
        pf.setOrientation(PageFormat.PORTRAIT);
    } else {
        pf.setOrientation(PageFormat.LANDSCAPE);
    }

    pjob.setPrintable(printable, pf);
    try {
        pjob.print();
    } catch (PrinterException e) {
    }
```

Printing Pages with Different Formats

A Book object is used when printing pages with different page formats. This example prints the first page in landscape and five more pages in portrait.

```
    public class PrintBook {
        public static void main(String[] args) {
            PrinterJob pjob = PrinterJob.getPrinterJob();
            Book book = new Book();

            // First part.
            PageFormat landscape = pjob.defaultPage();
            landscape.setOrientation(PageFormat.LANDSCAPE);
            book.append(new Printable1(), landscape);

            // Second part.
            PageFormat portrait = pjob.defaultPage();
            portrait.setOrientation(PageFormat.PORTRAIT);
            book.append(new Printable2(), portrait, 5);

            pjob.setPageable(book);
            try {
                pjob.print();
            } catch (PrinterException e) {
            }
        }
        static class Printable1 implements Printable {
            public int print(Graphics g, PageFormat pf, int pageIndex) {
                drawGraphics(g, pf);
                return Printable.PAGE_EXISTS;
            }
        }
        static class Printable2 implements Printable {
            public int print(Graphics g, PageFormat pf, int pageIndex) {
                drawGraphics(g, pf);
                return Printable.PAGE_EXISTS;
```

```
            }
        }
    }
```

Displaying the Page Format Dialog

The page format dialog allows the user to change the default page format values such as the orientation and paper size.

```
PrinterJob pjob = PrinterJob.getPrinterJob();

// Get and change default page format settings if necessary.
PageFormat pf = pjob.defaultPage();
pf.setOrientation(PageFormat.LANDSCAPE);

// Show page format dialog with page format settings.
pf = pjob.pageDialog(pf);
```

Displaying the Print Dialog

The print dialog allows the user to change the default printer settings such as the default printer, number of copies, range of pages, etc.

```
PrinterJob pjob = PrinterJob.getPrinterJob();
PageFormat pf = pjob.defaultPage();
pjob.setPrintable(new PrintableClass(), pf);
try {
    if (pjob.printDialog()) {
        pjob.print();
    }
} catch (PrinterException e) {
}
```

java.beans

This package contains classes related to JavaBeans development. Some classes in this package are used by beans while they run in an application. These include the property and vetoable change event and listener classes. Most of the other classes in this package are meant to be used by a bean editor (that is, a development environment for customizing and putting together beans to create an application). These classes help the bean editor create a user interface that the user can use to customize the bean. Information (descriptors) about a bean is obtained both explicitly via bean-infos, and implicitly via introspection. This information includes the events fired by a bean, its public methods and parameters, its properties, and so on.

java.lang.Object

1.1	├ Beans
1.1	├ FeatureDescriptor
1.1	│ ├ BeanDescriptor
1.1	│ ├ EventSetDescriptor
1.1	│ ├ MethodDescriptor
1.1	│ ├ ParameterDescriptor
1.1	│ └ PropertyDescriptor
1.1	│ └ IndexedPropertyDescriptor
1.1	├ Introspector
1.1	├ PropertyChangeSupport - *java.io.Serializable*
1.1	├ PropertyEditorManager
1.1	├ PropertyEditorSupport - *PropertyEditor*
1.1	├ SimpleBeanInfo - *BeanInfo*
1.1	├ VetoableChangeSupport - *java.io.Serializable*

Packages

43

	java.lang.Object — java.io.*Serializable*
1.1	‑ java.util.*EventObject* ‑
1.1	└ PropertyChangeEvent
	└ java.lang.Throwable ‑
	└ java.lang.Exception
1.1	‑ IntrospectionException
1.1	└ PropertyVetoException
1.2	*AppletInitializer*
1.1	*BeanInfo*
1.1	*Customizer*
1.2	*DesignMode*
1.1	*PropertyChangeListener* ——— java.util.*EventListener*
1.1	*PropertyEditor*
1.1	*VetoableChangeListener* ———
1.1	*Visibility*

The Quintessential Bean

This example bean has a single property called "property". If the property were not a boolean, it would not have an is*X()* method. Also, if the property were read-only, it would not have a set*X()* method.

```
import java.io.Serializable;

public class BasicBean implements Serializable {
    boolean property;
    public BasicBean() {
    }
    public boolean getProperty() {
        return property;
    }
    public boolean isProperty() {
        return property;
    }
    public void setProperty(boolean newValue) {
        property = newValue;
    }
}
```

Implementing a Bound Property

Bound properties fire a PropertyChangeEvent whenever its value is changed. This example bean implements a single bound integer property called "property".

```
int property;
public int getProperty() {
    return property;
}
public void setProperty(int newValue) {
    property = newValue;
    pceListeners.firePropertyChange("property", new Integer(property), new Integer(newValue));
}

// Create the listener list.
PropertyChangeSupport pceListeners = new PropertyChangeSupport(this);

// The listener list wrapper methods.
public synchronized void addPropertyChangeListener(PropertyChangeListener listener) {
    pceListeners.addPropertyChangeListener(listener);

}
public synchronized void removePropertyChangeListener(PropertyChangeListener listener) {
```

```
        pceListeners.removePropertyChangeListener(listener);
    }
```

Implementing a Constrained Property

Constrained properties fire a PropertyChangeEvent whenever its value is about to be changed. Any listener can veto the event, thereby preventing the change. This example bean implements a single constrained integer property called "property."

```
int property;
public int getProperty() {
    return property;
}
public void setProperty(int newValue) throws PropertyVetoException {
    try {
        vceListeners.fireVetoableChange("property", new Integer(property), new Integer(newValue));
        property = newValue;
    } catch (PropertyVetoException e) {
        throw e;
    }
}

// Create the listener list.
VetoableChangeSupport vceListeners = new VetoableChangeSupport(this);

// The listener list wrapper methods.
public synchronized void addVetoableChangeListener(VetoableChangeListener listener) {
    vceListeners.addVetoableChangeListener(listener);
}
public synchronized void removeVetoableChangeListener(VetoableChangeListener listener) {
    vceListeners.removeVetoableChangeListener(listener);
}
```

Instantiating a Bean

```
try {
    MyBean bean = (MyBean)Beans.instantiate(ClassLoader.getSystemClassLoader(), "MyBean");
} catch (ClassNotFoundException e) {
} catch (IOException e) {
}
```

Handling a Property Change Event

Property change events are fired when a bound property is changed.

```
bean.addPropertyChangeListener(new MyPropertyChangeListener());

class MyPropertyChangeListener implements PropertyChangeListener {
    public void propertyChange(PropertyChangeEvent evt) {
        Object oldValue = evt.getOldValue();
        Object newValue = evt.getNewValue();
        process(oldValue, newValue);
    }
}
```

Handling a Vetoable Property Change Event

Vetoable property change events are fired when a constrained property is changed. A listener can veto the change by throwing PropertyVetoException.

```
bean.addVetoableChangeListener(new MyVetoableChangeListener());

class MyVetoableChangeListener implements VetoableChangeListener {
    public void vetoableChange(PropertyChangeEvent evt) throws PropertyVetoException {
        Object oldValue = evt.getOldValue();
        Object newValue = evt.getNewValue();
        if (!process(oldValue, newValue)) {
```

```
                    throw new PropertyVetoException("message", evt);
                }
            }
        }
```

java.beans.beancontext

This package contains classes and interfaces relating to bean context. A bean context is a container for beans and defines the execution environment for the beans it contains. There can be several beans in a single bean context, and a bean context can be nested within another bean context. This package also contains events and listener interface for beans being added and removed from a bean context.

	java.lang.Object	
1.2	└ BeanContextChildSupport -	*BeanContextChild, BeanContextServicesListener, java.io.Serializable*
1.2	└ BeanContextSupport -	*BeanContext, java.beans ↵ .PropertyChangeListener, java.beans.VetoableChangeListener, java.io.Serializable*
1.2	└ BeanContextServicesSupport - - - - - - - - - - - - - - - -	*BeanContextServices*
1.2	└ BeanContextServicesSupport.BCSSProxyServiceProvider - - - -	*BeanContextServiceProvider, BeanContextServiceRevokedListener*
1.2	└ BeanContextServicesSupport.BCSSServiceProvider - - - - - - -	*java.io.Serializable*
1.2	└ BeanContextSupport.BCSChild - - - - - - - - - - - - - - - - -	
1.2	└ BeanContextServicesSupport.BCSSChild	
1.2 ●	└ BeanContextSupport.BCSIterator - - - - - - - - - - - - - - -	*java.util.Iterator*
1.1	└ java.util.EventObject -	*java.io.Serializable*
1.2 ○	└ BeanContextEvent	
1.2	├ BeanContextMembershipEvent	
1.2	├ BeanContextServiceAvailableEvent	
1.2	└ BeanContextServiceRevokedEvent	
1.2	*BeanContext* ————————————————	*BeanContextChild, java.beans.DesignMode, java.beans.Visibility, java.util.Collection*
1.2	*BeanContextChild*	
1.2	*BeanContextChildComponentProxy*	
1.2	*BeanContextContainerProxy*	
1.2	*BeanContextMembershipListener* ———————	*java.util.EventListener*
1.2	*BeanContextProxy*	
1.2	*BeanContextServiceProvider*	
1.2	*BeanContextServiceProviderBeanInfo* ———————	*java.beans.BeanInfo*
1.2	*BeanContextServiceRevokedListener* ———————	*java.util.EventListener*
1.2	*BeanContextServices* —————————————	*BeanContext, BeanContextServicesListener*
1.2	*BeanContextServicesListener* ————————	*BeanContextServiceRevokedListener*

Packages

java.io

This package contains three main groups of classes and interfaces. The first group is for building data streams. A data stream is either an input stream for reading bytes or characters, or an output stream for writing bytes or characters. The second group contains classes and interfaces for object serialization. Object serialization is the process of converting an object's state into a byte stream in such a way that the byte stream can be re-converted back into a copy of the object. The last group is for dealing with the file system.

Packages

java.lang.Object
```
├─ File --------------------------------------------------- Serializable, java.lang.Comparable
● ├─ FileDescriptor
○ ├─ InputStream
     ├─ ByteArrayInputStream
     ├─ FileInputStream
     ├─ FilterInputStream
          ├─ BufferedInputStream
          ├─ DataInputStream ---------------------------------- DataInput
```

java.lang.Object
- InputStream
  - FilterInputStream
    - LineNumberInputStream
    - PushbackInputStream
  1.1 - ObjectInputStream - *ObjectInput, ObjectStreamConstants*
  - PipedInputStream
  - SequenceInputStream
  - StringBufferInputStream
1.2 ○ - ObjectInputStream.GetField
1.2 ○ - ObjectOutputStream.PutField
1.1 - ObjectStreamClass - *Serializable*
1.2 - ObjectStreamField - *java.lang.Comparable*
○ - OutputStream
  - ByteArrayOutputStream
  - FileOutputStream
  - FilterOutputStream
    - BufferedOutputStream
    - DataOutputStream - *DataOutput*
    - PrintStream
  1.1 - ObjectOutputStream - *ObjectOutput, ObjectStreamConstants*
  - PipedOutputStream
- RandomAccessFile - *DataInput, DataOutput*
1.1 ○ - Reader
1.1 - BufferedReader
1.1 - LineNumberReader
1.1 - CharArrayReader
1.1 ○ - FilterReader
1.1 - PushbackReader
1.1 - InputStreamReader
1.1 - FileReader
1.1 - PipedReader
1.1 - StringReader
- StreamTokenizer
1.1 ○ - Writer
1.1 - BufferedWriter
1.1 - CharArrayWriter
1.1 ○ - FilterWriter
1.1 - OutputStreamWriter
1.1 - FileWriter
1.1 - PipedWriter
1.1 - PrintWriter
1.1 - StringWriter
1.2 ○ java.security.Permission - *Serializable, java.security.Guard*
1.2 ● - FilePermission - *Serializable*
1.2 ○ - java.security.BasicPermission - - - - - - - - - - - - - -
1.2 ● - SerializablePermission
java.lang.Throwable -
  - java.lang.Exception
    - IOException
    1.1 - CharConversionException

```
java.lang.Object
  └ java.lang.Throwable - - - - - - - - - - - - - - - - - - - - - - - - - - - - -┆- - Serializable
     └ java.lang.Exception
        └ IOException
              - EOFException
              - FileNotFoundException
              - InterruptedIOException
1.1 ○         - ObjectStreamException
1.1              - InvalidClassException
1.1              - InvalidObjectException
1.1              - NotActiveException
1.1              - NotSerializableException
1.1              - OptionalDataException
1.1              - StreamCorruptedException
1.1              └ WriteAbortedException
1.1           - SyncFailedException
              - UTFDataFormatException
1.1           └ UnsupportedEncodingException

      DataInput
      DataOutput
1.1   Externalizable ─────────────────────────────────────── Serializable
1.2   FileFilter
      FilenameFilter
1.1   ObjectInput ───────────────────────────────────────── DataInput
1.1   ObjectInputValidation
1.1   ObjectOutput ──────────────────────────────────────── DataOutput
1.2   ObjectStreamConstants
1.1   Serializable
```

Constructing a Path

On Windows, this example creates the path \a\b. On Unix, the path would be /a/b.

```
String path = File.separator + "a" + File.separator + "b";
```

Reading Text from Standard Input

```
try {
    BufferedReader in = new BufferedReader(new InputStreamReader(System.in));
    String str = "";
    while (str != null) {
        System.out.print("> prompt ");
        str = in.readLine();
        process(str);
    }
} catch (IOException e) {
}
```

Reading Text from a File

```
try {
    BufferedReader in = new BufferedReader(new FileReader("infilename"));
    String str;
    while ((str = in.readLine()) != null) {
        process(str);
    }
    in.close();
```

```
    } catch (IOException e) {
    }
```

Writing to a File

If the file does not already exist, it is automatically created.

```
    try {
        BufferedWriter out = new BufferedWriter(new FileWriter("outfilename"));
        out.write("aString");
        out.close();
    } catch (IOException e) {
    }
```

Creating a Directory

```
    (new File("directoryName")).mkdir();
```

Appending to a File

```
    try {
        BufferedWriter out = new BufferedWriter(new FileWriter("filename", true));
        out.write("aString");
        out.close();
    } catch (IOException e) {
    }
```

Deleting a File

```
    (new File("filename")).delete();
```

Deleting a Directory

```
    (new File("directoryName")).delete();
```

Creating a Temporary File

```
    try {
        // Create temp file.
        File temp = File.createTempFile("pattern", ".suffix");

        // Delete temp file when program exits.
        temp.deleteOnExit();

        // Write to temp file
        BufferedWriter out = new BufferedWriter(new FileWriter(temp));
        out.write("aString");
        out.close();
    } catch (IOException e) {
    }
```

Using a Random Access File

```
    try {
        File f = new File("filename");
        RandomAccessFile raf = new RandomAccessFile(f, "rw");

        // Read a character.
        char ch = raf.readChar();

        // Seek to end of file.
        raf.seek(f.length());

        // Append to the end.
        raf.writeChars("aString");
        raf.close();
```

```
    } catch (IOException e) {
    }
```

Serializing an Object

The object to be serialized must implement java.io.Serializable.

```
try {
    ObjectOutput out = new ObjectOutputStream(new FileOutputStream("filename.ser"));
    out.writeObject(object);
    out.close();
} catch (IOException e) {
}
```

Deserializing an Object

This example deserializes a java.awt.Button object.

```
try {
    ObjectInputStream in = new ObjectInputStream(new FileInputStream("filename.ser"));
    AnObject object = (AnObject) in.readObject();
    in.close();
} catch (ClassNotFoundException e) {
} catch (IOException e) {
}
```

Traversing a Directory

```
public static void traverse(File f) {
    process(f);

    if (f.isDirectory()) {
        String[] children = f.list();
        for (int i=0; i<children.length; i++) {
            traverse(new File(f, children[i]));
        }
    }
}
```

Reading UTF-8 Encoded Data

```
try {
    BufferedReader in = new BufferedReader(new InputStreamReader(new FileInputStream("infilename"), "UTF8"));
    String str = in.readLine();
} catch (UnsupportedEncodingException e) {
} catch (IOException e) {
}
```

Writing UTF-8 Encoded Data

```
try {
    Writer out = new BufferedWriter(new OutputStreamWriter(new FileOutputStream("outfilename"), "UTF8"));
    out.write(aString);
    out.close();
} catch (UnsupportedEncodingException e) {
} catch (IOException e) {
}
```

Reading ISO Latin-1 Encoded Data

```
try {
    BufferedReader in = new BufferedReader(new InputStreamReader(new FileInputStream("infilename"), "8859_1"));
    String str = in.readLine();
} catch (UnsupportedEncodingException e) {
} catch (IOException e) {
}
```

Writing ISO Latin-1 Encoded Data

```
try {
    Writer out = new BufferedWriter(new OutputStreamWriter(new FileOutputStream("outfilename"), "8859_1"));
    out.write(aString);
    out.close();
} catch (UnsupportedEncodingException e) {
} catch (IOException e) {
}
```

java.lang

This package contains classes and interfaces that are an integral part of the Java language. These include Object, Throwable, String and Thread. All errors and exceptions that can be thrown by the Java virtual machine appear in this package. Also included are classes for accessing system resources, primitive type object wrappers, and a math class.

Packages

Packages

```
        Object
    ●   ├ Boolean - - - - - - - - - - - - - - - - - - - - - - - - - - - - - java.io.Serializable
    ●   ├ Character - - - - - - - - - - - - - - - - - - - - - - - - - - - - Comparable, java.io.Serializable
1.2     ├ Character.Subset
1.2 ●   │  └ Character.UnicodeBlock
    ●   ├ Class - - - - - - - - - - - - - - - - - - - - - - - - - - - - - - ┐ java.io.Serializable
    ○   ├ ClassLoader                                                      │
    ●   ├ Compiler                                                         │
    ●   ├ Math                                                             │
    ○   ├ Number - - - - - - - - - - - - - - - - - - - - - - - - - - - - - ┘
1.1 ●   │  ├ Byte - - - - - - - - - - - - - - - - - - - - - - - - - - - ┬ Comparable
    ●   │  ├ Double - - - - - - - - - - - - - - - - - - - - - - - - - - ┤
    ●   │  ├ Float - - - - - - - - - - - - - - - - - - - - - - - - - - - ┤
    ●   │  ├ Integer - - - - - - - - - - - - - - - - - - - - - - - - - - ┤
    ●   │  ├ Long - - - - - - - - - - - - - - - - - - - - - - - - - - - ┤
1.1 ●   │  └ Short - - - - - - - - - - - - - - - - - - - - - - - - - - - ┘
1.2     ├ Package
    ○   ├ Process
        ├ Runtime
        ├ SecurityManager
    ●   ├ String - - - - - - - - - - - - - - - - - - - - - - - - - - - - Comparable, java.io.Serializable
    ●   ├ StringBuffer - - - - - - - - - - - - - - - - - - - - - - - - - java.io.Serializable
    ●   ├ System
        ├ Thread - - - - - - - - - - - - - - - - - - - - - - - - - - - - Runnable
        ├ ThreadGroup
1.2     ├ ThreadLocal
1.2     │  └ InheritableThreadLocal
1.1 ●   ├ Void
```

```
   Object
1.2 ○   ├ java.security.Permission --------------------------------- java.io.Serializable, java.security.Guard
1.2 ○   │  └ java.security.BasicPermission ------------------------ java.io.Serializable
1.2 ●   │     └ RuntimePermission
   └ Throwable --------------------------------------------┐
      ├ Error
      │  ├ LinkageError
      │  │  ├ ClassCircularityError
      │  │  ├ ClassFormatError
1.2   │  │  │  └ UnsupportedClassVersionError
1.1   │  │  ├ ExceptionInInitializerError
      │  │  ├ IncompatibleClassChangeError
      │  │  │  ├ AbstractMethodError
      │  │  │  ├ IllegalAccessError
      │  │  │  ├ InstantiationError
      │  │  │  ├ NoSuchFieldError
      │  │  │  └ NoSuchMethodError
      │  │  ├ NoClassDefFoundError
      │  │  ├ UnsatisfiedLinkError
      │  │  └ VerifyError
      │  ├ ThreadDeath
○     │  └ VirtualMachineError
      │     ├ InternalError
      │     ├ OutOfMemoryError
      │     ├ StackOverflowError
      │     └ UnknownError
      └ Exception
         ├ ClassNotFoundException
         ├ CloneNotSupportedException
         ├ IllegalAccessException
         ├ InstantiationException
         ├ InterruptedException
1.1      ├ NoSuchFieldException
         ├ NoSuchMethodException
         └ RuntimeException
            ├ ArithmeticException
            ├ ArrayStoreException
            ├ ClassCastException
            ├ IllegalArgumentException
            │  ├ IllegalThreadStateException
            │  └ NumberFormatException
            ├ IllegalMonitorStateException
1.1         ├ IllegalStateException
            ├ IndexOutOfBoundsException
            │  ├ ArrayIndexOutOfBoundsException
            │  └ StringIndexOutOfBoundsException
            ├ NegativeArraySizeException
            ├ NullPointerException
            ├ SecurityException
1.2         └ UnsupportedOperationException
```

Cloneable

The Quintessential Java Application

The parameters to the application are made available in "args".

```java
public class BasicApp {
    public static void main(String[] args) {
        for (int i=0; i<args.length; i++) {
            // process args[i];
        }
    }
}
```

This is the command to run the program:

```
>java BasicApp param1 param2 ...
```

Exiting a Java Program

```java
// Normal termination.
System.exit(0);

// Abnormal termination.
int errorCode = -1;
System.exit(errorCode);
```

The Quintessential Thread

There are two ways to declare a thread. The first way is to declare a class that extends Thread. Here is an example followed by code used to create and start the thread.

```java
class BasicThread1 extends Thread {
    public void run() {
        // This method is called when the thread runs.
    }
}
Thread thread = new BasicThread1();
thread.start();
```

The second way is to have a class implement Runnable. This method is typically used when a class makes use of a thread that is not shared with other classes. This example demonstrates the typical way in which such classes declare, create, and start a thread.

```java
class BasicThread2 implements Runnable {
    public void run() {
        // This method is called when the thread runs.
    }
    public void aMethod() {
        // Create and start a thread.
        Thread thread = new Thread(this);
        thread.start();
    }
}
```

Making an Object Cloneable

```java
class AnObject implements Cloneable {
    public AnObject() {
    }
    public Object clone() {
        AnObject theClone = new AnObject();
        // Initialize theClone.
        return theClone;
```

```
        }
    }
```

Here's some code to create a clone.

```
AnObject anObject = new AnObject();
AnObject copy = (AnObject)anObject.clone();
```

Constructing a String

If you are constructing a string with several appends, it may be more efficient to construct it using a StringBuffer and then convert it to an immutable String object.

```
StringBuffer buf = new StringBuffer("Initial Text");

// Modify
int index = 1;
buf.insert(index, "abc");
buf.append("def");

// Convert to string
String s = buf.toString();
```

Getting a Substring from a String

```
int start = 1;
int end = 4;
String substr = "aString".substring(start, end); // Str
```

Searching a String

```
String string = "aString";

// First occurrence.
int index = string.indexOf('S');        // 1

// Last occurrence.
index = string.lastIndexOf('i');        // 4

// Not found.
index = string.lastIndexOf('z');        // -1
```

Replacing Characters in a String

```
// Replace all occurrences of 'a' with 'o'
String newString = string.replace('a', 'o');
```

Replacing Substrings in a String

```
static String replace(String str, String pattern, String replace) {
    int s = 0;
    int e = 0;
    StringBuffer result = new StringBuffer();

    while ((e = str.indexOf(pattern, s)) >= 0) {
        result.append(str.substring(s, e));
        result.append(replace);
        s = e+pattern.length();
    }
    result.append(str.substring(s));
    return result.toString();
}
```

Converting a String to Upper or Lower Case

```
// Convert to upper case
String upper = string.toUpperCase();
```

```
// Convert to lower case
String lower = string.toLowerCase();
```

Converting a String to a Number

```
int i = Integer.parseInt("123");
long l = Long.parseLong("123");
float f = Float.parseFloat("123.4");
double d = Double.parseDouble("123.4e10");
```

Shifting Elements in an Array

```
// Shift all elements right by one
System.arraycopy(array, 0, array, 1, array.length-1);
```

```
// Shift all elements left by one
System.arraycopy(array, 1, array, 0, array.length-1);
```

Copying Elements from One Array to Another

```
System.arraycopy(src, 0, dst, 0, Math.min(src.length, dst.length));
```

Retrieving the SuperClass of an Object

```
Class supercls = object.getClass().getSuperclass();
```

Getting the Package of an Object

```
Package pkg = object.getClass().getPackage();
String pkgName = pkg.getName();
```

Implementing a Work Queue

The work queue is thread-safe so that multiple threads can simultaneously add and remove objects from it.

```
class WorkQueue {
    LinkedList queue = new LinkedList();
    public synchronized void addWork(Object o) {
        queue.addLast(o);
        notify();
    }
    public synchronized Object getWork() throws InterruptedException {
        while (queue.size() == 0) {
            wait();
        }
        return queue.removeFirst();
    }
}
```

Executes a Command

```
try {
    String command = "ls";
    Process child = Runtime.getRuntime().exec(command);
} catch (IOException e) {
}
```

Reading Output from a Command

```
try {
    // Execute command
    String command = "ls";
    Process child = Runtime.getRuntime().exec(command);

    // Get input stream to read from it
    InputStream in = child.getInputStream();
```

```
        int c;
        while ((c = in.read()) != -1) {
            process((char)c);
        }
        in.close();
    } catch (IOException e) {
    }
```

Sending Input to a Command

```
    try {
        // Execute command
        String command = "cat";
        Process child = Runtime.getRuntime().exec(command);

        // Get output stream to write from it
        OutputStream out = child.getOutputStream();

        out.write("some text".getBytes());
        out.close();
    } catch (IOException e) {
    }
```

Pausing

```
    try {
        Thread.sleep(5000); // 5 seconds
    } catch (InterruptedException e) {
    }
```

Getting the Current Time

There are two ways of getting the current time.

```
    // One way
    long time = System.currentTimeMillis();

    // Another way
    Date now = new Date();
```

Getting the Value of a System Property

```
    String dir = System.getProperty("user.dir");
```

Setting the Value of a System Property

```
    String previousValue = System.setProperty("application.property", "newValue");
```

Using a Thread-local Variable

```
    static ThreadLocal tlData = new ThreadLocal();

    public void m() {
        // Retrieve value.
        Object o = tlData.get();

        // Set value.
        tlData.set(o);
    }
```

Loading Native Code

On Windows, loadLibrary("s") loads s.dll. On Solaris, it loads s.so.

```
    System.loadLibrary("libraryName");
```

Converting Unicode to UTF-8

```
try {
    String string = "\u5639\u563b";
    byte[] utf8 = string.getBytes("UTF8");
} catch (UnsupportedEncodingException e) {
}
```

Converting UTF-8 to Unicode

```
public static String toUnicode(byte[] utf8buf) {
    try {
        return new String(utf8buf, "UTF8");
    } catch (UnsupportedEncodingException e) {
    }
    return null;
}
```

Determining a Character's Unicode Block

```
char ch = '\u5639';
Character.UnicodeBlock block = Character.UnicodeBlock.of(ch);
```

java.lang.ref

This package provides classes for obtaining information about references in the Java programming language. Reference objects are analogous to Class objects being used to represent a class. There are different types of references depending on their reachability. You can use a Reference in order to obtain information about the reference without hindering its corresponding object's eligibility for garbage-collection. References are useful for programs that cache objects.

```
java.lang.Object
1.2        ├ Reference
1.2        │  ├ PhantomReference
1.2        │  ├ SoftReference
1.2        │  └ WeakReference
1.2        └ ReferenceQueue
```

Holding onto an Object Until Memory Becomes Low

A soft reference holds onto its referent until memory becomes low.

```
// Create up the soft reference.
SoftReference sr = new SoftReference(object);

// Use the soft reference.
Object o = sr.get();
if (o != null) {
    process(o);
} else {
```

```
        // The object is being collected or has been reclaimed.
    }
```

Determining When an Object Is No Longer Used

A weak reference is used to determine when an object is no longer being referenced.

```
    // Create the weak reference.
    ReferenceQueue rq = new ReferenceQueue();
    WeakReference wr = new WeakReference(object, rq);

    // Wait for all the references to the object.
    try {
        while (true) {
            Reference r = rq.remove();
            if (r == wr) {
                // Object is no longer referenced.
            }
        }
    } catch (InterruptedException e) {
    }
```

Determining When an Object Is About to be Reclaimed

A phantom reference is used to determine when an object is just about to be reclaimed. Phantom references are safer to use than finalization because once an object is phantom reachable, it cannot be resurrected.

```
    // Create the phantom reference.
    ReferenceQueue rq = new ReferenceQueue();
    PhantomReference pr = new PhantomReference(object, rq);

    // Wait until the object is about to be reclaimed.
    try {
        while (true) {
            Reference r = rq.remove();
            if (r == pr) {
                // The object is about to be reclaimed.
                // Clear the referent so that it can be reclaimed.
                r.clear();
            }
        }
    } catch (InterruptedException e) {
    }
```

Packages

java.lang.reflect

This package provides classes and interfaces for obtaining reflective information about classes and objects. Reflective information includes information about the members a class has, the signatures of a class's constructors and methods, and the types of its fields. You can create new objects, access and change an object's fields, and invoke the object's methods. This package is typically used by programs such as debuggers, interpreters, object inspectors, class browsers, and by Java runtime services such as Object Serialization and JavaBeans.

java.lang.reflect

```
        java.lang.Object
1.2       └ AccessibleObject
1.1 ●        └ Constructor --------------------------------┬- Member
1.1 ●        ├ Field ---------------------------------------┊
1.1 ●        └ Method --------------------------------------┊
1.1 ●     ├ Array
1.1       ├ Modifier
1.2 ○     ├ java.security.Permission -------------------------- java.io.Serializable, java.security.Guard
1.2 ○        └ java.security.BasicPermission --------------------- java.io.Serializable
1.2 ●           └ ReflectPermission                              ┊
          └ java.lang.Throwable ---------------------------------┘
             └ java.lang.Exception
1.1             └ InvocationTargetException

1.1       Member
```

Getting a Class Object

There are three ways to retrieve a Class object.

```
// By way of an object.
Class cls = object.getClass();

// By way of a string
try {
    cls = Class.forName("java.lang.String");
} catch (ClassNotFoundException e) {
}

// By way of .class
cls = java.lang.String.class;
```

Getting the Modifiers of a Class Object

```
int mods = cls.getModifiers();
if (Modifier.isPublic(mods)) {
    // class is public
}
```

Getting the Interfaces of a Class Object

```
Class[] intfs = cls.getInterfaces();
for (int i=0; i<intfs.length; i++) {
    process(intfs[i]);
}
```

Getting the Methods of a Class Object

There are three ways of obtaining a Method object from a Class object.

```
Class cls = java.lang.String.class;

// By obtaining a list of all declared methods.
Method[] methods = cls.getDeclaredMethods();

// By obtaining a list of all public methods, both declared and inherited.
methods = cls.getMethods();
for (int i=0; i<methods.length; i++) {
    Class returnType = methods[i].getReturnType();
    Class[] paramTypes = methods[i].getParameterTypes();
    process(methods[i]);
}

// By obtaining a particular Method object.
// This example retrieves String.substring(int).
try {
    Method method = cls.getMethod("substring", new Class[] {int.class});
    process(method);
} catch (NoSuchMethodException e) {
}
```

Getting a Constructor of a Class Object

There are two ways of obtaining a Constructor object from a Class object.

```
// By obtaining a list of all Constructors object.
Constructor[] cons = cls.getDeclaredConstructors();
for (int i=0; i<cons.length; i++) {
    Class[] paramTypes = cons[i].getParameterTypes();
    process(cons[i]);
}

// By obtaining a particular Constructor object.
// This example retrieves java.awt.Point(int, int).
try {
    Constructor con = java.awt.Point.class.getConstructor(new Class[]{int.class, int.class});
    process(con);
} catch (NoSuchMethodException e) {
}
```

Creating an Object Using a Constructor Object

This example creates a new Point object from the constructor Point(int,int).

```
try {
    java.awt.Point obj = (java.awt.Point)con.newInstance(new Object[]{new Integer(123), new Integer(123)});
} catch (InstantiationException e) {
} catch (IllegalAccessException e) {
} catch (InvocationTargetException e) {
}
```

Getting the Field Objects of a Class Object

There are three ways of obtaining a Field object from a Class object.

```
Class cls = java.awt.Point.class;

// By obtaining a list of all declared fields.
Field[] fields = cls.getDeclaredFields();

// By obtaining a list of all public fields, both declared and inherited.
fields = cls.getFields();
for (int i=0; i<fields.length; i++) {
    Class type = fields[i].getType();
    process(fields[i]);
}

// By obtaining a particular Field object.
// This example retrieves java.awt.Point.x.
```

Packages

67

```
try {
    Field field = cls.getField("x");
    process(field);
} catch (NoSuchFieldException e) {
}
```

Getting and Setting the Value of a Field

This example assumes that the field has the type int.

```
try {
    // Get value
    field.getInt(object);

    // Set value
    field.setInt(object, 123);
} catch (IllegalAccessException e) {
}
```

Invoking a Method Using a Method Object

```
try {
    Object result = method.invoke(object, new Object[] {param1, param2, ..., paramN});
} catch (IllegalAccessException e) {
} catch (InvocationTargetException e) {
}
```

Getting the Modifiers of a Member Object

Field, Constructor, and Method are all subclasses of Member.

```
// Modifiers from a field.
int mods = member.getModifiers();
if (Modifier.isPublic(mods)) {
    // member is public
}
```

Getting the Name of a Class or Member Object

This example shows how to get the fully-qualified and non-fully-qualified name of a class and reflected objects.

```
// Non-fully-qualified names.
name = cls.getName().substring(cls.getPackage().getName().length()+1);
name = field.getName();
name = constructor.getName().substring(cls.getPackage().getName().length()+1);
name = method.getName();

// Fully-qualified names.
name = cls.getName();
name = cls.getName()+"."+field.getName();
name = constructor.getName();
name = cls.getName()+"."+method.getName();
```

Determining if an Object Is an Array

```
object.getClass().isArray();
```

Determining the Dimensions of an Array

```
public static int getDim(Object array) {
    int dim = 0;
    Class cls = array.getClass();
    while (cls.isArray()) {
        dim++;
        cls = cls.getComponentType();
    }
```

```
        return dim;
    }
```

Getting the Component Type of an Array

The component type of an array is the type of an array's elements. For example, the component type of int[] is int. The component type of int[][] is int[].

```
object.getClass().getComponentType();
```

Creating an Array

```
// An array of 10 ints.
int[] ints = (int[])Array.newInstance(int.class, 10);

// An array of 10 int-arrays.
int[][] ints2 = (int[][])Array.newInstance(int[].class, 10);

// A 10x20 2-dimenional int array.
ints2 = (int[][])Array.newInstance(int.class, new int[]{10, 20});
```

Expanding an Array

The length of an array cannot be changed. The closest thing to expanding an array is to create a larger one of the same type and copy the contents from the old array.

```
Object newArray = Array.newInstance(array.getClass().getComponentType(), Array.getLength(array)*2);
System.arraycopy(array, 0, newArray, 0, Array.getLength(array));
```

Getting and Setting the Value of an Element in an Array

```
// Get the value of the third element.
Object o = Array.get(array, 2);

// Set the value of the third element.
Array.set(array, 2, newValue);
```

Overriding Default Access

By default, a reflected object enforces the access as defined by the Java language. For example, by default you cannot retrieve the value from a Field object if the Field object represents a private field. To bypass these access checks, you call setAccessible() on the reflected object. However, the program may not have permission to call setAccessible(), in which case SecurityException is thrown.

```
field.setAccessible(true);
constructor.setAccessible(true);
method.setAccessible(true);
```

Packages

java.math

This package contains classes for performing arithmetic and bit manipulation on arbitrary precision decimal and integer numbers. BigInteger and BigDecimal are analogous to the primitive types long and double except that BigInteger and BigDecimal support arbitrary precision, and therefore operations on them do not overflow or lose precision.

```
    java.lang.Object
○     └ java.lang.Number - - - - - - - - - - - - - - - - - - - - - - - - - - - - - - java.io.Serializable
1.1       ├ BigDecimal - - - - - - - - - - - - - - - - - - - - - - - - - - - - - - - - - java.lang.Comparable
```

java.math

```
java.lang.Object
  └ java.lang.Number - - - - - - - - - - - - - - - - - - - - - - - - - - - java.io.Serializable
                                                              - - java.lang.Comparable
         └ BigInteger - - - - - - - - - - - - - - - - - - - - - - - -
```

Operating With Big Integer Values

```
// Create via a string.
BigInteger bi1 = new BigInteger("1234567890123456890");

// Create via a long.
BigInteger bi2 = BigInteger.valueOf(123);

bi1 = bi1.add(bi2);
bi1 = bi1.multiply(bi2);
bi1 = bi1.subtract(bi2);
bi1 = bi1.divide(bi2);
bi1 = bi1.negate();
int exponent = 2;
bi1 = bi1.pow(exponent);
```

Operating With Big Decimal Values

```
// Create via a string.
BigDecimal bd1 = new BigDecimal("123456789.0123456890");

// Create via a long.
BigDecimal bd2 = BigDecimal.valueOf(123);

bd1 = bd1.add(bd2);
bd1 = bd1.multiply(bd2);
bd1 = bd1.subtract(bd2);
bd1 = bd1.divide(bd2, BigDecimal.ROUND_UP);
bd1 = bd1.negate();
```

Setting the Decimal Place of a Big Decimal Value

```
int decimalPlaces = 2;

// Truncates the big decimal value.
bd = bd.setScale(decimalPlaces, BigDecimal.ROUND_DOWN);
String string = bd.toString();
```

java.net

This package contains classes for implementing networking applications. Using these classes, you can communicate with any server on the Internet or implement your own Internet server, within the restrictions placed by the security manager with respect to the servers to which the application can connect. A number of classes are provided to make it convenient to use URLs to retrieve data on the Internet.

Packages

```
      java.lang.Object
1.2 ○   ┌ Authenticator
    ○   ┌ ContentHandler
    ●   ┌ DatagramPacket
        ┌ DatagramSocket
1.1     │  └ MulticastSocket
1.1 ○   ┌ DatagramSocketImpl - - - - - - - - - - - - - - - - - - - - - - - - - SocketOptions
    ●   ┌ InetAddress - - - - - - - - - - - - - - - - - - - - - - - - - - - - java.io.Serializable
1.2 ●   ┌ PasswordAuthentication
        ┌ ServerSocket
        ┌ Socket
    ○   ┌ SocketImpl - - - - - - - - - - - - - - - - - - - - - - - - - - - - - SocketOptions
    ●   ┌ URL - - - - - - - - - - - - - - - - - - - - - - - - - - - - - - - - java.io.Serializable
    ○   ┌ URLConnection
1.1 ○   │  ┌ HttpURLConnection
1.2 ○   │  └ JarURLConnection
1.2     ┌ URLDecoder
        ┌ URLEncoder
        ┌ URLStreamHandler
    ○   ┌ java.lang.ClassLoader
1.2     │  └ java.security.SecureClassLoader
1.2     │     └ URLClassLoader
1.2 ○   ┌ java.security.Permission - - - - - - - - - - - - - - - java.io.Serializable,  java.security.Guard
1.2 ●   │  ┌ SocketPermission - - - - - - - - - - - - - - - - - - - - - java.io.Serializable
1.2 ○   │  ┌ java.security.BasicPermission - - - - - - - - - - - - ┐
1.2 ●   │  │  └ NetPermission                                     │
        └ java.lang.Throwable - - - - - - - - - - - - - - - - - - ┘
           └ java.lang.Exception
              └ java.io.IOException
                 ┌ MalformedURLException
                 ┌ ProtocolException
                 ┌ SocketException
1.1              │  ┌ BindException
1.1              │  ┌ ConnectException
1.1              │  └ NoRouteToHostException
                 ┌ UnknownHostException
                 └ UnknownServiceException

1.1   FileNameMap
      ContentHandlerFactory
      SocketImplFactory
1.2   SocketOptions
      URLStreamHandlerFactory
```

Creating a URL

```java
try {
    // With components.
    URL url = new URL("http", "hostname", 80, "index.html");

    // With a single string.
```

```
        url = new URL("http://hostname:80/index.html");
    } catch (MalformedURLException e) {
    }
```

Parsing a URL

```
    try {
        URL url = new URL("http://hostname:80/index.html#_top_");
        String protocol = url.getProtocol();      // http
        String host = url.getHost();        // hostname
        int port = url.getPort();      // 80
        String file = url.getFile();      // index.html
        String ref = url.getRef();        // _top_
    } catch (MalformedURLException e) {
    }
```

Reading Text from a URL

```
    try {
        URL url = new URL("http://hostname:80/index.html");
        BufferedReader in = new BufferedReader(new InputStreamReader(url.openStream()));

        String str;
        while ((str = in.readLine()) != null) {
            process(str);
        }
        in.close();
    } catch (MalformedURLException e) {
    } catch (IOException e) {
    }
```

Resolving a Hostname

```
    try {
        InetAddress addr = InetAddress.getByName("java.sun.com");
        process(addr);
    } catch (UnknownHostException e) {
    }
```

Creating a Client Socket

```
    try {
        InetAddress addr = InetAddress.getByName("java.sun.com");
        int port = 80;
        Socket sock = new Socket(addr, port);
    } catch (IOException e) {
    }
```

Creating a Server Socket

```
    try {
        int port = 2000;
        ServerSocket srv = new ServerSocket(port);

        // Wait for connection from client.
        Socket socket = srv.accept();
    } catch (IOException e) {
    }
```

Reading Text from a Socket

```
    try {
        BufferedReader rd = new BufferedReader(new InputStreamReader(socket.getInputStream()));

        String str;
```

Packages

73

```
        while ((str = rd.readLine()) != null) {
            process(str);
        }
        rd.close();
    } catch (IOException e) {
    }
```

Writing Text to a Socket

```
    try {
        BufferedWriter wr = new BufferedWriter(new OutputStreamWriter(socket.getOutputStream()));
        wr.write("aString");
        wr.flush();
    } catch (IOException e) {
    }
```

Sending a Datagram

```
    public static void send(InetAddress dst, int port, byte[] outbuf, int len) {
        try {
            DatagramPacket request = new DatagramPacket(outbuf, len, dst, port);
            DatagramSocket socket = new DatagramSocket();
            socket.send(request);
        } catch (SocketException e) {
        } catch (IOException e) {
        }
    }
```

Receiving a Datagram

```
    try {
        byte[] inbuf = new byte[256]; // default size
        DatagramSocket socket = new DatagramSocket();

        // Wait for packet
        DatagramPacket packet = new DatagramPacket(inbuf, inbuf.length);
        socket.receive(packet);

        // Data is now in inbuf
        int numBytesReceived = packet.getLength();
    } catch (SocketException e) {
    } catch (IOException e) {
    }
```

Joining a Multicast Group

```
    public void join(String groupName, int port) {
        try {
            MulticastSocket msocket = new MulticastSocket(port);
            group = InetAddress.getByName(groupName);
            msocket.joinGroup(group);
        } catch (IOException e) {
        }
    }
```

Receiving from a Multicast Group

Once you've created a multicast socket and joined the group, all datagrams sent to its corresponding multicast address will be available to be read from the socket. You can read from the socket just like you would from a unicast socket.

```
    public void read(MulticastSocket msocket, byte[] inbuf) {
        try {
            DatagramPacket packet = new DatagramPacket(inbuf, inbuf.length);
```

```
            // Wait for packet
            msocket.receive(packet);

            // Data is now in inbuf
            int numBytesReceived = packet.getLength();
        } catch (IOException e) {
        }
    }
```

Sending to a Multicast Group

You can send to a multicast socket using either a DatagramSocket or a MulticastSocket. What makes it multicast is the address that is in the datagram. If the address is a multicast address, the datagram will reach the multicast members in the group. You only need to use MulticastSocket if you want to control the time-to-live of the datagram.

```
byte[] outbuf = new byte[1024];
int port = 1234;
try {
    DatagramSocket socket = new DatagramSocket();
    InetAddress groupAddr = InetAddress.getByName("228.1.2.3");
    DatagramPacket packet = new DatagramPacket(outbuf, outbuf.length, groupAddr, port);
    socket.send(packet);
} catch (SocketException e) {
} catch (IOException e) {
}
```

This is the RMI package. RMI is Remote Method Invocation. It is a mechanism that enables an object on one Java virtual machine to invoke methods on an object in another Java virtual machine. Any object that can be invoked this way must implement the Remote interface. When such an object is invoked, its arguments are "marshalled" and sent from the local virtual machine to the remote one, where the arguments are "unmarshalled." When the method terminates, the results are marshalled from the remote machine and sent to the caller's virtual machine. If the method invocation results in an exception being thrown, the exception is indicated to the caller.

Packages

java.rmi

```
        java.lang.Object
1.2 ●   ├ MarshalledObject  - - - - - - - - - - - - - - - - - - - - - - java.io.Serializable
1.1 ●   ├ Naming
        ├ java.lang.SecurityManager
1.1     │   └ RMISecurityManager
        └ java.lang.Throwable  - - - - - - - - - - - - - - - - - - - - -
            └ java.lang.Exception
1.1         ├ AlreadyBoundException
1.1         ├ NotBoundException
            ├ java.io.IOException
1.1         │   └ RemoteException
1.1         │       ├ AccessException
1.1         │       ├ ConnectException
1.1         │       ├ ConnectIOException
1.1         │       ├ MarshalException
1.1         │       ├ NoSuchObjectException
1.1         │       ├ ServerError
1.1         │       ├ ServerException
1.1         │       ├ ServerRuntimeException
1.1         │       ├ StubNotFoundException
1.1         │       ├ UnexpectedException
1.1         │       ├ UnknownHostException
1.1         │       └ UnmarshalException
            └ java.lang.RuntimeException
                └ java.lang.SecurityException
1.1                 └ RMISecurityException

1.1     Remote
```

Starting Up the RMI Registry

Starting up the RMI registry allows you to create and export remote objects.

```
> rmiregistry
```

Defining and Exporting a Remote Object

1. Define the remote interface.

```
import java.rmi.*;

public interface RObject extends Remote {
    void aMethod() throws RemoteException;
}
```

2. Define the remote object implementation.

```
import java.rmi.*;
import java.rmi.server.UnicastRemoteObject;

public class RObjectImpl extends UnicastRemoteObject implements RObject {
    public RObjectImpl() throws RemoteException {
        super();
    }
    // All remote methods must throw RemoteException
    public void aMethod() throws RemoteException {
    }
}
```

3. Compile the remote object implementation.

```
> javac RObject.java RObjectImpl.java
```

4. Generate the skeletons and stubs.

```
> rmic RObjectImpl
```

5. Create an instance of RObjectImpl and bind it to the RMI Registry.

```
try {
    RObject robj = new RObjectImpl();
    Naming.rebind("//localhost/RObjectServer", robj);
} catch (MalformedURLException e) {
} catch (UnknownHostException e) {
} catch (RemoteException e) {
}
```

Looking Up a Remote Object and Invoking a Method

```
try {
    // Look up remote object
    RObject robj = (RObject) Naming.lookup("//localhost/RObjectServer");

    // Invoke method on remote object
    robj.aMethod();
} catch (MalformedURLException e) {
} catch (UnknownHostException e) {
} catch (NotBoundException e) {
} catch (RemoteException e) {
}
```

Passing Parameters to a Remote Method

Arguments to remote methods must be primitive, serializable, or Remote. This example demonstrates the declaration and use of all three parameter types.

1. Define the remote interface.

```
import java.rmi.*;
```

```
public interface RObject extends Remote {
    // This parameter is primitive.
    void primitiveArg(int num) throws RemoteException;

    // This parameter implements Serializable.
    void byValueArg(Integer num) throws RemoteException;

    // This parameter implements Remote.
    void byRefArg(ArgObject arg) throws RemoteException;
}

public interface ArgObject extends Remote {
    int aMethod() throws RemoteException;
}
```

2. Define the remote object implementation.

```
import java.rmi.*;
import java.rmi.server.UnicastRemoteObject;

public class RObjectImpl extends UnicastRemoteObject implements RObject {
    public RObjectImpl() throws RemoteException {
        super();
    }
    public void primitiveArg(int num) throws RemoteException {
    }
    public void byValueArg(Integer num) throws RemoteException {
    }
    public void byRefArg(ArgObject arg) throws RemoteException {
    }
}
```

3. Compile the remote object implementation.

```
> javac RObject.java RObjectImpl.java
```

4. Generate the skeletons and stubs.

```
> rmic RObjectImpl
```

5. Create an instance of RObjectImpl and bind it to the RMI Registry.

```
try {
    RObject robj = new RObjectImpl();
    Naming.rebind("//localhost/RObjectServer", robj);
} catch (MalformedURLException e) {
} catch (UnknownHostException e) {
} catch (RemoteException e) {
}
```

6. Look Up the Remote object and pass the parameters.

```
try {
    // Look up the remote object
    RObject robj = (RObject) Naming.lookup("//localhost/RObjectServer");

    // Pass a primitive value as argument
    robj.primitiveArg(1998);

    // Pass a serializable object as argument
    robj.byValueArg(new Integer(9));

    // Pass a Remote object as argument
    robj.byRefArg(new ArgObjectImpl());
} catch (MalformedURLException e) {
} catch (UnknownHostException e) {
} catch (NotBoundException e) {
} catch (RemoteException e) {
}
```

Returning Values from a Remote Method

Return values from remote methods must be primitive, serializable, or Remote. This example demonstrates the declaration and use of all three return types.

1. Define the remote interface.

```
import java.rmi.*;

public interface RObject extends Remote {
    // This return value is primitive.
    int primitiveRet() throws RemoteException;

    // This return value implements Serializable.
    Integer byValueRet() throws RemoteException;

    // This return value implements Remote.
    ArgObject byRefRet() throws RemoteException;
}

public interface ArgObject extends Remote {
    int aMethod() throws RemoteException;
}
```

2. Define the remote object implementation.

```
import java.rmi.*;
import java.rmi.server.UnicastRemoteObject;

public class RObjectImpl extends UnicastRemoteObject implements RObject {
    public RObjectImpl() throws RemoteException {
        super();
    }
    public int primitiveRet() throws RemoteException {
        return 3000;
    }
    public Integer byValueRet() throws RemoteException {
        return new Integer(2000);
    }
    public ArgObject byRefRet() throws RemoteException {
        return new ArgObjectImpl();
    }
}
```

3. Compile the remote object implementation.

```
> javac RObject.java RObjectImpl.java
```

4. Generate the skeletons and stubs.

```
> rmic RObjectImpl
```

5. Create an instance of RObjectImpl and bind it to the RMI Registry.

```
try {
    RObject robj = new RObjectImpl();
    Naming.rebind("//localhost/RObjectServer", robj);
} catch (MalformedURLException e) {
} catch (UnknownHostException e) {
} catch (RemoteException e) {
}
```

6. Look Up the Remote object, invoke the methods, and receive the return values.

```
try {
    // Look up the remote object
    RObject robj = (RObject) Naming.lookup("//localhost/RObjectServer");

    // Receive the primitive value as return value
    int r1 = robj.primitiveRet();

    // Receive the serializable object as return value
```

```
        Integer r2 = robj.byValueRet();

        // Receive the Remote Object as return value
        ArgObject aobj = robj.byRefRet();
    } catch (MalformedURLException e) {
    } catch (UnknownHostException e) {
    } catch (NotBoundException e) {
    } catch (RemoteException e) {
    }
```

Throwing an Exception from a Remote Method

1. Define the remote interface.

```
import java.rmi.*;

public interface RObject extends Remote {
    void aMethod() throws RemoteException;
}
```

2. Define the remote object implementation.

```
import java.rmi.*;
import java.rmi.server.UnicastRemoteObject;

public class RObjectImpl extends UnicastRemoteObject implements RObject {
    public RObjectImpl() throws RemoteException {
        super();
    }
    public void aMethod() throws RemoteException {
        // The actual exception must be wrapped in a RemoteException
        throw new RemoteException("message", new FileNotFoundException("message"));
    }
}
```

3. Compile the remote object implementation.

```
> javac RObject.java RObjectImpl.java
```

4. Generate the skeletons and stubs.

```
> rmic RObjectImpl
```

5. Create an instance of RObjectImpl and bind it to the RMI Registry.

```
try {
    RObject robj = new RObjectImpl();
    Naming.rebind("//localhost/RObjectServer", robj);
} catch (MalformedURLException e) {
} catch (UnknownHostException e) {
} catch (RemoteException e) {
}
```

6. Look up the Remote object, invoke the method, and catch the exception.

```
try {
    // Look up the remote object.
    RObject robj = (RObject) Naming.lookup("//localhost/RObjectServer");

    // Invoke the method.
    robj.aMethod();
} catch (MalformedURLException e) {
} catch (UnknownHostException e) {
} catch (NotBoundException e) {
} catch (RemoteException e) {
    // Get the actual exception that was thrown.
    Throwable realException = e.detail;
}
```

java.rmi.activation

This package provides support for RMI Object Activation. A remote object's reference can be made "persistent" and later activated into a "live" object using the RMI activation mechanism.

```
     java.lang.Object
1.2 ● ├ ActivationDesc - - - - - - - - - - - - - - - - - - - - - - - - - - - - - - - - - - - java.io.Serializable
1.2 ● ├ ActivationGroupDesc - - - - - - - - - - - - - - - - - - - - - - - - - -
1.2   ├ ActivationGroupDesc.CommandEnvironment - - - - - - - - - - - - -
1.2   ├ ActivationGroupID - - - - - - - - - - - - - - - - - - - - - - - - - - -
1.2   └ ActivationID - - - - - - - - - - - - - - - - - - - - - - - - - - - - -
1.1 ○ ├ java.rmi.server.RemoteObject - - - - - - - - - - - - - - - - - - - - - - java.io.Serializable, java.rmi.Remote
1.1 ○   ├ java.rmi.server.RemoteServer
1.2 ○   │ ├ Activatable
1.1     └ java.rmi.server.UnicastRemoteObject
1.2 ○       └ ActivationGroup - - - - - - - - - - - - - - - - - - - - - - - - ActivationInstantiator
```

java.rmi.activation

```
       java.lang.Object
1.1 ○    ├ java.rmi.server.RemoteObject ------------------------- java.io.Serializable,  java.rmi.Remote
1.1 ○    │  └ java.rmi.server.RemoteStub
1.2 ●    │     └ ActivationGroup_Stub ------------------------- ActivationInstantiator,  java.rmi.Remote
         └ java.lang.Throwable ------------------------------- java.io.Serializable
            └ java.lang.Exception
1.2         │  ├ ActivationException
1.2         │  │  ├ UnknownGroupException
1.2         │  │  └ UnknownObjectException
            │  └ java.io.IOException
1.1         │     └ java.rmi.RemoteException
1.2         │        └ ActivateFailedException

1.2    Activator ---------------------------------------- java.rmi.Remote
1.2    ActivationMonitor ------------------------------┐
1.2    ActivationInstantiator -------------------------┤
1.2    ActivationSystem -------------------------------┘
```

---

java.rmi.dgc

This package contains classes and interfaces for RMI distributed garbage-collection (DGC). When the RMI server returns an object to its client (caller of the remote method), it tracks the remote object's usage in the client. When there are no more references to the remote object on the client, or if the reference's "lease" expires and not renewed, the server garbage-collects the remote object.

```
       java.lang.Object
1.1 ●    ├ Lease --------------------------------------- java.io.Serializable
1.1 ●    └ VMID ----------------------------------------┘

1.1    DGC ----------------------------------------------- java.rmi.Remote
```

---

java.rmi.registry

This package contains a class and two interfaces for the RMI registry. A registry is a remote object that maps names to remote objects. A server registers its remote objects with the registry so that they can be looked up. When an object wants to invoke a method on a remote object, it must first look up the remote object using its name. The registry returns to the calling object a reference to the remote object, using which a remote method can be invoked.

java.rmi.server

This package contains classes and interfaces for supporting the server side of RMI. A group of classes are used by the stubs and skeletons generated by the rmic stub compiler. Another group of classes implements the RMI Transport protocol and HTTP tunneling.

Packages

java.rmi.server

java.lang.Object

1.1 ● ─ ObjID ─────────────────────────────── *java.io.Serializable*

1.1 ─ Operation

1.1 ─ RMIClassLoader

1.1 ○ ─ RMISocketFactory ───────────────── *RMIClientSocketFactory, RMIServerSocketFactory*

1.1 ○ ─ RemoteObject ───────────────── *java.io.Serializable*, *java.rmi.Remote*

1.1 ○ ─ RemoteServer

1.1 └ UnicastRemoteObject

1.1 ○ └ RemoteStub

1.1 ● ─ UID ─────────────────────────── *java.io.Serializable*

○ ─ *java.io.OutputStream*

└ *java.io.FilterOutputStream*

└ *java.io.PrintStream*

1.1 └ LogStream

└ *java.lang.Throwable*

└ *java.lang.Exception*

1.1 ─ ServerNotActiveException

─ *java.io.IOException*

1.1 └ *java.rmi.RemoteException*

1.1 ─ ExportException

1.1 └ SocketSecurityException

1.1 ─ SkeletonMismatchException

1.1 └ SkeletonNotFoundException

└ *java.lang.CloneNotSupportedException*

1.1 └ ServerCloneException

1.1 *LoaderHandler*

1.2 *RMIClientSocketFactory*

1.1 *RMIFailureHandler*

1.2 *RMIServerSocketFactory*

1.1 *RemoteCall*

1.1 *RemoteRef* ───────────────────────── *java.io.Externalizable*

1.1 *ServerRef* ───────────────────────── *RemoteRef*

1.1 *Skeleton*

1.1 *Unreferenced*

java.security

This package contains the classes and interfaces for the security framework. The security framework supports the use of certificates, public and private keys, message digests, secure class-loading, object signing, and policy-based fine-grained access control. These features are supported in an algorithm-independent way. For example, you can use the same interfaces but different algorithms for creating the message digest of a stream of data.

Packages

		java.lang.Object
1.2	●	– AccessControlContext
1.2	●	– AccessController
1.2		– AlgorithmParameterGenerator
1.2	○	– AlgorithmParameterGeneratorSpi
1.2		– AlgorithmParameters
1.2	○	– AlgorithmParametersSpi
1.2		– CodeSource - *java.io.Serializable*
1.2		– GuardedObject -┘
1.1	○	– Identity - *Principal, java.io.Serializable*
1.1	○	– IdentityScope
1.1	○	└ Signer
1.2		– KeyFactory
1.2	○	– KeyFactorySpi
1.1	●	– KeyPair - *java.io.Serializable*

java.security

		java.lang.Object
1.2	○	KeyPairGeneratorSpi
1.1	○	└ KeyPairGenerator
1.2		KeyStore
1.2	○	KeyStoreSpi
1.2	○	MessageDigestSpi
1.1	○	└ MessageDigest
1.2	○	Permission - *Guard, java.io.Serializable*
1.2	●	├ AllPermission
1.2	○	├ BasicPermission - *java.io.Serializable*
1.2	●	│ └ SecurityPermission
1.2	●	└ UnresolvedPermission - - - - - - - - - - - - - - - - - -
1.2	○	PermissionCollection -
1.2	●	└ Permissions -
1.2	○	Policy
1.2		ProtectionDomain
1.2	○	SecureRandomSpi -
1.1	●	Security
1.2	○	SignatureSpi
1.1	○	└ Signature
1.2	●	SignedObject -
	○	java.io.InputStream
		└ java.io.FilterInputStream
1.1		└ DigestInputStream
	○	java.io.OutputStream
		└ java.io.FilterOutputStream
1.1		└ DigestOutputStream
	○	java.lang.ClassLoader
1.2		└ SecureClassLoader
	○	java.util.Dictionary
		└ java.util.Hashtable - *java.io.Serializable, java.lang.Cloneable,*
			java.util.Map
		└ java.util.Properties
1.1	○	└ Provider
		java.util.Random - *java.io.Serializable*
1.1		└ SecureRandom
		└ java.lang.Throwable -
		└ java.lang.Exception
1.2		├ GeneralSecurityException
1.1		│ ├ DigestException
1.2		│ ├ InvalidAlgorithmParameterException
1.1		│ ├ KeyException
1.1		│ │ ├ InvalidKeyException
1.1		│ │ └ KeyManagementException
1.2		│ ├ KeyStoreException
1.1		│ ├ NoSuchAlgorithmException
1.1		│ ├ NoSuchProviderException
1.1		│ ├ SignatureException
1.2		│ └ UnrecoverableKeyException
1.2		├ PrivilegedActionException

```
        java.lang.Object
          └ java.lang.Throwable - - - - - - - - - - - - - - - - - - - - - - - - - - - - - - java.io.Serializable
              └ java.lang.Exception
                   └ java.lang.RuntimeException
1.1                    ├ ProviderException
                       ├ java.lang.IllegalArgumentException
1.1                    │   └ InvalidParameterException
                       ├ java.lang.SecurityException
1.2                    │   └ AccessControlException
                       ───────────────────────

1.1     Certificate
1.1     Key ──────────────────────────────────────────── java.io.Serializable
1.2     Guard
1.1     Principal
1.1     PrivateKey ─────────────────────────────────── Key
1.2     PrivilegedAction
1.2     PrivilegedExceptionAction
1.1     PublicKey ────────────────────────────────┘
```

Creating a New Key Pair and Self-signed Certificate

This example uses the keytool program to create a new key pair and self-signed certificate for the principal Duke.

```
> keytool -genkey -alias alias -keystore .keystore
Enter keystore password: password
What is your first and last name?
[Unknown]: Duke
What is the name of your organizational unit?
[Unknown]: JavaSoft
What is the name of your organization?
[Unknown]: Sun
What is the name of your City or Locality?
[Unknown]: Cupertino
What is the name of your State or Province?
[Unknown]: CA
What is the two-letter country code for this unit?
[Unknown]: US
Is <CN=Duke, OU=JavaSoft, O=Sun, L=Cupertino, ST=CA, C=US> correct?
[no]: yes
```

Creating and Signing a JAR File

```
> jar cf myjar.jar MyClass.class
```

```
> jarsigner -keystore .keystore -storepass password myjar.jar alias
```

Creating a New Policy File

Use policytool to create or edit an existing policy file. This is an example of a policy file created using policytool. It grants two permissions. It grants code signed by "Duke" permission to read files located in the user's home directory. It also grants code from the location "http://someserver/myjar.jar" (regardless of who signed it) to read the "file.encoding" system property.

```
> policytool -file .policy

keystore ".keystore";
    grant signedBy "Duke" {
        permission java.io.FilePermission "${user.dir}/-", "read";
    };
```

```
grant codeBase "http://someserver/myjar.jar" {
    permission java.util.PropertyPermission "file.encoding", "read";
}
```

Managing Policy Files

The Java Runtime provides default policy files to be used. See

http://java.sun.com/products/jdk/1.2/docs/guide/security/PolicyFiles.html

for more information. The location of these file is specified in the file "java.home/lib/security/java.security". By default, this file specifies two locations:

```
file:/java.home/lib/security/java.policy
file:/user.home/lib/security/.java.policy
```

The runtime's policy is the union of entries in these files. To specify an additional policy file, you can add entries to the java.security file:

```
> java -Djava.security.manager -Djava.security.policy=someURL MyApp
```

or specify the addition at runtime:

```
> appletviewer -J-Djava.security.policy=someURL HTMLfile
```

To ignore the policies in the "java.security" file, and only use the specified policy, use "==" instead of "=":

```
>java -Djava.security.manager -Djava.security.policy==someURL MyApp
```

Creating a Keyed Digest Using MD5

A "keyed" digest is one in which a secret key is used to create a digest for a buffer of bytes. You can use different keys to create different digests for the same buffer of bytes.

```java
public static byte[] getKeyedDigest(byte[] buffer, byte[] key) {
    try {
        MessageDigest md5 = MessageDigest.getInstance("MD5");
        md5.update(buffer);
        return md5.digest(key);
    } catch (NoSuchAlgorithmException e) {
    }
    return null;
}
```

Getting a Certificate from a Keystore

```java
try {
    KeyStore keyStore = KeyStore.getInstance(KeyStore.getDefaultType());

    InputStream in = new FileInputStream(".keystore");
    keyStore.load(in, "password".toCharArray());

    java.security.cert.Certificate cert = keyStore.getCertificate("Principal");
    process(cert);
} catch (KeyStoreException e) {
} catch (java.security.cert.CertificateException e) {
} catch (NoSuchAlgorithmException e) {
} catch (java.io.IOException e) {
}
```

Checking Read/Write Permission for a Directory

```java
AccessController.checkPermission(new FilePermission("/tmp/*", "read,write"));
```

Checking if One Permission Implies Another

```java
Permission perm1 = new FilePermission("/tmp/*", "read,write");
Permission perm2 = new FilePermission("/tmp/abc", "read");
```

```
if (perm1.implies(perm2)) {
    // perm1 implies perm2
}
```

Creating a Secure Random Number

```
public static float create(byte[] seed) {
    SecureRandom sr = new SecureRandom(seed);
    return sr.nextFloat();
}
```

---

java.security.acl

The classes and interfaces in this package have been superseded by classes in the java.security package. See java.security.Permission for details.

```
java.lang.Object
   └ java.lang.Throwable - - - - - - - - - - - - - - - - - - - - - - - - - - - - - java.io.Serializable
        └ java.lang.Exception
1.1           ├ AclNotFoundException
1.1           ├ LastOwnerException
1.1           └ NotOwnerException

1.1   Acl ——————————————————————— Owner
1.1   AclEntry ———————————————————— java.lang.Cloneable
1.1   Group ——————————————————————— java.security.Principal
1.1   Owner
1.1   Permission
```

---

java.security.cert

This package contains classes and interfaces for parsing and managing certifications. It contains support for X509 v3 certificates.

```
        java.lang.Object
1.2 ○    ├ CRL
1.2 ○    │  └ X509CRL - - - - - - - - - - - - - - - - - - - - - - - - - - - - ┐ X509Extension
1.2 ○    ├ Certificate                                                        ┊
1.2 ○    │  └ X509Certificate - - - - - - - - - - - - - - - - - - - - - - - ┐ ┊
1.2      ├ CertificateFactory                                              ┊ ┊
1.2 ○    ├ CertificateFactorySpi                                           ┊ ┊
1.2 ○    ├ X509CRLEntry - - - - - - - - - - - - - - - - - - - - - - - - - - ┘ ┊
         └ java.lang.Throwable - - - - - - - - - - - - - - - - - - - - - - - java.io.Serializable
            └ java.lang.Exception
1.2            └ java.security.GeneralSecurityException
1.2               ├ CRLException
1.2               └ CertificateException
1.2                  ├ CertificateEncodingException
1.2                  ├ CertificateExpiredException
1.2                  ├ CertificateNotYetValidException
1.2                  └ CertificateParsingException

1.2      X509Extension
```

java.security.interfaces

This package contains interfaces for generating DSA (Digital Signature Algorithm) keys as defined in NIST's FIPS-186.

java.security.spec

This package contains classes and interfaces for key specifications. Key specifications are transparent representations of the key material that constitutes a key. A key may be specified in either an algorithm-dependent way or an algorithm-independent way. This package contains key specifications for DSA public and private keys, PKCS #8 private keys in DER encoded format, and X509 public and private keys in DER encoded format.

Packages

java.security.spec

```
java.lang.Object
1.2    ├ DSAParameterSpec- - - - - - - - - - - - - - - - - - - - - - - - - - - - - AlgorithmParameterSpec,
                                                                          java.security.interfaces.DSAParams
1.2    ├ DSAPrivateKeySpec - - - - - - - - - - - - - - - - - - - - - - - - - ⊤ KeySpec
1.2    ├ DSAPublicKeySpec - - - - - - - - - - - - - - - - - - - - - - - - ┐ |
1.2 ○  ├ EncodedKeySpec - - - - - - - - - - - - - - - - - - - - - - - - - ┤ |
1.2    │ ├ PKCS8EncodedKeySpec                                           | |
1.2    │ └ X509EncodedKeySpec                                            | |
1.2    ├ RSAPrivateKeySpec - - - - - - - - - - - - - - - - - - - - - - - ┤ |
1.2    │ └ RSAPrivateCrtKeySpec                                          | |
1.2    ├ RSAPublicKeySpec - - - - - - - - - - - - - - - - - - - - - - - ┘ |
       └ java.lang.Throwable - - - - - - - - - - - - - - - - - - - - - - - java.io.Serializable
          └ java.lang.Exception
1.2          └ java.security.GeneralSecurityException
1.2             ├ InvalidKeySpecException
1.2             └ InvalidParameterSpecException

1.2  AlgorithmParameterSpec
1.2  KeySpec
```

java.sql

This is the JDBC package. JDBC is a standard API for executing SQL statements. It contains classes and interfaces for creating SQL statements, and retrieving the results of executing those statements against relational databases. JDBC has a framework whereby different "drivers" can be installed dynamically to access different databases.

java.lang.Object

1.1 ⌐ DriverManager
1.1 ⌐ DriverPropertyInfo
1.1 ⌐ Types
    ⌐ java.util.Date - java.io.Serializable, java.lang.Cloneable, java.lang.Comparable
1.1   ⌐ Date
1.1   ⌐ Time
1.1   ⌐ Timestamp
    ⌐ java.lang.Throwable - java.io.Serializable
      ⌐ java.lang.Exception
1.1   ⌐ SQLException
1.2   ⌐ BatchUpdateException
1.1   ⌐ SQLWarning
1.1   ⌐ DataTruncation

1.2 *Array*
1.2 *Blob*
1.1 *CallableStatement* ───────────────────── *PreparedStatement*
1.2 *Clob*
1.1 *Connection*
1.1 *DatabaseMetaData*
1.1 *Driver*
1.1 *PreparedStatement* ───────────────────── *Statement*
1.2 *Ref*
1.1 *ResultSet*

Packages

Connecting to a Database

This example uses the JDBC-ODBC bridge to connect to a database called "mydatabase".

```
try {
    Class.forName("sun.jdbc.odbc.JdbcOdbcDriver");

    String url = "jdbc:odbc:mydatabase";
    Connection con = DriverManager.getConnection(url, "login", "password");
} catch (ClassNotFoundException e) {
} catch (SQLException e) {
}
```

Creating a Table

This example creates a table called "mytable" with three columns: COL_A which holds strings, COL_B which holds integers, and COL_C which holds floating point numbers.

```
try {
    Statement stmt = con.createStatement();

    stmt.executeUpdate("CREATE TABLE mytable (COL_A VARCHAR(100), COL_B INTEGER, COL_C FLOAT)");
} catch (SQLException e) {
}
```

Entering a New Row into a Table

This example enters a row containing a string, an integer, and a floating point number into the table called "mytable".

```
try {
    Statement stmt = connection.createStatement();
    stmt.executeUpdate("INSERT INTO mytable VALUES ('Patrick Chan', 123, 1.23)");
    connection.close();
} catch (SQLException e) {
}
```

Getting All Rows from a Table

This example retrieves all the rows from a table called "mytable". A row in "mytable" consists of a string, integer, and floating point number.

```
try {
    Statement stmt = connection.createStatement();

    // Get data using colunm names.
    ResultSet rs = stmt.executeQuery("SELECT * FROM mytable");
    while (rs.next()) {
        String s = rs.getString("COL_A");
        int i = rs.getInt("COL_B");
        float f = rs.getFloat("COL_C");
        process(s, i, f);
    }

    // Get data using colunm numbers.
    rs = stmt.executeQuery("SELECT * FROM mytable");
    while (rs.next()) {
        String s = rs.getString(1);
        int i = rs.getInt(2);
```

```
            float f = rs.getFloat(3);
            process(s, i, f);
        }
    } catch (SQLException e) {
    }
```

Getting Particular Rows from a Table

This example retrieves all rows from a table called "mytable" whose column COL_A equals "Patrick Chan". A row in "mytable" consists of a string, integer, and floating point number.

```
    try {
        Statement stmt = connection.createStatement();
        ResultSet rs = stmt.executeQuery("SELECT * FROM mytable WHERE COL_A = 'Patrick Chan'");
        rs.next();
        String s = rs.getString("COL_A");
        int i = rs.getInt("COL_B");
        float f = rs.getFloat("COL_C");
        process(s, i, f);
    } catch (SQLException e) {
    }
```

Updating a Row of Data in a Table

This example updates a row in a table called "mytable". In particular, for all rows whose column COL_B equals 123, column COL_A is set to "John Doe".

```
    try {
        Statement stmt = connection.createStatement();
        int numUpdated = stmt.executeUpdate("UPDATE mytable SET COL_A = 'John Doe' WHERE COL_B = 123");
        connection.close();
    } catch (SQLException e) {
    }
```

Using a Prepared Statement

A prepared statement should be used in cases where a particular SQL statement is used frequently. The prepared statement is more expensive to set up but executes faster than a statement.

This example demonstrates a prepared statement for getting all rows from a table called "mytable" whose column COL_A equals "Patrick Chan". This example also demonstrates a prepared statement for updating data in the table. In particular, for all rows whose column COL_B equals 123, column COL_A is set to "John Doe".

```
    try {
        // Retrieving rows from the database.
        PreparedStatement stmt = connection.prepareStatement("SELECT * FROM mytable WHERE COL_A = ?");
        int colunm = 1;
        stmt.setString(colunm, "Patrick Chan");
        ResultSet rs = stmt.executeQuery();

        // Updating the database.
        stmt = connection.prepareStatement("UPDATE mytable SET COL_A = ? WHERE COL_B = ?");
        colunm = 1;
        stmt.setString(colunm, "John Doe");
        colunm = 2;
        stmt.setInt(colunm, 123);
        int numUpdated = stmt.executeUpdate();
    } catch (SQLException e) {
    }
```

java.text

This package contains classes and interfaces for handling text, dates, numbers and messages in a manner independent of natural language. This means your main application or applet can be written to be language-independent and to call upon separate, dynamically linked localized resources. This allows the flexibility of adding localization for new languages at any time. This package contains three groups of classes. The first group is for formatting dates, numbers, and messages. The second group is for parsing, searching, and sorting strings. The last group is for iterating over characters, words, sentences, and line breaks.

```
java.lang.Object
1.2     ├ Annotation
1.2     ├ AttributedCharacterIterator.Attribute - - - - - - - - - - - - - - - - java.io.Serializable
1.2     ├ AttributedString
1.1 ○   ├ BreakIterator - - - - - - - - - - - - - - - - - - - - - - - - - - - - - - - java.lang.Cloneable
1.1 ●   ├ CollationElementIterator
1.1 ●   ├ CollationKey - - - - - - - - - - - - - - - - - - - - - - - - - - - - - - - java.lang.Comparable
1.1 ○   ├ Collator - - - - - - - - - - - - - - - - - - - - - - - - - - - - - - - - java.lang.Cloneable, java.util.Comparator
1.1     │   └ RuleBasedCollator
1.1     ├ DateFormatSymbols - - - - - - - - - - - - - - - - - - - - - - - - - java.io.Serializable, java.lang.Cloneable
1.1 ●   ├ DecimalFormatSymbols - - - - - - - - - - - - - - - - - - - ┐
1.1     ├ FieldPosition                                             │
1.1 ○   ├ Format - - - - - - - - - - - - - - - - - - - - - - - - - - - ┘
1.1 ○   │   ├ DateFormat
1.1     │   │   └ SimpleDateFormat
1.1     │   ├ MessageFormat
1.1 ○   │   └ NumberFormat
1.1     │       ├ ChoiceFormat
1.1     │       └ DecimalFormat
1.1     ├ ParsePosition
1.1 ●   ├ StringCharacterIterator - - - - - - - - - - - - - - - - - - - - - CharacterIterator
        └ java.lang.Throwable - - - - - - - - - - - - - - - - - - - - - - - java.io.Serializable
            └ java.lang.Exception
1.1             └ ParseException

1.2     AttributedCharacterIterator ──────────────────── CharacterIterator
1.1     CharacterIterator ──────────────────── java.lang.Cloneable
```

Formatting and Parsing a Number

```
// Format
Locale locale = Locale.CANADA;
String string = NumberFormat.getNumberInstance(locale).format(123.45);

// Parse
try {
    Number number = NumberFormat.getNumberInstance(locale).parse("123.45");
    if (number instanceof Long) {
        // Long value
    } else {
        // Double value
    }
} catch (ParseException e) {
}
```

Formatting and Parsing Currency

```
// Format
Locale locale = Locale.CANADA;
String string = NumberFormat.getCurrencyInstance(locale).format(123.45);

// Parse
try {
```

```
              Number number = NumberFormat.getCurrencyInstance(locale).parse("$123.45");
              if (number instanceof Long) {
                  // Long value
              } else {
                  // Double value
              }
         } catch (ParseException e) {
         }
```

Formatting and Parsing a Percentage

```
         // Format
         Locale locale = Locale.CANADA;
         String string = NumberFormat.getPercentInstance(locale).format(123.45);

         // Parse
         try {
              Number number = NumberFormat.getPercentInstance(locale).parse("123.45%");
              if (number instanceof Long) {
                  // Long value
              } else {
                  // Double value
              }
         } catch (ParseException e) {
         }
```

Formatting and Parsing a Date

```
         // Format
         Locale locale = Locale.FRENCH;
         Date date = new Date();
         String string = DateFormat.getDateInstance(DateFormat.DEFAULT, locale).format(date);

         // Parse
         try {
              date = DateFormat.getDateInstance(DateFormat.DEFAULT, locale).parse("15 nov. 98");
         } catch (ParseException e) {
         }
```

Formatting and Parsing Time

```
         // Format
         Locale locale = Locale.FRENCH;
         Date date = new Date();
         String string = DateFormat.getTimeInstance(DateFormat.DEFAULT, locale).format(date);

         // Parse
         try {
              date = DateFormat.getTimeInstance(DateFormat.DEFAULT, locale).parse("01:37:11");
         } catch (ParseException e) {
         }
```

Formatting and Parsing a Date and Time

```
         // Format
         Locale locale = Locale.ITALIAN;
         Date date = new Date();
         String string = DateFormat.getDateTimeInstance(DateFormat.DEFAULT, DateFormat.DEFAULT, locale).format(date);

         // Parse
         try {
              date = DateFormat.getDateTimeInstance(
                      DateFormat.DEFAULT, DateFormat.DEFAULT, locale).parse("15-nov-98 1.45.12");
         } catch (ParseException e) {
         }
```

Determining the Type of a Character

You should use the methods in the class Character to determine the properties of a character. These methods work for the entire Unicode character set.

```
char ch = 'a';
if (Character.isLetter(ch)) {
} else if (Character.isDigit(ch)) {
} else if (Character.isLowerCase(ch)) {
} else if (Character.isUpperCase(ch)) {
}
// See Character for more methods.
```

Comparing Strings in a Locale-independent Way

```
Collator collator = Collator.getInstance(Locale.CANADA);
int compare = collator.compare(aString1, aString2);
if (compare < 0) {
    // aString1 < aString2
} else if (compare > 1) {
    // aString1 > aString2
} else {
    // aString1 = aString2
}
```

Determining the Character Boundaries in a Unicode String

```
BreakIterator iterator = BreakIterator.getCharacterInstance(Locale.CANADA);
iterator.setText("aString");
for (int index=iterator.first(); index != BreakIterator.DONE; index=iterator.next()) {
    process(index);
}
```

Determining the Word Boundaries in a Unicode String

The word break iterator finds both the beginning and end of words.

```
BreakIterator iterator = BreakIterator.getWordInstance(Locale.CANADA);
iterator.setText("a sentence");
for (int index=iterator.first(); index != BreakIterator.DONE; index=iterator.next()) {
    process(index);
}
```

Determining the Sentence Boundaries in a Unicode String

```
BreakIterator iterator = BreakIterator.getSentenceInstance(Locale.CANADA);
iterator.setText("A sentence. Another sentence.");
for (int index=iterator.first(); index != BreakIterator.DONE; index=iterator.next()) {
    process(index);
}
```

Determining Potential Line Breaks in a Unicode String

```
BreakIterator iterator = BreakIterator.getLineInstance(Locale.CANADA);
iterator.setText("line1\nline2");
for (int index=iterator.first(); index != BreakIterator.DONE; index=iterator.next()) {
    process(index);
}
```

java.util

This package contains a number of utility classes that are useful in typical Java applications. These include classes that implement useful data structures (the Collections framework), date- and time-related

java.util

classes, locale, root interfaces for events, and miscellaneous classes including a simple string tokenizer and pseudorandom-number generator.

java.lang.Object

```
1.2 ○   ├ AbstractCollection - - - - - - - - - - - - - - - - - - - - - - - - - - - - - - - - Collection
1.2 ○      ├ AbstractList - - - - - - - - - - - - - - - - - - - - - - - - - - - - - - - - List
1.2 ○         ├ AbstractSequentialList
1.2               └ LinkedList - - - - - - - - - - - - - - - - - - - - - - - - - - - - - - List, java.io.Serializable, java.lang.Cloneable
1.2            ├ ArrayList - - - - - - - - - - - - - - - - - - - - - - - - - - - - - - -
```

java.util

java.lang.Object

1.2 ○	├ AbstractCollection - *Collection*
1.2 ○	│ ├ AbstractList - *List*
	│ │ - *List, java.io.Serializable, java.lang.Cloneable*
	│ │ └ Vector - ┘
	│ │ └ Stack
1.2 ○	│ └ AbstractSet - *Set*
1.2	│ ├ HashSet - *Set, java.io.Serializable, java.lang.Cloneable*
1.2	│ └ TreeSet - *SortedSet, java.io.Serializable, java.lang.Cloneable*
1.2 ○	├ AbstractMap - *Map*
1.2	│ ├ HashMap - *Map, java.io.Serializable, java.lang.Cloneable*
1.2	│ ├ TreeMap - *SortedMap, java.io.Serializable, java.lang.Cloneable*
1.2	│ └ WeakHashMap - *Map*
1.2	├ Arrays
	├ BitSet - *java.io.Serializable, java.lang.Cloneable*
1.1 ○	├ Calendar - ┘
1.1	│ └ GregorianCalendar
1.2	├ Collections
	├ Date - *java.io.Serializable, java.lang.Cloneable, java.lang.Comparable*
○	├ Dictionary
	│ └ Hashtable - *Map, java.io.Serializable, java.lang.Cloneable*
	│ └ Properties
1.1	├ EventObject - *java.io.Serializable*
1.1 ●	├ Locale - *java.io.Serializable, java.lang.Cloneable*
	├ Observable
	├ Random - *java.io.Serializable*
1.1 ○	├ ResourceBundle
1.1 ○	│ ├ ListResourceBundle
1.1	│ └ PropertyResourceBundle
	├ StringTokenizer - *Enumeration*
1.1 ○	├ TimeZone - *java.io.Serializable, java.lang.Cloneable*
1.1	│ └ SimpleTimeZone
1.2 ○	├ java.security.Permission - - - - - - - - - - - - - - - - - - - *java.io.Serializable, java.security.Guard*
1.2 ○	│ └ java.security.BasicPermission - - - - - - - - - - - - - - - *java.io.Serializable*
1.2 ●	│ └ PropertyPermission
	└ java.lang.Throwable - ┘
	│ └ java.lang.Exception
1.1	│ ├ TooManyListenersException
	│ └ java.lang.RuntimeException
1.2	│ ├ ConcurrentModificationException
	│ ├ EmptyStackException
1.1	│ ├ MissingResourceException
	│ └ NoSuchElementException
1.2	*Collection*
1.2	*Comparator*
	Enumeration

java.util

Creating a Set

```
Set set = new HashSet();      // hash table
set = new TreeSet();       // sorted set

// Some operations.
set.add(value);
boolean b = set.contains(value);
set.remove(value);
```

Creating a List

```
List list = new LinkedList();       // doubly-linked list
list = new ArrayList();        // list implemented as growable array

// Some operations.
list.add(value);
list.get(0);
list.remove(value);
```

Creating a Hash Table

```
Map map = new HashMap();        // hash table
map = new TreeMap();       // sorted map

// Some operations.
map.put(key, value);
value = map.get(key);
map.remove(key);
```

Converting a Collection to an Array

```
Object[] objectArray = list.toArray();
AnObject[] array = (AnObject[])list.toArray(new AnObject[list.size()]);

objectArray = set.toArray();
array = (AnObject[])set.toArray(new AnObject[set.size()]);

objectArray = map.keySet().toArray();
array = (AnObject[])map.keySet().toArray(new AnObject[set.size()]);

objectArray = map.values().toArray();
array = (AnObject[])map.values().toArray(new AnObject[set.size()]);
```

Converting an Array to a Collection

```
// Ungrowable list.
List list = Arrays.asList(array);

// Growable list.
list = new LinkedList(Arrays.asList(array));

// Duplicate elements are discarded.
Set set = new HashSet(Arrays.asList(array));
```

Packages

Implementing a Queue

```
LinkedList queue = new LinkedList();

// Add to end of queue.
queue.add(object);

// Get head of queue.
Object o = queue.removeFirst();
```

Implementing a Stack

```
LinkedList stack = new LinkedList();

// Push on top of stack.
stack.addFirst(object);

// Pop off top of stack.
Object o = stack.getFirst();
```

Iterating the Elements of a Collection

```
// For sets and lists
for (Iterator it=collection.iterator(); it.hasNext(); ) {
    process(it.next());
}

// For keys of a map
for (Iterator it=map.keySet().iterator(); it.hasNext(); ) {
    process(it.next());
}

// For values of a map
for (Iterator it=map.values().iterator(); it.hasNext(); ) {
    process(it.next());
}
```

Sorting an Array

```
int[] intArray = new int[] {4, 1, 3, -23};
Arrays.sort(intArray);

String[] strArray = new String[] {"z", "a", "C"};
Arrays.sort(strArray);

// Case-insensitive sort.
Arrays.sort(strArray, String.CASE_INSENSITIVE_ORDER);
```

Finding an Element in a Sorted Array

This example also works if the object is a primitive type.

```
int index = Arrays.binarySearch(sortedArray, object);
if (index < 0) {
    // not found
}
```

Finding an Element in a Sorted List

```
int index = Collections.binarySearch(sortedList, object);
if (index < 0) {
    // not found
}
```

Inserting an Element into a Sorted List

```
int index = Collections.binarySearch(sortedList, object);
if (index < 0) {
```

```
        sortedList.add(-index-1, object);
    }
```

Generating a Random Number

```
Random rand = new Random();
int rnum = rand.nextInt();
// Continually call nextInt() for more random integers.
```

Breaking a String into Words

```
String aString = "word1 word2 word3";
StringTokenizer parser = new StringTokenizer(aString);
while (parser.hasMoreTokens()) {
    processWord(parser.nextToken());
}
```

Reading Properties from a Properties File

A properties filename has the form "basename_locale.properties". You only pass the string "basename" to getBundle().

```
ResourceBundle bundle = ResourceBundle.getBundle("basename");

// Enumerate contents of resource bundle
for (Enumeration props = bundle.getKeys(); props.hasMoreElements(); ) {
    String key = (String)props.nextElement();
    process(key, bundle.getObject(key));
}
```

Creating Date Object From a Particular Date

```
Calendar xmas = new GregorianCalendar(1998, Calendar.DECEMBER, 25);
Date date = xmas.getTime();
```

Creating a Date Object from a String

```
try {
    SimpleDateFormat formatter = new SimpleDateFormat("EEEE, MMMM dd, yyyy");
    Date d = formatter.parse("Tuesday, January 03, 1956");

    formatter = new SimpleDateFormat("EE, MMM d, yy");
    d = formatter.parse("Tue, Jan 3, 56");

    formatter = new SimpleDateFormat("EE, MM d, yy");
    d = formatter.parse("Tue, 01 3, 56");
    process(d);
} catch (ParseException e) {
}
```

Reading and Writing a Properties File

```
// Read properties file.
Properties properties = new Properties();
try {
    properties.load(new FileInputStream("infilename"));
} catch (IOException e) {
}
// Write properties file.
try {
    properties.store(new FileOutputStream("outfilename"), null);
} catch (IOException e) {
}
```

Here is an example of the contents of a properties file:

```
# a comment
! a comment

a = a string
b = a string with escape sequences \t \n \r \\ \" \' \ (space) \u0123
c = a string with a continuation line \
        contination line
d.e.f = another string
```

Getting and Setting Properties

```
String string = properties.getProperty("a.b");
properties.setProperty("a.b", "new value");
```

java.util.jar

This package contains classes for creating and reading JAR files. Its classes extend some of the classes in the java.util.zip package in order to support reading and storing meta-information about the JAR file contents in the form of a Manifest file.

```
       java.lang.Object
1.2      ├ Attributes - - - - - - - - - - - - - - - - - - - - - - - - - - - - - - - - - java.lang.Cloneable, java.util.Map
1.2      ├ Attributes.Name
1.2      ├ Manifest - - - - - - - - - - - - - - - - - - - - - - - - - - - - - - - - - - java.lang.Cloneable
   ○     ├ java.io.InputStream
            └ java.io.FilterInputStream
1.1            └ java.util.zip.InflaterInputStream
1.1               └ java.util.zip.ZipInputStream
1.2                  └ JarInputStream
   ○     ├ java.io.OutputStream
            └ java.io.FilterOutputStream
1.1            └ java.util.zip.DeflaterOutputStream
1.1               └ java.util.zip.ZipOutputStream
1.2                  └ JarOutputStream
1.1      ├ java.util.zip.ZipEntry - - - - - - - - - -
1.2         └ JarEntry
1.1      ├ java.util.zip.ZipFile
1.2         └ JarFile
```

```
java.lang.Object
  └ java.lang.Throwable ---------------------------------- java.io.Serializable
      └ java.lang.Exception
          └ java.io.IOException
1.1           └ java.util.zip.ZipException
1.2               └ JarException
```

Retrieving the Manifest of a JAR File

```
try {
    JarFile jarfile = new JarFile(filename);

    // Get manifest and write its contents
    jarfile.getManifest().write(System.out);
} catch (IOException e) {
}
```

java.util.zip

This package contains classes for computing checksums of data, and for compressing and decompressing data using standard ZIP and GZIP formats.

Packages

```
        java.lang.Object
1.1       ├ Adler32 ---------------------------------------· Checksum
1.1       ├ CRC32 ----------------------------------------·
1.1       ├ Deflater
1.1       ├ Inflater
1.1       ├ ZipEntry ------------------------------------ java.lang.Cloneable
1.1       ├ ZipFile
  ○       ├ java.io.InputStream
              └ java.io.FilterInputStream
1.1             ├ CheckedInputStream
1.1             └ InflaterInputStream
1.1               ├ GZIPInputStream
1.1               └ ZipInputStream
  ○       ├ java.io.OutputStream
              └ java.io.FilterOutputStream
1.1             ├ CheckedOutputStream
1.1             └ DeflaterOutputStream
1.1               ├ GZIPOutputStream
1.1               └ ZipOutputStream
          └ java.lang.Throwable ------------------------- java.io.Serializable
              └ java.lang.Exception
1.1             ├ DataFormatException
                └ java.io.IOException
1.1               └ ZipException

1.1     Checksum
```

Compressing a File

This example creates a ZIP file with one entry.

```java
try {
    String inFilename = "infile";
    String outFilename = "outfile.zip";
    FileInputStream in = new FileInputStream(inFilename);
    ZipOutputStream out = new ZipOutputStream(new FileOutputStream(outFilename));

    // Add ZIP entry to output stream.
    out.putNextEntry(new ZipEntry(inFilename));

    byte[] buf = new byte[1024];
    int len;
    while ((len = in.read(buf)) > 0) {
        out.write(buf, 0, len);
    }

    out.closeEntry();
    out.close();
    in.close();
} catch (IOException e) {
}
```

Decompressing a File

This example reads a ZIP file and decompresses the first entry.

```java
try {
```

```
        String inFilename = "infile.zip";
        String outFilename = "outfile";
        ZipInputStream in = new ZipInputStream(new FileInputStream(inFilename));
        OutputStream out = new FileOutputStream(outFilename);

        ZipEntry entry;
        byte[] buf = new byte[1024];
        int len;

        if ((entry = in.getNextEntry()) != null) {
            while ((len = in.read(buf)) > 0) {
                out.write(buf, 0, len);
            }
        }
        out.close();
        in.close();
    } catch (IOException e) {
    }
```

Listing the Contents of a ZIP file

```
    try {
        ZipFile zf = new ZipFile(filename);
        for (Enumeration entries = zf.entries(); entries.hasMoreElements();) {
            process(((ZipEntry)entries.nextElement()).getName());
        }
    } catch (IOException e) {
    }
```

Calculating the Checksum of a Byte Array

```
    public static long checksum(byte[] buf) {
        try {
            CheckedInputStream cis = new CheckedInputStream(new ByteArrayInputStream(buf), new Adler32());

            byte[] tempBuf = new byte[128];
            while (cis.read(tempBuf) >= 0) {
            }
            return cis.getChecksum().getValue();
        } catch (IOException e) {
            return -1;
        }
    }
```

Packages

javax.accessibility

This package provides support for building AWT and Swing user interfaces for use by people with and without physical disabilities. It provides an interface between UI objects and screen access products (such as screen readers and Braille terminals).

```
        java.lang.Object
1.2 ○    ├ AccessibleBundle
1.2      │  ├ AccessibleRole
1.2      │  └ AccessibleState
1.2 ○    ├ AccessibleContext
1.2 ○    ├ AccessibleHyperlink - - - - - - - - - - - - - - - - - - - - - - - - - - - AccessibleAction
1.2      ├ AccessibleStateSet
1.1 ○    ├ java.util.ResourceBundle
1.1 ○    │  └ java.util.ListResourceBundle
1.2      │     └ AccessibleResourceBundle

1.2      Accessible
1.2      AccessibleAction
1.2      AccessibleComponent
1.2      AccessibleHypertext ————————————————————————— AccessibleText
1.2      AccessibleSelection
1.2      AccessibleText
1.2      AccessibleValue
```

The Quintessential Accessible Object

You should try to subclass from JComponent or one of its descendents since that will automatically make your object accessible. If that is not possible, your object should implement Accessible.

```
import javax.accessibility.*;

public class BasicAccessible implements Accessible {
    public AccessibleContext getAccessibleContext() {
        return new AccessibleContext() {
            // Implement all the abstract methods in this abstract class.
        };
    }
}
```

Setting an Accessible Name for an Image Button

You should also set the accessible name for components that only show an image. The tool tip text, if set, serves as the accessible name for a component. However, if the tool tip text is being used for something else, set the component's accessible name.

```
JButton button = new JButton(new ImageIcon("image.gif"));
button.setToolTipText("Button Name");

// If tool tip is being used for something else, set the accessible name.
button.getAccessibleContext().setAccessibleName("Button Name");
```

Setting a Description for Image Icons

Image icons can be inserted in a variety of places such as in a text or tree component. You should set a description for image icons to help blind users.

```
ImageIcon icon = new ImageIcon("image.gif");
icon.setDescription("Description of Image");
```

Setting a Mnemomic for Buttons

```
JButton button = new JButton("Button");
button.setMnemonic('B');
JCheckBox checkBox = new JCheckBox("CheckBox");
checkBox.setMnemonic('C');
```

Setting a Mnemonic for a Menu

At least one menu in a menu bar should have a mnemonic. This makes all the menus and menu items accessible.

```
JMenu menu = new JMenu("Menu");
menu.setMnemonic('M');
```

Associating a Label with a Component

When a label is associated with a component, you should call setLabelFor() to make the association explicit and then set a mnemonic on the label. The associated component will get the focus when the mnemonic is activated.

```
JLabel label = new JLabel("Name:");
label.setDisplayedMnemonic('N');
label.setLabelFor(component);
```

Setting a Keyboard Accelerator for a Menu Item

At least one menu in a menu bar should have a mnemonic. This makes all the menus and menu items accessible.

```
JMenuItem item = new JMenuItem("Item");
item.setAccelerator(KeyStroke.getKeyStroke(KeyEvent.VK_I, KeyEvent.SHIFT_MASK));
```

javax.swing

This package extends the java.awt package by adding interfaces and classes for creating completely portable graphical user interfaces written entirely in Java (without any window-system-specific code). User interfaces built using this and related packages have a "pluggable" look and feel that can be changed dynamically by the user and/or application.

Packages

Packages

Packages

Packages

	java.lang.Object	
1.2 ○	├ AbstractAction -	*Action*, *java.io.Serializable*, *java.lang.Cloneable*
1.2	├ AbstractButton.ButtonChangeListener - - - - - - - - - - - - - - - - - - -	*java.io.Serializable*, *javax.swing.event ↵ .ChangeListener*
1.2 ○	├ AbstractListModel -	*ListModel*, *java.io.Serializable*
1.2	├ DefaultComboBoxModel -	*MutableComboBoxModel*, *java.io.Serializable*
1.2	└ DefaultListModel	
1.2	├ BorderFactory	
1.2	├ BoxLayout -	*java.awt.LayoutManager2*, *java.io.Serializable*
1.2	├ ButtonGroup -	*java.io.Serializable*
1.2	├ DefaultBoundedRangeModel -	*BoundedRangeModel*, *java.io.Serializable*
1.2	├ DefaultButtonModel -	*ButtonModel*, *java.io.Serializable*
1.2	└ JToggleButton.ToggleButtonModel	
1.2	├ DefaultCellEditor -	*java.io.Serializable*, *javax ↵ .swing.table.TableCellEditor*, *javax.swing.tree.TreeCellEditor*
1.2	├ DefaultCellEditor.EditorDelegate -	*java.awt.event.ActionListener*, *java.awt.event.ItemListener*, *java.io.Serializable*
1.2	├ DefaultDesktopManager -	*DesktopManager*, *java.io.Serializable*
1.2	├ DefaultListSelectionModel -	*ListSelectionModel*, *java.io.Serializable*, *java.lang.Cloneable*
1.2	├ DefaultSingleSelectionModel -	*SingleSelectionModel*, *java.io.Serializable*
1.2 ○	├ FocusManager	
1.2	└ DefaultFocusManager	
1.2	├ ImageIcon -	*Icon*, *java.io.Serializable*
1.2	├ JComponent.AccessibleJComponent ↵ .AccessibleContainerHandler	*java.awt.event.ContainerListener*
1.2	├ JRootPane.RootLayout -	*java.awt.LayoutManager2*, *java.io.Serializable*
1.2	├ JTabbedPane.ModelListener -	*java.io.Serializable*, *javax.swing.event ↵ .ChangeListener*
1.2	├ JTree.TreeModelHandler -	*javax.swing.event.TreeModelListener*
1.2	├ JTree.TreeSelectionRedirector -	*java.io.Serializable*, *javax.swing.event ↵ .TreeSelectionListener*
1.2	├ KeyStroke -	*java.io.Serializable*
1.2 ○	├ LookAndFeel	

java.lang.Object

1.2	MenuSelectionManager
1.2	OverlayLayout - *java.awt.LayoutManager2*, *java.io.Serializable*
1.2	ProgressMonitor
1.2	RepaintManager
1.2	ScrollPaneLayout - *ScrollPaneConstants*, *java.awt.LayoutManager*,
	java.io.Serializable
1.2	└ ScrollPaneLayout.UIResource - *javax.swing.plaf.UIResource*
1.2	SizeRequirements - *java.io.Serializable*
1.2	SwingUtilities - *SwingConstants*
1.2	Timer - *java.io.Serializable*
1.2	ToolTipManager.insideTimerAction - *java.awt.event.ActionListener*
1.2	ToolTipManager.outsideTimerAction - - - - - - - - - - - - - - - - - - - ┐
1.2	ToolTipManager.stillInsideTimerAction - - - - - - - - - - - - - - - - ┘
1.2	UIManager - *java.io.Serializable*
1.2	UIManager.LookAndFeelInfo
1.2	ViewportLayout - *java.awt.LayoutManager*, *java.io.Serializable*
○	java.awt.Component - *java.awt.MenuContainer*,
	java.awt.image.ImageObserver,
	java.io.Serializable
1.2	├ Box.Filler - *javax.accessibility.Accessible*
	└ java.awt.Container
1.2	├ Box - ┘
1.2	├ CellRendererPane - ┘
1.2 ○	├ JComponent - *java.io.Serializable*
1.2 ○	├ AbstractButton - *SwingConstants*, *java.awt.ItemSelectable*
1.2	├ JButton - *javax.accessibility.Accessible*
1.2	├ JMenuItem - *MenuElement*, *javax.accessibility.Accessible*
1.2	├ JCheckBoxMenuItem - *SwingConstants*, *javax.accessibility.Accessible*
1.2	├ JMenu - *MenuElement*, *javax.accessibility.Accessible*
1.2	└ JRadioButtonMenuItem - - - - - - - - - - - - - - - - - - *javax.accessibility.Accessible*
1.2	└ JToggleButton - ┐
1.2	├ JCheckBox - ┤
1.2	└ JRadioButton - ┘
1.2	├ JColorChooser - ┘
1.2	├ JComboBox - *java.awt.ItemSelectable*, *java ↵*
	.awt.event.ActionListener,
	javax.accessibility.Accessible,
	javax.swing.event.ListDataListener
1.2	├ JFileChooser - *javax.accessibility.Accessible*
1.2	├ JInternalFrame - *RootPaneContainer*, *WindowConstants*,
	javax.accessibility.Accessible
1.2	├ JInternalFrame.JDesktopIcon - *javax.accessibility.Accessible*
1.2	├ JLabel - *SwingConstants*, *javax.accessibility.Accessible*
1.2	└ DefaultListCellRenderer - *ListCellRenderer*, *java.io.Serializable*
1.2	└ DefaultListCellRenderer.UIResource - - - - - - - - - - - *javax.swing.plaf.UIResource*
1.2	├ JLayeredPane - *javax.accessibility.Accessible*
1.2	└ JDesktopPane - ┘
1.2	├ JList - *Scrollable*, *javax.accessibility.Accessible*

javax.swing

java.lang.Object

  ○ - java.awt.Component - *java.awt.MenuContainer* ,
                                                              java.awt.image.ImageObserver ,
                                                              java.io.Serializable

	└ java.awt.Container	
1.2 ○	└ JComponent -	*java.io.Serializable*
1.2	└ JMenuBar -	*MenuElement* , *javax . accessibility . Accessible*
1.2	├ JOptionPane -	*javax . accessibility . Accessible*
1.2	├ JPanel - ┐	
1.2	├ JPopupMenu -	*MenuElement* , *javax . accessibility . Accessible*
1.2	├ JProgressBar -	*SwingConstants* , *javax . accessibility . Accessible*
1.2	├ JRootPane -	*javax . accessibility . Accessible*
1.2	├ JScrollBar -	*java . awt . Adjustable* , *javax . accessibility* ↵ . *Accessible*
1.2	└ JScrollPane.ScrollBar -	*javax . swing . plaf . UIResource*
1.2	├ JScrollPane -	*ScrollPaneConstants* , *javax . accessibility* ↵ . *Accessible*
1.2	├ JSeparator - ┐	*SwingConstants* , *javax . accessibility . Accessible*
1.2	├ JPopupMenu.Separator	
1.2	└ JToolBar.Separator	
1.2	├ JSlider - ┘	
1.2	├ JSplitPane -	*javax . accessibility . Accessible*
1.2	├ JTabbedPane -	*SwingConstants* , *java . io . Serializable* , *javax . accessibility . Accessible*
1.2	├ JTable -	*Scrollable* , *javax . accessibility* ↵ . *Accessible* , *javax . swing . event* ↵ . *CellEditorListener* , *javax . swing . event* ↵ . *ListSelectionListener* , *javax . swing* ↵ . *event . TableColumnModelListener* , *javax . swing . event . TableModelListener*
1.2	├ JToolBar -	*SwingConstants* , *javax . accessibility . Accessible*
1.2	├ JToolTip -	*javax . accessibility . Accessible*
1.2	├ JTree -	*Scrollable* , *javax . accessibility . Accessible*
1.2	├ JViewport -	*javax . accessibility . Accessible*
1.2 ○	└ javax.swing.text.JTextComponent - - - - - - - - - - - - - - -	*Scrollable* , *javax . accessibility . Accessible*
1.2	├ JEditorPane	
1.2	└ JTextPane	
1.2	├ JTextArea	
1.2	├ JTextField -	*SwingConstants*
1.2	└ JPasswordField	
	├ java.awt.Panel	
	└ java.applet.Applet	
1.2	└ JApplet - ┐	*RootPaneContainer* , *javax . accessibility* ↵ . *Accessible*
	├ java.awt.Window	
1.2	├ JWindow - ┘	
	└ java.awt.Dialog	
1.2	└ JDialog -	*RootPaneContainer* , *WindowConstants* , *javax . accessibility . Accessible*

```
        java.lang.Object
  ○       java.awt.Component ------------------------------------- java.awt.MenuContainer,
                                                                    java.awt.image.ImageObserver,
                                                                    java.io.Serializable

              java.awt.Container
                └ java.awt.Window
                    └ java.awt.Frame ----------------------------- java.awt.MenuContainer
 1.2                    └ JFrame --------------------------------- RootPaneContainer, WindowConstants,
                                                                    javax.accessibility.Accessible
  ○       java.awt.Graphics
 1.2        └ DebugGraphics
1.1 ○     java.awt.event.ComponentAdapter ---------------------- java.awt.event.ComponentListener
 1.2        └ JViewport.ViewListener ------------------------------ java.io.Serializable
1.1 ○     java.awt.event.MouseAdapter ------------------------- java.awt.event.MouseListener
 1.2        └ ToolTipManager ------------------------------------- java.awt.event.MouseMotionListener
1.1 ○     java.awt.event.WindowAdapter ------------------------ java.awt.event.WindowListener
 1.2        └ JMenu.WinListener ---------------------------------- java.io.Serializable
  ○       java.awt.image.ImageFilter -------------------------- java.awt.image.ImageConsumer,
                                                                    java.lang.Cloneable

  ○           java.awt.image.RGBImageFilter
 1.2            └ GrayFilter
  ○       java.io.InputStream
              └ java.io.FilterInputStream
 1.2            └ ProgressMonitorInputStream
  ○       java.util.Dictionary
              └ java.util.Hashtable ------------------------------ java.io.Serializable, java.lang.Cloneable,
                                                                    java.util.Map

 1.2            └ UIDefaults
1.2 ○     javax.accessibility.AccessibleContext
 1.2        Box.AccessibleBox --------------------------------- java.io.Serializable, javax.accessibility ↵
                                                                    .AccessibleComponent

 1.2        Box.Filler.AccessibleBoxFiller ------------------
 1.2        CellRendererPane.AccessibleCellRendererPane -------
 1.2        JApplet.AccessibleJApplet -----------------------
1.2 ○       JComponent.AccessibleJComponent-----------------
1.2 ○           AbstractButton.AccessibleAbstractButton ------------- javax.accessibility.AccessibleAction,
                                                                    javax.accessibility.AccessibleValue
 1.2              JButton.AccessibleJButton
 1.2              JMenuItem.AccessibleJMenuItem ---------------- javax.swing.event.ChangeListener
 1.2                JCheckBoxMenuItem↵
                      .AccessibleJCheckBoxMenuItem
 1.2                JMenu.AccessibleJMenu --------------------- javax.accessibility.AccessibleSelection
 1.2                JRadioButtonMenuItem↵
                      .AccessibleJRadioButtonMenuItem
 1.2              JToggleButton.AccessibleJToggleButton ----------- java.awt.event.ItemListener
 1.2                JCheckBox.AccessibleJCheckBox
 1.2                JRadioButton.AccessibleJRadioButton
 1.2            JColorChooser.AccessibleJColorChooser
 1.2            JComboBox.AccessibleJComboBox ---------------- javax.accessibility.AccessibleAction
 1.2            JDesktopPane.AccessibleJDesktopPane
```

123

javax.swing

java.lang.Object

1.2 ○	├ javax.accessibility.AccessibleContext	
1.2 ○	│ ├ JComponent.AccessibleJComponent - - - - - - - - - - - - - - - - - - - ┊ -	*java.io.Serializable*, *javax.accessibility.AccessibleComponent*
1.2	│ │ ├ JFileChooser.AccessibleJFileChooser	
1.2	│ │ ├ JInternalFrame.AccessibleJInternalFrame - - - - - - - - - - - ┬ -	*javax . accessibility . AccessibleValue*
1.2	│ │ ├ JInternalFrame.JDesktopIcon.AccessibleJDesktopIcon - ┊	
1.2	│ │ ├ JLabel.AccessibleJLabel	
1.2	│ │ ├ JLayeredPane.AccessibleJLayeredPane	
1.2	│ │ ├ JList.AccessibleJList -	*java . beans . PropertyChangeListener*, *javax . accessibility . AccessibleSelection*, *javax . swing . event . ListDataListener*, *javax . swing . event . ListSelectionListener*
1.2	│ │ ├ JMenuBar.AccessibleJMenuBar - - - - - - - - - - - - - - - - - -	*javax . accessibility . AccessibleSelection*
1.2	│ │ ├ JOptionPane.AccessibleJOptionPane	
1.2	│ │ ├ JPanel.AccessibleJPanel	
1.2	│ │ ├ JPopupMenu.AccessibleJPopupMenu	
1.2	│ │ ├ JProgressBar.AccessibleJProgressBar - - - - - - - - - - - - - ┬ -	*javax . accessibility . AccessibleValue*
1.2	│ │ ├ JRootPane.AccessibleJRootPane	
1.2	│ │ ├ JScrollBar.AccessibleJScrollBar - - - - - - - - - - - - - - - - - ┊	
1.2	│ │ ├ JScrollPane.AccessibleJScrollPane - - - - - - - - - - - - - - - -	*javax . swing . event . ChangeListener*
1.2	│ │ ├ JSeparator.AccessibleJSeparator	
1.2	│ │ ├ JSlider.AccessibleJSlider - ┬ -	*javax . accessibility . AccessibleValue*
1.2	│ │ ├ JSplitPane.AccessibleJSplitPane - - - - - - - - - - - - - - - - ┊	
1.2	│ │ ├ JTabbedPane.AccessibleJTabbedPane - - - - - - - - - - - - -	*javax . accessibility . AccessibleSelection*, *javax . swing . event . ChangeListener*
1.2	│ │ ├ JTable.AccessibleJTable -	*java . beans . PropertyChangeListener*, *javax ↵ . accessibility . AccessibleSelection*, *javax ↵ . swing . event . CellEditorListener*, *javax ↵ . swing . event . ListSelectionListener*, *javax ↵ . swing . event . TableColumnModelListener*, *javax . swing . event . TableModelListener*
1.2	│ │ ├ JToolBar.AccessibleJToolBar	
1.2	│ │ ├ JToolTip.AccessibleJToolTip	
1.2	│ │ ├ JTree.AccessibleJTree -	*javax . accessibility . AccessibleSelection*, *javax . swing . event . TreeExpansionListener*, *javax . swing . event . TreeModelListener*, *javax . swing . event . TreeSelectionListener*
1.2	│ │ ├ JViewport.AccessibleJViewport	
1.2	│ │ └ javax.swing.text.JTextComponent ↵ - - - - - - - - - - - - - - - .AccessibleJTextComponent	*javax . accessibility . AccessibleText*, *javax . swing . event . CaretListener*, *javax . swing . event . DocumentListener*
1.2	│ │ ├ JEditorPane.AccessibleJEditorPane	
1.2	│ │ ├ JEditorPane.AccessibleJEditorPaneHTML	
1.2	│ │ └ JEditorPane.JEditorPaneAccessibleHypertextSupport	*javax . accessibility . AccessibleHypertext*
1.2	│ │ ├ JTextArea.AccessibleJTextArea	
1.2	│ │ └ JTextField.AccessibleJTextField	
1.2	│ │ └ JPasswordField.AccessibleJPasswordField	
1.2	│ ├ JDialog.AccessibleJDialog -	*java.io . Serializable*, *javax . accessibility ↵ . AccessibleComponent*
1.2	│ ├ JFrame.AccessibleJFrame - ┊	

java.lang.Object

1.2 ○ ├─ javax.accessibility.AccessibleContext

1.2 │ ├─ JList.AccessibleJList.AccessibleJListChild - - - - - - - - - - - - - *javax . accessibility . Accessible ,*
          javax . accessibility . AccessibleComponent

1.2 │ ├─ JPopupMenu.WindowPopup.AccessibleWindowPopup - - - - - *java.io. Serializable, javax . accessibility* ↵
          . AccessibleComponent

1.2 │ ├─ JTable.AccessibleJTable.AccessibleJTableCell - - - - - - - - - - - *javax . accessibility . Accessible ,*
          javax . accessibility . AccessibleComponent

1.2 │ ├─ JTree.AccessibleJTree.AccessibleJTreeNode - - - - - - - - - - - - *javax . accessibility . Accessible ,*
          javax . accessibility . AccessibleAction ,
          javax . accessibility . AccessibleComponent ,
          javax . accessibility . AccessibleSelection

1.2 │ └─ JWindow.AccessibleJWindow - *java.io. Serializable, javax . accessibility* ↵
          . AccessibleComponent

1.2 ○ ├─ javax.accessibility.AccessibleHyperlink - - - - - - - - - - - - - - - - - - - *javax . accessibility . AccessibleAction*

1.2 │ └─ JEditorPane.JEditorPaneAccessibleHypertextSupport ↵
        .HTMLLink

1.2 ├─ javax.swing.tree.DefaultMutableTreeNode - - - - - - - - - - - - - - - - *java.io. Serializable, java . lang . Cloneable ,*
          javax . swing . tree . MutableTreeNode

1.2 │ └─ JTree.DynamicUtilTreeNode

1.2 ├─ javax.swing.tree.DefaultTreeSelectionModel - - - - - - - - - - - - - - *java.io. Serializable, java . lang . Cloneable ,*
          javax . swing . tree . TreeSelectionModel

1.2 │ └─ JTree.EmptySelectionModel

1.2 ├─ java.lang.Throwable - *java.io. Serializable*

      └─ java.lang.Exception

1.2   └─ UnsupportedLookAndFeelException

1.2 *Action* ─── *java. awt . event . ActionListener*

1.2 *BoundedRangeModel*

1.2 *ButtonModel* ───────────────────────────────────── *java. awt . ItemSelectable*

1.2 *CellEditor*

1.2 *ComboBoxEditor*

1.2 *ComboBoxModel* ─────────────────────────────────── *ListModel*

1.2 *DesktopManager*

1.2 *Icon*

1.2 *JComboBox.KeySelectionManager*

1.2 *ListCellRenderer*

1.2 *ListModel*

1.2 *ListSelectionModel*

1.2 *MenuElement*

1.2 *MutableComboBoxModel* ─────────────────────────── *ComboBoxModel*

1.2 *Renderer*

1.2 *RootPaneContainer*

1.2 *ScrollPaneConstants*

1.2 *Scrollable*

1.2 *SingleSelectionModel*

1.2 *SwingConstants*

1.2 *UIDefaults.ActiveValue*

1.2 *UIDefaults.LazyValue*

1.2 *WindowConstants*

Packages

The Quintessential Swing User Interface

This example creates and shows a frame with a button.

```
import java.awt.*;
import javax.swing.*;

public class BasicUI {
    public static void main(String[] args) {
        JButton button = new JButton("Label");
        JFrame frame = new JFrame();

        // Add button to the frame.
        frame.getContentPane().add(button, BorderLayout.CENTER);

        // Set initial size.
        frame.setSize(300, 300);

        // Show the frame.
        frame.setVisible(true);
    }
}
```

Centering a Frame on the Screen

```
Dimension dim = Toolkit.getDefaultToolkit().getScreenSize();
int w = frame.getSize().width;
int h = frame.getSize().height;
int x = (dim.width-w)/2;
int y = (dim.height-h)/2;

frame.setBounds(x, y, w, h);
```

Exiting an Application When a Frame Is Closed

```
frame.addWindowListener(new WindowAdapter() {
    public void windowClosing(WindowEvent evt) {
        System.exit(0);
    }
});
```

Creating a Button

```
JButton button = new JButton("Label");
button.addActionListener(actionListener);
```

Creating a Checkbox Button

```
JCheckBox checkBox = new JCheckBox("Label");
checkBox.addActionListener(actionListener);

// Set the current state of the checkbox.
checkBox.setSelected(false);

// Get the current state of the checkbox.
boolean on = checkBox.isSelected();
```

Creating a Color Chooser Dialog

```
Color initialColor = Color.red;
Color newColor = JColorChooser.showDialog(frame, "Dialog Title", initialColor);
```

Creating a ComboBox

```
// A read-only combo box.
String[] items = {"item1", "item2"};
JComboBox readOnlyCB = new JComboBox(items);
readOnlyCB.addActionListener(actionListener);
```

```
// An editable combo box.
JComboBox editableCB = new JComboBox(items);
editableCB.setEditable(true);
editableCB.addActionListener(actionListener);
```

Creating a File Chooser Dialog

```
String filename = File.separator+"tmp";
JFileChooser fc = new JFileChooser(new File(filename));

// Open file dialog.
fc.showOpenDialog(frame);
openFile(fc.getSelectedFile());

// Save file dialog.
fc.showSaveDialog(frame);
saveFile(fc.getSelectedFile());
```

Displaying Only Directories in a File Chooser Dialog

```
JFileChooser fileChooser = new JFileChooser(file);
fileChooser.setFileSelectionMode(JFileChooser.DIRECTORIES_ONLY);
```

Creating an Internal Frame

```
boolean resizable = true;
boolean closeable = true;
boolean maximizable = true;
boolean iconifiable = true;
int width = 200;
int height = 50;
JInternalFrame iframe = new JInternalFrame("Title", resizable, closeable, maximizable, iconifiable);
iframe.setSize(width, height);

// Add component to internal frame.
iframe.getContentPane().add(childComponent, BorderLayout.CENTER);

// Add internal frame to desktop.
JDesktopPane desktop = new JDesktopPane();
desktop.add(iframe);
```

Creating a List

The list fires a list selection event whenever its set of selected items changes.

```
// A multiple selection list.
String[] items = {"item1", "item2"};
JList list = new JList(items);
list.addListSelectionListener(new MyListSelectionListener());

// Make the list single selection mode
list.setSelectionMode(ListSelectionModel.SINGLE_SELECTION);

class MyListSelectionListener implements ListSelectionListener {
    public void valueChanged(ListSelectionEvent evt) {
        if (!evt.getValueIsAdjusting()) {
            JList list = (JList)evt.getSource();
            Object[] selected = list.getSelectedValues();
            for (int i=0; i<selected.length; i++) {
                process(selected[i]);
            }
        }
    }
}
```

Creating a Menu Bar, Menu, and Menu Item

When the user selects a menu item, it fires an action event.

```
// Create the menu bar.
JMenuBar menuBar = new JMenuBar();

// Create a menu.
JMenu menu = new JMenu("Menu Label");
menuBar.add(menu);

// Create a menu item.
JMenuItem item = new JMenuItem("Item Label");
item.addActionListener(actionListener);
menu.add(item);

// Install the menu bar in the frame.
frame.setJMenuBar(menuBar);
```

Separating Menu Items in a Menu

```
menu.add(item1);
menu.add(new JSeparator());
menu.add(item2);
```

Creating a Popup Menu

```
final JPopupMenu menu = new JPopupMenu();

// Create and add a menu item.
JMenuItem item = new JMenuItem("Item Label");
item.addActionListener(actionListener);
menu.add(item);

// Set the component to show the popup menu.
component.addMouseListener(new MouseAdapter() {
    public void mousePressed(MouseEvent evt) {
        if (evt.isPopupTrigger()) {
            menu.show(evt.getComponent(), evt.getX(), evt.getY());
        }
    }
    public void mouseReleased(MouseEvent evt) {
        if (evt.isPopupTrigger()) {
            menu.show(evt.getComponent(), evt.getX(), evt.getY());
        }
    }
});
```

Creating a Progess Bar

```
int minimum = 0;
int maximum = 100;
JProgressBar progress = new JProgressBar(minimum, maximum);

// Change the progess bar's value.
int initValue = 50;
progress.setValue(initValue);
```

Creating Radio Buttons

```
ButtonGroup group = new ButtonGroup();

JRadioButton b1 = new JRadioButton("Label1");
b1.addActionListener(actionListener);
group.add(b1);

JRadioButton b2 = new JRadioButton("Label2");
b2.addActionListener(actionListener);
group.add(b2);

// Set one of the radio buttons on.
group.setSelected(b1.getModel(), true);
```

Creating a Scroll Pane

The Swing components do not typically have scroll bars. In order to automatically display scroll bars, you need to insert the component in a scroll pane.

```
JTextArea textArea = new JTextArea(10, 10);
JScrollPane scrollableTextArea = new JScrollPane(textArea);

JList list = new JList();
JScrollPane scrollableList = new JScrollPane(list);
```

Creating a Slider

```
int minimum = 0;
int maximum = 100;
int initValue = 50;

// A horizontal slider.
JSlider hSlider = new JSlider(JSlider.HORIZONTAL, minimum, maximum, initValue);
hSlider.addChangeListener(new MyChangeListener());

// A vertical slider.
JSlider vSlider = new JSlider(JSlider.VERTICAL, minimum, maximum, initValue);
vSlider.addChangeListener(new MyChangeListener());

class MyChangeListener implements ChangeListener {
    public void stateChanged(ChangeEvent evt) {
        JSlider slider = (JSlider)evt.getSource();

        if (!slider.getValueIsAdjusting()) {
            int value = slider.getValue();
            process(value);
        }
    }
}
```

Creating a Split Pane

```
// A left-right split pane.
JSplitPane hpane = new JSplitPane(JSplitPane.HORIZONTAL_SPLIT, leftComponent, rightComponent);

// A top-bottom split pane.
JSplitPane vpane = new JSplitPane(JSplitPane.VERTICAL_SPLIT, topComponent, bottomComponent);
```

Creating a Tabbed Pane

```
int location = JTabbedPane.TOP; // or BOTTOM, LEFT, RIGHT
JTabbedPane pane = new JTabbedPane(location);

ImageIcon icon = new ImageIcon("image.gif"); // or null;
pane.addTab("Tab Label", icon, panel, "Tool Tip Text");
```

Creating a Text Field

When the user hits RETURN, the text field fires an action event.

```
JTextField textfield = new JTextField("Initial Text");
textfield.addActionListener(new MyActionListener());

class MyActionListener implements ActionListener {
    public void actionPerformed(ActionEvent evt) {
        JTextField textfield = (JTextField)evt.getSource();
        process(textfield.getText());
    }
}
```

Creating a Password Text Field

When the user hits RETURN, the text field fires an action event.

```
JPasswordField textfield = new JPasswordField("Initial Text");
textfield.setEchoChar('#');
textfield.addActionListener(actionListener);
```

Creating a Table

A table fires change events when the contents of one of its cells is modified.

```
Object[][] cellData = {
    {"row1-col1", "row1-col2"},
    {"row2-col1", "row2-col2"}};
String[] columnNames = {"col1", "col2"};

JTable table = new JTable(cellData, columnNames);
table.getModel().addTableModelListener(new MyTableChangedListener());

// Make the table scrollable.
JScrollPane scrollPane = new JScrollPane(table);

class MyTableChangedListener implements TableModelListener {
    public void tableChanged(TableModelEvent evt) {
        int row = evt.getFirstRow();
        int column = evt.getColumn();
        Object data = ((TableModel)evt.getSource()).getValueAt(row, column);

        process(data);
    }
}
```

Creating a Text Area

The text area fires a document event whenever the text changes or some style on the text changes.

```
JTextArea textArea = new JTextArea("Line1\nLine2");
textArea.getDocument().addDocumentListener(new MyDocumentListener());

class MyDocumentListener implements DocumentListener {
    public void insertUpdate(DocumentEvent evt) {
        // Some text was inserted.
    }
    public void removeUpdate(DocumentEvent evt) {
        // Some text was inserted.
    }
    public void changedUpdate(DocumentEvent evt) {
        // The style of some text was changed.
    }
}
```

Displaying Simple HTML Files

```
try {
    String url = "http://java.sun.com";
    JEditorPane editorPane = new JEditorPane(url);
    editorPane.setEditable(false);

    JFrame frame = new JFrame();
    frame.getContentPane().add(editorPane, BorderLayout.CENTER);
    frame.setSize(width, height);
    frame.setVisible(true);
} catch (IOException e) {
}
```

Creating a Toolbar

This example adds an image button to the toolbar.

```
ImageIcon icon = new ImageIcon("image.gif");
JButton button = new JButton(icon);
button.addActionListener(actionListener);
```

```
JToolBar toolbar = new JToolBar();
toolbar.add(button);
```

Creating a Borderless Window

```
JWindow window = new JWindow();

// Add component to the window.
window.getContentPane().add(component, BorderLayout.CENTER);

// Set initial size.
window.setSize(300, 300);

// Show the window.
window.setVisible(true);
```

Showing a Dialog Box

```
// Modal dialog with OK button.
JOptionPane.showMessageDialog(frame, "Line1\nLine2");

// Modal dialog with yes/no button.
int answer = JOptionPane.showConfirmDialog(frame, "Line1\nLine2");
if (answer == JOptionPane.YES_OPTION) {
    // User clicked YES.
} else if (answer == JOptionPane.NO_OPTION) {
    // User clicked NO.
}

// Modal dialog with OK/cancel and a text field
String text = JOptionPane.showInputDialog(frame, "Line1\nLine2");
if (text == null) {
    // User clicked cancel
} else {
    process(text);
}
```

Setting a Tool Tip

```
component.setToolTipText("aString");
```

Laying Out Components in a Row or Column

```
// Use Y_AXIS for a vertical column.
Box box = new Box(BoxLayout.X_AXIS);
box.add(component1);
box.add(component2);
```

Separating Components in a Row or Column

```
Box box = new Box(BoxLayout.X_AXIS);

// Glue spreads the components as far apart as possible.
box.add(component1);
box.add(Box.createGlue());
box.add(component2);

// Strut spreads the components apart by a fixed distance.
int width = 10;
box.add(Box.createHorizontalStrut(width));
box.add(component3);
```

Laying Out Components in a Flow (Left-to-Right, Top-to-Bottom)

```
int align = FlowLayout.CENTER;      // or LEFT, RIGHT
JPanel panel = new JPanel(new FlowLayout(align));
```

```
panel.add(component1);
panel.add(component2);
```

Laying Out Components in a Grid

When components are added to the container, they fill the grid left-to-right, top-to-bottom.

```
int rows = 2;
int cols = 2;
JPanel panel = new JPanel(new GridLayout(rows, cols));
panel.add(component1);
panel.add(component2);
```

Laying Out Components Using Absolute Coordinates

```
JPanel panel = new JPanel(null);
component.setBounds(x, y, w, h);
panel.add(component);
```

Setting a Border

This example lists the various borders that are available.

```
component.setBorder(BorderFactory.createEmptyBorder());
component.setBorder(BorderFactory.createLineBorder(Color.black));
component.setBorder(BorderFactory.createEtchedBorder());
component.setBorder(BorderFactory.createRaisedBevelBorder());
component.setBorder(BorderFactory.createLoweredBevelBorder());

ImageIcon icon = new ImageIcon("image.gif");
component.setBorder(BorderFactory.createMatteBorder(-1, -1, -1, -1, icon));
```

Adding a Title to a Border

```
// Use default border.
TitledBorder titledBorder = BorderFactory.createTitledBorder("Title");

// Create around existing border.
titledBorder = BorderFactory.createTitledBorder(border, "Title");

// Also available: DEFAULT_JUSTIFICATION, LEFT, RIGHT
titledBorder.setTitleJustification(TitledBorder.CENTER);

// Also available: DEFAULT_POSITION, ABOVE_TOP, TOP, ABOVE_BOTTOM, BOTTOM, BELOW_BOTTOM
titledBorder.setTitlePosition(TitledBorder.BELOW_TOP);

component.setBorder(titledBorder);
```

Creating a Compound Border

```
// border1 is around border2
Border newBorder = BorderFactory.createCompoundBorder(border1, border2);
component.setBorder(newBorder);
```

Determining the Available Look and Feels

```
UIManager.LookAndFeelInfo[] info = UIManager.getInstalledLookAndFeels();
for (int i=0; i<info.length; i++) {
    String humanReadableName = info[i].getName();
    String className = info[i].getClassName();
    // The className is used with UIManager.setLookAndFeel()
}
```

Setting the Look and Feel

To change the look and feel, you need to know the class name of the new look and feel. This example changes it to the Windows look and feel.

```
try {
    UIManager.setLookAndFeel("com.sun.java.swing.plaf.windows.WindowsLookAndFeel");
} catch (InstantiationException e) {
} catch (ClassNotFoundException e) {
} catch (UnsupportedLookAndFeelException e) {
} catch (IllegalAccessException e) {
}
```

Firing Timer Events

```
// 1 second intervals.
Timer timer = new Timer(1000, new TimerActionListener());
timer.start();

class TimerActionListener implements ActionListener {
    public void actionPerformed(ActionEvent evt) {
        Timer timer = (Timer)evt.getSource();
        process();
    }
}
```

javax.swing.border

This package contains classes and interfaces for drawing specialized borders around a Swing component. You can subclass these classes to create customized borders for your components instead of using the default borders provided by the look-and-feel being used. If you want to create one of the default borders that Swing provides, used java.swing.BorderFactory.

```
java.lang.Object
1.2 ○  └ AbstractBorder ------------------------------------- Border, java.io.Serializable
1.2     ├ BevelBorder
1.2     │  └ SoftBevelBorder
1.2     ├ CompoundBorder
1.2     ├ EmptyBorder ------------------------------------- java.io.Serializable
1.2     │  └ MatteBorder
```

Packages

javax.swing.border

```
       java.lang.Object
1.2 ○    └ AbstractBorder - - - - - - - - - - - - - - - - - - - - - - - - - - - - - - Border, java.io.Serializable
1.2        ├ EtchedBorder
1.2        ├ LineBorder
1.2        └ TitledBorder

1.2    Border
```

javax.swing.colorchooser

```
       java.lang.Object
1.2      ├ ColorChooserComponentFactory
1.2      ├ DefaultColorSelectionModel - - - - - - - - - - - - - - - - - - - - - - - ColorSelectionModel, java.io.Serializable
     ○   └ java.awt.Component - - - - - - - - - - - - - - - - - - - - - - - - - - - java.awt.MenuContainer,
                                                                      java.awt.image.ImageObserver,
                                                                      java.io.Serializable

             └ java.awt.Container
1.2 ○           └ javax.swing.JComponent - - - - - - - - - - - - - - - - - - - - - - java.io.Serializable
1.2                └ javax.swing.JPanel - - - - - - - - - - - - - - - - - - - - - - javax.accessibility.Accessible
1.2 ○                 └ AbstractColorChooserPanel

1.2    ColorSelectionModel
```

javax.swing.event

This package contains event classes and corresponding event listener interfaces for events fired by Swing components.

Packages

javax.swing.event

```
       java.lang.Object
1.2 ●     ├ DocumentEvent.EventType
1.2       ├ EventListenerList - - - - - - - - - - - - - - - - - - - - - - - - - - - - - java.io.Serializable
1.2 ●     ├ HyperlinkEvent.EventType
1.2 ○     ├ InternalFrameAdapter - - - - - - - - - - - - - - - - - - - - - - - - InternalFrameListener
1.2 ○     ├ MouseInputAdapter - - - - - - - - - - - - - - - - - - - - - - - - - MouseInputListener
1.1       ├ java.beans.PropertyChangeSupport - - - - - - - - - - - - - -┐ java.io.Serializable
1.2 ●     │   └ SwingPropertyChangeSupport                              ┊
1.1 ●     └ java.util.EventObject - - - - - - - - - - - - - - - - - - - - - ┘
1.2 ○        ├ CaretEvent
1.2          ├ ChangeEvent
1.2          ├ HyperlinkEvent
1.2          ├ ListDataEvent
1.2          ├ ListSelectionEvent
1.2          ├ MenuEvent
1.2          ├ PopupMenuEvent
1.2          ├ TableColumnModelEvent
1.2          ├ TableModelEvent
1.2          ├ TreeExpansionEvent
1.2          ├ TreeModelEvent
1.2          ├ TreeSelectionEvent
1.2          ├ UndoableEditEvent
1.1 ○        └ java.awt.AWTEvent
1.2             ├ AncestorEvent
1.2             ├ InternalFrameEvent
1.1             └ java.awt.event.ComponentEvent
1.1 ○              └ java.awt.event.InputEvent
1.1                  ├ java.awt.event.KeyEvent
1.2                  │   └ MenuKeyEvent
1.1                  └ java.awt.event.MouseEvent
1.2                      └ MenuDragMouseEvent

1.2    AncestorListener ─────────────────────────────────┤ java.util.EventListener
```

java.util.EventListener

1.2	*CaretListener*	
1.2	*CellEditorListener*	
1.2	*ChangeListener*	
1.2	*DocumentEvent*	
1.2	*DocumentEvent.ElementChange*	
1.2	*DocumentListener*	
1.2	*HyperlinkListener*	
1.2	*InternalFrameListener*	
1.2	*ListDataListener*	
1.2	*ListSelectionListener*	
1.2	*MenuDragMouseListener*	
1.2	*MenuKeyListener*	
1.2	*MenuListener*	
1.2	*MouseInputListener*	*java.awt.event.MouseListener*, *java.awt.event.MouseMotionListener*
1.2	*PopupMenuListener*	*java.util.EventListener*
1.2	*TableColumnModelListener*	
1.2	*TableModelListener*	
1.2	*TreeExpansionListener*	
1.2	*TreeModelListener*	
1.2	*TreeSelectionListener*	
1.2	*TreeWillExpandListener*	
1.2	*UndoableEditListener*	

Handling Hyperlink Events

Hyperlink events are fired by a JEditorPane when the user clicks on a hyperlink.

```
try {
    String url = "http://java.sun.com";
    JEditorPane editorPane = new JEditorPane(url);
    editorPane.setEditable(false);
    editorPane.addHyperlinkListener(new MyHyperlinkListener());
} catch (IOException e) {
}

class MyHyperlinkListener implements HyperlinkListener {
    public void hyperlinkUpdate(HyperlinkEvent evt) {
        if (evt.getEventType() == HyperlinkEvent.EventType.ACTIVATED) {
            JEditorPane pane = (JEditorPane)evt.getSource();
            try {
                // Show the new page in the editor pane.
                pane.setPage(evt.getURL());
            } catch (IOException e) {
                e.printStackTrace();
            }
        }
    }
}
```

Packages

javax.swing.filechooser

PAGE

1.2 ○ **FileFilter** is used with a JFileChooser to keep unwanted files from appearing in the directory listing. 356

java.lang.Object

1.2 ○   ├ FileFilter

1.2 ○   ├ FileSystemView

1.2 ○   └ FileView

Adding a Filter to a File Chooser Dialog

This example add a filter for .java files to the file chooser.

```
JFileChooser fileChooser = new JFileChooser(new File(filename));
fileChooser.addChoosableFileFilter(new MyFilter());

// Open file dialog.
fileChooser.showOpenDialog(frame);
openFile(fileChooser.getSelectedFile());

class MyFilter extends javax.swing.filechooser.FileFilter {
    public boolean accept(File file) {
        String filename = file.getName();
        return filename.endsWith(".java");
    }
    public String getDescription() {
        return "*.java";
    }
}
```

javax.swing.plaf

This package contains one interface and many abstract classes that Swing uses to provide its pluggable look-and-feel capabilities. Its classes are subclassed and implemented by look-and-feel UIs like Basic and Metal. This package is used only by look-and-feel developers who cannot create a new look-and-feel by subclassing existing look-and-feel components.

Packages

java.lang.Object

1.2   └ BorderUIResource - *UIResource, java.io.Serializable,*
                                                             javax . swing . border . Border

1.2 ○ └ ComponentUI

1.2 ○   └ ButtonUI

1.2 ○   └ MenuItemUI

javax.swing.plaf

java.lang.Object

1.2 ○	ComponentUI	
1.2 ○	ColorChooserUI	
1.2 ○	ComboBoxUI	
1.2 ○	DesktopIconUI	
1.2 ○	DesktopPaneUI	
1.2 ○	FileChooserUI	
1.2 ○	InternalFrameUI	
1.2 ○	LabelUI	
1.2 ○	ListUI	
1.2 ○	MenuBarUI	
1.2 ○	OptionPaneUI	
1.2 ○	PanelUI	
1.2 ○	PopupMenuUI	
1.2 ○	ProgressBarUI	
1.2 ○	ScrollBarUI	
1.2 ○	ScrollPaneUI	
1.2 ○	SeparatorUI	
1.2 ○	SliderUI	
1.2 ○	SplitPaneUI	
1.2 ○	TabbedPaneUI	
1.2 ○	TableHeaderUI	
1.2 ○	TableUI	
1.2 ○	TextUI	
1.2 ○	ToolBarUI	
1.2 ○	ToolTipUI	
1.2 ○	TreeUI	
1.2 ○	ViewportUI	

1.2 IconUIResource - *UIResource*, *java.io.Serializable*,
javax.swing.Icon

1.2 java.awt.Color - *java.awt.Paint*, *java.io.Serializable*
1.2 └ ColorUIResource - *UIResource*

1.2 java.awt.Font - *java.io.Serializable*
1.2 └ FontUIResource - *UIResource*

1.2 java.awt.Insets - *java.io.Serializable*, *java.lang.Cloneable*
1.2 └ InsetsUIResource - *UIResource*

1.2 ○ java.awt.geom.Dimension2D - *java.lang.Cloneable*
1.2 └ java.awt.Dimension - *java.io.Serializable*
1.2 └ DimensionUIResource - - - - - - - - - - - - - - - - - - - *UIResource*

1.2 ○ javax.swing.border.AbstractBorder - - - - - - - - - - - - - - - - - - *java.io.Serializable*, *javax.swing.border.Border*
1.2 javax.swing.border.BevelBorder
1.2 └ BorderUIResource.BevelBorderUIResource - - - - - - - - - - - *UIResource*
1.2 javax.swing.border.CompoundBorder
1.2 └ BorderUIResource.CompoundBorderUIResource - - - - -
1.2 javax.swing.border.EmptyBorder - - - - - - - - - - - - - - - - - *java.io.Serializable*
1.2 BorderUIResource.EmptyBorderUIResource - - - - - - - - - - *UIResource*
1.2 javax.swing.border.MatteBorder
1.2 └ BorderUIResource.MatteBorderUIResource - - - - - - -
1.2 javax.swing.border.EtchedBorder
1.2 └ BorderUIResource.EtchedBorderUIResource - - - - - - - - -

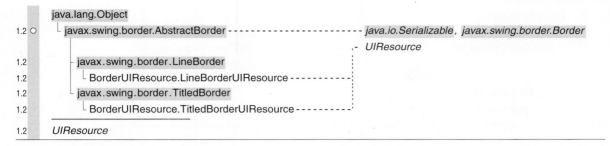

```
        java.lang.Object
1.2 ○      └ javax.swing.border.AbstractBorder - - - - - - - - - - - - - - - - - - - - - java.io.Serializable,  javax.swing.border.Border
                                                                            ┌ UIResource
1.2           ┌ javax.swing.border.LineBorder
1.2           │  └ BorderUIResource.LineBorderUIResource - - - - - - - - - - ┤
1.2           └ javax.swing.border.TitledBorder
1.2              └ BorderUIResource.TitledBorderUIResource - - - - - - - - - ┘

1.2     UIResource
```

javax.swing.table

This package contains classes and interfaces for dealing with javax.swing.JTable. You use these classes and interfaces if you want control over how tables are constructed, updated, and rendered, as well as how data associated with the tables are viewed and managed.

```
        java.lang.Object
1.2 ○    ┌ AbstractTableModel - - - - - - - - - - - - - - - - - - - - - - - TableModel, java.io.Serializable
1.2      │  └ DefaultTableModel - - - - - - - - - - - - - - - - - - - - - - java.io.Serializable
1.2      └ DefaultTableColumnModel - - - - - - - - - - - - - - - - - - - - TableColumnModel, java.beans ↵
                                                                          .PropertyChangeListener,
                                                                          java.io.Serializable, javax.swing.event ↵
                                                                          .ListSelectionListener
```

javax.swing.table

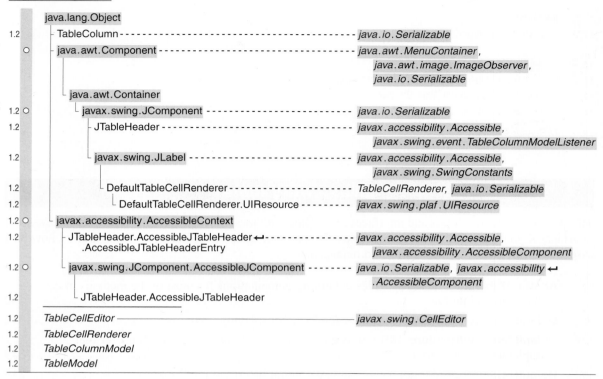

		java.lang.Object
1.2		└─ TableColumn - *java.io.Serializable*
	○	└─ java.awt.Component - *java.awt.MenuContainer,*
		java.awt.image.ImageObserver,
		java.io.Serializable
		└─ java.awt.Container
1.2	○	└─ javax.swing.JComponent - *java.io.Serializable*
1.2		└─ JTableHeader - *javax.accessibility.Accessible,*
		javax.swing.event.TableColumnModelListener
1.2		└─ javax.swing.JLabel - - - - - - - - - - - - - - - - - - *javax.accessibility.Accessible,*
		javax.swing.SwingConstants
1.2		└─ DefaultTableCellRenderer - - - - - - - - - - - - - - - - *TableCellRenderer, java.io.Serializable*
1.2		└─ DefaultTableCellRenderer.UIResource - - - - - - - - - *javax.swing.plaf.UIResource*
1.2	○	└─ javax.accessibility.AccessibleContext
1.2		├─ JTableHeader.AccessibleJTableHeader ↵ - - - - - - - - - - - *javax.accessibility.Accessible,*
		.AccessibleJTableHeaderEntry *javax.accessibility.AccessibleComponent*
1.2	○	└─ javax.swing.JComponent.AccessibleJComponent - - - - - - - *java.io.Serializable, javax.accessibility ↵*
		.AccessibleComponent
1.2		└─ JTableHeader.AccessibleJTableHeader
1.2		*TableCellEditor* ─────────────────────── *javax.swing.CellEditor*
1.2		*TableCellRenderer*
1.2		*TableColumnModel*
1.2		*TableModel*

javax.swing.text

This package contains classes and interfaces that deal with editable and noneditable text components. Examples of text components are text fields and text areas, of which password fields and document editors are special instantiations. Features that are supported by this package include selection/highlighting, editing, style, and key mapping.

Packages

java.lang.Object

1.2 ○   AbstractDocument - *Document, java.io.Serializable*

1.2   DefaultStyledDocument - *StyledDocument*

1.2   PlainDocument

1.2 ○   AbstractDocument.AbstractElement - - - - - - - - - - - - - - - - - *Element, MutableAttributeSet, java.io ↵*
                                                  .Serializable, javax.swing.tree.TreeNode

1.2   AbstractDocument.BranchElement

1.2   DefaultStyledDocument.SectionElement

1.2   AbstractDocument.LeafElement

1.2 ○   AbstractWriter

1.2   DefaultStyledDocument.ElementBuffer - - - - - - - - - - - - - - - - - - - *java.io.Serializable*

1.2   DefaultStyledDocument.ElementSpec

1.2 ○   EditorKit - *java.io.Serializable, java.lang.Cloneable*

1.2   DefaultEditorKit

1.2   StyledEditorKit

1.2   ElementIterator - *java.lang.Cloneable*

1.2   JTextComponent.KeyBinding

1.2 ○   LayeredHighlighter - *Highlighter*

1.2   DefaultHighlighter

1.2 ○   LayeredHighlighter.LayerPainter - *Highlighter.HighlightPainter*

1.2   DefaultHighlighter.DefaultHighlightPainter

1.2 ●   Position.Bias

1.2   Segment

1.2   SimpleAttributeSet - *MutableAttributeSet, java.io.Serializable,*
                                                  java.lang.Cloneable

1.2 ●   StringContent - *AbstractDocument.Content, java.io.Serializable*

1.2   StyleConstants

1.2   StyleConstants.CharacterConstants - - - - - - - - - - - - - - - - - - *AttributeSet.CharacterAttribute*

1.2   StyleConstants.ColorConstants - *AttributeSet.CharacterAttribute,*
                                                  AttributeSet.ColorAttribute

1.2   StyleConstants.FontConstants - *AttributeSet.CharacterAttribute,*
                                                  AttributeSet.FontAttribute

1.2   StyleConstants.ParagraphConstants - - - - - - - - - - - - - - - - - - *AttributeSet.ParagraphAttribute*

1.2   StyleContext - *AbstractDocument.AttributeContext,*
                                                  java.io.Serializable

1.2   StyleContext.NamedStyle - *Style, java.io.Serializable*

1.2   StyleContext.SmallAttributeSet - *AttributeSet*

1.2   TabSet - *java.io.Serializable*

1.2   TabStop -

1.2   Utilities

java.lang.Object

1.2 ○	├ View -	*javax . swing . SwingConstants*
1.2	├ ComponentView	
1.2 ○	├ CompositeView	
1.2	│ └ BoxView	
1.2	│ ├ ParagraphView -	*TabExpander*
1.2 ○	│ ├ TableView	
1.2	│ ├ TableView.TableCell	
1.2	│ ├ TableView.TableRow	
1.2	│ └ WrappedPlainView - - - - - - - - - - - - -	
1.2	├ IconView	
1.2	├ LabelView	
1.2	└ PlainView -	
1.2	│ └ FieldView	
1.2	│ └ PasswordView	
○	├ java.awt.Component -	*java.awt . MenuContainer ,*
		java.awt . image . ImageObserver ,
		java.io. Serializable
	│ └ java.awt.Container	
1.2 ○	│ └ javax.swing.JComponent -	*java.io. Serializable*
1.2 ○	│ └ JTextComponent -	*javax . accessibility . Accessible ,*
		javax . swing . Scrollable
1.2 ○	├ java.awt.geom.RectangularShape - - - - - - - - - - - - - - - - - - -	*java.awt . Shape , java.lang . Cloneable*
1.2 ○	│ └ java.awt.geom.Rectangle2D	
	│ └ java.awt.Rectangle -	*java.awt . Shape , java.io. Serializable*
1.2	│ └ DefaultCaret -	*Caret, java.awt . event . FocusListener ,*
		java.awt . event . MouseListener ,
		java.awt . event . MouseMotionListener
1.2 ○	├ javax.accessibility.AccessibleContext	
1.2 ○	│ └ javax . swing . JComponent . AccessibleJComponent - - - - - - - -	*java.io. Serializable , javax . accessibility* ↩
		. AccessibleComponent
1.2	│ └ JTextComponent.AccessibleJTextComponent - - - - - - - - - -	*javax . accessibility . AccessibleText ,*
		javax . swing . event . CaretListener ,
		javax . swing . event . DocumentListener
1.2 ○	├ javax . swing . AbstractAction -	*java.io. Serializable , java.lang . Cloneable ,*
		javax . swing . Action
1.2 ○	└ TextAction	
1.2	├ DefaultEditorKit.BeepAction	
1.2	├ DefaultEditorKit.CopyAction	
1.2	├ DefaultEditorKit.CutAction	
1.2	├ DefaultEditorKit.DefaultKeyTypedAction	
1.2	├ DefaultEditorKit.InsertBreakAction	
1.2	├ DefaultEditorKit.InsertContentAction	
1.2	├ DefaultEditorKit.InsertTabAction	
1.2	├ DefaultEditorKit.PasteAction	
1.2 ○	└ StyledEditorKit.StyledTextAction	
1.2	├ StyledEditorKit.AlignmentAction	
1.2	├ StyledEditorKit.BoldAction	
1.2	├ StyledEditorKit.FontFamilyAction	
1.2	├ StyledEditorKit.FontSizeAction	

Packages

javax.swing.text

java.lang.Object
- 1.2 ○   javax.swing.AbstractAction - *java.io.Serializable*, *java.lang.Cloneable*, *javax.swing.Action*

     1.2 ○   └ TextAction
     1.2 ○   └ StyledEditorKit.StyledTextAction
     1.2   ⊢ StyledEditorKit.ForegroundAction
     1.2   ⊢ StyledEditorKit.ItalicAction
     1.2   └ StyledEditorKit.UnderlineAction
- 1.2 ○   javax.swing.plaf.ComponentUI
     1.2 ○   └ javax.swing.plaf.TextUI
     1.2 ○   └ javax.swing.plaf.basic.BasicTextUI - - - - - - - - - - - - - - - - - - *ViewFactory*
     1.2 ○   └ DefaultTextUI
- 1.2   javax.swing.undo.AbstractUndoableEdit - - - - - - - - - - - - - - - - - - *java.io.Serializable*, *javax.swing.undo* ↩ *.UndoableEdit*
     1.2   ⊢ AbstractDocument.ElementEdit - *javax.swing.event.DocumentEvent* ↩ *.ElementChange*
     1.2   ⊢ DefaultStyledDocument.AttributeUndoableEdit
     1.2   └ javax.swing.undo.CompoundEdit
     1.2   └ AbstractDocument.DefaultDocumentEvent - - - - - - - - - - - - *javax.swing.event.DocumentEvent*
- 1.2   java.lang.Throwable - *java.io.Serializable*
     └ java.lang.Exception
     1.2   ⊢ BadLocationException
     └ java.io.IOException
     1.2   └ ChangedCharSetException

1.2	*AbstractDocument.AttributeContext*
1.2	*AbstractDocument.Content*
1.2	*AttributeSet*
1.2	*AttributeSet.CharacterAttribute*
1.2	*AttributeSet.ColorAttribute*
1.2	*AttributeSet.FontAttribute*
1.2	*AttributeSet.ParagraphAttribute*
1.2	*Caret*
1.2	*Document*
1.2	*Element*
1.2	*Highlighter*
1.2	*Highlighter.Highlight*
1.2	*Highlighter.HighlightPainter*
1.2	*Keymap*
1.2	*MutableAttributeSet* —————————————— *AttributeSet*
1.2	*Position*
1.2	*Style* ——————————————————— *MutableAttributeSet*
1.2	*StyledDocument* ————————————————— *Document*
1.2	*TabExpander*
1.2	*TabableView*
1.2	*ViewFactory*

javax.swing.text.html

This package contains the class (HTMLEditorKit) and supporting classes for creating HTML text editors.

javax.swing.text.html

```
      java.lang.Object
1.2     ├ CSS
1.2 ●   ├ CSS.Attribute
1.2     ├ HTML
1.2 ●   ├ HTML.Attribute
1.2     ├ HTML.Tag
1.2     │  └ HTML.UnknownTag - - - - - - - - - - - - - - - - - - - - - - - - - - java.io.Serializable
1.2     ├ HTMLDocument.HTMLReader.TagAction
1.2     │  ├ HTMLDocument.HTMLReader.BlockAction
1.2     │  │  ├ HTMLDocument.HTMLReader.ParagraphAction
1.2     │  │  └ HTMLDocument.HTMLReader.PreAction
1.2     │  ├ HTMLDocument.HTMLReader.CharacterAction
1.2     │  ├ HTMLDocument.HTMLReader.HiddenAction
1.2     │  ├ HTMLDocument.HTMLReader.IsindexAction
1.2     │  └ HTMLDocument.HTMLReader.SpecialAction
1.2     │     └ HTMLDocument.HTMLReader.FormAction
1.2 ○   ├ HTMLDocument.Iterator
1.2     ├ HTMLEditorKit.HTMLFactory - - - - - - - - - - - - - - - - - - - - - javax.swing.text.ViewFactory
1.2 ○   ├ HTMLEditorKit.Parser
```

	java.lang.Object
1.2	├ HTMLEditorKit.ParserCallback
1.2	│ └ HTMLDocument.HTMLReader
1.2	├ Option
1.2	├ StyleSheet.BoxPainter - *java.io.Serializable*
1.2	├ StyleSheet.ListPainter - ┘
1.1 ○	├ java.awt.event.MouseAdapter - *java.awt.event.MouseListener*
1.2	│ ├ FormView.MouseEventListener
1.2	│ └ HTMLEditorKit.LinkController - - - - - - - - - - - - - - - - - *java.io.Serializable*
1.1	├ java.util.EventObject - ┘
1.2	│ └ javax.swing.event.HyperlinkEvent
1.2	│ └ HTMLFrameHyperlinkEvent
1.2 ○	├ javax.swing.AbstractAction - *java.io.Serializable*, *java.lang.Cloneable*,
		javax.swing.Action
1.2 ○	│ └ javax.swing.text.TextAction
1.2 ○	│ └ javax.swing.text.StyledEditorKit.StyledTextAction
1.2 ○	│ └ HTMLEditorKit.HTMLTextAction
1.2	│ └ HTMLEditorKit.InsertHTMLTextAction
1.2 ○	├ javax.swing.text.AbstractDocument - - - - - - - - - - - - - - - - *java.io.Serializable*, *javax.swing.text.Document*
1.2	│ └ javax.swing.text.DefaultStyledDocument - - - - - - - - - - - - - - *javax.swing.text.StyledDocument*
1.2	│ └ HTMLDocument
1.2 ○	├ javax.swing.text.AbstractDocument.AbstractElement - - - - - - - - *java.io.Serializable*, *javax.swing.text.Element*,
		javax.swing.text.MutableAttributeSet,
		javax.swing.tree.TreeNode
1.2	│ ├ javax.swing.text.AbstractDocument.BranchElement
1.2	│ │ └ HTMLDocument.BlockElement
1.2	│ ├ javax.swing.text.AbstractDocument.LeafElement
1.2	│ │ └ HTMLDocument.RunElement
1.2 ○	├ javax.swing.text.AbstractWriter
1.2	│ ├ HTMLWriter
1.2	│ └ MinimalHTMLWriter
1.2 ○	├ javax.swing.text.EditorKit - *java.io.Serializable*, *java.lang.Cloneable*
1.2	│ └ javax.swing.text.DefaultEditorKit
1.2	│ └ javax.swing.text.StyledEditorKit
1.2	│ └ HTMLEditorKit
1.2	├ javax.swing.text.StyleContext - *java.io.Serializable*, *javax.swing.text ↵*
		.AbstractDocument.AttributeContext
1.2	│ └ StyleSheet
1.2 ○	└ javax.swing.text.View - *javax.swing.SwingConstants*
1.2	├ javax.swing.text.ComponentView
1.2	│ ├ FormView - *java.awt.event.ActionListener*
1.2	│ └ ObjectView
1.2 ○	├ javax.swing.text.CompositeView
1.2	│ └ javax.swing.text.BoxView
1.2	│ ├ BlockView
1.2	│ │ └ ListView
1.2	│ └ javax.swing.text.ParagraphView - - - - - - - - - - - - - - - - *javax.swing.text.TabExpander*
1.2	│ └ ParagraphView

Packages

javax.swing.text.html

javax.swing.text.html.parser

javax.swing.text.rtf

This package contains a class (RTFEditorKit) for creating Rich-Text-Format text editors.

```
      java.lang.Object
1.2 ○    └ javax.swing.text.EditorKit --------------------------------- java.io.Serializable,  java.lang.Cloneable
1.2        └ javax.swing.text.DefaultEditorKit
1.2           └ javax.swing.text.StyledEditorKit
1.2              └ RTFEditorKit
```

javax.swing.tree

This package contains classes and interfaces for dealing with javax.swing.JTree. You use these classes and interfaces if you want control over how trees are constructed, updated, and rendered, as well as how data associated with the tree nodes are viewed and managed.

```
      java.lang.Object
1.2 ○    ├ AbstractLayoutCache --------------------------------- RowMapper
1.2      │  ├ FixedHeightLayoutCache
1.2      │  └ VariableHeightLayoutCache
1.2 ○    ├ AbstractLayoutCache.NodeDimensions
```

Packages

javax.swing.tree

```
                 java.lang.Object
1.2                  DefaultMutableTreeNode - - - - - - - - - - - - - - - - - - - - - - - - - - - - - - - - - MutableTreeNode, java.io.Serializable,
                                                                                           java.lang.Cloneable
1.2                  DefaultTreeCellEditor - - - - - - - - - - - - - - - - - - - - - - - - - - - - - - - - - TreeCellEditor, java.awt.event.ActionListener,
                                                                                           javax.swing.event.TreeSelectionListener
1.2                  DefaultTreeModel - - - - - - - - - - - - - - - - - - - - - - - - - - - - - - - - - - - - TreeModel, java.io.Serializable
1.2                  DefaultTreeSelectionModel - - - - - - - - - - - - - - - - - - - - - - - - - - - - - - TreeSelectionModel, java.io.Serializable,
                                                                                           java.lang.Cloneable
1.2                  TreePath - - - - - - - - - - - - - - - - - - - - - - - - - - - - - - - - - - - - - - - - - - java.io.Serializable
      ○              java.awt.Component - - - - - - - - - - - - - - - - - - - - - - - - - - - - - - - - - - java.awt.MenuContainer,
                                                                                           java.awt.image.ImageObserver,
                                                                                           java.io.Serializable

                        java.awt.Container
1.2                        DefaultTreeCellEditor.EditorContainer
1.2 ○                      javax.swing.JComponent - - - - - - - - - - - - - - - - - - - - - - - - - java.io.Serializable
1.2                           javax.swing.JLabel - - - - - - - - - - - - - - - - - - - - - - - - - - - javax.accessibility.Accessible,
                                                                                           javax.swing.SwingConstants
1.2                              DefaultTreeCellRenderer - - - - - - - - - - - - - - - - - - - - - - TreeCellRenderer
1.2 ○                           javax.swing.text.JTextComponent - - - - - - - - - - - - - - - javax.accessibility.Accessible,
                                                                                           javax.swing.Scrollable
1.2                                 javax.swing.JTextField - - - - - - - - - - - - - - - - - - - - javax.swing.SwingConstants
1.2                                    DefaultTreeCellEditor.DefaultTextField
                        java.lang.Throwable - - - - - - - - - - - - - - - - - - - - - - - - - - - - - - - - java.io.Serializable
                           java.lang.Exception
1.2                           ExpandVetoException

1.2   MutableTreeNode ————————————————————————— TreeNode
1.2   RowMapper
1.2   TreeCellEditor ——————————————————————————— javax.swing.CellEditor
1.2   TreeCellRenderer
1.2   TreeModel
1.2   TreeNode
1.2   TreeSelectionModel
```

Creating a Tree

This example creates a tree component with a root node and a child of the root node. You build the tree hierarchy by adding nodes to nodes.

```
DefaultMutableTreeNode root = new DefaultMutableTreeNode("Root Label");
root.add(new DefaultMutableTreeNode("Node Label"));

JTree tree = new JTree(root);
```

Handling Selection Events in a Tree Component

This example adds a listener for selection events to a tree component.

```
tree.addTreeSelectionListener(new TreeSelectionListener() {
    public void valueChanged(TreeSelectionEvent evt) {
        DefaultMutableTreeNode node = (DefaultMutableTreeNode) (evt.getPath().getLastPathComponent());
        process(node);
    }
});
```

javax.swing.undo

This package provides support for undo/redo capabilities in an application such as a text editor. It is for developers that provide undo/redo capabilities in their application.

```
java.lang.Object
1.2   ├ AbstractUndoableEdit ------------------------------ UndoableEdit, java.io.Serializable
1.2   │  ├ CompoundEdit
1.2   │  │  └ UndoManager ------------------------------ javax.swing.event.UndoableEditListener
1.2   │  └ StateEdit
1.2   ├ UndoableEditSupport
      └ java.lang.Throwable ------------------------------ java.io.Serializable
         └ java.lang.Exception
            └ java.lang.RuntimeException
1.2            ├ CannotRedoException
1.2            └ CannotUndoException

1.2   StateEditable
1.2   UndoableEdit
```

org.omg.CORBA

This package contains classes and interfaces for use with programs that interact with CORBA services. CORBA is an object system that enables objects running on different platforms and possibly programmed using different programming languages to interoperate.

Packages

Packages

	java.lang.Object	
1.2 ○	Any	org.omg.CORBA.portable.IDLEntity
1.2 ●	AnyHolder	org.omg.CORBA.portable.Streamable
1.2 ●	BooleanHolder	
1.2 ●	ByteHolder	
1.2 ●	CharHolder	
1.2	CompletionStatus	org.omg.CORBA.portable.IDLEntity
1.2 ○	Context	
1.2 ○	ContextList	
1.2	DefinitionKind	
1.2 ●	DoubleHolder	org.omg.CORBA.portable.Streamable
1.2 ○	Environment	
1.2 ○	ExceptionList	
1.2 ●	FixedHolder	
1.2 ●	FloatHolder	
1.2 ●	IntHolder	
1.2 ●	LongHolder	
1.2 ○	NVList	
1.2 ●	NameValuePair	org.omg.CORBA.portable.IDLEntity
1.2 ○	NamedValue	
1.2 ○	ORB	
1.2 ●	ObjectHolder	org.omg.CORBA.portable.Streamable
1.2 ○	Principal	
1.2 ●	PrincipalHolder	
1.2 ○	Request	
1.2 ○	ServerRequest	
1.2 ●	ServiceDetail	org.omg.CORBA.portable.IDLEntity
1.2	ServiceDetailHelper	
1.2 ●	ServiceInformation	
1.2	ServiceInformationHelper	
1.2 ●	ServiceInformationHolder	org.omg.CORBA.portable.Streamable
1.2	SetOverrideType	org.omg.CORBA.portable.IDLEntity
1.2 ●	ShortHolder	org.omg.CORBA.portable.Streamable

Packages

org.omg.CORBA

	java.lang.Object	- *org.omg.CORBA.portable.Streamable*
1.2 ●	StringHolder	
1.2 ●	StructMember	*org . omg . CORBA . portable . IDLEntity*
1.2	TCKind	
1.2 ○	TypeCode	
1.2 ●	TypeCodeHolder	- *org . omg . CORBA . portable . Streamable*
1.2 ●	UnionMember	- *org . omg . CORBA . portable . IDLEntity*
1.2 ●	ValueMember	- -
1.2 ○	org.omg.CORBA.portable.ObjectImpl - *Object*
1.2 ○	└ DynamicImplementation	
	java.lang.Throwable - *java.io.Serializable*
	└ java.lang.Exception	
1.2 ○	UserException - *org . omg . CORBA . portable . IDLEntity*
1.2 ●	Bounds	
1.2 ●	PolicyError	
1.2 ●	UnknownUserException	
1.2	└ WrongTransaction	
	└ java.lang.RuntimeException	
1.2 ○	└ SystemException	
1.2 ●	BAD_CONTEXT	
1.2 ●	BAD_INV_ORDER	
1.2 ●	BAD_OPERATION	
1.2 ●	BAD_PARAM	
1.2 ●	BAD_TYPECODE	
1.2 ●	COMM_FAILURE	
1.2 ●	DATA_CONVERSION	
1.2 ●	FREE_MEM	
1.2 ●	IMP_LIMIT	
1.2 ●	INITIALIZE	
1.2 ●	INTERNAL	
1.2 ●	INTF_REPOS	
1.2 ●	INVALID_TRANSACTION	
1.2 ●	INV_FLAG	
1.2 ●	INV_IDENT	
1.2 ●	INV_OBJREF	
1.2	INV_POLICY	
1.2 ●	MARSHAL	
1.2 ●	NO_IMPLEMENT	
1.2 ●	NO_MEMORY	
1.2 ●	NO_PERMISSION	
1.2 ●	NO_RESOURCES	
1.2 ●	NO_RESPONSE	
1.2 ●	OBJECT_NOT_EXIST	
1.2 ●	OBJ_ADAPTER	
1.2 ●	PERSIST_STORE	
1.2 ●	TRANSACTION_REQUIRED	
1.2 ●	TRANSACTION_ROLLEDBACK	
1.2 ●	TRANSIENT	
1.2 ●	└ UNKNOWN	
1.2	*ARG_OUT*	

1.2	*ARG_IN*	
1.2	*ARG_INOUT*	
1.2	*BAD_POLICY*	
1.2	*BAD_POLICY_TYPE*	
1.2	*BAD_POLICY_VALUE*	
1.2	*CTX_RESTRICT_SCOPE*	
1.2	*Current* ——————————————	*Object*
1.2	*DomainManager* ———————————	
1.2	*DynAny*	
1.2	*DynArray* ————————————————	*DynAny, Object*
1.2	*DynEnum*	
1.2	*DynFixed*	
1.2	*DynSequence*	
1.2	*DynStruct*	
1.2	*DynUnion*	
1.2	*DynValue*	
1.2	*IDLType* —————————————————	*IRObject, Object,* org.omg.CORBA.portable ↩ .IDLEntity
1.2	*IRObject* ————————————————	*Object,* org.omg.CORBA.portable.IDLEntity
1.2	*Object*	
1.2	*PRIVATE_MEMBER*	
1.2	*PUBLIC_MEMBER*	
1.2	*Policy* ————————————————————	*Object*
1.2	*UNSUPPORTED_POLICY*	
1.2	*UNSUPPORTED_POLICY_VALUE*	
1.2	*VM_ABSTRACT*	
1.2	*VM_CUSTOM*	
1.2	*VM_NONE*	
1.2	*VM_TRUNCATABLE*	

org.omg.CORBA.DynAnyPackage

PAGE

```
java.lang.Object
  └ java.lang.Throwable ----------------------------------- java.io.Serializable
      └ java.lang.Exception
1.2 ○       └ org.omg.CORBA.UserException -------------------- org.omg.CORBA.portable.IDLEntity
1.2 ●           ├ Invalid
1.2 ●           ├ InvalidSeq
1.2 ●           ├ InvalidValue
```

Packages

org.omg.CORBA.DynAnyPackage

```
java.lang.Object
  └ java.lang.Throwable - - - - - - - - - - - - - - - - - - - - - - - - - - - - - - - - java.io.Serializable
      └ java.lang.Exception
1.2 ○      └ org.omg.CORBA.UserException - - - - - - - - - - - - - - - - - org.omg.CORBA.portable.IDLEntity
1.2 ●          └ TypeMismatch
```

org.omg.CORBA.ORBPackage

This package contains a class for the CORBA InvalidName exception, which can be thrown by the ORB.resolve_initial_references() method.

```
java.lang.Object
  └ java.lang.Throwable - - - - - - - - - - - - - - - - - - - - - - - - - - - - - - - - java.io.Serializable
      └ java.lang.Exception
1.2 ○      └ org.omg.CORBA.UserException - - - - - - - - - - - - - - - - - org.omg.CORBA.portable.IDLEntity
1.2 ●          ├ InconsistentTypeCode
1.2            └ InvalidName
```

org.omg.CORBA.TypeCodePackage

This package contains classes for the CORBA exceptions that can be thrown by the CORBA TypeCode operations.

```
java.lang.Object
  └ java.lang.Throwable - - - - - - - - - - - - - - - - - - - - - - - - - - - - - - - - java.io.Serializable
      └ java.lang.Exception
1.2 ○      └ org.omg.CORBA.UserException - - - - - - - - - - - - - - - - - org.omg.CORBA.portable.IDLEntity
1.2 ●          ├ BadKind
1.2 ●          └ Bounds
```

org.omg.CORBA.portable

This package contains classes and interfaces for developing ORB implementations.

```
     java.lang.Object
1.2 ○   ├ Delegate
1.2 ○   ├ ObjectImpl------------------------------------------ org.omg.CORBA.Object
1.2     ├ ServantObject
    ○   ├ java.io.InputStream
1.2 ○   │  └ InputStream
    ○   ├ java.io.OutputStream
1.2 ○   │  └ OutputStream
        └ java.lang.Throwable-------------------------------- java.io.Serializable
             └ java.lang.Exception
1.2            ├ ApplicationException
1.2 ●          └ RemarshalException

1.2    InvokeHandler
1.2    IDLEntity------------------------------------ java.io.Serializable
1.2    ResponseHandler
1.2    Streamable
```

org.omg.CosNaming

This package contains classes and interfaces for communicating with the COS naming server. The COS naming server provides a mapping of hierarchical names to CORBA object references.

Packages

org.omg.CosNaming

	java.lang.Object	
1.2 ●	├ Binding	*org.omg.CORBA.portable.IDLEntity*
1.2	├ BindingHelper	
1.2 ●	├ BindingHolder	*org.omg.CORBA.portable.Streamable*
1.2	├ BindingIteratorHelper	
1.2 ●	├ BindingIteratorHolder	
1.2	├ BindingListHelper	
1.2 ●	├ BindingListHolder	
1.2 ●	├ BindingType	*org.omg.CORBA.portable.IDLEntity*
1.2	├ BindingTypeHelper	
1.2 ●	├ BindingTypeHolder	*org.omg.CORBA.portable.Streamable*
1.2	├ IstringHelper	
1.2 ●	├ NameComponent	*org.omg.CORBA.portable.IDLEntity*
1.2	├ NameComponentHelper	
1.2 ●	├ NameComponentHolder	*org.omg.CORBA.portable.Streamable*
1.2	├ NameHelper	
1.2 ●	├ NameHolder	
1.2	├ NamingContextHelper	
1.2 ●	├ NamingContextHolder	
1.2 ○	└ org.omg.CORBA.portable.ObjectImpl	*org.omg.CORBA.Object*
1.2	├ _BindingIteratorStub	*BindingIterator*
1.2	├ _NamingContextStub	*NamingContext*
1.2 ○	└ org.omg.CORBA.DynamicImplementation	
1.2 ○	├ _BindingIteratorImplBase	*BindingIterator*
1.2 ○	└ _NamingContextImplBase	*NamingContext*
1.2	*BindingIterator*	*org.omg.CORBA.Object*, *org.omg.CORBA.portable.IDLEntity*
1.2	*NamingContext*	

org.omg.CosNaming.NamingContextPackage

This package contains helper and holder classes for CORBA exceptions that can be thrown by the COS naming server.

```
java.lang.Object
1.2      ├ AlreadyBoundHelper
1.2 ●    ├ AlreadyBoundHolder  - - - - - - - - - - - - - - - - - - - - - - -   org.omg.CORBA.portable.Streamable
1.2      ├ CannotProceedHelper
1.2 ●    ├ CannotProceedHolder  - - - - - - - - - - - - - - - -
1.2      ├ InvalidNameHelper
1.2 ●    ├ InvalidNameHolder  - - - - - - - - - - - - - - - - -
1.2      ├ NotEmptyHelper
1.2 ●    ├ NotEmptyHolder  - - - - - - - - - - - - - - - - - - -
1.2      ├ NotFoundHelper
1.2 ●    ├ NotFoundHolder  - - - - - - - - - - - - - - - - - - -
1.2 ●    ├ NotFoundReason  - - - - - - - - - - - - - - - - - - - - - - - - -   org.omg.CORBA.portable.IDLEntity
1.2      ├ NotFoundReasonHelper
1.2 ●    ├ NotFoundReasonHolder  - - - - - - - - - - - - - - - - - - - - - -   org.omg.CORBA.portable.Streamable
1.2      └ java.lang.Throwable  - - - - - - - - - - - - - - - - - - - - - - -   java.io.Serializable
1.2         └ java.lang.Exception
1.2 ○          └ org.omg.CORBA.UserException  - - - - - - - - - - - - - - - -   org.omg.CORBA.portable.IDLEntity
1.2 ●             ├ AlreadyBound  - - - - - - - - - - - - - - - - - - - - -
1.2 ●             ├ CannotProceed  - - - - - - - - - - - - - - - - - - - - -
1.2 ●             ├ InvalidName  - - - - - - - - - - - - - - - - - - - - - -
1.2 ●             ├ NotEmpty  - - - - - - - - - - - - - - - - - - - - - - -
```

Packages

165

org.omg.CosNaming.NamingContextPackage

```
     java.lang.Object
        └ java.lang.Throwable - - - - - - - - - - - - - - - - - - - - - - - - - - - java.io.Serializable
           └ java.lang.Exception
1.2 ○         └ org.omg.CORBA.UserException - - - - - - - - - - - - - - org.omg.CORBA.portable.IDLEntity
1.2 ●            └ NotFound - - - - - - - - - - - - - - - - - - - - - - - -
```

Part 2
CLASSES

This part contains information about each class in every package. For easy lookup, the classes are arranged alphabetically by class name without regard to package. The following legend describes the layout of the class information.

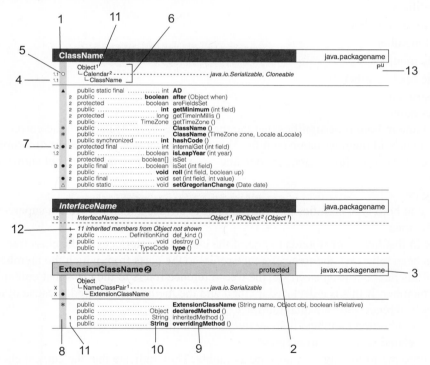

1. The class or interface name (interface names are italicized)
2. Class modifiers
   Currently, only the modifier "protected" can appear in this space.
3. Package name
   The name of the package that contains this class or interface
4. The version of Java in which this class or interface was introduced
   You need the specified version of Java or higher in order to use the class. If the field is blank, the class or interface was introduced in Java 1.0.

5. A symbolic representation of a class's modifier set:
   - ○ An abstract class
   - ● A final class
6. The class tree
   If the current entity is a class, the class tree shows the superclasses of the current class. Also shown are the interfaces that each class implements, if any. If the current entity is an interface, the class tree shows all of the interfaces from which the current interface extends, if any.
   A solid line means "extends" and a dotted line means "implements."
7. The version of Java in which this member was introduced
   You need the specified version of Java or higher in order to use the member. If the field is blank, the version is the same as that of the current class or interface. If the field contains a D, the member has been deprecated.
8. A symbolic representation of a member's modifier set, which is used to quickly locate members by their modifiers:
   - ○ An abstract member
   - ● A final member
   - △ A static member
   - ▲ A static final member
   - * A constructor
9. The member name
   A member name in bold type signifies that the member has been declared in the current class or interface. A non-bold member name signifies that the member was inherited from a superclass. Inherited members from `java.lang.Object` and `java.lang.Throwable` are not shown (in order to save space).
10. The return type
    A return type in bold type signifies that the member overrides a member from a superclass.
11. The tree-reference
    The number in this field corresponds to one of the classes or interfaces in the class tree. If this member has been inherited, the tree-reference refers to the class from which the member was inherited. If this member is an override, the tree-reference refers to the class that contains the overridden member. If this is a declared method and the method is required because of an interface, the tree-reference shows which interface.
12. The number of inherited members that are not shown in the member list
13. Any tags associated with the current class
    At present, only the following four tags are available. They indicate that the current class is part of the PersonalJava platform.
    P   A required class
    P[o]   An optional class
    P[m]   A modified class
    P[u]   An unsupported class
    For more details, see *http://java.sun.com/products/personaljava/*.

Note: For types appearing in a method's or constructor's signature, unless the type is from the same package or from the `java.lang` package, it is qualified with its package name.

Legend

A legend appears on all left-hand pages to remind you of the meanings of the symbols. Here are the symbols shown in the legend:

Class	Class names are not italicized
Interface	Interface names are italicized
○	An abstract member or class
●	A final member
△	A static member
▲	A static final member
*	A constructor
----	Implements
——	Extends
x x	Inherited
x **x**	Declared
x x	Overridden

The x x's represent the pattern of light and bold type for the return type and member name. Spelled out, this pattern is:

return type	member name	Inherited
return type	**member name**	Declared
return type	**member name**	Overridden

_BindingIteratorImplBase	org.omg.CosNaming

```
        Object
1.2 ○  └─org.omg.CORBA.portable.ObjectImpl 1 - - - - - - org.omg.CORBA.Object
1.2 ○     └─org.omg.CORBA.DynamicImplementation 2
1.2 ○        └─_BindingIteratorImplBase - - - - - - - - - - - - BindingIterator 3 (org.omg.CORBA.Object,
                                                    org.omg.CORBA.portable.IDLEntity (java.io.Serializable))
```

	1	*25 inherited members from org.omg.CORBA.portable.ObjectImpl not shown*
∗		public............................ **_BindingIteratorImplBase** ()
	1	public................. **String[]** **_ids** ()
○	3	public abstract.............void **destroy** ()
	2	public..................... **void** **invoke** (org.omg.CORBA.ServerRequest r)
○	3	public abstract........ boolean **next_n** (int, BindingListHolder)
○	3	public abstract........ boolean **next_one** (BindingHolder)

_BindingIteratorStub	org.omg.CosNaming

```
        Object
1.2 ○  └─org.omg.CORBA.portable.ObjectImpl 1 - - - - - - org.omg.CORBA.Object
1.2       └─_BindingIteratorStub - - - - - - - - - - - - - - - - - BindingIterator 2 (org.omg.CORBA.Object,
                                                    org.omg.CORBA.portable.IDLEntity (java.io.Serializable))
```

	1	*25 inherited members from org.omg.CORBA.portable.ObjectImpl not shown*
∗		public............................ **_BindingIteratorStub** (org.omg.CORBA.portable.Delegate d)
	1	public................. **String[]** **_ids** ()
	2	public......................void **destroy** ()
	2	public................. boolean **next_n** (int how_many, BindingListHolder bl)
	2	public................. boolean **next_one** (BindingHolder b)

_NamingContextImplBase	org.omg.CosNaming

```
        Object
1.2 ○  └─org.omg.CORBA.portable.ObjectImpl 1 - - - - - - org.omg.CORBA.Object
1.2 ○     └─org.omg.CORBA.DynamicImplementation 2
1.2 ○        └─_NamingContextImplBase - - - - - - - - - - - NamingContext 3 (org.omg.CORBA.Object,
                                                    org.omg.CORBA.portable.IDLEntity (java.io.Serializable))
```

	1	*25 inherited members from org.omg.CORBA.portable.ObjectImpl not shown*
	1	public................. **String[]** **_ids** ()
∗		public............................ **_NamingContextImplBase** ()
○	3	public abstract.............void **bind** (NameComponent[], *org. omg. CORBA. Object*)
		throws org. omg. CosNaming. NamingContextPackage. NotFound
		org. omg. CosNaming. NamingContextPackage. CannotProceed
		org. omg. CosNaming. NamingContextPackage. InvalidName
		org.omg.CosNaming.NamingContextPackage.AlreadyBound
○	3	public abstract.............void **bind_context** (NameComponent[], *NamingContext*)
		throws org. omg. CosNaming. NamingContextPackage. NotFound
		org. omg. CosNaming. NamingContextPackage. CannotProceed
		org. omg. CosNaming. NamingContextPackage. InvalidName
		org.omg.CosNaming.NamingContextPackage.AlreadyBound
○	3	public abstract *NamingContext* **bind_new_context** (NameComponent[]) throws org. omg ↵
		. CosNaming. NamingContextPackage. NotFound
		org. omg. CosNaming. NamingContextPackage. AlreadyBound
		org. omg. CosNaming. NamingContextPackage. CannotProceed
		org.omg.CosNaming.NamingContextPackage.InvalidName
○	3	public abstract.............void **destroy** () throws org.omg.CosNaming.NamingContextPackage.NotEmpty
	2	public..................... **void** **invoke** (org.omg.CORBA.ServerRequest r)
○	3	public abstract.............void **list** (int, BindingListHolder, BindingIteratorHolder)
○	3	public abstract *NamingContext* **new_context** ()
○	3	public abstract.............void **rebind** (NameComponent[], *org. omg. CORBA. Object*)
		throws org. omg. CosNaming. NamingContextPackage. NotFound
		org. omg. CosNaming. NamingContextPackage. CannotProceed
		org.omg.CosNaming.NamingContextPackage.InvalidName
○	3	public abstract.............void **rebind_context** (NameComponent[], *NamingContext*)
		throws org. omg. CosNaming. NamingContextPackage. NotFound
		org. omg. CosNaming. NamingContextPackage. CannotProceed
		org.omg.CosNaming.NamingContextPackage.InvalidName

Class *Interface* —extends - - -implements ○ abstract ● final △ static ▲ static final ∗ constructor x x—inherited x **x**—declared **x x**—overridden

O	3	public abstract . . . . *. . . . . . . org.omg.CORBA.Object*	**resolve** (NameComponent[]) throws org. omg. CosNaming ↵ . NamingContextPackage. NotFound org. omg ↵ . CosNaming. NamingContextPackage. CannotProceed org.omg.CosNaming.NamingContextPackage.InvalidName
O	3	public abstract . . . . void	**unbind** (NameComponent[]) throws org. omg. CosNaming ↵ . NamingContextPackage. NotFound org. omg ↵ . CosNaming. NamingContextPackage. CannotProceed org.omg.CosNaming.NamingContextPackage.InvalidName

---

_NamingContextStub   org.omg.CosNaming

Object
1.2 O	└org.omg.CORBA.portable.ObjectImpl [1] - - - - - - *org.omg.CORBA.Object*
1.2	└_NamingContextStub - - - - - - - - - - - - - - - - - *NamingContext* [2] (*org.omg.CORBA.Object*, *org.omg.CORBA.portable.IDLEntity* (*java.io.Serializable*))

	1	*25 inherited members from org.omg.CORBA.portable.ObjectImpl not shown*	
	1	public . . . . **String[]**	**_ids** ()
*		public	**_NamingContextStub** (org.omg.CORBA.portable.Delegate d)
	2	public . . . . void	**bind** (NameComponent[] n, *org. omg. CORBA. Object* obj) throws org. omg. CosNaming. NamingContextPackage. NotFound, org. omg. CosNaming. NamingContextPackage. CannotProceed, org. omg. CosNaming. NamingContextPackage. InvalidName, org.omg.CosNaming.NamingContextPackage.AlreadyBound
	2	public . . . . void	**bind_context** (NameComponent[] n, *NamingContext* nc) throws org. omg. CosNaming. NamingContextPackage. NotFound, org. omg. CosNaming. NamingContextPackage. CannotProceed, org. omg. CosNaming. NamingContextPackage. InvalidName, org.omg.CosNaming.NamingContextPackage.AlreadyBound
	2	public . . . . *NamingContext*	**bind_new_context** (NameComponent[] n) throws org. omg. CosNaming. NamingContextPackage. NotFound, org. omg. CosNaming. NamingContextPackage. AlreadyBound, org. omg. CosNaming. NamingContextPackage. CannotProceed, org.omg.CosNaming.NamingContextPackage.InvalidName
	2	public . . . . void	**destroy** () throws org.omg.CosNaming.NamingContextPackage.NotEmpty
	2	public . . . . void	**list** (int how_many, BindingListHolder bl, BindingIteratorHolder bi)
	2	public . . . . *NamingContext*	**new_context** ()
	2	public . . . . void	**rebind** (NameComponent[] n, *org. omg. CORBA. Object* obj) throws org. omg. CosNaming. NamingContextPackage. NotFound, org. omg. CosNaming. NamingContextPackage. CannotProceed, org.omg.CosNaming.NamingContextPackage.InvalidName
	2	public . . . . void	**rebind_context** (NameComponent[] n, *NamingContext* nc) throws org. omg. CosNaming. NamingContextPackage. NotFound, org. omg. CosNaming. NamingContextPackage. CannotProceed, org.omg.CosNaming.NamingContextPackage.InvalidName
	2	public *org.omg.CORBA.Object*	**resolve** (NameComponent[] n) throws org. omg ↵ . CosNaming. NamingContextPackage. NotFound, org. omg. CosNaming. NamingContextPackage. CannotProceed, org.omg.CosNaming.NamingContextPackage.InvalidName
	2	public . . . . void	**unbind** (NameComponent[] n) throws org. omg ↵ . CosNaming. NamingContextPackage. NotFound, org. omg. CosNaming. NamingContextPackage. CannotProceed, org.omg.CosNaming.NamingContextPackage.InvalidName

---

AbstractAction   javax.swing

Object [1]
1.2 O	└AbstractAction - *Action* [2] (*java.awt.event.ActionListener* [3] (*java.util.EventListener*)), *Cloneable, java.io.Serializable*

*		public	**AbstractAction** ()
*		public	**AbstractAction** (String name)
*		public	**AbstractAction** (String name, *Icon* icon)
O	3	public abstract . . . . void	**actionPerformed** (java.awt.event.ActionEvent)
	2	public synchronized . . . . void	**addPropertyChangeListener** (*java.beans.PropertyChangeListener* listener)
		protected . javax.swing.event ↵ .SwingPropertyChangeSupport	**changeSupport**
	1	protected . . . . **Object**	**clone** () throws CloneNotSupportedException
		protected . . . . boolean	**enabled**

AbstractAction

	protected	. . . . void	**firePropertyChange** (String propertyName, Object oldValue, Object newValue)
2	public	. . . . Object	**getValue** (String key)
2	public	. . . . boolean	**isEnabled** ()
2	public synchronized	. . . . . . void	**putValue** (String key, Object newValue)
2	public synchronized	. . . . . . void	**removePropertyChangeListener** (*java.beans.PropertyChangeListener* listener)
2	public synchronized	. . . . . . void	**setEnabled** (boolean newValue)

AbstractBorder   javax.swing.border

Object
1.2 ○ └AbstractBorder - *Border* [1], *java.io.Serializable*

✳	public	. . . .	**AbstractBorder** ()
1	public	. . . . java.awt.Insets	**getBorderInsets** (java.awt.Component c)
	public	. . . . java.awt.Insets	**getBorderInsets** (java.awt.Component c, java.awt.Insets insets)
	public	. . . . . . java.awt.Rectangle	**getInteriorRectangle** (java.awt.Component c, int x, int y, int width, int height)
△	public static	. . . . java.awt.Rectangle	**getInteriorRectangle** (java.awt.Component c, *Border* b, int x, int y, int width, int height)
1	public	. . . . boolean	**isBorderOpaque** ()
1	public	. . . . void	**paintBorder** (java.awt.Component c, java.awt.Graphics g, int x, int y, int width, int height)

AbstractButton   javax.swing

Object
○ └java.awt.Component [1] - *java.awt.image.ImageObserver*, *java.awt.MenuContainer*, *java.io.Serializable*
    └java.awt.Container [2]
1.2 ○   └JComponent [3] - *java.io.Serializable*
1.2 ○   └AbstractButton - - - - - - - - - - - - - - - - - - - *java.awt.ItemSelectable* [4], *SwingConstants*

1	*111 inherited members from java.awt.Component not shown*		
2	*39 inherited members from java.awt.Container not shown*		
3	*113 inherited members from JComponent not shown*		
✳	public	. . . .	**AbstractButton** ()
	protected	. . . . *java.awt.event.ActionListener*	**actionListener**
	public	. . . . void	**addActionListener** (*java.awt.event.ActionListener* l)
	public	. . . . void	**addChangeListener** (*javax.swing.event.ChangeListener* l)
4	public	. . . . void	**addItemListener** (*java.awt.event.ItemListener* l)
▲	public static final	. . . . String	**BORDER_PAINTED_CHANGED_PROPERTY** = "borderPainted"
	protected transient	. . . . . javax↩ .swing.event.ChangeEvent	**changeEvent**
	protected	. . . . *javax*↩ .*swing.event.ChangeListener*	**changeListener**
	protected	. . . . int	**checkHorizontalKey** (int key, String exception)
	protected	. . . . int	**checkVerticalKey** (int key, String exception)
▲	public static final	. . . . String	**CONTENT_AREA_FILLED_CHANGED_PROPERTY** = "contentAreaFilled"
	protected	. . . . *java.awt.event.ActionListener*	**createActionListener** ()
	protected	. . . . *javax*↩ .*swing.event.ChangeListener*	**createChangeListener** ()
	protected	. . . . *java.awt.event.ItemListener*	**createItemListener** ()
▲	public static final	. . . . String	**DISABLED_ICON_CHANGED_PROPERTY** = "disabledIcon"
▲	public static final	. . . . String	**DISABLED_SELECTED_ICON_CHANGED_PROPERTY** = "disabledSelectedIcon"
	public	. . . . void	**doClick** ()
	public	. . . . void	**doClick** (int pressTime)
	protected	. . . . void	**fireActionPerformed** (java.awt.event.ActionEvent event)
	protected	. . . . void	**fireItemStateChanged** (java.awt.event.ItemEvent event)
	protected	. . . . void	**fireStateChanged** ()
▲	public static final	. . . . String	**FOCUS_PAINTED_CHANGED_PROPERTY** = "focusPainted"
	public	. . . . String	**getActionCommand** ()
	public	. . . . *Icon*	**getDisabledIcon** ()
	public	. . . . *Icon*	**getDisabledSelectedIcon** ()
	public	. . . . int	**getHorizontalAlignment** ()
	public	. . . . int	**getHorizontalTextPosition** ()
	public	. . . . *Icon*	**getIcon** ()

Class   *Interface*   —extends   - - -implements   ○ abstract   ● final   △ static   ▲ static final   ✳ constructor   x x—inherited   x **x**—declared   **x x**—overridden

A

D	public	String	**getLabel** ()
	public	java.awt.Insets	**getMargin** ()
	public	int	**getMnemonic** ()
	public	*ButtonModel*	**getModel** ()
	public	*Icon*	**getPressedIcon** ()
	public	*Icon*	**getRolloverIcon** ()
	public	*Icon*	**getRolloverSelectedIcon** ()
	public	*Icon*	**getSelectedIcon** ()
4	public synchronized ..	Object[]	**getSelectedObjects** ()
	public	String	**getText** ()
	public		**getUI** ()
	...... javax.swing.plaf.ButtonUI		
	public	int	**getVerticalAlignment** ()
	public	int	**getVerticalTextPosition** ()
▲	public static final	String	**HORIZONTAL_ALIGNMENT_CHANGED_PROPERTY** = "horizontalAlignment"
▲	public static final	String	**HORIZONTAL_TEXT_POSITION_CHANGED_PROPERTY**
			= "horizontalTextPosition"
▲	public static final	String	**ICON_CHANGED_PROPERTY** = "icon"
	protected	void	**init** (String text, *Icon* icon)
	public	boolean	**isBorderPainted** ()
	public	boolean	**isContentAreaFilled** ()
	public	boolean	**isFocusPainted** ()
	public	boolean	**isRolloverEnabled** ()
	public	boolean	**isSelected** ()
	protected		**itemListener**
	.... java.awt.event.ItemListener		
▲	public static final	String	**MARGIN_CHANGED_PROPERTY** = "margin"
▲	public static final	String	**MNEMONIC_CHANGED_PROPERTY** = "mnemonic"
	protected	*ButtonModel*	**model**
▲	public static final	String	**MODEL_CHANGED_PROPERTY** = "model"
3	protected	**void**	**paintBorder** (java.awt.Graphics g)
3	protected	**String**	**paramString** ()
▲	public static final	String	**PRESSED_ICON_CHANGED_PROPERTY** = "pressedIcon"
	public	void	**removeActionListener** (*java.awt.event.ActionListener* l)
	public	void	**removeChangeListener** (*javax.swing.event.ChangeListener* l)
4	public	void	**removeItemListener** (*java.awt.event.ItemListener* l)
▲	public static final	String	**ROLLOVER_ENABLED_CHANGED_PROPERTY** = "rolloverEnabled"
▲	public static final	String	**ROLLOVER_ICON_CHANGED_PROPERTY** = "rolloverIcon"
▲	public static final	String	**ROLLOVER_SELECTED_ICON_CHANGED_PROPERTY** = "rolloverSelectedIcon"
▲	public static final	String	**SELECTED_ICON_CHANGED_PROPERTY** = "selectedIcon"
	public	void	**setActionCommand** (String actionCommand)
	public	void	**setBorderPainted** (boolean b)
	public	void	**setContentAreaFilled** (boolean b)
	public	void	**setDisabledIcon** (*Icon* disabledIcon)
	public	void	**setDisabledSelectedIcon** (*Icon* disabledSelectedIcon)
3	public	**void**	**setEnabled** (boolean b)
	public	void	**setFocusPainted** (boolean b)
	public	void	**setHorizontalAlignment** (int alignment)
	public	void	**setHorizontalTextPosition** (int textPosition)
	public	void	**setIcon** (*Icon* defaultIcon)
D	public	void	**setLabel** (String label)
	public	void	**setMargin** (java.awt.Insets m)
	public	void	**setMnemonic** (char mnemonic)
	public	void	**setMnemonic** (int mnemonic)
	public	void	**setModel** (*ButtonModel* newModel)
	public	void	**setPressedIcon** (*Icon* pressedIcon)
	public	void	**setRolloverEnabled** (boolean b)
	public	void	**setRolloverIcon** (*Icon* rolloverIcon)
	public	void	**setRolloverSelectedIcon** (*Icon* rolloverSelectedIcon)
	public	void	**setSelected** (boolean b)
	public	void	**setSelectedIcon** (*Icon* selectedIcon)
	public	void	**setText** (String text)
	public	void	**setUI** (javax.swing.plaf.ButtonUI ui)
	public	void	**setVerticalAlignment** (int alignment)
	public	void	**setVerticalTextPosition** (int textPosition)
▲	public static final	String	**TEXT_CHANGED_PROPERTY** = "text"
3	public	**void**	**updateUI** ()
▲	public static final	String	**VERTICAL_ALIGNMENT_CHANGED_PROPERTY** = "verticalAlignment"
▲	public static final	String	**VERTICAL_TEXT_POSITION_CHANGED_PROPERTY** = "verticalTextPosition"

Classes

A

AbstractButton.AccessibleAbstractButton	protected	javax.swing

Object
1.2 ○ └javax.accessibility.AccessibleContext[1]
1.2 ○ └JComponent.AccessibleJComponent[2] - - - - *java.io.Serializable, javax.accessibility.AccessibleComponent*
1.2 ○ └AbstractButton.AccessibleAbstractButton *javax.accessibility.AccessibleAction*[3],
javax.accessibility.AccessibleValue[4]

1	*19 inherited members from javax.accessibility.AccessibleContext not shown*		
2	*39 inherited members from JComponent.AccessibleJComponent not shown*		
✳	protected		**AccessibleAbstractButton** ()
3	public	boolean	**doAccessibleAction** (int i)
1	public... ***javax.accessibility↩***		**getAccessibleAction** ()
	.AccessibleAction		
3	public	int	**getAccessibleActionCount** ()
3	public	String	**getAccessibleActionDescription** (int i)
2	public	**String**	**getAccessibleName** ()
2	public... ***javax.accessibility↩***		**getAccessibleStateSet** ()
	.AccessibleStateSet		
1	public... ***javax.accessibility↩***		**getAccessibleValue** ()
	.AccessibleValue		
4	public	Number	**getCurrentAccessibleValue** ()
4	public	Number	**getMaximumAccessibleValue** ()
4	public	Number	**getMinimumAccessibleValue** ()
4	public	boolean	**setCurrentAccessibleValue** (Number n)

AbstractButton.ButtonChangeListener	protected	javax.swing

Object
1.2 └AbstractButton.ButtonChangeListener - - - - - - *javax.swing.event.ChangeListener*[1] (*java.util.EventListener*),
java.io.Serializable

1	public	void	**stateChanged** (javax.swing.event.ChangeEvent e)

AbstractCollection	java.util

Object[1]
P
1.2 ○ └AbstractCollection - *Collection*[2]

✳	protected		**AbstractCollection** ()
2	public	boolean	**add** (Object o)
2	public	boolean	**addAll** (*Collection* c)
2	public	void	**clear** ()
2	public	boolean	**contains** (Object o)
2	public	boolean	**containsAll** (*Collection* c)
2	public	boolean	**isEmpty** ()
○ 2	public abstract	*Iterator*	**iterator** ()
2	public	boolean	**remove** (Object o)
2	public	boolean	**removeAll** (*Collection* c)
2	public	boolean	**retainAll** (*Collection* c)
○ 2	public abstract	int	**size** ()
2	public	Object[]	**toArray** ()
2	public	Object[]	**toArray** (Object[] a)
1	public	**String**	**toString** ()

AbstractColorChooserPanel	javax.swing.colorchooser

Object
○ └java.awt.Component[1] - - - - - - - - - - - - - - - - - - - *java.awt.image.ImageObserver*, *java.awt.MenuContainer*,
java.io.Serializable
└java.awt.Container[2]
1.2 ○ └javax.swing.JComponent[3] - - - - - - - - - - - *java.io.Serializable*
1.2 └javax.swing.JPanel[4] - - - - - - - - - - - - - - - *javax.accessibility.Accessible*
1.2 ○ └AbstractColorChooserPanel

1	*111 inherited members from java.awt.Component not shown*
2	*39 inherited members from java.awt.Container not shown*

Class   *Interface*   —extends   - - -implements   ○ abstract   ● final   △ static   ▲ static final   ✳ constructor   x x—inherited   x **x**—declared   **x x**—overridden

3		*112 inherited members from javax.swing.JComponent not shown*	
✳	public		**AbstractColorChooserPanel** ()
○	protected abstract	void	**buildChooser** ()
4	public	javax.accessibility ↩	getAccessibleContext ()
	.AccessibleContext		
	protected	java.awt.Color	**getColorFromModel** ()
	public	*ColorSelectionModel*	**getColorSelectionModel** ()
○	public abstract	String	**getDisplayName** ()
○	public abstract		**getLargeDisplayIcon** ()
		javax.swing.Icon	
○	public abstract		**getSmallDisplayIcon** ()
		javax.swing.Icon	
4	public	String	getUIClassID ()
	public	void	**installChooserPanel** (javax.swing.JColorChooser enclosingChooser)
3	public	**void**	**paint** (java.awt.Graphics g)
4	protected	String	paramString ()
	public	void	**uninstallChooserPanel** (javax.swing.JColorChooser enclosingChooser)
○	public abstract	void	**updateChooser** ()
4	public	void	updateUI ()

Object
1.2 ○ └─AbstractDocument - *Document* [1], *java.io.Serializable*

✳	protected		**AbstractDocument** (*AbstractDocument.Content* data)
✳	protected		**AbstractDocument** (*AbstractDocument. Content* data,
			AbstractDocument.AttributeContext context)
1	public	void	**addDocumentListener** (*javax.swing.event.DocumentListener* listener)
1	public	void	**addUndoableEditListener** (*javax.swing.event.UndoableEditListener* listener)
▲	protected static final	String	**BAD_LOCATION**
▲	public static final	String	**BidiElementName** = "bidi level"
▲	public static final	String	**ContentElementName** = "content"
	protected	*Element*	**createBranchElement** (*Element* parent, *AttributeSet* a)
	protected	*Element*	**createLeafElement** (*Element* parent, *AttributeSet* a, int p0, int p1)
1	public synchronized	*Position*	**createPosition** (int offs) throws BadLocationException
	public	void	**dump** (java.io.PrintStream out)
▲	public static final	String	**ElementNameAttribute** = "$ename"
	protected	void	**fireChangedUpdate** (*javax.swing.event.DocumentEvent* e)
	protected	void	**fireInsertUpdate** (*javax.swing.event.DocumentEvent* e)
	protected	void	**fireRemoveUpdate** (*javax.swing.event.DocumentEvent* e)
	protected	void	**fireUndoableEditUpdate** (javax.swing.event.UndoableEditEvent e)
	public	int	**getAsynchronousLoadPriority** ()
●	protected final		**getAttributeContext** ()
		AbstractDocument↩	
	.AttributeContext		
	public	*Element*	**getBidiRootElement** ()
●	protected final		**getContent** ()
	.... *AbstractDocument.Content*		
●	protected final synchronized		**getCurrentWriter** ()
		Thread	
○ 1	public abstract	*Element*	**getDefaultRootElement** ()
	public	java.util.Dictionary	**getDocumentProperties** ()
● 1	public final	*Position*	**getEndPosition** ()
1	public	int	**getLength** ()
○	public abstract	*Element*	**getParagraphElement** (int pos)
● 1	public final	Object	**getProperty** (Object key)
1	public	*Element[]*	**getRootElements** ()
● 1	public final	*Position*	**getStartPosition** ()
1	public	String	**getText** (int offset, int length) throws BadLocationException
1	public	void	**getText** (int offset, int length, Segment txt) throws BadLocationException
1	public	void	**insertString** (int offs, String str, *AttributeSet* a) throws BadLocationException
	protected	void	**insertUpdate** (AbstractDocument.DefaultDocumentEvent chng, *AttributeSet* attr)
	protected	javax↩	**listenerList**
	.swing.event.EventListenerList		
▲	public static final	String	**ParagraphElementName** = "paragraph"
	protected	void	**postRemoveUpdate** (AbstractDocument.DefaultDocumentEvent chng)
● 1	public final	void	**putProperty** (Object key, Object value)
●	public final synchronized	void	**readLock** ()
●	public final synchronized	void	**readUnlock** ()
1	public	void	**remove** (int offs, int len) throws BadLocationException
1	public	void	**removeDocumentListener** (*javax.swing.event.DocumentListener* listener)
1	public	void	**removeUndoableEditListener** (*javax.swing.event.UndoableEditListener* listener)

AbstractDocument

	protected	.................void	**removeUpdate** (AbstractDocument.DefaultDocumentEvent chng)
1	public	.......................void	**render** (*Runnable* r)
▲	public static final	.........String	**SectionElementName** = "section"
	public	......................void	**setAsynchronousLoadPriority** (int p)
	public	......................void	**setDocumentProperties** (java.util.Dictionary x)
●	protected final synchronized . .		**writeLock** ()
		............................void	
●	protected final synchronized . .		**writeUnlock** ()
		............................void	

AbstractDocument.AbstractElement	javax.swing.text

Object[1]
1.2 ○ └─AbstractDocument.AbstractElement - - - - - - - *Element* [2], *MutableAttributeSet* [3] (*AttributeSet* [4]),
java.io.Serializable, javax.swing.tree.TreeNode [5]

✳	public	....	**AbstractElement** (*Element* parent, *AttributeSet* a)
3	public	........................void	**addAttribute** (Object name, Object value)
3	public	........................void	**addAttributes** (*AttributeSet* attr)
○ 5	public abstract	....	**children** ()
		.... *java.util.Enumeration*	
4	public	.... boolean	**containsAttribute** (Object name, Object value)
4	public	.... boolean	**containsAttributes** (*AttributeSet* attrs)
4	public	.... *AttributeSet*	**copyAttributes** ()
	public	........................void	**dump** (java.io.PrintStream psOut, int indentAmount)
1	protected	.... **void**	**finalize** () throws Throwable
○ 5	public abstract	.... boolean	**getAllowsChildren** ()
4	public	.... Object	**getAttribute** (Object attrName)
4	public	....................int	**getAttributeCount** ()
4	public	.... *java.util.Enumeration*	**getAttributeNames** ()
2	public	.... *AttributeSet*	**getAttributes** ()
5	public	....	**getChildAt** (int childIndex)
		..... *javax.swing.tree.TreeNode*	
5	public	....................int	**getChildCount** ()
2	public	.... *Document*	**getDocument** ()
○ 2	public abstract	.... *Element*	**getElement** (int index)
○ 2	public abstract	............int	**getElementCount** ()
○ 2	public abstract	............int	**getElementIndex** (int offset)
○ 2	public abstract	............int	**getEndOffset** ()
5	public	....................int	**getIndex** (*javax.swing.tree.TreeNode* node)
2	public	.... String	**getName** ()
5	public	....	**getParent** ()
		..... *javax.swing.tree.TreeNode*	
2	public	.... *Element*	**getParentElement** ()
4	public	.... *AttributeSet*	**getResolveParent** ()
○ 2	public abstract	............int	**getStartOffset** ()
4	public	.... boolean	**isDefined** (Object attrName)
4	public	.... boolean	**isEqual** (*AttributeSet* attr)
○ 2	public abstract	.... boolean	**isLeaf** ()
3	public	........................void	**removeAttribute** (Object name)
3	public	........................void	**removeAttributes** (*java.util.Enumeration* names)
3	public	........................void	**removeAttributes** (*AttributeSet* attrs)
3	public	........................void	**setResolveParent** (*AttributeSet* parent)

AbstractDocument.AttributeContext	javax.swing.text

1.2 *AbstractDocument.AttributeContext*

public	.... *AttributeSet*	**addAttribute** (*AttributeSet* old, Object name, Object value)
public	.... *AttributeSet*	**addAttributes** (*AttributeSet* old, *AttributeSet* attr)
public	.... *AttributeSet*	**getEmptySet** ()
public	.......................void	**reclaim** (*AttributeSet* a)
public	.... *AttributeSet*	**removeAttribute** (*AttributeSet* old, Object name)
public	.... *AttributeSet*	**removeAttributes** (*AttributeSet* old, *java.util.Enumeration* names)
public	.... *AttributeSet*	**removeAttributes** (*AttributeSet* old, *AttributeSet* attrs)

Class *Interface* —extends - - -implements ○ abstract ● final △ static ▲ static final ✳ constructor x x—inherited x **x**—declared **x x**—overridden

176

			AbstractDocument.BranchElement	javax.swing.text

```
          Object 1
1.2 ○       └─AbstractDocument.AbstractElement 2 ------- Element, MutableAttributeSet (AttributeSet), java.io.Serializable,
                                                         javax.swing.tree.TreeNode
1.2              └─AbstractDocument.BranchElement
```

2	public......................void	addAttribute (Object name, Object value)
2	public......................void	addAttributes (*AttributeSet* attr)
*	public..................	**BranchElement** (*Element* parent, *AttributeSet* a)
2	public.. ***java.util.Enumeration***	**children** ()
2	public.................. boolean	containsAttribute (Object name, Object value)
2	public.................. boolean	containsAttributes (*AttributeSet* attrs)
2	public............. *AttributeSet*	copyAttributes ()
2	public......................void	dump (java.io.PrintStream psOut, int indentAmount)
2	protected....................void	finalize () throws Throwable
2	public.............. **boolean**	**getAllowsChildren** ()
2	public............. Object	getAttribute (Object attrName)
2	public......................int	getAttributeCount ()
2	public.... *java.util.Enumeration*	getAttributeNames ()
2	public............. *AttributeSet*	getAttributes ()
2	public..........................	getChildAt (int childIndex)
	..... *javax.swing.tree.TreeNode*	
2	public......................int	getChildCount ()
2	public............. *Document*	getDocument ()
2	public............. ***Element***	**getElement** (int index)
2	public.............. **int**	**getElementCount** ()
2	public.............. **int**	**getElementIndex** (int offset)
2	public.............. **int**	**getEndOffset** ()
2	public......................int	getIndex (*javax.swing.tree.TreeNode* node)
2	public............. **String**	**getName** ()
2	public..........................	getParent ()
	..... *javax.swing.tree.TreeNode*	
2	public............. *Element*	getParentElement ()
2	public............. *AttributeSet*	getResolveParent ()
2	public.............. **int**	**getStartOffset** ()
2	public.............. boolean	isDefined (Object attrName)
2	public.............. boolean	isEqual (*AttributeSet* attr)
2	public............. **boolean**	**isLeaf** ()
	public............. *Element*	**positionToElement** (int pos)
2	public......................void	removeAttribute (Object name)
2	public......................void	removeAttributes (*java.util.Enumeration* names)
2	public......................void	removeAttributes (*AttributeSet* attrs)
	public......................void	**replace** (int offset, int length, *Element[]* elems)
2	public......................void	setResolveParent (*AttributeSet* parent)
1	public............. **String**	**toString** ()

AbstractDocument.Content	javax.swing.text

```
1.2    AbstractDocument.Content
```

	public..................*Position*	**createPosition** (int offset) throws BadLocationException
	public..................void	**getChars** (int where, int len, Segment txt) throws BadLocationException
	public..................String	**getString** (int where, int len) throws BadLocationException
	public..................*javax*↵	**insertString** (int where, String str) throws BadLocationException
	.*swing.undo.UndoableEdit*	
	public..................int	**length** ()
	public..................*javax*↵	**remove** (int where, int nitems) throws BadLocationException
	.*swing.undo.UndoableEdit*	

AbstractDocument.DefaultDocumentEvent	javax.swing.text

```
         Object
1.2      └─javax.swing.undo.AbstractUndoableEdit 1 ---- javax.swing.undo.UndoableEdit, java.io.Serializable
1.2         └─javax.swing.undo.CompoundEdit 2
1.2            └─AbstractDocument ↵ ---------------- javax.swing.event.DocumentEvent 3
                  .DefaultDocumentEvent
```

2	public............. **boolean**	**addEdit** (*javax.swing.undo.UndoableEdit* anEdit)
2	public.............. boolean	canRedo ()
2	public.............. boolean	canUndo ()

AbstractDocument.DefaultDocumentEvent

*	public		**DefaultDocumentEvent** (int offs, int len, javax.swing.event.DocumentEvent↵ .EventType type)
2	public	void	die ()
2	protected	java.util.Vector	edits
2	public	void	end ()
3	public	*javax.swing↵ .event.DocumentEvent↵ .ElementChange*	**getChange** (*Element* elem)
3	public	*Document*	**getDocument** ()
3	public	int	**getLength** ()
3	public	int	**getOffset** ()
2	public	**String**	**getPresentationName** ()
2	public	**String**	**getRedoPresentationName** ()
3	public	*javax.swing.event↵ .DocumentEvent.EventType*	**getType** ()
2	public	**String**	**getUndoPresentationName** ()
2	public	boolean	isInProgress ()
2	public	**boolean**	**isSignificant** ()
2	protected	*javax↵ .swing.undo.UndoableEdit*	lastEdit ()
2	public	**void**	**redo** () throws javax.swing.undo.CannotRedoException
1	public	boolean	replaceEdit (*javax.swing.undo.UndoableEdit* anEdit)
2	public	**String**	**toString** ()
2	public	**void**	**undo** () throws javax.swing.undo.CannotUndoException

AbstractDocument.ElementEdit — javax.swing.text

Object
1.2 └javax.swing.undo.AbstractUndoableEdit [1] - - - - *javax.swing.undo.UndoableEdit*, *java.io.Serializable*
1.2 └AbstractDocument.ElementEdit - - - - - - - - - *javax.swing.event.DocumentEvent.ElementChange* [2]

1	public	boolean	addEdit (*javax.swing.undo.UndoableEdit* anEdit)
1	public	boolean	canRedo ()
1	public	boolean	canUndo ()
1	public	void	die ()
*	public		**ElementEdit** (*Element* e, int index, *Element[]* removed, *Element[]* added)
2	public	*Element[]*	**getChildrenAdded** ()
2	public	*Element[]*	**getChildrenRemoved** ()
2	public	*Element*	**getElement** ()
2	public	int	**getIndex** ()
1	public	String	getPresentationName ()
1	public	String	getRedoPresentationName ()
1	public	String	getUndoPresentationName ()
1	public	boolean	isSignificant ()
1	public	**void**	**redo** () throws javax.swing.undo.CannotRedoException
1	public	boolean	replaceEdit (*javax.swing.undo.UndoableEdit* anEdit)
1	public	String	toString ()
1	public	**void**	**undo** () throws javax.swing.undo.CannotUndoException

AbstractDocument.LeafElement — javax.swing.text

Object [1]
1.2 ○ └AbstractDocument.AbstractElement [2] - - - - - - - *Element*, *MutableAttributeSet* (*AttributeSet*), *java.io.Serializable*, *javax.swing.tree.TreeNode*
1.2   └AbstractDocument.LeafElement

2	public	void	addAttribute (Object name, Object value)
2	public	void	addAttributes (*AttributeSet* attr)
2	public	***java.util.Enumeration***	**children** ()
2	public	boolean	containsAttribute (Object name, Object value)
2	public	boolean	containsAttributes (*AttributeSet* attrs)
2	public	*AttributeSet*	copyAttributes ()
2	public	void	dump (java.io.PrintStream psOut, int indentAmount)
2	protected	void	finalize () throws Throwable
2	public	**boolean**	**getAllowsChildren** ()
2	public	Object	getAttribute (Object attrName)
2	public	int	getAttributeCount ()
2	public	*java.util.Enumeration*	getAttributeNames ()
2	public	*AttributeSet*	getAttributes ()

Class *Interface* —extends - - -implements ○ abstract ● final △ static ▲ static final * constructor ×x—inherited ×**x**—declared **x x**—overridden

2	public	getChildAt (int childIndex)
	..... javax.swing.tree.TreeNode	
2	public......................int	getChildCount ()
2	public....................*Document*	getDocument ()
2	public..................***Element***	**getElement** (int index)
2	public.................. **int**	**getElementCount** ()
2	public.................. **int**	**getElementIndex** (int pos)
2	public.................. **int**	**getEndOffset** ()
2	public..................int	getIndex (*javax.swing.tree.TreeNode* node)
2	public.................. **String**	**getName** ()
2	public..................	getParent ()
	..... javax.swing.tree.TreeNode	
2	public................. *Element*	getParentElement ()
2	public......... *AttributeSet*	getResolveParent ()
2	public.................. **int**	**getStartOffset** ()
2	public................. boolean	isDefined (Object attrName)
2	public................. boolean	isEqual (*AttributeSet* attr)
2	public.................. **boolean**	**isLeaf** ()
*	public..................	**LeafElement** (*Element* parent, *AttributeSet* a, int offs0, int offs1)
2	public..................void	removeAttribute (Object name)
2	public..................void	removeAttributes (*java.util.Enumeration* names)
2	public..................void	removeAttributes (*AttributeSet* attrs)
2	public..................void	setResolveParent (*AttributeSet* parent)
1	public.................. **String**	**toString** ()

AbstractLayoutCache

	Object	
1.2 ○	└ AbstractLayoutCache - - - - - - - - - - - - - - - - - - *RowMapper* [1]	
*	public..........................	**AbstractLayoutCache** ()
○	public abstract.................	**getBounds** (TreePath path, java.awt.Rectangle placeIn)
	.... java.awt.Rectangle	
○	public abstract........ boolean	**getExpandedState** (TreePath path)
	public................*TreeModel*	**getModel** ()
	public AbstractLayoutCache ↵	**getNodeDimensions** ()
	.NodeDimensions	
	protected.. java.awt.Rectangle	**getNodeDimensions** (Object value, int row, int depth, boolean expanded, java.awt.Rectangle placeIn)
○	public abstract.......TreePath	**getPathClosestTo** (int x, int y)
○	public abstract........TreePath	**getPathForRow** (int row)
	public..........................int	**getPreferredHeight** ()
	public..........................int	**getPreferredWidth** (java.awt.Rectangle bounds)
○	public abstract...........int	**getRowCount** ()
○	public abstract...............int	**getRowForPath** (TreePath path)
	public..........................int	**getRowHeight** ()
1	public.......................int[]	**getRowsForPaths** (TreePath[] paths)
	public..... *TreeSelectionModel*	**getSelectionModel** ()
○	public abstract...............int	**getVisibleChildCount** (TreePath path)
○	public abstract.................	**getVisiblePathsFrom** (TreePath path)
	.... java.util.Enumeration	
○	public abstract.............void	**invalidatePathBounds** (TreePath path)
○	public abstract...........void	**invalidateSizes** ()
○	public abstract........ boolean	**isExpanded** (TreePath path)
	protected.............. boolean	**isFixedRowHeight** ()
	public................. boolean	**isRootVisible** ()
	protected......................	**nodeDimensions**
	.... AbstractLayoutCache ↵	
	.NodeDimensions	
	protected.............. boolean	**rootVisible**
	protected.....................int	**rowHeight**
○	public abstract.............void	**setExpandedState** (TreePath path, boolean isExpanded)
	public........................void	**setModel** (*TreeModel* newModel)
	public........................void	**setNodeDimensions** (AbstractLayoutCache.NodeDimensions nd)
	public........................void	**setRootVisible** (boolean rootVisible)
	public........................void	**setRowHeight** (int rowHeight)
	public........................void	**setSelectionModel** (*TreeSelectionModel* newLSM)
	protected.............*TreeModel*	**treeModel**
○	public abstract.............void	**treeNodesChanged** (javax.swing.event.TreeModelEvent e)
○	public abstract.............void	**treeNodesInserted** (javax.swing.event.TreeModelEvent e)
○	public abstract.............void	**treeNodesRemoved** (javax.swing.event.TreeModelEvent e)
	protected . *TreeSelectionModel*	**treeSelectionModel**

AbstractLayoutCache

○	public abstract . . . . void	**treeStructureChanged** (javax.swing.event.TreeModelEvent e)

A

AbstractLayoutCache.NodeDimensions   javax.swing.tree

Object
1.2 ○ └AbstractLayoutCache.NodeDimensions

○	public abstract . . . . java.awt.Rectangle	**getNodeDimensions** (Object value, int row, int depth, boolean expanded, java.awt.Rectangle bounds)
✳	public	**NodeDimensions** ()

AbstractList   java.util

Object [1]
1.2 ○ └AbstractCollection [2] - *Collection*
1.2 ○   └AbstractList - *List* [3] (*Collection*)

P

✳		protected	**AbstractList** ()
	2	public . . . . **boolean**	**add** (Object o)
	3	public . . . . void	**add** (int index, Object element)
	2	public . . . . boolean	addAll (*Collection* c)
	3	public . . . . boolean	**addAll** (int index, *Collection* c)
	2	public . . . . **void**	**clear** ()
	2	public . . . . boolean	contains (Object o)
	2	public . . . . boolean	containsAll (*Collection* c)
	1	public . . . . **boolean**	**equals** (Object o)
○	3	public abstract . . . . Object	**get** (int index)
	1	public . . . . **int**	**hashCode** ()
	3	public . . . . int	**indexOf** (Object o)
	2	public . . . . boolean	isEmpty ()
	2	public . . . . *Iterator*	**iterator** ()
	3	public . . . . int	**lastIndexOf** (Object o)
	3	public . . . .*ListIterator*	**listIterator** ()
	3	public . . . .*ListIterator*	**listIterator** (int index)
		protected transient . . . . int	**modCount**
	3	public . . . . Object	**remove** (int index)
	2	public . . . . boolean	remove (Object o)
	2	public . . . . boolean	removeAll (*Collection* c)
		protected . . . . void	**removeRange** (int fromIndex, int toIndex)
	2	public . . . . boolean	retainAll (*Collection* c)
	3	public . . . . Object	**set** (int index, Object element)
○	2	public abstract . . . . int	size ()
	3	public . . . . *List*	**subList** (int fromIndex, int toIndex)
	2	public . . . . Object[]	toArray ()
	2	public . . . . Object[]	toArray (Object[] a)
	2	public . . . . String	toString ()

AbstractListModel   javax.swing

Object
1.2 ○ └AbstractListModel - *ListModel* [1], *java.io.Serializable*

✳		public	**AbstractListModel** ()
	1	public . . . . void	**addListDataListener** (*javax.swing.event.ListDataListener* l)
		protected . . . . void	**fireContentsChanged** (Object source, int index0, int index1)
		protected . . . . void	**fireIntervalAdded** (Object source, int index0, int index1)
		protected . . . . void	**fireIntervalRemoved** (Object source, int index0, int index1)
○	1	public abstract . . . . Object	**getElementAt** (int)
○	1	public abstract . . . . int	**getSize** ()
		protected . . . . javax ↵ .swing.event.EventListenerList	**listenerList**
	1	public . . . . void	**removeListDataListener** (*javax.swing.event.ListDataListener* l)

Class *Interface* —extends - - -implements ○ abstract ● final △ static ▲ static final ✳ constructor x x—inherited x **x**—declared **x x**—overridden

180

		AbstractMap	java.util

P

A

```
       Object 1
1.2 ○    └ AbstractMap ------------------------- Map 2
```

∗	protected		**AbstractMap** ()
2	public . . . . void		**clear** ()
2	public . . . . boolean		**containsKey** (Object key)
2	public . . . . boolean		**containsValue** (Object value)
○ 2	public abstract . . . . *Set*		**entrySet** ()
1	public . . . . **boolean**		**equals** (Object o)
2	public . . . . Object		**get** (Object key)
1	public . . . . **int**		**hashCode** ()
2	public . . . . boolean		**isEmpty** ()
2	public . . . . *Set*		**keySet** ()
2	public . . . . Object		**put** (Object key, Object value)
2	public . . . . void		**putAll** (*Map* t)
2	public . . . . Object		**remove** (Object key)
2	public . . . . int		**size** ()
1	public . . . . **String**		**toString** ()
2	public . . . . *Collection*		**values** ()

		AbstractMethodError	java.lang

P

```
       Object
       └ Throwable --------------------------- java.io.Serializable
         └ Error
           └ LinkageError
             └ IncompatibleClassChangeError
               └ AbstractMethodError
```

∗	public		**AbstractMethodError** ()
∗	public		**AbstractMethodError** (String s)

		AbstractSequentialList	java.util

P

```
       Object
1.2 ○    └ AbstractCollection 1 --------------------- Collection
1.2 ○      └ AbstractList 2 ------------------------ List (Collection)
1.2 ○        └ AbstractSequentialList
```

∗	protected		**AbstractSequentialList** ()
2	public . . . . boolean		add (Object o)
2	public . . . . **void**		**add** (int index, Object element)
1	public . . . . boolean		addAll (*Collection* c)
2	public . . . . **boolean**		**addAll** (int index, *Collection* c)
2	public . . . . void		clear ()
1	public . . . . boolean		contains (Object o)
1	public . . . . boolean		containsAll (*Collection* c)
2	public . . . . boolean		equals (Object o)
2	public . . . . **Object**		**get** (int index)
2	public . . . . int		hashCode ()
2	public . . . . int		indexOf (Object o)
1	public . . . . boolean		isEmpty ()
2	public . . . . **Iterator**		**iterator** ()
2	public . . . . int		lastIndexOf (Object o)
2	public . . . . *ListIterator*		listIterator ()
○ 2	public abstract . . . . **ListIterator**		**listIterator** (int index)
2	protected transient . . . . int		modCount
2	public . . . . **Object**		**remove** (int index)
1	public . . . . boolean		remove (Object o)
1	public . . . . boolean		removeAll (*Collection* c)
2	protected . . . . void		removeRange (int fromIndex, int toIndex)
1	public . . . . boolean		retainAll (*Collection* c)
2	public . . . . **Object**		**set** (int index, Object element)
○ 1	public abstract . . . . int		size ()
2	public . . . . *List*		subList (int fromIndex, int toIndex)
1	public . . . . Object[]		toArray ()
1	public . . . . Object[]		toArray (Object[] a)
1	public . . . . String		toString ()

Classes

AbstractSet

			AbstractSet	java.util
				P

Object [1]
　└ AbstractCollection [2] - *Collection*
　　└ AbstractSet - *Set (Collection)*

1.2 ○
1.2 ○

✳		protected	**AbstractSet** ()	
	2	public .... boolean	add (Object o)	
	2	public .... boolean	addAll (*Collection* c)	
	2	public .... void	clear ()	
	2	public .... boolean	contains (Object o)	
	2	public .... boolean	containsAll (*Collection* c)	
	1	public .... **boolean**	**equals** (Object o)	
	1	public .... **int**	**hashCode** ()	
	2	public .... boolean	isEmpty ()	
○	2	public abstract .... *Iterator*	iterator ()	
	2	public .... boolean	remove (Object o)	
	2	public .... boolean	removeAll (*Collection* c)	
	2	public .... boolean	retainAll (*Collection* c)	
○	2	public abstract .... int	size ()	
	2	public .... Object[]	toArray ()	
	2	public .... Object[]	toArray (Object[] a)	
	2	public .... String	toString ()	

AbstractTableModel			javax.swing.table

Object
　└ AbstractTableModel - *TableModel* [1], *java.io.Serializable*

1.2 ○

✳		public	**AbstractTableModel** ()
	1	public .... void	**addTableModelListener** (*javax.swing.event.TableModelListener* l)
		public .... int	**findColumn** (String columnName)
		public .... void	**fireTableCellUpdated** (int row, int column)
		public .... void	**fireTableChanged** (javax.swing.event.TableModelEvent e)
		public .... void	**fireTableDataChanged** ()
		public .... void	**fireTableRowsDeleted** (int firstRow, int lastRow)
		public .... void	**fireTableRowsInserted** (int firstRow, int lastRow)
		public .... void	**fireTableRowsUpdated** (int firstRow, int lastRow)
		public .... void	**fireTableStructureChanged** ()
	1	public .... Class	**getColumnClass** (int columnIndex)
○	1	public abstract .... int	**getColumnCount** ()
	1	public .... String	**getColumnName** (int column)
○	1	public abstract .... int	**getRowCount** ()
○	1	public abstract .... Object	**getValueAt** (int, int)
	1	public .... boolean	**isCellEditable** (int rowIndex, int columnIndex)
		protected .... javax ↵	**listenerList**
		.swing.event.EventListenerList	
	1	public .... void	**removeTableModelListener** (*javax.swing.event.TableModelListener* l)
	1	public .... void	**setValueAt** (Object aValue, int rowIndex, int columnIndex)

AbstractUndoableEdit			javax.swing.undo

Object [1]
　└ AbstractUndoableEdit - *UndoableEdit* [2], *java.io.Serializable*

1.2

✳		public	**AbstractUndoableEdit** ()
	2	public .... boolean	**addEdit** (*UndoableEdit* anEdit)
	2	public .... boolean	**canRedo** ()
	2	public .... boolean	**canUndo** ()
	2	public .... void	**die** ()
	2	public .... String	**getPresentationName** ()
	2	public .... String	**getRedoPresentationName** ()
	2	public .... String	**getUndoPresentationName** ()
	2	public .... boolean	**isSignificant** ()
	2	public .... void	**redo** () throws CannotRedoException
▲		protected static final ..... String	**RedoName**
	2	public .... boolean	**replaceEdit** (*UndoableEdit* anEdit)
	1	public .... **String**	**toString** ()
	2	public .... void	**undo** () throws CannotUndoException

---

Class　*Interface*　—extends　- - -implements　○ abstract　● final　△ static　▲ static final　✳ constructor　x x—inherited　x **x**—declared　**x x**—overridden

▲   protected static final ..... String **UndoName**

AbstractWriter   javax.swing.text

Object
1.2 ○   └AbstractWriter

*	protected	**AbstractWriter** (java.io.Writer w, *Element* root)
*	protected	**AbstractWriter** (java.io.Writer w, *Document* doc)
*	protected	**AbstractWriter** (java.io.Writer w, *Document* doc, int pos, int len)
*	protected	**AbstractWriter** (java.io.Writer w, *Element* root, int pos, int len)
	protected ....void	**decrIndent** ()
	protected .... *Document*	**getDocument** ()
	protected ...... ElementIterator	**getElementIterator** ()
	protected ....String	**getText** (*Element* elem) throws BadLocationException
	protected ....void	**incrIndent** ()
	protected ....void	**indent** () throws java.io.IOException
	protected .... boolean	**inRange** (*Element* next)
▲	protected static final ..... char	**NEWLINE**
	protected ....void	**setIndentSpace** (int space)
	protected ....void	**setLineLength** (int l)
	protected ....void	**text** (*Element* elem) throws BadLocationException, java.io.IOException
○	protected abstract ....void	**write** () throws java.io.IOException, BadLocationException
	protected ....void	**write** (char ch) throws java.io.IOException
	protected ....void	**write** (String str) throws java.io.IOException
	protected ....void	**writeAttributes** (*AttributeSet* attr) throws java.io.IOException

---

AccessControlContext   java.security
P⁰

Object[1]
1.2 ●   └AccessControlContext

*	public	**AccessControlContext** (ProtectionDomain[] context)
	public ....void	**checkPermission** (Permission perm) throws AccessControlException
1	public ....boolean	**equals** (Object obj)
1	public .... int	**hashCode** ()

AccessControlException   java.security
P⁰

Object
└Throwable - *java.io.Serializable*
  └Exception
    └RuntimeException
      └SecurityException
1.2   └AccessControlException

*	public	**AccessControlException** (String s)
*	public	**AccessControlException** (String s, Permission p)
	public .... Permission	**getPermission** ()

AccessController   java.security
P⁰

Object
1.2 ●   └AccessController

△	public static ....void	**checkPermission** (Permission perm) throws AccessControlException
△	public static native ...... Object	**doPrivileged** (*PrivilegedAction* action)
△	public static native ...... Object	**doPrivileged** (*PrivilegedExceptionAction* action) throws PrivilegedActionException
△	public static native ...... Object	**doPrivileged** (*PrivilegedAction* action, AccessControlContext context)
△	public static native ...... Object	**doPrivileged** (*PrivilegedExceptionAction* action, AccessControlContext context) throws PrivilegedActionException
△	public static .... AccessControlContext	**getContext** ()

AccessException

AccessException			java.rmi
			P^O

P^O

```
Object
 └Throwable ------------------------------ java.io.Serializable
   └Exception
     └java.io.IOException
1.1     └RemoteException 1
1.1       └AccessException
```

✳	public.........................		**AccessException** (String s)
✳	public.........................		**AccessException** (String s, Exception ex)
1	public................Throwable	detail
1	public....................String	getMessage ()
1	public.......................void	printStackTrace ()
1	public.......................void	printStackTrace (java.io.PrintStream ps)
1	public.......................void	printStackTrace (java.io.PrintWriter pw)

Accessible	javax.accessibility

1.2 *Accessible*

public...... AccessibleContext **getAccessibleContext** ()

AccessibleAction	javax.accessibility

1.2 *AccessibleAction*

public.................. boolean **doAccessibleAction** (int i)
public............................int **getAccessibleActionCount** ()
public............................String **getAccessibleActionDescription** (int i)

AccessibleBundle	javax.accessibility

```
Object 1
1.2 ○  └AccessibleBundle
```

✳	public.........................		**AccessibleBundle** ()
	protected.................String	**key**
	public....................String	**toDisplayString** ()
	public....................String	**toDisplayString** (java.util.Locale locale)
	protected.................String	**toDisplayString** (String resourceBundleName, java.util.Locale locale)
1	public....................**String**	**toString** ()

AccessibleComponent	javax.accessibility

1.2 *AccessibleComponent*

public.......................void **addFocusListener** (*java.awt.event.FocusListener* l)
public.................. boolean **contains** (java.awt.Point p)
public............... *Accessible* **getAccessibleAt** (java.awt.Point p)
public...........java.awt.Color **getBackground** ()
public...... java.awt.Rectangle **getBounds** ()
public.......... java.awt.Cursor **getCursor** ()
public............. java.awt.Font **getFont** ()
public.... java.awt.FontMetrics **getFontMetrics** (java.awt.Font f)
public..........java.awt.Color **getForeground** ()
public........... java.awt.Point **getLocation** ()
public........... java.awt.Point **getLocationOnScreen** ()
public...... java.awt.Dimension **getSize** ()
public.................. boolean **isEnabled** ()
public.................. boolean **isFocusTraversable** ()
public.................. boolean **isShowing** ()
public.................. boolean **isVisible** ()
public.......................void **removeFocusListener** (*java.awt.event.FocusListener* l)
public.......................void **requestFocus** ()
public.......................void **setBackground** (java.awt.Color c)
public.......................void **setBounds** (java.awt.Rectangle r)
public.......................void **setCursor** (java.awt.Cursor cursor)

Class   *Interface*   —extends   - - -implements   ○ abstract   ● final   △ static   ▲ static final   ✳ constructor   x x—inherited   x **x**—declared   x **x**—overridden

```
public.....................void  setEnabled (boolean b)
public.....................void  setFont (java.awt.Font f)
public.....................void  setForeground (java.awt.Color c)
public.....................void  setLocation (java.awt.Point p)
public.....................void  setSize (java.awt.Dimension d)
public.....................void  setVisible (boolean b)
```

AccessibleContext · javax.accessibility

```
        Object
1.2 O   └─AccessibleContext
```

▲	public static final .... String	**ACCESSIBLE_ACTIVE_DESCENDANT_PROPERTY** = "AccessibleActiveDescendant"
▲	public static final .... String	**ACCESSIBLE_CARET_PROPERTY** = "AccessibleCaret"
▲	public static final .... String	**ACCESSIBLE_CHILD_PROPERTY** = "AccessibleChild"
▲	public static final .... String	**ACCESSIBLE_DESCRIPTION_PROPERTY** = "AccessibleDescription"
▲	public static final .... String	**ACCESSIBLE_NAME_PROPERTY** = "AccessibleName"
▲	public static final .... String	**ACCESSIBLE_SELECTION_PROPERTY** = "AccessibleSelection"
▲	public static final .... String	**ACCESSIBLE_STATE_PROPERTY** = "AccessibleState"
▲	public static final .... String	**ACCESSIBLE_TEXT_PROPERTY** = "AccessibleText"
▲	public static final .... String	**ACCESSIBLE_VALUE_PROPERTY** = "AccessibleValue"
▲	public static final .... String	**ACCESSIBLE_VISIBLE_DATA_PROPERTY** = "AccessibleVisibleData"
✱	public..........................	**AccessibleContext** ()
	protected .... String	**accessibleDescription**
	protected .... String	**accessibleName**
	protected .... *Accessible*	**accessibleParent**
	public.....................void	**addPropertyChangeListener** (*java.beans.PropertyChangeListener* listener)
	public.....................void	**firePropertyChange** (String propertyName, Object oldValue, Object newValue)
	public........ *AccessibleAction*	**getAccessibleAction** ()
O	public abstract ..... *Accessible*	**getAccessibleChild** (int i)
O	public abstract ....int	**getAccessibleChildrenCount** ()
	public.. *AccessibleComponent*	**getAccessibleComponent** ()
	public.....................String	**getAccessibleDescription** ()
O	public abstract ....int	**getAccessibleIndexInParent** ()
	public.....................String	**getAccessibleName** ()
	public................. *Accessible*	**getAccessibleParent** ()
O	public abstract AccessibleRole	**getAccessibleRole** ()
	public..... *AccessibleSelection*	**getAccessibleSelection** ()
O	public abstract .... AccessibleStateSet	**getAccessibleStateSet** ()
	public.......... *AccessibleText*	**getAccessibleText** ()
	public......... *AccessibleValue*	**getAccessibleValue** ()
O	public abstract . java.util.Locale	**getLocale** () throws java.awt.IllegalComponentStateException
	public.....................void	**removePropertyChangeListener** (*java.beans.PropertyChangeListener* listener)
	public.....................void	**setAccessibleDescription** (String s)
	public.....................void	**setAccessibleName** (String s)
	public.....................void	**setAccessibleParent** (*Accessible* a)

AccessibleHyperlink · javax.accessibility

```
        Object
1.2 O   └─AccessibleHyperlink - - - - - - - - - - - - - - - - - - - AccessibleAction ¹
```

✱		public..........................	**AccessibleHyperlink** ()
O	1	public abstract .... boolean	**doAccessibleAction** (int i)
O		public abstract .... Object	**getAccessibleActionAnchor** (int i)
O	1	public abstract ....int	**getAccessibleActionCount** ()
O	1	public abstract ....String	**getAccessibleActionDescription** (int i)
O		public abstract .... Object	**getAccessibleActionObject** (int i)
O		public abstract ....int	**getEndIndex** ()
O		public abstract ....int	**getStartIndex** ()
O		public abstract .... boolean	**isValid** ()

AccessibleHypertext · javax.accessibility

```
1.2   AccessibleHypertext──────────────── AccessibleText ¹
```

1	public.....................String	getAfterIndex (int part, int index)
1	public.....................String	getAtIndex (int part, int index)
1	public.....................String	getBeforeIndex (int part, int index)

Classes

AccessibleHypertext

1	public	int	getCaretPosition ()
1	public		getCharacterAttribute (int i)
	... *javax.swing.text.AttributeSet*		
1	public	java.awt.Rectangle	getCharacterBounds (int i)
1	public	int	getCharCount ()
1	public	int	getIndexAtPoint (java.awt.Point p)
	public	AccessibleHyperlink	**getLink** (int linkIndex)
	public	int	**getLinkCount** ()
	public	int	**getLinkIndex** (int charIndex)
1	public	String	getSelectedText ()
1	public	int	getSelectionEnd ()
1	public	int	getSelectionStart ()

AccessibleObject   java.lang.reflect

Object
  └AccessibleObject   P

1.2

✳	protected		**AccessibleObject** ()
	public	boolean	**isAccessible** ()
	public	void	**setAccessible** (boolean flag) throws SecurityException
△	public static	void	**setAccessible** (AccessibleObject[] array, boolean flag) throws SecurityException

---

AccessibleResourceBundle   javax.accessibility

Object
  └java.util.ResourceBundle [1]
    └java.util.ListResourceBundle [2]
      └AccessibleResourceBundle

1.1 ○
1.1 ○
1.2

✳	public		**AccessibleResourceBundle** ()
▲ *1*	public static final		getBundle (String baseName) throws java.util.MissingResourceException
	...... java.util.ResourceBundle		
▲ *1*	public static final		getBundle (String baseName, java.util.Locale locale)
	...... java.util.ResourceBundle		
△ *1*	public static		getBundle (String baseName, java.util.Locale locale, ClassLoader loader)
	...... java.util.ResourceBundle		throws java.util.MissingResourceException
2	public	**Object[][]**	**getContents** ()
2	public	*java.util.Enumeration*	getKeys ()
1	public	java.util.Locale	getLocale ()
● *1*	public final	Object	getObject (String key) throws java.util.MissingResourceException
● *1*	public final	String	getString (String key) throws java.util.MissingResourceException
● *1*	public final	String[]	getStringArray (String key) throws java.util.MissingResourceException
● *2*	public final	Object	handleGetObject (String key)
1	protected		parent
	...... java.util.ResourceBundle		
1	protected	void	setParent (java.util.ResourceBundle parent)

AccessibleRole   javax.accessibility

Object
  └AccessibleBundle [1]
    └AccessibleRole

1.2 ○
1.2

✳	protected		**AccessibleRole** (String key)
▲	public static final		**ALERT**
	.... AccessibleRole		
▲	public static final		**AWT_COMPONENT**
	.... AccessibleRole		
▲	public static final		**CHECK_BOX**
	.... AccessibleRole		
▲	public static final		**COLOR_CHOOSER**
	.... AccessibleRole		
▲	public static final		**COLUMN_HEADER**
	.... AccessibleRole		
▲	public static final		**COMBO_BOX**
	.... AccessibleRole		

Class *Interface* —extends - - -implements ○ abstract ● final △ static ▲ static final ✳ constructor x x—inherited x **x**—declared **x x**—overridden

Classes

AccessibleRole

▲	public static final	....	**TOGGLE_BUTTON**
	.... AccessibleRole		
▲	public static final	....	**TOOL_BAR**
	.... AccessibleRole		
▲	public static final	....	**TOOL_TIP**
	.... AccessibleRole		
1	public	.... String	toString ()
▲	public static final	....	**TREE**
	.... AccessibleRole		
▲	public static final	....	**UNKNOWN**
	.... AccessibleRole		
▲	public static final	....	**VIEWPORT**
	.... AccessibleRole		
▲	public static final	....	**WINDOW**
	.... AccessibleRole		

AccessibleSelection	javax.accessibility

1.2   *AccessibleSelection*

public	.... void	**addAccessibleSelection** (int i)
public	.... void	**clearAccessibleSelection** ()
public	.... *Accessible*	**getAccessibleSelection** (int i)
public	.... int	**getAccessibleSelectionCount** ()
public	.... boolean	**isAccessibleChildSelected** (int i)
public	.... void	**removeAccessibleSelection** (int i)
public	.... void	**selectAllAccessibleSelection** ()

AccessibleState	javax.accessibility

Object
1.2 ○   └AccessibleBundle[1]
1.2   └AccessibleState

✳	protected	....	**AccessibleState** (String key)
▲	public static final	....	**ACTIVE**
	.... AccessibleState		
▲	public static final	....	**ARMED**
	.... AccessibleState		
▲	public static final	....	**BUSY**
	.... AccessibleState		
▲	public static final	....	**CHECKED**
	.... AccessibleState		
▲	public static final	....	**COLLAPSED**
	.... AccessibleState		
▲	public static final	....	**EDITABLE**
	.... AccessibleState		
▲	public static final	....	**ENABLED**
	.... AccessibleState		
▲	public static final	....	**EXPANDABLE**
	.... AccessibleState		
▲	public static final	....	**EXPANDED**
	.... AccessibleState		
▲	public static final	....	**FOCUSABLE**
	.... AccessibleState		
▲	public static final	....	**FOCUSED**
	.... AccessibleState		
▲	public static final	....	**HORIZONTAL**
	.... AccessibleState		
▲	public static final	....	**ICONIFIED**
	.... AccessibleState		
1	protected	.... String	key
▲	public static final	....	**MODAL**
	.... AccessibleState		
▲	public static final	....	**MULTI_LINE**
	.... AccessibleState		
▲	public static final	....	**MULTISELECTABLE**
	.... AccessibleState		

Class   *Interface* —extends - - -implements ○ abstract ● final △ static ▲ static final ✳ constructor x x—inherited x **x**—declared **x x**—overridden

▲	public static final .... AccessibleState	**OPAQUE**
▲	public static final .... AccessibleState	**PRESSED**
▲	public static final .... AccessibleState	**RESIZABLE**
▲	public static final .... AccessibleState	**SELECTABLE**
▲	public static final .... AccessibleState	**SELECTED**
▲	public static final .... AccessibleState	**SHOWING**
▲	public static final .... AccessibleState	**SINGLE_LINE**
1	public .... String	toDisplayString ()
1	public .... String	toDisplayString (java.util.Locale locale)
1	protected .... String	toDisplayString (String resourceBundleName, java.util.Locale locale)
1	public .... String	toString ()
▲	public static final .... AccessibleState	**TRANSIENT**
▲	public static final .... AccessibleState	**VERTICAL**
▲	public static final .... AccessibleState	**VISIBLE**

AccessibleStateSet   javax.accessibility

Object [1]
1.2   └ AccessibleStateSet

*	public	**AccessibleStateSet** ()
*	public	**AccessibleStateSet** (AccessibleState[] states)
	public .... boolean	**add** (AccessibleState state)
	public ....void	**addAll** (AccessibleState[] states)
	public ....void	**clear** ()
	public .... boolean	**contains** (AccessibleState state)
	public .... boolean	**remove** (AccessibleState state)
	protected .... java.util.Vector	**states**
	public .... AccessibleState[]	**toArray** ()
1	public .... **String**	**toString** ()

AccessibleText   javax.accessibility

1.2   *AccessibleText*

▲	public static final ....int	**CHARACTER** = 1
	public .... String	**getAfterIndex** (int part, int index)
	public .... String	**getAtIndex** (int part, int index)
	public .... String	**getBeforeIndex** (int part, int index)
	public ....int	**getCaretPosition** ()
	public .... *javax.swing.text.AttributeSet*	**getCharacterAttribute** (int i)
	public ...... java.awt.Rectangle	**getCharacterBounds** (int i)
	public ....int	**getCharCount** ()
	public ....int	**getIndexAtPoint** (java.awt.Point p)
	public .... String	**getSelectedText** ()
	public ....int	**getSelectionEnd** ()
	public ....int	**getSelectionStart** ()
▲	public static final ....int	**SENTENCE** = 3
▲	public static final ....int	**WORD** = 2

AccessibleValue   javax.accessibility

1.2   *AccessibleValue*

	public .... Number	**getCurrentAccessibleValue** ()
	public .... Number	**getMaximumAccessibleValue** ()
	public .... Number	**getMinimumAccessibleValue** ()
	public .... boolean	**setCurrentAccessibleValue** (Number n)

Acl

		Acl	java.security.acl

1.1   *Acl*────────────────────── *Owner* [1]   P^U

	public	boolean	**addEntry** (*java.security.Principal* caller, *AclEntry* entry) throws NotOwnerException
1	public	boolean	addOwner (*java. security. Principal* caller, *java. security. Principal* owner) throws NotOwnerException
	public	boolean	**checkPermission** (*java.security.Principal* principal, *Permission* permission)
1	public	boolean	deleteOwner (*java. security. Principal* caller, *java. security. Principal* owner) throws NotOwnerException, LastOwnerException
	public	*java.util.Enumeration*	**entries** ()
	public	String	**getName** ()
	public	*java.util.Enumeration*	**getPermissions** (*java.security.Principal* user)
1	public	boolean	isOwner (*java.security.Principal* owner)
	public	boolean	**removeEntry** (*java. security. Principal* caller, *AclEntry* entry) throws NotOwnerException
	public	void	**setName** (*java.security.Principal* caller, String name) throws NotOwnerException
	public	String	**toString** ()

		AclEntry	java.security.acl

1.1   *AclEntry*────────────────────── *Cloneable*   P^U

public	boolean	**addPermission** (*Permission* permission)	
public	boolean	**checkPermission** (*Permission* permission)	
public	Object	**clone** ()	
public	*java.security.Principal*	**getPrincipal** ()	
public	boolean	**isNegative** ()	
public	*java.util.Enumeration*	**permissions** ()	
public	boolean	**removePermission** (*Permission* permission)	
public	void	**setNegativePermissions** ()	
public	boolean	**setPrincipal** (*java.security.Principal* user)	
public	String	**toString** ()	

		AclNotFoundException	java.security.acl

Object   P^U
  └Throwable - *java.io.Serializable*
    └Exception
1.1   └AclNotFoundException

✳	public	**AclNotFoundException** ()	

		Action	javax.swing

1.2   *Action*────────────────────── *java.awt.event.ActionListener* [1] (*java.util.EventListener*)

1	public	void	actionPerformed (java.awt.event.ActionEvent e)
	public	void	**addPropertyChangeListener** (*java.beans.PropertyChangeListener* listener)
▲	public static final	String	**DEFAULT** = "Default"
	public	Object	**getValue** (String key)
	public	boolean	**isEnabled** ()
▲	public static final	String	**LONG_DESCRIPTION** = "LongDescription"
▲	public static final	String	**NAME** = "Name"
	public	void	**putValue** (String key, Object value)
	public	void	**removePropertyChangeListener** (*java.beans.PropertyChangeListener* listener)
	public	void	**setEnabled** (boolean b)
▲	public static final	String	**SHORT_DESCRIPTION** = "ShortDescription"
▲	public static final	String	**SMALL_ICON** = "SmallIcon"

		ActionEvent	java.awt.event

Object   P
1.1   └java.util.EventObject [1] - - - - - - - - - - - - - - - - - - - *java.io.Serializable*
1.1 ○   └java.awt.AWTEvent [2]
1.1   └ActionEvent

▲	public static final	int	**ACTION_FIRST** = 1001
▲	public static final	int	**ACTION_LAST** = 1001

Class   *Interface*   ──extends   - - -implements   ○ abstract   ● final   △ static   ▲ static final   ✳ constructor   x x──inherited   x **x**──declared   **x x**──overridden

▲		public static final .... int	**ACTION_PERFORMED** = 1001	
✳		public	**ActionEvent** (Object source, int id, String command)	
✳		public	**ActionEvent** (Object source, int id, String command, int modifiers)	
▲		public static final .... int	**ALT_MASK** = 8	
	2	protected .... void	consume ()	
	2	protected .... boolean	consumed	
▲		public static final .... int	**CTRL_MASK** = 2	
	2	protected .... void	finalize () throws Throwable	
		public .... String	**getActionCommand** ()	
	2	public .... int	getID ()	
		public .... int	**getModifiers** ()	
	1	public .... Object	getSource ()	
	2	protected .... int	id	
	2	protected .... boolean	isConsumed ()	
▲		public static final .... int	**META_MASK** = 4	
	2	public .... **String**	**paramString** ()	
▲		public static final .... int	**SHIFT_MASK** = 1	
	1	protected transient ...... Object	source	
	2	public .... String	toString ()	

ActionListener
java.awt.event

1.1 *ActionListener————————————————java.util.EventListener*   P

---
public .... void **actionPerformed** (ActionEvent e)

Activatable
java.rmi.activation

Object
1.1 ○ └java.rmi.server.RemoteObject[1] - - - - - - - - - - *java.rmi.Remote, java.io.Serializable*
1.1 ○   └java.rmi.server.RemoteServer[2]
1.2 ○   └Activatable

✳		protected	**Activatable** (ActivationID id, int port) throws java.rmi.RemoteException
✳		protected	**Activatable** (String location, java.rmi.MarshalledObject data, boolean restart, int port) throws ActivationException, java.rmi.RemoteException
✳		protected	**Activatable** (ActivationID id, int port, *java.rmi.server.RMIClientSocketFactory* csf, *java.rmi.server.RMIServerSocketFactory* ssf) throws java.rmi.RemoteException
✳		protected	**Activatable** (String location, java.rmi. MarshalledObject data, boolean restart, int port, *java.rmi.server.RMIClientSocketFactory* csf, *java.rmi.server.RMIServerSocketFactory* ssf) throws ActivationException, java.rmi.RemoteException
	1	public .... boolean	equals (Object obj)
△		public static .. *java.rmi.Remote*	**exportObject** (*java.rmi.Remote* obj, ActivationID id, int port) throws java.rmi.RemoteException
△		public static .. *java.rmi.Remote*	**exportObject** (*java. rmi. Remote* obj, ActivationID id, int port, *java. rmi. server. RMIClientSocketFactory* csf, *java.rmi.server.RMIServerSocketFactory* ssf) throws java.rmi.RemoteException
△		public static .... ActivationID	**exportObject** (*java.rmi.Remote* obj, String location, java.rmi.MarshalledObject data, boolean restart, int port) throws ActivationException, java.rmi.RemoteException
△		public static .... ActivationID	**exportObject** (*java.rmi.Remote* obj, String location, java.rmi.MarshalledObject data, boolean restart, int port, *java. rmi. server. RMIClientSocketFactory* csf, *java.rmi.server.RMIServerSocketFactory* ssf) throws ActivationException, java.rmi.RemoteException
△	2	public static .... String	getClientHost () throws java.rmi.server.ServerNotActiveException
		protected .... ActivationID	**getID** ()
△	2	public static java.io.PrintStream	getLog ()
	1	public .... *java.rmi.server.RemoteRef*	getRef ()
	1	public .... int	hashCode ()
△		public static .... boolean	**inactive** (ActivationID id) throws UnknownObjectException, ActivationException, java.rmi.RemoteException
	1	protected transient .... *java.rmi.server.RemoteRef*	ref
△		public static .. *java.rmi.Remote*	**register** (ActivationDesc desc) throws UnknownGroupException, ActivationException, java.rmi.RemoteException
△	2	public static .... void	setLog (java.io.OutputStream out)
	1	public .... String	toString ()
△	1	public static .. *java.rmi.Remote*	toStub (*java.rmi.Remote* obj) throws java.rmi.NoSuchObjectException
△		public static .... boolean	**unexportObject** (*java. rmi. Remote* obj, boolean force) throws java.rmi.NoSuchObjectException

Activatable

△   public static .... void **unregister** (ActivationID id) throws UnknownObjectException, ActivationException,
                                            java.rmi.RemoteException

A

ActivateFailedException   java.rmi.activation

Object
└Throwable ---------------------------- *java.io.Serializable*
  └Exception
    └java.io.IOException
1.1   └java.rmi.RemoteException [1]
1.2   └ActivateFailedException

∗   public........................... **ActivateFailedException** (String s)
∗   public........................... **ActivateFailedException** (String s, Exception ex)
1   public................Throwable detail
1   public.....................String getMessage ()
1   public........................void printStackTrace ()
1   public........................void printStackTrace (java.io.PrintStream ps)
1   public........................void printStackTrace (java.io.PrintWriter pw)

ActivationDesc   java.rmi.activation

Object [1]
1.2 ● └ActivationDesc ------------------------ *java.io.Serializable*

∗   public........................... **ActivationDesc** (String className, String location, java.rmi.MarshalledObject data)
                                       throws ActivationException
∗   public........................... **ActivationDesc** (String className, String location, java.rmi.MarshalledObject data,
                                       boolean restart) throws ActivationException
∗   public........................... **ActivationDesc** (ActivationGroupID groupID, String className, String location,
                                       java.rmi.MarshalledObject data)
∗   public........................... **ActivationDesc** (ActivationGroupID groupID, String className, String location,
                                       java.rmi.MarshalledObject data, boolean restart)
1   public................. **boolean equals** (Object obj)
   public.......................String **getClassName** ()
   public........................ **getData** ()
  ..... java.rmi.MarshalledObject
   public....... ActivationGroupID **getGroupID** ()
   public.......................String **getLocation** ()
   public................. boolean **getRestartMode** ()
1   public...................... **int hashCode** ()

ActivationException   java.rmi.activation

Object
└Throwable [1] -------------------------- *java.io.Serializable*
  └Exception
1.2   └ActivationException

∗   public........................... **ActivationException** ()
∗   public........................... **ActivationException** (String s)
∗   public........................... **ActivationException** (String s, Throwable ex)
   public................Throwable **detail**
1   public................... **String getMessage** ()
1   public..................... **void printStackTrace** ()
1   public..................... **void printStackTrace** (java.io.PrintStream ps)
1   public..................... **void printStackTrace** (java.io.PrintWriter pw)

ActivationGroup   java.rmi.activation

Object
1.1 ○ └java.rmi.server.RemoteObject [1] ----------- *java.rmi.Remote, java.io.Serializable*
1.1 ○   └java.rmi.server.RemoteServer [2]
1.1   └java.rmi.server.UnicastRemoteObject [3]
1.2 ○   └ActivationGroup ------------------ *ActivationInstantiator [4]* (java.rmi.Remote)

Class   *Interface*   —extends   - - -implements   ○ abstract   ● final   △ static   ▲ static final   ∗ constructor   x x—inherited   x **x**—declared   **x x**—overridden

A

✳		protected	**ActivationGroup** (ActivationGroupID groupID) throws java.rmi.RemoteException
		protected . . . . void	**activeObject** (ActivationID id, java.rmi.MarshalledObject mobj) throws ActivationException, UnknownObjectException, java.rmi.RemoteException
○		public abstract . . . . void	**activeObject** (ActivationID id, *java.rmi.Remote* obj) throws ActivationException, UnknownObjectException, java.rmi.RemoteException
	3	public . . . . Object	clone () throws CloneNotSupportedException
△		public static synchronized . . . . ActivationGroup	**createGroup** (ActivationGroupID id, ActivationGroupDesc desc, long incarnation) throws ActivationException
△		public static synchronized . . . . ActivationGroupID	**currentGroupID** ()
	1	public . . . . boolean	equals (Object obj)
△	3	public static . . . . java.rmi.server.RemoteStub	exportObject (*java.rmi.Remote* obj) throws java.rmi.RemoteException
△	3	public static . . *java.rmi.Remote*	exportObject (*java.rmi.Remote* obj, int port) throws java.rmi.RemoteException
△	3	public static . . *java.rmi.Remote*	exportObject (*java.rmi.Remote* obj, int port, *java.rmi.server.RMIClientSocketFactory* csf, *java. rmi. server. RMIServerSocketFactory* ssf) throws java.rmi.RemoteException
△	2	public static . . . . String	getClientHost () throws java.rmi.server.ServerNotActiveException
△	2	public static java.io.PrintStream	getLog ()
	1	public . . . . *java.rmi.server.RemoteRef*	getRef ()
△		public static synchronized . . . . *ActivationSystem*	**getSystem** () throws ActivationException
	1	public . . . . int	hashCode ()
		protected . . . . void	**inactiveGroup** () throws UnknownGroupException, java.rmi.RemoteException
		public . . . . boolean	**inactiveObject** (ActivationID id) throws ActivationException, UnknownObjectException, java.rmi.RemoteException
○	4	public abstract . . . . java.rmi.MarshalledObject	**newInstance** (ActivationID, ActivationDesc) throws java.rmi.activation.ActivationException java.rmi.RemoteException
	1	protected transient . . . . *java.rmi.server.RemoteRef*	ref
△	2	public static . . . . void	setLog (java.io.OutputStream out)
△		public static synchronized void	**setSystem** (*ActivationSystem* system) throws ActivationException
	1	public . . . . String	toString ()
△	1	public static . . *java.rmi.Remote*	toStub (*java.rmi.Remote* obj) throws java.rmi.NoSuchObjectException
△	3	public static . . . . boolean	unexportObject (*java. rmi. Remote* obj, boolean force) throws java.rmi.NoSuchObjectException

ActivationGroup_Stub | java.rmi.activation

		Object	
1.1	○	└java.rmi.server.RemoteObject[1] - - - - - - - - - - - *java.rmi.Remote, java.io.Serializable*	
1.1	○	└java.rmi.server.RemoteStub	
1.2	●	└ActivationGroup_Stub - - - - - - - - - - - - - - *ActivationInstantiator* [2] (*java.rmi.Remote*), *java.rmi.Remote*	

✳		public	**ActivationGroup_Stub** (*java.rmi.server.RemoteRef*)
	1	public . . . . boolean	equals (Object obj)
	1	public . . . . *java.rmi.server.RemoteRef*	getRef ()
	1	public . . . . int	hashCode ()
	2	public . . . . java.rmi.MarshalledObject	**newInstance** (ActivationID, ActivationDesc) throws java.rmi.RemoteException java.rmi.activation.ActivationException
	1	protected transient . . . . *java.rmi.server.RemoteRef*	ref
	1	public . . . . String	toString ()
△	1	public static . . *java.rmi.Remote*	toStub (*java.rmi.Remote* obj) throws java.rmi.NoSuchObjectException

ActivationGroupDesc | java.rmi.activation

		Object[1]	
1.2	●	└ActivationGroupDesc - - - - - - - - - - - - - - - - - - - *java.io.Serializable*	

✳		public	**ActivationGroupDesc** (java. util. Properties overrides, ActivationGroupDesc.CommandEnvironment cmd)
✳		public	**ActivationGroupDesc** (String className, String location, java. rmi. MarshalledObject data, java. util. Properties overrides, ActivationGroupDesc.CommandEnvironment cmd)
	1	public . . . . **boolean**	**equals** (Object obj)
		public . . . . String	**getClassName** ()
		public . ActivationGroupDesc ↵ .CommandEnvironment	**getCommandEnvironment** ()

Classes

ActivationGroupDesc

public		**getData** ()
..... java.rmi.MarshalledObject		
public	String	**getLocation** ()
public	java.util.Properties	**getPropertyOverrides** ()
[1] public	int	**hashCode** ()

ActivationGroupDesc.CommandEnvironment — java.rmi.activation

Object[1]
1.2 └ActivationGroupDesc.CommandEnvironment - *java.io.Serializable*

* public		**CommandEnvironment** (String cmdpath, String[] argv)
[1] public	boolean	**equals** (Object obj)
public	String[]	**getCommandOptions** ()
public	String	**getCommandPath** ()
[1] public	int	**hashCode** ()

ActivationGroupID — java.rmi.activation

Object[1]
1.2 └ActivationGroupID - *java.io.Serializable*

* public		**ActivationGroupID** (*ActivationSystem* system)
[1] public	boolean	**equals** (Object obj)
public	*ActivationSystem*	**getSystem** ()
[1] public	int	**hashCode** ()

ActivationID — java.rmi.activation

Object[1]
1.2 └ActivationID - *java.io.Serializable*

public	*java.rmi.Remote*	**activate** (boolean force) throws ActivationException, UnknownObjectException, java.rmi.RemoteException
* public		**ActivationID** (*Activator* activator)
[1] public	boolean	**equals** (Object obj)
[1] public	int	**hashCode** ()

ActivationInstantiator — java.rmi.activation

1.2 *ActivationInstantiator*————————————*java.rmi.Remote*

public		**newInstance** (ActivationID id, ActivationDesc desc)
..... java.rmi.MarshalledObject		throws ActivationException, java.rmi.RemoteException

---

ActivationMonitor — java.rmi.activation

1.2 *ActivationMonitor*————————————*java.rmi.Remote*

public	void	**activeObject** (ActivationID id, java.rmi. MarshalledObject obj) throws UnknownObjectException, java.rmi.RemoteException
public	void	**inactiveGroup** (ActivationGroupID id, long incarnation) throws UnknownGroupException, java.rmi.RemoteException
public	void	**inactiveObject** (ActivationID id) throws UnknownObjectException, java.rmi.RemoteException

---

ActivationSystem — java.rmi.activation

1.2 *ActivationSystem*————————————*java.rmi.Remote*

public	*ActivationMonitor*	**activeGroup** (ActivationGroupID id, *ActivationInstantiator* group, long incarnation) throws UnknownGroupException, ActivationException, java.rmi.RemoteException
public	ActivationDesc	**getActivationDesc** (ActivationID id) throws ActivationException, UnknownObjectException, java.rmi.RemoteException
public	ActivationGroupDesc	**getActivationGroupDesc** (ActivationGroupID id) throws ActivationException, UnknownGroupException, java.rmi.RemoteException

---

Class *Interface* —extends - - -implements ○ abstract ● final △ static ▲ static final ＊ constructor x x—inherited x **x**—declared **x x**—overridden

public .... ActivationGroupID	**registerGroup** (ActivationGroupDesc desc) throws ActivationException,	
	java.rmi.RemoteException	
public .... ActivationID	**registerObject** (ActivationDesc desc) throws ActivationException,	
	UnknownGroupException, java.rmi.RemoteException	
public .... ActivationDesc	**setActivationDesc** (ActivationID id, ActivationDesc desc)	
	throws ActivationException, UnknownObjectException,	
	UnknownGroupException, java.rmi.RemoteException	
public .... ActivationGroupDesc	**setActivationGroupDesc** (ActivationGroupID id, ActivationGroupDesc desc)	
	throws ActivationException, UnknownGroupException, java.rmi.RemoteException	
public .... void	**shutdown** () throws java.rmi.RemoteException	
▲ public static final .... int	**SYSTEM_PORT** = 1098	
public .... void	**unregisterGroup** (ActivationGroupID id) throws ActivationException,	
	UnknownGroupException, java.rmi.RemoteException	
public .... void	**unregisterObject** (ActivationID id) throws ActivationException,	
	UnknownObjectException, java.rmi.RemoteException	

Activator   java.rmi.activation

1.2 *Activator*————————————————————*java.rmi.Remote*

public	**activate** (ActivationID id, boolean force) throws ActivationException,	
..... java.rmi.MarshalledObject	UnknownObjectException, java.rmi.RemoteException	

ActiveEvent   java.awt

1.2 *ActiveEvent*   P

public .... void	**dispatch** ()	

Adjustable   java.awt

1.1 *Adjustable*   P

public .... void	**addAdjustmentListener** (*java.awt.event.AdjustmentListener* l)	
public .... int	**getBlockIncrement** ()	
public .... int	**getMaximum** ()	
public .... int	**getMinimum** ()	
public .... int	**getOrientation** ()	
public .... int	**getUnitIncrement** ()	
public .... int	**getValue** ()	
public .... int	**getVisibleAmount** ()	
▲ public static final .... int	**HORIZONTAL** = 0	
public .... void	**removeAdjustmentListener** (*java.awt.event.AdjustmentListener* l)	
public .... void	**setBlockIncrement** (int b)	
public .... void	**setMaximum** (int max)	
public .... void	**setMinimum** (int min)	
public .... void	**setUnitIncrement** (int u)	
public .... void	**setValue** (int v)	
public .... void	**setVisibleAmount** (int v)	
▲ public static final .... int	**VERTICAL** = 1	

AdjustmentEvent   java.awt.event

Object   P
1.1 └java.util.EventObject[1] - - - - - - - - - - - - - - - - - - *java.io.Serializable*
1.1 ○   └java.awt.AWTEvent[2]
1.1   └AdjustmentEvent

▲	public static final .... int	**ADJUSTMENT_FIRST** = 601
▲	public static final .... int	**ADJUSTMENT_LAST** = 601
▲	public static final .... int	**ADJUSTMENT_VALUE_CHANGED** = 601
*	public	**AdjustmentEvent** (*java.awt.Adjustable* source, int id, int type, int value)
▲	public static final .... int	**BLOCK_DECREMENT** = 3
▲	public static final .... int	**BLOCK_INCREMENT** = 4
2	protected .... void	consume ()
2	protected .... boolean	consumed
2	protected .... void	finalize () throws Throwable
	public ...... *java.awt.Adjustable*	**getAdjustable** ()
	public .... int	**getAdjustmentType** ()
2	public .... int	getID ()
1	public .... Object	getSource ()

AdjustmentEvent

	public	int	**getValue** ()
2	protected	int	id
2	protected	boolean	isConsumed ()
2	public	**String**	**paramString** ()
1	protected transient	Object	source
2	public	String	toString ()
▲	public static final	int	**TRACK** = 5
▲	public static final	int	**UNIT_DECREMENT** = 2
▲	public static final	int	**UNIT_INCREMENT** = 1

AdjustmentListener   java.awt.event
P

1.1	*AdjustmentListener*————————————*java.util.EventListener*		
	public	void	**adjustmentValueChanged** (AdjustmentEvent e)

Adler32   java.util.zip
P O

Object
1.1 └─Adler32 - *Checksum* [1]

*	public		**Adler32** ()
1	public	long	**getValue** ()
1	public	void	**reset** ()
	public	void	**update** (byte[] b)
1	public	void	**update** (int b)
1	public	void	**update** (byte[] b, int off, int len)

AffineTransform   java.awt.geom

Object [1]
1.2 └─AffineTransform - *Cloneable, java.io.Serializable*

*	public		**AffineTransform** ()
*	public		**AffineTransform** (double[] flatmatrix)
*	public		**AffineTransform** (float[] flatmatrix)
*	public		**AffineTransform** (AffineTransform Tx)
*	public		**AffineTransform** (double m00, double m10, double m01, double m11, double m02, double m12)
*	public		**AffineTransform** (float m00, float m10, float m01, float m11, float m02, float m12)
1	public	**Object**	**clone** ()
	public	void	**concatenate** (AffineTransform Tx)
	public	AffineTransform	**createInverse** () throws NoninvertibleTransformException
	public	*java.awt.Shape*	**createTransformedShape** (*java.awt.Shape* pSrc)
	public	Point2D	**deltaTransform** (Point2D ptSrc, Point2D ptDst)
	public	void	**deltaTransform** (double[] srcPts, int srcOff, double[] dstPts, int dstOff, int numPts)
1	public	**boolean**	**equals** (Object obj)
	public	double	**getDeterminant** ()
	public	void	**getMatrix** (double[] flatmatrix)
△	public static	AffineTransform	**getRotateInstance** (double theta)
△	public static	AffineTransform	**getRotateInstance** (double theta, double x, double y)
△	public static	AffineTransform	**getScaleInstance** (double sx, double sy)
	public	double	**getScaleX** ()
	public	double	**getScaleY** ()
△	public static	AffineTransform	**getShearInstance** (double shx, double shy)
	public	double	**getShearX** ()
	public	double	**getShearY** ()
△	public static	AffineTransform	**getTranslateInstance** (double tx, double ty)
	public	double	**getTranslateX** ()
	public	double	**getTranslateY** ()
	public	int	**getType** ()
1	public	**int**	**hashCode** ()
	public	Point2D	**inverseTransform** (Point2D ptSrc, Point2D ptDst) throws NoninvertibleTransformException
	public	void	**inverseTransform** (double[] srcPts, int srcOff, double[] dstPts, int dstOff, int numPts) throws NoninvertibleTransformException
	public	boolean	**isIdentity** ()
	public	void	**preConcatenate** (AffineTransform Tx)
	public	void	**rotate** (double theta)

Class   *Interface*   —extends   - - -implements   ○ abstract   ● final   △ static   ▲ static final   * constructor   x x—inherited   x **x**—declared   **x x**—overridden

	public	void	**rotate** (double theta, double x, double y)
	public	void	**scale** (double sx, double sy)
	public	void	**setToIdentity** ()
	public	void	**setToRotation** (double theta)
	public	void	**setToRotation** (double theta, double x, double y)
	public	void	**setToScale** (double sx, double sy)
	public	void	**setToShear** (double shx, double shy)
	public	void	**setToTranslation** (double tx, double ty)
	public	void	**setTransform** (AffineTransform Tx)
	public	void	**setTransform** (double m00, double m10, double m01, double m11, double m02, double m12)
	public	void	**shear** (double shx, double shy)
1	public	**String**	**toString** ()
	public	Point2D	**transform** (Point2D ptSrc, Point2D ptDst)
	public	void	**transform** (double[] srcPts, int srcOff, float[] dstPts, int dstOff, int numPts)
	public	void	**transform** (double[] srcPts, int srcOff, double[] dstPts, int dstOff, int numPts)
	public	void	**transform** (float[] srcPts, int srcOff, double[] dstPts, int dstOff, int numPts)
	public	void	**transform** (float[] srcPts, int srcOff, float[] dstPts, int dstOff, int numPts)
	public	void	**transform** (Point2D[] ptSrc, int srcOff, Point2D[] ptDst, int dstOff, int numPts)
	public	void	**translate** (double tx, double ty)
▲	public static final	int	**TYPE_FLIP** = 64
▲	public static final	int	**TYPE_GENERAL_ROTATION** = 16
▲	public static final	int	**TYPE_GENERAL_SCALE** = 4
▲	public static final	int	**TYPE_GENERAL_TRANSFORM** = 32
▲	public static final	int	**TYPE_IDENTITY** = 0
▲	public static final	int	**TYPE_MASK_ROTATION** = 24
▲	public static final	int	**TYPE_MASK_SCALE** = 6
▲	public static final	int	**TYPE_QUADRANT_ROTATION** = 8
▲	public static final	int	**TYPE_TRANSLATION** = 1
▲	public static final	int	**TYPE_UNIFORM_SCALE** = 2

AffineTransformOp   java.awt.image

```
     Object                                                                P
1.2  └AffineTransformOp - - - - - - - - - - - - - - - - - - - - BufferedImageOp 1, RasterOp 2
```

*	public		**AffineTransformOp** (java. awt. geom. AffineTransform xform, java.awt.RenderingHints hints)
*	public		**AffineTransformOp** (java.awt.geom.AffineTransform xform, int interpolationType)
1	public	BufferedImage	**createCompatibleDestImage** (BufferedImage src, ColorModel destCM)
2	public	WritableRaster	**createCompatibleDestRaster** (Raster src)
● 1	public final	BufferedImage	**filter** (BufferedImage src, BufferedImage dst)
● 2	public final	WritableRaster	**filter** (Raster src, WritableRaster dst)
● 1	public final ... java.awt.geom.Rectangle2D		**getBounds2D** (BufferedImage src)
● 2	public final ... java.awt.geom.Rectangle2D		**getBounds2D** (Raster src)
●	public final	int	**getInterpolationType** ()
● 1	public final java.awt.geom.Point2D		**getPoint2D** (java.awt.geom.Point2D srcPt, java.awt.geom.Point2D dstPt)
● 1	public final ...... java.awt.RenderingHints		**getRenderingHints** ()
●	public final java.awt.geom.AffineTransform		**getTransform** ()
▲	public static final	int	**TYPE_BILINEAR** = 2
▲	public static final	int	**TYPE_NEAREST_NEIGHBOR** = 1

AlgorithmParameterGenerator   java.security

```
     Object                                                               PO
1.2  └AlgorithmParameterGenerator
```

*	protected		**AlgorithmParameterGenerator** (AlgorithmParameterGeneratorSpi paramGenSpi, Provider provider, String algorithm)
●	public final .... AlgorithmParameters		**generateParameters** ()
●	public final	String	**getAlgorithm** ()
△	public static ... . AlgorithmParameterGenerator		**getInstance** (String algorithm) throws NoSuchAlgorithmException
△	public static ... . AlgorithmParameterGenerator		**getInstance** (String algorithm, String provider) throws NoSuchAlgorithmException, NoSuchProviderException

A

Classes

AlgorithmParameterGenerator

- public final .... Provider **getProvider** ()
- public final ....void **init** (int size)
- public final ....void **init** (*java. security. spec. AlgorithmParameterSpec* genParamSpec)
  throws InvalidAlgorithmParameterException
- public final ....void **init** (int size, SecureRandom random)
- public final ....void **init** (*java. security. spec. AlgorithmParameterSpec* genParamSpec,
  SecureRandom random) throws InvalidAlgorithmParameterException

---

AlgorithmParameterGeneratorSpi	java.security
	P^O

Object
 └AlgorithmParameterGeneratorSpi   1.2 ○

✱	public..........................	**AlgorithmParameterGeneratorSpi** ()
○	protected abstract	**engineGenerateParameters** ()
	.... AlgorithmParameters	
○	protected abstract ....void	**engineInit** (int size, SecureRandom random)
○	protected abstract ....void	**engineInit** (*java. security. spec. AlgorithmParameterSpec* genParamSpec, SecureRandom random) throws InvalidAlgorithmParameterException

---

AlgorithmParameters	java.security
	P^O

Object[1]
 └AlgorithmParameters   1.2

✱	protected	**AlgorithmParameters** (AlgorithmParametersSpi paramSpi, Provider provider, String algorithm)
●	public final ....String	**getAlgorithm** ()
●	public final ....byte[]	**getEncoded** () throws java.io.IOException
●	public final ....byte[]	**getEncoded** (String format) throws java.io.IOException
△	public static	**getInstance** (String algorithm) throws NoSuchAlgorithmException
	.... AlgorithmParameters	
△	public static	**getInstance** (String algorithm, String provider) throws NoSuchAlgorithmException, NoSuchProviderException
	.... AlgorithmParameters	
●	public final	**getParameterSpec** (Class paramSpec) throws java. security. spec ↵ .InvalidParameterSpecException
	.... *java.security.spec* ↵ .*AlgorithmParameterSpec*	
●	public final .... Provider	**getProvider** ()
●	public final ....void	**init** (byte[] params) throws java.io.IOException
●	public final ....void	**init** (*java. security. spec. AlgorithmParameterSpec* paramSpec) throws java.security.spec.InvalidParameterSpecException
●	public final ....void	**init** (byte[] params, String format) throws java.io.IOException
● 1	public final .... **String**	**toString** ()

AlgorithmParameterSpec	java.security.spec

AlgorithmParameterSpec   1.2

AlgorithmParametersSpi	java.security
	P^O

Object
 └AlgorithmParametersSpi   1.2 ○

✱	public..........................	**AlgorithmParametersSpi** ()
○	protected abstract ....byte[]	**engineGetEncoded** () throws java.io.IOException
○	protected abstract ....byte[]	**engineGetEncoded** (String format) throws java.io.IOException
○	protected abstract	**engineGetParameterSpec** (Class paramSpec) throws java.security.spec.InvalidParameterSpecException
	.... *java.security.spec* ↵ .*AlgorithmParameterSpec*	
○	protected abstract ....void	**engineInit** (byte[] params) throws java.io.IOException
○	protected abstract ....void	**engineInit** (*java. security. spec. AlgorithmParameterSpec* paramSpec) throws java.security.spec.InvalidParameterSpecException
○	protected abstract ....void	**engineInit** (byte[] params, String format) throws java.io.IOException
○	protected abstract ....String	**engineToString** ()

Class   *Interface*   —extends   - - -implements   ○ abstract   ● final   △ static   ▲ static final   ✱ constructor   x x—inherited   x **x**—declared   **x x**—overridden

		AllPermission	java.security

P[o]

Object
1.2 ○ └ Permission [1] - *Guard, java.io.Serializable*
1.2 ●   └ AllPermission

*	public		**AllPermission** ()
*	public		**AllPermission** (String name, String actions)
1	public	void	checkGuard (Object object) throws SecurityException
1	public	**boolean**	**equals** (Object obj)
1	public	**String**	**getActions** ()
● 1	public final	String	getName ()
1	public	**int**	**hashCode** ()
1	public	**boolean**	**implies** (Permission p)
1	public	**PermissionCollection**	**newPermissionCollection** ()
1	public	String	toString ()

		AlphaComposite	java.awt

P

Object [1]
1.2 ● └ AlphaComposite - *Composite* [2]

▲	public static final		**Clear**
		AlphaComposite	
▲	public static final	int	**CLEAR** = 1
2	public	*CompositeContext*	**createContext** (java. awt. image. ColorModel srcColorModel, java.awt.image.ColorModel dstColorModel, RenderingHints hints)
▲	public static final	int	**DST_IN** = 6
▲	public static final	int	**DST_OUT** = 8
▲	public static final	int	**DST_OVER** = 4
▲	public static final		**DstIn**
		AlphaComposite	
▲	public static final		**DstOut**
		AlphaComposite	
▲	public static final		**DstOver**
		AlphaComposite	
1	public	**boolean**	**equals** (Object obj)
	public	float	**getAlpha** ()
△	public static	AlphaComposite	**getInstance** (int rule)
△	public static	AlphaComposite	**getInstance** (int rule, float alpha)
	public	int	**getRule** ()
1	public	**int**	**hashCode** ()
▲	public static final		**Src**
		AlphaComposite	
▲	public static final	int	**SRC** = 2
▲	public static final	int	**SRC_IN** = 5
▲	public static final	int	**SRC_OUT** = 7
▲	public static final	int	**SRC_OVER** = 3
▲	public static final		**SrcIn**
		AlphaComposite	
▲	public static final		**SrcOut**
		AlphaComposite	
▲	public static final		**SrcOver**
		AlphaComposite	

		AlreadyBound	org.omg.CosNaming.NamingContextPackage

Object
└ Throwable - *java.io.Serializable*
   └ Exception
1.2 ○   └ org.omg.CORBA.UserException - - - - - - - *org.omg.CORBA.portable.IDLEntity (java.io.Serializable)*
1.2 ●   └ AlreadyBound - *org.omg.CORBA.portable.IDLEntity (java.io.Serializable)*

*	public		**AlreadyBound** ()

A

Classes

AlreadyBoundException

AlreadyBoundException			java.rmi

Object
└Throwable - *java.io.Serializable*
1.1   └Exception
            └AlreadyBoundException

✳	public.........................	**AlreadyBoundException** ()
✳	public.........................	**AlreadyBoundException** (String s)

AlreadyBoundHelper	org.omg.CosNaming.NamingContextPackage

Object
1.2   └AlreadyBoundHelper

△	public static .... AlreadyBound	**extract** (org.omg.CORBA.Any a)
△	public static .... String	**id** ()
△	public static ....void	**insert** (org.omg.CORBA.Any a, AlreadyBound that)
△	public static .... AlreadyBound	**read** (org.omg.CORBA.portable.InputStream in)
△	public static synchronized .... org.omg.CORBA.TypeCode	**type** ()
△	public static ....void	**write** (org.omg.CORBA.portable.OutputStream out, AlreadyBound that)

AlreadyBoundHolder	org.omg.CosNaming.NamingContextPackage

Object
1.2 ●   └AlreadyBoundHolder - *org.omg.CORBA.portable.Streamable* [1]

1	public......................void	**_read** (org.omg.CORBA.portable.InputStream in)
1	public......................... ... org.omg.CORBA.TypeCode	**_type** ()
1	public......................void	**_write** (org.omg.CORBA.portable.OutputStream out)
✳	public.........................	**AlreadyBoundHolder** ()
✳	public.........................	**AlreadyBoundHolder** (AlreadyBound __arg)
	public............. AlreadyBound	**value**

AncestorEvent			javax.swing.event

Object
1.1   └java.util.EventObject [1] - - - - - - - - - - - - - - - - - - - *java.io.Serializable*
1.1 ○   └java.awt.AWTEvent [2]
1.2   └AncestorEvent

▲	public static final ....int	**ANCESTOR_ADDED** = 1
▲	public static final ....int	**ANCESTOR_MOVED** = 3
▲	public static final ....int	**ANCESTOR_REMOVED** = 2
✳	public.........................	**AncestorEvent** (javax. swing. JComponent source, int id, java.awt.Container ancestor, java.awt.Container ancestorParent)
2	protected ....void	consume ()
2	protected .... boolean	consumed
2	protected ....void	finalize () throws Throwable
	public.......java.awt.Container	**getAncestor** ()
	public.......java.awt.Container	**getAncestorParent** ()
	public......................... ...... javax.swing.JComponent	**getComponent** ()
2	public......................int	getID ()
1	public....................Object	getSource ()
2	protected ....int	id
2	protected .... boolean	isConsumed ()
2	public..................String	paramString ()
1	protected transient...... Object	source
2	public..................String	toString ()

Class   *Interface*   —extends   - - -implements   ○ abstract   ● final   △ static   ▲ static final   ✳ constructor   x x—inherited   x **x**—declared   **x x**—overridden

AncestorListener		javax.swing.event

1.2   *AncestorListener—————————————— java.util.EventListener*

- -

public......................void **ancestorAdded** (AncestorEvent event)
public......................void **ancestorMoved** (AncestorEvent event)
public......................void **ancestorRemoved** (AncestorEvent event)

- -

Annotation		java.text

Object[1]
1.2   └Annotation

P

*   public............................ **Annotation** (Object value)
    public....................Object **getValue** ()
 1 public....................**String** **toString** ()

Any		org.omg.CORBA

Object
1.2 ○ └Any - *org.omg.CORBA.portable.IDLEntity (java.io.Serializable)*

*   public............................ **Any** ()
○ public abstract ..... org.omg ↵ **create_input_stream** ()
    .CORBA.portable.InputStream
○ public abstract .... **create_output_stream** ()
    ....org.omg.CORBA ↵
    .portable.OutputStream
○ public abstract .... boolean **equal** (Any a)
○ public abstract .... Any **extract_any** () throws BAD_OPERATION
○ public abstract ..... boolean **extract_boolean** () throws BAD_OPERATION
○ public abstract .... char **extract_char** () throws BAD_OPERATION
○ public abstract ....double **extract_double** () throws BAD_OPERATION
    public... java.math.BigDecimal **extract_fixed** ()
○ public abstract ....float **extract_float** () throws BAD_OPERATION
○ public abstract ....int **extract_long** () throws BAD_OPERATION
○ public abstract .... long **extract_longlong** () throws BAD_OPERATION
○ public abstract .... *Object* **extract_Object** () throws BAD_OPERATION
○ public abstract .... byte **extract_octet** () throws BAD_OPERATION
D ○ public abstract ....Principal **extract_Principal** () throws BAD_OPERATION
○ public abstract ....short **extract_short** () throws BAD_OPERATION
○ public abstract ....String **extract_string** () throws BAD_OPERATION
○ public abstract ...... TypeCode **extract_TypeCode** () throws BAD_OPERATION
○ public abstract ....int **extract_ulong** () throws BAD_OPERATION
○ public abstract .... long **extract_ulonglong** () throws BAD_OPERATION
○ public abstract ....short **extract_ushort** () throws BAD_OPERATION
    public.......*java.io.Serializable* **extract_Value** () throws BAD_OPERATION
○ public abstract .... char **extract_wchar** () throws BAD_OPERATION
○ public abstract ....String **extract_wstring** () throws BAD_OPERATION
○ public abstract ....void **insert_any** (Any a)
○ public abstract ....void **insert_boolean** (boolean b)
○ public abstract ....void **insert_char** (char c) throws DATA_CONVERSION
○ public abstract ....void **insert_double** (double d)
    public...........................void **insert_fixed** (java.math.BigDecimal value)
    public...........................void **insert_fixed** (java.math.BigDecimal value, TypeCode type)
○ public abstract ....void **insert_float** (float f)
○ public abstract ....void **insert_long** (int l)
○ public abstract ....void **insert_longlong** (long l)
○ public abstract ....void **insert_Object** (*Object* o)
○ public abstract ....void **insert_Object** (*Object* o, TypeCode t) throws BAD_OPERATION
○ public abstract ....void **insert_octet** (byte b)
D ○ public abstract ....void **insert_Principal** (Principal p)
○ public abstract ....void **insert_short** (short s)
○ public abstract ....void **insert_Streamable** (*org.omg.CORBA.portable.Streamable* s)
○ public abstract ....void **insert_string** (String s) throws DATA_CONVERSION, MARSHAL
○ public abstract ....void **insert_TypeCode** (TypeCode t)
○ public abstract ....void **insert_ulong** (int l)
○ public abstract ....void **insert_ulonglong** (long l)
○ public abstract ....void **insert_ushort** (short s)
    public...........................void **insert_Value** (*java.io.Serializable* v)
    public...........................void **insert_Value** (*java.io.Serializable* v, TypeCode t) throws MARSHAL
○ public abstract ....void **insert_wchar** (char c)

Any

○	public abstract . . . . void	**insert_wstring** (String s) throws MARSHAL
○	public abstract . . . . void	**read_value** (org.omg.CORBA.portable.InputStream is, TypeCode t) throws MARSHAL
○	public abstract . . . . . . TypeCode	**type** ()
○	public abstract . . . . void	**type** (TypeCode t)
○	public abstract . . . . void	**write_value** (org.omg.CORBA.portable.OutputStream os)

AnyHolder   org.omg.CORBA

Object
1.2 ● └─AnyHolder - *org.omg.CORBA.portable.Streamable* [1]

1	public . . . . void	**_read** (org.omg.CORBA.portable.InputStream input)
1	public . . . . TypeCode	**_type** ()
1	public . . . . void	**_write** (org.omg.CORBA.portable.OutputStream output)
✻	public	**AnyHolder** ()
✻	public	**AnyHolder** (Any initial)
	public . . . . Any	**value**

Applet   java.applet

P

Object
○ └─*java.awt.Component* [1] - *java.awt.image.ImageObserver*, *java.awt.MenuContainer*, *java.io.Serializable*

   └─*java.awt.Container* [2]
     └─*java.awt.Panel* [3]
      └─Applet

	1	*134 inherited members from java.awt.Component not shown*	
	2	*50 inherited members from java.awt.Container not shown*	
	3	public . . . . void	addNotify ()
✻		public	**Applet** ()
		public . . . . void	**destroy** ()
		public . . . . *AppletContext*	**getAppletContext** ()
		public : . . . . String	**getAppletInfo** ()
		public . . . . *AudioClip*	**getAudioClip** (java.net.URL url)
		public . . . . *AudioClip*	**getAudioClip** (java.net.URL url, String name)
		public . . . . java.net.URL	**getCodeBase** ()
		public . . . . java.net.URL	**getDocumentBase** ()
		public . . . . java.awt.Image	**getImage** (java.net.URL url)
		public . . . . java.awt.Image	**getImage** (java.net.URL url, String name)
1.1	1	public . . . . **java.util.Locale**	**getLocale** ()
		public . . . . String	**getParameter** (String name)
		public . . . . String[][]	**getParameterInfo** ()
		public . . . . void	**init** ()
		public . . . . boolean	**isActive** ()
1.2 ▲		public static final . . . . *AudioClip*	**newAudioClip** (java.net.URL url)
		public . . . . void	**play** (java.net.URL url)
		public . . . . void	**play** (java.net.URL url, String name)
	1	public . . . . **void**	**resize** (java.awt.Dimension d)
	1	public . . . . **void**	**resize** (int width, int height)
●		public final . . . . void	**setStub** (*AppletStub* stub)
		public . . . . void	**showStatus** (String msg)
		public . . . . void	**start** ()
		public . . . . void	**stop** ()

AppletContext   java.applet

P

AppletContext

public . . . . Applet	**getApplet** (String name)
public . . . . *java.util.Enumeration*	**getApplets** ()
public . . . . *AudioClip*	**getAudioClip** (java.net.URL url)
public . . . . java.awt.Image	**getImage** (java.net.URL url)
public . . . . void	**showDocument** (java.net.URL url)
public . . . . void	**showDocument** (java.net.URL url, String target)
public . . . . void	**showStatus** (String status)

Class   *Interface*   —extends   - - -implements   ○ abstract   ● final   △ static   ▲ static final   ✻ constructor   x x—inherited   x **x**—declared   **x x**—overridden

AppletInitializer

		java.beans

1.2   *AppletInitializer*

    public......................void **activate** (java.applet.Applet newApplet)
    public......................void **initialize** (java.applet.Applet newAppletBean, *java.beans.beancontext↵*
                                .BeanContext bCtxt)

AppletStub

		java.applet

     AppletStub   P

    public......................void **appletResize** (int width, int height)
    public............. *AppletContext* **getAppletContext** ()
    public............. java.net.URL **getCodeBase** ()
    public............. java.net.URL **getDocumentBase** ()
    public......................String **getParameter** (String name)
    public.................. boolean **isActive** ()

ApplicationException

		org.omg.CORBA.portable

    Object
    └Throwable - *java.io.Serializable*
      └Exception
        └ApplicationException

1.2

*   public......................... **ApplicationException** (String id, InputStream ins)
     public......................String **getId** ()
     public............. InputStream **getInputStream** ()

Arc2D

		java.awt.geom

    Object
1.2 ○   └RectangularShape[1] - *java.awt.Shape, Cloneable*
1.2 ○   └Arc2D

*   protected............................. **Arc2D** (int type)
▲   public static final.............int **CHORD** = 1
   1   public....................Object clone ()
   1   public.................. boolean contains (Point2D p)
   1   public.................. **boolean contains** (Rectangle2D r)
   1   public.................. **boolean contains** (double x, double y)
   1   public.................. **boolean contains** (double x, double y, double w, double h)
     public.................. boolean **containsAngle** (double angle)
○   public abstract..........double **getAngleExtent** ()
○   public abstract..........double **getAngleStart** ()
     public.......................int **getArcType** ()
   1   public...... java.awt.Rectangle getBounds ()
   1   public............. **Rectangle2D getBounds2D** ()
   1   public....................double getCenterX ()
   1   public....................double getCenterY ()
     public....................Point2D **getEndPoint** ()
   1   public....................Rectangle2D getFrame ()
○ 1   public abstract..........double getHeight ()
   1   public....................double getMaxX ()
   1   public....................double getMaxY ()
   1   public....................double getMinX ()
   1   public....................double getMinY ()
   1   public............. *PathIterator* **getPathIterator** (AffineTransform at)
   1   public............. *PathIterator* getPathIterator (AffineTransform at, double flatness)
     public....................Point2D **getStartPoint** ()
○ 1   public abstract..........double getWidth ()
○ 1   public abstract..........double getX ()
○ 1   public abstract..........double getY ()
   1   public.................. boolean intersects (Rectangle2D r)
   1   public.................. **boolean intersects** (double x, double y, double w, double h)
○ 1   public abstract........ boolean isEmpty ()
○   protected abstract............. **makeBounds** (double x, double y, double w, double h)
                   ....Rectangle2D
▲   public static final.............int **OPEN** = 0
▲   public static final.............int **PIE** = 2

Arc2D

○	public abstract . . . . void	**setAngleExtent** (double angExt)
	public . . . . void	**setAngles** (Point2D p1, Point2D p2)
	public . . . . void	**setAngles** (double x1, double y1, double x2, double y2)
○	public abstract . . . . void	**setAngleStart** (double angSt)
	public . . . . void	**setAngleStart** (Point2D p)
	public . . . . void	**setArc** (Arc2D a)
	public . . . . void	**setArc** (Rectangle2D rect, double angSt, double angExt, int closure)
	public . . . . void	**setArc** (Point2D loc, Dimension2D size, double angSt, double angExt, int closure)
○	public abstract . . . . void	**setArc** (double x, double y, double w, double h, double angSt, double angExt, int closure)
	public . . . . void	**setArcByCenter** (double x, double y, double radius, double angSt, double angExt, int closure)
	public . . . . void	**setArcByTangent** (Point2D p1, Point2D p2, Point2D p3, double radius)
	public . . . . void	**setArcType** (int type)
1	public . . . . void	setFrame (Rectangle2D r)
1	public . . . . void	setFrame (Point2D loc, Dimension2D size)
1	public . . . . **void**	**setFrame** (double x, double y, double w, double h)
1	public . . . . void	setFrameFromCenter (Point2D center, Point2D corner)
1	public . . . . void	setFrameFromCenter (double centerX, double centerY, double cornerX, double cornerY)
1	public . . . . void	setFrameFromDiagonal (Point2D p1, Point2D p2)
1	public . . . . void	setFrameFromDiagonal (double x1, double y1, double x2, double y2)

Arc2D.Double   java.awt.geom

```
        Object
1.2 ○   └─RectangularShape¹ - - - - - - - - - - - - - - - - - - - - java.awt.Shape, Cloneable
1.2 ○     └─Arc2D²
1.2         └─Arc2D.Double
```

1	public . . . . Object	clone ()
1	public . . . . boolean	contains (Point2D p)
2	public . . . . boolean	contains (Rectangle2D r)
2	public . . . . boolean	contains (double x, double y)
2	public . . . . boolean	contains (double x, double y, double w, double h)
2	public . . . . boolean	containsAngle (double angle)
*	public	**Double** ()
*	public	**Double** (int type)
*	public	**Double** (Rectangle2D ellipseBounds, double start, double extent, int type)
*	public	**Double** (double x, double y, double w, double h, double start, double extent, int type)
	public . . . . double	**extent**
2	public . . . . **double**	**getAngleExtent** ()
2	public . . . . **double**	**getAngleStart** ()
2	public . . . . int	getArcType ()
1	public . . . . . . java.awt.Rectangle	getBounds ()
2	public Rectangle2D	getBounds2D ()
1	public . . . . double	getCenterX ()
1	public . . . . double	getCenterY ()
2	public Point2D	getEndPoint ()
1	public Rectangle2D	getFrame ()
1	public . . . . **double getHeight** ()
1	public . . . . double	getMaxX ()
1	public . . . . double	getMaxY ()
1	public . . . . double	getMinX ()
1	public . . . . double	getMinY ()
2	public . . . . PathIterator	getPathIterator (AffineTransform at)
1	public . . . . PathIterator	getPathIterator (AffineTransform at, double flatness)
2	public Point2D	getStartPoint ()
1	public . . . . **double getWidth** ()
1	public . . . . **double getX** ()
1	public . . . . **double getY** ()
	public . . . . double	**height**
1	public . . . . boolean	intersects (Rectangle2D r)
2	public . . . . boolean	intersects (double x, double y, double w, double h)
1	public . . . . **boolean isEmpty** ()
2	protected . . . . **Rectangle2D makeBounds** (double x, double y, double w, double h)
2	public . . . . **void setAngleExtent** (double angExt)
2	public . . . . void	setAngles (Point2D p1, Point2D p2)
2	public . . . . void	setAngles (double x1, double y1, double x2, double y2)
2	public . . . . **void setAngleStart** (double angSt)
2	public . . . . void	setAngleStart (Point2D p)

Class *Interface* —extends - - -implements ○ abstract ● final △ static ▲ static final ✻ constructor x x—inherited x **x**—declared **x x**—overridden

A

2	public	void	setArc (Arc2D a)
2	public	void	setArc (Rectangle2D rect, double angSt, double angExt, int closure)
2	public	void	setArc (Point2D loc, Dimension2D size, double angSt, double angExt, int closure)
2	public	**void**	**setArc** (double x, double y, double w, double h, double angSt, double angExt, int closure)
2	public	void	setArcByCenter (double x, double y, double radius, double angSt, double angExt, int closure)
2	public	void	setArcByTangent (Point2D p1, Point2D p2, Point2D p3, double radius)
2	public	void	setArcType (int type)
1	public	void	setFrame (Rectangle2D r)
1	public	void	setFrame (Point2D loc, Dimension2D size)
2	public	void	setFrame (double x, double y, double w, double h)
1	public	void	setFrameFromCenter (Point2D center, Point2D corner)
1	public	void	setFrameFromCenter (double centerX, double centerY, double cornerX, double cornerY)
1	public	void	setFrameFromDiagonal (Point2D p1, Point2D p2)
1	public	void	setFrameFromDiagonal (double x1, double y1, double x2, double y2)
	public	double	**start**
	public	double	**width**
	public	double	**x**
	public	double	**y**

Arc2D.Float

```
      Object
1.2 ○  └ RectangularShape 1 --------------------- java.awt.Shape, Cloneable
1.2 ○     └ Arc2D 2
1.2          └ Arc2D.Float
```

1	public	Object	clone ()
1	public	boolean	contains (Point2D p)
2	public	boolean	contains (Rectangle2D r)
2	public	boolean	contains (double x, double y)
2	public	boolean	contains (double x, double y, double w, double h)
2	public	boolean	containsAngle (double angle)
	public	float	**extent**
✱	public		**Float** ()
✱	public		**Float** (int type)
✱	public		**Float** (Rectangle2D ellipseBounds, float start, float extent, int type)
✱	public		**Float** (float x, float y, float w, float h, float start, float extent, int type)
2	public	**double**	**getAngleExtent** ()
2	public	**double**	**getAngleStart** ()
2	public	int	getArcType ()
1	public	java.awt.Rectangle	getBounds ()
2	public	Rectangle2D	getBounds2D ()
1	public	double	getCenterX ()
1	public	double	getCenterY ()
2	public	Point2D	getEndPoint ()
1	public	Rectangle2D	getFrame ()
1	public	**double**	**getHeight** ()
1	public	double	getMaxX ()
1	public	double	getMaxY ()
1	public	double	getMinX ()
1	public	double	getMinY ()
2	public	*PathIterator*	getPathIterator (AffineTransform at)
1	public	*PathIterator*	getPathIterator (AffineTransform at, double flatness)
2	public	Point2D	getStartPoint ()
1	public	**double**	**getWidth** ()
1	public	**double**	**getX** ()
1	public	**double**	**getY** ()
	public	float	**height**
1	public	boolean	intersects (Rectangle2D r)
2	public	boolean	intersects (double x, double y, double w, double h)
1	public	**boolean**	**isEmpty** ()
2	protected	**Rectangle2D**	**makeBounds** (double x, double y, double w, double h)
2	public	**void**	**setAngleExtent** (double angExt)
2	public	void	setAngles (Point2D p1, Point2D p2)
2	public	void	setAngles (double x1, double y1, double x2, double y2)
2	public	**void**	**setAngleStart** (double angSt)
2	public	void	setAngleStart (Point2D p)
2	public	void	setArc (Arc2D a)
2	public	void	setArc (Rectangle2D rect, double angSt, double angExt, int closure)
2	public	void	setArc (Point2D loc, Dimension2D size, double angSt, double angExt, int closure)

Classes

Arc2D.Float

2	public	**void**	**setArc**	(double x, double y, double w, double h, double angSt, double angExt, int closure)
2	public	void	setArcByCenter	(double x, double y, double radius, double angSt, double angExt, int closure)
2	public	void	setArcByTangent	(Point2D p1, Point2D p2, Point2D p3, double radius)
2	public	void	setArcType	(int type)
1	public	void	setFrame	(Rectangle2D r)
1	public	void	setFrame	(Point2D loc, Dimension2D size)
2	public	void	setFrame	(double x, double y, double w, double h)
1	public	void	setFrameFromCenter	(Point2D center, Point2D corner)
1	public	void	setFrameFromCenter	(double centerX, double centerY, double cornerX, double cornerY)
1	public	void	setFrameFromDiagonal	(Point2D p1, Point2D p2)
1	public	void	setFrameFromDiagonal	(double x1, double y1, double x2, double y2)
	public	float	**start**	
	public	float	**width**	
	public	float	**x**	
	public	float	**y**	

Area   java.awt.geom

```
Object 1
1.2   └─Area ------------------------------- java.awt.Shape 2, Cloneable
```

	public	void	**add**	(Area rhs)
*	public		**Area**	()
*	public		**Area**	(*java.awt.Shape* g)
1	public	**Object**	**clone**	()
2	public	boolean	**contains**	(Point2D p)
2	public	boolean	**contains**	(Rectangle2D r)
2	public	boolean	**contains**	(double x, double y)
2	public	boolean	**contains**	(double x, double y, double w, double h)
	public	Area	**createTransformedArea**	(AffineTransform t)
	public	boolean	**equals**	(Area rhs)
	public	void	**exclusiveOr**	(Area rhs)
2	public	java.awt.Rectangle	**getBounds**	()
2	public	Rectangle2D	**getBounds2D**	()
2	public	*PathIterator*	**getPathIterator**	(AffineTransform t)
2	public	*PathIterator*	**getPathIterator**	(AffineTransform t, double f)
	public	void	**intersect**	(Area rhs)
2	public	boolean	**intersects**	(Rectangle2D r)
2	public	boolean	**intersects**	(double x, double y, double w, double h)
	public	boolean	**isEmpty**	()
	public	boolean	**isPolygonal**	()
	public	boolean	**isRectangular**	()
	public	boolean	**isSingular**	()
	public	void	**reset**	()
	public	void	**subtract**	(Area rhs)
	public	void	**transform**	(AffineTransform t)

AreaAveragingScaleFilter   java.awt.image

P

```
Object
  └─ImageFilter 1 ------------------------- ImageConsumer, Cloneable
1.1   └─ReplicateScaleFilter 2
1.1      └─AreaAveragingScaleFilter
```

*	public		**AreaAveragingScaleFilter**	(int width, int height)
1	public	Object	clone	()
1	protected	*ImageConsumer*	consumer	
2	protected	int	destHeight	
2	protected	int	destWidth	
1	public	ImageFilter	getFilterInstance	(*ImageConsumer* ic)
1	public	void	imageComplete	(int status)
2	protected	Object	outpixbuf	
1	public	void	resendTopDownLeftRight	(*ImageProducer* ip)
1	public	void	setColorModel	(ColorModel model)
2	public	void	setDimensions	(int w, int h)
1	public	**void**	**setHints**	(int hints)

Class   *Interface*   —extends   - - -implements   O abstract   ● final   △ static   ▲ static final   ✳ constructor   x x—inherited   x **x**—declared   **x x**—overridden

2	public	**void**	**setPixels** (int x, int y, int w, int h, ColorModel model, byte[] pixels, int off, int scansize)
2	public	**void**	**setPixels** (int x, int y, int w, int h, ColorModel model, int[] pixels, int off, int scansize)
2	public	void	setProperties (java.util.Hashtable props)
2	protected	int[]	srccols
2	protected	int	srcHeight
2	protected	int[]	srcrows
2	protected	int	srcWidth

A

ARG_IN
org.omg.CORBA

1.2	*ARG_IN*	
▲	public static final .... int **value** = 1	

ARG_INOUT
org.omg.CORBA

1.2	*ARG_INOUT*	
▲	public static final .... int **value** = 3	

ARG_OUT
org.omg.CORBA

1.2	*ARG_OUT*	
▲	public static final .... int **value** = 2	

ArithmeticException
java.lang

P

```
Object
└Throwable --------------------------- java.io.Serializable
  └Exception
    └RuntimeException
      └ArithmeticException
```

∗	public	**ArithmeticException** ()
∗	public	**ArithmeticException** (String s)

Array❶
java.lang.reflect

P

```
Object
└Array
```
1.1 ●

△	public static native ...... Object	**get** (Object array, int index) throws IllegalArgumentException, ArrayIndexOutOfBoundsException
△	public static native .... boolean	**getBoolean** (Object array, int index) throws IllegalArgumentException, ArrayIndexOutOfBoundsException
△	public static native .... byte	**getByte** (Object array, int index) throws IllegalArgumentException, ArrayIndexOutOfBoundsException
△	public static native .... char	**getChar** (Object array, int index) throws IllegalArgumentException, ArrayIndexOutOfBoundsException
△	public static native ......double	**getDouble** (Object array, int index) throws IllegalArgumentException, ArrayIndexOutOfBoundsException
△	public static native ....float	**getFloat** (Object array, int index) throws IllegalArgumentException, ArrayIndexOutOfBoundsException
△	public static native ....int	**getInt** (Object array, int index) throws IllegalArgumentException, ArrayIndexOutOfBoundsException
△	public static native ....int	**getLength** (Object array) throws IllegalArgumentException
△	public static native .... long	**getLong** (Object array, int index) throws IllegalArgumentException, ArrayIndexOutOfBoundsException
△	public static native ....short	**getShort** (Object array, int index) throws IllegalArgumentException, ArrayIndexOutOfBoundsException
△	public static .... Object	**newInstance** (Class componentType, int length) throws NegativeArraySizeException
△	public static .... Object	**newInstance** (Class componentType, int[] dimensions) throws IllegalArgumentException, NegativeArraySizeException
△	public static native ....void	**set** (Object array, int index, Object value) throws IllegalArgumentException, ArrayIndexOutOfBoundsException
△	public static native ....void	**setBoolean** (Object array, int index, boolean z) throws IllegalArgumentException, ArrayIndexOutOfBoundsException

Classes

Array❶

△	public static native.........void	**setByte** (Object array, int index, byte b) throws IllegalArgumentException, ArrayIndexOutOfBoundsException	
△	public static native.........void	**setChar** (Object array, int index, char c) throws IllegalArgumentException, ArrayIndexOutOfBoundsException	
△	public static native.........void	**setDouble** (Object array, int index, double d) throws IllegalArgumentException, ArrayIndexOutOfBoundsException	
△	public static native.........void	**setFloat** (Object array, int index, float f) throws IllegalArgumentException, ArrayIndexOutOfBoundsException	
△	public static native.........void	**setInt** (Object array, int index, int i) throws IllegalArgumentException, ArrayIndexOutOfBoundsException	
△	public static native.........void	**setLong** (Object array, int index, long l) throws IllegalArgumentException, ArrayIndexOutOfBoundsException	
△	public static native.........void	**setShort** (Object array, int index, short s) throws IllegalArgumentException, ArrayIndexOutOfBoundsException	

Array❷   java.sql

1.2   *Array*   P○

```
public....................Object  getArray () throws SQLException
public....................Object  getArray (java.util.Map map) throws SQLException
public....................Object  getArray (long index, int count) throws SQLException
public....................Object  getArray (long index, int count, java.util.Map map) throws SQLException
public.........................int  getBaseType () throws SQLException
public....................String  getBaseTypeName () throws SQLException
public.................ResultSet  getResultSet () throws SQLException
public.................ResultSet  getResultSet (java.util.Map map) throws SQLException
public.................ResultSet  getResultSet (long index, int count) throws SQLException
public.................ResultSet  getResultSet (long index, int count, java.util.Map map) throws SQLException
```

ArrayIndexOutOfBoundsException   java.lang

P

```
Object
└Throwable ------------------------- java.io.Serializable
  └Exception
    └RuntimeException
      └IndexOutOfBoundsException
        └ArrayIndexOutOfBoundsException
```

✳	public...........................	**ArrayIndexOutOfBoundsException** ()
✳	public...........................	**ArrayIndexOutOfBoundsException** (int index)
✳	public...........................	**ArrayIndexOutOfBoundsException** (String s)

ArrayList   java.util

P

```
      Object 1
1.2 ○  └AbstractCollection 2 --------------------- Collection
1.2 ○    └AbstractList 3 --------------------- List (Collection)
1.2        └ArrayList ------------------------- List (Collection), Cloneable, java.io.Serializable
```

3	public..................**boolean**	**add** (Object o)	
3	public........................**void**	**add** (int index, Object element)	
2	public..................**boolean**	**addAll** (*Collection* c)	
3	public..................**boolean**	**addAll** (int index, *Collection* c)	
✳	public............................	**ArrayList** ()	
✳	public............................	**ArrayList** (int initialCapacity)	
✳	public............................	**ArrayList** (*Collection* c)	
3	public........................**void**	**clear** ()	
1	public....................**Object**	**clone** ()	
2	public..................**boolean**	**contains** (Object elem)	
2	public.................. boolean	containsAll (*Collection* c)	
	public........................**void**	**ensureCapacity** (int minCapacity)	
3	public.................. boolean	equals (Object o)	
3	public....................**Object**	**get** (int index)	
3	public.............................int	hashCode ()	
3	public............................ **int**	**indexOf** (Object elem)	
2	public..................**boolean**	**isEmpty** ()	
3	public................. *Iterator*	iterator ()	

Class   *Interface* —extends - - -implements ○ abstract ● final △ static ▲ static final ✳ constructor x x—inherited x **x**—declared **x x**—overridden

3	public	**int**	**lastIndexOf** (Object elem)
3	public	*ListIterator*	listIterator ()
3	public	*ListIterator*	listIterator (int index)
3	protected transient	int	modCount
3	public	**Object**	**remove** (int index)
2	public	boolean	remove (Object o)
2	public	boolean	removeAll (*Collection* c)
3	protected	**void**	**removeRange** (int fromIndex, int toIndex)
2	public	boolean	retainAll (*Collection* c)
3	public	**Object**	**set** (int index, Object element)
2	public	**int**	**size** ()
3	public	*List*	subList (int fromIndex, int toIndex)
2	public	**Object[]**	**toArray** ()
2	public	**Object[]**	**toArray** (Object[] a)
2	public	String	toString ()
	public	void	**trimToSize** ()

Arrays
java.util

Object
  └Arrays

1.2

P

△	public static	*List*	**asList** (Object[] a)
△	public static	int	**binarySearch** (byte[] a, byte key)
△	public static	int	**binarySearch** (char[] a, char key)
△	public static	int	**binarySearch** (double[] a, double key)
△	public static	int	**binarySearch** (float[] a, float key)
△	public static	int	**binarySearch** (int[] a, int key)
△	public static	int	**binarySearch** (Object[] a, Object key)
△	public static	int	**binarySearch** (long[] a, long key)
△	public static	int	**binarySearch** (short[] a, short key)
△	public static	int	**binarySearch** (Object[] a, Object key, *Comparator* c)
△	public static	boolean	**equals** (boolean[] a, boolean[] a2)
△	public static	boolean	**equals** (byte[] a, byte[] a2)
△	public static	boolean	**equals** (char[] a, char[] a2)
△	public static	boolean	**equals** (double[] a, double[] a2)
△	public static	boolean	**equals** (float[] a, float[] a2)
△	public static	boolean	**equals** (int[] a, int[] a2)
△	public static	boolean	**equals** (Object[] a, Object[] a2)
△	public static	boolean	**equals** (long[] a, long[] a2)
△	public static	boolean	**equals** (short[] a, short[] a2)
△	public static	void	**fill** (boolean[] a, boolean val)
△	public static	void	**fill** (byte[] a, byte val)
△	public static	void	**fill** (char[] a, char val)
△	public static	void	**fill** (double[] a, double val)
△	public static	void	**fill** (float[] a, float val)
△	public static	void	**fill** (int[] a, int val)
△	public static	void	**fill** (Object[] a, Object val)
△	public static	void	**fill** (long[] a, long val)
△	public static	void	**fill** (short[] a, short val)
△	public static	void	**fill** (boolean[] a, int fromIndex, int toIndex, boolean val)
△	public static	void	**fill** (byte[] a, int fromIndex, int toIndex, byte val)
△	public static	void	**fill** (char[] a, int fromIndex, int toIndex, char val)
△	public static	void	**fill** (double[] a, int fromIndex, int toIndex, double val)
△	public static	void	**fill** (float[] a, int fromIndex, int toIndex, float val)
△	public static	void	**fill** (int[] a, int fromIndex, int toIndex, int val)
△	public static	void	**fill** (Object[] a, int fromIndex, int toIndex, Object val)
△	public static	void	**fill** (long[] a, int fromIndex, int toIndex, long val)
△	public static	void	**fill** (short[] a, int fromIndex, int toIndex, short val)
△	public static	void	**sort** (byte[] a)
△	public static	void	**sort** (char[] a)
△	public static	void	**sort** (double[] a)
△	public static	void	**sort** (float[] a)
△	public static	void	**sort** (int[] a)
△	public static	void	**sort** (Object[] a)
△	public static	void	**sort** (long[] a)
△	public static	void	**sort** (short[] a)
△	public static	void	**sort** (Object[] a, *Comparator* c)
△	public static	void	**sort** (byte[] a, int fromIndex, int toIndex)
△	public static	void	**sort** (char[] a, int fromIndex, int toIndex)
△	public static	void	**sort** (double[] a, int fromIndex, int toIndex)
△	public static	void	**sort** (float[] a, int fromIndex, int toIndex)
△	public static	void	**sort** (int[] a, int fromIndex, int toIndex)

Classes

Arrays

△	public static ....void	**sort** (Object[] a, int fromIndex, int toIndex)
△	public static ....void	**sort** (long[] a, int fromIndex, int toIndex)
△	public static ....void	**sort** (short[] a, int fromIndex, int toIndex)
△	public static ....void	**sort** (Object[] a, int fromIndex, int toIndex, *Comparator* c)

ArrayStoreException   java.lang
P

Object
└ Throwable - *java.io.Serializable*
  └ Exception
    └ RuntimeException
      └ ArrayStoreException

*	public........................	**ArrayStoreException** ()
*	public........................	**ArrayStoreException** (String s)

AttributedCharacterIterator   java.text
P

1.2 *AttributedCharacterIterator*————————————— *CharacterIterator* [1] (*Cloneable*)

1	public....................Object	clone ()
1	public.................... char	current ()
1	public.................... char	first ()
	public....................*java.util.Set*	**getAllAttributeKeys** ()
	public....................Object	**getAttribute** (AttributedCharacterIterator.Attribute attribute)
	public....................*java.util.Map*	**getAttributes** ()
1	public.................... int	getBeginIndex ()
1	public.................... int	getEndIndex ()
1	public.................... int	getIndex ()
	public.................... int	**getRunLimit** ()
	public.................... int	**getRunLimit** (AttributedCharacterIterator.Attribute attribute)
	public.................... int	**getRunLimit** (*java.util.Set* attributes)
	public.................... int	**getRunStart** ()
	public.................... int	**getRunStart** (AttributedCharacterIterator.Attribute attribute)
	public.................... int	**getRunStart** (*java.util.Set* attributes)
1	public.................... char	last ()
1	public.................... char	next ()
1	public.................... char	previous ()
1	public.................... char	setIndex (int position)

AttributedCharacterIterator.Attribute   java.text
P

Object [1]
└ AttributedCharacterIterator.Attribute - - - - - - - *java.io.Serializable*
1.2

*	protected......................	**Attribute** (String name)
● *1*	public final ....**boolean**	**equals** (Object obj)
	protected ....String	**getName** ()
● *1*	public final .... **int**	**hashCode** ()
▲	public static final..............	**INPUT_METHOD_SEGMENT**
	.. AttributedCharacterIterator ↵	
	.Attribute	
▲	public static final..............	**LANGUAGE**
	.. AttributedCharacterIterator ↵	
	.Attribute	
▲	public static final..............	**READING**
	.. AttributedCharacterIterator ↵	
	.Attribute	
	protected ....Object	**readResolve** () throws java.io.InvalidObjectException
1	public.................... **String**	**toString** ()

AttributedString   java.text
P

Object
└ AttributedString
1.2

Class *Interface* —extends - - -implements ○ abstract ● final △ static ▲ static final ✳ constructor x x—inherited x **x**—declared **x x**—overridden

210

	public	void	**addAttribute** (AttributedCharacterIterator.Attribute attribute, Object value)
	public	void	**addAttribute** (AttributedCharacterIterator.Attribute attribute, Object value, int beginIndex, int endIndex)
	public	void	**addAttributes** (*java.util.Map* attributes, int beginIndex, int endIndex)
✳	public		**AttributedString** (String text)
✳	public		**AttributedString** (*AttributedCharacterIterator* text)
✳ ✳	public		**AttributedString** (String text, *java.util.Map* attributes)
✳	public		**AttributedString** (*AttributedCharacterIterator* text, int beginIndex, int endIndex)
✳	public		**AttributedString** (*AttributedCharacterIterator* text, int beginIndex, int endIndex, AttributedCharacterIterator.Attribute[] attributes)
	public .... *AttributedCharacterIterator*		**getIterator** ()
	public .... *AttributedCharacterIterator*		**getIterator** (AttributedCharacterIterator.Attribute[] attributes)
	public .... *AttributedCharacterIterator*		**getIterator** (AttributedCharacterIterator.Attribute[] attributes, int beginIndex, int endIndex)

AttributeList
javax.swing.text.html.parser

Object [1]
└AttributeList - *DTDConstants, java.io.Serializable*

1.2 ●

✳	public		**AttributeList** (String name)
✳	public		**AttributeList** (String name, int type, int modifier, String value, java.util.Vector values, AttributeList next)
	public	int	**getModifier** ()
	public	String	**getName** ()
	public	AttributeList	**getNext** ()
	public	int	**getType** ()
	public	String	**getValue** ()
	public	*java.util.Enumeration*	**getValues** ()
	public	int	**modifier**
	public	String	**name**
△	public static	int	**name2type** (String nm)
	public	AttributeList	**next**
1	public	**String**	**toString** ()
	public	int	**type**
△	public static	String	**type2name** (int tp)
	public	String	**value**
	public	java.util.Vector	**values**

Attributes
java.util.jar

Object [1]
└Attributes - *java.util.Map* [2], *Cloneable*

1.2

✳	public		**Attributes** ()
✳	public		**Attributes** (int size)
✳	public		**Attributes** (Attributes attr)
2	public	void	**clear** ()
1	public	**Object**	**clone** ()
2	public	boolean	**containsKey** (Object name)
2	public	boolean	**containsValue** (Object value)
2	public	*java.util.Set*	**entrySet** ()
1	public	**boolean**	**equals** (Object o)
2	public	Object	**get** (Object name)
	public	String	**getValue** (String name)
	public	String	**getValue** (Attributes.Name name)
1	public	**int**	**hashCode** ()
2	public	boolean	**isEmpty** ()
2	public	*java.util.Set*	**keySet** ()
	protected	*java.util.Map*	**map**
2	public	Object	**put** (Object name, Object value)
2	public	void	**putAll** (*java.util.Map* attr)
	public	String	**putValue** (String name, String value)
2	public	Object	**remove** (Object name)
2	public	int	**size** ()
2	public	*java.util.Collection*	**values** ()

Classes

Attributes.Name			java.util.jar

A

1.2

Object [1]
└ Attributes.Name

▲	public static final .... Attributes.Name		**CLASS_PATH**
▲	public static final .... Attributes.Name		**CONTENT_TYPE**
1	public	**boolean**	**equals** (Object o)
1	public	**int**	**hashCode** ()
▲	public static final .... Attributes.Name		**IMPLEMENTATION_TITLE**
▲	public static final .... Attributes.Name		**IMPLEMENTATION_VENDOR**
▲	public static final .... Attributes.Name		**IMPLEMENTATION_VERSION**
▲	public static final .... Attributes.Name		**MAIN_CLASS**
▲	public static final .... Attributes.Name		**MANIFEST_VERSION**
✳	public		**Name** (String name)
▲	public static final .... Attributes.Name		**SEALED**
▲	public static final .... Attributes.Name		**SIGNATURE_VERSION**
▲	public static final .... Attributes.Name		**SPECIFICATION_TITLE**
▲	public static final .... Attributes.Name		**SPECIFICATION_VENDOR**
▲	public static final .... Attributes.Name		**SPECIFICATION_VERSION**
1	public	**String**	**toString** ()

AttributeSet			javax.swing.text

1.2   *AttributeSet*

	public	boolean	**containsAttribute** (Object name, Object value)
	public	boolean	**containsAttributes** (*AttributeSet* attributes)
	public	*AttributeSet*	**copyAttributes** ()
	public	Object	**getAttribute** (Object key)
	public	int	**getAttributeCount** ()
	public .... *java.util.Enumeration*		**getAttributeNames** ()
	public	*AttributeSet*	**getResolveParent** ()
	public	boolean	**isDefined** (Object attrName)
	public	boolean	**isEqual** (*AttributeSet* attr)
▲	public static final	Object	**NameAttribute**
▲	public static final	Object	**ResolveAttribute**

AttributeSet.CharacterAttribute			javax.swing.text

1.2   *AttributeSet.CharacterAttribute*

AttributeSet.ColorAttribute			javax.swing.text

1.2   *AttributeSet.ColorAttribute*

AttributeSet.FontAttribute			javax.swing.text

1.2   *AttributeSet.FontAttribute*

AttributeSet.ParagraphAttribute			javax.swing.text

1.2   *AttributeSet.ParagraphAttribute*

Class *Interface* —extends - - -implements ○ abstract ● final △ static ▲ static final ✳ constructor x x—inherited x **x**—declared **x x**—overridden

AudioClip — java.applet

	AudioClip	P

public	void	**loop** ()
public	void	**play** ()
public	void	**stop** ()

Authenticator — java.net

Object
　└Authenticator   *(1.2 ○)*   P

✳	public	**Authenticator** ()
	protected PasswordAuthentication	**getPasswordAuthentication** ()
●	protected final int	**getRequestingPort** ()
●	protected final String	**getRequestingPrompt** ()
●	protected final String	**getRequestingProtocol** ()
●	protected final String	**getRequestingScheme** ()
●	protected final InetAddress	**getRequestingSite** ()
△	public static PasswordAuthentication	**requestPasswordAuthentication** (InetAddress addr, int port, String protocol, String prompt, String scheme)
△	public static synchronized void	**setDefault** (Authenticator a)

Autoscroll — java.awt.dnd

Autoscroll   *(1.2)*

public	void	**autoscroll** (java.awt.Point cursorLocn)
public	java.awt.Insets	**getAutoscrollInsets** ()

AWTError — java.awt

Object
　└Throwable - *java.io.Serializable*
　　└Error
　　　└AWTError   P

✳	public	**AWTError** (String msg)

AWTEvent — java.awt

Object[1]
　└java.util.EventObject[2] - *java.io.Serializable*   *(1.1)*
　　└AWTEvent   *(1.1 ○)*   P

▲		public static final long	**ACTION_EVENT_MASK** = 128
▲		public static final long	**ADJUSTMENT_EVENT_MASK** = 256
✳		public	**AWTEvent** (Event event)
✳		public	**AWTEvent** (Object source, int id)
▲		public static final long	**COMPONENT_EVENT_MASK** = 1
		protected void	**consume** ()
		protected boolean	**consumed**
▲		public static final long	**CONTAINER_EVENT_MASK** = 2
	1	protected void	**finalize** () throws Throwable
▲		public static final long	**FOCUS_EVENT_MASK** = 4
		public int	**getID** ()
	2	public Object	**getSource** ()
		protected int	**id**
1.2 ▲		public static final long	**INPUT_METHOD_EVENT_MASK** = 2048
		protected boolean	**isConsumed** ()
▲		public static final long	**ITEM_EVENT_MASK** = 512
▲		public static final long	**KEY_EVENT_MASK** = 8
▲		public static final long	**MOUSE_EVENT_MASK** = 16
▲		public static final long	**MOUSE_MOTION_EVENT_MASK** = 32
		public String	**paramString** ()
▲		public static final int	**RESERVED_ID_MAX** = 1999
	2	protected transient Object	**source**
▲		public static final long	**TEXT_EVENT_MASK** = 1024

A

Classes

AWTEvent

2	public	**String**	**toString** ()
▲	public static final	long	**WINDOW_EVENT_MASK** = 64

AWTEventListener — java.awt.event

1.2   *AWTEventListener*————————————— *java.util.EventListener*

- -

public..........................void **eventDispatched** (java.awt.AWTEvent event)

- -

AWTEventMulticaster — java.awt

Object
1.1   └AWTEventMulticaster - - - - - - - - - - - - - - - *java.awt.event.ComponentListener [1]* (*java.util.EventListener*),
                                    java.awt.event.ContainerListener [2] (*java.util.EventListener*),
                                      java.awt.event.FocusListener [3] (*java.util.EventListener*),
                                      java.awt.event.KeyListener [4] (*java.util.EventListener*),
                                      java.awt.event.MouseListener [5] (*java.util.EventListener*),
                                      java.awt.event.MouseMotionListener [6] (*java.util.EventListener*),
                                      java.awt.event.WindowListener [7] (*java.util.EventListener*),
                                      java.awt.event.ActionListener [8] (*java.util.EventListener*),
                                      java.awt.event.ItemListener [9] (*java.util.EventListener*),
                                      java.awt.event.AdjustmentListener [10] (*java.util.EventListener*),
                                      java.awt.event.TextListener [11] (*java.util.EventListener*),
                                      java.awt.event.InputMethodListener [12] (*java.util.EventListener*)

●	protected final .... *java.util.EventListener*	**a**	
8	public......................void	**actionPerformed** (java.awt.event.ActionEvent e)	
△	public static .... *.. java.awt.event.ActionListener*	**add** (*java.awt.event.ActionListener* a, *java.awt.event.ActionListener* b)	
△	public static .... *java↵ .awt.event.AdjustmentListener*	**add** (*java.awt.event.AdjustmentListener* a, *java.awt.event.AdjustmentListener* b)	
△	public static .... *java↵ .awt.event.ComponentListener*	**add** (*java.awt.event.ComponentListener* a, *java.awt.event.ComponentListener* b)	
△	public static .... *java↵ .awt.event.ContainerListener*	**add** (*java.awt.event.ContainerListener* a, *java.awt.event.ContainerListener* b)	
△	public static .... *.. java.awt.event.FocusListener*	**add** (*java.awt.event.FocusListener* a, *java.awt.event.FocusListener* b)	
1.2 △	public static .... *java.awt↵ .event.InputMethodListener*	**add** (*java.awt.event.InputMethodListener* a, *java.awt.event.InputMethodListener* b)	
△	public static .... *.... java.awt.event.ItemListener*	**add** (*java.awt.event.ItemListener* a, *java.awt.event.ItemListener* b)	
△	public static .... *..... java.awt.event.KeyListener*	**add** (*java.awt.event.KeyListener* a, *java.awt.event.KeyListener* b)	
△	public static .... *. java.awt.event.MouseListener*	**add** (*java.awt.event.MouseListener* a, *java.awt.event.MouseListener* b)	
△	public static .... *java.awt↵ .event.MouseMotionListener*	**add** (*java.awt.event.MouseMotionListener* a, *java.awt.event.MouseMotionListener* b)	
△	public static .... *.... java.awt.event.TextListener*	**add** (*java.awt.event.TextListener* a, *java.awt.event.TextListener* b)	
△	public static .... *java.awt.event.WindowListener*	**add** (*java.awt.event.WindowListener* a, *java.awt.event.WindowListener* b)	
△	protected static .... *.......... java.util.EventListener*	**addInternal** (*java.util.EventListener* a, *java.util.EventListener* b)	
10	public......................void	**adjustmentValueChanged** (java.awt.event.AdjustmentEvent e)	
✳	protected......................	**AWTEventMulticaster** (*java.util.EventListener* a, *java.util.EventListener* b)	
●	protected final .... *.......... java.util.EventListener*	**b**	
1.2	12 public......................void	**caretPositionChanged** (java.awt.event.InputMethodEvent e)	
2	public......................void	**componentAdded** (java.awt.event.ContainerEvent e)	
1	public......................void	**componentHidden** (java.awt.event.ComponentEvent e)	
1	public......................void	**componentMoved** (java.awt.event.ComponentEvent e)	
2	public......................void	**componentRemoved** (java.awt.event.ContainerEvent e)	
1	public......................void	**componentResized** (java.awt.event.ComponentEvent e)	
1	public......................void	**componentShown** (java.awt.event.ComponentEvent e)	
3	public......................void	**focusGained** (java.awt.event.FocusEvent e)	
3	public......................void	**focusLost** (java.awt.event.FocusEvent e)	
1.2	12 public......................void	**inputMethodTextChanged** (java.awt.event.InputMethodEvent e)	

Class   *Interface*   —extends   - - -implements   ○ abstract   ● final   △ static   ▲ static final   ✳ constructor   x x—inherited   x **x**—declared   **x x**—overridden

	9	public.........................void	**itemStateChanged** (java.awt.event.ItemEvent e)
	4	public.........................void	**keyPressed** (java.awt.event.KeyEvent e)
	4	public.........................void	**keyReleased** (java.awt.event.KeyEvent e)
	4	public.........................void	**keyTyped** (java.awt.event.KeyEvent e)
	5	public.........................void	**mouseClicked** (java.awt.event.MouseEvent e)
	6	public.........................void	**mouseDragged** (java.awt.event.MouseEvent e)
	5	public.........................void	**mouseEntered** (java.awt.event.MouseEvent e)
	5	public.........................void	**mouseExited** (java.awt.event.MouseEvent e)
	6	public.........................void	**mouseMoved** (java.awt.event.MouseEvent e)
	5	public.........................void	**mousePressed** (java.awt.event.MouseEvent e)
	5	public.........................void	**mouseReleased** (java.awt.event.MouseEvent e)

protected........................ *java.util.EventListener* **remove** (*java.util.EventListener* oldl)

△ public static .... *.. java.awt.event.ActionListener* **remove** (*java.awt.event.ActionListener* l, *java.awt.event.ActionListener* oldl)

△ public static .... *java↵* *.awt.event.AdjustmentListener* **remove** (*java.awt.event.AdjustmentListener* l, *java.awt.event.AdjustmentListener* oldl)

△ public static .... *java↵* *.awt.event.ComponentListener* **remove** (*java.awt.event.ComponentListener* l, *java.awt.event.ComponentListener* oldl)

△ public static .... *java↵* *.awt.event.ContainerListener* **remove** (*java.awt.event.ContainerListener* l, *java.awt.event.ContainerListener* oldl)

△ public static .... *.. java.awt.event.FocusListener* **remove** (*java.awt.event.FocusListener* l, *java.awt.event.FocusListener* oldl)

1.2 △ public static .... *java.awt↵* *.event.InputMethodListener* **remove** (*java.awt.event.InputMethodListener* l, *java.awt.event.InputMethodListener* oldl)

△ public static .... *.... java.awt.event.ItemListener* **remove** (*java.awt.event.ItemListener* l, *java.awt.event.ItemListener* oldl)

△ public static .... *..... java.awt.event.KeyListener* **remove** (*java.awt.event.KeyListener* l, *java.awt.event.KeyListener* oldl)

△ public static .... *. java.awt.event.MouseListener* **remove** (*java.awt.event.MouseListener* l, *java.awt.event.MouseListener* oldl)

△ public static .... *java.awt↵* *.event.MouseMotionListener* **remove** (*java. awt. event. MouseMotionListener* l, *java. awt. event↵* *.MouseMotionListener* oldl)

△ public static .... *.... java.awt.event.TextListener* **remove** (*java.awt.event.TextListener* l, *java.awt.event.TextListener* oldl)

△ public static .... *java.awt.event.WindowListener* **remove** (*java.awt.event.WindowListener* l, *java.awt.event.WindowListener* oldl)

△ protected static .... *.......... java.util.EventListener* **removeInternal** (*java.util.EventListener* l, *java.util.EventListener* oldl)

△ protected static ....void **save** (java. io. ObjectOutputStream s, String k, *java. util. EventListener* l) throws java.io.IOException

protected....................void **saveInternal** (java.io.ObjectOutputStream s, String k) throws java.io.IOException

	11	public.........................void	**textValueChanged** (java.awt.event.TextEvent e)
	7	public.........................void	**windowActivated** (java.awt.event.WindowEvent e)
	7	public.........................void	**windowClosed** (java.awt.event.WindowEvent e)
	7	public.........................void	**windowClosing** (java.awt.event.WindowEvent e)
	7	public.........................void	**windowDeactivated** (java.awt.event.WindowEvent e)
	7	public.........................void	**windowDeiconified** (java.awt.event.WindowEvent e)
	7	public.........................void	**windowIconified** (java.awt.event.WindowEvent e)
	7	public.........................void	**windowOpened** (java.awt.event.WindowEvent e)

AWTException
java.awt

Object
└Throwable - *java.io.Serializable*
  └Exception
    └AWTException

P

* public........................ **AWTException** (String msg)

AWTPermission
java.awt

Object
1.2 ○ └java.security.Permission [1] - - - - - - - - - - - - - - - - *java.security.Guard*, *java.io.Serializable*
1.2 ○   └java.security.BasicPermission [2] - - - - - - - - - - *java.io.Serializable*
1.2 ●   └AWTPermission

P

*	public........................		**AWTPermission** (String name)
*	public........................		**AWTPermission** (String name, String actions)
1	public.....................void		checkGuard (Object object) throws SecurityException
2	public................. boolean		equals (Object obj)

AWTPermission

A

2	public	String	getActions ()
● 1	public final	String	getName ()
2	public	int	hashCode ()
2	public	boolean	implies (java.security.Permission p)
2	public	java ↵	newPermissionCollection ()
	.security.PermissionCollection		
1	public	String	toString ()

BAD_CONTEXT   org.omg.CORBA

```
Object
 └Throwable ----------------------------- java.io.Serializable
    └Exception
       └RuntimeException
1.2 ○        └SystemException¹
1.2 ●           └BAD_CONTEXT
```

∗	public		**BAD_CONTEXT** ()
∗	public		**BAD_CONTEXT** (String s)
∗	public		**BAD_CONTEXT** (int minor, CompletionStatus completed)
∗	public		**BAD_CONTEXT** (String s, int minor, CompletionStatus completed)
1	public	CompletionStatus	completed
1	public	int	minor
1	public	String	toString ()

BAD_INV_ORDER   org.omg.CORBA

```
Object
 └Throwable ----------------------------- java.io.Serializable
    └Exception
       └RuntimeException
1.2 ○        └SystemException¹
1.2 ●           └BAD_INV_ORDER
```

∗	public		**BAD_INV_ORDER** ()
∗	public		**BAD_INV_ORDER** (String s)
∗	public		**BAD_INV_ORDER** (int minor, CompletionStatus completed)
∗	public		**BAD_INV_ORDER** (String s, int minor, CompletionStatus completed)
1	public	CompletionStatus	completed
1	public	int	minor
1	public	String	toString ()

BAD_OPERATION   org.omg.CORBA

```
Object
 └Throwable ----------------------------- java.io.Serializable
    └Exception
       └RuntimeException
1.2 ○        └SystemException¹
1.2 ●           └BAD_OPERATION
```

∗	public		**BAD_OPERATION** ()
∗	public		**BAD_OPERATION** (String s)
∗	public		**BAD_OPERATION** (int minor, CompletionStatus completed)
∗	public		**BAD_OPERATION** (String s, int minor, CompletionStatus completed)
1	public	CompletionStatus	completed
1	public	int	minor
1	public	String	toString ()

Class *Interface* —extends - - -implements ○ abstract ● final △ static ▲ static final ∗ constructor x x—inherited x **x**—declared **x x**—overridden

BAD_PARAM — org.omg.CORBA

```
Object
 └ Throwable ------------------------------ java.io.Serializable
    └ Exception
       └ RuntimeException
          └ SystemException [1]
1.2 ○
1.2 ●        └ BAD_PARAM
```

*	public	**BAD_PARAM** ()	
*	public	**BAD_PARAM** (String s)	
*	public	**BAD_PARAM** (int minor, CompletionStatus completed)	
*	public	**BAD_PARAM** (String s, int minor, CompletionStatus completed)	
1	public	CompletionStatus completed	
1	public	int minor	
1	public	String toString ()	

BAD_POLICY — org.omg.CORBA

```
1.2   BAD_POLICY
```

▲	public static final	short **value** = 0

BAD_POLICY_TYPE — org.omg.CORBA

```
1.2   BAD_POLICY_TYPE
```

▲	public static final	short **value** = 2

BAD_POLICY_VALUE — org.omg.CORBA

```
1.2   BAD_POLICY_VALUE
```

▲	public static final	short **value** = 3

BAD_TYPECODE — org.omg.CORBA

```
Object
 └ Throwable ------------------------------ java.io.Serializable
    └ Exception
       └ RuntimeException
          └ SystemException [1]
1.2 ○
1.2 ●        └ BAD_TYPECODE
```

*	public	**BAD_TYPECODE** ()	
*	public	**BAD_TYPECODE** (String s)	
*	public	**BAD_TYPECODE** (int minor, CompletionStatus completed)	
*	public	**BAD_TYPECODE** (String s, int minor, CompletionStatus completed)	
1	public	CompletionStatus completed	
1	public	int minor	
1	public	String toString ()	

BadKind — org.omg.CORBA.TypeCodePackage

```
Object
 └ Throwable ------------------------------ java.io.Serializable
    └ Exception
1.2 ○    └ org.omg.CORBA.UserException ------- org.omg.CORBA.portable.IDLEntity (java.io.Serializable)
1.2 ●       └ BadKind
```

*	public	**BadKind** ()
*	public	**BadKind** (String reason)

BadLocationException

BadLocationException	javax.swing.text

```
      Object
      └Throwable ------------------------------ java.io.Serializable
         └Exception
 1.2        └BadLocationException
```

*	public		**BadLocationException** (String s, int offs)
	public	int	**offsetRequested** ()

BandCombineOp	java.awt.image

P

```
      Object
 1.2  └BandCombineOp ---------------------- RasterOp 1
```

*	public		**BandCombineOp** (float[][] matrix, java.awt.RenderingHints hints)
	1	public	WritableRaster	**createCompatibleDestRaster** (Raster src)
	1	public	WritableRaster	**filter** (Raster src, WritableRaster dst)
●	1	public final		**getBounds2D** (Raster src)
		... java.awt.geom.Rectangle2D		
●		public final	float[][]	**getMatrix** ()
●	1	public final		**getPoint2D** (java.awt.geom.Point2D srcPt, java.awt.geom.Point2D dstPt)
		.... java.awt.geom.Point2D		
●	1	public final		**getRenderingHints** ()
		.... java.awt.RenderingHints		

BandedSampleModel	java.awt.image

P

```
       Object
 1.2 ○ └SampleModel 1
 1.2    └ComponentSampleModel 2
 1.2 ●     └BandedSampleModel
```

	1	*26 inherited members from SampleModel not shown*		
*		public		**BandedSampleModel** (int dataType, int w, int h, int numBands)
*		public		**BandedSampleModel** (int dataType, int w, int h, int scanlineStride,
				int[] bankIndices, int[] bandOffsets)
	2	protected	int[]	bandOffsets
	2	protected	int[]	bankIndices
	2	public	**SampleModel**	**createCompatibleSampleModel** (int w, int h)
	2	public	**DataBuffer**	**createDataBuffer** ()
	2	public	**SampleModel**	**createSubsetSampleModel** (int[] bands)
●	2	public final	int[]	getBandOffsets ()
●	2	public final	int[]	getBankIndices ()
	2	public	**Object**	**getDataElements** (int x, int y, Object obj, DataBuffer data)
●	2	public final	int	getNumDataElements ()
	2	public	int	getOffset (int x, int y)
	2	public	int	getOffset (int x, int y, int b)
	2	public	**int[]**	**getPixel** (int x, int y, int[] iArray, DataBuffer data)
	2	public	**int[]**	**getPixels** (int x, int y, int w, int h, int[] iArray, DataBuffer data)
●	2	public final	int	getPixelStride ()
	2	public	**int**	**getSample** (int x, int y, int b, DataBuffer data)
	2	public	**int[]**	**getSamples** (int x, int y, int w, int h, int b, int[] iArray, DataBuffer data)
●	2	public final	int[]	getSampleSize ()
●	2	public final	int	getSampleSize (int band)
●	2	public final	int	getScanlineStride ()
	2	protected	int	numBands
	2	protected	int	numBanks
	2	protected	int	pixelStride
	2	protected	int	scanlineStride
	2	public	**void**	**setDataElements** (int x, int y, Object obj, DataBuffer data)
	2	public	**void**	**setPixel** (int x, int y, int[] iArray, DataBuffer data)
	2	public	**void**	**setPixels** (int x, int y, int w, int h, int[] iArray, DataBuffer data)
	2	public	**void**	**setSample** (int x, int y, int b, int s, DataBuffer data)
	2	public	**void**	**setSamples** (int x, int y, int w, int h, int b, int[] iArray, DataBuffer data)

Class *Interface* —extends - - -implements ○ abstract ● final △ static ▲ static final ✳ constructor x x—inherited x **x**—declared **x x**—overridden

BasicPermission | java.security

1.2	O		Object	P^O
			└─Permission [1] - *Guard*, *java.io.Serializable*	
1.2	O		└─BasicPermission - *java.io.Serializable*	

*		public		**BasicPermission** (String name)
*		public		**BasicPermission** (String name, String actions)
	1	public	void	checkGuard (Object object) throws SecurityException
	1	public	**boolean**	**equals** (Object obj)
	1	public	**String**	**getActions** ()
●	1	public final	String	getName ()
	1	public	**int**	**hashCode** ()
	1	public	**boolean**	**implies** (Permission p)
	1	public	**PermissionCollection**	**newPermissionCollection** ()
	1	public	String	toString ()

BasicStroke | java.awt

			Object [1]	P
1.2			└─BasicStroke - *Stroke* [2]	

*		public		**BasicStroke** ()
*		public		**BasicStroke** (float width)
*		public		**BasicStroke** (float width, int cap, int join)
*		public		**BasicStroke** (float width, int cap, int join, float miterlimit)
*		public		**BasicStroke** (float width, int cap, int join, float miterlimit, float[] dash, float dash_phase)
▲		public static final	int	**CAP_BUTT** = 0
▲		public static final	int	**CAP_ROUND** = 1
▲		public static final	int	**CAP_SQUARE** = 2
	2	public	*Shape*	**createStrokedShape** (*Shape* s)
	1	public	**boolean**	**equals** (Object obj)
		public	float[]	**getDashArray** ()
		public	float	**getDashPhase** ()
		public	int	**getEndCap** ()
		public	int	**getLineJoin** ()
		public	float	**getLineWidth** ()
		public	float	**getMiterLimit** ()
	1	public	**int**	**hashCode** ()
▲		public static final	int	**JOIN_BEVEL** = 2
▲		public static final	int	**JOIN_MITER** = 0
▲		public static final	int	**JOIN_ROUND** = 1

BatchUpdateException | java.sql

			Object	P^O
			└─Throwable - *java.io.Serializable*	
			└─Exception	
1.1			└─SQLException [1]	
1.2			└─BatchUpdateException	

*		public		**BatchUpdateException** ()
*		public		**BatchUpdateException** (int[] updateCounts)
*		public		**BatchUpdateException** (String reason, int[] updateCounts)
*		public		**BatchUpdateException** (String reason, String SQLState, int[] updateCounts)
*		public		**BatchUpdateException** (String reason, String SQLState, int vendorCode, int[] updateCounts)
	1	public	int	getErrorCode ()
	1	public	SQLException	getNextException ()
	1	public	String	getSQLState ()
		public	int[]	**getUpdateCounts** ()
	1	public synchronized	void	setNextException (SQLException ex)

BeanContext

BeanContext	java.beans.beancontext

B

1.2   *BeanContext*————————————*BeanContextChild* [1], *java.util.Collection* [2], *java.beans.DesignMode* [3],
                                               java.beans.Visibility [4]

2	public	boolean	add (Object o)
2	public	boolean	addAll (*java.util.Collection* c)
	public	void	**addBeanContextMembershipListener** (*BeanContextMembershipListener* bcml)
1	public	void	addPropertyChangeListener (String name, *java.beans.PropertyChangeListener* pcl)
1	public	void	addVetoableChangeListener (String name, *java.beans.VetoableChangeListener* vcl)
4	public	boolean	avoidingGui ()
2	public	void	clear ()
2	public	boolean	contains (Object o)
2	public	boolean	containsAll (*java.util.Collection* c)
4	public	void	dontUseGui ()
2	public	boolean	equals (Object o)
1	public	*BeanContext*	getBeanContext ()
	public	java.net.URL	**getResource** (String name, *BeanContextChild* bcc) throws IllegalArgumentException
	public	java.io.InputStream	**getResourceAsStream** (String name, *BeanContextChild* bcc) throws IllegalArgumentException
▲	public static final	Object	**globalHierarchyLock**
2	public	int	hashCode ()
	public	Object	**instantiateChild** (String beanName) throws java. io. IOException, ClassNotFoundException
3	public	boolean	isDesignTime ()
2	public	boolean	isEmpty ()
2	public	*java.util.Iterator*	iterator ()
4	public	boolean	needsGui ()
4	public	void	okToUseGui ()
2	public	boolean	remove (Object o)
2	public	boolean	removeAll (*java.util.Collection* c)
	public	void	**removeBeanContextMembershipListener** (*BeanContextMembershipListener* bcml)
1	public	void	removePropertyChangeListener (String name, *java.beans.PropertyChangeListener* pcl)
1	public	void	removeVetoableChangeListener (String name, *java.beans.VetoableChangeListener* vcl)
2	public	boolean	retainAll (*java.util.Collection* c)
1	public	void	setBeanContext (*BeanContext* bc) throws java.beans.PropertyVetoException
3	public	void	setDesignTime (boolean designTime)
2	public	int	size ()
2	public	Object[]	toArray ()
2	public	Object[]	toArray (Object[] a)

BeanContextChild	java.beans.beancontext

1.2   *BeanContextChild*

	public	void	**addPropertyChangeListener** (String name, *java.beans.PropertyChangeListener* pcl)
	public	void	**addVetoableChangeListener** (String name, *java.beans.VetoableChangeListener* vcl)
	public	*BeanContext*	**getBeanContext** ()
	public	void	**removePropertyChangeListener** (String name, *java. beans ↵ .PropertyChangeListener* pcl)
	public	void	**removeVetoableChangeListener** (String name, *java. beans ↵ .VetoableChangeListener* vcl)
	public	void	**setBeanContext** (*BeanContext* bc) throws java.beans.PropertyVetoException

BeanContextChildComponentProxy	java.beans.beancontext

1.2   *BeanContextChildComponentProxy*

	public	java.awt.Component	**getComponent** ()

Class   *Interface*   —extends   - - -implements   ○ abstract   ● final   △ static   ▲ static final   ✳ constructor   x x—inherited   x **x**—declared   **x x**—overridden

BeanContextChildSupport

B

```
      Object
1.2   └─BeanContextChildSupport ─ ─ ─ ─ ─ ─ ─ ─ ─ ─ ─ ─ ─ BeanContextChild 1, BeanContextServicesListener 2
                                                        (BeanContextServiceRevokedListener 3
                                                        (java.util.EventListener)), java.io.Serializable
```

	1	public......................void	**addPropertyChangeListener** (String name, *java.beans.PropertyChangeListener* pcl)
	1	public......................void	**addVetoableChangeListener** (String name, *java.beans.VetoableChangeListener* vcl)
		protected transient............ ....*BeanContext*	**beanContext**
		public....... *BeanContextChild*	**beanContextChildPeer**
*		public............................	**BeanContextChildSupport** ()
*		public............................	**BeanContextChildSupport** (*BeanContextChild* bcc)
		public......................void	**firePropertyChange** (String name, Object oldValue, Object newValue)
		public......................void	**fireVetoableChange** (String name, Object oldValue, Object newValue) throws java.beans.PropertyVetoException
	1	public synchronized ....*BeanContext*	**getBeanContext** ()
		public....... *BeanContextChild*	**getBeanContextChildPeer** ()
		protected ....void	**initializeBeanContextResources** ()
		public.................. boolean	**isDelegated** ()
		protected .... java.beans↩ .PropertyChangeSupport	**pcSupport**
		protected transient.... boolean	**rejectedSetBCOnce**
		protected ....void	**releaseBeanContextResources** ()
	1	public......................void	**removePropertyChangeListener** (String name, *java. beans↩ .PropertyChangeListener* pcl)
	1	public......................void	**removeVetoableChangeListener** (String name, *java. beans↩ .VetoableChangeListener* vcl)
	2	public......................void	**serviceAvailable** (BeanContextServiceAvailableEvent bcsae)
	3	public......................void	**serviceRevoked** (BeanContextServiceRevokedEvent bcsre)
	1	public synchronized ....void	**setBeanContext** (*BeanContext* bc) throws java.beans.PropertyVetoException
		public.................. boolean	**validatePendingSetBeanContext** (*BeanContext* newValue)
		protected .... java.beans↩ .VetoableChangeSupport	**vcSupport**

BeanContextContainerProxy

```
1.2   BeanContextContainerProxy
```

	public....... java.awt.Container	**getContainer** ()

BeanContextEvent

```
      Object
1.1   └─java.util.EventObject 1 ─ ─ ─ ─ ─ ─ ─ ─ ─ ─ ─ ─ ─ java.io.Serializable
1.2 ○   └─BeanContextEvent
```

*		protected	**BeanContextEvent** (*BeanContext* bc)
		public............. *BeanContext*	**getBeanContext** ()
		public synchronized ....*BeanContext*	**getPropagatedFrom** ()
	1	public....................Object	getSource ()
		public synchronized .. boolean	**isPropagated** ()
		protected .... *BeanContext*	**propagatedFrom**
		public synchronized ....void	**setPropagatedFrom** (*BeanContext* bc)
	1	protected transient...... Object	source
	1	public....................String	toString ()

BeanContextMembershipEvent

```
      Object
1.1   └─java.util.EventObject 1 ─ ─ ─ ─ ─ ─ ─ ─ ─ ─ ─ ─ ─ java.io.Serializable
1.2 ○   └─BeanContextEvent 2
1.2       └─BeanContextMembershipEvent
```

BeanContextMembershipEvent

*	public		**BeanContextMembershipEvent** (*BeanContext* bc, *java.util.Collection* changes)
*	public		**BeanContextMembershipEvent** (*BeanContext* bc, Object[] changes)
	protected ... *java.util.Collection*	**children**	
	public	boolean	**contains** (Object child)
2	public	*BeanContext*	getBeanContext ()
2	public synchronized		getPropagatedFrom ()
		BeanContext	
1	public	Object	getSource ()
2	public synchronized .. boolean		isPropagated ()
	public	*java.util.Iterator*	**iterator** ()
2	protected	*BeanContext*	propagatedFrom
2	public synchronized	void	setPropagatedFrom (*BeanContext* bc)
	public	int	**size** ()
1	protected transient	Object	source
	public	Object[]	**toArray** ()
1	public	String	toString ()

BeanContextMembershipListener   java.beans.beancontext

1.2	*BeanContextMembershipListener*————————*java.util.EventListener*

	public	void	**childrenAdded** (BeanContextMembershipEvent bcme)
	public	void	**childrenRemoved** (BeanContextMembershipEvent bcme)

BeanContextProxy   java.beans.beancontext

1.2	*BeanContextProxy*

	public	*BeanContextChild*	**getBeanContextProxy** ()

BeanContextServiceAvailableEvent   java.beans.beancontext

```
        Object
 1.1     └java.util.EventObject 1 ------------------- java.io.Serializable
 1.2 O      └BeanContextEvent 2
 1.2           └BeanContextServiceAvailableEvent
```

*	public		**BeanContextServiceAvailableEvent** (*BeanContextServices* bcs, Class sc)
2	public	*BeanContext*	getBeanContext ()
	public	*java.util.Iterator*	**getCurrentServiceSelectors** ()
2	public synchronized		getPropagatedFrom ()
		BeanContext	
	public	Class	**getServiceClass** ()
1	public	Object	getSource ()
	public ... *BeanContextServices*	**getSourceAsBeanContextServices** ()	
2	public synchronized .. boolean		isPropagated ()
2	protected	*BeanContext*	propagatedFrom
	protected	Class	**serviceClass**
2	public synchronized	void	setPropagatedFrom (*BeanContext* bc)
1	protected transient	Object	source
1	public	String	toString ()

BeanContextServiceProvider   java.beans.beancontext

1.2	*BeanContextServiceProvider*

	public	*java.util.Iterator*	**getCurrentServiceSelectors** (*BeanContextServices* bcs, Class serviceClass)
	public	Object	**getService** (*BeanContextServices* bcs, Object requestor, Class serviceClass, Object serviceSelector)
	public	void	**releaseService** (*BeanContextServices* bcs, Object requestor, Object service)

BeanContextServiceProviderBeanInfo   java.beans.beancontext

1.2	*BeanContextServiceProviderBeanInfo*————————*java.beans.BeanInfo* [1]

1	public... *java.beans.BeanInfo[]*	getAdditionalBeanInfo ()	
1	public		getBeanDescriptor ()
	.... java.beans.BeanDescriptor		

Class   *Interface*   —extends   - - -implements   O abstract   ● final   △ static   ▲ static final   * constructor   x x—inherited   x **x**—declared   **x x**—overridden

1	public	int	getDefaultEventIndex ()
1	public	int	getDefaultPropertyIndex ()
1	public	java ↵ .beans.EventSetDescriptor[]	getEventSetDescriptors ()
1	public	java.awt.Image	getIcon (int iconKind)
1	public java.beans.MethodDescriptor[]		getMethodDescriptors ()
1	public	java ↵ .beans.PropertyDescriptor[]	getPropertyDescriptors ()
	public	*java.beans.BeanInfo[]*	**getServicesBeanInfo** ()

BeanContextServiceRevokedEvent   java.beans.beancontext

```
      Object
1.1    └java.util.EventObject 1 - - - - - - - - - - - - - - - - - - java.io.Serializable
1.2 ○     └BeanContextEvent 2
1.2        └BeanContextServiceRevokedEvent
```

*	public		**BeanContextServiceRevokedEvent** (*BeanContextServices* bcs, Class sc, boolean invalidate)
2	public	*BeanContext*	getBeanContext ()
2	public synchronized *BeanContext*		getPropagatedFrom ()
	public	Class	**getServiceClass** ()
1	public	Object	getSource ()
	public	*BeanContextServices*	**getSourceAsBeanContextServices** ()
	public	boolean	**isCurrentServiceInvalidNow** ()
2	public synchronized	boolean	isPropagated ()
	public	boolean	**isServiceClass** (Class service)
2	protected	*BeanContext*	propagatedFrom
	protected	Class	**serviceClass**
2	public synchronized	void	setPropagatedFrom (*BeanContext* bc)
1	protected transient	Object	source
1	public	String	toString ()

BeanContextServiceRevokedListener   java.beans.beancontext

```
1.2    BeanContextServiceRevokedListener————java.util.EventListener
```

	public	void	**serviceRevoked** (BeanContextServiceRevokedEvent bcsre)

BeanContextServices   java.beans.beancontext

```
1.2    BeanContextServices————————BeanContext 1 (BeanContextChild 2,
                                   java.util.Collection 3, java.beans.DesignMode 4,
                                   java.beans.Visibility 5), BeanContextServicesListener 6
                                   (BeanContextServiceRevokedListener 7 (java.util.EventListener))
```

3	public	boolean	add (Object o)
3	public	boolean	addAll (*java.util.Collection* c)
1	public	void	addBeanContextMembershipListener (*BeanContextMembershipListener* bcml)
	public	void	**addBeanContextServicesListener** (*BeanContextServicesListener* bcsl)
2	public	void	addPropertyChangeListener (String name, *java.beans.PropertyChangeListener* pcl)
	public	boolean	**addService** (Class serviceClass, *BeanContextServiceProvider* serviceProvider)
2	public	void	addVetoableChangeListener (String name, *java.beans.VetoableChangeListener* vcl)
5	public	boolean	avoidingGui ()
3	public	void	clear ()
3	public	boolean	contains (Object o)
3	public	boolean	containsAll (*java.util.Collection* c)
5	public	void	dontUseGui ()
3	public	boolean	equals (Object o)
2	public	*BeanContext*	getBeanContext ()
	public	*java.util.Iterator*	**getCurrentServiceClasses** ()
	public	*java.util.Iterator*	**getCurrentServiceSelectors** (Class serviceClass)
1	public	java.net.URL	getResource (String name, *BeanContextChild* bcc) throws IllegalArgumentException
1	public	java.io.InputStream	getResourceAsStream (String name, *BeanContextChild* bcc) throws IllegalArgumentException
	public	Object	**getService** (*BeanContextChild* child, Object requestor, Class serviceClass, Object serviceSelector, *BeanContextServiceRevokedListener* bcsrl) throws java.util.TooManyListenersException
3	public	int	hashCode ()

BeanContextServices

	public	boolean	**hasService** (Class serviceClass)
1	public	Object	instantiateChild (String beanName) throws java. io. IOException, ClassNotFoundException
4	public	boolean	isDesignTime ()
3	public	boolean	isEmpty ()
3	public	*java.util.Iterator*	iterator ()
5	public	boolean	needsGui ()
5	public	void	okToUseGui ()
	public	void	**releaseService** (*BeanContextChild* child, Object requestor, Object service)
3	public	boolean	remove (Object o)
3	public	boolean	removeAll (*java.util.Collection* c)
1	public	void	removeBeanContextMembershipListener (*BeanContextMembershipListener* bcml)
	public	void	**removeBeanContextServicesListener** (*BeanContextServicesListener* bcsl)
2	public	void	removePropertyChangeListener (String name, *java.beans.PropertyChangeListener* pcl)
2	public	void	removeVetoableChangeListener (String name, *java.beans.VetoableChangeListener* vcl)
3	public	boolean	retainAll (*java.util.Collection* c)
	public	void	**revokeService** (Class serviceClass, *BeanContextServiceProvider* serviceProvider, boolean revokeCurrentServicesNow)
6	public	void	serviceAvailable (BeanContextServiceAvailableEvent bcsae)
7	public	void	serviceRevoked (BeanContextServiceRevokedEvent bcsre)
2	public	void	setBeanContext (*BeanContext* bc) throws java.beans.PropertyVetoException
4	public	void	setDesignTime (boolean designTime)
3	public	int	size ()
3	public	Object[]	toArray ()
3	public	Object[]	toArray (Object[] a)

BeanContextServicesListener
java.beans.beancontext

1.2	*BeanContextServicesListener*—————————	*BeanContextServiceRevokedListener* [1] (*java.util.EventListener*)

	public	void	**serviceAvailable** (BeanContextServiceAvailableEvent bcsae)
1	public	void	serviceRevoked (BeanContextServiceRevokedEvent bcsre)

BeanContextServicesSupport
java.beans.beancontext

Object
1.2	└BeanContextChildSupport [1] - - - - - - - - - - - - - - -	*BeanContextChild*, *BeanContextServicesListener* (*BeanContextServiceRevokedListener* (*java.util.EventListener*)), *java.io.Serializable*
1.2	└BeanContextSupport [2] - - - - - - - - - - - - - - -	*BeanContext* (*BeanContextChild*, *java.util.Collection*, *java↵.beans.DesignMode*, *java.beans.Visibility*), *java.io.Serializable*, *java.beans.PropertyChangeListener* (*java.util.EventListener*), *java.beans.VetoableChangeListener* (*java.util.EventListener*)
1.2	└BeanContextServicesSupport - - - - - - - - -	*BeanContextServices* [3] (*BeanContext* (*BeanContextChild*, *java.util.Collection*, *java.beans.DesignMode*, *java.beans.Visibility*), *BeanContextServicesListener* (*BeanContextServiceRevokedListener* (*java.util.EventListener*)))

2	*56 inherited members from BeanContextSupport not shown*		
3	public	void	**addBeanContextServicesListener** (*BeanContextServicesListener* bcsl)
1	public	void	addPropertyChangeListener (String name, *java.beans.PropertyChangeListener* pcl)
3	public	boolean	**addService** (Class serviceClass, *BeanContextServiceProvider* bcsp)
	protected	boolean	**addService** (Class serviceClass, *BeanContextServiceProvider* bcsp, boolean fireEvent)
1	public	void	addVetoableChangeListener (String name, *java.beans.VetoableChangeListener* vcl)
	protected transient		**bcsListeners**
		java.util.ArrayList	
2	protected synchronized	**void**	**bcsPreDeserializationHook** (java. io. ObjectInputStream ois) throws java.io.IOException, ClassNotFoundException
2	protected synchronized	**void**	**bcsPreSerializationHook** (java. io. ObjectOutputStream oos) throws java.io.IOException
1	protected transient		beanContext
		BeanContext	
1	public	*BeanContextChild*	beanContextChildPeer
✱	public		**BeanContextServicesSupport** ()
✱	public		**BeanContextServicesSupport** (*BeanContextServices* peer)
✱	public		**BeanContextServicesSupport** (*BeanContextServices* peer, java.util.Locale lcle)

Class   *Interface*   —extends   - - -implements   ○ abstract   ● final   △ static   ▲ static final   ✱ constructor   x x—inherited   x **x**—declared   **x x**—overridden

*	public		**BeanContextServicesSupport** (*BeanContextServices* peer, java.util.Locale lcle, boolean dtime)
*	public		**BeanContextServicesSupport** (*BeanContextServices* peer, java.util.Locale lcle, boolean dTime, boolean visible)
2	protected	**void**	**childJustRemovedHook** (Object child, BeanContextSupport.BCSChild bcsc)
2	protected ......**BeanContextSupport↩ .BCSChild**		**createBCSChild** (Object targetChild, Object peer)
	protected BeanContextServicesSupport↩ .BCSSServiceProvider		**createBCSSServiceProvider** (Class sc, *BeanContextServiceProvider* bcsp)
1	public	void	firePropertyChange (String name, Object oldValue, Object newValue)
●	protected final	void	**fireServiceAdded** (BeanContextServiceAvailableEvent bcssae)
●	protected final	void	**fireServiceAdded** (Class serviceClass)
●	protected final	void	**fireServiceRevoked** (BeanContextServiceRevokedEvent bcsre)
●	protected final	void	**fireServiceRevoked** (Class serviceClass, boolean revokeNow)
1	public	void	fireVetoableChange (String name, Object oldValue, Object newValue) throws java.beans.PropertyVetoException
1	public synchronized ....*BeanContext*		getBeanContext ()
1	public....... *BeanContextChild*		getBeanContextChildPeer ()
	public... *BeanContextServices*		**getBeanContextServicesPeer** ()
▲	protected static final ....*BeanContextServicesListener*		**getChildBeanContextServicesListener** (Object child)
3	public.........*java.util.Iterator*		**getCurrentServiceClasses** ()
3	public.........*java.util.Iterator*		**getCurrentServiceSelectors** (Class serviceClass)
3	public....................Object		**getService** (*BeanContextChild* child, Object requestor, Class serviceClass, Object serviceSelector, *BeanContextServiceRevokedListener* bcsrl) throws java.util.TooManyListenersException
3	public synchronized .. boolean		**hasService** (Class serviceClass)
2	public	**void**	**initialize** ()
1	protected synchronized .. **void**		**initializeBeanContextResources** ()
1	public	boolean	isDelegated ()
1	protected .... java.beans↩ .PropertyChangeSupport		pcSupport
	protected transient ....BeanContextServicesSupport↩ .BCSSProxyServiceProvider		**proxy**
1	protected transient.... boolean		rejectedSetBCOnce
1	protected synchronized .. **void**		**releaseBeanContextResources** ()
3	public	void	**releaseService** (*BeanContextChild* child, Object requestor, Object service)
3	public	void	**removeBeanContextServicesListener** (*BeanContextServicesListener* bcsl)
1	public	void	removePropertyChangeListener (String name, *java.beans.PropertyChangeListener* pcl)
1	public	void	removeVetoableChangeListener (String name, *java.beans.VetoableChangeListener* vcl)
3	public	void	**revokeService** (Class serviceClass, *BeanContextServiceProvider* bcsp, boolean revokeCurrentServicesNow)
	protected transient...........int		**serializable**
1	public	**void**	**serviceAvailable** (BeanContextServiceAvailableEvent bcssae)
1	public	**void**	**serviceRevoked** (BeanContextServiceRevokedEvent bcssre)
	protected transient.............. java.util.HashMap		**services**
1	public synchronized ....void		setBeanContext (*BeanContext* bc) throws java.beans.PropertyVetoException
1	public	boolean	validatePendingSetBeanContext (*BeanContext* newValue)
1	protected .... java.beans↩ .VetoableChangeSupport		vcSupport

---

BeanContextServicesSupport.BCSSChild	protected	java.beans.beancontext

```
     Object
1.2  └BeanContextSupport.BCSChild ----------- java.io.Serializable
1.2      └BeanContextServicesSupport.BCSSChild
```

BeanContextServicesSupport.BCSSProxyServiceProvider	protected	java.beans.beancontext

B

1.2
```
Object
 └─BeanContextServicesSupport ↵ - - - - - - - - - - - BeanContextServiceProvider ¹, BeanContextServiceRevokedListener ²
    .BCSSProxyServiceProvider                         (java.util.EventListener)
```

1	public . . . . *java.util.Iterator*	**getCurrentServiceSelectors** (*BeanContextServices* bcs, Class serviceClass)
1	public . . . . Object	**getService** (*BeanContextServices* bcs, Object requestor, Class serviceClass, Object serviceSelector)
1	public . . . . void	**releaseService** (*BeanContextServices* bcs, Object requestor, Object service)
2	public . . . . void	**serviceRevoked** (BeanContextServiceRevokedEvent bcsre)

BeanContextServicesSupport.BCSSServiceProvider	protected	java.beans.beancontext

1.2
```
Object
 └─BeanContextServicesSupport ↵ - - - - - - - - - - - java.io.Serializable
    .BCSSServiceProvider
```

protected	**getServiceProvider** ()
.. *BeanContextServiceProvider*	
protected	**serviceProvider**
.. *BeanContextServiceProvider*	

BeanContextSupport	java.beans.beancontext

1.2

1.2
```
Object
 └─BeanContextChildSupport¹ - - - - - - - - - - - - - BeanContextChild, BeanContextServicesListener
                                                      (BeanContextServiceRevokedListener (java.util.EventListener)),
                                                      java.io.Serializable
      └─BeanContextSupport - - - - - - - - - - - - - - BeanContext ² (BeanContextChild, java.util.Collection ³, java↵
                                                      .beans.DesignMode ⁴, java.beans.Visibility ⁵), java.io.Serializable,
                                                      java.beans.PropertyChangeListener ⁶ (java.util.EventListener),
                                                      java.beans.VetoableChangeListener ⁷ (java.util.EventListener)
```

	3	public . . . . boolean	**add** (Object targetChild)
	3	public . . . . boolean	**addAll** (*java.util.Collection* c)
	2	public . . . . void	**addBeanContextMembershipListener** (*BeanContextMembershipListener* bcml)
	1	public . . . . void	addPropertyChangeListener (String name, *java.beans.PropertyChangeListener* pcl)
	1	public . . . . void	addVetoableChangeListener (String name, *java.beans.VetoableChangeListener* vcl)
	5	public . . . . boolean	**avoidingGui** ()
		protected transient	**bcmListeners**
		. . . . java.util.ArrayList	
		protected . . . . . . *java.util.Iterator*	**bcsChildren** ()
		protected . . . . void	**bcsPreDeserializationHook** (java. io. ObjectInputStream ois) throws java.io.IOException, ClassNotFoundException
		protected . . . . void	**bcsPreSerializationHook** (java. io. ObjectOutputStream oos) throws java.io.IOException
	1	protected transient	beanContext
		. . . . *BeanContext*	
	1	public . . . . *BeanContextChild*	beanContextChildPeer
✳		public	**BeanContextSupport** ()
✳		public	**BeanContextSupport** (*BeanContext* peer)
✳		public	**BeanContextSupport** (*BeanContext* peer, java.util.Locale lcle)
✳		public	**BeanContextSupport** (*BeanContext* peer, java.util.Locale lcle, boolean dtime)
✳		public	**BeanContextSupport** (*BeanContext* peer, java.util.Locale lcle, boolean dTime, boolean visible)
		protected . . . . void	**childDeserializedHook** (Object child, BeanContextSupport.BCSChild bcsc)
		protected . . . . void	**childJustAddedHook** (Object child, BeanContextSupport.BCSChild bcsc)
		protected . . . . void	**childJustRemovedHook** (Object child, BeanContextSupport.BCSChild bcsc)
		protected transient	**children**
		. . . . java.util.HashMap	
▲		protected static final . . boolean	**classEquals** (Class first, Class second)
	3	public . . . . void	**clear** ()
	3	public . . . . boolean	**contains** (Object o)
	3	public . . . . boolean	**containsAll** (*java.util.Collection* c)
		public . . . . boolean	**containsKey** (Object o)
●		protected final . . . . Object[]	**copyChildren** ()
		protected	**createBCSChild** (Object targetChild, Object peer)
		BeanContextSupport.BCSChild	

Class *Interface* —extends - - -implements ○ abstract ● final △ static ▲ static final ✳ constructor x x—inherited x **x**—declared **x x**—overridden

● protected final.............void **deserialize** (java.io.ObjectInputStream ois, *java.util.Collection* coll)
throws java.io.IOException, ClassNotFoundException

protected.............. boolean **designTime**

5 public synchronized ....void **dontUseGui** ()

● protected final.............void **fireChildrenAdded** (BeanContextMembershipEvent bcme)

● protected final.............void **fireChildrenRemoved** (BeanContextMembershipEvent bcme)

1 public.....................void firePropertyChange (String name, Object oldValue, Object newValue)

1 public.....................void fireVetoableChange (String name, Object oldValue, Object newValue)
throws java.beans.PropertyVetoException

1 public synchronized ....
.... *BeanContext* getBeanContext ()

1 public....... *BeanContextChild* getBeanContextChildPeer ()

public....... *BeanContext* **getBeanContextPeer** ()

▲ protected static final ....
.... *BeanContextChild* **getChildBeanContextChild** (Object child)

▲ protected static final ..... *Bean-* **getChildBeanContextMembershipListener** (Object child)
ContextMembershipListener

▲ protected static final ....
.... *java.beans↩* **getChildPropertyChangeListener** (Object child)
.PropertyChangeListener

▲ protected static final ....
..............*java.io.Serializable* **getChildSerializable** (Object child)

▲ protected static final ....
.... *java.beans↩* **getChildVetoableChangeListener** (Object child)
.VetoableChangeListener

▲ protected static final ....
.... *java.beans.Visibility* **getChildVisibility** (Object child)

public synchronized ....
.................java.util.Locale **getLocale** ()

2 public............. java.net.URL **getResource** (String name, *BeanContextChild* bcc)

2 public...... java.io.InputStream **getResourceAsStream** (String name, *BeanContextChild* bcc)

protected synchronized ...void **initialize** ()

1 protected....................void initializeBeanContextResources ()

2 public................. Object **instantiateChild** (String beanName) throws java.io.IOException,
ClassNotFoundException

1 public................. boolean isDelegated ()

4 public synchronized .. boolean **isDesignTime** ()

3 public................. boolean **isEmpty** ()

public................. boolean **isSerializing** ()

3 public......... *java.util.Iterator* **iterator** ()

protected.......java.util.Locale **locale**

5 public synchronized .. boolean **needsGui** ()

5 public synchronized ....void **okToUseGui** ()

protected.............. boolean **okToUseGui**

1 protected........ java.beans↩ pcSupport
.PropertyChangeSupport

6 public.....................void **propertyChange** (java.beans.PropertyChangeEvent pce)

● public final ....void **readChildren** (java.io.ObjectInputStream ois) throws java.io.IOException,
ClassNotFoundException

1 protected transient.... boolean rejectedSetBCOnce

1 protected....................void releaseBeanContextResources ()

3 public.............. boolean **remove** (Object targetChild)

protected.............. boolean **remove** (Object targetChild, boolean callChildSetBC)

3 public.............. boolean **removeAll** (*java.util.Collection* c)

2 public.....................void **removeBeanContextMembershipListener** (*BeanContextMembershipListener*
bcml)

1 public.....................void removePropertyChangeListener (String name, *java.beans.PropertyChangeListener*
pcl)

1 public.....................void removeVetoableChangeListener (String name, *java.beans.VetoableChangeListener*
vcl)

3 public.............. boolean **retainAll** (*java.util.Collection* c)

● protected final.............void **serialize** (java.io.ObjectOutputStream oos, *java.util.Collection* coll)
throws java.io.IOException

1 public.....................void serviceAvailable (BeanContextServiceAvailableEvent bcsae)

1 public.....................void serviceRevoked (BeanContextServiceRevokedEvent bcsre)

1 public synchronized ....void setBeanContext (*BeanContext* bc) throws java.beans.PropertyVetoException

4 public synchronized ....void **setDesignTime** (boolean dTime)

public synchronized ....void **setLocale** (java.util.Locale newLocale) throws java.beans.PropertyVetoException

3 public.....................int **size** ()

3 public.................. Object[] **toArray** ()

3 public.................. Object[] **toArray** (Object[] arry)

protected.............. boolean **validatePendingAdd** (Object targetChild)

protected.............. boolean **validatePendingRemove** (Object targetChild)

BeanContextSupport

1	public	boolean	validatePendingSetBeanContext (*BeanContext* newValue)
1	protected	java.beans ↵	vcSupport
	.VetoableChangeSupport		
7	public	void	**vetoableChange** (java. beans. PropertyChangeEvent pce)
			throws java.beans.PropertyVetoException
●	public final	void	**writeChildren** (java.io.ObjectOutputStream oos) throws java.io.IOException

---

BeanContextSupport.BCSChild   protected   java.beans.beancontext

```
      Object
1.2   └─BeanContextSupport.BCSChild - - - - - - - - - - - java.io.Serializable
```

BeanContextSupport.BCSIterator   protected   java.beans.beancontext

```
      Object
1.2 ● └─BeanContextSupport.BCSIterator - - - - - - - - - java.util.Iterator 1
```

1	public	boolean	**hasNext** ()
1	public	Object	**next** ()
1	public	void	**remove** ()

BeanDescriptor   java.beans

```
      Object
1.1   └─FeatureDescriptor 1
1.1     └─BeanDescriptor
```

1	public.... *java.util.Enumeration*	attributeNames ()	
*	public	**BeanDescriptor** (Class beanClass)	
*	public	**BeanDescriptor** (Class beanClass, Class customizerClass)	
	public	Class	**getBeanClass** ()
	public	Class	**getCustomizerClass** ()
1	public	String	getDisplayName ()
1	public	String	getName ()
1	public	String	getShortDescription ()
1	public	Object	getValue (String attributeName)
1	public	boolean	isExpert ()
1	public	boolean	isHidden ()
1.2 1	public	boolean	isPreferred ()
1	public	void	setDisplayName (String displayName)
1	public	void	setExpert (boolean expert)
1	public	void	setHidden (boolean hidden)
1	public	void	setName (String name)
1.2 1	public	void	setPreferred (boolean preferred)
1	public	void	setShortDescription (String text)
1	public	void	setValue (String attributeName, Object value)

BeanInfo   java.beans

```
1.1   BeanInfo
```

	public	*BeanInfo[]*	**getAdditionalBeanInfo** ()
	public	BeanDescriptor	**getBeanDescriptor** ()
	public	int	**getDefaultEventIndex** ()
	public	int	**getDefaultPropertyIndex** ()
	public	EventSetDescriptor[]	**getEventSetDescriptors** ()
	public	java.awt.Image	**getIcon** (int iconKind)
	public	MethodDescriptor[]	**getMethodDescriptors** ()
	public	PropertyDescriptor[]	**getPropertyDescriptors** ()
▲	public static final	int	**ICON_COLOR_16x16** = 1
▲	public static final	int	**ICON_COLOR_32x32** = 2
▲	public static final	int	**ICON_MONO_16x16** = 3
▲	public static final	int	**ICON_MONO_32x32** = 4

Class   *Interface*   —extends   - - -implements   ○ abstract   ● final   △ static   ▲ static final   * constructor   x x—inherited   x **x**—declared   **x x**—overridden

Beans

java.beans

```
        Object
1.1     └Beans
```

✳	public		**Beans** ()
△	public static	Object	**getInstanceOf** (Object bean, Class targetType)
△	public static	Object	**instantiate** (ClassLoader cls, String beanName) throws java.io.IOException, ClassNotFoundException
1.2 △	public static	Object	**instantiate** (ClassLoader cls, String beanName, *java.beans.beancontext*↵ *.BeanContext* beanContext) throws java.io.IOException, ClassNotFoundException
1.2 △	public static	Object	**instantiate** (ClassLoader cls, String beanName, *java.beans*↵ *.beancontext.BeanContext* beanContext, *AppletInitializer* initializer) throws java.io.IOException, ClassNotFoundException
△	public static	boolean	**isDesignTime** ()
△	public static	boolean	**isGuiAvailable** ()
△	public static	boolean	**isInstanceOf** (Object bean, Class targetType)
△	public static	void	**setDesignTime** (boolean isDesignTime) throws SecurityException
△	public static	void	**setGuiAvailable** (boolean isGuiAvailable) throws SecurityException

BevelBorder

javax.swing.border

```
        Object
1.2 ○   └AbstractBorder 1 ----------------------- Border, java.io.Serializable
1.2       └BevelBorder
```

✳	public		**BevelBorder** (int bevelType)
✳	public		**BevelBorder** (int bevelType, java.awt.Color highlight, java.awt.Color shadow)
✳	public		**BevelBorder** (int bevelType, java.awt.Color highlightOuter, java.awt.Color highlightInner, java.awt.Color shadowOuter, java.awt.Color shadowInner)
	protected	int	**bevelType**
	public	int	**getBevelType** ()
1	public	**java.awt.Insets**	**getBorderInsets** (java.awt.Component c)
1	public	**java.awt.Insets**	**getBorderInsets** (java.awt.Component c, java.awt.Insets insets)
	public	java.awt.Color	**getHighlightInnerColor** (java.awt.Component c)
	public	java.awt.Color	**getHighlightOuterColor** (java.awt.Component c)
1	public	java.awt.Rectangle	getInteriorRectangle (java.awt.Component c, int x, int y, int width, int height)
△ 1	public static	java.awt.Rectangle	getInteriorRectangle (java.awt.Component c, *Border* b, int x, int y, int width, int height)
	public	java.awt.Color	**getShadowInnerColor** (java.awt.Component c)
	public	java.awt.Color	**getShadowOuterColor** (java.awt.Component c)
	protected	java.awt.Color	**highlightInner**
	protected	java.awt.Color	**highlightOuter**
1	public	**boolean**	**isBorderOpaque** ()
▲	public static final	int	**LOWERED** = 1
1	public	**void**	**paintBorder** (java.awt.Component c, java.awt.Graphics g, int x, int y, int width, int height)
	protected	void	**paintLoweredBevel** (java.awt.Component c, java.awt.Graphics g, int x, int y, int width, int height)
	protected	void	**paintRaisedBevel** (java.awt.Component c, java.awt.Graphics g, int x, int y, int width, int height)
▲	public static final	int	**RAISED** = 0
	protected	java.awt.Color	**shadowInner**
	protected	java.awt.Color	**shadowOuter**

BigDecimal

java.math
P^O

```
        Object 1
   ○    └Number 2 --------------------------- java.io.Serializable
1.1       └BigDecimal -------------------------- Comparable 3
```

	public	BigDecimal	**abs** ()
	public	BigDecimal	**add** (BigDecimal val)
✳	public		**BigDecimal** (double val)
✳	public		**BigDecimal** (String val)
✳	public		**BigDecimal** (BigInteger val)
✳	public		**BigDecimal** (BigInteger unscaledVal, int scale)
2	public	byte	byteValue ()
1.2	3 public	int	**compareTo** (Object o)
	public	int	**compareTo** (BigDecimal val)
	public	BigDecimal	**divide** (BigDecimal val, int roundingMode)

BigDecimal

	public	BigDecimal	**divide** (BigDecimal val, int scale, int roundingMode)
2	public	**double**	**doubleValue** ()
1	public	**boolean**	**equals** (Object x)
2	public	**float**	**floatValue** ()
1	public	**int**	**hashCode** ()
2	public	**int**	**intValue** ()
2	public	**long**	**longValue** ()
	public	BigDecimal	**max** (BigDecimal val)
	public	BigDecimal	**min** (BigDecimal val)
	public	BigDecimal	**movePointLeft** (int n)
	public	BigDecimal	**movePointRight** (int n)
	public	BigDecimal	**multiply** (BigDecimal val)
	public	BigDecimal	**negate** ()
▲	public static final	int	**ROUND_CEILING** = 2
▲	public static final	int	**ROUND_DOWN** = 1
▲	public static final	int	**ROUND_FLOOR** = 3
▲	public static final	int	**ROUND_HALF_DOWN** = 5
▲	public static final	int	**ROUND_HALF_EVEN** = 6
▲	public static final	int	**ROUND_HALF_UP** = 4
▲	public static final	int	**ROUND_UNNECESSARY** = 7
▲	public static final	int	**ROUND_UP** = 0
	public	int	**scale** ()
	public	BigDecimal	**setScale** (int scale)
	public	BigDecimal	**setScale** (int scale, int roundingMode)
2	public	short	shortValue ()
	public	int	**signum** ()
	public	BigDecimal	**subtract** (BigDecimal val)
	public	BigInteger	**toBigInteger** ()
1	public	**String**	**toString** ()
1.2	public	BigInteger	**unscaledValue** ()
△	public static	BigDecimal	**valueOf** (long val)
△	public static	BigDecimal	**valueOf** (long unscaledVal, int scale)

BigInteger   java.math

P⁰

○	Object[1]	
	└─Number[2] - *java.io.Serializable*	
1.1	└─BigInteger - *Comparable*[3]	

	public	BigInteger	**abs** ()
	public	BigInteger	**add** (BigInteger val)
	public	BigInteger	**and** (BigInteger val)
	public	BigInteger	**andNot** (BigInteger val)
✱	public		**BigInteger** (byte[] val)
✱	public		**BigInteger** (String val)
✱	public		**BigInteger** (int numBits, java.util.Random rnd)
✱	public		**BigInteger** (int signum, byte[] magnitude)
✱	public		**BigInteger** (String val, int radix)
✱	public		**BigInteger** (int bitLength, int certainty, java.util.Random rnd)
	public	int	**bitCount** ()
	public	int	**bitLength** ()
2	public	byte	byteValue ()
	public	BigInteger	**clearBit** (int n)
1.2 3	public	int	**compareTo** (Object o)
	public	int	**compareTo** (BigInteger val)
	public	BigInteger	**divide** (BigInteger val)
	public	BigInteger[]	**divideAndRemainder** (BigInteger val)
2	public	**double**	**doubleValue** ()
1	public	**boolean**	**equals** (Object x)
	public	BigInteger	**flipBit** (int n)
2	public	**float**	**floatValue** ()
	public	BigInteger	**gcd** (BigInteger val)
	public	int	**getLowestSetBit** ()
1	public	**int**	**hashCode** ()
2	public	**int**	**intValue** ()
	public	boolean	**isProbablePrime** (int certainty)
2	public	**long**	**longValue** ()
	public	BigInteger	**max** (BigInteger val)
	public	BigInteger	**min** (BigInteger val)
	public	BigInteger	**mod** (BigInteger m)
	public	BigInteger	**modInverse** (BigInteger m)

Class   *Interface*   —extends   - - -implements   ○ abstract   ● final   △ static   ▲ static final   ✱ constructor   x x—inherited   x **x**—declared   **x x**—overridden

		public	...............BigInteger	**modPow** (BigInteger exponent, BigInteger m)
		public	...............BigInteger	**multiply** (BigInteger val)
		public	...............BigInteger	**negate** ()
		public	...............BigInteger	**not** ()
1.2 ▲		public static final	....BigInteger	**ONE**
		public	...............BigInteger	**or** (BigInteger val)
		public	...............BigInteger	**pow** (int exponent)
		public	...............BigInteger	**remainder** (BigInteger val)
		public	...............BigInteger	**setBit** (int n)
		public	...............BigInteger	**shiftLeft** (int n)
		public	...............BigInteger	**shiftRight** (int n)
	2	public	..................short	shortValue ()
		public	.....................int	**signum** ()
		public	...............BigInteger	**subtract** (BigInteger val)
		public	...............boolean	**testBit** (int n)
		public	................byte[]	**toByteArray** ()
	1	public	................**String**	**toString** ()
		public	................String	**toString** (int radix)
△		public static	.........BigInteger	**valueOf** (long val)
		public	...............BigInteger	**xor** (BigInteger val)
1.2 ▲		public static final	....BigInteger	**ZERO**

BindException   java.net

P

```
Object
 └Throwable ------------------------------ java.io.Serializable
   └Exception
     └java.io.IOException
       └SocketException
```
1.1
```
         └BindException
```

✳		public	....	**BindException** ()
✳		public	....	**BindException** (String msg)

Binding   org.omg.CosNaming

```
Object
```
1.2 ●
```
 └Binding ----------------------------- org.omg.CORBA.portable.IDLEntity (java.io.Serializable)
```

✳	public	....	**Binding** ()
✳	public	....	**Binding** (NameComponent[] __binding_name, BindingType __binding_type)
	public	...... NameComponent[]	**binding_name**
	public	.... BindingType	**binding_type**

BindingHelper   org.omg.CosNaming

```
Object
```
1.2
```
 └BindingHelper
```

△	public static	............Binding	**extract** (org.omg.CORBA.Any a)
△	public static	..............String	**id** ()
△	public static	................void	**insert** (org.omg.CORBA.Any a, Binding that)
△	public static	.............Binding	**read** (org.omg.CORBA.portable.InputStream in)
△	public static synchronized	.... org.omg.CORBA.TypeCode	**type** ()
△	public static	................void	**write** (org.omg.CORBA.portable.OutputStream out, Binding that)

BindingHolder   org.omg.CosNaming

```
Object
```
1.2 ●
```
 └BindingHolder ------------------------- org.omg.CORBA.portable.Streamable 1
```

1	public	.......................void	**_read** (org.omg.CORBA.portable.InputStream in)
1	public	.... org.omg.CORBA.TypeCode	**_type** ()
1	public	.......................void	**_write** (org.omg.CORBA.portable.OutputStream out)
✳	public	....	**BindingHolder** ()
✳	public	....	**BindingHolder** (Binding __arg)
	public	.................Binding	**value**

BindingIterator

org.omg.CosNaming

1.2 | *BindingIterator*————————————————— *org.omg.CORBA.Object* [1], *org.omg.CORBA.portable.IDLEntity*
(*java.io.Serializable*)

- -

    1 13 inherited members from org.omg.CORBA.Object not shown
    public........................void **destroy** ()
    public................... boolean **next_n** (int how_many, BindingListHolder bl)
    public................... boolean **next_one** (BindingHolder b)

- -

BindingIteratorHelper

org.omg.CosNaming

Object
1.2 | └BindingIteratorHelper

△   public static .... *BindingIterator* **extract** (org.omg.CORBA.Any a)
△   public static .... String **id** ()
△   public static ....void **insert** (org.omg.CORBA.Any a, *BindingIterator* that)
△   public static .... *BindingIterator* **narrow** (*org.omg.CORBA.Object* that) throws org.omg.CORBA.BAD_PARAM
△   public static .... *BindingIterator* **read** (org.omg.CORBA.portable.InputStream in)
△   public static synchronized .... **type** ()
    ... org.omg.CORBA.TypeCode
△   public static ....void **write** (org.omg.CORBA.portable.OutputStream out, *BindingIterator* that)

BindingIteratorHolder

org.omg.CosNaming

Object
1.2 ● | └BindingIteratorHolder - - - - - - - - - - - - - - - - - - - *org.omg.CORBA.portable.Streamable* [1]

1   public........................void **_read** (org.omg.CORBA.portable.InputStream in)
1   public............................. **_type** ()
    ... org.omg.CORBA.TypeCode
1   public........................void **_write** (org.omg.CORBA.portable.OutputStream out)
✳   public............................. **BindingIteratorHolder** ()
✳   public............................. **BindingIteratorHolder** (*BindingIterator* __arg)
   public.......... *BindingIterator* **value**

BindingListHelper

org.omg.CosNaming

Object
1.2 | └BindingListHelper

△   public static .... Binding[] **extract** (org.omg.CORBA.Any a)
△   public static .... String **id** ()
△   public static ....void **insert** (org.omg.CORBA.Any a, Binding[] that)
△   public static .... Binding[] **read** (org.omg.CORBA.portable.InputStream in)
△   public static synchronized .... **type** ()
    ... org.omg.CORBA.TypeCode
△   public static ....void **write** (org.omg.CORBA.portable.OutputStream out, Binding[] that)

BindingListHolder

org.omg.CosNaming

Object
1.2 ● | └BindingListHolder - - - - - - - - - - - - - - - - - - - *org.omg.CORBA.portable.Streamable* [1]

1   public........................void **_read** (org.omg.CORBA.portable.InputStream in)
1   public............................. **_type** ()
    ... org.omg.CORBA.TypeCode
1   public........................void **_write** (org.omg.CORBA.portable.OutputStream out)
✳   public............................. **BindingListHolder** ()
✳   public............................. **BindingListHolder** (Binding[] __arg)
   public................ Binding[] **value**

Class   *Interface*   —extends   - - -implements   ○ abstract   ● final   △ static   ▲ static final   ✳ constructor   x x—inherited   x **x**—declared   **x x**—overridden

B

BindingType | org.omg.CosNaming

1.2 ●		Object		
		└ BindingType - *org.omg.CORBA.portable.IDLEntity* (*java.io.Serializable*)		

B

▲	public static final	int	**_ncontext**	= 1
▲	public static final	int	**_nobject**	= 0
▲	public static final	BindingType	**from_int** (int i) throws org.omg.CORBA.BAD_PARAM	
▲	public static final	BindingType	**ncontext**	
▲	public static final	BindingType	**nobject**	
	public	int	**value** ()	

BindingTypeHelper | org.omg.CosNaming

1.2		Object	
		└ BindingTypeHelper	

△	public static	BindingType	**extract** (org.omg.CORBA.Any a)
△	public static	String	**id** ()
△	public static	void	**insert** (org.omg.CORBA.Any a, BindingType that)
△	public static	BindingType	**read** (org.omg.CORBA.portable.InputStream in)
△	public static synchronized		**type** ()
	... org.omg.CORBA.TypeCode		
△	public static	void	**write** (org.omg.CORBA.portable.OutputStream out, BindingType that)

BindingTypeHolder | org.omg.CosNaming

1.2 ●		Object	
		└ BindingTypeHolder - *org.omg.CORBA.portable.Streamable* [1]	

1	public	void	**_read** (org.omg.CORBA.portable.InputStream in)
1	public		**_type** ()
	... org.omg.CORBA.TypeCode		
1	public	void	**_write** (org.omg.CORBA.portable.OutputStream out)
＊	public		**BindingTypeHolder** ()
＊	public		**BindingTypeHolder** (BindingType __arg)
	public	BindingType	**value**

BitSet | java.util

		Object [1]	P
		└ BitSet - *Cloneable, java.io.Serializable*	

	public	void	**and** (BitSet set)
1.2	public	void	**andNot** (BitSet set)
＊	public		**BitSet** ()
＊	public		**BitSet** (int nbits)
	public	void	**clear** (int bitIndex)
1	public	Object	**clone** ()
1	public	boolean	**equals** (Object obj)
	public	boolean	**get** (int bitIndex)
1	public	int	**hashCode** ()
1.2	public	int	**length** ()
	public	void	**or** (BitSet set)
	public	void	**set** (int bitIndex)
	public	int	**size** ()
1	public	String	**toString** ()
	public	void	**xor** (BitSet set)

Blob | java.sql

1.2	*Blob*	P^O

	public	java.io.InputStream	**getBinaryStream** () throws SQLException
	public	byte[]	**getBytes** (long pos, int length) throws SQLException
	public	long	**length** () throws SQLException
	public	long	**position** (byte[] pattern, long start) throws SQLException
	public	long	**position** (*Blob* pattern, long start) throws SQLException

BlockView

<table>
<tr><td></td><td colspan="2">**BlockView**</td><td>javax.swing.text.html</td></tr>
</table>

```
         Object
1.2 ○    └─javax.swing.text.View 1 - - - - - - - - - - - - - - - - - -  javax.swing.SwingConstants
1.2 ○       └─javax.swing.text.CompositeView 2
1.2            └─javax.swing.text.BoxView 3
1.2               └─BlockView
```

	3	*29 inherited members from javax.swing.text.BoxView not shown*	
	2	public......................void	append (javax.swing.text.View v)
*		public..........................	**BlockView** (*javax.swing.text.Element* elem, int axis)
	1	public....javax.swing.text.View	breakView (int axis, int offset, float pos, float len)
	1	public....javax.swing.text.View	createFragment (int p0, int p1)
	3	public......................**float**	**getAlignment** (int axis)
	1	public..........................	**getAttributes** ()
		. javax.swing.text.AttributeSet	
●	2	protected final.............short	getBottomInset ()
	1	public..........................int	getBreakWeight (int axis, float pos, float len)
	2	public......... *java.awt.Shape*	getChildAllocation (int index, *java.awt.Shape* a)
	1	public.......java.awt.Container	getContainer ()
	1	public..........................	getDocument ()
		.... javax.swing.text.Document	
	1	public..........................	getElement ()
		.... javax.swing.text.Element	
	1	public..........................int	getEndOffset ()
	2	protected .. java.awt.Rectangle	getInsideAllocation (*java.awt.Shape* a)
●	2	protected final.............short	getLeftInset ()
	2	protected......................int	getNextEastWestVisualPositionFrom (int pos, javax.swing.text.Position.Bias b,
			java.awt.Shape a, int direction, javax.swing.text.Position.Bias[] biasRet)
			throws javax.swing.text.BadLocationException
	2	protected......................int	getNextNorthSouthVisualPositionFrom (int pos, javax.swing.text.Position.Bias b,
			java.awt.Shape a, int direction, javax.swing.text.Position.Bias[] biasRet)
			throws javax.swing.text.BadLocationException
	2	public..........................int	getNextVisualPositionFrom (int pos, javax.swing.text.Position.Bias b,
			java.awt.Shape a, int direction, javax.swing.text.Position.Bias[] biasRet)
			throws javax.swing.text.BadLocationException
	1	public....javax.swing.text.View	getParent ()
	3	public.....................**int**	**getResizeWeight** (int axis)
●	2	protected final.............short	getRightInset ()
	1	public..........................int	getStartOffset ()
		protected.............StyleSheet	**getStyleSheet** ()
●	2	protected final.............short	getTopInset ()
	2	public....javax.swing.text.View	getView (int n)
	2	protected......................	getViewAtPosition (int pos, java.awt.Rectangle a)
		.... javax.swing.text.View	
	2	public..........................int	getViewCount ()
	1	public..........................	getViewFactory ()
		.. javax.swing.text.ViewFactory	
	2	protected......................int	getViewIndexAtPosition (int pos)
	2	public......................void	insert (int offs, javax.swing.text.View v)
	1	public.................. boolean	isVisible ()
	2	protected...................void	loadChildren (*javax.swing.text.ViewFactory* f)
	2	public.......... *java.awt.Shape*	modelToView (int p0, javax. swing. text. Position. Bias b0, int p1,
			javax. swing. text. Position. Bias b1, *java. awt. Shape* a)
			throws javax.swing.text.BadLocationException
	3	public......................**void paint** (java.awt.Graphics g, *java.awt.Shape* allocation)	
	2	public......................void	removeAll ()
●	2	protected final.............void	setInsets (short top, short left, short bottom, short right)
●	2	protected final.............void	setParagraphInsets (*javax.swing.text.AttributeSet* attr)
	2	public......................void	setParent (javax.swing.text.View parent)
		protected...................void	**setPropertiesFromAttributes** ()

<table>
<tr><td colspan="3">**Book**</td><td>java.awt.print</td></tr>
</table>

```
         Object
1.2      └─Book - - - - - - - - - - - - - - - - - - - - - - - - - - - - - Pageable 1
```

	public......................void	**append** (*Printable* painter, PageFormat page)
	public......................void	**append** (*Printable* painter, PageFormat page, int numPages)
*	public..........................	**Book** ()

Class   *Interface*   —extends   - - -implements   ○ abstract   ● final   △ static   ▲ static final   ✳ constructor   x x—inherited   x **x**—declared   **x x**—overridden

1	public	int	**getNumberOfPages** ()	
1	public	PageFormat	**getPageFormat** (int pageIndex) throws IndexOutOfBoundsException	
1	public	*Printable*	**getPrintable** (int pageIndex) throws IndexOutOfBoundsException	
	public	void	**setPage** (int pageIndex, *Printable* painter, PageFormat page) throws IndexOutOfBoundsException	

Boolean

java.lang

Object [1]
     P
●   └Boolean ---------------------------- *java.io.Serializable*

✱	public		**Boolean** (boolean value)
✱	public		**Boolean** (String s)
	public	boolean	**booleanValue** ()
1	public	**boolean**	**equals** (Object obj)
▲	public static final	Boolean	**FALSE** = new Boolean(false)
△	public static	boolean	**getBoolean** (String name)
1	public	**int**	**hashCode** ()
1	public	**String**	**toString** ()
▲	public static final	Boolean	**TRUE** = new Boolean(true)
1.1 ▲	public static final	Class	**TYPE**
△	public static	Boolean	**valueOf** (String s)

BooleanHolder

org.omg.CORBA

Object
1.2 ●   └BooleanHolder ---------------------- *org.omg.CORBA.portable.Streamable* [1]

1	public	void	**_read** (org.omg.CORBA.portable.InputStream input)
1	public	TypeCode	**_type** ()
1	public	void	**_write** (org.omg.CORBA.portable.OutputStream output)
✱	public		**BooleanHolder** ()
✱	public		**BooleanHolder** (boolean initial)
	public	boolean	**value**

Border

javax.swing.border

1.2   *Border*

public	java.awt.Insets	**getBorderInsets** (java.awt.Component c)
public	boolean	**isBorderOpaque** ()
public	void	**paintBorder** (java.awt.Component c, java.awt.Graphics g, int x, int y, int width, int height)

BorderFactory

javax.swing

Object
1.2   └BorderFactory

△	public static *javax.swing.border.Border*		**createBevelBorder** (int type)
△	public static *javax.swing.border.Border*		**createBevelBorder** (int type, java.awt.Color highlight, java.awt.Color shadow)
△	public static *javax.swing.border.Border*		**createBevelBorder** (int type, java.awt.Color highlightOuter, java.awt.Color highlightInner, java.awt.Color shadowOuter, java.awt.Color shadowInner)
△	public static *javax.swing* ↵ *.border.CompoundBorder*		**createCompoundBorder** ()
△	public static *javax.swing* ↵ *.border.CompoundBorder*		**createCompoundBorder** (*javax.swing.border.Border* outsideBorder, *javax.swing.border.Border* insideBorder)
△	public static *javax.swing.border.Border*		**createEmptyBorder** ()
△	public static *javax.swing.border.Border*		**createEmptyBorder** (int top, int left, int bottom, int right)
△	public static *javax.swing.border.Border*		**createEtchedBorder** ()
△	public static *javax.swing.border.Border*		**createEtchedBorder** (java.awt.Color highlight, java.awt.Color shadow)
△	public static *javax.swing.border.Border*		**createLineBorder** (java.awt.Color color)

BorderFactory

△	public static .... *javax.swing.border.Border*	**createLineBorder** (java.awt.Color color, int thickness)
△	public static .... *javax.swing.border.Border*	**createLoweredBevelBorder** ()
△	public static ....javax ↩ .swing.border.MatteBorder	**createMatteBorder** (int top, int left, int bottom, int right, *Icon* tileIcon)
△	public static ....javax ↩ .swing.border.MatteBorder	**createMatteBorder** (int top, int left, int bottom, int right, java.awt.Color color)
△	public static .... *javax.swing.border.Border*	**createRaisedBevelBorder** ()
△	public static ....javax ↩ .swing.border.TitledBorder	**createTitledBorder** (String title)
△	public static ....javax ↩ .swing.border.TitledBorder	**createTitledBorder** (*javax.swing.border.Border* border)
△	public static ....javax ↩ .swing.border.TitledBorder	**createTitledBorder** (*javax.swing.border.Border* border, String title)
△	public static ....javax ↩ .swing.border.TitledBorder	**createTitledBorder** (*javax. swing. border. Border* border, String title, int titleJustification, int titlePosition)
△	public static ....javax ↩ .swing.border.TitledBorder	**createTitledBorder** (*javax. swing. border. Border* border, String title, int titleJustification, int titlePosition, java.awt.Font titleFont)
△	public static ....javax ↩ .swing.border.TitledBorder	**createTitledBorder** (*javax. swing. border. Border* border, String title, int titleJustification, int titlePosition, java.awt.Font titleFont, java.awt.Color titleColor)

BorderLayout   java.awt

P

Object [1]
└ BorderLayout - *LayoutManager2* [2] (*LayoutManager* [3]), *java.io.Serializable*

1.1	2	public......................void	**addLayoutComponent** (Component comp, Object constraints)
D	3	public......................void	**addLayoutComponent** (String name, Component comp)
1.2 ▲		public static final........String	**AFTER_LAST_LINE** = "Last"
1.2 ▲		public static final........String	**AFTER_LINE_ENDS** = "After"
1.2 ▲		public static final........String	**BEFORE_FIRST_LINE** = "First"
1.2 ▲		public static final........String	**BEFORE_LINE_BEGINS** = "Before"
✳		public..........................	**BorderLayout** ()
✳		public..........................	**BorderLayout** (int hgap, int vgap)
1.1 ▲		public static final........String	**CENTER** = "Center"
1.1 ▲		public static final........String	**EAST** = "East"
1.1		public........................int	**getHgap** ()
1.1	2	public......................float	**getLayoutAlignmentX** (Container parent)
1.1	2	public......................float	**getLayoutAlignmentY** (Container parent)
1.1		public........................int	**getVgap** ()
1.1	2	public......................void	**invalidateLayout** (Container target)
	3	public......................void	**layoutContainer** (Container target)
1.1	2	public.................Dimension	**maximumLayoutSize** (Container target)
	3	public.................Dimension	**minimumLayoutSize** (Container target)
1.1 ▲		public static final........String	**NORTH** = "North"
	3	public.................Dimension	**preferredLayoutSize** (Container target)
	3	public......................void	**removeLayoutComponent** (Component comp)
1.1		public......................void	**setHgap** (int hgap)
1.1		public......................void	**setVgap** (int vgap)
1.1 ▲		public static final........String	**SOUTH** = "South"
	1	public................**String**	**toString** ()
1.1 ▲		public static final........String	**WEST** = "West"

BorderUIResource   javax.swing.plaf

Object
└ BorderUIResource - *javax.swing.border.Border* [1], *UIResource*, *java.io.Serializable*

1.2			
✳		public..........................	**BorderUIResource** (*javax.swing.border.Border* delegate)
△		public static .... *javax.swing.border.Border*	**getBlackLineBorderUIResource** ()
	1	public..........java.awt.Insets	**getBorderInsets** (java.awt.Component c)
△		public static .... *javax.swing.border.Border*	**getEtchedBorderUIResource** ()
△		public static .... *javax.swing.border.Border*	**getLoweredBevelBorderUIResource** ()

Class *Interface* —extends - - -implements ○ abstract ● final △ static ▲ static final ✳ constructor x x—inherited x **x**—declared **x x**—overridden

△	public static	**getRaisedBevelBorderUIResource** ()	
	..... *javax.swing.border.Border*		
1	public .... boolean	**isBorderOpaque** ()	
1	public .... void	**paintBorder** (java.awt.Component c, java.awt.Graphics g, int x, int y, int width, int height)	

BorderUIResource.BevelBorderUIResource   javax.swing.plaf

Object
- 1.2 ○ └javax.swing.border.AbstractBorder [1] - - - - - - - *javax.swing.border.Border* , *java.io.Serializable*
- 1.2   └javax.swing.border.BevelBorder [2]
- 1.2   └BorderUIResource ↩ - - - - - - - - - - - - - - - *UIResource*
       .BevelBorderUIResource

1	*2 inherited members from javax.swing.border.AbstractBorder not shown*	
2	*18 inherited members from javax.swing.border.BevelBorder not shown*	
*	public	**BevelBorderUIResource** (int bevelType)
*	public	**BevelBorderUIResource** (int bevelType, java. awt. Color highlight, java.awt.Color shadow)
*	public	**BevelBorderUIResource** (int bevelType, java.awt.Color highlightOuter, java.awt ↩ .Color highlightInner, java.awt.Color shadowOuter, java.awt.Color shadowInner)

BorderUIResource.CompoundBorderUIResource   javax.swing.plaf

Object
- 1.2 ○ └javax.swing.border.AbstractBorder [1] - - - - - - - *javax.swing.border.Border* , *java.io.Serializable*
- 1.2   └javax.swing.border.CompoundBorder [2]
- 1.2   └BorderUIResource ↩ - - - - - - - - - - - - - - - *UIResource*
       .CompoundBorderUIResource

1	*2 inherited members from javax.swing.border.AbstractBorder not shown*	
2	*8 inherited members from javax.swing.border.CompoundBorder not shown*	
*	public	**CompoundBorderUIResource** (*javax. swing. border. Border* outsideBorder, *javax.swing.border.Border* insideBorder)

BorderUIResource.EmptyBorderUIResource   javax.swing.plaf

Object
- 1.2 ○ └javax.swing.border.AbstractBorder [1] - - - - - - - *javax.swing.border.Border* , *java.io.Serializable*
- 1.2   └javax.swing.border.EmptyBorder [2] - - - - - - - *java.io.Serializable*
- 1.2   └BorderUIResource ↩ - - - - - - - - - - - - - - - *UIResource*
       .EmptyBorderUIResource

1	*2 inherited members from javax.swing.border.AbstractBorder not shown*	
2	*8 inherited members from javax.swing.border.EmptyBorder not shown*	
*	public	**EmptyBorderUIResource** (java.awt.Insets insets)
*	public	**EmptyBorderUIResource** (int top, int left, int bottom, int right)

BorderUIResource.EtchedBorderUIResource   javax.swing.plaf

Object
- 1.2 ○ └javax.swing.border.AbstractBorder [1] - - - - - - - *javax.swing.border.Border* , *java.io.Serializable*
- 1.2   └javax.swing.border.EtchedBorder [2]
- 1.2   └BorderUIResource ↩ - - - - - - - - - - - - - - - *UIResource*
       .EtchedBorderUIResource

1	*2 inherited members from javax.swing.border.AbstractBorder not shown*	
2	*12 inherited members from javax.swing.border.EtchedBorder not shown*	
*	public	**EtchedBorderUIResource** ()
*	public	**EtchedBorderUIResource** (int etchType)
*	public	**EtchedBorderUIResource** (java.awt.Color highlight, java.awt.Color shadow)
*	public	**EtchedBorderUIResource** (int etchType, java. awt. Color highlight, java.awt.Color shadow)

BorderUIResource.LineBorderUIResource	javax.swing.plaf

```
       Object
1.2 ○   └─javax.swing.border.AbstractBorder[1] ------- javax.swing.border.Border, java.io.Serializable
1.2        └─javax.swing.border.LineBorder[2]
1.2           └─BorderUIResource↵ ---------------- UIResource
                 .LineBorderUIResource
```

1	*2 inherited members from javax.swing.border.AbstractBorder not shown*		
2	*11 inherited members from javax.swing.border.LineBorder not shown*		
✻	public..........................	**LineBorderUIResource** (java.awt.Color color)	
✻	public..........................	**LineBorderUIResource** (java.awt.Color color, int thickness)	

BorderUIResource.MatteBorderUIResource	javax.swing.plaf

```
       Object
1.2 ○   └─javax.swing.border.AbstractBorder[1] ------- javax.swing.border.Border, java.io.Serializable
1.2        └─javax.swing.border.EmptyBorder[2] -------- java.io.Serializable
1.2           └─javax.swing.border.MatteBorder[3]
1.2              └─BorderUIResource↵ -------------- UIResource
                    .MatteBorderUIResource
```

1	*2 inherited members from javax.swing.border.AbstractBorder not shown*	
2	*5 inherited members from javax.swing.border.EmptyBorder not shown*	
3	*5 inherited members from javax.swing.border.MatteBorder not shown*	
✻	public..........................	**MatteBorderUIResource** (*javax.swing.Icon* tileIcon)
✻	public..........................	**MatteBorderUIResource** (int top, int left, int bottom, int right, java.awt.Color color)
✻	public..........................	**MatteBorderUIResource** (int top, int left, int bottom, int right, *javax.swing.Icon* tileIcon)

BorderUIResource.TitledBorderUIResource	javax.swing.plaf

```
       Object
1.2 ○   └─javax.swing.border.AbstractBorder[1] ------- javax.swing.border.Border, java.io.Serializable
1.2        └─javax.swing.border.TitledBorder[2]
1.2           └─BorderUIResource↵ ---------------- UIResource
                 .TitledBorderUIResource
```

1	*2 inherited members from javax.swing.border.AbstractBorder not shown*	
2	*38 inherited members from javax.swing.border.TitledBorder not shown*	
✻	public..........................	**TitledBorderUIResource** (String title)
✻	public..........................	**TitledBorderUIResource** (*javax.swing.border.Border* border)
✻	public..........................	**TitledBorderUIResource** (*javax.swing.border.Border* border, String title)
✻	public..........................	**TitledBorderUIResource** (*javax.swing.border.Border* border, String title, int titleJustification, int titlePosition)
✻	public..........................	**TitledBorderUIResource** (*javax.swing.border.Border* border, String title, int titleJustification, int titlePosition, java.awt.Font titleFont)
✻	public..........................	**TitledBorderUIResource** (*javax.swing.border.Border* border, String title, int titleJustification, int titlePosition, java.awt.Font titleFont, java.awt.Color titleColor)

BoundedRangeModel	javax.swing

```
1.2    BoundedRangeModel
```

public.......................void	**addChangeListener** (*javax.swing.event.ChangeListener* x)	
public.......................int	**getExtent** ()	
public.......................int	**getMaximum** ()	
public.......................int	**getMinimum** ()	
public.......................int	**getValue** ()	
public....................boolean	**getValueIsAdjusting** ()	
public.......................void	**removeChangeListener** (*javax.swing.event.ChangeListener* x)	
public.......................void	**setExtent** (int newExtent)	
public.......................void	**setMaximum** (int newMaximum)	
public.......................void	**setMinimum** (int newMinimum)	
public.......................void	**setRangeProperties** (int value, int extent, int min, int max, boolean adjusting)	
public.......................void	**setValue** (int newValue)	
public.......................void	**setValueIsAdjusting** (boolean b)	

Class   *Interface*   —extends   - - -implements   ○ abstract   ● final   △ static   ▲ static final   ✻ constructor   x x—inherited   x **x**—declared   **x x**—overridden

Bounds➊ · org.omg.CORBA.TypeCodePackage

```
Object
└Throwable ---------------------------- java.io.Serializable
  └Exception
```
1.2 ○	└org.omg.CORBA.UserException -------	org.omg.CORBA.portable.IDLEntity (java.io.Serializable)
1.2 ●	└Bounds	

✳	public........................	**Bounds** ()
✳	public........................	**Bounds** (String reason)

Bounds➋ · org.omg.CORBA

```
Object
└Throwable -------------------------- java.io.Serializable
  └Exception
```
1.2 ○	└UserException -------------------	org.omg.CORBA.portable.IDLEntity (java.io.Serializable)
1.2 ●	└Bounds	

✳	public........................	**Bounds** ()
✳	public........................	**Bounds** (String reason)

Box · javax.swing

```
Object
```
○	└java.awt.Component[1] ------------------	java.awt.image.ImageObserver, java.awt.MenuContainer, java.io.Serializable
	└java.awt.Container[2]	
1.2	└Box ----------------------------	javax.accessibility.Accessible[3]

1	*137 inherited members from java.awt.Component not shown*		
2	*50 inherited members from java.awt.Container not shown*		
	protected javax.accessibility ↩ .AccessibleContext	**accessibleContext**	
✳	public........................	**Box** (int axis)	
△	public static .... java.awt.Component	**createGlue** ()	
△	public static .... Box	**createHorizontalBox** ()	
△	public static .... java.awt.Component	**createHorizontalGlue** ()	
△	public static .... java.awt.Component	**createHorizontalStrut** (int width)	
△	public static .... java.awt.Component	**createRigidArea** (java.awt.Dimension d)	
△	public static .... Box	**createVerticalBox** ()	
△	public static .... java.awt.Component	**createVerticalGlue** ()	
△	public static .... java.awt.Component	**createVerticalStrut** (int height)	
3	public.... javax.accessibility ↩ .AccessibleContext	**getAccessibleContext** ()	
2	public........................ **void**	**setLayout** (java.awt.LayoutManager l)	

Box.AccessibleBox · protected · javax.swing

```
Object
```
1.2 ○	└javax.accessibility.AccessibleContext[1]	
1.2	└Box.AccessibleBox -------------------	java.io.Serializable, javax.accessibility.AccessibleComponent[2]

1	*25 inherited members from javax.accessibility.AccessibleContext not shown*	
✳	protected......................	**AccessibleBox** ()
2	public......................void	**addFocusListener** (java.awt.event.FocusListener l)
2	public................. boolean	**contains** (java.awt.Point p)
2	public........................ *javax.accessibility.Accessible*	**getAccessibleAt** (java.awt.Point p)
1	public................. *javax↩ .accessibility.Accessible*	**getAccessibleChild** (int i)
1	public........................ **int**	**getAccessibleChildrenCount** ()

Box.AccessibleBox

1	public...	**javax.accessibility↵**	**getAccessibleComponent** ()
		.AccessibleComponent	
1	public.....................	**int**	**getAccessibleIndexInParent** ()
1	public.....................	**javax↵**	**getAccessibleParent** ()
		.accessibility.Accessible	
1	public.....................	**javax↵**	**getAccessibleRole** ()
		.accessibility.AccessibleRole	
1	public...	**javax.accessibility↵**	**getAccessibleStateSet** ()
		.AccessibleStateSet	
2	public............java.awt.Color		**getBackground** ()
2	public......java.awt.Rectangle		**getBounds** ()
2	public............java.awt.Cursor		**getCursor** ()
2	public...............java.awt.Font		**getFont** ()
2	public.....java.awt.FontMetrics		**getFontMetrics** (java.awt.Font f)
2	public............java.awt.Color		**getForeground** ()
1	public.............**java.util.Locale**		**getLocale** ()
2	public............java.awt.Point		**getLocation** ()
2	public............java.awt.Point		**getLocationOnScreen** ()
2	public......java.awt.Dimension		**getSize** ()
2	public..................boolean		**isEnabled** ()
2	public..................boolean		**isFocusTraversable** ()
2	public..................boolean		**isShowing** ()
2	public..................boolean		**isVisible** ()
2	public..................void		**removeFocusListener** (*java.awt.event.FocusListener* l)
2	public..................void		**requestFocus** ()
2	public..................void		**setBackground** (java.awt.Color c)
2	public..................void		**setBounds** (java.awt.Rectangle r)
2	public..................void		**setCursor** (java.awt.Cursor cursor)
2	public..................void		**setEnabled** (boolean b)
2	public..................void		**setFont** (java.awt.Font f)
2	public..................void		**setForeground** (java.awt.Color c)
2	public..................void		**setLocation** (java.awt.Point p)
2	public..................void		**setSize** (java.awt.Dimension d)
2	public..................void		**setVisible** (boolean b)

Box.Filler   javax.swing

Object
  ○ └java.awt.Component[1] - - - - - - - - - - - - - - - - - - - *java.awt.image.ImageObserver*, *java.awt.MenuContainer*,
                                        java.io.Serializable
1.2   └Box.Filler - *javax.accessibility.Accessible* [2]

1	*159 inherited members from java.awt.Component not shown*		
	protected javax.accessibility↵		**accessibleContext**
	.AccessibleContext		
	public......................void		**changeShape** (java.awt.Dimension min, java.awt.Dimension pref,
			java.awt.Dimension max)
*	public.........................		**Filler** (java.awt.Dimension min, java.awt.Dimension pref, java.awt.Dimension max)
2	public.... javax.accessibility↵		**getAccessibleContext** ()
	.AccessibleContext		
1	public.... **java.awt.Dimension**		**getMaximumSize** ()
1	public.... **java.awt.Dimension**		**getMinimumSize** ()
1	public.... **java.awt.Dimension**		**getPreferredSize** ()

Box.Filler.AccessibleBoxFiller   protected   javax.swing

Object
1.2 ○ └javax.accessibility.AccessibleContext[1]
1.2   └Box.Filler.AccessibleBoxFiller - - - - - - - - - - - *java.io.Serializable*, *javax.accessibility.AccessibleComponent* [2]

1	*25 inherited members from javax.accessibility.AccessibleContext not shown*		
*	protected......................		**AccessibleBoxFiller** ()
2	public......................void		**addFocusListener** (*java.awt.event.FocusListener* l)
2	public.............. boolean		**contains** (java.awt.Point p)
2	public..........................		**getAccessibleAt** (java.awt.Point p)
	. *javax.accessibility.Accessible*		
1	public.....................**javax↵**		**getAccessibleChild** (int i)
	.accessibility.Accessible		
1	public......................**int**		**getAccessibleChildrenCount** ()

Class   *Interface*   —extends   - - -implements   ○ abstract   ● final   △ static   ▲ static final   ✳ constructor   x x—inherited   x **x**—declared   **x x**—overridden

1	public...	***javax.accessibility↩***	**getAccessibleComponent** ()
		.AccessibleComponent	
1	public.....................	**int**	**getAccessibleIndexInParent** ()
1	public.................	***javax↩***	**getAccessibleParent** ()
		.accessibility.Accessible	
1	public..............	***javax↩***	**getAccessibleRole** ()
		.accessibility.AccessibleRole	
1	public...	***javax.accessibility↩***	**getAccessibleStateSet** ()
		.AccessibleStateSet	
2	public...........	java.awt.Color	**getBackground** ()
2	public......	java.awt.Rectangle	**getBounds** ()
2	public.........	java.awt.Cursor	**getCursor** ()
2	public...........	java.awt.Font	**getFont** ()
2	public....	java.awt.FontMetrics	**getFontMetrics** (java.awt.Font f)
2	public...........	java.awt.Color	**getForeground** ()
1	public..........	**java.util.Locale**	**getLocale** ()
2	public...........	java.awt.Point	**getLocation** ()
2	public...........	java.awt.Point	**getLocationOnScreen** ()
2	public......	java.awt.Dimension	**getSize** ()
2	public.................	boolean	**isEnabled** ()
2	public.................	boolean	**isFocusTraversable** ()
2	public.................	boolean	**isShowing** ()
2	public.................	boolean	**isVisible** ()
2	public.....................	void	**removeFocusListener** (*java.awt.event.FocusListener* l)
2	public.....................	void	**requestFocus** ()
2	public.....................	void	**setBackground** (java.awt.Color c)
2	public.....................	void	**setBounds** (java.awt.Rectangle r)
2	public.....................	void	**setCursor** (java.awt.Cursor cursor)
2	public.....................	void	**setEnabled** (boolean b)
2	public.....................	void	**setFont** (java.awt.Font f)
2	public.....................	void	**setForeground** (java.awt.Color c)
2	public.....................	void	**setLocation** (java.awt.Point p)
2	public.....................	void	**setSize** (java.awt.Dimension d)
2	public.....................	void	**setVisible** (boolean b)

BoxLayout

javax.swing

Object
1.2 └BoxLayout - *java.awt.LayoutManager2* [1] (*java.awt.LayoutManager* [2]), *java.io.Serializable*

1	public.....................	void	**addLayoutComponent** (java.awt.Component comp, Object constraints)
2	public.....................	void	**addLayoutComponent** (String name, java.awt.Component comp)
*	public.....................		**BoxLayout** (java.awt.Container target, int axis)
1	public.....................	float	**getLayoutAlignmentX** (java.awt.Container target)
1	public.....................	float	**getLayoutAlignmentY** (java.awt.Container target)
1	public.....................	void	**invalidateLayout** (java.awt.Container target)
2	public.....................	void	**layoutContainer** (java.awt.Container target)
1	public......	java.awt.Dimension	**maximumLayoutSize** (java.awt.Container target)
2	public......	java.awt.Dimension	**minimumLayoutSize** (java.awt.Container target)
2	public......	java.awt.Dimension	**preferredLayoutSize** (java.awt.Container target)
2	public.....................	void	**removeLayoutComponent** (java.awt.Component comp)
▲	public static final..............	int	**X_AXIS** = 0
▲	public static final..............	int	**Y_AXIS** = 1

Classes

BoxView

javax.swing.text

Object
1.2 ○ └View [1] - *javax.swing.SwingConstants*
1.2 ○ └CompositeView [2]
1.2 └BoxView

2	public.....................	void	append (View v)
	protected	void	**baselineLayout** (int targetSpan, int axis, int[] offsets, int[] spans)
	protected......................		**baselineRequirements** (int axis, javax.swing.SizeRequirements r)
	.javax.swing.SizeRequirements		
*	public........................		**BoxView** (*Element* elem, int axis)
1	public.....................	View	breakView (int axis, int offset, float pos, float len)
	protected......................		**calculateMajorAxisRequirements** (int axis, javax.swing.SizeRequirements r)
	.javax.swing.SizeRequirements		

BoxView

		protected . . . . .javax.swing.SizeRequirements	**calculateMinorAxisRequirements** (int axis, javax.swing.SizeRequirements r)
	1	public . . . . **void**	**changedUpdate** (*javax. swing. event. DocumentEvent* e, *java. awt. Shape* a, *ViewFactory* f)
	2	protected . . . . **void**	**childAllocation** (int index, java.awt.Rectangle alloc)
	1	public . . . . View	createFragment (int p0, int p1)
	2	protected . . . . **boolean**	**flipEastAndWestAtEnds** (int position, Position.Bias bias)
	1	public . . . . **float**	**getAlignment** (int axis)
	1	public . . . . *AttributeSet*	getAttributes ()
●	2	protected final . . . . short	getBottomInset ()
	1	public . . . . int	getBreakWeight (int axis, float pos, float len)
	2	public . . . . *java.awt.Shape*	getChildAllocation (int index, *java.awt.Shape* a)
	1	public . . . . java.awt.Container	getContainer ()
	1	public . . . . *Document*	getDocument ()
	1	public . . . . *Element*	getElement ()
	1	public . . . . int	getEndOffset ()
●		public final . . . . int	**getHeight** ()
	2	protected .. java.awt.Rectangle	getInsideAllocation (*java.awt.Shape* a)
●	2	protected final . . . . short	getLeftInset ()
	1	public . . . . **float**	**getMaximumSpan** (int axis)
	1	public . . . . **float**	**getMinimumSpan** (int axis)
	2	protected . . . . int	getNextEastWestVisualPositionFrom (int pos, Position.Bias b, *java.awt.Shape* a, int direction, Position.Bias[] biasRet) throws BadLocationException
	2	protected . . . . int	getNextNorthSouthVisualPositionFrom (int pos, Position.Bias b, *java.awt.Shape* a, int direction, Position.Bias[] biasRet) throws BadLocationException
	2	public . . . . int	getNextVisualPositionFrom (int pos, Position.Bias b, *java.awt.Shape* a, int direction, Position.Bias[] biasRet) throws BadLocationException
●		protected final . . . . int	**getOffset** (int axis, int childIndex)
	1	public . . . . View	getParent ()
	1	public . . . . **float**	**getPreferredSpan** (int axis)
	1	public . . . . **int**	**getResizeWeight** (int axis)
●	2	protected final . . . . short	getRightInset ()
●	2	protected final . . . . int	**getSpan** (int axis, int childIndex)
	1	public . . . . int	getStartOffset ()
●	2	protected final . . . . short	getTopInset ()
	2	public . . . . View	getView (int n)
	2	protected . . . . **View**	**getViewAtPoint** (int x, int y, java.awt.Rectangle alloc)
	2	protected . . . . View	getViewAtPosition (int pos, java.awt.Rectangle a)
	2	public . . . . int	getViewCount ()
	1	public . . . . *ViewFactory*	getViewFactory ()
	2	protected . . . . int	getViewIndexAtPosition (int pos)
●		public final . . . . int	**getWidth** ()
	2	public . . . . void	insert (int offs, View v)
	1	public . . . . **void**	**insertUpdate** (*javax. swing. event. DocumentEvent* e, *java. awt. Shape* a, *ViewFactory* f)
	2	protected . . . . **boolean**	**isAfter** (int x, int y, java.awt.Rectangle innerAlloc)
		protected . . . . boolean	**isAllocationValid** ()
	2	protected . . . . **boolean**	**isBefore** (int x, int y, java.awt.Rectangle innerAlloc)
	1	public . . . . boolean	isVisible ()
		protected . . . . void	**layout** (int width, int height)
		protected . . . . void	**layoutMajorAxis** (int targetSpan, int axis, int[] offsets, int[] spans)
		protected . . . . void	**layoutMinorAxis** (int targetSpan, int axis, int[] offsets, int[] spans)
	2	protected . . . . void	loadChildren (*ViewFactory* f)
	2	public . . . . *java.awt.Shape*	**modelToView** (int pos, *java. awt. Shape* a, Position. Bias b) throws BadLocationException
	2	public . . . . *java.awt.Shape*	modelToView (int p0, Position.Bias b0, int p1, Position.Bias b1, *java.awt.Shape* a) throws BadLocationException
	1	public . . . . **void**	**paint** (java.awt.Graphics g, *java.awt.Shape* allocation)
		protected . . . . void	**paintChild** (java.awt.Graphics g, java.awt.Rectangle alloc, int index)
	1	public . . . . **void**	**preferenceChanged** (View child, boolean width, boolean height)
	2	public . . . . void	removeAll ()
	1	public . . . . **void**	**removeUpdate** (*javax. swing. event. DocumentEvent* e, *java. awt. Shape* a, *ViewFactory* f)
	2	public . . . . **void**	**replace** (int offset, int length, View[] elems)
●	2	protected final . . . . void	setInsets (short top, short left, short bottom, short right)
●	2	protected final . . . . void	setParagraphInsets (*AttributeSet* attr)
	2	public . . . . void	setParent (View parent)
	1	public . . . . **void**	**setSize** (float width, float height)
	2	public . . . . **int**	**viewToModel** (float x, float y, *java.awt.Shape* a, Position.Bias[] bias)

Class   *Interface*   —extends   - - -implements   ○ abstract   ● final   △ static   ▲ static final   ✳ constructor   x x—inherited   x **x**—declared   **x x**—overridden

242

BreakIterator

```
Object 1
1.1  O  └ BreakIterator ------------------------- Cloneable                    P
```

B

*	protected	**BreakIterator** ()
1	public . . . . **Object**	**clone** ()
O	public abstract . . . . .int	**current** ()
▲	public static final . . . . .int	**DONE** = -1
O	public abstract . . . . .int	**first** ()
O	public abstract . . . . .int	**following** (int offset)
△	public static synchronized	**getAvailableLocales** ()
	. . . . java.util.Locale[]	
△	public static . . . . . . BreakIterator	**getCharacterInstance** ()
△	public static . . . . . . BreakIterator	**getCharacterInstance** (java.util.Locale where)
△	public static . . . . . . BreakIterator	**getLineInstance** ()
△	public static . . . . . . BreakIterator	**getLineInstance** (java.util.Locale where)
△	public static . . . . . . BreakIterator	**getSentenceInstance** ()
△	public static . . . . . . BreakIterator	**getSentenceInstance** (java.util.Locale where)
O	public abstract	**getText** ()
	. . . . *CharacterIterator*	
△	public static . . . . . . BreakIterator	**getWordInstance** ()
△	public static . . . . . . BreakIterator	**getWordInstance** (java.util.Locale where)
1.2	public . . . . boolean	**isBoundary** (int offset)
O	public abstract . . . . .int	**last** ()
O	public abstract . . . . .int	**next** ()
O	public abstract . . . . .int	**next** (int n)
1.2	public . . . . .int	**preceding** (int offset)
O	public abstract . . . . .int	**previous** ()
	public .void	**setText** (String newText)
O	public abstract . . . . .void	**setText** (*CharacterIterator* newText)

BufferedImage

```
Object 1
O  └ java.awt.Image 2                                                         P
1.2     └ BufferedImage ------------------- WritableRenderedImage 3 (RenderedImage 4)
```

3	public . . . . .void	**addTileObserver** (*TileObserver* to)
*	public	**BufferedImage** (int width, int height, int imageType)
*	public	**BufferedImage** (int width, int height, int imageType, IndexColorModel cm)
*	public	**BufferedImage** (ColorModel cm, WritableRaster raster,
		boolean isRasterPremultiplied, java.util.Hashtable properties)
	public . . . . .void	**coerceData** (boolean isAlphaPremultiplied)
4	public . . . . WritableRaster	**copyData** (WritableRaster outRaster)
	public java.awt.Graphics2D	**createGraphics** ()
2	public . . . . **void**	**flush** ()
	public . . . . WritableRaster	**getAlphaRaster** ()
4	public . . . . ColorModel	**getColorModel** ()
4	public . . . . Raster	**getData** ()
4	public . . . . Raster	**getData** (java.awt.Rectangle rect)
2	public . . . . . . **java.awt.Graphics**	**getGraphics** ()
4	public . . . . .int	**getHeight** ()
2	public . . . . **int**	**getHeight** (*ImageObserver* observer)
4	public . . . . .int	**getMinTileX** ()
4	public . . . . .int	**getMinTileY** ()
4	public . . . . .int	**getMinX** ()
4	public . . . . .int	**getMinY** ()
4	public . . . . .int	**getNumXTiles** ()
4	public . . . . .int	**getNumYTiles** ()
4	public . . . . Object	**getProperty** (String name)
2	public . . . . **Object**	**getProperty** (String name, *ImageObserver* observer)
4	public . . . . String[]	**getPropertyNames** ()
	public . . . . WritableRaster	**getRaster** ()
	public . . . . .int	**getRGB** (int x, int y)
	public . . . . .int[]	**getRGB** (int startX, int startY, int w, int h, int[] rgbArray, int offset, int scansize)
4	public . . . . SampleModel	**getSampleModel** ()
2	public . . . . java.awt.Image	getScaledInstance (int width, int height, int hints)
2	public . . . . **ImageProducer**	**getSource** ()
4	public . . . . java.util.Vector	**getSources** ()
	public . . . . BufferedImage	**getSubimage** (int x, int y, int w, int h)
4	public . . . . Raster	**getTile** (int tileX, int tileY)

BufferedImage

4	public	int	**getTileGridXOffset** ()
4	public	int	**getTileGridYOffset** ()
4	public	int	**getTileHeight** ()
4	public	int	**getTileWidth** ()
	public	int	**getType** ()
4	public	int	**getWidth** ()
2	public	**int**	**getWidth** (*ImageObserver* observer)
3	public	WritableRaster	**getWritableTile** (int tileX, int tileY)
3	public	java.awt.Point[]	**getWritableTileIndices** ()
3	public	boolean	**hasTileWriters** ()
	public	boolean	**isAlphaPremultiplied** ()
3	public	boolean	**isTileWritable** (int tileX, int tileY)
3	public	void	**releaseWritableTile** (int tileX, int tileY)
3	public	void	**removeTileObserver** (*TileObserver* to)
3	public	void	**setData** (Raster r)
	public synchronized	void	**setRGB** (int x, int y, int rgb)
	public	void	**setRGB** (int startX, int startY, int w, int h, int[] rgbArray, int offset, int scansize)
1	public	**String**	**toString** ()
▲	public static final	int	**TYPE_3BYTE_BGR** = 5
▲	public static final	int	**TYPE_4BYTE_ABGR** = 6
▲	public static final	int	**TYPE_4BYTE_ABGR_PRE** = 7
▲	public static final	int	**TYPE_BYTE_BINARY** = 12
▲	public static final	int	**TYPE_BYTE_GRAY** = 10
▲	public static final	int	**TYPE_BYTE_INDEXED** = 13
▲	public static final	int	**TYPE_CUSTOM** = 0
▲	public static final	int	**TYPE_INT_ARGB** = 2
▲	public static final	int	**TYPE_INT_ARGB_PRE** = 3
▲	public static final	int	**TYPE_INT_BGR** = 4
▲	public static final	int	**TYPE_INT_RGB** = 1
▲	public static final	int	**TYPE_USHORT_555_RGB** = 9
▲	public static final	int	**TYPE_USHORT_565_RGB** = 8
▲	public static final	int	**TYPE_USHORT_GRAY** = 11

BufferedImageFilter
java.awt.image

P

```
Object
 └ImageFilter¹ - - - - - - - - - - - - - - - - - - - - - - - - - ImageConsumer, Cloneable
1.2    └BufferedImageFilter - - - - - - - - - - - - - - - - - - Cloneable
```

*	public		**BufferedImageFilter** (*BufferedImageOp* op)
1	public	Object	clone ()
1	protected	*ImageConsumer*	consumer
	public	*BufferedImageOp*	**getBufferedImageOp** ()
1	public	ImageFilter	getFilterInstance (*ImageConsumer* ic)
1	public	**void**	**imageComplete** (int status)
1	public	void	resendTopDownLeftRight (*ImageProducer* ip)
1	public	**void**	**setColorModel** (ColorModel model)
1	public	**void**	**setDimensions** (int width, int height)
1	public	void	setHints (int hints)
1	public	**void**	**setPixels** (int x, int y, int w, int h, ColorModel model, int[] pixels, int off, int scansize)
1	public	**void**	**setPixels** (int x, int y, int w, int h, ColorModel model, byte[] pixels, int off, int scansize)
1	public	void	setProperties (java.util.Hashtable props)

BufferedImageOp
java.awt.image

P

```
1.2    BufferedImageOp
```

public	BufferedImage	**createCompatibleDestImage** (BufferedImage src, ColorModel destCM)
public	BufferedImage	**filter** (BufferedImage src, BufferedImage dest)
public		**getBounds2D** (BufferedImage src)
	java.awt.geom.Rectangle2D	
public	java.awt.geom.Point2D	**getPoint2D** (java.awt.geom.Point2D srcPt, java.awt.geom.Point2D dstPt)
public	java.awt.RenderingHints	**getRenderingHints** ()

Class   *Interface*   —extends   - - -implements   ○ abstract   ● final   △ static   ▲ static final   ✳ constructor   x x—inherited   x **x**—declared   **x x**—overridden

BufferedInputStream			java.io

Object
○ └InputStream
　　└FilterInputStream [1]
　　　└BufferedInputStream

1	public synchronized .... **int**	**available** () throws IOException
	protected .... byte[]	**buf**
*	public...........................	**BufferedInputStream** (InputStream in)
*	public...........................	**BufferedInputStream** (InputStream in, int size)
1	public synchronized ...... **void**	**close** () throws IOException
	protected .... int	**count**
1	protected .... InputStream	in
1	public synchronized ...... **void**	**mark** (int readlimit)
	protected .... int	**marklimit**
	protected .... int	**markpos**
1	public................. **boolean**	**markSupported** ()
	protected .... int	**pos**
1	public synchronized .... **int**	**read** () throws IOException
1	public..................... int	read (byte[] b) throws IOException
1	public synchronized .... **int**	**read** (byte[] b, int off, int len) throws IOException
1	public synchronized ...... **void**	**reset** () throws IOException
1	public synchronized ...... **long**	**skip** (long n) throws IOException

BufferedOutputStream			java.io

Object
○ └OutputStream
　　└FilterOutputStream [1]
　　　└BufferedOutputStream

	protected .... byte[]	**buf**
*	public...........................	**BufferedOutputStream** (OutputStream out)
*	public...........................	**BufferedOutputStream** (OutputStream out, int size)
1	public....................... void	close () throws IOException
	protected .... int	**count**
1	public synchronized ...... **void**	**flush** () throws IOException
1	protected .... OutputStream	out
1	public....................... void	write (byte[] b) throws IOException
1	public synchronized ...... **void**	**write** (int b) throws IOException
1	public synchronized ...... **void**	**write** (byte[] b, int off, int len) throws IOException

BufferedReader			java.io

Object
1.1 ○ └Reader [1]
1.1 　└BufferedReader

*	public...........................	**BufferedReader** (Reader in)
*	public...........................	**BufferedReader** (Reader in, int sz)
1	public..................... **void**	**close** () throws IOException
1	protected .... Object	lock
1	public..................... **void**	**mark** (int readAheadLimit) throws IOException
1	public................. **boolean**	**markSupported** ()
1	public...................... **int**	**read** () throws IOException
1	public..................... int	read (char[] cbuf) throws IOException
1	public...................... **int**	**read** (char[] cbuf, int off, int len) throws IOException
	public................. String	**readLine** () throws IOException
1	public................. **boolean**	**ready** () throws IOException
1	public..................... **void**	**reset** () throws IOException
1	public..................... **long**	**skip** (long n) throws IOException

BufferedWriter			java.io

Object
1.1 ○ └Writer [1]
1.1 　└BufferedWriter

BufferedWriter

*	public		**BufferedWriter** (Writer out)
*	public		**BufferedWriter** (Writer out, int sz)
1	public	**void**	**close** () throws IOException
1	public	**void**	**flush** () throws IOException
	protected	Object	lock
	public	void	**newLine** () throws IOException
	public	void	write (char[] cbuf) throws IOException
1	public	**void**	**write** (int c) throws IOException
1	public	void	write (String str) throws IOException
1	public	**void**	**write** (char[] cbuf, int off, int len) throws IOException
1	public	**void**	**write** (String s, int off, int len) throws IOException

Button   java.awt
P

```
        Object
  ○     └Component¹ - - - - - - - - - - - - - - - - - - - - - - java.awt.image.ImageObserver, MenuContainer,
                                                                java.io.Serializable
          └Button
```

	1	*159 inherited members from Component not shown*	
1.1	public synchronized	void	**addActionListener** (*java.awt.event.ActionListener* l)
	1 public	**void**	**addNotify** ()
*	public		**Button** ()
*	public		**Button** (String label)
1.1	public	String	**getActionCommand** ()
	public	String	**getLabel** ()
	1 protected	**String**	**paramString** ()
1.1	protected	void	**processActionEvent** (java.awt.event.ActionEvent e)
1.1	1 protected	**void**	**processEvent** (AWTEvent e)
1.1	public synchronized	void	**removeActionListener** (*java.awt.event.ActionListener* l)
1.1	public	void	**setActionCommand** (String command)
	public	void	**setLabel** (String label)

ButtonGroup   javax.swing

```
        Object
  1.2   └ButtonGroup - - - - - - - - - - - - - - - - - - - - - - java.io.Serializable
```

	public	void	**add** (AbstractButton b)
*	public		**ButtonGroup** ()
	protected	java.util.Vector	**buttons**
	public	*java.util.Enumeration*	**getElements** ()
	public	*ButtonModel*	**getSelection** ()
	public	boolean	**isSelected** (*ButtonModel* m)
	public	void	**remove** (AbstractButton b)
	public	void	**setSelected** (*ButtonModel* m, boolean b)

ButtonModel   javax.swing

```
  1.2   ButtonModel───────────────────── java.awt.ItemSelectable ¹
```

	public	void	**addActionListener** (*java.awt.event.ActionListener* l)
	public	void	**addChangeListener** (*javax.swing.event.ChangeListener* l)
	1 public	**void**	**addItemListener** (*java.awt.event.ItemListener* l)
	public	String	**getActionCommand** ()
	public	int	**getMnemonic** ()
	1 public	Object[]	getSelectedObjects ()
	public	boolean	**isArmed** ()
	public	boolean	**isEnabled** ()
	public	boolean	**isPressed** ()
	public	boolean	**isRollover** ()
	public	boolean	**isSelected** ()
	public	void	**removeActionListener** (*java.awt.event.ActionListener* l)
	public	void	**removeChangeListener** (*javax.swing.event.ChangeListener* l)
	1 public	**void**	**removeItemListener** (*java.awt.event.ItemListener* l)
	public	void	**setActionCommand** (String s)
	public	void	**setArmed** (boolean b)
	public	void	**setEnabled** (boolean b)
	public	void	**setGroup** (ButtonGroup group)

Class   *Interface*   —extends   - - -implements   ○ abstract   ● final   △ static   ▲ static final   * constructor   x x—inherited   x **x**—declared   **x x**—overridden

```
        public.....................void  setMnemonic (int key)
        public.....................void  setPressed (boolean b)
        public.....................void  setRollover (boolean b)
        public.....................void  setSelected (boolean b)
```

ButtonPeer   java.awt.peer

```
        ButtonPeer——————————————————ComponentPeer 1
```

```
    1   32 inherited members from ComponentPeer not shown
        public.....................void  setLabel (String)
```

ButtonUI   javax.swing.plaf

```
        Object
1.2 ○   └ComponentUI 1
1.2 ○     └ButtonUI
```

```
    1   11 inherited members from ComponentUI not shown
  *     public..........................  ButtonUI ()
```

Byte   java.lang
                                                                              P

```
        Object 1
    ○   └Number 2 --------------------------- java.io.Serializable
1.1 ●     └Byte --------------------------- Comparable 3
```

```
  *     public..........................        Byte (byte value)
  *     public..........................        Byte (String s) throws NumberFormatException
    2   public.....................byte  byteValue ()
1.2     public......................int  compareTo (Byte anotherByte)
1.2 3   public......................int  compareTo (Object o)
  △     public static .............Byte  decode (String nm) throws NumberFormatException
    2   public...................double  doubleValue ()
    1   public..................boolean  equals (Object obj)
    2   public....................float  floatValue ()
    1   public......................int  hashCode ()
    2   public......................int  intValue ()
    2   public.....................long  longValue ()
  ▲     public static final ........byte  MAX_VALUE = 127
  ▲     public static final ........byte  MIN_VALUE = -128
  △     public static ..............byte  parseByte (String s) throws NumberFormatException
  △     public static ..............byte  parseByte (String s, int radix) throws NumberFormatException
    2   public....................short  shortValue ()
    1   public...................String  toString ()
  △     public static ...........String  toString (byte b)
  ▲     public static final ........Class  TYPE
  △     public static ..............Byte  valueOf (String s) throws NumberFormatException
  △     public static ..............Byte  valueOf (String s, int radix) throws NumberFormatException
```

ByteArrayInputStream   java.io

```
        Object
    ○   └InputStream 1
          └ByteArrayInputStream
```

```
    1   public synchronized ........int  available ()
        protected................byte[]  buf
  *     public..........................  ByteArrayInputStream (byte[] buf)
  *     public..........................  ByteArrayInputStream (byte[] buf, int offset, int length)
    1   public synchronized ......void  close () throws IOException
        protected...................int  count
1.1     protected...................int  mark
    1   public....................void  mark (int readAheadLimit)
    1   public..................boolean  markSupported ()
        protected...................int  pos
    1   public synchronized ........int  read ()
    1   public......................int  read (byte[] b) throws IOException
    1   public synchronized ........int  read (byte[] b, int off, int len)
    1   public synchronized ......void  reset ()
```

ByteArrayInputStream

1	public synchronized ...... **long skip** (long n)	

ByteArrayOutputStream   java.io

Object [1]
○ └OutputStream [2]
   └ByteArrayOutputStream

	protected .... byte[]	**buf**
*	public..........................	**ByteArrayOutputStream** ()
*	public..........................	**ByteArrayOutputStream** (int size)
2	public synchronized ...... **void**	**close** () throws IOException
	protected .... int	**count**
2	public......................... void	flush () throws IOException
	public synchronized ...... void	**reset** ()
	public......................... int	**size** ()
	public synchronized ..... byte[]	**toByteArray** ()
1	public.................. **String**	**toString** ()
D	public.................. String	**toString** (int hibyte)
1.1	public.................. String	**toString** (String enc) throws UnsupportedEncodingException
2	public......................... void	write (byte[] b) throws IOException
2	public synchronized ...... **void**	**write** (int b)
2	public synchronized ...... **void**	**write** (byte[] b, int off, int len)
	public synchronized .... void	**writeTo** (OutputStream out) throws IOException

---

ByteHolder   org.omg.CORBA

Object
1.2 ● └ByteHolder - *org.omg.CORBA.portable.Streamable* [1]

1	public..................... void	**_read** (org.omg.CORBA.portable.InputStream input)
1	public............... TypeCode	**_type** ()
1	public..................... void	**_write** (org.omg.CORBA.portable.OutputStream output)
*	public..........................	**ByteHolder** ()
*	public..........................	**ByteHolder** (byte initial)
	public..................... byte	**value**

ByteLookupTable   java.awt.image
P

Object
1.2 ○ └LookupTable [1]
1.2   └ByteLookupTable

*	public..........................	**ByteLookupTable** (int offset, byte[][] data)
*	public..........................	**ByteLookupTable** (int offset, byte[] data)
1	public......................... int	getNumComponents ()
1	public......................... int	getOffset ()
●	public final .... byte[][]	**getTable** ()
	public.....................byte[]	**lookupPixel** (byte[] src, byte[] dst)
1	public......................... **int[]**	**lookupPixel** (int[] src, int[] dst)

Calendar   java.util
P

Object [1]
1.1 ○ └Calendar - *java.io.Serializable*, *Cloneable*

○	public abstract .... void	**add** (int field, int amount)
	public.................. boolean	**after** (Object when)
▲	public static final .... int	**AM** = 0
▲	public static final .... int	**AM_PM** = 9
▲	public static final .... int	**APRIL** = 3
	protected .... boolean	**areFieldsSet**
▲	public static final .... int	**AUGUST** = 7
	public.................. boolean	**before** (Object when)
*	protected	**Calendar** ()
*	protected	**Calendar** (TimeZone zone, Locale aLocale)
●	public final .... void	**clear** ()

Class *Interface* —extends - - -implements ○ abstract ● final △ static ▲ static final ✳ constructor x x—inherited x **x**—declared **x x**—overridden

Calendar

|---|---|---|---|---|
●		public final	void	**clear** (int field)
	1	public	Object	**clone** ()
		protected	void	**complete** ()
○		protected abstract	void	**computeFields** ()
○		protected abstract	void	**computeTime** ()
▲		public static final	int	**DATE** = 5
▲		public static final	int	**DAY_OF_MONTH** = 5
▲		public static final	int	**DAY_OF_WEEK** = 7
▲		public static final	int	**DAY_OF_WEEK_IN_MONTH** = 8
▲		public static final	int	**DAY_OF_YEAR** = 6
▲		public static final	int	**DECEMBER** = 11
▲		public static final	int	**DST_OFFSET** = 16
	1	public	boolean	**equals** (Object obj)
▲		public static final	int	**ERA** = 0
▲		public static final	int	**FEBRUARY** = 1
▲		public static final	int	**FIELD_COUNT** = 17
		protected	int[]	**fields**
▲		public static final	int	**FRIDAY** = 6
●		public final	int	**get** (int field)
1.2		public	int	**getActualMaximum** (int field)
1.2		public	int	**getActualMinimum** (int field)
△		public static synchronized	Locale[]	**getAvailableLocales** ()
		public	int	**getFirstDayOfWeek** ()
○		public abstract	int	**getGreatestMinimum** (int field)
△		public static synchronized	Calendar	**getInstance** ()
△		public static synchronized	Calendar	**getInstance** (Locale aLocale)
△		public static synchronized	Calendar	**getInstance** (TimeZone zone)
△		public static synchronized	Calendar	**getInstance** (TimeZone zone, Locale aLocale)
○		public abstract	int	**getLeastMaximum** (int field)
○		public abstract	int	**getMaximum** (int field)
		public	int	**getMinimalDaysInFirstWeek** ()
○		public abstract	int	**getMinimum** (int field)
●		public final	Date	**getTime** ()
		protected	long	**getTimeInMillis** ()
		public	TimeZone	**getTimeZone** ()
	1	public	int	**hashCode** ()
▲		public static final	int	**HOUR** = 10
▲		public static final	int	**HOUR_OF_DAY** = 11
●		protected final	int	**internalGet** (int field)
		public	boolean	**isLenient** ()
		protected	boolean[]	**isSet**
●		public final	boolean	**isSet** (int field)
		protected	boolean	**isTimeSet**
▲		public static final	int	**JANUARY** = 0
▲		public static final	int	**JULY** = 6
▲		public static final	int	**JUNE** = 5
▲		public static final	int	**MARCH** = 2
▲		public static final	int	**MAY** = 4
▲		public static final	int	**MILLISECOND** = 14
▲		public static final	int	**MINUTE** = 12
▲		public static final	int	**MONDAY** = 2
▲		public static final	int	**MONTH** = 2
▲		public static final	int	**NOVEMBER** = 10
▲		public static final	int	**OCTOBER** = 9
○		public static final	int	**PM** = 1
○		public abstract	void	**roll** (int field, boolean up)
1.2		public	void	**roll** (int field, int amount)
▲		public static final	int	**SATURDAY** = 7
▲		public static final	int	**SECOND** = 13
▲		public static final	int	**SEPTEMBER** = 8
●		public final	void	**set** (int field, int value)
●		public final	void	**set** (int year, int month, int date)
●		public final	void	**set** (int year, int month, int date, int hour, int minute)
●		public final	void	**set** (int year, int month, int date, int hour, int minute, int second)
		public	void	**setFirstDayOfWeek** (int value)
		public	void	**setLenient** (boolean lenient)
		public	void	**setMinimalDaysInFirstWeek** (int value)
●		public final	void	**setTime** (Date date)
		protected	void	**setTimeInMillis** (long millis)

Calendar

C

Classes

249

Calendar

	public	void	**setTimeZone** (TimeZone value)	
▲	public static final	int	**SUNDAY** = 1	
▲	public static final	int	**THURSDAY** = 5	
	protected	long	**time**	
1	public	**String**	**toString** ()	
▲	public static final	int	**TUESDAY** = 3	
▲	public static final	int	**UNDECIMBER** = 12	
▲	public static final	int	**WEDNESDAY** = 4	
▲	public static final	int	**WEEK_OF_MONTH** = 4	
▲	public static final	int	**WEEK_OF_YEAR** = 3	
▲	public static final	int	**YEAR** = 1	
▲	public static final	int	**ZONE_OFFSET** = 15	

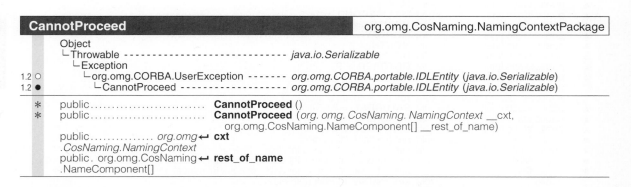

CallableStatement — java.sql

1.1   *CallableStatement*————————————*PreparedStatement [1]* (*Statement [2]*)   P^O

   2   *28 inherited members from Statement not shown*
   1   *35 inherited members from PreparedStatement not shown*

1.2	public	*Array*	**getArray** (int i) throws SQLException
1.2	public... java.math.BigDecimal		**getBigDecimal** (int parameterIndex) throws SQLException
D	public... java.math.BigDecimal		**getBigDecimal** (int parameterIndex, int scale) throws SQLException
1.2	public	*Blob*	**getBlob** (int i) throws SQLException
	public	boolean	**getBoolean** (int parameterIndex) throws SQLException
	public	byte	**getByte** (int parameterIndex) throws SQLException
	public	byte[]	**getBytes** (int parameterIndex) throws SQLException
1.2	public	*Clob*	**getClob** (int i) throws SQLException
	public	Date	**getDate** (int parameterIndex) throws SQLException
1.2	public	Date	**getDate** (int parameterIndex, java.util.Calendar cal) throws SQLException
	public	double	**getDouble** (int parameterIndex) throws SQLException
	public	float	**getFloat** (int parameterIndex) throws SQLException
	public	int	**getInt** (int parameterIndex) throws SQLException
	public	long	**getLong** (int parameterIndex) throws SQLException
	public	Object	**getObject** (int parameterIndex) throws SQLException
1.2	public	Object	**getObject** (int i, *java.util.Map* map) throws SQLException
1.2	public	*Ref*	**getRef** (int i) throws SQLException
	public	short	**getShort** (int parameterIndex) throws SQLException
	public	String	**getString** (int parameterIndex) throws SQLException
	public	Time	**getTime** (int parameterIndex) throws SQLException
1.2	public	Time	**getTime** (int parameterIndex, java.util.Calendar cal) throws SQLException
	public	Timestamp	**getTimestamp** (int parameterIndex) throws SQLException
1.2	public	Timestamp	**getTimestamp** (int parameterIndex, java.util.Calendar cal) throws SQLException
	public	void	**registerOutParameter** (int parameterIndex, int sqlType) throws SQLException
1.2	public	void	**registerOutParameter** (int paramIndex, int sqlType, String typeName) throws SQLException
	public	void	**registerOutParameter** (int parameterIndex, int sqlType, int scale) throws SQLException
	public	boolean	**wasNull** () throws SQLException

CannotProceed — org.omg.CosNaming.NamingContextPackage

Object
  └Throwable - *java.io.Serializable*
    └Exception
1.2 ○   └org.omg.CORBA.UserException - - - - - - *org.omg.CORBA.portable.IDLEntity* (*java.io.Serializable*)
1.2 ●   └CannotProceed - - - - - - - - - - - - - - - *org.omg.CORBA.portable.IDLEntity* (*java.io.Serializable*)

*	public		**CannotProceed** ()
*	public		**CannotProceed** (*org. omg. CosNaming. NamingContext* __cxt, org.omg.CosNaming.NameComponent[] __rest_of_name)
	public	*org.omg*↵ *.CosNaming.NamingContext*	**cxt**
	public	org.omg.CosNaming↵ .NameComponent[]	**rest_of_name**

Class   *Interface*   —extends   - - -implements   ○ abstract   ● final   △ static   ▲ static final   ✳ constructor   x x—inherited   x **x**—declared   **x x**—overridden

C

CannotProceedHelper | org.omg.CosNaming.NamingContextPackage

Object
1.2 └CannotProceedHelper

△	public static ... CannotProceed **extract** (org.omg.CORBA.Any a)
△	public static .... String **id** ()
△	public static .... void **insert** (org.omg.CORBA.Any a, CannotProceed that)
△	public static ... CannotProceed **read** (org.omg.CORBA.portable.InputStream in)
△	public static synchronized .... **type** ()
	... org.omg.CORBA.TypeCode
△	public static .... void **write** (org.omg.CORBA.portable.OutputStream out, CannotProceed that)

CannotProceedHolder | org.omg.CosNaming.NamingContextPackage

Object
1.2 ● └CannotProceedHolder ------------------- *org.omg.CORBA.portable.Streamable* [1]

1	public....................... void **_read** (org.omg.CORBA.portable.InputStream in)
1	public........................... **_type** ()
	... org.omg.CORBA.TypeCode
1	public....................... void **_write** (org.omg.CORBA.portable.OutputStream out)
∗	public.......................... **CannotProceedHolder** ()
∗	public.......................... **CannotProceedHolder** (CannotProceed __arg)
	public.......... CannotProceed **value**

CannotRedoException | javax.swing.undo

Object
└Throwable -------------------------- *java.io.Serializable*
  └Exception
    └RuntimeException
1.2   └CannotRedoException

∗	public......................... **CannotRedoException** ()

CannotUndoException | javax.swing.undo

Object
└Throwable -------------------------- *java.io.Serializable*
  └Exception
    └RuntimeException
1.2   └CannotUndoException

∗	public......................... **CannotUndoException** ()

Canvas | java.awt

P

Object
○ └Component [1] -------------------------- *java.awt.image.ImageObserver*, *MenuContainer*,
                                         java.io.Serializable
   └Canvas

1	*160 inherited members from Component not shown*
1	public...................... **void addNotify** ()
∗	public.......................... **Canvas** ()
1.2 ∗	public.......................... **Canvas** (GraphicsConfiguration config)
1	public...................... **void paint** (Graphics g)

CanvasPeer | java.awt.peer

CanvasPeer——————————————————— ComponentPeer [1]

1 *32 inherited members from ComponentPeer not shown*

Classes

CardLayout

			CardLayout		java.awt

P

Object[1]
└CardLayout - *LayoutManager2* [2] (*LayoutManager* [3]), *java.io.Serializable*

1.1	2	public.....................void	**addLayoutComponent** (Component comp, Object constraints)
D	3	public.....................void	**addLayoutComponent** (String name, Component comp)
*		public.........................	**CardLayout** ()
*		public.........................	**CardLayout** (int hgap, int vgap)
		public.....................void	**first** (Container parent)
1.1		public.......................int	**getHgap** ()
1.1	2	public.....................float	**getLayoutAlignmentX** (Container parent)
1.1	2	public.....................float	**getLayoutAlignmentY** (Container parent)
1.1		public.......................int	**getVgap** ()
1.1	2	public.....................void	**invalidateLayout** (Container target)
		public.....................void	**last** (Container parent)
	3	public.....................void	**layoutContainer** (Container parent)
1.1	2	public................Dimension	**maximumLayoutSize** (Container target)
	3	public................Dimension	**minimumLayoutSize** (Container parent)
		public.....................void	**next** (Container parent)
	3	public................Dimension	**preferredLayoutSize** (Container parent)
		public.....................void	**previous** (Container parent)
	3	public.....................void	**removeLayoutComponent** (Component comp)
1.1		public.....................void	**setHgap** (int hgap)
1.1		public.....................void	**setVgap** (int vgap)
		public.....................void	**show** (Container parent, String name)
	1	public..................... **String**	**toString** ()

			Caret	javax.swing.text

1.2		*Caret*

	public.....................void	**addChangeListener** (*javax.swing.event.ChangeListener* l)
	public.....................void	**deinstall** (JTextComponent c)
	public.......................int	**getBlinkRate** ()
	public.......................int	**getDot** ()
	public............java.awt.Point	**getMagicCaretPosition** ()
	public.......................int	**getMark** ()
	public.....................void	**install** (JTextComponent c)
	public..................boolean	**isSelectionVisible** ()
	public..................boolean	**isVisible** ()
	public.....................void	**moveDot** (int dot)
	public.....................void	**paint** (java.awt.Graphics g)
	public.....................void	**removeChangeListener** (*javax.swing.event.ChangeListener* l)
	public.....................void	**setBlinkRate** (int rate)
	public.....................void	**setDot** (int dot)
	public.....................void	**setMagicCaretPosition** (java.awt.Point p)
	public.....................void	**setSelectionVisible** (boolean v)
	public.....................void	**setVisible** (boolean v)

			CaretEvent	javax.swing.event

Object
1.1 └java.util.EventObject[1] - - - - - - - - - - - - - - - - - - - *java.io.Serializable*
1.2 ○ └CaretEvent

*		public.........................	**CaretEvent** (Object source)
○		public abstract...............int	**getDot** ()
○		public abstract...............int	**getMark** ()
	1	public..................Object	getSource ()
	1	protected transient......Object	source
	1	public...................String	toString ()

			CaretListener	javax.swing.event

1.2		*CaretListener*—————————————————*java.util.EventListener*

public.....................void	**caretUpdate** (CaretEvent e)

Class   *Interface*   —extends   - - -implements   ○ abstract   ● final   △ static   ▲ static final   ✳ constructor   x x—inherited   x **x**—declared   **x x**—overridden

CellEditor
javax.swing

1.2 *CellEditor*

```
public.....................void  addCellEditorListener (javax.swing.event.CellEditorListener l)
public.....................void  cancelCellEditing ()
public...................Object  getCellEditorValue ()
public..................boolean  isCellEditable (java.util.EventObject anEvent)
public.....................void  removeCellEditorListener (javax.swing.event.CellEditorListener l)
public..................boolean  shouldSelectCell (java.util.EventObject anEvent)
public..................boolean  stopCellEditing ()
```

CellEditorListener
javax.swing.event

1.2 *CellEditorListener*────────────────────────*java.util.EventListener*

```
public.....................void  editingCanceled (ChangeEvent e)
public.....................void  editingStopped (ChangeEvent e)
```

CellRendererPane
javax.swing

Object
○ └java.awt.Component[1] - - - - - - - - - - - - - - - - - - *java.awt.image.ImageObserver*, *java.awt.MenuContainer*,
java.io.Serializable
  └java.awt.Container[2]
1.2   └CellRendererPane - - - - - - - - - - - - - - - - - - *javax.accessibility.Accessible*[3]

```
      1  137 inherited members from java.awt.Component not shown
      2  47 inherited members from java.awt.Container not shown
         protected  javax.accessibility ↩  accessibleContext
         .AccessibleContext
      2  protected.................  void  addImpl (java.awt.Component x, Object constraints, int index)
*        public...................        CellRendererPane ()
      3  public.... javax.accessibility ↩  getAccessibleContext ()
         .AccessibleContext
      2  public....................  void  invalidate ()
      2  public....................  void  paint (java.awt.Graphics g)
         public.....................void  paintComponent (java. awt. Graphics g, java. awt. Component c,
                                           java.awt.Container p, java.awt.Rectangle r)
         public.....................void  paintComponent (java. awt. Graphics g, java. awt. Component c,
                                           java.awt.Container p, int x, int y, int w, int h)
         public.....................void  paintComponent (java. awt. Graphics g, java. awt. Component c,
                                           java.awt.Container p, int x, int y, int w, int h, boolean shouldValidate)
      2  public....................  void  update (java.awt.Graphics g)
```

CellRendererPane.AccessibleCellRendererPane
protected
javax.swing

Object
1.2 ○ └javax.accessibility.AccessibleContext[1]
1.2   └CellRendererPane ↩ - - - - - - - - - - - - - - - - - - *java.io.Serializable*, *javax.accessibility.AccessibleComponent*[2]
         .AccessibleCellRendererPane

```
      1  25 inherited members from javax.accessibility.AccessibleContext not shown
*        protected.....................      AccessibleCellRendererPane ()
      2  public.....................void  addFocusListener (java.awt.event.FocusListener l)
      2  public..................boolean  contains (java.awt.Point p)
      2  public...................        getAccessibleAt (java.awt.Point p)
         . javax.accessibility.Accessible
      1  public.................  javax ↩  getAccessibleChild (int i)
         .accessibility.Accessible
      1  public.................... int  getAccessibleChildrenCount ()
      1  public... javax.accessibility ↩  getAccessibleComponent ()
         .AccessibleComponent
      1  public.................... int  getAccessibleIndexInParent ()
      1  public.............. javax ↩  getAccessibleParent ()
         .accessibility.Accessible
      1  public.............. javax ↩  getAccessibleRole ()
         .accessibility.AccessibleRole
      1  public... javax.accessibility ↩  getAccessibleStateSet ()
         .AccessibleStateSet
```

CellRendererPane.AccessibleCellRendererPane

2	public	java.awt.Color	**getBackground** ()	
2	public	java.awt.Rectangle	**getBounds** ()	
2	public	java.awt.Cursor	**getCursor** ()	
2	public	java.awt.Font	**getFont** ()	
2	public	java.awt.FontMetrics	**getFontMetrics** (java.awt.Font f)	
2	public	java.awt.Color	**getForeground** ()	
1	public	**java.util.Locale**	**getLocale** ()	
2	public	java.awt.Point	**getLocation** ()	
2	public	java.awt.Point	**getLocationOnScreen** ()	
2	public	java.awt.Dimension	**getSize** ()	
2	public	boolean	**isEnabled** ()	
2	public	boolean	**isFocusTraversable** ()	
2	public	boolean	**isShowing** ()	
2	public	boolean	**isVisible** ()	
2	public	void	**removeFocusListener** (*java.awt.event.FocusListener* l)	
2	public	void	**requestFocus** ()	
2	public	void	**setBackground** (java.awt.Color c)	
2	public	void	**setBounds** (java.awt.Rectangle r)	
2	public	void	**setCursor** (java.awt.Cursor cursor)	
2	public	void	**setEnabled** (boolean b)	
2	public	void	**setFont** (java.awt.Font f)	
2	public	void	**setForeground** (java.awt.Color c)	
2	public	void	**setLocation** (java.awt.Point p)	
2	public	void	**setSize** (java.awt.Dimension d)	
2	public	void	**setVisible** (boolean b)	

Certificate ❶   java.security.cert

Object[1]
1.2 ○ └─Certificate

✻		protected	**Certificate** (String type)	
	1	public	**boolean**	**equals** (Object other)
○		public abstract	byte[]	**getEncoded** () throws CertificateEncodingException
○		public abstract		**getPublicKey** ()
			java.security.PublicKey	
●		public final	String	**getType** ()
	1	public	**int**	**hashCode** ()
○	1	public abstract	**String**	**toString** ()
○		public abstract	void	**verify** (*java.security.PublicKey* key) throws CertificateException, java.security.NoSuchAlgorithmException, java.security.InvalidKeyException, java.security.NoSuchProviderException, java.security.SignatureException
○		public abstract	void	**verify** (*java.security.PublicKey* key, String sigProvider) throws CertificateException, java.security.NoSuchAlgorithmException, java.security.InvalidKeyException, java.security.NoSuchProviderException, java.security.SignatureException

Certificate ❷   java.security

1.1 *Certificate*   P[O]

public	void	**decode** (java.io.InputStream stream) throws KeyException, java.io.IOException	
public	void	**encode** (java.io.OutputStream stream) throws KeyException, java.io.IOException	
public	String	**getFormat** ()	
public	*Principal*	**getGuarantor** ()	
public	*Principal*	**getPrincipal** ()	
public	*PublicKey*	**getPublicKey** ()	
public	String	**toString** (boolean detailed)	

CertificateEncodingException   java.security.cert

Object
└─Throwable ------------------------------ *java.io.Serializable*
   └─Exception
1.2   └─java.security.GeneralSecurityException
1.2   └─CertificateException
1.2   └─CertificateEncodingException

Class   *Interface*   —extends   - - -implements   ○ abstract   ● final   △ static   ▲ static final   ✻ constructor   x x—inherited   x **x**—declared   x **x**—overridden

✳	public.........................	**CertificateEncodingException** ()
✳	public.........................	**CertificateEncodingException** (String message)

CertificateException
java.security.cert

```
Object
 └Throwable ------------------------------ java.io.Serializable
    └Exception
```
1.2   `└java.security.GeneralSecurityException`
1.2   `└CertificateException`

✳	public.........................	**CertificateException** ()
✳	public.........................	**CertificateException** (String msg)

CertificateExpiredException
java.security.cert

```
Object
 └Throwable ------------------------------ java.io.Serializable
    └Exception
```
1.2   `└java.security.GeneralSecurityException`
1.2   `└CertificateException`
1.2   `└CertificateExpiredException`

✳	public.........................	**CertificateExpiredException** ()
✳	public.........................	**CertificateExpiredException** (String message)

CertificateFactory
java.security.cert

```
Object
```
1.2   `└CertificateFactory`

✳	protected	**CertificateFactory** (CertificateFactorySpi certFacSpi, java.security.Provider provider, String type)
●	public final ....Certificate	**generateCertificate** (java.io.InputStream inStream) throws CertificateException
●	public final . java.util.Collection	**generateCertificates** (java.io.InputStream inStream) throws CertificateException
●	public final .... CRL	**generateCRL** (java.io.InputStream inStream) throws CRLException
●	public final . java.util.Collection	**generateCRLs** (java.io.InputStream inStream) throws CRLException
▲	public static final ....CertificateFactory	**getInstance** (String type) throws CertificateException
▲	public static final ....CertificateFactory	**getInstance** (String type, String provider) throws CertificateException, java.security.NoSuchProviderException
●	public final .... java.security.Provider	**getProvider** ()
●	public final ....String	**getType** ()

CertificateFactorySpi
java.security.cert

```
Object
```
1.2 ○   `└CertificateFactorySpi`

✳	public.........................	**CertificateFactorySpi** ()
○	public abstract ...... Certificate	**engineGenerateCertificate** (java. io. InputStream inStream) throws CertificateException
○	public abstract .... java.util.Collection	**engineGenerateCertificates** (java. io. InputStream inStream) throws CertificateException
○	public abstract .... CRL	**engineGenerateCRL** (java.io.InputStream inStream) throws CRLException
○	public abstract .... java.util.Collection	**engineGenerateCRLs** (java.io.InputStream inStream) throws CRLException

---

CertificateNotYetValidException
java.security.cert

```
Object
 └Throwable ------------------------------ java.io.Serializable
    └Exception
```
1.2   `└java.security.GeneralSecurityException`
1.2   `└CertificateException`
1.2   `└CertificateNotYetValidException`

CertificateNotYetValidException

✳	public..........................		**CertificateNotYetValidException** ()
✳	public..........................		**CertificateNotYetValidException** (String message)

CertificateParsingException   java.security.cert

```
Object
 └Throwable  - - - - - - - - - - - - - - - - - - - - - - - - - - - java.io.Serializable
    └Exception
1.2     └java.security.GeneralSecurityException
1.2        └CertificateException
1.2           └CertificateParsingException
```

✳	public..........................		**CertificateParsingException** ()
✳	public..........................		**CertificateParsingException** (String message)

ChangedCharSetException   javax.swing.text

```
Object
 └Throwable  - - - - - - - - - - - - - - - - - - - - - - - - - - - java.io.Serializable
    └Exception
       └java.io.IOException
1.2        └ChangedCharSetException
```

✳	public..........................		**ChangedCharSetException** (String charSetSpec, boolean charSetKey)
	public.....................	String	**getCharSetSpec** ()
	public.................	boolean	**keyEqualsCharSet** ()

ChangeEvent   javax.swing.event

```
     Object
1.1   └java.util.EventObject¹  - - - - - - - - - - - - - - - - - - - java.io.Serializable
1.2      └ChangeEvent
```

✳	public.....................		**ChangeEvent** (Object source)
1	public.....................	Object	getSource ()
1	protected transient......	Object	source
1	public...................	String	toString ()

ChangeListener   javax.swing.event

1.2	*ChangeListener*———————————*java.util.EventListener*
	public......................void **stateChanged** (ChangeEvent e)

Character   java.lang
                                                                           P

```
     Object¹
 ●    └Character  - - - - - - - - - - - - - - - - - - - - - - - - - java.io.Serializable, Comparable²
```

✳		public..........................		**Character** (char value)
		public..........................	char	**charValue** ()
1.1	▲	public static final..........	byte	**COMBINING_SPACING_MARK** = 8
1.2		public..........................	int	**compareTo** (Character anotherCharacter)
1.2	2	public..........................	int	**compareTo** (Object o)
1.1	▲	public static final..........	byte	**CONNECTOR_PUNCTUATION** = 23
1.1	▲	public static final..........	byte	**CONTROL** = 15
1.1	▲	public static final..........	byte	**CURRENCY_SYMBOL** = 26
1.1	▲	public static final..........	byte	**DASH_PUNCTUATION** = 20
1.1	▲	public static final..........	byte	**DECIMAL_DIGIT_NUMBER** = 9
	△	public static	int	**digit** (char ch, int radix)
1.1	▲	public static final..........	byte	**ENCLOSING_MARK** = 7
1.1	▲	public static final..........	byte	**END_PUNCTUATION** = 22
	1	public..................	boolean	**equals** (Object obj)
	△	public static	char	**forDigit** (int digit, int radix)
1.1	▲	public static final..........	byte	**FORMAT** = 16
1.1	△	public static	int	**getNumericValue** (char ch)

Class *Interface* ——extends - - -implements ○ abstract ● final △ static ▲ static final ✳ constructor x x—inherited x **x**—declared **x x**—overridden

1.1 △	public static	..............int	**getType**	(char ch)
1	public	.... **int**	**hashCode**	()
△	public static	..........boolean	**isDefined**	(char ch)
△	public static	..........boolean	**isDigit**	(char ch)
1.1 △	public static	..........boolean	**isIdentifierIgnorable**	(char ch)
1.1 △	public static	..........boolean	**isISOControl**	(char ch)
1.1 △	public static	..........boolean	**isJavaIdentifierPart**	(char ch)
1.1 △	public static	..........boolean	**isJavaIdentifierStart**	(char ch)
D △	public static	..........boolean	**isJavaLetter**	(char ch)
D △	public static	..........boolean	**isJavaLetterOrDigit**	(char ch)
△	public static	..........boolean	**isLetter**	(char ch)
△	public static	..........boolean	**isLetterOrDigit**	(char ch)
△	public static	..........boolean	**isLowerCase**	(char ch)
D △	public static	..........boolean	**isSpace**	(char ch)
1.1 △	public static	..........boolean	**isSpaceChar**	(char ch)
△	public static	..........boolean	**isTitleCase**	(char ch)
1.1 △	public static	..........boolean	**isUnicodeIdentifierPart**	(char ch)
1.1 △	public static	..........boolean	**isUnicodeIdentifierStart**	(char ch)
△	public static	..........boolean	**isUpperCase**	(char ch)
1.1 △	public static	..........boolean	**isWhitespace**	(char ch)
1.1 ▲	public static final	..........byte	**LETTER_NUMBER**	= 10
1.1 ▲	public static final	..........byte	**LINE_SEPARATOR**	= 13
1.1 ▲	public static final	..........byte	**LOWERCASE_LETTER**	= 2
1.1 ▲	public static final	..........byte	**MATH_SYMBOL**	= 25
▲	public static final	..............int	**MAX_RADIX**	= 36
▲	public static final	..........char	**MAX_VALUE**	= '?'
▲	public static final	..............int	**MIN_RADIX**	= 2
▲	public static final	..........char	**MIN_VALUE**	
1.1 ▲	public static final	..........byte	**MODIFIER_LETTER**	= 4
1.1 ▲	public static final	..........byte	**MODIFIER_SYMBOL**	= 27
1.1 ▲	public static final	..........byte	**NON_SPACING_MARK**	= 6
1.1 ▲	public static final	..........byte	**OTHER_LETTER**	= 5
1.1 ▲	public static final	..........byte	**OTHER_NUMBER**	= 11
1.1 ▲	public static final	..........byte	**OTHER_PUNCTUATION**	= 24
1.1 ▲	public static final	..........byte	**OTHER_SYMBOL**	= 28
1.1 ▲	public static final	..........byte	**PARAGRAPH_SEPARATOR**	= 14
1.1 ▲	public static final	..........byte	**PRIVATE_USE**	= 18
1.1 ▲	public static final	..........byte	**SPACE_SEPARATOR**	= 12
1.1 ▲	public static final	..........byte	**START_PUNCTUATION**	= 21
1.1 ▲	public static final	..........byte	**SURROGATE**	= 19
1.1 ▲	public static final	..........byte	**TITLECASE_LETTER**	= 3
△	public static	..............char	**toLowerCase**	(char ch)
1	public	.... **String**	**toString**	()
△	public static	..............char	**toTitleCase**	(char ch)
△	public static	..............char	**toUpperCase**	(char ch)
1.1 ▲	public static final	..........Class	**TYPE**	
1.1 ▲	public static final	..........byte	**UNASSIGNED**	= 0
1.1 ▲	public static final	..........byte	**UPPERCASE_LETTER**	= 1

Character.Subset | java.lang

```
      Object 1
1.2    └Character.Subset
```
P

● 1	public final	.............**boolean**	**equals** (Object obj)
● 1	public final	.... **int**	**hashCode** ()
✳	protected	....	**Subset** (String name)
● 1	public final	.............**String**	**toString** ()

Character.UnicodeBlock | java.lang

```
      Object
1.2    └Character.Subset 1
1.2 ●    └Character.UnicodeBlock
```
P

▲	public static final...............	**ALPHABETIC_PRESENTATION_FORMS**
	.......Character.UnicodeBlock	
▲	public static final...............	**ARABIC**
	.......Character.UnicodeBlock	
▲	public static final...............	**ARABIC_PRESENTATION_FORMS_A**
	.......Character.UnicodeBlock	

Character.UnicodeBlock

▲	public static final .... Character.UnicodeBlock	**ARABIC_PRESENTATION_FORMS_B**
▲	public static final .... Character.UnicodeBlock	**ARMENIAN**
▲	public static final .... Character.UnicodeBlock	**ARROWS**
▲	public static final .... Character.UnicodeBlock	**BASIC_LATIN**
▲	public static final .... Character.UnicodeBlock	**BENGALI**
▲	public static final .... Character.UnicodeBlock	**BLOCK_ELEMENTS**
▲	public static final .... Character.UnicodeBlock	**BOPOMOFO**
▲	public static final .... Character.UnicodeBlock	**BOX_DRAWING**
▲	public static final .... Character.UnicodeBlock	**CJK_COMPATIBILITY**
▲	public static final .... Character.UnicodeBlock	**CJK_COMPATIBILITY_FORMS**
▲	public static final .... Character.UnicodeBlock	**CJK_COMPATIBILITY_IDEOGRAPHS**
▲	public static final .... Character.UnicodeBlock	**CJK_SYMBOLS_AND_PUNCTUATION**
▲	public static final .... Character.UnicodeBlock	**CJK_UNIFIED_IDEOGRAPHS**
▲	public static final .... Character.UnicodeBlock	**COMBINING_DIACRITICAL_MARKS**
▲	public static final .... Character.UnicodeBlock	**COMBINING_HALF_MARKS**
▲	public static final .... Character.UnicodeBlock	**COMBINING_MARKS_FOR_SYMBOLS**
▲	public static final .... Character.UnicodeBlock	**CONTROL_PICTURES**
▲	public static final .... Character.UnicodeBlock	**CURRENCY_SYMBOLS**
▲	public static final .... Character.UnicodeBlock	**CYRILLIC**
▲	public static final .... Character.UnicodeBlock	**DEVANAGARI**
▲	public static final .... Character.UnicodeBlock	**DINGBATS**
▲	public static final .... Character.UnicodeBlock	**ENCLOSED_ALPHANUMERICS**
▲	public static final .... Character.UnicodeBlock	**ENCLOSED_CJK_LETTERS_AND_MONTHS**
● 1	public final .... boolean	equals (Object obj)
▲	public static final .... Character.UnicodeBlock	**GENERAL_PUNCTUATION**
▲	public static final .... Character.UnicodeBlock	**GEOMETRIC_SHAPES**
▲	public static final .... Character.UnicodeBlock	**GEORGIAN**
▲	public static final .... Character.UnicodeBlock	**GREEK**
▲	public static final .... Character.UnicodeBlock	**GREEK_EXTENDED**
▲	public static final .... Character.UnicodeBlock	**GUJARATI**
▲	public static final .... Character.UnicodeBlock	**GURMUKHI**
▲	public static final .... Character.UnicodeBlock	**HALFWIDTH_AND_FULLWIDTH_FORMS**
▲	public static final .... Character.UnicodeBlock	**HANGUL_COMPATIBILITY_JAMO**
▲	public static final .... Character.UnicodeBlock	**HANGUL_JAMO**
▲	public static final .... Character.UnicodeBlock	**HANGUL_SYLLABLES**
● 1	public final .... int	hashCode ()

C

Class *Interface* —extends - - -implements ○ abstract ● final △ static ▲ static final ✳ constructor x x—inherited x **x**—declared **x x**—overridden

C

▲	public static final		**HEBREW**	
	...... Character.UnicodeBlock			
▲	public static final		**HIRAGANA**	
	...... Character.UnicodeBlock			
▲	public static final		**IPA_EXTENSIONS**	
	...... Character.UnicodeBlock			
▲	public static final		**KANBUN**	
	...... Character.UnicodeBlock			
▲	public static final		**KANNADA**	
	...... Character.UnicodeBlock			
▲	public static final		**KATAKANA**	
	...... Character.UnicodeBlock			
▲	public static final		**LAO**	
	...... Character.UnicodeBlock			
▲	public static final		**LATIN_1_SUPPLEMENT**	
	...... Character.UnicodeBlock			
▲	public static final		**LATIN_EXTENDED_A**	
	...... Character.UnicodeBlock			
▲	public static final		**LATIN_EXTENDED_ADDITIONAL**	
	...... Character.UnicodeBlock			
▲	public static final		**LATIN_EXTENDED_B**	
	...... Character.UnicodeBlock			
▲	public static final		**LETTERLIKE_SYMBOLS**	
	...... Character.UnicodeBlock			
▲	public static final		**MALAYALAM**	
	...... Character.UnicodeBlock			
▲	public static final		**MATHEMATICAL_OPERATORS**	
	...... Character.UnicodeBlock			
▲	public static final		**MISCELLANEOUS_SYMBOLS**	
	...... Character.UnicodeBlock			
▲	public static final		**MISCELLANEOUS_TECHNICAL**	
	...... Character.UnicodeBlock			
▲	public static final		**NUMBER_FORMS**	
	...... Character.UnicodeBlock			
△	public static		**of** (char c)	
	...... Character.UnicodeBlock			
▲	public static final		**OPTICAL_CHARACTER_RECOGNITION**	
	...... Character.UnicodeBlock			
▲	public static final		**ORIYA**	
	...... Character.UnicodeBlock			
▲	public static final		**PRIVATE_USE_AREA**	
	...... Character.UnicodeBlock			
▲	public static final		**SMALL_FORM_VARIANTS**	
	...... Character.UnicodeBlock			
▲	public static final		**SPACING_MODIFIER_LETTERS**	
	...... Character.UnicodeBlock			
▲	public static final		**SPECIALS**	
	...... Character.UnicodeBlock			
▲	public static final		**SUPERSCRIPTS_AND_SUBSCRIPTS**	
	...... Character.UnicodeBlock			
▲	public static final		**SURROGATES_AREA**	
	...... Character.UnicodeBlock			
▲	public static final		**TAMIL**	
	...... Character.UnicodeBlock			
▲	public static final		**TELUGU**	
	...... Character.UnicodeBlock			
▲	public static final		**THAI**	
	...... Character.UnicodeBlock			
▲	public static final		**TIBETAN**	
	...... Character.UnicodeBlock			
● 1	public final .... String		toString ()	

CharacterIterator		java.text
1.1	*CharacterIterator*————————————*Cloneable*	P

	public.................... Object	**clone** ()
	public..................... char	**current** ()
▲	public static final .... char	**DONE** = '?'
	public..................... char	**first** ()
	public........................int	**getBeginIndex** ()

CharacterIterator

```
public.........................int getEndIndex ()
public.........................int getIndex ()
public...................... char last ()
public...................... char next ()
public...................... char previous ()
public...................... char setIndex (int position)
```

CharArrayReader   java.io

```
       Object
1.1 ○  └Reader¹
1.1       └CharArrayReader
```

	protected ....char[]	**buf**	
*	public..........................	**CharArrayReader** (char[] buf)	
*	public..........................	**CharArrayReader** (char[] buf, int offset, int length)	
1	public...................... **void**	**close** ()	
	protected ....int	**count**	
1	protected ....Object	lock	
1	public...................... **void**	**mark** (int readAheadLimit) throws IOException	
	protected ....int	**markedPos**	
1	public......................**boolean**	**markSupported** ()	
	protected ....int	**pos**	
1	public...................... **int**	**read** () throws IOException	
1	public......................int	read (char[] cbuf) throws IOException	
1	public...................... **int**	**read** (char[] b, int off, int len) throws IOException	
1	public......................**boolean**	**ready** () throws IOException	
1	public...................... **void**	**reset** () throws IOException	
1	public...................... **long**	**skip** (long n) throws IOException	

CharArrayWriter   java.io

```
       Object¹
1.1 ○  └Writer²
1.1       └CharArrayWriter
```

	protected ....char[]	**buf**	
*	public..........................	**CharArrayWriter** ()	
*	public..........................	**CharArrayWriter** (int initialSize)	
2	public...................... **void**	**close** ()	
	protected ....int	**count**	
2	public...................... **void**	**flush** ()	
2	protected ....Object	lock	
	public......................void	**reset** ()	
	public......................int	**size** ()	
	public......................char[]	**toCharArray** ()	
1	public................... **String**	**toString** ()	
2	public......................void	write (char[] cbuf) throws IOException	
2	public...................... **void**	**write** (int c)	
2	public......................void	write (String str) throws IOException	
2	public...................... **void**	**write** (char[] c, int off, int len)	
2	public...................... **void**	**write** (String str, int off, int len)	
	public......................void	**writeTo** (Writer out) throws IOException	

CharConversionException   java.io

```
       Object
       └Throwable  - - - - - - - - - - - - - - - - - - - - - - - -  Serializable
         └Exception
           └IOException
1.1          └CharConversionException
```

*	public..........................	**CharConversionException** ()
*	public..........................	**CharConversionException** (String s)

Class *Interface* —extends - - -implements ○ abstract ● final △ static ▲ static final ✳ constructor x x—inherited x **x**—declared **x x**—overridden

		CharHolder	org.omg.CORBA

Object
1.2 ● └CharHolder ------------------------- *org.omg.CORBA.portable.Streamable* [1]

	1	public.....................void	**_read** (org.omg.CORBA.portable.InputStream input)
	1	public...............TypeCode	**_type** ()
	1	public.....................void	**_write** (org.omg.CORBA.portable.OutputStream output)
✳		public...........................	**CharHolder** ()
✳		public...........................	**CharHolder** (char initial)
		public.....................char	**value**

		Checkbox	java.awt
			P

Object
○ └Component [1] ------------------------- *java.awt.image.ImageObserver*, *MenuContainer*,
　　　　　　　　　　　　　　　　　　　　　　　java.io.Serializable
　　└Checkbox ------------------------- *ItemSelectable* [2]

	1	*159 inherited members from Component not shown*
1.1	2	public synchronized ....void	**addItemListener** (*java.awt.event.ItemListener* l)
	1	public..................**void**	**addNotify** ()
✳		public...........................	**Checkbox** ()
✳		public...........................	**Checkbox** (String label)
1.1 ✳		public...........................	**Checkbox** (String label, boolean state)
1.1 ✳		public...........................	**Checkbox** (String label, boolean state, CheckboxGroup group)
✳		public...........................	**Checkbox** (String label, CheckboxGroup group, boolean state)
		public........CheckboxGroup	**getCheckboxGroup** ()
		public.....................String	**getLabel** ()
1.1	2	public...................Object[]	**getSelectedObjects** ()
		public..................boolean	**getState** ()
	1	protected ....**String**	**paramString** ()
1.1	1	protected ....**void**	**processEvent** (AWTEvent e)
1.1		protected ....void	**processItemEvent** (java.awt.event.ItemEvent e)
1.1	2	public synchronized ....void	**removeItemListener** (*java.awt.event.ItemListener* l)
		public.....................void	**setCheckboxGroup** (CheckboxGroup g)
		public.....................void	**setLabel** (String label)
		public.....................void	**setState** (boolean state)

		CheckboxGroup	java.awt
			P

Object [1]
└CheckboxGroup ----------------------- *java.io.Serializable*

✳		public...........................	**CheckboxGroup** ()
D		public...............Checkbox	**getCurrent** ()
1.1		public...............Checkbox	**getSelectedCheckbox** ()
D		public synchronized ....void	**setCurrent** (Checkbox box)
1.1		public.....................void	**setSelectedCheckbox** (Checkbox box)
	1	public..................**String**	**toString** ()

		CheckboxMenuItem	java.awt
			P○

Object
○ └MenuComponent [1] --------------------- *java.io.Serializable*
　└MenuItem [2]
　　└CheckboxMenuItem ----------------- *ItemSelectable* [3]

1.1	2	public synchronized ....void	addActionListener (*java.awt.event.ActionListener* l)
1.1	3	public synchronized ....void	**addItemListener** (*java.awt.event.ItemListener* l)
	2	public..................**void**	**addNotify** ()
1.1 ✳		public...........................	**CheckboxMenuItem** ()
✳		public...........................	**CheckboxMenuItem** (String label)
1.1 ✳		public...........................	**CheckboxMenuItem** (String label, boolean state)
1.1	2	public.....................void	deleteShortcut ()
1.1 ●	2	protected final.............void	disableEvents (long eventsToDisable)
1.1 ●	1	public final ....void	dispatchEvent (AWTEvent e)
1.1 ●	2	protected final.............void	enableEvents (long eventsToEnable)
1.1	2	public.....................String	getActionCommand ()
	1	public.......................Font	getFont ()

CheckboxMenuItem

	2	public	String	getLabel ()
1.1	1	public	String	getName ()
		public	*MenuContainer*	getParent ()
1.1	3	public synchronized ..	Object[]	**getSelectedObjects** ()
1.1	2	public	MenuShortcut	getShortcut ()
		public	boolean	**getState** ()
1.2 ●	1	protected final	Object	getTreeLock ()
	2	public	boolean	isEnabled ()
	2	public	**String**	**paramString** ()
1.1	2	protected	void	processActionEvent (java.awt.event.ActionEvent e)
1.1	2	protected	**void**	**processEvent** (AWTEvent e)
1.1		protected	void	**processItemEvent** (java.awt.event.ItemEvent e)
1.1	2	public synchronized	void	removeActionListener (*java.awt.event.ActionListener* l)
1.1	3	public synchronized	void	**removeItemListener** (*java.awt.event.ItemListener* l)
	1	public	void	removeNotify ()
1.1	2	public	void	setActionCommand (String command)
1.1	2	public synchronized	void	setEnabled (boolean b)
	1	public	void	setFont (Font f)
	2	public synchronized	void	setLabel (String label)
1.1	1	public	void	setName (String name)
1.1	2	public	void	setShortcut (MenuShortcut s)
		public synchronized	void	**setState** (boolean b)
	1	public	String	toString ()

CheckboxMenuItemPeer — java.awt.peer

CheckboxMenuItemPeer ——————————— *MenuItemPeer* [1] (*MenuComponentPeer* [2])

- -

2		*1 inherited members from MenuComponentPeer not shown*		
1		*4 inherited members from MenuItemPeer not shown*		
		public	void	**setState** (boolean)

- -

CheckboxPeer — java.awt.peer

CheckboxPeer ——————————————— *ComponentPeer* [1]

- -

1		*32 inherited members from ComponentPeer not shown*		
	public	void	**setCheckboxGroup** (java.awt.CheckboxGroup)
	public	void	**setLabel** (String)
	public	void	**setState** (boolean)

- -

CheckedInputStream — java.util.zip
P

```
Object
 └─java.io.InputStream
     └─java.io.FilterInputStream 1
         └─CheckedInputStream
```
1.1

	1	public	int	available () throws java.io.IOException
*		public	**CheckedInputStream**	(java.io.InputStream in, *Checksum* cksum)
	1	public	void	close () throws java.io.IOException
		public	*Checksum*	**getChecksum** ()
	1	protected .. java.io.InputStream		in
	1	public synchronized	void	mark (int readlimit)
	1	public	boolean	markSupported ()
	1	public	**int**	**read** () throws java.io.IOException
	1	public	int	read (byte[] b) throws java.io.IOException
	1	public	**int**	read (byte[] buf, int off, int len) throws java.io.IOException
	1	public synchronized	void	reset () throws java.io.IOException
	1	public	**long**	**skip** (long n) throws java.io.IOException

---

CheckedOutputStream — java.util.zip
P

```
Object
 └─java.io.OutputStream
     └─java.io.FilterOutputStream 1
         └─CheckedOutputStream
```
1.1

Class *Interface* —extends - - -implements ○ abstract ● final △ static ▲ static final ✳ constructor x x—inherited x **x**—declared **x x**—overridden

*		public		**CheckedOutputStream** (java.io.OutputStream out, *Checksum* cksum)
	1	public	void	close () throws java.io.IOException
	1	public	void	flush () throws java.io.IOException
		public	*Checksum*	**getChecksum** ()
	1	protected java.io.OutputStream		out
	1	public	void	write (byte[] b) throws java.io.IOException
	1	public	**void**	**write** (int b) throws java.io.IOException
	1	public	**void**	**write** (byte[] b, int off, int len) throws java.io.IOException

C

Checksum — java.util.zip

1.1		*Checksum*		P
		public	long	**getValue** ()
		public	void	**reset** ()
		public	void	**update** (int b)
		public	void	**update** (byte[] b, int off, int len)

Choice — java.awt

```
       Object
   o    └Component¹ ------------------------ java.awt.image.ImageObserver, MenuContainer,
                                                java.io.Serializable
              └Choice ------------------------ ItemSelectable²
```

	1	*159 inherited members from Component not shown*		
1.1		public	void	**add** (String item)
		public	void	**addItem** (String item)
1.1	2	public synchronized	void	**addItemListener** (*java.awt.event.ItemListener* l)
	1	public	**void**	**addNotify** ()
*		public		**Choice** ()
D		public	int	**countItems** ()
		public	String	**getItem** (int index)
1.1		public	int	**getItemCount** ()
		public	int	**getSelectedIndex** ()
		public synchronized	String	**getSelectedItem** ()
1.1	2	public synchronized	Object[]	**getSelectedObjects** ()
1.1		public	void	**insert** (String item, int index)
	1	protected	**String**	**paramString** ()
1.1	1	protected	**void**	**processEvent** (AWTEvent e)
1.1		protected	void	**processItemEvent** (java.awt.event.ItemEvent e)
1.1		public	void	**remove** (int position)
1.1		public	void	**remove** (String item)
1.1		public	void	**removeAll** ()
1.1	2	public synchronized	void	**removeItemListener** (*java.awt.event.ItemListener* l)
		public synchronized	void	**select** (int pos)
		public synchronized	void	**select** (String str)

ChoiceFormat — java.text

```
        Object
  1.1 o └Format¹ ----------------------------- java.io.Serializable, Cloneable
  1.1 o    └NumberFormat²
  1.1         └ChoiceFormat
```

	2	*28 inherited members from NumberFormat not shown*		
		public	void	**applyPattern** (String newPattern)
*		public		**ChoiceFormat** (String newPattern)
*		public		**ChoiceFormat** (double[] limits, String[] formats)
	2	public	**Object**	**clone** ()
	2	public	**boolean**	**equals** (Object obj)
●	1	public final	String	format (Object obj)
	2	public	**StringBuffer**	**format** (double number, StringBuffer toAppendTo, FieldPosition status)
	2	public	**StringBuffer**	**format** (long number, StringBuffer toAppendTo, FieldPosition status)
		public	Object[]	**getFormats** ()
		public	double[]	**getLimits** ()
	2	public	**int**	**hashCode** ()
▲		public static final	double	**nextDouble** (double d)
△		public static	double	**nextDouble** (double d, boolean positive)
	2	public	**Number**	**parse** (String text, ParsePosition status)
	1	public	Object	parseObject (String source) throws ParseException

Classes

ChoiceFormat

▲	public static final	double	**previousDouble** (double d)
	public	void	**setChoices** (double[] limits, String[] formats)
	public	String	**toPattern** ()

ChoicePeer   java.awt.peer

ChoicePeer ———————————————— *ComponentPeer* [1]

	1	*32 inherited members from ComponentPeer not shown*		
1.1		public	void	**add** (String, int)
		public	void	**addItem** (String, int)
1.1		public	void	**remove** (int)
		public	void	**select** (int)

Class   java.lang

Object [1]

    P

●   └─Class - *java.io.Serializable*

△	public static	Class	**forName** (String className) throws ClassNotFoundException
1.2 △	public static	Class	**forName** (String name, boolean initialize, ClassLoader loader) throws ClassNotFoundException
1.1	public	Class[]	**getClasses** ()
	public	ClassLoader	**getClassLoader** ()
1.1	public native	Class	**getComponentType** ()
1.1	public ... java.lang.reflect.Constructor		**getConstructor** (Class[] parameterTypes) throws NoSuchMethodException, SecurityException
1.1	public . java.lang.reflect.Constructor[]		**getConstructors** () throws SecurityException
1.1	public	Class[]	**getDeclaredClasses** () throws SecurityException
1.1	public ... java.lang.reflect.Constructor		**getDeclaredConstructor** (Class[] parameterTypes) throws NoSuchMethodException, SecurityException
1.1	public . java.lang.reflect.Constructor[]		**getDeclaredConstructors** () throws SecurityException
1.1	public ....java.lang.reflect.Field		**getDeclaredField** (String name) throws NoSuchFieldException, SecurityException
1.1	public .. java.lang.reflect.Field[]		**getDeclaredFields** () throws SecurityException
1.1	public .java.lang.reflect.Method		**getDeclaredMethod** (String name, Class[] parameterTypes) throws NoSuchMethodException, SecurityException
1.1	public ...... java.lang.reflect.Method[]		**getDeclaredMethods** () throws SecurityException
1.1	public native	Class	**getDeclaringClass** ()
1.1	public ....java.lang.reflect.Field		**getField** (String name) throws NoSuchFieldException, SecurityException
1.1	public .. java.lang.reflect.Field[]		**getFields** () throws SecurityException
	public native	Class[]	**getInterfaces** ()
1.1	public .java.lang.reflect.Method		**getMethod** (String name, Class[] parameterTypes) throws NoSuchMethodException, SecurityException
1.1	public ...... java.lang.reflect.Method[]		**getMethods** () throws SecurityException
1.1	public native	int	**getModifiers** ()
	public native	String	**getName** ()
1.2	public	Package	**getPackage** ()
1.2	public java.security.ProtectionDomain		**getProtectionDomain** ()
1.1	public	java.net.URL	**getResource** (String name)
1.1	public	java.io.InputStream	**getResourceAsStream** (String name)
	public native	Object[]	**getSigners** ()
	public native	Class	**getSuperclass** ()
1.1	public native	boolean	**isArray** ()
1.1	public native	boolean	**isAssignableFrom** (Class cls)
1.1	public native	boolean	**isInstance** (Object obj)
	public native	boolean	**isInterface** ()
1.1	public native	boolean	**isPrimitive** ()
	public	Object	**newInstance** () throws InstantiationException, IllegalAccessException
1	public	**String**	**toString** ()

Class   *Interface*   —extends   - - -implements   ○ abstract   ● final   △ static   ▲ static final   ✳ constructor   x x—inherited   x **x**—declared   **x x**—overridden

ClassCastException | java.lang
P

```
Object
└Throwable - - - - - - - - - - - - - - - - - - - - - - - - - - java.io.Serializable
   └Exception
      └RuntimeException
         └ClassCastException
```

✱	public.........................	**ClassCastException** ()
✱	public.........................	**ClassCastException** (String s)

ClassCircularityError | java.lang
P

```
Object
└Throwable - - - - - - - - - - - - - - - - - - - - - - - - - - java.io.Serializable
   └Error
      └LinkageError
         └ClassCircularityError
```

✱	public.........................	**ClassCircularityError** ()
✱	public.........................	**ClassCircularityError** (String s)

ClassFormatError | java.lang
P

```
Object
└Throwable - - - - - - - - - - - - - - - - - - - - - - - - - - java.io.Serializable
   └Error
      └LinkageError
         └ClassFormatError
```

✱	public.........................	**ClassFormatError** ()
✱	public.........................	**ClassFormatError** (String s)

ClassLoader | java.lang
P

```
Object
└ClassLoader
```

	✱	protected......................	**ClassLoader** ()
1.2	✱	protected......................	**ClassLoader** (ClassLoader parent)
D	●	protected final............Class	**defineClass** (byte[] b, int off, int len) throws ClassFormatError
1.1	●	protected final............Class	**defineClass** (String name, byte[] b, int off, int len) throws ClassFormatError
1.2	●	protected final............Class	**defineClass** (String name, byte[] b, int off, int len, java.security.ProtectionDomain protectionDomain) throws ClassFormatError
1.2		protected............. Package	**definePackage** (String name, String specTitle, String specVersion, String specVendor, String implTitle, String implVersion, String implVendor, java.net.URL sealBase) throws IllegalArgumentException
1.2		protected.................Class	**findClass** (String name) throws ClassNotFoundException
1.2		protected................String	**findLibrary** (String libname)
1.1	●	protected final native ....Class	**findLoadedClass** (String name)
1.2		protected........ java.net.URL	**findResource** (String name)
1.2		protected *java.util.Enumeration*	**findResources** (String name) throws java.io.IOException
	●	protected final............Class	**findSystemClass** (String name) throws ClassNotFoundException
1.2		protected............. Package	**getPackage** (String name)
1.2		protected............Package[]	**getPackages** ()
1.2	●	public final .... ClassLoader	**getParent** ()
1.1		public............. java.net.URL	**getResource** (String name)
1.1		public.... java.io.InputStream	**getResourceAsStream** (String name)
1.2	●	public final *java.util.Enumeration*	**getResources** (String name) throws java.io.IOException
1.2	△	public static ...... ClassLoader	**getSystemClassLoader** ()
1.1	△	public static ...... java.net.URL	**getSystemResource** (String name)
1.1	△	public static *java.io.InputStream*	**getSystemResourceAsStream** (String name)
1.2	△	public static *java.util.Enumeration*	**getSystemResources** (String name) throws java.io.IOException
1.1		public.....................Class	**loadClass** (String name) throws ClassNotFoundException
		protected synchronized . Class	**loadClass** (String name, boolean resolve) throws ClassNotFoundException
	●	protected final.............void	**resolveClass** (Class c)
1.1	●	protected final.............void	**setSigners** (Class c, Object[] signers)

C

Classes

265

ClassNotFoundException

ClassNotFoundException				java.lang
				P

```
Object
└Throwable ¹ -------------------------- java.io.Serializable
  └Exception
    └ClassNotFoundException
```

C

*	public...........................	**ClassNotFoundException** ()	
*	public...........................	**ClassNotFoundException** (String s)	
1.2 *	public...........................	**ClassNotFoundException** (String s, Throwable ex)	
1.2	public...............Throwable	**getException** ()	
1	public.....................**void**	**printStackTrace** ()	
1	public.....................**void**	**printStackTrace** (java.io.PrintStream ps)	
1.1	1	public.....................**void**	**printStackTrace** (java.io.PrintWriter pw)

Clipboard			java.awt.datatransfer
			P

```
Object
1.1 └Clipboard
```

*	public...........................	**Clipboard** (String name)
	protected..........*Transferable*	**contents**
	public synchronized...........	**getContents** (Object requestor)
	..................*Transferable*	
	public.....................String	**getName** ()
	protected.....*ClipboardOwner*	**owner**
	public synchronized.......void	**setContents** (*Transferable* contents, *ClipboardOwner* owner)

ClipboardOwner			java.awt.datatransfer
1.1	*ClipboardOwner*		P

	public........................void	**lostOwnership** (Clipboard clipboard, *Transferable* contents)

Clob			java.sql
1.2	*Clob*		P○

	public......java.io.InputStream	**getAsciiStream** () throws SQLException
	public...........java.io.Reader	**getCharacterStream** () throws SQLException
	public.....................String	**getSubString** (long pos, int length) throws SQLException
	public.......................long	**length** () throws SQLException
	public.......................long	**position** (String searchstr, long start) throws SQLException
	public.......................long	**position** (*Clob* searchstr, long start) throws SQLException

Cloneable			java.lang
	Cloneable		P

CloneNotSupportedException			java.lang
			P

```
Object
└Throwable -------------------------- java.io.Serializable
  └Exception
    └CloneNotSupportedException
```

*	public...........................	**CloneNotSupportedException** ()
*	public...........................	**CloneNotSupportedException** (String s)

Class *Interface* —extends - - -implements ○ abstract ● final △ static ▲ static final * constructor x x—inherited x **x**—declared **x x**—overridden

CMMException
java.awt.color

```
Object
 └Throwable -------------------------- java.io.Serializable
   └Exception
     └RuntimeException
1.2    └CMMException
```

✳	public.........................	**CMMException** (String s)

CodeSource
java.security
P○

```
Object 1
1.2  └CodeSource -------------------------- java.io.Serializable
```

✳		public.........................	**CodeSource** (java.net.URL url, java.security.cert.Certificate[] certs)
	1	public................**boolean**	**equals** (Object obj)
●		public final	**getCertificates** ()
		..java.security.cert.Certificate[]	
●		public final .... java.net.URL	**getLocation** ()
	1	public...................... **int**	**hashCode** ()
		public................ boolean	**implies** (CodeSource codesource)
	1	public.................. **String**	**toString** ()

CollationElementIterator
java.text
P

```
Object
1.1 ● └CollationElementIterator
```

1.2	public......................int	**getMaxExpansion** (int order)
1.2	public......................int	**getOffset** ()
	public......................int	**next** ()
▲	public static final ....int	**NULLORDER** = -1
1.2	public......................int	**previous** ()
▲	public static final ....int	**primaryOrder** (int order)
	public...................void	**reset** ()
▲	public static final ....short	**secondaryOrder** (int order)
1.2	public...................void	**setOffset** (int newOffset)
1.2	public...................void	**setText** (String source)
1.2	public...................void	**setText** (*CharacterIterator* source)
▲	public static final ....short	**tertiaryOrder** (int order)

CollationKey
java.text
P

```
Object 1
1.1 ●  └CollationKey -------------------------- Comparable 2
```

1.2	2	public......................int	**compareTo** (Object o)
		public......................int	**compareTo** (CollationKey target)
	1	public................**boolean**	**equals** (Object target)
		public..................String	**getSourceString** ()
	1	public.................. **int**	**hashCode** ()
		public..................byte[]	**toByteArray** ()

Collator
java.text
P

```
Object 1
1.1 ○ └Collator -------------------------- java.util.Comparator 2, Cloneable
```

▲		public static final ....int	**CANONICAL_DECOMPOSITION** = 1
	1	public..................**Object**	**clone** ()
✳		protected	**Collator** ()
1.2	2	public......................int	**compare** (Object o1, Object o2)
○		public abstract ....int	**compare** (String source, String target)
	1	public................**boolean**	**equals** (Object that)
		public................ boolean	**equals** (String source, String target)
▲		public static final ....int	**FULL_DECOMPOSITION** = 2
△		public static synchronized	**getAvailableLocales** ()
		.... java.util.Locale[]	

C

Classes

Collator

○	public abstract ... CollationKey	**getCollationKey** (String source)	
	public synchronized ....int	**getDecomposition** ()	
△	public static synchronized ....Collator	**getInstance** ()	
△	public static synchronized ....Collator	**getInstance** (java.util.Locale desiredLocale)	
	public synchronized ....int	**getStrength** ()	
○ 1	public abstract .... int	**hashCode** ()	
▲	public static final.............int	**IDENTICAL** = 3	
▲	public static final.............int	**NO_DECOMPOSITION** = 0	
▲	public static final.............int	**PRIMARY** = 0	
▲	public static final.............int	**SECONDARY** = 1	
	public synchronized ......void	**setDecomposition** (int decompositionMode)	
	public synchronized ......void	**setStrength** (int newStrength)	
▲	public static final.............int	**TERTIARY** = 2	

Collections   java.util

P

1.2   *Collection*

public................. boolean	**add** (Object o)
public................. boolean	**addAll** (*Collection* c)
public.....................void	**clear** ()
public................. boolean	**contains** (Object o)
public................. boolean	**containsAll** (*Collection* c)
public................. boolean	**equals** (Object o)
public.....................int	**hashCode** ()
public................. boolean	**isEmpty** ()
public................. *Iterator*	**iterator** ()
public................. boolean	**remove** (Object o)
public................. boolean	**removeAll** (*Collection* c)
public................. boolean	**retainAll** (*Collection* c)
public.....................int	**size** ()
public................. Object[]	**toArray** ()
public................. Object[]	**toArray** (Object[] a)

Collections   java.util

P

Object
└Collections

1.2

△	public static ....int	**binarySearch** (*List* list, Object key)
△	public static ....int	**binarySearch** (*List* list, Object key, *Comparator* c)
△	public static ....void	**copy** (*List* dest, *List* src)
▲	public static final .... *List*	**EMPTY_LIST**
▲	public static final .... *Set*	**EMPTY_SET**
△	public static ...... *Enumeration*	**enumeration** (*Collection* c)
△	public static ....void	**fill** (*List* list, Object o)
△	public static .... Object	**max** (*Collection* coll)
△	public static .... Object	**max** (*Collection* coll, *Comparator* comp)
△	public static .... Object	**min** (*Collection* coll)
△	public static .... Object	**min** (*Collection* coll, *Comparator* comp)
△	public static .... *List*	**nCopies** (int n, Object o)
△	public static ....void	**reverse** (*List* l)
△	public static .... *Comparator*	**reverseOrder** ()
△	public static ....void	**shuffle** (*List* list)
△	public static ....void	**shuffle** (*List* list, Random rnd)
△	public static ....*Set*	**singleton** (Object o)
△	public static ....void	**sort** (*List* list)
△	public static ....void	**sort** (*List* list, *Comparator* c)
△	public static .... *Collection*	**synchronizedCollection** (*Collection* c)
△	public static .... *List*	**synchronizedList** (*List* list)
△	public static .... *Map*	**synchronizedMap** (*Map* m)
△	public static .... *Set*	**synchronizedSet** (*Set* s)
△	public static ..... *SortedMap*	**synchronizedSortedMap** (*SortedMap* m)
△	public static .... *SortedSet*	**synchronizedSortedSet** (*SortedSet* s)
△	public static .... *Collection*	**unmodifiableCollection** (*Collection* c)
△	public static .... *List*	**unmodifiableList** (*List* list)
△	public static .... *Map*	**unmodifiableMap** (*Map* m)
△	public static ....*Set*	**unmodifiableSet** (*Set* s)

Class   *Interface*   —extends   - - -implements   ○ abstract   ● final   △ static   ▲ static final   ✳ constructor   x x—inherited   x **x**—declared   **x x**—overridden

△	public static	SortedMap	**unmodifiableSortedMap**	(SortedMap m)
△	public static	SortedSet	**unmodifiableSortedSet**	(SortedSet s)

Color — java.awt

Object[1]
└Color `- - - - - - - - - - - - - - - - - - - - - - - - - - - - - -` Paint[2] (Transparency[3]), java.io.Serializable

▲	public static final	Color	**black**	= new Color(0, 0, 0)
▲	public static final	Color	**blue**	= new Color(0, 0, 255)
	public	Color	**brighter** ()	
*	public	Color	**Color** (int rgb)	
1.2 *	public	Color	**Color** (int rgba, boolean hasalpha)	
*	public	Color	**Color** (float r, float g, float b)	
*	public	Color	**Color** (int r, int g, int b)	
1.2 *	public	Color	**Color** (java.awt.color.ColorSpace cspace, float[] components, float alpha)	
1.2 *	public	Color	**Color** (float r, float g, float b, float a)	
1.2 *	public	Color	**Color** (int r, int g, int b, int a)	
1.2 2	public synchronized	PaintContext	**createContext** (java.awt.image.ColorModel cm, Rectangle r, java.awt.geom↵ .Rectangle2D r2d, java.awt.geom.AffineTransform xform, RenderingHints hints)	
▲	public static final	Color	**cyan**	= new Color(0, 255, 255)
	public	Color	**darker** ()	
▲	public static final	Color	**darkGray**	= new Color(64, 64, 64)
1.1 △	public static	Color	**decode** (String nm) throws NumberFormatException	
1	public	boolean	**equals** (Object obj)	
1.2	public	int	**getAlpha** ()	
	public	int	**getBlue** ()	
△	public static	Color	**getColor** (String nm)	
△	public static	Color	**getColor** (String nm, Color v)	
△	public static	Color	**getColor** (String nm, int v)	
1.2	public	float[]	**getColorComponents** (float[] compArray)	
1.2	public	float[]	**getColorComponents** (java.awt.color.ColorSpace cspace, float[] compArray)	
1.2	public	java.awt.color.ColorSpace	**getColorSpace** ()	
1.2	public	float[]	**getComponents** (float[] compArray)	
1.2	public	float[]	**getComponents** (java.awt.color.ColorSpace cspace, float[] compArray)	
	public	int	**getGreen** ()	
△	public static	Color	**getHSBColor** (float h, float s, float b)	
	public	int	**getRed** ()	
	public	int	**getRGB** ()	
1.2	public	float[]	**getRGBColorComponents** (float[] compArray)	
1.2	public	float[]	**getRGBComponents** (float[] compArray)	
1.2 3	public	int	**getTransparency** ()	
▲	public static final	Color	**gray**	= new Color(128, 128, 128)
▲	public static final	Color	**green**	= new Color(0, 255, 0)
1	public	int	**hashCode** ()	
△	public static	int	**HSBtoRGB** (float hue, float saturation, float brightness)	
▲	public static final	Color	**lightGray**	= new Color(192, 192, 192)
▲	public static final	Color	**magenta**	= new Color(255, 0, 255)
▲	public static final	Color	**orange**	= new Color(255, 200, 0)
▲	public static final	Color	**pink**	= new Color(255, 175, 175)
▲	public static final	Color	**red**	= new Color(255, 0, 0)
△	public static	float[]	**RGBtoHSB** (int r, int g, int b, float[] hsbvals)	
1	public	String	**toString** ()	
▲	public static final	Color	**white**	= new Color(255, 255, 255)
▲	public static final	Color	**yellow**	= new Color(255, 255, 0)

ColorChooserComponentFactory — javax.swing.colorchooser

Object
└ColorChooserComponentFactory

△	public static	AbstractColorChooserPanel[]	**getDefaultChooserPanels** ()
△	public static	javax.swing.JComponent	**getPreviewPanel** ()

ColorChooserUI | javax.swing.plaf

```
        Object
1.2 ○   └ComponentUI 1
1.2 ○     └ColorChooserUI
```

	1	*11 inherited members from ComponentUI not shown*	
✳		public............................	**ColorChooserUI** ()

ColorConvertOp | java.awt.image
P

```
        Object
1.2     └ColorConvertOp ----------------------- BufferedImageOp 1, RasterOp 2
```

✳		public...........................	**ColorConvertOp** (java.awt.RenderingHints hints)
✳		public...........................	**ColorConvertOp** (java. awt. color. ColorSpace cspace, java.awt.RenderingHints hints)
✳		public...........................	**ColorConvertOp** (java. awt. color. ICC_Profile[] profiles, java.awt.RenderingHints hints)
✳		public...........................	**ColorConvertOp** (java. awt. color. ColorSpace srcCspace, java.awt.color.ColorSpace dstCspace, java.awt.RenderingHints hints)
	1	public........... BufferedImage	**createCompatibleDestImage** (BufferedImage src, ColorModel destCM)
	2	public........... WritableRaster	**createCompatibleDestRaster** (Raster src)
●	1	public final ..... BufferedImage	**filter** (BufferedImage src, BufferedImage dest)
●	2	public final ..... WritableRaster	**filter** (Raster src, WritableRaster dest)
●	1	public final java.awt.geom.Rectangle2D	**getBounds2D** (BufferedImage src)
●	2	public final java.awt.geom.Rectangle2D	**getBounds2D** (Raster src)
●		public final .... java.awt.color.ICC_Profile[]	**getICC_Profiles** ()
●	1	public final java.awt.geom.Point2D	**getPoint2D** (java.awt.geom.Point2D srcPt, java.awt.geom.Point2D dstPt)
●	1	public final .... java.awt.RenderingHints	**getRenderingHints** ()

ColorModel | java.awt.image
P

```
        Object 1
 ○      └ColorModel -------------------------- java.awt.Transparency 2
```

1.2		public.............. ColorModel	**coerceData** (WritableRaster raster, boolean isAlphaPremultiplied)
1.2	✳	public...........................	**ColorModel** (int bits)
1.2	✳	protected......................	**ColorModel** (int pixel_bits, int[] bits, java.awt.color.ColorSpace cspace, boolean hasAlpha, boolean isAlphaPremultiplied, int transparency, int transferType)
1.2		public........... SampleModel	**createCompatibleSampleModel** (int w, int h)
1.2		public........... WritableRaster	**createCompatibleWritableRaster** (int w, int h)
	1	public................. **boolean**	**equals** (Object obj)
	1	public..................... **void**	**finalize** ()
○		public abstract ....int	**getAlpha** (int pixel)
1.2		public........................int	**getAlpha** (Object inData)
1.2		public........... WritableRaster	**getAlphaRaster** (WritableRaster raster)
○		public abstract ....int	**getBlue** (int pixel)
1.2		public........................int	**getBlue** (Object inData)
1.2	●	public final .... java.awt.color.ColorSpace	**getColorSpace** ()
1.2		public........................int[]	**getComponents** (int pixel, int[] components, int offset)
1.2		public........................int[]	**getComponents** (Object pixel, int[] components, int offset)
1.2		public........................int[]	**getComponentSize** ()
1.2		public........................int	**getComponentSize** (int componentIdx)
1.2		public........................int	**getDataElement** (int[] components, int offset)
1.2		public...................Object	**getDataElements** (int rgb, Object pixel)
1.2		public...................Object	**getDataElements** (int[] components, int offset, Object obj)
○		public abstract ....int	**getGreen** (int pixel)
1.2		public........................int	**getGreen** (Object inData)
1.2		public...................float[]	**getNormalizedComponents** (int[] components, int offset, float[] normComponents, int normOffset)
1.2		public........................int	**getNumColorComponents** ()
1.2		public........................int	**getNumComponents** ()

Class *Interface* —extends - - -implements ○ abstract ● final △ static ▲ static final ✳ constructor x x—inherited x **x**—declared **x x**—overridden

	public	int	**getPixelSize** ()
○	public abstract	int	**getRed** (int pixel)
1.2	public	int	**getRed** (Object inData)
	public	int	**getRGB** (int pixel)
1.2	public	int	**getRGB** (Object inData)
△	public static	ColorModel	**getRGBdefault** ()
1.2 2	public	int	**getTransparency** ()
1.2	public	int[]	**getUnnormalizedComponents** (float[] normComponents, int normOffset, int[] components, int offset)
1.2 ●	public final	boolean	**hasAlpha** ()
1.2 ●	public final	boolean	**isAlphaPremultiplied** ()
1.2	public	boolean	**isCompatibleRaster** (Raster raster)
1.2	public	boolean	**isCompatibleSampleModel** (SampleModel sm)
	protected	int	**pixel_bits**
1	public	String	**toString** ()
1.2	protected	int	**transferType**

C

ColorSelectionModel

1.2	*ColorSelectionModel*		

	public	void	**addChangeListener** (*javax.swing.event.ChangeListener* listener)
	public	java.awt.Color	**getSelectedColor** ()
	public	void	**removeChangeListener** (*javax.swing.event.ChangeListener* listener)
	public	void	**setSelectedColor** (java.awt.Color color)

ColorSpace

	Object		
1.2 ○	└ColorSpace		

✳	protected		**ColorSpace** (int type, int numcomponents)
▲	public static final	int	**CS_CIEXYZ** = 1001
▲	public static final	int	**CS_GRAY** = 1003
▲	public static final	int	**CS_LINEAR_RGB** = 1004
▲	public static final	int	**CS_PYCC** = 1002
▲	public static final	int	**CS_sRGB** = 1000
○	public abstract	float[]	**fromCIEXYZ** (float[] colorvalue)
○	public abstract	float[]	**fromRGB** (float[] rgbvalue)
△	public static	ColorSpace	**getInstance** (int colorspace)
	public	String	**getName** (int idx)
	public	int	**getNumComponents** ()
	public	int	**getType** ()
	public	boolean	**isCS_sRGB** ()
○	public abstract	float[]	**toCIEXYZ** (float[] colorvalue)
○	public abstract	float[]	**toRGB** (float[] colorvalue)
▲	public static final	int	**TYPE_2CLR** = 12
▲	public static final	int	**TYPE_3CLR** = 13
▲	public static final	int	**TYPE_4CLR** = 14
▲	public static final	int	**TYPE_5CLR** = 15
▲	public static final	int	**TYPE_6CLR** = 16
▲	public static final	int	**TYPE_7CLR** = 17
▲	public static final	int	**TYPE_8CLR** = 18
▲	public static final	int	**TYPE_9CLR** = 19
▲	public static final	int	**TYPE_ACLR** = 20
▲	public static final	int	**TYPE_BCLR** = 21
▲	public static final	int	**TYPE_CCLR** = 22
▲	public static final	int	**TYPE_CMY** = 11
▲	public static final	int	**TYPE_CMYK** = 9
▲	public static final	int	**TYPE_DCLR** = 23
▲	public static final	int	**TYPE_ECLR** = 24
▲	public static final	int	**TYPE_FCLR** = 25
▲	public static final	int	**TYPE_GRAY** = 6
▲	public static final	int	**TYPE_HLS** = 8
▲	public static final	int	**TYPE_HSV** = 7
▲	public static final	int	**TYPE_Lab** = 1
▲	public static final	int	**TYPE_Luv** = 2
▲	public static final	int	**TYPE_RGB** = 5
▲	public static final	int	**TYPE_XYZ** = 0
▲	public static final	int	**TYPE_YCbCr** = 3
▲	public static final	int	**TYPE_Yxy** = 4

Classes

ColorUIResource

ColorUIResource	javax.swing.plaf

```
       Object
       └java.awt.Color 1 ----------------------- java.awt.Paint (java.awt.Transparency), java.io.Serializable
1.2          └ColorUIResource --------------------- UIResource
```

	1	*39 inherited members from java.awt.Color not shown*
*		public........................... **ColorUIResource** (int rgb)
*		public........................... **ColorUIResource** (java.awt.Color c)
*		public........................... **ColorUIResource** (float r, float g, float b)
*		public........................... **ColorUIResource** (int r, int g, int b)

ComboBoxEditor	javax.swing

```
1.2    ComboBoxEditor
```

public.........................void **addActionListener** (*java.awt.event.ActionListener* l)
public.... java.awt.Component **getEditorComponent** ()
public.....................Object **getItem** ()
public.........................void **removeActionListener** (*java.awt.event.ActionListener* l)
public.........................void **selectAll** ()
public.........................void **setItem** (Object anObject)

ComboBoxModel	javax.swing

```
1.2    ComboBoxModel————————————————ListModel 1
```

1	public.........................void addListDataListener (*javax.swing.event.ListDataListener* l)
1	public.....................Object getElementAt (int index)
	public.....................Object **getSelectedItem** ()
1	public.........................int getSize ()
1	public.........................void removeListDataListener (*javax.swing.event.ListDataListener* l)
	public.........................void **setSelectedItem** (Object anItem)

ComboBoxUI	javax.swing.plaf

```
         Object
1.2 ○    └ComponentUI 1
1.2 ○       └ComboBoxUI
```

	1	*11 inherited members from ComponentUI not shown*
*		public........................... **ComboBoxUI** ()
○		public abstract .... boolean **isFocusTraversable** (javax.swing.JComboBox c)
○		public abstract .... boolean **isPopupVisible** (javax.swing.JComboBox c)
○		public abstract ....void **setPopupVisible** (javax.swing.JComboBox c, boolean v)

COMM_FAILURE	org.omg.CORBA

```
       Object
       └Throwable ------------------------- java.io.Serializable
         └Exception
           └RuntimeException
1.2 ○        └SystemException 1
1.2 ●          └COMM_FAILURE
```

*		public........................... **COMM_FAILURE** ()
*		public........................... **COMM_FAILURE** (String s)
*		public........................... **COMM_FAILURE** (int minor, CompletionStatus completed)
*		public........................... **COMM_FAILURE** (String s, int minor, CompletionStatus completed)
	1	public........CompletionStatus completed
	1	public.........................int minor
	1	public...................String toString ()

Class   *Interface*   —extends   - - -implements   ○ abstract   ● final   △ static   ▲ static final   ✳ constructor   x x—inherited   x **x**—declared   **x x**—overridden

Comparable — java.lang

1.2	*Comparable*	P

```
public.......................int compareTo (Object o)
```

Comparator — java.util

1.2	*Comparator*	P

```
public........................int compare (Object o1, Object o2)
public.................. boolean equals (Object obj)
```

Compiler — java.lang

```
Object
● └─Compiler                                                    P
```

```
△  public static native...... Object command (Object any)
△  public static native.... boolean compileClass (Class clazz)
△  public static native.... boolean compileClasses (String string)
△  public static native........void disable ()
△  public static native........void enable ()
```

CompletionStatus — org.omg.CORBA

```
Object
1.2 └─CompletionStatus ---------------------- org.omg.CORBA.portable.IDLEntity (java.io.Serializable)
```

```
▲  public static final.............int _COMPLETED_MAYBE = 2
▲  public static final.............int _COMPLETED_NO = 1
▲  public static final.............int _COMPLETED_YES = 0
▲  public static final...............  COMPLETED_MAYBE
   ................CompletionStatus
▲  public static final...............  COMPLETED_NO
   ................CompletionStatus
▲  public static final...............  COMPLETED_YES
   ................CompletionStatus
✳  protected......................  CompletionStatus (int _value)
△  public static .CompletionStatus from_int (int i) throws BAD_PARAM
   public.........................int value ()
```

Component — java.awt

```
Object¹
○ └─Component ------------------------- java.awt.image.ImageObserver ², MenuContainer ³,
                                         java.io.Serializable                              Pᵐ
```

D	public.................. boolean **action** (Event evt, Object what)
1.1	public synchronized ....void **add** (PopupMenu popup)
1.1	public synchronized ......void **addComponentListener** (*java.awt.event.ComponentListener* l)
1.1	public synchronized ......void **addFocusListener** (*java.awt.event.FocusListener* l)
1.2	public synchronized ......void **addInputMethodListener** (*java.awt.event.InputMethodListener* l)
1.1	public synchronized ......void **addKeyListener** (*java.awt.event.KeyListener* l)
1.1	public synchronized ......void **addMouseListener** (*java.awt.event.MouseListener* l)
1.1	public synchronized ......void **addMouseMotionListener** (*java.awt.event.MouseMotionListener* l)
	public.........................void **addNotify** ()
1.2	public synchronized ......void **addPropertyChangeListener** (*java.beans.PropertyChangeListener* listener)
1.2	public synchronized ......void **addPropertyChangeListener** (String propertyName, *java.beans.PropertyChangeListener* listener)
1.1 ▲	public static final..........float **BOTTOM_ALIGNMENT** = 1.0
D	public...................... Rectangle **bounds** ()
1.1 ▲	public static final..........float **CENTER_ALIGNMENT** = 0.5
	public.........................int **checkImage** (Image image, *java.awt.image.ImageObserver* observer)
	public.........................int **checkImage** (Image image, int width, int height, *java.awt.image.ImageObserver* observer)
1.2	protected........... AWTEvent **coalesceEvents** (AWTEvent existingEvent, AWTEvent newEvent)
1.1 ✳	protected...................... **Component** ()
1.1	public.................. boolean **contains** (Point p)
1.1	public.................. boolean **contains** (int x, int y)

	public	Image	**createImage** (*java.awt.image.ImageProducer* producer)
	public	Image	**createImage** (int width, int height)
D	public	void	**deliverEvent** (Event e)
D	public	void	**disable** ()
1.1 ●	protected final	void	**disableEvents** (long eventsToDisable)
1.1 ●	public final	void	**dispatchEvent** (AWTEvent e)
1.1	public	void	**doLayout** ()
D	public	void	**enable** ()
D	public	void	**enable** (boolean b)
1.1 ●	protected final	void	**enableEvents** (long eventsToEnable)
1.2	public	void	**enableInputMethods** (boolean enable)
1.2	protected	void	**firePropertyChange** (String propertyName, Object oldValue, Object newValue)
1.1	public	float	**getAlignmentX** ()
1.1	public	float	**getAlignmentY** ()
	public	Color	**getBackground** ()
1.1	public	Rectangle	**getBounds** ()
1.2	public	Rectangle	**getBounds** (Rectangle rv)
	public		**getColorModel** ()
	.... java.awt.image.ColorModel		
1.1	public	Component	**getComponentAt** (Point p)
1.1	public	Component	**getComponentAt** (int x, int y)
1.2	public	ComponentOrientation	**getComponentOrientation** ()
1.1	public	Cursor	**getCursor** ()
1.2	public synchronized		**getDropTarget** ()
	.... java.awt.dnd.DropTarget		
3	public	Font	**getFont** ()
	public	FontMetrics	**getFontMetrics** (Font font)
	public	Color	**getForeground** ()
	public	Graphics	**getGraphics** ()
1.2	public	int	**getHeight** ()
1.2	public		**getInputContext** ()
	.... java.awt.im.InputContext		
1.2	public	*java* ↩	**getInputMethodRequests** ()
	.awt.im.InputMethodRequests		
1.1	public	java.util.Locale	**getLocale** ()
1.1	public	Point	**getLocation** ()
1.2	public	Point	**getLocation** (Point rv)
1.1	public	Point	**getLocationOnScreen** ()
1.1	public	Dimension	**getMaximumSize** ()
1.1	public	Dimension	**getMinimumSize** ()
1.1	public	String	**getName** ()
	public	Container	**getParent** ()
D	public		**getPeer** ()
	.java.awt.peer.ComponentPeer		
1.1	public	Dimension	**getPreferredSize** ()
1.1	public	Dimension	**getSize** ()
1.2	public	Dimension	**getSize** (Dimension rv)
	public	Toolkit	**getToolkit** ()
1.1 ●	public final	Object	**getTreeLock** ()
1.2	public	int	**getWidth** ()
1.2	public	int	**getX** ()
1.2	public	int	**getY** ()
D	public	boolean	**gotFocus** (Event evt, Object what)
D	public	boolean	**handleEvent** (Event evt)
1.2	public	boolean	**hasFocus** ()
D	public	void	**hide** ()
2	public	boolean	**imageUpdate** (Image img, int flags, int x, int y, int w, int h)
D	public	boolean	**inside** (int x, int y)
	public	void	**invalidate** ()
1.2	public	boolean	**isDisplayable** ()
1.2	public	boolean	**isDoubleBuffered** ()
	public	boolean	**isEnabled** ()
1.1	public	boolean	**isFocusTraversable** ()
1.2	public	boolean	**isLightweight** ()
1.2	public	boolean	**isOpaque** ()
	public	boolean	**isShowing** ()
	public	boolean	**isValid** ()
	public	boolean	**isVisible** ()
D	public	boolean	**keyDown** (Event evt, int key)
D	public	boolean	**keyUp** (Event evt, int key)
D	public	void	**layout** ()
1.1 ▲	public static final	float	**LEFT_ALIGNMENT** = 0.0

Class   *Interface*   —extends   - - -implements   ○ abstract   ● final   △ static   ▲ static final   ✱ constructor   x x—inherited   x **x**—declared   **x x**—overridden

	public	void	**list**	()
	public	void	**list**	(java.io.PrintStream out)
1.1	public	void	**list**	(java.io.PrintWriter out)
	public	void	**list**	(java.io.PrintStream out, int indent)
1.1	public	void	**list**	(java.io.PrintWriter out, int indent)
D	public	Component	**locate**	(int x, int y)
D	public	Point	**location**	()
D	public	boolean	**lostFocus**	(Event evt, Object what)
D	public	Dimension	**minimumSize**	()
D	public	boolean	**mouseDown**	(Event evt, int x, int y)
D	public	boolean	**mouseDrag**	(Event evt, int x, int y)
D	public	boolean	**mouseEnter**	(Event evt, int x, int y)
D	public	boolean	**mouseExit**	(Event evt, int x, int y)
D	public	boolean	**mouseMove**	(Event evt, int x, int y)
D	public	boolean	**mouseUp**	(Event evt, int x, int y)
D	public	void	**move**	(int x, int y)
D	public	void	**nextFocus**	()
	public	void	**paint**	(Graphics g)
	public	void	**paintAll**	(Graphics g)
	protected	String	**paramString**	()
D 3	public	boolean	**postEvent**	(Event e)
D	public	Dimension	**preferredSize**	()
	public	boolean	**prepareImage**	(Image image, *java.awt.image.ImageObserver* observer)
	public	boolean	**prepareImage**	(Image image, int width, int height, *java.awt.image.ImageObserver* observer)
	public	void	**print**	(Graphics g)
	public	void	**printAll**	(Graphics g)
1.1	protected	void	**processComponentEvent**	(java.awt.event.ComponentEvent e)
1.1	protected	void	**processEvent**	(AWTEvent e)
1.1	protected	void	**processFocusEvent**	(java.awt.event.FocusEvent e)
1.2	protected	void	**processInputMethodEvent**	(java.awt.event.InputMethodEvent e)
1.1	protected	void	**processKeyEvent**	(java.awt.event.KeyEvent e)
1.1	protected	void	**processMouseEvent**	(java.awt.event.MouseEvent e)
1.1	protected	void	**processMouseMotionEvent**	(java.awt.event.MouseEvent e)
1.1 3	public synchronized	void	**remove**	(MenuComponent popup)
1.1	public synchronized	void	**removeComponentListener**	(*java.awt.event.ComponentListener* l)
1.1	public synchronized	void	**removeFocusListener**	(*java.awt.event.FocusListener* l)
1.2	public synchronized	void	**removeInputMethodListener**	(*java.awt.event.InputMethodListener* l)
1.1	public synchronized	void	**removeKeyListener**	(*java.awt.event.KeyListener* l)
1.1	public synchronized	void	**removeMouseListener**	(*java.awt.event.MouseListener* l)
1.1	public synchronized	void	**removeMouseMotionListener**	(*java.awt.event.MouseMotionListener* l)
	public	void	**removeNotify**	()
1.2	public synchronized	void	**removePropertyChangeListener**	(*java.beans.PropertyChangeListener* listener)
1.2	public synchronized	void	**removePropertyChangeListener**	(String propertyName, *java.beans.PropertyChangeListener* listener)
	public	void	**repaint**	()
	public	void	**repaint**	(long tm)
	public	void	**repaint**	(int x, int y, int width, int height)
	public	void	**repaint**	(long tm, int x, int y, int width, int height)
	public	void	**requestFocus**	()
D	public	void	**reshape**	(int x, int y, int width, int height)
D	public	void	**resize**	(Dimension d)
D	public	void	**resize**	(int width, int height)
1.1 ▲	public static final	float	**RIGHT_ALIGNMENT**	= 1.0
	public	void	**setBackground**	(Color c)
1.1	public	void	**setBounds**	(Rectangle r)
1.1	public	void	**setBounds**	(int x, int y, int width, int height)
1.2	public	void	**setComponentOrientation**	(ComponentOrientation o)
1.1	public synchronized	void	**setCursor**	(Cursor cursor)
1.2	public synchronized	void	**setDropTarget**	(java.awt.dnd.DropTarget dt)
1.1	public	void	**setEnabled**	(boolean b)
	public	void	**setFont**	(Font f)
	public	void	**setForeground**	(Color c)
1.1	public	void	**setLocale**	(java.util.Locale l)
1.1	public	void	**setLocation**	(Point p)
1.1	public	void	**setLocation**	(int x, int y)
1.1	public	void	**setName**	(String name)
1.1	public	void	**setSize**	(Dimension d)
1.1	public	void	**setSize**	(int width, int height)
1.1	public	void	**setVisible**	(boolean b)
D	public	void	**show**	()
D	public	void	**show**	(boolean b)
D	public	Dimension	**size**	()
1.1 ▲	public static final	float	**TOP_ALIGNMENT**	= 0.0

C

Classes

Component

	1	public....................	**String**	**toString** ()
1.1		public.....................	void	**transferFocus** ()
		public.....................	void	**update** (Graphics g)
		public.....................	void	**validate** ()

ComponentAdapter   java.awt.event

Object

P

1.1 ○		└─ComponentAdapter - *ComponentListener* [1] (*java.util.EventListener*)

✳	public............................	**ComponentAdapter** ()	
1	public..................... void	**componentHidden** (ComponentEvent e)	
1	public..................... void	**componentMoved** (ComponentEvent e)	
1	public..................... void	**componentResized** (ComponentEvent e)	
1	public..................... void	**componentShown** (ComponentEvent e)	

ComponentColorModel   java.awt.image

Object

P

	└─ColorModel [1] - *java.awt.Transparency*

1.2   └─ComponentColorModel

	1	public.............. **ColorModel**	**coerceData** (WritableRaster raster, boolean isAlphaPremultiplied)	
✳		public............................	**ComponentColorModel** (java.awt.color.ColorSpace colorSpace, int[] bits, boolean hasAlpha, boolean isAlphaPremultiplied, int transparency, int transferType)	
	1	public.......... **SampleModel**	**createCompatibleSampleModel** (int w, int h)	
	1	public....... **WritableRaster**	**createCompatibleWritableRaster** (int w, int h)	
	1	public.......... **boolean**	**equals** (Object obj)	
	1	public..................... void	finalize ()	
	1	public.......... **int**	**getAlpha** (int pixel)	
	1	public.......... **int**	**getAlpha** (Object inData)	
	1	public....... **WritableRaster**	**getAlphaRaster** (WritableRaster raster)	
	1	public.......... **int**	**getBlue** (int pixel)	
	1	public.......... **int**	**getBlue** (Object inData)	
●	1	public final	getColorSpace ()	
		.... java.awt.color.ColorSpace		
	1	public..................... **int[]**	**getComponents** (int pixel, int[] components, int offset)	
	1	public..................... **int[]**	**getComponents** (Object pixel, int[] components, int offset)	
	1	public..................... int[]	getComponentSize ()	
	1	public..................... int	getComponentSize (int componentIdx)	
	1	public.......... **int**	**getDataElement** (int[] components, int offset)	
	1	public.......... **Object**	**getDataElements** (int rgb, Object pixel)	
	1	public.......... **Object**	**getDataElements** (int[] components, int offset, Object obj)	
	1	public.......... **int**	**getGreen** (int pixel)	
	1	public.......... **int**	**getGreen** (Object inData)	
	1	public..................... float[]	getNormalizedComponents (int[] components, int offset, float[] normComponents, int normOffset)	
	1	public..................... int	getNumColorComponents ()	
	1	public..................... int	getNumComponents ()	
	1	public..................... int	getPixelSize ()	
	1	public.......... **int**	**getRed** (int pixel)	
	1	public.......... **int**	**getRed** (Object inData)	
	1	public.......... **int**	**getRGB** (int pixel)	
	1	public.......... **int**	**getRGB** (Object inData)	
△	1	public static .... ColorModel	getRGBdefault ()	
	1	public..................... int	getTransparency ()	
	1	public..................... int[]	getUnnormalizedComponents (float[] normComponents, int normOffset, int[] components, int offset)	
●	1	public final .... boolean	hasAlpha ()	
●	1	public final .... boolean	isAlphaPremultiplied ()	
	1	public.................. **boolean**	**isCompatibleRaster** (Raster raster)	
	1	public.................. **boolean**	**isCompatibleSampleModel** (SampleModel sm)	
	1	protected .... int	pixel_bits	
	1	public..................... String	toString ()	
	1	protected .... int	transferType	

Class   *Interface*   —extends   - - -implements   ○ abstract   ● final   △ static   ▲ static final   ✳ constructor   x x—inherited   x **x**—declared   **x x**—overridden

ComponentEvent

java.awt.event

P

```
         Object
1.1      └─java.util.EventObject 1 - - - - - - - - - - - - - - - - - - java.io.Serializable
1.1  ○     └─java.awt.AWTEvent 2
1.1          └─ComponentEvent
```

C

▲	public static final............int	**COMPONENT_FIRST** = 100
▲	public static final............int	**COMPONENT_HIDDEN** = 103
▲	public static final............int	**COMPONENT_LAST** = 103
▲	public static final............int	**COMPONENT_MOVED** = 100
▲	public static final............int	**COMPONENT_RESIZED** = 101
▲	public static final............int	**COMPONENT_SHOWN** = 102
*	public.............................	**ComponentEvent** (java.awt.Component source, int id)
2	protected.................void	consume ()
2	protected..............boolean	consumed
2	protected.................void	finalize () throws Throwable
	public.... java.awt.Component	**getComponent** ()
2	public............................int	getID ()
1	public....................Object	getSource ()
2	protected....................int	id
2	protected..............boolean	isConsumed ()
2	public.............**String**	**paramString** ()
1	protected transient......Object	source
2	public....................String	toString ()

ComponentListener

java.awt.event

P

```
1.1   ComponentListener————————————java.util.EventListener
```

	public.....................void	**componentHidden** (ComponentEvent e)
	public.....................void	**componentMoved** (ComponentEvent e)
	public.....................void	**componentResized** (ComponentEvent e)
	public.....................void	**componentShown** (ComponentEvent e)

ComponentOrientation

java.awt

P

```
       Object
1.2 ●  └─ComponentOrientation - - - - - - - - - - - - - - - - - - java.io.Serializable
```

△	public static .... ComponentOrientation	**getOrientation** (java.util.Locale locale)
△	public static .... ComponentOrientation	**getOrientation** (java.util.ResourceBundle bdl)
	public.................boolean	**isHorizontal** ()
	public.................boolean	**isLeftToRight** ()
▲	public static final............... .... ComponentOrientation	**LEFT_TO_RIGHT**
▲	public static final............... .... ComponentOrientation	**RIGHT_TO_LEFT**
▲	public static final............... .... ComponentOrientation	**UNKNOWN**

ComponentPeer

java.awt.peer

Classes

```
    ComponentPeer
```

	public............................int	**checkImage** (java.awt.Image, int, int, *java.awt.image.ImageObserver*)
	public.......... java.awt.Image	**createImage** (*java.awt.image.ImageProducer*)
	public.......... java.awt.Image	**createImage** (int, int)
	public.....................void	**disable** ()
	public.....................void	**dispose** ()
	public.....................void	**enable** ()
	public............................. .... java.awt.image.ColorModel	**getColorModel** ()
	public.... java.awt.FontMetrics	**getFontMetrics** (java.awt.Font)
	public....... java.awt.Graphics	**getGraphics** ()
1.1	public.........java.awt.Point	**getLocationOnScreen** ()
1.1	public.....java.awt.Dimension	**getMinimumSize** ()
1.1	public.....java.awt.Dimension	**getPreferredSize** ()
	public...........java.awt.Toolkit	**getToolkit** ()

ComponentPeer

1.1	public	void	**handleEvent** (java.awt.AWTEvent)
	public	void	**hide** ()
1.1	public	boolean	**isFocusTraversable** ()
	public	java.awt.Dimension	**minimumSize** ()
	public	void	**paint** (java.awt.Graphics)
	public	java.awt.Dimension	**preferredSize** ()
	public	boolean	**prepareImage** (java.awt.Image, int, int, *java.awt.image.ImageObserver*)
	public	void	**print** (java.awt.Graphics)
	public	void	**repaint** (long, int, int, int, int)
	public	void	**requestFocus** ()
	public	void	**reshape** (int, int, int, int)
	public	void	**setBackground** (java.awt.Color)
1.1	public	void	**setBounds** (int, int, int, int)
1.1	public	void	**setCursor** (java.awt.Cursor)
1.1	public	void	**setEnabled** (boolean)
	public	void	**setFont** (java.awt.Font)
	public	void	**setForeground** (java.awt.Color)
1.1	public	void	**setVisible** (boolean)
	public	void	**show** ()

ComponentSampleModel

java.awt.image
P

		Object
1.2 O		└SampleModel [1]
1.2		└ComponentSampleModel

	1		*26 inherited members from SampleModel not shown*
		protected int[]	**bandOffsets**
		protected int[]	**bankIndices**
*		public	**ComponentSampleModel** (int dataType, int w, int h, int pixelStride, int scanlineStride, int[] bandOffsets)
*		public	**ComponentSampleModel** (int dataType, int w, int h, int pixelStride, int scanlineStride, int[] bankIndices, int[] bandOffsets)
	1	public SampleModel	**createCompatibleSampleModel** (int w, int h)
	1	public DataBuffer	**createDataBuffer** ()
	1	public SampleModel	**createSubsetSampleModel** (int[] bands)
●		public final int[]	**getBandOffsets** ()
●		public final int[]	**getBankIndices** ()
	1	public Object	**getDataElements** (int x, int y, Object obj, DataBuffer data)
●	1	public final int	**getNumDataElements** ()
		public int	**getOffset** (int x, int y)
		public int	**getOffset** (int x, int y, int b)
	1	public int[]	**getPixel** (int x, int y, int[] iArray, DataBuffer data)
	1	public int[]	**getPixels** (int x, int y, int w, int h, int[] iArray, DataBuffer data)
●		public final int	**getPixelStride** ()
	1	public int	**getSample** (int x, int y, int b, DataBuffer data)
	1	public int[]	**getSamples** (int x, int y, int w, int h, int b, int[] iArray, DataBuffer data)
●	1	public final int[]	**getSampleSize** ()
●	1	public final int	**getSampleSize** (int band)
●		public final int	**getScanlineStride** ()
	1	protected int	**numBands**
		protected int	**numBanks**
		protected int	**pixelStride**
		protected int	**scanlineStride**
	1	public void	**setDataElements** (int x, int y, Object obj, DataBuffer data)
	1	public void	**setPixel** (int x, int y, int[] iArray, DataBuffer data)
	1	public void	**setPixels** (int x, int y, int w, int h, int[] iArray, DataBuffer data)
	1	public void	**setSample** (int x, int y, int b, int s, DataBuffer data)
	1	public void	**setSamples** (int x, int y, int w, int h, int b, int[] iArray, DataBuffer data)

ComponentUI

javax.swing.plaf

		Object
1.2 O		└ComponentUI

*		public	**ComponentUI** ()
		public boolean	**contains** (javax.swing.JComponent c, int x, int y)
△		public static ComponentUI	**createUI** (javax.swing.JComponent c)
		public	**getAccessibleChild** (javax.swing.JComponent c, int i)
		. *javax.accessibility.Accessible*	

Class   *Interface*   —extends   - - implements   O abstract   ● final   △ static   ▲ static final   * constructor   x x—inherited   x **x**—declared   **x x**—overridden

public	int	**getAccessibleChildrenCount** (javax.swing.JComponent c)
public	java.awt.Dimension	**getMaximumSize** (javax.swing.JComponent c)
public	java.awt.Dimension	**getMinimumSize** (javax.swing.JComponent c)
public	java.awt.Dimension	**getPreferredSize** (javax.swing.JComponent c)
public	void	**installUI** (javax.swing.JComponent c)
public	void	**paint** (java.awt.Graphics g, javax.swing.JComponent c)
public	void	**uninstallUI** (javax.swing.JComponent c)
public	void	**update** (java.awt.Graphics g, javax.swing.JComponent c)

C

ComponentView
javax.swing.text

Object
1.2 ○ └View[1] - *javax.swing.SwingConstants*
1.2   └ComponentView

1   *30 inherited members from View not shown*
*   public .... **ComponentView** (*Element* elem)
    protected java.awt.Component **createComponent** ()
1   public .... **float** **getAlignment** (int axis)
●   public final .... **getComponent** ()
    .... java.awt.Component
1   public .... **float** **getMaximumSpan** (int axis)
1   public .... **float** **getMinimumSpan** (int axis)
1   public .... **float** **getPreferredSpan** (int axis)
1   public .... ***java.awt.Shape*** **modelToView** (int pos, *java. awt. Shape* a, Position. Bias b)
                                         throws BadLocationException
1   public .... **void** **paint** (java.awt.Graphics g, *java.awt.Shape* a)
1   public .... **void** **setParent** (View p)
1   public .... **void** **setSize** (float width, float height)
1   public .... **int** **viewToModel** (float x, float y, *java.awt.Shape* a, Position.Bias[] bias)

Composite
java.awt

1.2   *Composite*   P

public .... *CompositeContext* **createContext** (java. awt. image. ColorModel srcColorModel,
                        java.awt.image.ColorModel dstColorModel, RenderingHints hints)

CompositeContext
java.awt

1.2   *CompositeContext*   P

public .... void **compose** (java. awt. image. Raster src, java. awt. image. Raster dstIn,
                        java.awt.image.WritableRaster dstOut)
public .... void **dispose** ()

CompositeView
javax.swing.text

Object
1.2 ○ └View[1] - *javax.swing.SwingConstants*
1.2 ○   └CompositeView

1   *31 inherited members from View not shown*
    public .... void **append** (View v)
○   protected abstract .... void **childAllocation** (int index, java.awt.Rectangle a)
*   public .... **CompositeView** (*Element* elem)
    protected .... boolean **flipEastAndWestAtEnds** (int position, Position.Bias bias)
●   protected final .... short **getBottomInset** ()
1   public .... ***java.awt.Shape*** **getChildAllocation** (int index, *java.awt.Shape* a)
    protected .. java.awt.Rectangle **getInsideAllocation** (*java.awt.Shape* a)
●   protected final .... short **getLeftInset** ()
    protected .... int **getNextEastWestVisualPositionFrom** (int pos, Position.Bias b, *java.awt.Shape* a,
                        int direction, Position.Bias[] biasRet) throws BadLocationException
    protected .... int **getNextNorthSouthVisualPositionFrom** (int pos, Position.Bias b, *java.awt.Shape*
                        a, int direction, Position.Bias[] biasRet) throws BadLocationException
1   public .... **int** **getNextVisualPositionFrom** (int pos, Position.Bias b, *java.awt.Shape* a,
                        int direction, Position.Bias[] biasRet) throws BadLocationException
●   protected final .... short **getRightInset** ()
●   protected final .... short **getTopInset** ()
1   public .... **View** **getView** (int n)

Classes

CompositeView

○	protected abstract	View	**getViewAtPoint** (int x, int y, java.awt.Rectangle alloc)
	protected	View	**getViewAtPosition** (int pos, java.awt.Rectangle a)
1	public	**int**	**getViewCount** ()
	protected	int	**getViewIndexAtPosition** (int pos)
	public	void	**insert** (int offs, View v)
○	protected abstract	boolean	**isAfter** (int x, int y, java.awt.Rectangle alloc)
○	protected abstract	boolean	**isBefore** (int x, int y, java.awt.Rectangle alloc)
	protected	void	**loadChildren** (*ViewFactory* f)
1	public	*java.awt.Shape*	**modelToView** (int pos, *java. awt. Shape* a, Position. Bias b) throws BadLocationException
1	public	*java.awt.Shape*	**modelToView** (int p0, Position.Bias b0, int p1, Position.Bias b1, *java.awt.Shape* a) throws BadLocationException
	public	void	**removeAll** ()
	public	void	**replace** (int offset, int length, View[] views)
●	protected final	void	**setInsets** (short top, short left, short bottom, short right)
●	protected final	void	**setParagraphInsets** (*AttributeSet* attr)
1	public	**void**	**setParent** (View parent)
1	public	**int**	**viewToModel** (float x, float y, *java.awt.Shape* a, Position.Bias[] bias)

CompoundBorder
javax.swing.border

Object
1.2 ○ └─AbstractBorder[1] ----------------------- *Border*, *java.io.Serializable*
1.2   └─CompoundBorder

✳	public		**CompoundBorder** ()
✳	public		**CompoundBorder** (*Border* outsideBorder, *Border* insideBorder)
1	public	**java.awt.Insets**	**getBorderInsets** (java.awt.Component c)
1	public	**java.awt.Insets**	**getBorderInsets** (java.awt.Component c, java.awt.Insets insets)
	public	*Border*	**getInsideBorder** ()
1	public	java.awt.Rectangle	getInteriorRectangle (java.awt.Component c, int x, int y, int width, int height)
△ 1	public static		getInteriorRectangle (java.awt.Component c, *Border* b, int x, int y, int width, int height)
		java.awt.Rectangle	
	public	*Border*	**getOutsideBorder** ()
	protected	*Border*	**insideBorder**
1	public	**boolean**	**isBorderOpaque** ()
	protected	*Border*	**outsideBorder**
1	public	**void**	**paintBorder** (java.awt.Component c, java.awt.Graphics g, int x, int y, int width, int height)

CompoundEdit
javax.swing.undo

Object
1.2 └─AbstractUndoableEdit[1] ------------------ *UndoableEdit*, *java.io.Serializable*
1.2   └─CompoundEdit

1	public	**boolean**	**addEdit** (*UndoableEdit* anEdit)
1	public	**boolean**	**canRedo** ()
1	public	**boolean**	**canUndo** ()
✳	public		**CompoundEdit** ()
1	public	**void**	**die** ()
	protected	java.util.Vector	**edits**
	public	void	**end** ()
1	public	**String**	**getPresentationName** ()
1	public	**String**	**getRedoPresentationName** ()
1	public	**String**	**getUndoPresentationName** ()
	public	boolean	**isInProgress** ()
1	public	**boolean**	**isSignificant** ()
	protected	*UndoableEdit*	**lastEdit** ()
1	public	**void**	**redo** () throws CannotRedoException
1	public	boolean	replaceEdit (*UndoableEdit* anEdit)
1	public	**String**	**toString** ()
1	public	**void**	**undo** () throws CannotUndoException

Class   *Interface* —extends   - - -implements   ○ abstract   ● final   △ static   ▲ static final   ✳ constructor   x x—inherited   x **x**—declared   **x x**—overridden

280

ConcurrentModificationException			java.util

        P

```
Object
 └Throwable ------------------------- java.io.Serializable
   └Exception
     └RuntimeException
```
1.2   `└ConcurrentModificationException`

✻	public.........................	**ConcurrentModificationException** ()
✻	public.........................	**ConcurrentModificationException** (String message)

ConcurrentModificationException			java.util

C

ConnectException❶			java.rmi

        P⁰

```
Object
 └Throwable ------------------------- java.io.Serializable
   └Exception
     └java.io.IOException
```
1.1   `└RemoteException`[1]
1.1   `└ConnectException`

✻	public.........................	**ConnectException** (String s)
✻	public.........................	**ConnectException** (String s, Exception ex)
1	public...............Throwable	detail
1	public.....................String	getMessage ()
1	public.......................void	printStackTrace ()
1	public.......................void	printStackTrace (java.io.PrintStream ps)
1	public.......................void	printStackTrace (java.io.PrintWriter pw)

ConnectException❷			java.net

        P

```
Object
 └Throwable ------------------------- java.io.Serializable
   └Exception
     └java.io.IOException
       └SocketException
```
1.1   `└ConnectException`

✻	public.........................	**ConnectException** ()
✻	public.........................	**ConnectException** (String msg)

ConnectIOException			java.rmi

        P⁰

```
Object
 └Throwable ------------------------- java.io.Serializable
   └Exception
     └java.io.IOException
```
1.1   `└RemoteException`[1]
1.1   `└ConnectIOException`

✻	public.........................	**ConnectIOException** (String s)
✻	public.........................	**ConnectIOException** (String s, Exception ex)
1	public...............Throwable	detail
1	public.....................String	getMessage ()
1	public.......................void	printStackTrace ()
1	public.......................void	printStackTrace (java.io.PrintStream ps)
1	public.......................void	printStackTrace (java.io.PrintWriter pw)

Connection			java.sql

        P⁰

1.1   *Connection*

	public.......................void	**clearWarnings** () throws SQLException
	public.......................void	**close** () throws SQLException
	public.......................void	**commit** () throws SQLException
	public...............*Statement*	**createStatement** () throws SQLException
1.2	public...............*Statement*	**createStatement** (int resultSetType, int resultSetConcurrency) throws SQLException
	public.................boolean	**getAutoCommit** () throws SQLException
	public.....................String	**getCatalog** () throws SQLException
	public......*DatabaseMetaData*	**getMetaData** () throws SQLException

Connection

	public	int	**getTransactionIsolation** () throws SQLException
1.2	public	*java.util.Map*	**getTypeMap** () throws SQLException
	public	SQLWarning	**getWarnings** () throws SQLException
	public	boolean	**isClosed** () throws SQLException
	public	boolean	**isReadOnly** () throws SQLException
	public	String	**nativeSQL** (String sql) throws SQLException
	public	*CallableStatement*	**prepareCall** (String sql) throws SQLException
1.2	public	*CallableStatement*	**prepareCall** (String sql, int resultSetType, int resultSetConcurrency) throws SQLException
	public	*PreparedStatement*	**prepareStatement** (String sql) throws SQLException
1.2	public	*PreparedStatement*	**prepareStatement** (String sql, int resultSetType, int resultSetConcurrency) throws SQLException
	public	void	**rollback** () throws SQLException
	public	void	**setAutoCommit** (boolean autoCommit) throws SQLException
	public	void	**setCatalog** (String catalog) throws SQLException
	public	void	**setReadOnly** (boolean readOnly) throws SQLException
	public	void	**setTransactionIsolation** (int level) throws SQLException
1.2	public	void	**setTypeMap** (*java.util.Map* map) throws SQLException
▲	public static final	int	**TRANSACTION_NONE** = 0
▲	public static final	int	**TRANSACTION_READ_COMMITTED** = 2
▲	public static final	int	**TRANSACTION_READ_UNCOMMITTED** = 1
▲	public static final	int	**TRANSACTION_REPEATABLE_READ** = 4
▲	public static final	int	**TRANSACTION_SERIALIZABLE** = 8

Constructor — java.lang.reflect
P

Object [1]
  └AccessibleObject [2]   (1.2)
    └Constructor - *Member* [3]   (1.1 ●)

	1	public	**boolean**	**equals** (Object obj)
	3	public	Class	**getDeclaringClass** ()
		public	Class[]	**getExceptionTypes** ()
	3	public	int	**getModifiers** ()
	3	public	String	**getName** ()
		public	Class[]	**getParameterTypes** ()
	1	public	**int**	**hashCode** ()
1.2	2	public	boolean	isAccessible ()
		public native	Object	**newInstance** (Object[] initargs) throws InstantiationException, IllegalAccessException, IllegalArgumentException, InvocationTargetException
1.2	2	public	void	setAccessible (boolean flag) throws SecurityException
1.2 △	2	public static	void	setAccessible (AccessibleObject[] array, boolean flag) throws SecurityException
	1	public	**String**	**toString** ()

Container — java.awt
P

Object
  └Component [1] - *java.awt.image.ImageObserver*, *MenuContainer*,   (○)
                                          java.io.Serializable
      └Container

	1	*137 inherited members from Component not shown*		
		public	Component	**add** (Component comp)
1.1		public	void	**add** (Component comp, Object constraints)
		public	Component	**add** (Component comp, int index)
		public	Component	**add** (String name, Component comp)
1.1		public	void	**add** (Component comp, Object constraints, int index)
1.1		public synchronized	void	**addContainerListener** (*java.awt.event.ContainerListener* l)
1.1		protected	void	**addImpl** (Component comp, Object constraints, int index)
	1	public	**void**	**addNotify** ()
1.1 ✳		public		**Container** ()
D		public	int	**countComponents** ()
D	1	public	**void**	**deliverEvent** (Event e)
1.1	1	public	**void**	**doLayout** ()
1.2		public	Component	**findComponentAt** (Point p)
1.2		public	Component	**findComponentAt** (int x, int y)
1.1	1	public	**float**	**getAlignmentX** ()
1.1	1	public	**float**	**getAlignmentY** ()
		public	Component	**getComponent** (int n)
1.1	1	public	**Component**	**getComponentAt** (Point p)

Class *Interface* —extends - - -implements ○ abstract ● final △ static ▲ static final ✳ constructor x x—inherited x **x**—declared **x x**—overridden

1.1	1	public	**Component**	**getComponentAt** (int x, int y)
1.1		public	int	**getComponentCount** ()
		public	Component[]	**getComponents** ()
1.1		public	Insets	**getInsets** ()
		public	*LayoutManager*	**getLayout** ()
1.1	1	public	**Dimension**	**getMaximumSize** ()
1.1	1	public	**Dimension**	**getMinimumSize** ()
1.1	1	public	**Dimension**	**getPreferredSize** ()
D		public	Insets	**insets** ()
	1	public	**void**	**invalidate** ()
1.1		public	boolean	**isAncestorOf** (Component c)
D	1	public	**void**	**layout** ()
	1	public	**void**	**list** (java.io.PrintStream out, int indent)
1.1	1	public	**void**	**list** (java.io.PrintWriter out, int indent)
D	1	public	**Component**	**locate** (int x, int y)
D	1	public	**Dimension**	**minimumSize** ()
	1	public	**void**	**paint** (Graphics g)
		public	void	**paintComponents** (Graphics g)
	1	protected	**String**	**paramString** ()
D	1	public	**Dimension**	**preferredSize** ()
	1	public	**void**	**print** (Graphics g)
		public	void	**printComponents** (Graphics g)
1.1		protected	void	**processContainerEvent** (java.awt.event.ContainerEvent e)
1.1	1	protected	**void**	**processEvent** (AWTEvent e)
1.1		public	void	**remove** (int index)
		public	void	**remove** (Component comp)
		public	void	**removeAll** ()
1.1		public synchronized	void	**removeContainerListener** (*java.awt.event.ContainerListener* l)
	1	public	**void**	**removeNotify** ()
	1	public	**void**	**setFont** (Font f)
		public :	void	**setLayout** (*LayoutManager* mgr)
	1	public	**void**	**update** (Graphics g)
	1	public	**void**	**validate** ()
1.1		protected	void	**validateTree** ()

ContainerAdapter java.awt.event

P

Object
1.1 O └ContainerAdapter ---------------------- *ContainerListener* [1] (*java.util.EventListener*)

	1	public	void	**componentAdded** (ContainerEvent e)
	1	public	void	**componentRemoved** (ContainerEvent e)
*		public		**ContainerAdapter** ()

ContainerEvent java.awt.event

P

Object
1.1 └java.util.EventObject[1] -------------------- *java.io.Serializable*
1.1 O   └java.awt.AWTEvent[2]
1.1   └ComponentEvent[3]
1.1   └ContainerEvent

▲		public static final	int	**COMPONENT_ADDED** = 300
▲		public static final	int	**COMPONENT_REMOVED** = 301
	2	protected	void	consume ()
	2	protected	boolean	consumed
▲		public static final	int	**CONTAINER_FIRST** = 300
▲		public static final	int	**CONTAINER_LAST** = 301
*		public		**ContainerEvent** (java.awt.Component source, int id, java.awt.Component child)
	2	protected	void	finalize () throws Throwable
		public	java.awt.Component	**getChild** ()
	3	public	java.awt.Component	getComponent ()
		public	java.awt.Container	**getContainer** ()
	2	public	int	getID ()
	1	public	Object	getSource ()
	2	protected	int	id
	2	protected	boolean	isConsumed ()
	3	public	**String**	**paramString** ()
	1	protected transient	Object	source
	2	public	String	toString ()

C

ContainerListener — java.awt.event

| | | | | |
1.1 *ContainerListener*————————————*java.util.EventListener*   P

    public......................void **componentAdded** (ContainerEvent e)
    public......................void **componentRemoved** (ContainerEvent e)

ContainerPeer — java.awt.peer

ContainerPeer————————————*ComponentPeer* [1]

  1 32 inherited members from ComponentPeer not shown
1.1 public......................void **beginValidate** ()
1.1 public......................void **endValidate** ()
1.1 public..........java.awt.Insets **getInsets** ()
    public..........java.awt.Insets **insets** ()

ContentHandler — java.net

  Object
○ └ContentHandler   P

∗ public.......................... **ContentHandler** ()
○ public abstract..........Object **getContent** (URLConnection urlc) throws java.io.IOException

ContentHandlerFactory — java.net

ContentHandlerFactory   P

    public..........ContentHandler **createContentHandler** (String mimetype)

ContentModel — javax.swing.text.html.parser

  Object [1]
1.2 ● └ContentModel - - - - - - - - - - - - - - - - - *java.io.Serializable*

    public....................Object **content**
∗ public.......................... **ContentModel** ()
∗ public.......................... **ContentModel** (Element content)
∗ public.......................... **ContentModel** (int type, ContentModel content)
∗ public.......................... **ContentModel** (int type, Object content, ContentModel next)
    public..................boolean **empty** ()
    public..................Element **first** ()
    public..................boolean **first** (Object token)
    public......................void **getElements** (java.util.Vector elemVec)
    public............ContentModel **next**
1 public.................. **String toString** ()
    public.......................int **type**

Context — org.omg.CORBA

  Object
1.2 ○ └Context

∗ public.......................... **Context** ()
○ public abstract..........String **context_name** ()
○ public abstract.........Context **create_child** (String child_ctx_name)
○ public abstract............void **delete_values** (String propname)
○ public abstract..........NVList **get_values** (String start_scope, int op_flags, String pattern)
○ public abstract.........Context **parent** ()
○ public abstract............void **set_one_value** (String propname, Any propvalue)
○ public abstract............void **set_values** (NVList values)

Class *Interface* —extends - - -implements ○ abstract ● final △ static ▲ static final ∗ constructor x x—inherited x **x**—declared **x x**—overridden

ContextList | org.omg.CORBA

1.2 ○	Object └ContextList	

○	public abstract	void	**add** (String ctx)
✳	public		**ContextList** ()
○	public abstract	int	**count** ()
○	public abstract	String	**item** (int index) throws Bounds
○	public abstract	void	**remove** (int index) throws Bounds

C

ContextualRenderedImageFactory | java.awt.image.renderable

1.2 | *ContextualRenderedImageFactory*————————*RenderedImageFactory* [1]

	1	public ...... *java*↵ *.awt.image.RenderedImage*	create (ParameterBlock paramBlock, java.awt.RenderingHints hints)
		public ...... *java*↵ *.awt.image.RenderedImage*	**create** (RenderContext renderContext, ParameterBlock paramBlock)
		public ... java.awt.geom.Rectangle2D	**getBounds2D** (ParameterBlock paramBlock)
		public ...... Object	**getProperty** (ParameterBlock paramBlock, String name)
		public ...... String[]	**getPropertyNames** ()
		public ...... boolean	**isDynamic** ()
		public ...... RenderContext	**mapRenderContext** (int i, RenderContext renderContext, ParameterBlock paramBlock, *RenderableImage* image)

ConvolveOp | java.awt.image

P

1.2	Object └ConvolveOp - *BufferedImageOp* [1], *RasterOp* [2]	

✳		public	**ConvolveOp** (Kernel kernel)
✳		public	**ConvolveOp** (Kernel kernel, int edgeCondition, java.awt.RenderingHints hints)
	1	public ...... BufferedImage	**createCompatibleDestImage** (BufferedImage src, ColorModel destCM)
	2	public ...... WritableRaster	**createCompatibleDestRaster** (Raster src)
▲		public static final ...... int	**EDGE_NO_OP** = 1
▲		public static final ...... int	**EDGE_ZERO_FILL** = 0
●	1	public final ..... BufferedImage	**filter** (BufferedImage src, BufferedImage dst)
●	2	public final ..... WritableRaster	**filter** (Raster src, WritableRaster dst)
●	1	public final ... java.awt.geom.Rectangle2D	**getBounds2D** (BufferedImage src)
●	2	public final ... java.awt.geom.Rectangle2D	**getBounds2D** (Raster src)
		public ...... int	**getEdgeCondition** ()
●		public final ...... Kernel	**getKernel** ()
●	1	public final java.awt.geom.Point2D	**getPoint2D** (java.awt.geom.Point2D srcPt, java.awt.geom.Point2D dstPt)
●	1	public final .... java.awt.RenderingHints	**getRenderingHints** ()

CRC32 | java.util.zip

P

1.1	Object └CRC32 - *Checksum* [1]	

✳		public	**CRC32** ()
	1	public ...... long	**getValue** ()
	1	public ...... void	**reset** ()
		public ...... void	**update** (byte[] b)
	1	public ...... void	**update** (int b)
	1	public ...... void	**update** (byte[] b, int off, int len)

CRL | java.security.cert

1.2 ○	Object [1] └CRL	

✳		protected	**CRL** (String type)
●		public final ...... String	**getType** ()

Classes

CRL

○	public abstract .... boolean	**isRevoked** (Certificate cert)
○ 1	public abstract .... **String**	**toString** ()

CRLException

java.security.cert

Object
└Throwable `- - - - - - - - - - - - - - - - - - - - - - - - - -` *java.io.Serializable*
  └Exception
1.2   └java.security.GeneralSecurityException
1.2   └CRLException

✱	public..........................	**CRLException** ()
✱	public..........................	**CRLException** (String message)

CropImageFilter

java.awt.image

P

Object
└ImageFilter[1] `- - - - - - - - - - - - - - - - - - - - - - - - -` *ImageConsumer*, *Cloneable*
  └CropImageFilter

1	public.................... Object	clone ()
1	protected ..... *ImageConsumer*	consumer
✱	public..........................	**CropImageFilter** (int x, int y, int w, int h)
1	public............... ImageFilter	getFilterInstance (*ImageConsumer* ic)
1	public....................void	imageComplete (int status)
1	public....................void	resendTopDownLeftRight (*ImageProducer* ip)
1	public....................void	setColorModel (ColorModel model)
1	public.............. **void**	**setDimensions** (int w, int h)
1	public....................void	setHints (int hints)
1	public.............. **void**	**setPixels** (int x, int y, int w, int h, ColorModel model, byte[] pixels, int off, int scansize)
1	public.............. **void**	**setPixels** (int x, int y, int w, int h, ColorModel model, int[] pixels, int off, int scansize)
1	public.............. **void**	**setProperties** (java.util.Hashtable props)

CSS

javax.swing.text.html

Object
1.2 └CSS

✱	public..........................	**CSS** ()
△	public static .... CSS.Attribute[]	**getAllAttributeKeys** ()
▲	public static final CSS.Attribute	**getAttribute** (String name)

CSS.Attribute

javax.swing.text.html

Object[1]
1.2 ● └CSS.Attribute

▲	public static final CSS.Attribute	**BACKGROUND**
▲	public static final CSS.Attribute	**BACKGROUND_ATTACHMENT**
▲	public static final CSS.Attribute	**BACKGROUND_COLOR**
▲	public static final CSS.Attribute	**BACKGROUND_IMAGE**
▲	public static final CSS.Attribute	**BACKGROUND_POSITION**
▲	public static final CSS.Attribute	**BACKGROUND_REPEAT**
▲	public static final CSS.Attribute	**BORDER**
▲	public static final CSS.Attribute	**BORDER_BOTTOM**
▲	public static final CSS.Attribute	**BORDER_BOTTOM_WIDTH**
▲	public static final CSS.Attribute	**BORDER_COLOR**
▲	public static final CSS.Attribute	**BORDER_LEFT**
▲	public static final CSS.Attribute	**BORDER_LEFT_WIDTH**
▲	public static final CSS.Attribute	**BORDER_RIGHT**
▲	public static final CSS.Attribute	**BORDER_RIGHT_WIDTH**
▲	public static final CSS.Attribute	**BORDER_STYLE**
▲	public static final CSS.Attribute	**BORDER_TOP**
▲	public static final CSS.Attribute	**BORDER_TOP_WIDTH**
▲	public static final CSS.Attribute	**BORDER_WIDTH**
▲	public static final CSS.Attribute	**CLEAR**
▲	public static final CSS.Attribute	**COLOR**
▲	public static final CSS.Attribute	**DISPLAY**

Class *Interface* —extends - - -implements ○ abstract ● final △ static ▲ static final ✱ constructor x x—inherited x **x**—declared **x x**—overridden

▲	public static final	CSS.Attribute	**FLOAT**
▲	public static final	CSS.Attribute	**FONT**
▲	public static final	CSS.Attribute	**FONT_FAMILY**
▲	public static final	CSS.Attribute	**FONT_SIZE**
▲	public static final	CSS.Attribute	**FONT_STYLE**
▲	public static final	CSS.Attribute	**FONT_VARIANT**
▲	public static final	CSS.Attribute	**FONT_WEIGHT**
	public	String	**getDefaultValue** ()
▲	public static final	CSS.Attribute	**HEIGHT**
	public	boolean	**isInherited** ()
▲	public static final	CSS.Attribute	**LETTER_SPACING**
▲	public static final	CSS.Attribute	**LINE_HEIGHT**
▲	public static final	CSS.Attribute	**LIST_STYLE**
▲	public static final	CSS.Attribute	**LIST_STYLE_IMAGE**
▲	public static final	CSS.Attribute	**LIST_STYLE_POSITION**
▲	public static final	CSS.Attribute	**LIST_STYLE_TYPE**
▲	public static final	CSS.Attribute	**MARGIN**
▲	public static final	CSS.Attribute	**MARGIN_BOTTOM**
▲	public static final	CSS.Attribute	**MARGIN_LEFT**
▲	public static final	CSS.Attribute	**MARGIN_RIGHT**
▲	public static final	CSS.Attribute	**MARGIN_TOP**
▲	public static final	CSS.Attribute	**PADDING**
▲	public static final	CSS.Attribute	**PADDING_BOTTOM**
▲	public static final	CSS.Attribute	**PADDING_LEFT**
▲	public static final	CSS.Attribute	**PADDING_RIGHT**
▲	public static final	CSS.Attribute	**PADDING_TOP**
▲	public static final	CSS.Attribute	**TEXT_ALIGN**
▲	public static final	CSS.Attribute	**TEXT_DECORATION**
▲	public static final	CSS.Attribute	**TEXT_INDENT**
▲	public static final	CSS.Attribute	**TEXT_TRANSFORM**
1	public	String	**toString** ()
▲	public static final	CSS.Attribute	**VERTICAL_ALIGN**
▲	public static final	CSS.Attribute	**WHITE_SPACE**
▲	public static final	CSS.Attribute	**WIDTH**
▲	public static final	CSS.Attribute	**WORD_SPACING**

CTX_RESTRICT_SCOPE
org.omg.CORBA

1.2 *CTX_RESTRICT_SCOPE*

▲	public static final	int **value** = 15	

CubicCurve2D
java.awt.geom

Object[1]
1.2 ○ └CubicCurve2D ------------------------- *java.awt.Shape*[2], *Cloneable*

1	public	**Object**	**clone** ()
2	public	boolean	**contains** (Point2D p)
2	public	boolean	**contains** (Rectangle2D r)
2	public	boolean	**contains** (double x, double y)
2	public	boolean	**contains** (double x, double y, double w, double h)
*	protected		**CubicCurve2D** ()
2	public	java.awt.Rectangle	**getBounds** ()
○ 2	public abstract	Rectangle2D	**getBounds2D** ()
○	public abstract	Point2D	**getCtrlP1** ()
○	public abstract	Point2D	**getCtrlP2** ()
○	public abstract	double	**getCtrlX1** ()
○	public abstract	double	**getCtrlX2** ()
○	public abstract	double	**getCtrlY1** ()
○	public abstract	double	**getCtrlY2** ()
	public	double	**getFlatness** ()
△	public static	double	**getFlatness** (double[] coords, int offset)
△	public static	double	**getFlatness** (double x1, double y1, double ctrlx1, double ctrly1, double ctrlx2, double ctrly2, double x2, double y2)
	public	double	**getFlatnessSq** ()
△	public static	double	**getFlatnessSq** (double[] coords, int offset)
△	public static	double	**getFlatnessSq** (double x1, double y1, double ctrlx1, double ctrly1, double ctrlx2, double ctrly2, double x2, double y2)
○	public abstract	Point2D	**getP1** ()
○	public abstract	Point2D	**getP2** ()
2	public	*PathIterator*	**getPathIterator** (AffineTransform at)

Classes

CubicCurve2D

	2	public	PathIterator	**getPathIterator** (AffineTransform at, double flatness)
○		public abstract	double	**getX1** ()
○		public abstract	double	**getX2** ()
○		public abstract	double	**getY1** ()
○		public abstract	double	**getY2** ()
	2	public	boolean	**intersects** (Rectangle2D r)
	2	public	boolean	**intersects** (double x, double y, double w, double h)
		public	void	**setCurve** (CubicCurve2D c)
		public	void	**setCurve** (double[] coords, int offset)
		public	void	**setCurve** (Point2D[] pts, int offset)
		public	void	**setCurve** (Point2D p1, Point2D cp1, Point2D cp2, Point2D p2)
○		public abstract	void	**setCurve** (double x1, double y1, double ctrlx1, double ctrly1, double ctrlx2, double ctrly2, double x2, double y2)
△		public static	int	**solveCubic** (double[] eqn)
		public	void	**subdivide** (CubicCurve2D left, CubicCurve2D right)
△		public static	void	**subdivide** (CubicCurve2D src, CubicCurve2D left, CubicCurve2D right)
△		public static	void	**subdivide** (double[] src, int srcoff, double[] left, int leftoff, double[] right, int rightoff)

CubicCurve2D.Double   java.awt.geom

Object
1.2 ○ └CubicCurve2D [1] - *java.awt.Shape, Cloneable*
1.2   └CubicCurve2D.Double

	1	public	Object	clone ()
	1	public	boolean	contains (Point2D p)
	1	public	boolean	contains (Rectangle2D r)
	1	public	boolean	contains (double x, double y)
	1	public	boolean	contains (double x, double y, double w, double h)
		public	double	**ctrlx1**
		public	double	**ctrlx2**
		public	double	**ctrly1**
		public	double	**ctrly2**
✻		public		**Double** ()
✻		public		**Double** (double x1, double y1, double ctrlx1, double ctrly1, double ctrlx2, double ctrly2, double x2, double y2)
	1	public	java.awt.Rectangle	getBounds ()
	1	public	**Rectangle2D**	**getBounds2D** ()
	1	public	**Point2D**	**getCtrlP1** ()
	1	public	**Point2D**	**getCtrlP2** ()
	1	public	**double**	**getCtrlX1** ()
	1	public	**double**	**getCtrlX2** ()
	1	public	**double**	**getCtrlY1** ()
	1	public	**double**	**getCtrlY2** ()
	1	public	double	getFlatness ()
△	1	public static	double	getFlatness (double[] coords, int offset)
△	1	public static	double	getFlatness (double x1, double y1, double ctrlx1, double ctrly1, double ctrlx2, double ctrly2, double x2, double y2)
	1	public	double	getFlatnessSq ()
△	1	public static	double	getFlatnessSq (double[] coords, int offset)
△	1	public static	double	getFlatnessSq (double x1, double y1, double ctrlx1, double ctrly1, double ctrlx2, double ctrly2, double x2, double y2)
	1	public	**Point2D**	**getP1** ()
	1	public	**Point2D**	**getP2** ()
	1	public	PathIterator	getPathIterator (AffineTransform at)
	1	public	PathIterator	getPathIterator (AffineTransform at, double flatness)
	1	public	**double**	**getX1** ()
	1	public	**double**	**getX2** ()
	1	public	**double**	**getY1** ()
	1	public	**double**	**getY2** ()
	1	public	boolean	intersects (Rectangle2D r)
	1	public	boolean	intersects (double x, double y, double w, double h)
	1	public	void	setCurve (CubicCurve2D c)
	1	public	void	setCurve (double[] coords, int offset)
	1	public	void	setCurve (Point2D[] pts, int offset)
	1	public	void	setCurve (Point2D p1, Point2D cp1, Point2D cp2, Point2D p2)
	1	public	**void**	**setCurve** (double x1, double y1, double ctrlx1, double ctrly1, double ctrlx2, double ctrly2, double x2, double y2)
△	1	public static	int	solveCubic (double[] eqn)
	1	public	void	subdivide (CubicCurve2D left, CubicCurve2D right)
△	1	public static	void	subdivide (CubicCurve2D src, CubicCurve2D left, CubicCurve2D right)

Class *Interface* —extends - - -implements ○ abstract ● final △ static ▲ static final ✻ constructor x x—inherited x **x**—declared **x x**—overridden

△ 1	public static	.............void	subdivide (double[] src, int srcoff, double[] left, int leftoff, double[] right, int rightoff)
	public	..................double	**x1**
	public	..................double	**x2**
	public	..................double	**y1**
	public	..................double	**y2**

C

CubicCurve2D.Float   java.awt.geom

Object
1.2 ○ └CubicCurve2D [1] - *java.awt.Shape*, *Cloneable*
1.2   └CubicCurve2D.Float

	1	public	.....................Object	clone ()
	1	public	..................boolean	contains (Point2D p)
	1	public	..................boolean	contains (Rectangle2D r)
	1	public	..................boolean	contains (double x, double y)
	1	public	..................boolean	contains (double x, double y, double w, double h)
		public	.....................float	**ctrlx1**
		public	.....................float	**ctrlx2**
		public	.....................float	**ctrly1**
		public	.....................float	**ctrly2**
∗		public	....	**Float** ()
∗		public	....	**Float** (float x1, float y1, float ctrlx1, float ctrly1, float ctrlx2, float ctrly2, float x2, float y2)
	1	public	......java.awt.Rectangle	getBounds ()
	1	public	............**Rectangle2D**	**getBounds2D** ()
	1	public	..................**Point2D**	**getCtrlP1** ()
	1	public	..................**Point2D**	**getCtrlP2** ()
	1	public	...................**double**	**getCtrlX1** ()
	1	public	...................**double**	**getCtrlX2** ()
	1	public	...................**double**	**getCtrlY1** ()
	1	public	...................**double**	**getCtrlY2** ()
	1	public	...................double	getFlatness ()
△	1	public static	.............double	getFlatness (double[] coords, int offset)
△	1	public static	.............double	getFlatness (double x1, double y1, double ctrlx1, double ctrly1, double ctrlx2, double ctrly2, double x2, double y2)
	1	public	...................double	getFlatnessSq ()
△	1	public static	.............double	getFlatnessSq (double[] coords, int offset)
△	1	public static	.............double	getFlatnessSq (double x1, double y1, double ctrlx1, double ctrly1, double ctrlx2, double ctrly2, double x2, double y2)
	1	public	..................**Point2D**	**getP1** ()
	1	public	..................**Point2D**	**getP2** ()
	1	public	............*PathIterator*	getPathIterator (AffineTransform at)
	1	public	............*PathIterator*	getPathIterator (AffineTransform at, double flatness)
	1	public	...................**double**	**getX1** ()
	1	public	...................**double**	**getX2** ()
	1	public	...................**double**	**getY1** ()
	1	public	...................**double**	**getY2** ()
	1	public	..................boolean	intersects (Rectangle2D r)
	1	public	..................boolean	intersects (double x, double y, double w, double h)
	1	public	.....................void	setCurve (CubicCurve2D c)
	1	public	.....................void	setCurve (double[] coords, int offset)
	1	public	.....................void	setCurve (Point2D[] pts, int offset)
	1	public	.....................void	setCurve (Point2D p1, Point2D cp1, Point2D cp2, Point2D p2)
	1	public	.....................**void**	**setCurve** (double x1, double y1, double ctrlx1, double ctrly1, double ctrlx2, double ctrly2, double x2, double y2)
		public	.....................void	**setCurve** (float x1, float y1, float ctrlx1, float ctrly1, float ctrlx2, float ctrly2, float x2, float y2)
△	1	public static	..................int	solveCubic (double[] eqn)
	1	public	.....................void	subdivide (CubicCurve2D left, CubicCurve2D right)
△	1	public static	.............void	subdivide (CubicCurve2D src, CubicCurve2D left, CubicCurve2D right)
△	1	public static	.............void	subdivide (double[] src, int srcoff, double[] left, int leftoff, double[] right, int rightoff)
		public	.....................float	**x1**
		public	.....................float	**x2**
		public	.....................float	**y1**
		public	.....................float	**y2**

Classes

Current

			org.omg.CORBA

1.2 *Current*──────────────── *Object* [1]

　　　　1　*13 inherited members from Object not shown*

D

Cursor

			java.awt
			P

Object [1]

1.1 └Cursor - *java.io.Serializable*

▲		public static final . . . . int	**CROSSHAIR_CURSOR** = 1	
✳		public	**Cursor** (int type)	
1.2 ✳		protected	**Cursor** (String name)	
1.2 ▲		public static final . . . . int	**CUSTOM_CURSOR** = -1	
▲		public static final . . . . int	**DEFAULT_CURSOR** = 0	
▲		public static final . . . . int	**E_RESIZE_CURSOR** = 11	
△		public static . . . . Cursor	**getDefaultCursor** ()	
1.2		public . . . . String	**getName** ()	
△		public static . . . . Cursor	**getPredefinedCursor** (int type)	
1.2 △		public static . . . . Cursor	**getSystemCustomCursor** (String name) throws AWTException	
		public . . . . int	**getType** ()	
▲		public static final . . . . int	**HAND_CURSOR** = 12	
▲		public static final . . . . int	**MOVE_CURSOR** = 13	
▲		public static final . . . . int	**N_RESIZE_CURSOR** = 8	
1.2		protected . . . . String	**name**	
▲		public static final . . . . int	**NE_RESIZE_CURSOR** = 7	
▲		public static final . . . . int	**NW_RESIZE_CURSOR** = 6	
△		protected static . . . . Cursor[]	**predefined**	
▲		public static final . . . . int	**S_RESIZE_CURSOR** = 9	
▲		public static final . . . . int	**SE_RESIZE_CURSOR** = 5	
▲		public static final . . . . int	**SW_RESIZE_CURSOR** = 4	
▲		public static final . . . . int	**TEXT_CURSOR** = 2	
	1	public . . . . **String**	**toString** ()	
▲		public static final . . . . int	**W_RESIZE_CURSOR** = 10	
▲		public static final . . . . int	**WAIT_CURSOR** = 3	

Customizer

			java.beans

1.1 *Customizer*

public . . . . void	**addPropertyChangeListener** (*PropertyChangeListener* listener)	
public . . . . void	**removePropertyChangeListener** (*PropertyChangeListener* listener)	
public . . . . void	**setObject** (Object bean)	

DATA_CONVERSION

			org.omg.CORBA

Object

└Throwable - *java.io.Serializable*

　└Exception

　　└RuntimeException

1.2 ○　　　└SystemException [1]

1.2 ●　　　　└DATA_CONVERSION

	1	public . . . . CompletionStatus	**completed**
✳		public	**DATA_CONVERSION** ()
✳		public	**DATA_CONVERSION** (String s)
✳		public	**DATA_CONVERSION** (int minor, CompletionStatus completed)
✳		public	**DATA_CONVERSION** (String s, int minor, CompletionStatus completed)
	1	public . . . . int	**minor**
	1	public . . . . String	**toString** ()

DatabaseMetaData

			java.sql
			P○

1.1 *DatabaseMetaData*

public . . . . boolean	**allProceduresAreCallable** () throws SQLException	
public . . . . boolean	**allTablesAreSelectable** () throws SQLException	

Class　*Interface*　──extends　- - -implements　○ abstract　● final　△ static　▲ static final　✳ constructor　x x──inherited　x **x**──declared　**x x**──overridden

▲ public static final . . . . int **bestRowNotPseudo** = 1
▲ public static final . . . . int **bestRowPseudo** = 2
▲ public static final . . . . int **bestRowSession** = 2
▲ public static final . . . . int **bestRowTemporary** = 0
▲ public static final . . . . int **bestRowTransaction** = 1
▲ public static final . . . . int **bestRowUnknown** = 0
▲ public static final . . . . int **columnNoNulls** = 0
▲ public static final . . . . int **columnNullable** = 1
▲ public static final . . . . int **columnNullableUnknown** = 2
public . . . . boolean **dataDefinitionCausesTransactionCommit** () throws SQLException
public . . . . boolean **dataDefinitionIgnoredInTransactions** () throws SQLException
1.2 public . . . . boolean **deletesAreDetected** (int type) throws SQLException
public . . . . boolean **doesMaxRowSizeIncludeBlobs** () throws SQLException
public . . . . ResultSet **getBestRowIdentifier** (String catalog, String schema, String table, int scope,
        boolean nullable) throws SQLException
public . . . . ResultSet **getCatalogs** () throws SQLException
public . . . . String **getCatalogSeparator** () throws SQLException
public . . . . String **getCatalogTerm** () throws SQLException
public . . . . ResultSet **getColumnPrivileges** (String catalog, String schema, String table,
        String columnNamePattern) throws SQLException
public . . . . ResultSet **getColumns** (String catalog, String schemaPattern, String tableNamePattern,
        String columnNamePattern) throws SQLException
1.2 public . . . . Connection **getConnection** () throws SQLException
public . . . . ResultSet **getCrossReference** (String primaryCatalog, String primarySchema,
        String primaryTable, String foreignCatalog, String foreignSchema,
        String foreignTable) throws SQLException
public . . . . String **getDatabaseProductName** () throws SQLException
public . . . . String **getDatabaseProductVersion** () throws SQLException
public . . . . int **getDefaultTransactionIsolation** () throws SQLException
public . . . . int **getDriverMajorVersion** ()
public . . . . int **getDriverMinorVersion** ()
public . . . . String **getDriverName** () throws SQLException
public . . . . String **getDriverVersion** () throws SQLException
public . . . . ResultSet **getExportedKeys** (String catalog, String schema, String table)
        throws SQLException
public . . . . String **getExtraNameCharacters** () throws SQLException
public . . . . String **getIdentifierQuoteString** () throws SQLException
public . . . . ResultSet **getImportedKeys** (String catalog, String schema, String table)
        throws SQLException
public . . . . ResultSet **getIndexInfo** (String catalog, String schema, String table, boolean unique,
        boolean approximate) throws SQLException
public . . . . int **getMaxBinaryLiteralLength** () throws SQLException
public . . . . int **getMaxCatalogNameLength** () throws SQLException
public . . . . int **getMaxCharLiteralLength** () throws SQLException
public . . . . int **getMaxColumnNameLength** () throws SQLException
public . . . . int **getMaxColumnsInGroupBy** () throws SQLException
public . . . . int **getMaxColumnsInIndex** () throws SQLException
public . . . . int **getMaxColumnsInOrderBy** () throws SQLException
public . . . . int **getMaxColumnsInSelect** () throws SQLException
public . . . . int **getMaxColumnsInTable** () throws SQLException
public . . . . int **getMaxConnections** () throws SQLException
public . . . . int **getMaxCursorNameLength** () throws SQLException
public . . . . int **getMaxIndexLength** () throws SQLException
public . . . . int **getMaxProcedureNameLength** () throws SQLException
public . . . . int **getMaxRowSize** () throws SQLException
public . . . . int **getMaxSchemaNameLength** () throws SQLException
public . . . . int **getMaxStatementLength** () throws SQLException
public . . . . int **getMaxStatements** () throws SQLException
public . . . . int **getMaxTableNameLength** () throws SQLException
public . . . . int **getMaxTablesInSelect** () throws SQLException
public . . . . int **getMaxUserNameLength** () throws SQLException
public . . . . String **getNumericFunctions** () throws SQLException
public . . . . ResultSet **getPrimaryKeys** (String catalog, String schema, String table) throws SQLException
public . . . . ResultSet **getProcedureColumns** (String catalog, String schemaPattern,
        String procedureNamePattern, String columnNamePattern) throws SQLException
public . . . . ResultSet **getProcedures** (String catalog, String schemaPattern,
        String procedureNamePattern) throws SQLException
public . . . . String **getProcedureTerm** () throws SQLException
public . . . . ResultSet **getSchemas** () throws SQLException
public . . . . String **getSchemaTerm** () throws SQLException
public . . . . String **getSearchStringEscape** () throws SQLException
public . . . . String **getSQLKeywords** () throws SQLException
public . . . . String **getStringFunctions** () throws SQLException

D

Classes

DatabaseMetaData

	public	String	**getSystemFunctions** () throws SQLException
	public	ResultSet	**getTablePrivileges** (String catalog, String schemaPattern, String tableNamePattern) throws SQLException
	public	ResultSet	**getTables** (String catalog, String schemaPattern, String tableNamePattern, String[] types) throws SQLException
	public	ResultSet	**getTableTypes** () throws SQLException
	public	String	**getTimeDateFunctions** () throws SQLException
	public	ResultSet	**getTypeInfo** () throws SQLException
1.2	public	ResultSet	**getUDTs** (String catalog, String schemaPattern, String typeNamePattern, int[] types) throws SQLException
	public	String	**getURL** () throws SQLException
	public	String	**getUserName** () throws SQLException
	public	ResultSet	**getVersionColumns** (String catalog, String schema, String table) throws SQLException
▲	public static final	int	**importedKeyCascade** = 0
▲	public static final	int	**importedKeyInitiallyDeferred** = 5
▲	public static final	int	**importedKeyInitiallyImmediate** = 6
▲	public static final	int	**importedKeyNoAction** = 3
▲	public static final	int	**importedKeyNotDeferrable** = 7
▲	public static final	int	**importedKeyRestrict** = 1
▲	public static final	int	**importedKeySetDefault** = 4
▲	public static final	int	**importedKeySetNull** = 2
1.2	public	boolean	**insertsAreDetected** (int type) throws SQLException
	public	boolean	**isCatalogAtStart** () throws SQLException
	public	boolean	**isReadOnly** () throws SQLException
	public	boolean	**nullPlusNonNullIsNull** () throws SQLException
	public	boolean	**nullsAreSortedAtEnd** () throws SQLException
	public	boolean	**nullsAreSortedAtStart** () throws SQLException
	public	boolean	**nullsAreSortedHigh** () throws SQLException
	public	boolean	**nullsAreSortedLow** () throws SQLException
1.2	public	boolean	**othersDeletesAreVisible** (int type) throws SQLException
1.2	public	boolean	**othersInsertsAreVisible** (int type) throws SQLException
1.2	public	boolean	**othersUpdatesAreVisible** (int type) throws SQLException
1.2	public	boolean	**ownDeletesAreVisible** (int type) throws SQLException
1.2	public	boolean	**ownInsertsAreVisible** (int type) throws SQLException
1.2	public	boolean	**ownUpdatesAreVisible** (int type) throws SQLException
▲	public static final	int	**procedureColumnIn** = 1
▲	public static final	int	**procedureColumnInOut** = 2
▲	public static final	int	**procedureColumnOut** = 4
▲	public static final	int	**procedureColumnResult** = 3
▲	public static final	int	**procedureColumnReturn** = 5
▲	public static final	int	**procedureColumnUnknown** = 0
▲	public static final	int	**procedureNoNulls** = 0
▲	public static final	int	**procedureNoResult** = 1
▲	public static final	int	**procedureNullable** = 1
▲	public static final	int	**procedureNullableUnknown** = 2
▲	public static final	int	**procedureResultUnknown** = 0
▲	public static final	int	**procedureReturnsResult** = 2
	public	boolean	**storesLowerCaseIdentifiers** () throws SQLException
	public	boolean	**storesLowerCaseQuotedIdentifiers** () throws SQLException
	public	boolean	**storesMixedCaseIdentifiers** () throws SQLException
	public	boolean	**storesMixedCaseQuotedIdentifiers** () throws SQLException
	public	boolean	**storesUpperCaseIdentifiers** () throws SQLException
	public	boolean	**storesUpperCaseQuotedIdentifiers** () throws SQLException
	public	boolean	**supportsAlterTableWithAddColumn** () throws SQLException
	public	boolean	**supportsAlterTableWithDropColumn** () throws SQLException
	public	boolean	**supportsANSI92EntryLevelSQL** () throws SQLException
	public	boolean	**supportsANSI92FullSQL** () throws SQLException
	public	boolean	**supportsANSI92IntermediateSQL** () throws SQLException
1.2	public	boolean	**supportsBatchUpdates** () throws SQLException
	public	boolean	**supportsCatalogsInDataManipulation** () throws SQLException
	public	boolean	**supportsCatalogsInIndexDefinitions** () throws SQLException
	public	boolean	**supportsCatalogsInPrivilegeDefinitions** () throws SQLException
	public	boolean	**supportsCatalogsInProcedureCalls** () throws SQLException
	public	boolean	**supportsCatalogsInTableDefinitions** () throws SQLException
	public	boolean	**supportsColumnAliasing** () throws SQLException
	public	boolean	**supportsConvert** () throws SQLException
	public	boolean	**supportsConvert** (int fromType, int toType) throws SQLException
	public	boolean	**supportsCoreSQLGrammar** () throws SQLException
	public	boolean	**supportsCorrelatedSubqueries** () throws SQLException
	public	boolean	**supportsDataDefinitionAndDataManipulationTransactions** () throws SQLException

Class *Interface* —extends - - -implements ○ abstract ● final △ static ▲ static final ✳ constructor x x—inherited x **x**—declared **x x**—overridden

D

public	boolean	**supportsDataManipulationTransactionsOnly** () throws SQLException	
public	boolean	**supportsDifferentTableCorrelationNames** () throws SQLException	
public	boolean	**supportsExpressionsInOrderBy** () throws SQLException	
public	boolean	**supportsExtendedSQLGrammar** () throws SQLException	
public	boolean	**supportsFullOuterJoins** () throws SQLException	
public	boolean	**supportsGroupBy** () throws SQLException	
public	boolean	**supportsGroupByBeyondSelect** () throws SQLException	
public	boolean	**supportsGroupByUnrelated** () throws SQLException	
public	boolean	**supportsIntegrityEnhancementFacility** () throws SQLException	
public	boolean	**supportsLikeEscapeClause** () throws SQLException	
public	boolean	**supportsLimitedOuterJoins** () throws SQLException	
public	boolean	**supportsMinimumSQLGrammar** () throws SQLException	
public	boolean	**supportsMixedCaseIdentifiers** () throws SQLException	
public	boolean	**supportsMixedCaseQuotedIdentifiers** () throws SQLException	
public	boolean	**supportsMultipleResultSets** () throws SQLException	
public	boolean	**supportsMultipleTransactions** () throws SQLException	
public	boolean	**supportsNonNullableColumns** () throws SQLException	
public	boolean	**supportsOpenCursorsAcrossCommit** () throws SQLException	
public	boolean	**supportsOpenCursorsAcrossRollback** () throws SQLException	
public	boolean	**supportsOpenStatementsAcrossCommit** () throws SQLException	
public	boolean	**supportsOpenStatementsAcrossRollback** () throws SQLException	
public	boolean	**supportsOrderByUnrelated** () throws SQLException	
public	boolean	**supportsOuterJoins** () throws SQLException	
public	boolean	**supportsPositionedDelete** () throws SQLException	
public	boolean	**supportsPositionedUpdate** () throws SQLException	

1.2 public boolean **supportsResultSetConcurrency** (int type, int concurrency) throws SQLException
1.2 public boolean **supportsResultSetType** (int type) throws SQLException

public	boolean	**supportsSchemasInDataManipulation** () throws SQLException
public	boolean	**supportsSchemasInIndexDefinitions** () throws SQLException
public	boolean	**supportsSchemasInPrivilegeDefinitions** () throws SQLException
public	boolean	**supportsSchemasInProcedureCalls** () throws SQLException
public	boolean	**supportsSchemasInTableDefinitions** () throws SQLException
public	boolean	**supportsSelectForUpdate** () throws SQLException
public	boolean	**supportsStoredProcedures** () throws SQLException
public	boolean	**supportsSubqueriesInComparisons** () throws SQLException
public	boolean	**supportsSubqueriesInExists** () throws SQLException
public	boolean	**supportsSubqueriesInIns** () throws SQLException
public	boolean	**supportsSubqueriesInQuantifieds** () throws SQLException
public	boolean	**supportsTableCorrelationNames** () throws SQLException
public	boolean	**supportsTransactionIsolationLevel** (int level) throws SQLException
public	boolean	**supportsTransactions** () throws SQLException
public	boolean	**supportsUnion** () throws SQLException
public	boolean	**supportsUnionAll** () throws SQLException

- ▲ public static final short **tableIndexClustered** = 1
- ▲ public static final short **tableIndexHashed** = 2
- ▲ public static final short **tableIndexOther** = 3
- ▲ public static final short **tableIndexStatistic** = 0
- ▲ public static final int **typeNoNulls** = 0
- ▲ public static final int **typeNullable** = 1
- ▲ public static final int **typeNullableUnknown** = 2
- ▲ public static final int **typePredBasic** = 2
- ▲ public static final int **typePredChar** = 1
- ▲ public static final int **typePredNone** = 0
- ▲ public static final int **typeSearchable** = 3

1.2 public boolean **updatesAreDetected** (int type) throws SQLException
public boolean **usesLocalFilePerTable** () throws SQLException
public boolean **usesLocalFiles** () throws SQLException
- ▲ public static final int **versionColumnNotPseudo** = 1
- ▲ public static final int **versionColumnPseudo** = 2
- ▲ public static final int **versionColumnUnknown** = 0

DataBuffer | java.awt.image

Object
  └DataBuffer   P

1.2 ○

protected	int	**banks**
* protected		**DataBuffer** (int dataType, int size)
* protected		**DataBuffer** (int dataType, int size, int numBanks)
* protected		**DataBuffer** (int dataType, int size, int numBanks, int[] offsets)
* protected		**DataBuffer** (int dataType, int size, int numBanks, int offset)
protected	int	**dataType**
public	int	**getDataType** ()

DataBuffer

△	public static	int	**getDataTypeSize** (int type)
	public	int	**getElem** (int i)
○	public abstract	int	**getElem** (int bank, int i)
	public	double	**getElemDouble** (int i)
	public	double	**getElemDouble** (int bank, int i)
	public	float	**getElemFloat** (int i)
	public	float	**getElemFloat** (int bank, int i)
	public	int	**getNumBanks** ()
	public	int	**getOffset** ()
	public	int[]	**getOffsets** ()
	public	int	**getSize** ()
	protected	int	**offset**
	protected	int[]	**offsets**
	public	void	**setElem** (int i, int val)
○	public abstract	void	**setElem** (int bank, int i, int val)
	public	void	**setElemDouble** (int i, double val)
	public	void	**setElemDouble** (int bank, int i, double val)
	public	void	**setElemFloat** (int i, float val)
	public	void	**setElemFloat** (int bank, int i, float val)
	protected	int	**size**
▲	public static final	int	**TYPE_BYTE** = 0
▲	public static final	int	**TYPE_DOUBLE** = 5
▲	public static final	int	**TYPE_FLOAT** = 4
▲	public static final	int	**TYPE_INT** = 3
▲	public static final	int	**TYPE_SHORT** = 2
▲	public static final	int	**TYPE_UNDEFINED** = 32
▲	public static final	int	**TYPE_USHORT** = 1

DataBufferByte
java.awt.image
P

Object
1.2 ○ └DataBuffer [1]
1.2 ●   └DataBufferByte

1	*26 inherited members from DataBuffer not shown*		
✱	public		**DataBufferByte** (int size)
✱	public		**DataBufferByte** (byte[] dataArray, int size)
✱	public		**DataBufferByte** (byte[][] dataArray, int size)
✱	public		**DataBufferByte** (int size, int numBanks)
✱	public		**DataBufferByte** (byte[] dataArray, int size, int offset)
✱	public		**DataBufferByte** (byte[][] dataArray, int size, int[] offsets)
	public	byte[][]	**getBankData** ()
	public	byte[]	**getData** ()
	public	byte[]	**getData** (int bank)
1	public	int	**getElem** (int i)
1	public	int	**getElem** (int bank, int i)
1	public	void	**setElem** (int i, int val)
1	public	void	**setElem** (int bank, int i, int val)

DataBufferInt
java.awt.image
P

Object
1.2 ○ └DataBuffer [1]
1.2 ●   └DataBufferInt

1	*26 inherited members from DataBuffer not shown*		
✱	public		**DataBufferInt** (int size)
✱	public		**DataBufferInt** (int size, int numBanks)
✱	public		**DataBufferInt** (int[] dataArray, int size)
✱	public		**DataBufferInt** (int[][] dataArray, int size)
✱	public		**DataBufferInt** (int[] dataArray, int size, int offset)
✱	public		**DataBufferInt** (int[][] dataArray, int size, int[] offsets)
	public	int[][]	**getBankData** ()
	public	int[]	**getData** ()
	public	int[]	**getData** (int bank)
1	public	int	**getElem** (int i)
1	public	int	**getElem** (int bank, int i)
1	public	void	**setElem** (int i, int val)
1	public	void	**setElem** (int bank, int i, int val)

Class   *Interface*   —extends   - - -implements   ○ abstract   ● final   △ static   ▲ static final   ✱ constructor   x x—inherited   x **x**—declared   **x x**—overridden

DataBufferShort

java.awt.image

```
        Object                                                              P
1.2 ○   └DataBuffer 1
1.2 ●     └DataBufferShort
```

	1	*26 inherited members from DataBuffer not shown*		
*		public.....................	**DataBufferShort** (int size)	
*		public.....................	**DataBufferShort** (int size, int numBanks)	
*		public.....................	**DataBufferShort** (short[] dataArray, int size)	
*		public.....................	**DataBufferShort** (short[][] dataArray, int size)	
*		public.....................	**DataBufferShort** (short[] dataArray, int size, int offset)	
*		public.....................	**DataBufferShort** (short[][] dataArray, int size, int[] offsets)	
		public............ short[][]	**getBankData** ()	
		public............ short[]	**getData** ()	
		public............ short[]	**getData** (int bank)	
	1	public............ **int**	**getElem** (int i)	
	1	public............ **int**	**getElem** (int bank, int i)	
	1	public............ **void**	**setElem** (int i, int val)	
	1	public............ **void**	**setElem** (int bank, int i, int val)	

DataBufferUShort

java.awt.image

```
        Object                                                              P
1.2 ○   └DataBuffer 1
1.2 ●     └DataBufferUShort
```

	1	*26 inherited members from DataBuffer not shown*		
*		public.....................	**DataBufferUShort** (int size)	
*		public.....................	**DataBufferUShort** (int size, int numBanks)	
*		public.....................	**DataBufferUShort** (short[] dataArray, int size)	
*		public.....................	**DataBufferUShort** (short[][] dataArray, int size)	
*		public.....................	**DataBufferUShort** (short[] dataArray, int size, int offset)	
*		public.....................	**DataBufferUShort** (short[][] dataArray, int size, int[] offsets)	
		public............ short[][]	**getBankData** ()	
		public............ short[]	**getData** ()	
		public............ short[]	**getData** (int bank)	
	1	public............ **int**	**getElem** (int i)	
	1	public............ **int**	**getElem** (int bank, int i)	
	1	public............ **void**	**setElem** (int i, int val)	
	1	public............ **void**	**setElem** (int bank, int i, int val)	

DataFlavor

java.awt.datatransfer

```
        Object 1                                                            P
1.1     └DataFlavor - - - - - - - - - - - - - - - - - - - - - - - - - - java.io.Externalizable 2 (java.io.Serializable), Cloneable
```

	1	public............ **Object**	**clone** () throws CloneNotSupportedException	
1.2 *		public.....................	**DataFlavor** ()	
1.2 *		public.....................	**DataFlavor** (String mimeType) throws ClassNotFoundException	
*		public.....................	**DataFlavor** (Class representationClass, String humanPresentableName)	
*		public.....................	**DataFlavor** (String mimeType, String humanPresentableName)	
1.2 *		public.....................	**DataFlavor** (String mimeType, String humanPresentableName, ClassLoader classLoader) throws ClassNotFoundException	
		public............ boolean	**equals** (DataFlavor dataFlavor)	
	1	public............ **boolean**	**equals** (Object o)	
1.2		public............ boolean	**equals** (String s)	
		public............ String	**getHumanPresentableName** ()	
		public............ String	**getMimeType** ()	
1.2		public............ String	**getParameter** (String paramName)	
1.2		public............ String	**getPrimaryType** ()	
		public............ Class	**getRepresentationClass** ()	
1.2		public............ String	**getSubType** ()	
1.2		public............ boolean	**isFlavorJavaFileListType** ()	
1.2		public............ boolean	**isFlavorRemoteObjectType** ()	
1.2		public............ boolean	**isFlavorSerializedObjectType** ()	
	●	public final .... boolean	**isMimeTypeEqual** (DataFlavor dataFlavor)	
		public............ boolean	**isMimeTypeEqual** (String mimeType)	
1.2		public............ boolean	**isMimeTypeSerializedObject** ()	
1.2		public............ boolean	**isRepresentationClassInputStream** ()	
1.2		public............ boolean	**isRepresentationClassRemote** ()	

DataFlavor

1.2		public .... boolean	**isRepresentationClassSerializable** ()
1.2	▲	public static final ... DataFlavor	**javaFileListFlavor**
1.2	▲	public static final .... String	**javaJVMLocalObjectMimeType** = "application/x-java-jvm-local-objectref"
1.2	▲	public static final .... String	**javaRemoteObjectMimeType** = "application/x-java-remote-object"
1.2	▲	public static final .... String	**javaSerializedObjectMimeType** = "application/x-java-serialized-object"
D		protected .... String	**normalizeMimeType** (String mimeType)
D		protected .... String	**normalizeMimeTypeParameter** (String parameterName, String parameterValue)
	▲	public static final ... DataFlavor	**plainTextFlavor**
1.2	2	public synchronized .... void	**readExternal** (*java.io.ObjectInput* is) throws java.io.IOException, ClassNotFoundException
		public.........................void	**setHumanPresentableName** (String humanPresentableName)
	▲	public static final ... DataFlavor	**stringFlavor**
1.2	▲	protected static final ..... Class	**tryToLoadClass** (String className, ClassLoader fallback) throws ClassNotFoundException
1.2	2	public synchronized .... void	**writeExternal** (*java.io.ObjectOutput* os) throws java.io.IOException

---

DataFormatException · java.util.zip
P

```
Object
└ Throwable - - - - - - - - - - - - - - - - - - - - - - - - - - - java.io.Serializable
   └ Exception
      └ DataFormatException
```
1.1

*		public...........................	**DataFormatException** ()
*		public...........................	**DataFormatException** (String s)

DatagramPacket · java.net
P

```
Object
● └ DatagramPacket
```

*		public...........................	**DatagramPacket** (byte[] buf, int length)
1.2	*	public...........................	**DatagramPacket** (byte[] buf, int offset, int length)
*		public...........................	**DatagramPacket** (byte[] buf, int length, InetAddress address, int port)
1.2	*	public...........................	**DatagramPacket** (byte[] buf, int offset, int length, InetAddress address, int port)
		public synchronized .... InetAddress	**getAddress** ()
		public synchronized ..... byte[]	**getData** ()
		public synchronized .... int	**getLength** ()
1.2		public synchronized .... int	**getOffset** ()
		public synchronized .... int	**getPort** ()
1.1		public synchronized ...... void	**setAddress** (InetAddress iaddr)
1.1		public synchronized ...... void	**setData** (byte[] buf)
1.2		public synchronized ...... void	**setData** (byte[] buf, int offset, int length)
1.1		public synchronized ...... void	**setLength** (int length)
1.1		public synchronized ...... void	**setPort** (int iport)

DatagramSocket · java.net
P

```
Object
└ DatagramSocket
```

		public........................void	**close** ()
1.2		public........................void	**connect** (InetAddress address, int port)
	*	public...........................	**DatagramSocket** () throws SocketException
	*	public...........................	**DatagramSocket** (int port) throws SocketException
1.1	*	public...........................	**DatagramSocket** (int port, InetAddress laddr) throws SocketException
1.2		public........................void	**disconnect** ()
1.2		public............... InetAddress	**getInetAddress** ()
1.1		public............... InetAddress	**getLocalAddress** ()
		public.........................int	**getLocalPort** ()
1.2		public.........................int	**getPort** ()
1.2		public synchronized .... int	**getReceiveBufferSize** () throws SocketException
1.2		public synchronized .... int	**getSendBufferSize** () throws SocketException
1.1		public synchronized .... int	**getSoTimeout** () throws SocketException
		public.........................void	**receive** (DatagramPacket p) throws java.io.IOException
		public.........................void	**send** (DatagramPacket p) throws java.io.IOException
1.2		public synchronized ...... void	**setReceiveBufferSize** (int size) throws SocketException
1.2		public synchronized ...... void	**setSendBufferSize** (int size) throws SocketException

---

Class *Interface* —extends - - -implements ○ abstract ● final △ static ▲ static final ✳ constructor x x—inherited x **x**—declared **x x**—overridden

| 1.1 | public synchronized ....void **setSoTimeout** (int timeout) throws SocketException |

DatagramSocketImpl

D

Object
                                                                 P

1.1 ○	└ DatagramSocketImpl - - - - - - - - - - - - - - - - - - - *SocketOptions [1]*
○ protected abstract ....void **bind** (int lport, InetAddress laddr) throws SocketException
○ protected abstract ....void **close** ()
○ protected abstract ....void **create** () throws SocketException
✱ public.............................. **DatagramSocketImpl** ()
protected java.io.FileDescriptor **fd**
protected java.io.FileDescriptor **getFileDescriptor** ()
protected ....int **getLocalPort** ()
○ 1 public abstract ....Object **getOption** (int) throws SocketException
1.2 ○ protected abstract ....int **getTimeToLive** () throws java.io.IOException
D ○ protected abstract .... byte **getTTL** () throws java.io.IOException
○ protected abstract ....void **join** (InetAddress inetaddr) throws java.io.IOException
○ protected abstract ....void **leave** (InetAddress inetaddr) throws java.io.IOException
protected ....int **localPort**
○ protected abstract ....int **peek** (InetAddress i) throws java.io.IOException
○ protected abstract ....void **receive** (DatagramPacket p) throws java.io.IOException
○ protected abstract ....void **send** (DatagramPacket p) throws java.io.IOException
○ 1 public abstract ....void **setOption** (int, Object) throws SocketException
1.2 ○ protected abstract ....void **setTimeToLive** (int ttl) throws java.io.IOException
D ○ protected abstract ....void **setTTL** (byte ttl) throws java.io.IOException

DataInput

DataInput

public.................... boolean **readBoolean** () throws IOException
public.................... byte **readByte** () throws IOException
public.................... char **readChar** () throws IOException
public....................double **readDouble** () throws IOException
public....................float **readFloat** () throws IOException
public....................void **readFully** (byte[] b) throws IOException
public....................void **readFully** (byte[] b, int off, int len) throws IOException
public....................int **readInt** () throws IOException
public.................... String **readLine** () throws IOException
public.................... long **readLong** () throws IOException
public....................short **readShort** () throws IOException
public....................int **readUnsignedByte** () throws IOException
public....................int **readUnsignedShort** () throws IOException
public.................... String **readUTF** () throws IOException
public....................int **skipBytes** (int n) throws IOException

DataInputStream

Object
      └ InputStream
          └ FilterInputStream [1]
              └ DataInputStream - - - - - - - - - - - - - - - - - - - *DataInput [2]*

1 public.........................int available () throws IOException
1 public.........................void close () throws IOException
✱ public......................... **DataInputStream** (InputStream in)
1 protected ....InputStream in
1 public synchronized ....void mark (int readlimit)
1 public.................... boolean markSupported ()
1 public.........................int read () throws IOException
● 1 public final .... **int read** (byte[] b) throws IOException
● 1 public final .... **int read** (byte[] b, int off, int len) throws IOException
● 2 public final .... boolean **readBoolean** () throws IOException
● 2 public final .... byte **readByte** () throws IOException
● 2 public final .... char **readChar** () throws IOException
● 2 public final ....double **readDouble** () throws IOException
● 2 public final ....float **readFloat** () throws IOException
● 2 public final ....void **readFully** (byte[] b) throws IOException
● 2 public final ....void **readFully** (byte[] b, int off, int len) throws IOException
● 2 public final ....int **readInt** () throws IOException

Classes

DataInputStream

D	●	2	public final	.... String	**readLine** () throws IOException
	●	2	public final	.... long	**readLong** () throws IOException
	●	2	public final	.... short	**readShort** () throws IOException
	●	2	public final	.... int	**readUnsignedByte** () throws IOException
	●	2	public final	.... int	**readUnsignedShort** () throws IOException
	●	2	public final	.... String	**readUTF** () throws IOException
	▲		public static final	.... String	**readUTF** (*DataInput* in) throws IOException
		1	public synchronized	.... void	reset () throws IOException
		1	public	.... long	skip (long n) throws IOException
	●	2	public final	.... int	**skipBytes** (int n) throws IOException

---

DataOutput   java.io

DataOutput

- -

public	.... void	**write** (byte[] b) throws IOException
public	.... void	**write** (int b) throws IOException
public	.... void	**write** (byte[] b, int off, int len) throws IOException
public	.... void	**writeBoolean** (boolean v) throws IOException
public	.... void	**writeByte** (int v) throws IOException
public	.... void	**writeBytes** (String s) throws IOException
public	.... void	**writeChar** (int v) throws IOException
public	.... void	**writeChars** (String s) throws IOException
public	.... void	**writeDouble** (double v) throws IOException
public	.... void	**writeFloat** (float v) throws IOException
public	.... void	**writeInt** (int v) throws IOException
public	.... void	**writeLong** (long v) throws IOException
public	.... void	**writeShort** (int v) throws IOException
public	.... void	**writeUTF** (String str) throws IOException

- -

DataOutputStream   java.io

```
     Object
○    └OutputStream
        └FilterOutputStream 1
           └DataOutputStream - - - - - - - - - - - - - - - - - - - DataOutput 2
```

		1	public	.... void	close () throws IOException
✳			public	.... **DataOutputStream** (OutputStream out)
		1	public	.... **void flush** () throws IOException
		1	protected	.... OutputStream	out
●			public final	.... int	**size** ()
		1	public	.... void	write (byte[] b) throws IOException
		1	public synchronized	...... **void write** (int b) throws IOException
		1	public synchronized	...... **void write** (byte[] b, int off, int len) throws IOException
	●	2	public final	.... void	**writeBoolean** (boolean v) throws IOException
	●	2	public final	.... void	**writeByte** (int v) throws IOException
	●	2	public final	.... void	**writeBytes** (String s) throws IOException
	●	2	public final	.... void	**writeChar** (int v) throws IOException
	●	2	public final	.... void	**writeChars** (String s) throws IOException
	●	2	public final	.... void	**writeDouble** (double v) throws IOException
	●	2	public final	.... void	**writeFloat** (float v) throws IOException
	●	2	public final	.... void	**writeInt** (int v) throws IOException
	●	2	public final	.... void	**writeLong** (long v) throws IOException
	●	2	public final	.... void	**writeShort** (int v) throws IOException
	●	2	public final	.... void	**writeUTF** (String str) throws IOException
			protected	.... int	**written**

DataTruncation   java.sql
                                                                                                   P○

```
       Object
       └Throwable - - - - - - - - - - - - - - - - - - - - - - - - - - java.io.Serializable
          └Exception
1.1          └SQLException 1
1.1             └SQLWarning 2
1.1                └DataTruncation
```

Class   *Interface*   —extends   - - -implements   ○ abstract   ● final   △ static   ▲ static final   ✳ constructor   x x—inherited   x **x**—declared   **x x**—overridden

298

*	public		**DataTruncation** (int index, boolean parameter, boolean read, int dataSize, int transferSize)
	public	int	**getDataSize** ()
1	public	int	getErrorCode ()
	public	int	**getIndex** ()
1	public	SQLException	getNextException ()
2	public	SQLWarning	getNextWarning ()
	public	boolean	**getParameter** ()
	public	boolean	**getRead** ()
1	public	String	getSQLState ()
	public	int	**getTransferSize** ()
1	public synchronized	void	setNextException (SQLException ex)
2	public	void	setNextWarning (SQLWarning w)

D

Date [1]   java.util

P

Object [1]
└─Date ------------------------------ *java.io.Serializable, Cloneable, Comparable* [2]

		public	boolean	**after** (Date when)
		public	boolean	**before** (Date when)
	1	public	**Object**	**clone** ()
1.2	2	public	int	**compareTo** (Object o)
1.2		public	int	**compareTo** (Date anotherDate)
	*	public		**Date** ()
D	*	public		**Date** (String s)
	*	public		**Date** (long date)
D	*	public		**Date** (int year, int month, int date)
D	*	public		**Date** (int year, int month, int date, int hrs, int min)
D	*	public		**Date** (int year, int month, int date, int hrs, int min, int sec)
	1	public	**boolean**	**equals** (Object obj)
D		public	int	**getDate** ()
D		public	int	**getDay** ()
D		public	int	**getHours** ()
D		public	int	**getMinutes** ()
D		public	int	**getMonth** ()
D		public	int	**getSeconds** ()
		public	long	**getTime** ()
D		public	int	**getTimezoneOffset** ()
D		public	int	**getYear** ()
	1	public	**int**	**hashCode** ()
D	△	public static	long	**parse** (String s)
D		public	void	**setDate** (int date)
D		public	void	**setHours** (int hours)
D		public	void	**setMinutes** (int minutes)
D		public	void	**setMonth** (int month)
D		public	void	**setSeconds** (int seconds)
		public	void	**setTime** (long time)
D		public	void	**setYear** (int year)
D		public	String	**toGMTString** ()
D		public	String	**toLocaleString** ()
	1	public	**String**	**toString** ()
D	△	public static	long	**UTC** (int year, int month, int date, int hrs, int min, int sec)

Classes

Date [2]   java.sql

P O

Object
└─java.util.Date [1] ------------------------ *java.io.Serializable, Cloneable, Comparable*
   └─Date

1.1

	1	public	boolean	after (java.util.Date when)
	1	public	boolean	before (java.util.Date when)
	1	public	Object	clone ()
1.2	1	public	int	compareTo (Object o)
1.2	1	public	int	compareTo (java.util.Date anotherDate)
	*	public		**Date** (long date)
D	*	public		**Date** (int year, int month, int day)
	1	public	boolean	equals (Object obj)
D	1	public	**int**	**getHours** ()
D	1	public	**int**	**getMinutes** ()
D	1	public	**int**	**getSeconds** ()

Date⊘

	1	public	long	**getTime** ()	
	1	public	int	**hashCode** ()	
D	1	public	**void**	**setHours** (int i)	
D	1	public	**void**	**setMinutes** (int i)	
D	1	public	**void**	**setSeconds** (int i)	
	1	public	**void**	**setTime** (long date)	
	1	public	**String**	**toString** ()	
△		public static	Date	**valueOf** (String s)	

DateFormat   java.text

```
        Object 1                                                          P
1.1 ○     └─ Format 2 ------------------------------- java.io.Serializable, Cloneable
1.1 ○          └─ DateFormat
```

▲		public static final	int	**AM_PM_FIELD** = 14	
		protected	java.util.Calendar	**calendar**	
	2	public	**Object**	**clone** ()	
▲		public static final	int	**DATE_FIELD** = 3	
✳		protected		**DateFormat** ()	
▲		public static final	int	**DAY_OF_WEEK_FIELD** = 9	
▲		public static final	int	**DAY_OF_WEEK_IN_MONTH_FIELD** = 11	
▲		public static final	int	**DAY_OF_YEAR_FIELD** = 10	
▲		public static final	int	**DEFAULT** = 2	
	1	public	**boolean**	**equals** (Object obj)	
▲		public static final	int	**ERA_FIELD** = 0	
●	2	public final	String	**format** (Object obj)	
●		public final	String	**format** (java.util.Date date)	
●	2	public final	**StringBuffer**	**format** (Object obj, StringBuffer toAppendTo, FieldPosition fieldPosition)	
○		public abstract	StringBuffer	**format** (java.util.Date date, StringBuffer toAppendTo, FieldPosition fieldPosition)	
▲		public static final	int	**FULL** = 0	
△		public static	java.util.Locale[]	**getAvailableLocales** ()	
		public	java.util.Calendar	**getCalendar** ()	
▲		public static final	DateFormat	**getDateInstance** ()	
▲		public static final	DateFormat	**getDateInstance** (int style)	
▲		public static final	DateFormat	**getDateInstance** (int style, java.util.Locale aLocale)	
▲		public static final	DateFormat	**getDateTimeInstance** ()	
▲		public static final	DateFormat	**getDateTimeInstance** (int dateStyle, int timeStyle)	
▲		public static final	DateFormat	**getDateTimeInstance** (int dateStyle, int timeStyle, java.util.Locale aLocale)	
▲		public static final	DateFormat	**getInstance** ()	
		public	NumberFormat	**getNumberFormat** ()	
▲		public static final	DateFormat	**getTimeInstance** ()	
▲		public static final	DateFormat	**getTimeInstance** (int style)	
▲		public static final	DateFormat	**getTimeInstance** (int style, java.util.Locale aLocale)	
		public	java.util.TimeZone	**getTimeZone** ()	
	1	public	**int**	**hashCode** ()	
▲		public static final	int	**HOUR0_FIELD** = 16	
▲		public static final	int	**HOUR1_FIELD** = 15	
▲		public static final	int	**HOUR_OF_DAY0_FIELD** = 5	
▲		public static final	int	**HOUR_OF_DAY1_FIELD** = 4	
		public	boolean	**isLenient** ()	
▲		public static final	int	**LONG** = 1	
▲		public static final	int	**MEDIUM** = 2	
▲		public static final	int	**MILLISECOND_FIELD** = 8	
▲		public static final	int	**MINUTE_FIELD** = 6	
▲		public static final	int	**MONTH_FIELD** = 2	
		protected	NumberFormat	**numberFormat**	
		public	java.util.Date	**parse** (String text) throws ParseException	
○		public abstract	java.util.Date	**parse** (String text, ParsePosition pos)	
	2	public	Object	**parseObject** (String source) throws ParseException	
	2	public	**Object**	**parseObject** (String source, ParsePosition pos)	
▲		public static final	int	**SECOND_FIELD** = 7	
		public	void	**setCalendar** (java.util.Calendar newCalendar)	
		public	void	**setLenient** (boolean lenient)	
		public	void	**setNumberFormat** (NumberFormat newNumberFormat)	
		public	void	**setTimeZone** (java.util.TimeZone zone)	
▲		public static final	int	**SHORT** = 3	
▲		public static final	int	**TIMEZONE_FIELD** = 17	
▲		public static final	int	**WEEK_OF_MONTH_FIELD** = 13	
▲		public static final	int	**WEEK_OF_YEAR_FIELD** = 12	

Class   *Interface*   —extends   - - -implements   ○ abstract   ● final   △ static   ▲ static final   ✳ constructor   x x—inherited   x **x**—declared   x **x**—overridden

▲   public static final . . . . int **YEAR_FIELD** = 1

DebugGraphics — DateFormatSymbols

DateFormatSymbols   java.text

Object [1]

1.1   └DateFormatSymbols - *java.io.Serializable*, *Cloneable*   P

1	public . . . . **Object**	**clone** ()
*	public	**DateFormatSymbols** ()
*	public	**DateFormatSymbols** (java.util.Locale locale)
1	public . . . . **boolean**	**equals** (Object obj)
	public . . . . String[]	**getAmPmStrings** ()
	public . . . . String[]	**getEras** ()
	public . . . . String	**getLocalPatternChars** ()
	public . . . . String[]	**getMonths** ()
	public . . . . String[]	**getShortMonths** ()
	public . . . . String[]	**getShortWeekdays** ()
	public . . . . String[]	**getWeekdays** ()
	public . . . . String[][]	**getZoneStrings** ()
1	public . . . . **int**	**hashCode** ()
	public . . . . void	**setAmPmStrings** (String[] newAmpms)
	public . . . . void	**setEras** (String[] newEras)
	public . . . . void	**setLocalPatternChars** (String newLocalPatternChars)
	public . . . . void	**setMonths** (String[] newMonths)
	public . . . . void	**setShortMonths** (String[] newShortMonths)
	public . . . . void	**setShortWeekdays** (String[] newShortWeekdays)
	public . . . . void	**setWeekdays** (String[] newWeekdays)
	public . . . . void	**setZoneStrings** (String[][] newZoneStrings)

DebugGraphics   javax.swing

Object

○   └java.awt.Graphics [1]

1.2   └DebugGraphics

▲	public static final . . . . int	**BUFFERED_OPTION** = 4
1	public . . . . **void**	**clearRect** (int x, int y, int width, int height)
1	public . . . . **void**	**clipRect** (int x, int y, int width, int height)
1	public . . . . **void**	**copyArea** (int x, int y, int width, int height, int destX, int destY)
1	public . . . . . . **java.awt.Graphics**	**create** ()
1	public . . . . . . **java.awt.Graphics**	**create** (int x, int y, int width, int height)
*	public	**DebugGraphics** ()
*	public	**DebugGraphics** (java.awt.Graphics graphics)
*	public	**DebugGraphics** (java.awt.Graphics graphics, JComponent component)
1	public . . . . **void**	**dispose** ()
1	public . . . . **void**	**draw3DRect** (int x, int y, int width, int height, boolean raised)
1	public . . . . **void**	**drawArc** (int x, int y, int width, int height, int startAngle, int arcAngle)
1	public . . . . **void**	**drawBytes** (byte[] data, int offset, int length, int x, int y)
1	public . . . . **void**	**drawChars** (char[] data, int offset, int length, int x, int y)
1	public . . . . **boolean**	**drawImage** (java.awt.Image img, int x, int y, *java.awt.image.ImageObserver* observer)
1	public . . . . **boolean**	**drawImage** (java.awt.Image img, int x, int y, java.awt.Color bgcolor, *java.awt.image.ImageObserver* observer)
1	public . . . . **boolean**	**drawImage** (java.awt.Image img, int x, int y, int width, int height, *java.awt.image.ImageObserver* observer)
1	public . . . . **boolean**	**drawImage** (java.awt.Image img, int x, int y, int width, int height, java.awt.Color bgcolor, *java.awt.image.ImageObserver* observer)
1	public . . . . **boolean**	**drawImage** (java.awt.Image img, int dx1, int dy1, int dx2, int dy2, int sx1, int sy1, int sx2, int sy2, *java.awt.image.ImageObserver* observer)
1	public . . . . **boolean**	**drawImage** (java.awt.Image img, int dx1, int dy1, int dx2, int dy2, int sx1, int sy1, int sx2, int sy2, java.awt.Color bgcolor, *java.awt.image.ImageObserver* observer)
1	public . . . . **void**	**drawLine** (int x1, int y1, int x2, int y2)
1	public . . . . **void**	**drawOval** (int x, int y, int width, int height)
1	public . . . . void	drawPolygon (java.awt.Polygon p)
1	public . . . . **void**	**drawPolygon** (int[] xPoints, int[] yPoints, int nPoints)
1	public . . . . **void**	**drawPolyline** (int[] xPoints, int[] yPoints, int nPoints)
1	public . . . . **void**	**drawRect** (int x, int y, int width, int height)
1	public . . . . **void**	**drawRoundRect** (int x, int y, int width, int height, int arcWidth, int arcHeight)
1	public . . . . **void**	**drawString** (String aString, int x, int y)
1	public . . . . **void**	**drawString** (*java.text.AttributedCharacterIterator* iterator, int x, int y)
1	public . . . . **void**	**fill3DRect** (int x, int y, int width, int height, boolean raised)

DebugGraphics

1	public	**void**	**fillArc**	(int x, int y, int width, int height, int startAngle, int arcAngle)
1	public	**void**	**fillOval**	(int x, int y, int width, int height)
1	public	void	fillPolygon	(java.awt.Polygon p)
1	public	**void**	**fillPolygon**	(int[] xPoints, int[] yPoints, int nPoints)
1	public	**void**	**fillRect**	(int x, int y, int width, int height)
1	public	**void**	**fillRoundRect**	(int x, int y, int width, int height, int arcWidth, int arcHeight)
1	public	void	finalize	()
▲	public static final	int	**FLASH_OPTION**	= 2
△	public static	java.awt.Color	**flashColor**	()
△	public static	int	**flashCount**	()
△	public static	int	**flashTime**	()
1	public	*java.awt.Shape*	**getClip**	()
1	public	**java.awt.Rectangle**	**getClipBounds**	()
1	public	java.awt.Rectangle	getClipBounds	(java.awt.Rectangle r)
1	public	**java.awt.Color**	**getColor**	()
	public	int	**getDebugOptions**	()
1	public	**java.awt.Font**	**getFont**	()
1	public	**java.awt.FontMetrics**	**getFontMetrics**	()
1	public	**java.awt.FontMetrics**	**getFontMetrics**	(java.awt.Font f)
1	public	boolean	hitClip	(int x, int y, int width, int height)
	public	boolean	**isDrawingBuffer**	()
▲	public static final	int	**LOG_OPTION**	= 1
△	public static	java.io.PrintStream	**logStream**	()
▲	public static final	int	**NONE_OPTION**	= -1
1	public	**void**	**setClip**	(*java.awt.Shape* clip)
1	public	**void**	**setClip**	(int x, int y, int width, int height)
1	public	**void**	**setColor**	(java.awt.Color aColor)
	public	void	**setDebugOptions**	(int options)
△	public static	void	**setFlashColor**	(java.awt.Color flashColor)
△	public static	void	**setFlashCount**	(int flashCount)
△	public static	void	**setFlashTime**	(int flashTime)
1	public	**void**	**setFont**	(java.awt.Font aFont)
△	public static	void	**setLogStream**	(java.io.PrintStream stream)
1	public	**void**	**setPaintMode**	()
1	public	**void**	**setXORMode**	(java.awt.Color aColor)
1	public	String	toString	()
1	public	**void**	**translate**	(int x, int y)

DecimalFormat — java.text

P

```
        Object
1.1 O   └Format¹ - - - - - - - - - - - - - - - - - - - - - - - - - - - - java.io.Serializable, Cloneable
1.1 O     └NumberFormat²
1.1         └DecimalFormat
```

	public	void	**applyLocalizedPattern**	(String pattern)
	public	void	**applyPattern**	(String pattern)
2	public	**Object**	**clone**	()
*	public		**DecimalFormat**	()
*	public		**DecimalFormat**	(String pattern)
*	public		**DecimalFormat**	(String pattern, DecimalFormatSymbols symbols)
2	public	**boolean**	**equals**	(Object obj)
● 2	public final	String	format	(double number)
● 1	public final	String	format	(Object obj)
● 2	public final	String	format	(long number)
2	public	**StringBuffer**	**format**	(double number, StringBuffer result, FieldPosition fieldPosition)
● 2	public final	StringBuffer	format	(Object number, StringBuffer toAppendTo, FieldPosition pos)
2	public	**StringBuffer**	**format**	(long number, StringBuffer result, FieldPosition fieldPosition)
△ 2	public static	java.util.Locale[]	getAvailableLocales	()
▲ 2	public static final	NumberFormat	getCurrencyInstance	()
△ 2	public static	NumberFormat	getCurrencyInstance	(java.util.Locale inLocale)
	public	DecimalFormatSymbols	**getDecimalFormatSymbols**	()
	public	int	**getGroupingSize**	()
▲ 2	public static final	NumberFormat	getInstance	()
△ 2	public static	NumberFormat	getInstance	(java.util.Locale inLocale)
2	public	int	getMaximumFractionDigits	()
2	public	int	getMaximumIntegerDigits	()
2	public	int	getMinimumFractionDigits	()
2	public	int	getMinimumIntegerDigits	()

Class *Interface* —extends - - -implements O abstract ● final △ static ▲ static final ✳ constructor x x—inherited x **x**—declared **x x**—overridden

	public	int	**getMultiplier** ()
	public	String	**getNegativePrefix** ()
	public	String	**getNegativeSuffix** ()
▲ 2	public static final		getNumberInstance ()
		NumberFormat	
△ 2	public static	NumberFormat	getNumberInstance (java.util.Locale inLocale)
▲ 2	public static final		getPercentInstance ()
		NumberFormat	
△ 2	public static	NumberFormat	getPercentInstance (java.util.Locale inLocale)
	public	String	**getPositivePrefix** ()
	public	String	**getPositiveSuffix** ()
2	public	**int**	**hashCode** ()
	public	boolean	**isDecimalSeparatorAlwaysShown** ()
2	public	boolean	isGroupingUsed ()
2	public	boolean	isParseIntegerOnly ()
2	public	Number	parse (String text) throws ParseException
2	public	**Number**	**parse** (String text, ParsePosition parsePosition)
1	public	Object	parseObject (String source) throws ParseException
● 2	public final	Object	parseObject (String source, ParsePosition parsePosition)
	public	void	**setDecimalFormatSymbols** (DecimalFormatSymbols newSymbols)
	public	void	**setDecimalSeparatorAlwaysShown** (boolean newValue)
	public	void	**setGroupingSize** (int newValue)
2	public	void	setGroupingUsed (boolean newValue)
2	public	**void**	**setMaximumFractionDigits** (int newValue)
2	public	**void**	**setMaximumIntegerDigits** (int newValue)
2	public	**void**	**setMinimumFractionDigits** (int newValue)
2	public	**void**	**setMinimumIntegerDigits** (int newValue)
	public	void	**setMultiplier** (int newValue)
	public	void	**setNegativePrefix** (String newValue)
	public	void	**setNegativeSuffix** (String newValue)
2	public	void	setParseIntegerOnly (boolean value)
	public	void	**setPositivePrefix** (String newValue)
	public	void	**setPositiveSuffix** (String newValue)
	public	String	**toLocalizedPattern** ()
	public	String	**toPattern** ()

DecimalFormatSymbols   java.text

Object[1]
P
1.1 ● └DecimalFormatSymbols ----------------- *Cloneable, java.io.Serializable*

1	public	**Object**	**clone** ()
*	public		**DecimalFormatSymbols** ()
*	public		**DecimalFormatSymbols** (java.util.Locale locale)
1	public	**boolean**	**equals** (Object obj)
1.2	public	String	**getCurrencySymbol** ()
	public	char	**getDecimalSeparator** ()
	public	char	**getDigit** ()
	public	char	**getGroupingSeparator** ()
	public	String	**getInfinity** ()
1.2	public	String	**getInternationalCurrencySymbol** ()
	public	char	**getMinusSign** ()
1.2	public	char	**getMonetaryDecimalSeparator** ()
	public	String	**getNaN** ()
	public	char	**getPatternSeparator** ()
	public	char	**getPercent** ()
	public	char	**getPerMill** ()
	public	char	**getZeroDigit** ()
1	public	**int**	**hashCode** ()
1.2	public	void	**setCurrencySymbol** (String currency)
	public	void	**setDecimalSeparator** (char decimalSeparator)
	public	void	**setDigit** (char digit)
	public	void	**setGroupingSeparator** (char groupingSeparator)
	public	void	**setInfinity** (String infinity)
1.2	public	void	**setInternationalCurrencySymbol** (String currency)
	public	void	**setMinusSign** (char minusSign)
1.2	public	void	**setMonetaryDecimalSeparator** (char sep)
	public	void	**setNaN** (String NaN)
	public	void	**setPatternSeparator** (char patternSeparator)
	public	void	**setPercent** (char percent)
	public	void	**setPerMill** (char perMill)
	public	void	**setZeroDigit** (char zeroDigit)

DefaultBoundedRangeModel

	DefaultBoundedRangeModel		javax.swing

Object[1]
1.2 └─DefaultBoundedRangeModel ------------- *BoundedRangeModel* [2], *java.io.Serializable*

2	public......................void	**addChangeListener** (*javax.swing.event.ChangeListener* l)
	protected transient.....javax↩	**changeEvent**
	.swing.event.ChangeEvent	
*	public...........................	**DefaultBoundedRangeModel** ()
*	public...........................	**DefaultBoundedRangeModel** (int value, int extent, int min, int max)
	protected...................void	**fireStateChanged** ()
2	public.............................int	**getExtent** ()
2	public.............................int	**getMaximum** ()
2	public.............................int	**getMinimum** ()
2	public.............................int	**getValue** ()
2	public....................boolean	**getValueIsAdjusting** ()
	protected..................javax↩	**listenerList**
	.swing.event.EventListenerList	
2	public......................void	**removeChangeListener** (*javax.swing.event.ChangeListener* l)
2	public......................void	**setExtent** (int n)
2	public......................void	**setMaximum** (int n)
2	public......................void	**setMinimum** (int n)
2	public......................void	**setRangeProperties** (int newValue, int newExtent, int newMin, int newMax, boolean adjusting)
2	public......................void	**setValue** (int n)
2	public......................void	**setValueIsAdjusting** (boolean b)
1	public..................**String**	**toString** ()

	DefaultButtonModel		javax.swing

Object
1.2 └─DefaultButtonModel --------------------- *ButtonModel* [1] (*java.awt.ItemSelectable* [2]), *java.io.Serializable*

	protected.................String	**actionCommand**
1	public......................void	**addActionListener** (*java.awt.event.ActionListener* l)
1	public......................void	**addChangeListener** (*javax.swing.event.ChangeListener* l)
1	public......................void	**addItemListener** (*java.awt.event.ItemListener* l)
▲	public static final.............int	**ARMED** = 1
	protected transient.....javax↩	**changeEvent**
	.swing.event.ChangeEvent	
*	public...........................	**DefaultButtonModel** ()
▲	public static final.............int	**ENABLED** = 8
	protected...................void	**fireActionPerformed** (java.awt.event.ActionEvent e)
	protected...................void	**fireItemStateChanged** (java.awt.event.ItemEvent e)
	protected...................void	**fireStateChanged** ()
1	public....................String	**getActionCommand** ()
1	public.............................int	**getMnemonic** ()
2	public.................Object[]	**getSelectedObjects** ()
	protected.........ButtonGroup	**group**
1	public....................boolean	**isArmed** ()
1	public....................boolean	**isEnabled** ()
1	public....................boolean	**isPressed** ()
1	public....................boolean	**isRollover** ()
1	public....................boolean	**isSelected** ()
	protected..................javax↩	**listenerList**
	.swing.event.EventListenerList	
	protected..........................int	**mnemonic**
▲	public static final.............int	**PRESSED** = 4
1	public......................void	**removeActionListener** (*java.awt.event.ActionListener* l)
1	public......................void	**removeChangeListener** (*javax.swing.event.ChangeListener* l)
1	public......................void	**removeItemListener** (*java.awt.event.ItemListener* l)
▲	public static final.............int	**ROLLOVER** = 16
▲	public static final.............int	**SELECTED** = 2
1	public......................void	**setActionCommand** (String actionCommand)
1	public......................void	**setArmed** (boolean b)
1	public......................void	**setEnabled** (boolean b)
1	public......................void	**setGroup** (ButtonGroup group)
1	public......................void	**setMnemonic** (int key)
1	public......................void	**setPressed** (boolean b)
1	public......................void	**setRollover** (boolean b)
1	public......................void	**setSelected** (boolean b)

Class   *Interface*   —extends   - - -implements   ○ abstract   ● final   △ static   ▲ static final   ✳ constructor   x x—inherited   x **x**—declared   **x x**—overridden

protected .int **stateMask**

DefaultCaret · javax.swing.text

Object
1.2 ○ └java.awt.geom.RectangularShape [1] - - - - - - - - *java.awt.Shape, Cloneable*
1.2 ○ └java.awt.geom.Rectangle2D [2]
  └java.awt.Rectangle [3] - - - - - - - - - - - - - - - - *java.awt.Shape, java.io.Serializable*
1.2   └DefaultCaret - *Caret [4], java.awt.event.FocusListener [5] (java.util.EventListener),*
    java.awt.event.MouseListener [6] (java.util.EventListener),
    java.awt.event.MouseMotionListener [7] (java.util.EventListener)

3			*40 inherited members from java.awt.Rectangle not shown*
2	public	void	add (java.awt.geom.Point2D pt)
2	public	void	add (java.awt.geom.Rectangle2D r)
2	public	void	add (double newx, double newy)
4	public	void	**addChangeListener** (*javax.swing.event.ChangeListener* l)
	protected	void	**adjustVisibility** (java.awt.Rectangle nloc)
	protected transient	javax↵ .swing.event.ChangeEvent	**changeEvent**
1	public	Object	clone ()
1	public	boolean	contains (java.awt.geom.Point2D p)
1	public	boolean	contains (java.awt.geom.Rectangle2D r)
2	public	boolean	contains (double x, double y)
2	public	boolean	contains (double x, double y, double w, double h)
	protected synchronized	void	**damage** (java.awt.Rectangle r)
*	public		**DefaultCaret** ()
4	public	void	**deinstall** (JTextComponent c)
	protected	void	**fireStateChanged** ()
5	public	void	**focusGained** (java.awt.event.FocusEvent e)
5	public	void	**focusLost** (java.awt.event.FocusEvent e)
4	public	int	**getBlinkRate** ()
1	public	double	getCenterX ()
1	public	double	getCenterY ()
●	protected final	JTextComponent	**getComponent** ()
4	public	int	**getDot** ()
1	public	java.awt.geom.Rectangle2D	getFrame ()
4	public	java.awt.Point	**getMagicCaretPosition** ()
4	public	int	**getMark** ()
1	public	double	getMaxX ()
1	public	double	getMaxY ()
1	public	double	getMinX ()
1	public	double	getMinY ()
2	public	*java.awt.geom.PathIterator*	getPathIterator (java.awt.geom.AffineTransform at)
2	public	*java.awt.geom.PathIterator*	getPathIterator (java.awt.geom.AffineTransform at, double flatness)
	protected	*Highlighter.HighlightPainter*	**getSelectionPainter** ()
2	public	int	hashCode ()
4	public	void	**install** (JTextComponent c)
△ 2	public static	void	intersect (java.awt.geom.Rectangle2D src1, java.awt.geom.Rectangle2D src2, java.awt.geom.Rectangle2D dest)
1	public	boolean	intersects (java.awt.geom.Rectangle2D r)
2	public	boolean	intersects (double x, double y, double w, double h)
2	public	boolean	intersectsLine (java.awt.geom.Line2D l)
2	public	boolean	intersectsLine (double x1, double y1, double x2, double y2)
4	public	boolean	**isSelectionVisible** ()
4	public	boolean	**isVisible** ()
	protected	javax↵ .swing.event.EventListenerList	**listenerList**
6	public	void	**mouseClicked** (java.awt.event.MouseEvent e)
7	public	void	**mouseDragged** (java.awt.event.MouseEvent e)
6	public	void	**mouseEntered** (java.awt.event.MouseEvent e)
6	public	void	**mouseExited** (java.awt.event.MouseEvent e)
7	public	void	**mouseMoved** (java.awt.event.MouseEvent e)
6	public	void	**mousePressed** (java.awt.event.MouseEvent e)
6	public	void	**mouseReleased** (java.awt.event.MouseEvent e)
	protected	void	**moveCaret** (java.awt.event.MouseEvent e)
4	public	void	**moveDot** (int dot)

D

Classes

DefaultCaret

	2	public........................int	outcode (java.awt.geom.Point2D p)
	4	public........................void	**paint** (java.awt.Graphics g)
		protected.....................void	**positionCaret** (java.awt.event.MouseEvent e)
	4	public........................void	**removeChangeListener** (*javax.swing.event.ChangeListener* l)
●		protected final synchronized .. ..void	**repaint** ()
	4	public........................void	**setBlinkRate** (int rate)
	4	public........................void	**setDot** (int dot)
	1	public........................void	setFrame (java.awt.geom.Rectangle2D r)
	1	public........................void	setFrame (java.awt.geom.Point2D loc, java.awt.geom.Dimension2D size)
	2	public........................void	setFrame (double x, double y, double w, double h)
	1	public........................void	setFrameFromCenter (java. awt. geom. Point2D center, java.awt.geom.Point2D corner)
	1	public........................void	setFrameFromCenter (double centerX, double centerY, double cornerX, double cornerY)
	1	public........................void	setFrameFromDiagonal (java.awt.geom.Point2D p1, java.awt.geom.Point2D p2)
	1	public........................void	setFrameFromDiagonal (double x1, double y1, double x2, double y2)
	4	public........................void	**setMagicCaretPosition** (java.awt.Point p)
	2	public........................void	setRect (java.awt.geom.Rectangle2D r)
	4	public........................void	**setSelectionVisible** (boolean vis)
	4	public........................void	**setVisible** (boolean e)
	3	public................**String**	**toString** ()
△	2	public static ....void	union (java.awt.geom.Rectangle2D src1, java.awt.geom.Rectangle2D src2, java.awt.geom.Rectangle2D dest)

DefaultCellEditor   javax.swing

Object
 └─DefaultCellEditor - *javax.swing.table.TableCellEditor [1] (CellEditor [2]), javax.swing↵ .tree.TreeCellEditor [3] (CellEditor [2]), java.io.Serializable*

1.2

	2	public........................void	**addCellEditorListener** (*javax.swing.event.CellEditorListener* l)
	2	public........................void	**cancelCellEditing** ()
		protected transient..... javax↵ .swing.event.ChangeEvent	**changeEvent**
		protected....................int	**clickCountToStart**
✳		public........................	**DefaultCellEditor** (JCheckBox x)
✳		public........................	**DefaultCellEditor** (JComboBox x)
✳		public........................	**DefaultCellEditor** (JTextField x)
		protected .. DefaultCellEditor↵ .EditorDelegate	**delegate**
		protected .... JComponent	**editorComponent**
		protected...................void	**fireEditingCanceled** ()
		protected...................void	**fireEditingStopped** ()
	2	public....................Object	**getCellEditorValue** ()
		public........................int	**getClickCountToStart** ()
		public.... java.awt.Component	**getComponent** ()
	1	public.... java.awt.Component	**getTableCellEditorComponent** (JTable table, Object value, boolean isSelected, int row, int column)
	3	public.... java.awt.Component	**getTreeCellEditorComponent** (JTree tree, Object value, boolean isSelected, boolean expanded, boolean leaf, int row)
	2	public................ boolean	**isCellEditable** (java.util.EventObject anEvent)
		protected .... javax↵ .swing.event.EventListenerList	**listenerList**
	2	public........................void	**removeCellEditorListener** (*javax.swing.event.CellEditorListener* l)
		public........................void	**setClickCountToStart** (int count)
	2	public................ boolean	**shouldSelectCell** (java.util.EventObject anEvent)
	2	public................ boolean	**stopCellEditing** ()

DefaultCellEditor.EditorDelegate   protected   javax.swing

Object
 └─DefaultCellEditor.EditorDelegate - - - - - - - - - - *java.awt.event.ActionListener [1] (java.util.EventListener), java.awt↵ .event.ItemListener [2] (java.util.EventListener), java.io.Serializable*

1.2

	1	public........................void	**actionPerformed** (java.awt.event.ActionEvent e)
		public........................void	**cancelCellEditing** ()
✳		protected	**EditorDelegate** ()
		public....................Object	**getCellEditorValue** ()

Class *Interface* ──extends - - -implements ○ abstract ● final △ static ▲ static final ✳ constructor x x──inherited x **x**──declared **x x**──overridden

```
       public.................boolean  isCellEditable (java.util.EventObject anEvent)
    2  public.....................void  itemStateChanged (java.awt.event.ItemEvent e)
       public.....................void  setValue (Object x)
       public.................boolean  startCellEditing (java.util.EventObject anEvent)
       public.................boolean  stopCellEditing ()
       protected...............Object  value
```

DefaultColorSelectionModel   javax.swing.colorchooser

```
       Object
1.2    └─DefaultColorSelectionModel -------------- ColorSelectionModel 1, java.io.Serializable
```

```
    1  public.....................void  addChangeListener (javax.swing.event.ChangeListener l)
       protected transient.....javax↵  changeEvent
       .swing.event.ChangeEvent
 *     public...........................  DefaultColorSelectionModel ()
 *     public...........................  DefaultColorSelectionModel (java.awt.Color color)
       protected..................void  fireStateChanged ()
    1  public............java.awt.Color  getSelectedColor ()
       protected................javax↵  listenerList
       .swing.event.EventListenerList
    1  public.....................void  removeChangeListener (javax.swing.event.ChangeListener l)
    1  public.....................void  setSelectedColor (java.awt.Color color)
```

DefaultComboBoxModel   javax.swing

```
       Object
1.2 ○  └─AbstractListModel 1 ---------------------- ListModel, java.io.Serializable
1.2         └─DefaultComboBoxModel --------------- MutableComboBoxModel 2 (ComboBoxModel 3 (ListModel)),
                                                       java.io.Serializable
```

```
    2  public.....................void  addElement (Object anObject)
    1  public.....................void  addListDataListener (javax.swing.event.ListDataListener l)
 *     public...........................  DefaultComboBoxModel ()
 *     public...........................  DefaultComboBoxModel (Object[] items)
 *     public...........................  DefaultComboBoxModel (java.util.Vector v)
    1  protected..................void  fireContentsChanged (Object source, int index0, int index1)
    1  protected..................void  fireIntervalAdded (Object source, int index0, int index1)
    1  protected..................void  fireIntervalRemoved (Object source, int index0, int index1)
    1  public...................Object  getElementAt (int index)
       public......................int  getIndexOf (Object anObject)
    3  public...................Object  getSelectedItem ()
    1  public......................int  getSize ()
    2  public.....................void  insertElementAt (Object anObject, int index)
    1  protected................javax↵  listenerList
       .swing.event.EventListenerList
       public.....................void  removeAllElements ()
    2  public.....................void  removeElement (Object anObject)
    2  public.....................void  removeElementAt (int index)
    1  public.....................void  removeListDataListener (javax.swing.event.ListDataListener l)
    3  public.....................void  setSelectedItem (Object anObject)
```

DefaultDesktopManager   javax.swing

```
       Object
1.2    └─DefaultDesktopManager ----------------- DesktopManager 1, java.io.Serializable
```

```
    1  public.....................void  activateFrame (JInternalFrame f)
    1  public.....................void  beginDraggingFrame (JComponent f)
    1  public.....................void  beginResizingFrame (JComponent f, int direction)
    1  public.....................void  closeFrame (JInternalFrame f)
    1  public.....................void  deactivateFrame (JInternalFrame f)
 *     public...........................  DefaultDesktopManager ()
    1  public.....................void  deiconifyFrame (JInternalFrame f)
    1  public.....................void  dragFrame (JComponent f, int newX, int newY)
    1  public.....................void  endDraggingFrame (JComponent f)
    1  public.....................void  endResizingFrame (JComponent f)
       protected .. java.awt.Rectangle  getBoundsForIconOf (JInternalFrame f)
       protected .. java.awt.Rectangle  getPreviousBounds (JInternalFrame f)
    1  public.....................void  iconifyFrame (JInternalFrame f)
```

DefaultDesktopManager

1	public	void	**maximizeFrame** (JInternalFrame f)
1	public	void	**minimizeFrame** (JInternalFrame f)
1	public	void	**openFrame** (JInternalFrame f)
	protected	void	**removeIconFor** (JInternalFrame f)
1	public	void	**resizeFrame** (JComponent f, int newX, int newY, int newWidth, int newHeight)
1	public	void	**setBoundsForFrame** (JComponent f, int newX, int newY, int newWidth, int newHeight)
	protected	void	**setPreviousBounds** (JInternalFrame f, java.awt.Rectangle r)
	protected	void	**setWasIcon** (JInternalFrame f, Boolean value)
	protected	boolean	**wasIcon** (JInternalFrame f)

D

DefaultEditorKit | javax.swing.text

Object
└ EditorKit[1] - *Cloneable, java.io.Serializable*   (1.2 O)
  └ DefaultEditorKit   (1.2)

▲	public static final	String	**backwardAction** = "caret-backward"
▲	public static final	String	**beepAction** = "beep"
▲	public static final	String	**beginAction** = "caret-begin"
▲	public static final	String	**beginLineAction** = "caret-begin-line"
▲	public static final	String	**beginParagraphAction** = "caret-begin-paragraph"
▲	public static final	String	**beginWordAction** = "caret-begin-word"
1	public	*Object*	**clone** ()
▲	public static final	String	**copyAction** = "copy-to-clipboard"
1	public	*Caret*	**createCaret** ()
1	public	*Document*	**createDefaultDocument** ()
▲	public static final	String	**cutAction** = "cut-to-clipboard"
✳	public		**DefaultEditorKit** ()
▲	public static final	String	**defaultKeyTypedAction** = "default-typed"
1	public	void	**deinstall** (javax.swing.JEditorPane c)
▲	public static final	String	**deleteNextCharAction** = "delete-next"
▲	public static final	String	**deletePrevCharAction** = "delete-previous"
▲	public static final	String	**downAction** = "caret-down"
▲	public static final	String	**endAction** = "caret-end"
▲	public static final	String	**endLineAction** = "caret-end-line"
▲	public static final	String	**EndOfLineStringProperty** = "__EndOfLine__"
▲	public static final	String	**endParagraphAction** = "caret-end-paragraph"
▲	public static final	String	**endWordAction** = "caret-end-word"
▲	public static final	String	**forwardAction** = "caret-forward"
1	public	*javax.swing.Action[]*	**getActions** ()
1	public	**String**	**getContentType** ()
1	public	*ViewFactory*	**getViewFactory** ()
▲	public static final	String	**insertBreakAction** = "insert-break"
▲	public static final	String	**insertContentAction** = "insert-content"
▲	public static final	String	**insertTabAction** = "insert-tab"
1	public	void	**install** (javax.swing.JEditorPane c)
▲	public static final	String	**nextWordAction** = "caret-next-word"
▲	public static final	String	**pageDownAction** = "page-down"
▲	public static final	String	**pageUpAction** = "page-up"
▲	public static final	String	**pasteAction** = "paste-from-clipboard"
▲	public static final	String	**previousWordAction** = "caret-previous-word"
1	public	**void**	**read** (java.io.InputStream in, *Document* doc, int pos) throws java.io.IOException, BadLocationException
1	public	**void**	**read** (java.io.Reader in, *Document* doc, int pos) throws java.io.IOException, BadLocationException
▲	public static final	String	**readOnlyAction** = "set-read-only"
▲	public static final	String	**selectAllAction** = "select-all"
▲	public static final	String	**selectionBackwardAction** = "selection-backward"
▲	public static final	String	**selectionBeginAction** = "selection-begin"
▲	public static final	String	**selectionBeginLineAction** = "selection-begin-line"
▲	public static final	String	**selectionBeginParagraphAction** = "selection-begin-paragraph"
▲	public static final	String	**selectionBeginWordAction** = "selection-begin-word"
▲	public static final	String	**selectionDownAction** = "selection-down"
▲	public static final	String	**selectionEndAction** = "selection-end"
▲	public static final	String	**selectionEndLineAction** = "selection-end-line"
▲	public static final	String	**selectionEndParagraphAction** = "selection-end-paragraph"
▲	public static final	String	**selectionEndWordAction** = "selection-end-word"
▲	public static final	String	**selectionForwardAction** = "selection-forward"
▲	public static final	String	**selectionNextWordAction** = "selection-next-word"
▲	public static final	String	**selectionPreviousWordAction** = "selection-previous-word"

Class *Interface* —extends - - -implements O abstract ● final △ static ▲ static final ✳ constructor x x—inherited x **x**—declared **x x**—overridden

▲	public static final .... String	**selectionUpAction**	= "selection-up"
▲	public static final .... String	**selectLineAction**	= "select-line"
▲	public static final .... String	**selectParagraphAction**	= "select-paragraph"
▲	public static final .... String	**selectWordAction**	= "select-word"
▲	public static final .... String	**upAction**	= "caret-up"
▲	public static final .... String	**writableAction**	= "set-writable"
1	public .... **void**	**write** (java. io. OutputStream out, *Document* doc, int pos, int len)
		throws java.io.IOException, BadLocationException
1	public .... **void**	**write** (java. io. Writer out, *Document* doc, int pos, int len)
		throws java.io.IOException, BadLocationException

DefaultEditorKit.BeepAction javax.swing.text

Object
    1.2 ○   └ javax.swing.AbstractAction [1] - - - - - - - - - - - - - - *javax.swing.Action (java.awt.event.ActionListener*
                                                   (java.util.EventListener)), *Cloneable, java.io.Serializable*
    1.2 ○   └ TextAction [2]
    1.2   └ DefaultEditorKit.BeepAction

	1	public .... **void**	**actionPerformed** (java.awt.event.ActionEvent e)
	1	public synchronized .... void	addPropertyChangeListener (*java.beans.PropertyChangeListener* listener)
▲	2	public static final	augmentList (*javax.swing.Action[]* list1, *javax.swing.Action[]* list2)
		.... *javax.swing.Action[]*	
*		public	**BeepAction** ()
	1	protected . javax.swing.event ↵	changeSupport
		.SwingPropertyChangeSupport	
	1	protected .... Object	clone () throws CloneNotSupportedException
	1	protected .... boolean	enabled
	1	protected .... void	firePropertyChange (String propertyName, Object oldValue, Object newValue)
●	2	protected final..................	getFocusedComponent ()
		.... JTextComponent	
●	2	protected final..................	getTextComponent (java.awt.event.ActionEvent e)
		.... JTextComponent	
	1	public .... Object	getValue (String key)
	1	public .... boolean	isEnabled ()
	1	public synchronized .... void	putValue (String key, Object newValue)
	1	public synchronized .... void	removePropertyChangeListener (*java.beans.PropertyChangeListener* listener)
	1	public synchronized .... void	setEnabled (boolean newValue)

DefaultEditorKit.CopyAction javax.swing.text

Object
    1.2 ○   └ javax.swing.AbstractAction [1] - - - - - - - - - - - - - - *javax.swing.Action (java.awt.event.ActionListener*
                                                   (java.util.EventListener)), *Cloneable, java.io.Serializable*
    1.2 ○   └ TextAction [2]
    1.2   └ DefaultEditorKit.CopyAction

	1	public .... **void**	**actionPerformed** (java.awt.event.ActionEvent e)
	1	public synchronized .... void	addPropertyChangeListener (*java.beans.PropertyChangeListener* listener)
▲	2	public static final	augmentList (*javax.swing.Action[]* list1, *javax.swing.Action[]* list2)
		.... *javax.swing.Action[]*	
	1	protected . javax.swing.event ↵	changeSupport
		.SwingPropertyChangeSupport	
	1	protected .... Object	clone () throws CloneNotSupportedException
*		public	**CopyAction** ()
	1	protected .... boolean	enabled
	1	protected .... void	firePropertyChange (String propertyName, Object oldValue, Object newValue)
●	2	protected final..................	getFocusedComponent ()
		.... JTextComponent	
●	2	protected final..................	getTextComponent (java.awt.event.ActionEvent e)
		.... JTextComponent	
	1	public .... Object	getValue (String key)
	1	public .... boolean	isEnabled ()
	1	public synchronized .... void	putValue (String key, Object newValue)
	1	public synchronized .... void	removePropertyChangeListener (*java.beans.PropertyChangeListener* listener)
	1	public synchronized .... void	setEnabled (boolean newValue)

Classes

DefaultEditorKit.CutAction

		DefaultEditorKit.CutAction	javax.swing.text

```
        Object
1.2 ○   └javax.swing.AbstractAction¹ - - - - - - - - - - - - - javax.swing.Action (java.awt.event.ActionListener
                                                              (java.util.EventListener)), Cloneable, java.io.Serializable
1.2 ○       └TextAction²
1.2           └DefaultEditorKit.CutAction
```

	1	public **void**	**actionPerformed** (java.awt.event.ActionEvent e)
	1	public synchronized void	addPropertyChangeListener (*java.beans.PropertyChangeListener* listener)
▲	2	public static final *javax.swing.Action[]*	augmentList (*javax.swing.Action[]* list1, *javax.swing.Action[]* list2)
	1	protected . java.swing.event↩ .SwingPropertyChangeSupport	changeSupport
	1	protected Object	clone () throws CloneNotSupportedException
✳		public	**CutAction** ()
	1	protected boolean	enabled
	1	protected void	firePropertyChange (String propertyName, Object oldValue, Object newValue)
●	2	protected final JTextComponent	getFocusedComponent ()
●	2	protected final JTextComponent	getTextComponent (java.awt.event.ActionEvent e)
	1	public Object	getValue (String key)
	1	public boolean	isEnabled ()
	1	public synchronized void	putValue (String key, Object newValue)
	1	public synchronized void	removePropertyChangeListener (*java.beans.PropertyChangeListener* listener)
	1	public synchronized void	setEnabled (boolean newValue)

		DefaultEditorKit.DefaultKeyTypedAction	javax.swing.text

```
        Object
1.2 ○   └javax.swing.AbstractAction¹ - - - - - - - - - - - - - javax.swing.Action (java.awt.event.ActionListener
                                                              (java.util.EventListener)), Cloneable, java.io.Serializable
1.2 ○       └TextAction²
1.2           └DefaultEditorKit.DefaultKeyTypedAction
```

	1	public **void**	**actionPerformed** (java.awt.event.ActionEvent e)
	1	public synchronized void	addPropertyChangeListener (*java.beans.PropertyChangeListener* listener)
▲	2	public static final *javax.swing.Action[]*	augmentList (*javax.swing.Action[]* list1, *javax.swing.Action[]* list2)
	1	protected . java.swing.event↩ .SwingPropertyChangeSupport	changeSupport
	1	protected Object	clone () throws CloneNotSupportedException
✳		public	**DefaultKeyTypedAction** ()
	1	protected boolean	enabled
	1	protected void	firePropertyChange (String propertyName, Object oldValue, Object newValue)
●	2	protected final JTextComponent	getFocusedComponent ()
●	2	protected final JTextComponent	getTextComponent (java.awt.event.ActionEvent e)
	1	public Object	getValue (String key)
	1	public boolean	isEnabled ()
	1	public synchronized void	putValue (String key, Object newValue)
	1	public synchronized void	removePropertyChangeListener (*java.beans.PropertyChangeListener* listener)
	1	public synchronized void	setEnabled (boolean newValue)

		DefaultEditorKit.InsertBreakAction	javax.swing.text

```
        Object
1.2 ○   └javax.swing.AbstractAction¹ - - - - - - - - - - - - - javax.swing.Action (java.awt.event.ActionListener
                                                              (java.util.EventListener)), Cloneable, java.io.Serializable
1.2 ○       └TextAction²
1.2           └DefaultEditorKit.InsertBreakAction
```

	1	public **void**	**actionPerformed** (java.awt.event.ActionEvent e)
	1	public synchronized void	addPropertyChangeListener (*java.beans.PropertyChangeListener* listener)
▲	2	public static final *javax.swing.Action[]*	augmentList (*javax.swing.Action[]* list1, *javax.swing.Action[]* list2)

Class *Interface* —extends - - -implements ○ abstract ● final △ static ▲ static final ✳ constructor x x—inherited x **x**—declared **x x**—overridden

	1	protected . javax.swing.event ↵	changeSupport
		.SwingPropertyChangeSupport	
	1	protected . . . . Object	clone () throws CloneNotSupportedException
	1	protected . . . . boolean	enabled
	1	protected . . . . void	firePropertyChange (String propertyName, Object oldValue, Object newValue)
●	2	protected final . . . . JTextComponent	getFocusedComponent ()
●	2	protected final . . . . JTextComponent	getTextComponent (java.awt.event.ActionEvent e)
	1	public . . . . Object	getValue (String key)
*		public	**InsertBreakAction** ()
	1	public . . . . boolean	isEnabled ()
	1	public synchronized . . . . . . .void	putValue (String key, Object newValue)
	1	public synchronized . . . . . . .void	removePropertyChangeListener (*java.beans.PropertyChangeListener* listener)
	1	public synchronized . . . . . . .void	setEnabled (boolean newValue)

DefaultEditorKit.InsertContentAction javax.swing.text

Object
1.2 ○ └─javax.swing.AbstractAction [1] - - - - - - - - - - - - - - *javax.swing.Action* (*java.awt.event.ActionListener*
  (*java.util.EventListener*)), *Cloneable, java.io.Serializable*
1.2 ○   └─TextAction [2]
1.2   └─DefaultEditorKit.InsertContentAction

	1	public . . . . **void**	**actionPerformed** (java.awt.event.ActionEvent e)
	1	public synchronized . . . . . . .void	addPropertyChangeListener (*java.beans.PropertyChangeListener* listener)
▲	2	public static final . . . . *javax.swing.Action[]*	augmentList (*javax.swing.Action[]* list1, *javax.swing.Action[]* list2)
	1	protected . javax.swing.event ↵	changeSupport
		.SwingPropertyChangeSupport	
	1	protected . . . . Object	clone () throws CloneNotSupportedException
	1	protected . . . . boolean	enabled
	1	protected . . . . void	firePropertyChange (String propertyName, Object oldValue, Object newValue)
●	2	protected final . . . . JTextComponent	getFocusedComponent ()
●	2	protected final . . . . JTextComponent	getTextComponent (java.awt.event.ActionEvent e)
	1	public . . . . Object	getValue (String key)
*		public	**InsertContentAction** ()
	1	public . . . . boolean	isEnabled ()
	1	public synchronized . . . . . . .void	putValue (String key, Object newValue)
	1	public synchronized . . . . . . .void	removePropertyChangeListener (*java.beans.PropertyChangeListener* listener)
	1	public synchronized . . . . . . .void	setEnabled (boolean newValue)

DefaultEditorKit.InsertTabAction javax.swing.text

Object
1.2 ○ └─javax.swing.AbstractAction [1] - - - - - - - - - - - - - - *javax.swing.Action* (*java.awt.event.ActionListener*
  (*java.util.EventListener*)), *Cloneable, java.io.Serializable*
1.2 ○   └─TextAction [2]
1.2   └─DefaultEditorKit.InsertTabAction

	1	public . . . . **void**	**actionPerformed** (java.awt.event.ActionEvent e)
	1	public synchronized . . . . . . .void	addPropertyChangeListener (*java.beans.PropertyChangeListener* listener)
▲	2	public static final . . . . *javax.swing.Action[]*	augmentList (*javax.swing.Action[]* list1, *javax.swing.Action[]* list2)
	1	protected . javax.swing.event ↵	changeSupport
		.SwingPropertyChangeSupport	
	1	protected . . . . Object	clone () throws CloneNotSupportedException
	1	protected . . . . boolean	enabled
	1	protected . . . . void	firePropertyChange (String propertyName, Object oldValue, Object newValue)
●	2	protected final . . . . JTextComponent	getFocusedComponent ()
●	2	protected final . . . . JTextComponent	getTextComponent (java.awt.event.ActionEvent e)
	1	public . . . . Object	getValue (String key)
*		public	**InsertTabAction** ()
	1	public . . . . boolean	isEnabled ()
	1	public synchronized . . . . . . .void	putValue (String key, Object newValue)
	1	public synchronized . . . . . . .void	removePropertyChangeListener (*java.beans.PropertyChangeListener* listener)

D

Classes

DefaultEditorKit.InsertTabAction

	1	public synchronized ....void	setEnabled (boolean newValue)

DefaultEditorKit.PasteAction   `javax.swing.text`

Object
 └javax.swing.AbstractAction [1] - - - - - - - - - - - - - - *javax.swing.Action* (*java.awt.event.ActionListener*
  1.2 ○   (*java.util.EventListener*)), *Cloneable, java.io.Serializable*
  1.2 ○   └TextAction [2]
  1.2   └DefaultEditorKit.PasteAction

	1	public...................... **void**	**actionPerformed** (java.awt.event.ActionEvent e)
	1	public synchronized ....void	addPropertyChangeListener (*java.beans.PropertyChangeListener* listener)
▲	2	public static final .... *javax.swing.Action[]*	augmentList (*javax.swing.Action[]* list1, *javax.swing.Action[]* list2)
	1	protected . javax.swing.event↵ .SwingPropertyChangeSupport	changeSupport
	1	protected...................Object	clone () throws CloneNotSupportedException
	1	protected............. boolean	enabled
	1	protected...................void	firePropertyChange (String propertyName, Object oldValue, Object newValue)
●	2	protected final................... ....JTextComponent	getFocusedComponent ()
●	2	protected final................... ....JTextComponent	getTextComponent (java.awt.event.ActionEvent e)
	1	public...................Object	getValue (String key)
	1	public................. boolean	isEnabled ()
*		public....................	**PasteAction** ()
	1	public synchronized ....void	putValue (String key, Object newValue)
	1	public synchronized ....void	removePropertyChangeListener (*java.beans.PropertyChangeListener* listener)
	1	public synchronized ....void	setEnabled (boolean newValue)

DefaultFocusManager   `javax.swing`

Object
 └FocusManager [1]
  1.2 ○   └DefaultFocusManager
  1.2

		public................. boolean	**compareTabOrder** (java.awt.Component a, java.awt.Component b)
*		public....................	**DefaultFocusManager** ()
△	1	public static ....void	disableSwingFocusManager ()
	1	public...................... **void**	**focusNextComponent** (java.awt.Component aComponent)
	1	public...................... **void**	**focusPreviousComponent** (java.awt.Component aComponent)
		public.... java.awt.Component	**getComponentAfter** (java. awt. Container aContainer, java.awt.Component aComponent)
		public.... java.awt.Component	**getComponentBefore** (java. awt. Container aContainer, java.awt.Component aComponent)
△	1	public static ....FocusManager	getCurrentManager ()
		public.... java.awt.Component	**getFirstComponent** (java.awt.Container aContainer)
		public.... java.awt.Component	**getLastComponent** (java.awt.Container aContainer)
△	1	public static .... boolean	isFocusManagerEnabled ()
	1	public...................... **void**	**processKeyEvent** (java. awt. Component focusedComponent, java.awt.event.KeyEvent anEvent)
△	1	public static ....void	setCurrentManager (FocusManager aFocusManager)

DefaultHighlighter   `javax.swing.text`

Object
 └LayeredHighlighter [1] - *Highlighter*
  1.2 ○   └DefaultHighlighter
  1.2

	1	public...................**Object**	**addHighlight** (int p0, int p1, *Highlighter. HighlightPainter* p) throws BadLocationException
	1	public...................... **void**	**changeHighlight** (Object tag, int p0, int p1) throws BadLocationException
*		public....................	**DefaultHighlighter** ()
△		public static .... LayeredHighlighter↵ .LayerPainter	**DefaultPainter**
		public................. **void**	**deinstall** (JTextComponent c)
		public................. boolean	**getDrawsLayeredHighlights** ()

Class   *Interface*   —extends   - - -implements   ○ abstract   ● final   △ static   ▲ static final   ✳ constructor   x x—inherited   x **x**—declared   **x x**—overridden

1	public .	***Highlighter.Highlight[]***	**getHighlights** ()
1	public......................	**void**	**install** (JTextComponent c)
1	public......................	**void**	**paint** (java.awt.Graphics g)
1	public......................	**void**	**paintLayeredHighlights** (java. awt. Graphics g, int p0, int p1, *java.awt.Shape* viewBounds, JTextComponent editor, View view)
1	public......................	**void**	**removeAllHighlights** ()
1	public......................	**void**	**removeHighlight** (Object tag)
	public......................	void	**setDrawsLayeredHighlights** (boolean newValue)

DefaultHighlighter.DefaultHighlightPainter   javax.swing.text

```
     Object
1.2 O └ LayeredHighlighter.LayerPainter 1 --------- Highlighter.HighlightPainter
1.2        └ DefaultHighlighter.DefaultHighlightPainter
```

*	public...........................		**DefaultHighlightPainter** (java.awt.Color c)
	public............java.awt.Color		**getColor** ()
1	public......................	**void**	**paint** (java. awt. Graphics g, int offs0, int offs1, *java. awt. Shape* bounds, JTextComponent c)
1	public..........	***java.awt.Shape***	**paintLayer** (java.awt. Graphics g, int offs0, int offs1, *java. awt. Shape* bounds, JTextComponent c, View view)

DefaultListCellRenderer   javax.swing

```
     Object
  O └ java.awt.Component 1 ------------------- java.awt.image.ImageObserver, java.awt.MenuContainer,
                                                java.io.Serializable
       └ java.awt.Container 2
1.2 O     └ JComponent 3 --------------------- java.io.Serializable
1.2          └ JLabel 4 ------------------------ SwingConstants, javax.accessibility.Accessible
1.2             └ DefaultListCellRenderer ---------- ListCellRenderer 5, java.io.Serializable
```

1	*111 inherited members from java.awt.Component not shown*
2	*39 inherited members from java.awt.Container not shown*
3	*113 inherited members from JComponent not shown*
4	*30 inherited members from JLabel not shown*

*	public...........................	**DefaultListCellRenderer** ()
5	public.... java.awt.Component	**getListCellRendererComponent** (JList list, Object value, int index, boolean isSelected, boolean cellHasFocus)
△	protected static	**noFocusBorder**
	..... javax.swing.border.Border	

DefaultListCellRenderer.UIResource   javax.swing

```
     Object
  O └ java.awt.Component 1 ------------------- java.awt.image.ImageObserver, java.awt.MenuContainer,
                                                java.io.Serializable
       └ java.awt.Container 2
1.2 O     └ JComponent 3 --------------------- java.io.Serializable
1.2          └ JLabel 4 ------------------------ SwingConstants, javax.accessibility.Accessible
1.2             └ DefaultListCellRenderer 5 --------- ListCellRenderer, java.io.Serializable
1.2                └ DefaultListCellRenderer ↵ ------- javax.swing.plaf.UIResource
                      .UIResource
```

1	*111 inherited members from java.awt.Component not shown*
2	*39 inherited members from java.awt.Container not shown*
3	*113 inherited members from JComponent not shown*
4	*30 inherited members from JLabel not shown*

5	public.... java.awt.Component	getListCellRendererComponent (JList list, Object value, int index, boolean isSelected, boolean cellHasFocus)
△ 5	protected static	noFocusBorder
	..... javax.swing.border.Border	
*	public...........................	**UIResource** ()

DefaultListModel

		DefaultListModel	javax.swing

```
            Object 1
1.2  ○      └ AbstractListModel 2 - - - - - - - - - - - - - - - - - - - - - ListModel, java.io.Serializable
1.2               └ DefaultListModel
```

	public	void	**add** (int index, Object element)
	public	void	**addElement** (Object obj)
2	public	void	addListDataListener (*javax.swing.event.ListDataListener* l)
	public	int	**capacity** ()
	public	void	**clear** ()
	public	boolean	**contains** (Object elem)
	public	void	**copyInto** (Object[] anArray)
*	public		**DefaultListModel** ()
	public	Object	**elementAt** (int index)
	public	*java.util.Enumeration*	**elements** ()
	public	void	**ensureCapacity** (int minCapacity)
2	protected	void	fireContentsChanged (Object source, int index0, int index1)
2	protected	void	fireIntervalAdded (Object source, int index0, int index1)
2	protected	void	fireIntervalRemoved (Object source, int index0, int index1)
	public	Object	**firstElement** ()
	public	Object	**get** (int index)
2	public	**Object**	**getElementAt** (int index)
2	public	**int**	**getSize** ()
	public	int	**indexOf** (Object elem)
	public	int	**indexOf** (Object elem, int index)
	public	void	**insertElementAt** (Object obj, int index)
	public	boolean	**isEmpty** ()
	public	Object	**lastElement** ()
	public	int	**lastIndexOf** (Object elem)
	public	int	**lastIndexOf** (Object elem, int index)
2	protected	javax ↩ .swing.event.EventListenerList	listenerList
	public	Object	**remove** (int index)
	public	void	**removeAllElements** ()
	public	boolean	**removeElement** (Object obj)
	public	void	**removeElementAt** (int index)
2	public	void	removeListDataListener (*javax.swing.event.ListDataListener* l)
	public	void	**removeRange** (int fromIndex, int toIndex)
	public	Object	**set** (int index, Object element)
	public	void	**setElementAt** (Object obj, int index)
	public	void	**setSize** (int newSize)
	public	int	**size** ()
	public	Object[]	**toArray** ()
1	public	**String**	**toString** ()
	public	void	**trimToSize** ()

		DefaultListSelectionModel	javax.swing

```
            Object 1
1.2         └ DefaultListSelectionModel - - - - - - - - - - - - - - - ListSelectionModel 2, Cloneable, java.io.Serializable
```

2	public	void	**addListSelectionListener** (*javax.swing.event.ListSelectionListener* l)
2	public	void	**addSelectionInterval** (int index0, int index1)
2	public	void	**clearSelection** ()
1	public	**Object**	**clone** () throws CloneNotSupportedException
*	public		**DefaultListSelectionModel** ()
	protected	void	**fireValueChanged** (boolean isAdjusting)
	protected	void	**fireValueChanged** (int firstIndex, int lastIndex)
	protected	void	**fireValueChanged** (int firstIndex, int lastIndex, boolean isAdjusting)
2	public	int	**getAnchorSelectionIndex** ()
2	public	int	**getLeadSelectionIndex** ()
2	public	int	**getMaxSelectionIndex** ()
2	public	int	**getMinSelectionIndex** ()
2	public	int	**getSelectionMode** ()
2	public	boolean	**getValueIsAdjusting** ()
2	public	void	**insertIndexInterval** (int index, int length, boolean before)
	public	boolean	**isLeadAnchorNotificationEnabled** ()
2	public	boolean	**isSelectedIndex** (int index)
2	public	boolean	**isSelectionEmpty** ()
	protected	boolean	**leadAnchorNotificationEnabled**

Class *Interface* —extends - - -implements ○ abstract ● final △ static ▲ static final * constructor x x—inherited x **x**—declared **x x**—overridden

	protected . . . . javax↵	**listenerList**	
	.swing.event.EventListenerList		
2	public . . . . void	**removeIndexInterval** (int index0, int index1)	
2	public . . . . void	**removeListSelectionListener** (*javax.swing.event.ListSelectionListener* l)	
2	public . . . . void	**removeSelectionInterval** (int index0, int index1)	
2	public . . . . void	**setAnchorSelectionIndex** (int anchorIndex)	
	public . . . . void	**setLeadAnchorNotificationEnabled** (boolean flag)	
2	public . . . . void	**setLeadSelectionIndex** (int leadIndex)	
2	public . . . . void	**setSelectionInterval** (int index0, int index1)	
2	public . . . . void	**setSelectionMode** (int selectionMode)	
2	public . . . . void	**setValueIsAdjusting** (boolean isAdjusting)	
1	public . . . . **String**	**toString** ()	

D

DefaultMutableTreeNode

javax.swing.tree

Object[1]

1.2   └ DefaultMutableTreeNode - - - - - - - - - - - - - - - - - *Cloneable, MutableTreeNode[2] (TreeNode[3]), java.io.Serializable*

	public . . . . void	**add** (*MutableTreeNode* newChild)
	protected . . . . boolean	**allowsChildren**
	public . . . . *java.util.Enumeration*	**breadthFirstEnumeration** ()
3	public . . . . *java.util.Enumeration*	**children** ()
	protected . . . . java.util.Vector	**children**
1	public . . . . **Object**	**clone** ()
**	public	**DefaultMutableTreeNode** ()
**	public	**DefaultMutableTreeNode** (Object userObject)
**	public	**DefaultMutableTreeNode** (Object userObject, boolean allowsChildren)
	public . . . . *java.util.Enumeration*	**depthFirstEnumeration** ()
▲	public·static final	**EMPTY_ENUMERATION**
	. . . . *java.util.Enumeration*	
3	public . . . . boolean	**getAllowsChildren** ()
	public . . . . *TreeNode*	**getChildAfter** (*TreeNode* aChild)
3	public . . . . *TreeNode*	**getChildAt** (int index)
	public . . . . *TreeNode*	**getChildBefore** (*TreeNode* aChild)
3	public . . . . int	**getChildCount** ()
	public . . . . int	**getDepth** ()
	public . . . . *TreeNode*	**getFirstChild** ()
	public	**getFirstLeaf** ()
	. . . . DefaultMutableTreeNode	
3	public . . . . int	**getIndex** (*TreeNode* aChild)
	public . . . . *TreeNode*	**getLastChild** ()
	public	**getLastLeaf** ()
	. . . . DefaultMutableTreeNode	
	public . . . . int	**getLeafCount** ()
	public . . . . int	**getLevel** ()
	public	**getNextLeaf** ()
	. . . . DefaultMutableTreeNode	
	public	**getNextNode** ()
	. . . . DefaultMutableTreeNode	
	public	**getNextSibling** ()
	. . . . DefaultMutableTreeNode	
3	public . . . . *TreeNode*	**getParent** ()
	public . . . . *TreeNode[]*	**getPath** ()
	protected . . . . *TreeNode[]*	**getPathToRoot** (*TreeNode* aNode, int depth)
	public	**getPreviousLeaf** ()
	. . . . DefaultMutableTreeNode	
	public	**getPreviousNode** ()
	. . . . DefaultMutableTreeNode	
	public	**getPreviousSibling** ()
	. . . . DefaultMutableTreeNode	
	public . . . . *TreeNode*	**getRoot** ()
	public . . . . *TreeNode*	**getSharedAncestor** (DefaultMutableTreeNode aNode)
	public . . . . int	**getSiblingCount** ()
	public . . . . **Object**	**getUserObject** ()
	public . . . . **Object[]**	**getUserObjectPath** ()
2	public . . . . void	**insert** (*MutableTreeNode* newChild, int childIndex)
3	public . . . . boolean	**isLeaf** ()
	public . . . . boolean	**isNodeAncestor** (*TreeNode* anotherNode)
	public . . . . boolean	**isNodeChild** (*TreeNode* aNode)
	public . . . . boolean	**isNodeDescendant** (DefaultMutableTreeNode anotherNode)
	public . . . . boolean	**isNodeRelated** (DefaultMutableTreeNode aNode)
	public . . . . boolean	**isNodeSibling** (*TreeNode* anotherNode)

Classes

DefaultMutableTreeNode

	public	boolean	**isRoot** ()
	protected	*MutableTreeNode*	**parent**
	public	*java.util.Enumeration*	**pathFromAncestorEnumeration** (*TreeNode* ancestor)
	public	*java.util.Enumeration*	**postorderEnumeration** ()
	public	*java.util.Enumeration*	**preorderEnumeration** ()
2	public	void	**remove** (int childIndex)
2	public	void	**remove** (*MutableTreeNode* aChild)
	public	void	**removeAllChildren** ()
2	public	void	**removeFromParent** ()
	public	void	**setAllowsChildren** (boolean allows)
2	public	void	**setParent** (*MutableTreeNode* newParent)
2	public	void	**setUserObject** (Object userObject)
1	public	**String**	**toString** ()
	protected transient	Object	**userObject**

D

DefaultSingleSelectionModel

Object
1.2 └─DefaultSingleSelectionModel - - - - - - - - - - - - - *SingleSelectionModel* [1], *java.io.Serializable*

1	public	void	**addChangeListener** (*javax.swing.event.ChangeListener* l)
	protected transient	javax ↵ .swing.event.ChangeEvent	**changeEvent**
1	public	void	**clearSelection** ()
*	public		**DefaultSingleSelectionModel** ()
	protected	void	**fireStateChanged** ()
1	public	int	**getSelectedIndex** ()
1	public	boolean	**isSelected** ()
	protected	javax ↵ .swing.event.EventListenerList	**listenerList**
1	public	void	**removeChangeListener** (*javax.swing.event.ChangeListener* l)
1	public	void	**setSelectedIndex** (int index)

DefaultStyledDocument

Object
1.2 ○ └─AbstractDocument [1] - *Document*, *java.io.Serializable*
1.2 └─DefaultStyledDocument - - - - - - - - - - - - - - *StyledDocument* [2] (*Document*)

	1		*41 inherited members from AbstractDocument not shown*
	1	public **void**	**addDocumentListener** (*javax.swing.event.DocumentListener* listener)
	2	public *Style*	**addStyle** (String nm, *Style* parent)
		protected	**buffer**
		..... DefaultStyledDocument ↵ .ElementBuffer	
▲		public static final int	**BUFFER_SIZE_DEFAULT** = 4096
		protected void	**create** (DefaultStyledDocument.ElementSpec[] data)
		protected	**createDefaultRoot** ()
		..........AbstractDocument ↵ .AbstractElement	
*		public	**DefaultStyledDocument** ()
*		public	**DefaultStyledDocument** (StyleContext styles)
*		public	**DefaultStyledDocument** (*AbstractDocument.Content* c, StyleContext styles)
	2	public java.awt.Color	**getBackground** (*AttributeSet* attr)
	2	public *Element*	**getCharacterElement** (int pos)
	1	public **Element**	**getDefaultRootElement** ()
	2	public java.awt.Font	**getFont** (*AttributeSet* attr)
	2	public java.awt.Color	**getForeground** (*AttributeSet* attr)
	2	public *Style*	**getLogicalStyle** (int p)
	1	public **Element**	**getParagraphElement** (int pos)
	2	public *Style*	**getStyle** (String nm)
		public *java.util.Enumeration*	**getStyleNames** ()
		protected void	**insert** (int offset, DefaultStyledDocument. ElementSpec[] data) throws BadLocationException
	1	protected **void**	**insertUpdate** (AbstractDocument.DefaultDocumentEvent chng, *AttributeSet* attr)
	1	public **void**	**removeDocumentListener** (*javax.swing.event.DocumentListener* listener)
	2	public void	**removeStyle** (String nm)
	1	protected **void**	**removeUpdate** (AbstractDocument.DefaultDocumentEvent chng)
	2	public void	**setCharacterAttributes** (int offset, int length, *AttributeSet* s, boolean replace)

Class   *Interface*   —extends   - - -implements   ○ abstract   ● final   △ static   ▲ static final   ✳ constructor   x x—inherited   x **x**—declared   **x x**—overridden

2	public	void	**setLogicalStyle** (int pos, *Style* s)
2	public	void	**setParagraphAttributes** (int offset, int length, *AttributeSet* s, boolean replace)
	protected	void	**styleChanged** (*Style* style)

DefaultStyledDocument.AttributeUndoableEdit   javax.swing.text

Object
1.2 └javax.swing.undo.AbstractUndoableEdit[1] - - - - *javax.swing.undo.UndoableEdit*, *java.io.Serializable*
1.2   └ DefaultStyledDocument ↵
            .AttributeUndoableEdit

1	public	boolean	addEdit (*javax.swing.undo.UndoableEdit* anEdit)
*	public		**AttributeUndoableEdit** (*Element* element, *AttributeSet* newAttributes, boolean isReplacing)
1	public	boolean	canRedo ()
1	public	boolean	canUndo ()
	protected	*AttributeSet*	**copy**
1	public	void	die ()
	protected	*Element*	**element**
1	public	String	getPresentationName ()
1	public	String	getRedoPresentationName ()
1	public	String	getUndoPresentationName ()
	protected	boolean	**isReplacing**
1	public	boolean	isSignificant ()
	protected	*AttributeSet*	**newAttributes**
* 1	public	**void**	redo () throws javax.swing.undo.CannotRedoException
1	public	boolean	replaceEdit (*javax.swing.undo.UndoableEdit* anEdit)
1	public	String	toString ()
1	public	**void**	undo () throws javax.swing.undo.CannotUndoException

---

DefaultStyledDocument.ElementBuffer   javax.swing.text

Object
1.2 └ DefaultStyledDocument.ElementBuffer - - - - - - *java.io.Serializable*

	public	void	**change** (int offset, int length, AbstractDocument.DefaultDocumentEvent de)
	protected	void	**changeUpdate** ()
	public	*Element*	**clone** (*Element* parent, *Element* clonee)
*	public		**ElementBuffer** (*Element* root)
	public	*Element*	**getRootElement** ()
	public	void	**insert** (int offset, int length, DefaultStyledDocument.ElementSpec[] data, AbstractDocument.DefaultDocumentEvent de)
	protected	void	**insertUpdate** (DefaultStyledDocument.ElementSpec[] data)
	public	void	**remove** (int offset, int length, AbstractDocument.DefaultDocumentEvent de)
	protected	void	**removeUpdate** ()

DefaultStyledDocument.ElementSpec   javax.swing.text

Object[1]
1.2 └ DefaultStyledDocument.ElementSpec

▲	public static final	short	**ContentType**
*	public		**ElementSpec** (*AttributeSet* a, short type)
*	public		**ElementSpec** (*AttributeSet* a, short type, int len)
*	public		**ElementSpec** (*AttributeSet* a, short type, char[] txt, int offs, int len)
▲	public static final	short	**EndTagType**
	public	char[]	**getArray** ()
	public	*AttributeSet*	**getAttributes** ()
	public	short	**getDirection** ()
	public	int	**getLength** ()
	public	int	**getOffset** ()
	public	short	**getType** ()
▲	public static final	short	**JoinFractureDirection**
▲	public static final	short	**JoinNextDirection**
▲	public static final	short	**JoinPreviousDirection**
▲	public static final	short	**OriginateDirection**
	public	void	**setDirection** (short direction)
	public	void	**setType** (short type)
▲	public static final	short	**StartTagType**
1	public	**String**	**toString** ()

D

Classes

DefaultStyledDocument.SectionElement

DefaultStyledDocument.SectionElement	protected	javax.swing.text

Object
└AbstractDocument.AbstractElement [1] - - - - - - - *Element*, *MutableAttributeSet* (*AttributeSet*), *java.io.Serializable*,
                                                        javax.swing.tree.TreeNode

1.2 ○

1.2 └AbstractDocument.BranchElement [2]
1.2   └DefaultStyledDocument.SectionElement

1	public	void	addAttribute (Object name, Object value)
1	public	void	addAttributes (*AttributeSet* attr)
2	public	*java.util.Enumeration*	children ()
1	public	boolean	containsAttribute (Object name, Object value)
1	public	boolean	containsAttributes (*AttributeSet* attrs)
1	public	*AttributeSet*	copyAttributes ()
1	public	void	dump (java.io.PrintStream psOut, int indentAmount)
1	protected	void	finalize () throws Throwable
2	public	boolean	getAllowsChildren ()
1	public	Object	getAttribute (Object attrName)
1	public	int	getAttributeCount ()
1	public	*java.util.Enumeration*	getAttributeNames ()
1	public	*AttributeSet*	getAttributes ()
1	public ..... *javax.swing.tree.TreeNode*		getChildAt (int childIndex)
1	public	int	getChildCount ()
1	public	*Document*	getDocument ()
2	public	*Element*	getElement (int index)
2	public	int	getElementCount ()
2	public	int	getElementIndex (int offset)
2	public	int	getEndOffset ()
1	public	int	getIndex (*javax.swing.tree.TreeNode* node)
2	public	**String**	**getName** ()
1	public ..... *javax.swing.tree.TreeNode*		getParent ()
1	public	*Element*	getParentElement ()
1	public	*AttributeSet*	getResolveParent ()
2	public	int	getStartOffset ()
1	public	boolean	isDefined (Object attrName)
1	public	boolean	isEqual (*AttributeSet* attr)
2	public	boolean	isLeaf ()
2	public	*Element*	positionToElement (int pos)
1	public	void	removeAttribute (Object name)
1	public	void	removeAttributes (*java.util.Enumeration* names)
1	public	void	removeAttributes (*AttributeSet* attrs)
2	public	void	replace (int offset, int length, *Element[]* elems)
*	public	**SectionElement**	()
1	public	void	setResolveParent (*AttributeSet* parent)
2	public	String	toString ()

DefaultTableCellRenderer	javax.swing.table

Object
└java.awt.Component [1] - - - - - - - - - - - - - - - - - *java.awt.image.ImageObserver*, *java.awt.MenuContainer*,
                                                            java.io.Serializable

○

        └java.awt.Container [2]
1.2 ○   └javax.swing.JComponent [3] - - - - - - - - - - - *java.io.Serializable*
1.2   └javax.swing.JLabel [4] - - - - - - - - - - - - - *javax.swing.SwingConstants*, *javax.accessibility.Accessible*
1.2   └DefaultTableCellRenderer - - - - - - - - - *TableCellRenderer* [5], *java.io.Serializable*

1	*111 inherited members from java.awt.Component not shown*		
2	*39 inherited members from java.awt.Container not shown*		
3	*111 inherited members from javax.swing.JComponent not shown*		
4	*29 inherited members from javax.swing.JLabel not shown*		
*	public	**DefaultTableCellRenderer**	()
5	public .... java.awt.Component	**getTableCellRendererComponent**	(javax.swing.JTable table, Object value, boolean isSelected, boolean hasFocus, int row, int column)
△	protected static ..... *javax.swing.border.Border*	**noFocusBorder**	
3	public	**void**	**setBackground** (java.awt.Color c)
3	public	**void**	**setForeground** (java.awt.Color c)
	protected	void	**setValue** (Object value)

Class   *Interface*   —extends   - - -implements   ○ abstract   ● final   △ static   ▲ static final   ✳ constructor   x x—inherited   x **x**—declared   **x x**—overridden

318

4	public	**void updateUI** ()	

DefaultTableCellRenderer.UIResource | javax.swing.table

Object
- └─java.awt.Component[1] - - - - - - - - - - - - - - - - - - - *java.awt.image.ImageObserver*, *java.awt.MenuContainer*, *java.io.Serializable*

○

  └─java.awt.Container[2]

1.2 ○
    └─javax.swing.JComponent[3] - - - - - - - - - - - *java.io.Serializable*
1.2
      └─javax.swing.JLabel[4] - - - - - - - - - - - - - *javax.swing.SwingConstants*, *javax.accessibility.Accessible*
1.2
        └─DefaultTableCellRenderer[5] - - - - - - - - *TableCellRenderer*, *java.io.Serializable*
1.2
          └─DefaultTableCellRenderer↩ - - - - - *javax.swing.plaf.UIResource*
           .UIResource

	1	*111 inherited members from java.awt.Component not shown*	
	2	*39 inherited members from java.awt.Container not shown*	
	3	*111 inherited members from javax.swing.JComponent not shown*	
	4	*29 inherited members from javax.swing.JLabel not shown*	
	5	public.... java.awt.Component	getTableCellRendererComponent (javax.swing.JTable table, Object value, boolean isSelected, boolean hasFocus, int row, int column)
△	5	protected static .... *..... javax.swing.border.Border*	noFocusBorder
	5	public......................void	setBackground (java.awt.Color c)
	5	public......................void	setForeground (java.awt.Color c)
	5	protected ....void	setValue (Object value)
*		public.........................	**UIResource** ()
	5	public......................void	updateUI ()

DefaultTableColumnModel | javax.swing.table

Object
1.2
- └─DefaultTableColumnModel - - - - - - - - - - - - - - - *TableColumnModel*[1], *java.beans.PropertyChangeListener*[2] (*java↩ .util.EventListener*), *javax.swing.event.ListSelectionListener*[3] (*java.util.EventListener*), *java.io.Serializable*

	1	public......................void	**addColumn** (TableColumn aColumn)
	1	public......................void	**addColumnModelListener** (*javax.swing.event.TableColumnModelListener* x)
		protected transient.....javax↩ .swing.event.ChangeEvent	**changeEvent**
		protected ....int	**columnMargin**
		protected .... boolean	**columnSelectionAllowed**
		protected .... *javax.swing.ListSelectionModel*	**createSelectionModel** ()
*		public...........................	**DefaultTableColumnModel** ()
		protected ....void	**fireColumnAdded** (javax.swing.event.TableColumnModelEvent e)
		protected ....void	**fireColumnMarginChanged** ()
		protected ....void	**fireColumnMoved** (javax.swing.event.TableColumnModelEvent e)
		protected ....void	**fireColumnRemoved** (javax.swing.event.TableColumnModelEvent e)
		protected ....void	**fireColumnSelectionChanged** (javax.swing.event.ListSelectionEvent e)
	1	public.............TableColumn	**getColumn** (int columnIndex)
	1	public......................int	**getColumnCount** ()
	1	public......................int	**getColumnIndex** (Object identifier)
	1	public......................int	**getColumnIndexAtX** (int xPosition)
	1	public......................int	**getColumnMargin** ()
	1	public.... *java.util.Enumeration*	**getColumns** ()
	1	public................. boolean	**getColumnSelectionAllowed** ()
	1	public......................int	**getSelectedColumnCount** ()
	1	public.....................int[]	**getSelectedColumns** ()
	1	public......................... *javax.swing.ListSelectionModel*	**getSelectionModel** ()
	1	public......................int	**getTotalColumnWidth** ()
		protected ....javax↩ .swing.event.EventListenerList	**listenerList**
	1	public......................void	**moveColumn** (int columnIndex, int newIndex)
	2	public......................void	**propertyChange** (java.beans.PropertyChangeEvent evt)
		protected ....void	**recalcWidthCache** ()
	1	public......................void	**removeColumn** (TableColumn column)
	1	public......................void	**removeColumnModelListener** (*javax.swing.event.TableColumnModelListener* x)
		protected .... *javax.swing.ListSelectionModel*	**selectionModel**

DefaultTableColumnModel

1	public	void	**setColumnMargin** (int newMargin)
1	public	void	**setColumnSelectionAllowed** (boolean flag)
1	public	void	**setSelectionModel** (*javax.swing.ListSelectionModel* newModel)
	protected	java.util.Vector	**tableColumns**
	protected	int	**totalColumnWidth**
3	public	void	**valueChanged** (javax.swing.event.ListSelectionEvent e)

D

DefaultTableModel   javax.swing.table

Object
- 1.2 ○ └AbstractTableModel[1] - - - - - - - - - - - - - - - - - - - *TableModel*, *java.io.Serializable*
- 1.2   └DefaultTableModel - - - - - - - - - - - - - - - - - - - *java.io.Serializable*

	public	void	**addColumn** (Object columnName)
	public	void	**addColumn** (Object columnName, java.util.Vector columnData)
	public	void	**addColumn** (Object columnName, Object[] columnData)
	public	void	**addRow** (Object[] rowData)
	public	void	**addRow** (java.util.Vector rowData)
1	public	void	addTableModelListener (*javax.swing.event.TableModelListener* l)
	protected	java.util.Vector	**columnIdentifiers**
△	protected static	java.util.Vector	**convertToVector** (Object[] anArray)
△	protected static	java.util.Vector	**convertToVector** (Object[][] anArray)
	protected	java.util.Vector	**dataVector**
✻	public		**DefaultTableModel** ()
✻	public		**DefaultTableModel** (int numRows, int numColumns)
✻	public		**DefaultTableModel** (Object[] columnNames, int numRows)
✻	public		**DefaultTableModel** (Object[][] data, Object[] columnNames)
✻	public		**DefaultTableModel** (java.util.Vector columnNames, int numRows)
✻	public		**DefaultTableModel** (java.util.Vector data, java.util.Vector columnNames)
1	public	int	findColumn (String columnName)
1	public	void	fireTableCellUpdated (int row, int column)
1	public	void	fireTableChanged (javax.swing.event.TableModelEvent e)
1	public	void	fireTableDataChanged ()
1	public	void	fireTableRowsDeleted (int firstRow, int lastRow)
1	public	void	fireTableRowsInserted (int firstRow, int lastRow)
1	public	void	fireTableRowsUpdated (int firstRow, int lastRow)
1	public	void	fireTableStructureChanged ()
1	public	Class	getColumnClass (int columnIndex)
1	public	**int**	**getColumnCount** ()
1	public	**String**	**getColumnName** (int column)
	public	java.util.Vector	**getDataVector** ()
1	public	**int**	**getRowCount** ()
1	public	**Object**	**getValueAt** (int row, int column)
	public	void	**insertRow** (int row, java.util.Vector rowData)
	public	void	**insertRow** (int row, Object[] rowData)
1	public	**boolean**	**isCellEditable** (int row, int column)
1	protected	javax↵ .swing.event.EventListenerList	listenerList
	public	void	**moveRow** (int startIndex, int endIndex, int toIndex)
	public	void	**newDataAvailable** (javax.swing.event.TableModelEvent event)
	public	void	**newRowsAdded** (javax.swing.event.TableModelEvent event)
	public	void	**removeRow** (int row)
1	public	void	removeTableModelListener (*javax.swing.event.TableModelListener* l)
	public	void	**rowsRemoved** (javax.swing.event.TableModelEvent event)
	public	void	**setColumnIdentifiers** (Object[] newIdentifiers)
	public	void	**setColumnIdentifiers** (java.util.Vector newIdentifiers)
	public	void	**setDataVector** (Object[][] newData, Object[] columnNames)
	public	void	**setDataVector** (java.util.Vector newData, java.util.Vector columnNames)
	public	void	**setNumRows** (int newSize)
1	public	**void**	**setValueAt** (Object aValue, int row, int column)

DefaultTextUI   javax.swing.text

Object
- 1.2 ○ └javax.swing.plaf.ComponentUI[1]
- 1.2 ○   └javax.swing.plaf.TextUI
- 1.2 ○   └javax.swing.plaf.basic.BasicTextUI[2] - - - - - *ViewFactory*
- 1.2 ○   └DefaultTextUI

Class   *Interface*   —extends   - - -implements   ○ abstract   ● final   △ static   ▲ static final   ✻ constructor   x x—inherited   x **x**—declared   **x x**—overridden

1 *5 inherited members from javax.swing.plaf.ComponentUI not shown*
2 *35 inherited members from javax.swing.plaf.basic.BasicTextUI not shown*
*   public . . . .   **DefaultTextUI** ()

DefaultTreeCellEditor   javax.swing.tree

Object
1.2 └─DefaultTreeCellEditor - - - - - - - - - - - - - - - - - - - *java.awt.event.ActionListener* [1] (*java.util.EventListener*),
                                                                TreeCellEditor [2] (*javax.swing.CellEditor* [3]), *javax.swing.event*↩
                                                                . *TreeSelectionListener* [4] (*java.util.EventListener*)

1	public . . . . void	**actionPerformed** (java.awt.event.ActionEvent e)
3	public . . . . void	**addCellEditorListener** (*javax.swing.event.CellEditorListener* l)
	protected . . . . java.awt.Color	**borderSelectionColor**
3	public . . . . void	**cancelCellEditing** ()
	protected . . . . boolean	**canEdit**
	protected . . . . boolean	**canEditImmediately** (java.util.EventObject event)
	protected . . . java.awt.Container	**createContainer** ()
	protected . . . . *TreeCellEditor*	**createTreeCellEditor** ()
**	public	**DefaultTreeCellEditor** (javax.swing.JTree tree, DefaultTreeCellRenderer renderer)
**	public	**DefaultTreeCellEditor** (javax.swing.JTree tree, DefaultTreeCellRenderer renderer, *TreeCellEditor* editor)
	protected . . . . void	**determineOffset** (javax.swing.JTree tree, Object value, boolean isSelected, boolean expanded, boolean leaf, int row)
	protected transient . . . . java.awt.Component	**editingComponent**
	protected . . . java.awt.Container	**editingContainer**
	protected transient . . . . *javax.swing.Icon*	**editingIcon**
	protected . . . . java.awt.Font	**font**
	public . . . . java.awt.Color	**getBorderSelectionColor** ()
3	public . . . . Object	**getCellEditorValue** ()
	public . . . . java.awt.Font	**getFont** ()
2	public . . . . java.awt.Component	**getTreeCellEditorComponent** (javax.swing.JTree tree, Object value, boolean isSelected, boolean expanded, boolean leaf, int row)
	protected . . . . boolean	**inHitRegion** (int x, int y)
3	public . . . . boolean	**isCellEditable** (java.util.EventObject event)
	protected transient . . . . TreePath	**lastPath**
	protected transient . . . . int	**lastRow**
	protected transient . . . . int	**offset**
	protected . . . . void	**prepareForEditing** ()
	protected . . . . *TreeCellEditor*	**realEditor**
3	public . . . . void	**removeCellEditorListener** (*javax.swing.event.CellEditorListener* l)
	protected . . . . DefaultTreeCellRenderer	**renderer**
	public . . . . void	**setBorderSelectionColor** (java.awt.Color newColor)
	public . . . . void	**setFont** (java.awt.Font font)
	protected . . . . void	**setTree** (javax.swing.JTree newTree)
3	public . . . . boolean	**shouldSelectCell** (java.util.EventObject event)
	protected . . . . boolean	**shouldStartEditingTimer** (java.util.EventObject event)
	protected . . . . void	**startEditingTimer** ()
3	public . . . . boolean	**stopCellEditing** ()
	protected transient . . . . javax.swing.Timer	**timer**
	protected transient . . . . javax.swing.JTree	**tree**
4	public . . . . void	**valueChanged** (javax.swing.event.TreeSelectionEvent e)

DefaultTreeCellEditor.DefaultTextField   javax.swing.tree

Object
○   └─java.awt.Component [1] - - - - - - - - - - - - - - - - - - - *java.awt.image.ImageObserver*, *java.awt.MenuContainer*,
                                                                java.io.Serializable
        └─java.awt.Container [2]
1.2 ○   └─javax.swing.JComponent [3] - - - - - - - - - - - *java.io.Serializable*
1.2 ○   └─javax.swing.text.JTextComponent [4] - - - - *javax.swing.Scrollable*, *javax.accessibility.Accessible*
1.2   └─javax.swing.JTextField [5] - - - - - - - - - - - *javax.swing.SwingConstants*
1.2   └─DefaultTreeCellEditor↩
                        .DefaultTextField

DefaultTreeCellEditor.DefaultTextField

1	*108 inherited members from java.awt.Component not shown*	
2	*39 inherited members from java.awt.Container not shown*	
3	*102 inherited members from javax.swing.JComponent not shown*	
4	*68 inherited members from javax.swing.text.JTextComponent not shown*	
5	public synchronized ....void	addActionListener (*java.awt.event.ActionListener* l)
	protected	**border**
	..... *javax.swing.border.Border*	
5	protected	createDefaultModel ()
	.... *javax.swing.text.Document*	
✳	public............................	**DefaultTextField** (*javax.swing.border.Border* border)
5	protected ....void	fireActionPerformed ()
5	public.... *javax.accessibility* ↩	getAccessibleContext ()
	.AccessibleContext	
5	public..... *javax.swing.Action[]*	getActions ()
3	public..........................	**getBorder** ()
	... *javax.swing.border.Border*	
5	public...........................int	getColumns ()
5	protected ....int	getColumnWidth ()
1	public........... **java.awt.Font**	**getFont** ()
5	public..........................int	getHorizontalAlignment ()
5	public.....................*javax* ↩	getHorizontalVisibility ()
	.*swing.BoundedRangeModel*	
5	public.... **java.awt.Dimension**	**getPreferredSize** ()
5	public..........................int	getScrollOffset ()
5	public................... String	getUIClassID ()
5	public.................. boolean	isValidateRoot ()
5	protected ....String	paramString ()
5	public.......................void	postActionEvent ()
5	public synchronized ....void	removeActionListener (*java.awt.event.ActionListener* l)
5	public.......................void	scrollRectToVisible (java.awt.Rectangle r)
5	public.......................void	setActionCommand (String command)
5	public.......................void	setColumns (int columns)
5	public.......................void	setFont (java.awt.Font f)
5	public.......................void	setHorizontalAlignment (int alignment)
5	public.......................void	setScrollOffset (int scrollOffset)

DefaultTreeCellEditor.EditorContainer   javax.swing.tree

```
       Object
 ○     └─java.awt.Component¹ - - - - - - - - - - - - - - - - - - - - - java.awt.image.ImageObserver, java.awt.MenuContainer,
                                                                      java.io.Serializable
          └─java.awt.Container²
 1.2         └─DefaultTreeCellEditor.EditorContainer
```

1	*137 inherited members from java.awt.Component not shown*	
2	*48 inherited members from java.awt.Container not shown*	
2	public...................... **void**	**doLayout** ()
	public......................void	**EditorContainer** ()
✳	public............................	**EditorContainer** ()
2	public.... **java.awt.Dimension**	**getPreferredSize** ()
2	public...................... **void**	**paint** (java.awt.Graphics g)

DefaultTreeCellRenderer   javax.swing.tree

```
       Object
 ○     └─java.awt.Component¹ - - - - - - - - - - - - - - - - - - - - - java.awt.image.ImageObserver, java.awt.MenuContainer,
                                                                      java.io.Serializable
          └─java.awt.Container²
 1.2 ○      └─javax.swing.JComponent³ - - - - - - - - - - - - java.io.Serializable
 1.2          └─javax.swing.JLabel⁴ - - - - - - - - - - - - - - - javax.swing.SwingConstants, javax.accessibility.Accessible
 1.2             └─DefaultTreeCellRenderer - - - - - - - - - - TreeCellRenderer⁵
```

1	*111 inherited members from java.awt.Component not shown*	
2	*39 inherited members from java.awt.Container not shown*	
3	*109 inherited members from javax.swing.JComponent not shown*	
4	*30 inherited members from javax.swing.JLabel not shown*	
	protected ....java.awt.Color	**backgroundNonSelectionColor**
	protected ....java.awt.Color	**backgroundSelectionColor**

Class   *Interface*   —extends   - - -implements   ○ abstract   ● final   △ static   ▲ static final   ✳ constructor   x x—inherited   x **x**—declared   **x x**—overridden

	protected........java.awt.Color	**borderSelectionColor**
	protected transient.............	**closedIcon**
	...............*javax.swing.Icon*	
*	public...........................	**DefaultTreeCellRenderer** ()
	public...........java.awt.Color	**getBackgroundNonSelectionColor** ()
	public...........java.awt.Color	**getBackgroundSelectionColor** ()
	public...........java.awt.Color	**getBorderSelectionColor** ()
	public.........*javax.swing.Icon*	**getClosedIcon** ()
	public.........*javax.swing.Icon*	**getDefaultClosedIcon** ()
	public.........*javax.swing.Icon*	**getDefaultLeafIcon** ()
	public.........*javax.swing.Icon*	**getDefaultOpenIcon** ()
	public.........*javax.swing.Icon*	**getLeafIcon** ()
	public.........*javax.swing.Icon*	**getOpenIcon** ()
3	public.... **java.awt.Dimension**	**getPreferredSize** ()
	public...........java.awt.Color	**getTextNonSelectionColor** ()
	public...........java.awt.Color	**getTextSelectionColor** ()
5	public.... java.awt.Component	**getTreeCellRendererComponent** (javax.swing.JTree tree, Object value, boolean sel, boolean expanded, boolean leaf, int row, boolean hasFocus)
	protected transient.............	**leafIcon**
	...............*javax.swing.Icon*	
	protected transient.............	**openIcon**
	...............*javax.swing.Icon*	
3	public................... **void**	**paint** (java.awt.Graphics g)
	protected.............. boolean	**selected**
3	public................... **void**	**setBackground** (java.awt.Color color)
	public....................void	**setBackgroundNonSelectionColor** (java.awt.Color newColor)
	public....................void	**setBackgroundSelectionColor** (java.awt.Color newColor)
	public....................void	**setBorderSelectionColor** (java.awt.Color newColor)
	public....................void	**setClosedIcon** (*javax.swing.Icon* newIcon)
3	public................... **void**	**setFont** (java.awt.Font font)
	public....................void	**setLeafIcon** (*javax.swing.Icon* newIcon)
	public....................void	**setOpenIcon** (*javax.swing.Icon* newIcon)
	public....................void	**setTextNonSelectionColor** (java.awt.Color newColor)
	public....................void	**setTextSelectionColor** (java.awt.Color newColor)
	protected........java.awt.Color	**textNonSelectionColor**
	protected........java.awt.Color	**textSelectionColor**

DefaultTreeModel

Object
1.2 └DefaultTreeModel ---------------------- *java.io.Serializable, TreeModel* [1]

1	public.......................void	**addTreeModelListener** (*javax.swing.event.TreeModelListener* l)
	protected.............. boolean	**asksAllowsChildren**
	public................. boolean	**asksAllowsChildren** ()
**	public...........................	**DefaultTreeModel** (*TreeNode* root)
**	public...........................	**DefaultTreeModel** (*TreeNode* root, boolean asksAllowsChildren)
	protected.................void	**fireTreeNodesChanged** (Object source, Object[] path, int[] childIndices, Object[] children)
	protected.................void	**fireTreeNodesInserted** (Object source, Object[] path, int[] childIndices, Object[] children)
	protected.................void	**fireTreeNodesRemoved** (Object source, Object[] path, int[] childIndices, Object[] children)
	protected.................void	**fireTreeStructureChanged** (Object source, Object[] path, int[] childIndices, Object[] children)
1	public...................Object	**getChild** (Object parent, int index)
1	public......................int	**getChildCount** (Object parent)
1	public......................int	**getIndexOfChild** (Object parent, Object child)
	public..............*TreeNode[]*	**getPathToRoot** (*TreeNode* aNode)
	protected...........*TreeNode[]*	**getPathToRoot** (*TreeNode* aNode, int depth)
	public...................Object	**getRoot** ()
	public....................void	**insertNodeInto** (*MutableTreeNode* newChild, *MutableTreeNode* parent, int index)
1	public................. boolean	**isLeaf** (Object node)
	protected..............javax↩	**listenerList**
	.swing.event.EventListenerList	
	public....................void	**nodeChanged** (*TreeNode* node)
	public....................void	**nodesChanged** (*TreeNode* node, int[] childIndices)
	public....................void	**nodeStructureChanged** (*TreeNode* node)
	public....................void	**nodesWereInserted** (*TreeNode* node, int[] childIndices)
	public....................void	**nodesWereRemoved** (*TreeNode* node, int[] childIndices, Object[] removedChildren)
	public....................void	**reload** ()
	public....................void	**reload** (*TreeNode* node)

DefaultTreeModel

	public	void	**removeNodeFromParent** (*MutableTreeNode* node)
1	public	void	**removeTreeModelListener** (*javax.swing.event.TreeModelListener* l)
	protected	*TreeNode*	**root**
	public	void	**setAsksAllowsChildren** (boolean newValue)
	public	void	**setRoot** (*TreeNode* root)
1	public	void	**valueForPathChanged** (TreePath path, Object newValue)

DefaultTreeSelectionModel   javax.swing.tree

Object [1]
1.2 └DefaultTreeSelectionModel - - - - - - - - - - - - - - - - *Cloneable, java.io.Serializable, TreeSelectionModel* [2]

2	public synchronized	void	**addPropertyChangeListener** (*java.beans.PropertyChangeListener* listener)
2	public	void	**addSelectionPath** (TreePath path)
2	public	void	**addSelectionPaths** (TreePath[] paths)
2	public	void	**addTreeSelectionListener** (*javax.swing.event.TreeSelectionListener* x)
	protected	boolean	**arePathsContiguous** (TreePath[] paths)
	protected	boolean	**canPathsBeAdded** (TreePath[] paths)
	protected	boolean	**canPathsBeRemoved** (TreePath[] paths)
	protected . javax.swing.event ↵ .SwingPropertyChangeSupport		**changeSupport**
2	public	void	**clearSelection** ()
1	public	**Object**	**clone** () throws CloneNotSupportedException
*	public		**DefaultTreeSelectionModel** ()
	protected	void	**fireValueChanged** (javax.swing.event.TreeSelectionEvent e)
2	public	TreePath	**getLeadSelectionPath** ()
2	public	int	**getLeadSelectionRow** ()
2	public	int	**getMaxSelectionRow** ()
2	public	int	**getMinSelectionRow** ()
2	public	*RowMapper*	**getRowMapper** ()
2	public	int	**getSelectionCount** ()
2	public	int	**getSelectionMode** ()
2	public	TreePath	**getSelectionPath** ()
2	public	TreePath[]	**getSelectionPaths** ()
2	public	int[]	**getSelectionRows** ()
	protected	void	**insureRowContinuity** ()
	protected	void	**insureUniqueness** ()
2	public	boolean	**isPathSelected** (TreePath path)
2	public	boolean	**isRowSelected** (int row)
2	public	boolean	**isSelectionEmpty** ()
	protected	int	**leadIndex**
	protected	TreePath	**leadPath**
	protected	int	**leadRow**
	protected	javax ↵ .swing.event.EventListenerList	**listenerList**
	protected	javax.swing ↵ .DefaultListSelectionModel	**listSelectionModel**
	protected	void	**notifyPathChange** (java.util.Vector changedPaths, TreePath oldLeadSelection)
2	public synchronized	void	**removePropertyChangeListener** (*java.beans.PropertyChangeListener* listener)
2	public	void	**removeSelectionPath** (TreePath path)
2	public	void	**removeSelectionPaths** (TreePath[] paths)
2	public	void	**removeTreeSelectionListener** (*javax.swing.event.TreeSelectionListener* x)
2	public	void	**resetRowSelection** ()
	protected transient	*RowMapper*	**rowMapper**
	protected	TreePath[]	**selection**
▲	public static final	String	**SELECTION_MODE_PROPERTY** = "selectionMode"
	protected	int	**selectionMode**
2	public	void	**setRowMapper** (*RowMapper* newMapper)
2	public	void	**setSelectionMode** (int mode)
2	public	void	**setSelectionPath** (TreePath path)
2	public	void	**setSelectionPaths** (TreePath[] pPaths)
1	public	**String**	**toString** ()
	protected	void	**updateLeadIndex** ()

DefinitionKind   org.omg.CORBA

Object
1.2 └DefinitionKind - *org.omg.CORBA.portable.IDLEntity* (*java.io.Serializable*)

Class *Interface* —extends - - -implements ○ abstract ● final △ static ▲ static final ✱ constructor x x—inherited x **x**—declared **x x**—overridden

▲	public static final	int	**_dk_Alias** = 9
▲	public static final	int	**_dk_all** = 1
▲	public static final	int	**_dk_Array** = 16
▲	public static final	int	**_dk_Attribute** = 2
▲	public static final	int	**_dk_Constant** = 3
▲	public static final	int	**_dk_Enum** = 12
▲	public static final	int	**_dk_Exception** = 4
▲	public static final	int	**_dk_Fixed** = 19
▲	public static final	int	**_dk_Interface** = 5
▲	public static final	int	**_dk_Module** = 6
▲	public static final	int	**_dk_Native** = 23
▲	public static final	int	**_dk_none** = 0
▲	public static final	int	**_dk_Operation** = 7
▲	public static final	int	**_dk_Primitive** = 13
▲	public static final	int	**_dk_Repository** = 17
▲	public static final	int	**_dk_Sequence** = 15
▲	public static final	int	**_dk_String** = 14
▲	public static final	int	**_dk_Struct** = 10
▲	public static final	int	**_dk_Typedef** = 8
▲	public static final	int	**_dk_Union** = 11
▲	public static final	int	**_dk_Value** = 20
▲	public static final	int	**_dk_ValueBox** = 21
▲	public static final	int	**_dk_ValueMember** = 22
▲	public static final	int	**_dk_Wstring** = 18
*	protected		**DefinitionKind** (int _value)
▲	public static final DefinitionKind		**dk_Alias**
▲	public static final DefinitionKind		**dk_all**
▲	public static final DefinitionKind		**dk_Array**
▲	public static final DefinitionKind		**dk_Attribute**
▲	public static final DefinitionKind		**dk_Constant**
▲	public static final DefinitionKind		**dk_Enum**
▲	public static final DefinitionKind		**dk_Exception**
▲	public static final DefinitionKind		**dk_Fixed**
▲	public static final DefinitionKind		**dk_Interface**
▲	public static final DefinitionKind		**dk_Module**
▲	public static final DefinitionKind		**dk_Native**
▲	public static final DefinitionKind		**dk_none**
▲	public static final DefinitionKind		**dk_Operation**
▲	public static final DefinitionKind		**dk_Primitive**
▲	public static final DefinitionKind		**dk_Repository**
▲	public static final DefinitionKind		**dk_Sequence**
▲	public static final DefinitionKind		**dk_String**
▲	public static final DefinitionKind		**dk_Struct**
▲	public static final DefinitionKind		**dk_Typedef**
▲	public static final DefinitionKind		**dk_Union**
▲	public static final DefinitionKind		**dk_Value**
▲	public static final DefinitionKind		**dk_ValueBox**
▲	public static final DefinitionKind		**dk_ValueMember**
▲	public static final DefinitionKind		**dk_Wstring**
△	public static DefinitionKind		**from_int** (int i) throws BAD_PARAM
	public	int	**value** ()

Deflater   java.util.zip

P○

Classes

```
Object 1
1.1    └ Deflater
```

▲	public static final	int	**BEST_COMPRESSION** = 9
▲	public static final	int	**BEST_SPEED** = 1
▲	public static final	int	**DEFAULT_COMPRESSION** = -1
▲	public static final	int	**DEFAULT_STRATEGY** = 0
	public	int	**deflate** (byte[] b)
	public synchronized	int	**deflate** (byte[] b, int off, int len)
▲	public static final	int	**DEFLATED** = 8
*	public		**Deflater** ()
*	public		**Deflater** (int level)
*	public		**Deflater** (int level, boolean nowrap)
	public synchronized	void	**end** ()
▲	public static final	int	**FILTERED** = 1
1	protected	void	**finalize** ()
	public synchronized	void	**finish** ()
	public synchronized	boolean	**finished** ()
	public synchronized	int	**getAdler** ()

Deflater

	public synchronized ....int	**getTotalIn** ()
	public synchronized ....int	**getTotalOut** ()
▲	public static final.............int	**HUFFMAN_ONLY** = 2
	public................ boolean	**needsInput** ()
▲	public static final.............int	**NO_COMPRESSION** = 0
	public synchronized ....void	**reset** ()
	public...................void	**setDictionary** (byte[] b)
	public synchronized ....void	**setDictionary** (byte[] b, int off, int len)
	public...................void	**setInput** (byte[] b)
	public synchronized ....void	**setInput** (byte[] b, int off, int len)
	public synchronized ....void	**setLevel** (int level)
	public synchronized ....void	**setStrategy** (int strategy)

DeflaterOutputStream   java.util.zip

P○

Object
  └java.io.OutputStream
    └java.io.FilterOutputStream [1]

1.1   └DeflaterOutputStream

	protected ....byte[]	**buf**
1	public..................... **void**	**close** () throws java.io.IOException
	protected ....Deflater	**def**
	protected ....void	**deflate** () throws java.io.IOException
✳	public..........................	**DeflaterOutputStream** (java.io.OutputStream out)
✳	public..........................	**DeflaterOutputStream** (java.io.OutputStream out, Deflater def)
✳	public..........................	**DeflaterOutputStream** (java.io.OutputStream out, Deflater def, int size)
	public...................void	**finish** () throws java.io.IOException
1	public...................void	flush () throws java.io.IOException
1	protected java.io.OutputStream	out
1	public...................void	write (byte[] b) throws java.io.IOException
1	public..................... **void**	**write** (int b) throws java.io.IOException
1	public..................... **void**	**write** (byte[] b, int off, int len) throws java.io.IOException

---

Delegate   org.omg.CORBA.portable

Object
1.2 ○ └Delegate

○	public abstract ....org.omg.CORBA.Request	**create_request** (*org.omg.CORBA.Object* obj, org.omg.CORBA.Context ctx, String operation, org.omg.CORBA.NVList arg_list, org.omg.CORBA.NamedValue result)
○	public abstract ....org.omg.CORBA.Request	**create_request** (*org.omg.CORBA.Object* obj, org.omg.CORBA.Context ctx, String operation, org.omg.CORBA.NVList arg_list, org.omg.CORBA.NamedValue result, org.omg.CORBA.ExceptionList exclist, org.omg.CORBA.ContextList ctxlist)
✳	public..........................	**Delegate** ()
○	public abstract .... *org.omg.CORBA.Object*	**duplicate** (*org.omg.CORBA.Object* obj)
	public................ boolean	**equals** (*org.omg.CORBA.Object* self, Object obj)
	public.............. *org.omg*↩ .CORBA.DomainManager[]	**get_domain_managers** (*org.omg.CORBA.Object* self)
	public. *org.omg.CORBA.Object*	**get_interface_def** (*org.omg.CORBA.Object* self)
	public. *org.omg.CORBA.Policy*	**get_policy** (*org.omg.CORBA.Object* self, int policy_type)
○	public abstract ....int	**hash** (*org.omg.CORBA.Object* obj, int max)
	public.....................int	**hashCode** (*org.omg.CORBA.Object* self)
	public.............. InputStream	**invoke** (*org. omg. CORBA. Object* self, OutputStream output) throws ApplicationException, RemarshalException
○	public abstract .... boolean	**is_a** (*org.omg.CORBA.Object* obj, String repository_id)
○	public abstract .... boolean	**is_equivalent** (*org.omg.CORBA.Object* obj, *org.omg.CORBA.Object* other)
	public................ boolean	**is_local** (*org.omg.CORBA.Object* self)
○	public abstract .... boolean	**non_existent** (*org.omg.CORBA.Object* obj)
	public...org.omg.CORBA.ORB	**orb** (*org.omg.CORBA.Object* obj)
○	public abstract ....void	**release** (*org.omg.CORBA.Object* obj)
	public...................void	**releaseReply** (*org.omg.CORBA.Object* self, InputStream input)
○	public abstract ....org.omg.CORBA.Request	**request** (*org.omg.CORBA.Object* obj, String operation)
	public............ OutputStream	**request** (*org. omg. CORBA. Object* self, String operation, boolean responseExpected)
	public...................void	**servant_postinvoke** (*org.omg.CORBA.Object* self, ServantObject servant)

Class *Interface* —extends - - -implements ○ abstract ● final △ static ▲ static final ✳ constructor x x—inherited x **x**—declared **x x**—overridden

public . . . . ServantObject **servant_preinvoke** (*org. omg. CORBA. Object* self, String operation,
                              Class expectedType)
public *org.omg.CORBA.Object* **set_policy_override** (*org. omg. CORBA. Object* self,
                              org.omg.CORBA.Policy[] policies, org.omg.CORBA.SetOverrideType set_add)
public . . . . String **toString** (*org.omg.CORBA.Object* self)

DesignMode   java.beans

1.2	*DesignMode*

- -
```
       public . . . . . . . . . . . . . . . . boolean  isDesignTime ()
   ▲   public static final . . . . . . . . String   PROPERTYNAME  = "designTime"
       public . . . . . . . . . . . . . . . . . . . void   setDesignTime (boolean designTime)
```
- -

DesktopIconUI   javax.swing.plaf

Object
1.2 ○	└ComponentUI [1]
1.2 ○	└ DesktopIconUI

```
      1  11 inherited members from ComponentUI not shown
   *   public . . . . . . . . . . . . . . . . . . . . . . . . . . DesktopIconUI ()
```

DesktopManager   javax.swing

1.2	*DesktopManager*

- -
```
   public . . . . . . . . . . . . . . . . . . . . void  activateFrame (JInternalFrame f)
   public . . . . . . . . . . . . . . . . . . . . void  beginDraggingFrame (JComponent f)
   public . . . . . . . . . . . . . . . . . . . . void  beginResizingFrame (JComponent f, int direction)
   public . . . . . . . . . . . . . . . . . . . . void  closeFrame (JInternalFrame f)
   public . . . . . . . . . . . . . . . . . . . . void  deactivateFrame (JInternalFrame f)
   public . . . . . . . . . . . . . . . . . . . . void  deiconifyFrame (JInternalFrame f)
   public . . . . . . . . . . . . . . . . . . . . void  dragFrame (JComponent f, int newX, int newY)
   public . . . . . . . . . . . . . . . . . . . . void  endDraggingFrame (JComponent f)
   public . . . . . . . . . . . . . . . . . . . . void  endResizingFrame (JComponent f)
   public . . . . . . . . . . . . . . . . . . . . void  iconifyFrame (JInternalFrame f)
   public . . . . . . . . . . . . . . . . . . . . void  maximizeFrame (JInternalFrame f)
   public . . . . . . . . . . . . . . . . . . . . void  minimizeFrame (JInternalFrame f)
   public . . . . . . . . . . . . . . . . . . . . void  openFrame (JInternalFrame f)
   public . . . . . . . . . . . . . . . . . . . . void  resizeFrame (JComponent f, int newX, int newY, int newWidth, int newHeight)
   public . . . . . . . . . . . . . . . . . . . . void  setBoundsForFrame (JComponent f, int newX, int newY, int newWidth,
                              int newHeight)
```
- -

DesktopPaneUI   javax.swing.plaf

Object
1.2 ○	└ComponentUI [1]
1.2 ○	└ DesktopPaneUI

```
      1  11 inherited members from ComponentUI not shown
   *   public . . . . . . . . . . . . . . . . . . . . . . . . . . DesktopPaneUI ()
```

DGC   java.rmi.dgc

1.1	*DGC*————————————————————*java.rmi.Remote* P○

- -
```
   public . . . . . . . . . . . . . . . . . . . . void  clean (java.rmi.server.ObjID[] ids, long sequenceNum, VMID vmid, boolean strong)
                              throws java.rmi.RemoteException
   public . . . . . . . . . . . . . . . . Lease  dirty (java.rmi.server.ObjID[] ids, long sequenceNum, Lease lease)
                              throws java.rmi.RemoteException
```
- -

Dialog

Dialog				java.awt
				Pᵐ

```
Object
 ○  └─Component¹ ─────────────────────────── java.awt.image.ImageObserver, MenuContainer,
                                              java.io.Serializable
        └─Container²
           └─Window³
              └─Dialog
```

	1	*131 inherited members from Component not shown*	
	2	*48 inherited members from Container not shown*	
	3	public...................... **void addNotify** ()	
1.1	3	public synchronized ....void addWindowListener (*java.awt.event.WindowListener* l)	
1.2	3	public.......................void applyResourceBundle (String rbName)	
1.2	3	public.......................void applyResourceBundle (java.util.ResourceBundle rb)	
1.2 ✳		public.......................... **Dialog** (Dialog owner)	
1.1 ✳		public.......................... **Dialog** (Frame owner)	
1.2 ✳		public.......................... **Dialog** (Dialog owner, String title)	
1.1 ✳		public.......................... **Dialog** (Frame owner, String title)	
✳		public.......................... **Dialog** (Frame owner, boolean modal)	
1.2 ✳		public.......................... **Dialog** (Dialog owner, String title, boolean modal)	
✳		public.......................... **Dialog** (Frame owner, String title, boolean modal)	
	3	public.......................void dispose ()	
	3	protected ....void finalize () throws Throwable	
1.1	3	public.............. Component getFocusOwner ()	
1.2	3	public.......................... getInputContext ()	
		.... java.awt.im.InputContext	
1.1	3	public...........java.util.Locale getLocale ()	
1.2	3	public.................Window[] getOwnedWindows ()	
1.2	3	public................. Window getOwner ()	
		public.................String **getTitle** ()	
	3	public................. Toolkit getToolkit ()	
●	3	public final .... String getWarningString ()	
		public................. boolean **isModal** ()	
		public................. boolean **isResizable** ()	
	3	public................. boolean isShowing ()	
	3	public.......................void pack ()	
	2	protected .... **String paramString** ()	
1.1	3	protected ....void processEvent (AWTEvent e)	
1.1	3	protected ....void processWindowEvent (java.awt.event.WindowEvent e)	
1.1	3	public synchronized ....void removeWindowListener (*java.awt.event.WindowListener* l)	
1.1		public.......................void **setModal** (boolean b)	
		public.......................void **setResizable** (boolean resizable)	
		public synchronized ....void **setTitle** (String title)	
	3	public....................... **void show** ()	
	3	public.......................void toBack ()	
	3	public.......................void toFront ()	

DialogPeer		java.awt.peer

```
DialogPeer─────────────────────── WindowPeer ¹ (ContainerPeer ² (ComponentPeer ³))
```

3	*32 inherited members from ComponentPeer not shown*	
1	*7 inherited members from WindowPeer not shown*	
2	*4 inherited members from ContainerPeer not shown*	
	public.......................void **setResizable** (boolean)	
	public.......................void **setTitle** (String)	

Dictionary			java.util
			P

```
Object
 ○  └─Dictionary
```

✳	public.......................... **Dictionary** ()	
○	public abstract ... *Enumeration* **elements** ()	
○	public abstract .... Object **get** (Object key)	
○	public abstract .... boolean **isEmpty** ()	
○	public abstract ... *Enumeration* **keys** ()	
○	public abstract ....Object **put** (Object key, Object value)	
○	public abstract ....Object **remove** (Object key)	

Class   *Interface*   ──extends   - - -implements   ○ abstract   ● final   △ static   ▲ static final   ✳ constructor   x x──inherited   x **x**──declared   **x x**──overridden

○ public abstract . . . . int **size** ()

DigestException java.security

```
Object                                                    P⁰
└Throwable - - - - - - - - - - - - - - - - - - - - - - - - - java.io.Serializable
  └Exception
```
1.2 └GeneralSecurityException
1.1   └DigestException

---

* public . . . . **DigestException** ()
* public . . . . **DigestException** (String msg)

DigestInputStream java.security

```
Object¹                                                   P⁰
```
○ └java.io.InputStream
    └java.io.FilterInputStream²
1.1   └DigestInputStream

---

2 public . . . . int available () throws java.io.IOException
2 public . . . . void close () throws java.io.IOException
   protected . . . . . . MessageDigest **digest**
* public . . . . **DigestInputStream** (java.io.InputStream stream, MessageDigest digest)
   public . . . . MessageDigest **getMessageDigest** ()
2 protected . . java.io.InputStream in
2 public synchronized . . . . void mark (int readlimit)
2 public . . . . boolean markSupported ()
   public . . . . void **on** (boolean on)
2 public . . . . **int read** () throws java.io.IOException
2 public . . . . int read (byte[] b) throws java.io.IOException
2 public . . . . **int read** (byte[] b, int off, int len) throws java.io.IOException
2 public synchronized . . . . void reset () throws java.io.IOException
   public . . . . void **setMessageDigest** (MessageDigest digest)
2 public . . . . long skip (long n) throws java.io.IOException
1 public . . . . **String toString** ()

DigestOutputStream java.security

```
Object¹                                                   P⁰
```
○ └java.io.OutputStream
    └java.io.FilterOutputStream²
1.1   └DigestOutputStream

---

2 public . . . . void close () throws java.io.IOException
   protected . . . . . . MessageDigest **digest**
* public . . . . **DigestOutputStream** (java.io.OutputStream stream, MessageDigest digest)
2 public . . . . void flush () throws java.io.IOException
   public . . . . MessageDigest **getMessageDigest** ()
   public . . . . void **on** (boolean on)
2 protected java.io.OutputStream out
   public . . . . void **setMessageDigest** (MessageDigest digest)
1 public . . . . **String toString** ()
2 public . . . . void write (byte[] b) throws java.io.IOException
2 public . . . . **void write** (int b) throws java.io.IOException
2 public . . . . **void write** (byte[] b, int off, int len) throws java.io.IOException

---

Dimension java.awt

```
Object¹                                                   P
```
1.2 ○ └java.awt.geom.Dimension2D² - - - - - - - - - - - - Cloneable
      └Dimension - java.io.Serializable

---

* 2 public . . . . Object clone ()
* public . . . . **Dimension** ()
* public . . . . **Dimension** (Dimension d)
* public . . . . **Dimension** (int width, int height)
   1 public . . . . **boolean equals** (Object obj)
1.2 2 public . . . . **double getHeight** ()

Dimension

1.1		public.............Dimension	**getSize** ()	
1.2	2	public.................**double**	**getWidth** ()	
		public.........................int	**height**	
1.1		public.....................void	**setSize** (Dimension d)	
1.2	2	public.....................void	setSize (java.awt.geom.Dimension2D d)	
1.2	2	public.................**void**	**setSize** (double width, double height)	
1.1		public.....................void	**setSize** (int width, int height)	
	1	public.................**String**	**toString** ()	
		public.........................int	**width**	

D

Dimension2D   java.awt.geom

```
Object 1
 └Dimension2D - - - - - - - - - - - - - - - - - - - - - - - - - Cloneable
```
1.2 ○

	1	public.................**Object**	**clone** ()	
✳		protected.....................**Dimension2D** ()		
○		public abstract..........double	**getHeight** ()	
○		public abstract..........double	**getWidth** ()	
		public.....................void	**setSize** (Dimension2D d)	
○		public abstract.............void	**setSize** (double width, double height)	

DimensionUIResource   javax.swing.plaf

```
Object
 └java.awt.geom.Dimension2D 1 - - - - - - - - - - - - Cloneable
    └java.awt.Dimension 2 - - - - - - - - - - - - - - - - - java.io.Serializable
       └DimensionUIResource - - - - - - - - - - - - - - UIResource
```
1.2 ○

1.2

	1	*2 inherited members from java.awt.geom.Dimension2D not shown*	
	2	*10 inherited members from java.awt.Dimension not shown*	
✳		public.........................**DimensionUIResource** (int width, int height)	

DirectColorModel   java.awt.image
P

```
Object
 └ColorModel 1 - - - - - - - - - - - - - - - - - - - - - - - - java.awt.Transparency
    └PackedColorModel 2
       └DirectColorModel
```
○
1.2 ○

1.2	● 1	public final ....**ColorModel**	**coerceData** (WritableRaster raster, boolean isAlphaPremultiplied)	
1.2	2	public............SampleModel	createCompatibleSampleModel (int w, int h)	
1.2	● 1	public final ....**WritableRaster**	**createCompatibleWritableRaster** (int w, int h)	
✳		public.........................**DirectColorModel** (int bits, int rmask, int gmask, int bmask)		
✳		public.........................**DirectColorModel** (int bits, int rmask, int gmask, int bmask, int amask)		
1.2	✳	public.........................**DirectColorModel** (java.awt.color.ColorSpace space, int bits, int rmask, int gmask, int bmask, int amask, boolean isAlphaPremultiplied, int transferType)		
	2	public................. boolean	equals (Object obj)	
	1	public.....................void	finalize ()	
●	1	public final ....**int**	**getAlpha** (int pixel)	
1.2	1	public.....................**int**	**getAlpha** (Object inData)	
●		public final ....int	**getAlphaMask** ()	
1.2	2	public......... WritableRaster	getAlphaRaster (WritableRaster raster)	
●	1	public final ....**int**	**getBlue** (int pixel)	
1.2	1	public.....................**int**	**getBlue** (Object inData)	
●		public final ....int	**getBlueMask** ()	
1.2	● 1	public final .... java.awt.color.ColorSpace	getColorSpace ()	
1.2	● 1	public final ....**int[]**	**getComponents** (int pixel, int[] components, int offset)	
1.2	● 1	public final ....**int[]**	**getComponents** (Object pixel, int[] components, int offset)	
1.2	1	public.....................int[]	getComponentSize ()	
1.2	1	public.........................int	getComponentSize (int componentIdx)	
1.2	1	public.....................**int**	**getDataElement** (int[] components, int offset)	
1.2	1	public.................**Object**	**getDataElements** (int rgb, Object pixel)	
1.2	1	public.................**Object**	**getDataElements** (int[] components, int offset, Object obj)	
●	1	public final ....**int**	**getGreen** (int pixel)	
1.2	1	public.....................**int**	**getGreen** (Object inData)	
●		public final ....int	**getGreenMask** ()	

Class   *Interface*   —extends   - - -implements   ○ abstract   ● final   △ static   ▲ static final   ✳ constructor   x x—inherited   x **x**—declared   **x x**—overridden

1.2	●	2	public final	int	getMask (int index)
1.2	●	2	public final	int[]	getMasks ()
1.2		1	public	float[]	getNormalizedComponents (int[] components, int offset, float[] normComponents, int normOffset)
1.2		1	public	int	getNumColorComponents ()
1.2		1	public	int	getNumComponents ()
		1	public	int	getPixelSize ()
	●	1	public final	**int**	**getRed** (int pixel)
1.2		1	public	**int**	**getRed** (Object inData)
	●		public final	**int**	**getRedMask** ()
	●	1	public final	**int**	**getRGB** (int pixel)
1.2		1	public	**int**	**getRGB** (Object inData)
	△	1	public static	ColorModel	getRGBdefault ()
1.2		1	public	int	getTransparency ()
1.2		1	public	int[]	getUnnormalizedComponents (float[] normComponents, int normOffset, int[] components, int offset)
1.2	●	1	public final	boolean	hasAlpha ()
1.2	●	1	public final	boolean	isAlphaPremultiplied ()
1.2		1	public	**boolean**	**isCompatibleRaster** (Raster raster)
1.2		2	public	boolean	isCompatibleSampleModel (SampleModel sm)
		1	protected	int	pixel_bits
		1	public	**String**	**toString** ()
1.2		1	protected	int	transferType

DnDConstants   java.awt.dnd

Object
1.2 ● └ DnDConstants

▲	public static final	int	**ACTION_COPY**	= 1
▲	public static final	int	**ACTION_COPY_OR_MOVE**	= 3
▲	public static final	int	**ACTION_LINK**	= 1073741824
▲	public static final	int	**ACTION_MOVE**	= 2
▲	public static final	int	**ACTION_NONE**	= 0
▲	public static final	int	**ACTION_REFERENCE**	= 1073741824

Document   javax.swing.text

1.2 *Document*

	public	void	**addDocumentListener** (*javax.swing.event.DocumentListener* listener)
	public	void	**addUndoableEditListener** (*javax.swing.event.UndoableEditListener* listener)
	public	*Position*	**createPosition** (int offs) throws BadLocationException
	public	*Element*	**getDefaultRootElement** ()
	public	*Position*	**getEndPosition** ()
	public	int	**getLength** ()
	public	Object	**getProperty** (Object key)
	public	*Element[]*	**getRootElements** ()
	public	*Position*	**getStartPosition** ()
	public	String	**getText** (int offset, int length) throws BadLocationException
	public	void	**getText** (int offset, int length, Segment txt) throws BadLocationException
	public	void	**insertString** (int offset, String str, *AttributeSet* a) throws BadLocationException
	public	void	**putProperty** (Object key, Object value)
	public	void	**remove** (int offs, int len) throws BadLocationException
	public	void	**removeDocumentListener** (*javax.swing.event.DocumentListener* listener)
	public	void	**removeUndoableEditListener** (*javax.swing.event.UndoableEditListener* listener)
	public	void	**render** (*Runnable* r)
▲	public static final	String	**StreamDescriptionProperty** = "stream"
▲	public static final	String	**TitleProperty** = "title"

DocumentEvent   javax.swing.event

1.2 *DocumentEvent*

	public	*DocumentEvent*↵ .*ElementChange*	**getChange** (*javax.swing.text.Element* elem)
	public	.... *javax.swing.text.Document*	**getDocument** ()
	public	int	**getLength** ()
	public	int	**getOffset** ()

DocumentEvent

public............................	**getType** ()	
.... DocumentEvent.EventType		

DocumentEvent.ElementChange

javax.swing.event

1.2 *DocumentEvent.ElementChange*

public............................	**getChildrenAdded** ()	
.... *javax.swing.text.Element[]*		
public............................	**getChildrenRemoved** ()	
.... *javax.swing.text.Element[]*		
public............................	**getElement** ()	
.... *javax.swing.text.Element*		
public............................int	**getIndex** ()	

DocumentEvent.EventType

javax.swing.event

Object[1]
1.2 ● └DocumentEvent.EventType

▲	public static final	**CHANGE**	
	.... DocumentEvent.EventType		
▲	public static final	**INSERT**	
	.... DocumentEvent.EventType		
▲	public static final	**REMOVE**	
	.... DocumentEvent.EventType		
1	public.................. **String**	**toString** ()	

DocumentListener

javax.swing.event

1.2 *DocumentListener*────────────────────*java.util.EventListener*

public......................void	**changedUpdate** (*DocumentEvent* e)	
public......................void	**insertUpdate** (*DocumentEvent* e)	
public......................void	**removeUpdate** (*DocumentEvent* e)	

DocumentParser

javax.swing.text.html.parser

Object
1.2 └Parser[1] - *DTDConstants*
1.2 └DocumentParser

✳	public............................	**DocumentParser** (DTD dtd)	
1	protected .... DTD	dtd	
1	protected ....void	endTag (boolean omitted)	
1	protected ....void	error (String err)	
1	protected ....void	error (String err, String arg1)	
1	protected ....void	error (String err, String arg1, String arg2)	
1	protected ....void	error (String err, String arg1, String arg2, String arg3)	
1	protected ....void	flushAttributes ()	
1	protected ....javax↩	getAttributes ()	
	.swing.text.SimpleAttributeSet		
1	protected ....int	getCurrentLine ()	
1	protected ....int	getCurrentPos ()	
1	protected .... **void handleComment** (char[] text)		
1	protected .... **void handleEmptyTag** (TagElement tag) throws javax. swing. text↩		
	.ChangedCharSetException		
1	protected .... **void handleEndTag** (TagElement tag)		
1	protected ....void	handleEOFInComment ()	
1	protected .... **void handleError** (int ln, String errorMsg)		
1	protected .... **void handleStartTag** (TagElement tag)		
1	protected .... **void handleText** (char[] data)		
1	protected ....void	handleTitle (char[] text)	
1	protected .... TagElement	makeTag (Element elem)	
1	protected .... TagElement	makeTag (Element elem, boolean fictional)	
1	protected ....void	markFirstTime (Element elem)	
1	public synchronized ....void	parse (java.io.Reader in) throws java.io.IOException	
	public......................void	**parse** (java.io.Reader in, javax.swing.text.html.HTMLEditorKit.ParserCallback	
		callback, boolean ignoreCharSet) throws java.io.IOException	

Class *Interface* —extends - - -implements ○ abstract ● final △ static ▲ static final ✳ constructor x x—inherited x **x**—declared **x x**—overridden

1	public	String	parseDTDMarkup	() throws java.io.IOException
1	protected	boolean	parseMarkupDeclarations	(StringBuffer strBuff) throws java.io.IOException
1	protected	void	startTag	(TagElement tag) throws javax.swing.text.ChangedCharSetException
1	protected	boolean	strict	

DomainManager — org.omg.CORBA

D

1.2 *DomainManager*——————————— *Object* [1]

- 1 *13 inherited members from Object not shown*

	public .... *Policy*	**get_domain_policy** (int policy_type)

Double — java.lang

P

Object [1]
○ └ Number [2] ---------------------- *java.io.Serializable*
●   └ Double ---------------------- *Comparable* [3]

1.1	2	public	**byte**	**byteValue** ()
1.2		public	int	**compareTo** (Double anotherDouble)
1.2	3	public	int	**compareTo** (Object o)
*		public		**Double** (double value)
*		public		**Double** (String s) throws NumberFormatException
△		public static native	long	**doubleToLongBits** (double value)
	2	public	**double**	**doubleValue** ()
	1	public	**boolean**	**equals** (Object obj)
	2	public	**float**	**floatValue** ()
	1	public	**int**	**hashCode** ()
	2	public	**int**	**intValue** ()
		public	boolean	**isInfinite** ()
△		public static	boolean	**isInfinite** (double v)
		public	boolean	**isNaN** ()
△		public static	boolean	**isNaN** (double v)
△		public static native	double	**longBitsToDouble** (long bits)
	2	public	**long**	**longValue** ()
▲		public static final	double	**MAX_VALUE** = 1.7976931348623157E308
▲		public static final	double	**MIN_VALUE** = 4.9E-324
▲		public static final	double	**NaN** = NaN
▲		public static final	double	**NEGATIVE_INFINITY** = -Infinity
1.2 △		public static	double	**parseDouble** (String s) throws NumberFormatException
▲		public static final	double	**POSITIVE_INFINITY** = Infinity
1.1	2	public	**short**	**shortValue** ()
	1	public	**String**	**toString** ()
△		public static	String	**toString** (double d)
1.1 ▲		public static final	Class	**TYPE**
△		public static	Double	**valueOf** (String s) throws NumberFormatException

DoubleHolder — org.omg.CORBA

Object
1.2 ● └ DoubleHolder ---------------------- *org.omg.CORBA.portable.Streamable* [1]

	1	public	void	**_read** (org.omg.CORBA.portable.InputStream input)
	1	public	TypeCode	**_type** ()
	1	public	void	**_write** (org.omg.CORBA.portable.OutputStream output)
*		public		**DoubleHolder** ()
*		public		**DoubleHolder** (double initial)
		public	double	**value**

DragGestureEvent — java.awt.dnd

Object
1.1 └ java.util.EventObject [1] ---------------------- *java.io.Serializable*
1.2   └ DragGestureEvent

*	public		**DragGestureEvent** (DragGestureRecognizer dgr, int act, java.awt.Point ori, *java.util.List* evs)
	public .... java.awt.Component	**getComponent** ()	
	public	int	**getDragAction** ()
	public	java.awt.Point	**getDragOrigin** ()

DragGestureEvent

	public	DragSource	**getDragSource** ()
1	public	Object	getSource ()
	public DragGestureRecognizer		**getSourceAsDragGestureRecognizer** ()
	public		**getTriggerEvent** ()
		java.awt.event.InputEvent	
	public	*java.util.Iterator*	**iterator** ()
1	protected transient	Object	source
	public	void	**startDrag** (java.awt.Cursor dragCursor, *java.awt.datatransfer.Transferable* transferable, *DragSourceListener* dsl) throws InvalidDnDOperationException
	public	void	**startDrag** (java.awt.Cursor dragCursor, java.awt.Image dragImage, java.awt.Point imageOffset, *java.awt.datatransfer.Transferable* transferable, *DragSourceListener* dsl) throws InvalidDnDOperationException
	public	Object[]	**toArray** ()
	public	Object[]	**toArray** (Object[] array)
1	public	String	toString ()

DragGestureListener — java.awt.dnd

1.2   *DragGestureListener* ────────────── *java.util.EventListener*

public	void	**dragGestureRecognized** (DragGestureEvent dge)

DragGestureRecognizer — java.awt.dnd

Object
└ DragGestureRecognizer   1.2 ○

	public synchronized	void	**addDragGestureListener** (*DragGestureListener* dgl) throws java.util.TooManyListenersException
	protected synchronized	void	**appendEvent** (java.awt.event.InputEvent awtie)
	protected java.awt.Component		**component**
	protected *DragGestureListener*		**dragGestureListener**
*	protected		**DragGestureRecognizer** (DragSource ds)
*	protected		**DragGestureRecognizer** (DragSource ds, java.awt.Component c)
*	protected		**DragGestureRecognizer** (DragSource ds, java.awt.Component c, int sa)
*	protected		**DragGestureRecognizer** (DragSource ds, java.awt.Component c, int sa, *DragGestureListener* dgl)
	protected	DragSource	**dragSource**
	protected	java.util.ArrayList	**events**
	protected synchronized	void	**fireDragGestureRecognized** (int dragAction, java.awt.Point p)
	public synchronized	java.awt.Component	**getComponent** ()
	public	DragSource	**getDragSource** ()
	public synchronized	int	**getSourceActions** ()
	public		**getTriggerEvent** ()
		java.awt.event.InputEvent	
○	protected abstract	void	**registerListeners** ()
	public synchronized	void	**removeDragGestureListener** (*DragGestureListener* dgl)
	public	void	**resetRecognizer** ()
	public synchronized	void	**setComponent** (java.awt.Component c)
	public synchronized	void	**setSourceActions** (int actions)
	protected	int	**sourceActions**
○	protected abstract	void	**unregisterListeners** ()

DragSource — java.awt.dnd

Object
└ DragSource   1.2

	public DragGestureRecognizer		**createDefaultDragGestureRecognizer** (java.awt.Component c, int actions, *DragGestureListener* dgl)
	public DragGestureRecognizer		**createDragGestureRecognizer** (Class recognizerAbstractClass, java.awt.Component c, int actions, *DragGestureListener* dgl)
	protected . DragSourceContext		**createDragSourceContext** (java.awt.dnd.peer.DragSourceContextPeer dscp, DragGestureEvent dgl, java.awt.Cursor dragCursor, java.awt.Image dragImage, java.awt.Point imageOffset, *java.awt.datatransfer.Transferable* t, *DragSourceListener* dsl)
▲	public static final		**DefaultCopyDrop**
		java.awt.Cursor	

Class   *Interface*   —extends   - - -implements   ○ abstract   ● final   △ static   ▲ static final   ✳ constructor   x x—inherited   x **x**—declared   **x x**—overridden

▲	public static final . . . . java.awt.Cursor	**DefaultCopyNoDrop**	
▲	public static final . . . . java.awt.Cursor	**DefaultLinkDrop**	
▲	public static final . . . . java.awt.Cursor	**DefaultLinkNoDrop**	
▲	public static final . . . . java.awt.Cursor	**DefaultMoveDrop**	
▲	public static final . . . . java.awt.Cursor	**DefaultMoveNoDrop**	
✳	public	**DragSource** ()	
△	public static . . . . DragSource	**getDefaultDragSource** ()	
	public . . . . *java↩* *.awt.datatransfer.FlavorMap*	**getFlavorMap** ()	
△	public static . . . . boolean	**isDragImageSupported** ()	

public . . . . void **startDrag** (DragGestureEvent trigger, java.awt.Cursor dragCursor,
java.awt.datatransfer.Transferable transferable, *DragSourceListener* dsl)
throws InvalidDnDOperationException

public . . . . void **startDrag** (DragGestureEvent trigger, java.awt.Cursor dragCursor,
java.awt.datatransfer.Transferable transferable, *DragSourceListener* dsl, *java↩*
.awt.datatransfer.FlavorMap flavorMap) throws InvalidDnDOperationException

public . . . . void **startDrag** (DragGestureEvent trigger, java.awt.Cursor dragCursor, java.awt.Image
dragImage, java.awt.Point dragOffset, *java.awt.datatransfer.Transferable*
transferable, *DragSourceListener* dsl) throws InvalidDnDOperationException

public . . . . void **startDrag** (DragGestureEvent trigger, java.awt.Cursor dragCursor, java.awt.Image
dragImage, java.awt.Point imageOffset, *java.awt.datatransfer.Transferable*
transferable, *DragSourceListener* dsl, *java.awt.datatransfer.FlavorMap* flavorMap)
throws InvalidDnDOperationException

DragSourceContext java.awt.dnd

Object
1.2　└DragSourceContext - *DragSourceListener* [1] (*java.util.EventListener*)

	public synchronized . . . . void	**addDragSourceListener** (*DragSourceListener* dsl) throws java.util.TooManyListenersException	
▲	protected static final . . . . int	**CHANGED**	
▲	protected static final . . . . int	**DEFAULT**	
1	public synchronized . . . . void	**dragDropEnd** (DragSourceDropEvent dsde)	
1	public synchronized . . . . void	**dragEnter** (DragSourceDragEvent dsde)	
1	public synchronized . . . . void	**dragExit** (DragSourceEvent dse)	
1	public synchronized . . . . void	**dragOver** (DragSourceDragEvent dsde)	
✳	public	**DragSourceContext** (java.awt.dnd.peer.DragSourceContextPeer dscp, DragGestureEvent trigger, java.awt.Cursor dragCursor, java.awt.Image dragImage, java.awt.Point offset, *java.awt.datatransfer.Transferable* t, *DragSourceListener* dsl)	
1	public synchronized . . . . void	**dropActionChanged** (DragSourceDragEvent dsde)	
▲	protected static final . . . . int	**ENTER**	
	public . . . . java.awt.Component	**getComponent** ()	
	public . . . . java.awt.Cursor	**getCursor** ()	
	public . . . . DragSource	**getDragSource** ()	
	public . . . . int	**getSourceActions** ()	
	public . . . . *java↩* *.awt.datatransfer.Transferable*	**getTransferable** ()	
	public . . . . DragGestureEvent	**getTrigger** ()	
▲	protected static final . . . . int	**OVER**	
	public synchronized . . . . void	**removeDragSourceListener** (*DragSourceListener* dsl)	
	public . . . . void	**setCursor** (java.awt.Cursor c)	
	public . . . . void	**transferablesFlavorsChanged** ()	
	protected . . . . void	**updateCurrentCursor** (int dropOp, int targetAct, int status)	

DragSourceDragEvent java.awt.dnd

Object
1.1　└java.util.EventObject [1] - *java.io.Serializable*
1.2　　└DragSourceEvent [2]
1.2　　　└DragSourceDragEvent

Classes

DragSourceDragEvent

*	public		**DragSourceDragEvent** (DragSourceContext dsc, int dropAction, int actions,
			int modifiers)
2	public	DragSourceContext	getDragSourceContext ()
	public	int	**getDropAction** ()
	public	int	**getGestureModifiers** ()
1	public	Object	getSource ()
	public	int	**getTargetActions** ()
	public	int	**getUserAction** ()
1	protected transient	Object	source
1	public	String	toString ()

DragSourceDropEvent java.awt.dnd

```
Object
1.1  └java.util.EventObject¹ - - - - - - - - - - - - - - - - - - - java.io.Serializable
1.2     └DragSourceEvent²
1.2        └DragSourceDropEvent
```

*	public		**DragSourceDropEvent** (DragSourceContext dsc)
*	public		**DragSourceDropEvent** (DragSourceContext dsc, int action, boolean success)
2	public	DragSourceContext	getDragSourceContext ()
	public	int	**getDropAction** ()
	public	boolean	**getDropSuccess** ()
1	public	Object	getSource ()
1	protected transient	Object	source
1	public	String	toString ()

DragSourceEvent java.awt.dnd

```
Object
1.1  └java.util.EventObject¹ - - - - - - - - - - - - - - - - - - - java.io.Serializable
1.2     └DragSourceEvent
```

*	public		**DragSourceEvent** (DragSourceContext dsc)
	public	DragSourceContext	**getDragSourceContext** ()
1	public	Object	getSource ()
1	protected transient	Object	source
1	public	String	toString ()

DragSourceListener java.awt.dnd

```
1.2  DragSourceListener─────────────────java.util.EventListener
```

	public	void	**dragDropEnd** (DragSourceDropEvent dsde)
	public	void	**dragEnter** (DragSourceDragEvent dsde)
	public	void	**dragExit** (DragSourceEvent dse)
	public	void	**dragOver** (DragSourceDragEvent dsde)
	public	void	**dropActionChanged** (DragSourceDragEvent dsde)

Driver java.sql
P⁰

```
1.1  Driver
```

	public	boolean	**acceptsURL** (String url) throws SQLException
	public	*Connection*	**connect** (String url, java.util.Properties info) throws SQLException
	public	int	**getMajorVersion** ()
	public	int	**getMinorVersion** ()
	public	DriverPropertyInfo[]	**getPropertyInfo** (String url, java.util.Properties info) throws SQLException
	public	boolean	**jdbcCompliant** ()

DriverManager java.sql
P⁰

```
Object
1.1  └DriverManager
```

Class *Interface* —extends - - -implements ○ abstract ● final △ static ▲ static final ✳ constructor x x—inherited x **x**—declared **x x**—overridden

336

D

△	public static synchronized void	**deregisterDriver** (*Driver* driver) throws SQLException
△	public static synchronized .... Connection	**getConnection** (String url) throws SQLException
△	public static synchronized .... Connection	**getConnection** (String url, java.util.Properties info) throws SQLException
△	public static synchronized .... Connection	**getConnection** (String url, String user, String password) throws SQLException
△	public static synchronized .... Driver	**getDriver** (String url) throws SQLException
△	public static synchronized .... java.util.Enumeration	**getDrivers** ()
△	public static ....int	**getLoginTimeout** ()
D △	public static java.io.PrintStream	**getLogStream** ()
1.2 △	public static . java.io.PrintWriter	**getLogWriter** ()
△	public static synchronized void	**println** (String message)
△	public static synchronized void	**registerDriver** (*Driver* driver) throws SQLException
△	public static ....void	**setLoginTimeout** (int seconds)
D △	public static synchronized void	**setLogStream** (java.io.PrintStream out)
1.2 △	public static synchronized void	**setLogWriter** (java.io.PrintWriter out)

DriverPropertyInfo

P^O

Object
1.1 └DriverPropertyInfo

	public..................String[]	**choices**
	public...................String	**description**
*	public.......................	**DriverPropertyInfo** (String name, String value)
	public...................String	**name**
	public..................boolean	**required**
	public...................String	**value**

DropTarget

Object
1.2 └DropTarget - *DropTargetListener* [1] (*java.util.EventListener*), *java.io.Serializable*

		public synchronized ....void	**addDropTargetListener** (*DropTargetListener* dtl) throws java.util.TooManyListenersException
		public.......................void	**addNotify** (*java.awt.peer.ComponentPeer* peer)
		protected ....void	**clearAutoscroll** ()
		protected .... DropTarget ↵ .DropTargetAutoScroller	**createDropTargetAutoScroller** (java.awt.Component c, java.awt.Point p)
		protected .. DropTargetContext	**createDropTargetContext** ()
	1	public synchronized ....void	**dragEnter** (DropTargetDragEvent dtde)
	1	public synchronized ....void	**dragExit** (DropTargetEvent dte)
	1	public synchronized ....void	**dragOver** (DropTargetDragEvent dtde)
	1	public synchronized ....void	**drop** (DropTargetDropEvent dtde)
	1	public.......................void	**dropActionChanged** (DropTargetDragEvent dtde)
*		public.......................	**DropTarget** ()
*		public.......................	**DropTarget** (java.awt.Component c, *DropTargetListener* dtl)
*		public.......................	**DropTarget** (java.awt.Component c, int ops, *DropTargetListener* dtl)
*		public.......................	**DropTarget** (java.awt.Component c, int ops, *DropTargetListener* dtl, boolean act)
*		public.......................	**DropTarget** (java.awt.Component c, int ops, *DropTargetListener* dtl, boolean act, *java.awt.datatransfer.FlavorMap* fm)
		public synchronized .... java.awt.Component	**getComponent** ()
		public synchronized ....int	**getDefaultActions** ()
		public...... DropTargetContext	**getDropTargetContext** ()
		public....................*java* ↵ .awt.datatransfer.FlavorMap	**getFlavorMap** ()
		protected ....void	**initializeAutoscrolling** (java.awt.Point p)
		public synchronized .. boolean	**isActive** ()
		public synchronized ....void	**removeDropTargetListener** (*DropTargetListener* dtl)
		public.......................void	**removeNotify** (*java.awt.peer.ComponentPeer* peer)
		public synchronized ....void	**setActive** (boolean isActive)
		public synchronized ....void	**setComponent** (java.awt.Component c)
		public synchronized ....void	**setDefaultActions** (int ops)
		public.......................void	**setFlavorMap** (*java.awt.datatransfer.FlavorMap* fm)
		protected ....void	**updateAutoscroll** (java.awt.Point dragCursorLocn)

Classes

		DropTarget.DropTargetAutoScroller	protected	java.awt.dnd

Object

1.2 └ DropTarget.DropTargetAutoScroller - - - - - - - - - *java.awt.event.ActionListener [1]* (*java.util.EventListener*)

	1	public synchronized ....void	**actionPerformed** (java.awt.event.ActionEvent e)
*		protected	**DropTargetAutoScroller** (java.awt.Component c, java.awt.Point p)
		protected ....void	**stop** ()
		protected synchronized ...void	**updateLocation** (java.awt.Point newLocn)

D

DropTargetContext	java.awt.dnd

Object

1.2 └ DropTargetContext

protected ....void	**acceptDrag** (int dragOperation)
protected ....void	**acceptDrop** (int dropOperation)
public synchronized ....void	**addNotify** (java.awt.dnd.peer.DropTargetContextPeer dtcp)
protected .... *java↵* *.awt.datatransfer.Transferable*	**createTransferableProxy** (*java.awt.datatransfer.Transferable* t, boolean local)
public......................void	**dropComplete** (boolean success) throws InvalidDnDOperationException
public.... java.awt.Component	**getComponent** ()
protected .... *java↵* *.awt.datatransfer.DataFlavor[]*	**getCurrentDataFlavors** ()
protected .... *java.util.List*	**getCurrentDataFlavorsAsList** ()
public.............. DropTarget	**getDropTarget** ()
protected ....int	**getTargetActions** ()
protected synchronized *java↵* *.awt.datatransfer.Transferable*	**getTransferable** () throws InvalidDnDOperationException
protected .... boolean	**isDataFlavorSupported** (java.awt.datatransfer.DataFlavor df)
protected ....void	**rejectDrag** ()
protected ....void	**rejectDrop** ()
public synchronized ....void	**removeNotify** ()
protected ....void	**setTargetActions** (int actions)

		DropTargetContext.TransferableProxy	protected	java.awt.dnd

Object

1.2 └ DropTargetContext.TransferableProxy - - - - - - *java.awt.datatransfer.Transferable [1]*

	1	public synchronized .... Object	**getTransferData** (java. awt. datatransfer. DataFlavor df)
			throws java.awt.datatransfer.UnsupportedFlavorException, java.io.IOException
	1	public synchronized .... *java↵* *.awt.datatransfer.DataFlavor[]*	**getTransferDataFlavors** ()
	1	public synchronized .. boolean	**isDataFlavorSupported** (java.awt.datatransfer.DataFlavor flavor)
		protected .... boolean	**isLocal**
		protected .... *java↵* *.awt.datatransfer.Transferable*	**transferable**

DropTargetDragEvent	java.awt.dnd

Object

1.1 └ java.util.EventObject [1] - *java.io.Serializable*
1.2   └ DropTargetEvent [2]
1.2   └ DropTargetDragEvent

		public........................void	**acceptDrag** (int dragOperation)
	2	protected .. DropTargetContext	context
*		public........................	**DropTargetDragEvent** (DropTargetContext dtc, java.awt.Point cursorLocn,
			int dropAction, int srcActions)
		public.................. *java↵* *.awt.datatransfer.DataFlavor[]*	**getCurrentDataFlavors** ()
		public.............. *java.util.List*	**getCurrentDataFlavorsAsList** ()
		public........................int	**getDropAction** ()
	2	public...... DropTargetContext	getDropTargetContext ()
		public............. java.awt.Point	**getLocation** ()
	1	public........................Object	getSource ()
		public........................int	**getSourceActions** ()

Class   *Interface*   —extends   - - -implements   ○ abstract   ● final   △ static   ▲ static final   ✳ constructor   x x—inherited   x **x**—declared   **x x**—overridden

	public	boolean	**isDataFlavorSupported** (java.awt.datatransfer.DataFlavor df)
	public	void	**rejectDrag** ()
1	protected transient	Object	source
1	public	String	toString ()

DropTargetDropEvent

java.awt.dnd

D

```
Object
1.1  └java.util.EventObject¹ ------------------- java.io.Serializable
1.2      └DropTargetEvent²
1.2          └DropTargetDropEvent
```

	public	void	**acceptDrop** (int dropAction)
2	protected ..	DropTargetContext	context
	public	void	**dropComplete** (boolean success)
*	public		**DropTargetDropEvent** (DropTargetContext dtc, java.awt.Point cursorLocn, int dropAction, int srcActions)
*	public		**DropTargetDropEvent** (DropTargetContext dtc, java.awt.Point cursorLocn, int dropAction, int srcActions, boolean isLocal)
	public	java↵ .awt.datatransfer.DataFlavor[]	**getCurrentDataFlavors** ()
	public	java.util.List	**getCurrentDataFlavorsAsList** ()
	public	int	**getDropAction** ()
2	public	DropTargetContext	getDropTargetContext ()
	public	java.awt.Point	**getLocation** ()
1	public	Object	getSource ()
	public	int	**getSourceActions** ()
	public	java↵ .awt.datatransfer.Transferable	**getTransferable** ()
	public	boolean	**isDataFlavorSupported** (java.awt.datatransfer.DataFlavor df)
	public	boolean	**isLocalTransfer** ()
	public	void	**rejectDrop** ()
1	protected transient	Object	source
1	public	String	toString ()

DropTargetEvent

java.awt.dnd

```
Object
1.1  └java.util.EventObject¹ ------------------- java.io.Serializable
1.2      └DropTargetEvent
```

	protected ..	DropTargetContext	**context**
*	public		**DropTargetEvent** (DropTargetContext dtc)
	public	DropTargetContext	**getDropTargetContext** ()
1	public	Object	getSource ()
1	protected transient	Object	source
1	public	String	toString ()

DropTargetListener

java.awt.dnd

```
1.2  DropTargetListener─────────────────java.util.EventListener
```

	public	void	**dragEnter** (DropTargetDragEvent dtde)
	public	void	**dragExit** (DropTargetEvent dte)
	public	void	**dragOver** (DropTargetDragEvent dtde)
	public	void	**drop** (DropTargetDropEvent dtde)
	public	void	**dropActionChanged** (DropTargetDragEvent dtde)

DSAKey

java.security.interfaces

```
1.1  DSAKey                                                      Pᴼ
```

	public	DSAParams	**getParams** ()

DSAKeyPairGenerator

DSAKeyPairGenerator	java.security.interfaces

1.1   *DSAKeyPairGenerator*   P^O

```
public....................void initialize (DSAParams params, java.security.SecureRandom random)
                              throws java.security.InvalidParameterException
public....................void initialize (int modlen, boolean genParams, java.security.SecureRandom random)
                              throws java.security.InvalidParameterException
```

DSAParameterSpec	java.security.spec

Object
└DSAParameterSpec - - - - - - - - - - - - - - - - - - *AlgorithmParameterSpec, java.security.interfaces.DSAParams* [1]

1.2

```
 *  public........................... DSAParameterSpec (java.math.BigInteger p, java.math.BigInteger q,
                                        java.math.BigInteger g)
 1  public.... java.math.BigInteger getG ()
 1  public.... java.math.BigInteger getP ()
 1  public.... java.math.BigInteger getQ ()
```

DSAParams	java.security.interfaces

1.1   *DSAParams*   P^O

```
public.... java.math.BigInteger getG ()
public.... java.math.BigInteger getP ()
public.... java.math.BigInteger getQ ()
```

DSAPrivateKey	java.security.interfaces

1.1   *DSAPrivateKey*─────────────── *DSAKey* [1], *java.security.PrivateKey* [2] *(java.security.Key* [3]   P^O
                       (java.io.Serializable))

```
 3  public.....................String getAlgorithm ()
 3  public.....................byte[] getEncoded ()
 3  public.....................String getFormat ()
 1  public.............DSAParams getParams ()
    public.... java.math.BigInteger getX ()
```
1.2 ▲ 2   public static final.......... **long serialVersionUID** = 7776497482533790279

DSAPrivateKeySpec	java.security.spec

Object
└DSAPrivateKeySpec - - - - - - - - - - - - - - - - - - - *KeySpec*

1.2

```
 *  public........................... DSAPrivateKeySpec (java.math.BigInteger x, java.math.BigInteger p,
                                        java.math.BigInteger q, java.math.BigInteger g)
    public.... java.math.BigInteger getG ()
    public.... java.math.BigInteger getP ()
    public.... java.math.BigInteger getQ ()
    public.... java.math.BigInteger getX ()
```

DSAPublicKey	java.security.interfaces

1.1   *DSAPublicKey*─────────────── *DSAKey* [1], *java.security.PublicKey* [2] *(java.security.Key* [3]   P^O
                       (java.io.Serializable))

```
 3  public.....................String getAlgorithm ()
 3  public.....................byte[] getEncoded ()
 3  public.....................String getFormat ()
 1  public.............DSAParams getParams ()
    public.... java.math.BigInteger getY ()
```
1.2 ▲ 2   public static final.......... **long serialVersionUID** = 1234526332779022332

Class   *Interface*   —extends   - - -implements   ○ abstract   ● final   △ static   ▲ static final   ✳ constructor   x x—inherited   x **x**—declared   **x x**—overridden

DSAPublicKeySpec

```
       Object
1.2    └─DSAPublicKeySpec - - - - - - - - - - - - - - - - - - - - - KeySpec
```

*	public.............................	**DSAPublicKeySpec** (java. math. BigInteger y, java. math. BigInteger p, java.math.BigInteger q, java.math.BigInteger g)
	public.... java.math.BigInteger	**getG** ()
	public.... java.math.BigInteger	**getP** ()
	public.... java.math.BigInteger	**getQ** ()
	public.... java.math.BigInteger	**getY** ()

D

DTD

```
       Object¹
1.2    └─DTD - - - - - - - - - - - - - - - - - - - - - - - - - - - DTDConstants
```

●	public final	Element	**applet**
●	public final	Element	**base**
●	public final	Element	**body**
	protected	AttributeList	**defAttributeList** (String name, int type, int modifier, String value, String values, AttributeList atts)
	protected	ContentModel	**defContentModel** (int type, Object obj, ContentModel next)
	protected	Element	**defElement** (String name, int type, boolean omitStart, boolean omitEnd, ContentModel content, String[] exclusions, String[] inclusions, AttributeList atts)
	public	Entity	**defEntity** (String name, int type, int ch)
	protected	Entity	**defEntity** (String name, int type, String str)
	public	void	**defineAttributes** (String name, AttributeList atts)
	public	Element	**defineElement** (String name, int type, boolean omitStart, boolean omitEnd, ContentModel content, java.util.BitSet exclusions, java.util.BitSet inclusions, AttributeList atts)
	public	Entity	**defineEntity** (String name, int type, char[] data)
*	protected		**DTD** (String name)
	public	java.util.Hashtable	**elementHash**
	public	java.util.Vector	**elements**
	public	java.util.Hashtable	**entityHash**
△	public static	int	**FILE_VERSION**
△	public static	DTD	**getDTD** (String name) throws java.io.IOException
	public	Element	**getElement** (int index)
	public	Element	**getElement** (String name)
	public	Entity	**getEntity** (int ch)
	public	Entity	**getEntity** (String name)
	public	String	**getName** ()
●	public final	Element	**head**
●	public final	Element	**html**
●	public final	Element	**isindex**
●	public final	Element	**meta**
	public	String	**name**
●	public final	Element	**p**
●	public final	Element	**param**
●	public final	Element	**pcdata**
△	public static	void	**putDTDHash** (String name, DTD dtd)
	public	void	**read** (java.io.DataInputStream in) throws java.io.IOException
●	public final	Element	**title**
1	public	String	**toString** ()

DTDConstants

```
1.2    DTDConstants
```

▲	public static final	int	**ANY** = 19
▲	public static final	int	**CDATA** = 1
▲	public static final	int	**CONREF** = 4
▲	public static final	int	**CURRENT** = 3
▲	public static final	int	**DEFAULT** = 131072
▲	public static final	int	**EMPTY** = 17
▲	public static final	int	**ENDTAG** = 14
▲	public static final	int	**ENTITIES** = 3
▲	public static final	int	**ENTITY** = 2
▲	public static final	int	**FIXED** = 1
▲	public static final	int	**GENERAL** = 65536
▲	public static final	int	**ID** = 4

DTDConstants

▲	public static final	int	**IDREF** = 5
▲	public static final	int	**IDREFS** = 6
▲	public static final	int	**IMPLIED** = 5
▲	public static final	int	**MD** = 16
▲	public static final	int	**MODEL** = 18
▲	public static final	int	**MS** = 15
▲	public static final	int	**NAME** = 7
▲	public static final	int	**NAMES** = 8
▲	public static final	int	**NMTOKEN** = 9
▲	public static final	int	**NMTOKENS** = 10
▲	public static final	int	**NOTATION** = 11
▲	public static final	int	**NUMBER** = 12
▲	public static final	int	**NUMBERS** = 13
▲	public static final	int	**NUTOKEN** = 14
▲	public static final	int	**NUTOKENS** = 15
▲	public static final	int	**PARAMETER** = 262144
▲	public static final	int	**PI** = 12
▲	public static final	int	**PUBLIC** = 10
▲	public static final	int	**RCDATA** = 16
▲	public static final	int	**REQUIRED** = 2
▲	public static final	int	**SDATA** = 11
▲	public static final	int	**STARTTAG** = 13
▲	public static final	int	**SYSTEM** = 17

DynamicImplementation
org.omg.CORBA

Object
1.2 ○ └org.omg.CORBA.portable.ObjectImpl [1] - - - - - - Object
1.2 ○ └DynamicImplementation

---

1 *26 inherited members from org.omg.CORBA.portable.ObjectImpl not shown*
* public .... **DynamicImplementation** ()
○ public abstract .... void **invoke** (ServerRequest request)

DynAny
org.omg.CORBA

1.2 *DynAny* ────────────────────── *Object* [1]

---

1 *13 inherited members from Object not shown*
public .... void **assign** (*DynAny* dyn_any) throws org.omg.CORBA.DynAnyPackage.Invalid
public .... *DynAny* **copy** ()
public .... *DynAny* **current_component** ()
public .... void **destroy** ()
public .... void **from_any** (Any value) throws org.omg.CORBA.DynAnyPackage.Invalid
public .... Any **get_any** () throws org.omg.CORBA.DynAnyPackage.TypeMismatch
public .... boolean **get_boolean** () throws org.omg.CORBA.DynAnyPackage.TypeMismatch
public .... char **get_char** () throws org.omg.CORBA.DynAnyPackage.TypeMismatch
public .... double **get_double** () throws org.omg.CORBA.DynAnyPackage.TypeMismatch
public .... float **get_float** () throws org.omg.CORBA.DynAnyPackage.TypeMismatch
public .... int **get_long** () throws org.omg.CORBA.DynAnyPackage.TypeMismatch
public .... long **get_longlong** () throws org.omg.CORBA.DynAnyPackage.TypeMismatch
public .... byte **get_octet** () throws org.omg.CORBA.DynAnyPackage.TypeMismatch
public .... *Object* **get_reference** () throws org.omg.CORBA.DynAnyPackage.TypeMismatch
public .... short **get_short** () throws org.omg.CORBA.DynAnyPackage.TypeMismatch
public .... String **get_string** () throws org.omg.CORBA.DynAnyPackage.TypeMismatch
public .... TypeCode **get_typecode** () throws org.omg.CORBA.DynAnyPackage.TypeMismatch
public .... int **get_ulong** () throws org.omg.CORBA.DynAnyPackage.TypeMismatch
public .... long **get_ulonglong** () throws org.omg.CORBA.DynAnyPackage.TypeMismatch
public .... short **get_ushort** () throws org.omg.CORBA.DynAnyPackage.TypeMismatch
public .... *java.io.Serializable* **get_val** () throws org.omg.CORBA.DynAnyPackage.TypeMismatch
public .... char **get_wchar** () throws org.omg.CORBA.DynAnyPackage.TypeMismatch
public .... String **get_wstring** () throws org.omg.CORBA.DynAnyPackage.TypeMismatch
public .... void **insert_any** (Any value) throws org.omg.CORBA.DynAnyPackage.InvalidValue
public .... void **insert_boolean** (boolean value) throws org.omg.CORBA.DynAnyPackage ↩
.InvalidValue
public .... void **insert_char** (char value) throws org.omg.CORBA.DynAnyPackage.InvalidValue
public .... void **insert_double** (double value) throws org.omg.CORBA.DynAnyPackage ↩
.InvalidValue
public .... void **insert_float** (float value) throws org.omg.CORBA.DynAnyPackage.InvalidValue
public .... void **insert_long** (int value) throws org.omg.CORBA.DynAnyPackage.InvalidValue

---

Class *Interface* —extends - - -implements ○ abstract ● final △ static ▲ static final ✻ constructor x x—inherited x **x**—declared **x x**—overridden

public	void	**insert_longlong**	(long value) throws org.omg.CORBA.DynAnyPackage.InvalidValue
public	void	**insert_octet**	(byte value) throws org.omg.CORBA.DynAnyPackage.InvalidValue
public	void	**insert_reference**	(*Object* value) throws org.omg.CORBA.DynAnyPackage↵.InvalidValue
public	void	**insert_short**	(short value) throws org.omg.CORBA.DynAnyPackage.InvalidValue
public	void	**insert_string**	(String value) throws org.omg.CORBA.DynAnyPackage.InvalidValue
public	void	**insert_typecode**	(TypeCode value) throws org.omg.CORBA.DynAnyPackage↵.InvalidValue
public	void	**insert_ulong**	(int value) throws org.omg.CORBA.DynAnyPackage.InvalidValue
public	void	**insert_ulonglong**	(long value) throws org.omg.CORBA.DynAnyPackage↵.InvalidValue
public	void	**insert_ushort**	(short value) throws org.omg.CORBA.DynAnyPackage.InvalidValue
public	void	**insert_val**	(*java.io.Serializable* value) throws org.omg.CORBA.DynAnyPackage↵.InvalidValue
public	void	**insert_wchar**	(char value) throws org.omg.CORBA.DynAnyPackage.InvalidValue
public	void	**insert_wstring**	(String value) throws org.omg.CORBA.DynAnyPackage.InvalidValue
public	boolean	**next**	()
public	void	**rewind**	()
public	boolean	**seek**	(int index)
public	Any	**to_any**	() throws org.omg.CORBA.DynAnyPackage.Invalid
public	TypeCode	**type**	()

D

DynArray
org.omg.CORBA

1.2   *DynArray*——————————————— *Object* [1], *DynAny* [2] (*Object* [1])

[2] *46 inherited members from DynAny not shown*
[1] *13 inherited members from Object not shown*

public	Any[]	**get_elements**	()
public	void	**set_elements**	(Any[] value) throws org.omg.CORBA.DynAnyPackage.InvalidSeq

DynEnum
org.omg.CORBA

1.2   *DynEnum*——————————————— *Object* [1], *DynAny* [2] (*Object* [1])

[2] *46 inherited members from DynAny not shown*
[1] *13 inherited members from Object not shown*

public	String	**value_as_string**	()
public	void	**value_as_string**	(String arg)
public	int	**value_as_ulong**	()
public	void	**value_as_ulong**	(int arg)

DynFixed
org.omg.CORBA

1.2   *DynFixed*——————————————— *Object* [1], *DynAny* [2] (*Object* [1])

[2] *46 inherited members from DynAny not shown*
[1] *13 inherited members from Object not shown*

public	byte[]	**get_value**	()
public	void	**set_value**	(byte[] val) throws org.omg.CORBA.DynAnyPackage.InvalidValue

DynSequence
org.omg.CORBA

1.2   *DynSequence*——————————————— *Object* [1], *DynAny* [2] (*Object* [1])

[2] *46 inherited members from DynAny not shown*
[1] *13 inherited members from Object not shown*

public	Any[]	**get_elements**	()
public	int	**length**	()
public	void	**length**	(int arg)
public	void	**set_elements**	(Any[] value) throws org.omg.CORBA.DynAnyPackage.InvalidSeq

DynStruct
org.omg.CORBA

1.2   *DynStruct*——————————————— *Object* [1], *DynAny* [2] (*Object* [1])

[2] *46 inherited members from DynAny not shown*
[1] *13 inherited members from Object not shown*

public	TCKind	**current_member_kind**	()
public	String	**current_member_name**	()
public	NameValuePair[]	**get_members**	()

Classes

DynStruct

public......................void **set_members** (NameValuePair[] value) throws org. omg. CORBA↵
.DynAnyPackage.InvalidSeq

DynUnion

1.2 *DynUnion*——————————————— *Object*[1], *DynAny*[2] (*Object*[1])

[2] *46 inherited members from DynAny not shown*
[1] *13 inherited members from Object not shown*
public...................*DynAny* **discriminator** ()
public....................TCKind **discriminator_kind** ()
public...................*DynAny* **member** ()
public....................TCKind **member_kind** ()
public......................String **member_name** ()
public......................void **member_name** (String arg)
public..................boolean **set_as_default** ()
public......................void **set_as_default** (boolean arg)

DynValue

1.2 *DynValue*——————————————— *Object*[1], *DynAny*[2] (*Object*[1])

[2] *46 inherited members from DynAny not shown*
[1] *13 inherited members from Object not shown*
public....................TCKind **current_member_kind** ()
public....................String **current_member_name** ()
public.........NameValuePair[] **get_members** ()
public......................void **set_members** (NameValuePair[] value) throws org. omg. CORBA↵
.DynAnyPackage.InvalidSeq

EditorKit

Object[1]
1.2 ○ └EditorKit - *Cloneable, java.io.Serializable*

○ 1 public abstract..........**Object clone** ()
○ public abstract.......... *Caret* **createCaret** ()
○ public abstract...... *Document* **createDefaultDocument** ()
public......................void **deinstall** (javax.swing.JEditorPane c)
✳ public............................. **EditorKit** ()
○ public abstract................. **getActions** ()
...........*javax.swing.Action[]*
○ public abstract..........String **getContentType** ()
○ public abstract.... *ViewFactory* **getViewFactory** ()
public......................void **install** (javax.swing.JEditorPane c)
○ public abstract.............void **read** (java. io. InputStream in, *Document* doc, int pos)
throws java.io.IOException, BadLocationException
○ public abstract.............void **read** (java. io. Reader in, *Document* doc, int pos)
throws java.io.IOException, BadLocationException
○ public abstract.............void **write** (java. io. OutputStream out, *Document* doc, int pos, int len)
throws java.io.IOException, BadLocationException
○ public abstract.............void **write** (java. io. Writer out, *Document* doc, int pos, int len)
throws java.io.IOException, BadLocationException

Element●

Object[1]
1.2 ● └Element - *DTDConstants, java.io.Serializable*

public.............AttributeList **atts**
public...........ContentModel **content**
public....................Object **data**
public............java.util.BitSet **exclusions**
public.............AttributeList **getAttribute** (String name)
public.............AttributeList **getAttributeByValue** (String name)
public.............AttributeList **getAttributes** ()
public...........ContentModel **getContent** ()
public....................int **getIndex** ()
public....................String **getName** ()

Class *Interface* ——extends - - -implements ○ abstract ● final △ static ▲ static final ✳ constructor x x—inherited x **x**—declared **x x**—overridden

```
         public..........................int  getType ()
         public...........java.util.BitSet  inclusions
         public..........................int  index
         public................. boolean  isEmpty ()
         public.....................String  name
△        public static ................int  name2type (String nm)
         public................. boolean  oEnd
         public................. boolean  omitEnd ()
         public................. boolean  omitStart ()
         public................. boolean  oStart
    1    public.................... String  toString ()
         public..........................int  type
```

Element❷   javax.swing.text

```
1.2    Element
- - - - - - - - - - - - - - - - - - - - - - - - - - - - - - - - - - - - - - - -
       public.............. AttributeSet  getAttributes ()
       public................ Document  getDocument ()
       public................... Element  getElement (int index)
       public..........................int  getElementCount ()
       public..........................int  getElementIndex (int offset)
       public..........................int  getEndOffset ()
       public.....................String  getName ()
       public................... Element  getParentElement ()
       public..........................int  getStartOffset ()
       public................. boolean  isLeaf ()
```

ElementIterator   javax.swing.text

```
       Object 1
1.2    └ElementIterator - - - - - - - - - - - - - - - - - - - - - - Cloneable
    1  public synchronized ....Object  clone ()
       public.................. Element  current ()
       public..........................int  depth ()
*      public.........................  ElementIterator (Document document)
*      public.........................  ElementIterator (Element root)
       public.................. Element  first ()
       public.................. Element  next ()
       public.................. Element  previous ()
```

Ellipse2D   java.awt.geom

```
       Object
1.2 ○  └RectangularShape 1 - - - - - - - - - - - - - - - - - - - - java.awt.Shape, Cloneable
1.2 ○     └Ellipse2D
    1  26 inherited members from RectangularShape not shown
    1  public.................. boolean  contains (double x, double y)
    1  public.................. boolean  contains (double x, double y, double w, double h)
*      protected ......................  Ellipse2D ()
    1  public............. PathIterator  getPathIterator (AffineTransform at)
    1  public.................. boolean  intersects (double x, double y, double w, double h)
```

Ellipse2D.Double   java.awt.geom

```
       Object
1.2 ○  └RectangularShape 1 - - - - - - - - - - - - - - - - - - - - java.awt.Shape, Cloneable
1.2 ○     └Ellipse2D 2
1.2         └Ellipse2D.Double
    1  public.................. Object  clone ()
    1  public.................. boolean  contains (Point2D p)
    1  public.................. boolean  contains (Rectangle2D r)
    2  public.................. boolean  contains (double x, double y)
    2  public.................. boolean  contains (double x, double y, double w, double h)
*      public.........................  Double ()
*      public.........................  Double (double x, double y, double w, double h)
    1  public...... java.awt.Rectangle  getBounds ()
```

Ellipse2D.Double

1	public	**Rectangle2D**	**getBounds2D** ()
1	public	double	getCenterX ()
1	public	double	getCenterY ()
1	public	Rectangle2D	getFrame ()
1	public	**double**	**getHeight** ()
1	public	double	getMaxX ()
1	public	double	getMaxY ()
1	public	double	getMinX ()
1	public	double	getMinY ()
2	public	*PathIterator*	getPathIterator (AffineTransform at)
1	public	*PathIterator*	getPathIterator (AffineTransform at, double flatness)
1	public	**double**	**getWidth** ()
1	public	**double**	**getX** ()
1	public	**double**	**getY** ()
	public	double	**height**
1	public	boolean	intersects (Rectangle2D r)
2	public	boolean	intersects (double x, double y, double w, double h)
1	public	**boolean**	**isEmpty** ()
1	public	void	setFrame (Rectangle2D r)
1	public	void	setFrame (Point2D loc, Dimension2D size)
1	public	**void**	**setFrame** (double x, double y, double w, double h)
1	public	void	setFrameFromCenter (Point2D center, Point2D corner)
1	public	void	setFrameFromCenter (double centerX, double centerY, double cornerX, double cornerY)
1	public	void	setFrameFromDiagonal (Point2D p1, Point2D p2)
1	public	void	setFrameFromDiagonal (double x1, double y1, double x2, double y2)
	public	double	**width**
	public	double	**x**
	public	double	**y**

Ellipse2D.Float   java.awt.geom

```
        Object
1.2 O   └─RectangularShape 1 - - - - - - - - - - - - - - - - - - - - - java.awt.Shape, Cloneable
1.2 O      └─Ellipse2D 2
1.2          └─Ellipse2D.Float
```

1	public	Object	clone ()
1	public	boolean	contains (Point2D p)
1	public	boolean	contains (Rectangle2D r)
2	public	boolean	contains (double x, double y)
2	public	boolean	contains (double x, double y, double w, double h)
*	public		**Float** ()
*	public		**Float** (float x, float y, float w, float h)
1	public	java.awt.Rectangle	getBounds ()
1	public	**Rectangle2D**	**getBounds2D** ()
1	public	double	getCenterX ()
1	public	double	getCenterY ()
1	public	Rectangle2D	getFrame ()
1	public	**double**	**getHeight** ()
1	public	double	getMaxX ()
1	public	double	getMaxY ()
1	public	double	getMinX ()
1	public	double	getMinY ()
2	public	*PathIterator*	getPathIterator (AffineTransform at)
1	public	*PathIterator*	getPathIterator (AffineTransform at, double flatness)
1	public	**double**	**getWidth** ()
1	public	**double**	**getX** ()
1	public	**double**	**getY** ()
	public	float	**height**
1	public	boolean	intersects (Rectangle2D r)
2	public	boolean	intersects (double x, double y, double w, double h)
1	public	**boolean**	**isEmpty** ()
1	public	void	setFrame (Rectangle2D r)
1	public	void	setFrame (Point2D loc, Dimension2D size)
1	public	**void**	**setFrame** (double x, double y, double w, double h)
	public	void	**setFrame** (float x, float y, float w, float h)
1	public	void	setFrameFromCenter (Point2D center, Point2D corner)
1	public	void	setFrameFromCenter (double centerX, double centerY, double cornerX, double cornerY)
1	public	void	setFrameFromDiagonal (Point2D p1, Point2D p2)

Class   *Interface*   —extends   - - -implements   O abstract   ● final   △ static   ▲ static final   ✳ constructor   x x—inherited   x **x**—declared   **x x**—overridden

1	public	void	setFrameFromDiagonal (double x1, double y1, double x2, double y2)
	public	float	**width**
	public	float	**x**
	public	float	**y**

EmptyBorder

```
        Object
1.2 ○   └AbstractBorder¹ ---------------------- Border, java.io.Serializable
1.2         └EmptyBorder ---------------------- java.io.Serializable
```

	protected	int	**bottom**
*	public		**EmptyBorder** (java.awt.Insets insets)
*	public		**EmptyBorder** (int top, int left, int bottom, int right)
1	public	**java.awt.Insets**	**getBorderInsets** (java.awt.Component c)
1	public	**java.awt.Insets**	**getBorderInsets** (java.awt.Component c, java.awt.Insets insets)
1	public	java.awt.Rectangle	getInteriorRectangle (java.awt.Component c, int x, int y, int width, int height)
△ 1	public static	java.awt.Rectangle	getInteriorRectangle (java.awt.Component c, *Border* b, int x, int y, int width, int height)
1	public	**boolean**	**isBorderOpaque** ()
	protected	int	**left**
1	public	**void**	**paintBorder** (java.awt.Component c, java.awt.Graphics g, int x, int y, int width, int height)
	protected	int	**right**
	protected	int	**top**

EmptyStackException

P

```
        Object
        └Throwable -------------------------- java.io.Serializable
          └Exception
            └RuntimeException
              └EmptyStackException
```

*	public		**EmptyStackException** ()

EncodedKeySpec

```
        Object
1.2 ○   └EncodedKeySpec ---------------------- KeySpec
```

*	public		**EncodedKeySpec** (byte[] encodedKey)
	public	byte[]	**getEncoded** ()
○	public abstract	String	**getFormat** ()

Entity

```
        Object
1.2 ●   └Entity ------------------------------ DTDConstants
```

	public	char[]	**data**
*	public		**Entity** (String name, int type, char[] data)
	public	char[]	**getData** ()
	public	String	**getName** ()
	public	String	**getString** ()
	public	int	**getType** ()
	public	boolean	**isGeneral** ()
	public	boolean	**isParameter** ()
	public	String	**name**
△	public static	int	**name2type** (String nm)
	public	int	**type**

Enumeration

```
        Enumeration
```

P

	public	boolean	**hasMoreElements** ()
	public	Object	**nextElement** ()

Environment — org.omg.CORBA

1.2 ○	Object	└ Environment

○	public abstract ....void	**clear** ()	
✳	public..........................	**Environment** ()	
○	public abstract ...... Exception	**exception** ()	
○	public abstract ....void	**exception** (Exception except)	

E

EOFException — java.io

Object	
└ Throwable - *Serializable*	
└ Exception	
└ IOException	
└ EOFException	

✳	public..........................	**EOFException** ()
✳	public..........................	**EOFException** (String s)

Error — java.lang
P

Object
└ Throwable - *java.io.Serializable*
└ Error

✳	public..........................	**Error** ()
✳	public..........................	**Error** (String s)

EtchedBorder — javax.swing.border

1.2 ○	Object	
1.2	└ AbstractBorder[1] - *Border*, *java.io.Serializable*	
	└ EtchedBorder	

✳	public..........................	**EtchedBorder** ()	
✳	public..........................	**EtchedBorder** (int etchType)	
✳	public..........................	**EtchedBorder** (java.awt.Color highlight, java.awt.Color shadow)	
✳	public..........................	**EtchedBorder** (int etchType, java.awt.Color highlight, java.awt.Color shadow)	
	protected ....int	**etchType**	
1	public......... **java.awt.Insets**	**getBorderInsets** (java.awt.Component c)	
1	public......... **java.awt.Insets**	**getBorderInsets** (java.awt.Component c, java.awt.Insets insets)	
	public.........................int	**getEtchType** ()	
	public.............java.awt.Color	**getHighlightColor** (java.awt.Component c)	
1	public ...... java.awt.Rectangle	getInteriorRectangle (java.awt.Component c, int x, int y, int width, int height)	
△ 1	public static	getInteriorRectangle (java.awt.Component c, *Border* b, int x, int y, int width,	
	.... java.awt.Rectangle	int height)	
	public.............java.awt.Color	**getShadowColor** (java.awt.Component c)	
	protected ....java.awt.Color	**highlight**	
1	public................. **boolean**	**isBorderOpaque** ()	
▲	public static final ....int	**LOWERED** = 1	
1	public..................... **void**	**paintBorder** (java.awt.Component c, java.awt.Graphics g, int x, int y, int width,	
		int height)	
▲	public static final ....int	**RAISED** = 0	
	protected ....java.awt.Color	**shadow**	

Event — java.awt
P

Object[1]
└ Event - *java.io.Serializable*

▲	public static final ....int	**ACTION_EVENT** = 1001
▲	public static final ....int	**ALT_MASK** = 8
	public.....................Object	**arg**
1.1 ▲	public static final ....int	**BACK_SPACE** = 8
1.1 ▲	public static final ....int	**CAPS_LOCK** = 1022

Class *Interface* —extends - - -implements ○ abstract ● final △ static ▲ static final ✳ constructor x x—inherited x **x**—declared **x x**—overridden

E

	public	int	**clickCount**
	public	boolean	**controlDown** ()
▲	public static final	int	**CTRL_MASK** = 2
1.1 ▲	public static final	int	**DELETE** = 127
▲	public static final	int	**DOWN** = 1005
▲	public static final	int	**END** = 1001
1.1 ▲	public static final	int	**ENTER** = 10
1.1 ▲	public static final	int	**ESCAPE** = 27
*	public		**Event** (Object target, int id, Object arg)
* *	public		**Event** (Object target, long when, int id, int x, int y, int key, int modifiers)
*	public		**Event** (Object target, long when, int id, int x, int y, int key, int modifiers, Object arg)
	public	Event	**evt**
▲	public static final	int	**F1** = 1008
▲	public static final	int	**F10** = 1017
▲	public static final	int	**F11** = 1018
▲	public static final	int	**F12** = 1019
▲	public static final	int	**F2** = 1009
▲	public static final	int	**F3** = 1010
▲	public static final	int	**F4** = 1011
▲	public static final	int	**F5** = 1012
▲	public static final	int	**F6** = 1013
▲	public static final	int	**F7** = 1014
▲	public static final	int	**F8** = 1015
▲	public static final	int	**F9** = 1016
▲	public static final	int	**GOT_FOCUS** = 1004
▲	public static final	int	**HOME** = 1000
	public	int	**id**
1.1 ▲	public static final	int	**INSERT** = 1025
	public	int	**key**
▲	public static final	int	**KEY_ACTION** = 403
▲	public static final	int	**KEY_ACTION_RELEASE** = 404
▲	public static final	int	**KEY_PRESS** = 401
▲	public static final	int	**KEY_RELEASE** = 402
▲	public static final	int	**LEFT** = 1006
▲	public static final	int	**LIST_DESELECT** = 702
▲	public static final	int	**LIST_SELECT** = 701
▲	public static final	int	**LOAD_FILE** = 1002
▲	public static final	int	**LOST_FOCUS** = 1005
▲	public static final	int	**META_MASK** = 4
	public	boolean	**metaDown** ()
	public	int	**modifiers**
▲	public static final	int	**MOUSE_DOWN** = 501
▲	public static final	int	**MOUSE_DRAG** = 506
▲	public static final	int	**MOUSE_ENTER** = 504
▲	public static final	int	**MOUSE_EXIT** = 505
▲	public static final	int	**MOUSE_MOVE** = 503
▲	public static final	int	**MOUSE_UP** = 502
1.1 ▲	public static final	int	**NUM_LOCK** = 1023
	protected	String	**paramString** ()
1.1 ▲	public static final	int	**PAUSE** = 1024
▲	public static final	int	**PGDN** = 1003
▲	public static final	int	**PGUP** = 1002
1.1 ▲	public static final	int	**PRINT_SCREEN** = 1020
▲	public static final	int	**RIGHT** = 1007
▲	public static final	int	**SAVE_FILE** = 1003
▲	public static final	int	**SCROLL_ABSOLUTE** = 605
1.1 ▲	public static final	int	**SCROLL_BEGIN** = 606
1.1 ▲	public static final	int	**SCROLL_END** = 607
▲	public static final	int	**SCROLL_LINE_DOWN** = 602
▲	public static final	int	**SCROLL_LINE_UP** = 601
1.1 ▲	public static final	int	**SCROLL_LOCK** = 1021
▲	public static final	int	**SCROLL_PAGE_DOWN** = 604
▲	public static final	int	**SCROLL_PAGE_UP** = 603
▲	public static final	int	**SHIFT_MASK** = 1
	public	boolean	**shiftDown** ()
1.1 ▲	public static final	int	**TAB** = 9
	public	Object	**target**
1	public	String	**toString** ()
	public	void	**translate** (int x, int y)
▲	public static final	int	**UP** = 1004
	public	long	**when**
▲	public static final	int	**WINDOW_DEICONIFY** = 204
▲	public static final	int	**WINDOW_DESTROY** = 201
▲	public static final	int	**WINDOW_EXPOSE** = 202

Classes

Event

▲	public static final .... int	**WINDOW_ICONIFY** = 203
▲	public static final .... int	**WINDOW_MOVED** = 205
	public .... int	**x**
	public .... int	**y**

EventListener   java.util

1.1	*EventListener*	P

- -

EventListenerList   java.swing.event... javax.swing.event

	Object [1]	
1.2	└─EventListenerList - *java.io.Serializable*	

	public synchronized .... void	**add** (Class t, *java.util.EventListener* l)
✳	public	**EventListenerList** ()
	public .... int	**getListenerCount** ()
	public .... int	**getListenerCount** (Class t)
	public .... Object[]	**getListenerList** ()
	protected transient .... Object[]	**listenerList**
	public synchronized .... void	**remove** (Class t, *java.util.EventListener* l)
1	public .... **String**	**toString** ()

EventObject   java.util

	Object [1]	P
1.1	└─EventObject - *java.io.Serializable*	

✳	public	**EventObject** (Object source)
	public .... Object	**getSource** ()
	protected transient ...... Object	**source**
1	public .... **String**	**toString** ()

EventQueue   java.awt

	Object	P
1.1	└─EventQueue	

1.1	protected .... void	**dispatchEvent** (AWTEvent event)
✳	public	**EventQueue** ()
	public synchronized AWTEvent	**getNextEvent** () throws InterruptedException
1.2 △	public static .... void	**invokeAndWait** (*Runnable* runnable) throws InterruptedException, java.lang.reflect.InvocationTargetException
1.2 △	public static .... void	**invokeLater** (*Runnable* runnable)
1.2 △	public static .... boolean	**isDispatchThread** ()
	public synchronized AWTEvent	**peekEvent** ()
	public synchronized AWTEvent	**peekEvent** (int id)
1.2	protected .... void	**pop** () throws java.util.EmptyStackException
	public synchronized ...... void	**postEvent** (AWTEvent theEvent)
1.2	public synchronized ...... void	**push** (EventQueue newEventQueue)

EventSetDescriptor   java.beans

1.1	Object	
1.1	└─FeatureDescriptor [1]	
	└─EventSetDescriptor	

1	public .... *java.util.Enumeration*	attributeNames ()
✳	public	**EventSetDescriptor** (Class sourceClass, String eventSetName, Class listenerType, String listenerMethodName) throws IntrospectionException
✳	public	**EventSetDescriptor** (String eventSetName, Class listenerType, MethodDescriptor[] listenerMethodDescriptors, java.lang.reflect.Method addListenerMethod, java.lang.reflect.Method removeListenerMethod) throws IntrospectionException
✳	public	**EventSetDescriptor** (String eventSetName, Class listenerType, java.lang ↵ .reflect.Method[] listenerMethods, java.lang.reflect.Method addListenerMethod, java.lang.reflect.Method removeListenerMethod) throws IntrospectionException

---

Class   *Interface*   —extends   - - -implements   ○ abstract   ● final   △ static   ▲ static final   ✳ constructor   x x—inherited   x **x**—declared   **x x**—overridden

*		public	**EventSetDescriptor** (Class sourceClass, String eventSetName, Class listenerType, String[] listenerMethodNames, String addListenerMethodName, String removeListenerMethodName) throws IntrospectionException
		public . java.lang.reflect.Method	**getAddListenerMethod** ()
	1	public String	getDisplayName ()
		public MethodDescriptor[]	**getListenerMethodDescriptors** ()
		public ...... java.lang.reflect.Method[]	**getListenerMethods** ()
		public Class	**getListenerType** ()
	1	public String	getName ()
		public . java.lang.reflect.Method	**getRemoveListenerMethod** ()
	1	public String	getShortDescription ()
	1	public Object	getValue (String attributeName)
	1	public boolean	isExpert ()
	1	public boolean	isHidden ()
		public boolean	**isInDefaultEventSet** ()
1.2	1	public boolean	isPreferred ()
		public boolean	**isUnicast** ()
	1	public void	setDisplayName (String displayName)
	1	public void	setExpert (boolean expert)
	1	public void	setHidden (boolean hidden)
		public void	**setInDefaultEventSet** (boolean inDefaultEventSet)
	1	public void	setName (String name)
1.2	1	public void	setPreferred (boolean preferred)
	1	public void	setShortDescription (String text)
		public void	**setUnicast** (boolean unicast)
	1	public void	setValue (String attributeName, Object value)

Exception   java.lang

P

```
Object
└Throwable - - - - - - - - - - - - - - - - - - - - - - - - - - java.io.Serializable
   └Exception
```

*	public	**Exception** ()
*	public	**Exception** (String s)

ExceptionInInitializerError   java.lang

P

```
Object
└Throwable 1 - - - - - - - - - - - - - - - - - - - - - - - - - - java.io.Serializable
   └Error
      └LinkageError
         └ExceptionInInitializerError
1.1
```

*	public	**ExceptionInInitializerError** ()
*	public	**ExceptionInInitializerError** (String s)
*	public	**ExceptionInInitializerError** (Throwable thrown)
	public Throwable	**getException** ()
1	public **void**	**printStackTrace** ()
1	public **void**	**printStackTrace** (java.io.PrintStream ps)
1	public **void**	**printStackTrace** (java.io.PrintWriter pw)

Classes

ExceptionList   org.omg.CORBA

```
    Object
1.2 O  └ExceptionList
```

O	public abstract void	**add** (TypeCode exc)
O	public abstract int	**count** ()
*	public	**ExceptionList** ()
O	public abstract TypeCode	**item** (int index) throws Bounds
O	public abstract void	**remove** (int index) throws Bounds

ExpandVetoException			javax.swing.tree

```
        Object
         └Throwable --------------------------- java.io.Serializable
          └Exception
1.2        └ExpandVetoException
```

	protected........javax.swing↵	**event**	
	.event.TreeExpansionEvent		
*	public...........................	**ExpandVetoException** (javax.swing.event.TreeExpansionEvent event)	
*	public...........................	**ExpandVetoException** (javax.swing.event.TreeExpansionEvent event,	
		String message)	

F

ExportException			java.rmi.server
			P^O

```
        Object
         └Throwable --------------------------- java.io.Serializable
          └Exception
           └java.io.IOException
1.1         └java.rmi.RemoteException 1
1.1          └ExportException
```

1	public...............Throwable	detail	
*	public........................	**ExportException** (String s)	
*	public........................	**ExportException** (String s, Exception ex)	
1	public...............String	getMessage ()	
1	public...............void	printStackTrace ()	
1	public...............void	printStackTrace (java.io.PrintStream ps)	
1	public...............void	printStackTrace (java.io.PrintWriter pw)	

Externalizable			java.io

```
1.1     Externalizable──────────────── Serializable
```

	public........................void	**readExternal** (*ObjectInput* in) throws IOException, ClassNotFoundException	
	public........................void	**writeExternal** (*ObjectOutput* out) throws IOException	

FeatureDescriptor			java.beans

```
        Object
1.1      └FeatureDescriptor
```

	public.... java.util.Enumeration	**attributeNames** ()	
*	public...........................	**FeatureDescriptor** ()	
	public...............String	**getDisplayName** ()	
	public...............String	**getName** ()	
	public...............String	**getShortDescription** ()	
	public...............Object	**getValue** (String attributeName)	
	public...............boolean	**isExpert** ()	
	public...............boolean	**isHidden** ()	
1.2	public...............boolean	**isPreferred** ()	
	public...............void	**setDisplayName** (String displayName)	
	public...............void	**setExpert** (boolean expert)	
	public...............void	**setHidden** (boolean hidden)	
	public...............void	**setName** (String name)	
1.2	public...............void	**setPreferred** (boolean preferred)	
	public...............void	**setShortDescription** (String text)	
	public...............void	**setValue** (String attributeName, Object value)	

Field			java.lang.reflect
			P

```
        Object 1
1.2      └AccessibleObject 2
1.1 ●     └Field --------------------------- Member 3
```

1	public...............**boolean**	**equals** (Object obj)	
	public native...........Object	**get** (Object obj) throws IllegalArgumentException, IllegalAccessException	
	public native..........boolean	**getBoolean** (Object obj) throws IllegalArgumentException, IllegalAccessException	

Class   *Interface*   —extends   - - -implements   ○ abstract   ● final   △ static   ▲ static final   ✳ constructor   x x—inherited   x **x**—declared   **x x**—overridden

		public native	.... byte	**getByte** (Object obj) throws IllegalArgumentException, IllegalAccessException
		public native	.... char	**getChar** (Object obj) throws IllegalArgumentException, IllegalAccessException
	3	public	.... Class	**getDeclaringClass** ()
		public native	.... double	**getDouble** (Object obj) throws IllegalArgumentException, IllegalAccessException
		public native	.... float	**getFloat** (Object obj) throws IllegalArgumentException, IllegalAccessException
		public native	.... int	**getInt** (Object obj) throws IllegalArgumentException, IllegalAccessException
		public native	.... long	**getLong** (Object obj) throws IllegalArgumentException, IllegalAccessException
	3	public	.... int	**getModifiers** ()
	3	public	.... String	**getName** ()
		public native	.... short	**getShort** (Object obj) throws IllegalArgumentException, IllegalAccessException
		public	.... Class	**getType** ()
	1	public	.... **int**	**hashCode** ()
1.2	2	public	.... boolean	**isAccessible** ()
		public native	.... void	**set** (Object obj, Object value) throws IllegalArgumentException, IllegalAccessException
1.2	2	public	.... void	**setAccessible** (boolean flag) throws SecurityException
1.2 △	2	public static	.... void	**setAccessible** (AccessibleObject[] array, boolean flag) throws SecurityException
		public native	.... void	**setBoolean** (Object obj, boolean z) throws IllegalArgumentException, IllegalAccessException
		public native	.... void	**setByte** (Object obj, byte b) throws IllegalArgumentException, IllegalAccessException
		public native	.... void	**setChar** (Object obj, char c) throws IllegalArgumentException, IllegalAccessException
		public native	.... void	**setDouble** (Object obj, double d) throws IllegalArgumentException, IllegalAccessException
		public native	.... void	**setFloat** (Object obj, float f) throws IllegalArgumentException, IllegalAccessException
		public native	.... void	**setInt** (Object obj, int i) throws IllegalArgumentException, IllegalAccessException
		public native	.... void	**setLong** (Object obj, long l) throws IllegalArgumentException, IllegalAccessException
		public native	.... void	**setShort** (Object obj, short s) throws IllegalArgumentException, IllegalAccessException
	1	public	.... **String**	**toString** ()

FieldPosition　　　　　　　　　　　　　　　　　　　　java.text

```
     Object 1
1.1   └ FieldPosition
```
P

	1	public	.... **boolean**	**equals** (Object obj)
*		public	....	**FieldPosition** (int field)
		public	.... int	**getBeginIndex** ()
		public	.... int	**getEndIndex** ()
		public	.... int	**getField** ()
	1	public	.... **int**	**hashCode** ()
1.2		public	.... void	**setBeginIndex** (int bi)
1.2		public	.... void	**setEndIndex** (int ei)
	1	public	.... **String**	**toString** ()

FieldView　　　　　　　　　　　　　　　　　　　javax.swing.text

```
     Object
1.2 ○  └ View 1 - - - - - - - - - - - - - - - - - - - - - - - - - - - javax.swing.SwingConstants
1.2     └ PlainView 2 - - - - - - - - - - - - - - - - - - - - - - - TabExpander
1.2       └ FieldView
```

Classes

	1	*30 inherited members from View not shown*		
		protected	...... *java.awt.Shape*	**adjustAllocation** (*java.awt.Shape* a)
	2	public	.... void	changedUpdate (*javax.swing.event.DocumentEvent* changes, *java.awt.Shape* a, *ViewFactory* f)
	2	protected	.... void	drawLine (int lineIndex, java.awt.Graphics g, int x, int y)
	2	protected	.... int	drawSelectedText (java.awt.Graphics g, int x, int y, int p0, int p1) throws BadLocationException
	2	protected	.... int	drawUnselectedText (java.awt.Graphics g, int x, int y, int p0, int p1) throws BadLocationException
*		public	....	**FieldView** (*Element* elem)
		protected	java.awt.FontMetrics	**getFontMetrics** ()
●	2	protected final	.... Segment	getLineBuffer ()
	2	public	.... **float**	**getPreferredSpan** (int axis)
	1	public	.... **int**	**getResizeWeight** (int axis)
	2	protected	.... int	getTabSize ()

FieldView

2	public	**void**	**insertUpdate** (*javax.swing.event.DocumentEvent* changes, *java.awt.Shape* a, *ViewFactory* f)
2	protected java.awt.FontMetrics	metrics	
2	public	***java.awt.Shape***	**modelToView** (int pos, *java. awt. Shape* a, Position. Bias b) throws BadLocationException
2	public	float	nextTabStop (float x, int tabOffset)
2	public	**void**	**paint** (java.awt.Graphics g, *java.awt.Shape* a)
2	public	void	preferenceChanged (View child, boolean width, boolean height)
2	public	**void**	**removeUpdate** (*javax.swing.event.DocumentEvent* changes, *java.awt.Shape* a, *ViewFactory* f)
2	public	**int**	**viewToModel** (float fx, float fy, *java.awt.Shape* a, Position.Bias[] bias)

File   java.io

P⁰

Object[1]
└File - *Serializable, Comparable*[2]

		public	boolean	**canRead** ()
		public	boolean	**canWrite** ()
1.2		public	int	**compareTo** (File pathname)
1.2	2	public	int	**compareTo** (Object o)
1.2		public	boolean	**createNewFile** () throws IOException
1.2	△	public static	File	**createTempFile** (String prefix, String suffix) throws IOException
1.2	△	public static	File	**createTempFile** (String prefix, String suffix, File directory) throws IOException
		public	boolean	**delete** ()
1.2		public	void	**deleteOnExit** ()
	1	public	**boolean**	**equals** (Object obj)
		public	boolean	**exists** ()
	*	public	**File**	**File** (String pathname)
	*	public	**File**	**File** (File parent, String child)
	*	public	**File**	**File** (String parent, String child)
1.2		public	File	**getAbsoluteFile** ()
		public	String	**getAbsolutePath** ()
1.2		public	File	**getCanonicalFile** () throws IOException
1.1		public	String	**getCanonicalPath** () throws IOException
		public	String	**getName** ()
		public	String	**getParent** ()
1.2		public	File	**getParentFile** ()
		public	String	**getPath** ()
	1	public	**int**	**hashCode** ()
		public	boolean	**isAbsolute** ()
		public	boolean	**isDirectory** ()
		public	boolean	**isFile** ()
1.2		public	boolean	**isHidden** ()
		public	long	**lastModified** ()
		public	long	**length** ()
		public	String[]	**list** ()
		public	String[]	**list** (*FilenameFilter* filter)
1.2		public	File[]	**listFiles** ()
1.2		public	File[]	**listFiles** (*FileFilter* filter)
1.2		public	File[]	**listFiles** (*FilenameFilter* filter)
1.2	△	public static	File[]	**listRoots** ()
		public	boolean	**mkdir** ()
		public	boolean	**mkdirs** ()
	▲	public static final	String	**pathSeparator** = ";"
	▲	public static final	char	**pathSeparatorChar** = ';'
		public	boolean	**renameTo** (File dest)
	▲	public static final	String	**separator** = "\"
	▲	public static final	char	**separatorChar** = '\'
1.2		public	boolean	**setLastModified** (long time)
1.2		public	boolean	**setReadOnly** ()
	1	public	**String**	**toString** ()
1.2		public	java.net.URL	**toURL** () throws java.net.MalformedURLException

---

FileChooserUI   javax.swing.plaf

Object
1.2 ○ └ComponentUI[1]
1.2 ○   └FileChooserUI

Class *Interface* —extends - - -implements ○ abstract ● final △ static ▲ static final ✳ constructor x x—inherited x **x**—declared **x x**—overridden

○ 1 *11 inherited members from ComponentUI not shown*
○ public abstract ....void **ensureFileIsVisible** (javax.swing.JFileChooser fc, java.io.File f)
✳ public............................ **FileChooserUI** ()
○ public abstract ....javax ↩ **getAcceptAllFileFilter** (javax.swing.JFileChooser fc)
.swing.filechooser.FileFilter
○ public abstract ....String **getApproveButtonText** (javax.swing.JFileChooser fc)
○ public abstract ....String **getDialogTitle** (javax.swing.JFileChooser fc)
○ public abstract ....javax ↩ **getFileView** (javax.swing.JFileChooser fc)
.swing.filechooser.FileView
○ public abstract ....void **rescanCurrentDirectory** (javax.swing.JFileChooser fc)

FileDescriptor
java.io

Object
● └FileDescriptor

▲ public static final FileDescriptor **err**
✳ public............................ **FileDescriptor** ()
▲ public static final FileDescriptor **in**
▲ public static final FileDescriptor **out**
1.1 public native ....void **sync** () throws SyncFailedException
public................boolean **valid** ()

FileDialog
java.awt
P○

Object
○ └Component[1] - *java.awt.image.ImageObserver*, *MenuContainer*,
java.io.Serializable

└Container[2]
└Window[3]
└Dialog[4]
└FileDialog

---

1 *131 inherited members from Component not shown*
2 *48 inherited members from Container not shown*
4 public................ **void addNotify** ()
1.1 3 public synchronized ....void addWindowListener (*java.awt.event.WindowListener* l)
1.2 3 public........................void applyResourceBundle (String rbName)
1.2 3 public........................void applyResourceBundle (java.util.ResourceBundle rb)
3 public........................void dispose ()
1.1 ✳ public............................ **FileDialog** (Frame parent)
✳ public............................ **FileDialog** (Frame parent, String title)
✳ public............................ **FileDialog** (Frame parent, String title, int mode)
3 protected....................void finalize () throws Throwable
public....................String **getDirectory** ()
public....................String **getFile** ()
public.... *java.io.FilenameFilter* **getFilenameFilter** ()
1.1 3 public.............. Component getFocusOwner ()
1.2 3 public............................ getInputContext ()
.... java.awt.im.InputContext
1.1 3 public...........java.util.Locale getLocale ()
public........................int **getMode** ()
1.2 3 public................. Window[] getOwnedWindows ()
1.2 3 public.................. Window getOwner ()
4 public....................String getTitle ()
3 public.................... Toolkit getToolkit ()
● 3 public final ....String getWarningString ()
4 public.............. boolean isModal ()
4 public.............. boolean isResizable ()
3 public.............. boolean isShowing ()
▲ public static final.............int **LOAD** = 0
3 public........................void pack ()
4 protected.............. **String paramString** ()
1.1 3 protected ....void processEvent (AWTEvent e)
1.1 3 protected ....void processWindowEvent (java.awt.event.WindowEvent e)
1.1 3 public synchronized ....void removeWindowListener (*java.awt.event.WindowListener* l)
▲ public static final.............int **SAVE** = 1
public........................void **setDirectory** (String dir)
public........................void **setFile** (String file)
public synchronized ....void **setFilenameFilter** (*java.io.FilenameFilter* filter)
1.1 4 public........................void setModal (boolean b)

F

Classes

FileDialog

1.1	public	void	**setMode** (int mode)
4	public	void	setResizable (boolean resizable)
4	public synchronized	void	setTitle (String title)
4	public	void	show ()
3	public	void	toBack ()
3	public	void	toFront ()

FileDialogPeer
java.awt.peer

FileDialogPeer ———————————— *DialogPeer* [1] (*WindowPeer* [2] (*ContainerPeer* [3] (*ComponentPeer* [4])))

4	*32 inherited members from ComponentPeer not shown*		
1	*2 inherited members from DialogPeer not shown*		
2	*7 inherited members from WindowPeer not shown*		
3	*4 inherited members from ContainerPeer not shown*		
	public	void	**setDirectory** (String)
	public	void	**setFile** (String)
	public	void	**setFilenameFilter** (*java.io.FilenameFilter*)

FileFilter ❶
java.io

FileFilter

1.2	*FileFilter*		
	public	boolean	**accept** (File pathname)

FileFilter ❷
javax.swing.filechooser

Object
└*FileFilter*

1.2 ○			
○	public abstract	boolean	**accept** (java.io.File f)
✳	public		**FileFilter** ()
○	public abstract	String	**getDescription** ()

FileInputStream
java.io
P○

Object [1]
└InputStream [2]
  └FileInputStream

2	public native	**int**	**available** () throws IOException
2	public native	**void**	**close** () throws IOException
✳	public		**FileInputStream** (File file) throws FileNotFoundException
✳	public		**FileInputStream** (FileDescriptor fdObj)
✳	public		**FileInputStream** (String name) throws FileNotFoundException
1	protected	**void**	**finalize** () throws IOException
●	public final	FileDescriptor	**getFD** () throws IOException
2	public synchronized	void	mark (int readlimit)
2	public	boolean	markSupported ()
2	public native	**int**	**read** () throws IOException
2	public	**int**	**read** (byte[] b) throws IOException
2	public	**int**	**read** (byte[] b, int off, int len) throws IOException
2	public synchronized	void	reset () throws IOException
2	public native	**long**	**skip** (long n) throws IOException

---

FilenameFilter
java.io
P○

FilenameFilter

	public	boolean	**accept** (File dir, String name)

FileNameMap
java.net
P

FileNameMap

1.1	*FileNameMap*		
	public	String	**getContentTypeFor** (String fileName)

Class   *Interface*   —extends   - - -implements   ○ abstract   ● final   △ static   ▲ static final   ✳ constructor   x x—inherited   x **x**—declared   **x x**—overridden

F

FileNotFoundException

java.io
P O

```
Object
 └Throwable - - - - - - - - - - - - - - - - - - - - - - - - - - Serializable
   └Exception
     └IOException
       └FileNotFoundException
```

*	public.........................	**FileNotFoundException** ()
*	public.........................	**FileNotFoundException** (String s)

F

FileOutputStream

java.io
P O

```
Object 1
 └OutputStream 2
   └FileOutputStream
```

	2	public native .... **void**	**close** () throws IOException
*		public.........................	**FileOutputStream** (File file) throws IOException
*		public.........................	**FileOutputStream** (FileDescriptor fdObj)
*		public.........................	**FileOutputStream** (String name) throws FileNotFoundException
1.1 *		public.........................	**FileOutputStream** (String name, boolean append) throws FileNotFoundException
	1	protected .... **void**	**finalize** () throws IOException
	2	public......................void	flush () throws IOException
●		public final ...... FileDescriptor	**getFD** () throws IOException
`	2	public......................... **void**	**write** (byte[] b) throws IOException
	2	public native .... **void**	**write** (int b) throws IOException
	2	public......................... **void**	**write** (byte[] b, int off, int len) throws IOException

FilePermission

java.io

```
Object
 └java.security.Permission 1 - - - - - - - - - - - - - - - - java.security.Guard, Serializable
   └FilePermission - - - - - - - - - - - - - - - - - - - - - Serializable
```

	1	public......................void	checkGuard (Object object) throws SecurityException
	1	public................. **boolean**	**equals** (Object obj)
*	1	public.........................	**FilePermission** (String path, String actions)
	1	public................. **String**	**getActions** ()
●	1	public final ....String	getName ()
	1	public................. **int**	**hashCode** ()
	1	public................. **boolean**	**implies** (java.security.Permission p)
	1	public..........**java.security** ↵	**newPermissionCollection** ()
		.PermissionCollection	
	1	public.................... String	toString ()

FileReader

java.io
P O

```
Object
 └Reader 1
   └InputStreamReader 2
     └FileReader
```
1.1
1.1
1.1

	2	public......................void	close () throws IOException
*		public.........................	**FileReader** (File file) throws FileNotFoundException
*		public.........................	**FileReader** (FileDescriptor fd)
*		public.........................	**FileReader** (String fileName) throws FileNotFoundException
	2	public......................String	getEncoding ()
	1	protected .... Object	lock
	1	public......................void	mark (int readAheadLimit) throws IOException
	1	public................. boolean	markSupported ()
	2	public......................int	read () throws IOException
	1	public......................int	read (char[] cbuf) throws IOException
	2	public......................int	read (char[] cbuf, int off, int len) throws IOException
	2	public................. boolean	ready () throws IOException
	1	public......................void	reset () throws IOException
	1	public................. long	skip (long n) throws IOException

Classes

FileSystemView

		javax.swing.filechooser

```
        Object
1.2 ○    └FileSystemView
```

	public.................java.io.File	**createFileObject** (String path)
	public.................java.io.File	**createFileObject** (java.io.File dir, String filename)
○	public abstract ......java.io.File	**createNewFolder** (java.io.File containingDir) throws java.io.IOException
*	public............................	**FileSystemView** ()
	public..............java.io.File[]	**getFiles** (java.io.File dir, boolean useFileHiding)
△	public static ... FileSystemView	**getFileSystemView** ()
	public.................java.io.File	**getHomeDirectory** ()
	public.................java.io.File	**getParentDirectory** (java.io.File dir)
○	public abstract .... java.io.File[]	**getRoots** ()
○	public abstract .... boolean	**isHiddenFile** (java.io.File f)
○	public abstract .... boolean	**isRoot** (java.io.File f)

FileView

		javax.swing.filechooser

```
        Object
1.2 ○    └FileView
```

*	public..........................	**FileView** ()
○	public abstract ....String	**getDescription** (java.io.File f)
○	public abstract	**getIcon** (java.io.File f)
	...............javax.swing.Icon	
○	public abstract ....String	**getName** (java.io.File f)
○	public abstract ....String	**getTypeDescription** (java.io.File f)
○	public abstract .... Boolean	**isTraversable** (java.io.File f)

FileWriter

		java.io
		P○

```
        Object
1.1 ○    └Writer 1
1.1          └OutputStreamWriter 2
1.1              └FileWriter
```

2	public.......................void	close () throws IOException
*	public..........................	**FileWriter** (File file) throws IOException
*	public..........................	**FileWriter** (FileDescriptor fd)
*	public..........................	**FileWriter** (String fileName) throws IOException
*	public..........................	**FileWriter** (String fileName, boolean append) throws IOException
2	public.......................void	flush () throws IOException
2	public.....................String	getEncoding ()
1	protected.................Object	lock
1	public.......................void	write (char[] cbuf) throws IOException
2	public.......................void	write (int c) throws IOException
1	public.......................void	write (String str) throws IOException
2	public.......................void	write (char[] cbuf, int off, int len) throws IOException
2	public.......................void	write (String str, int off, int len) throws IOException

FilteredImageSource

		java.awt.image
		P

```
        Object
        └FilteredImageSource - - - - - - - - - - - - - - - - - - - ImageProducer 1
```

1	public synchronized ....void	**addConsumer** (*ImageConsumer* ic)
*	public..........................	**FilteredImageSource** (*ImageProducer* orig, ImageFilter imgf)
1	public synchronized .. boolean	**isConsumer** (*ImageConsumer* ic)
1	public synchronized ....void	**removeConsumer** (*ImageConsumer* ic)
1	public.......................void	**requestTopDownLeftRightResend** (*ImageConsumer* ic)
1	public.......................void	**startProduction** (*ImageConsumer* ic)

Class   *Interface*   —extends   - - -implements   ○ abstract   ● final   △ static   ▲ static final   ✳ constructor   x x—inherited   x **x**—declared   **x x**—overridden

FilterInputStream

```
      Object
  ○   └InputStream 1
           └FilterInputStream
```

1	public	**int**	**available** () throws IOException
1	public	**void**	**close** () throws IOException
*	protected		**FilterInputStream** (InputStream in)
	protected	InputStream	**in**
1	public synchronized	**void**	**mark** (int readlimit)
1	public	**boolean**	**markSupported** ()
1	public	**int**	**read** () throws IOException
1	public	**int**	**read** (byte[] b) throws IOException
1	public	**int**	**read** (byte[] b, int off, int len) throws IOException
1	public synchronized	**void**	**reset** () throws IOException
1	public	**long**	**skip** (long n) throws IOException

FilterOutputStream

```
      Object
  ○   └OutputStream 1
           └FilterOutputStream
```

1	public	**void**	**close** () throws IOException
*	public		**FilterOutputStream** (OutputStream out)
1	public	**void**	**flush** () throws IOException
	protected	OutputStream	**out**
1	public	**void**	**write** (byte[] b) throws IOException
1	public	**void**	**write** (int b) throws IOException
1	public	**void**	**write** (byte[] b, int off, int len) throws IOException

FilterReader

```
        Object
1.1 ○   └Reader 1
1.1 ○        └FilterReader
```

1	public	**void**	**close** () throws IOException
*	protected		**FilterReader** (Reader in)
	protected	Reader	**in**
1	protected	Object	lock
1	public	**void**	**mark** (int readAheadLimit) throws IOException
1	public	**boolean**	**markSupported** ()
1	public	**int**	**read** () throws IOException
1	public	int	read (char[] cbuf) throws IOException
1	public	**int**	**read** (char[] cbuf, int off, int len) throws IOException
1	public	**boolean**	**ready** () throws IOException
1	public	**void**	**reset** () throws IOException
1	public	**long**	**skip** (long n) throws IOException

FilterWriter

```
        Object
1.1 ○   └Writer 1
1.1 ○        └FilterWriter
```

1	public	**void**	**close** () throws IOException
*	protected		**FilterWriter** (Writer out)
1	public	**void**	**flush** () throws IOException
1	protected	Object	lock
	protected	Writer	**out**
1	public	void	write (char[] cbuf) throws IOException
1	public	**void**	**write** (int c) throws IOException
1	public	void	write (String str) throws IOException
1	public	**void**	**write** (char[] cbuf, int off, int len) throws IOException
1	public	**void**	**write** (String str, int off, int len) throws IOException

F

Classes

FixedHeightLayoutCache

			javax.swing.tree

```
        Object
1.2 ○   └AbstractLayoutCache¹ - - - - - - - - - - - - - - - - - - RowMapper
1.2        └FixedHeightLayoutCache
```

*	public		**FixedHeightLayoutCache** ()
1	public..... **java.awt.Rectangle**	**getBounds** (TreePath path, java.awt.Rectangle placeIn)
1	public	**boolean**	**getExpandedState** (TreePath path)
1	public	*TreeModel*	getModel ()
1	public AbstractLayoutCache ↵	getNodeDimensions ()
	.NodeDimensions	
1	protected .. java.awt.Rectangle	getNodeDimensions (Object value, int row, int depth, boolean expanded,
		java.awt.Rectangle placeIn)
1	public................. **TreePath**	**getPathClosestTo** (int x, int y)
1	public................. **TreePath**	**getPathForRow** (int row)
1	public....................int	getPreferredHeight ()
1	public....................int	getPreferredWidth (java.awt.Rectangle bounds)
1	public................... **int**	**getRowCount** ()
1	public................... **int**	**getRowForPath** (TreePath path)
1	public....................int	getRowHeight ()
1	public.................... int[]	getRowsForPaths (TreePath[] paths)
1	public..... *TreeSelectionModel*	getSelectionModel ()
1	public................... **int**	**getVisibleChildCount** (TreePath path)
1	public.. ***java.util.Enumeration***	**getVisiblePathsFrom** (TreePath path)
1	public................... **void**	**invalidatePathBounds** (TreePath path)
1	public................... **void**	**invalidateSizes** ()
1	public................ **boolean**	**isExpanded** (TreePath path)
1	protected .... boolean	isFixedRowHeight ()
1	public................. boolean	isRootVisible ()
1	protected	nodeDimensions
	.... AbstractLayoutCache ↵	
	.NodeDimensions	
1	protected .... boolean	rootVisible
1	protected ....int	rowHeight
1	public................... **void**	**setExpandedState** (TreePath path, boolean isExpanded)
1	public................... **void**	**setModel** (*TreeModel* newModel)
1	public....................void	setNodeDimensions (AbstractLayoutCache.NodeDimensions nd)
1	public................... **void**	**setRootVisible** (boolean rootVisible)
1	public................... **void**	**setRowHeight** (int rowHeight)
1	public....................void	setSelectionModel (*TreeSelectionModel* newLSM)
1	protected .... *TreeModel*	treeModel
1	public................... **void**	**treeNodesChanged** (javax.swing.event.TreeModelEvent e)
1	public................... **void**	**treeNodesInserted** (javax.swing.event.TreeModelEvent e)
1	public................... **void**	**treeNodesRemoved** (javax.swing.event.TreeModelEvent e)
1	protected . *TreeSelectionModel*	treeSelectionModel
1	public................... **void**	**treeStructureChanged** (javax.swing.event.TreeModelEvent e)

FixedHolder

			org.omg.CORBA

```
        Object
1.2 ●   └FixedHolder - - - - - - - - - - - - - - - - - - - - - - - - - - - org.omg.CORBA.portable.Streamable¹
```

1	public.....................void	**_read** (org.omg.CORBA.portable.InputStream input)
1	public.................TypeCode	**_type** ()
1	public.....................void	**_write** (org.omg.CORBA.portable.OutputStream output)
*	public.....................	**FixedHolder** ()
*	public.....................	**FixedHolder** (java.math.BigDecimal initial)
	public... java.math.BigDecimal	**value**

FlatteningPathIterator

			java.awt.geom

```
        Object
1.2     └FlatteningPathIterator - - - - - - - - - - - - - - - - - - - - PathIterator¹
```

1	public.......................int	**currentSegment** (double[] coords)
1	public.......................int	**currentSegment** (float[] coords)
*	public.....................	**FlatteningPathIterator** (*PathIterator* src, double flatness)
*	public.....................	**FlatteningPathIterator** (*PathIterator* src, double flatness, int limit)

Class   *Interface*   —extends   - - -implements   ○ abstract   ● final   △ static   ▲ static final   ✳ constructor   x x—inherited   x **x**—declared   **x x**—overridden

	public	double	**getFlatness** ()
	public	int	**getRecursionLimit** ()
1	public	int	**getWindingRule** ()
1	public	boolean	**isDone** ()
1	public	void	**next** ()

FlavorMap
java.awt.datatransfer

1.2	*FlavorMap*		P

	public	*java.util.Map*	**getFlavorsForNatives** (String[] natives)
	public	*java.util.Map*	**getNativesForFlavors** (DataFlavor[] flavors)

Float
java.lang

Object [1]
○ └ Number [2] ----------------------------- *java.io.Serializable*
●   └ Float ----------------------------- *Comparable* [3]

P

1.1	2	public	**byte**	**byteValue** ()
1.2		public	int	**compareTo** (Float anotherFloat)
1.2	3	public	int	**compareTo** (Object o)
	2	public	**double**	**doubleValue** ()
	1	public	**boolean**	**equals** (Object obj)
✳		public		**Float** (double value)
✳		public		**Float** (float value)
✳		public		**Float** (String s) throws NumberFormatException
△		public static native	int	**floatToIntBits** (float value)
	2	public	**float**	**floatValue** ()
	1	public	**int**	**hashCode** ()
△		public static native	float	**intBitsToFloat** (int bits)
	2	public	**int**	**intValue** ()
		public	boolean	**isInfinite** ()
△		public static	boolean	**isInfinite** (float v)
		public	boolean	**isNaN** ()
△		public static	boolean	**isNaN** (float v)
	2	public	**long**	**longValue** ()
▲		public static final	float	**MAX_VALUE** = 3.4028235E38
▲		public static final	float	**MIN_VALUE** = 1.4E-45
▲		public static final	float	**NaN** = NaN
▲		public static final	float	**NEGATIVE_INFINITY** = -Infinity
1.2 △		public static	float	**parseFloat** (String s) throws NumberFormatException
▲		public static final	float	**POSITIVE_INFINITY** = Infinity
1.1 ▲	2	public	**short**	**shortValue** ()
	1	public	**String**	**toString** ()
△		public static	String	**toString** (float f)
1.1 ▲		public static final	Class	**TYPE**
△		public static	Float	**valueOf** (String s) throws NumberFormatException

FloatHolder
org.omg.CORBA

Object
1.2 ● └ FloatHolder ------------------------- *org.omg.CORBA.portable.Streamable* [1]

	1	public	void	**_read** (org.omg.CORBA.portable.InputStream input)
	1	public	TypeCode	**_type** ()
	1	public	void	**_write** (org.omg.CORBA.portable.OutputStream output)
✳		public		**FloatHolder** ()
✳		public		**FloatHolder** (float initial)
		public	float	**value**

FlowLayout
java.awt

Object [1]
└ FlowLayout ------------------------- *LayoutManager* [2], *java.io.Serializable*

P

	2	public	void	**addLayoutComponent** (String name, Component comp)
▲		public static final	int	**CENTER** = 1
✳		public		**FlowLayout** ()
✳		public		**FlowLayout** (int align)

F

Classes

FlowLayout

✳	public		**FlowLayout**	(int align, int hgap, int vgap)
1.1	public	int	**getAlignment**	()
1.1	public	int	**getHgap**	()
1.1	public	int	**getVgap**	()
2	public	void	**layoutContainer**	(Container target)
1.2 ▲	public static final	int	**LEADING**	= 3
▲	public static final	int	**LEFT**	= 0
2	public	Dimension	**minimumLayoutSize**	(Container target)
2	public	Dimension	**preferredLayoutSize**	(Container target)
2	public	void	**removeLayoutComponent**	(Component comp)
▲	public static final	int	**RIGHT**	= 2
1.1	public	void	**setAlignment**	(int align)
1.1	public	void	**setHgap**	(int hgap)
1.1	public	void	**setVgap**	(int vgap)
1	public	String	**toString**	()
1.2 ▲	public static final	int	**TRAILING**	= 4

F

FocusAdapter
java.awt.event
P

Object
└FocusAdapter - *FocusListener* [1] (*java.util.EventListener*)
1.1 ○

✳	public		**FocusAdapter**	()
1	public	void	**focusGained**	(FocusEvent e)
1	public	void	**focusLost**	(FocusEvent e)

FocusEvent
java.awt.event
P

Object
1.1 └java.util.EventObject [1] - - - - - - - - - - - - - - - - - - - *java.io.Serializable*
1.1 ○   └java.awt.AWTEvent [2]
1.1   └ComponentEvent [3]
1.1   └FocusEvent

2	protected	void	consume	()
2	protected	boolean	consumed	
2	protected	void	finalize	() throws Throwable
▲	public static final	int	**FOCUS_FIRST**	= 1004
▲	public static final	int	**FOCUS_GAINED**	= 1004
▲	public static final	int	**FOCUS_LAST**	= 1005
▲	public static final	int	**FOCUS_LOST**	= 1005
✳	public		**FocusEvent**	(java.awt.Component source, int id)
✳	public		**FocusEvent**	(java.awt.Component source, int id, boolean temporary)
3	public	java.awt.Component	getComponent	()
2	public	int	getID	()
1	public	Object	getSource	()
2	protected	int	id	
2	protected	boolean	isConsumed	()
	public	boolean	**isTemporary**	()
3	public	String	**paramString**	()
1	protected transient	Object	source	
2	public	String	toString	()

FocusListener
java.awt.event
P

1.1 *FocusListener*————————————*java.util.EventListener*

	public	void	**focusGained**	(FocusEvent e)
	public	void	**focusLost**	(FocusEvent e)

FocusManager
javax.swing

Object
1.2 ○ └FocusManager

△	public static	void	**disableSwingFocusManager**	()
▲	public static final	String	**FOCUS_MANAGER_CLASS_PROPERTY**	= "FocusManagerClassName"
✳	public		**FocusManager**	()

Class   *Interface*   —extends   - - -implements   ○ abstract   ● final   △ static   ▲ static final   ✳ constructor   x x—inherited   x **x**—declared   x **x**—overridden

○	public abstract.............void	**focusNextComponent** (java.awt.Component aComponent)	
○	public abstract.............void	**focusPreviousComponent** (java.awt.Component aComponent)	
△	public static ....FocusManager	**getCurrentManager** ()	
△	public static ....boolean	**isFocusManagerEnabled** ()	
○	public abstract.............void	**processKeyEvent** (java. awt. Component focusedComponent,	
		java.awt.event.KeyEvent anEvent)	
△	public static ....void	**setCurrentManager** (FocusManager aFocusManager)	

Font

java.awt

P

Object[1]
└ Font - *java.io.Serializable*

	▲	public static final.............int	**BOLD** = 1
1.2		public.................boolean	**canDisplay** (char c)
1.2		public.....................int	**canDisplayUpTo** (String str)
1.2		public.....................int	**canDisplayUpTo** (char[] text, int start, int limit)
1.2		public.....................int	**canDisplayUpTo** (*java.text.CharacterIterator* iter, int start, int limit)
1.2	▲	public static final.............int	**CENTER_BASELINE** = 1
1.2		public.....................	**createGlyphVector** (java.awt.font.FontRenderContext frc, int[] glyphCodes)
		......java.awt.font.GlyphVector	
1.2		public.....................	**createGlyphVector** (java. awt. font. FontRenderContext frc,
		......java.awt.font.GlyphVector	*java.text.CharacterIterator* ci)
1.2		public.....................	**createGlyphVector** (java.awt.font.FontRenderContext frc, String str)
		......java.awt.font.GlyphVector	
1.2		public.....................	**createGlyphVector** (java.awt.font.FontRenderContext frc, char[] chars)
		......java.awt.font.GlyphVector	
1.1	△	public static ....Font	**decode** (String str)
1.2		public: ....Font	**deriveFont** (float size)
1.2		public....................Font	**deriveFont** (int style)
1.2		public....................Font	**deriveFont** (java.awt.geom.AffineTransform trans)
1.2		public....................Font	**deriveFont** (*java.util.Map* attributes)
1.2		public....................Font	**deriveFont** (int style, float size)
1.2		public....................Font	**deriveFont** (int style, java.awt.geom.AffineTransform trans)
	1	public..................**boolean**	**equals** (Object obj)
	1	protected ....**void**	**finalize** () throws Throwable
1.2	∗	public.....................	**Font** (*java.util.Map* attributes)
	∗	public.....................	**Font** (String name, int style, int size)
1.2		public.............*java.util.Map*	**getAttributes** ()
1.2		public..............java.text ↩	**getAvailableAttributes** ()
		.AttributedCharacterIterator ↩	
		.Attribute[]	
1.2		public.....................byte	**getBaselineFor** (char c)
		public....................String	**getFamily** ()
1.2		public....................String	**getFamily** (java.util.Locale l)
1.2	△	public static ....Font	**getFont** (String nm)
1.2	△	public static ....Font	**getFont** (*java.util.Map* attributes)
	△	public static ....Font	**getFont** (String nm, Font font)
1.2		public....................String	**getFontName** ()
1.2		public....................String	**getFontName** (java.util.Locale l)
1.2		public....................float	**getItalicAngle** ()
1.2		public.....................	**getLineMetrics** (String str, java.awt.font.FontRenderContext frc)
		......java.awt.font.LineMetrics	
1.2		public.....................	**getLineMetrics** (char[] chars, int beginIndex, int limit,
		......java.awt.font.LineMetrics	java.awt.font.FontRenderContext frc)
1.2		public.....................	**getLineMetrics** (String str, int beginIndex, int limit,
		......java.awt.font.LineMetrics	java.awt.font.FontRenderContext frc)
1.2		public.....................	**getLineMetrics** (*java. text. CharacterIterator* ci, int beginIndex, int limit,
		......java.awt.font.LineMetrics	java.awt.font.FontRenderContext frc)
1.2		public.....................	**getMaxCharBounds** (java.awt.font.FontRenderContext frc)
		...java.awt.geom.Rectangle2D	
1.2		public.....................int	**getMissingGlyphCode** ()
		public....................String	**getName** ()
1.2		public.....................int	**getNumGlyphs** ()
D		public..*java.awt.peer.FontPeer*	**getPeer** ()
1.2		public....................String	**getPSName** ()
		public.....................int	**getSize** ()
1.2		public....................float	**getSize2D** ()
1.2		public.....................	**getStringBounds** (String str, java.awt.font.FontRenderContext frc)
		...java.awt.geom.Rectangle2D	
1.2		public.....................	**getStringBounds** (char[] chars, int beginIndex, int limit,
		...java.awt.geom.Rectangle2D	java.awt.font.FontRenderContext frc)

F

Classes

Font

1.2		public............................ ...java.awt.geom.Rectangle2D	**getStringBounds** (String str, int beginIndex, int limit, java.awt.font.FontRenderContext frc)
1.2		public............................ ...java.awt.geom.Rectangle2D	**getStringBounds** (*java.text.CharacterIterator* ci, int beginIndex, int limit, java.awt.font.FontRenderContext frc)
		public..................int	**getStyle** ()
1.2		public............................ java.awt.geom.AffineTransform	**getTransform** ()
1.2	▲	public static final.............int	**HANGING_BASELINE** = 2
	1	public.....................**int**	**hashCode** ()
1.2		public.................boolean	**hasUniformLineMetrics** ()
		public.................boolean	**isBold** ()
		public.................boolean	**isItalic** ()
		public.................boolean	**isPlain** ()
	▲	public static final.............int	**ITALIC** = 2
		protected..................String	**name**
	▲	public static final.............int	**PLAIN** = 0
1.2		protected...................float	**pointSize**
1.2	▲	public static final.............int	**ROMAN_BASELINE** = 0
		protected......................int	**size**
		protected......................int	**style**
	1	public...................**String**	**toString** ()

FontMetrics   java.awt

P

Object[1]
  ○ └FontMetrics - *java.io.Serializable*

	public........................int	**bytesWidth** (byte[] data, int off, int len)
	public........................int	**charsWidth** (char[] data, int off, int len)
	public........................int	**charWidth** (char ch)
	public........................int	**charWidth** (int ch)
	protected .... Font	**font**
✳	protected......................	**FontMetrics** (Font font)
	public........................int	**getAscent** ()
	public........................int	**getDescent** ()
	public........................ Font	**getFont** ()
	public........................int	**getHeight** ()
	public........................int	**getLeading** ()
1.2	public...................... ....java.awt.font.LineMetrics	**getLineMetrics** (String str, Graphics context)
1.2	public...................... ....java.awt.font.LineMetrics	**getLineMetrics** (char[] chars, int beginIndex, int limit, Graphics context)
1.2	public...................... ....java.awt.font.LineMetrics	**getLineMetrics** (String str, int beginIndex, int limit, Graphics context)
1.2	public...................... ....java.awt.font.LineMetrics	**getLineMetrics** (*java.text.CharacterIterator* ci, int beginIndex, int limit, Graphics context)
	public...................int	**getMaxAdvance** ()
	public...................int	**getMaxAscent** ()
1.2	public...................... ...java.awt.geom.Rectangle2D	**getMaxCharBounds** (Graphics context)
D	public...................int	**getMaxDecent** ()
	public...................int	**getMaxDescent** ()
1.2	public...................... ...java.awt.geom.Rectangle2D	**getStringBounds** (String str, Graphics context)
1.2	public...................... ...java.awt.geom.Rectangle2D	**getStringBounds** (char[] chars, int beginIndex, int limit, Graphics context)
1.2	public...................... ...java.awt.geom.Rectangle2D	**getStringBounds** (String str, int beginIndex, int limit, Graphics context)
1.2	public...................... ...java.awt.geom.Rectangle2D	**getStringBounds** (*java.text.CharacterIterator* ci, int beginIndex, int limit, Graphics context)
	public......................int[]	**getWidths** ()
1.2	public.................boolean	**hasUniformLineMetrics** ()
	public......................int	**stringWidth** (String str)
1	public...................**String**	**toString** ()

FontPeer   java.awt.peer

1.1	*FontPeer*

- -

Class   *Interface*   —extends   - - -implements   ○ abstract   ● final   △ static   ▲ static final   ✳ constructor   x x—inherited   x **x**—declared   **x x**—overridden

FontRenderContext

java.awt.font

Object
1.2 └FontRenderContext

*	protected	**FontRenderContext** ()
*	public	**FontRenderContext** (java.awt.geom.AffineTransform tx, boolean isAntiAliased, boolean usesFractionalMetrics)
	public . . . . java.awt.geom.AffineTransform	**getTransform** ()
	public . . . . boolean	**isAntiAliased** ()
	public . . . . boolean	**usesFractionalMetrics** ()

FontUIResource

javax.swing.plaf

Object
└java.awt.Font [1] - *java.io.Serializable*
1.2 └FontUIResource - *UIResource*

	[1]	*62 inherited members from java.awt.Font not shown*
*	public	**FontUIResource** (java.awt.Font font)
*	public	**FontUIResource** (String name, int style, int size)

Format

java.text

P

Object [1]
1.1 ○ └Format - *java.io.Serializable, Cloneable*

	[1] public . . . . **Object**	**clone** ()
*	public	**Format** ()
●	public final . . . . String	**format** (Object obj)
○	public abstract . . . . StringBuffer	**format** (Object obj, StringBuffer toAppendTo, FieldPosition pos)
	public . . . . Object	**parseObject** (String source) throws ParseException
○	public abstract . . . . Object	**parseObject** (String source, ParsePosition status)

FormView

javax.swing.text.html

Object
1.2 ○ └javax.swing.text.View [1] - - - - - - - - - - - - - - - - - - *javax.swing.SwingConstants*
1.2 └javax.swing.text.ComponentView [2]
1.2 └FormView - *java.awt.event.ActionListener* [3] (*java.util.EventListener*)

	[1]		*30 inherited members from javax.swing.text.View not shown*
	[3]	public . . . . void	**actionPerformed** (java.awt.event.ActionEvent evt)
	[2]	protected	**createComponent** ()
		. . . . **java.awt.Component**	
*		public	**FormView** (*javax.swing.text.Element* elem)
	[2]	public . . . . float	getAlignment (int axis)
●	[2]	public final	getComponent ()
		. . . . java.awt.Component	
	[2]	public . . . . float	getMaximumSpan (int axis)
	[2]	public . . . . float	getMinimumSpan (int axis)
	[2]	public . . . . float	getPreferredSpan (int axis)
		protected . . . . void	**imageSubmit** (String imageData)
	[2]	public . . . . *java.awt.Shape*	modelToView (int pos, *java.awt.Shape* a, javax.swing.text.Position.Bias b) throws javax.swing.text.BadLocationException
	[2]	public . . . . void	paint (java.awt.Graphics g, *java.awt.Shape* a)
▲		public static final . . . . String	**RESET** = "Reset"
	[2]	public . . . . void	setParent (javax.swing.text.View p)
	[2]	public . . . . void	setSize (float width, float height)
▲		public static final . . . . String	**SUBMIT** = "Submit Query"
		protected . . . . void	**submitData** (String data)
	[2]	public . . . . int	viewToModel (float x, float y, *java.awt.Shape* a, javax.swing.text.Position.Bias[] bias)

F

Classes

FormView.MouseEventListener	protected	javax.swing.text.html

Object
1.1 ○ └java.awt.event.MouseAdapter[1] - - - - - - - - - - - *java.awt.event.MouseListener* (*java.util.EventListener*)
1.2   └FormView.MouseEventListener

	1	public......................void	mouseClicked (java.awt.event.MouseEvent e)
	1	public......................void	mouseEntered (java.awt.event.MouseEvent e)
*		protected......................	**MouseEventListener** ()
	1	public......................void	mouseExited (java.awt.event.MouseEvent e)
	1	public......................void	mousePressed (java.awt.event.MouseEvent e)
	1	public......................**void**	**mouseReleased** (java.awt.event.MouseEvent evt)

F

Frame		java.awt
		P^m

Object
 ○ └Component[1] - *java.awt.image.ImageObserver*, *MenuContainer*,
                                          java.io.Serializable
    └Container[2]
     └Window[3]
      └Frame - *MenuContainer*

	1	*130 inherited members from Component not shown*	
	2	*47 inherited members from Container not shown*	
	3	public......................**void**	**addNotify** ()
1.1	3	public synchronized ....void	addWindowListener (*java.awt.event.WindowListener* l)
1.2	3	public......................void	applyResourceBundle (String rbName)
1.2	3	public......................void	applyResourceBundle (java.util.ResourceBundle rb)
D ▲		public static final.............int	**CROSSHAIR_CURSOR** = 1
D ▲		public static final.............int	**DEFAULT_CURSOR** = 0
	3	public......................void	dispose ()
D ▲		public static final.............int	**E_RESIZE_CURSOR** = 11
	3	protected...................**void**	**finalize** () throws Throwable
*		public......................	**Frame** ()
*		public......................	**Frame** (String title)
D		public......................int	**getCursorType** ()
1.1	3	public............ Component	getFocusOwner ()
1.2 △		public static ....Frame[]	**getFrames** ()
		public............ Image	**getIconImage** ()
1.2	3	public......................	getInputContext ()
		.... java.awt.im.InputContext	
1.1	3	public............java.util.Locale	getLocale ()
		public............ MenuBar	**getMenuBar** ()
1.2	3	public................Window[]	getOwnedWindows ()
1.2	3	public................ Window	getOwner ()
1.2		public synchronized ....int	**getState** ()
		public................String	**getTitle** ()
	3	public................ Toolkit	getToolkit ()
●	3	public final .... String	getWarningString ()
D ▲		public static final.............int	**HAND_CURSOR** = 12
1.2 ▲		public static final.............int	**ICONIFIED** = 1
		public................ boolean	**isResizable** ()
	3	public................ boolean	isShowing ()
D ▲		public static final.............int	**MOVE_CURSOR** = 13
D ▲		public static final.............int	**N_RESIZE_CURSOR** = 8
D ▲		public static final.............int	**NE_RESIZE_CURSOR** = 7
1.2 ▲		public static final.............int	**NORMAL** = 0
D ▲		public static final.............int	**NW_RESIZE_CURSOR** = 6
	3	public......................void	pack ()
	2	protected...............**String**	**paramString** ()
1.1	3	protected...................void	processEvent (AWTEvent e)
1.1	3	protected...................void	processWindowEvent (java.awt.event.WindowEvent e)
	1	public......................**void**	**remove** (MenuComponent m)
	2	public......................**void**	**removeNotify** ()
1.1	3	public synchronized ....void	removeWindowListener (*java.awt.event.WindowListener* l)
D ▲		public static final.............int	**S_RESIZE_CURSOR** = 9
D ▲		public static final.............int	**SE_RESIZE_CURSOR** = 5
D		public synchronized ....void	**setCursor** (int cursorType)
		public synchronized ....void	**setIconImage** (Image image)
		public......................void	**setMenuBar** (MenuBar mb)

Class   *Interface*   —extends   - - -implements   ○ abstract   ● final   △ static   ▲ static final   ✳ constructor   x x—inherited   x **x**—declared   **x x**—overridden

	1.2	public....................void	**setResizable** (boolean resizable)	
		public synchronized ....void	**setState** (int state)	
		public synchronized ....void	**setTitle** (String title)	
	3	public....................void	show ()	
D ▲		public static final ....int	**SW_RESIZE_CURSOR** = 4	
D ▲		public static final ....int	**TEXT_CURSOR** = 2	
	3	public....................void	toBack ()	
	3	public....................void	toFront ()	
D ▲		public static final ....int	**W_RESIZE_CURSOR** = 10	
D ▲		public static final ....int	**WAIT_CURSOR** = 3	

FramePeer   java.awt.peer

FramePeer————————————————— *WindowPeer* [1] (*ContainerPeer* [2] (*ComponentPeer* [3]))

- -

	3	*32 inherited members from ComponentPeer not shown*	
	1	*7 inherited members from WindowPeer not shown*	
	2	*4 inherited members from ContainerPeer not shown*	
1.2		public........................int	**getState** ()
		public....................void	**setIconImage** (java.awt.Image)
		public....................void	**setMenuBar** (java.awt.MenuBar)
		public....................void	**setResizable** (boolean)
1.2		public....................void	**setState** (int)
		public....................void	**setTitle** (String)

- -

FREE_MEM   org.omg.CORBA

Object
└Throwable - *java.io.Serializable*
  └Exception
    └RuntimeException
1.2 ○   └SystemException [1]
1.2 ●   └FREE_MEM

1	public........CompletionStatus	completed	
✳	public.........................	**FREE_MEM** ()	
✳	public.........................	**FREE_MEM** (String s)	
✳	public.........................	**FREE_MEM** (int minor, CompletionStatus completed)	
✳	public.........................	**FREE_MEM** (String s, int minor, CompletionStatus completed)	
1	public........................int	minor	
1	public....................String	toString ()	

GapContent   javax.swing.text

1.2   GapContent - *AbstractDocument.Content* [1], *java.io.Serializable*

		protected ....**Object**	**allocateArray** (int len)
1		public...................*Position*	**createPosition** (int offset) throws BadLocationException
✳		public.........................	**GapContent** ()
✳		public.........................	**GapContent** (int initialLength)
		protected ....**int**	**getArrayLength** ()
1		public....................void	**getChars** (int where, int len, Segment chars) throws BadLocationException
		protected .... java.util.Vector	**getPositionsInRange** (java.util.Vector v, int offset, int length)
1		public....................String	**getString** (int where, int len) throws BadLocationException
1		public......................*javax↵*	**insertString** (int where, String str) throws BadLocationException
		.swing.undo.UndoableEdit	
1		public........................int	**length** ()
1		public......................*javax↵*	**remove** (int where, int nitems) throws BadLocationException
		.swing.undo.UndoableEdit	
		protected ....void	**resetMarksAtZero** ()
		protected ....**void**	**shiftEnd** (int newSize)
		protected ....**void**	**shiftGap** (int newGapStart)
		protected ....**void**	**shiftGapEndUp** (int newGapEnd)
		protected ....**void**	**shiftGapStartDown** (int newGapStart)
		protected ....void	**updateUndoPositions** (java.util.Vector positions, int offset, int length)

GeneralPath

				java.awt.geom
GeneralPath				

Object[1]
└─GeneralPath - *java.awt.Shape*[2], *Cloneable*

1.2 ●

	public.......................void	**append** (*java.awt.Shape* s, boolean connect)
	public.......................void	**append** (*PathIterator* pi, boolean connect)
1	public........................**Object**	**clone** ()
	public synchronized ....void	**closePath** ()
2	public................. boolean	**contains** (Point2D p)
2	public................. boolean	**contains** (Rectangle2D r)
2	public................. boolean	**contains** (double x, double y)
2	public................. boolean	**contains** (double x, double y, double w, double h)
	public synchronized	**createTransformedShape** (AffineTransform at)
	.... *java.awt.Shape*	
	public synchronized ....void	**curveTo** (float x1, float y1, float x2, float y2, float x3, float y3)
✳	public.......................	**GeneralPath** ()
✳	public.......................	**GeneralPath** (int rule)
✳	public.......................	**GeneralPath** (*java.awt.Shape* s)
✳	public.......................	**GeneralPath** (int rule, int initialCapacity)
2	public...... java.awt.Rectangle	**getBounds** ()
2	public synchronized	**getBounds2D** ()
	.... Rectangle2D	
	public synchronized ...Point2D	**getCurrentPoint** ()
2	public.............. *PathIterator*	**getPathIterator** (AffineTransform at)
2	public.............. *PathIterator*	**getPathIterator** (AffineTransform at, double flatness)
	public synchronized ....int	**getWindingRule** ()
2	public................. boolean	**intersects** (Rectangle2D r)
2	public................. boolean	**intersects** (double x, double y, double w, double h)
	public synchronized ......void	**lineTo** (float x, float y)
	public synchronized ......void	**moveTo** (float x, float y)
	public synchronized ......void	**quadTo** (float x1, float y1, float x2, float y2)
	public synchronized ......void	**reset** ()
	public.......................void	**setWindingRule** (int rule)
	public.......................void	**transform** (AffineTransform at)
▲	public static final.............int	**WIND_EVEN_ODD** = 0
▲	public static final.............int	**WIND_NON_ZERO** = 1

---

				java.security
GeneralSecurityException				P[o]

Object
└─Throwable - *java.io.Serializable*
 └─Exception
  └─GeneralSecurityException

1.2

✳	public.........................	**GeneralSecurityException** ()
✳	public.........................	**GeneralSecurityException** (String msg)

---

				java.awt.font
GlyphJustificationInfo				

Object
└─GlyphJustificationInfo

1.2 ●

✳	public.........................	**GlyphJustificationInfo** (float weight, boolean growAbsorb, int growPriority, float growLeftLimit, float growRightLimit, boolean shrinkAbsorb, int shrinkPriority, float shrinkLeftLimit, float shrinkRightLimit)
●	public final .... boolean	**growAbsorb**
●	public final ....float	**growLeftLimit**
●	public final ....int	**growPriority**
●	public final ....float	**growRightLimit**
▲	public static final.............int	**PRIORITY_INTERCHAR** = 2
▲	public static final.............int	**PRIORITY_KASHIDA** = 0
▲	public static final.............int	**PRIORITY_NONE** = 3
▲	public static final.............int	**PRIORITY_WHITESPACE** = 1
●	public final .... boolean	**shrinkAbsorb**
●	public final ....float	**shrinkLeftLimit**
●	public final ....int	**shrinkPriority**
●	public final ....float	**shrinkRightLimit**
●	public final ....float	**weight**

Class   *Interface*   —extends   - - -implements   ○ abstract   ● final   △ static   ▲ static final   ✳ constructor   x x—inherited   x **x**—declared   **x x**—overridden

GlyphMetrics		java.awt.font

Object
 └─GlyphMetrics

1.2 ●

▲	public static final .... byte	**COMBINING** = 2
▲	public static final .... byte	**COMPONENT** = 3
	public......................float	**getAdvance** ()
	public..........................	**getBounds2D** ()
	... java.awt.geom.Rectangle2D	
	public......................float	**getLSB** ()
	public......................float	**getRSB** ()
	public........................int	**getType** ()
*	public..........................	**GlyphMetrics** (float advance, java.awt.geom.Rectangle2D bounds, byte glyphType)
	public.............. boolean	**isCombining** ()
	public.............. boolean	**isComponent** ()
	public.............. boolean	**isLigature** ()
	public.............. boolean	**isStandard** ()
	public.............. boolean	**isWhitespace** ()
▲	public static final .... byte	**LIGATURE** = 1
▲	public static final .... byte	**STANDARD** = 0
▲	public static final .... byte	**WHITESPACE** = 4

G

GlyphVector		java.awt.font

Object
 └─GlyphVector - *Cloneable*

1.2 ○

○	public abstract .... boolean	**equals** (GlyphVector set)
○	public abstract ...java.awt.Font	**getFont** ()
○	public abstract	**getFontRenderContext** ()
	............FontRenderContext	
○	public abstract ....int	**getGlyphCode** (int glyphIndex)
○	public abstract .... int[]	**getGlyphCodes** (int beginGlyphIndex, int numEntries, int[] codeReturn)
○	public abstract	**getGlyphJustificationInfo** (int glyphIndex)
	.... GlyphJustificationInfo	
○	public abstract *java.awt.Shape*	**getGlyphLogicalBounds** (int glyphIndex)
○	public abstract .. GlyphMetrics	**getGlyphMetrics** (int glyphIndex)
○	public abstract *java.awt.Shape*	**getGlyphOutline** (int glyphIndex)
○	public abstract	**getGlyphPosition** (int glyphIndex)
	.........java.awt.geom.Point2D	
○	public abstract .... float[]	**getGlyphPositions** (int beginGlyphIndex, int numEntries, float[] positionReturn)
○	public abstract	**getGlyphTransform** (int glyphIndex)
	java.awt.geom.AffineTransform	
○	public abstract *java.awt.Shape*	**getGlyphVisualBounds** (int glyphIndex)
○	public abstract	**getLogicalBounds** ()
	... java.awt.geom.Rectangle2D	
○	public abstract ....int	**getNumGlyphs** ()
○	public abstract *java.awt.Shape*	**getOutline** ()
○	public abstract *java.awt.Shape*	**getOutline** (float x, float y)
○	public abstract	**getVisualBounds** ()
	... java.awt.geom.Rectangle2D	
*	public..........................	**GlyphVector** ()
○	public abstract ....void	**performDefaultLayout** ()
○	public abstract ....void	**setGlyphPosition** (int glyphIndex, java.awt.geom.Point2D newPos)
○	public abstract ....void	**setGlyphTransform** (int glyphIndex, java.awt.geom.AffineTransform newTX)

Classes

GradientPaint		java.awt

Object
 └─GradientPaint - *Paint [1]* (*Transparency [2]*)

1.2

P

1	public............. *PaintContext*	**createContext** (java.awt.image.ColorModel cm, Rectangle deviceBounds, java.awt.geom.Rectangle2D userBounds, java.awt.geom.AffineTransform xform, RenderingHints hints)
	public.................... Color	**getColor1** ()
	public.................... Color	**getColor2** ()
	public.. java.awt.geom.Point2D	**getPoint1** ()
	public.. java.awt.geom.Point2D	**getPoint2** ()
2	public......................int	**getTransparency** ()

GradientPaint

*	public		**GradientPaint** (java. awt. geom. Point2D pt1, Color color1, java.awt.geom.Point2D pt2, Color color2)
*	public		**GradientPaint** (java. awt. geom. Point2D pt1, Color color1, java.awt.geom.Point2D pt2, Color color2, boolean cyclic)
*	public		**GradientPaint** (float x1, float y1, Color color1, float x2, float y2, Color color2)
*	public		**GradientPaint** (float x1, float y1, Color color1, float x2, float y2, Color color2, boolean cyclic)
	public	boolean	**isCyclic** ()

GraphicAttribute

java.awt.font

Object
└GraphicAttribute
1.2 ○

▲	public static final	int	**BOTTOM_ALIGNMENT** = -2
▲	public static final	int	**CENTER_BASELINE** = 1
○	public abstract	void	**draw** (java.awt.Graphics2D graphics, float x, float y)
○	public abstract	float	**getAdvance** ()
●	public final	int	**getAlignment** ()
○	public abstract	float	**getAscent** ()
	public		**getBounds** ()
	... java.awt.geom.Rectangle2D		
○	public abstract	float	**getDescent** ()
	public...	GlyphJustificationInfo	**getJustificationInfo** ()
*	protected		**GraphicAttribute** (int alignment)
▲	public static final	int	**HANGING_BASELINE** = 2
▲	public static final	int	**ROMAN_BASELINE** = 0
▲	public static final	int	**TOP_ALIGNMENT** = -1

Graphics

java.awt

P○

Object[1]
└Graphics
○

○	public abstract	void	**clearRect** (int x, int y, int width, int height)
○	public abstract	void	**clipRect** (int x, int y, int width, int height)
○	public abstract	void	**copyArea** (int x, int y, int width, int height, int dx, int dy)
○	public abstract	Graphics	**create** ()
	public	Graphics	**create** (int x, int y, int width, int height)
○	public abstract	void	**dispose** ()
	public	void	**draw3DRect** (int x, int y, int width, int height, boolean raised)
○	public abstract	void	**drawArc** (int x, int y, int width, int height, int startAngle, int arcAngle)
	public	void	**drawBytes** (byte[] data, int offset, int length, int x, int y)
	public	void	**drawChars** (char[] data, int offset, int length, int x, int y)
○	public abstract	boolean	**drawImage** (Image img, int x, int y, *java.awt.image.ImageObserver* observer)
○	public abstract	boolean	**drawImage** (Image img, int x, int y, Color bgcolor, *java.awt.image.ImageObserver* observer)
○	public abstract	boolean	**drawImage** (Image img, int x, int y, int width, int height, *java.awt.image.ImageObserver* observer)
○	public abstract	boolean	**drawImage** (Image img, int x, int y, int width, int height, Color bgcolor, *java.awt.image.ImageObserver* observer)
1.1 ○	public abstract	boolean	**drawImage** (Image img, int dx1, int dy1, int dx2, int dy2, int sx1, int sy1, int sx2, int sy2, *java.awt.image.ImageObserver* observer)
1.1 ○	public abstract	boolean	**drawImage** (Image img, int dx1, int dy1, int dx2, int dy2, int sx1, int sy1, int sx2, int sy2, Color bgcolor, *java.awt.image.ImageObserver* observer)
○	public abstract	void	**drawLine** (int x1, int y1, int x2, int y2)
○	public abstract	void	**drawOval** (int x, int y, int width, int height)
	public	void	**drawPolygon** (Polygon p)
○	public abstract	void	**drawPolygon** (int[] xPoints, int[] yPoints, int nPoints)
1.1 ○	public abstract	void	**drawPolyline** (int[] xPoints, int[] yPoints, int nPoints)
	public	void	**drawRect** (int x, int y, int width, int height)
○	public abstract	void	**drawRoundRect** (int x, int y, int width, int height, int arcWidth, int arcHeight)
○	public abstract	void	**drawString** (String str, int x, int y)
1.2 ○	public abstract	void	**drawString** (*java.text.AttributedCharacterIterator* iterator, int x, int y)
	public	void	**fill3DRect** (int x, int y, int width, int height, boolean raised)
○	public abstract	void	**fillArc** (int x, int y, int width, int height, int startAngle, int arcAngle)
○	public abstract	void	**fillOval** (int x, int y, int width, int height)
	public	void	**fillPolygon** (Polygon p)
○	public abstract	void	**fillPolygon** (int[] xPoints, int[] yPoints, int nPoints)

Class   *Interface*   —extends   - - -implements   ○ abstract   ● final   △ static   ▲ static final   ✳ constructor   x x—inherited   x **x**—declared   **x x**—overridden

	○	public abstract . . . . .void	**fillRect** (int x, int y, int width, int height)
	○	public abstract . . . . .void	**fillRoundRect** (int x, int y, int width, int height, int arcWidth, int arcHeight)
	1	public. **void**	**finalize** ()
1.1	○	public abstract . . . . *Shape*	**getClip** ()
1.1	○	public abstract . . . . . . Rectangle	**getClipBounds** ()
1.2		public. . . . . Rectangle	**getClipBounds** (Rectangle r)
D		public. . . . . Rectangle	**getClipRect** ()
	○	public abstract . . . . Color	**getColor** ()
	○	public abstract . . . . Font	**getFont** ()
		public. . . . . FontMetrics	**getFontMetrics** ()
	○	public abstract . . . . FontMetrics	**getFontMetrics** (Font f)
	*	protected	**Graphics** ()
1.2		public. . . . . boolean	**hitClip** (int x, int y, int width, int height)
1.1	○	public abstract . . . . .void	**setClip** (*Shape* clip)
1.1	○	public abstract . . . . .void	**setClip** (int x, int y, int width, int height)
	○	public abstract . . . . .void	**setColor** (Color c)
	○	public abstract . . . . .void	**setFont** (Font font)
	○	public abstract . . . . .void	**setPaintMode** ()
	○	public abstract . . . . .void	**setXORMode** (Color c1)
	1	public. . . . . **String**	**toString** ()
	○	public abstract . . . . .void	**translate** (int x, int y)

G

Graphics2D

```
Object
└─Graphics 1
    └─Graphics2D
```

	○		
1.2	○		

	1	*45 inherited members from Graphics not shown*	
	○	public abstract . . . . .void	**addRenderingHints** (*java.util.Map* hints)
	○	public abstract . . . . .void	**clip** (*Shape* s)
	○	public abstract . . . . .void	**draw** (*Shape* s)
	1	public. **void**	**draw3DRect** (int x, int y, int width, int height, boolean raised)
	○	public abstract . . . . .void	**drawGlyphVector** (java.awt.font.GlyphVector g, float x, float y)
	○	public abstract . . . . boolean	**drawImage** (Image img, java.awt.geom.AffineTransform xform, *java.awt.image.ImageObserver* obs)
	○	public abstract . . . . .void	**drawImage** (java.awt.image.BufferedImage img, java.awt.image.BufferedImageOp op, int x, int y)
	○	public abstract . . . . .void	**drawRenderableImage** (*java.awt.image.renderable.RenderableImage* img, java.awt.geom.AffineTransform xform)
	○	public abstract . . . . .void	**drawRenderedImage** (*java.awt.image.RenderedImage* img, java.awt.geom.AffineTransform xform)
	○	public abstract . . . . .void	**drawString** (String s, float x, float y)
	○ 1	public abstract . . . . **void**	**drawString** (String str, int x, int y)
	○ 1	public abstract . . . . **void**	**drawString** (*java.text.AttributedCharacterIterator* iterator, int x, int y)
	○	public abstract . . . . .void	**drawString** (*java.text.AttributedCharacterIterator* iterator, float x, float y)
	○	public abstract . . . . .void	**fill** (*Shape* s)
	1	public. **void**	**fill3DRect** (int x, int y, int width, int height, boolean raised)
	○	public abstract . . . . Color	**getBackground** ()
	○	public abstract . . . . . . *Composite*	**getComposite** ()
	○	public abstract . . . . GraphicsConfiguration	**getDeviceConfiguration** ()
	○	public abstract . . . . java↵ .awt.font.FontRenderContext	**getFontRenderContext** ()
	○	public abstract . . . . *Paint*	**getPaint** ()
	○	public abstract . . . . Object	**getRenderingHint** (RenderingHints.Key hintKey)
	○	public abstract RenderingHints	**getRenderingHints** ()
	○	public abstract . . . . *Stroke*	**getStroke** ()
	○	public abstract . . . . java.awt.geom.AffineTransform	**getTransform** ()
	*	protected	**Graphics2D** ()
	○	public abstract . . . . boolean	**hit** (Rectangle rect, *Shape* s, boolean onStroke)
	○	public abstract . . . . .void	**rotate** (double theta)
	○	public abstract . . . . .void	**rotate** (double theta, double x, double y)
	○	public abstract . . . . .void	**scale** (double sx, double sy)
	○	public abstract . . . . .void	**setBackground** (Color color)
	○	public abstract . . . . .void	**setComposite** (*Composite* comp)
	○	public abstract . . . . .void	**setPaint** (*Paint* paint)
	○	public abstract . . . . .void	**setRenderingHint** (RenderingHints.Key hintKey, Object hintValue)
	○	public abstract . . . . .void	**setRenderingHints** (*java.util.Map* hints)
	○	public abstract . . . . .void	**setStroke** (*Stroke* s)
	○	public abstract . . . . .void	**setTransform** (java.awt.geom.AffineTransform Tx)

Classes

Graphics2D

O	public abstract .... void	**shear** (double shx, double shy)
O	public abstract .... void	**transform** (java.awt.geom.AffineTransform Tx)
O	public abstract .... void	**translate** (double tx, double ty)
O 1	public abstract .... **void**	**translate** (int x, int y)

GraphicsConfigTemplate — java.awt

P

Object
1.2 O └GraphicsConfigTemplate - - - - - - - - - - - - - - - - *java.io.Serializable*

O	public abstract .... GraphicsConfiguration	**getBestConfiguration** (GraphicsConfiguration[] gc)
✳	public.......................	**GraphicsConfigTemplate** ()
O	public abstract .... boolean	**isGraphicsConfigSupported** (GraphicsConfiguration gc)
▲	public static final .... int	**PREFERRED** = 2
▲	public static final .... int	**REQUIRED** = 1
▲	public static final .... int	**UNNECESSARY** = 3

GraphicsConfiguration — java.awt

P

Object
1.2 O └GraphicsConfiguration

O	public abstract .... java.awt.image.BufferedImage	**createCompatibleImage** (int width, int height)
O	public abstract .... java.awt.image.BufferedImage	**createCompatibleImage** (int width, int height, int transparency)
O	public abstract .... java.awt.image.ColorModel	**getColorModel** ()
O	public abstract .... java.awt.image.ColorModel	**getColorModel** (int transparency)
O	public abstract .... java.awt.geom.AffineTransform	**getDefaultTransform** ()
O	public abstract .... GraphicsDevice	**getDevice** ()
O	public abstract .... java.awt.geom.AffineTransform	**getNormalizingTransform** ()
✳	protected......................	**GraphicsConfiguration** ()

GraphicsDevice — java.awt

P

Object
1.2 O └GraphicsDevice

	public.. GraphicsConfiguration	**getBestConfiguration** (GraphicsConfigTemplate gct)
O	public abstract .... GraphicsConfiguration[]	**getConfigurations** ()
O	public abstract .... GraphicsConfiguration	**getDefaultConfiguration** ()
O	public abstract .... String	**getIDstring** ()
O	public abstract .... int	**getType** ()
✳	protected......................	**GraphicsDevice** ()
▲	public static final .... int	**TYPE_IMAGE_BUFFER** = 2
▲	public static final .... int	**TYPE_PRINTER** = 1
▲	public static final .... int	**TYPE_RASTER_SCREEN** = 0

GraphicsEnvironment — java.awt

P

Object
1.2 O └GraphicsEnvironment

O	public abstract Graphics2D	**createGraphics** (java.awt.image.BufferedImage img)
O	public abstract ....Font[]	**getAllFonts** ()
O	public abstract .... String[]	**getAvailableFontFamilyNames** ()
O	public abstract .... String[]	**getAvailableFontFamilyNames** (java.util.Locale l)
O	public abstract .... GraphicsDevice	**getDefaultScreenDevice** ()

Class *Interface* —extends - - -implements O abstract ● final △ static ▲ static final ✳ constructor x x—inherited x **x**—declared **x x**—overridden

△	public static	**getLocalGraphicsEnvironment** ()
	. . . . GraphicsEnvironment	
○	public abstract	**getScreenDevices** ()
	. . . . GraphicsDevice[]	
*	protected	**GraphicsEnvironment** ()

GrayFilter

Object
└java.awt.image.ImageFilter[1] - - - - - - - - - - - - - *java.awt.image.ImageConsumer* , *Cloneable*
　　└java.awt.image.RGBImageFilter[2]
○　　　└GrayFilter
1.2

2	protected . . . . boolean	canFilterIndexColorModel
1	public . . . . Object	clone ()
1	protected . . . . *java↵*	consumer
	.awt.image.ImageConsumer	
△	public static . . . java.awt.Image	**createDisabledImage** (java.awt.Image i)
2	public . . . . *java↵*	filterIndexColorModel (java.awt.image.IndexColorModel icm)
	.awt.image.IndexColorModel	
2	public . . . . **int**	**filterRGB** (int x, int y, int rgb)
2	public . . . . void	filterRGBPixels (int x, int y, int w, int h, int[] pixels, int off, int scansize)
1	public	getFilterInstance (*java.awt.image.ImageConsumer* ic)
	. . . . java.awt.image.ImageFilter	
*	public	**GrayFilter** (boolean b, int p)
1	public . . . . void	imageComplete (int status)
2	protected	newmodel
	. . . . java.awt.image.ColorModel	
2	protected	origmodel
	. . . . java.awt.image.ColorModel	
1	public . . . . void	resendTopDownLeftRight (*java.awt.image.ImageProducer* ip)
2	public . . . . void	setColorModel (java.awt.image.ColorModel model)
1	public . . . . void	setDimensions (int width, int height)
1	public . . . . void	setHints (int hints)
2	public . . . . void	setPixels (int x, int y, int w, int h, java.awt.image.ColorModel model, int[] pixels, int off, int scansize)
2	public . . . . void	setPixels (int x, int y, int w, int h, java.awt.image.ColorModel model, byte[] pixels, int off, int scansize)
1	public . . . . void	setProperties (java.util.Hashtable props)
2	public . . . . void	substituteColorModel (java. awt. image. ColorModel oldcm, java.awt.image.ColorModel newcm)

GregorianCalendar

P

Object
1.1 ○　└Calendar[1] - *java.io.Serializable* , *Cloneable*
1.1　　　└GregorianCalendar

▲		public static final . . . . int	**AD** = 1
	1	public . . . . **void**	**add** (int field, int amount)
	1	public . . . . boolean	after (Object when)
	1	protected . . . . boolean	areFieldsSet
▲		public static final . . . . int	**BC** = 0
	1	public . . . . boolean	before (Object when)
●	1	public final . . . . void	clear ()
●	1	public final . . . . void	clear (int field)
	1	public . . . . Object	clone ()
	1	protected . . . . void	complete ()
	1	protected . . . . **void**	**computeFields** ()
	1	protected . . . . **void**	**computeTime** ()
	1	public . . . . **boolean**	**equals** (Object obj)
	1	protected . . . . int[]	fields
●	1	public final . . . . int	get (int field)
1.2	1	public . . . . **int**	**getActualMaximum** (int field)
1.2	1	public . . . . **int**	**getActualMinimum** (int field)
△	1	public static synchronized	getAvailableLocales ()
		. . . . Locale[]	
	1	public . . . . int	getFirstDayOfWeek ()
	1	public . . . . **int**	**getGreatestMinimum** (int field)
●		public final . . . . Date	**getGregorianChange** ()

GregorianCalendar

△	1	public static synchronized .... Calendar	getInstance ()
△	1	public static synchronized .... Calendar	getInstance (Locale aLocale)
△	1	public static synchronized .... Calendar	getInstance (TimeZone zone)
△	1	public static synchronized .... Calendar	getInstance (TimeZone zone, Locale aLocale)
	1	public...... **int getLeastMaximum** (int field)	
	1	public...... **int getMaximum** (int field)	
	1	public......int getMinimalDaysInFirstWeek ()	
	1	public...... **int getMinimum** (int field)	
●	1	public final ...... Date getTime ()	
	1	protected...... long getTimeInMillis ()	
	1	public...... TimeZone getTimeZone ()	
*		public...... **GregorianCalendar** ()	
*		public...... **GregorianCalendar** (Locale aLocale)	
*		public...... **GregorianCalendar** (TimeZone zone)	
*		public...... **GregorianCalendar** (TimeZone zone, Locale aLocale)	
*		public...... **GregorianCalendar** (int year, int month, int date)	
*		public...... **GregorianCalendar** (int year, int month, int date, int hour, int minute)	
*		public...... **GregorianCalendar** (int year, int month, int date, int hour, int minute, int second)	
	1	public...... **int hashCode** ()	
●	1	protected final......int internalGet (int field)	
		public...... boolean **isLeapYear** (int year)	
	1	public...... boolean isLenient ()	
	1	protected......boolean[] isSet	
●	1	public final ...... boolean isSet (int field)	
	1	protected......boolean isTimeSet	
1.2	1	public...... **void roll** (int field, int amount)	
	1	public...... **void roll** (int field, boolean up)	
●	1	public final ......void set (int field, int value)	
●	1	public final ......void set (int year, int month, int date)	
●	1	public final ......void set (int year, int month, int date, int hour, int minute)	
●	1	public final ......void set (int year, int month, int date, int hour, int minute, int second)	
	1	public......void setFirstDayOfWeek (int value)	
		public......void **setGregorianChange** (Date date)	
	1	public......void setLenient (boolean lenient)	
	1	public......void setMinimalDaysInFirstWeek (int value)	
●	1	public final ......void setTime (Date date)	
	1	protected......void setTimeInMillis (long millis)	
	1	public......void setTimeZone (TimeZone value)	
	1	protected......long time	
	1	public......String toString ()	

GridBagConstraints java.awt P

Object[1]
└ GridBagConstraints - *Cloneable, java.io.Serializable*

		public......int **anchor**	
▲		public static final......int **BOTH** = 1	
▲		public static final......int **CENTER** = 10	
	1	public......**Object clone** ()	
▲		public static final......int **EAST** = 13	
		public......int **fill**	
*		public...... **GridBagConstraints** ()	
1.2 *		public...... **GridBagConstraints** (int gridx, int gridy, int gridwidth, int gridheight, double weightx, double weighty, int anchor, int fill, Insets insets, int ipadx, int ipady)	
		public......int **gridheight**	
		public......int **gridwidth**	
		public......int **gridx**	
		public......int **gridy**	
▲		public static final......int **HORIZONTAL** = 2	
		public......Insets **insets**	
		public......int **ipadx**	
		public......int **ipady**	
▲		public static final......int **NONE** = 0	
▲		public static final......int **NORTH** = 11	
▲		public static final......int **NORTHEAST** = 12	
▲		public static final......int **NORTHWEST** = 18	

Class *Interface* —extends - - -implements ○ abstract ● final △ static ▲ static final * constructor x x—inherited x **x**—declared **x x**—overridden

▲		public static final	int	**RELATIVE** = -1
▲		public static final	int	**REMAINDER** = 0
▲		public static final	int	**SOUTH** = 15
▲		public static final	int	**SOUTHEAST** = 14
▲		public static final	int	**SOUTHWEST** = 16
▲		public static final	int	**VERTICAL** = 3
		public	double	**weightx**
		public	double	**weighty**
▲		public static final	int	**WEST** = 17

GridBagLayout — java.awt — P

Object [1]
└ GridBagLayout - *LayoutManager2* [2] (*LayoutManager* [3]), *java.io.Serializable*

1.1	2	public	void	**addLayoutComponent** (Component comp, Object constraints)
	3	public	void	**addLayoutComponent** (String name, Component comp)
		protected	void	**AdjustForGravity** (GridBagConstraints constraints, Rectangle r)
		protected	void	**ArrangeGrid** (Container parent)
		public	double[]	**columnWeights**
		public	int[]	**columnWidths**
		protected	java.util.Hashtable	**comptable**
		protected	GridBagConstraints	**defaultConstraints**
		public	GridBagConstraints	**getConstraints** (Component comp)
1.1	2	public	float	**getLayoutAlignmentX** (Container parent)
1.1	2	public	float	**getLayoutAlignmentY** (Container parent)
		public	int[][]	**getLayoutDimensions** ()
		protected		**GetLayoutInfo** (Container parent, int sizeflag)
		... java.awt.GridBagLayoutInfo		
		public	Point	**getLayoutOrigin** ()
		public	double[][]	**getLayoutWeights** ()
		protected	Dimension	**GetMinSize** (Container parent, java.awt.GridBagLayoutInfo info)
*		public		**GridBagLayout** ()
1.1	2	public	void	**invalidateLayout** (Container target)
	3	public	void	**layoutContainer** (Container parent)
		protected		**layoutInfo**
		... java.awt.GridBagLayoutInfo		
		public	Point	**location** (int x, int y)
		protected	GridBagConstraints	**lookupConstraints** (Component comp)
▲		protected static final	int	**MAXGRIDSIZE**
1.1	2	public	Dimension	**maximumLayoutSize** (Container target)
	3	public	Dimension	**minimumLayoutSize** (Container parent)
▲		protected static final	int	**MINSIZE**
	3	public	Dimension	**preferredLayoutSize** (Container parent)
▲		protected static final	int	**PREFERREDSIZE**
	3	public	void	**removeLayoutComponent** (Component comp)
		public	int[]	**rowHeights**
		public	double[]	**rowWeights**
		public	void	**setConstraints** (Component comp, GridBagConstraints constraints)
	1	public	String	**toString** ()

GridLayout — java.awt — P

Object [1]
└ GridLayout - *LayoutManager* [2], *java.io.Serializable*

	2	public	void	**addLayoutComponent** (String name, Component comp)
1.1		public	int	**getColumns** ()
1.1		public	int	**getHgap** ()
1.1		public	int	**getRows** ()
1.1		public	int	**getVgap** ()
1.1	*	public		**GridLayout** ()
	*	public		**GridLayout** (int rows, int cols)
	*	public		**GridLayout** (int rows, int cols, int hgap, int vgap)
	2	public	void	**layoutContainer** (Container parent)
	2	public	Dimension	**minimumLayoutSize** (Container parent)
	2	public	Dimension	**preferredLayoutSize** (Container parent)
	2	public	void	**removeLayoutComponent** (Component comp)
1.1		public	void	**setColumns** (int cols)
1.1		public	void	**setHgap** (int hgap)
1.1		public	void	**setRows** (int rows)
1.1		public	void	**setVgap** (int vgap)

G

Classes

GridLayout

	1	public.................... **String toString** ()

Group   java.security.acl
P^u

1.1		*Group*————————————————————*java.security.Principal* [1]
		public.................... boolean **addMember** (*java.security.Principal* user)
	1	public.................... boolean equals (Object another)
	1	public....................String getName ()
	1	public........................int hashCode ()
		public.................... boolean **isMember** (*java.security.Principal* member)
		public.... *java.util.Enumeration* **members** ()
		public.................... boolean **removeMember** (*java.security.Principal* user)
	1	public....................String toString ()

Guard   java.security
P^o

1.2		*Guard*
		public....................void **checkGuard** (Object object) throws SecurityException

---

GuardedObject   java.security
P^o

1.2		Object └GuardedObject - *java.io.Serializable*
		public.................... Object **getObject** () throws SecurityException
	*	public.......................... **GuardedObject** (Object object, *Guard* guard)

GZIPInputStream   java.util.zip
P

	○	Object └java.io.InputStream └java.io.FilterInputStream [1]
1.1		└InflaterInputStream [2]
1.1		└GZIPInputStream
	2	public........................int available () throws java.io.IOException
	2	protected.................byte[] buf
	2	public.................... **void close** () throws java.io.IOException
		protected..............CRC32 **crc**
		protected.............. boolean **eos**
	2	protected....................void fill () throws java.io.IOException
▲		public static final ....int **GZIP_MAGIC** = 35615
*		public.......................... **GZIPInputStream** (java.io.InputStream in) throws java.io.IOException
*		public.......................... **GZIPInputStream** (java.io.InputStream in, int size) throws java.io.IOException
	1	protected .. java.io.InputStream in
	2	protected ....Inflater inf
	2	protected ....int len
	1	public synchronized ....void mark (int readlimit)
	1	public.................... boolean markSupported ()
	2	public........................int read () throws java.io.IOException
	1	public........................int read (byte[] b) throws java.io.IOException
	2	public.................... **int read** (byte[] buf, int off, int len) throws java.io.IOException
	1	public synchronized ....void reset () throws java.io.IOException
	2	public.................... long skip (long n) throws java.io.IOException

---

GZIPOutputStream   java.util.zip
P^o

	○	Object └java.io.OutputStream └java.io.FilterOutputStream [1]
1.1		└DeflaterOutputStream [2]
1.1		└GZIPOutputStream
	2	protected.................byte[] buf
	2	public.................... **void close** () throws java.io.IOException

---

Class   *Interface*   —extends   - - -implements   ○ abstract   ● final   △ static   ▲ static final   ✱ constructor   x x—inherited   x **x**—declared   **x x**—overridden

	protected	CRC32	**crc**
2	protected	Deflater	def
2	protected	void	deflate () throws java.io.IOException
2	public	**void**	**finish** () throws java.io.IOException
1	public	void	flush () throws java.io.IOException
*	public	**GZIPOutputStream**	(java.io.OutputStream out) throws java.io.IOException
*	public	**GZIPOutputStream**	(java.io.OutputStream out, int size) throws java.io.IOException
1	protected java.io.OutputStream		out
1	public	void	write (byte[] b) throws java.io.IOException
2	public	void	write (int b) throws java.io.IOException
2	public synchronized	**void**	**write** (byte[] buf, int off, int len) throws java.io.IOException

HashMap
java.util

P

```
      Object 1
1.2 O └ AbstractMap 2 ------------------------- Map
1.2       └ HashMap ------------------------- Map, Cloneable, java.io.Serializable
```

2	public	void	**clear** ()
1	public	**Object**	**clone** ()
2	public	**boolean**	**containsKey** (Object key)
2	public	**boolean**	**containsValue** (Object value)
2	public	*Set*	**entrySet** ()
2	public	boolean	equals (Object o)
2	public	**Object**	**get** (Object key)
2	public	int	hashCode ()
*	public		**HashMap** ()
*	public		**HashMap** (int initialCapacity)
*	public		**HashMap** (*Map* t)
*	public		**HashMap** (int initialCapacity, float loadFactor)
2	public	**boolean**	**isEmpty** ()
2	public	*Set*	**keySet** ()
2	public	**Object**	**put** (Object key, Object value)
2	public	**void**	**putAll** (*Map* t)
2	public	**Object**	**remove** (Object key)
2	public	**int**	**size** ()
2	public	String	toString ()
2	public	*Collection*	**values** ()

HashSet
java.util

P

```
      Object 1
1.2 O └ AbstractCollection 2 ------------------- Collection
1.2 O    └ AbstractSet 3 ------------------- Set (Collection)
1.2          └ HashSet ------------------- Set (Collection), Cloneable, java.io.Serializable
```

2	public	**boolean**	**add** (Object o)
2	public	boolean	addAll (*Collection* c)
2	public	**void**	**clear** ()
1	public	**Object**	**clone** ()
2	public	**boolean**	**contains** (Object o)
2	public	boolean	containsAll (*Collection* c)
3	public	boolean	equals (Object o)
3	public	int	hashCode ()
*	public		**HashSet** ()
*	public		**HashSet** (int initialCapacity)
*	public		**HashSet** (*Collection* c)
*	public		**HashSet** (int initialCapacity, float loadFactor)
2	public	**boolean**	**isEmpty** ()
2	public	*Iterator*	**iterator** ()
2	public	**boolean**	**remove** (Object o)
2	public	boolean	removeAll (*Collection* c)
2	public	boolean	retainAll (*Collection* c)
2	public	**int**	**size** ()
2	public	Object[]	toArray ()
2	public	Object[]	toArray (Object[] a)
2	public	String	toString ()

Hashtable

				java.util
				P

		Object [1]		
○		└ Dictionary [2]		
		└ Hashtable - *Map* [3], *Cloneable*, *java.io.Serializable*		

	3	public synchronized . . . . void	**clear** ()	
	1	public synchronized . . . . **Object**	**clone** ()	
		public synchronized . . boolean	**contains** (Object value)	
	3	public synchronized . . boolean	**containsKey** (Object key)	
1.2	3	public . . . . boolean	**containsValue** (Object value)	
	2	public synchronized	**elements** ()	
		. . . . ***Enumeration***		
1.2	3	public . . . . *Set*	**entrySet** ()	
	1	public synchronized . . **boolean**	**equals** (Object o)	
	2	public synchronized . . . . **Object**	**get** (Object key)	
	1	public synchronized . . . . **int**	**hashCode** ()	
✳		public	**Hashtable** ()	
✳		public	**Hashtable** (int initialCapacity)	
1.2 ✳		public	**Hashtable** (*Map* t)	
✳		public	**Hashtable** (int initialCapacity, float loadFactor)	
	2	public . . . . **boolean**	**isEmpty** ()	
	2	public synchronized	**keys** ()	
		. . . . ***Enumeration***		
1.2	3	public . . . . *Set*	**keySet** ()	
	2	public synchronized . . . . **Object**	**put** (Object key, Object value)	
1.2	3	public synchronized . . . . void	**putAll** (*Map* t)	
		protected . . . . void	**rehash** ()	
	2	public synchronized . . . . **Object**	**remove** (Object key)	
	2	public . . . . **int**	**size** ()	
	1	public synchronized . . . . **String**	**toString** ()	
1.2	3	public . . . . *Collection*	**values** ()	

Highlighter

			javax.swing.text

1.2		*Highlighter*	
	public . . . . Object	**addHighlight** (int p0, int p1, *Highlighter. HighlightPainter* p)	
		throws BadLocationException	
	public . . . . void	**changeHighlight** (Object tag, int p0, int p1) throws BadLocationException	
	public . . . . void	**deinstall** (JTextComponent c)	
	public . . . *Highlighter.Highlight[]*	**getHighlights** ()	
	public . . . . void	**install** (JTextComponent c)	
	public . . . . void	**paint** (java.awt.Graphics g)	
	public . . . . void	**removeAllHighlights** ()	
	public . . . . void	**removeHighlight** (Object tag)	

Highlighter.Highlight

			javax.swing.text

1.2		*Highlighter.Highlight*	
	public . . . . int	**getEndOffset** ()	
	public	**getPainter** ()	
	. . . . *Highlighter.HighlightPainter*		
	public . . . . int	**getStartOffset** ()	

Highlighter.HighlightPainter

			javax.swing.text

1.2		*Highlighter.HighlightPainter*	
	public . . . . void	**paint** (java. awt. Graphics g, int p0, int p1, *java. awt. Shape* bounds,	
		JTextComponent c)	

HTML

			javax.swing.text.html

		Object	
1.2		└ HTML	

Class   *Interface*   —extends   - - -implements   ○ abstract   ● final   △ static   ▲ static final   ✳ constructor   x x—inherited   x **x**—declared   **x x**—overridden

△	public static .. HTML.Attribute[]	**getAllAttributeKeys** ()
△	public static .... HTML.Tag[]	**getAllTags** ()
△	public static ....HTML.Attribute	**getAttributeKey** (String attName)
△	public static .... int	**getIntegerAttributeValue** (*javax.swing.text.AttributeSet* attr, HTML.Attribute key, int def)
△	public static .... HTML.Tag	**getTag** (String tagName)
✳	public..........................	**HTML** ()
▲	public static final .... String	**NULL_ATTRIBUTE_VALUE** = "#DEFAULT"

HTML.Attribute

Object [1]
1.2 ● └HTML.Attribute

H

▲	public static final ....HTML.Attribute	**ACTION**
▲	public static final ....HTML.Attribute	**ALIGN**
▲	public static final ....HTML.Attribute	**ALINK**
▲	public static final ....HTML.Attribute	**ALT**
▲	public static final ....HTML.Attribute	**ARCHIVE**
▲	public static final ....HTML.Attribute	**BACKGROUND**
▲	public static final ....HTML.Attribute	**BGCOLOR**
▲	public·static final ....HTML.Attribute	**BORDER**
▲	public static final ....HTML.Attribute	**CELLPADDING**
▲	public static final ....HTML.Attribute	**CELLSPACING**
▲	public static final ....HTML.Attribute	**CHECKED**
▲	public static final ....HTML.Attribute	**CLASS**
▲	public static final ....HTML.Attribute	**CLASSID**
▲	public static final ....HTML.Attribute	**CLEAR**
▲	public static final ....HTML.Attribute	**CODE**
▲	public static final ....HTML.Attribute	**CODEBASE**
▲	public static final ....HTML.Attribute	**CODETYPE**
▲	public static final ....HTML.Attribute	**COLOR**
▲	public static final ....HTML.Attribute	**COLS**
▲	public static final ....HTML.Attribute	**COLSPAN**
▲	public static final ....HTML.Attribute	**COMMENT**
▲	public static final ....HTML.Attribute	**COMPACT**
▲	public static final ....HTML.Attribute	**CONTENT**
▲	public static final ....HTML.Attribute	**COORDS**
▲	public static final ....HTML.Attribute	**DATA**
▲	public static final ....HTML.Attribute	**DECLARE**
▲	public static final ....HTML.Attribute	**DIR**
▲	public static final ....HTML.Attribute	**DUMMY**
▲	public static final ....HTML.Attribute	**ENCTYPE**

Classes

HTML.Attribute

▲	public static final . . . . HTML.Attribute	**ENDTAG**	
▲	public static final . . . . HTML.Attribute	**FACE**	
▲	public static final . . . . HTML.Attribute	**FRAMEBORDER**	
▲	public static final . . . . HTML.Attribute	**HALIGN**	
▲	public static final . . . . HTML.Attribute	**HEIGHT**	
▲	public static final . . . . HTML.Attribute	**HREF**	
▲	public static final . . . . HTML.Attribute	**HSPACE**	
▲	public static final . . . . HTML.Attribute	**HTTPEQUIV**	
▲	public static final . . . . HTML.Attribute	**ID**	
▲	public static final . . . . HTML.Attribute	**ISMAP**	
▲	public static final . . . . HTML.Attribute	**LANG**	
▲	public static final . . . . HTML.Attribute	**LANGUAGE**	
▲	public static final . . . . HTML.Attribute	**LINK**	
▲	public static final . . . . HTML.Attribute	**LOWSRC**	
▲	public static final . . . . HTML.Attribute	**MARGINHEIGHT**	
▲	public static final . . . . HTML.Attribute	**MARGINWIDTH**	
▲	public static final . . . . HTML.Attribute	**MAXLENGTH**	
▲	public static final . . . . HTML.Attribute	**METHOD**	
▲	public static final . . . . HTML.Attribute	**MULTIPLE**	
▲	public static final . . . . HTML.Attribute	**N**	
▲	public static final . . . . HTML.Attribute	**NAME**	
▲	public static final . . . . HTML.Attribute	**NOHREF**	
▲	public static final . . . . HTML.Attribute	**NORESIZE**	
▲	public static final . . . . HTML.Attribute	**NOSHADE**	
▲	public static final . . . . HTML.Attribute	**NOWRAP**	
▲	public static final . . . . HTML.Attribute	**PROMPT**	
▲	public static final . . . . HTML.Attribute	**REL**	
▲	public static final . . . . HTML.Attribute	**REV**	
▲	public static final . . . . HTML.Attribute	**ROWS**	
▲	public static final . . . . HTML.Attribute	**ROWSPAN**	
▲	public static final . . . . HTML.Attribute	**SCROLLING**	
▲	public static final . . . . HTML.Attribute	**SELECTED**	
▲	public static final . . . . HTML.Attribute	**SHAPE**	
▲	public static final . . . . HTML.Attribute	**SHAPES**	
▲	public static final . . . . HTML.Attribute	**SIZE**	

Class *Interface* —extends - - -implements ○ abstract ● final △ static ▲ static final ✳ constructor x x—inherited x **x**—declared **x x**—overridden

▲ public static final .... **SRC**
................HTML.Attribute
▲ public static final .... **STANDBY**
................HTML.Attribute
▲ public static final .... **START**
................HTML.Attribute
▲ public static final .... **STYLE**
................HTML.Attribute
▲ public static final .... **TARGET**
................HTML.Attribute
▲ public static final .... **TEXT**
................HTML.Attribute
▲ public static final .... **TITLE**
................HTML.Attribute
  1 public................. **String toString** ()
▲ public static final .... **TYPE**
................HTML.Attribute
▲ public static final .... **USEMAP**
................HTML.Attribute
▲ public static final .... **VALIGN**
................HTML.Attribute
▲ public static final .... **VALUE**
................HTML.Attribute
▲ public static final .... **VALUETYPE**
................HTML.Attribute
▲ public static final .... **VERSION**
................HTML.Attribute
▲ public static final .... **VLINK**
................HTML.Attribute
▲ public static final .... **VSPACE**
................HTML.Attribute
▲ public static final .... **WIDTH**
................HTML.Attribute

HTML.Tag

javax.swing.text.html

Object [1]
  └HTML.Tag

1.2

▲ public static final .... HTML.Tag **A**
▲ public static final .... HTML.Tag **ADDRESS**
▲ public static final .... HTML.Tag **APPLET**
▲ public static final .... HTML.Tag **AREA**
▲ public static final .... HTML.Tag **B**
▲ public static final .... HTML.Tag **BASE**
▲ public static final .... HTML.Tag **BASEFONT**
▲ public static final .... HTML.Tag **BIG**
▲ public static final .... HTML.Tag **BLOCKQUOTE**
▲ public static final .... HTML.Tag **BODY**
▲ public static final .... HTML.Tag **BR**
   public................. boolean **breaksFlow** ()
▲ public static final .... HTML.Tag **CAPTION**
▲ public static final .... HTML.Tag **CENTER**
▲ public static final .... HTML.Tag **CITE**
▲ public static final .... HTML.Tag **CODE**
▲ public static final .... HTML.Tag **COMMENT**
▲ public static final .... HTML.Tag **CONTENT**
▲ public static final .... HTML.Tag **DD**
▲ public static final .... HTML.Tag **DFN**
▲ public static final .... HTML.Tag **DIR**
▲ public static final .... HTML.Tag **DIV**
▲ public static final .... HTML.Tag **DL**
▲ public static final .... HTML.Tag **DT**
▲ public static final .... HTML.Tag **EM**
▲ public static final .... HTML.Tag **FONT**
▲ public static final .... HTML.Tag **FORM**
▲ public static final .... HTML.Tag **FRAME**
▲ public static final .... HTML.Tag **FRAMESET**
▲ public static final .... HTML.Tag **H1**
▲ public static final .... HTML.Tag **H2**
▲ public static final .... HTML.Tag **H3**
▲ public static final .... HTML.Tag **H4**

H

Classes

HTML.Tag

▲	public static final	HTML.Tag	**H5**
▲	public static final	HTML.Tag	**H6**
▲	public static final	HTML.Tag	**HEAD**
▲	public static final	HTML.Tag	**HR**
▲	public static final	HTML.Tag	**HTML**
▲	public static final	HTML.Tag	**I**
▲	public static final	HTML.Tag	**IMG**
▲	public static final	HTML.Tag	**IMPLIED**
▲	public static final	HTML.Tag	**INPUT**
	public	boolean	**isBlock** ()
▲	public static final	HTML.Tag	**ISINDEX**
	public	boolean	**isPreformatted** ()
▲	public static final	HTML.Tag	**KBD**
▲	public static final	HTML.Tag	**LI**
▲	public static final	HTML.Tag	**LINK**
▲	public static final	HTML.Tag	**MAP**
▲	public static final	HTML.Tag	**MENU**
▲	public static final	HTML.Tag	**META**
▲	public static final	HTML.Tag	**NOFRAMES**
▲	public static final	HTML.Tag	**OBJECT**
▲	public static final	HTML.Tag	**OL**
▲	public static final	HTML.Tag	**OPTION**
▲	public static final	HTML.Tag	**P**
▲	public static final	HTML.Tag	**PARAM**
▲	public static final	HTML.Tag	**PRE**
▲	public static final	HTML.Tag	**S**
▲	public static final	HTML.Tag	**SAMP**
▲	public static final	HTML.Tag	**SCRIPT**
▲	public static final	HTML.Tag	**SELECT**
▲	public static final	HTML.Tag	**SMALL**
▲	public static final	HTML.Tag	**STRIKE**
▲	public static final	HTML.Tag	**STRONG**
▲	public static final	HTML.Tag	**STYLE**
▲	public static final	HTML.Tag	**SUB**
▲	public static final	HTML.Tag	**SUP**
▲	public static final	HTML.Tag	**TABLE**
✳	protected		**Tag** (String id)
✳	protected		**Tag** (String id, boolean causesBreak, boolean isBlock)
▲	public static final	HTML.Tag	**TD**
▲	public static final	HTML.Tag	**TEXTAREA**
▲	public static final	HTML.Tag	**TH**
▲	public static final	HTML.Tag	**TITLE**
1	public	String	**toString** ()
▲	public static final	HTML.Tag	**TR**
▲	public static final	HTML.Tag	**TT**
▲	public static final	HTML.Tag	**U**
▲	public static final	HTML.Tag	**UL**
▲	public static final	HTML.Tag	**VAR**

HTML.UnknownTag　　　　　　　　　　　　　　　　　　javax.swing.text.html

```
      Object 1
1.2   └HTML.Tag 2
1.2      └HTML.UnknownTag - - - - - - - - - - - - - - - - - - - java.io.Serializable
```

2	*79 inherited members from HTML.Tag not shown*		
1	public	**boolean**	**equals** (Object obj)
1	public	**int**	**hashCode** ()
✳	public		**UnknownTag** (String id)

HTMLDocument　　　　　　　　　　　　　　　　　　　　javax.swing.text.html

```
        Object
1.2 ○   └javax.swing.text.AbstractDocument 1 - - - - - - - - javax.swing.text.Document, java.io.Serializable
1.2        └javax.swing.text.DefaultStyledDocument 2 - - javax.swing.text.StyledDocument (javax.swing.text.Document)
1.2           └HTMLDocument
```

1	*39 inherited members from javax.swing.text.AbstractDocument not shown*		
2	public	void	addDocumentListener (*javax.swing.event.DocumentListener* listener)
▲	public static final	String	**AdditionalComments** = "AdditionalComments"

Class　*Interface*　—extends　- - -implements　○ abstract　● final　△ static　▲ static final　✳ constructor　x x—inherited　x **x**—declared　**x x**—overridden

2	public.....	*javax.swing.text.Style*	addStyle	(String nm, *javax.swing.text.Style* parent)
2	protected.......	**javax.swing**↵ .text.DefaultStyledDocument↵ .ElementBuffer	buffer	
2	protected...............	**void**	**create**	(javax.swing.text.DefaultStyledDocument.ElementSpec[] data)
1	protected....................	***javax.swing.text.Element***	**createBranchElement**	(*javax. swing. text. Element* parent, *javax.swing.text.AttributeSet* a)
2	protected.......	**javax.swing**↵ **.text.AbstractDocument**↵ **.AbstractElement**	**createDefaultRoot**	()
1	protected..................	***javax.swing.text.Element***	**createLeafElement**	(*javax. swing. text. Element* parent, *javax.swing.text.AttributeSet* a, int p0, int p1)
2	public............	java.awt.Color	getBackground	(*javax.swing.text.AttributeSet* attr)
	public.............	java.net.URL	**getBase**	()
2	public....................	*javax.swing.text.Element*	getCharacterElement	(int pos)
2	public....................	*javax.swing.text.Element*	getDefaultRootElement	()
2	public............	java.awt.Font	getFont	(*javax.swing.text.AttributeSet* attr)
2	public............	java.awt.Color	getForeground	(*javax.swing.text.AttributeSet* attr)
	public.	HTMLDocument.Iterator	**getIterator**	(HTML.Tag t)
2	public....	*javax.swing.text.Style*	getLogicalStyle	(int p)
2	public....................	*javax.swing.text.Element*	getParagraphElement	(int pos)
	public................	boolean	**getPreservesUnknownTags**	()
	public....................	.HTMLEditorKit.ParserCallback	**getReader**	(int pos)
	public....................	.HTMLEditorKit.ParserCallback	**getReader**	(int pos, int popDepth, int pushDepth, HTML.Tag insertTag)
2	public....	*javax.swing.text.Style*	getStyle	(String nm)
2	public....	*java.util.Enumeration*	getStyleNames	()
	public................	StyleSheet	**getStyleSheet**	()
	public................	int	**getTokenThreshold**	()
*	public....................		**HTMLDocument**	()
*	public....................		**HTMLDocument**	(StyleSheet styles)
*	public....................		**HTMLDocument**	(*javax.swing.text.AbstractDocument.Content* c, StyleSheet styles)
2	protected...............	**void**	**insert**	(int offset, javax.swing.text.DefaultStyledDocument.ElementSpec[] data) throws javax.swing.text.BadLocationException
2	protected...............	**void**	**insertUpdate**	(javax.swing.text.AbstractDocument.DefaultDocumentEvent chng, *javax.swing.text.AttributeSet* attr)
	public....................	void	**processHTMLFrameHyperlinkEvent**	(HTMLFrameHyperlinkEvent e)
2	public....................	void	removeDocumentListener	(*javax.swing.event.DocumentListener* listener)
2	public....................	void	removeStyle	(String nm)
2	protected...............	void	removeUpdate	(javax.swing.text.AbstractDocument.DefaultDocumentEvent chng)
	public....................	void	**setBase**	(java.net.URL u)
2	public....................	void	setCharacterAttributes	(int offset, int length, *javax. swing. text. AttributeSet* s, boolean replace)
2	public....................	void	setLogicalStyle	(int pos, *javax.swing.text.Style* s)
2	public....................	void	setParagraphAttributes	(int offset, int length, *javax. swing. text. AttributeSet* s, boolean replace)
	public....................	void	**setPreservesUnknownTags**	(boolean preservesTags)
	public....................	void	**setTokenThreshold**	(int n)
2	protected...............	void	styleChanged	(*javax.swing.text.Style* style)

HTMLDocument.BlockElement   javax.swing.text.html

```
     Object
1.2 ○  └─javax.swing.text.AbstractDocument ↵ - - - - - - javax.swing.text.Element, javax.swing.text.MutableAttributeSet
            .AbstractElement¹                              (javax.swing.text.AttributeSet), java.io.Serializable,
                                                           javax.swing.tree.TreeNode
1.2        └─javax.swing.text.AbstractDocument ↵
              │ .BranchElement²
1.2           └─HTMLDocument.BlockElement
```

1	public....................	void	addAttribute	(Object name, Object value)
1	public....................	void	addAttributes	(*javax.swing.text.AttributeSet* attr)
*	public....................		**BlockElement**	(*javax.swing.text.Element* parent, *javax.swing.text.AttributeSet* a)
2	public....	*java.util.Enumeration*	children	()
1	public................	boolean	containsAttribute	(Object name, Object value)
1	public................	boolean	containsAttributes	(*javax.swing.text.AttributeSet* attrs)
1	public.................... ...	*javax.swing.text.AttributeSet*	copyAttributes	()

HTMLDocument.BlockElement

1	public . . . . void	dump (java.io.PrintStream psOut, int indentAmount)
1	protected . . . . void	finalize () throws Throwable
2	public . . . . boolean	getAllowsChildren ()
1	public . . . . Object	getAttribute (Object attrName)
1	public . . . . int	getAttributeCount ()
1	public . . . . . *java.util.Enumeration*	getAttributeNames ()
1	public	getAttributes ()
	. . . javax.swing.text.AttributeSet	
1	public	getChildAt (int childIndex)
	. . . . . javax.swing.tree.TreeNode	
1	public . . . . int	getChildCount ()
1	public	getDocument ()
	. . . . javax.swing.text.Document	
2	public	getElement (int index)
	. . . . javax.swing.text.Element	
2	public . . . . int	getElementCount ()
2	public . . . . int	getElementIndex (int offset)
2	public . . . . int	getEndOffset ()
1	public . . . . int	getIndex (*javax.swing.tree.TreeNode* node)
2	public . . . . **String**	**getName** ()
1	public	getParent ()
	. . . . . javax.swing.tree.TreeNode	
1	public	getParentElement ()
	. . . . javax.swing.text.Element	
1	public	**getResolveParent** ()
	*. **javax.swing.text.AttributeSet***	
2	public . . . . int	getStartOffset ()
1	public . . . . boolean	isDefined (Object attrName)
1	public . . . . boolean	isEqual (*javax.swing.text.AttributeSet* attr)
2	public . . . . boolean	isLeaf ()
2	public	positionToElement (int pos)
	. . . . javax.swing.text.Element	
1	public . . . . void	removeAttribute (Object name)
1	public . . . . void	removeAttributes (*java.util.Enumeration* names)
1	public . . . . void	removeAttributes (*javax.swing.text.AttributeSet* attrs)
2	public . . . . void	replace (int offset, int length, *javax.swing.text.Element[]* elems)
1	public . . . . void	setResolveParent (*javax.swing.text.AttributeSet* parent)
2	public . . . . String	toString ()

HTMLDocument.HTMLReader

```
        Object
1.2     └─HTMLEditorKit.ParserCallback¹
1.2         └─HTMLDocument.HTMLReader
```

	protected . . . . void	**addContent** (char[] data, int offs, int length)
	protected . . . . void	**addContent** (char[] data, int offs, int length, boolean generateImpliedPIfNecessary)
	protected . . . . void	**addSpecialElement** (HTML.Tag t, *javax.swing.text.MutableAttributeSet* a)
	protected . . . . void	**blockClose** (HTML.Tag t)
	protected . . . . void	**blockOpen** (HTML.Tag t, *javax.swing.text.MutableAttributeSet* attr)
	protected . . . . *javax*↵	**charAttr**
	.swing.text.MutableAttributeSet	
1	public . . . . **void**	**flush** () throws javax.swing.text.BadLocationException
1	public . . . . **void**	**handleComment** (char[] data, int pos)
1	public . . . . **void**	**handleEndTag** (HTML.Tag t, int pos)
1	public . . . . void	handleError (String errorMsg, int pos)
1	public . . . . **void**	**handleSimpleTag** (HTML.Tag t, *javax.swing.text.MutableAttributeSet* a, int pos)
1	public . . . . **void**	**handleStartTag** (HTML.Tag t, *javax.swing.text.MutableAttributeSet* a, int pos)
1	public . . . . **void**	**handleText** (char[] data, int pos)
*	public	**HTMLReader** (int offset)
*	public	**HTMLReader** (int offset, int popDepth, int pushDepth, HTML.Tag insertTag)
	protected . . . . java.util.Vector	**parseBuffer**
	protected . . . . void	**popCharacterStyle** ()
	protected . . . . void	**preContent** (char[] data)
	protected . . . . void	**pushCharacterStyle** ()
	protected . . . . void	**registerTag** (HTML.Tag t, HTMLDocument.HTMLReader.TagAction a)
	protected . . . . void	**textAreaContent** (char[] data)

Class   *Interface*   —extends   - - -implements   ○ abstract   ● final   △ static   ▲ static final   ✳ constructor   x x—inherited   x **x**—declared   **x x**—overridden

HTMLDocument.HTMLReader.BlockAction

javax.swing.text.html

```
     Object
1.2   └HTMLDocument.HTMLReader.TagAction ¹
1.2     └HTMLDocument.HTMLReader.BlockAction
```

*   public..........................**BlockAction** ()
1   public....................**void end** (HTML.Tag t)
1   public....................**void start** (HTML.Tag t, *javax.swing.text.MutableAttributeSet* attr)

HTMLDocument.HTMLReader.CharacterAction

javax.swing.text.html

```
     Object
1.2   └HTMLDocument.HTMLReader.TagAction ¹
1.2     └HTMLDocument.HTMLReader ↵
         .CharacterAction
```

*   public..........................**CharacterAction** ()
1   public....................**void end** (HTML.Tag t)
1   public....................**void start** (HTML.Tag t, *javax.swing.text.MutableAttributeSet* attr)

HTMLDocument.HTMLReader.FormAction

javax.swing.text.html

```
     Object
1.2   └HTMLDocument.HTMLReader.TagAction ¹
1.2     └HTMLDocument.HTMLReader ↵
           .SpecialAction ²
1.2       └HTMLDocument.HTMLReader ↵
           .FormAction
```

1   public....................**void end** (HTML.Tag t)
*   public..........................**FormAction** ()
2   public....................**void start** (HTML.Tag t, *javax.swing.text.MutableAttributeSet* attr)

HTMLDocument.HTMLReader.HiddenAction

javax.swing.text.html

```
     Object
1.2   └HTMLDocument.HTMLReader.TagAction ¹
1.2     └HTMLDocument.HTMLReader ↵
         .HiddenAction
```

1   public....................**void end** (HTML.Tag t)
*   public..........................**HiddenAction** ()
1   public....................**void start** (HTML.Tag t, *javax.swing.text.MutableAttributeSet* a)

HTMLDocument.HTMLReader.IsindexAction

javax.swing.text.html

```
     Object
1.2   └HTMLDocument.HTMLReader.TagAction ¹
1.2     └HTMLDocument.HTMLReader ↵
         .IsindexAction
```

1   public....................void end (HTML.Tag t)
*   public..........................**IsindexAction** ()
1   public....................**void start** (HTML.Tag t, *javax.swing.text.MutableAttributeSet* a)

HTMLDocument.HTMLReader.ParagraphAction

javax.swing.text.html

```
     Object
1.2   └HTMLDocument.HTMLReader.TagAction
1.2     └HTMLDocument.HTMLReader ↵
           .BlockAction ¹
1.2       └HTMLDocument.HTMLReader ↵
           .ParagraphAction
```

1   public....................**void end** (HTML.Tag t)
*   public..........................**ParagraphAction** ()

HTMLDocument.HTMLReader.ParagraphAction

| 1 public | **void** **start** (HTML.Tag t, *javax.swing.text.MutableAttributeSet* a) |

HTMLDocument.HTMLReader.PreAction `javax.swing.text.html`

```
       Object
1.2    └─HTMLDocument.HTMLReader.TagAction
1.2      └─HTMLDocument.HTMLReader ↵
            .BlockAction 1
1.2           └─HTMLDocument.HTMLReader.PreAction
```

1	public	**void** **end** (HTML.Tag t)
*	public	**PreAction** ()
1	public	**void** **start** (HTML.Tag t, *javax.swing.text.MutableAttributeSet* attr)

HTMLDocument.HTMLReader.SpecialAction `javax.swing.text.html`

```
       Object
1.2    └─HTMLDocument.HTMLReader.TagAction 1
1.2      └─HTMLDocument.HTMLReader ↵
            .SpecialAction
```

1	public	void end (HTML.Tag t)
*	public	**SpecialAction** ()
1	public	**void** **start** (HTML.Tag t, *javax.swing.text.MutableAttributeSet* a)

HTMLDocument.HTMLReader.TagAction `javax.swing.text.html`

```
       Object
1.2    └─HTMLDocument.HTMLReader.TagAction
```

	public	void **end** (HTML.Tag t)
	public	void **start** (HTML.Tag t, *javax.swing.text.MutableAttributeSet* a)
*	public	**TagAction** ()

HTMLDocument.Iterator `javax.swing.text.html`

```
         Object
1.2 ○    └─HTMLDocument.Iterator
```

○	public abstract	**getAttributes** ()
	... *javax.swing.text.AttributeSet*	
○	public abstract .... int	**getEndOffset** ()
○	public abstract .... int	**getStartOffset** ()
○	public abstract ...... HTML.Tag	**getTag** ()
○	public abstract .... boolean	**isValid** ()
*	public	**Iterator** ()
○	public abstract .... void	**next** ()

HTMLDocument.RunElement `javax.swing.text.html`

```
         Object
1.2 ○    └─javax.swing.text.AbstractDocument ↵ - - - - - - -  javax.swing.text.Element, javax.swing.text.MutableAttributeSet
            .AbstractElement 1                                (javax.swing.text.AttributeSet), java.io.Serializable,
                                                              javax.swing.tree.TreeNode
1.2         └─javax.swing.text.AbstractDocument ↵
               .LeafElement 2
1.2              └─HTMLDocument.RunElement
```

1	public	void addAttribute (Object name, Object value)
1	public	void addAttributes (*javax.swing.text.AttributeSet* attr)
2	public .... *java.util.Enumeration*	children ()
1	public	boolean containsAttribute (Object name, Object value)
1	public	boolean containsAttributes (*javax.swing.text.AttributeSet* attrs)
1	public	copyAttributes ()
	... *javax.swing.text.AttributeSet*	
1	public	void dump (java.io.PrintStream psOut, int indentAmount)

Class *Interface* —extends - - -implements ○ abstract ● final △ static ▲ static final ✳ constructor x x—inherited x **x**—declared **x x**—overridden

1	protected	. . . . void	finalize () throws Throwable
2	public	. . . . boolean	getAllowsChildren ()
1	public	. . . . Object	getAttribute (Object attrName)
1	public	. . . . int	getAttributeCount ()
1	public	. . . . *java.util.Enumeration*	getAttributeNames ()
1	public	. . . . *. . . javax.swing.text.AttributeSet*	getAttributes ()
1	public	. . . . *. . . . . javax.swing.tree.TreeNode*	getChildAt (int childIndex)
1	public	. . . . int	getChildCount ()
1	public	. . . . *. . . . javax.swing.text.Document*	getDocument ()
2	public	. . . . *. . . . . . javax.swing.text.Element*	getElement (int index)
2	public	. . . . int	getElementCount ()
2	public	. . . . int	getElementIndex (int pos)
2	public	. . . . int	getEndOffset ()
1	public	. . . . int	getIndex (*javax.swing.tree.TreeNode* node)
2	public	. . . . **String**	**getName** ()
1	public	. . . . *. . . . . javax.swing.tree.TreeNode*	getParent ()
1	public	. . . . *. . . . . javax.swing.text.Element*	getParentElement ()
1	public	. . . . *. javax.swing.text.AttributeSet*	**getResolveParent** ()
2	public	. . . . int	getStartOffset ()
1	public	. . . . boolean	isDefined (Object attrName)
1	public	. . . . boolean	isEqual (*javax.swing.text.AttributeSet* attr)
2	public	. . . . boolean	isLeaf ()
1	public	. . . . void	removeAttribute (Object name)
1	public	. . . . void	removeAttributes (*java.util.Enumeration* names)
1	public	. . . . void	removeAttributes (*javax.swing.text.AttributeSet* attrs)
*	public	. . . .	**RunElement** (*javax.swing.text.Element* parent, *javax.swing.text.AttributeSet* a, int offs0, int offs1)
1	public	. . . . void	setResolveParent (*javax.swing.text.AttributeSet* parent)
2	public	. . . . String	toString ()

HTMLEditorKit   javax.swing.text.html

```
        Object
1.2 ○   └─javax.swing.text.EditorKit - - - - - - - - - - - - - - - - Cloneable, java.io.Serializable
1.2        └─javax.swing.text.DefaultEditorKit 1
1.2            └─javax.swing.text.StyledEditorKit 2
1.2                └─HTMLEditorKit
```

1	*50 inherited members from javax.swing.text.DefaultEditorKit not shown*		
▲	public static final	. . . . String	**BOLD_ACTION** = "html-bold-action"
2	public	. . . . **Object**	**clone** ()
▲	public static final	. . . . String	**COLOR_ACTION** = "html-color-action"
2	public	. . . . *. . . javax.swing.text.Document*	**createDefaultDocument** ()
2	protected	. . . . **void**	**createInputAttributes** (*javax. swing. text. Element* element, *javax.swing.text.MutableAttributeSet* set)
▲	public static final	. . . . String	**DEFAULT_CSS** = "default.css"
2	public	. . . . **void**	**deinstall** (javax.swing.JEditorPane c)
▲	public static final	. . . . String	**FONT_CHANGE_BIGGER** = "html-font-bigger"
▲	public static final	. . . . String	**FONT_CHANGE_SMALLER** = "html-font-smaller"
2	public	. . . **javax.swing.Action[]**	**getActions** ()
2	public	. . . . *. . . . . . . javax.swing.text.Element*	getCharacterAttributeRun ()
1	public	. . . . **String**	**getContentType** ()
2	public	. . . . *javax*↩ *.swing.text.MutableAttributeSet*	getInputAttributes ()
	protected	. . . . HTMLEditorKit.Parser	**getParser** ()
	public	. . . . StyleSheet	**getStyleSheet** ()
2	public	. . . . *javax.swing.text.ViewFactory*	**getViewFactory** ()
*	public	. . . .	**HTMLEditorKit** ()
▲	public static final	. . . . String	**IMG_ALIGN_BOTTOM** = "html-image-align-bottom"
▲	public static final	. . . . String	**IMG_ALIGN_MIDDLE** = "html-image-align-middle"
▲	public static final	. . . . String	**IMG_ALIGN_TOP** = "html-image-align-top"

H

Classes

HTMLEditorKit

▲	public static final	String	**IMG_BORDER**	= "html-image-border"
	public	void	**insertHTML** (HTMLDocument doc, int offset, String html,
			int popDepth, int pushDepth, HTML. Tag insertTag)
			throws javax.swing.text.BadLocationException, java.io.IOException
2	public	**void install** (javax.swing.JEditorPane c)
▲	public static final	String	**ITALIC_ACTION**	= "html-italic-action"
▲	public static final	String	**LOGICAL_STYLE_ACTION**	= "html-logical-style-action"
▲	public static final	String	**PARA_INDENT_LEFT**	= "html-para-indent-left"
▲	public static final	String	**PARA_INDENT_RIGHT**	= "html-para-indent-right"
1	public	**void read** (java. io. Reader in, *javax. swing. text. Document* doc, int pos)
			throws java.io.IOException, javax.swing.text.BadLocationException
	public	void	**setStyleSheet** (StyleSheet s)
1	public	**void write** (java.io. Writer out, *javax. swing. text. Document* doc, int pos, int len)
			throws java.io.IOException, javax.swing.text.BadLocationException

H

HTMLEditorKit.HTMLFactory   javax.swing.text.html

Object
1.2 └─HTMLEditorKit.HTMLFactory - - - - - - - - - - - - - *javax.swing.text.ViewFactory* [1]

1	public	javax.swing.text.View	**create** (*javax.swing.text.Element* elem)
✻	public		**HTMLFactory** ()

HTMLEditorKit.HTMLTextAction   javax.swing.text.html

Object
1.2 ○ └─javax.swing.AbstractAction [1] - - - - - - - - - - - - - *javax.swing.Action (java.awt.event.ActionListener*
                                              (*java.util.EventListener*)), *Cloneable, java.io.Serializable*

1.2 ○   └─javax.swing.text.TextAction [2]
1.2 ○   └─javax.swing.text.StyledEditorKit ↵
        | .StyledTextAction [3]
        └─HTMLEditorKit.HTMLTextAction

○ 1	public abstract	void	actionPerformed (java.awt.event.ActionEvent)
1	public synchronized	void	addPropertyChangeListener (*java.beans.PropertyChangeListener* listener)
▲ 2	public static final		augmentList (*javax.swing.Action[]* list1, *javax.swing.Action[]* list2)
		javax.swing.Action[]	
1	protected . javax.swing.event ↵		changeSupport
	.SwingPropertyChangeSupport	
1	protected	Object	clone () throws CloneNotSupportedException
	protected	int	**elementCountToTag** (HTMLDocument doc, int offset, HTML.Tag tag)
1	protected	boolean	enabled
	protected		**findElementMatchingTag** (HTMLDocument doc, int offset, HTML.Tag tag)
		javax.swing.text.Element	
1	protected	void	firePropertyChange (String propertyName, Object oldValue, Object newValue)
● 3	protected final		getEditor (java.awt.event.ActionEvent e)
		javax.swing.JEditorPane	
	protected		**getElementsAt** (HTMLDocument doc, int offset)
		javax.swing.text.Element[]	
● 2	protected final	*javax* ↵	getFocusedComponent ()
	.swing.text.JTextComponent	
	protected	HTMLDocument	**getHTMLDocument** (javax.swing.JEditorPane e)
	protected	HTMLEditorKit	**getHTMLEditorKit** (javax.swing.JEditorPane e)
● 3	protected final	*javax* ↵	getStyledDocument (javax.swing.JEditorPane e)
	.swing.text.StyledDocument	
● 3	protected final		getStyledEditorKit (javax.swing.JEditorPane e)
	javax.swing.text.StyledEditorKit	
● 2	protected final	*javax* ↵	getTextComponent (java.awt.event.ActionEvent e)
	.swing.text.JTextComponent	
1	public	Object	getValue (String key)
✻	public		**HTMLTextAction** (String name)
1	public	boolean	isEnabled ()
1	public synchronized	void	putValue (String key, Object newValue)
1	public synchronized	void	removePropertyChangeListener (*java.beans.PropertyChangeListener* listener)
● 3	protected final	void	setCharacterAttributes (javax. swing. JEditorPane editor,
			javax.swing.text.AttributeSet attr, boolean replace)
1	public synchronized	void	setEnabled (boolean newValue)

Class   *Interface*   —extends   - - -implements   ○ abstract   ● final   △ static   ▲ static final   ✻ constructor   x x—inherited   x **x**—declared   **x x**—overridden

388

● 3　protected final . . . . void　setParagraphAttributes (javax. swing. JEditorPane editor,
javax.swing.text.AttributeSet attr, boolean replace)

HTMLEditorKit.InsertHTMLTextAction　　　　　　　　　　　　　javax.swing.text.html

Object
　└javax.swing.AbstractAction [1] - - - - - - - - - - - - - *javax.swing.Action (java.awt.event.ActionListener*
1.2 ○
　　　　　　　　　　　　　　　　　　　　　　　　　　　(java.util.EventListener)), Cloneable, java.io.Serializable
1.2 ○　　└javax.swing.text.TextAction [2]
1.2 ○　　　└javax.swing.text.StyledEditorKit ↵
　　　　　　.StyledTextAction [3]
1.2 ○　　　　└HTMLEditorKit.HTMLTextAction [4]
1.2　　　　　　└HTMLEditorKit ↵
　　　　　　　　　.InsertHTMLTextAction

	1	public . . . . **void**	**actionPerformed** (java.awt.event.ActionEvent ae)
	1	public synchronized . . . . void	addPropertyChangeListener (*java.beans.PropertyChangeListener* listener)
		protected . . . . HTML.Tag	**addTag**
		protected . . . . HTML.Tag	**alternateAddTag**
		protected . . . . HTML.Tag	**alternateParentTag**
▲	2	public static final . . . . *. . . . . javax.swing.Action[]*	augmentList (*javax.swing.Action[]* list1, *javax.swing.Action[]* list2)
	1	protected . javax.swing.event ↵ .SwingPropertyChangeSupport	changeSupport
	1	protected . . . . Object	clone () throws CloneNotSupportedException
	4	protected . . . . int	elementCountToTag (HTMLDocument doc, int offset, HTML.Tag tag)
	1	protected . . . . boolean	enabled
	4	protected . . . . *javax.swing.text.Element*	findElementMatchingTag (HTMLDocument doc, int offset, HTML.Tag tag)
	1	protected . . . . void	firePropertyChange (String propertyName, Object oldValue, Object newValue)
●	3	protected final . . . . javax.swing.JEditorPane	getEditor (java.awt.event.ActionEvent e)
	4	protected . . . . *javax.swing.text.Element[]*	getElementsAt (HTMLDocument doc, int offset)
●	2	protected final . . . . javax ↵ .swing.text.JTextComponent	getFocusedComponent ()
	4	protected . . . . . HTMLDocument	getHTMLDocument (javax.swing.JEditorPane e)
	4	protected . . . . HTMLEditorKit	getHTMLEditorKit (javax.swing.JEditorPane e)
●	3	protected final . . . . *javax↵* .swing.text.StyledDocument	getStyledDocument (javax.swing.JEditorPane e)
●	3	protected final . . . . javax.swing.text.StyledEditorKit	getStyledEditorKit (javax.swing.JEditorPane e)
●	2	protected final . . . . javax ↵ .swing.text.JTextComponent	getTextComponent (java.awt.event.ActionEvent e)
	1	public . . . . Object	getValue (String key)
		protected . . . . String	**html**
		protected . . . . void	**insertAtBoundry** (javax.swing.JEditorPane editor, HTMLDocument doc, int offset, *javax.swing.text.Element* insertElement, String html, HTML.Tag parentTag, HTML.Tag addTag)
		protected . . . . void	**insertHTML** (javax.swing.JEditorPane editor, HTMLDocument doc, int offset, String html, int popDepth, int pushDepth, HTML.Tag addTag)
＊		public	**InsertHTMLTextAction** (String name, String html, HTML.Tag parentTag, HTML.Tag addTag)
＊		public	**InsertHTMLTextAction** (String name, String html, HTML.Tag parentTag, HTML.Tag addTag, HTML.Tag alternateParentTag, HTML.Tag alternateAddTag)
	1	public . . . . boolean	isEnabled ()
		protected . . . . HTML.Tag	**parentTag**
	1	public synchronized . . . . void	putValue (String key, Object newValue)
	1	public synchronized . . . . void	removePropertyChangeListener (*java.beans.PropertyChangeListener* listener)
●	3	protected final . . . . void	setCharacterAttributes (javax. swing. JEditorPane editor, *javax.swing.text.AttributeSet* attr, boolean replace)
	1	public synchronized . . . . void	setEnabled (boolean newValue)
●	3	protected final . . . . void	setParagraphAttributes (javax. swing. JEditorPane editor, *javax.swing.text.AttributeSet* attr, boolean replace)

H

Classes

HTMLEditorKit.LinkController

		javax.swing.text.html

```
      Object
1.1 ○  └java.awt.event.MouseAdapter¹ ------------ java.awt.event.MouseListener (java.util.EventListener)
1.2         └HTMLEditorKit.LinkController ------------ java.io.Serializable
```

	protected . . . . .void	**activateLink** (int pos, javax.swing.JEditorPane html)
✳	public.	**LinkController** ()
1	public. . . . . void	**mouseClicked** (java.awt.event.MouseEvent e)
1	public. . . . . .void	mouseEntered (java.awt.event.MouseEvent e)
1	public. . . . . .void	mouseExited (java.awt.event.MouseEvent e)
1	public. . . . . .void	mousePressed (java.awt.event.MouseEvent e)
1	public. . . . . .void	mouseReleased (java.awt.event.MouseEvent e)

HTMLEditorKit.Parser

		javax.swing.text.html

```
      Object
1.2 ○  └HTMLEditorKit.Parser
```

○	public abstract . . . . .void	**parse** (java.io.Reader r, HTMLEditorKit.ParserCallback cb, boolean ignoreCharSet)
		throws java.io.IOException
✳	public.	**Parser** ()

HTMLEditorKit.ParserCallback

		javax.swing.text.html

```
      Object
1.2    └HTMLEditorKit.ParserCallback
```

	public. . . . . .void	**flush** () throws javax.swing.text.BadLocationException
	public. . . . . .void	**handleComment** (char[] data, int pos)
	public. . . . . .void	**handleEndTag** (HTML.Tag t, int pos)
	public. . . . . .void	**handleError** (String errorMsg, int pos)
	public. . . . . .void	**handleSimpleTag** (HTML.Tag t, *javax.swing.text.MutableAttributeSet* a, int pos)
	public. . . . . .void	**handleStartTag** (HTML.Tag t, *javax.swing.text.MutableAttributeSet* a, int pos)
	public. . . . . .void	**handleText** (char[] data, int pos)
✳	public.	**ParserCallback** ()

HTMLFrameHyperlinkEvent

		javax.swing.text.html

```
      Object
1.1  └java.util.EventObject¹ -------------------- java.io.Serializable
1.2     └javax.swing.event.HyperlinkEvent²
1.2        └HTMLFrameHyperlinkEvent
```

2	public. . . . . String	getDescription ()
2	public. . . . . . javax.swing.event ↵	getEventType ()
	.HyperlinkEvent.EventType	
1	public. . . . . Object	getSource ()
	public.	**getSourceElement** ()
	. . . . . . *javax.swing.text.Element*	
	public. . . . . String	**getTarget** ()
2	public. . . . . java.net.URL	getURL ()
✳	public.	**HTMLFrameHyperlinkEvent** (Object source, javax.swing.event.HyperlinkEvent ↵
		.EventType type, java.net.URL targetURL, String targetFrame)
✳	public.	**HTMLFrameHyperlinkEvent** (Object source, javax. swing. event ↵
		. HyperlinkEvent. EventType type, java. net. URL targetURL,
		javax.swing.text.Element sourceElement, String targetFrame)
✳	public.	**HTMLFrameHyperlinkEvent** (Object source, javax.swing.event.HyperlinkEvent ↵
		.EventType type, java.net.URL targetURL, String desc, String targetFrame)
✳	public.	**HTMLFrameHyperlinkEvent** (Object source, javax. swing. event ↵
		. HyperlinkEvent. EventType type, java. net. URL targetURL, String desc,
		javax.swing.text.Element sourceElement, String targetFrame)
1	protected transient. . . . . . Object	source
1	public. . . . . String	toString ()

Class	*Interface*	—extends	- - -implements	○ abstract	● final	△ static	▲ static final	✳ constructor	x x—inherited	x **x**—declared	**x x**—overridden

		HTMLWriter	

```
      Object
1.2 ○  └java.swing.text.AbstractWriter 1
1.2       └HTMLWriter
```

		protected................void	**closeOutUnwantedEmbeddedTags** (*javax. swing. text. AttributeSet* attr) throws java.io.IOException	
		protected................void	**comment** (*javax. swing. text. Element* elem) throws javax.swing.text.BadLocationException, java.io.IOException	
	1	protected................void	decrIndent ()	
		protected................void	**emptyTag** (*javax. swing. text. Element* elem) throws javax.swing.text.BadLocationException, java.io.IOException	
		protected................void	**endTag** (*javax.swing.text.Element* elem) throws java.io.IOException	
	1	protected...................... .... *javax.swing.text.Document*	getDocument ()	
	1	protected..............java ↵ .swing.text.ElementIterator	getElementIterator ()	
	1	protected.............. String	getText (*javax. swing. text. Element* elem) throws javax. swing. text ↵ .BadLocationException	
*		public......	**HTMLWriter** (java.io.Writer w, HTMLDocument doc)	
*		public......	**HTMLWriter** (java.io.Writer w, HTMLDocument doc, int pos, int len)	
	1	protected................void	incrIndent ()	
	1	protected................void	indent () throws java.io.IOException	
	1	protected.............. boolean	inRange (*javax.swing.text.Element* next)	
		protected.............. boolean	**isBlockTag** (*javax.swing.text.AttributeSet* attr)	
		protected.............. boolean	**matchNameAttribute** (*javax.swing.text.AttributeSet* attr, HTML.Tag tag)	
		protected................void	**selectContent** (*javax.swing.text.AttributeSet* attr) throws java.io.IOException	
	1	protected................void	setIndentSpace (int space)	
	1	protected................void	setLineLength (int l)	
		protected................void	**startTag** (*javax. swing. text. Element* elem) throws java. io. IOException, javax.swing.text.BadLocationException	
		protected.............. boolean	**synthesizedElement** (*javax.swing.text.Element* elem)	
	1	protected.............. **void**	**text** (*javax.swing.text.Element* elem) throws javax.swing.text.BadLocationException, java.io.IOException	
		protected................void	**textAreaContent** (*javax. swing. text. AttributeSet* attr) throws javax.swing.text.BadLocationException, java.io.IOException	
	1	public.............. **void**	**write** () throws java.io.IOException, javax.swing.text.BadLocationException	
	1	protected................void	write (char ch) throws java.io.IOException	
	1	protected.............. **void**	**write** (String content) throws java.io.IOException	
	1	protected................void	**writeAttributes** (*javax.swing.text.AttributeSet* attr) throws java.io.IOException	
		protected................void	**writeEmbeddedTags** (*javax.swing.text.AttributeSet* attr) throws java.io.IOException	
		protected................void	**writeOption** (Option option) throws java.io.IOException	

		HttpURLConnection	

```
      Object
  ○  └URLConnection 1
1.1 ○       └HttpURLConnection
```

P

	1	protected.............. boolean	allowUserInteraction	
○	1	public abstract.............void	connect () throws java.io.IOException	
	1	protected.............. boolean	connected	
○		public abstract.............void	**disconnect** ()	
	1	protected.............. boolean	doInput	
	1	protected.............. boolean	doOutput	
	1	public.............. boolean	getAllowUserInteraction ()	
	1	public.................. Object	getContent () throws java.io.IOException	
	1	public.................. String	getContentEncoding ()	
	1	public.....................int	getContentLength ()	
	1	public.................. String	getContentType ()	
	1	public.................... long	getDate ()	
△	1	public static .... boolean	getDefaultAllowUserInteraction ()	
△	1	public static .... String	getDefaultRequestProperty (String key)	
	1	public.............. boolean	getDefaultUseCaches ()	
	1	public.............. boolean	getDoInput ()	
	1	public.............. boolean	getDoOutput ()	
1.2		public...... java.io.InputStream	**getErrorStream** ()	
	1	public.................... long	getExpiration ()	
1.2 △	1	public static ..... *FileNameMap*	getFileNameMap ()	
△		public static .... boolean	**getFollowRedirects** ()	
	1	public.................... String	getHeaderField (int n)	

HttpURLConnection

	1	public	String	getHeaderField (String name)
	1	public	long	getHeaderFieldDate (String name, long Default)
	1	public	int	getHeaderFieldInt (String name, int Default)
	1	public	String	getHeaderFieldKey (int n)
	1	public	long	getIfModifiedSince ()
	1	public	java.io.InputStream	getInputStream () throws java.io.IOException
	1	public	long	getLastModified ()
	1	public	java.io.OutputStream	getOutputStream () throws java.io.IOException
1.2	1	public		**getPermission** () throws java.io.IOException
			..... **java.security.Permission**	
		public	String	**getRequestMethod** ()
	1	public	String	getRequestProperty (String key)
		public	int	**getResponseCode** () throws java.io.IOException
		public	String	**getResponseMessage** () throws java.io.IOException
	1	public	URL	getURL ()
	1	public	boolean	getUseCaches ()
△	1	protected static	String	guessContentTypeFromName (String fname)
△	1	public static	String	guessContentTypeFromStream (java.io.InputStream is) throws java.io.IOException
▲		public static final	int	**HTTP_ACCEPTED** = 202
▲		public static final	int	**HTTP_BAD_GATEWAY** = 502
▲		public static final	int	**HTTP_BAD_METHOD** = 405
▲		public static final	int	**HTTP_BAD_REQUEST** = 400
▲		public static final	int	**HTTP_CLIENT_TIMEOUT** = 408
▲		public static final	int	**HTTP_CONFLICT** = 409
▲		public static final	int	**HTTP_CREATED** = 201
▲		public static final	int	**HTTP_ENTITY_TOO_LARGE** = 413
▲		public static final	int	**HTTP_FORBIDDEN** = 403
▲		public static final	int	**HTTP_GATEWAY_TIMEOUT** = 504
▲		public static final	int	**HTTP_GONE** = 410
▲		public static final	int	**HTTP_INTERNAL_ERROR** = 501
▲		public static final	int	**HTTP_LENGTH_REQUIRED** = 411
▲		public static final	int	**HTTP_MOVED_PERM** = 301
▲		public static final	int	**HTTP_MOVED_TEMP** = 302
▲		public static final	int	**HTTP_MULT_CHOICE** = 300
▲		public static final	int	**HTTP_NO_CONTENT** = 204
▲		public static final	int	**HTTP_NOT_ACCEPTABLE** = 406
▲		public static final	int	**HTTP_NOT_AUTHORITATIVE** = 203
▲		public static final	int	**HTTP_NOT_FOUND** = 404
▲		public static final	int	**HTTP_NOT_MODIFIED** = 304
▲		public static final	int	**HTTP_OK** = 200
▲		public static final	int	**HTTP_PARTIAL** = 206
▲		public static final	int	**HTTP_PAYMENT_REQUIRED** = 402
▲		public static final	int	**HTTP_PRECON_FAILED** = 412
▲		public static final	int	**HTTP_PROXY_AUTH** = 407
▲		public static final	int	**HTTP_REQ_TOO_LONG** = 414
▲		public static final	int	**HTTP_RESET** = 205
▲		public static final	int	**HTTP_SEE_OTHER** = 303
▲		public static final	int	**HTTP_SERVER_ERROR** = 500
▲		public static final	int	**HTTP_UNAUTHORIZED** = 401
▲		public static final	int	**HTTP_UNAVAILABLE** = 503
▲		public static final	int	**HTTP_UNSUPPORTED_TYPE** = 415
▲		public static final	int	**HTTP_USE_PROXY** = 305
▲		public static final	int	**HTTP_VERSION** = 505
✳		protected		**HttpURLConnection** (URL u)
	1	protected	long	ifModifiedSince
		protected	String	**method**
		protected	int	**responseCode**
		protected	String	**responseMessage**
	1	public	void	setAllowUserInteraction (boolean allowuserinteraction)
△	1	public static synchronized	void	setContentHandlerFactory (*ContentHandlerFactory* fac)
△	1	public static	void	setDefaultAllowUserInteraction (boolean defaultallowuserinteraction)
△	1	public static	void	setDefaultRequestProperty (String key, String value)
	1	public	void	setDefaultUseCaches (boolean defaultusecaches)
	1	public	void	setDoInput (boolean doinput)
	1	public	void	setDoOutput (boolean dooutput)
1.2	△ 1	public static	void	setFileNameMap (*FileNameMap* map)
△		public static	void	**setFollowRedirects** (boolean set)
	1	public	void	setIfModifiedSince (long ifmodifiedsince)
		public	void	**setRequestMethod** (String method) throws ProtocolException
	1	public	void	setRequestProperty (String key, String value)
	1	public	void	setUseCaches (boolean usecaches)
	1	public	String	toString ()

Class   *Interface*   —extends   - - -implements   ○ abstract   ● final   △ static   ▲ static final   ✳ constructor   x x—inherited   x **x**—declared   **x x**—overridden

1	protected . . . . URL	url	
1	protected . . . . boolean	useCaches	
○	public abstract . . . . boolean	**usingProxy** ()	

HyperlinkEvent
javax.swing.event

Object
1.1 └java.util.EventObject [1] - - - - - - - - - - - - - - - - - - - *java.io.Serializable*
1.2   └HyperlinkEvent

	public . . . . String	**getDescription** ()	
	public	**getEventType** ()	
	. . . . . HyperlinkEvent.EventType		
1	public . . . . Object	getSource ()	
	public . . . . java.net.URL	**getURL** ()	
*	public	**HyperlinkEvent** (Object source, HyperlinkEvent.EventType type, java.net.URL u)	
*	public	**HyperlinkEvent** (Object source, HyperlinkEvent.EventType type, java.net.URL u, String desc)	
1	protected transient . . . . . . Object	source	
1	public . . . . String	toString ()	

HyperlinkEvent.EventType
javax.swing.event

Object [1]
1.2 ● └HyperlinkEvent.EventType

▲	public static final	**ACTIVATED**	
	. . . . . HyperlinkEvent.EventType		
▲	public static final	**ENTERED**	
	. . . . . HyperlinkEvent.EventType		
▲	public static final	**EXITED**	
	. . . . . HyperlinkEvent.EventType		
1	public . . . . **String**	**toString** ()	

HyperlinkListener
javax.swing.event

1.2 *HyperlinkListener*————————————————*java.util.EventListener*

	public . . . . void	**hyperlinkUpdate** (HyperlinkEvent e)	

ICC_ColorSpace
java.awt.color

Object
1.2 ○ └ColorSpace [1]
1.2   └ICC_ColorSpace

1	*35 inherited members from ColorSpace not shown*		
1	public . . . . **float[]**	**fromCIEXYZ** (float[] colorvalue)	
1	public . . . . **float[]**	**fromRGB** (float[] rgbvalue)	
	public . . . . ICC_Profile	**getProfile** ()	
*	public	**ICC_ColorSpace** (ICC_Profile profile)	
1	public . . . . **float[]**	**toCIEXYZ** (float[] colorvalue)	
1	public . . . . **float[]**	**toRGB** (float[] colorvalue)	

ICC_Profile
java.awt.color

Object [1]
1.2 └ICC_Profile

▲	public static final . . . . int	**CLASS_ABSTRACT** = 5	
▲	public static final . . . . int	**CLASS_COLORSPACECONVERSION** = 4	
▲	public static final . . . . int	**CLASS_DEVICELINK** = 3	
▲	public static final . . . . int	**CLASS_DISPLAY** = 1	
▲	public static final . . . . int	**CLASS_INPUT** = 0	
▲	public static final . . . . int	**CLASS_NAMEDCOLOR** = 6	
▲	public static final . . . . int	**CLASS_OUTPUT** = 2	
1	protected . . . . **void**	**finalize** ()	
	public . . . . int	**getColorSpaceType** ()	
	public . . . . byte[]	**getData** ()	

ICC_Profile

	public	byte[]	**getData** (int tagSignature)
△	public static	ICC_Profile	**getInstance** (byte[] data)
△	public static	ICC_Profile	**getInstance** (int cspace)
△	public static	ICC_Profile	**getInstance** (java.io.InputStream s) throws java.io.IOException
△	public static	ICC_Profile	**getInstance** (String fileName) throws java.io.IOException
	public	int	**getMajorVersion** ()
	public	int	**getMinorVersion** ()
	public	int	**getNumComponents** ()
	public	int	**getPCSType** ()
	public	int	**getProfileClass** ()
▲	public static final	int	**icAbsoluteColorimetric** = 3
▲	public static final	int	**icCurveCount** = 8
▲	public static final	int	**icCurveData** = 12
▲	public static final	int	**icHdrAttributes** = 56
▲	public static final	int	**icHdrCmmId** = 4
▲	public static final	int	**icHdrColorSpace** = 16
▲	public static final	int	**icHdrCreator** = 80
▲	public static final	int	**icHdrDate** = 24
▲	public static final	int	**icHdrDeviceClass** = 12
▲	public static final	int	**icHdrFlags** = 44
▲	public static final	int	**icHdrIlluminant** = 68
▲	public static final	int	**icHdrMagic** = 36
▲	public static final	int	**icHdrManufacturer** = 48
▲	public static final	int	**icHdrModel** = 52
▲	public static final	int	**icHdrPcs** = 20
▲	public static final	int	**icHdrPlatform** = 40
▲	public static final	int	**icHdrRenderingIntent** = 64
▲	public static final	int	**icHdrSize** = 0
▲	public static final	int	**icHdrVersion** = 8
▲	public static final	int	**icPerceptual** = 0
▲	public static final	int	**icRelativeColorimetric** = 1
▲	public static final	int	**icSaturation** = 2
▲	public static final	int	**icSigAbstractClass** = 1633842036
▲	public static final	int	**icSigAToB0Tag** = 1093812784
▲	public static final	int	**icSigAToB1Tag** = 1093812785
▲	public static final	int	**icSigAToB2Tag** = 1093812786
▲	public static final	int	**icSigBlueColorantTag** = 1649957210
▲	public static final	int	**icSigBlueTRCTag** = 1649693251
▲	public static final	int	**icSigBToA0Tag** = 1110589744
▲	public static final	int	**icSigBToA1Tag** = 1110589745
▲	public static final	int	**icSigBToA2Tag** = 1110589746
▲	public static final	int	**icSigCalibrationDateTimeTag** = 1667329140
▲	public static final	int	**icSigCharTargetTag** = 1952543335
▲	public static final	int	**icSigCmyData** = 1129142560
▲	public static final	int	**icSigCmykData** = 1129142603
▲	public static final	int	**icSigColorSpaceClass** = 1936744803
▲	public static final	int	**icSigCopyrightTag** = 1668313716
▲	public static final	int	**icSigDeviceMfgDescTag** = 1684893284
▲	public static final	int	**icSigDeviceModelDescTag** = 1684890724
▲	public static final	int	**icSigDisplayClass** = 1835955314
▲	public static final	int	**icSigGamutTag** = 1734438260
▲	public static final	int	**icSigGrayData** = 1196573017
▲	public static final	int	**icSigGrayTRCTag** = 1800688195
▲	public static final	int	**icSigGreenColorantTag** = 1733843290
▲	public static final	int	**icSigGreenTRCTag** = 1733579331
▲	public static final	int	**icSigHead** = 1751474532
▲	public static final	int	**icSigHlsData** = 1212961568
▲	public static final	int	**icSigHsvData** = 1213421088
▲	public static final	int	**icSigInputClass** = 1935896178
▲	public static final	int	**icSigLabData** = 1281450528
▲	public static final	int	**icSigLinkClass** = 1818848875
▲	public static final	int	**icSigLuminanceTag** = 1819635049
▲	public static final	int	**icSigLuvData** = 1282766368
▲	public static final	int	**icSigMeasurementTag** = 1835360627
▲	public static final	int	**icSigMediaBlackPointTag** = 1651208308
▲	public static final	int	**icSigMediaWhitePointTag** = 2004119668
▲	public static final	int	**icSigNamedColor2Tag** = 1852009522
▲	public static final	int	**icSigNamedColorClass** = 1852662636
▲	public static final	int	**icSigOutputClass** = 1886549106
▲	public static final	int	**icSigPreview0Tag** = 1886545200
▲	public static final	int	**icSigPreview1Tag** = 1886545201
▲	public static final	int	**icSigPreview2Tag** = 1886545202

▲ public static final . . . . int **icSigProfileDescriptionTag** = 1684370275
▲ public static final . . . . int **icSigProfileSequenceDescTag** = 1886610801
▲ public static final . . . . int **icSigPs2CRD0Tag** = 1886610480
▲ public static final . . . . int **icSigPs2CRD1Tag** = 1886610481
▲ public static final . . . . int **icSigPs2CRD2Tag** = 1886610482
▲ public static final . . . . int **icSigPs2CRD3Tag** = 1886610483
▲ public static final . . . . int **icSigPs2CSATag** = 1886597747
▲ public static final . . . . int **icSigPs2RenderingIntentTag** = 1886597737
▲ public static final . . . . int **icSigRedColorantTag** = 1918392666
▲ public static final . . . . int **icSigRedTRCTag** = 1918128707
▲ public static final . . . . int **icSigRgbData** = 1380401696
▲ public static final . . . . int **icSigScreeningDescTag** = 1935897188
▲ public static final . . . . int **icSigScreeningTag** = 1935897198
▲ public static final . . . . int **icSigSpace2CLR** = 843271250
▲ public static final . . . . int **icSigSpace3CLR** = 860048466
▲ public static final . . . . int **icSigSpace4CLR** = 876825682
▲ public static final . . . . int **icSigSpace5CLR** = 893602898
▲ public static final . . . . int **icSigSpace6CLR** = 910380114
▲ public static final . . . . int **icSigSpace7CLR** = 927157330
▲ public static final . . . . int **icSigSpace8CLR** = 943934546
▲ public static final . . . . int **icSigSpace9CLR** = 960711762
▲ public static final . . . . int **icSigSpaceACLR** = 1094929490
▲ public static final . . . . int **icSigSpaceBCLR** = 1111706706
▲ public static final . . . . int **icSigSpaceCCLR** = 1128483922
▲ public static final . . . . int **icSigSpaceDCLR** = 1145261138
▲ public static final . . . . int **icSigSpaceECLR** = 1162038354
▲ public static final . . . . int **icSigSpaceFCLR** = 1178815570
▲ public static final . . . . int **icSigTechnologyTag** = 1952801640
▲ public static final . . . . int **icSigUcrBgTag** = 1650877472
▲ public static final . . . . int **icSigViewingCondDescTag** = 1987405156
▲ public static final . . . . int **icSigViewingConditionsTag** = 1986618743
▲ public static final . . . . int **icSigXYZData** = 1482250784
▲ public static final . . . . int **icSigYCbCrData** = 1497588338
▲ public static final . . . . int **icSigYxyData** = 1501067552
▲ public static final . . . . int **icTagReserved** = 4
▲ public static final . . . . int **icTagType** = 0
▲ public static final . . . . int **icXYZNumberX** = 8
  public . . . . void **setData** (int tagSignature, byte[] tagData)
  public . . . . void **write** (java.io.OutputStream s) throws java.io.IOException
  public . . . . void **write** (String fileName) throws java.io.IOException

---

ICC_ProfileGray
java.awt.color

Object
1.2 └ICC_Profile [1]
1.2   └ICC_ProfileGray

  [1] *122 inherited members from ICC_Profile not shown*
    public . . . . float **getGamma** ()
    public . . . . float[] **getMediaWhitePoint** ()
    public . . . . short[] **getTRC** ()

ICC_ProfileRGB
java.awt.color

Object
1.2 └ICC_Profile [1]
1.2   └ICC_ProfileRGB

  [1] *122 inherited members from ICC_Profile not shown*
▲ public static final . . . . int **BLUECOMPONENT** = 2
  public . . . . float **getGamma** (int component)
  public . . . . float[][] **getMatrix** ()
  public . . . . float[] **getMediaWhitePoint** ()
  public . . . . short[] **getTRC** (int component)
▲ public static final . . . . int **GREENCOMPONENT** = 1
▲ public static final . . . . int **REDCOMPONENT** = 0

Icon — javax.swing

1.2		*Icon*	
	public	int	**getIconHeight** ()
	public	int	**getIconWidth** ()
	public	void	**paintIcon** (java.awt.Component c, java.awt.Graphics g, int x, int y)

IconUIResource — javax.swing.plaf

Object
└IconUIResource - *javax.swing.Icon [1], UIResource, java.io.Serializable*

1.2

1	public	int	**getIconHeight** ()
1	public	int	**getIconWidth** ()
*	public		**IconUIResource** (*javax.swing.Icon* delegate)
1	public	void	**paintIcon** (java.awt.Component c, java.awt.Graphics g, int x, int y)

IconView — javax.swing.text

Object
1.2 ○ └*View [1]* - *javax.swing.SwingConstants*
1.2   └IconView

1	*33 inherited members from View not shown*		
1	public	**float**	**getAlignment** (int axis)
1	public	**float**	**getPreferredSpan** (int axis)
*	public		**IconView** (*Element* elem)
1	public	***java.awt.Shape***	**modelToView** (int pos, *java. awt. Shape* a, Position. Bias b)
			throws BadLocationException
1	public	**void**	**paint** (java.awt.Graphics g, *java.awt.Shape* a)
1	public	**void**	**setSize** (float width, float height)
1	public	**int**	**viewToModel** (float x, float y, *java.awt.Shape* a, Position.Bias[] bias)

Identity — java.security

P○

Object [1]
1.1 ○ └Identity - *Principal [2], java.io.Serializable*

		public	void	**addCertificate** (*Certificate* certificate) throws KeyManagementException
		public	*Certificate[]*	**certificates** ()
●	1	public final	**boolean**	**equals** (Object identity)
		public	String	**getInfo** ()
●	2	public final	String	**getName** ()
		public	*PublicKey*	**getPublicKey** ()
●		public final	IdentityScope	**getScope** ()
	1	public	**int**	**hashCode** ()
*		protected		**Identity** ()
*		public		**Identity** (String name)
*		public		**Identity** (String name, IdentityScope scope) throws KeyManagementException
		protected	boolean	**identityEquals** (Identity identity)
		public	void	**removeCertificate** (*Certificate* certificate) throws KeyManagementException
		public	void	**setInfo** (String info)
		public	void	**setPublicKey** (*PublicKey* key) throws KeyManagementException
	1	public	**String**	**toString** ()
		public	String	**toString** (boolean detailed)

IdentityScope — java.security

P○

Object
1.1 ○ └Identity [1] - *Principal, java.io.Serializable*
1.1 ○   └IdentityScope

	1	public	void	addCertificate (*Certificate* certificate) throws KeyManagementException
○		public abstract	void	**addIdentity** (Identity identity) throws KeyManagementException
	1	public	*Certificate[]*	certificates ()
●	1	public final	boolean	equals (Object identity)
○		public abstract	Identity	**getIdentity** (String name)

Class   *Interface*   —extends   - - -implements   ○ abstract   ● final   △ static   ▲ static final   ✳ constructor   x x—inherited   x **x**—declared   **x x**—overridden

		public	Identity	**getIdentity** (*Principal* principal)
○		public abstract	Identity	**getIdentity** (*PublicKey* key)
	1	public	String	getInfo ()
●	1	public final	String	getName ()
	1	public	*PublicKey*	getPublicKey ()
●	1	public final	IdentityScope	getScope ()
△		public static	IdentityScope	**getSystemScope** ()
	1	public	int	hashCode ()
○		public abstract		**identities** ()
			java.util.Enumeration	
	1	protected	boolean	identityEquals (Identity identity)
*		protected		**IdentityScope** ()
*		public		**IdentityScope** (String name)
*		public		**IdentityScope** (String name, IdentityScope scope)
				throws KeyManagementException
	1	public	void	removeCertificate (*Certificate* certificate) throws KeyManagementException
○		public abstract	void	**removeIdentity** (Identity identity) throws KeyManagementException
	1	public	void	setInfo (String info)
	1	public	void	setPublicKey (*PublicKey* key) throws KeyManagementException
△		protected static	void	**setSystemScope** (IdentityScope scope)
○		public abstract	int	**size** ()
	1	public	**String**	**toString** ()
	1	public	String	toString (boolean detailed)

IDLEntity   org.omg.CORBA.portable

1.2 *IDLEntity* ——————————————— *java.io.Serializable*

IDLType   org.omg.CORBA

1.2 *IDLType* ——————— *Object*[1], *org.omg.CORBA.portable.IDLEntity (java.io.Serializable)*, *IRObject*[2] (*Object*[1], *org.omg.CORBA.portable.IDLEntity* (*java.io.Serializable*))

1	*13 inherited members from Object not shown*		
2	public	DefinitionKind	def_kind ()
2	public	void	destroy ()
	public	TypeCode	**type** ()

IllegalAccessError   java.lang

Object   P
└Throwable - *java.io.Serializable*
　└Error
　　└LinkageError
　　　└IncompatibleClassChangeError
　　　　└IllegalAccessError

*	public	**IllegalAccessError** ()
*	public	**IllegalAccessError** (String s)

IllegalAccessException   java.lang

Object   P
└Throwable - *java.io.Serializable*
　└Exception
　　└IllegalAccessException

*	public	**IllegalAccessException** ()
*	public	**IllegalAccessException** (String s)

IllegalArgumentException   java.lang

Object   P
└Throwable - *java.io.Serializable*
　└Exception
　　└RuntimeException
　　　└IllegalArgumentException

I

Classes

IllegalArgumentException

*	public........................	**IllegalArgumentException** ()
*	public........................	**IllegalArgumentException** (String s)

IllegalComponentStateException   java.awt

P

```
Object
└Throwable --------------------------- java.io.Serializable
  └Exception
    └RuntimeException
1.1    └IllegalStateException
1.1      └IllegalComponentStateException
```

*	public........................	**IllegalComponentStateException** ()
*	public........................	**IllegalComponentStateException** (String s)

IllegalMonitorStateException   java.lang

P

```
Object
└Throwable --------------------------- java.io.Serializable
  └Exception
    └RuntimeException
      └IllegalMonitorStateException
```

*	public........................	**IllegalMonitorStateException** ()
*	public........................	**IllegalMonitorStateException** (String s)

IllegalPathStateException   java.awt.geom

P

```
Object
└Throwable --------------------------- java.io.Serializable
  └Exception
    └RuntimeException
1.2    └IllegalPathStateException
```

*	public........................	**IllegalPathStateException** ()
*	public........................	**IllegalPathStateException** (String s)

IllegalStateException   java.lang

P

```
Object
└Throwable --------------------------- java.io.Serializable
  └Exception
    └RuntimeException
1.1    └IllegalStateException
```

*	public........................	**IllegalStateException** ()
*	public........................	**IllegalStateException** (String s)

IllegalThreadStateException   java.lang

P

```
Object
└Throwable --------------------------- java.io.Serializable
  └Exception
    └RuntimeException
      └IllegalArgumentException
        └IllegalThreadStateException
```

*	public........................	**IllegalThreadStateException** ()
*	public........................	**IllegalThreadStateException** (String s)

Image   java.awt

P

```
   Object
○  └Image
```

Class   *Interface*   —extends   - - -implements   ○ abstract   ● final   △ static   ▲ static final   * constructor   x x—inherited   x **x**—declared   **x x**—overridden

○	public abstract	void	**flush** ()	
○	public abstract	Graphics	**getGraphics** ()	
○	public abstract	int	**getHeight** (*java.awt.image.ImageObserver* observer)	
○	public abstract	Object	**getProperty** (String name, *java.awt.image.ImageObserver* observer)	
1.1	public	Image	**getScaledInstance** (int width, int height, int hints)	
○	public abstract		**getSource** ()	
	java.awt.image.ImageProducer			
○	public abstract	int	**getWidth** (*java.awt.image.ImageObserver* observer)	
∗	public		**Image** ()	
1.1 ▲	public static final	int	**SCALE_AREA_AVERAGING** = 16	
1.1 ▲	public static final	int	**SCALE_DEFAULT** = 1	
1.1 ▲	public static final	int	**SCALE_FAST** = 2	
1.1 ▲	public static final	int	**SCALE_REPLICATE** = 8	
1.1 ▲	public static final	int	**SCALE_SMOOTH** = 4	
▲	public static final	Object	**UndefinedProperty**	

ImageConsumer — java.awt.image

ImageConsumer — P

▲	public static final	int	**COMPLETESCANLINES** = 4
▲	public static final	int	**IMAGEABORTED** = 4
	public	void	**imageComplete** (int status)
▲	public static final	int	**IMAGEERROR** = 1
▲	public static final	int	**RANDOMPIXELORDER** = 1
	public	void	**setColorModel** (ColorModel model)
	public	void	**setDimensions** (int width, int height)
	public	void	**setHints** (int hintflags)
	public	void	**setPixels** (int x, int y, int w, int h, ColorModel model, int[] pixels, int off, int scansize)
	public	void	**setPixels** (int x, int y, int w, int h, ColorModel model, byte[] pixels, int off, int scansize)
	public	void	**setProperties** (java.util.Hashtable props)
▲	public static final	int	**SINGLEFRAME** = 16
▲	public static final	int	**SINGLEFRAMEDONE** = 2
▲	public static final	int	**SINGLEPASS** = 8
▲	public static final	int	**STATICIMAGEDONE** = 3
▲	public static final	int	**TOPDOWNLEFTRIGHT** = 2

ImageFilter — java.awt.image

Object [1]
  └ ImageFilter - *ImageConsumer* [2], *Cloneable*   P

1	public	**Object**	**clone** ()
	protected	*ImageConsumer*	**consumer**
	public	ImageFilter	**getFilterInstance** (*ImageConsumer* ic)
2	public	void	**imageComplete** (int status)
∗	public		**ImageFilter** ()
	public	void	**resendTopDownLeftRight** (*ImageProducer* ip)
2	public	void	**setColorModel** (ColorModel model)
2	public	void	**setDimensions** (int width, int height)
2	public	void	**setHints** (int hints)
2	public	void	**setPixels** (int x, int y, int w, int h, ColorModel model, byte[] pixels, int off, int scansize)
2	public	void	**setPixels** (int x, int y, int w, int h, ColorModel model, int[] pixels, int off, int scansize)
2	public	void	**setProperties** (java.util.Hashtable props)

ImageGraphicAttribute — java.awt.font

Object [1]
1.2 ○ └ GraphicAttribute [2]
1.2 ●   └ ImageGraphicAttribute

2	public	**void**	**draw** (java.awt.Graphics2D graphics, float x, float y)
	public	boolean	**equals** (ImageGraphicAttribute rhs)
1	public	**boolean**	**equals** (Object rhs)
2	public	**float**	**getAdvance** ()
● 2	public final	int	**getAlignment** ()
2	public	**float**	**getAscent** ()
2	public		**getBounds** ()
	java.awt.geom.Rectangle2D		
2	public	**float**	**getDescent** ()
2	public	GlyphJustificationInfo	**getJustificationInfo** ()

ImageGraphicAttribute

	1	public .... int	**hashCode** ()
	*	public	**ImageGraphicAttribute** (java.awt.Image image, int alignment)
	*	public	**ImageGraphicAttribute** (java.awt.Image image, int alignment, float originX,
			float originY)

ImageIcon | javax.swing

Object
  └ImageIcon - Icon[1], *java.io.Serializable*

1.2

▲		protected static final	**component**
		.... java.awt.Component	
		public .... String	**getDescription** ()
	1	public .... int	**getIconHeight** ()
	1	public .... int	**getIconWidth** ()
		public .... java.awt.Image	**getImage** ()
		public .... int	**getImageLoadStatus** ()
		public .... java↵	**getImageObserver** ()
		.awt.image.ImageObserver	
	*	public	**ImageIcon** ()
	*	public	**ImageIcon** (byte[] imageData)
	*	public	**ImageIcon** (java.awt.Image image)
	*	public	**ImageIcon** (String filename)
	*	public	**ImageIcon** (java.net.URL location)
	*	public	**ImageIcon** (byte[] imageData, String description)
	*	public	**ImageIcon** (java.awt.Image image, String description)
	*	public	**ImageIcon** (String filename, String description)
	*	public	**ImageIcon** (java.net.URL location, String description)
		protected .... void	**loadImage** (java.awt.Image image)
	1	public synchronized ...... void	**paintIcon** (java.awt.Component c, java.awt.Graphics g, int x, int y)
		public .... void	**setDescription** (String description)
		public .... void	**setImage** (java.awt.Image image)
		public .... void	**setImageObserver** (*java.awt.image.ImageObserver* observer)
▲		protected static final	**tracker**
		.... java.awt.MediaTracker	

ImageObserver | java.awt.image
P

ImageObserver

▲	public static final .... int	**ABORT** = 128
▲	public static final .... int	**ALLBITS** = 32
▲	public static final .... int	**ERROR** = 64
▲	public static final .... int	**FRAMEBITS** = 16
▲	public static final .... int	**HEIGHT** = 2
	public .... boolean	**imageUpdate** (java.awt.Image img, int infoflags, int x, int y, int width, int height)
▲	public static final .... int	**PROPERTIES** = 4
▲	public static final .... int	**SOMEBITS** = 8
▲	public static final .... int	**WIDTH** = 1

ImageProducer | java.awt.image
P

ImageProducer

	public .... void	**addConsumer** (*ImageConsumer* ic)
	public .... boolean	**isConsumer** (*ImageConsumer* ic)
	public .... void	**removeConsumer** (*ImageConsumer* ic)
	public .... void	**requestTopDownLeftRightResend** (*ImageConsumer* ic)
	public .... void	**startProduction** (*ImageConsumer* ic)

ImagingOpException | java.awt.image
P

Object
  └Throwable - *java.io.Serializable*
    └Exception
      └RuntimeException
        └ImagingOpException

1.2

Class *Interface* —extends - - -implements ○ abstract ● final △ static ▲ static final ✳ constructor x x—inherited x **x**—declared **x x**—overridden

*	public	**ImagingOpException** (String s)	

IMP_LIMIT

```
Object
 └ Throwable ------------------------- java.io.Serializable
    └ Exception
       └ RuntimeException
          └ SystemException¹
             └ IMP_LIMIT
```

	1	public	CompletionStatus	completed
*		public	**IMP_LIMIT** ()	
*		public	**IMP_LIMIT** (String s)	
*		public	**IMP_LIMIT** (int minor, CompletionStatus completed)	
*		public	**IMP_LIMIT** (String s, int minor, CompletionStatus completed)	
	1	public	int	minor
	1	public	String	toString ()

IncompatibleClassChangeError
P

```
Object
 └ Throwable ------------------------- java.io.Serializable
    └ Error
       └ LinkageError
          └ IncompatibleClassChangeError
```

*	public	**IncompatibleClassChangeError** ()	
*	public	**IncompatibleClassChangeError** (String s)	

InconsistentTypeCode

```
Object
 └ Throwable ------------------------- java.io.Serializable
    └ Exception
       └ org.omg.CORBA.UserException ------- org.omg.CORBA.portable.IDLEntity (java.io.Serializable)
          └ InconsistentTypeCode
```

*	public	**InconsistentTypeCode** ()	
*	public	**InconsistentTypeCode** (String reason)	

IndexColorModel
P

```
Object
 └ ColorModel¹ ------------------------- java.awt.Transparency
    └ IndexColorModel
```

1.2	1	public	ColorModel	coerceData (WritableRaster raster, boolean isAlphaPremultiplied)
1.2		public	BufferedImage	**convertToIntDiscrete** (Raster raster, boolean forceARGB)
1.2	1	public	**SampleModel**	**createCompatibleSampleModel** (int w, int h)
1.2	1	public	**WritableRaster**	**createCompatibleWritableRaster** (int w, int h)
	1	public	boolean	equals (Object obj)
	1	public	**void**	**finalize** ()
●	1	public final	**int**	**getAlpha** (int pixel)
1.2	1	public	int	getAlpha (Object inData)
1.2	1	public	WritableRaster	getAlphaRaster (WritableRaster raster)
●	1	public final	void	**getAlphas** (byte[] a)
●	1	public final	**int**	**getBlue** (int pixel)
1.2	1	public	int	getBlue (Object inData)
●	1	public final	void	**getBlues** (byte[] b)
1.2 ●	1	public final java.awt.color.ColorSpace		getColorSpace ()
1.2	1	public	**int[]**	**getComponents** (int pixel, int[] components, int offset)
1.2	1	public	**int[]**	**getComponents** (Object pixel, int[] components, int offset)
1.2	1	public	**int[]**	**getComponentSize** ()
1.2	1	public	int	getComponentSize (int componentIdx)
1.2	1	public	**int**	**getDataElement** (int[] components, int offset)
1.2	1	public	**Object**	**getDataElements** (int rgb, Object pixel)
1.2	1	public	**Object**	**getDataElements** (int[] components, int offset, Object pixel)

I

Classes

IndexColorModel

●	1	public final	**int**	**getGreen** (int pixel)
1.2	1	public..........................	int	getGreen (Object inData)
●		public final ....void		**getGreens** (byte[] g)
●		public final	**int**	**getMapSize** ()
1.2	1	public....................float[]		getNormalizedComponents (int[] components, int offset, float[] normComponents, int normOffset)
1.2	1	public..........................	int	getNumColorComponents ()
1.2	1	public..........................	int	getNumComponents ()
	1	public..........................	int	getPixelSize ()
●	1	public final	**int**	**getRed** (int pixel)
1.2	1	public..........................	int	getRed (Object inData)
		public.........................void		**getReds** (byte[] r)
●	1	public final	**int**	**getRGB** (int pixel)
1.2	1	public..........................	int	getRGB (Object inData)
△	1	public static .... ColorModel		getRGBdefault ()
1.2 ●	1	public final ....void		**getRGBs** (int[] rgb)
1.2	1	public..........................	**int**	**getTransparency** ()
●		public final ....int		**getTransparentPixel** ()
1.2	1	public........................int[]		getUnnormalizedComponents (float[] normComponents, int normOffset, int[] components, int offset)
1.2 ●	1	public final .... boolean		hasAlpha ()
*		public..........................		**IndexColorModel** (int bits, int size, byte[] r, byte[] g, byte[] b)
*		public..........................		**IndexColorModel** (int bits, int size, byte[] cmap, int start, boolean hasalpha)
*		public..........................		**IndexColorModel** (int bits, int size, byte[] cmap, int start, boolean hasalpha, int trans)
*		public..........................		**IndexColorModel** (int bits, int size, byte[] r, byte[] g, byte[] b, byte[] a)
*		public..........................		**IndexColorModel** (int bits, int size, byte[] r, byte[] g, byte[] b, int trans)
1.2 *		public..........................		**IndexColorModel** (int bits, int size, int[] cmap, int start, boolean hasalpha, int trans, int transferType)
1.2 ●	1	public final .... boolean		isAlphaPremultiplied ()
1.2	1	public....................	**boolean**	**isCompatibleRaster** (Raster raster)
1.2	1	public....................	**boolean**	**isCompatibleSampleModel** (SampleModel sm)
	1	protected ....int		pixel_bits
	1	public....................	**String**	**toString** ()
1.2	1	protected ....int		transferType

IndexedPropertyDescriptor | java.beans

```
      Object
1.1   └FeatureDescriptor¹
1.1      └PropertyDescriptor²
1.1         └IndexedPropertyDescriptor
```

	1	public.... *java.util.Enumeration*		attributeNames ()
	1	public....................String		getDisplayName ()
		public....................Class		**getIndexedPropertyType** ()
		public.java.lang.reflect.Method		**getIndexedReadMethod** ()
		public.java.lang.reflect.Method		**getIndexedWriteMethod** ()
	1	public....................String		getName ()
	2	public....................Class		getPropertyEditorClass ()
	2	public....................Class		getPropertyType ()
	2	public.java.lang.reflect.Method		getReadMethod ()
	1	public....................String		getShortDescription ()
	1	public....................Object		getValue (String attributeName)
	2	public.java.lang.reflect.Method		getWriteMethod ()
*		public..........................		**IndexedPropertyDescriptor** (String propertyName, Class beanClass) throws IntrospectionException
*		public..........................		**IndexedPropertyDescriptor** (String propertyName, java.lang.reflect.Method getter, java.lang.reflect.Method setter, java.lang.reflect.Method indexedGetter, java.lang.reflect.Method indexedSetter) throws IntrospectionException
*		public..........................		**IndexedPropertyDescriptor** (String propertyName, Class beanClass, String getterName, String setterName, String indexedGetterName, String indexedSetterName) throws IntrospectionException
	2	public.................. boolean		isBound ()
	2	public.................. boolean		isConstrained ()
	1	public.................. boolean		isExpert ()
	1	public.................. boolean		isHidden ()
1.2	1	public.................. boolean		isPreferred ()
	2	public....................void		setBound (boolean bound)
	2	public....................void		setConstrained (boolean constrained)

Class *Interface* —extends - - -implements O abstract ● final △ static ▲ static final * constructor x x—inherited x **x**—declared **x x**—overridden

	1	public.....................void	setDisplayName (String displayName)
	1	public.....................void	setExpert (boolean expert)
	1	public.....................void	setHidden (boolean hidden)
1.2		public.....................void	**setIndexedReadMethod** (java. lang. reflect. Method getter)
			throws IntrospectionException
1.2		public.....................void	**setIndexedWriteMethod** (java. lang. reflect. Method setter)
			throws IntrospectionException
	1	public.....................void	setName (String name)
1.2	1	public.....................void	setPreferred (boolean preferred)
	2	public.....................void	setPropertyEditorClass (Class propertyEditorClass)
1.2	2	public.....................void	setReadMethod (java.lang.reflect.Method getter) throws IntrospectionException
	1	public.....................void	setShortDescription (String text)
	1	public.....................void	setValue (String attributeName, Object value)
1.2	2	public.....................void	setWriteMethod (java.lang.reflect.Method setter) throws IntrospectionException

---

IndexOfBoundsException

IndexOutOfBoundsException — java.lang

Object
  └Throwable - *java.io.Serializable*
    └Exception
      └RuntimeException
        └IndexOutOfBoundsException

*	public.........................	**IndexOutOfBoundsException** ()
*	public.........................	**IndexOutOfBoundsException** (String s)

InetAddress

InetAddress — java.net

● Object[1]
  └InetAddress - *java.io.Serializable*

	1	public..................**boolean**	**equals** (Object obj)
		public.....................byte[]	**getAddress** ()
△		public static ..... InetAddress[]	**getAllByName** (String host) throws UnknownHostException
△		public static ....InetAddress	**getByName** (String host) throws UnknownHostException
		public.....................String	**getHostAddress** ()
		public.....................String	**getHostName** ()
△		public static synchronized .... InetAddress	**getLocalHost** () throws UnknownHostException
	1	public.....................**int**	**hashCode** ()
1.1		public...................boolean	**isMulticastAddress** ()
	1	public...................**String**	**toString** ()

Inflater

Inflater — java.util.zip

P[m]

Object[1]
1.1 └Inflater

		public synchronized ....void	**end** ()
	1	protected..................**void**	**finalize** ()
		public synchronized .. boolean	**finished** ()
		public synchronized ....int	**getAdler** ()
		public synchronized ....int	**getRemaining** ()
		public synchronized ....int	**getTotalIn** ()
		public synchronized ....int	**getTotalOut** ()
		public.....................int	**inflate** (byte[] b) throws DataFormatException
		public synchronized ....int	**inflate** (byte[] b, int off, int len) throws DataFormatException
*		public.........................	**Inflater** ()
*		public.........................	**Inflater** (boolean nowrap)
		public synchronized .. boolean	**needsDictionary** ()
		public synchronized .. boolean	**needsInput** ()
		public synchronized ......void	**reset** ()
		public.....................void	**setDictionary** (byte[] b)
		public synchronized ......void	**setDictionary** (byte[] b, int off, int len)
		public.....................void	**setInput** (byte[] b)
		public synchronized ......void	**setInput** (byte[] b, int off, int len)

I

Classes

403

InflaterInputStream

P

```
Object
  └java.io.InputStream
     └java.io.FilterInputStream 1
        └InflaterInputStream
```
1.1

1	public	int	**available** () throws java.io.IOException
	protected	byte[]	**buf**
1	public	**void**	**close** () throws java.io.IOException
	protected	void	**fill** () throws java.io.IOException
1	protected	java.io.InputStream	in
	protected	Inflater	**inf**
*	public		**InflaterInputStream** (java.io.InputStream in)
*	public		**InflaterInputStream** (java.io.InputStream in, Inflater inf)
*	public		**InflaterInputStream** (java.io.InputStream in, Inflater inf, int size)
	protected	int	**len**
1	public synchronized	void	mark (int readlimit)
1	public	boolean	markSupported ()
1	public	int	read () throws java.io.IOException
1	public	int	read (byte[] b) throws java.io.IOException
1	public	int	read (byte[] b, int off, int len) throws java.io.IOException
1	public synchronized	void	reset () throws java.io.IOException
1	public	long	skip (long n) throws java.io.IOException

InheritableThreadLocal

P

```
Object
  └ThreadLocal 1
     └InheritableThreadLocal
```
1.2
1.2

	protected	Object	**childValue** (Object parentValue)
1	public	Object	get ()
*	public		**InheritableThreadLocal** ()
1	protected	Object	initialValue ()
1	public	void	set (Object value)

INITIALIZE

```
Object
  └Throwable ---------------------------- java.io.Serializable
     └Exception
        └RuntimeException
           └SystemException 1
              └INITIALIZE
```
1.2 ○
1.2 ●

1	public	CompletionStatus	completed
*	public		**INITIALIZE** ()
*	public		**INITIALIZE** (String s)
*	public		**INITIALIZE** (int minor, CompletionStatus completed)
*	public		**INITIALIZE** (String s, int minor, CompletionStatus completed)
1	public	int	minor
1	public	String	toString ()

InlineView

```
Object
  └javax.swing.text.View 1 ------------------- javax.swing.SwingConstants
     └javax.swing.text.LabelView 2
        └InlineView
```
1.2 ○
1.2
1.2

1	*25 inherited members from javax.swing.text.View not shown*		
2	public	javax.swing.text.View	breakView (int axis, int p0, float pos, float len)
2	public	void	changedUpdate (*javax.swing.event.DocumentEvent* e, *java.awt.Shape* a, *javax.swing.text.ViewFactory* f)
2	public	javax.swing.text.View	createFragment (int p0, int p1)
2	public	float	getAlignment (int axis)

Class   *Interface*   —extends   - - -implements   ○ abstract   ● final   △ static   ▲ static final   ✳ constructor   x x—inherited   x **x**—declared   **x x**—overridden

1	public		**getAttributes** ()
		.javax.swing.text.AttributeSet	
2	public	int	getBreakWeight (int axis, float pos, float len)
2	protected	java.awt.Font	getFont ()
2	protected	java.awt.FontMetrics	getFontMetrics ()
2	public	int	getNextVisualPositionFrom (int pos, javax. swing. text. Position. Bias b, *java. awt. Shape* a, int direction, javax. swing. text. Position. Bias[] biasRet) throws javax.swing.text.BadLocationException
2	public	float	getPreferredSpan (int axis)
	protected	StyleSheet	**getStyleSheet** ()
*	public		**InlineView** (*javax.swing.text.Element* elem)
2	public	void	insertUpdate (*javax. swing. event. DocumentEvent* e, *java. awt. Shape* a, *javax. swing. text. ViewFactory* f)
1	public	**boolean**	**isVisible** ()
2	public	*java.awt.Shape*	modelToView (int pos, *java. awt. Shape* a, javax. swing. text. Position. Bias b) throws javax.swing.text.BadLocationException
2	public	void	paint (java.awt.Graphics g, *java.awt.Shape* a)
2	public	void	removeUpdate (*javax. swing. event. DocumentEvent* changes, *java. awt. Shape* a, *javax. swing. text. ViewFactory* f)
2	protected	**void**	**setPropertiesFromAttributes** ()
2	protected	void	setStrikeThrough (boolean s)
2	protected	void	setSubscript (boolean s)
2	protected	void	setSuperscript (boolean s)
2	protected	void	setUnderline (boolean u)
2	public	String	toString ()
2	public	int	viewToModel (float x, float y, *java. awt. Shape* a, javax. swing. text. Position. Bias[] biasReturn)

InputContext

Object
1.2 └InputContext

	public synchronized	void	**dispatchEvent** (java.awt.AWTEvent event)
	public	void	**dispose** ()
	public synchronized	void	**endComposition** ()
	public	Object	**getInputMethodControlObject** ()
△	public static	InputContext	**getInstance** ()
*	protected		**InputContext** ()
	public	void	**removeNotify** (java.awt.Component client)
	public	boolean	**selectInputMethod** (java.util.Locale locale)
	public	void	**setCharacterSubsets** (Character.Subset[] subsets)

InputEvent

P

Object
1.1 └java.util.EventObject[1] - - - - - - - - - - - - - - - - - - - *java.io.Serializable*
1.1 ○   └java.awt.AWTEvent[2]
1.1   └ComponentEvent[3]
1.1 ○   └InputEvent

1.2 ▲	public static final	int	**ALT_GRAPH_MASK** = 32
▲	public static final	int	**ALT_MASK** = 8
▲	public static final	int	**BUTTON1_MASK** = 16
▲	public static final	int	**BUTTON2_MASK** = 8
▲	public static final	int	**BUTTON3_MASK** = 4
2	public	**void**	**consume** ()
2	protected	boolean	consumed
▲	public static final	int	**CTRL_MASK** = 2
2	protected	void	finalize () throws Throwable
3	public	java.awt.Component	getComponent ()
2	public	int	getID ()
	public	int	**getModifiers** ()
1	public	Object	getSource ()
	public	long	**getWhen** ()
2	protected	int	id
	public	boolean	**isAltDown** ()
1.2	public	boolean	**isAltGraphDown** ()
2	public	**boolean**	**isConsumed** ()
	public	boolean	**isControlDown** ()
	public	boolean	**isMetaDown** ()

I

Classes

InputEvent

	public	boolean	**isShiftDown** ()
▲	public static final	int	**META_MASK** = 4
3	public	String	paramString ()
▲	public static final	int	**SHIFT_MASK** = 1
1	protected transient	Object	source
2	public	String	toString ()

InputMethodEvent java.awt.event

P

```
      Object
1.1   └─java.util.EventObject¹ ------------------- java.io.Serializable
1.1 O    └─java.awt.AWTEvent²
1.2         └─InputMethodEvent
```

▲	public static final	int	**CARET_POSITION_CHANGED** = 1101
2	public	**void**	**consume** ()
2	protected	boolean	consumed
2	protected	void	finalize () throws Throwable
	public . java.awt.font.TextHitInfo		**getCaret** ()
	public	int	**getCommittedCharacterCount** ()
2	public	int	getID ()
1	public	Object	getSource ()
	public	*java.text*↩	**getText** ()
	.*AttributedCharacterIterator*		
	public . java.awt.font.TextHitInfo		**getVisiblePosition** ()
2	protected	int	id
▲	public static final	int	**INPUT_METHOD_FIRST** = 1100
▲	public static final	int	**INPUT_METHOD_LAST** = 1101
▲	public static final	int	**INPUT_METHOD_TEXT_CHANGED** = 1100
✳	public		**InputMethodEvent** (java. awt. Component source, int id, java.awt.font.TextHitInfo caret, java.awt.font.TextHitInfo visiblePosition)
✳	public		**InputMethodEvent** (java. awt. Component source, int id, *java.text.AttributedCharacterIterator* text, int committedCharacterCount, java.awt.font.TextHitInfo caret, java.awt.font.TextHitInfo visiblePosition)
2	public	**boolean**	**isConsumed** ()
2	public	**String**	**paramString** ()
1	protected transient	Object	source
2	public	String	toString ()

InputMethodHighlight java.awt.im

```
      Object
1.2   └─InputMethodHighlight
```

▲	public static final	int	**CONVERTED_TEXT** = 1
	public	int	**getState** ()
	public	int	**getVariation** ()
✳	public		**InputMethodHighlight** (boolean selected, int state)
✳	public		**InputMethodHighlight** (boolean selected, int state, int variation)
	public	boolean	**isSelected** ()
▲	public static final	int	**RAW_TEXT** = 0
▲	public static final .... InputMethodHighlight		**SELECTED_CONVERTED_TEXT_HIGHLIGHT**
▲	public static final .... InputMethodHighlight		**SELECTED_RAW_TEXT_HIGHLIGHT**
▲	public static final .... InputMethodHighlight		**UNSELECTED_CONVERTED_TEXT_HIGHLIGHT**
▲	public static final .... InputMethodHighlight		**UNSELECTED_RAW_TEXT_HIGHLIGHT**

InputMethodListener java.awt.event

P

```
1.2   InputMethodListener───────────────java.util.EventListener
```

	public	void	**caretPositionChanged** (InputMethodEvent event)
	public	void	**inputMethodTextChanged** (InputMethodEvent event)

Class *Interface* ──extends - - -implements O abstract ● final △ static ▲ static final ✳ constructor x x──inherited x **x**──declared **x x**──overridden

InputMethodRequests

java.awt.im

1.2   *InputMethodRequests*

public.............. *java.text*↵ *.AttributedCharacterIterator*	**cancelLatestCommittedText** (java.text.AttributedCharacterIterator.Attribute[] attributes)
public.............. *java.text*↵ *.AttributedCharacterIterator*	**getCommittedText** (int beginIndex, int endIndex, java.text.AttributedCharacterIterator.Attribute[] attributes)
public.........................int	**getCommittedTextLength** ()
public.........................int	**getInsertPositionOffset** ()
public. java.awt.font.TextHitInfo	**getLocationOffset** (int x, int y)
public.............. *java.text*↵ *.AttributedCharacterIterator*	**getSelectedText** (java.text.AttributedCharacterIterator.Attribute[] attributes)
public...... java.awt.Rectangle	**getTextLocation** (java.awt.font.TextHitInfo offset)

InputStream ⓘ

org.omg.CORBA.portable

Object
   ○   └java.io.InputStream [1]
1.2 ○   └InputStream

	1	public.........................int available () throws java.io.IOException
	1	public.........................void close () throws java.io.IOException
*		public............................ **InputStream** ()
	1	public synchronized ....void mark (int readlimit)
	1	public.................. boolean markSupported ()
		public...org.omg.CORBA.ORB **orb** ()
	1	public............................ **int read** () throws java.io.IOException
	1	public.........................int read (byte[] b) throws java.io.IOException
	1	public.........................int read (byte[] b, int off, int len) throws java.io.IOException
○		public abstract ....org.omg.CORBA.Any **read_any** ()
○		public abstract .... boolean **read_boolean** ()
○		public abstract ....void **read_boolean_array** (boolean[] value, int offset, int length)
○		public abstract .... char **read_char** ()
○		public abstract ....void **read_char_array** (char[] value, int offset, int length)
		public............................ ...... org.omg.CORBA.Context **read_Context** ()
○		public abstract...........double **read_double** ()
○		public abstract ....void **read_double_array** (double[] value, int offset, int length)
		public... java.math.BigDecimal **read_fixed** ()
○		public abstract ....float **read_float** ()
○		public abstract ....void **read_float_array** (float[] value, int offset, int length)
○		public abstract ....int **read_long** ()
○		public abstract ....void **read_long_array** (int[] value, int offset, int length)
○		public abstract .... long **read_longlong** ()
○		public abstract ....void **read_longlong_array** (long[] value, int offset, int length)
○		public abstract .... *org.omg.CORBA.Object* **read_Object** ()
		public *org.omg.CORBA.Object* **read_Object** (Class clz)
○		public abstract .... byte **read_octet** ()
○		public abstract ....void **read_octet_array** (byte[] value, int offset, int length)
D ○		public abstract .... org.omg.CORBA.Principal **read_Principal** ()
○		public abstract ....short **read_short** ()
○		public abstract ....void **read_short_array** (short[] value, int offset, int length)
○		public abstract ....String **read_string** ()
○		public abstract .... org.omg.CORBA.TypeCode **read_TypeCode** ()
○		public abstract ....int **read_ulong** ()
○		public abstract ....void **read_ulong_array** (int[] value, int offset, int length)
○		public abstract .... long **read_ulonglong** ()
○		public abstract ....void **read_ulonglong_array** (long[] value, int offset, int length)
○		public abstract ....short **read_ushort** ()
○		public abstract ....void **read_ushort_array** (short[] value, int offset, int length)
○		public abstract .... char **read_wchar** ()
○		public abstract ....void **read_wchar_array** (char[] value, int offset, int length)
○		public abstract ....String **read_wstring** ()
	1	public synchronized ....void reset () throws java.io.IOException
	1	public.........................long skip (long n) throws java.io.IOException

InputStream⊘

InputStream⊘					java.io

```
       Object
  ○    └─InputStream
```

public	int	**available** () throws IOException
public	void	**close** () throws IOException
✳ public		**InputStream** ()
public synchronized	void	**mark** (int readlimit)
public	boolean	**markSupported** ()
○ public abstract	int	**read** () throws IOException
public	int	**read** (byte[] b) throws IOException
public	int	**read** (byte[] b, int off, int len) throws IOException
public synchronized	void	**reset** () throws IOException
public	long	**skip** (long n) throws IOException

InputStreamReader					java.io

```
        Object
  1.1 ○ └─Reader 1
  1.1      └─InputStreamReader
```

1	public	**void**	**close** () throws IOException
	public	String	**getEncoding** ()
✳	public		**InputStreamReader** (InputStream in)
✳	public		**InputStreamReader** (InputStream in, String enc) throws UnsupportedEncodingException
1	protected	Object	lock
1	public	void	mark (int readAheadLimit) throws IOException
1	public	boolean	markSupported ()
1	public	**int**	**read** () throws IOException
1	public	int	read (char[] cbuf) throws IOException
1	public	**int**	**read** (char[] cbuf, int off, int len) throws IOException
1	public	**boolean**	**ready** () throws IOException
1	public	void	reset () throws IOException
1	public	long	skip (long n) throws IOException

InputSubset					java.awt.im

```
        Object
  1.2   └─Character.Subset 1
  1.2 ● └─InputSubset
```

●	1	public final	boolean	equals (Object obj)
▲		public static final	InputSubset	**HALFWIDTH_KATAKANA**
▲		public static final	InputSubset	**HANJA**
●	1	public final	int	hashCode ()
▲		public static final	InputSubset	**KANJI**
▲		public static final	InputSubset	**LATIN**
▲		public static final	InputSubset	**LATIN_DIGITS**
▲		public static final	InputSubset	**SIMPLIFIED_HANZI**
●	1	public final	String	toString ()
▲		public static final	InputSubset	**TRADITIONAL_HANZI**

Insets					java.awt

```
        Object 1                                                    P
        └─Insets  - - - - - - - - - - - - - - - - - - - - - Cloneable, java.io.Serializable
```

	public	int	**bottom**
1	public	**Object**	**clone** ()
1	public	**boolean**	**equals** (Object obj)
✳	public		**Insets** (int top, int left, int bottom, int right)
	public	int	**left**
	public	int	**right**
	public	int	**top**
1	public	**String**	**toString** ()

Class   *Interface*   —extends   - - -implements   ○ abstract   ● final   △ static   ▲ static final   ✳ constructor   x x—inherited   x **x**—declared   **x x**—overridden

InsetsUIResource
javax.swing.plaf

```
Object
└java.awt.Insets 1 ----------------------- Cloneable, java.io.Serializable
1.2    └InsetsUIResource -------------------- UIResource
```

	1	*7 inherited members from java.awt.Insets not shown*
*		public........................... **InsetsUIResource** (int top, int left, int bottom, int right)

InstantiationError
java.lang
P

```
Object
└Throwable -------------------------- java.io.Serializable
  └Error
    └LinkageError
      └IncompatibleClassChangeError
        └InstantiationError
```

*	public........................... **InstantiationError** ()
*	public........................... **InstantiationError** (String s)

InstantiationException
java.lang
P

```
Object
└Throwable -------------------------- java.io.Serializable
  └Exception
    └InstantiationException
```

*	public........................... **InstantiationException** ()
*	public........................... **InstantiationException** (String s)

Integer
java.lang
P

```
Object 1
○ └Number 2 ----------------------- java.io.Serializable
● └Integer ----------------------- Comparable 3
```

1.1	2	public...................... **byte**	**byteValue** ()
1.2		public...................... int	**compareTo** (Integer anotherInteger)
1.2	3	public...................... int	**compareTo** (Object o)
1.1	△	public static .... Integer	**decode** (String nm) throws NumberFormatException
	2	public...................... **double**	**doubleValue** ()
	1	public...................... **boolean**	**equals** (Object obj)
	2	public...................... **float**	**floatValue** ()
	△	public static .... Integer	**getInteger** (String nm)
	△	public static .... Integer	**getInteger** (String nm, int val)
	△	public static .... Integer	**getInteger** (String nm, Integer val)
	1	public...................... **int**	**hashCode** ()
*		public...........................	**Integer** (int value)
*		public...........................	**Integer** (String s) throws NumberFormatException
	2	public...................... **int**	**intValue** ()
	2	public...................... **long**	**longValue** ()
▲		public static final ....int	**MAX_VALUE** = 2147483647
▲		public static final ....int	**MIN_VALUE** = -2147483648
	△	public static ....int	**parseInt** (String s) throws NumberFormatException
	△	public static ....int	**parseInt** (String s, int radix) throws NumberFormatException
1.1	2	public...................... **short**	**shortValue** ()
	△	public static .... String	**toBinaryString** (int i)
	△	public static .... String	**toHexString** (int i)
	△	public static .... String	**toOctalString** (int i)
	1	public...................... **String**	**toString** ()
	△	public static .... String	**toString** (int i)
	△	public static .... String	**toString** (int i, int radix)
1.1	▲	public static final .... Class	**TYPE**
	△	public static .... Integer	**valueOf** (String s) throws NumberFormatException
	△	public static .... Integer	**valueOf** (String s, int radix) throws NumberFormatException

INTERNAL — org.omg.CORBA

```
Object
└Throwable ------------------------- java.io.Serializable
  └Exception
    └RuntimeException
      └SystemException 1
        └INTERNAL
```

	1	public........CompletionStatus	completed	
✳		public.........................	**INTERNAL** ()	
✳		public.........................	**INTERNAL** (String s)	
✳		public.........................	**INTERNAL** (int minor, CompletionStatus completed)	
✳		public.........................	**INTERNAL** (String s, int minor, CompletionStatus completed)	
	1	public.....................int	minor	
	1	public....................String	toString ()	

1.2 ○ (SystemException)
1.2 ● (INTERNAL)

I

InternalError — java.lang
P

```
Object
└Throwable ------------------------- java.io.Serializable
  └Error
    └VirtualMachineError
      └InternalError
```

○ (VirtualMachineError)

✳	public.........................	**InternalError** ()	
✳	public.........................	**InternalError** (String s)	

InternalFrameAdapter — javax.swing.event

```
Object
└InternalFrameAdapter ------------------ InternalFrameListener 1 (java.util.EventListener)
```

1.2 ○

	1	public.....................void	**internalFrameActivated** (InternalFrameEvent e)
✳		public.....................	**InternalFrameAdapter** ()
	1	public.....................void	**internalFrameClosed** (InternalFrameEvent e)
	1	public.....................void	**internalFrameClosing** (InternalFrameEvent e)
	1	public.....................void	**internalFrameDeactivated** (InternalFrameEvent e)
	1	public.....................void	**internalFrameDeiconified** (InternalFrameEvent e)
	1	public.....................void	**internalFrameIconified** (InternalFrameEvent e)
	1	public.....................void	**internalFrameOpened** (InternalFrameEvent e)

InternalFrameEvent — javax.swing.event

```
Object
└java.util.EventObject 1 ------------------ java.io.Serializable
  └java.awt.AWTEvent 2
    └InternalFrameEvent
```

1.1 (EventObject)
1.1 ○ (AWTEvent)
1.2 (InternalFrameEvent)

	2	protected.................void	consume ()
	2	protected............. boolean	consumed
	2	protected.................void	finalize () throws Throwable
	2	public.........................int	getID ()
	1	public...................Object	getSource ()
	2	protected.....................int	id
▲		public static final............int	**INTERNAL_FRAME_ACTIVATED** = 25554
▲		public static final............int	**INTERNAL_FRAME_CLOSED** = 25551
▲		public static final............int	**INTERNAL_FRAME_CLOSING** = 25550
▲		public static final............int	**INTERNAL_FRAME_DEACTIVATED** = 25555
▲		public static final............int	**INTERNAL_FRAME_DEICONIFIED** = 25553
▲		public static final............int	**INTERNAL_FRAME_FIRST** = 25549
▲		public static final............int	**INTERNAL_FRAME_ICONIFIED** = 25552
▲		public static final............int	**INTERNAL_FRAME_LAST** = 25555
▲		public static final............int	**INTERNAL_FRAME_OPENED** = 25549
✳		public.........................	**InternalFrameEvent** (javax.swing.JInternalFrame source, int id)
	2	protected............. boolean	isConsumed ()
	2	public.........................	**String paramString** ()
	1	protected transient......Object	source

Class   *Interface*   —extends   - - -implements   ○ abstract   ● final   △ static   ▲ static final   ✳ constructor   x x—inherited   x **x**—declared   **x x**—overridden

	2	public . . . . String toString ()

InternalFrameListener   javax.swing.event

1.2	*InternalFrameListener* ———————————— *java.util.EventListener*
	public . . . . void **internalFrameActivated** (InternalFrameEvent e)
	public . . . . void **internalFrameClosed** (InternalFrameEvent e)
	public . . . . void **internalFrameClosing** (InternalFrameEvent e)
	public . . . . void **internalFrameDeactivated** (InternalFrameEvent e)
	public . . . . void **internalFrameDeiconified** (InternalFrameEvent e)
	public . . . . void **internalFrameIconified** (InternalFrameEvent e)
	public . . . . void **internalFrameOpened** (InternalFrameEvent e)

InternalFrameUI   javax.swing.plaf

Object
1.2 ○ └ ComponentUI [1]
1.2 ○   └ InternalFrameUI

[1] *11 inherited members from ComponentUI not shown*
*   public . . . . **InternalFrameUI** ()

InterruptedException   java.lang
P

Object
└ Throwable - *java.io.Serializable*
   └ Exception
     └ InterruptedException

*   public . . . . **InterruptedException** ()
*   public . . . . **InterruptedException** (String s)

InterruptedIOException   java.io

Object
└ Throwable - *Serializable*
   └ Exception
     └ IOException
       └ InterruptedIOException

   public . . . . int **bytesTransferred**
*   public . . . . **InterruptedIOException** ()
*   public . . . . **InterruptedIOException** (String s)

INTF_REPOS   org.omg.CORBA

Object
└ Throwable - *java.io.Serializable*
   └ Exception
     └ RuntimeException
1.2 ○   └ SystemException [1]
1.2 ●   └ INTF_REPOS

	1	public . . . . CompletionStatus completed
*		public . . . . **INTF_REPOS** ()
*		public . . . . **INTF_REPOS** (String s)
*		public . . . . **INTF_REPOS** (int minor, CompletionStatus completed)
*		public . . . . **INTF_REPOS** (String s, int minor, CompletionStatus completed)
	1	public . . . . int minor
	1	public . . . . String toString ()

IntHolder   org.omg.CORBA

Object
1.2 ● └ IntHolder - *org.omg.CORBA.portable.Streamable* [1]

IntHolder

	1	public	void	**_read** (org.omg.CORBA.portable.InputStream input)
	1	public	TypeCode	**_type** ()
	1	public	void	**_write** (org.omg.CORBA.portable.OutputStream output)
✳		public		**IntHolder** ()
✳		public		**IntHolder** (int initial)
		public	int	**value**

IntrospectionException java.beans

```
Object
└ Throwable ---------------------------- java.io.Serializable
   └ Exception
      └ IntrospectionException
```
1.1

✳		public		**IntrospectionException** (String mess)

Introspector java.beans

```
Object
└ Introspector
```
1.1

△	public static	String	**decapitalize** (String name)
1.2	△	public static	void	**flushCaches** ()
1.2	△	public static	void	**flushFromCaches** (Class clz)
△	public static	BeanInfo	**getBeanInfo** (Class beanClass) throws IntrospectionException
△	public static	BeanInfo	**getBeanInfo** (Class beanClass, Class stopClass) throws IntrospectionException
1.2	△	public static	BeanInfo	**getBeanInfo** (Class beanClass, int flags) throws IntrospectionException
△	public static synchronized	String[]	**getBeanInfoSearchPath** ()
1.2	▲	public static final	int	**IGNORE_ALL_BEANINFO** = 3
1.2	▲	public static final	int	**IGNORE_IMMEDIATE_BEANINFO** = 2
△	public static synchronized	void	**setBeanInfoSearchPath** (String[] path)
1.2	▲	public static final	int	**USE_ALL_BEANINFO** = 1

INV_FLAG org.omg.CORBA

```
Object
└ Throwable ---------------------------- java.io.Serializable
   └ Exception
      └ RuntimeException
         └ SystemException [1]
            └ INV_FLAG
```
1.2 ○
1.2 ●

	1	public	CompletionStatus	completed
✳		public		**INV_FLAG** ()
✳		public		**INV_FLAG** (String s)
✳		public		**INV_FLAG** (int minor, CompletionStatus completed)
✳		public		**INV_FLAG** (String s, int minor, CompletionStatus completed)
	1	public	int	minor
	1	public	String	toString ()

INV_IDENT org.omg.CORBA

```
Object
└ Throwable ---------------------------- java.io.Serializable
   └ Exception
      └ RuntimeException
         └ SystemException [1]
            └ INV_IDENT
```
1.2 ○
1.2 ●

	1	public	CompletionStatus	completed
✳		public		**INV_IDENT** ()
✳		public		**INV_IDENT** (String s)
✳		public		**INV_IDENT** (int minor, CompletionStatus completed)
✳		public		**INV_IDENT** (String s, int minor, CompletionStatus completed)
	1	public	int	minor
	1	public	String	toString ()

Class   *Interface*   —extends   - - -implements   ○ abstract   ● final   △ static   ▲ static final   ✳ constructor   x x—inherited   x **x**—declared   **x x**—overridden

INV_OBJREF

org.omg.CORBA

```
Object
 └Throwable ------------------------- java.io.Serializable
    └Exception
       └RuntimeException
1.2 ○        └SystemException 1
1.2 ●           └INV_OBJREF
```

	1	public........CompletionStatus	completed
*		public...........................	**INV_OBJREF** ()
*		public...........................	**INV_OBJREF** (String s)
*		public...........................	**INV_OBJREF** (int minor, CompletionStatus completed)
*		public...........................	**INV_OBJREF** (String s, int minor, CompletionStatus completed)
	1	public...........................int	minor
	1	public....................String	toString ()

I

INV_POLICY

org.omg.CORBA

```
Object
 └Throwable ------------------------- java.io.Serializable
    └Exception
       └RuntimeException
1.2 ○        └SystemException 1
1.2           └INV_POLICY
```

	1	public........CompletionStatus	completed
*		public...........................	**INV_POLICY** ()
*		public...........................	**INV_POLICY** (String s)
*		public...........................	**INV_POLICY** (int minor, CompletionStatus completed)
*		public...........................	**INV_POLICY** (String s, int minor, CompletionStatus completed)
	1	public...........................int	minor
	1	public....................String	toString ()

Invalid

org.omg.CORBA.DynAnyPackage

```
Object
 └Throwable ------------------------- java.io.Serializable
    └Exception
1.2 ○     └org.omg.CORBA.UserException ------- org.omg.CORBA.portable.IDLEntity (java.io.Serializable)
1.2 ●        └Invalid
```

*	public...........................	**Invalid** ()
*	public...........................	**Invalid** (String reason)

INVALID_TRANSACTION

org.omg.CORBA

```
Object
 └Throwable ------------------------- java.io.Serializable
    └Exception
       └RuntimeException
1.2 ○        └SystemException 1
1.2 ●           └INVALID_TRANSACTION
```

	1	public........CompletionStatus	completed
*		public...........................	**INVALID_TRANSACTION** ()
*		public...........................	**INVALID_TRANSACTION** (String s)
*		public...........................	**INVALID_TRANSACTION** (int minor, CompletionStatus completed)
*		public...........................	**INVALID_TRANSACTION** (String s, int minor, CompletionStatus completed)
	1	public...........................int	minor
	1	public....................String	toString ()

InvalidAlgorithmParameterException

InvalidAlgorithmParameterException	java.security

```
Object
└─Throwable ------------------------- java.io.Serializable
   └─Exception
```
	└─GeneralSecurityException
1.2	
1.2	└─InvalidAlgorithmParameterException

✳	public.........................	**InvalidAlgorithmParameterException** ()
✳	public.........................	**InvalidAlgorithmParameterException** (String msg)

InvalidClassException	java.io

```
Object
└─Throwable ¹ ------------------------- Serializable
   └─Exception
      └─IOException
```
	└─ObjectStreamException
1.1 ○	
1.1	└─InvalidClassException

	public....................String	**classname**
1	public....................**String**	**getMessage** ()
✳	public.........................	**InvalidClassException** (String reason)
✳	public.........................	**InvalidClassException** (String cname, String reason)

InvalidDnDOperationException	java.awt.dnd

```
Object
└─Throwable ------------------------- java.io.Serializable
   └─Exception
      └─RuntimeException
```
	└─IllegalStateException
1.1	
1.2	└─InvalidDnDOperationException

✳	public.........................	**InvalidDnDOperationException** ()
✳	public.........................	**InvalidDnDOperationException** (String msg)

InvalidKeyException	java.security

```
Object
└─Throwable ------------------------- java.io.Serializable
   └─Exception
      └─GeneralSecurityException
```
	└─KeyException
1.2	
1.1	
1.1	└─InvalidKeyException

✳	public.........................	**InvalidKeyException** ()
✳	public.........................	**InvalidKeyException** (String msg)

InvalidKeySpecException	java.security.spec

```
Object
└─Throwable ------------------------- java.io.Serializable
   └─Exception
      └─java.security.GeneralSecurityException
```
	└─InvalidKeySpecException
1.2	
1.2	

✳	public.........................	**InvalidKeySpecException** ()
✳	public.........................	**InvalidKeySpecException** (String msg)

Class   *Interface*   —extends   - - -implements   ○ abstract   ● final   △ static   ▲ static final   ✳ constructor   x x—inherited   x **x**—declared   **x x**—overridden

I

InvalidName❶	org.omg.CosNaming.NamingContextPackage

```
     Object
     └ Throwable --------------------------- java.io.Serializable
        └ Exception
```
1.2 ○   `└ org.omg.CORBA.UserException ------- org.omg.CORBA.portable.IDLEntity (java.io.Serializable)`
1.2 ●   `└ InvalidName --------------------- org.omg.CORBA.portable.IDLEntity (java.io.Serializable)`

*	public.........................	**InvalidName** ()

InvalidName❷	org.omg.CORBA.ORBPackage

```
     Object
     └ Throwable --------------------------- java.io.Serializable
        └ Exception
```
1.2 ○   `└ org.omg.CORBA.UserException ------- org.omg.CORBA.portable.IDLEntity (java.io.Serializable)`
1.2   `└ InvalidName`

*	public.........................	**InvalidName** ()
*	public.........................	**InvalidName** (String reason)

InvalidNameHelper	org.omg.CosNaming.NamingContextPackage

```
     Object
```
1.2   `└ InvalidNameHelper`

△	public static ...... InvalidName	**extract** (org.omg.CORBA.Any a)
△	public static .... String	**id** ()
△	public static ....void	**insert** (org.omg.CORBA.Any a, InvalidName that)
△	public static ...... InvalidName	**read** (org.omg.CORBA.portable.InputStream in)
△	public static synchronized .... org.omg.CORBA.TypeCode	**type** ()
△	public static ....void	**write** (org.omg.CORBA.portable.OutputStream out, InvalidName that)

InvalidNameHolder	org.omg.CosNaming.NamingContextPackage

```
     Object
```
1.2 ● `└ InvalidNameHolder --------------------- org.omg.CORBA.portable.Streamable` [1]

1	public......................void	**_read** (org.omg.CORBA.portable.InputStream in)
1	public......................... ... org.omg.CORBA.TypeCode	**_type** ()
1	public......................void	**_write** (org.omg.CORBA.portable.OutputStream out)
*	public.........................	**InvalidNameHolder** ()
*	public.........................	**InvalidNameHolder** (InvalidName __arg)
	public............. InvalidName	**value**

InvalidObjectException	java.io

```
     Object
     └ Throwable --------------------------- Serializable
        └ Exception
           └ IOException
```
1.1 ○   `└ ObjectStreamException`
1.1   `└ InvalidObjectException`

*	public.........................	**InvalidObjectException** (String reason)

InvalidParameterException	java.security
	P⁰

```
     Object
     └ Throwable --------------------------- java.io.Serializable
        └ Exception
           └ RuntimeException
              └ IllegalArgumentException
```
1.1   `└ InvalidParameterException`

I

Classes

InvalidParameterException

✳	public		**InvalidParameterException** ()
✳	public		**InvalidParameterException** (String msg)

InvalidParameterSpecException java.security.spec

Object
└ Throwable - *java.io.Serializable*
    └ Exception
1.2   └ java.security.GeneralSecurityException
1.2   └ InvalidParameterSpecException

✳	public		**InvalidParameterSpecException** ()
✳	public		**InvalidParameterSpecException** (String msg)

InvalidSeq org.omg.CORBA.DynAnyPackage

Object
└ Throwable - *java.io.Serializable*
    └ Exception
1.2 ○   └ org.omg.CORBA.UserException - - - - - - - *org.omg.CORBA.portable.IDLEntity* (*java.io.Serializable*)
1.2 ●   └ InvalidSeq

✳	public		**InvalidSeq** ()
✳	public		**InvalidSeq** (String reason)

InvalidValue org.omg.CORBA.DynAnyPackage

Object
└ Throwable - *java.io.Serializable*
    └ Exception
1.2 ○   └ org.omg.CORBA.UserException - - - - - - - *org.omg.CORBA.portable.IDLEntity* (*java.io.Serializable*)
1.2 ●   └ InvalidValue

✳	public		**InvalidValue** ()
✳	public		**InvalidValue** (String reason)

InvocationEvent java.awt.event

P

Object
1.1   └ java.util.EventObject [1] - - - - - - - - - - - - - - - - - - - *java.io.Serializable*
1.1 ○   └ java.awt.AWTEvent [2]
1.2   └ InvocationEvent - *java.awt.ActiveEvent* [3]

		protected	boolean	**catchExceptions**
	2	protected	void	consume ()
	2	protected	boolean	consumed
	3	public	void	**dispatch** ()
	2	protected	void	finalize () throws Throwable
		public	Exception	**getException** ()
	2	public	int	getID ()
	1	public	Object	getSource ()
	2	protected	int	id
▲		public static final	int	**INVOCATION_DEFAULT** = 1200
▲		public static final	int	**INVOCATION_FIRST** = 1200
▲		public static final	int	**INVOCATION_LAST** = 1200
✳		public		**InvocationEvent** (Object source, *Runnable* runnable)
✳		public		**InvocationEvent** (Object source, *Runnable* runnable, Object notifier, boolean catchExceptions)
✳		protected		**InvocationEvent** (Object source, int id, *Runnable* runnable, Object notifier, boolean catchExceptions)
	2	protected	boolean	isConsumed ()
		protected	Object	**notifier**
	2	public	String	**paramString** ()
		protected	*Runnable*	**runnable**
	1	protected transient	Object	source
	2	public	String	toString ()

Class   *Interface*   —extends   - - -implements   ○ abstract   ● final   △ static   ▲ static final   ✳ constructor   x x—inherited   x **x**—declared   **x x**—overridden

InvocationTargetException — java.lang.reflect

P

```
Object
 └Throwable 1 - - - - - - - - - - - - - - - - - - - - - - - - - java.io.Serializable
    └Exception
1.1     └InvocationTargetException
```

	public..............Throwable	**getTargetException** ()
✳	protected.......................	**InvocationTargetException** ()
✳	public...........................	**InvocationTargetException** (Throwable target)
✳	public...........................	**InvocationTargetException** (Throwable target, String s)
1	public....................**void**	**printStackTrace** ()
1	public....................**void**	**printStackTrace** (java.io.PrintStream ps)
1	public....................**void**	**printStackTrace** (java.io.PrintWriter pw)

InvokeHandler — org.omg.CORBA.portable

I

1.2 *InvokeHandler*

```
public............OutputStream  _invoke (String method, InputStream input, ResponseHandler handler)
                       throws org.omg.CORBA.SystemException
```

IOException — java.io

```
Object
 └Throwable - - - - - - - - - - - - - - - - - - - - - - - - - Serializable
    └Exception
      └IOException
```

✳	public...........................	**IOException** ()
✳	public...........................	**IOException** (String s)

IRObject — org.omg.CORBA

1.2 *IRObject* ———————————————— *Object 1, org.omg.CORBA.portable.IDLEntity (java.io.Serializable)*

```
1  13 inherited members from Object not shown
   public............DefinitionKind  def_kind ()
   public.....................void  destroy ()
```

IstringHelper — org.omg.CosNaming

```
Object
1.2 └IstringHelper
```

△	public static ....String	**extract** (org.omg.CORBA.Any a)
△	public static ....String	**id** ()
△	public static ....void	**insert** (org.omg.CORBA.Any a, String that)
△	public static ....String	**read** (org.omg.CORBA.portable.InputStream in)
△	public static synchronized .... org.omg.CORBA.TypeCode	**type** ()
△	public static ....void	**write** (org.omg.CORBA.portable.OutputStream out, String that)

ItemEvent — java.awt.event

P

```
Object
1.1 └java.util.EventObject 1 - - - - - - - - - - - - - - - - - - - java.io.Serializable
1.1 O   └java.awt.AWTEvent 2
1.1       └ItemEvent
```

2	protected...................void	consume ()
2	protected.............. boolean	consumed
▲	public static final.............int	**DESELECTED** = 2
2	protected...................void	finalize () throws Throwable
2	public.......................int	getID ()
	public....................Object	**getItem** ()
	public . *java.awt.ItemSelectable*	**getItemSelectable** ()
1	public....................Object	getSource ()
	public.......................int	**getStateChange** ()

Classes

417

ItemEvent

2	protected	int	id
2	protected	boolean	isConsumed ()
▲	public static final	int	**ITEM_FIRST** = 701
▲	public static final	int	**ITEM_LAST** = 701
▲	public static final	int	**ITEM_STATE_CHANGED** = 701
✳	public		**ItemEvent** (*java.awt.ItemSelectable* source, int id, Object item, int stateChange)
2	public	String	**paramString** ()
▲	public static final	int	**SELECTED** = 1
1	protected transient	Object	source
2	public	String	toString ()

ItemListener   java.awt.event

P

1.1 *ItemListener ————————————————————— java.util.EventListener*

	public	void	**itemStateChanged** (ItemEvent e)

ItemSelectable   java.awt

P

1.1 *ItemSelectable*

	public	void	**addItemListener** (*java.awt.event.ItemListener* l)
	public	Object[]	**getSelectedObjects** ()
	public	void	**removeItemListener** (*java.awt.event.ItemListener* l)

Iterator   java.util

P

1.2 *Iterator*

	public	boolean	**hasNext** ()
	public	Object	**next** ()
	public	void	**remove** ()

JApplet   javax.swing

Object
  ○ └java.awt.Component [1] - *java.awt.image.ImageObserver*, *java.awt.MenuContainer*,
                                                                                     java.io.Serializable
      └java.awt.Container [2]
        └java.awt.Panel [3]
          └java.applet.Applet [4]
1.2   └JApplet - *javax.accessibility.Accessible* [5], *RootPaneContainer* [6]

1	*133 inherited members from java.awt.Component not shown*		
2	*46 inherited members from java.awt.Container not shown*		
	protected javax.accessibility ↩		**accessibleContext**
	.AccessibleContext		
2	protected	**void**	**addImpl** (java.awt.Component comp, Object constraints, int index)
3	public	void	addNotify ()
	protected	JRootPane	**createRootPane** ()
4	public	void	destroy ()
5	public	javax.accessibility ↩	**getAccessibleContext** ()
	.AccessibleContext		
4	public		getAppletContext ()
		java.applet.AppletContext	
4	public	String	getAppletInfo ()
4	public	*java.applet.AudioClip*	getAudioClip (java.net.URL url)
4	public	*java.applet.AudioClip*	getAudioClip (java.net.URL url, String name)
4	public	java.net.URL	getCodeBase ()
6	public	java.awt.Container	**getContentPane** ()
4	public	java.net.URL	getDocumentBase ()
6	public	java.awt.Component	**getGlassPane** ()
4	public	java.awt.Image	getImage (java.net.URL url)
4	public	java.awt.Image	getImage (java.net.URL url, String name)
	public	JMenuBar	**getJMenuBar** ()
6	public	JLayeredPane	**getLayeredPane** ()
4	public	java.util.Locale	getLocale ()
4	public	String	getParameter (String name)

Class   *Interface*   —extends   - - -implements   ○ abstract   ● final   △ static   ▲ static final   ✳ constructor   x x—inherited   x **x**—declared   **x x**—overridden

	4	public	String[][]	getParameterInfo ()
	6	public	JRootPane	**getRootPane** ()
	4	public	void	init ()
	4	public	boolean	isActive ()
		protected	boolean	**isRootPaneCheckingEnabled** ()
✱		public		**JApplet** ()
▲	4	public static final		newAudioClip (java.net.URL url)
		java.applet.AudioClip		
	2	protected	**String**	**paramString** ()
	4	public	void	play (java.net.URL url)
	4	public	void	play (java.net.URL url, String name)
	1	protected	**void**	**processKeyEvent** (java.awt.event.KeyEvent e)
	4	public	void	resize (java.awt.Dimension d)
	4	public	void	resize (int width, int height)
		protected	JRootPane	**rootPane**
		protected	boolean	**rootPaneCheckingEnabled**
	6	public	void	**setContentPane** (java.awt.Container contentPane)
	6	public	void	**setGlassPane** (java.awt.Component glassPane)
		public	void	**setJMenuBar** (JMenuBar menuBar)
	6	public	void	**setLayeredPane** (JLayeredPane layeredPane)
	2	public	**void**	**setLayout** (_java.awt.LayoutManager_ manager)
		protected	void	**setRootPane** (JRootPane root)
		protected	void	**setRootPaneCheckingEnabled** (boolean enabled)
●	4	public final	void	setStub (_java.applet.AppletStub_ stub)
	4	public	void	showStatus (String msg)
	4	public	void	start ()
	4	public	void	stop ()
	2	public	**void**	**update** (java.awt.Graphics g)

JApplet.AccessibleJApplet — protected — javax.swing

Object
1.2 └─ javax.accessibility.AccessibleContext [1]
1.2   └─ JApplet.AccessibleJApplet - - - - - - - - - - - - - _java.io.Serializable, javax.accessibility.AccessibleComponent_ [2]

	1	_25 inherited members from javax.accessibility.AccessibleContext not shown_		
✱		protected		**AccessibleJApplet** ()
	2	public	void	**addFocusListener** (_java.awt.event.FocusListener_ l)
	2	public	boolean	**contains** (java.awt.Point p)
	2	public		**getAccessibleAt** (java.awt.Point p)
		. _javax.accessibility.Accessible_		
	1	public	_javax↩_	**getAccessibleChild** (int i)
		.accessibility.Accessible		
	1	public	**int**	**getAccessibleChildrenCount** ()
	1	public	_javax.accessibility↩_	**getAccessibleComponent** ()
		.AccessibleComponent		
	1	public	**int**	**getAccessibleIndexInParent** ()
	1	public	_javax↩_	**getAccessibleParent** ()
		.accessibility.Accessible		
	1	public	_javax↩_	**getAccessibleRole** ()
		.accessibility.AccessibleRole		
	1	public	_javax.accessibility↩_	**getAccessibleStateSet** ()
		.AccessibleStateSet		
	2	public	java.awt.Color	**getBackground** ()
	2	public	java.awt.Rectangle	**getBounds** ()
	2	public	java.awt.Cursor	**getCursor** ()
	2	public	java.awt.Font	**getFont** ()
	2	public	java.awt.FontMetrics	**getFontMetrics** (java.awt.Font f)
	2	public	java.awt.Color	**getForeground** ()
	1	public	**java.util.Locale**	**getLocale** ()
	2	public	java.awt.Point	**getLocation** ()
	2	public	java.awt.Point	**getLocationOnScreen** ()
	2	public	java.awt.Dimension	**getSize** ()
	2	public	boolean	**isEnabled** ()
	2	public	boolean	**isFocusTraversable** ()
	2	public	boolean	**isShowing** ()
	2	public	boolean	**isVisible** ()
	2	public	void	**removeFocusListener** (_java.awt.event.FocusListener_ l)
	2	public	void	**requestFocus** ()
	2	public	void	**setBackground** (java.awt.Color c)
	2	public	void	**setBounds** (java.awt.Rectangle r)
	2	public	void	**setCursor** (java.awt.Cursor cursor)

J

Classes

JApplet.AccessibleJApplet

2	public	void	**setEnabled**	(boolean b)
2	public	void	**setFont**	(java.awt.Font f)
2	public	void	**setForeground**	(java.awt.Color c)
2	public	void	**setLocation**	(java.awt.Point p)
2	public	void	**setSize**	(java.awt.Dimension d)
2	public	void	**setVisible**	(boolean b)

JarEntry
java.util.jar

```
Object
1.1  └java.util.zip.ZipEntry 1 - - - - - - - - - - - - - - - - - - - - java.util.zip.ZipConstants, Cloneable
1.2      └JarEntry
```

1	public	Object	clone	()
	public	Attributes	**getAttributes**	() throws java.io.IOException
	public		**getCertificates**	()
	..java.security.cert.Certificate[]			
1	public	String	getComment	()
1	public	long	getCompressedSize	()
1	public	long	getCrc	()
1	public	byte[]	getExtra	()
1	public	int	getMethod	()
1	public	String	getName	()
1	public	long	getSize	()
1	public	long	getTime	()
1	public	int	hashCode	()
1	public	boolean	isDirectory	()
✳	public		**JarEntry**	(String name)
✳	public		**JarEntry**	(JarEntry je)
✳	public		**JarEntry**	(java.util.zip.ZipEntry ze)
1	public	void	setComment	(String comment)
1	public	void	setCompressedSize	(long csize)
1	public	void	setCrc	(long crc)
1	public	void	setExtra	(byte[] extra)
1	public	void	setMethod	(int method)
1	public	void	setSize	(long size)
1	public	void	setTime	(long time)
1	public	String	toString	()

JarException
java.util.jar

```
Object
 └Throwable - - - - - - - - - - - - - - - - - - - - - - - - - - - java.io.Serializable
     └Exception
         └java.io.IOException
1.1          └java.util.zip.ZipException
1.2              └JarException
```

✳	public	**JarException**	()
✳	public	**JarException**	(String s)

JarFile
java.util.jar

```
Object
1.1  └java.util.zip.ZipFile 1 - - - - - - - - - - - - - - - - - - - - java.util.zip.ZipConstants
1.2      └JarFile
```

1	public	void	close	() throws java.io.IOException
1	public	*java.util.Enumeration*	**entries**	()
1	public	*java.util.zip.ZipEntry*	**getEntry**	(String name)
1	public synchronized		**getInputStream**	(java.util.zip.ZipEntry ze) throws java.io.IOException
		java.io.InputStream		
	public	JarEntry	**getJarEntry**	(String name)
	public	Manifest	**getManifest**	() throws java.io.IOException
1	public	String	getName	()
✳	public		**JarFile**	(java.io.File file) throws java.io.IOException
✳	public		**JarFile**	(String name) throws java.io.IOException
✳	public		**JarFile**	(java.io.File file, boolean verify) throws java.io.IOException

---

Class   *Interface*   —extends   - - -implements   ○ abstract   ● final   △ static   ▲ static final   ✳ constructor   x x—inherited   x **x**—declared   **x x**—overridden

*	public	**JarFile** (String name, boolean verify) throws java.io.IOException
▲	public static final .... String	**MANIFEST_NAME** = "META-INF/MANIFEST.MF"
1	public .... int	size ()

JarInputStream java.util.jar

```
Object
○  └java.io.InputStream
        └java.io.FilterInputStream 1
1.1         └java.util.zip.InflaterInputStream 2
1.1             └java.util.zip.ZipInputStream 3 - - - - - - - - java.util.zip.ZipConstants
1.2                 └JarInputStream
```

3	public .... int	available () throws java.io.IOException
2	protected .... byte[]	buf
3	public .... void	close () throws java.io.IOException
3	public .... void	closeEntry () throws java.io.IOException
3	protected	**createZipEntry** (String name)
	.... **java.util.zip.ZipEntry**	
2	protected .... void	fill () throws java.io.IOException
	public .... Manifest	**getManifest** ()
3	public ... **java.util.zip.ZipEntry**	**getNextEntry** () throws java.io.IOException
	public .... JarEntry	**getNextJarEntry** () throws java.io.IOException
1	protected .. java.io.InputStream	in
2	protected ...java.util.zip.Inflater	inf
*	public	**JarInputStream** (java.io.InputStream in) throws java.io.IOException
*	public	**JarInputStream** (java.io.InputStream in, boolean verify) throws java.io.IOException
2	protected	len
1	public synchronized ......void	mark (int readlimit)
1	public .... boolean	markSupported ()
2	public .... int	read () throws java.io.IOException
1	public .... int	read (byte[] b) throws java.io.IOException
3	public .... **int read** (byte[] b, int off, int len) throws java.io.IOException
1	public synchronized ......void	reset () throws java.io.IOException
3	public .... long	skip (long n) throws java.io.IOException

JarOutputStream java.util.jar

```
Object
○  └java.io.OutputStream
        └java.io.FilterOutputStream 1
1.1         └java.util.zip.DeflaterOutputStream 2
1.1             └java.util.zip.ZipOutputStream 3 - - - - - - java.util.zip.ZipConstants
1.2                 └JarOutputStream
```

2	protected .... byte[]	buf
3	public .... void	close () throws java.io.IOException
3	public .... void	closeEntry () throws java.io.IOException
2	protected . java.util.zip.Deflater	def
2	protected .... void	deflate () throws java.io.IOException
3	public .... void	finish () throws java.io.IOException
1	public .... void	flush () throws java.io.IOException
*	public	**JarOutputStream** (java.io.OutputStream out) throws java.io.IOException
*	public	**JarOutputStream** (java. io. OutputStream out, Manifest man)
		throws java.io.IOException
1	protected java.io.OutputStream	out
3	public .... **void putNextEntry** (java.util.zip.ZipEntry ze) throws java.io.IOException
3	public .... void	setComment (String comment)
3	public .... void	setLevel (int level)
3	public .... void	setMethod (int method)
1	public .... void	write (byte[] b) throws java.io.IOException
2	public .... void	write (int b) throws java.io.IOException
3	public synchronized ......void	write (byte[] b, int off, int len) throws java.io.IOException

JarURLConnection java.net

```
     Object                                                          P
○  └URLConnection 1
1.2 ○     └JarURLConnection
```

JarURLConnection

	1	protected	boolean	allowUserInteraction
○	1	public abstract	void	connect () throws java.io.IOException
	1	protected	boolean	connected
	1	protected	boolean	doInput
	1	protected	boolean	doOutput
	1	public	boolean	getAllowUserInteraction ()
		public	java.util.jar.Attributes	**getAttributes** () throws java.io.IOException
		public	java.security.cert.Certificate[]	**getCertificates** () throws java.io.IOException
	1	public	Object	getContent () throws java.io.IOException
	1	public	String	getContentEncoding ()
	1	public	int	getContentLength ()
	1	public	String	getContentType ()
	1	public	long	getDate ()
△	1	public static	boolean	getDefaultAllowUserInteraction ()
△	1	public static	String	getDefaultRequestProperty (String key)
	1	public	boolean	getDefaultUseCaches ()
	1	public	boolean	getDoInput ()
	1	public	boolean	getDoOutput ()
	1	public	String	**getEntryName** ()
	1	public	long	getExpiration ()
△	1	public static	*FileNameMap*	getFileNameMap ()
	1	public	String	getHeaderField (int n)
	1	public	String	getHeaderField (String name)
	1	public	long	getHeaderFieldDate (String name, long Default)
	1	public	int	getHeaderFieldInt (String name, int Default)
	1	public	String	getHeaderFieldKey (int n)
	1	public	long	getIfModifiedSince ()
	1	public	java.io.InputStream	getInputStream () throws java.io.IOException
		public	java.util.jar.JarEntry	**getJarEntry** () throws java.io.IOException
○		public abstract	java.util.jar.JarFile	**getJarFile** () throws java.io.IOException
		public	URL	**getJarFileURL** ()
	1	public	long	getLastModified ()
		public	java.util.jar.Attributes	**getMainAttributes** () throws java.io.IOException
		public	java.util.jar.Manifest	**getManifest** () throws java.io.IOException
	1	public	java.io.OutputStream	getOutputStream () throws java.io.IOException
	1	public	java.security.Permission	getPermission () throws java.io.IOException
	1	public	String	getRequestProperty (String key)
	1	public	URL	getURL ()
	1	public	boolean	getUseCaches ()
△	1	protected static	String	guessContentTypeFromName (String fname)
△	1	public static	String	guessContentTypeFromStream (java.io.InputStream is) throws java.io.IOException
	1	protected	long	ifModifiedSince
		protected	URLConnection	**jarFileURLConnection**
✳		protected		**JarURLConnection** (URL url) throws MalformedURLException
	1	public	void	setAllowUserInteraction (boolean allowuserinteraction)
△	1	public static synchronized	void	setContentHandlerFactory (*ContentHandlerFactory* fac)
△	1	public static	void	setDefaultAllowUserInteraction (boolean defaultallowuserinteraction)
△	1	public static	void	setDefaultRequestProperty (String key, String value)
	1	public	void	setDefaultUseCaches (boolean defaultusecaches)
	1	public	void	setDoInput (boolean doinput)
	1	public	void	setDoOutput (boolean dooutput)
△	1	public static	void	setFileNameMap (*FileNameMap* map)
	1	public	void	setIfModifiedSince (long ifmodifiedsince)
	1	public	void	setRequestProperty (String key, String value)
	1	public	void	setUseCaches (boolean usecaches)
	1	public	String	toString ()
	1	protected	URL	url
	1	protected	boolean	useCaches

Class   *Interface*   —extends   - - -implements   ○ abstract   ● final   △ static   ▲ static final   ✳ constructor   x x—inherited   x **x**—declared   **x x**—overridden

422

JButton | javax.swing

```
            Object
  O         └java.awt.Component¹ ------------------ java.awt.image.ImageObserver, java.awt.MenuContainer,
                                                     java.io.Serializable
            └java.awt.Container²
1.2 O        └JComponent³ --------------------- java.io.Serializable
1.2 O         └AbstractButton⁴ ------------- java.awt.ItemSelectable, SwingConstants
1.2            └JButton -------------------- javax.accessibility.Accessible
```

1	*111 inherited members from java.awt.Component not shown*		
2	*39 inherited members from java.awt.Container not shown*		
3	*111 inherited members from JComponent not shown*		
4	*91 inherited members from AbstractButton not shown*		
3	public...	**javax.accessibility ↵ .AccessibleContext**	**getAccessibleContext** ()
3	public..................	**String**	**getUIClassID** ()
	public.................	boolean	**isDefaultButton** ()
	public.................	boolean	**isDefaultCapable** ()
*	public.......................		**JButton** ()
*	public.......................		**JButton** (String text)
*	public.......................		**JButton** (*Icon* icon)
*	public.......................		**JButton** (String text, *Icon* icon)
4	protected..............	**String**	**paramString** ()
	public....................void		**setDefaultCapable** (boolean defaultCapable)
4	public....................	**void**	**updateUI** ()

JButton.AccessibleJButton | protected | javax.swing

```
            Object
1.2 O       └javax.accessibility.AccessibleContext¹
1.2 O        └JComponent.AccessibleJComponent² ---- java.io.Serializable, javax.accessibility.AccessibleComponent
1.2 O         └AbstractButton↵ ------------------- javax.accessibility.AccessibleAction,
                .AccessibleAbstractButton³            javax.accessibility.AccessibleValue
1.2            └JButton.AccessibleJButton
```

1	*19 inherited members from javax.accessibility.AccessibleContext not shown*		
2	*38 inherited members from JComponent.AccessibleJComponent not shown*		
*	protected......................		**AccessibleJButton** ()
3	public.................	boolean	doAccessibleAction (int i)
3	public...................	*javax↵ .accessibility.AccessibleAction*	getAccessibleAction ()
3	public.......................int		getAccessibleActionCount ()
3	public...................	String	getAccessibleActionDescription (int i)
3	public...................	String	getAccessibleName ()
2	public................	**javax↵ .accessibility.AccessibleRole**	**getAccessibleRole** ()
3	public....	javax.accessibility↵ .AccessibleStateSet	getAccessibleStateSet ()
3	public.................	*javax↵ .accessibility.AccessibleValue*	getAccessibleValue ()
3	public.................	Number	getCurrentAccessibleValue ()
3	public.................	Number	getMaximumAccessibleValue ()
3	public.................	Number	getMinimumAccessibleValue ()
3	public.................	boolean	setCurrentAccessibleValue (Number n)

JCheckBox | javax.swing

```
            Object
  O         └java.awt.Component¹ ------------------ java.awt.image.ImageObserver, java.awt.MenuContainer,
                                                     java.io.Serializable
            └java.awt.Container²
1.2 O        └JComponent³ --------------------- java.io.Serializable
1.2 O         └AbstractButton⁴ ------------- java.awt.ItemSelectable, SwingConstants
1.2            └JToggleButton⁵ --------------- javax.accessibility.Accessible
1.2             └JCheckBox ---------------- javax.accessibility.Accessible
```

1	*111 inherited members from java.awt.Component not shown*
2	*39 inherited members from java.awt.Container not shown*
3	*111 inherited members from JComponent not shown*

JCheckBox

4	*91 inherited members from AbstractButton not shown*		
5	public... **javax.accessibility** ↩	**getAccessibleContext** ()	
	.AccessibleContext		
5	public.................... **String**	**getUIClassID** ()	
*	public...........................	**JCheckBox** ()	
*	public...........................	**JCheckBox** (String text)	
*	public...........................	**JCheckBox** (*Icon* icon)	
*	public...........................	**JCheckBox** (String text, *Icon* icon)	
*	public...........................	**JCheckBox** (String text, boolean selected)	
*	public...........................	**JCheckBox** (*Icon* icon, boolean selected)	
*	public...........................	**JCheckBox** (String text, *Icon* icon, boolean selected)	
5	protected .... **String**	**paramString** ()	
5	public.................... **void**	**updateUI** ()	

JCheckBox.AccessibleJCheckBox   protected   javax.swing

```
Object
1.2 ○  └javax.accessibility.AccessibleContext 1
1.2 ○    └JComponent.AccessibleJComponent 2 - - - - java.io.Serializable, javax.accessibility.AccessibleComponent
1.2 ○      └AbstractButton ↩ - - - - - - - - - - - - - - - - - - - javax.accessibility.AccessibleAction,
              .AccessibleAbstractButton 3                         javax.accessibility.AccessibleValue
1.2        └JToggleButton ↩ - - - - - - - - - - - - - - - java.awt.event.ItemListener (java.util.EventListener)
                .AccessibleJToggleButton 4
1.2          └JCheckBox.AccessibleJCheckBox
```

1	*19 inherited members from javax.accessibility.AccessibleContext not shown*		
2	*38 inherited members from JComponent.AccessibleJComponent not shown*		
*	protected	**AccessibleJCheckBox** ()	
3	public................. boolean	doAccessibleAction (int i)	
3	public....................*javax* ↩	getAccessibleAction ()	
	.accessibility.AccessibleAction		
3	public.......................int	getAccessibleActionCount ()	
3	public....................String	getAccessibleActionDescription (int i)	
3	public....................String	getAccessibleName ()	
4	public................. **javax** ↩	**getAccessibleRole** ()	
	.accessibility.AccessibleRole		
3	public.... javax.accessibility ↩	getAccessibleStateSet ()	
	.AccessibleStateSet		
3	public...................*javax* ↩	getAccessibleValue ()	
	.accessibility.AccessibleValue		
3	public................. Number	getCurrentAccessibleValue ()	
3	public................. Number	getMaximumAccessibleValue ()	
3	public................. Number	getMinimumAccessibleValue ()	
4	public.....................void	itemStateChanged (java.awt.event.ItemEvent e)	
3	public................. boolean	setCurrentAccessibleValue (Number n)	

JCheckBoxMenuItem   javax.swing

```
Object
  ○  └java.awt.Component 1 - - - - - - - - - - - - - - - - - - - - java.awt.image.ImageObserver, java.awt.MenuContainer,
                                                                    java.io.Serializable
        └java.awt.Container 2
1.2 ○      └JComponent 3 - - - - - - - - - - - - - - - - - - - - - java.io.Serializable
1.2 ○        └AbstractButton 4 - - - - - - - - - - - - - - - - - - java.awt.ItemSelectable, SwingConstants
1.2          └JMenuItem 5 - - - - - - - - - - - - - - - - - - - javax.accessibility.Accessible, MenuElement
1.2            └JCheckBoxMenuItem - - - - - - - - - - - SwingConstants, javax.accessibility.Accessible
```

1	*111 inherited members from java.awt.Component not shown*		
2	*39 inherited members from java.awt.Container not shown*		
3	*110 inherited members from JComponent not shown*		
4	*88 inherited members from AbstractButton not shown*		
5	public.....................void	addMenuDragMouseListener (*javax.swing.event.MenuDragMouseListener* l)	
5	public.....................void	addMenuKeyListener (*javax.swing.event.MenuKeyListener* l)	
5	protected ....void	fireMenuDragMouseDragged (javax.swing.event.MenuDragMouseEvent event)	
5	protected ....void	fireMenuDragMouseEntered (javax.swing.event.MenuDragMouseEvent event)	
5	protected ....void	fireMenuDragMouseExited (javax.swing.event.MenuDragMouseEvent event)	
5	protected ....void	fireMenuDragMouseReleased (javax.swing.event.MenuDragMouseEvent event)	
5	protected ....void	fireMenuKeyPressed (javax.swing.event.MenuKeyEvent event)	

Class   *Interface*   —extends   - - -implements   ○ abstract   ● final   △ static   ▲ static final   ✱ constructor   x x—inherited   x **x**—declared   **x x**—overridden

5	protected	void	fireMenuKeyReleased (javax.swing.event.MenuKeyEvent event)
5	protected	void	fireMenuKeyTyped (javax.swing.event.MenuKeyEvent event)
5	public	KeyStroke	getAccelerator ()
5	public	**javax.accessibility ↩**	**getAccessibleContext** ()
		.AccessibleContext	
5	public	java.awt.Component	getComponent ()
4	public synchronized	**Object[]**	**getSelectedObjects** ()
	public	boolean	getState ()
5	public	*MenuElement[]*	getSubElements ()
5	public	**String**	**getUIClassID** ()
5	protected	**void**	**init** (String text, *Icon* icon)
5	public	boolean	isArmed ()
*	public		**JCheckBoxMenuItem** ()
*	public		**JCheckBoxMenuItem** (String text)
*	public		**JCheckBoxMenuItem** (*Icon* icon)
*	public		**JCheckBoxMenuItem** (String text, *Icon* icon)
*	public		**JCheckBoxMenuItem** (String text, boolean b)
*	public		**JCheckBoxMenuItem** (String text, *Icon* icon, boolean b)
5	public	void	menuSelectionChanged (boolean isIncluded)
5	protected	**String**	**paramString** ()
5	public	void	processKeyEvent (java.awt.event.KeyEvent e, *MenuElement[]* path, MenuSelectionManager manager)
5	public	void	processMenuDragMouseEvent (javax.swing.event.MenuDragMouseEvent e)
5	public	void	processMenuKeyEvent (javax.swing.event.MenuKeyEvent e)
5	public	void	processMouseEvent (java.awt.event.MouseEvent e, *MenuElement[]* path, MenuSelectionManager manager)
5	public	void	removeMenuDragMouseListener (*javax.swing.event.MenuDragMouseListener* l)
5	public	void	removeMenuKeyListener (*javax.swing.event.MenuKeyListener* l)
3	public	**void**	**requestFocus** ()
5	public	void	setAccelerator (KeyStroke keyStroke)
5	public	void	setArmed (boolean b)
5	public	void	setEnabled (boolean b)
	public synchronized	void	**setState** (boolean b)
5	public	void	setUI (javax.swing.plaf.MenuItemUI ui)
5	public	**void**	**updateUI** ()

J

JCheckBoxMenuItem.AccessibleJCheckBoxMenuItem　　　protected　　　javax.swing

```
     Object
1.2 ○ └─javax.accessibility.AccessibleContext 1
1.2 ○    └─JComponent.AccessibleJComponent 2 - - - - java.io.Serializable, javax.accessibility.AccessibleComponent
1.2 ○       └─AbstractButton ↩ - - - - - - - - - - - - - - - - javax.accessibility.AccessibleAction,
                 .AccessibleAbstractButton 3                    javax.accessibility.AccessibleValue
1.2          └─JMenuItem.AccessibleJMenuItem 4 - - - javax.swing.event.ChangeListener (java.util.EventListener)
1.2             └─JCheckBoxMenuItem ↩
                    .AccessibleJCheckBoxMenuItem
```

1	*19 inherited members from javax.accessibility.AccessibleContext not shown*		
2	*38 inherited members from JComponent.AccessibleJComponent not shown*		
*	protected		**AccessibleJCheckBoxMenuItem** ()
3	public	boolean	doAccessibleAction (int i)
3	public	*javax ↩*	getAccessibleAction ()
		.accessibility.AccessibleAction	
3	public	int	getAccessibleActionCount ()
3	public	String	getAccessibleActionDescription (int i)
3	public	String	getAccessibleName ()
4	public	**javax ↩**	**getAccessibleRole** ()
		.accessibility.AccessibleRole	
3	public	javax.accessibility ↩	getAccessibleStateSet ()
		.AccessibleStateSet	
3	public	*javax ↩*	getAccessibleValue ()
		.accessibility.AccessibleValue	
3	public	Number	getCurrentAccessibleValue ()
3	public	Number	getMaximumAccessibleValue ()
3	public	Number	getMinimumAccessibleValue ()
3	public	boolean	setCurrentAccessibleValue (Number n)
4	public	void	stateChanged (javax.swing.event.ChangeEvent e)

Classes

JColorChooser		javax.swing

Object
 O └java.awt.Component[1] - - - - - - - - - - - - - - - - - - - *java.awt.image.ImageObserver*, *java.awt.MenuContainer*,
                                                               java.io.Serializable

       └java.awt.Container[2]
 1.2 O   └JComponent[3] - - - - - - - - - - - - - - - - - - - *java.io.Serializable*
 1.2   └JColorChooser - - - - - - - - - - - - - - - - - - - *javax.accessibility.Accessible*

1			*111 inherited members from java.awt.Component not shown*
2			*39 inherited members from java.awt.Container not shown*
3			*112 inherited members from JComponent not shown*
3	protected		**accessibleContext**
	. . . . **javax.accessibility** ↵		
	.AccessibleContext		
	public . . . . void		**addChooserPanel** (javax.swing.colorchooser.AbstractColorChooserPanel panel)
▲	public static final . . . . String		**CHOOSER_PANELS_PROPERTY** = "chooserPanels"
△	public static . . . . JDialog		**createDialog** (java. awt. Component c, String title, boolean modal,
			JColorChooser chooserPane, *java.awt.event.ActionListener* okListener,
			java.awt.event.ActionListener cancelListener)
3	public . . . **javax.accessibility** ↵		**getAccessibleContext** ()
	.AccessibleContext		
	public		**getChooserPanels** ()
	. . . javax.swing.colorchooser ↵		
	.AbstractColorChooserPanel[]		
	public . . . . java.awt.Color		**getColor** ()
	public . . . . JComponent		**getPreviewPanel** ()
	public		**getSelectionModel** ()
	. . . *javax.swing.colorchooser* ↵		
	.ColorSelectionModel		
	public . . . . javax ↵		**getUI** ()
	.swing.plaf.ColorChooserUI		
3	public . . . . **String**		**getUIClassID** ()
*	public		**JColorChooser** ()
*	public		**JColorChooser** (java.awt.Color initialColor)
*	public		**JColorChooser** (*javax.swing.colorchooser.ColorSelectionModel* model)
3	protected . . . . **String**		**paramString** ()
▲	public static final . . . . String		**PREVIEW_PANEL_PROPERTY** = "previewPanel"
	public		**removeChooserPanel** (javax.swing.colorchooser.AbstractColorChooserPanel
	. . . javax.swing.colorchooser ↵		panel)
	.AbstractColorChooserPanel		
▲	public static final . . . . String		**SELECTION_MODEL_PROPERTY** = "selectionModel"
	public . . . . void		**setChooserPanels** (javax.swing.colorchooser.AbstractColorChooserPanel[]
			panels)
	public . . . . void		**setColor** (int c)
	public . . . . void		**setColor** (java.awt.Color color)
	public . . . . void		**setColor** (int r, int g, int b)
	public . . . . void		**setPreviewPanel** (JComponent preview)
	public . . . . void		**setSelectionModel** (*javax.swing.colorchooser.ColorSelectionModel* newModel)
	public . . . . void		**setUI** (javax.swing.plaf.ColorChooserUI ui)
△	public static . . . . . java.awt.Color		**showDialog** (java. awt. Component component, String title,
			java.awt.Color initialColor)
3	public . . . . **void**		**updateUI** ()

JColorChooser.AccessibleJColorChooser	protected	javax.swing

Object
 1.2 O └javax.accessibility.AccessibleContext[1]
 1.2 O   └JComponent.AccessibleJComponent[2] - - - - *java.io.Serializable*, *javax.accessibility.AccessibleComponent*
 1.2   └JColorChooser ↵
                 .AccessibleJColorChooser

1			*21 inherited members from javax.accessibility.AccessibleContext not shown*
2			*40 inherited members from JComponent.AccessibleJComponent not shown*
*	protected		**AccessibleJColorChooser** ()
2	public . . . . javax ↵		**getAccessibleRole** ()
	.accessibility.AccessibleRole		

Class   *Interface*   —extends   - - -implements   O abstract   ● final   △ static   ▲ static final   ✳ constructor   x x—inherited   x **x**—declared   **x x**—overridden

```
        Object
    ○   └─java.awt.Component¹ ------------------- java.awt.image.ImageObserver, java.awt.MenuContainer,
                                                              java.io.Serializable
            └─java.awt.Container²
1.2 ○           └─JComponent³ -------------------- java.io.Serializable
1.2             └─JComboBox ------------------- java.awt.ItemSelectable⁴, javax.swing.event.ListDataListener⁵
                                                       (java.util.EventListener), java.awt.event.ActionListener⁶
                                                       (java.util.EventListener), javax.accessibility.Accessible
```

1	*111 inherited members from java.awt.Component not shown*		
2	*39 inherited members from java.awt.Container not shown*		
3	*110 inherited members from JComponent not shown*		
	protected	String	**actionCommand**
6	public	void	**actionPerformed** (java.awt.event.ActionEvent e)
	public	void	**addActionListener** (*java.awt.event.ActionListener* l)
	public	void	**addItem** (Object anObject)
4	public	void	**addItemListener** (*java.awt.event.ItemListener* aListener)
	public	void	**configureEditor** (*ComboBoxEditor* anEditor, Object anItem)
5	public	void	**contentsChanged** (javax.swing.event.ListDataEvent e)
	protected	*JComboBox↩*	**createDefaultKeySelectionManager** ()
	.KeySelectionManager		
	protected	*ComboBoxModel*	**dataModel**
	protected	*ComboBoxEditor*	**editor**
	protected	void	**fireActionEvent** ()
	protected	void	**fireItemStateChanged** (java.awt.event.ItemEvent e)
3	public	**javax.accessibility↩**	**getAccessibleContext** ()
	.AccessibleContext		
	public	String	**getActionCommand** ()
	public	*ComboBoxEditor*	**getEditor** ()
	public	Object	**getItemAt** (int index)
	public	int	**getItemCount** ()
	public	*JComboBox↩*	**getKeySelectionManager** ()
	.KeySelectionManager		
	public	int	**getMaximumRowCount** ()
	public	*ComboBoxModel*	**getModel** ()
	public	*ListCellRenderer*	**getRenderer** ()
	public	int	**getSelectedIndex** ()
	public	Object	**getSelectedItem** ()
4	public	Object[]	**getSelectedObjects** ()
	public		**getUI** ()
	. javax.swing.plaf.ComboBoxUI		
3	public	**String**	**getUIClassID** ()
	public	void	**hidePopup** ()
	public	void	**insertItemAt** (Object anObject, int index)
	protected	void	**installAncestorListener** ()
5	public	void	**intervalAdded** (javax.swing.event.ListDataEvent e)
5	public	void	**intervalRemoved** (javax.swing.event.ListDataEvent e)
	public	boolean	**isEditable** ()
	protected	boolean	**isEditable**
3	public	**boolean**	**isFocusTraversable** ()
	public	boolean	**isLightWeightPopupEnabled** ()
	public	boolean	**isPopupVisible** ()
*	public		**JComboBox** ()
*	public		**JComboBox** (Object[] items)
*	public		**JComboBox** (java.util.Vector items)
*	public		**JComboBox** (*ComboBoxModel* aModel)
	protected	*JComboBox↩*	**keySelectionManager**
	.KeySelectionManager		
	protected	boolean	**lightWeightPopupEnabled**
	protected	int	**maximumRowCount**
3	protected	**String**	**paramString** ()
3	public	**void**	**processKeyEvent** (java.awt.event.KeyEvent e)
	public	void	**removeActionListener** (*java.awt.event.ActionListener* l)
	public	void	**removeAllItems** ()
	public	void	**removeItem** (Object anObject)
	public	void	**removeItemAt** (int anIndex)
4	public	void	**removeItemListener** (*java.awt.event.ItemListener* aListener)
	protected	*ListCellRenderer*	**renderer**
	protected	void	**selectedItemChanged** ()
	protected	Object	**selectedItemReminder**
	public	boolean	**selectWithKeyChar** (char keyChar)

J

Classes

JComboBox

	public	void	**setActionCommand** (String aCommand)	
	public	void	**setEditable** (boolean aFlag)	
	public	void	**setEditor** (*ComboBoxEditor* anEditor)	
3	public	**void**	**setEnabled** (boolean b)	
	public	void	**setKeySelectionManager** (*JComboBox.KeySelectionManager* aManager)	
	public	void	**setLightWeightPopupEnabled** (boolean aFlag)	
	public	void	**setMaximumRowCount** (int count)	
	public	void	**setModel** (*ComboBoxModel* aModel)	
	public	void	**setPopupVisible** (boolean v)	
	public	void	**setRenderer** (*ListCellRenderer* aRenderer)	
	public	void	**setSelectedIndex** (int anIndex)	
	public	void	**setSelectedItem** (Object anObject)	
	public	void	**setUI** (javax.swing.plaf.ComboBoxUI ui)	
	public	void	**showPopup** ()	
3	public	**void**	**updateUI** ()	

JComboBox.AccessibleJComboBox   protected   javax.swing

Object
  └─javax.accessibility.AccessibleContext [1]   *(1.2 ○)*
      └─JComponent.AccessibleJComponent [2] - - - - *java.io.Serializable, javax.accessibility.AccessibleComponent*   *(1.2 ○)*
          └─JComboBox.AccessibleJComboBox - - - - *javax.accessibility.AccessibleAction* [3]   *(1.2)*

1	*20 inherited members from javax.accessibility.AccessibleContext not shown*		
2	*40 inherited members from JComponent.AccessibleJComponent not shown*		
✳	protected	**AccessibleJComboBox** ()	
3	public	boolean	**doAccessibleAction** (int i)
1	public... ***javax.accessibility*** ↩ ***.AccessibleAction***	**getAccessibleAction** ()	
3	public	int	**getAccessibleActionCount** ()
3	public	String	**getAccessibleActionDescription** (int i)
2	public	**javax** ↩ **.accessibility.AccessibleRole**	**getAccessibleRole** ()

JComboBox.KeySelectionManager   javax.swing

JComboBox.KeySelectionManager   *(1.2)*

	public	int	**selectionForKey** (char aKey, *ComboBoxModel* aModel)

JComponent   javax.swing

Object
  └─java.awt.Component [1] - - - - - - - - - - - - - - - - - - *java.awt.image.ImageObserver*, *java.awt.MenuContainer*,   *(○)*
                                                              java.io.Serializable
      └─java.awt.Container [2]
          └─JComponent - - - - - - - - - - - - - - - - - - - *java.io.Serializable*   *(1.2 ○)*

	protected javax.accessibility ↩ .AccessibleContext	**accessibleContext**	
2	public.... java.awt.Component	add (java.awt.Component comp)	
1	public synchronized .... void	add (java.awt.PopupMenu popup)	
2	public.... java.awt.Component	add (java.awt.Component comp, int index)	
2	public..... void	add (java.awt.Component comp, Object constraints)	
2	public.... java.awt.Component	add (String name, java.awt.Component comp)	
2	public..... void	add (java.awt.Component comp, Object constraints, int index)	
	public..... void	**addAncestorListener** (*javax.swing.event.AncestorListener* listener)	
1	public synchronized ....void	addComponentListener (*java.awt.event.ComponentListener* l)	
2	public synchronized .... void	addContainerListener (*java.awt.event.ContainerListener* l)	
1	public synchronized ....void	addFocusListener (*java.awt.event.FocusListener* l)	
2	protected..... void	addImpl (java.awt.Component comp, Object constraints, int index)	
1	public synchronized ....void	addInputMethodListener (*java.awt.event.InputMethodListener* l)	
1	public synchronized ....void	addKeyListener (*java.awt.event.KeyListener* l)	
1	public synchronized ....void	addMouseListener (*java.awt.event.MouseListener* l)	
1	public synchronized ....void	addMouseMotionListener (*java.awt.event.MouseMotionListener* l)	
2	public..... **void**	**addNotify** ()	
1	public synchronized ...... **void**	**addPropertyChangeListener** (*java.beans.PropertyChangeListener* listener)	
1	public synchronized ....void	addPropertyChangeListener (String propertyName,	
		java.beans.PropertyChangeListener listener)	

Class   *Interface*   —extends   - - -implements   ○ abstract   ● final   △ static   ▲ static final   ✳ constructor   x x—inherited   x **x**—declared   **x x**—overridden

	public synchronized ....void	**addVetoableChangeListener** (*java.beans.VetoableChangeListener* listener)
1	public..........................int	checkImage (java.awt.Image image, *java.awt.image.ImageObserver* observer)
1	public..........................int	checkImage (java. awt. Image image, int width, int height, *java.awt.image.ImageObserver* observer)
1	protected .. java.awt.AWTEvent	coalesceEvents (java.awt.AWTEvent existingEvent, java.awt.AWTEvent newEvent)
	public.......................void	**computeVisibleRect** (java.awt.Rectangle visibleRect)
1	public................. boolean	contains (java.awt.Point p)
1	public................. **boolean**	**contains** (int x, int y)
1	public.......... java.awt.Image	createImage (*java.awt.image.ImageProducer* producer)
1	public.......... java.awt.Image	createImage (int width, int height)
	public................. JToolTip	**createToolTip** ()
● 1	protected final..............void	disableEvents (long eventsToDisable)
● 1	public final ....void	dispatchEvent (java.awt.AWTEvent e)
2	public.......................void	doLayout ()
● 1	protected final..............void	enableEvents (long eventsToEnable)
1	public.......................void	enableInputMethods (boolean enable)
2	public.... java.awt.Component	findComponentAt (java.awt.Point p)
2	public.... java.awt.Component	findComponentAt (int x, int y)
	public.......................void	**firePropertyChange** (String propertyName, float oldValue, float newValue)
	public.......................void	**firePropertyChange** (String propertyName, boolean oldValue, boolean newValue)
	public.......................void	**firePropertyChange** (String propertyName, int oldValue, int newValue)
	public.......................void	**firePropertyChange** (String propertyName, byte oldValue, byte newValue)
	public.......................void	**firePropertyChange** (String propertyName, char oldValue, char newValue)
1	protected .... **void**	**firePropertyChange** (String propertyName, Object oldValue, Object newValue)
	public.......................void	**firePropertyChange** (String propertyName, short oldValue, short newValue)
	public.......................void	**firePropertyChange** (String propertyName, double oldValue, double newValue)
	public.......................void	**firePropertyChange** (String propertyName, long oldValue, long newValue)
	protected ....void	**fireVetoableChange** (String propertyName, Object oldValue, Object newValue) throws java.beans.PropertyVetoException
	public.... javax.accessibility ↩ .AccessibleContext	**getAccessibleContext** ()
	public.......................... .. *java.awt.event.ActionListener*	**getActionForKeyStroke** (KeyStroke aKeyStroke)
2	public................. **float**	**getAlignmentX** ()
2	public................. **float**	**getAlignmentY** ()
	public................. boolean	**getAutoscrolls** ()
1	public..........java.awt.Color	getBackground ()
	public.......................... .... *javax.swing.border.Border*	**getBorder** ()
1	public...... java.awt.Rectangle	getBounds ()
● 1	public.... **java.awt.Rectangle**	**getBounds** (java.awt.Rectangle rv)
	public final ....Object	**getClientProperty** (Object key)
1	public.......................... .... java.awt.image.ColorModel	getColorModel ()
2	public.... java.awt.Component	getComponent (int n)
2	public.... java.awt.Component	getComponentAt (java.awt.Point p)
2	public.... java.awt.Component	getComponentAt (int x, int y)
2	public.......................int	getComponentCount ()
	protected ... java.awt.Graphics	**getComponentGraphics** (java.awt.Graphics g)
1	public.................... java ↩ .awt.ComponentOrientation	getComponentOrientation ()
2	public...java.awt.Component[]	getComponents ()
	public.......................int	**getConditionForKeyStroke** (KeyStroke aKeyStroke)
1	public.......... java.awt.Cursor	getCursor ()
	public.......................int	**getDebugGraphicsOptions** ()
1	public synchronized .... java.awt.dnd.DropTarget	getDropTarget ()
1	public..............java.awt.Font	getFont ()
1	public..... java.awt.FontMetrics	getFontMetrics (java.awt.Font font)
1	public..........java.awt.Color	getForeground ()
1	public..... **java.awt.Graphics**	**getGraphics** ()
1	public....................... **int**	**getHeight** ()
1	public.......................... .... java.awt.im.InputContext	getInputContext ()
1	public.................... *java* ↩ .*awt.im.InputMethodRequests*	getInputMethodRequests ()
2	public...... **java.awt.Insets**	**getInsets** ()
	public.......... java.awt.Insets	**getInsets** (java.awt.Insets insets)
2	public *java.awt.LayoutManager*	getLayout ()
1	public.......... java.util.Locale	getLocale ()
1	public.......... java.awt.Point	getLocation ()
1	public.......... **java.awt.Point**	**getLocation** (java.awt.Point rv)
1	public.......... java.awt.Point	getLocationOnScreen ()
2	public.... **java.awt.Dimension**	**getMaximumSize** ()

JComponent

2	public....	**java.awt.Dimension**	**getMinimumSize** ()
1	public.....................	String	getName ()
	public....	java.awt.Component	**getNextFocusableComponent** ()
1	public.......	java.awt.Container	getParent ()
2	public....	**java.awt.Dimension**	**getPreferredSize** ()
	public..............	KeyStroke[]	**getRegisteredKeyStrokes** ()
	public..............	JRootPane	**getRootPane** ()
1	public......	java.awt.Dimension	getSize ()
1	public....	**java.awt.Dimension**	**getSize** (java.awt.Dimension rv)
1	public..........	java.awt.Toolkit	getToolkit ()
	public......	java.awt.Point	**getToolTipLocation** (java.awt.event.MouseEvent event)
	public.....................	String	**getToolTipText** ()
	public.....................	String	**getToolTipText** (java.awt.event.MouseEvent event)
	public......	java.awt.Container	**getTopLevelAncestor** ()
● 1	public final	Object	getTreeLock ()
	public.....................	String	**getUIClassID** ()
	public......	java.awt.Rectangle	**getVisibleRect** ()
1	public........................	**int**	**getWidth** ()
1	public........................	**int**	**getX** ()
1	public........................	**int**	**getY** ()
	public.....................void		**grabFocus** ()
1	public........................	**boolean**	**hasFocus** ()
1	public.................	boolean	imageUpdate (java.awt.Image img, int flags, int x, int y, int w, int h)
2	public.....................void		invalidate ()
2	public.................	boolean	isAncestorOf (java.awt.Component c)
1	public.................	boolean	isDisplayable ()
1	public.................	**boolean**	**isDoubleBuffered** ()
1	public.................	boolean	isEnabled ()
	public.................	boolean	**isFocusCycleRoot** ()
1	public.................	**boolean**	**isFocusTraversable** ()
1	public.................	boolean	isLightweight ()
△	public static	boolean	**isLightweightComponent** (java.awt.Component c)
	public.................	boolean	**isManagingFocus** ()
1	public.................	**boolean**	**isOpaque** ()
	public.................	boolean	**isOptimizedDrawingEnabled** ()
	public.................	boolean	**isPaintingTile** ()
	public.................	boolean	**isRequestFocusEnabled** ()
1	public.................	boolean	isShowing ()
1	public.................	boolean	isValid ()
	public.................	boolean	**isValidateRoot** ()
1	public.................	boolean	isVisible ()
✳	public.................	**JComponent**	()
1	public.....................void		list ()
1	public.....................void		list (java.io.PrintStream out)
1	public.....................void		list (java.io.PrintWriter out)
2	public.....................void		list (java.io.PrintStream out, int indent)
2	public.....................void		list (java.io.PrintWriter out, int indent)
	protected .... javax↵		**listenerList**
	.swing.event.EventListenerList		
2	public.....................	**void**	**paint** (java.awt.Graphics g)
1	public.....................	void	paintAll (java.awt.Graphics g)
	protected ....void		**paintBorder** (java.awt.Graphics g)
	protected ....void		**paintChildren** (java.awt.Graphics g)
	protected ....void		**paintComponent** (java.awt.Graphics g)
2	public.....................	void	paintComponents (java.awt.Graphics g)
	public.....................	void	**paintImmediately** (java.awt.Rectangle r)
	public.....................	void	**paintImmediately** (int x, int y, int w, int h)
2	protected	**String**	**paramString** ()
1	public.................	boolean	prepareImage (java.awt.Image image, *java.awt.image.ImageObserver* observer)
1	public.................	boolean	prepareImage (java. awt. Image image, int width, int height, *java.awt.image.ImageObserver* observer)
2	public.....................	void	print (java.awt.Graphics g)
1	public.....................	void	printAll (java.awt.Graphics g)
2	public.....................	void	printComponents (java.awt.Graphics g)
	protected	void	processComponentEvent (java.awt.event.ComponentEvent e)
	protected	void	**processComponentKeyEvent** (java.awt.event.KeyEvent e)
2	protected	void	processContainerEvent (java.awt.event.ContainerEvent e)
2	protected	void	processEvent (java.awt.AWTEvent e)
1	protected	**void**	**processFocusEvent** (java.awt.event.FocusEvent e)
1	protected	void	processInputMethodEvent (java.awt.event.InputMethodEvent e)
1	protected	**void**	**processKeyEvent** (java.awt.event.KeyEvent e)
1	protected	void	processMouseEvent (java.awt.event.MouseEvent e)

J

Class *Interface* —extends - - -implements ○ abstract ● final △ static ▲ static final ✳ constructor x x—inherited x **x**—declared **x x**—overridden

1	protected	**void**	**processMouseMotionEvent** (java.awt.event.MouseEvent e)
●	public final	void	**putClientProperty** (Object key, Object value)
	public	void	**registerKeyboardAction** (*java. awt. event. ActionListener* anAction, KeyStroke aKeyStroke, int aCondition)
	public	void	**registerKeyboardAction** (*java. awt. event. ActionListener* anAction, String aCommand, KeyStroke aKeyStroke, int aCondition)
2	public	void	remove (int index)
2	public	void	remove (java.awt.Component comp)
1	public synchronized	void	remove (java.awt.MenuComponent popup)
2	public	void	removeAll ()
	public	void	**removeAncestorListener** (*javax.swing.event.AncestorListener* listener)
1	public synchronized	void	removeComponentListener (*java.awt.event.ComponentListener* l)
2	public synchronized	void	removeContainerListener (*java.awt.event.ContainerListener* l)
1	public synchronized	void	removeFocusListener (*java.awt.event.FocusListener* l)
1	public synchronized	void	removeInputMethodListener (*java.awt.event.InputMethodListener* l)
1	public synchronized	void	removeKeyListener (*java.awt.event.KeyListener* l)
1	public synchronized	void	removeMouseListener (*java.awt.event.MouseListener* l)
1	public synchronized	void	removeMouseMotionListener (*java.awt.event.MouseMotionListener* l)
2	public	**void**	**removeNotify** ()
1	public synchronized	**void**	**removePropertyChangeListener** (*java.beans.PropertyChangeListener* listener)
1	public synchronized	void	removePropertyChangeListener (String propertyName, *java.beans.PropertyChangeListener* listener)
	public synchronized	void	**removeVetoableChangeListener** (*java.beans.VetoableChangeListener* listener)
1	public	void	repaint ()
	public	void	**repaint** (java.awt.Rectangle r)
1	public	void	repaint (long tm)
1	public	void	repaint (int x, int y, int width, int height)
1	public	**void**	**repaint** (long tm, int x, int y, int width, int height)
	public	boolean	**requestDefaultFocus** ()
1	public	**void**	**requestFocus** ()
	public	void	**resetKeyboardActions** ()
1	public	**void**	**reshape** (int x, int y, int w, int h)
	public	void	**revalidate** ()
	public	void	**scrollRectToVisible** (java.awt.Rectangle aRect)
	public	void	**setAlignmentX** (float alignmentX)
	public	void	**setAlignmentY** (float alignmentY)
	public	void	**setAutoscrolls** (boolean autoscrolls)
1	public	**void**	**setBackground** (java.awt.Color bg)
	public	void	**setBorder** (*javax.swing.border.Border* border)
1	public	void	setBounds (java.awt.Rectangle r)
1	public	void	setBounds (int x, int y, int width, int height)
1	public	void	setComponentOrientation (java.awt.ComponentOrientation o)
1	public synchronized	void	setCursor (java.awt.Cursor cursor)
	public	void	**setDebugGraphicsOptions** (int debugOptions)
	public	void	**setDoubleBuffered** (boolean aFlag)
1	public synchronized	void	setDropTarget (java.awt.dnd.DropTarget dt)
1	public	**void**	**setEnabled** (boolean enabled)
2	public	**void**	**setFont** (java.awt.Font font)
1	public	**void**	**setForeground** (java.awt.Color fg)
2	public	void	setLayout (*java.awt.LayoutManager* mgr)
1	public	void	setLocale (java.util.Locale l)
1	public	void	setLocation (java.awt.Point p)
1	public	void	setLocation (int x, int y)
	public	void	**setMaximumSize** (java.awt.Dimension maximumSize)
	public	void	**setMinimumSize** (java.awt.Dimension minimumSize)
1	public	void	setName (String name)
	public	void	**setNextFocusableComponent** (java.awt.Component aComponent)
	public	void	**setOpaque** (boolean isOpaque)
	public	void	**setPreferredSize** (java.awt.Dimension preferredSize)
	public	void	**setRequestFocusEnabled** (boolean aFlag)
1	public	void	setSize (java.awt.Dimension d)
1	public	void	setSize (int width, int height)
	public	void	**setToolTipText** (String text)
	protected	void	**setUI** (javax.swing.plaf.ComponentUI newUI)
1	public	**void**	**setVisible** (boolean aFlag)
▲	public static final	String	**TOOL_TIP_TEXT_KEY** = "ToolTipText"
1	public	String	toString ()
1	public	void	transferFocus ()
	protected transient		**ui**
	javax.swing.plaf.ComponentUI		
▲	public static final	int	**UNDEFINED_CONDITION** = -1
	public	void	**unregisterKeyboardAction** (KeyStroke aKeyStroke)
2	public	**void**	**update** (java.awt.Graphics g)
	public	void	**updateUI** ()

JComponent

2	public	void	validate ()
2	protected	void	validateTree ()
▲	public static final	int	**WHEN_ANCESTOR_OF_FOCUSED_COMPONENT** = 1
▲	public static final	int	**WHEN_FOCUSED** = 0
▲	public static final	int	**WHEN_IN_FOCUSED_WINDOW** = 2

JComponent.AccessibleJComponent — javax.swing

```
        Object
1.2 ○   └─javax.accessibility.AccessibleContext 1
1.2 ○      └─JComponent.AccessibleJComponent - - - - - java.io.Serializable, javax.accessibility.AccessibleComponent 2
```

1	*21 inherited members from javax.accessibility.AccessibleContext not shown*		
	protected	*java↵.awt.event.ContainerListener*	**accessibleContainerHandler**
✳	protected		**AccessibleJComponent** ()
2	public	void	**addFocusListener** (*java.awt.event.FocusListener* l)
1	public	**void**	**addPropertyChangeListener** (*java.beans.PropertyChangeListener* listener)
2	public	boolean	**contains** (java.awt.Point p)
2	public	*javax.accessibility.Accessible*	**getAccessibleAt** (java.awt.Point p)
1	public	***javax↵.accessibility.Accessible***	**getAccessibleChild** (int i)
1	public	int	**getAccessibleChildrenCount** ()
1	public	***javax.accessibility↵.AccessibleComponent***	**getAccessibleComponent** ()
1	public	**String**	**getAccessibleDescription** ()
1	public	int	**getAccessibleIndexInParent** ()
1	public	**String**	**getAccessibleName** ()
1	public	***javax↵.accessibility.Accessible***	**getAccessibleParent** ()
1	public	***javax↵.accessibility.AccessibleRole***	**getAccessibleRole** ()
1	public	***javax.accessibility↵.AccessibleStateSet***	**getAccessibleStateSet** ()
2	public	java.awt.Color	**getBackground** ()
	protected	String	**getBorderTitle** (*javax.swing.border.Border* b)
2	public	java.awt.Rectangle	**getBounds** ()
2	public	java.awt.Cursor	**getCursor** ()
2	public	java.awt.Font	**getFont** ()
2	public	java.awt.FontMetrics	**getFontMetrics** (java.awt.Font f)
2	public	java.awt.Color	**getForeground** ()
1	public	**java.util.Locale**	**getLocale** ()
2	public	java.awt.Point	**getLocation** ()
2	public	java.awt.Point	**getLocationOnScreen** ()
2	public	java.awt.Dimension	**getSize** ()
2	public	boolean	**isEnabled** ()
2	public	boolean	**isFocusTraversable** ()
2	public	boolean	**isShowing** ()
2	public	boolean	**isVisible** ()
2	public	void	**removeFocusListener** (*java.awt.event.FocusListener* l)
1	public	**void**	**removePropertyChangeListener** (*java.beans.PropertyChangeListener* listener)
2	public	void	**requestFocus** ()
2	public	void	**setBackground** (java.awt.Color c)
2	public	void	**setBounds** (java.awt.Rectangle r)
2	public	void	**setCursor** (java.awt.Cursor cursor)
2	public	void	**setEnabled** (boolean b)
2	public	void	**setFont** (java.awt.Font f)
2	public	void	**setForeground** (java.awt.Color c)
2	public	void	**setLocation** (java.awt.Point p)
2	public	void	**setSize** (java.awt.Dimension d)
2	public	void	**setVisible** (boolean b)

JComponent.AccessibleJComponent.AccessibleContainerHandler — protecte — javax.swing

```
        Object
1.2     └─JComponent.AccessibleJComponent↵ - - - - - java.awt.event.ContainerListener 1 (java.util.EventListener)
           .AccessibleContainerHandler
```

Class   *Interface*   —extends   - - -implements   ○ abstract   ● final   △ static   ▲ static final   ✳ constructor   x x—inherited   x **x**—declared   **x x**—overridden

*	protected		**AccessibleContainerHandler** ()
1	public . . . . void		**componentAdded** (java.awt.event.ContainerEvent e)
1	public . . . . void		**componentRemoved** (java.awt.event.ContainerEvent e)

JDesktopPane   javax.swing

Object
   └java.awt.Component[1] - - - - - - - - - - - - - - - - - - - *java.awt.image.ImageObserver*, *java.awt.MenuContainer*,
                                   java.io.Serializable
     └java.awt.Container[2]
1.2 ○   └JComponent[3] - - - - - - - - - - - - - - - - - - - *java.io.Serializable*
1.2   └JLayeredPane[4] - - - - - - - - - - - - - - - - *javax.accessibility.Accessible*
1.2   └JDesktopPane - - - - - - - - - - - - - - - - *javax.accessibility.Accessible*

1	*111 inherited members from java.awt.Component not shown*		
2	*37 inherited members from java.awt.Container not shown*		
3	*110 inherited members from JComponent not shown*		
4	*29 inherited members from JLayeredPane not shown*		
4	public . . . **javax.accessibility** ↵		**getAccessibleContext** ()
	.AccessibleContext		
	public . . . . JInternalFrame[]		**getAllFrames** ()
	public . . . . JInternalFrame[]		**getAllFramesInLayer** (int layer)
	public . . . . *DesktopManager*		**getDesktopManager** ()
	public . . . . javax ↵		**getUI** ()
	.swing.plaf.DesktopPaneUI		
3	public . . . . **String**		**getUIClassID** ()
3	public . . . . **boolean**		**isOpaque** ()
*	public		**JDesktopPane** ()
4	protected . . . . **String**		**paramString** ()
	public . . . . void		**setDesktopManager** (*DesktopManager* d)
	public . . . . void		**setUI** (javax.swing.plaf.DesktopPaneUI ui)
3	public . . . . **void**		**updateUI** ()

JDesktopPane.AccessibleJDesktopPane   protected   javax.swing

Object
1.2 ○ └javax.accessibility.AccessibleContext[1]
1.2 ○   └JComponent.AccessibleJComponent[2] - - - - *java.io.Serializable*, *javax.accessibility.AccessibleComponent*
1.2   └JDesktopPane.AccessibleJDesktopPane

1	*21 inherited members from javax.accessibility.AccessibleContext not shown*		
2	*40 inherited members from JComponent.AccessibleJComponent not shown*		
*	protected		**AccessibleJDesktopPane** ()
2	public . . . . **javax** ↵		**getAccessibleRole** ()
	.accessibility.AccessibleRole		

JDialog   javax.swing

Object
   └java.awt.Component[1] - - - - - - - - - - - - - - - - - - - *java.awt.image.ImageObserver*, *java.awt.MenuContainer*,
                                   java.io.Serializable
     └java.awt.Container[2]
      └java.awt.Window[3]
       └java.awt.Dialog[4]
1.2   └JDialog - *WindowConstants*, *javax.accessibility.Accessible*[5],
                                RootPaneContainer[6]

1	*131 inherited members from java.awt.Component not shown*		
2	*45 inherited members from java.awt.Container not shown*		
	protected javax.accessibility ↵		**accessibleContext**
	.AccessibleContext		
2	protected . . . . **void**		**addImpl** (java.awt.Component comp, Object constraints, int index)
4	public . . . . void		addNotify ()
3	public synchronized . . . . . . void		addWindowListener (*java.awt.event.WindowListener* l)
3	public . . . . void		applyResourceBundle (String rbName)
3	public . . . . void		applyResourceBundle (java.util.ResourceBundle rb)
	protected . . . . JRootPane		**createRootPane** ()
	protected . . . . void		**dialogInit** ()
3	public . . . . void		dispose ()

JDialog

	3	protected . . . . .void	finalize () throws Throwable
	5	public. . . . . javax.accessibility ↵	**getAccessibleContext** ()
		.AccessibleContext	
	6	public. . . . . . . java.awt.Container	**getContentPane** ()
		public. . . . . .int	**getDefaultCloseOperation** ()
	3	public. . . . . java.awt.Component	getFocusOwner ()
	6	public. . . . java.awt.Component	**getGlassPane** ()
	3	public.	getInputContext ()
		. . . . . . java.awt.im.InputContext	
		public. . . . . JMenuBar	**getJMenuBar** ()
	6	public. . . . . JLayeredPane	**getLayeredPane** ()
	3	public. . . . . .java.util.Locale	getLocale ()
	3	public. . . . . . . java.awt.Window[]	getOwnedWindows ()
	3	public. . . . . .java.awt.Window	getOwner ()
	6	public. . . . . JRootPane	**getRootPane** ()
	4	public. .String	getTitle ()
	3	public. . . . . .java.awt.Toolkit	getToolkit ()
●	3	public final . . . . .String	getWarningString ()
	4	public. . . . . boolean	isModal ()
	4	public. . . . . boolean	isResizable ()
		protected . . . . boolean	**isRootPaneCheckingEnabled** ()
	3	public. . . . . boolean	isShowing ()
*		public.	**JDialog** ()
*		public.	**JDialog** (java.awt.Dialog owner)
*		public.	**JDialog** (java.awt.Frame owner)
*		public.	**JDialog** (java.awt.Dialog owner, boolean modal)
*		public.	**JDialog** (java.awt.Dialog owner, String title)
*		public.	**JDialog** (java.awt.Frame owner, boolean modal)
*		public.	**JDialog** (java.awt.Frame owner, String title)
*		public.	**JDialog** (java.awt.Dialog owner, String title, boolean modal)
*		public.	**JDialog** (java.awt.Frame owner, String title, boolean modal)
	3	public. . . . . .void	pack ()
	4	protected . . . . **String**	**paramString** ()
	3	protected . . . . .void	processEvent (java.awt.AWTEvent e)
	3	protected . . . . **void**	**processWindowEvent** (java.awt.event.WindowEvent e)
	3	public synchronized . . . . . . .void	removeWindowListener (*java.awt.event.WindowListener* l)
		protected . . . . JRootPane	**rootPane**
		protected . . . . boolean	**rootPaneCheckingEnabled**
	6	public. . . . . .void	**setContentPane** (java.awt.Container contentPane)
		public. . . . . .void	**setDefaultCloseOperation** (int operation)
	6	public. . . . . .void	**setGlassPane** (java.awt.Component glassPane)
		public. . . . . .void	**setJMenuBar** (JMenuBar menu)
	6	public. . . . . .void	**setLayeredPane** (JLayeredPane layeredPane)
	2	public. . . . . **void**	**setLayout** (*java.awt.LayoutManager* manager)
		public. . . . . .void	**setLocationRelativeTo** (java.awt.Component c)
	4	public. . . . . .void	setModal (boolean b)
	4	public. . . . . .void	setResizable (boolean resizable)
		protected . . . . .void	**setRootPane** (JRootPane root)
		protected . . . . .void	**setRootPaneCheckingEnabled** (boolean enabled)
	4	public synchronized . . . . . . .void	setTitle (String title)
	4	public. . . . . .void	show ()
	3	public. . . . . .void	toBack ()
	3	public. . . . . .void	toFront ()
	2	public. . . . . **void**	**update** (java.awt.Graphics g)

JDialog.AccessibleJDialog	protected	javax.swing

Object
1.2 ○ └─javax.accessibility.AccessibleContext [1]
1.2   └─JDialog.AccessibleJDialog - - - - - - - - - - - - - *java.io.Serializable, javax.accessibility.AccessibleComponent* [2]

	1	*24 inherited members from javax.accessibility.AccessibleContext not shown*	
*		protected	**AccessibleJDialog** ()
	2	public. . . . . .void	**addFocusListener** (*java.awt.event.FocusListener* l)
	2	public. . . . . boolean	**contains** (java.awt.Point p)
	2	public.	**getAccessibleAt** (java.awt.Point p)
		. *javax.accessibility.Accessible*	
	1	public. . . . . *javax* ↵	**getAccessibleChild** (int i)
		.accessibility.Accessible	
	1	public. . . . . **int**	**getAccessibleChildCount** ()

Class   *Interface*   —extends   - - -implements   ○ abstract   ● final   △ static   ▲ static final   ✳ constructor   x x—inherited   x **x**—declared   **x x**—overridden

1	public...	***javax.accessibility↩*** *.AccessibleComponent*	**getAccessibleComponent** ()
1	public......................	**int**	**getAccessibleIndexInParent** ()
1	public..................	**String**	**getAccessibleName** ()
1	public...................	***javax↩*** *.accessibility.Accessible*	**getAccessibleParent** ()
1	public.................	***javax↩*** *.accessibility.AccessibleRole*	**getAccessibleRole** ()
1	public...	***javax.accessibility↩*** *.AccessibleStateSet*	**getAccessibleStateSet** ()
2	public............	java.awt.Color	**getBackground** ()
2	public......	java.awt.Rectangle	**getBounds** ()
2	public..........	java.awt.Cursor	**getCursor** ()
2	public............	java.awt.Font	**getFont** ()
2	public...	java.awt.FontMetrics	**getFontMetrics** (java.awt.Font f)
2	public...........	java.awt.Color	**getForeground** ()
1	public..........	**java.util.Locale**	**getLocale** ()
2	public.........	java.awt.Point	**getLocation** ()
2	public.........	java.awt.Point	**getLocationOnScreen** ()
2	public......	java.awt.Dimension	**getSize** ()
2	public........	boolean	**isEnabled** ()
2	public........	boolean	**isFocusTraversable** ()
2	public........	boolean	**isShowing** ()
2	public........	boolean	**isVisible** ()
2	public........	void	**removeFocusListener** (*java.awt.event.FocusListener* l)
2	public........	void	**requestFocus** ()
2	public........	void	**setBackground** (java.awt.Color c)
2	public........	void	**setBounds** (java.awt.Rectangle r)
2	public........	void	**setCursor** (java.awt.Cursor cursor)
2	public........	void	**setEnabled** (boolean b)
2	public........	void	**setFont** (java.awt.Font f)
2	public........	void	**setForeground** (java.awt.Color c)
2	public........	void	**setLocation** (java.awt.Point p)
2	public........	void	**setSize** (java.awt.Dimension d)
2	public........	void	**setVisible** (boolean b)

JEditorPane   javax.swing

```
         Object
    ○    └java.awt.Component 1 ------------------ java.awt.image.ImageObserver, java.awt.MenuContainer,
                                                   java.io.Serializable
           └java.awt.Container 2
1.2 ○        └JComponent 3 --------------------- java.io.Serializable
1.2 ○          └javax.swing.text.JTextComponent 4 ---- Scrollable, javax.accessibility.Accessible
1.2              └JEditorPane
```

1		*109 inherited members from java.awt.Component not shown*	
2		*39 inherited members from java.awt.Container not shown*	
3		*105 inherited members from JComponent not shown*	
4		*63 inherited members from javax.swing.text.JTextComponent not shown*	
	public synchronized	void	**addHyperlinkListener** (*javax.swing.event.HyperlinkListener* listener)
	protected ....javax.swing.text.EditorKit		**createDefaultEditorKit** ()
△	public static ....javax.swing.text.EditorKit		**createEditorKitForContentType** (String type)
	public.....................	void	**fireHyperlinkUpdate** (javax.swing.event.HyperlinkEvent e)
4	public...	**javax.accessibility↩** *.AccessibleContext*	**getAccessibleContext** ()
●	public final	String	**getContentType** ()
●	public final ....javax.swing.text.EditorKit		**getEditorKit** ()
	public..................... ....javax.swing.text.EditorKit		**getEditorKitForContentType** (String type)
	public.............	java.net.URL	**getPage** ()
3	public....	**java.awt.Dimension**	**getPreferredSize** ()
4	public..................	**boolean**	**getScrollableTracksViewportHeight** ()
4	public..................	**boolean**	**getScrollableTracksViewportWidth** ()
	protected ..	java.io.InputStream	**getStream** (java.net.URL page) throws java.io.IOException
4	public..................	**String**	**getText** ()
3	public..................	**String**	**getUIClassID** ()
3	public..................	**boolean**	**isManagingFocus** ()
*	public.........................		**JEditorPane** ()

JEditorPane

✳	public...........................	**JEditorPane**	(String url) throws java.io.IOException
✳	public...........................	**JEditorPane**	(java.net.URL initialPage) throws java.io.IOException
✳	public...........................	**JEditorPane**	(String type, String text)
4	protected .... **String**	**paramString**	()
4	protected .... **void**	**processComponentKeyEvent**	(java.awt.event.KeyEvent e)
	public........................void	**read**	(java.io.InputStream in, Object desc) throws java.io.IOException
△	public static ....void	**registerEditorKitForContentType**	(String type, String classname)
△	public static ....void	**registerEditorKitForContentType**	(String type, String classname, ClassLoader loader)
	public synchronized ....void	**removeHyperlinkListener**	(*javax.swing.event.HyperlinkListener* listener)
4	public........................ **void**	**replaceSelection**	(String content)
	protected ....void	**scrollToReference**	(String reference)
●	public final ....void	**setContentType**	(String type)
	public........................void	**setEditorKit**	(javax.swing.text.EditorKit kit)
	public........................void	**setEditorKitForContentType**	(String type, javax.swing.text.EditorKit k)
	public........................void	**setPage**	(String url) throws java.io.IOException
	public........................void	**setPage**	(java.net.URL page) throws java.io.IOException
4	public........................ **void**	**setText**	(String t)

JEditorPane.AccessibleJEditorPane	protected	javax.swing

Object
1.2 ○ └javax.accessibility.AccessibleContext[1]
1.2 ○ └JComponent.AccessibleJComponent[2] - - - - *java.io.Serializable, javax.accessibility.AccessibleComponent*
1.2 └javax.swing.text.JTextComponent↵ - - - - - *javax.accessibility.AccessibleText, javax.swing.event.CaretListener*
.AccessibleJTextComponent[3] *(java.util.EventListener), javax.swing.event.DocumentListener*
(java.util.EventListener)
1.2 └JEditorPane.AccessibleJEditorPane

1	*20 inherited members from javax.accessibility.AccessibleContext not shown*		
2	*38 inherited members from JComponent.AccessibleJComponent not shown*		
✳	protected	**AccessibleJEditorPane**	()
3	public........................void	caretUpdate	(javax.swing.event.CaretEvent e)
3	public........................void	changedUpdate	(*javax.swing.event.DocumentEvent* e)
2	public................. **String**	**getAccessibleDescription**	()
3	public.................javax↵	getAccessibleRole	()
	.accessibility.AccessibleRole		
3	public... **javax.accessibility↵**	**getAccessibleStateSet**	()
	.AccessibleStateSet		
3	public.................*javax↵*	getAccessibleText	()
	.accessibility.AccessibleText		
3	public...................String	getAfterIndex	(int part, int index)
3	public...................String	getAtIndex	(int part, int index)
3	public...................String	getBeforeIndex	(int part, int index)
3	public.......................int	getCaretPosition	()
3	public.......................	getCharacterAttribute	(int i)
	... javax.swing.text.AttributeSet		
3	public...... java.awt.Rectangle	getCharacterBounds	(int i)
3	public.......................int	getCharCount	()
3	public.......................int	getIndexAtPoint	(java.awt.Point p)
3	public...................String	getSelectedText	()
3	public.......................int	getSelectionEnd	()
3	public.......................int	getSelectionStart	()
3	public........................void	insertUpdate	(*javax.swing.event.DocumentEvent* e)
3	public........................void	removeUpdate	(*javax.swing.event.DocumentEvent* e)

JEditorPane.AccessibleJEditorPaneHTML	protected	javax.swing

Object
1.2 ○ └javax.accessibility.AccessibleContext[1]
1.2 ○ └JComponent.AccessibleJComponent[2] - - - - *java.io.Serializable, javax.accessibility.AccessibleComponent*
1.2 └javax.swing.text.JTextComponent↵ - - - - - *javax.accessibility.AccessibleText, javax.swing.event.CaretListener*
.AccessibleJTextComponent[3] *(java.util.EventListener), javax.swing.event.DocumentListener*
(java.util.EventListener)
1.2 └JEditorPane.AccessibleJEditorPane[4]
1.2 └JEditorPane↵
.AccessibleJEditorPaneHTML

Class   *Interface*   —extends   - - -implements   ○ abstract   ● final   △ static   ▲ static final   ✳ constructor   x x—inherited   x **x**—declared   **x x**—overridden

	1	*20 inherited members from javax.accessibility.AccessibleContext not shown*	
	2	*38 inherited members from JComponent.AccessibleJComponent not shown*	
*		protected	**AccessibleJEditorPaneHTML** ()
	3	public . . . . void	caretUpdate (javax.swing.event.CaretEvent e)
	3	public . . . . void	changedUpdate (*javax.swing.event.DocumentEvent* e)
	4	public . . . . String	getAccessibleDescription ()
	3	public . . . . javax←	getAccessibleRole ()
		.accessibility.AccessibleRole	
	4	public . . . . javax.accessibility←	getAccessibleStateSet ()
		.AccessibleStateSet	
	3	public . . . . *javax←*	**getAccessibleText** ()
		.accessibility.AccessibleText	
	3	public . . . . String	getAfterIndex (int part, int index)
	3	public . . . . String	getAtIndex (int part, int index)
	3	public . . . . String	getBeforeIndex (int part, int index)
	3	public . . . . int	getCaretPosition ()
	3	public	getCharacterAttribute (int i)
		. . . *javax.swing.text.AttributeSet*	
	3	public . . . . . . java.awt.Rectangle	getCharacterBounds (int i)
	3	public . . . . int	getCharCount ()
	3	public . . . . int	getIndexAtPoint (java.awt.Point p)
	3	public . . . . String	getSelectedText ()
	3	public . . . . int	getSelectionEnd ()
	3	public . . . . int	getSelectionStart ()
	3	public . . . . void	insertUpdate (*javax.swing.event.DocumentEvent* e)
	3	public . . . . void	removeUpdate (*javax.swing.event.DocumentEvent* e)

J

JEditorPane.JEditorPaneAccessibleHypertextSupport   protected   javax.swing

```
      Object
1.2 ○   └javax.accessibility.AccessibleContext 1
1.2 ○     └JComponent.AccessibleJComponent 2 - - - - java.io.Serializable, javax.accessibility.AccessibleComponent
1.2         └javax.swing.text.JTextComponent ← - - - - - javax.accessibility.AccessibleText, javax.swing.event.CaretListener
              .AccessibleJTextComponent 3               (java.util.EventListener), javax.swing.event.DocumentListener
                                                         (java.util.EventListener)
1.2           └JEditorPane.AccessibleJEditorPane 4
1.2             └JEditorPane ← - - - - - - - - - - - - - - - - - javax.accessibility.AccessibleHypertext 5
                  .JEditorPaneAccessibleHypertextSupport (javax.accessibility.AccessibleText)
```

	1	*20 inherited members from javax.accessibility.AccessibleContext not shown*	
	2	*38 inherited members from JComponent.AccessibleJComponent not shown*	
	3	public . . . . void	caretUpdate (javax.swing.event.CaretEvent e)
	3	public . . . . void	changedUpdate (*javax.swing.event.DocumentEvent* e)
	4	public . . . . String	getAccessibleDescription ()
	3	public . . . . javax←	getAccessibleRole ()
		.accessibility.AccessibleRole	
	4	public . . . . javax.accessibility←	getAccessibleStateSet ()
		.AccessibleStateSet	
	3	public . . . . *javax←*	getAccessibleText ()
		.accessibility.AccessibleText	
	3	public . . . . String	getAfterIndex (int part, int index)
	3	public . . . . String	getAtIndex (int part, int index)
	3	public . . . . String	getBeforeIndex (int part, int index)
	3	public . . . . int	getCaretPosition ()
	3	public	getCharacterAttribute (int i)
		. . . *javax.swing.text.AttributeSet*	
	3	public . . . . . . java.awt.Rectangle	getCharacterBounds (int i)
	3	public . . . . int	getCharCount ()
	3	public . . . . int	getIndexAtPoint (java.awt.Point p)
	5	public . . . . javax.accessibility←	**getLink** (int linkIndex)
		.AccessibleHyperlink	
	5	public . . . . int	**getLinkCount** ()
	5	public . . . . int	**getLinkIndex** (int charIndex)
		public . . . . String	**getLinkText** (int linkIndex)
	3	public . . . . String	getSelectedText ()
	3	public . . . . int	getSelectionEnd ()
	3	public . . . . int	getSelectionStart ()
	3	public . . . . void	insertUpdate (*javax.swing.event.DocumentEvent* e)
*		public	**JEditorPaneAccessibleHypertextSupport** ()
	3	public . . . . void	removeUpdate (*javax.swing.event.DocumentEvent* e)

Classes

		JEditorPane.JEditorPaneAccessibleHypertextSupport.HTMLLink	javax.swing

Object
```
1.2 ○  └javax.accessibility.AccessibleHyperlink¹ - - - - - javax.accessibility.AccessibleAction
1.2        └JEditorPane↵
              .JEditorPaneAccessibleHypertextSupport↵
              .HTMLLink
```

1	public..................	**boolean**	**doAccessibleAction** (int i)
1	public....................	**Object**	**getAccessibleActionAnchor** (int i)
1	public......................	**int**	**getAccessibleActionCount** ()
1	public.................	**String**	**getAccessibleActionDescription** (int i)
1	public...................	**Object**	**getAccessibleActionObject** (int i)
1	public......................	**int**	**getEndIndex** ()
1	public......................	**int**	**getStartIndex** ()
*	public.................		**HTMLLink** (*javax.swing.text.Element* e)
1	public..................	**boolean**	**isValid** ()

J

	JFileChooser		javax.swing

Object
```
   ○  └java.awt.Component¹ - - - - - - - - - - - - - - - - - - - java.awt.image.ImageObserver, java.awt.MenuContainer,
                                                                         java.io.Serializable
           └java.awt.Container²
1.2 ○        └JComponent³ - - - - - - - - - - - - - - - - - - - java.io.Serializable
1.2             └JFileChooser - - - - - - - - - - - - - - - - - - - javax.accessibility.Accessible
```

1	*111 inherited members from java.awt.Component not shown*		
2	*39 inherited members from java.awt.Container not shown*		
3	*112 inherited members from JComponent not shown*		
	public.................	boolean	**accept** (java.io.File f)
3	protected......................		**accessibleContext**
	.... **javax.accessibility**↵		
	.AccessibleContext		
▲	public static final........	String	**ACCESSORY_CHANGED_PROPERTY** = "AccessoryChangedProperty"
	public.......................	void	**addActionListener** (*java.awt.event.ActionListener* l)
	public.......................	void	**addChoosableFileFilter** (javax.swing.filechooser.FileFilter filter)
▲	public static final........	String	**APPROVE_BUTTON_MNEMONIC_CHANGED_PROPERTY**
			= "ApproveButtonMnemonicChangedProperty"
▲	public static final........	String	**APPROVE_BUTTON_TEXT_CHANGED_PROPERTY**
			= "ApproveButtonTextChangedProperty"
▲	public static final........	String	**APPROVE_BUTTON_TOOL_TIP_TEXT_CHANGED_PROPERTY**
			= "ApproveButtonToolTipTextChangedProperty"
▲	public static final...........	int	**APPROVE_OPTION** = 0
▲	public static final........	String	**APPROVE_SELECTION** = "ApproveSelection"
	public......................void		**approveSelection** ()
▲	public static final...........	int	**CANCEL_OPTION** = 1
▲	public static final........	String	**CANCEL_SELECTION** = "CancelSelection"
	public......................void		**cancelSelection** ()
	public......................void		**changeToParentDirectory** ()
▲	public static final........	String	**CHOOSABLE_FILE_FILTER_CHANGED_PROPERTY**
			= "ChoosableFileFilterChangedProperty"
▲	public static final...........	int	**CUSTOM_DIALOG** = 2
▲	public static final........	String	**DIALOG_TITLE_CHANGED_PROPERTY** = "DialogTitleChangedProperty"
▲	public static final........	String	**DIALOG_TYPE_CHANGED_PROPERTY** = "DialogTypeChangedProperty"
▲	public static final...........	int	**DIRECTORIES_ONLY** = 1
▲	public static final........	String	**DIRECTORY_CHANGED_PROPERTY** = "directoryChanged"
	public......................void		**ensureFileIsVisible** (java.io.File f)
▲	public static final...........	int	**ERROR_OPTION** = -1
▲	public static final........	String	**FILE_FILTER_CHANGED_PROPERTY** = "fileFilterChanged"
▲	public static final........	String	**FILE_HIDING_CHANGED_PROPERTY** = "FileHidingChanged"
▲	public static final........	String	**FILE_SELECTION_MODE_CHANGED_PROPERTY** = "fileSelectionChanged"
▲	public static final........	String	**FILE_SYSTEM_VIEW_CHANGED_PROPERTY** = "FileSystemViewChanged"
▲	public static final........	String	**FILE_VIEW_CHANGED_PROPERTY** = "fileViewChanged"
▲	public static final...........	int	**FILES_AND_DIRECTORIES** = 2
▲	public static final...........	int	**FILES_ONLY** = 0
	protected....................void		**fireActionPerformed** (String command)
	public...................javax↵		**getAcceptAllFileFilter** ()
	.swing.filechooser.FileFilter		

Class *Interface* —extends - - -implements ○ abstract ● final △ static ▲ static final ✳ constructor x x—inherited x **x**—declared **x x**—overridden

3	public...	**javax.accessibility ↵ .AccessibleContext**	getAccessibleContext ()
	public	JComponent	**getAccessory** ()
	public	int	**getApproveButtonMnemonic** ()
	public	String	**getApproveButtonText** ()
	public	String	**getApproveButtonToolTipText** ()
	public	javax ↵ .swing.filechooser.FileFilter[]	**getChoosableFileFilters** ()
	public	java.io.File	**getCurrentDirectory** ()
	public	String	**getDescription** (java.io.File f)
	public	String	**getDialogTitle** ()
	public	int	**getDialogType** ()
	public	javax ↵ .swing.filechooser.FileFilter	**getFileFilter** ()
	public	int	**getFileSelectionMode** ()
	public	javax.swing ↵ .filechooser.FileSystemView	**getFileSystemView** ()
	public	javax ↵ .swing.filechooser.FileView	**getFileView** ()
	public	Icon	**getIcon** (java.io.File f)
	public	String	**getName** (java.io.File f)
	public	java.io.File	**getSelectedFile** ()
	public	java.io.File[]	**getSelectedFiles** ()
	public	String	**getTypeDescription** (java.io.File f)
	public	javax.swing.plaf.FileChooserUI	**getUI** ()
3	public	**String**	**getUIClassID** ()
	public	boolean	**isDirectorySelectionEnabled** ()
	public	boolean	**isFileHidingEnabled** ()
	public	boolean	**isFileSelectionEnabled** ()
	public	boolean	**isMultiSelectionEnabled** ()
	public	boolean	**isTraversable** (java.io.File f)
✳	public		**JFileChooser** ()
✳	public		**JFileChooser** (java.io.File currentDirectory)
✳	public		**JFileChooser** (String currentDirectoryPath)
✳	public		**JFileChooser** (javax.swing.filechooser.FileSystemView fsv)
✳	public		**JFileChooser** (java.io.File currentDirectory, javax.swing.filechooser.FileSystemView fsv)
✳	public		**JFileChooser** (String currentDirectoryPath, javax.swing.filechooser.FileSystemView fsv)
▲	public static final	String	**MULTI_SELECTION_ENABLED_CHANGED_PROPERTY** = "fileFilterChanged"
▲	public static final	int	**OPEN_DIALOG** = 0
3	protected	**String**	**paramString** ()
	public	void	**removeActionListener** (*java.awt.event.ActionListener* l)
	public	boolean	**removeChoosableFileFilter** (javax.swing.filechooser.FileFilter f)
	public	void	**rescanCurrentDirectory** ()
	public	void	**resetChoosableFileFilters** ()
▲	public static final	int	**SAVE_DIALOG** = 1
▲	public static final	String	**SELECTED_FILE_CHANGED_PROPERTY** = "SelectedFileChangedProperty"
▲	public static final	String	**SELECTED_FILES_CHANGED_PROPERTY** = "SelectedFilesChangedProperty"
	public	void	**setAccessory** (JComponent newAccessory)
	public	void	**setApproveButtonMnemonic** (char mnemonic)
	public	void	**setApproveButtonMnemonic** (int mnemonic)
	public	void	**setApproveButtonText** (String approveButtonText)
	public	void	**setApproveButtonToolTipText** (String toolTipText)
	public	void	**setCurrentDirectory** (java.io.File dir)
	public	void	**setDialogTitle** (String dialogTitle)
	public	void	**setDialogType** (int dialogType)
	public	void	**setFileFilter** (javax.swing.filechooser.FileFilter filter)
	public	void	**setFileHidingEnabled** (boolean b)
	public	void	**setFileSelectionMode** (int mode)
	public	void	**setFileSystemView** (javax.swing.filechooser.FileSystemView fsv)
	public	void	**setFileView** (javax.swing.filechooser.FileView fileView)
	public	void	**setMultiSelectionEnabled** (boolean b)
	public	void	**setSelectedFile** (java.io.File selectedFile)
	public	void	**setSelectedFiles** (java.io.File[] selectedFiles)
	protected	void	**setup** (javax.swing.filechooser.FileSystemView view)
	public	int	**showDialog** (java.awt.Component parent, String approveButtonText)
	public	int	**showOpenDialog** (java.awt.Component parent)
	public	int	**showSaveDialog** (java.awt.Component parent)
3	public	**void**	**updateUI** ()

J

Classes

JFileChooser.AccessibleJFileChooser			protected	javax.swing

Object
1.2 ○ └javax.accessibility.AccessibleContext [1]
1.2 ○   └JComponent.AccessibleJComponent [2] - - - - *java.io.Serializable, javax.accessibility.AccessibleComponent*
1.2   └JFileChooser.AccessibleJFileChooser

	1	*21 inherited members from javax.accessibility.AccessibleContext not shown*	
	2	*40 inherited members from JComponent.AccessibleJComponent not shown*	
✳		protected	**AccessibleJFileChooser** ()
	2	public . . . . **javax** ↵	**getAccessibleRole** ()
		.accessibility.AccessibleRole	

JFrame		javax.swing

Object
○ └java.awt.Component [1] - - - - - - - - - - - - - - - - - - - *java.awt.image.ImageObserver*, *java.awt.MenuContainer*,
                                            java.io.Serializable
  └java.awt.Container [2]
    └java.awt.Window [3]
      └java.awt.Frame [4] - - - - - - - - - - - - - - - - - *java.awt.MenuContainer*
1.2   └JFrame - *WindowConstants, javax.accessibility.Accessible* [5],
                                          RootPaneContainer [6]

	1	*129 inherited members from java.awt.Component not shown*	
	2	*44 inherited members from java.awt.Container not shown*	
	4	*33 inherited members from java.awt.Frame not shown*	
		protected javax.accessibility ↵	**accessibleContext**
		.AccessibleContext	
	2	protected . . . . **void**	**addImpl** (java.awt.Component comp, Object constraints, int index)
	3	public synchronized . . . . . . .void	addWindowListener (*java.awt.event.WindowListener* l)
	3	public . . . . .void	applyResourceBundle (String rbName)
	3	public . . . . .void	applyResourceBundle (java.util.ResourceBundle rb)
		protected . . . . JRootPane	**createRootPane** ()
	3	public . . . . .void	dispose ()
		protected . . . . .void	**frameInit** ()
	5	public . . . . javax.accessibility ↵	**getAccessibleContext** ()
		.AccessibleContext	
	6	public . . . . . . .java.awt.Container	**getContentPane** ()
		public . . . . int	**getDefaultCloseOperation** ()
	3	public . . . . java.awt.Component	getFocusOwner ()
	6	public . . . . java.awt.Component	**getGlassPane** ()
	3	public	getInputContext ()
		. . . . java.awt.im.InputContext	
		public . . . . JMenuBar	**getJMenuBar** ()
	6	public . . . . JLayeredPane	**getLayeredPane** ()
	3	public . . . . .java.util.Locale	getLocale ()
	3	public . . . . java.awt.Window[]	getOwnedWindows ()
	3	public . . . . .java.awt.Window	getOwner ()
	6	public . . . . JRootPane	**getRootPane** ()
	3	public . . . . . . .java.awt.Toolkit	getToolkit ()
●	3	public final . . . . .String	getWarningString ()
		protected . . . . boolean	**isRootPaneCheckingEnabled** ()
	3	public . . . . boolean	isShowing ()
✳		public	**JFrame** ()
✳		public	**JFrame** (String title)
	3	public . . . . .void	pack ()
	4	protected . . . . String	**paramString** ()
	3	protected . . . . .void	processEvent (java.awt.AWTEvent e)
	1	protected . . . . **void**	**processKeyEvent** (java.awt.event.KeyEvent e)
	3	protected . . . . **void**	**processWindowEvent** (java.awt.event.WindowEvent e)
	3	public synchronized . . . . . . .void	removeWindowListener (*java.awt.event.WindowListener* l)
		protected . . . . JRootPane	**rootPane**
		protected . . . . boolean	**rootPaneCheckingEnabled**
	6	public . . . . .void	**setContentPane** (java.awt.Container contentPane)
		public . . . . .void	**setDefaultCloseOperation** (int operation)
	6	public . . . . .void	**setGlassPane** (java.awt.Component glassPane)
		public . . . . .void	**setJMenuBar** (JMenuBar menubar)
	6	public . . . . .void	**setLayeredPane** (JLayeredPane layeredPane)
	2	public . . . . **void**	**setLayout** (*java.awt.LayoutManager* manager)

Class   *Interface*   —extends   - - -implements   ○ abstract   ● final   △ static   ▲ static final   ✳ constructor   x x—inherited   x **x**—declared   **x x**—overridden

	protected...................	void	**setRootPane** (JRootPane root)
	protected...................	void	**setRootPaneCheckingEnabled** (boolean enabled)
3	public......................	void	show ()
3	public......................	void	toBack ()
3	public......................	void	toFront ()
2	public......................	**void**	**update** (java.awt.Graphics g)

JFrame.AccessibleJFrame ␣␣␣␣␣␣␣␣␣␣␣␣ protected ␣␣␣␣␣␣ javax.swing

Object
1.2 ○ └javax.accessibility.AccessibleContext [1]
1.2 └JFrame.AccessibleJFrame - - - - - - - - - - - - - *java.io.Serializable, javax.accessibility.AccessibleComponent* [2]

1	*24 inherited members from javax.accessibility.AccessibleContext not shown*		
✱	protected......................		**AccessibleJFrame** ()
2	public......................	void	**addFocusListener** (*java.awt.event.FocusListener* l)
2	public.................	boolean	**contains** (java.awt.Point p)
2	public...................... *. javax.accessibility.Accessible*		**getAccessibleAt** (java.awt.Point p)
1	public................. *javax↩* *.accessibility.Accessible*		**getAccessibleChild** (int i)
1	public......................	**int**	**getAccessibleChildrenCount** ()
1	public... *javax.accessibility↩* *.AccessibleComponent*		**getAccessibleComponent** ()
1	public......................	**int**	**getAccessibleIndexInParent** ()
1	public.................	**String**	**getAccessibleName** ()
1	public................. *javax↩* *.accessibility.Accessible*		**getAccessibleParent** ()
1	public................. *javax↩* *.accessibility.AccessibleRole*		**getAccessibleRole** ()
1	public... *javax.accessibility↩* *.AccessibleStateSet*		**getAccessibleStateSet** ()
2	public...........java.awt.Color		**getBackground** ()
2	public...... java.awt.Rectangle		**getBounds** ()
2	public........... java.awt.Cursor		**getCursor** ()
2	public...........java.awt.Font		**getFont** ()
2	public.... java.awt.FontMetrics		**getFontMetrics** (java.awt.Font f)
2	public...........java.awt.Color		**getForeground** ()
1	public...........**java.util.Locale**		**getLocale** ()
2	public...........java.awt.Point		**getLocation** ()
2	public...........java.awt.Point		**getLocationOnScreen** ()
2	public......java.awt.Dimension		**getSize** ()
2	public.................	boolean	**isEnabled** ()
2	public.................	boolean	**isFocusTraversable** ()
2	public.................	boolean	**isShowing** ()
2	public.................	boolean	**isVisible** ()
2	public......................	void	**removeFocusListener** (*java.awt.event.FocusListener* l)
2	public......................	void	**requestFocus** ()
2	public......................	void	**setBackground** (java.awt.Color c)
2	public......................	void	**setBounds** (java.awt.Rectangle r)
2	public......................	void	**setCursor** (java.awt.Cursor cursor)
2	public......................	void	**setEnabled** (boolean b)
2	public......................	void	**setFont** (java.awt.Font f)
2	public......................	void	**setForeground** (java.awt.Color c)
2	public......................	void	**setLocation** (java.awt.Point p)
2	public......................	void	**setSize** (java.awt.Dimension d)
2	public......................	void	**setVisible** (boolean b)

JInternalFrame ␣␣␣␣␣␣␣␣␣␣␣␣␣␣␣␣ javax.swing

Object
○ └java.awt.Component [1] - - - - - - - - - - - - - - - - - - - *java.awt.image.ImageObserver, java.awt.MenuContainer,*
java.io.Serializable
└java.awt.Container [2]
1.2 ○ └JComponent [3] - *java.io.Serializable*
1.2 └JInternalFrame - - - - - - - - - - - - - - - - - - *javax.accessibility.Accessible, WindowConstants,*
RootPaneContainer [4]

1	*108 inherited members from java.awt.Component not shown*
2	*37 inherited members from java.awt.Container not shown*
3	*108 inherited members from JComponent not shown*

J

Classes

JInternalFrame

		modifier	type	member
	2	protected	**void**	**addImpl** (java.awt.Component comp, Object constraints, int index)
		public	void	**addInternalFrameListener** (*javax.swing.event.InternalFrameListener* l)
		protected	boolean	**closable**
▲		public static final	String	**CONTENT_PANE_PROPERTY** = "contentPane"
		protected	JRootPane	**createRootPane** ()
		protected	..JInternalFrame.JDesktopIcon	**desktopIcon**
		public	void	**dispose** ()
		protected	void	**fireInternalFrameEvent** (int id)
▲		public static final	String	**FRAME_ICON_PROPERTY** = "frameIcon"
		protected	*Icon*	**frameIcon**
	3	public	**javax.accessibility** ↩ **.AccessibleContext**	**getAccessibleContext** ()
	1	public	**java.awt.Color**	**getBackground** ()
	4	public	java.awt.Container	**getContentPane** ()
		public	int	**getDefaultCloseOperation** ()
		public	..JInternalFrame.JDesktopIcon	**getDesktopIcon** ()
		public	JDesktopPane	**getDesktopPane** ()
	1	public	**java.awt.Color**	**getForeground** ()
		public	*Icon*	**getFrameIcon** ()
	4	public	java.awt.Component	**getGlassPane** ()
		public	JMenuBar	**getJMenuBar** ()
		public	int	**getLayer** ()
	4	public	JLayeredPane	**getLayeredPane** ()
D		public	JMenuBar	**getMenuBar** ()
	3	public	**JRootPane**	**getRootPane** ()
		public	String	**getTitle** ()
		public	javax ↩ .swing.plaf.InternalFrameUI	**getUI** ()
	3	public	**String**	**getUIClassID** ()
●		public final	String	**getWarningString** ()
▲		public static final	String	**GLASS_PANE_PROPERTY** = "glassPane"
		protected	boolean	**iconable**
▲		public static final	String	**IS_CLOSED_PROPERTY** = "closed"
▲		public static final	String	**IS_ICON_PROPERTY** = "icon"
▲		public static final	String	**IS_MAXIMUM_PROPERTY** = "maximum"
▲		public static final	String	**IS_SELECTED_PROPERTY** = "selected"
		public	boolean	**isClosable** ()
		public	boolean	**isClosed** ()
		protected	boolean	**isClosed**
		public	boolean	**isIcon** ()
		protected	boolean	**isIcon**
		public	boolean	**isIconifiable** ()
		public	boolean	**isMaximizable** ()
		public	boolean	**isMaximum** ()
		protected	boolean	**isMaximum**
		public	boolean	**isResizable** ()
		protected	boolean	**isRootPaneCheckingEnabled** ()
		public	boolean	**isSelected** ()
		protected	boolean	**isSelected**
✳		public		**JInternalFrame** ()
✳		public		**JInternalFrame** (String title)
✳		public		**JInternalFrame** (String title, boolean resizable)
✳		public		**JInternalFrame** (String title, boolean resizable, boolean closable)
✳		public		**JInternalFrame** (String title, boolean resizable, boolean closable, boolean maximizable)
✳		public		**JInternalFrame** (String title, boolean resizable, boolean closable, boolean maximizable, boolean iconifiable)
▲		public static final	String	**LAYERED_PANE_PROPERTY** = "layeredPane"
		protected	boolean	**maximizable**
▲		public static final	String	**MENU_BAR_PROPERTY** = "menuBar"
		public	void	**moveToBack** ()
		public	void	**moveToFront** ()
		public	void	**pack** ()
	3	protected	**String**	**paramString** ()
		public	void	**removeInternalFrameListener** (*javax.swing.event.InternalFrameListener* l)
	3	public	**void**	**reshape** (int x, int y, int width, int height)
		protected	boolean	**resizable**
▲		public static final	String	**ROOT_PANE_PROPERTY** = "rootPane"
		protected	JRootPane	**rootPane**
		protected	boolean	**rootPaneCheckingEnabled**

Class   *Interface*   —extends   - - -implements   ○ abstract   ● final   △ static   ▲ static final   ✳ constructor   x x—inherited   x **x**—declared   **x x**—overridden

3	public	**void**	**setBackground**	(java.awt.Color c)
	public	void	**setClosable**	(boolean b)
	public	void	**setClosed**	(boolean b) throws java.beans.PropertyVetoException
4	public	void	**setContentPane**	(java.awt.Container c)
	public	void	**setDefaultCloseOperation**	(int operation)
	public	void	**setDesktopIcon**	(JInternalFrame.JDesktopIcon d)
3	public	**void**	**setForeground**	(java.awt.Color c)
	public	void	**setFrameIcon**	(*Icon* icon)
4	public	void	**setGlassPane**	(java.awt.Component glass)
	public	void	**setIcon**	(boolean b) throws java.beans.PropertyVetoException
	public	void	**setIconifiable**	(boolean b)
	public	void	**setJMenuBar**	(JMenuBar m)
	public	void	**setLayer**	(Integer layer)
4	public	void	**setLayeredPane**	(JLayeredPane layered)
2	public	**void**	**setLayout**	(*java.awt.LayoutManager* manager)
	public	void	**setMaximizable**	(boolean b)
	public	void	**setMaximum**	(boolean b) throws java.beans.PropertyVetoException
D	public	void	**setMenuBar**	(JMenuBar m)
	public	void	**setResizable**	(boolean b)
	protected	void	**setRootPane**	(JRootPane root)
	protected	void	**setRootPaneCheckingEnabled**	(boolean enabled)
	public	void	**setSelected**	(boolean selected) throws java.beans.PropertyVetoException
	public	void	**setTitle**	(String title)
	public	void	**setUI**	(javax.swing.plaf.InternalFrameUI ui)
3	public	**void**	**setVisible**	(boolean b)
1	public	**void**	**show**	()
	protected	String	**title**	
▲	public static final	String	**TITLE_PROPERTY**	= "title"
	public	void	**toBack**	()
	public	void	**toFront**	()
3	public	**void**	**updateUI**	()

JInternalFrame.AccessibleJInternalFrame   protected   javax.swing

```
      Object
1.2 ○  └─javax.accessibility.AccessibleContext¹
1.2 ○    └─JComponent.AccessibleJComponent² ---- java.io.Serializable, javax.accessibility.AccessibleComponent
1.2       └─JInternalFrame↩ ------------------ javax.accessibility.AccessibleValue³
                .AccessibleJInternalFrame
```

1	*20 inherited members from javax.accessibility.AccessibleContext not shown*			
2	*39 inherited members from JComponent.AccessibleJComponent not shown*			
*	protected		**AccessibleJInternalFrame**	()
2	public	**String**	**getAccessibleName**	()
2	public	**javax** ↩	**getAccessibleRole**	()
	.accessibility.AccessibleRole			
1	public	*javax.accessibility*↩	**getAccessibleValue**	()
	.AccessibleValue			
3	public	Number	**getCurrentAccessibleValue**	()
3	public	Number	**getMaximumAccessibleValue**	()
3	public	Number	**getMinimumAccessibleValue**	()
3	public	boolean	**setCurrentAccessibleValue**	(Number n)

JInternalFrame.JDesktopIcon   javax.swing

```
      Object
  ○  └─java.awt.Component¹ ------------------- java.awt.image.ImageObserver, java.awt.MenuContainer,
                                                       java.io.Serializable
        └─java.awt.Container²
1.2 ○      └─JComponent³ ----------------------- java.io.Serializable
1.2         └─JInternalFrame.JDesktopIcon -------- javax.accessibility.Accessible
```

1	*111 inherited members from java.awt.Component not shown*			
2	*39 inherited members from java.awt.Container not shown*			
3	*114 inherited members from JComponent not shown*			
3	public	**javax.accessibility** ↩	**getAccessibleContext**	()
	.AccessibleContext			
	public	JDesktopPane	**getDesktopPane**	()
	public	JInternalFrame	**getInternalFrame**	()
	public	javax ↩	**getUI**	()
	.swing.plaf.DesktopIconUI			

JInternalFrame.JDesktopIcon

3	public	**String**	**getUIClassID** ()
*	public		**JDesktopIcon** (JInternalFrame f)
	public	void	**setInternalFrame** (JInternalFrame f)
	public	void	**setUI** (javax.swing.plaf.DesktopIconUI ui)
3	public	**void**	**updateUI** ()

JInternalFrame.JDesktopIcon.AccessibleJDesktopIcon   protected   javax.swing

Object
1.2 O └javax.accessibility.AccessibleContext[1]
1.2 O   └JComponent.AccessibleJComponent[2] - - - - *java.io.Serializable*, *javax.accessibility.AccessibleComponent*
1.2   └JInternalFrame.JDesktopIcon↵ - - - - - - - - *javax.accessibility.AccessibleValue[3]*
       .AccessibleJDesktopIcon

1	*20 inherited members from javax.accessibility.AccessibleContext not shown*		
2	*40 inherited members from JComponent.AccessibleJComponent not shown*		
*	protected		**AccessibleJDesktopIcon** ()
2	public	**javax** ↵	**getAccessibleRole** ()
	.accessibility.AccessibleRole		
1	public	*javax.accessibility* ↵	**getAccessibleValue** ()
	.AccessibleValue		
3	public	Number	**getCurrentAccessibleValue** ()
3	public	Number	**getMaximumAccessibleValue** ()
3	public	Number	**getMinimumAccessibleValue** ()
3	public	boolean	**setCurrentAccessibleValue** (Number n)

JLabel   javax.swing

Object
O └java.awt.Component[1] - - - - - - - - - - - - - - - - - - - *java.awt.image.ImageObserver*, *java.awt.MenuContainer*,
                                          java.io.Serializable
  └java.awt.Container[2]
1.2 O   └JComponent[3] - *java.io.Serializable*
1.2   └JLabel - *SwingConstants*, *javax.accessibility.Accessible*

1	*111 inherited members from java.awt.Component not shown*		
2	*39 inherited members from java.awt.Container not shown*		
3	*113 inherited members from JComponent not shown*		
	protected	int	**checkHorizontalKey** (int key, String message)
	protected	int	**checkVerticalKey** (int key, String message)
3	public	**javax.accessibility** ↵	**getAccessibleContext** ()
	.AccessibleContext		
	public	*Icon*	**getDisabledIcon** ()
	public	int	**getDisplayedMnemonic** ()
	public	int	**getHorizontalAlignment** ()
	public	int	**getHorizontalTextPosition** ()
	public	*Icon*	**getIcon** ()
	public	int	**getIconTextGap** ()
	public	java.awt.Component	**getLabelFor** ()
	public	String	**getText** ()
	public javax.swing.plaf.LabelUI		**getUI** ()
3	public	**String**	**getUIClassID** ()
	public	int	**getVerticalAlignment** ()
	public	int	**getVerticalTextPosition** ()
*	public		**JLabel** ()
*	public		**JLabel** (String text)
*	public		**JLabel** (*Icon* image)
*	public		**JLabel** (String text, int horizontalAlignment)
*	public		**JLabel** (*Icon* image, int horizontalAlignment)
*	public		**JLabel** (String text, *Icon* icon, int horizontalAlignment)
	protected	java.awt.Component	**labelFor**
3	protected	**String**	**paramString** ()
	public	void	**setDisabledIcon** (*Icon* disabledIcon)
	public	void	**setDisplayedMnemonic** (char aChar)
	public	void	**setDisplayedMnemonic** (int key)
	public	void	**setHorizontalAlignment** (int alignment)
	public	void	**setHorizontalTextPosition** (int textPosition)
	public	void	**setIcon** (*Icon* icon)
	public	void	**setIconTextGap** (int iconTextGap)

Class   *Interface*   —extends   - - -implements   O abstract   ● final   △ static   ▲ static final   ✳ constructor   x x—inherited   x **x**—declared   **x x**—overridden

```
      public.....................void  setLabelFor (java.awt.Component c)
      public.....................void  setText (String text)
      public.....................void  setUI (javax.swing.plaf.LabelUI ui)
      public.....................void  setVerticalAlignment (int alignment)
      public.....................void  setVerticalTextPosition (int textPosition)
   3  public.....................void  updateUI ()
```

JLabel.AccessibleJLabel   protected   javax.swing

```
          Object
1.2 ○     └javax.accessibility.AccessibleContext¹
1.2 ○        └JComponent.AccessibleJComponent² ---- java.io.Serializable, javax.accessibility.AccessibleComponent
1.2              └JLabel.AccessibleJLabel
```

```
   1  21 inherited members from javax.accessibility.AccessibleContext not shown
   2  39 inherited members from JComponent.AccessibleJComponent not shown
*     protected.....................  AccessibleJLabel ()
   2  public.................. String  getAccessibleName ()
   2  public.................. javax↵  getAccessibleRole ()
      .accessibility.AccessibleRole
```

JLayeredPane   javax.swing

```
          Object
    ○     └java.awt.Component¹ ------------------- java.awt.image.ImageObserver, java.awt.MenuContainer,
                                                   java.io.Serializable
          └java.awt.Container²
1.2 ○        └JComponent³ -------------------- java.io.Serializable
1.2              └JLayeredPane -------------------- javax.accessibility.Accessible
```

```
   1  111 inherited members from java.awt.Component not shown
   2  37 inherited members from java.awt.Container not shown
   3  113 inherited members from JComponent not shown
   2  protected.................. void  addImpl (java.awt.Component comp, Object constraints, int index)
▲     public static final....... Integer  DEFAULT_LAYER  = new Integer(0)
▲     public static final....... Integer  DRAG_LAYER  = new Integer(400)
▲     public static final....... Integer  FRAME_CONTENT_LAYER  = new Integer(-30000)
   3  public... javax.accessibility↵  getAccessibleContext ()
      .AccessibleContext
      public.....................int  getComponentCountInLayer (int layer)
      public... java.awt.Component[]  getComponentsInLayer (int layer)
      protected... java.util.Hashtable  getComponentToLayer ()
      public.....................int  getIndexOf (java.awt.Component c)
      public.....................int  getLayer (java.awt.Component c)
△     public static.............int  getLayer (JComponent c)
△     public static .... JLayeredPane  getLayeredPaneAbove (java.awt.Component c)
      protected............... Integer  getObjectForLayer (int layer)
      public.....................int  getPosition (java.awt.Component c)
      public.....................int  highestLayer ()
      protected.................int  insertIndexForLayer (int layer, int position)
   3  public.................. boolean  isOptimizedDrawingEnabled ()
*     public.....................  JLayeredPane ()
▲     public static final......... String  LAYER_PROPERTY  = "layeredContainerLayer"
      public.....................int  lowestLayer ()
▲     public static final....... Integer  MODAL_LAYER  = new Integer(200)
      public.....................void  moveToBack (java.awt.Component c)
      public.....................void  moveToFront (java.awt.Component c)
   3  public.................. void  paint (java.awt.Graphics g)
▲     public static final....... Integer  PALETTE_LAYER  = new Integer(100)
   3  protected............... String  paramString ()
▲     public static final....... Integer  POPUP_LAYER  = new Integer(300)
△     public static .............void  putLayer (JComponent c, int layer)
   2  public.................. void  remove (int index)
      public.....................void  setLayer (java.awt.Component c, int layer)
      public.....................void  setLayer (java.awt.Component c, int layer, int position)
      public.....................void  setPosition (java.awt.Component c, int position)
```

Classes

JLayeredPane.AccessibleJLayeredPane	protected	javax.swing

Object
1.2 ○ └javax.accessibility.AccessibleContext [1]
1.2 ○   └JComponent.AccessibleJComponent [2] - - - - *java.io.Serializable, javax.accessibility.AccessibleComponent*
1.2   └JLayeredPane.AccessibleJLayeredPane

	1	*21 inherited members from javax.accessibility.AccessibleContext not shown*	
	2	*40 inherited members from JComponent.AccessibleJComponent not shown*	
*		protected....................	**AccessibleJLayeredPane** ()
	2	public................. **javax** ↵	**getAccessibleRole** ()
		.accessibility.AccessibleRole	

JList		javax.swing

Object
○ └java.awt.Component [1] - - - - - - - - - - - - - - - - - - *java.awt.image.ImageObserver, java.awt.MenuContainer,*
                                                                     java.io.Serializable
  └java.awt.Container [2]
1.2 ○   └JComponent [3] - *java.io.Serializable*
1.2   └JList - *Scrollable [4], javax.accessibility.Accessible*

	1	*111 inherited members from java.awt.Component not shown*
	2	*39 inherited members from java.awt.Container not shown*
	3	*113 inherited members from JComponent not shown*
		public......................void **addListSelectionListener** (*javax.swing.event.ListSelectionListener* listener)
		public......................void **addSelectionInterval** (int anchor, int lead)
		public......................void **clearSelection** ()
		protected.. *ListSelectionModel* **createSelectionModel** ()
		public......................void **ensureIndexIsVisible** (int index)
		protected......................void **fireSelectionValueChanged** (int firstIndex, int lastIndex, boolean isAdjusting)
	3	public... **javax.accessibility** ↵ **getAccessibleContext** ()
		.AccessibleContext
		public.......................int **getAnchorSelectionIndex** ()
		public...... java.awt.Rectangle **getCellBounds** (int index1, int index2)
		public......... *ListCellRenderer* **getCellRenderer** ()
		public.......................int **getFirstVisibleIndex** ()
		public.......................int **getFixedCellHeight** ()
		public.......................int **getFixedCellWidth** ()
		public.......................int **getLastVisibleIndex** ()
		public.......................int **getLeadSelectionIndex** ()
		public.......................int **getMaxSelectionIndex** ()
		public.......................int **getMinSelectionIndex** ()
		public.................. *ListModel* **getModel** ()
	4	public...... java.awt.Dimension **getPreferredScrollableViewportSize** ()
		public....................Object **getPrototypeCellValue** ()
	4	public.......................int **getScrollableBlockIncrement** (java.awt.Rectangle visibleRect, int orientation,
		int direction)
	4	public.................. boolean **getScrollableTracksViewportHeight** ()
	4	public.................. boolean **getScrollableTracksViewportWidth** ()
	4	public.......................int **getScrollableUnitIncrement** (java.awt.Rectangle visibleRect, int orientation,
		int direction)
		public.......................int **getSelectedIndex** ()
		public......................int[] **getSelectedIndices** ()
		public....................Object **getSelectedValue** ()
		public...................Object[] **getSelectedValues** ()
		public............java.awt.Color **getSelectionBackground** ()
		public............java.awt.Color **getSelectionForeground** ()
		public.......................int **getSelectionMode** ()
		public..... *ListSelectionModel* **getSelectionModel** ()
		public.. javax.swing.plaf.ListUI **getUI** ()
	3	public.................. **String** **getUIClassID** ()
		public.................. boolean **getValueIsAdjusting** ()
		public.......................int **getVisibleRowCount** ()
		public...........java.awt.Point **indexToLocation** (int index)
		public.................. boolean **isSelectedIndex** (int index)
		public.................. boolean **isSelectionEmpty** ()
*		public............................ **JList** ()
*		public............................ **JList** (Object[] listData)
*		public............................ **JList** (java.util.Vector listData)

Class   *Interface*   —extends   - - -implements   ○ abstract   ● final   △ static   ▲ static final   ✳ constructor   x x—inherited   x **x**—declared   **x x**—overridden

446

	public...........................		**JList** (*ListModel* dataModel)
	public...........................int		**locationToIndex** (java.awt.Point location)
3	protected............... **String**		**paramString** ()
	public...........................void		**removeListSelectionListener** (*javax.swing.event.ListSelectionListener* listener)
	public...........................void		**removeSelectionInterval** (int index0, int index1)
	public...........................void		**setCellRenderer** (*ListCellRenderer* cellRenderer)
	public...........................void		**setFixedCellHeight** (int height)
	public...........................void		**setFixedCellWidth** (int width)
	public...........................void		**setListData** (Object[] listData)
	public...........................void		**setListData** (java.util.Vector listData)
	public...........................void		**setModel** (*ListModel* model)
	public...........................void		**setPrototypeCellValue** (Object prototypeCellValue)
	public...........................void		**setSelectedIndex** (int index)
	public...........................void		**setSelectedIndices** (int[] indices)
	public...........................void		**setSelectedValue** (Object anObject, boolean shouldScroll)
	public...........................void		**setSelectionBackground** (java.awt.Color selectionBackground)
	public...........................void		**setSelectionForeground** (java.awt.Color selectionForeground)
	public...........................void		**setSelectionInterval** (int anchor, int lead)
	public...........................void		**setSelectionMode** (int selectionMode)
	public...........................void		**setSelectionModel** (*ListSelectionModel* selectionModel)
	public...........................void		**setUI** (javax.swing.plaf.ListUI ui)
	public...........................void		**setValueIsAdjusting** (boolean b)
	public...........................void		**setVisibleRowCount** (int visibleRowCount)
3	public........................... **void**		**updateUI** ()

JList.AccessibleJList   protected   javax.swing

```
        Object
1.2 ○   └javax.accessibility.AccessibleContext 1
1.2 ○     └JComponent.AccessibleJComponent 2 ---- java.io.Serializable, javax.accessibility.AccessibleComponent
1.2         └JList.AccessibleJList - - - - - - - - - - - - - javax.accessibility.AccessibleSelection 3, java.beans↩
                                                            .PropertyChangeListener 4 (java.util.EventListener), javax↩
                                                            .swing.event.ListSelectionListener 5 (java.util.EventListener),
                                                            javax.swing.event.ListDataListener 6 (java.util.EventListener)
```

1	*20 inherited members from javax.accessibility.AccessibleContext not shown*		
2	*36 inherited members from JComponent.AccessibleJComponent not shown*		
*	public...........................		**AccessibleJList** ()
3	public...........................void		**addAccessibleSelection** (int i)
3	public...........................void		**clearAccessibleSelection** ()
6	public...........................void		**contentsChanged** (javax.swing.event.ListDataEvent e)
2	public.................. *javax↩* *.accessibility.Accessible*		**getAccessibleAt** (java.awt.Point p)
2	public.................. *javax↩* *.accessibility.Accessible*		**getAccessibleChild** (int i)
2	public.................. **int**		**getAccessibleChildrenCount** ()
2	public.................. **javax ↩** *.accessibility.AccessibleRole*		**getAccessibleRole** ()
1	public... *javax.accessibility↩* *.AccessibleSelection*		**getAccessibleSelection** ()
3	public........................... *. javax.accessibility.Accessible*		**getAccessibleSelection** (int i)
3	public..........................int		**getAccessibleSelectionCount** ()
2	public... **javax.accessibility ↩** *.AccessibleStateSet*		**getAccessibleStateSet** ()
6	public...........................void		**intervalAdded** (javax.swing.event.ListDataEvent e)
6	public...........................void		**intervalRemoved** (javax.swing.event.ListDataEvent e)
3	public.................. boolean		**isAccessibleChildSelected** (int i)
4	public...........................void		**propertyChange** (java.beans.PropertyChangeEvent e)
3	public...........................void		**removeAccessibleSelection** (int i)
3	public...........................void		**selectAllAccessibleSelection** ()
5	public...........................void		**valueChanged** (javax.swing.event.ListSelectionEvent e)

JList.AccessibleJList.AccessibleJListChild   protected   javax.swing

```
        Object
1.2 ○   └javax.accessibility.AccessibleContext 1
1.2       └JList.AccessibleJList.AccessibleJListChild - javax.accessibility.Accessible 2, javax.accessibility↩
                                                        .AccessibleComponent 3
```

JList.AccessibleJList.AccessibleJListChild

	1	*16 inherited members from javax.accessibility.AccessibleContext not shown*	
＊		public............................	**AccessibleJListChild** (JList parent, int indexInParent)
	3	public........................void	**addFocusListener** (*java.awt.event.FocusListener* l)
	1	public.......................**void**	**addPropertyChangeListener** (*java.beans.PropertyChangeListener* l)
	3	public........................boolean	**contains** (java.awt.Point p)
	1	public...*javax.accessibility*↵ *.AccessibleAction*	**getAccessibleAction** ()
	3	public............................ *. javax.accessibility.Accessible*	**getAccessibleAt** (java.awt.Point p)
	1	public..................**javax**↵ *.accessibility.Accessible*	**getAccessibleChild** (int i)
	1	public........................**int**	**getAccessibleChildrenCount** ()
	1	public...*javax.accessibility*↵ *.AccessibleComponent*	**getAccessibleComponent** ()
	2	public.... javax.accessibility ↵ *.AccessibleContext*	**getAccessibleContext** ()
	1	public...................**String**	**getAccessibleDescription** ()
	1	public........................**int**	**getAccessibleIndexInParent** ()
	1	public....................**String**	**getAccessibleName** ()
	1	public.................**javax**↵ *.accessibility.AccessibleRole*	**getAccessibleRole** ()
	1	public...*javax.accessibility*↵ *.AccessibleSelection*	**getAccessibleSelection** ()
	1	public...*javax.accessibility*↵ *.AccessibleStateSet*	**getAccessibleStateSet** ()
	1	public.................**javax**↵ *.accessibility.AccessibleText*	**getAccessibleText** ()
	1	public...*javax.accessibility*↵ *.AccessibleValue*	**getAccessibleValue** ()
	3	public...........java.awt.Color	**getBackground** ()
	3	public.........java.awt.Rectangle	**getBounds** ()
	3	public..........java.awt.Cursor	**getCursor** ()
	3	public.............java.awt.Font	**getFont** ()
	3	public.... java.awt.FontMetrics	**getFontMetrics** (java.awt.Font f)
	3	public.........java.awt.Color	**getForeground** ()
	1	public................**java.util.Locale**	**getLocale** ()
	3	public..........java.awt.Point	**getLocation** ()
	3	public..........java.awt.Point	**getLocationOnScreen** ()
	3	public......java.awt.Dimension	**getSize** ()
	3	public...............boolean	**isEnabled** ()
	3	public...............boolean	**isFocusTraversable** ()
	3	public...............boolean	**isShowing** ()
	3	public...............boolean	**isVisible** ()
	3	public.....................void	**removeFocusListener** (*java.awt.event.FocusListener* l)
	1	public.......................**void**	**removePropertyChangeListener** (*java.beans.PropertyChangeListener* l)
	3	public.....................void	**requestFocus** ()
	1	public.................**void**	**setAccessibleDescription** (String s)
	1	public.................**void**	**setAccessibleName** (String s)
	3	public.....................void	**setBackground** (java.awt.Color c)
	3	public.....................void	**setBounds** (java.awt.Rectangle r)
	3	public.....................void	**setCursor** (java.awt.Cursor c)
	3	public.....................void	**setEnabled** (boolean b)
	3	public.....................void	**setFont** (java.awt.Font f)
	3	public.....................void	**setForeground** (java.awt.Color c)
	3	public.....................void	**setLocation** (java.awt.Point p)
	3	public.....................void	**setSize** (java.awt.Dimension d)
	3	public.....................void	**setVisible** (boolean b)

JMenu

javax.swing

```
Object
○  └java.awt.Component¹ - - - - - - - - - - - - - - - - - - - java.awt.image.ImageObserver, java.awt.MenuContainer,
                                                             java.io.Serializable
       └java.awt.Container²
1.2 ○     └JComponent³ - - - - - - - - - - - - - - - - - - - - java.io.Serializable
1.2 ○       └AbstractButton⁴ - - - - - - - - - - - - - - - - - java.awt.ItemSelectable, SwingConstants
1.2           └JMenuItem⁵ - - - - - - - - - - - - - - - - - - javax.accessibility.Accessible, MenuElement
1.2             └JMenu - - - - - - - - - - - - - - - - - - - javax.accessibility.Accessible, MenuElement
```

Class   *Interface*   —extends   - - -implements   ○ abstract   ● final   △ static   ▲ static final   ＊ constructor   x x—inherited   x **x**—declared   **x x**—overridden

1		*111 inherited members from java.awt.Component not shown*	
2		*35 inherited members from java.awt.Container not shown*	
3		*110 inherited members from JComponent not shown*	
4		*85 inherited members from AbstractButton not shown*	
2	public...	**java.awt.Component**	**add** (java.awt.Component c)
	public..............	JMenuItem	**add** (String s)
	public..............	JMenuItem	**add** (*Action* a)
	public..............	JMenuItem	**add** (JMenuItem menuItem)
5	public.....................	void	addMenuDragMouseListener (*javax.swing.event.MenuDragMouseListener* l)
5	public.....................	void	addMenuKeyListener (*javax.swing.event.MenuKeyListener* l)
	public.....................	void	**addMenuListener** (*javax.swing.event.MenuListener* l)
	public.....................	void	**addSeparator** ()
	protected........	*java.beans*↵ *.PropertyChangeListener*	**createActionChangeListener** (JMenuItem b)
	protected..	JMenu.WinListener	**createWinListener** (JPopupMenu p)
4	public.....................	**void**	**doClick** (int pressTime)
	protected.................	void	**fireMenuCanceled** ()
	protected.................	void	**fireMenuDeselected** ()
5	protected.................	void	fireMenuDragMouseDragged (javax.swing.event.MenuDragMouseEvent event)
5	protected.................	void	fireMenuDragMouseEntered (javax.swing.event.MenuDragMouseEvent event)
5	protected.................	void	fireMenuDragMouseExited (javax.swing.event.MenuDragMouseEvent event)
5	protected.................	void	fireMenuDragMouseReleased (javax.swing.event.MenuDragMouseEvent event)
5	protected.................	void	fireMenuKeyPressed (javax.swing.event.MenuKeyEvent event)
5	protected.................	void	fireMenuKeyReleased (javax.swing.event.MenuKeyEvent event)
5	protected.................	void	fireMenuKeyTyped (javax.swing.event.MenuKeyEvent event)
	protected.................	void	**fireMenuSelected** ()
5	public..............	KeyStroke	getAccelerator ()
5	public...	**javax.accessibility**↵ **.AccessibleContext**	**getAccessibleContext** ()
5	public...	**java.awt.Component**	**getComponent** ()
	public.....................	int	**getDelay** ()
	public..............	JMenuItem	**getItem** (int pos)
	public.....................	int	**getItemCount** ()
	public....	java.awt.Component	**getMenuComponent** (int n)
	public.....................	int	**getMenuComponentCount** ()
	public...	java.awt.Component[]	**getMenuComponents** ()
	public..........	JPopupMenu	**getPopupMenu** ()
5	public.........	*MenuElement[]*	**getSubElements** ()
5	public................	**String**	**getUIClassID** ()
5	protected.................	void	init (String text, *Icon* icon)
	public.................	void	**insert** (String s, int pos)
	public..............	JMenuItem	**insert** (*Action* a, int pos)
	public..............	JMenuItem	**insert** (JMenuItem mi, int pos)
	public.................	void	**insertSeparator** (int index)
5	public................	boolean	isArmed ()
	public................	boolean	**isMenuComponent** (java.awt.Component c)
	public................	boolean	**isPopupMenuVisible** ()
4	public................	**boolean**	**isSelected** ()
	public................	boolean	**isTearOff** ()
	public................	boolean	**isTopLevelMenu** ()
*	public.....................		**JMenu** ()
*	public.....................		**JMenu** (String s)
*	public.....................		**JMenu** (String s, boolean b)
5	public.................	**void**	**menuSelectionChanged** (boolean isIncluded)
5	protected................	**String**	**paramString** ()
	protected..	JMenu.WinListener	**popupListener**
3	protected.................	**void**	**processKeyEvent** (java.awt.event.KeyEvent e)
5	public.....................	void	processKeyEvent (java.awt.event.KeyEvent e, *MenuElement[]* path, MenuSelectionManager manager)
5	public.....................	void	processMenuDragMouseEvent (javax.swing.event.MenuDragMouseEvent e)
5	public.....................	void	processMenuKeyEvent (javax.swing.event.MenuKeyEvent e)
5	public.....................	void	processMouseEvent (java.awt.event.MouseEvent e, *MenuElement[]* path, MenuSelectionManager manager)
2	public.....................	**void**	**remove** (int pos)
2	public.....................	**void**	**remove** (java.awt.Component c)
	public.....................	void	**remove** (JMenuItem item)
2	public.....................	**void**	**removeAll** ()
5	public.....................	void	removeMenuDragMouseListener (*javax.swing.event.MenuDragMouseListener* l)
5	public.....................	void	removeMenuKeyListener (*javax.swing.event.MenuKeyListener* l)
	public.....................	void	**removeMenuListener** (*javax.swing.event.MenuListener* l)
5	public.....................	**void**	**setAccelerator** (KeyStroke keyStroke)
	public.....................	void	setArmed (boolean b)
	public.....................	void	**setDelay** (int d)
5	public.....................	void	setEnabled (boolean b)

Classes

449

JMenu

	public	void	**setMenuLocation** (int x, int y)
4	public	**void**	**setModel** (*ButtonModel* newModel)
	public	void	**setPopupMenuVisible** (boolean b)
4	public	**void**	**setSelected** (boolean b)
5	public	void	setUI (javax.swing.plaf.MenuItemUI ui)
5	public	**void**	**updateUI** ()

JMenu.AccessibleJMenu   protected   javax.swing

```
      Object
1.2 ○ └─javax.accessibility.AccessibleContext 1
1.2 ○    └─JComponent.AccessibleJComponent 2 - - - - java.io.Serializable, javax.accessibility.AccessibleComponent
1.2 ○       └─AbstractButton ←- - - - - - - - - - - - - - - javax.accessibility.AccessibleAction,
                .AccessibleAbstractButton 3                     javax.accessibility.AccessibleValue
1.2          └─JMenuItem.AccessibleJMenuItem 4 - - - javax.swing.event.ChangeListener (java.util.EventListener)
1.2             └─JMenu.AccessibleJMenu - - - - - - - - - javax.accessibility.AccessibleSelection 5
```

	1	*18 inherited members from javax.accessibility.AccessibleContext not shown*	
	2	*36 inherited members from JComponent.AccessibleJComponent not shown*	
✳		protected	**AccessibleJMenu** ()
5	public	void	**addAccessibleSelection** (int i)
5	public	void	**clearAccessibleSelection** ()
3	public	boolean	doAccessibleAction (int i)
3	public	*javax*←	getAccessibleAction ()
	.accessibility.AccessibleAction		
3	public	int	getAccessibleActionCount ()
3	public	String	getAccessibleActionDescription (int i)
2	public	***javax*←**	**getAccessibleChild** (int i)
	.accessibility.Accessible		
2	public	**int**	**getAccessibleChildrenCount** ()
3	public	String	getAccessibleName ()
4	public	**javax ←**	**getAccessibleRole** ()
	.accessibility.AccessibleRole		
1	public...	***javax.accessibility*←**	**getAccessibleSelection** ()
	.AccessibleSelection		
5	public		**getAccessibleSelection** (int i)
	. javax.accessibility.Accessible		
5	public	int	**getAccessibleSelectionCount** ()
3	public...	javax.accessibility ←	getAccessibleStateSet ()
	.AccessibleStateSet		
3	public	*javax*←	getAccessibleValue ()
	.accessibility.AccessibleValue		
3	public	Number	getCurrentAccessibleValue ()
3	public	Number	getMaximumAccessibleValue ()
3	public	Number	getMinimumAccessibleValue ()
5	public	boolean	**isAccessibleChildSelected** (int i)
5	public	void	**removeAccessibleSelection** (int i)
5	public	void	**selectAllAccessibleSelection** ()
3	public	boolean	setCurrentAccessibleValue (Number n)
4	public	void	stateChanged (javax.swing.event.ChangeEvent e)

JMenu.WinListener   protected   javax.swing

```
      Object
1.1 ○ └─java.awt.event.WindowAdapter 1 - - - - - - - - - - java.awt.event.WindowListener (java.util.EventListener)
1.2    └─JMenu.WinListener - - - - - - - - - - - - - - - - - - java.io.Serializable
```

	1	public	void	windowActivated (java.awt.event.WindowEvent e)
	1	public	void	windowClosed (java.awt.event.WindowEvent e)
	1	public	**void**	**windowClosing** (java.awt.event.WindowEvent e)
	1	public	void	windowDeactivated (java.awt.event.WindowEvent e)
	1	public	void	windowDeiconified (java.awt.event.WindowEvent e)
	1	public	void	windowIconified (java.awt.event.WindowEvent e)
	1	public	void	windowOpened (java.awt.event.WindowEvent e)
✳		public		**WinListener** (JPopupMenu p)

Class   *Interface*   —extends   - - -implements   ○ abstract   ● final   △ static   ▲ static final   ✳ constructor   x x—inherited   x **x**—declared   **x x**—overridden

JMenuBar
javax.swing

```
        Object
  ○     └java.awt.Component 1 - - - - - - - - - - - - - - - - - - - java.awt.image.ImageObserver, java.awt.MenuContainer,
                                                                    java.io.Serializable
          └java.awt.Container 2
1.2 ○       └JComponent 3 - - - - - - - - - - - - - - - - - - - - java.io.Serializable
1.2           └JMenuBar - - - - - - - - - - - - - - - - - - - - javax.accessibility.Accessible, MenuElement 4
```

1	*111 inherited members from java.awt.Component not shown*		
2	*39 inherited members from java.awt.Container not shown*		
3	*109 inherited members from JComponent not shown*		
	public	JMenu	**add** (JMenu c)
3	public	**void**	**addNotify** ()
3	public	**javax.accessibility** ↵ **.AccessibleContext**	**getAccessibleContext** ()
4	public	java.awt.Component	**getComponent** ()
	public	java.awt.Component	**getComponentAtIndex** (int i)
	public	int	**getComponentIndex** (java.awt.Component c)
	public	JMenu	**getHelpMenu** ()
	public	java.awt.Insets	**getMargin** ()
	public	JMenu	**getMenu** (int index)
	public	int	**getMenuCount** ()
	public	*SingleSelectionModel*	**getSelectionModel** ()
4	public	*MenuElement[]*	**getSubElements** ()
	public	*... javax.swing.plaf.MenuBarUI*	**getUI** ()
3	public	**String**	**getUIClassID** ()
	public	boolean	**isBorderPainted** ()
3	public	**boolean**	**isManagingFocus** ()
	public	boolean	**isSelected** ()
∗	public		**JMenuBar** ()
4	public	void	**menuSelectionChanged** (boolean isIncluded)
3	protected	**void**	**paintBorder** (java.awt.Graphics g)
3	protected	**String**	**paramString** ()
4	public	void	**processKeyEvent** (java.awt.event.KeyEvent e, *MenuElement[]* path, MenuSelectionManager manager)
4	public	void	**processMouseEvent** (java.awt.event.MouseEvent event, *MenuElement[]* path, MenuSelectionManager manager)
3	public	**void**	**removeNotify** ()
	public	void	**setBorderPainted** (boolean s)
	public	void	**setHelpMenu** (JMenu menu)
	public	void	**setMargin** (java.awt.Insets margin)
	public	void	**setSelected** (java.awt.Component sel)
	public	void	**setSelectionModel** (*SingleSelectionModel* model)
	public	void	**setUI** (javax.swing.plaf.MenuBarUI ui)
3	public	**void**	**updateUI** ()

JMenuBar.AccessibleJMenuBar
protected
javax.swing

```
        Object
1.2 ○   └javax.accessibility.AccessibleContext 1
1.2 ○     └JComponent.AccessibleJComponent 2 - - - - java.io.Serializable, javax.accessibility.AccessibleComponent
1.2         └JMenuBar.AccessibleJMenuBar - - - - - - - javax.accessibility.AccessibleSelection 3
```

1	*20 inherited members from javax.accessibility.AccessibleContext not shown*		
2	*39 inherited members from JComponent.AccessibleJComponent not shown*		
∗	protected		**AccessibleJMenuBar** ()
3	public	void	**addAccessibleSelection** (int i)
3	public	void	**clearAccessibleSelection** ()
2	public	**javax** ↵ **.accessibility.AccessibleRole**	**getAccessibleRole** ()
1	public	**javax.accessibility** ↵ **.AccessibleSelection**	**getAccessibleSelection** ()
3	public	*. javax.accessibility.Accessible*	**getAccessibleSelection** (int i)
3	public	int	**getAccessibleSelectionCount** ()
2	public	**javax.accessibility** ↵ **.AccessibleStateSet**	**getAccessibleStateSet** ()
3	public	boolean	**isAccessibleChildSelected** (int i)
3	public	void	**removeAccessibleSelection** (int i)

J

Classes

JMenuBar.AccessibleJMenuBar

public......................void **selectAllAccessibleSelection** ()

JMenuItem	javax.swing

Object
    ○   └java.awt.Component[1] - *java.awt.image.ImageObserver*, *java.awt.MenuContainer*,
                                          java.io.Serializable
           └java.awt.Container[2]
1.2 ○   └JComponent[3] - *java.io.Serializable*
1.2 ○   └AbstractButton[4] - - - - - - - - - - - - - - - - - *java.awt.ItemSelectable*, *SwingConstants*
1.2   └JMenuItem - *javax.accessibility.Accessible*, *MenuElement*[5]

    1 *111 inherited members from java.awt.Component not shown*
    2 *39 inherited members from java.awt.Container not shown*
    3 *111 inherited members from JComponent not shown*
    4 *89 inherited members from AbstractButton not shown*
      public......................void **addMenuDragMouseListener** (*javax.swing.event.MenuDragMouseListener* l)
      public......................void **addMenuKeyListener** (*javax.swing.event.MenuKeyListener* l)
      protected..................void **fireMenuDragMouseDragged** (javax.swing.event.MenuDragMouseEvent event)
      protected..................void **fireMenuDragMouseEntered** (javax.swing.event.MenuDragMouseEvent event)
      protected..................void **fireMenuDragMouseExited** (javax.swing.event.MenuDragMouseEvent event)
      protected..................void **fireMenuDragMouseReleased** (javax.swing.event.MenuDragMouseEvent event)
      protected..................void **fireMenuKeyPressed** (javax.swing.event.MenuKeyEvent event)
      protected..................void **fireMenuKeyReleased** (javax.swing.event.MenuKeyEvent event)
      protected..................void **fireMenuKeyTyped** (javax.swing.event.MenuKeyEvent event)
      public...............KeyStroke **getAccelerator** ()
    3 public... **javax.accessibility** ↩ **getAccessibleContext** ()
      .AccessibleContext
    5 public.... java.awt.Component **getComponent** ()
    5 public........... *MenuElement[]* **getSubElements** ()
    3 public....................**String** **getUIClassID** ()
    4 protected..................**void** **init** (String text, *Icon* icon)
      public................boolean **isArmed** ()
  * public............... **JMenuItem** ()
  * public............... **JMenuItem** (String text)
  * public............... **JMenuItem** (*Icon* icon)
  * public............... **JMenuItem** (String text, *Icon* icon)
  * public............... **JMenuItem** (String text, int mnemonic)
    5 public......................void **menuSelectionChanged** (boolean isIncluded)
    4 protected...........**String** **paramString** ()
    5 public......................void **processKeyEvent** (java.awt.event.KeyEvent e, *MenuElement[]* path,
                         MenuSelectionManager manager)
      public......................void **processMenuDragMouseEvent** (javax.swing.event.MenuDragMouseEvent e)
      public......................void **processMenuKeyEvent** (javax.swing.event.MenuKeyEvent e)
    5 public......................void **processMouseEvent** (java.awt.event.MouseEvent e, *MenuElement[]* path,
                         MenuSelectionManager manager)
      public......................void **removeMenuDragMouseListener** (*javax.swing.event.MenuDragMouseListener* l)
      public......................void **removeMenuKeyListener** (*javax.swing.event.MenuKeyListener* l)
      public......................void **setAccelerator** (KeyStroke keyStroke)
      public......................void **setArmed** (boolean b)
    4 public....................**void** **setEnabled** (boolean b)
      public......................void **setUI** (javax.swing.plaf.MenuItemUI ui)
    4 public....................**void** **updateUI** ()

JMenuItem.AccessibleJMenuItem	protected	javax.swing

Object
1.2 ○ └javax.accessibility.AccessibleContext[1]
1.2 ○   └JComponent.AccessibleJComponent[2] - - - - *java.io.Serializable*, *javax.accessibility.AccessibleComponent*
1.2 ○   └AbstractButton↩ - - - - - - - - - - - - - - - - - *javax.accessibility.AccessibleAction*,
        .AccessibleAbstractButton[3]   *javax.accessibility.AccessibleValue*
1.2   └JMenuItem.AccessibleJMenuItem - - - - *javax.swing.event.ChangeListener*[4] (*java.util.EventListener*)

    1 *19 inherited members from javax.accessibility.AccessibleContext not shown*
    2 *38 inherited members from JComponent.AccessibleJComponent not shown*
    3 public................. boolean **doAccessibleAction** (int i)
    3 public....................*javax*↩ **getAccessibleAction** ()
      .accessibility.AccessibleAction
    3 public........................int **getAccessibleActionCount** ()

Class   *Interface* —extends - - -implements ○ abstract ● final △ static ▲ static final ✳ constructor x x—inherited x **x**—declared **x x**—overridden

3	public	String	getAccessibleActionDescription (int i)
3	public	String	getAccessibleName ()
2	public	**javax ↵ .accessibility.AccessibleRole**	**getAccessibleRole** ()
3	public	javax.accessibility ↵ .AccessibleStateSet	getAccessibleStateSet ()
3	public	*javax ↵ .accessibility.AccessibleValue*	getAccessibleValue ()
3	public	Number	getCurrentAccessibleValue ()
3	public	Number	getMaximumAccessibleValue ()
3	public	Number	getMinimumAccessibleValue ()
3	public	boolean	setCurrentAccessibleValue (Number n)
4	public	void	**stateChanged** (javax.swing.event.ChangeEvent e)

JOptionPane   javax.swing

```
        Object
    ○   └─java.awt.Component¹ - - - - - - - - - - - - - - - - - - - - java.awt.image.ImageObserver, java.awt.MenuContainer,
                                                                      java.io.Serializable
            └─java.awt.Container²
1.2 ○         └─JComponent³ - - - - - - - - - - - - - - - - - - - java.io.Serializable
1.2             └─JOptionPane - - - - - - - - - - - - - - - - - - javax.accessibility.Accessible
```

1	*111 inherited members from java.awt.Component not shown*		
2	*39 inherited members from java.awt.Container not shown*		
3	*113 inherited members from JComponent not shown*		
▲	public static final	int	**CANCEL_OPTION** = 2
▲	public static final	int	**CLOSED_OPTION** = -1
	public	JDialog	**createDialog** (java.awt.Component parentComponent, String title)
	public	JInternalFrame	**createInternalFrame** (java.awt.Component parentComponent, String title)
▲	public static final	int	**DEFAULT_OPTION** = -1
▲	public static final	int	**ERROR_MESSAGE** = 0
3	public	**javax.accessibility ↵ .AccessibleContext**	**getAccessibleContext** ()
△	public static	JDesktopPane	**getDesktopPaneForComponent** (java.awt.Component parentComponent)
△	public static	java.awt.Frame	**getFrameForComponent** (java.awt.Component parentComponent)
	public	*Icon*	**getIcon** ()
	public	Object	**getInitialSelectionValue** ()
	public	Object	**getInitialValue** ()
	public	Object	**getInputValue** ()
	public	int	**getMaxCharactersPerLineCount** ()
	public	Object	**getMessage** ()
	public	int	**getMessageType** ()
	public	Object[]	**getOptions** ()
	public	int	**getOptionType** ()
△	public static	java.awt.Frame	**getRootFrame** ()
	public	Object[]	**getSelectionValues** ()
	public	javax.swing.plaf.OptionPaneUI	**getUI** ()
3	public	**String**	**getUIClassID** ()
	public	Object	**getValue** ()
	public	boolean	**getWantsInput** ()
	protected transient	*Icon*	**icon**
▲	public static final	String	**ICON_PROPERTY** = "icon"
▲	public static final	int	**INFORMATION_MESSAGE** = 1
▲	public static final	String	**INITIAL_SELECTION_VALUE_PROPERTY** = "initialSelectionValue"
▲	public static final	String	**INITIAL_VALUE_PROPERTY** = "initialValue"
	protected transient	Object	**initialSelectionValue**
	protected transient	Object	**initialValue**
▲	public static final	String	**INPUT_VALUE_PROPERTY** = "inputValue"
	protected transient	Object	**inputValue**
*	public		**JOptionPane** ()
*	public		**JOptionPane** (Object message)
*	public		**JOptionPane** (Object message, int messageType)
*	public		**JOptionPane** (Object message, int messageType, int optionType)
*	public		**JOptionPane** (Object message, int messageType, int optionType, *Icon* icon)
*	public		**JOptionPane** (Object message, int messageType, int optionType, *Icon* icon, Object[] options)
*	public		**JOptionPane** (Object message, int messageType, int optionType, *Icon* icon, Object[] options, Object initialValue)
	protected transient	Object	**message**
▲	public static final	String	**MESSAGE_PROPERTY** = "message"

J

Classes

JOptionPane

▲	public static final	String	**MESSAGE_TYPE_PROPERTY** = "messageType"
	protected	int	**messageType**
▲	public static final	int	**NO_OPTION** = 1
▲	public static final	int	**OK_CANCEL_OPTION** = 2
▲	public static final	int	**OK_OPTION** = 0
▲	public static final	String	**OPTION_TYPE_PROPERTY** = "optionType"
	protected transient	Object[]	**options**
▲	public static final	String	**OPTIONS_PROPERTY** = "options"
	protected	int	**optionType**
3	protected	**String**	**paramString** ()
▲	public static final	int	**PLAIN_MESSAGE** = -1
▲	public static final	int	**QUESTION_MESSAGE** = 3
	public	void	**selectInitialValue** ()
▲	public static final	String	**SELECTION_VALUES_PROPERTY** = "selectionValues"
	protected transient	Object[]	**selectionValues**
	public	void	**setIcon** (*Icon* newIcon)
	public	void	**setInitialSelectionValue** (Object newValue)
	public	void	**setInitialValue** (Object newInitialValue)
	public	void	**setInputValue** (Object newValue)
	public	void	**setMessage** (Object newMessage)
	public	void	**setMessageType** (int newType)
	public	void	**setOptions** (Object[] newOptions)
	public	void	**setOptionType** (int newType)
△	public static	void	**setRootFrame** (java.awt.Frame newRootFrame)
	public	void	**setSelectionValues** (Object[] newValues)
	public	void	**setUI** (javax.swing.plaf.OptionPaneUI ui)
	public	void	**setValue** (Object newValue)
	public	void	**setWantsInput** (boolean newValue)
△	public static	int	**showConfirmDialog** (java.awt.Component parentComponent, Object message)
△	public static	int	**showConfirmDialog** (java.awt.Component parentComponent, Object message, String title, int optionType)
△	public static	int	**showConfirmDialog** (java.awt.Component parentComponent, Object message, String title, int optionType, int messageType)
△	public static	int	**showConfirmDialog** (java.awt.Component parentComponent, Object message, String title, int optionType, int messageType, *Icon* icon)
△	public static	String	**showInputDialog** (Object message)
△	public static	String	**showInputDialog** (java.awt.Component parentComponent, Object message)
△	public static	String	**showInputDialog** (java.awt.Component parentComponent, Object message, String title, int messageType)
△	public static	Object	**showInputDialog** (java.awt.Component parentComponent, Object message, String title, int messageType, *Icon* icon, Object[] selectionValues, Object initialSelectionValue)
△	public static	int	**showInternalConfirmDialog** (java.awt.Component parentComponent, Object message)
△	public static	int	**showInternalConfirmDialog** (java.awt.Component parentComponent, Object message, String title, int optionType)
△	public static	int	**showInternalConfirmDialog** (java.awt.Component parentComponent, Object message, String title, int optionType, int messageType)
△	public static	int	**showInternalConfirmDialog** (java.awt.Component parentComponent, Object message, String title, int optionType, int messageType, *Icon* icon)
△	public static	String	**showInternalInputDialog** (java.awt.Component parentComponent, Object message)
△	public static	String	**showInternalInputDialog** (java.awt.Component parentComponent, Object message, String title, int messageType)
△	public static	Object	**showInternalInputDialog** (java.awt.Component parentComponent, Object message, String title, int messageType, *Icon* icon, Object[] selectionValues, Object initialSelectionValue)
△	public static	void	**showInternalMessageDialog** (java.awt.Component parentComponent, Object message)
△	public static	void	**showInternalMessageDialog** (java.awt.Component parentComponent, Object message, String title, int messageType)
△	public static	void	**showInternalMessageDialog** (java.awt.Component parentComponent, Object message, String title, int messageType, *Icon* icon)
△	public static	int	**showInternalOptionDialog** (java.awt.Component parentComponent, Object message, String title, int optionType, int messageType, *Icon* icon, Object[] options, Object initialValue)
△	public static	void	**showMessageDialog** (java.awt.Component parentComponent, Object message)
△	public static	void	**showMessageDialog** (java.awt.Component parentComponent, Object message, String title, int messageType)
△	public static	void	**showMessageDialog** (java.awt.Component parentComponent, Object message, String title, int messageType, *Icon* icon)

Class *Interface* —extends - - -implements ○ abstract ● final △ static ▲ static final ✳ constructor x x—inherited x **x**—declared **x x**—overridden

△	public static .... int	**showOptionDialog** (java.awt.Component parentComponent, Object message, String title, int optionType, int messageType, *Icon* icon, Object[] options, Object initialValue)	
▲	public static final .... Object	**UNINITIALIZED_VALUE**	
3	public..................... **void**	**updateUI** ()	
	protected transient...... Object	**value**	
▲	public static final .... String	**VALUE_PROPERTY** = "value"	
▲	public static final .... String	**WANTS_INPUT_PROPERTY** = "wantsInput"	
	protected .... boolean	**wantsInput**	
▲	public static final .... int	**WARNING_MESSAGE** = 2	
▲	public static final .... int	**YES_NO_CANCEL_OPTION** = 1	
▲	public static final .... int	**YES_NO_OPTION** = 0	
▲	public static final .... int	**YES_OPTION** = 0	

JOptionPane.AccessibleJOptionPane   protected   javax.swing   **J**

Object
- 1.2 ○ └javax.accessibility.AccessibleContext [1]
- 1.2 ○   └JComponent.AccessibleJComponent [2] ---- *java.io.Serializable, javax.accessibility.AccessibleComponent*
- 1.2   └JOptionPane.AccessibleJOptionPane

1	*21 inherited members from javax.accessibility.AccessibleContext not shown*		
2	*40 inherited members from JComponent.AccessibleJComponent not shown*		
*	protected	**AccessibleJOptionPane** ()	
2	public................. **javax** ← .accessibility.AccessibleRole	**getAccessibleRole** ()	

JPanel   javax.swing

Object
- ○ └java.awt.Component [1] ------------------ *java.awt.image.ImageObserver, java.awt.MenuContainer, java.io.Serializable*
-   └java.awt.Container [2]
- 1.2 ○   └JComponent [3] ----------------------- *java.io.Serializable*
- 1.2   └JPanel ------------------------ *javax.accessibility.Accessible*

1	*111 inherited members from java.awt.Component not shown*		
2	*39 inherited members from java.awt.Container not shown*		
3	*113 inherited members from JComponent not shown*		
3	public... **javax.accessibility** ← .AccessibleContext	**getAccessibleContext** ()	
3	public....................... **String**	**getUIClassID** ()	
*	public..........................	**JPanel** ()	
*	public..........................	**JPanel** (boolean isDoubleBuffered)	
*	public..........................	**JPanel** (*java.awt.LayoutManager* layout)	
*	public..........................	**JPanel** (*java.awt.LayoutManager* layout, boolean isDoubleBuffered)	
3	protected .... **String**	**paramString** ()	
3	public..................... **void**	**updateUI** ()	

Classes

JPanel.AccessibleJPanel   protected   javax.swing

Object
- 1.2 ○ └javax.accessibility.AccessibleContext [1]
- 1.2 ○   └JComponent.AccessibleJComponent [2] ---- *java.io.Serializable, javax.accessibility.AccessibleComponent*
- 1.2   └JPanel.AccessibleJPanel

1	*21 inherited members from javax.accessibility.AccessibleContext not shown*		
2	*40 inherited members from JComponent.AccessibleJComponent not shown*		
*	protected	**AccessibleJPanel** ()	
2	public................. **javax** ← .accessibility.AccessibleRole	**getAccessibleRole** ()	

JPasswordField

JPasswordField	javax.swing

Object
  ○ └java.awt.Component[1] - - - - - - - - - - - - - - - - - - - *java.awt.image.ImageObserver*, *java.awt.MenuContainer*,
                           java.io.Serializable
         └java.awt.Container[2]
1.2 ○   └JComponent[3] - - - - - - - - - - - - - - - - - - - *java.io.Serializable*
1.2 ○   └javax.swing.text.JTextComponent[4] - - - - *Scrollable*, *javax.accessibility.Accessible*
1.2   └JTextField[5] - - - - - - - - - - - - - - - - - - - *SwingConstants*
1.2   └JPasswordField

1	*109 inherited members from java.awt.Component not shown*	
2	*39 inherited members from java.awt.Container not shown*	
3	*103 inherited members from JComponent not shown*	
4	*64 inherited members from javax.swing.text.JTextComponent not shown*	
5	public synchronized ....void	addActionListener (*java.awt.event.ActionListener* l)
4	public...................... **void**	**copy** ()
5	protected......................	createDefaultModel ()
	.... *javax.swing.text.Document*	
4	public...................... **void**	**cut** ()
	public................... boolean	**echoCharIsSet** ()
5	protected...................void	fireActionPerformed ()
5	public... **javax.accessibility** ↩	**getAccessibleContext** ()
	.AccessibleContext	
5	public...................... *Action[]*	getActions ()
5	public......................int	getColumns ()
5	protected......................int	getColumnWidth ()
	public...................... char	**getEchoChar** ()
5	public......................int	getHorizontalAlignment ()
5	public... *BoundedRangeModel*	getHorizontalVisibility ()
	public......................char[]	**getPassword** ()
5	public......java.awt.Dimension	getPreferredSize ()
5	public......................int	getScrollOffset ()
D 4	public...................... **String**	**getText** ()
D 4	public...................... **String**	**getText** (int offs, int len) throws javax.swing.text.BadLocationException
5	public...................... **String**	**getUIClassID** ()
5	public................... boolean	isValidateRoot ()
*	public...................... **JPasswordField**	**JPasswordField** ()
*	public...................... **JPasswordField**	**JPasswordField** (int columns)
*	public...................... **JPasswordField**	**JPasswordField** (String text)
*	public...................... **JPasswordField**	**JPasswordField** (String text, int columns)
*	public...................... **JPasswordField**	**JPasswordField** (*javax.swing.text.Document* doc, String txt, int columns)
5	protected............... **String**	**paramString** ()
5	public......................void	postActionEvent ()
5	public synchronized ....void	removeActionListener (*java.awt.event.ActionListener* l)
5	public......................void	scrollRectToVisible (java.awt.Rectangle r)
5	public......................void	setActionCommand (String command)
5	public......................void	setColumns (int columns)
	public......................void	**setEchoChar** (char c)
5	public......................void	setFont (java.awt.Font f)
5	public......................void	setHorizontalAlignment (int alignment)
5	public......................void	setScrollOffset (int scrollOffset)

JPasswordField.AccessibleJPasswordField	protected	javax.swing

Object
1.2 ○ └javax.accessibility.AccessibleContext[1]
1.2 ○   └JComponent.AccessibleJComponent[2] - - - - *java.io.Serializable*, *javax.accessibility.AccessibleComponent*
1.2   └javax.swing.text.JTextComponent↩ - - - - - *javax.accessibility.AccessibleText*, *javax.swing.event.CaretListener*
           .AccessibleJTextComponent[3]   (*java.util.EventListener*), *javax.swing.event.DocumentListener*
                                (*java.util.EventListener*)
1.2   └JTextField.AccessibleJTextField[4]
1.2   └JPasswordField↩
             .AccessibleJPasswordField

1	*20 inherited members from javax.accessibility.AccessibleContext not shown*	
2	*39 inherited members from JComponent.AccessibleJComponent not shown*	
*	protected......................	**AccessibleJPasswordField** ()
3	public......................void	caretUpdate (javax.swing.event.CaretEvent e)

Class   *Interface* —extends - - -implements ○ abstract ● final △ static ▲ static final ✳ constructor x x—inherited x **x**—declared **x x**—overridden

3	public	void	changedUpdate (*javax.swing.event.DocumentEvent* e)
3	public	**javax↩ .accessibility.AccessibleRole**	**getAccessibleRole** ()
4	public	javax.accessibility↩ .AccessibleStateSet	getAccessibleStateSet ()
3	public	*javax↩ .accessibility.AccessibleText*	getAccessibleText ()
3	public	String	getAfterIndex (int part, int index)
3	public	String	getAtIndex (int part, int index)
3	public	String	getBeforeIndex (int part, int index)
3	public	int	getCaretPosition ()
3	public	*... javax.swing.text.AttributeSet*	getCharacterAttribute (int i)
3	public	java.awt.Rectangle	getCharacterBounds (int i)
3	public	int	getCharCount ()
3	public	int	getIndexAtPoint (java.awt.Point p)
3	public	String	getSelectedText ()
3	public	int	getSelectionEnd ()
3	public	int	getSelectionStart ()
3	public	void	insertUpdate (*javax.swing.event.DocumentEvent* e)
3	public	void	removeUpdate (*javax.swing.event.DocumentEvent* e)

JPopupMenu
javax.swing

```
       Object
  ○     └─java.awt.Component 1 - - - - - - - - - - - - - - -  java.awt.image.ImageObserver, java.awt.MenuContainer,
                                                                 java.io.Serializable
          └─java.awt.Container 2
1.2 ○       └─JComponent 3 - - - - - - - - - - - - - - - -  java.io.Serializable
1.2           └─JPopupMenu - - - - - - - - - - - - - - - -  javax.accessibility.Accessible, MenuElement 4
```

1	*109 inherited members from java.awt.Component not shown*		
2	*38 inherited members from java.awt.Container not shown*		
3	*111 inherited members from JComponent not shown*		
	public	JMenuItem	**add** (String s)
	public	JMenuItem	**add** (*Action* a)
	public	JMenuItem	**add** (JMenuItem menuItem)
	public	void	**addPopupMenuListener** (*javax.swing.event.PopupMenuListener* l)
	public	void	**addSeparator** ()
	protected	*java.beans↩ .PropertyChangeListener*	**createActionChangeListener** (JMenuItem b)
	protected	void	**firePopupMenuCanceled** ()
	protected	void	**firePopupMenuWillBecomeInvisible** ()
	protected	void	**firePopupMenuWillBecomeVisible** ()
3	public	**javax.accessibility↩ .AccessibleContext**	**getAccessibleContext** ()
4	public	java.awt.Component	**getComponent** ()
	public	java.awt.Component	**getComponentAtIndex** (int i)
	public	int	**getComponentIndex** (java.awt.Component c)
△	public static	boolean	**getDefaultLightWeightPopupEnabled** ()
	public	java.awt.Component	**getInvoker** ()
	public	String	**getLabel** ()
	public	java.awt.Insets	**getMargin** ()
	public	*SingleSelectionModel*	**getSelectionModel** ()
4	public	*MenuElement[]*	**getSubElements** ()
	public	*javax.swing.plaf.PopupMenuUI*	**getUI** ()
3	public	**String**	**getUIClassID** ()
	public	void	**insert** (java.awt.Component component, int index)
	public	void	**insert** (*Action* a, int index)
	public	boolean	**isBorderPainted** ()
	public	boolean	**isLightWeightPopupEnabled** ()
1	public	**boolean**	**isVisible** ()
*	public		**JPopupMenu** ()
*	public		**JPopupMenu** (String label)
4	public	void	**menuSelectionChanged** (boolean isIncluded)
	public	void	**pack** ()
3	protected	**void**	**paintBorder** (java.awt.Graphics g)
3	protected	**String**	**paramString** ()
4	public	void	**processKeyEvent** (java.awt.event.KeyEvent e, *MenuElement[]* path, MenuSelectionManager manager)

JPopupMenu

4	public	void	**processMouseEvent** (java.awt.event.MouseEvent event, *MenuElement[]* path, MenuSelectionManager manager)
2	public	**void**	**remove** (java.awt.Component comp)
	public	void	**removePopupMenuListener** (*javax.swing.event.PopupMenuListener* l)
	public	void	**setBorderPainted** (boolean b)
△	public static	void	**setDefaultLightWeightPopupEnabled** (boolean aFlag)
	public	void	**setInvoker** (java.awt.Component invoker)
	public	void	**setLabel** (String label)
	public	void	**setLightWeightPopupEnabled** (boolean aFlag)
1	public	**void**	**setLocation** (int x, int y)
	public	void	**setPopupSize** (java.awt.Dimension d)
	public	void	**setPopupSize** (int width, int height)
	public	void	**setSelected** (java.awt.Component sel)
	public	void	**setSelectionModel** (*SingleSelectionModel* model)
	public	void	**setUI** (javax.swing.plaf.PopupMenuUI ui)
3	public	**void**	**setVisible** (boolean b)
	public	void	**show** (java.awt.Component invoker, int x, int y)
3	public	**void**	**updateUI** ()

JPopupMenu.AccessibleJPopupMenu   protected   javax.swing

Object
```
1.2 ○  └─javax.accessibility.AccessibleContext 1
1.2 ○     └─JComponent.AccessibleJComponent 2 ---- java.io.Serializable, javax.accessibility.AccessibleComponent
1.2        └─JPopupMenu.AccessibleJPopupMenu
```

1	*21 inherited members from javax.accessibility.AccessibleContext not shown*		
2	*40 inherited members from JComponent.AccessibleJComponent not shown*		
✳	protected		**AccessibleJPopupMenu** ()
2	public	**javax ↵ .accessibility.AccessibleRole**	**getAccessibleRole** ()

JPopupMenu.Separator   javax.swing

Object
```
  ○  └─java.awt.Component 1 ------------------- java.awt.image.ImageObserver, java.awt.MenuContainer,
                                                        java.io.Serializable
        └─java.awt.Container 2
1.2 ○       └─JComponent 3 --------------------- java.io.Serializable
1.2          └─JSeparator 4 ------------------- SwingConstants, javax.accessibility.Accessible
1.2             └─JPopupMenu.Separator
```

1	*111 inherited members from java.awt.Component not shown*		
2	*39 inherited members from java.awt.Container not shown*		
3	*112 inherited members from JComponent not shown*		
4	public	javax.accessibility ↵ .AccessibleContext	getAccessibleContext ()
4	public	int	getOrientation ()
4	public	getUI () .. javax.swing.plaf.SeparatorUI	
4	public	**String**	**getUIClassID** ()
4	public	boolean	isFocusTraversable ()
4	protected	String	paramString ()
✳	public		**Separator** ()
4	public	void	setOrientation (int orientation)
4	public	void	setUI (javax.swing.plaf.SeparatorUI ui)
4	public	void	updateUI ()

JPopupMenu.WindowPopup.AccessibleWindowPopup   protected   javax.swing

Object
```
1.2 ○  └─javax.accessibility.AccessibleContext 1
1.2       └─JPopupMenu.WindowPopup ↵ ---------- java.io.Serializable, javax.accessibility.AccessibleComponent 2
            .AccessibleWindowPopup
```

1	*25 inherited members from javax.accessibility.AccessibleContext not shown*		
✳	protected		**AccessibleWindowPopup** (javax.swing.JPopupMenu.WindowPopup)

Class   *Interface*   —extends   - - -implements   ○ abstract   ● final   △ static   ▲ static final   ✳ constructor   x x—inherited   x **x**—declared   **x x**—overridden

2	public	void	**addFocusListener** (*java.awt.event.FocusListener*)
2	public	boolean	**contains** (*java.awt.Point*)
2	public		**getAccessibleAt** (*java.awt.Point*)
	. javax.accessibility.Accessible		
1	public	*javax* ↵	**getAccessibleChild** (int)
	.accessibility.Accessible		
1	public	int	**getAccessibleChildrenCount** ()
1	public	*javax.accessibility* ↵	**getAccessibleComponent** ()
	.AccessibleComponent		
1	public	int	**getAccessibleIndexInParent** ()
1	public	*javax* ↵	**getAccessibleParent** ()
	.accessibility.Accessible		
1	public	*javax* ↵	**getAccessibleRole** ()
	.accessibility.AccessibleRole		
1	public	*javax.accessibility* ↵	**getAccessibleStateSet** ()
	.AccessibleStateSet		
2	public	java.awt.Color	**getBackground** ()
2	public	java.awt.Rectangle	**getBounds** ()
2	public	java.awt.Cursor	**getCursor** ()
2	public	java.awt.Font	**getFont** ()
2	public	java.awt.FontMetrics	**getFontMetrics** (*java.awt.Font*)
2	public	java.awt.Color	**getForeground** ()
1	public	**java.util.Locale**	**getLocale** ()
2	public	java.awt.Point	**getLocation** ()
2	public	java.awt.Point	**getLocationOnScreen** ()
2	public	java.awt.Dimension	**getSize** ()
2	public	boolean	**isEnabled** ()
2	public	boolean	**isFocusTraversable** ()
2	public	boolean	**isShowing** ()
2	public	boolean	**isVisible** ()
2	public	void	**removeFocusListener** (*java.awt.event.FocusListener*)
2	public	void	**requestFocus** ()
2	public	void	**setBackground** (java.awt.Color)
2	public	void	**setBounds** (java.awt.Rectangle)
2	public	void	**setCursor** (java.awt.Cursor)
2	public	void	**setEnabled** (boolean)
2	public	void	**setFont** (java.awt.Font)
2	public	void	**setForeground** (java.awt.Color)
2	public	void	**setLocation** (java.awt.Point)
2	public	void	**setSize** (java.awt.Dimension)
2	public	void	**setVisible** (boolean)

JProgressBar

javax.swing

```
Object
 └java.awt.Component1 ------------------- java.awt.image.ImageObserver, java.awt.MenuContainer,
                                                         java.io.Serializable
      └java.awt.Container2
           └JComponent3 --------------------- java.io.Serializable
                └JProgressBar -------------------- SwingConstants, javax.accessibility.Accessible
```

1	*111 inherited members from java.awt.Component not shown*		
2	*39 inherited members from java.awt.Container not shown*		
3	*112 inherited members from JComponent not shown*		
	public	void	**addChangeListener** (*javax.swing.event.ChangeListener* l)
	protected transient	javax ↵	**changeEvent**
	.swing.event.ChangeEvent		
	protected	*javax* ↵	**changeListener**
	.swing.event.ChangeListener		
	protected	*javax* ↵	**createChangeListener** ()
	.swing.event.ChangeListener		
	protected	void	**fireStateChanged** ()
3	public	**javax.accessibility** ↵	**getAccessibleContext** ()
	.AccessibleContext		
	public	int	**getMaximum** ()
	public	int	**getMinimum** ()
	public	*BoundedRangeModel*	**getModel** ()
	public	int	**getOrientation** ()
	public	double	**getPercentComplete** ()
	public	String	**getString** ()
	public		**getUI** ()
	javax.swing.plaf.ProgressBarUI		

JProgressBar

3	public	**String**	**getUIClassID** ()
	public	int	**getValue** ()
	public	boolean	**isBorderPainted** ()
	public	boolean	**isStringPainted** ()
*	public		**JProgressBar** ()
*	public		**JProgressBar** (int orient)
*	public		**JProgressBar** (*BoundedRangeModel* newModel)
*	public		**JProgressBar** (int min, int max)
*	public		**JProgressBar** (int orient, int min, int max)
	protected		**model**
		BoundedRangeModel	
	protected	int	**orientation**
	protected	boolean	**paintBorder**
3	protected	**void**	**paintBorder** (java.awt.Graphics g)
	protected	boolean	**paintString**
3	protected	**String**	**paramString** ()
	protected	String	**progressString**
	public	void	**removeChangeListener** (*javax.swing.event.ChangeListener* l)
	public	void	**setBorderPainted** (boolean b)
	public	void	**setMaximum** (int n)
	public	void	**setMinimum** (int n)
	public	void	**setModel** (*BoundedRangeModel* newModel)
	public	void	**setOrientation** (int newOrientation)
	public	void	**setString** (String s)
	public	void	**setStringPainted** (boolean b)
	public	void	**setUI** (javax.swing.plaf.ProgressBarUI ui)
	public	void	**setValue** (int n)
3	public	**void**	**updateUI** ()

JProgressBar.AccessibleJProgressBar   protected   javax.swing

Object
1.2 ○	└javax.accessibility.AccessibleContext [1]
1.2 ○	└JComponent.AccessibleJComponent [2] - - - - *java.io.Serializable, javax.accessibility.AccessibleComponent*
1.2	└JProgressBar.AccessibleJProgressBar - - *javax.accessibility.AccessibleValue* [3]

1	*20 inherited members from javax.accessibility.AccessibleContext not shown*		
2	*39 inherited members from JComponent.AccessibleJComponent not shown*		
*	protected		**AccessibleJProgressBar** ()
2	public	**javax ↩**	**getAccessibleRole** ()
	.accessibility.AccessibleRole		
2	public	**javax.accessibility ↩**	**getAccessibleStateSet** ()
	.AccessibleStateSet		
1	public	*javax.accessibility ↩*	**getAccessibleValue** ()
	.AccessibleValue		
3	public	Number	**getCurrentAccessibleValue** ()
3	public	Number	**getMaximumAccessibleValue** ()
3	public	Number	**getMinimumAccessibleValue** ()
3	public	boolean	**setCurrentAccessibleValue** (Number n)

JRadioButton   javax.swing

Object
○	└java.awt.Component [1] - - - - - - - - - - - - - - - - - - - *java.awt.image.ImageObserver, java.awt.MenuContainer,*
		java.io.Serializable
	└java.awt.Container [2]
1.2 ○	└JComponent [3] - *java.io.Serializable*
1.2 ○	└AbstractButton [4] - - - - - - - - - - - - - - - - - - *java.awt.ItemSelectable, SwingConstants*
1.2	└JToggleButton [5] - - - - - - - - - - - - - - - - *javax.accessibility.Accessible*
1.2	└JRadioButton - - - - - - - - - - - - - - - - *javax.accessibility.Accessible*

1	*111 inherited members from java.awt.Component not shown*		
2	*39 inherited members from java.awt.Container not shown*		
3	*111 inherited members from JComponent not shown*		
4	*91 inherited members from AbstractButton not shown*		
5	public	**javax.accessibility ↩**	**getAccessibleContext** ()
	.AccessibleContext		
5	public	**String**	**getUIClassID** ()

Class *Interface* —extends - - -implements ○ abstract ● final △ static ▲ static final ✳ constructor x x—inherited x **x**—declared **x x**—overridden

*	public		**JRadioButton** ()
*	public		**JRadioButton** (String text)
*	public		**JRadioButton** (*Icon* icon)
*	public		**JRadioButton** (String text, boolean selected)
*	public		**JRadioButton** (String text, *Icon* icon)
*	public		**JRadioButton** (*Icon* icon, boolean selected)
*	public		**JRadioButton** (String text, *Icon* icon, boolean selected)
5	protected	**String**	**paramString** ()
5	public	**void**	**updateUI** ()

JRadioButton.AccessibleJRadioButton   protected   javax.swing

Object
```
1.2 ○  └─javax.accessibility.AccessibleContext¹
1.2 ○      └─JComponent.AccessibleJComponent² ---- java.io.Serializable, javax.accessibility.AccessibleComponent
1.2 ○          └─AbstractButton↵ ------------------- javax.accessibility.AccessibleAction,
                  .AccessibleAbstractButton³                javax.accessibility.AccessibleValue
1.2              └─JToggleButton↵ ----------------- java.awt.event.ItemListener (java.util.EventListener)
                    .AccessibleJToggleButton⁴
1.2                  └─JRadioButton↵
                      .AccessibleJRadioButton
```

1	*19 inherited members from javax.accessibility.AccessibleContext not shown*		
2	*38 inherited members from JComponent.AccessibleJComponent not shown*		
*	protected		**AccessibleJRadioButton** ()
3	public	boolean	doAccessibleAction (int i)
3	public	*javax*↵	getAccessibleAction ()
	.accessibility.AccessibleAction		
3	public	int	getAccessibleActionCount ()
3	public	String	getAccessibleActionDescription (int i)
3	public	String	getAccessibleName ()
4	public	**javax**↵	**getAccessibleRole** ()
	.accessibility.AccessibleRole		
3	public	javax.accessibility↵	getAccessibleStateSet ()
	.AccessibleStateSet		
3	public	*javax*↵	getAccessibleValue ()
	.accessibility.AccessibleValue		
3	public	Number	getCurrentAccessibleValue ()
3	public	Number	getMaximumAccessibleValue ()
3	public	Number	getMinimumAccessibleValue ()
4	public	void	itemStateChanged (java.awt.event.ItemEvent e)
3	public	boolean	setCurrentAccessibleValue (Number n)

JRadioButtonMenuItem   javax.swing

Object
```
     ○  └─java.awt.Component¹ -------------------- java.awt.image.ImageObserver, java.awt.MenuContainer,
                                                    java.io.Serializable
             └─java.awt.Container²
1.2 ○            └─JComponent³ ---------------------- java.io.Serializable
1.2 ○                └─AbstractButton⁴ ------------------ java.awt.ItemSelectable, SwingConstants
1.2                      └─JMenuItem⁵ ------------------- javax.accessibility.Accessible, MenuElement
1.2                          └─JRadioButtonMenuItem --------- javax.accessibility.Accessible
```

1	*111 inherited members from java.awt.Component not shown*		
2	*39 inherited members from java.awt.Container not shown*		
3	*110 inherited members from JComponent not shown*		
4	*89 inherited members from AbstractButton not shown*		
5	public	void	addMenuDragMouseListener (*javax.swing.event.MenuDragMouseListener* l)
5	public	void	addMenuKeyListener (*javax.swing.event.MenuKeyListener* l)
5	protected	void	fireMenuDragMouseDragged (javax.swing.event.MenuDragMouseEvent event)
5	protected	void	fireMenuDragMouseEntered (javax.swing.event.MenuDragMouseEvent event)
5	protected	void	fireMenuDragMouseExited (javax.swing.event.MenuDragMouseEvent event)
5	protected	void	fireMenuDragMouseReleased (javax.swing.event.MenuDragMouseEvent event)
5	protected	void	fireMenuKeyPressed (javax.swing.event.MenuKeyEvent event)
5	protected	void	fireMenuKeyReleased (javax.swing.event.MenuKeyEvent event)
5	protected	void	fireMenuKeyTyped (javax.swing.event.MenuKeyEvent event)
5	public	KeyStroke	getAccelerator ()
5	public	**javax.accessibility**↵	**getAccessibleContext** ()
	.AccessibleContext		

Classes

JRadioButtonMenuItem

5	public....	java.awt.Component	getComponent ()
5	public.........	*MenuElement[]*	getSubElements ()
5	public..................	**String**	**getUIClassID** ()
5	protected.................	**void**	**init** (String text, *Icon* icon)
5	public.................	boolean	isArmed ()
*	public............................		**JRadioButtonMenuItem** ()
*	public............................		**JRadioButtonMenuItem** (String text)
*	public............................		**JRadioButtonMenuItem** (*Icon* icon)
*	public............................		**JRadioButtonMenuItem** (String text, boolean b)
*	public............................		**JRadioButtonMenuItem** (String text, *Icon* icon)
*	public............................		**JRadioButtonMenuItem** (*Icon* icon, boolean selected)
*	public............................		**JRadioButtonMenuItem** (String text, *Icon* icon, boolean selected)
5	public....................	void	menuSelectionChanged (boolean isIncluded)
5	protected.................	**String**	**paramString** ()
5	public....................	void	processKeyEvent (java. awt. event. KeyEvent e, *MenuElement[]* path, MenuSelectionManager manager)
5	public....................	void	processMenuDragMouseEvent (javax.swing.event.MenuDragMouseEvent e)
5	public....................	void	processMenuKeyEvent (javax.swing.event.MenuKeyEvent e)
5	public....................	void	processMouseEvent (java. awt. event. MouseEvent e, *MenuElement[]* path, MenuSelectionManager manager)
5	public....................	void	removeMenuDragMouseListener (*javax.swing.event.MenuDragMouseListener* l)
5	public....................	void	removeMenuKeyListener (*javax.swing.event.MenuKeyListener* l)
3	public....................	**void**	**requestFocus** ()
5	public....................	void	setAccelerator (KeyStroke keyStroke)
5	public....................	void	setArmed (boolean b)
5	public....................	void	setEnabled (boolean b)
5	public....................	void	setUI (javax.swing.plaf.MenuItemUI ui)
5	public....................	**void**	**updateUI** ()

J

JRadioButtonMenuItem.AccessibleJRadioButtonMenuItem protected · · · · · · · · · · · · · · · · · · · `javax.swing`

Object
- 1.2 ○ └─javax.accessibility.AccessibleContext [1]
- 1.2 ○   └─JComponent.AccessibleJComponent [2] - - - - *java.io.Serializable, javax.accessibility.AccessibleComponent*
- 1.2 ○   └─AbstractButton ↩ - - - - - - - - - - - - - - - - - - - *javax.accessibility.AccessibleAction,*
-         │ .AccessibleAbstractButton [3]   *javax.accessibility.AccessibleValue*
- 1.2   └─JMenuItem.AccessibleJMenuItem [4] - - - *javax.swing.event.ChangeListener (java.util.EventListener)*
- 1.2   └─JRadioButtonMenuItem ↩
-             .AccessibleJRadioButtonMenuItem

1	*19 inherited members from javax.accessibility.AccessibleContext not shown*		
2	*38 inherited members from JComponent.AccessibleJComponent not shown*		
*	protected......................		**AccessibleJRadioButtonMenuItem** ()
3	public.................	boolean	doAccessibleAction (int i)
3	public....................	*javax↩ .accessibility.AccessibleAction*	getAccessibleAction ()
3	public........................	int	getAccessibleActionCount ()
3	public....................	String	getAccessibleActionDescription (int i)
3	public....................	String	getAccessibleName ()
4	public.................	**javax ↩ .accessibility.AccessibleRole**	**getAccessibleRole** ()
3	public....	javax.accessibility↩ .AccessibleStateSet	getAccessibleStateSet ()
3	public....................	*javax↩ .accessibility.AccessibleValue*	getAccessibleValue ()
3	public.................	Number	getCurrentAccessibleValue ()
3	public.................	Number	getMaximumAccessibleValue ()
3	public.................	Number	getMinimumAccessibleValue ()
3	public.................	boolean	setCurrentAccessibleValue (Number n)
4	public......................	void	stateChanged (javax.swing.event.ChangeEvent e)

Class *Interface* —extends - - -implements ○ abstract ● final △ static ▲ static final ✳ constructor x x—inherited x **x**—declared **x x**—overridden

		JRootPane	javax.swing

```
        Object
   ○    └─java.awt.Component¹ ------------------ java.awt.image.ImageObserver, java.awt.MenuContainer,
                                                      java.io.Serializable
            └─java.awt.Container²
1.2 ○          └─JComponent³ --------------------- java.io.Serializable
1.2               └─JRootPane --------------------- javax.accessibility.Accessible
```

	1		*111 inherited members from java.awt.Component not shown*	
	2		*38 inherited members from java.awt.Container not shown*	
	3		*111 inherited members from JComponent not shown*	
	2	protected	**void addImpl**	(java.awt.Component comp, Object constraints, int index)
	3	public	**void addNotify** ()	
		protected...java.awt.Container	**contentPane**	
		protected...java.awt.Container	**createContentPane** ()	
		protected java.awt.Component	**createGlassPane** ()	
		protected...... JLayeredPane	**createLayeredPane** ()	
		protected......................	**createRootLayout** ()	
		.... *java.awt.LayoutManager*		
		protected..............JButton	**defaultButton**	
		protected.......javax.swing ↵	**defaultPressAction**	
		.JRootPane.DefaultAction		
		protected.......javax.swing ↵	**defaultReleaseAction**	
		.JRootPane.DefaultAction		
	3	public... **javax.accessibility** ↵	**getAccessibleContext** ()	
		.AccessibleContext		
		public.......java.awt.Container	**getContentPane** ()	
		public.................JButton	**getDefaultButton** ()	
		public.... java.awt.Component	**getGlassPane** ()	
		public..............JMenuBar	**getJMenuBar** ()	
		public........... JLayeredPane	**getLayeredPane** ()	
D		public..............JMenuBar	**getMenuBar** ()	
		protected java.awt.Component	**glassPane**	
	3	public.................**boolean**	**isFocusCycleRoot** ()	
	3	public.................**boolean**	**isValidateRoot** ()	
*		public..........................	**JRootPane** ()	
		protected....... JLayeredPane	**layeredPane**	
		protected............ JMenuBar	**menuBar**	
	3	protected.............. **String**	**paramString** ()	
	3	public.................... **void**	**removeNotify** ()	
		public....................void	**setContentPane** (java.awt.Container content)	
		public....................void	**setDefaultButton** (JButton defaultButton)	
		public....................void	**setGlassPane** (java.awt.Component glass)	
		public....................void	**setJMenuBar** (JMenuBar menu)	
		public....................void	**setLayeredPane** (JLayeredPane layered)	
D		public....................void	**setMenuBar** (JMenuBar menu)	

	JRootPane.AccessibleJRootPane	protected	javax.swing

```
        Object
1.2 ○   └─javax.accessibility.AccessibleContext¹
1.2 ○      └─JComponent.AccessibleJComponent² ---- java.io.Serializable, javax.accessibility.AccessibleComponent
1.2           └─JRootPane.AccessibleJRootPane
```

	1		*21 inherited members from javax.accessibility.AccessibleContext not shown*	
	2		*40 inherited members from JComponent.AccessibleJComponent not shown*	
*		protected......................	**AccessibleJRootPane** ()	
	2	public.................. **javax** ↵	**getAccessibleRole** ()	
		.accessibility.AccessibleRole		

	JRootPane.RootLayout	protected	javax.swing

```
        Object
1.2     └─JRootPane.RootLayout ------------------ java.awt.LayoutManager2¹ (java.awt.LayoutManager²),
                                                      java.io.Serializable
```

	1	public.....................void	**addLayoutComponent** (java.awt.Component comp, Object constraints)	
	2	public.....................void	**addLayoutComponent** (String name, java.awt.Component comp)	
	1	public.....................float	**getLayoutAlignmentX** (java.awt.Container target)	
	1	public.....................float	**getLayoutAlignmentY** (java.awt.Container target)	

JRootPane.RootLayout

	1	public.....................void	**invalidateLayout** (java.awt.Container target)
	2	public.....................void	**layoutContainer** (java.awt.Container parent)
	1	public......java.awt.Dimension	**maximumLayoutSize** (java.awt.Container target)
	2	public......java.awt.Dimension	**minimumLayoutSize** (java.awt.Container parent)
	2	public......java.awt.Dimension	**preferredLayoutSize** (java.awt.Container parent)
	2	public.....................void	**removeLayoutComponent** (java.awt.Component comp)
✳		protected......................	**RootLayout** ()

JScrollBar   javax.swing

```
      Object
 ○    └─java.awt.Component¹ - - - - - - - - - - - - - - - - - - java.awt.image.ImageObserver, java.awt.MenuContainer,
                                                                java.io.Serializable
          └─java.awt.Container²
1.2 ○        └─JComponent³ - - - - - - - - - - - - - - - - - - java.io.Serializable
1.2            └─JScrollBar - - - - - - - - - - - - - - - - - - java.awt.Adjustable⁴, javax.accessibility.Accessible
```

	1	*111 inherited members from java.awt.Component not shown*
	2	*39 inherited members from java.awt.Container not shown*
	3	*110 inherited members from JComponent not shown*
	4	public.....................void	**addAdjustmentListener** (*java.awt.event.AdjustmentListener* l)
		protected...................int	**blockIncrement**
		protected.................void	**fireAdjustmentValueChanged** (int id, int type, int value)
	3	public... **javax.accessibility↵**	**getAccessibleContext** ()
		.AccessibleContext	
	4	public.......................int	**getBlockIncrement** ()
		public.......................int	**getBlockIncrement** (int direction)
	4	public.......................int	**getMaximum** ()
	3	public.... **java.awt.Dimension**	**getMaximumSize** ()
	4	public.......................int	**getMinimum** ()
	3	public.... **java.awt.Dimension**	**getMinimumSize** ()
		public... *BoundedRangeModel*	**getModel** ()
	4	public.......................int	**getOrientation** ()
		public......................	**getUI** ()
		... javax.swing.plaf.ScrollBarUI	
	3	public................. **String**	**getUIClassID** ()
	4	public.......................int	**getUnitIncrement** ()
		public.......................int	**getUnitIncrement** (int direction)
	4	public.......................int	**getValue** ()
		public.................boolean	**getValueIsAdjusting** ()
	4	public.......................int	**getVisibleAmount** ()
✳		public......................	**JScrollBar** ()
✳		public......................	**JScrollBar** (int orientation)
✳		public......................	**JScrollBar** (int orientation, int value, int extent, int min, int max)
		protected......................	**model**
		.... *BoundedRangeModel*	
		protected...................int	**orientation**
	3	protected............... **String**	**paramString** ()
	4	public.....................void	**removeAdjustmentListener** (*java.awt.event.AdjustmentListener* l)
	4	public.....................void	**setBlockIncrement** (int blockIncrement)
	3	public..................... **void**	**setEnabled** (boolean x)
	4	public.....................void	**setMaximum** (int maximum)
	4	public.....................void	**setMinimum** (int minimum)
		public.....................void	**setModel** (*BoundedRangeModel* newModel)
		public.....................void	**setOrientation** (int orientation)
	4	public.....................void	**setUnitIncrement** (int unitIncrement)
	4	public.....................void	**setValue** (int value)
		public.....................void	**setValueIsAdjusting** (boolean b)
		public.....................void	**setValues** (int newValue, int newExtent, int newMin, int newMax)
	4	public.....................void	**setVisibleAmount** (int extent)
		protected...................int	**unitIncrement**
	3	public..................... **void**	**updateUI** ()

Class   *Interface*   —extends   - - -implements   ○ abstract   ● final   △ static   ▲ static final   ✳ constructor   x x—inherited   x **x**—declared   **x x**—overridden

JScrollBar.AccessibleJScrollBar

	protected		javax.swing

```
    Object
1.2 O  └ javax.accessibility.AccessibleContext 1
1.2 O      └ JComponent.AccessibleJComponent 2 ---- java.io.Serializable, javax.accessibility.AccessibleComponent
1.2          └ JScrollBar.AccessibleJScrollBar -------- javax.accessibility.AccessibleValue 3
```

	1	20 inherited members from javax.accessibility.AccessibleContext not shown	
	2	39 inherited members from JComponent.AccessibleJComponent not shown	
*		protected	**AccessibleJScrollBar** ()
	2	public .... **javax** ↵	**getAccessibleRole** ()
		.accessibility.AccessibleRole	
	2	public ... **javax.accessibility** ↵	**getAccessibleStateSet** ()
		.AccessibleStateSet	
	1	public ... **javax.accessibility** ↵	**getAccessibleValue** ()
		.AccessibleValue	
	3	public .... Number	**getCurrentAccessibleValue** ()
	3	public .... Number	**getMaximumAccessibleValue** ()
	3	public .... Number	**getMinimumAccessibleValue** ()
	3	public .... boolean	**setCurrentAccessibleValue** (Number n)

JScrollPane

		javax.swing

```
    Object
  O  └ java.awt.Component 1 ------------------- java.awt.image.ImageObserver, java.awt.MenuContainer,
                                                    java.io.Serializable
      └ java.awt.Container 2
1.2 O      └ JComponent 3 --------------------- java.io.Serializable
1.2          └ JScrollPane --------------------- ScrollPaneConstants, javax.accessibility.Accessible
```

	1	111 inherited members from java.awt.Component not shown	
	2	38 inherited members from java.awt.Container not shown	
	3	111 inherited members from JComponent not shown	
		protected .... JViewport	**columnHeader**
		public .... JScrollBar	**createHorizontalScrollBar** ()
		public .... JScrollBar	**createVerticalScrollBar** ()
		protected .... JViewport	**createViewport** ()
	3	public ... **javax.accessibility** ↵	**getAccessibleContext** ()
		.AccessibleContext	
		public .... JViewport	**getColumnHeader** ()
		public .... java.awt.Component	**getCorner** (String key)
		public .... JScrollBar	**getHorizontalScrollBar** ()
		public .... int	**getHorizontalScrollBarPolicy** ()
		public .... JViewport	**getRowHeader** ()
		public	**getUI** ()
		. javax.swing.plaf.ScrollPaneUI	
	3	public .... **String**	**getUIClassID** ()
		public .... JScrollBar	**getVerticalScrollBar** ()
		public .... int	**getVerticalScrollBarPolicy** ()
		public .... JViewport	**getViewport** ()
		public	**getViewportBorder** ()
		..... javax.swing.border.Border	
		public ...... java.awt.Rectangle	**getViewportBorderBounds** ()
		protected .... JScrollBar	**horizontalScrollBar**
		protected .... int	**horizontalScrollBarPolicy**
	3	public .... **boolean**	**isOpaque** ()
	3	public .... **boolean**	**isValidateRoot** ()
*		public .... **JScrollPane**	**JScrollPane** ()
*		public	**JScrollPane** (java.awt.Component view)
*		public	**JScrollPane** (int vsbPolicy, int hsbPolicy)
*		public	**JScrollPane** (java.awt.Component view, int vsbPolicy, int hsbPolicy)
		protected java.awt.Component	**lowerLeft**
		protected java.awt.Component	**lowerRight**
	3	protected .... **String**	**paramString** ()
		protected .... JViewport	**rowHeader**
		public .... void	**setColumnHeader** (JViewport columnHeader)
		public .... void	**setColumnHeaderView** (java.awt.Component view)
		public .... void	**setCorner** (String key, java.awt.Component corner)
		public .... void	**setHorizontalScrollBar** (JScrollBar horizontalScrollBar)
		public .... void	**setHorizontalScrollBarPolicy** (int policy)
	2	public .... **void**	**setLayout** (java.awt.LayoutManager layout)
		public .... void	**setRowHeader** (JViewport rowHeader)

JScrollPane

public		void	**setRowHeaderView** (java.awt.Component view)
public		void	**setUI** (javax.swing.plaf.ScrollPaneUI ui)
public		void	**setVerticalScrollBar** (JScrollBar verticalScrollBar)
public		void	**setVerticalScrollBarPolicy** (int policy)
public		void	**setViewport** (JViewport viewport)
public		void	**setViewportBorder** (*javax.swing.border.Border* viewportBorder)
public		void	**setViewportView** (java.awt.Component view)
3	public	**void**	**updateUI** ()
protected	java.awt.Component	**upperLeft**	
protected	java.awt.Component	**upperRight**	
protected	JScrollBar	**verticalScrollBar**	
protected	int	**verticalScrollBarPolicy**	
protected	JViewport	**viewport**	

JScrollPane.AccessibleJScrollPane · protected · javax.swing

Object
 └java.accessibility.AccessibleContext[1]   *1.2* ○
  └JComponent.AccessibleJComponent[2] - - - - *java.io.Serializable, javax.accessibility.AccessibleComponent*   *1.2* ○
   └JScrollPane.AccessibleJScrollPane - - - - - *javax.swing.event.ChangeListener[3] (java.util.EventListener)*   *1.2*

1	*21 inherited members from javax.accessibility.AccessibleContext not shown*		
2	*40 inherited members from JComponent.AccessibleJComponent not shown*		
*	public		**AccessibleJScrollPane** ()
2	public	**javax ↩**	**getAccessibleRole** ()
	.accessibility.AccessibleRole		
	public	void	**resetViewPort** ()
3	public	void	**stateChanged** (javax.swing.event.ChangeEvent e)
	protected	JViewport	**viewPort**

JScrollPane.ScrollBar · protected · javax.swing

Object
 └java.awt.Component[1] - - - - - - - - - - - - - - - - - - - *java.awt.image.ImageObserver, java.awt.MenuContainer,*   ○
                  java.io.Serializable
  └java.awt.Container[2]
   └JComponent[3] - *java.io.Serializable*   *1.2* ○
    └JScrollBar[4] - - - - - - - - - - - - - - - - - - - *java.awt.Adjustable, javax.accessibility.Accessible*   *1.2*
     └JScrollPane.ScrollBar - - - - - - - - - - - *javax.swing.plaf.UIResource*   *1.2*

1	*111 inherited members from java.awt.Component not shown*		
2	*39 inherited members from java.awt.Container not shown*		
3	*110 inherited members from JComponent not shown*		
4	*32 inherited members from JScrollBar not shown*		
4	public	**int**	**getBlockIncrement** (int direction)
4	public	**int**	**getUnitIncrement** (int direction)
*	public	**ScrollBar**	(int orientation)
4	public	**void**	**setBlockIncrement** (int blockIncrement)
4	public	**void**	**setUnitIncrement** (int unitIncrement)

JSeparator · javax.swing

Object
 └java.awt.Component[1] - - - - - - - - - - - - - - - - - - - *java.awt.image.ImageObserver, java.awt.MenuContainer,*   ○
                  java.io.Serializable
  └java.awt.Container[2]
   └JComponent[3] - *java.io.Serializable*   *1.2* ○
    └JSeparator - *SwingConstants, javax.accessibility.Accessible*   *1.2*

1	*111 inherited members from java.awt.Component not shown*		
2	*39 inherited members from java.awt.Container not shown*		
3	*112 inherited members from JComponent not shown*		
3	public…	**javax.accessibility ↩**	**getAccessibleContext** ()
	.AccessibleContext		
	public	int	**getOrientation** ()
	public		**getUI** ()
	.. javax.swing.plaf.SeparatorUI		

Class *Interface* —extends - - -implements ○ abstract ● final △ static ▲ static final ✳ constructor x x—inherited x **x**—declared **x x**—overridden

3	public	**String**	**getUIClassID** ()
3	public	**boolean**	**isFocusTraversable** ()
*	public		**JSeparator** ()
*	public		**JSeparator** (int orientation)
3	protected	**String**	**paramString** ()
	public	void	**setOrientation** (int orientation)
	public	void	**setUI** (javax.swing.plaf.SeparatorUI ui)
3	public	**void**	**updateUI** ()

JSeparator.AccessibleJSeparator | protected | javax.swing

Object
- 1.2 ○ └javax.accessibility.AccessibleContext[1]
- 1.2 ○   └JComponent.AccessibleJComponent[2] - - - - *java.io.Serializable, javax.accessibility.AccessibleComponent*
- 1.2   └JSeparator.AccessibleJSeparator

1	*21 inherited members from javax.accessibility.AccessibleContext not shown*		
2	*40 inherited members from JComponent.AccessibleJComponent not shown*		
*	protected		**AccessibleJSeparator** ()
2	public	**javax ↵**	**getAccessibleRole** ()
	.accessibility.AccessibleRole		

JSlider | javax.swing

Object
- ○ └java.awt.Component[1] - - - - - - - - - - - - - - - - - - *java.awt.image.ImageObserver, java.awt.MenuContainer,*
                                    java.io.Serializable
-   └java.awt.Container[2]
- 1.2 ○   └JComponent[3] - - - - - - - - - - - - - - - - - - - *java.io.Serializable*
- 1.2   └JSlider - *SwingConstants, javax.accessibility.Accessible*

1	*111 inherited members from java.awt.Component not shown*		
2	*39 inherited members from java.awt.Container not shown*		
3	*113 inherited members from JComponent not shown*		
	public	void	**addChangeListener** (*javax.swing.event.ChangeListener* l)
	protected transient	javax ↵	**changeEvent**
	.swing.event.ChangeEvent		
	protected	*javax ↵*	**changeListener**
	.swing.event.ChangeListener		
	protected	*javax ↵*	**createChangeListener** ()
	.swing.event.ChangeListener		
	public	java.util.Hashtable	**createStandardLabels** (int increment)
	public	java.util.Hashtable	**createStandardLabels** (int increment, int start)
	protected	void	**fireStateChanged** ()
3	public	**javax.accessibility ↵**	**getAccessibleContext** ()
	.AccessibleContext		
	public	int	**getExtent** ()
	public	boolean	**getInverted** ()
	public	java.util.Dictionary	**getLabelTable** ()
	public	int	**getMajorTickSpacing** ()
	public	int	**getMaximum** ()
	public	int	**getMinimum** ()
	public	int	**getMinorTickSpacing** ()
	public	*BoundedRangeModel*	**getModel** ()
	public	int	**getOrientation** ()
	public	boolean	**getPaintLabels** ()
	public	boolean	**getPaintTicks** ()
	public	boolean	**getPaintTrack** ()
	public	boolean	**getSnapToTicks** ()
	public		**getUI** ()
	javax.swing.plaf.SliderUI		
3	public	**String**	**getUIClassID** ()
	public	int	**getValue** ()
	public	boolean	**getValueIsAdjusting** ()
*	public		**JSlider** ()
*	public		**JSlider** (int orientation)
*	public		**JSlider** (*BoundedRangeModel* brm)
*	public		**JSlider** (int min, int max)
*	public		**JSlider** (int min, int max, int value)
*	public		**JSlider** (int orientation, int min, int max, int value)
	protected	int	**majorTickSpacing**

JSlider

```
        protected . . . . . . . . . . . . . . . . . . . . int  minorTickSpacing
        protected . . . . . . . . . . . . . . . . . . . . int  orientation
    3   protected . . . . . . . . . . . . . . String  paramString ()
        public . . . . . . . . . . . . . . . . . . . . . . void  removeChangeListener (javax.swing.event.ChangeListener l)
        public . . . . . . . . . . . . . . . . . . . . . . void  setExtent (int extent)
        public . . . . . . . . . . . . . . . . . . . . . . void  setInverted (boolean b)
        public . . . . . . . . . . . . . . . . . . . . . . void  setLabelTable (java.util.Dictionary labels)
        public . . . . . . . . . . . . . . . . . . . . . . void  setMajorTickSpacing (int n)
        public . . . . . . . . . . . . . . . . . . . . . . void  setMaximum (int maximum)
        public . . . . . . . . . . . . . . . . . . . . . . void  setMinimum (int minimum)
        public . . . . . . . . . . . . . . . . . . . . . . void  setMinorTickSpacing (int n)
        public . . . . . . . . . . . . . . . . . . . . . . void  setModel (BoundedRangeModel newModel)
        public . . . . . . . . . . . . . . . . . . . . . . void  setOrientation (int orientation)
        public . . . . . . . . . . . . . . . . . . . . . . void  setPaintLabels (boolean b)
        public . . . . . . . . . . . . . . . . . . . . . . void  setPaintTicks (boolean b)
        public . . . . . . . . . . . . . . . . . . . . . . void  setPaintTrack (boolean b)
        public . . . . . . . . . . . . . . . . . . . . . . void  setSnapToTicks (boolean b)
        public . . . . . . . . . . . . . . . . . . . . . . void  setUI (javax.swing.plaf.SliderUI ui)
        public . . . . . . . . . . . . . . . . . . . . . . void  setValue (int n)
        public . . . . . . . . . . . . . . . . . . . . . . void  setValueIsAdjusting (boolean b)
        protected . . . . . . . . . . . . . . . . . . . .       sliderModel
        . . . . . . . . . . BoundedRangeModel
        protected . . . . . . . . . . . . . . . . boolean  snapToTicks
        protected . . . . . . . . . . . . . . . . . . . . void  updateLabelUIs ()
    3   public . . . . . . . . . . . . . . . . . . . . void  updateUI ()
```

JSlider.AccessibleJSlider   protected   javax.swing

```
        Object
1.2 O   └javax.accessibility.AccessibleContext 1
1.2 O       └JComponent.AccessibleJComponent 2 - - - - java.io.Serializable, javax.accessibility.AccessibleComponent
1.2           └JSlider.AccessibleJSlider - - - - - - - - - - - - javax.accessibility.AccessibleValue 3
```

```
    1   20 inherited members from javax.accessibility.AccessibleContext not shown
    2   39 inherited members from JComponent.AccessibleJComponent not shown
*       protected . . . . . . . . . . . . . . . . . . . . .  AccessibleJSlider ()
    2   public . . . . . . . . . . . . . . . . javax ↵  getAccessibleRole ()
        .accessibility.AccessibleRole
    2   public . . . javax.accessibility ↵  getAccessibleStateSet ()
        .AccessibleStateSet
    1   public . . . javax.accessibility ↵  getAccessibleValue ()
        .AccessibleValue
    3   public . . . . . . . . . . . . . . . . Number  getCurrentAccessibleValue ()
    3   public . . . . . . . . . . . . . . . . Number  getMaximumAccessibleValue ()
    3   public . . . . . . . . . . . . . . . . Number  getMinimumAccessibleValue ()
    3   public . . . . . . . . . . . . . . . . boolean  setCurrentAccessibleValue (Number n)
```

JSplitPane   javax.swing

```
        Object
O       └java.awt.Component 1 - - - - - - - - - - - - - - - - - - - java.awt.image.ImageObserver, java.awt.MenuContainer,
                                                                      java.io.Serializable
          └java.awt.Container 2
1.2 O       └JComponent 3 - - - - - - - - - - - - - - - - - - - - java.io.Serializable
1.2           └JSplitPane - - - - - - - - - - - - - - - - - - - - - javax.accessibility.Accessible
```

```
    1   111 inherited members from java.awt.Component not shown
    2   35 inherited members from java.awt.Container not shown
    3   112 inherited members from JComponent not shown
    2   protected . . . . . . . . . . . . . . . . . void  addImpl (java.awt.Component comp, Object constraints, int index)
▲       public static final . . . . . . . . String  BOTTOM = "bottom"
▲       public static final . . . . . . . . String  CONTINUOUS_LAYOUT_PROPERTY = "continuousLayout"
        protected . . . . . . . . . . . . . . boolean  continuousLayout
▲       public static final . . . . . . . . String  DIVIDER = "divider"
▲       public static final . . . . . . . . String  DIVIDER_SIZE_PROPERTY = "dividerSize"
        protected . . . . . . . . . . . . . . . . . . . . int  dividerSize
    3   public . . . javax.accessibility ↵  getAccessibleContext ()
        .AccessibleContext
        public . . . . java.awt.Component  getBottomComponent ()
```

Class *Interface* —extends - - -implements O abstract ● final △ static ▲ static final ✴ constructor x x—inherited x **x**—declared **x x**—overridden

468

	public	int	**getDividerLocation** ()
	public	int	**getDividerSize** ()
	public	int	**getLastDividerLocation** ()
	public	java.awt.Component	**getLeftComponent** ()
	public	int	**getMaximumDividerLocation** ()
	public	int	**getMinimumDividerLocation** ()
	public	int	**getOrientation** ()
	public	java.awt.Component	**getRightComponent** ()
	public	java.awt.Component	**getTopComponent** ()
	public		**getUI** ()
	...javax.swing.plaf.SplitPaneUI		
3	public	**String**	**getUIClassID** ()
▲	public static final	int	**HORIZONTAL_SPLIT** = 1
	public	boolean	**isContinuousLayout** ()
	public	boolean	**isOneTouchExpandable** ()
*	public		**JSplitPane** ()
*	public		**JSplitPane** (int newOrientation)
*	public		**JSplitPane** (int newOrientation, boolean newContinuousLayout)
*	public		**JSplitPane** (int newOrientation, java.awt.Component newLeftComponent, java.awt.Component newRightComponent)
*	public		**JSplitPane** (int newOrientation, boolean newContinuousLayout, java.awt↵.Component newLeftComponent, java.awt.Component newRightComponent)
▲	public static final	String	**LAST_DIVIDER_LOCATION_PROPERTY** = "lastDividerLocation"
	protected	int	**lastDividerLocation**
▲	public static final	String	**LEFT** = "left"
	protected java.awt.Component		**leftComponent**
▲	public static final	String	**ONE_TOUCH_EXPANDABLE_PROPERTY** = "oneTouchExpandable"
	protected	boolean	**oneTouchExpandable**
	protected	int	**orientation**
▲	public static final	String	**ORIENTATION_PROPERTY** = "orientation"
3	protected	**void**	**paintChildren** (java.awt.Graphics g)
3	protected	**String**	**paramString** ()
2	public	**void**	**remove** (int index)
2	public	**void**	**remove** (java.awt.Component component)
2	public	**void**	**removeAll** ()
	public	void	**resetToPreferredSizes** ()
▲	public static final	String	**RIGHT** = "right"
	protected java.awt.Component		**rightComponent**
	public	void	**setBottomComponent** (java.awt.Component comp)
	public	void	**setContinuousLayout** (boolean newContinuousLayout)
	public	void	**setDividerLocation** (double proportionalLocation)
	public	void	**setDividerLocation** (int location)
	public	void	**setDividerSize** (int newSize)
	public	void	**setLastDividerLocation** (int newLastLocation)
	public	void	**setLeftComponent** (java.awt.Component comp)
	public	void	**setOneTouchExpandable** (boolean newValue)
	public	void	**setOrientation** (int orientation)
	public	void	**setRightComponent** (java.awt.Component comp)
	public	void	**setTopComponent** (java.awt.Component comp)
	public	void	**setUI** (javax.swing.plaf.SplitPaneUI ui)
▲	public static final	String	**TOP** = "top"
3	public	**void**	**updateUI** ()
▲	public static final	int	**VERTICAL_SPLIT** = 0

JSplitPane.AccessibleJSplitPane	protected	javax.swing

Object
1.2 O └javax.accessibility.AccessibleContext [1]
1.2 O   └JComponent.AccessibleJComponent [2] - - - - java.io.Serializable, javax.accessibility.AccessibleComponent
1.2   └JSplitPane.AccessibleJSplitPane - - - - - - - javax.accessibility.AccessibleValue [3]

1	*20 inherited members from javax.accessibility.AccessibleContext not shown*		
2	*39 inherited members from JComponent.AccessibleJComponent not shown*		
*	protected		**AccessibleJSplitPane** ()
2	public	**javax↵.accessibility.AccessibleRole**	**getAccessibleRole** ()
2	public	**javax.accessibility↵.AccessibleStateSet**	**getAccessibleStateSet** ()
1	public	***javax.accessibility↵.AccessibleValue***	**getAccessibleValue** ()
3	public	Number	**getCurrentAccessibleValue** ()
3	public	Number	**getMaximumAccessibleValue** ()

JSplitPane.AccessibleJSplitPane

3	public	Number	**getMinimumAccessibleValue** ()
3	public	boolean	**setCurrentAccessibleValue** (Number n)

JTabbedPane	javax.swing

```
Object
 └─java.awt.Component¹ ------------------- java.awt.image.ImageObserver, java.awt.MenuContainer,
                                                        java.io.Serializable
        │
        └─java.awt.Container²
1.2 ○       └─JComponent³ -------------------- java.io.Serializable
1.2            └─JTabbedPane -------------------- java.io.Serializable, javax.accessibility.Accessible, SwingConstants
```

1		*111 inherited members from java.awt.Component not shown*	
2		*32 inherited members from java.awt.Container not shown*	
3		*112 inherited members from JComponent not shown*	
2	public...	**java.awt.Component**	**add** (java.awt.Component component)
2	public...	**java.awt.Component**	**add** (java.awt.Component component, int index)
2	public...	**void**	**add** (java.awt.Component component, Object constraints)
2	public...	**java.awt.Component**	**add** (String title, java.awt.Component component)
2	public...	**void**	**add** (java.awt.Component component, Object constraints, int index)
	public	void	**addChangeListener** (*javax.swing.event.ChangeListener* l)
	public	void	**addTab** (String title, java.awt.Component component)
	public	void	**addTab** (String title, *Icon* icon, java.awt.Component component)
	public	void	**addTab** (String title, *Icon* icon, java.awt.Component component, String tip)
	protected transient.....	javax↵ .swing.event.ChangeEvent	**changeEvent**
	protected...............	*javax↵ .swing.event.ChangeListener*	**changeListener**
	protected...............	*javax↵ .swing.event.ChangeListener*	**createChangeListener** ()
	protected...................	void	**fireStateChanged** ()
3	public...	**javax.accessibility↵ .AccessibleContext**	**getAccessibleContext** ()
	public.............	java.awt.Color	**getBackgroundAt** (int index)
	public.....	java.awt.Rectangle	**getBoundsAt** (int index)
	public....	java.awt.Component	**getComponentAt** (int index)
	public..................	*Icon*	**getDisabledIconAt** (int index)
	public.............	java.awt.Color	**getForegroundAt** (int index)
	public..................	*Icon*	**getIconAt** (int index)
	public...	*SingleSelectionModel*	**getModel** ()
	public....	java.awt.Component	**getSelectedComponent** ()
	public.......................	int	**getSelectedIndex** ()
	public.......................	int	**getTabCount** ()
	public.......................	int	**getTabPlacement** ()
	public.......................	int	**getTabRunCount** ()
	public...................	String	**getTitleAt** (int index)
3	public..............	**String**	**getToolTipText** (java.awt.event.MouseEvent event)
	public.................	javax↵ .swing.plaf.TabbedPaneUI	**getUI** ()
3	public..............	**String**	**getUIClassID** ()
	public.......................	int	**indexOfComponent** (java.awt.Component component)
	public.......................	int	**indexOfTab** (String title)
	public.......................	int	**indexOfTab** (*Icon* icon)
	public...................	void	**insertTab** (String title, *Icon* icon, java.awt.Component component, String tip, int index)
	public.................	boolean	**isEnabledAt** (int index)
✱	public..................		**JTabbedPane** ()
✱	public..................		**JTabbedPane** (int tabPlacement)
	protected.................... .... *SingleSelectionModel*		**model**
3	protected..............	**String**	**paramString** ()
2	public..................	**void**	**remove** (java.awt.Component component)
2	public..................	**void**	**removeAll** ()
	public..................	void	**removeChangeListener** (*javax.swing.event.ChangeListener* l)
	public..................	void	**removeTabAt** (int index)
	public..................	void	**setBackgroundAt** (int index, java.awt.Color background)
	public..................	void	**setComponentAt** (int index, java.awt.Component component)
	public..................	void	**setDisabledIconAt** (int index, *Icon* disabledIcon)
	public..................	void	**setEnabledAt** (int index, boolean enabled)
	public..................	void	**setForegroundAt** (int index, java.awt.Color foreground)

Class   *Interface*   —extends   - - -implements   ○ abstract   ● final   △ static   ▲ static final   ✱ constructor   x x—inherited   x **x**—declared   **x x**—overridden

	public	void	**setIconAt** (int index, *Icon* icon)	
	public	void	**setModel** (*SingleSelectionModel* model)	
	public	void	**setSelectedComponent** (java.awt.Component c)	
	public	void	**setSelectedIndex** (int index)	
	public	void	**setTabPlacement** (int tabPlacement)	
	public	void	**setTitleAt** (int index, String title)	
	public	void	**setUI** (javax.swing.plaf.TabbedPaneUI ui)	
	protected	int	**tabPlacement**	
3	public	**void**	**updateUI** ()	

JTabbedPane.AccessibleJTabbedPane	protected	javax.swing

Object
1.2 ○	└javax.accessibility.AccessibleContext[1]
1.2 ○	└JComponent.AccessibleJComponent[2] - - - - *java.io.Serializable, javax.accessibility.AccessibleComponent*
1.2	└JTabbedPane.AccessibleJTabbedPane - - *javax.accessibility.AccessibleSelection[3],*
	javax.swing.event.ChangeListener[4] (*java.util.EventListener*)

1	*20 inherited members from javax.accessibility.AccessibleContext not shown*		
2	*37 inherited members from JComponent.AccessibleJComponent not shown*		
*	public		**AccessibleJTabbedPane** ()
3	public	void	**addAccessibleSelection** (int i)
3	public	void	**clearAccessibleSelection** ()
2	public	*javax↩*	**getAccessibleAt** (java.awt.Point p)
	.accessibility.Accessible		
2	public	*javax↩*	**getAccessibleChild** (int i)
	.accessibility.Accessible		
2	public	int	**getAccessibleChildrenCount** ()
2	public	javax ↩	**getAccessibleRole** ()
	.accessibility.AccessibleRole		
1	public	*javax.accessibility↩*	**getAccessibleSelection** ()
	.AccessibleSelection		
3	public		**getAccessibleSelection** (int i)
	. *javax.accessibility.Accessible*		
3	public	int	**getAccessibleSelectionCount** ()
3	public	boolean	**isAccessibleChildSelected** (int i)
3	public	void	**removeAccessibleSelection** (int i)
3	public	void	**selectAllAccessibleSelection** ()
4	public	void	**stateChanged** (javax.swing.event.ChangeEvent e)

JTabbedPane.ModelListener	protected	javax.swing

Object
1.2	└JTabbedPane.ModelListener - - - - - - - - - - - - - *javax.swing.event.ChangeListener[1]* (*java.util.EventListener*),
	java.io.Serializable

*	protected		**ModelListener** ()
1	public	void	**stateChanged** (javax.swing.event.ChangeEvent e)

JTable	javax.swing

Object
○	└java.awt.Component[1] - - - - - - - - - - - - - - - - - - - *java.awt.image.ImageObserver, java.awt.MenuContainer,*
	java.io.Serializable
	└java.awt.Container[2]
1.2 ○	└JComponent[3] - *java.io.Serializable*
1.2	└JTable - *javax.swing.event.TableModelListener[4]* (*java.util.EventListener*),
	Scrollable[5], javax.swing.event.TableColumnModelListener[6]
	(*java.util.EventListener*), *javax.swing.event↩*
	.ListSelectionListener[7] (*java.util.EventListener*),
	javax.swing.event.CellEditorListener[8] (*java.util.EventListener*),
	javax.accessibility.Accessible

1	*111 inherited members from java.awt.Component not shown*		
3	*109 inherited members from JComponent not shown*		
2	public	java.awt.Component	**add** (java.awt.Component comp)
2	public	void	**add** (java.awt.Component comp, Object constraints)
2	public	java.awt.Component	**add** (java.awt.Component comp, int index)
2	public	java.awt.Component	**add** (String name, java.awt.Component comp)

JTable

<table>
<tr><td></td><td>2</td><td>public</td><td>void</td><td>add (java.awt.Component comp, Object constraints, int index)</td></tr>
<tr><td></td><td></td><td>public</td><td>void</td><td>addColumn (javax.swing.table.TableColumn aColumn)</td></tr>
<tr><td></td><td></td><td>public</td><td>void</td><td>addColumnSelectionInterval (int index0, int index1)</td></tr>
<tr><td></td><td>2</td><td>public synchronized</td><td>void</td><td>addContainerListener (java.awt.event.ContainerListener l)</td></tr>
<tr><td></td><td>2</td><td>protected</td><td>void</td><td>addImpl (java.awt.Component comp, Object constraints, int index)</td></tr>
<tr><td></td><td>3</td><td>public</td><td>void</td><td>addNotify ()</td></tr>
<tr><td></td><td></td><td>public</td><td>void</td><td>addRowSelectionInterval (int index0, int index1)</td></tr>
<tr><td>▲</td><td></td><td>public static final</td><td>int</td><td>AUTO_RESIZE_ALL_COLUMNS = 4</td></tr>
<tr><td>▲</td><td></td><td>public static final</td><td>int</td><td>AUTO_RESIZE_LAST_COLUMN = 3</td></tr>
<tr><td>▲</td><td></td><td>public static final</td><td>int</td><td>AUTO_RESIZE_NEXT_COLUMN = 1</td></tr>
<tr><td>▲</td><td></td><td>public static final</td><td>int</td><td>AUTO_RESIZE_OFF = 0</td></tr>
<tr><td>▲</td><td></td><td>public static final</td><td>int</td><td>AUTO_RESIZE_SUBSEQUENT_COLUMNS = 2</td></tr>
<tr><td></td><td></td><td>protected</td><td>boolean</td><td>autoCreateColumnsFromModel</td></tr>
<tr><td></td><td></td><td>protected</td><td>int</td><td>autoResizeMode</td></tr>
<tr><td></td><td></td><td>protected transient</td><td>javax↵
.swing.table.TableCellEditor</td><td>cellEditor</td></tr>
<tr><td></td><td></td><td>protected</td><td>boolean</td><td>cellSelectionEnabled</td></tr>
<tr><td></td><td></td><td>public</td><td>void</td><td>clearSelection ()</td></tr>
<tr><td></td><td>6</td><td>public</td><td>void</td><td>columnAdded (javax.swing.event.TableColumnModelEvent e)</td></tr>
<tr><td></td><td></td><td>public</td><td>int</td><td>columnAtPoint (java.awt.Point point)</td></tr>
<tr><td></td><td>6</td><td>public</td><td>void</td><td>columnMarginChanged (javax.swing.event.ChangeEvent e)</td></tr>
<tr><td></td><td></td><td>protected</td><td>javax.swing↵
.table.TableColumnModel</td><td>columnModel</td></tr>
<tr><td></td><td>6</td><td>public</td><td>void</td><td>columnMoved (javax.swing.event.TableColumnModelEvent e)</td></tr>
<tr><td></td><td>6</td><td>public</td><td>void</td><td>columnRemoved (javax.swing.event.TableColumnModelEvent e)</td></tr>
<tr><td></td><td>6</td><td>public</td><td>void</td><td>columnSelectionChanged (javax.swing.event.ListSelectionEvent e)</td></tr>
<tr><td></td><td></td><td>protected</td><td>void</td><td>configureEnclosingScrollPane ()</td></tr>
<tr><td></td><td></td><td>public</td><td>int</td><td>convertColumnIndexToModel (int viewColumnIndex)</td></tr>
<tr><td></td><td></td><td>public</td><td>int</td><td>convertColumnIndexToView (int modelColumnIndex)</td></tr>
<tr><td></td><td></td><td>protected</td><td>javax.swing↵
.table.TableColumnModel</td><td>createDefaultColumnModel ()</td></tr>
<tr><td></td><td></td><td>public</td><td>void</td><td>createDefaultColumnsFromModel ()</td></tr>
<tr><td></td><td></td><td>protected</td><td>. . javax.swing.table.TableModel</td><td>createDefaultDataModel ()</td></tr>
<tr><td></td><td></td><td>protected</td><td>void</td><td>createDefaultEditors ()</td></tr>
<tr><td></td><td></td><td>protected</td><td>void</td><td>createDefaultRenderers ()</td></tr>
<tr><td></td><td></td><td>protected</td><td>ListSelectionModel</td><td>createDefaultSelectionModel ()</td></tr>
<tr><td></td><td></td><td>protected</td><td>javax↵
.swing.table.JTableHeader</td><td>createDefaultTableHeader ()</td></tr>
<tr><td>D △</td><td></td><td>public static</td><td>JScrollPane</td><td>createScrollPaneForTable (JTable aTable)</td></tr>
<tr><td></td><td></td><td>protected</td><td>. . javax.swing.table.TableModel</td><td>dataModel</td></tr>
<tr><td></td><td></td><td>protected transient</td><td>. . . . . java.util.Hashtable</td><td>defaultEditorsByColumnClass</td></tr>
<tr><td></td><td></td><td>protected transient</td><td>. . . . . java.util.Hashtable</td><td>defaultRenderersByColumnClass</td></tr>
<tr><td></td><td>2</td><td>public</td><td>void</td><td>doLayout ()</td></tr>
<tr><td></td><td></td><td>public</td><td>boolean</td><td>editCellAt (int row, int column)</td></tr>
<tr><td></td><td></td><td>public</td><td>boolean</td><td>editCellAt (int row, int column, java.util.EventObject e)</td></tr>
<tr><td></td><td>8</td><td>public</td><td>void</td><td>editingCanceled (javax.swing.event.ChangeEvent e)</td></tr>
<tr><td></td><td></td><td>protected transient</td><td>int</td><td>editingColumn</td></tr>
<tr><td></td><td></td><td>protected transient</td><td>int</td><td>editingRow</td></tr>
<tr><td></td><td>8</td><td>public</td><td>void</td><td>editingStopped (javax.swing.event.ChangeEvent e)</td></tr>
<tr><td></td><td></td><td>protected transient</td><td>. . . . . java.awt.Component</td><td>editorComp</td></tr>
<tr><td></td><td>2</td><td>public</td><td>java.awt.Component</td><td>findComponentAt (java.awt.Point p)</td></tr>
<tr><td></td><td>2</td><td>public</td><td>java.awt.Component</td><td>findComponentAt (int x, int y)</td></tr>
<tr><td></td><td>3</td><td>public</td><td>javax.accessibility↵
.AccessibleContext</td><td>getAccessibleContext ()</td></tr>
<tr><td></td><td></td><td>public</td><td>boolean</td><td>getAutoCreateColumnsFromModel ()</td></tr>
<tr><td></td><td></td><td>public</td><td>int</td><td>getAutoResizeMode ()</td></tr>
<tr><td></td><td></td><td>public</td><td>javax↵
.swing.table.TableCellEditor</td><td>getCellEditor ()</td></tr>
<tr><td></td><td></td><td>public</td><td>javax↵
.swing.table.TableCellEditor</td><td>getCellEditor (int row, int column)</td></tr>
<tr><td></td><td></td><td>public</td><td>java.awt.Rectangle</td><td>getCellRect (int row, int column, boolean includeSpacing)</td></tr>
<tr><td></td><td></td><td>public</td><td>javax↵
.swing.table.TableCellRenderer</td><td>getCellRenderer (int row, int column)</td></tr>
<tr><td></td><td></td><td>public</td><td>boolean</td><td>getCellSelectionEnabled ()</td></tr>
<tr><td></td><td></td><td>public</td><td>javax.swing.table.TableColumn</td><td>getColumn (Object identifier)</td></tr>
</table>

J

Class   *Interface*   —extends   - - -implements   ○ abstract   ● final   △ static   ▲ static final   ✳ constructor   x x—inherited   x **x**—declared   **x x**—overridden

public	Class	**getColumnClass** (int column)
public	int	**getColumnCount** ()
public	*javax.swing↵*	**getColumnModel** ()
.table.TableColumnModel		
public	String	**getColumnName** (int column)
public	boolean	**getColumnSelectionAllowed** ()
2 public	java.awt.Component	getComponent (int n)
2 public	java.awt.Component	getComponentAt (java.awt.Point p)
2 public	java.awt.Component	getComponentAt (int x, int y)
2 public	int	getComponentCount ()
2 public	java.awt.Component[]	getComponents ()
public	*javax↵*	**getDefaultEditor** (Class columnClass)
.swing.table.TableCellEditor		
public	*javax↵*	**getDefaultRenderer** (Class columnClass)
.swing.table.TableCellRenderer		
public	int	**getEditingColumn** ()
public	int	**getEditingRow** ()
public	java.awt.Component	**getEditorComponent** ()
public	java.awt.Color	**getGridColor** ()
public	java.awt.Dimension	**getIntercellSpacing** ()
2 public	*java.awt.LayoutManager*	getLayout ()
public		**getModel** ()
..javax.swing.table.TableModel		
5 public	java.awt.Dimension	**getPreferredScrollableViewportSize** ()
public	int	**getRowCount** ()
public	int	**getRowHeight** ()
public	int	**getRowMargin** ()
public	boolean	**getRowSelectionAllowed** ()
5 public	int	**getScrollableBlockIncrement** (java.awt.Rectangle visibleRect, int orientation, int direction)
5 public	boolean	**getScrollableTracksViewportHeight** ()
5 public	boolean	**getScrollableTracksViewportWidth** ()
5 public	int	**getScrollableUnitIncrement** (java.awt.Rectangle visibleRect, int orientation, int direction)
public	int	**getSelectedColumn** ()
public	int	**getSelectedColumnCount** ()
public	int[]	**getSelectedColumns** ()
public	int	**getSelectedRow** ()
public	int	**getSelectedRowCount** ()
public	int[]	**getSelectedRows** ()
public	java.awt.Color	**getSelectionBackground** ()
public	java.awt.Color	**getSelectionForeground** ()
public	*ListSelectionModel*	**getSelectionModel** ()
public	boolean	**getShowHorizontalLines** ()
public	boolean	**getShowVerticalLines** ()
public	*javax↵*	**getTableHeader** ()
.swing.table.JTableHeader		
3 public	**String**	**getToolTipText** (java.awt.event.MouseEvent event)
public javax.swing.plaf.TableUI		getUI ()
3 public	**String**	**getUIClassID** ()
public	Object	**getValueAt** (int row, int column)
protected	java.awt.Color	**gridColor**
protected	void	**initializeLocalVars** ()
2 public	void	invalidate ()
2 public	boolean	isAncestorOf (java.awt.Component c)
public	boolean	**isCellEditable** (int row, int column)
public	boolean	**isCellSelected** (int row, int column)
public	boolean	**isColumnSelected** (int column)
public	boolean	**isEditing** ()
3 public	**boolean**	**isManagingFocus** ()
public	boolean	**isRowSelected** (int row)
* public	**JTable**	**JTable** ()
* public	**JTable**	**JTable** (*javax.swing.table.TableModel* dm)
* public	**JTable**	**JTable** (int numRows, int numColumns)
* public	**JTable**	**JTable** (Object[][] rowData, Object[] columnNames)
* public	**JTable**	**JTable** (java.util.Vector rowData, java.util.Vector columnNames)
* public	**JTable**	**JTable** (*javax.swing.table.TableModel* dm, *javax.swing.table.TableColumnModel* cm)
* public	**JTable**	**JTable** (*javax.swing.table.TableModel* dm, *javax.swing.table.TableColumnModel* cm, *ListSelectionModel* sm)
2 public	void	list (java.io.PrintStream out, int indent)
2 public	void	list (java.io.PrintWriter out, int indent)
public	void	**moveColumn** (int column, int targetColumn)
2 public	void	paintComponents (java.awt.Graphics g)

JTable

3	protected	**String**	**paramString** ()
	protected	java.awt.Dimension	**preferredViewportSize**
	public	java.awt.Component	**prepareEditor** (*javax.swing.table.TableCellEditor* editor, int row, int column)
	public	java.awt.Component	**prepareRenderer** (*javax.swing.table.TableCellRenderer* renderer, int row, int column)
2	public	void	print (java.awt.Graphics g)
2	public	void	printComponents (java.awt.Graphics g)
2	protected	void	processContainerEvent (java.awt.event.ContainerEvent e)
2	protected	void	processEvent (java.awt.AWTEvent e)
2	public	void	remove (int index)
2	public	void	remove (java.awt.Component comp)
2	public	void	removeAll ()
	public	void	**removeColumn** (javax.swing.table.TableColumn aColumn)
	public	void	**removeColumnSelectionInterval** (int index0, int index1)
2	public synchronized	void	removeContainerListener (*java.awt.event.ContainerListener* l)
	public	void	**removeEditor** ()
	public	void	**removeRowSelectionInterval** (int index0, int index1)
3	public	**void**	**reshape** (int x, int y, int width, int height)
	protected	void	**resizeAndRepaint** ()
	public	int	**rowAtPoint** (java.awt.Point point)
	protected	int	**rowHeight**
	protected	int	**rowMargin**
	protected	boolean	**rowSelectionAllowed**
	public	void	**selectAll** ()
	protected	java.awt.Color	**selectionBackground**
	protected	java.awt.Color	**selectionForeground**
	protected	*ListSelectionModel*	**selectionModel**
	public	void	**setAutoCreateColumnsFromModel** (boolean createColumns)
	public	void	**setAutoResizeMode** (int mode)
	public	void	**setCellEditor** (*javax.swing.table.TableCellEditor* anEditor)
	public	void	**setCellSelectionEnabled** (boolean flag)
	public	void	**setColumnModel** (*javax.swing.table.TableColumnModel* newModel)
	public	void	**setColumnSelectionAllowed** (boolean flag)
	public	void	**setColumnSelectionInterval** (int index0, int index1)
	public	void	**setDefaultEditor** (Class columnClass, *javax.swing.table.TableCellEditor* editor)
	public	void	**setDefaultRenderer** (Class columnClass, *javax.swing.table.TableCellRenderer* renderer)
	public	void	**setEditingColumn** (int aColumn)
	public	void	**setEditingRow** (int aRow)
	public	void	**setGridColor** (java.awt.Color newColor)
	public	void	**setIntercellSpacing** (java.awt.Dimension newSpacing)
2	public	void	setLayout (*java.awt.LayoutManager* mgr)
	public	void	**setModel** (*javax.swing.table.TableModel* newModel)
	public	void	**setPreferredScrollableViewportSize** (java.awt.Dimension size)
	public	void	**setRowHeight** (int newHeight)
	public	void	**setRowMargin** (int rowMargin)
	public	void	**setRowSelectionAllowed** (boolean flag)
	public	void	**setRowSelectionInterval** (int index0, int index1)
	public	void	**setSelectionBackground** (java.awt.Color selectionBackground)
	public	void	**setSelectionForeground** (java.awt.Color selectionForeground)
	public	void	**setSelectionMode** (int selectionMode)
	public	void	**setSelectionModel** (*ListSelectionModel* newModel)
	public	void	**setShowGrid** (boolean b)
	public	void	**setShowHorizontalLines** (boolean b)
	public	void	**setShowVerticalLines** (boolean b)
	public	void	**setTableHeader** (javax.swing.table.JTableHeader newHeader)
	public	void	**setUI** (javax.swing.plaf.TableUI ui)
	public	void	**setValueAt** (Object aValue, int row, int column)
	protected	boolean	**showHorizontalLines**
	protected	boolean	**showVerticalLines**
D	public	void	**sizeColumnsToFit** (boolean lastColumnOnly)
	public	void	**sizeColumnsToFit** (int resizingColumn)
4	public	void	**tableChanged** (javax.swing.event.TableModelEvent e)
	protected	javax↵ .swing.table.JTableHeader	**tableHeader**
3	public	**void**	**updateUI** ()
2	public	void	validate ()
2	protected	void	validateTree ()
7	public	void	**valueChanged** (javax.swing.event.ListSelectionEvent e)

Class   *Interface*   —extends   - - -implements   ○ abstract   ● final   △ static   ▲ static final   ✳ constructor   x x—inherited   x **x**—declared   **x x**—overridden

JTable.AccessibleJTable	protected	javax.swing

Object
1.2 ○ └─javax.accessibility.AccessibleContext[1]
1.2 ○   └─JComponent.AccessibleJComponent[2] ---- *java.io.Serializable, javax.accessibility.AccessibleComponent*
1.2   └─JTable.AccessibleJTable ------------- *javax.accessibility.AccessibleSelection[3], javax.swing↩*
      .event.ListSelectionListener[4] (java.util.EventListener),
      javax.swing.event.TableModelListener[5] (java.util.EventListener),
      javax.swing.event.TableColumnModelListener[6]
      (java.util.EventListener), javax.swing.event.CellEditorListener[7]
      (java.util.EventListener), java.beans.PropertyChangeListener[8]
      (java.util.EventListener)

1	*20 inherited members from javax.accessibility.AccessibleContext not shown*		
2	*37 inherited members from JComponent.AccessibleJComponent not shown*		
3	public	void	**addAccessibleSelection** (int i)
3	public	void	**clearAccessibleSelection** ()
6	public	void	**columnAdded** (javax.swing.event.TableColumnModelEvent e)
6	public	void	**columnMarginChanged** (javax.swing.event.ChangeEvent e)
6	public	void	**columnMoved** (javax.swing.event.TableColumnModelEvent e)
6	public	void	**columnRemoved** (javax.swing.event.TableColumnModelEvent e)
6	public	void	**columnSelectionChanged** (javax.swing.event.ListSelectionEvent e)
7	public	void	**editingCanceled** (javax.swing.event.ChangeEvent e)
7	public	void	**editingStopped** (javax.swing.event.ChangeEvent e)
2	public	*javax↩ .accessibility.Accessible*	**getAccessibleAt** (java.awt.Point p)
2	public	*javax↩ .accessibility.Accessible*	**getAccessibleChild** (int i)
2	public	int	**getAccessibleChildrenCount** ()
2	public	*javax↩ .accessibility.AccessibleRole*	**getAccessibleRole** ()
1	public	*javax.accessibility↩ .AccessibleSelection*	**getAccessibleSelection** ()
3	public	*. javax.accessibility.Accessible*	**getAccessibleSelection** (int i)
3	public	int	**getAccessibleSelectionCount** ()
3	public	boolean	**isAccessibleChildSelected** (int i)
8	public	void	**propertyChange** (java.beans.PropertyChangeEvent e)
3	public	void	**removeAccessibleSelection** (int i)
3	public	void	**selectAllAccessibleSelection** ()
5	public	void	**tableChanged** (javax.swing.event.TableModelEvent e)
	public	void	**tableRowsDeleted** (javax.swing.event.TableModelEvent e)
	public	void	**tableRowsInserted** (javax.swing.event.TableModelEvent e)
4	public	void	**valueChanged** (javax.swing.event.ListSelectionEvent e)

JTable.AccessibleJTable.AccessibleJTableCell	protected	javax.swing

Object
1.2 ○ └─javax.accessibility.AccessibleContext[1]
1.2   └─JTable.AccessibleJTable ↩ ------------- *javax.accessibility.Accessible[2], javax.accessibility↩*
    .AccessibleJTableCell   *.AccessibleComponent[3]*

1	*15 inherited members from javax.accessibility.AccessibleContext not shown*		
*	public		**AccessibleJTableCell** (JTable t, int r, int c, int i)
3	public	void	**addFocusListener** (*java.awt.event.FocusListener* l)
1	public	**void**	**addPropertyChangeListener** (*java.beans.PropertyChangeListener* l)
3	public	boolean	**contains** (java.awt.Point p)
1	public	*javax.accessibility↩ .AccessibleAction*	**getAccessibleAction** ()
3	public	*. javax.accessibility.Accessible*	**getAccessibleAt** (java.awt.Point p)
1	public	*javax↩ .accessibility.Accessible*	**getAccessibleChild** (int i)
1	public	int	**getAccessibleChildrenCount** ()
1	public	*javax.accessibility↩ .AccessibleComponent*	**getAccessibleComponent** ()
2	public	javax.accessibility↩ .AccessibleContext	**getAccessibleContext** ()
1	public	**String**	**getAccessibleDescription** ()
1	public	int	**getAccessibleIndexInParent** ()
1	public	**String**	**getAccessibleName** ()

J

Classes

JTable.AccessibleJTable.AccessibleJTableCell

1	public	*javax↵* *.accessibility.Accessible*	**getAccessibleParent** ()
1	public	*javax↵* *.accessibility.AccessibleRole*	**getAccessibleRole** ()
1	public	*javax.accessibility↵* *.AccessibleSelection*	**getAccessibleSelection** ()
1	public	*javax.accessibility↵* *.AccessibleStateSet*	**getAccessibleStateSet** ()
1	public	*javax↵* *.accessibility.AccessibleText*	**getAccessibleText** ()
1	public	*javax.accessibility↵* *.AccessibleValue*	**getAccessibleValue** ()
3	public	java.awt.Color	**getBackground** ()
3	public	java.awt.Rectangle	**getBounds** ()
3	public	java.awt.Cursor	**getCursor** ()
3	public	java.awt.Font	**getFont** ()
3	public	java.awt.FontMetrics	**getFontMetrics** (java.awt.Font f)
3	public	java.awt.Color	**getForeground** ()
1	public	**java.util.Locale**	**getLocale** ()
3	public	java.awt.Point	**getLocation** ()
3	public	java.awt.Point	**getLocationOnScreen** ()
3	public	java.awt.Dimension	**getSize** ()
3	public	boolean	**isEnabled** ()
3	public	boolean	**isFocusTraversable** ()
3	public	boolean	**isShowing** ()
3	public	boolean	**isVisible** ()
3	public	void	**removeFocusListener** (*java.awt.event.FocusListener* l)
1	public	**void**	**removePropertyChangeListener** (*java.beans.PropertyChangeListener* l)
3	public	void	**requestFocus** ()
1	public	**void**	**setAccessibleDescription** (String s)
1	public	**void**	**setAccessibleName** (String s)
3	public	void	**setBackground** (java.awt.Color c)
3	public	void	**setBounds** (java.awt.Rectangle r)
3	public	void	**setCursor** (java.awt.Cursor c)
3	public	void	**setEnabled** (boolean b)
3	public	void	**setFont** (java.awt.Font f)
3	public	void	**setForeground** (java.awt.Color c)
3	public	void	**setLocation** (java.awt.Point p)
3	public	void	**setSize** (java.awt.Dimension d)
3	public	void	**setVisible** (boolean b)

JTableHeader   javax.swing.table

```
Object
 └─java.awt.Component¹ ------------------- java.awt.image.ImageObserver, java.awt.MenuContainer,
                                                    java.io.Serializable
     └─java.awt.Container²
         └─javax.swing.JComponent³ ----------- java.io.Serializable
             └─JTableHeader ------------------- javax.swing.event.TableColumnModelListener⁴
                                             (java.util.EventListener), javax.accessibility.Accessible
```

1	*111 inherited members from java.awt.Component not shown*		
2	*39 inherited members from java.awt.Container not shown*		
3	*112 inherited members from javax.swing.JComponent not shown*		
4	public	void	**columnAdded** (javax.swing.event.TableColumnModelEvent e)
	public	int	**columnAtPoint** (java.awt.Point point)
4	public	void	**columnMarginChanged** (javax.swing.event.ChangeEvent e)
	protected	*TableColumnModel*	**columnModel**
4	public	void	**columnMoved** (javax.swing.event.TableColumnModelEvent e)
4	public	void	**columnRemoved** (javax.swing.event.TableColumnModelEvent e)
4	public	void	**columnSelectionChanged** (javax.swing.event.ListSelectionEvent e)
	protected	*TableColumnModel*	**createDefaultColumnModel** ()
	protected transient	*TableColumn*	**draggedColumn**
	protected transient	int	**draggedDistance**
3	public	*javax.accessibility↵* *.AccessibleContext*	**getAccessibleContext** ()
	public	*TableColumnModel*	**getColumnModel** ()
	public	TableColumn	**getDraggedColumn** ()
	public	int	**getDraggedDistance** ()

Class   *Interface*   —extends   - - -implements   ○ abstract   ● final   △ static   ▲ static final   ✳ constructor   x x—inherited   x **x**—declared   **x x**—overridden

476

	public	java.awt.Rectangle	**getHeaderRect** (int columnIndex)
	public	boolean	**getReorderingAllowed** ()
	public	boolean	**getResizingAllowed** ()
	public	TableColumn	**getResizingColumn** ()
	public	javax.swing.JTable	**getTable** ()
3	public	String	**getToolTipText** (java.awt.event.MouseEvent event)
	public	javax↩ .swing.plaf.TableHeaderUI	**getUI** ()
3	public	String	**getUIClassID** ()
	public	boolean	**getUpdateTableInRealTime** ()
	protected	void	**initializeLocalVars** ()
*	public		**JTableHeader** ()
*	public		**JTableHeader** (*TableColumnModel* cm)
3	protected	String	**paramString** ()
	protected	boolean	**reorderingAllowed**
	public	void	**resizeAndRepaint** ()
	protected	boolean	**resizingAllowed**
	protected transient	TableColumn	**resizingColumn**
	public	void	**setColumnModel** (*TableColumnModel* newModel)
	public	void	**setDraggedColumn** (TableColumn aColumn)
	public	void	**setDraggedDistance** (int distance)
	public	void	**setReorderingAllowed** (boolean b)
	public	void	**setResizingAllowed** (boolean b)
	public	void	**setResizingColumn** (TableColumn aColumn)
	public	void	**setTable** (javax.swing.JTable aTable)
	public	void	**setUI** (javax.swing.plaf.TableHeaderUI ui)
	public	void	**setUpdateTableInRealTime** (boolean flag)
	protected	javax.swing.JTable	**table**
	protected	boolean	**updateTableInRealTime**
3	public	void	**updateUI** ()

JTableHeader.AccessibleJTableHeader   protected   javax.swing.table

Object
- 1.2 ○ └─javax.accessibility.AccessibleContext [1]
- 1.2 ○   └─javax.swing.JComponent ↩ - - - - - - - - - - - - *java.io.Serializable*, *javax.accessibility.AccessibleComponent*
          .AccessibleJComponent [2]
- 1.2   └─JTableHeader.AccessibleJTableHeader

1	*21 inherited members from javax.accessibility.AccessibleContext not shown*		
2	*37 inherited members from javax.swing.JComponent.AccessibleJComponent not shown*		
*	protected		**AccessibleJTableHeader** ()
2	public	javax↩ .accessibility.Accessible	**getAccessibleAt** (java.awt.Point p)
2	public	javax↩ .accessibility.Accessible	**getAccessibleChild** (int i)
2	public	int	**getAccessibleChildrenCount** ()
2	public	javax↩ .accessibility.AccessibleRole	**getAccessibleRole** ()

JTableHeader.AccessibleJTableHeader.AccessibleJTableHeaderEntry   protect[ed]   javax.swing.table

Object
- 1.2 ○ └─javax.accessibility.AccessibleContext [1]
- 1.2   └─JTableHeader.AccessibleJTableHeader ↩ - - *javax.accessibility.Accessible* [2], *javax.accessibility* ↩
            .AccessibleJTableHeaderEntry   .AccessibleComponent [3]

1	*16 inherited members from javax.accessibility.AccessibleContext not shown*		
*	public		**AccessibleJTableHeaderEntry** (int c, JTableHeader p, javax.swing.JTable t)
3	public	void	**addFocusListener** (*java.awt.event.FocusListener* l)
1	public	void	**addPropertyChangeListener** (*java.beans.PropertyChangeListener* l)
3	public	boolean	**contains** (java.awt.Point p)
1	public	*javax.accessibility*↩ *.AccessibleAction*	**getAccessibleAction** ()
3	public	*javax.accessibility.Accessible*	**getAccessibleAt** (java.awt.Point p)
1	public	javax↩ *.accessibility.Accessible*	**getAccessibleChild** (int i)
1	public	int	**getAccessibleChildrenCount** ()

JTableHeader.AccessibleJTableHeader.AccessibleJTableHeaderEntry

1	public...	***javax.accessibility↵.AccessibleComponent***	**getAccessibleComponent** ()
2	public....	javax.accessibility↵.AccessibleContext	**getAccessibleContext** ()
1	public....................	**String**	**getAccessibleDescription** ()
1	public....................	**int**	**getAccessibleIndexInParent** ()
1	public....................	**String**	**getAccessibleName** ()
1	public....................	**javax↵.accessibility.AccessibleRole**	**getAccessibleRole** ()
1	public...	***javax.accessibility↵.AccessibleSelection***	**getAccessibleSelection** ()
1	public...	***javax.accessibility↵.AccessibleStateSet***	**getAccessibleStateSet** ()
1	public....................	***javax↵.accessibility.AccessibleText***	**getAccessibleText** ()
1	public...	***javax.accessibility↵.AccessibleValue***	**getAccessibleValue** ()
3	public..........java.awt.Color	**getBackground** ()
3	public......java.awt.Rectangle	**getBounds** ()
3	public..........java.awt.Cursor	**getCursor** ()
3	public..............java.awt.Font	**getFont** ()
3	public...java.awt.FontMetrics	**getFontMetrics** (java.awt.Font f)
3	public..........java.awt.Color	**getForeground** ()
1	public............**java.util.Locale**	**getLocale** ()
3	public..........java.awt.Point	**getLocation** ()
3	public..........java.awt.Point	**getLocationOnScreen** ()
3	public......java.awt.Dimension	**getSize** ()
3	public....................boolean	**isEnabled** ()
3	public....................boolean	**isFocusTraversable** ()
3	public....................boolean	**isShowing** ()
3	public....................boolean	**isVisible** ()
3	public......................void	**removeFocusListener** (*java.awt.event.FocusListener* l)
1	public......................void	**removePropertyChangeListener** (*java.beans.PropertyChangeListener* l)
3	public......................void	**requestFocus** ()
1	public......................void	**setAccessibleDescription** (String s)
1	public......................void	**setAccessibleName** (String s)
3	public......................void	**setBackground** (java.awt.Color c)
3	public......................void	**setBounds** (java.awt.Rectangle r)
3	public......................void	**setCursor** (java.awt.Cursor c)
3	public......................void	**setEnabled** (boolean b)
3	public......................void	**setFont** (java.awt.Font f)
3	public......................void	**setForeground** (java.awt.Color c)
3	public......................void	**setLocation** (java.awt.Point p)
3	public......................void	**setSize** (java.awt.Dimension d)
3	public......................void	**setVisible** (boolean b)

JTextArea   javax.swing

```
Object
 └─java.awt.Component 1 ------------------- java.awt.image.ImageObserver, java.awt.MenuContainer,
                                                              java.io.Serializable
       └─java.awt.Container 2
          └─JComponent 3 ----------------------- java.io.Serializable
             └─javax.swing.text.JTextComponent 4 ---- Scrollable, javax.accessibility.Accessible
                └─JTextArea
```

1	*109 inherited members from java.awt.Component not shown*		
2	*39 inherited members from java.awt.Container not shown*		
3	*104 inherited members from JComponent not shown*		
4	*65 inherited members from javax.swing.text.JTextComponent not shown*		
	public......................void	**append** (String str)
	protected......................	**createDefaultModel** ()
	....*javax.swing.text.Document*	
4	public... **javax.accessibility↵.AccessibleContext**	**getAccessibleContext** ()
	public..........................int	**getColumns** ()
	protected.....................int	**getColumnWidth** ()
	public..........................int	**getLineCount** ()
	public..........................int	**getLineEndOffset** (int line) throws javax.swing.text.BadLocationException
	public..........................int	**getLineOfOffset** (int offset) throws javax.swing.text.BadLocationException

---

Class   *Interface*   —extends   - - -implements   ○ abstract   ● final   △ static   ▲ static final   ✳ constructor   x x—inherited   x **x**—declared   **x x**—overridden

	public	int	**getLineStartOffset** (int line) throws javax.swing.text.BadLocationException
	public	boolean	**getLineWrap** ()
4	public	**java.awt.Dimension**	**getPreferredScrollableViewportSize** ()
3	public	**java.awt.Dimension**	**getPreferredSize** ()
	protected	int	**getRowHeight** ()
	public	int	**getRows** ()
4	public	**boolean**	**getScrollableTracksViewportWidth** ()
4	public	**int**	**getScrollableUnitIncrement** (java.awt.Rectangle visibleRect, int orientation, int direction)
	public	int	**getTabSize** ()
3	public	**String**	**getUIClassID** ()
	public	boolean	**getWrapStyleWord** ()
	public	void	**insert** (String str, int pos)
3	public	**boolean**	**isManagingFocus** ()
*	public		**JTextArea** ()
*	public		**JTextArea** (String text)
*	public		**JTextArea** (*javax.swing.text.Document* doc)
*	public		**JTextArea** (int rows, int columns)
*	public		**JTextArea** (String text, int rows, int columns)
*	public		**JTextArea** (*javax.swing.text.Document* doc, String text, int rows, int columns)
4	protected	**String**	**paramString** ()
4	protected	**void**	**processComponentKeyEvent** (java.awt.event.KeyEvent e)
	public	void	**replaceRange** (String str, int start, int end)
	public	void	**setColumns** (int columns)
3	public	**void**	**setFont** (java.awt.Font f)
	public	void	**setLineWrap** (boolean wrap)
	public	void	**setRows** (int rows)
	public	void	**setTabSize** (int size)
	public	void	**setWrapStyleWord** (boolean word)

J

JTextArea.AccessibleJTextArea	protected	javax.swing

	Object
1.2 ○	└javax.accessibility.AccessibleContext[1]
1.2 ○	└JComponent.AccessibleJComponent[2] - - - - *java.io.Serializable, javax.accessibility.AccessibleComponent*
1.2	└javax.swing.text.JTextComponent ← - - - - *javax.accessibility.AccessibleText, javax.swing.event.CaretListener*
	.AccessibleJTextComponent[3] *(java.util.EventListener), javax.swing.event.DocumentListener*
	(java.util.EventListener))
1.2	└JTextArea.AccessibleJTextArea

1	*20 inherited members from javax.accessibility.AccessibleContext not shown*		
2	*39 inherited members from JComponent.AccessibleJComponent not shown*		
*	protected		**AccessibleJTextArea** ()
3	public	void	caretUpdate (javax.swing.event.CaretEvent e)
3	public	void	changedUpdate (*javax.swing.event.DocumentEvent* e)
3	public	*javax* ←	getAccessibleRole ()
	.accessibility.AccessibleRole		
3	public	**javax.accessibility** ←	**getAccessibleStateSet** ()
	.AccessibleStateSet		
3	public	*javax* ←	getAccessibleText ()
	.*accessibility.AccessibleText*		
3	public	String	getAfterIndex (int part, int index)
3	public	String	getAtIndex (int part, int index)
3	public	String	getBeforeIndex (int part, int index)
3	public	int	getCaretPosition ()
3	public		getCharacterAttribute (int i)
	... *javax.swing.text.AttributeSet*		
3	public	java.awt.Rectangle	getCharacterBounds (int i)
3	public	int	getCharCount ()
3	public	int	getIndexAtPoint (java.awt.Point p)
3	public	String	getSelectedText ()
3	public	int	getSelectionEnd ()
3	public	int	getSelectionStart ()
3	public	void	insertUpdate (*javax.swing.event.DocumentEvent* e)
3	public	void	removeUpdate (*javax.swing.event.DocumentEvent* e)

Classes

JTextComponent

	JTextComponent		javax.swing.text

```
        Object
  ○     └─java.awt.Component¹ ─ ─ ─ ─ ─ ─ ─ ─ ─ ─ java.awt.image.ImageObserver, java.awt.MenuContainer,
                                                    java.io.Serializable
          └─java.awt.Container²
  1.2 ○     └─javax.swing.JComponent³ ─ ─ ─ ─ ─ ─ java.io.Serializable
  1.2 ○       └─JTextComponent ─ ─ ─ ─ ─ ─ ─ ─ ─ javax.swing.Scrollable⁴, javax.accessibility.Accessible
```

	1	*109 inherited members from java.awt.Component not shown*	
	2	*39 inherited members from java.awt.Container not shown*	
	3	*108 inherited members from javax.swing.JComponent not shown*	
		public.....................void	**addCaretListener** (*javax.swing.event.CaretListener* listener)
△		public static .... *Keymap*	**addKeymap** (String nm, *Keymap* parent)
		public.....................void	**copy** ()
		public.....................void	**cut** ()
▲		public static final ....String	**DEFAULT_KEYMAP** = "default"
		protected..................void	**fireCaretUpdate** (*javax.swing.event.CaretEvent* e)
▲		public static final ....String	**FOCUS_ACCELERATOR_KEY** = "focusAcceleratorKey"
	3	public... **javax.accessibility ↵** **.AccessibleContext**	**getAccessibleContext** ()
		public..... *javax.swing.Action[]*	**getActions** ()
		public..................... *Caret*	**getCaret** ()
		public............java.awt.Color	**getCaretColor** ()
		public.......................int	**getCaretPosition** ()
		public............java.awt.Color	**getDisabledTextColor** ()
		public................. *Document*	**getDocument** ()
		public...................... char	**getFocusAccelerator** ()
		public............... *Highlighter*	**getHighlighter** ()
	1	public............... *java.awt ↵* **.im.InputMethodRequests**	**getInputMethodRequests** ()
		public................. *Keymap*	**getKeymap** ()
△		public static .... *Keymap*	**getKeymap** (String nm)
		public............java.awt.Insets	**getMargin** ()
	4	public........java.awt.Dimension	**getPreferredScrollableViewportSize** ()
	4	public.......................int	**getScrollableBlockIncrement** (java.awt.Rectangle visibleRect, int orientation, int direction)
	4	public................... boolean	**getScrollableTracksViewportHeight** ()
	4	public................... boolean	**getScrollableTracksViewportWidth** ()
	4	public.......................int	**getScrollableUnitIncrement** (java.awt.Rectangle visibleRect, int orientation, int direction)
		public....................String	**getSelectedText** ()
		public............java.awt.Color	**getSelectedTextColor** ()
		public............java.awt.Color	**getSelectionColor** ()
		public.......................int	**getSelectionEnd** ()
		public.......................int	**getSelectionStart** ()
		public....................String	**getText** ()
		public....................String	**getText** (int offs, int len) throws BadLocationException
		public.. javax.swing.plaf.TextUI	**getUI** ()
		public................... boolean	**isEditable** ()
	3	public................... **boolean**	**isFocusTraversable** ()
	3	public................... **boolean**	**isOpaque** ()
*		public...	**JTextComponent** ()
△		public static ....void	**loadKeymap** (*Keymap* map, JTextComponent. KeyBinding[] bindings, *javax.swing.Action[]* actions)
		public..... java.awt.Rectangle	**modelToView** (int pos) throws BadLocationException
		public.....................void	**moveCaretPosition** (int pos)
	3	protected .... **String**	**paramString** ()
		public.....................void	**paste** ()
	3	protected .... **void**	**processComponentKeyEvent** (java.awt.event.KeyEvent e)
	1	protected .... **void**	**processInputMethodEvent** (java.awt.event.InputMethodEvent e)
		public.....................void	**read** (java.io.Reader in, Object desc) throws java.io.IOException
		public.....................void	**removeCaretListener** (*javax.swing.event.CaretListener* listener)
△		public static .... *Keymap*	**removeKeymap** (String nm)
	3	public................... **void**	**removeNotify** ()
		public.....................void	**replaceSelection** (String content)
		public.....................void	**select** (int selectionStart, int selectionEnd)
		public.....................void	**selectAll** ()
		public.....................void	**setCaret** (*Caret* c)
		public.....................void	**setCaretColor** (java.awt.Color c)
		public.....................void	**setCaretPosition** (int position)

Class   *Interface*   —extends   - - -implements   ○ abstract   ● final   △ static   ▲ static final   ✳ constructor   x x—inherited   x **x**—declared   **x x**—overridden

	public	...................void	**setDisabledTextColor** (java.awt.Color c)
	public	...................void	**setDocument** (*Document* doc)
	public	...................void	**setEditable** (boolean b)
3	public	**void**	**setEnabled** (boolean b)
	public	...................void	**setFocusAccelerator** (char aKey)
	public	...................void	**setHighlighter** (*Highlighter* h)
	public	...................void	**setKeymap** (*Keymap* map)
	public	...................void	**setMargin** (java.awt.Insets m)
3	public	**void**	**setOpaque** (boolean o)
	public	...................void	**setSelectedTextColor** (java.awt.Color c)
	public	...................void	**setSelectionColor** (java.awt.Color c)
	public	...................void	**setSelectionEnd** (int selectionEnd)
	public	...................void	**setSelectionStart** (int selectionStart)
	public	...................void	**setText** (String t)
	public	...................void	**setUI** (javax.swing.plaf.TextUI ui)
3	public	**void**	**updateUI** ()
	public	...................int	**viewToModel** (java.awt.Point pt)
	public	...................void	**write** (java.io.Writer out) throws java.io.IOException

J

JTextComponent.AccessibleJTextComponent
javax.swing.text

Object
1.2 O	└ javax.accessibility.AccessibleContext [1]
1.2 O	└ javax.swing.JComponent ↩ - - - - - - - - - - - - java.io.Serializable, javax.accessibility.AccessibleComponent
	.AccessibleJComponent [2]
1.2	└ JTextComponent ↩ - - - - - - - - - - - - - - - javax.accessibility.AccessibleText [3],
	.AccessibleJTextComponent javax.swing.event.CaretListener [4] (java.util.EventListener),
	javax.swing.event.DocumentListener [5] (java.util.EventListener)

	1	*20 inherited members from javax.accessibility.AccessibleContext not shown*	
	2	*39 inherited members from javax.swing.JComponent.AccessibleJComponent not shown*	
*	public	....	**AccessibleJTextComponent** ()
4	public	...................void	**caretUpdate** (javax.swing.event.CaretEvent e)
5	public	...................void	**changedUpdate** (*javax.swing.event.DocumentEvent* e)
2	public	**javax** ↩	**getAccessibleRole** ()
	.accessibility.AccessibleRole		
2	public	**javax.accessibility** ↩	**getAccessibleStateSet** ()
	.AccessibleStateSet		
1	public	**javax** ↩	**getAccessibleText** ()
	.accessibility.AccessibleText		
3	public	...................String	**getAfterIndex** (int part, int index)
3	public	...................String	**getAtIndex** (int part, int index)
3	public	...................String	**getBeforeIndex** (int part, int index)
3	public	...................int	**getCaretPosition** ()
3	public	...........*AttributeSet*	**getCharacterAttribute** (int i)
3	public	......java.awt.Rectangle	**getCharacterBounds** (int i)
3	public	...................int	**getCharCount** ()
3	public	...................int	**getIndexAtPoint** (java.awt.Point p)
3	public	...................String	**getSelectedText** ()
3	public	...................int	**getSelectionEnd** ()
3	public	...................int	**getSelectionStart** ()
5	public	...................void	**insertUpdate** (*javax.swing.event.DocumentEvent* e)
5	public	...................void	**removeUpdate** (*javax.swing.event.DocumentEvent* e)

Classes

JTextComponent.KeyBinding
javax.swing.text

Object
1.2	└ JTextComponent.KeyBinding

	public	...................String	**actionName**
	public	..javax.swing.KeyStroke	**key**
*	public	....	**KeyBinding** (javax.swing.KeyStroke key, String actionName)

JTextField		javax.swing

```
        Object
  ○     └─java.awt.Component¹ - - - - - - - - - - - - - - - - - -  java.awt.image.ImageObserver, java.awt.MenuContainer,
                                                                    java.io.Serializable
              └─java.awt.Container² - - - - - - - - - - - - - - - - -  java.io.Serializable
1.2 ○           └─JComponent³ - - - - - - - - - - - - - - - - - - -  java.io.Serializable
1.2 ○             └─javax.swing.text.JTextComponent⁴ - - - -  Scrollable, javax.accessibility.Accessible
1.2                 └─JTextField - - - - - - - - - - - - - - - - - - -  SwingConstants
```

1			*109 inherited members from java.awt.Component not shown*
2			*39 inherited members from java.awt.Container not shown*
3			*103 inherited members from JComponent not shown*
4			*68 inherited members from javax.swing.text.JTextComponent not shown*
	public synchronized	void	**addActionListener** (*java.awt.event.ActionListener* l)
	protected		**createDefaultModel** ()
	.... javax.swing.text.Document		
	protected	void	**fireActionPerformed** ()
4	public...	**javax.accessibility** ↵	**getAccessibleContext** ()
	.AccessibleContext		
4	public	***Action[]***	**getActions** ()
	public	int	**getColumns** ()
	protected	int	**getColumnWidth** ()
	public	int	**getHorizontalAlignment** ()
	public...	*BoundedRangeModel*	**getHorizontalVisibility** ()
3	public....	**java.awt.Dimension**	**getPreferredSize** ()
	public	int	**getScrollOffset** ()
3	public	**String**	**getUIClassID** ()
3	public	**boolean**	**isValidateRoot** ()
*	public		**JTextField** ()
*	public		**JTextField** (int columns)
*	public		**JTextField** (String text)
*	public		**JTextField** (String text, int columns)
*	public		**JTextField** (*javax.swing.text.Document* doc, String text, int columns)
▲	public static final	String	**notifyAction** = "notify-field-accept"
4	protected	**String**	**paramString** ()
	public	void	**postActionEvent** ()
	public synchronized	void	**removeActionListener** (*java.awt.event.ActionListener* l)
3	public	**void**	**scrollRectToVisible** (java.awt.Rectangle r)
	public	void	**setActionCommand** (String command)
	public	void	**setColumns** (int columns)
3	public	**void**	**setFont** (java.awt.Font f)
	public	void	**setHorizontalAlignment** (int alignment)
	public	void	**setScrollOffset** (int scrollOffset)

JTextField.AccessibleJTextField	protected	javax.swing

```
        Object
1.2 ○   └─javax.accessibility.AccessibleContext¹
1.2 ○     └─JComponent.AccessibleJComponent² - - - -  java.io.Serializable, javax.accessibility.AccessibleComponent
1.2         └─javax.swing.text.JTextComponent ↵ - - - - -  javax.accessibility.AccessibleText, javax.swing.event.CaretListener
                  .AccessibleJTextComponent³             (java.util.EventListener), javax.swing.event.DocumentListener
                                                          (java.util.EventListener)
1.2           └─JTextField.AccessibleJTextField
```

1			*20 inherited members from javax.accessibility.AccessibleContext not shown*
2			*39 inherited members from JComponent.AccessibleJComponent not shown*
*	protected		**AccessibleJTextField** ()
3	public	void	caretUpdate (javax.swing.event.CaretEvent e)
3	public	void	changedUpdate (*javax.swing.event.DocumentEvent* e)
3	public	*javax* ↵	getAccessibleRole ()
	.accessibility.AccessibleRole		
3	public...	**javax.accessibility** ↵	**getAccessibleStateSet** ()
	.AccessibleStateSet		
3	public	*javax* ↵	getAccessibleText ()
	.accessibility.AccessibleText		
3	public	String	getAfterIndex (int part, int index)
3	public	String	getAtIndex (int part, int index)
3	public	String	getBeforeIndex (int part, int index)
3	public	int	getCaretPosition ()

Class   *Interface*   —extends   - - -implements   ○ abstract   ● final   △ static   ▲ static final   ✳ constructor   x x—inherited   x **x**—declared   **x x**—overridden

J

3	public	....	getCharacterAttribute (int i)

    ... *javax.swing.text.AttributeSet*

3	public	java.awt.Rectangle	getCharacterBounds (int i)
3	public	int	getCharCount ()
3	public	int	getIndexAtPoint (java.awt.Point p)
3	public	String	getSelectedText ()
3	public	int	getSelectionEnd ()
3	public	int	getSelectionStart ()
3	public	void	insertUpdate (*javax.swing.event.DocumentEvent* e)
3	public	void	removeUpdate (*javax.swing.event.DocumentEvent* e)

JTextPane
                                                                                   javax.swing

```
Object
 └java.awt.Component 1 ------------------- java.awt.image.ImageObserver, java.awt.MenuContainer,
                                                         java.io.Serializable
      └java.awt.Container 2
          └JComponent 3 ------------------ java.io.Serializable
              └javax.swing.text.JTextComponent 4 ---- Scrollable, javax.accessibility.Accessible
                  └JEditorPane 5
                      └JTextPane
```

  1 *109 inherited members from java.awt.Component not shown*
  2 *39 inherited members from java.awt.Container not shown*
  3 *105 inherited members from JComponent not shown*
  4 *62 inherited members from javax.swing.text.JTextComponent not shown*

5	public synchronized	void	addHyperlinkListener (*javax.swing.event.HyperlinkListener* listener)
	public	*javax.swing.text.Style*	**addStyle** (String nm, *javax.swing.text.Style* parent)
	protected		**createDefaultEditorKit** ()

    .... **javax.swing.text.EditorKit**

△ 5	public static		createEditorKitForContentType (String type)

    ...... javax.swing.text.EditorKit

5	public	void	fireHyperlinkUpdate (javax.swing.event.HyperlinkEvent e)
5	public	*javax.accessibility* ↵ .AccessibleContext	getAccessibleContext ()
	public		**getCharacterAttributes** ()

    ... *javax.swing.text.AttributeSet*

● 5	public final	String	getContentType ()
● 5	public final		getEditorKit ()

    ...... javax.swing.text.EditorKit

	public		getEditorKitForContentType (String type)

    ...... javax.swing.text.EditorKit

	public	*javax* ↵	**getInputAttributes** ()

    .swing.text.MutableAttributeSet

	public	*javax.swing.text.Style*	**getLogicalStyle** ()
5	public	java.net.URL	getPage ()
	public		**getParagraphAttributes** ()

    ... *javax.swing.text.AttributeSet*

5	public	java.awt.Dimension	getPreferredSize ()
5	public	boolean	getScrollableTracksViewportHeight ()
5	public	**boolean**	**getScrollableTracksViewportWidth** ()
5	protected	java.io.InputStream	getStream (java.net.URL page) throws java.io.IOException
	public	*javax.swing.text.Style*	**getStyle** (String nm)
	public	*javax* ↵	**getStyledDocument** ()

    .swing.text.StyledDocument

●	protected final		**getStyledEditorKit** ()

    javax.swing.text.StyledEditorKit

5	public	String	getText ()
5	public	**String**	**getUIClassID** ()
	public	void	**insertComponent** (java.awt.Component c)
	public	void	**insertIcon** (*Icon* g)
5	public	boolean	isManagingFocus ()
*	public		**JTextPane** ()
*	public		**JTextPane** (*javax.swing.text.StyledDocument* doc)
5	protected	**String**	**paramString** ()
5	protected	void	processComponentKeyEvent (java.awt.event.KeyEvent e)
5	public	void	read (java.io.InputStream in, Object desc) throws java.io.IOException
△ 5	public static	void	registerEditorKitForContentType (String type, String classname)
△ 5	public static	void	registerEditorKitForContentType (String type, String classname, ClassLoader loader)
5	public synchronized	void	removeHyperlinkListener (*javax.swing.event.HyperlinkListener* listener)
	public	void	**removeStyle** (String nm)

Classes

JTextPane

	5	public	**void**	**replaceSelection** (String content)
	5	protected	void	scrollToReference (String reference)
		public	void	**setCharacterAttributes** (*javax.swing.text.AttributeSet* attr, boolean replace)
●	5	public final	void	setContentType (String type)
	4	public	**void**	**setDocument** (*javax.swing.text.Document* doc)
●	5	public final	**void**	**setEditorKit** (javax.swing.text.EditorKit kit)
	5	public	void	setEditorKitForContentType (String type, javax.swing.text.EditorKit k)
		public	**void**	**setLogicalStyle** (*javax.swing.text.Style* s)
	5	public	void	setPage (String url) throws java.io.IOException
	5	public	void	setPage (java.net.URL page) throws java.io.IOException
		public	void	**setParagraphAttributes** (*javax.swing.text.AttributeSet* attr, boolean replace)
		public	void	**setStyledDocument** (*javax.swing.text.StyledDocument* doc)
	5	public	void	setText (String t)

JToggleButton

javax.swing

```
        Object
  ○     └─java.awt.Component 1 ─────────────── java.awt.image.ImageObserver , java.awt.MenuContainer ,
                                                java.io.Serializable
           └─java.awt.Container 2
1.2 ○        └─JComponent 3 ──────────────── java.io.Serializable
1.2 ○          └─AbstractButton 4 ──────────── java.awt.ItemSelectable , SwingConstants
1.2              └─JToggleButton ─────────── javax.accessibility.Accessible
```

	1	*111 inherited members from java.awt.Component not shown*		
	2	*39 inherited members from java.awt.Container not shown*		
	3	*111 inherited members from JComponent not shown*		
	4	*91 inherited members from AbstractButton not shown*		
	3	public... **javax.accessibility** ↵ **.AccessibleContext**		**getAccessibleContext** ()
	3	public	**String**	getUIClassID ()
✳		public	**JToggleButton**	**JToggleButton** ()
✳		public	**JToggleButton**	**JToggleButton** (String text)
✳		public	**JToggleButton**	**JToggleButton** (*Icon* icon)
✳		public	**JToggleButton**	**JToggleButton** (String text, boolean selected)
✳		public	**JToggleButton**	**JToggleButton** (String text, *Icon* icon)
✳		public	**JToggleButton**	**JToggleButton** (*Icon* icon, boolean selected)
✳		public	**JToggleButton**	**JToggleButton** (String text, *Icon* icon, boolean selected)
	4	protected	**String**	**paramString** ()
	4	public	**void**	updateUI ()

JToggleButton.AccessibleJToggleButton

protected   javax.swing

```
        Object
1.2 ○   └─javax.accessibility.AccessibleContext 1
1.2 ○     └─JComponent.AccessibleJComponent 2 ──── java.io.Serializable , javax.accessibility.AccessibleComponent
1.2 ○       └─AbstractButton ↵ ─────────────── javax.accessibility.AccessibleAction ,
               .AccessibleAbstractButton 3          javax.accessibility.AccessibleValue
1.2            └─JToggleButton ↵ ────────────── java.awt.event.ItemListener 4 (java.util.EventListener)
                  .AccessibleJToggleButton
```

	1	*19 inherited members from javax.accessibility.AccessibleContext not shown*		
	2	*38 inherited members from JComponent.AccessibleJComponent not shown*		
✳		public		**AccessibleJToggleButton** ()
	3	public	boolean	doAccessibleAction (int i)
	3	public	*javax* ↵ *.accessibility.AccessibleAction*	getAccessibleAction ()
	3	public	int	getAccessibleActionCount ()
	3	public	String	getAccessibleActionDescription (int i)
	3	public	String	getAccessibleName ()
	2	public	**javax** ↵ **.accessibility.AccessibleRole**	**getAccessibleRole** ()
	3	public	javax.accessibility ↵ .AccessibleStateSet	getAccessibleStateSet ()
	3	public	*javax* ↵ *.accessibility.AccessibleValue*	getAccessibleValue ()
	3	public	Number	getCurrentAccessibleValue ()
	3	public	Number	getMaximumAccessibleValue ()
	3	public	Number	getMinimumAccessibleValue ()

Class   *Interface*   —extends   - - -implements   ○ abstract   ● final   △ static   ▲ static final   ✳ constructor   x x—inherited   x **x**—declared   **x x**—overridden

J

4	public	void	**itemStateChanged** (java.awt.event.ItemEvent e)
3	public	boolean	setCurrentAccessibleValue (Number n)

JToggleButton.ToggleButtonModel

Object
```
1.2  └─DefaultButtonModel 1 - - - - - - - - - - - - - - - - ButtonModel (java.awt.ItemSelectable), java.io.Serializable
1.2     └─JToggleButton.ToggleButtonModel
```

1	*33 inherited members from DefaultButtonModel not shown*		
1	public	**boolean**	**isSelected** ()
1	public	**void**	**setPressed** (boolean b)
1	public	**void**	**setSelected** (boolean b)
*	public		**ToggleButtonModel** ()

JToolBar

Object
```
     ○  └─java.awt.Component 1 - - - - - - - - - - - - - - - - - java.awt.image.ImageObserver, java.awt.MenuContainer,
                                                                java.io.Serializable
           └─java.awt.Container 2
1.2  ○       └─JComponent 3 - - - - - - - - - - - - - - - - - java.io.Serializable
1.2           └─JToolBar - - - - - - - - - - - - - - - - - - SwingConstants, javax.accessibility.Accessible
```

1	*111 inherited members from java.awt.Component not shown*		
2	*37 inherited members from java.awt.Container not shown*		
3	*112 inherited members from JComponent not shown*		
	public	JButton	**add** (*Action* a)
2	protected	**void**	**addImpl** (java.awt.Component comp, Object constraints, int index)
	public	void	**addSeparator** ()
	public	void	**addSeparator** (java.awt.Dimension size)
	protected	*java.beans* ↵ *.PropertyChangeListener*	**createActionChangeListener** (JButton b)
3	public	**javax.accessibility** ↵ **.AccessibleContext**	**getAccessibleContext** ()
	public	java.awt.Component	**getComponentAtIndex** (int i)
	public	int	**getComponentIndex** (java.awt.Component c)
	public	java.awt.Insets	**getMargin** ()
	public	int	**getOrientation** ()
	public	..... javax.swing.plaf.ToolBarUI	**getUI** ()
3	public	**String**	**getUIClassID** ()
	public	boolean	**isBorderPainted** ()
	public	boolean	**isFloatable** ()
*	public		**JToolBar** ()
*	public		**JToolBar** (int orientation)
3	protected	**void**	**paintBorder** (java.awt.Graphics g)
3	protected	**String**	**paramString** ()
2	public	**void**	**remove** (java.awt.Component comp)
	public	void	**setBorderPainted** (boolean b)
	public	void	**setFloatable** (boolean b)
	public	void	**setMargin** (java.awt.Insets m)
	public	void	**setOrientation** (int o)
	public	void	**setUI** (javax.swing.plaf.ToolBarUI ui)
3	public	**void**	**updateUI** ()

Classes

JToolBar.AccessibleJToolBar
protected

Object
```
1.2  ○  └─javax.accessibility.AccessibleContext 1
1.2  ○     └─JComponent.AccessibleJComponent 2 - - - - java.io.Serializable, javax.accessibility.AccessibleComponent
1.2           └─JToolBar.AccessibleJToolBar
```

1	*21 inherited members from javax.accessibility.AccessibleContext not shown*		
2	*39 inherited members from JComponent.AccessibleJComponent not shown*		
*	protected		**AccessibleJToolBar** ()
2	public	**javax** ↵ **.accessibility.AccessibleRole**	**getAccessibleRole** ()

JToolBar.AccessibleJToolBar

```
2  public...  javax.accessibility ↩  getAccessibleStateSet ()
   .AccessibleStateSet
```

JToolBar.Separator   javax.swing

```
       Object
   ○   └java.awt.Component 1 - - - - - - - - - - - - - - - - - - - java.awt.image.ImageObserver, java.awt.MenuContainer,
                                                                   java.io.Serializable
           └java.awt.Container 2
1.2 ○        └JComponent 3 - - - - - - - - - - - - - - - - - - - java.io.Serializable
1.2            └JSeparator 4 - - - - - - - - - - - - - - - - - - SwingConstants, javax.accessibility.Accessible
1.2              └JToolBar.Separator
```

```
   1  111 inherited members from java.awt.Component not shown
   2  39 inherited members from java.awt.Container not shown
   3  109 inherited members from JComponent not shown
   4  public....  javax.accessibility ↩  getAccessibleContext ()
      .AccessibleContext
   3  public....  java.awt.Dimension  getMaximumSize ()
   3  public....  java.awt.Dimension  getMinimumSize ()
   4  public..........................int  getOrientation ()
   3  public....  java.awt.Dimension  getPreferredSize ()
      public.....java.awt.Dimension  getSeparatorSize ()
   4  public..........................  getUI ()
      .. javax.swing.plaf.SeparatorUI
   4  public..................  String  getUIClassID ()
   4  public.............. boolean  isFocusTraversable ()
   4  protected ................String  paramString ()
 *    public..........................  Separator ()
 *    public..........................  Separator (java.awt.Dimension size)
   4  public....................void  setOrientation (int orientation)
      public....................void  setSeparatorSize (java.awt.Dimension size)
   4  public....................void  setUI (javax.swing.plaf.SeparatorUI ui)
   4  public....................void  updateUI ()
```

JToolTip   javax.swing

```
       Object
   ○   └java.awt.Component 1 - - - - - - - - - - - - - - - - - - java.awt.image.ImageObserver, java.awt.MenuContainer,
                                                                 java.io.Serializable
           └java.awt.Container 2
1.2 ○        └JComponent 3 - - - - - - - - - - - - - - - - - - - java.io.Serializable
1.2            └JToolTip - - - - - - - - - - - - - - - - - - - - javax.accessibility.Accessible
```

```
   1  111 inherited members from java.awt.Component not shown
   2  39 inherited members from java.awt.Container not shown
   3  113 inherited members from JComponent not shown
   3  public...  javax.accessibility ↩  getAccessibleContext ()
      .AccessibleContext
      public.............JComponent  getComponent ()
      public....................String  getTipText ()
      public..........................  getUI ()
      ..... javax.swing.plaf.ToolTipUI
   3  public..................  String  getUIClassID ()
 *    public..........................  JToolTip ()
   3  protected ..............  String  paramString ()
      public....................void  setComponent (JComponent c)
      public....................void  setTipText (String tipText)
   3  public..................  void  updateUI ()
```

JToolTip.AccessibleJToolTip   protected   javax.swing

```
       Object
1.2 ○  └javax.accessibility.AccessibleContext 1
1.2 ○    └JComponent.AccessibleJComponent 2 - - - - java.io.Serializable, javax.accessibility.AccessibleComponent
1.2        └JToolTip.AccessibleJToolTip
```

Class   *Interface*   —extends   - - -implements   ○ abstract   ● final   △ static   ▲ static final   ✳ constructor   x x—inherited   x **x**—declared   **x x**—overridden

1			*21 inherited members from javax.accessibility.AccessibleContext not shown*
2			*39 inherited members from JComponent.AccessibleJComponent not shown*
*	protected		**AccessibleJToolTip** ()
2	public	**String**	**getAccessibleDescription** ()
2	public	**javax** ↵	**getAccessibleRole** ()
	.accessibility.AccessibleRole		

JTree javax.swing

```
Object
  └─java.awt.Component¹ - - - - - - - - - - - - - - - - - - - java.awt.image.ImageObserver, java.awt.MenuContainer,
                                                                 java.io.Serializable
        └─java.awt.Container²
```

1.2	○	└─JComponent³ - *java.io.Serializable*
1.2		└─JTree - *Scrollable⁴, javax.accessibility.Accessible*

	1		*111 inherited members from java.awt.Component not shown*
	3		*112 inherited members from JComponent not shown*
	2	public.... java.awt.Component	add (java.awt.Component comp)
	2	public.... java.awt.Component	add (java.awt.Component comp, int index)
	2	public......................void	add (java.awt.Component comp, Object constraints)
	2	public.... java.awt.Component	add (String name, java.awt.Component comp)
	2	public......................void	add (java.awt.Component comp, Object constraints, int index)
	2	public synchronized ....void	addContainerListener (*java.awt.event.ContainerListener* l)
	2	protected.....................void	addImpl (java.awt.Component comp, Object constraints, int index)
		public......................void	**addSelectionInterval** (int index0, int index1)
		public......................void	**addSelectionPath** (javax.swing.tree.TreePath path)
		public......................void	**addSelectionPaths** (javax.swing.tree.TreePath[] paths)
		public......................void	**addSelectionRow** (int row)
		public......................void	**addSelectionRows** (int[] rows)
		public......................void	**addTreeExpansionListener** (*javax.swing.event.TreeExpansionListener* tel)
		public......................void	**addTreeSelectionListener** (*javax.swing.event.TreeSelectionListener* tsl)
		public......................void	**addTreeWillExpandListener** (*javax.swing.event.TreeWillExpandListener* tel)
		public......................void	**cancelEditing** ()
▲		public static final ....String	**CELL_EDITOR_PROPERTY** = "cellEditor"
▲		public static final ....String	**CELL_RENDERER_PROPERTY** = "cellRenderer"
		protected transient............	**cellEditor**
		javax.swing.tree.TreeCellEditor	
		protected transient.....*javax*↵	**cellRenderer**
		.swing.tree.TreeCellRenderer	
		public......................void	**clearSelection** ()
		protected....................void	**clearToggledPaths** ()
		public......................void	**collapsePath** (javax.swing.tree.TreePath path)
		public......................void	**collapseRow** (int row)
		public......................String	**convertValueToText** (Object value, boolean selected, boolean expanded,
			boolean leaf, int row, boolean hasFocus)
△		protected static	**createTreeModel** (Object value)
		.... javax.swing.tree.TreeModel	
		protected.......*javax.swing*↵	**createTreeModelListener** ()
		.event.TreeModelListener	
	2	public......................void	doLayout ()
		protected .... boolean	**editable**
▲		public static final ....String	**EDITABLE_PROPERTY** = "editable"
		public......................void	**expandPath** (javax.swing.tree.TreePath path)
		public......................void	**expandRow** (int row)
	2	public.... java.awt.Component	findComponentAt (java.awt.Point p)
	2	public.... java.awt.Component	findComponentAt (int x, int y)
		public......................void	**fireTreeCollapsed** (javax.swing.tree.TreePath path)
		public......................void	**fireTreeExpanded** (javax.swing.tree.TreePath path)
		public......................void	**fireTreeWillCollapse** (javax. swing. tree. TreePath path)
			throws javax.swing.tree.ExpandVetoException
		public......................void	**fireTreeWillExpand** (javax. swing. tree. TreePath path)
			throws javax.swing.tree.ExpandVetoException
		protected....................void	**fireValueChanged** (javax.swing.event.TreeSelectionEvent e)
	3	public... **javax.accessibility**↵	**getAccessibleContext** ()
		.AccessibleContext	
		public.........................	**getCellEditor** ()
		javax.swing.tree.TreeCellEditor	
		public......................*javax*↵	**getCellRenderer** ()
		.swing.tree.TreeCellRenderer	
		public.........................	**getClosestPathForLocation** (int x, int y)
		...... javax.swing.tree.TreePath	

Classes

JTree

	public	int	**getClosestRowForLocation** (int x, int y)
2	public	java.awt.Component	getComponent (int n)
2	public	java.awt.Component	getComponentAt (java.awt.Point p)
2	public	java.awt.Component	getComponentAt (int x, int y)
2	public	int	getComponentCount ()
2	public	java.awt.Component[]	getComponents ()
△	protected static *javax.swing.tree.TreeModel*		**getDefaultTreeModel** ()
	protected *java.util.Enumeration*		**getDescendantToggledPaths** (javax.swing.tree.TreePath parent)
	public *javax.swing.tree.TreePath*		**getEditingPath** ()
	public *java.util.Enumeration*		**getExpandedDescendants** (javax.swing.tree.TreePath parent)
	public	boolean	**getInvokesStopCellEditing** ()
	public	Object	**getLastSelectedPathComponent** ()
2	public *java.awt.LayoutManager*		getLayout ()
	public *javax.swing.tree.TreePath*		**getLeadSelectionPath** ()
	public	int	**getLeadSelectionRow** ()
	public	int	**getMaxSelectionRow** ()
	public	int	**getMinSelectionRow** ()
	public *javax.swing.tree.TreeModel*		**getModel** ()
	protected *javax.swing.tree.TreePath[]*		**getPathBetweenRows** (int index0, int index1)
	public	java.awt.Rectangle	**getPathBounds** (javax.swing.tree.TreePath path)
	public *javax.swing.tree.TreePath*		**getPathForLocation** (int x, int y)
	public *javax.swing.tree.TreePath*		**getPathForRow** (int row)
4	public	java.awt.Dimension	**getPreferredScrollableViewportSize** ()
	public	java.awt.Rectangle	**getRowBounds** (int row)
	public	int	**getRowCount** ()
	public	int	**getRowForLocation** (int x, int y)
	public	int	**getRowForPath** (javax.swing.tree.TreePath path)
	public	int	**getRowHeight** ()
4	public	int	**getScrollableBlockIncrement** (java.awt.Rectangle visibleRect, int orientation, int direction)
4	public	boolean	**getScrollableTracksViewportHeight** ()
4	public	boolean	**getScrollableTracksViewportWidth** ()
4	public	int	**getScrollableUnitIncrement** (java.awt.Rectangle visibleRect, int orientation, int direction)
	public	boolean	**getScrollsOnExpand** ()
	public	int	**getSelectionCount** ()
	public *javax.swing.tree.TreeSelectionModel*		**getSelectionModel** ()
	public *javax.swing.tree.TreePath*		**getSelectionPath** ()
	public *javax.swing.tree.TreePath[]*		**getSelectionPaths** ()
	public	int[]	**getSelectionRows** ()
	public	boolean	**getShowsRootHandles** ()
3	public	String	**getToolTipText** (java.awt.event.MouseEvent event)
	public	javax.swing.plaf.TreeUI	**getUI** ()
3	public	String	**getUIClassID** ()
	public	int	**getVisibleRowCount** ()
	public	boolean	**hasBeenExpanded** (javax.swing.tree.TreePath path)
2	public	void	invalidate ()
▲	public static final	String	**INVOKES_STOP_CELL_EDITING_PROPERTY** = "messagesStopCellEditing"
	protected	boolean	**invokesStopCellEditing**
2	public	boolean	isAncestorOf (java.awt.Component c)
	public	boolean	**isCollapsed** (int row)
	public	boolean	**isCollapsed** (javax.swing.tree.TreePath path)
	public	boolean	**isEditable** ()
	public	boolean	**isEditing** ()
	public	boolean	**isExpanded** (int row)
	public	boolean	**isExpanded** (javax.swing.tree.TreePath path)
	public	boolean	**isFixedRowHeight** ()
	public	boolean	**isLargeModel** ()
	public	boolean	**isPathEditable** (javax.swing.tree.TreePath path)
	public	boolean	**isPathSelected** (javax.swing.tree.TreePath path)
	public	boolean	**isRootVisible** ()
	public	boolean	**isRowSelected** (int row)

Class   *Interface*   —extends   - - -implements   ○ abstract   ● final   △ static   ▲ static final   ✳ constructor   x x—inherited   x **x**—declared   **x x**—overridden

	public	boolean	**isSelectionEmpty** ()
	public	boolean	**isVisible** (javax.swing.tree.TreePath path)
*	public		**JTree** ()
*	public		**JTree** (Object[] value)
*	public		**JTree** (java.util.Hashtable value)
*	public		**JTree** (java.util.Vector value)
*	public		**JTree** (*javax.swing.tree.TreeModel* newModel)
*	public		**JTree** (*javax.swing.tree.TreeNode* root)
*	public		**JTree** (*javax.swing.tree.TreeNode* root, boolean asksAllowsChildren)
▲	public static final	String	**LARGE_MODEL_PROPERTY** = "largeModel"
	protected	boolean	**largeModel**
2	public	void	list (java.io.PrintStream out, int indent)
2	public	void	list (java.io.PrintWriter out, int indent)
	public	void	**makeVisible** (javax.swing.tree.TreePath path)
2	public	void	paintComponents (java.awt.Graphics g)
3	protected	**String**	**paramString** ()
2	public	void	print (java.awt.Graphics g)
2	public	void	printComponents (java.awt.Graphics g)
2	protected	void	processContainerEvent (java.awt.event.ContainerEvent e)
2	protected	void	processEvent (java.awt.AWTEvent e)
2	public	void	remove (int index)
2	public	void	remove (java.awt.Component comp)
2	public	void	removeAll ()
2	public synchronized	void	removeContainerListener (*java.awt.event.ContainerListener* l)
	protected	void	**removeDescendantToggledPaths** (*java.util.Enumeration* toRemove)
	public	void	**removeSelectionInterval** (int index0, int index1)
	public	void	**removeSelectionPath** (javax.swing.tree.TreePath path)
	public	void	**removeSelectionPaths** (javax.swing.tree.TreePath[] paths)
	public	void	**removeSelectionRow** (int row)
	public	void	**removeSelectionRows** (int[] rows)
	public	void	**removeTreeExpansionListener** (*javax.swing.event.TreeExpansionListener* tel)
	public	void	**removeTreeSelectionListener** (*javax.swing.event.TreeSelectionListener* tsl)
	public	void	**removeTreeWillExpandListener** (*javax.swing.event.TreeWillExpandListener* tel)
▲	public static final	String	**ROOT_VISIBLE_PROPERTY** = "rootVisible"
	protected	boolean	**rootVisible**
▲	public static final	String	**ROW_HEIGHT_PROPERTY** = "rowHeight"
	protected	int	**rowHeight**
	public	void	**scrollPathToVisible** (javax.swing.tree.TreePath path)
	public	void	**scrollRowToVisible** (int row)
▲	public static final	String	**SCROLLS_ON_EXPAND_PROPERTY** = "scrollsOnExpand"
	protected	boolean	**scrollsOnExpand**
▲	public static final	String	**SELECTION_MODEL_PROPERTY** = "selectionModel"
	protected transient	*javax⤸ .swing.tree.TreeSelectionModel*	**selectionModel**
	protected transient	. JTree.TreeSelectionRedirector	**selectionRedirector**
	public	void	**setCellEditor** (*javax.swing.tree.TreeCellEditor* cellEditor)
	public	void	**setCellRenderer** (*javax.swing.tree.TreeCellRenderer* x)
	public	void	**setEditable** (boolean flag)
	protected	void	**setExpandedState** (javax.swing.tree.TreePath path, boolean state)
	public	void	**setInvokesStopCellEditing** (boolean newValue)
	public	void	**setLargeModel** (boolean newValue)
2	public	void	setLayout (*java.awt.LayoutManager* mgr)
	public	void	**setModel** (*javax.swing.tree.TreeModel* newModel)
	public	void	**setRootVisible** (boolean rootVisible)
	public	void	**setRowHeight** (int rowHeight)
	public	void	**setScrollsOnExpand** (boolean newValue)
	public	void	**setSelectionInterval** (int index0, int index1)
	public	void	**setSelectionModel** (*javax.swing.tree.TreeSelectionModel* selectionModel)
	public	void	**setSelectionPath** (javax.swing.tree.TreePath path)
	public	void	**setSelectionPaths** (javax.swing.tree.TreePath[] paths)
	public	void	**setSelectionRow** (int row)
	public	void	**setSelectionRows** (int[] rows)
	public	void	**setShowsRootHandles** (boolean newValue)
	public	void	**setUI** (javax.swing.plaf.TreeUI ui)
	public	void	**setVisibleRowCount** (int newCount)
▲	public static final	String	**SHOWS_ROOT_HANDLES_PROPERTY** = "showsRootHandles"
	protected	boolean	**showsRootHandles**
	public	void	**startEditingAtPath** (javax.swing.tree.TreePath path)
	public	boolean	**stopEditing** ()
	protected	int	**toggleClickCount**
▲	public static final	String	**TREE_MODEL_PROPERTY** = "treeModel"
	public	void	**treeDidChange** ()

J

Classes

JTree

	protected transient.............		**treeModel**	
	.... *javax.swing.tree.TreeModel*			
	protected transient.............		**treeModelListener**	
	.................*javax.swing*↩			
	.event.TreeModelListener			
3	public.....................	**void**	**updateUI** ()	
2	public.....................	void	validate ()	
2	protected..................	void	validateTree ()	
▲	public static final	String	**VISIBLE_ROW_COUNT_PROPERTY**	= "visibleRowCount"
	protected	int	**visibleRowCount**	

JTree.AccessibleJTree   protected   javax.swing

Object
1.2 ○ └javax.accessibility.AccessibleContext [1]
1.2 ○   └JComponent.AccessibleJComponent [2] - - - - *java.io.Serializable, javax.accessibility.AccessibleComponent*
1.2   └JTree.AccessibleJTree - - - - - - - - - - - - - - *javax.accessibility.AccessibleSelection [3], javax.swing.event*↩
                                      .TreeSelectionListener [4] (java.util.EventListener), javax.swing↩
                                      .event.TreeModelListener [5] (java.util.EventListener), javax↩
                                      .swing.event.TreeExpansionListener [6] (java.util.EventListener)

1	*20 inherited members from javax.accessibility.AccessibleContext not shown*		
2	*36 inherited members from JComponent.AccessibleJComponent not shown*		
✳	public.....................		**AccessibleJTree** ()
3	public.....................	void	**addAccessibleSelection** (int i)
3	public.....................	void	**clearAccessibleSelection** ()
	public.....................	void	**fireVisibleDataPropertyChange** ()
2	public..................	*javax*↩	**getAccessibleAt** (java.awt.Point p)
	.accessibility.Accessible		
2	public..................	*javax*↩	**getAccessibleChild** (int i)
	.accessibility.Accessible		
2	public.....................	int	**getAccessibleChildrenCount** ()
2	public.....................	int	**getAccessibleIndexInParent** ()
2	public..................	*javax*↩	**getAccessibleRole** ()
	.accessibility.AccessibleRole		
1	public...	*javax.accessibility*↩	**getAccessibleSelection** ()
	.AccessibleSelection		
3	public.....................		**getAccessibleSelection** (int i)
	. javax.accessibility.Accessible		
3	public.....................	int	**getAccessibleSelectionCount** ()
3	public.....................	boolean	**isAccessibleChildSelected** (int i)
3	public.....................	void	**removeAccessibleSelection** (int i)
3	public.....................	void	**selectAllAccessibleSelection** ()
6	public.....................	void	**treeCollapsed** (javax.swing.event.TreeExpansionEvent e)
6	public.....................	void	**treeExpanded** (javax.swing.event.TreeExpansionEvent e)
5	public.....................	void	**treeNodesChanged** (javax.swing.event.TreeModelEvent e)
5	public.....................	void	**treeNodesInserted** (javax.swing.event.TreeModelEvent e)
5	public.....................	void	**treeNodesRemoved** (javax.swing.event.TreeModelEvent e)
5	public.....................	void	**treeStructureChanged** (javax.swing.event.TreeModelEvent e)
4	public.....................	void	**valueChanged** (javax.swing.event.TreeSelectionEvent e)

JTree.AccessibleJTree.AccessibleJTreeNode   protected   javax.swing

Object
1.2 ○ └javax.accessibility.AccessibleContext [1]
1.2   └JTree.AccessibleJTree↩ - - - - - - - - - - - - - *javax.accessibility.Accessible [2], javax.accessibility*↩
    .AccessibleJTreeNode   *.AccessibleComponent [3], javax.accessibility*↩
                                      .AccessibleSelection [4], javax.accessibility.AccessibleAction [5]

1	*15 inherited members from javax.accessibility.AccessibleContext not shown*		
✳	public.....................		**AccessibleJTreeNode** (JTree t, javax. swing. tree. TreePath p,
			javax.accessibility.Accessible ap)
4	public.....................	void	**addAccessibleSelection** (int i)
3	public.....................	void	**addFocusListener** (*java.awt.event.FocusListener* l)
1	public.....................	**void**	**addPropertyChangeListener** (*java.beans.PropertyChangeListener* l)
4	public.....................	void	**clearAccessibleSelection** ()
3	public.....................	boolean	**contains** (java.awt.Point p)
5	public.....................	boolean	**doAccessibleAction** (int i)

Class   *Interface*   —extends   - - -implements   ○ abstract   ● final   △ static   ▲ static final   ✳ constructor   x x—inherited   x **x**—declared   **x x**—overridden

1	public... ***javax.accessibility***↩ **.AccessibleAction**	**getAccessibleAction** ()
5	public.........................int	**getAccessibleActionCount** ()
5	public........................String	**getAccessibleActionDescription** (int i)
3	public............................ *. javax.accessibility.Accessible*	**getAccessibleAt** (java.awt.Point p)
1	public..................... ***javax***↩ **.accessibility.Accessible**	**getAccessibleChild** (int i)
1	public..................... **int**	**getAccessibleChildrenCount** ()
1	public... ***javax.accessibility***↩ **.AccessibleComponent**	**getAccessibleComponent** ()
2	public.... javax.accessibility↩ .AccessibleContext	**getAccessibleContext** ()
1	public.................... **String**	**getAccessibleDescription** ()
1	public.................... **int**	**getAccessibleIndexInParent** ()
1	public.................... **String**	**getAccessibleName** ()
1	public.................... ***javax***↩ **.accessibility.Accessible**	**getAccessibleParent** ()
1	public.................... **javax**↩ **.accessibility.AccessibleRole**	**getAccessibleRole** ()
1	public... ***javax.accessibility***↩ **.AccessibleSelection**	**getAccessibleSelection** ()
4	public............................ *. javax.accessibility.Accessible*	**getAccessibleSelection** (int i)
4	public.........................int	**getAccessibleSelectionCount** ()
1	public... **javax.accessibility**↩ **.AccessibleStateSet**	**getAccessibleStateSet** ()
1	public.................. ***javax***↩ **.accessibility.AccessibleText**	**getAccessibleText** ()
1	public... ***javax.accessibility***↩ **.AccessibleValue**	**getAccessibleValue** ()
3	public............java.awt.Color	**getBackground** ()
3	public...... java.awt.Rectangle	**getBounds** ()
3	public.........java.awt.Cursor	**getCursor** ()
3	public............java.awt.Font	**getFont** ()
3	public.... java.awt.FontMetrics	**getFontMetrics** (java.awt.Font f)
3	public............java.awt.Color	**getForeground** ()
1	public......... **java.util.Locale**	**getLocale** ()
3	public............ java.awt.Point	**getLocation** ()
	protected .... java.awt.Point	**getLocationInJTree** ()
3	public............ java.awt.Point	**getLocationOnScreen** ()
3	public......java.awt.Dimension	**getSize** ()
4	public.............. boolean	**isAccessibleChildSelected** (int i)
3	public.............. boolean	**isEnabled** ()
3	public.............. boolean	**isFocusTraversable** ()
3	public.............. boolean	**isShowing** ()
3	public.............. boolean	**isVisible** ()
4	public...................void	**removeAccessibleSelection** (int i)
3	public...................void	**removeFocusListener** (*java.awt.event.FocusListener* l)
1	public............... **void**	**removePropertyChangeListener** (*java.beans.PropertyChangeListener* l)
3	public...................void	**requestFocus** ()
4	public...................void	**selectAllAccessibleSelection** ()
1	public............... **void**	**setAccessibleDescription** (String s)
1	public............... **void**	**setAccessibleName** (String s)
3	public...................void	**setBackground** (java.awt.Color c)
3	public...................void	**setBounds** (java.awt.Rectangle r)
3	public...................void	**setCursor** (java.awt.Cursor c)
3	public...................void	**setEnabled** (boolean b)
3	public...................void	**setFont** (java.awt.Font f)
3	public...................void	**setForeground** (java.awt.Color c)
3	public...................void	**setLocation** (java.awt.Point p)
3	public...................void	**setSize** (java.awt.Dimension d)
3	public...................void	**setVisible** (boolean b)

JTree.DynamicUtilTreeNode   javax.swing

Object
  1.2 └javax.swing.tree.DefaultMutableTreeNode¹ - - *Cloneable, javax.swing.tree.MutableTreeNode*
                                    (javax.swing.tree.TreeNode), java.io.Serializable
  1.2   └JTree.DynamicUtilTreeNode

JTree.DynamicUtilTreeNode

	1	*52 inherited members from javax.swing.tree.DefaultMutableTreeNode not shown*	
	1	public.. ***java.util.Enumeration***	**children** ()
		protected .... Object	**childValue**
△		public static ....void	**createChildren** (javax.swing.tree.DefaultMutableTreeNode parent, Object children)
✱		public..........................	**DynamicUtilTreeNode** (Object value, Object children)
	1	public..........................	**getChildAt** (int index)
		... javax.swing.tree.TreeNode	
	1	public...................... **int**	**getChildCount** ()
		protected .... boolean	**hasChildren**
	1	public................. **boolean**	**isLeaf** ()
		protected ....void	**loadChildren** ()
		protected .... boolean	**loadedChildren**

JTree.EmptySelectionModel   protected   javax.swing

Object
└javax.swing.tree.DefaultTreeSelectionModel[1] - *Cloneable, java.io.Serializable, javax.swing.tree↵*
.TreeSelectionModel
1.2

1.2   └JTree.EmptySelectionModel

	1	*44 inherited members from javax.swing.tree.DefaultTreeSelectionModel not shown*	
	1	public.................... **void**	**addSelectionPaths** (javax.swing.tree.TreePath[] paths)
✱		protected	**EmptySelectionModel** ()
	1	public.................... **void**	**removeSelectionPaths** (javax.swing.tree.TreePath[] paths)
	1	public.................... **void**	**setSelectionPaths** (javax.swing.tree.TreePath[] pPaths)
△		public static	**sharedInstance** ()
		... JTree.EmptySelectionModel	
▲		protected static final	**sharedInstance**
		... JTree.EmptySelectionModel	

JTree.TreeModelHandler   protected   javax.swing

Object
1.2   └JTree.TreeModelHandler - - - - - - - - - - - - - - - - - *javax.swing.event.TreeModelListener*[1] (*java.util.EventListener*)

✱		protected	**TreeModelHandler** ()
	1	public....................void	**treeNodesChanged** (javax.swing.event.TreeModelEvent e)
	1	public....................void	**treeNodesInserted** (javax.swing.event.TreeModelEvent e)
	1	public....................void	**treeNodesRemoved** (javax.swing.event.TreeModelEvent e)
	1	public....................void	**treeStructureChanged** (javax.swing.event.TreeModelEvent e)

JTree.TreeSelectionRedirector   protected   javax.swing

Object
1.2   └JTree.TreeSelectionRedirector - - - - - - - - - - - - *java.io.Serializable, javax.swing.event.TreeSelectionListener*[1]
(*java.util.EventListener*)

✱		protected	**TreeSelectionRedirector** ()
	1	public....................void	**valueChanged** (javax.swing.event.TreeSelectionEvent e)

JViewport   javax.swing

Object
○   └java.awt.Component[1] - - - - - - - - - - - - - - - - - - - *java.awt.image.ImageObserver, java.awt.MenuContainer,*
java.io.Serializable

└java.awt.Container[2]
1.2 ○   └JComponent[3] - *java.io.Serializable*
1.2   └JViewport - *javax.accessibility.Accessible*

	1	*111 inherited members from java.awt.Component not shown*	
	2	*37 inherited members from java.awt.Container not shown*	
	3	*107 inherited members from JComponent not shown*	
		public....................void	**addChangeListener** (*javax.swing.event.ChangeListener* l)
	2	protected .... **void**	**addImpl** (java.awt.Component child, Object constraints, int index)
		protected .... boolean	**backingStore**
		protected transient............	**backingStoreImage**
		.... java.awt.Image	

Class *Interface* —extends - - -implements ○ abstract ● final △ static ▲ static final ✱ constructor x x—inherited x **x**—declared **x x**—overridden

J

	protected .... boolean	**computeBlit** (int dx, int dy, java.awt.Point blitFrom, java.awt.Point blitTo,
		java.awt.Dimension blitSize, java.awt.Rectangle blitPaint)
	protected	**createLayoutManager** ()
	.... *java.awt.LayoutManager*	
	protected	**createViewListener** ()
	.........JViewport.ViewListener	
	protected .... void	**fireStateChanged** ()
3	public... **javax.accessibility** ↩	**getAccessibleContext** ()
	.AccessibleContext	
	public...... java.awt.Dimension	**getExtentSize** ()
● 3	public final .... **java.awt.Insets**	**getInsets** ()
● 3	public final .... **java.awt.Insets**	**getInsets** (java.awt.Insets insets)
	public.... java.awt.Component	**getView** ()
	public............ java.awt.Point	**getViewPosition** ()
	public...... java.awt.Rectangle	**getViewRect** ()
	public...... java.awt.Dimension	**getViewSize** ()
	public................. boolean	**isBackingStoreEnabled** ()
3	public.................. **boolean**	**isOptimizedDrawingEnabled** ()
	protected .... boolean	**isViewSizeSet**
✳	public.................	**JViewport** ()
	protected .... java.awt.Point	**lastPaintPosition**
3	public.................... **void**	**paint** (java.awt.Graphics g)
3	protected .... **String**	**paramString** ()
2	public................... **void**	**remove** (java.awt.Component child)
	public....................void	**removeChangeListener** (*javax.swing.event.ChangeListener* l)
3	public................... **void**	**repaint** (long tm, int x, int y, int w, int h)
3	public................... **void**	**reshape** (int x, int y, int w, int h)
3	public................... **void**	**scrollRectToVisible** (java.awt.Rectangle contentRect)
	protected .... boolean	**scrollUnderway**
	public....................void	**setBackingStoreEnabled** (boolean x)
● 3	public final .... **void**	**setBorder** (*javax.swing.border.Border* border)
	public....................void	**setExtentSize** (java.awt.Dimension newExtent)
	public....................void	**setView** (java.awt.Component view)
	public....................void	**setViewPosition** (java.awt.Point p)
	public....................void	**setViewSize** (java.awt.Dimension newSize)
	public...... java.awt.Dimension	**toViewCoordinates** (java.awt.Dimension size)
	public............ java.awt.Point	**toViewCoordinates** (java.awt.Point p)

JViewport.AccessibleJViewport		protected	javax.swing

	Object
1.2 ○	└javax.accessibility.AccessibleContext [1]
1.2 ○	└JComponent.AccessibleJComponent [2] ---- *java.io.Serializable, javax.accessibility.AccessibleComponent*
1.2	└JViewport.AccessibleJViewport

1	*21 inherited members from javax.accessibility.AccessibleContext not shown*	
2	*40 inherited members from JComponent.AccessibleJComponent not shown*	
✳	protected	**AccessibleJViewport** ()
2	public................. **javax** ↩	**getAccessibleRole** ()
	.accessibility.AccessibleRole	

Classes

JViewport.ViewListener		protected	javax.swing

	Object
1.1 ○	└java.awt.event.ComponentAdapter [1] ------- *java.awt.event.ComponentListener* (*java.util.EventListener*)
1.2	└JViewport.ViewListener ---------------- *java.io.Serializable*

1	public....................void	componentHidden (java.awt.event.ComponentEvent e)
1	public....................void	componentMoved (java.awt.event.ComponentEvent e)
1	public.................... **void**	**componentResized** (java.awt.event.ComponentEvent e)
1	public....................void	componentShown (java.awt.event.ComponentEvent e)
✳	protected	**ViewListener** ()

JWindow	javax.swing

Object
　○　└java.awt.Component[1] - java.awt.image.ImageObserver, java.awt.MenuContainer,
　　　　　　　　　　　　　　　　　　　　　　　　　　　　java.io.Serializable
　　　　└java.awt.Container[2]
　　　　　　└java.awt.Window[3]
　1.2　　　　└JWindow - javax.accessibility.Accessible[4], RootPaneContainer[5]

1	*131 inherited members from java.awt.Component not shown*	
2	*46 inherited members from java.awt.Container not shown*	
	protected javax.accessibility↵	**accessibleContext**
	.AccessibleContext	
2	protected................. **void**	**addImpl** (java.awt.Component comp, Object constraints, int index)
3	public.......................void	addNotify ()
3	public synchronized ....void	addWindowListener (*java.awt.event.WindowListener* l)
3	public.......................void	applyResourceBundle (String rbName)
3	public.......................void	applyResourceBundle (java.util.ResourceBundle rb)
	protected .... JRootPane	**createRootPane** ()
3	public.......................void	dispose ()
3	protected..................void	finalize () throws Throwable
4	public.... javax.accessibility↵	**getAccessibleContext** ()
	.AccessibleContext	
5	public...... java.awt.Container	**getContentPane** ()
3	public.... java.awt.Component	getFocusOwner ()
5	public.... java.awt.Component	**getGlassPane** ()
3	public...........................	getInputContext ()
	.... java.awt.im.InputContext	
5	public........... JLayeredPane	**getLayeredPane** ()
3	public..........java.util.Locale	getLocale ()
3	public...... java.awt.Window[]	getOwnedWindows ()
3	public........java.awt.Window	getOwner ()
5	public................JRootPane	**getRootPane** ()
3	public........java.awt.Toolkit	getToolkit ()
● 3	public final ....String	getWarningString ()
	protected.............. boolean	**isRootPaneCheckingEnabled** ()
3	public.................. boolean	isShowing ()
✳	public...........................	**JWindow** ()
✳	public...........................	**JWindow** (java.awt.Frame owner)
✳	public...........................	**JWindow** (java.awt.Window owner)
3	public.......................void	pack ()
2	protected .... **String**	**paramString** ()
3	protected..................void	processEvent (java.awt.AWTEvent e)
3	protected..................void	processWindowEvent (java.awt.event.WindowEvent e)
3	public synchronized ....void	removeWindowListener (*java.awt.event.WindowListener* l)
	protected .... JRootPane	**rootPane**
	protected .... boolean	**rootPaneCheckingEnabled**
5	public.......................void	**setContentPane** (java.awt.Container contentPane)
5	public.......................void	**setGlassPane** (java.awt.Component glassPane)
5	public.......................void	**setLayeredPane** (JLayeredPane layeredPane)
2	public.................. **void**	**setLayout** (*java.awt.LayoutManager* manager)
	protected..................void	**setRootPane** (JRootPane root)
	protected..................void	**setRootPaneCheckingEnabled** (boolean enabled)
3	public.......................void	show ()
3	public.......................void	toBack ()
3	public.......................void	toFront ()
	protected..................void	**windowInit** ()

JWindow.AccessibleJWindow	protected	javax.swing

Object
　1.2　○　└javax.accessibility.AccessibleContext[1]
　1.2　　　　└JWindow.AccessibleJWindow - - - - - - - - - - java.io.Serializable, javax.accessibility.AccessibleComponent[2]

1	*25 inherited members from javax.accessibility.AccessibleContext not shown*	
✳	protected.......................	**AccessibleJWindow** ()
2	public.......................void	**addFocusListener** (*java.awt.event.FocusListener* l)
2	public.................. boolean	**contains** (java.awt.Point p)
2	public...........................	**getAccessibleAt** (java.awt.Point p)
	. javax.accessibility.Accessible	

Class　*Interface*　—extends　- - -implements　○ abstract　● final　△ static　▲ static final　✳ constructor　× x—inherited　× **x**—declared　**x x**—overridden

1	public	*javax*↩	**getAccessibleChild** (int i)	
	.accessibility.Accessible			
1	public	**int**	**getAccessibleChildrenCount** ()	
1	public	*javax.accessibility*↩	**getAccessibleComponent** ()	
	.AccessibleComponent			
1	public	**int**	**getAccessibleIndexInParent** ()	
1	public	*javax*↩	**getAccessibleParent** ()	
	.accessibility.Accessible			
1	public	*javax*↩	**getAccessibleRole** ()	
	.accessibility.AccessibleRole			
1	public	*javax.accessibility*↩	**getAccessibleStateSet** ()	
	.AccessibleStateSet			
2	public	java.awt.Color	**getBackground** ()	
2	public	java.awt.Rectangle	**getBounds** ()	
2	public	java.awt.Cursor	**getCursor** ()	
2	public	java.awt.Font	**getFont** ()	
2	public	java.awt.FontMetrics	**getFontMetrics** (java.awt.Font f)	
2	public	java.awt.Color	**getForeground** ()	
1	public	**java.util.Locale**	**getLocale** ()	
2	public	java.awt.Point	**getLocation** ()	
2	public	java.awt.Point	**getLocationOnScreen** ()	
2	public	java.awt.Dimension	**getSize** ()	
2	public	boolean	**isEnabled** ()	
2	public	boolean	**isFocusTraversable** ()	
2	public	boolean	**isShowing** ()	
2	public	boolean	**isVisible** ()	
2	public	void	**removeFocusListener** (*java.awt.event.FocusListener* l)	
2	public	void	**requestFocus** ()	
2	public	void	**setBackground** (java.awt.Color c)	
2	public	void	**setBounds** (java.awt.Rectangle r)	
2	public	void	**setCursor** (java.awt.Cursor cursor)	
2	public	void	**setEnabled** (boolean b)	
2	public	void	**setFont** (java.awt.Font f)	
2	public	void	**setForeground** (java.awt.Color c)	
2	public	void	**setLocation** (java.awt.Point p)	
2	public	void	**setSize** (java.awt.Dimension d)	
2	public	void	**setVisible** (boolean b)	

K

Kernel
java.awt.image

Object[1]   P

1.2 └─Kernel - *Cloneable*

1	public	**Object**	**clone** ()
●	public final	int	**getHeight** ()
●	public final	float[]	**getKernelData** (float[] data)
●	public final	int	**getWidth** ()
●	public final	int	**getXOrigin** ()
●	public final	int	**getYOrigin** ()
✳	public		**Kernel** (int width, int height, float[] data)

Key
java.security

1.1 *Key*─────────────────────────────── *java.io.Serializable*[1]   P○

	public	String	**getAlgorithm** ()
	public	byte[]	**getEncoded** ()
	public	String	**getFormat** ()
1.2 ▲ 1	public static final	**long**	**serialVersionUID** = 6603384152749567654

KeyAdapter
java.awt.event

Object   P

1.1 ○ └─KeyAdapter - *KeyListener*[1] (*java.util.EventListener*)

✳	public		**KeyAdapter** ()
1	public	void	**keyPressed** (KeyEvent e)
1	public	void	**keyReleased** (KeyEvent e)
1	public	void	**keyTyped** (KeyEvent e)

Classes

KeyEvent

P

```
        Object
1.1     └java.util.EventObject 1 - - - - - - - - - - - - - - - - - - - java.io.Serializable
1.1  ○      └java.awt.AWTEvent 2
1.1          └ComponentEvent 3
1.1  ○          └InputEvent 4
1.1              └KeyEvent
```

▲		public static final .... char	**CHAR_UNDEFINED** = '?'
	4	public......................void	consume ()
	2	protected .... boolean	consumed
	2	protected ....void	finalize () throws Throwable
	3	public.... java.awt.Component	getComponent ()
	2	public........................int	getID ()
		public...................... char	**getKeyChar** ()
		public........................int	**getKeyCode** ()
△		public static ....String	**getKeyModifiersText** (int modifiers)
△		public static ....String	**getKeyText** (int keyCode)
	4	public........................int	getModifiers ()
	1	public.................. Object	getSource ()
	4	public........................ long	getWhen ()
	2	protected ....int	id
		public.................. boolean	**isActionKey** ()
	4	public.................. boolean	isAltDown ()
1.2	4	public.................. boolean	isAltGraphDown ()
	4	public.................. boolean	isConsumed ()
	4	public.................. boolean	isControlDown ()
	4	public.................. boolean	isMetaDown ()
	4	public.................. boolean	isShiftDown ()
▲		public static final ....int	**KEY_FIRST** = 400
▲		public static final ....int	**KEY_LAST** = 402
▲		public static final ....int	**KEY_PRESSED** = 401
▲		public static final ....int	**KEY_RELEASED** = 402
▲		public static final ....int	**KEY_TYPED** = 400
✳		public............................	**KeyEvent** (java.awt.Component source, int id, long when, int modifiers, int keyCode)
✳		public............................	**KeyEvent** (java.awt.Component source, int id, long when, int modifiers, int keyCode, char keyChar)
	3	public.................. **String**	**paramString** ()
		public......................void	**setKeyChar** (char keyChar)
		public......................void	**setKeyCode** (int keyCode)
		public......................void	**setModifiers** (int modifiers)
	1	protected transient...... Object	source
	2	public..................... String	toString ()
▲		public static final ....int	**VK_0** = 48
▲		public static final ....int	**VK_1** = 49
▲		public static final ....int	**VK_2** = 50
▲		public static final ....int	**VK_3** = 51
▲		public static final ....int	**VK_4** = 52
▲		public static final ....int	**VK_5** = 53
▲		public static final ....int	**VK_6** = 54
▲		public static final ....int	**VK_7** = 55
▲		public static final ....int	**VK_8** = 56
▲		public static final ....int	**VK_9** = 57
▲		public static final ....int	**VK_A** = 65
▲		public static final ....int	**VK_ACCEPT** = 30
▲		public static final ....int	**VK_ADD** = 107
1.2 ▲		public static final ....int	**VK_AGAIN** = 65481
1.2 ▲		public static final ....int	**VK_ALL_CANDIDATES** = 256
1.2 ▲		public static final ....int	**VK_ALPHANUMERIC** = 240
▲		public static final ....int	**VK_ALT** = 18
1.2 ▲		public static final ....int	**VK_ALT_GRAPH** = 65406
1.2 ▲		public static final ....int	**VK_AMPERSAND** = 150
1.2 ▲		public static final ....int	**VK_ASTERISK** = 151
1.2 ▲		public static final ....int	**VK_AT** = 512
▲		public static final ....int	**VK_B** = 66
▲		public static final ....int	**VK_BACK_QUOTE** = 192
▲		public static final ....int	**VK_BACK_SLASH** = 92
▲		public static final ....int	**VK_BACK_SPACE** = 8
1.2 ▲		public static final ....int	**VK_BRACELEFT** = 161
1.2 ▲		public static final ....int	**VK_BRACERIGHT** = 162

Class *Interface* —extends - - -implements ○ abstract ● final △ static ▲ static final ✳ constructor x x—inherited x **x**—declared **x x**—overridden

	▲	public static final............int	**VK_C** = 67
	▲	public static final............int	**VK_CANCEL** = 3
	▲	public static final............int	**VK_CAPS_LOCK** = 20
1.2	▲	public static final............int	**VK_CIRCUMFLEX** = 514
	▲	public static final............int	**VK_CLEAR** = 12
	▲	public static final............int	**VK_CLOSE_BRACKET** = 93
1.2	▲	public static final............int	**VK_CODE_INPUT** = 258
1.2	▲	public static final............int	**VK_COLON** = 513
	▲	public static final............int	**VK_COMMA** = 44
1.2	▲	public static final............int	**VK_COMPOSE** = 65312
	▲	public static final............int	**VK_CONTROL** = 17
	▲	public static final............int	**VK_CONVERT** = 28
1.2	▲	public static final............int	**VK_COPY** = 65485
1.2	▲	public static final............int	**VK_CUT** = 65489
	▲	public static final............int	**VK_D** = 68
1.2	▲	public static final............int	**VK_DEAD_ABOVEDOT** = 134
1.2	▲	public static final............int	**VK_DEAD_ABOVERING** = 136
1.2	▲	public static final............int	**VK_DEAD_ACUTE** = 129
1.2	▲	public static final............int	**VK_DEAD_BREVE** = 133
1.2	▲	public static final............int	**VK_DEAD_CARON** = 138
1.2	▲	public static final............int	**VK_DEAD_CEDILLA** = 139
1.2	▲	public static final............int	**VK_DEAD_CIRCUMFLEX** = 130
1.2	▲	public static final............int	**VK_DEAD_DIAERESIS** = 135
1.2	▲	public static final............int	**VK_DEAD_DOUBLEACUTE** = 137
1.2	▲	public static final............int	**VK_DEAD_GRAVE** = 128
1.2	▲	public static final............int	**VK_DEAD_IOTA** = 141
1.2	▲	public static final............int	**VK_DEAD_MACRON** = 132
1.2	▲	public static final............int	**VK_DEAD_OGONEK** = 140
1.2	▲	public static final............int	**VK_DEAD_SEMIVOICED_SOUND** = 143
1.2	▲	public static final............int	**VK_DEAD_TILDE** = 131
1.2	▲	public static final............int	**VK_DEAD_VOICED_SOUND** = 142
	▲	public static final............int	**VK_DECIMAL** = 110
	▲	public static final............int	**VK_DELETE** = 127
	▲	public static final............int	**VK_DIVIDE** = 111
1.2	▲	public static final............int	**VK_DOLLAR** = 515
	▲	public static final............int	**VK_DOWN** = 40
	▲	public static final............int	**VK_E** = 69
	▲	public static final............int	**VK_END** = 35
	▲	public static final............int	**VK_ENTER** = 10
	▲	public static final............int	**VK_EQUALS** = 61
	▲	public static final............int	**VK_ESCAPE** = 27
1.2	▲	public static final............int	**VK_EURO_SIGN** = 516
1.2	▲	public static final............int	**VK_EXCLAMATION_MARK** = 517
	▲	public static final............int	**VK_F** = 70
	▲	public static final............int	**VK_F1** = 112
	▲	public static final............int	**VK_F10** = 121
	▲	public static final............int	**VK_F11** = 122
	▲	public static final............int	**VK_F12** = 123
1.2	▲	public static final............int	**VK_F13** = 61440
1.2	▲	public static final............int	**VK_F14** = 61441
1.2	▲	public static final............int	**VK_F15** = 61442
1.2	▲	public static final............int	**VK_F16** = 61443
1.2	▲	public static final............int	**VK_F17** = 61444
1.2	▲	public static final............int	**VK_F18** = 61445
1.2	▲	public static final............int	**VK_F19** = 61446
	▲	public static final............int	**VK_F2** = 113
1.2	▲	public static final............int	**VK_F20** = 61447
1.2	▲	public static final............int	**VK_F21** = 61448
1.2	▲	public static final............int	**VK_F22** = 61449
1.2	▲	public static final............int	**VK_F23** = 61450
1.2	▲	public static final............int	**VK_F24** = 61451
	▲	public static final............int	**VK_F3** = 114
	▲	public static final............int	**VK_F4** = 115
	▲	public static final............int	**VK_F5** = 116
	▲	public static final............int	**VK_F6** = 117
	▲	public static final............int	**VK_F7** = 118
	▲	public static final............int	**VK_F8** = 119
	▲	public static final............int	**VK_F9** = 120
	▲	public static final............int	**VK_FINAL** = 24
1.2	▲	public static final............int	**VK_FIND** = 65488
1.2	▲	public static final............int	**VK_FULL_WIDTH** = 243
	▲	public static final............int	**VK_G** = 71
1.2	▲	public static final............int	**VK_GREATER** = 160
	▲	public static final............int	**VK_H** = 72

K

Classes

KeyEvent

1.2	▲	public static final . . . . .int	**VK_HALF_WIDTH** = 244
	▲	public static final . . . . .int	**VK_HELP** = 156
1.2	▲	public static final . . . . .int	**VK_HIRAGANA** = 242
	▲	public static final . . . . .int	**VK_HOME** = 36
	▲	public static final . . . . .int	**VK_I** = 73
	▲	public static final . . . . .int	**VK_INSERT** = 155
1.2	▲	public static final . . . . .int	**VK_INVERTED_EXCLAMATION_MARK** = 518
	▲	public static final . . . . .int	**VK_J** = 74
1.2	▲	public static final . . . . .int	**VK_JAPANESE_HIRAGANA** = 260
1.2	▲	public static final . . . . .int	**VK_JAPANESE_KATAKANA** = 259
1.2	▲	public static final . . . . .int	**VK_JAPANESE_ROMAN** = 261
	▲	public static final . . . . .int	**VK_K** = 75
	▲	public static final . . . . .int	**VK_KANA** = 21
	▲	public static final . . . . .int	**VK_KANJI** = 25
1.2	▲	public static final . . . . .int	**VK_KATAKANA** = 241
1.2	▲	public static final . . . . .int	**VK_KP_DOWN** = 225
1.2	▲	public static final . . . . .int	**VK_KP_LEFT** = 226
1.2	▲	public static final . . . . .int	**VK_KP_RIGHT** = 227
1.2	▲	public static final . . . . .int	**VK_KP_UP** = 224
	▲	public static final . . . . .int	**VK_L** = 76
	▲	public static final . . . . .int	**VK_LEFT** = 37
1.2	▲	public static final . . . . .int	**VK_LEFT_PARENTHESIS** = 519
1.2	▲	public static final . . . . .int	**VK_LESS** = 153
	▲	public static final . . . . .int	**VK_M** = 77
	▲	public static final . . . . .int	**VK_META** = 157
1.2	▲	public static final . . . . .int	**VK_MINUS** = 45
	▲	public static final . . . . .int	**VK_MODECHANGE** = 31
	▲	public static final . . . . .int	**VK_MULTIPLY** = 106
	▲	public static final . . . . .int	**VK_N** = 78
	▲	public static final . . . . .int	**VK_NONCONVERT** = 29
	▲	public static final . . . . .int	**VK_NUM_LOCK** = 144
1.2	▲	public static final . . . . .int	**VK_NUMBER_SIGN** = 520
	▲	public static final . . . . .int	**VK_NUMPAD0** = 96
	▲	public static final . . . . .int	**VK_NUMPAD1** = 97
	▲	public static final . . . . .int	**VK_NUMPAD2** = 98
	▲	public static final . . . . .int	**VK_NUMPAD3** = 99
	▲	public static final . . . . .int	**VK_NUMPAD4** = 100
	▲	public static final . . . . .int	**VK_NUMPAD5** = 101
	▲	public static final . . . . .int	**VK_NUMPAD6** = 102
	▲	public static final . . . . .int	**VK_NUMPAD7** = 103
	▲	public static final . . . . .int	**VK_NUMPAD8** = 104
	▲	public static final . . . . .int	**VK_NUMPAD9** = 105
	▲	public static final . . . . .int	**VK_O** = 79
	▲	public static final . . . . .int	**VK_OPEN_BRACKET** = 91
	▲	public static final . . . . .int	**VK_P** = 80
	▲	public static final . . . . .int	**VK_PAGE_DOWN** = 34
	▲	public static final . . . . .int	**VK_PAGE_UP** = 33
1.2	▲	public static final . . . . .int	**VK_PASTE** = 65487
	▲	public static final . . . . .int	**VK_PAUSE** = 19
	▲	public static final . . . . .int	**VK_PERIOD** = 46
1.2	▲	public static final . . . . .int	**VK_PLUS** = 521
1.2	▲	public static final . . . . .int	**VK_PREVIOUS_CANDIDATE** = 257
	▲	public static final . . . . .int	**VK_PRINTSCREEN** = 154
1.2	▲	public static final . . . . .int	**VK_PROPS** = 65482
	▲	public static final . . . . .int	**VK_Q** = 81
	▲	public static final . . . . .int	**VK_QUOTE** = 222
1.2	▲	public static final . . . . .int	**VK_QUOTEDBL** = 152
	▲	public static final . . . . .int	**VK_R** = 82
	▲	public static final . . . . .int	**VK_RIGHT** = 39
1.2	▲	public static final . . . . .int	**VK_RIGHT_PARENTHESIS** = 522
1.2	▲	public static final . . . . .int	**VK_ROMAN_CHARACTERS** = 245
	▲	public static final . . . . .int	**VK_S** = 83
	▲	public static final . . . . .int	**VK_SCROLL_LOCK** = 145
	▲	public static final . . . . .int	**VK_SEMICOLON** = 59
	▲	public static final . . . . .int	**VK_SEPARATER** = 108
	▲	public static final . . . . .int	**VK_SHIFT** = 16
	▲	public static final . . . . .int	**VK_SLASH** = 47
	▲	public static final . . . . .int	**VK_SPACE** = 32
1.2	▲	public static final . . . . .int	**VK_STOP** = 65480
	▲	public static final . . . . .int	**VK_SUBTRACT** = 109
	▲	public static final . . . . .int	**VK_T** = 84
	▲	public static final . . . . .int	**VK_TAB** = 9

K

Class *Interface* —extends - - -implements ○ abstract ● final △ static ▲ static final ✳ constructor x x—inherited x **x**—declared **x x**—overridden

▲	public static final ....int	**VK_U** = 85
▲	public static final ....int	**VK_UNDEFINED** = 0
1.2 ▲	public static final ....int	**VK_UNDERSCORE** = 523
1.2 ▲	public static final ....int	**VK_UNDO** = 65483
▲	public static final ....int	**VK_UP** = 38
▲	public static final ....int	**VK_V** = 86
▲	public static final ....int	**VK_W** = 87
▲	public static final ....int	**VK_X** = 88
▲	public static final ....int	**VK_Y** = 89
▲	public static final ....int	**VK_Z** = 90

KeyException   java.security

P⁰

```
Object
 └Throwable - - - - - - - - - - - - - - - - - - - - - - - - - - java.io.Serializable
   └Exception
```
1.2   └GeneralSecurityException
1.1   └KeyException

∗	public..........................	**KeyException** ()
∗	public..........................	**KeyException** (String msg)

KeyFactory   java.security

P⁰

```
Object
```
1.2 └KeyFactory

●	public final .... *PrivateKey*	**generatePrivate** (*java. security. spec. KeySpec* keySpec)
		throws java.security.spec.InvalidKeySpecException
●	public final .... *PublicKey*	**generatePublic** (*java. security. spec. KeySpec* keySpec)
		throws java.security.spec.InvalidKeySpecException
●	public final ....String	**getAlgorithm** ()
△	public static ....KeyFactory	**getInstance** (String algorithm) throws NoSuchAlgorithmException
△	public static ....KeyFactory	**getInstance** (String algorithm, String provider) throws NoSuchAlgorithmException,
		NoSuchProviderException
●	public final	**getKeySpec** (*Key* key, Class keySpec) throws java. security. spec ↩
	... *java.security.spec.KeySpec*	.InvalidKeySpecException
●	public final .... Provider	**getProvider** ()
∗	protected	**KeyFactory** (KeyFactorySpi keyFacSpi, Provider provider, String algorithm)
●	public final .... *Key*	**translateKey** (*Key* key) throws InvalidKeyException

---

KeyFactorySpi   java.security

P⁰

```
Object
```
1.2 ○ └KeyFactorySpi

○	protected abstract . *PrivateKey*	**engineGeneratePrivate** (*java. security. spec. KeySpec* keySpec)
		throws java.security.spec.InvalidKeySpecException
○	protected abstract .. *PublicKey*	**engineGeneratePublic** (*java. security. spec. KeySpec* keySpec)
		throws java.security.spec.InvalidKeySpecException
○	protected abstract	**engineGetKeySpec** (*Key* key, Class keySpec) throws
	... *java.security.spec.KeySpec*	java.security.spec.InvalidKeySpecException
○	protected abstract .... *Key*	**engineTranslateKey** (*Key* key) throws InvalidKeyException
∗	public..........................	**KeyFactorySpi** ()

KeyListener   java.awt.event

P

1.1 *KeyListener* ———————————— *java.util.EventListener*

	public.......................void	**keyPressed** (KeyEvent e)
	public.......................void	**keyReleased** (KeyEvent e)
	public.......................void	**keyTyped** (KeyEvent e)

KeyManagementException

	KeyManagementException			java.security
				P^O

```
        Object
        └ Throwable - - - - - - - - - - - - - - - - - - - - - - - - - - java.io.Serializable
1.2       └ Exception
1.1         └ GeneralSecurityException
1.1           └ KeyException
                └ KeyManagementException
```

*	public............................	**KeyManagementException** ()	
*	public............................	**KeyManagementException** (String msg)	

	Keymap		javax.swing.text

1.2	*Keymap*

public....................void	**addActionForKeyStroke** (javax.swing.KeyStroke key, *javax.swing.Action* a)
public.......*javax.swing.Action*	**getAction** (javax.swing.KeyStroke key)
public.....*javax.swing.Action[]*	**getBoundActions** ()
public.javax.swing.KeyStroke[]	**getBoundKeyStrokes** ()
public.......*javax.swing.Action*	**getDefaultAction** ()
public.javax.swing.KeyStroke[]	**getKeyStrokesForAction** (*javax.swing.Action* a)
public...................String	**getName** ()
public..................*Keymap*	**getResolveParent** ()
public..................boolean	**isLocallyDefined** (javax.swing.KeyStroke key)
public.....................void	**removeBindings** ()
public.....................void	**removeKeyStrokeBinding** (javax.swing.KeyStroke keys)
public.....................void	**setDefaultAction** (*javax.swing.Action* a)
public.....................void	**setResolveParent** (*Keymap* parent)

	KeyPair		java.security
			P^O

```
        Object
1.1 ●   └ KeyPair - - - - - - - - - - - - - - - - - - - - - - - - - - - java.io.Serializable
```

public.............. *PrivateKey*	**getPrivate** ()
public.............. *PublicKey*	**getPublic** ()
*	public............................	**KeyPair** (*PublicKey* publicKey, *PrivateKey* privateKey)

	KeyPairGenerator		java.security
			P^O

```
          Object
1.2 O     └ KeyPairGeneratorSpi 1
1.1 O       └ KeyPairGenerator
```

1.2 O	1	public abstract ....KeyPair	generateKeyPair ()
1.2 ●		public final ....KeyPair	**genKeyPair** ()
		public.....................String	**getAlgorithm** ()
△		public static .KeyPairGenerator	**getInstance** (String algorithm) throws NoSuchAlgorithmException
△		public static .KeyPairGenerator	**getInstance** (String algorithm, String provider) throws NoSuchAlgorithmException, NoSuchProviderException
1.2 ●		public final .... Provider	**getProvider** ()
		public.....................void	**initialize** (int keysize)
1.2		public.....................void	**initialize** (*java. security. spec. AlgorithmParameterSpec* params) throws InvalidAlgorithmParameterException
	1	public..................... **void**	**initialize** (int keysize, SecureRandom random)
1.2	1	public..................... **void**	**initialize** (*java. security. spec. AlgorithmParameterSpec* params, SecureRandom random) throws InvalidAlgorithmParameterException
*		protected	**KeyPairGenerator** (String algorithm)

	KeyPairGeneratorSpi		java.security
			P^O

```
          Object
1.2 O     └ KeyPairGeneratorSpi
```

O	public abstract ....KeyPair	**generateKeyPair** ()
O	public abstract ....void	**initialize** (int keysize, SecureRandom random)

Class *Interface* —extends - - -implements O abstract ● final △ static ▲ static final ✳ constructor x x—inherited x **x**—declared **x x**—overridden

public	void	**initialize** (*java. security. spec. AlgorithmParameterSpec* params, SecureRandom random) throws InvalidAlgorithmParameterException
* public		**KeyPairGeneratorSpi** ()

KeySpec
java.security.spec

1.2 *KeySpec*

- -

KeyStore
java.security

Object P⁰
1.2 └KeyStore

●	public final .... *java.util.Enumeration*	**aliases** () throws KeyStoreException
●	public final .... boolean	**containsAlias** (String alias) throws KeyStoreException
●	public final .... void	**deleteEntry** (String alias) throws KeyStoreException
●	public final .... java.security.cert.Certificate	**getCertificate** (String alias) throws KeyStoreException
●	public final .... String	**getCertificateAlias** (java.security.cert.Certificate cert) throws KeyStoreException
●	public final .... java.security.cert.Certificate[]	**getCertificateChain** (String alias) throws KeyStoreException
●	public final .... java.util.Date	**getCreationDate** (String alias) throws KeyStoreException
▲	public static final .... String	**getDefaultType** ()
△	public static .... KeyStore	**getInstance** (String type) throws KeyStoreException
△	public static .... KeyStore	**getInstance** (String type, String provider) throws KeyStoreException, NoSuchProviderException
●	public final .... *Key*	**getKey** (String alias, char[] password) throws KeyStoreException, NoSuchAlgorithmException, UnrecoverableKeyException
●	public final .... Provider	**getProvider** ()
●	public final .... String	**getType** ()
●	public final .... boolean	**isCertificateEntry** (String alias) throws KeyStoreException
●	public final .... boolean	**isKeyEntry** (String alias) throws KeyStoreException
*	protected	**KeyStore** (KeyStoreSpi keyStoreSpi, Provider provider, String type)
●	public final .... void	**load** (java.io.InputStream stream, char[] password) throws java.io.IOException, NoSuchAlgorithmException, java.security.cert.CertificateException
●	public final .... void	**setCertificateEntry** (String alias, java. security. cert. Certificate cert) throws KeyStoreException
●	public final .... void	**setKeyEntry** (String alias, byte[] key, java. security. cert. Certificate[] chain) throws KeyStoreException
●	public final .... void	**setKeyEntry** (String alias, *Key* key, char[] password, java.security.cert.Certificate[] chain) throws KeyStoreException
●	public final .... int	**size** () throws KeyStoreException
●	public final .... void	**store** (java. io. OutputStream stream, char[] password) throws KeyStoreException, java.io.IOException, NoSuchAlgorithmException, java.security.cert.CertificateException

---

KeyStoreException
java.security

Object P⁰
└Throwable - *java.io.Serializable*
└Exception
1.2 └GeneralSecurityException
1.2 └KeyStoreException

*	public	**KeyStoreException** ()
*	public	**KeyStoreException** (String msg)

KeyStoreSpi
java.security

Object P⁰
1.2 ○ └KeyStoreSpi

○	public abstract .... *java.util.Enumeration*	**engineAliases** ()
○	public abstract .... boolean	**engineContainsAlias** (String alias)
○	public abstract .... void	**engineDeleteEntry** (String alias) throws KeyStoreException
○	public abstract .... java.security.cert.Certificate	**engineGetCertificate** (String alias)

KeyStoreSpi

○	public abstract . . . . String	**engineGetCertificateAlias** (java.security.cert.Certificate cert)
○	public abstract . . . . java.security.cert.Certificate[]	**engineGetCertificateChain** (String alias)
○	public abstract . . . java.util.Date	**engineGetCreationDate** (String alias)
○	public abstract . . . . *Key*	**engineGetKey** (String alias, char[] password) throws NoSuchAlgorithmException, UnrecoverableKeyException
○	public abstract . . . . boolean	**engineIsCertificateEntry** (String alias)
○	public abstract . . . . boolean	**engineIsKeyEntry** (String alias)
○	public abstract . . . . void	**engineLoad** (java.io.InputStream stream, char[] password) throws java.io↵ .IOException, NoSuchAlgorithmException, java.security.cert.CertificateException
○	public abstract . . . . void	**engineSetCertificateEntry** (String alias, java.security.cert.Certificate cert) throws KeyStoreException
○	public abstract . . . . void	**engineSetKeyEntry** (String alias, byte[] key, java.security.cert.Certificate[] chain) throws KeyStoreException
○	public abstract . . . . void	**engineSetKeyEntry** (String alias, *Key* key, char[] password, java.security.cert.Certificate[] chain) throws KeyStoreException
○	public abstract . . . . int	**engineSize** ()
○	public abstract . . . . void	**engineStore** (java.io.OutputStream stream, char[] password) throws java.io↵ .IOException, NoSuchAlgorithmException, java.security.cert.CertificateException
✳	public	**KeyStoreSpi** ()

K

KeyStroke javax.swing

Object[1]
1.2 └KeyStroke - *java.io.Serializable*

	1	public . . . . **boolean**	**equals** (Object anObject)
		public . . . . char	**getKeyChar** ()
		public . . . . int	**getKeyCode** ()
△		public static . . . . KeyStroke	**getKeyStroke** (char keyChar)
△		public static . . . . KeyStroke	**getKeyStroke** (String representation)
D △		public static . . . . KeyStroke	**getKeyStroke** (char keyChar, boolean onKeyRelease)
△		public static . . . . KeyStroke	**getKeyStroke** (int keyCode, int modifiers)
△		public static . . . . KeyStroke	**getKeyStroke** (int keyCode, int modifiers, boolean onKeyRelease)
△		public static . . . . KeyStroke	**getKeyStrokeForEvent** (java.awt.event.KeyEvent anEvent)
		public . . . . int	**getModifiers** ()
	1	public . . . . **int**	**hashCode** ()
		public . . . . boolean	**isOnKeyRelease** ()
	1	public . . . . **String**	**toString** ()

Label java.awt

P

Object
○ └Component[1] - *java.awt.image.ImageObserver*, *MenuContainer*,
            └Label *java.io.Serializable*

	1	*160 inherited members from Component not shown*	
	1	public . . . . **void**	**addNotify** ()
▲		public static final . . . . int	**CENTER** = 1
		public . . . . int	**getAlignment** ()
		public . . . . String	**getText** ()
✳		public	**Label** ()
✳		public	**Label** (String text)
✳		public	**Label** (String text, int alignment)
▲		public static final . . . . int	**LEFT** = 0
	1	protected . . . . **String**	**paramString** ()
▲		public static final . . . . int	**RIGHT** = 2
		public synchronized . . . . void	**setAlignment** (int alignment)
		public . . . . void	**setText** (String text)

LabelPeer java.awt.peer

LabelPeer————————————— *ComponentPeer*[1]

	1	*32 inherited members from ComponentPeer not shown*	
		public . . . . void	**setAlignment** (int)
		public . . . . void	**setText** (String)

Class   *Interface*   —extends   - - -implements   ○ abstract   ● final   △ static   ▲ static final   ✳ constructor   x x—inherited   x **x**—declared   **x x**—overridden

LabelUI

javax.swing.plaf

```
         Object
1.2 O    └ComponentUI 1
1.2 O       └LabelUI
```

	1	11 inherited members from ComponentUI not shown
✳		public........................ **LabelUI** ()

LabelView

javax.swing.text

```
         Object 1
1.2 O    └ View 2 - - - - - - - - - - - - - - - - - - - - - - - - - - - - javax.swing.SwingConstants
1.2         └ LabelView
```

	2	*27 inherited members from View not shown*
	2	public..................... **View breakView** (int axis, int p0, float pos, float len)
	2	public..................... **void changedUpdate** (*javax. swing. event. DocumentEvent* e, *java.awt.Shape* a, *ViewFactory* f)
	2	public..................... **View createFragment** (int p0, int p1)
	2	public..................... **float getAlignment** (int axis)
	2	public........................ **int getBreakWeight** (int axis, float pos, float len)
		protected ....java.awt.Font **getFont** ()
		protected java.awt.FontMetrics **getFontMetrics** ()
	2	public........................ **int getNextVisualPositionFrom** (int pos, Position.Bias b, *java.awt.Shape* a, int direction, Position.Bias[] biasRet) throws BadLocationException
	2	public..................... **float getPreferredSpan** (int axis)
	2	public..................... **void insertUpdate** (*javax. swing. event. DocumentEvent* e, *java.awt.Shape* a, *ViewFactory* f)
✳		public........................ **LabelView** (*Element* elem)
	2	public......... ***java.awt.Shape* modelToView** (int pos, *java. awt. Shape* a, Position. Bias b) throws BadLocationException
	2	public..................... **void paint** (java.awt.Graphics g, *java.awt.Shape* a)
	2	public..................... **void removeUpdate** (*javax. swing. event. DocumentEvent* changes, *java.awt.Shape* a, *ViewFactory* f)
		protected ....void **setPropertiesFromAttributes** ()
		protected ....void **setStrikeThrough** (boolean s)
		protected ....void **setSubscript** (boolean s)
		protected ....void **setSuperscript** (boolean s)
		protected ....void **setUnderline** (boolean u)
	1	public.............. **String toString** ()
	2	public........................ **int viewToModel** (float x, float y, *java.awt.Shape* a, Position.Bias[] biasReturn)

LastOwnerException

java.security.acl

P^U

```
         Object
         └ Throwable - - - - - - - - - - - - - - - - - - - - - - - - - - java.io.Serializable
            └ Exception
1.1            └ LastOwnerException
```

✳		public........................ **LastOwnerException** ()

LayeredHighlighter

javax.swing.text

```
         Object
1.2 O    └ LayeredHighlighter - - - - - - - - - - - - - - - - - - - - - Highlighter 1
```

O	1	public abstract .... Object **addHighlight** (int, int, *Highlighter.HighlightPainter*) throws BadLocationException
O	1	public abstract ....void **changeHighlight** (Object, int, int) throws BadLocationException
O	1	public abstract ....void **deinstall** (JTextComponent)
O	1	public abstract .... **getHighlights** () .... *Highlighter.Highlight[]*
O	1	public abstract ....void **install** (JTextComponent)
✳		public........................ **LayeredHighlighter** ()
O	1	public abstract ....void **paint** (java.awt.Graphics)
O		public abstract ....void **paintLayeredHighlights** (java. awt. Graphics g, int p0, int p1, *java.awt.Shape* viewBounds, JTextComponent editor, View view)
O	1	public abstract ....void **removeAllHighlights** ()
O	1	public abstract ....void **removeHighlight** (Object)

LayeredHighlighter.LayerPainter — javax.swing.text

Object
  └LayeredHighlighter.LayerPainter `---------- ` *Highlighter.HighlightPainter* [1]

1.2 ○

✳	public.........................		**LayerPainter** ()
○ 1	public abstract ....void		**paint** (java.awt.Graphics, int, int, *java.awt.Shape*, JTextComponent)
○	public abstract *java.awt.Shape*		**paintLayer** (java.awt.Graphics g, int p0, int p1, *java.awt.Shape* viewBounds, JTextComponent editor, View view)

LayoutManager — java.awt

P

LayoutManager

public........................void	**addLayoutComponent** (String name, Component comp)
public........................void	**layoutContainer** (Container parent)
public..............Dimension	**minimumLayoutSize** (Container parent)
public..............Dimension	**preferredLayoutSize** (Container parent)
public........................void	**removeLayoutComponent** (Component comp)

LayoutManager2 — java.awt

P

1.1 *LayoutManager2*————————————*LayoutManager* [1]

	public........................void	**addLayoutComponent** (Component comp, Object constraints)
1	public........................void	addLayoutComponent (String name, Component comp)
	public........................float	**getLayoutAlignmentX** (Container target)
	public........................float	**getLayoutAlignmentY** (Container target)
	public........................void	**invalidateLayout** (Container target)
1	public........................void	layoutContainer (Container parent)
	public..............Dimension	**maximumLayoutSize** (Container target)
1	public..............Dimension	minimumLayoutSize (Container parent)
1	public..............Dimension	preferredLayoutSize (Container parent)
1	public........................void	removeLayoutComponent (Component comp)

Lease — java.rmi.dgc

P°

Object
  └Lease `----------------------------- ` *java.io.Serializable*

1.1 ●

public.................... long	**getValue** ()
public.................... VMID	**getVMID** ()
✳ public..........................	**Lease** (VMID id, long duration)

LightweightPeer — java.awt.peer

1.1 *LightweightPeer*————————————*ComponentPeer* [1]

1 *32 inherited members from ComponentPeer not shown*

Line2D — java.awt.geom

Object [1]

1.2 ○
  └Line2D `----------------------------- ` *java.awt.Shape* [2], *Cloneable*

1	public.................... **Object**	**clone** ()
2	public.................... boolean	**contains** (Point2D p)
2	public.................... boolean	**contains** (Rectangle2D r)
2	public.................... boolean	**contains** (double x, double y)
2	public.................... boolean	**contains** (double x, double y, double w, double h)
2	public...... java.awt.Rectangle	**getBounds** ()
○ 2	public abstract ... Rectangle2D	**getBounds2D** ()
○	public abstract Point2D	**getP1** ()
○	public abstract Point2D	**getP2** ()
2	public.............. *PathIterator*	**getPathIterator** (AffineTransform at)
2	public.............. *PathIterator*	**getPathIterator** (AffineTransform at, double flatness)
○	public abstract ....double	**getX1** ()
○	public abstract ....double	**getX2** ()

Class *Interface* —extends ---implements ○ abstract ● final △ static ▲ static final ✳ constructor x x—inherited x **x**—declared **x x**—overridden

○	public abstract	double	**getY1** ()	
○	public abstract	double	**getY2** ()	
2	public	boolean	**intersects** (Rectangle2D r)	
2	public	boolean	**intersects** (double x, double y, double w, double h)	
	public	boolean	**intersectsLine** (Line2D l)	
	public	boolean	**intersectsLine** (double X1, double Y1, double X2, double Y2)	
*	protected		**Line2D** ()	
△	public static	boolean	**linesIntersect** (double X1, double Y1, double X2, double Y2, double X3, double Y3, double X4, double Y4)	
	public	double	**ptLineDist** (Point2D pt)	
	public	double	**ptLineDist** (double PX, double PY)	
△	public static	double	**ptLineDist** (double X1, double Y1, double X2, double Y2, double PX, double PY)	
	public	double	**ptLineDistSq** (Point2D pt)	
	public	double	**ptLineDistSq** (double PX, double PY)	
△	public static	double	**ptLineDistSq** (double X1, double Y1, double X2, double Y2, double PX, double PY)	
	public	double	**ptSegDist** (Point2D pt)	
	public	double	**ptSegDist** (double PX, double PY)	
△	public static	double	**ptSegDist** (double X1, double Y1, double X2, double Y2, double PX, double PY)	
	public	double	**ptSegDistSq** (Point2D pt)	
	public	double	**ptSegDistSq** (double PX, double PY)	
△	public static	double	**ptSegDistSq** (double X1, double Y1, double X2, double Y2, double PX, double PY)	
	public	int	**relativeCCW** (Point2D p)	
	public	int	**relativeCCW** (double PX, double PY)	
△	public static	int	**relativeCCW** (double X1, double Y1, double X2, double Y2, double PX, double PY)	
	public	void	**setLine** (Line2D l)	
	public	void	**setLine** (Point2D p1, Point2D p2)	
○	public abstract	void	**setLine** (double X1, double Y1, double X2, double Y2)	

Line2D.Double — java.awt.geom

```
Object
└ Line2D¹ - - - - - - - - - - - - - - - - - - - - - - - - - - - - java.awt.Shape, Cloneable
    └ Line2D.Double
```

1	*30 inherited members from Line2D not shown*			
*	public		**Double** ()	
*	public		**Double** (Point2D p1, Point2D p2)	
*	public		**Double** (double X1, double Y1, double X2, double Y2)	
1	public	Rectangle2D	**getBounds2D** ()	
1	public	Point2D	**getP1** ()	
1	public	Point2D	**getP2** ()	
1	public	double	**getX1** ()	
1	public	double	**getX2** ()	
1	public	double	**getY1** ()	
1	public	double	**getY2** ()	
1	public	void	**setLine** (double X1, double Y1, double X2, double Y2)	
	public	double	**x1**	
	public	double	**x2**	
	public	double	**y1**	
	public	double	**y2**	

Line2D.Float — java.awt.geom

```
Object
└ Line2D¹ - - - - - - - - - - - - - - - - - - - - - - - - - - - - java.awt.Shape, Cloneable
    └ Line2D.Float
```

1	*30 inherited members from Line2D not shown*			
*	public		**Float** ()	
*	public		**Float** (Point2D p1, Point2D p2)	
*	public		**Float** (float X1, float Y1, float X2, float Y2)	
1	public	Rectangle2D	**getBounds2D** ()	
1	public	Point2D	**getP1** ()	
1	public	Point2D	**getP2** ()	
1	public	double	**getX1** ()	
1	public	double	**getX2** ()	
1	public	double	**getY1** ()	
1	public	double	**getY2** ()	
1	public	void	**setLine** (double X1, double Y1, double X2, double Y2)	
	public	void	**setLine** (float X1, float Y1, float X2, float Y2)	
	public	float	**x1**	
	public	float	**x2**	

Line2D.Float

public	float	**y1**
public	float	**y2**

LineBorder

Object
1.2 ○ └ AbstractBorder[1] ----------------------- *Border, java.io.Serializable*
1.2   └ LineBorder

△	public static	*Border*	**createBlackLineBorder** ()
△	public static	*Border*	**createGrayLineBorder** ()
1	public	**java.awt.Insets**	**getBorderInsets** (java.awt.Component c)
1	public	**java.awt.Insets**	**getBorderInsets** (java.awt.Component c, java.awt.Insets insets)
1	public	java.awt.Rectangle	getInteriorRectangle (java.awt.Component c, int x, int y, int width, int height)
△ 1	public static	java.awt.Rectangle	getInteriorRectangle (java.awt.Component c, *Border* b, int x, int y, int width, int height)
	public	java.awt.Color	**getLineColor** ()
	public	int	**getThickness** ()
1	public	**boolean**	**isBorderOpaque** ()
*	public		**LineBorder** (java.awt.Color color)
*	public		**LineBorder** (java.awt.Color color, int thickness)
	protected	java.awt.Color	**lineColor**
1	public	**void**	**paintBorder** (java.awt.Component c, java.awt.Graphics g, int x, int y, int width, int height)
	protected	boolean	**roundedCorners**
	protected	int	**thickness**

LineBreakMeasurer
java.awt.font

Object
1.2 ● └ LineBreakMeasurer

	public	void	**deleteChar** (*java.text.AttributedCharacterIterator* newParagraph, int deletePos)
	public	int	**getPosition** ()
	public	void	**insertChar** (*java.text.AttributedCharacterIterator* newParagraph, int insertPos)
*	public		**LineBreakMeasurer** (*java.text. AttributedCharacterIterator* text, FontRenderContext frc)
*	public		**LineBreakMeasurer** (*java.text. AttributedCharacterIterator* text, java.text.BreakIterator breakIter, FontRenderContext frc)
	public	TextLayout	**nextLayout** (float maxAdvance)
	public	TextLayout	**nextLayout** (float wrappingWidth, int offsetLimit, boolean requireNextWord)
	public	int	**nextOffset** (float maxAdvance)
	public	int	**nextOffset** (float wrappingWidth, int offsetLimit, boolean requireNextWord)
	public	void	**setPosition** (int newPosition)

LineMetrics
java.awt.font

Object
1.2 ○ └ LineMetrics

○	public abstract	float	**getAscent** ()
○	public abstract	int	**getBaselineIndex** ()
○	public abstract	float[]	**getBaselineOffsets** ()
○	public abstract	float	**getDescent** ()
○	public abstract	float	**getHeight** ()
○	public abstract	float	**getLeading** ()
○	public abstract	int	**getNumChars** ()
○	public abstract	float	**getStrikethroughOffset** ()
○	public abstract	float	**getStrikethroughThickness** ()
○	public abstract	float	**getUnderlineOffset** ()
○	public abstract	float	**getUnderlineThickness** ()
*	public		**LineMetrics** ()

Class   *Interface*   —extends   - - -implements   ○ abstract   ● final   △ static   ▲ static final   ✳ constructor   x x—inherited   x **x**—declared   **x x**—overridden

LineNumberInputStream   java.io

```
      Object
  ○   └InputStream
         └FilterInputStream¹
            └LineNumberInputStream
```

1	public	**int**	**available**	() throws IOException
1	public	void	close	() throws IOException
	public	int	**getLineNumber**	()
1	protected	InputStream	in	
*	public		**LineNumberInputStream**	(InputStream in)
1	public	**void**	**mark**	(int readlimit)
1	public	boolean	markSupported	()
1	public	**int**	**read**	() throws IOException
1	public	int	read	(byte[] b) throws IOException
1	public	**int**	**read**	(byte[] b, int off, int len) throws IOException
1	public	**void**	**reset**	() throws IOException
	public	void	**setLineNumber**	(int lineNumber)
1	public	**long**	**skip**	(long n) throws IOException

LineNumberReader   java.io

```
        Object
1.1 ○   └Reader¹
1.1        └BufferedReader²
1.1           └LineNumberReader
```

2	public	void	close	() throws IOException
	public	int	**getLineNumber**	()
*	public		**LineNumberReader**	(Reader in)
*	public		**LineNumberReader**	(Reader in, int sz)
1	protected	Object	lock	
2	public	**void**	**mark**	(int readAheadLimit) throws IOException
2	public	boolean	markSupported	()
2	public	**int**	**read**	() throws IOException
1	public	int	read	(char[] cbuf) throws IOException
2	public	**int**	**read**	(char[] cbuf, int off, int len) throws IOException
2	public	**String**	**readLine**	() throws IOException
2	public	boolean	ready	() throws IOException
2	public	**void**	**reset**	() throws IOException
	public	void	**setLineNumber**	(int lineNumber)
2	public	**long**	**skip**	(long n) throws IOException

LinkageError   java.lang
P

```
      Object
      └Throwable ----------------------------- java.io.Serializable
         └Error
            └LinkageError
```

*	public		**LinkageError**	()
*	public		**LinkageError**	(String s)

LinkedList   java.util
P

```
        Object¹
1.2 ○   └AbstractCollection² ---------------------- Collection
1.2 ○      └AbstractList³ ----------------------- List (Collection)
1.2 ○         └AbstractSequentialList⁴
1.2            └LinkedList ---------------------- List (Collection), Cloneable, java.io.Serializable
```

3	public	**boolean**	**add**	(Object o)
4	public	**void**	**add**	(int index, Object element)
2	public	**boolean**	**addAll**	(Collection c)
4	public	**boolean**	**addAll**	(int index, Collection c)
	public	void	**addFirst**	(Object o)
	public	void	**addLast**	(Object o)
3	public	**void**	**clear**	()
1	public	**Object**	**clone**	()

LinkedList

2	public	**boolean contains**	(Object o)
2	public	boolean containsAll	(*Collection* c)
3	public	boolean equals	(Object o)
4	public	**Object get**	(int index)
	public	Object **getFirst**	()
	public	Object **getLast**	()
3	public	int hashCode	()
3	public	**int indexOf**	(Object o)
2	public	boolean isEmpty	()
4	public	*Iterator* iterator	()
3	public	**int lastIndexOf**	(Object o)
*	public	**LinkedList**	()
*	public	**LinkedList**	(*Collection* c)
3	public	*ListIterator* listIterator	()
4	public	*ListIterator* **listIterator**	(int index)
3	protected transient	int modCount	
4	public	**Object remove**	(int index)
2	public	**boolean remove**	(Object o)
2	public	boolean removeAll	(*Collection* c)
	public	Object **removeFirst**	()
	public	Object **removeLast**	()
3	protected	void removeRange	(int fromIndex, int toIndex)
2	public	boolean retainAll	(*Collection* c)
4	public	**Object set**	(int index, Object element)
2	public	**int size**	()
3	public	*List* subList	(int fromIndex, int toIndex)
2	public	**Object[] toArray**	()
2	public	**Object[] toArray**	(Object[] a)
2	public	String toString	()

List ❶ — java.util

P

1.2   *List* ──────────────────────── *Collection* [1]

1	public	**boolean add**	(Object o)
	public	void **add**	(int index, Object element)
1	public	**boolean addAll**	(*Collection* c)
	public	boolean **addAll**	(int index, *Collection* c)
1	public	**void clear**	()
1	public	**boolean contains**	(Object o)
1	public	**boolean containsAll**	(*Collection* c)
1	public	**boolean equals**	(Object o)
	public	Object **get**	(int index)
1	public	**int hashCode**	()
	public	int **indexOf**	(Object o)
1	public	**boolean isEmpty**	()
1	public	***Iterator* iterator**	()
	public	int **lastIndexOf**	(Object o)
	public	*ListIterator* **listIterator**	()
	public	*ListIterator* **listIterator**	(int index)
	public	Object **remove**	(int index)
1	public	**boolean remove**	(Object o)
1	public	**boolean removeAll**	(*Collection* c)
1	public	**boolean retainAll**	(*Collection* c)
	public	Object **set**	(int index, Object element)
1	public	**int size**	()
	public	*List* **subList**	(int fromIndex, int toIndex)
1	public	**Object[] toArray**	()
1	public	**Object[] toArray**	(Object[] a)

List ❷ — java.awt

P

```
    Object
 ○  └─Component [1] ----------------------- java.awt.image.ImageObserver, MenuContainer,
                                             java.io.Serializable
          └─List ------------------------- ItemSelectable [2]
```

	1	*154 inherited members from Component not shown*	
1.1	public	void **add**	(String item)
1.1	public	void **add**	(String item, int index)

Class   *Interface*   ──extends   ‑ ‑ ‑implements   ○ abstract   ● final   △ static   ▲ static final   ✳ constructor   x x─inherited   x **x**─declared   **x x**─overridden

1.1		public synchronized ....void	**addActionListener** (*java.awt.event.ActionListener* l)
D		public........................void	**addItem** (String item)
D		public synchronized ......void	**addItem** (String item, int index)
1.1	2	public synchronized ......void	**addItemListener** (*java.awt.event.ItemListener* l)
	1	public........................ **void**	**addNotify** ()
D		public................. boolean	**allowsMultipleSelections** ()
D		public synchronized ......void	**clear** ()
D		public.........................int	**countItems** ()
D		public........................void	**delItem** (int position)
D		public synchronized ......void	**delItems** (int start, int end)
		public synchronized ......void	**deselect** (int index)
		public.....................String	**getItem** (int index)
1.1		public.........................int	**getItemCount** ()
1.1		public synchronized ... String[]	**getItems** ()
1.1	1	public..............**Dimension**	**getMinimumSize** ()
1.1		public................Dimension	**getMinimumSize** (int rows)
1.1	1	public..............**Dimension**	**getPreferredSize** ()
1.1		public................Dimension	**getPreferredSize** (int rows)
		public.........................int	**getRows** ()
		public synchronized ....int	**getSelectedIndex** ()
		public synchronized ...... int[]	**getSelectedIndexes** ()
		public synchronized .....String	**getSelectedItem** ()
		public synchronized ... String[]	**getSelectedItems** ()
1.1	2	public................. Object[]	**getSelectedObjects** ()
		public.........................int	**getVisibleIndex** ()
1.1		public................. boolean	**isIndexSelected** (int index)
1.1		public................. boolean	**isMultipleMode** ()
D		public................. boolean	**isSelected** (int index)
	*	public.............................	**List** ()
1.1	*	public.............................	**List** (int rows)
	*	public.............................	**List** (int rows, boolean multipleMode)
		public synchronized ....void	**makeVisible** (int index)
D	1	public..............**Dimension**	**minimumSize** ()
D		public................Dimension	**minimumSize** (int rows)
	1	protected .... **String**	**paramString** ()
D	1	public..............**Dimension**	**preferredSize** ()
D		public................Dimension	**preferredSize** (int rows)
1.1		protected....................void	**processActionEvent** (java.awt.event.ActionEvent e)
1.1	1	protected................. **void**	**processEvent** (AWTEvent e)
1.1		protected....................void	**processItemEvent** (java.awt.event.ItemEvent e)
1.1		public........................void	**remove** (int position)
1.1		public synchronized ......void	**remove** (String item)
1.1		public synchronized ......void	**removeActionListener** (*java.awt.event.ActionListener* l)
1.1		public........................void	**removeAll** ()
1.1	2	public synchronized ......void	**removeItemListener** (*java.awt.event.ItemListener* l)
	1	public........................ **void**	**removeNotify** ()
		public synchronized ......void	**replaceItem** (String newValue, int index)
		public........................void	**select** (int index)
1.1		public........................void	**setMultipleMode** (boolean b)
D		public synchronized ......void	**setMultipleSelections** (boolean b)

ListCellRenderer — javax.swing

1.2		*ListCellRenderer*
	public.... java.awt.Component	**getListCellRendererComponent** (JList list, Object value, int index, boolean isSelected, boolean cellHasFocus)

ListDataEvent — javax.swing.event

Object
- 1.1 └java.util.EventObject [1] -------------------- *java.io.Serializable*
- 1.2   └ListDataEvent

▲		public static final ....int	**CONTENTS_CHANGED** = 0
		public.........................int	**getIndex0** ()
		public.........................int	**getIndex1** ()
	1	public.....................Object	getSource ()
		public.........................int	**getType** ()
▲		public static final ....int	**INTERVAL_ADDED** = 1
▲		public static final ....int	**INTERVAL_REMOVED** = 2
	*	public.............................	**ListDataEvent** (Object source, int type, int index0, int index1)

ListDataEvent

1	protected transient......	Object	source
1	public...................	String	toString ()

1.2	*ListDataListener*————————————*java.util.EventListener*

public...................void	**contentsChanged** (ListDataEvent e)
public...................void	**intervalAdded** (ListDataEvent e)
public...................void	**intervalRemoved** (ListDataEvent e)

1.2	*ListIterator*———————————— *Iterator* [1]

	public...................void	**add** (Object o)
1	public................**boolean**	**hasNext** ()
	public................ boolean	**hasPrevious** ()
1	public................**Object**	**next** ()
	public...................int	**nextIndex** ()
	public................... Object	**previous** ()
	public...................int	**previousIndex** ()
1	public................**void**	**remove** ()
	public...................void	**set** (Object o)

1.2	*ListModel*

public...................void	**addListDataListener** (*javax.swing.event.ListDataListener* l)
public................ Object	**getElementAt** (int index)
public...................int	**getSize** ()
public...................void	**removeListDataListener** (*javax.swing.event.ListDataListener* l)

	ListPeer———————————— *ComponentPeer* [1]

	1 32 inherited members from ComponentPeer not shown
1.1	public...................void	**add** (String, int)
	public...................void	**addItem** (String, int)
	public...................void	**clear** ()
	public...................void	**delItems** (int, int)
	public...................void	**deselect** (int)
1.1	public...... java.awt.Dimension	**getMinimumSize** (int)
1.1	public...... java.awt.Dimension	**getPreferredSize** (int)
	public...................int[]	**getSelectedIndexes** ()
	public...................void	**makeVisible** (int)
	public...... java.awt.Dimension	**minimumSize** (int)
	public...... java.awt.Dimension	**preferredSize** (int)
1.1	public...................void	**removeAll** ()
	public...................void	**select** (int)
1.1	public...................void	**setMultipleMode** (boolean)
	public...................void	**setMultipleSelections** (boolean)

	Object
1.1 ○	└ ResourceBundle [1]
1.1 ○	└ ListResourceBundle

▲ 1	public static final...............		getBundle (String baseName) throws MissingResourceException
	.... ResourceBundle		
▲ 1	public static final...............		getBundle (String baseName, Locale locale)
	.... ResourceBundle		
1.2 △ 1	public static .. ResourceBundle		getBundle (String baseName, Locale locale, ClassLoader loader)
			throws MissingResourceException
○	protected abstract .. Object[][]	**getContents** ()

Class   *Interface*   —extends   - - -implements   ○ abstract   ● final   △ static   ▲ static final   ✳ constructor   x x—inherited   x **x**—declared   **x x**—overridden

1.2	1	public .... **Enumeration**	**getKeys** ()
	1	public .... Locale	getLocale ()
●	1	public final .... Object	getObject (String key) throws MissingResourceException
●	1	public final .... String	getString (String key) throws MissingResourceException
●	1	public final .... String[]	getStringArray (String key) throws MissingResourceException
●	1	public final .... **Object**	**handleGetObject** (String key)
*		public	**ListResourceBundle** ()
	1	protected ..... ResourceBundle	parent
	1	protected .... void	setParent (ResourceBundle parent)

ListSelectionEvent javax.swing.event

```
      Object
1.1   └─java.util.EventObject¹ - - - - - - - - - - - - - - - - java.io.Serializable
1.2       └─ListSelectionEvent
```

		public .... int	**getFirstIndex** ()
		public .... int	**getLastIndex** ()
	1	public .... Object	getSource ()
		public .... boolean	**getValueIsAdjusting** ()
*		public	**ListSelectionEvent** (Object source, int firstIndex, int lastIndex, boolean isAdjusting)
	1	protected transient ...... Object	source
	1	public .... **String**	**toString** ()

L

ListSelectionListener javax.swing.event

```
1.2   ListSelectionListener—————————————java.util.EventListener
```

	public .... void	**valueChanged** (ListSelectionEvent e)

ListSelectionModel javax.swing

```
1.2   ListSelectionModel
```

		public .... void	**addListSelectionListener** (*javax.swing.event.ListSelectionListener* x)
		public .... void	**addSelectionInterval** (int index0, int index1)
		public .... void	**clearSelection** ()
		public .... int	**getAnchorSelectionIndex** ()
		public .... int	**getLeadSelectionIndex** ()
		public .... int	**getMaxSelectionIndex** ()
		public .... int	**getMinSelectionIndex** ()
		public .... int	**getSelectionMode** ()
		public .... boolean	**getValueIsAdjusting** ()
		public .... void	**insertIndexInterval** (int index, int length, boolean before)
		public .... boolean	**isSelectedIndex** (int index)
		public .... boolean	**isSelectionEmpty** ()
▲		public static final .... int	**MULTIPLE_INTERVAL_SELECTION** = 2
		public .... void	**removeIndexInterval** (int index0, int index1)
		public .... void	**removeListSelectionListener** (*javax.swing.event.ListSelectionListener* x)
		public .... void	**removeSelectionInterval** (int index0, int index1)
		public .... void	**setAnchorSelectionIndex** (int index)
		public .... void	**setLeadSelectionIndex** (int index)
		public .... void	**setSelectionInterval** (int index0, int index1)
		public .... void	**setSelectionMode** (int selectionMode)
		public .... void	**setValueIsAdjusting** (boolean valueIsAdjusting)
▲		public static final .... int	**SINGLE_INTERVAL_SELECTION** = 1
▲		public static final .... int	**SINGLE_SELECTION** = 0

Classes

ListUI javax.swing.plaf

```
       Object
1.2 ○  └─ComponentUI¹
1.2 ○      └─ListUI
```

	1	*11 inherited members from ComponentUI not shown*	
○		public abstract	**getCellBounds** (javax.swing.JList list, int index1, int index2)
		.... java.awt.Rectangle	
○		public abstract .. java.awt.Point	**indexToLocation** (javax.swing.JList list, int index)
*		public	**ListUI** ()
○		public abstract .... int	**locationToIndex** (javax.swing.JList list, java.awt.Point location)

ListView

```
        Object
1.2 ○   └javax.swing.text.View 1 - - - - - - - - - - - - - - - - - - javax.swing.SwingConstants
1.2 ○       └javax.swing.text.CompositeView 2
1.2           └javax.swing.text.BoxView 3
1.2             └BlockView 4
1.2               └ListView
```

	3	*28 inherited members from javax.swing.text.BoxView not shown*	
	2	public......................void	append (javax.swing.text.View v)
	1	public....javax.swing.text.View	breakView (int axis, int offset, float pos, float len)
	1	public....javax.swing.text.View	createFragment (int p0, int p1)
	4	public......................**float**	**getAlignment** (int axis)
	4	public.......................... ....*javax.swing.text.AttributeSet*	getAttributes ()
●	2	protected final.............short	getBottomInset ()
	1	public.............................int	getBreakWeight (int axis, float pos, float len)
	2	public..........*java.awt.Shape*	getChildAllocation (int index, *java.awt.Shape* a)
	1	public.......java.awt.Container	getContainer ()
	1	public.......................... ....*javax.swing.text.Document*	getDocument ()
	1	public.......................... ....*javax.swing.text.Element*	getElement ()
	1	public.............................int	getEndOffset ()
	2	protected .. java.awt.Rectangle	getInsideAllocation (*java.awt.Shape* a)
●	2	protected final.............short	getLeftInset ()
	2	protected.......................int	getNextEastWestVisualPositionFrom (int pos, javax.swing.text.Position.Bias b, *java.awt.Shape* a, int direction, javax.swing.text.Position.Bias[] biasRet) throws javax.swing.text.BadLocationException
	2	protected.......................int	getNextNorthSouthVisualPositionFrom (int pos, javax.swing.text.Position.Bias b, *java.awt.Shape* a, int direction, javax.swing.text.Position.Bias[] biasRet) throws javax.swing.text.BadLocationException
	2	public.............................int	getNextVisualPositionFrom (int pos, javax.swing.text.Position.Bias b, *java.awt.Shape* a, int direction, javax.swing.text.Position.Bias[] biasRet) throws javax.swing.text.BadLocationException
	1	public....javax.swing.text.View	getParent ()
	4	public.............................int	getResizeWeight (int axis)
●	2	protected final.............short	getRightInset ()
	1	public.............................int	getStartOffset ()
	4	protected............StyleSheet	getStyleSheet ()
●	2	protected final.............short	getTopInset ()
	2	public....javax.swing.text.View	getView (int n)
	2	protected...................... ....*javax.swing.text.View*	getViewAtPosition (int pos, java.awt.Rectangle a)
	2	public.............................int	getViewCount ()
	1	public.......................... .. *javax.swing.text.ViewFactory*	getViewFactory ()
	2	protected.......................int	getViewIndexAtPosition (int pos)
	2	public......................void	insert (int offs, javax.swing.text.View v)
	1	public...................boolean	isVisible ()
*		public..........................	**ListView** (*javax.swing.text.Element* elem)
	2	protected...................void	loadChildren (*javax.swing.text.ViewFactory* f)
	2	public..........*java.awt.Shape*	modelToView (int p0, javax.swing.text.Position.Bias b0, int p1, javax.swing.text.Position.Bias b1, *java.awt.Shape* a) throws javax.swing.text.BadLocationException
	4	public......................**void**	**paint** (java.awt.Graphics g, *java.awt.Shape* allocation)
	3	protected..................**void**	**paintChild** (java.awt.Graphics g, java.awt.Rectangle alloc, int index)
	2	public......................void	removeAll ()
●	2	protected final.............void	setInsets (short top, short left, short bottom, short right)
●	2	protected final.............void	setParagraphInsets (*javax.swing.text.AttributeSet* attr)
	2	public......................void	setParent (javax.swing.text.View parent)
	4	protected..................void	setPropertiesFromAttributes ()

Class   *Interface*   —extends   - - -implements   ○ abstract   ● final   △ static   ▲ static final   ✳ constructor   x x—inherited   x **x**—declared   **x x**—overridden

LoaderHandler | java.rmi.server

1.1		*LoaderHandler*	P^O

D	public	Object	**getSecurityContext** (ClassLoader loader)
D	public	Class	**loadClass** (String name) throws java. net. MalformedURLException, ClassNotFoundException
D	public	Class	**loadClass** (java. net. URL codebase, String name) throws java.net.MalformedURLException, ClassNotFoundException
▲	public static final	String	**packagePrefix** = "sun.rmi.server"

Locale | java.util

Object[1]
└Locale - *Cloneable, java.io.Serializable*

1.1	●			P

▲		public static final	Locale	**CANADA** = new Locale("en", "CA", "")
▲		public static final	Locale	**CANADA_FRENCH** = new Locale("fr", "CA", "")
▲		public static final	Locale	**CHINA** = new Locale("zh", "CN", "")
▲		public static final	Locale	**CHINESE** = new Locale("zh", "", "")
	1	public	**Object**	**clone** ()
▲		public static final	Locale	**ENGLISH** = new Locale("en", "", "")
	1	public	**boolean**	**equals** (Object obj)
▲		public static final	Locale	**FRANCE** = new Locale("fr", "FR", "")
▲		public static final	Locale	**FRENCH** = new Locale("fr", "", "")
▲		public static final	Locale	**GERMAN** = new Locale("de", "", "")
▲		public static final	Locale	**GERMANY** = new Locale("de", "DE", "")
1.2	△	public static	Locale[]	**getAvailableLocales** ()
		public	String	**getCountry** ()
	△	public static	Locale	**getDefault** ()
	●	public final	String	**getDisplayCountry** ()
		public	String	**getDisplayCountry** (Locale inLocale)
	●	public final	String	**getDisplayLanguage** ()
		public	String	**getDisplayLanguage** (Locale inLocale)
	●	public final	String	**getDisplayName** ()
		public	String	**getDisplayName** (Locale inLocale)
	●	public final	String	**getDisplayVariant** ()
		public	String	**getDisplayVariant** (Locale inLocale)
		public	String	**getISO3Country** () throws MissingResourceException
		public	String	**getISO3Language** () throws MissingResourceException
1.2	△	public static	String[]	**getISOCountries** ()
1.2	△	public static	String[]	**getISOLanguages** ()
		public	String	**getLanguage** ()
		public	String	**getVariant** ()
	1	public synchronized	**int**	**hashCode** ()
▲		public static final	Locale	**ITALIAN** = new Locale("it", "", "")
▲		public static final	Locale	**ITALY** = new Locale("it", "IT", "")
▲		public static final	Locale	**JAPAN** = new Locale("ja", "JP", "")
▲		public static final	Locale	**JAPANESE** = new Locale("ja", "", "")
▲		public static final	Locale	**KOREA** = new Locale("ko", "KR", "")
▲		public static final	Locale	**KOREAN** = new Locale("ko", "", "")
✱		public		**Locale** (String language, String country)
✱		public		**Locale** (String language, String country, String variant)
▲		public static final	Locale	**PRC** = new Locale("zh", "CN", "")
	△	public static synchronized void		**setDefault** (Locale newLocale)
▲		public static final	Locale	**SIMPLIFIED_CHINESE** = new Locale("zh", "CN", "")
▲		public static final	Locale	**TAIWAN** = new Locale("zh", "TW", "")
●	1	public final	**String**	**toString** ()
▲		public static final	Locale	**TRADITIONAL_CHINESE** = new Locale("zh", "TW", "")
▲		public static final	Locale	**UK** = new Locale("en", "GB", "")
▲		public static final	Locale	**US** = new Locale("en", "US", "")

LocateRegistry | java.rmi.registry

Object
└LocateRegistry

1.1	●			P^O

	△	public static	*Registry*	**createRegistry** (int port) throws java.rmi.RemoteException
1.2	△	public static	*Registry*	**createRegistry** (int port, *java. rmi. server. RMIClientSocketFactory* csf, *java.rmi.server.RMIServerSocketFactory* ssf) throws java.rmi.RemoteException
	△	public static	*Registry*	**getRegistry** () throws java.rmi.RemoteException
	△	public static	*Registry*	**getRegistry** (int port) throws java.rmi.RemoteException

L

Classes

LocateRegistry

△	public static .... *Registry* **getRegistry** (String host) throws java.rmi.RemoteException	
△	public static .... *Registry* **getRegistry** (String host, int port) throws java.rmi.RemoteException	
1.2 △	public static .... *Registry* **getRegistry** (String host, int port, *java.rmi.server.RMIClientSocketFactory* csf) throws java.rmi.RemoteException	

LogStream		java.rmi.server
		P[o]

```
    Object¹
○   └java.io.OutputStream
        └java.io.FilterOutputStream²
            └java.io.PrintStream³
1.1          └LogStream
```

▲		public static final ....int	**BRIEF** = 10
	3	public.................. boolean	checkError ()
	3	public........................void	close ()
	3	public........................void	flush ()
D △		public static synchronized ....java.io.PrintStream	**getDefaultStream** ()
D		public synchronized .... java.io.OutputStream	**getOutputStream** ()
D △		public static .... LogStream	**log** (String name)
	2	protected java.io.OutputStream	out
D △		public static ....int	**parseLevel** (String s)
	3	public........................void	print (boolean b)
	3	public........................void	print (char c)
	3	public........................void	print (char[] s)
	3	public........................void	print (double d)
	3	public........................void	print (float f)
	3	public........................void	print (int i)
	3	public........................void	print (Object obj)
	3	public........................void	print (String s)
	3	public........................void	print (long l)
	3	public........................void	println ()
	3	public........................void	println (boolean x)
	3	public........................void	println (char x)
	3	public........................void	println (char[] x)
	3	public........................void	println (double x)
	3	public........................void	println (float x)
	3	public........................void	println (int x)
	3	public........................void	println (Object x)
	3	public........................void	println (String x)
	3	public........................void	println (long x)
D △		public static synchronized void	**setDefaultStream** (java.io.PrintStream newDefault)
	3	protected ....void	setError ()
D		public synchronized ....void	**setOutputStream** (java.io.OutputStream out)
▲		public static final.............int	**SILENT** = 0
D	1	public...................... **String**	**toString** ()
▲		public static final.............int	**VERBOSE** = 20
	2	public........................void	write (byte[] b) throws java.io.IOException
D	3	public...................... **void**	**write** (int b)
D	3	public...................... **void**	**write** (byte[] b, int off, int len)

Long		java.lang
		P

```
    Object¹
○   └Number² - - - - - - - - - - - - - - - - - - - - - - - - - - - *java.io.Serializable*
●       └Long - - - - - - - - - - - - - - - - - - - - - - - - - - - *Comparable³*
```

1.1	2	public.................... **byte**	**byteValue** ()
1.2		public........................int	**compareTo** (Long anotherLong)
1.2	3	public........................int	**compareTo** (Object o)
1.2 △		public static ....Long	**decode** (String nm) throws NumberFormatException
	2	public.................. **double**	**doubleValue** ()
	1	public.................. **boolean**	**equals** (Object obj)
	2	public.................... **float**	**floatValue** ()
△		public static ....Long	**getLong** (String nm)
△		public static ....Long	**getLong** (String nm, long val)
△		public static ....Long	**getLong** (String nm, Long val)

Class   *Interface*   —extends   - - -implements   ○ abstract   ● final   △ static   ▲ static final   ✳ constructor   x x—inherited   x **x**—declared   **x x**—overridden

1	public	int	**hashCode** ()	
2	public	int	**intValue** ()	
✳	public		**Long** (String s) throws NumberFormatException	
✳	public		**Long** (long value)	
2	public	long	**longValue** ()	
▲	public static final	long	**MAX_VALUE** = 9223372036854775807	
▲	public static final	long	**MIN_VALUE** = -9223372036854775808	
△	public static	long	**parseLong** (String s) throws NumberFormatException	
△	public static	long	**parseLong** (String s, int radix) throws NumberFormatException	
1.1 2	public	short	**shortValue** ()	
△	public static	String	**toBinaryString** (long i)	
△	public static	String	**toHexString** (long i)	
△	public static	String	**toOctalString** (long i)	
1	public	String	**toString** ()	
△	public static	String	**toString** (long i)	
△	public static	String	**toString** (long i, int radix)	
1.1 ▲	public static final	Class	**TYPE**	
△	public static	Long	**valueOf** (String s) throws NumberFormatException	
△	public static	Long	**valueOf** (String s, int radix) throws NumberFormatException	

LongHolder

L

Object
1.2 ● └LongHolder - *org.omg.CORBA.portable.Streamable [1]*

1	public	void	**_read** (org.omg.CORBA.portable.InputStream input)
1	public	TypeCode	**_type** ()
1	public	void	**_write** (org.omg.CORBA.portable.OutputStream output)
✳	public		**LongHolder** ()
✳	public		**LongHolder** (long initial)
	public	long	**value**

LookAndFeel

Object [1]
1.2 ○ └LookAndFeel

	public	UIDefaults	**getDefaults** ()
○	public abstract	String	**getDescription** ()
○	public abstract	String	**getID** ()
○	public abstract	String	**getName** ()
	public	void	**initialize** ()
△	public static	void	**installBorder** (JComponent c, String defaultBorderName)
△	public static	void	**installColors** (JComponent c, String defaultBgName, String defaultFgName)
△	public static	void	**installColorsAndFont** (JComponent c, String defaultBgName, String defaultFgName, String defaultFontName)
○	public abstract	boolean	**isNativeLookAndFeel** ()
○	public abstract	boolean	**isSupportedLookAndFeel** ()
✳	public		**LookAndFeel** ()
△	public static	Object	**makeIcon** (Class baseClass, String gifFile)
△	public static javax.swing.text↵ .JTextComponent.KeyBinding[]		**makeKeyBindings** (Object[] keyBindingList)
1	public	String	**toString** ()
	public	void	**uninitialize** ()
△	public static	void	**uninstallBorder** (JComponent c)

LookupOp

P

Object
1.2 └LookupOp - *BufferedImageOp [1], RasterOp [2]*

1	public	BufferedImage	**createCompatibleDestImage** (BufferedImage src, ColorModel destCM)
2	public	WritableRaster	**createCompatibleDestRaster** (Raster src)
● 1	public final	BufferedImage	**filter** (BufferedImage src, BufferedImage dst)
● 2	public final	WritableRaster	**filter** (Raster src, WritableRaster dst)
● 1	public final ...java.awt.geom.Rectangle2D		**getBounds2D** (BufferedImage src)
● 2	public final ...java.awt.geom.Rectangle2D		**getBounds2D** (Raster src)
● 1	public final java.awt.geom.Point2D		**getPoint2D** (java.awt.geom.Point2D srcPt, java.awt.geom.Point2D dstPt)

LookupOp

●	*1*	public final	....	**getRenderingHints** ()
			java.awt.RenderingHints	
●		public final	.... LookupTable	**getTable** ()
✻		public	....	**LookupOp** (LookupTable lookup, java.awt.RenderingHints hints)

LookupTable
java.awt.image
P

Object
└LookupTable

`1.2` ○

	public	........................int	**getNumComponents** ()
	public	........................int	**getOffset** ()
○	public abstract	.... int[]	**lookupPixel** (int[] src, int[] dest)
✻	protected	....	**LookupTable** (int offset, int numComponents)

MalformedURLException
java.net
P

Object
└Throwable - *java.io.Serializable*
 └Exception
  └java.io.IOException
   └MalformedURLException

✻	public	....	**MalformedURLException** ()
✻	public	....	**MalformedURLException** (String msg)

Manifest
java.util.jar

Object[1]
└Manifest - *Cloneable*

`1.2`

		public	........................void	**clear** ()
	1	public	....................**Object**	**clone** ()
	1	public	.... **boolean**	**equals** (Object o)
		public	....................Attributes	**getAttributes** (String name)
		public	.... *java.util.Map*	**getEntries** ()
		public	....................Attributes	**getMainAttributes** ()
	1	public	.... **int**	**hashCode** ()
✻		public	....	**Manifest** ()
✻		public	....	**Manifest** (java.io.InputStream is) throws java.io.IOException
✻		public	....	**Manifest** (Manifest man)
		public	........................void	**read** (java.io.InputStream is) throws java.io.IOException
		public	........................void	**write** (java.io.OutputStream out) throws java.io.IOException

---

Map
java.util
P

Map

`1.2`

	public	........................void	**clear** ()
	public	.... boolean	**containsKey** (Object key)
	public	.... boolean	**containsValue** (Object value)
	public	........................*Set*	**entrySet** ()
	public	.... boolean	**equals** (Object o)
	public	....................Object	**get** (Object key)
	public	........................int	**hashCode** ()
	public	.... boolean	**isEmpty** ()
	public	........................*Set*	**keySet** ()
	public	....................Object	**put** (Object key, Object value)
	public	........................void	**putAll** (*Map* t)
	public	....................Object	**remove** (Object key)
	public	........................int	**size** ()
	public	.... *Collection*	**values** ()

Class *Interface* —extends - - -implements ○ abstract ● final △ static ▲ static final ✻ constructor x x—inherited x **x**—declared **x x**—overridden

Map.Entry

java.util

1.2		*Map.Entry*	P

public	boolean	**equals** (Object o)
public	Object	**getKey** ()
public	Object	**getValue** ()
public	int	**hashCode** ()
public	Object	**setValue** (Object value)

MARSHAL

org.omg.CORBA

```
Object
└Throwable ------------------------- java.io.Serializable
  └Exception
    └RuntimeException
      └SystemException ¹
        └MARSHAL
```

1.2 ○			
1.2 ●			

1	public	CompletionStatus	completed
*	public		**MARSHAL** ()
*	public		**MARSHAL** (String s)
*	public		**MARSHAL** (int minor, CompletionStatus completed)
*	public		**MARSHAL** (String s, int minor, CompletionStatus completed)
1	public	int	minor
1	public	String	toString ()

MarshalException

java.rmi

P°

```
Object
└Throwable ------------------------- java.io.Serializable
  └Exception
    └java.io.IOException
      └RemoteException ¹
        └MarshalException
```

1.1			
1.1			

1	public	Throwable	detail
1	public	String	getMessage ()
*	public		**MarshalException** (String s)
*	public		**MarshalException** (String s, Exception ex)
1	public	void	printStackTrace ()
1	public	void	printStackTrace (java.io.PrintStream ps)
1	public	void	printStackTrace (java.io.PrintWriter pw)

MarshalledObject

java.rmi

P°

```
Object ¹
└MarshalledObject -------------------- java.io.Serializable
```

1.2 ●			

1	public	boolean	**equals** (Object obj)
	public	Object	**get** () throws java.io.IOException, ClassNotFoundException
1	public	int	**hashCode** ()
*	public		**MarshalledObject** (Object obj) throws java.io.IOException

Math

java.lang

P

```
Object
└Math
```

●			

△	public static	double	**abs** (double a)
△	public static	float	**abs** (float a)
△	public static	int	**abs** (int a)
△	public static	long	**abs** (long a)
△	public static native	double	**acos** (double a)
△	public static native	double	**asin** (double a)
△	public static native	double	**atan** (double a)
△	public static native	double	**atan2** (double a, double b)
△	public static native	double	**ceil** (double a)
△	public static native	double	**cos** (double a)
▲	public static final	double	**E** = 2.718281828459045

Math

△	public static native......double	**exp** (double a)
△	public static native......double	**floor** (double a)
△	public static native......double	**IEEEremainder** (double f1, double f2)
△	public static native......double	**log** (double a)
△	public static ....double	**max** (double a, double b)
△	public static ....float	**max** (float a, float b)
△	public static ....int	**max** (int a, int b)
△	public static .... long	**max** (long a, long b)
△	public static ....double	**min** (double a, double b)
△	public static ....float	**min** (float a, float b)
△	public static ....int	**min** (int a, int b)
△	public static .... long	**min** (long a, long b)
▲	public static final.......double	**PI** = 3.141592653589793
△	public static native......double	**pow** (double a, double b)
△	public static synchronized	**random** ()
	...................................double	
△	public static native......double	**rint** (double a)
△	public static .... long	**round** (double a)
△	public static ....int	**round** (float a)
△	public static native......double	**sin** (double a)
△	public static native......double	**sqrt** (double a)
△	public static native......double	**tan** (double a)
1.2 △	public static ....double	**toDegrees** (double angrad)
1.2 △	public static ....double	**toRadians** (double angdeg)

M

MatteBorder

javax.swing.border

```
Object
 └AbstractBorder¹ ------------------------ Border, java.io.Serializable
    └EmptyBorder² ---------------------- java.io.Serializable
       └MatteBorder
```

1.2 ○
1.2
1.2

2	protected ....int	bottom
	protected ....java.awt.Color	**color**
2	public.........**java.awt.Insets**	**getBorderInsets** (java.awt.Component c)
2	public......... java.awt.Insets	getBorderInsets (java.awt.Component c, java.awt.Insets insets)
1	public...... java.awt.Rectangle	getInteriorRectangle (java.awt.Component c, int x, int y, int width, int height)
△ 1	public static	getInteriorRectangle (java.awt.Component c, Border b, int x, int y, int width,
	.... java.awt.Rectangle	int height)
2	public...............**boolean**	**isBorderOpaque** ()
2	protected ....int	left
∗	public..........................	**MatteBorder** (javax.swing.Icon tileIcon)
∗	public..........................	**MatteBorder** (int top, int left, int bottom, int right, javax.swing.Icon tileIcon)
∗	public..........................	**MatteBorder** (int top, int left, int bottom, int right, java.awt.Color color)
2	public......................**void**	**paintBorder** (java.awt.Component c, java.awt.Graphics g, int x, int y, int width,
		int height)
2	protected ....int	right
	protected .....javax.swing.Icon	**tileIcon**
2	protected ....int	top

MediaTracker

java.awt
P

```
Object
 └MediaTracker ------------------------- java.io.Serializable
```

▲	public static final.............int	**ABORTED** = 2
	public.....................void	**addImage** (Image image, int id)
	public synchronized ....void	**addImage** (Image image, int id, int w, int h)
	public.................. boolean	**checkAll** ()
	public.................. boolean	**checkAll** (boolean load)
	public.................. boolean	**checkID** (int id)
	public.................. boolean	**checkID** (int id, boolean load)
▲	public static final.............int	**COMPLETE** = 8
▲	public static final.............int	**ERRORED** = 4
	public synchronized .. Object[]	**getErrorsAny** ()
	public synchronized .. Object[]	**getErrorsID** (int id)
	public synchronized .. boolean	**isErrorAny** ()
	public synchronized .. boolean	**isErrorID** (int id)
▲	public static final.............int	**LOADING** = 1
∗	public..........................	**MediaTracker** (Component comp)

Class *Interface* —extends - - -implements ○ abstract ● final △ static ▲ static final ∗ constructor x x—inherited x **x**—declared x **x**—overridden

1.1		public synchronized ....void	**removeImage** (Image image)
1.1		public synchronized ......void	**removeImage** (Image image, int id)
1.1		public synchronized ......void	**removeImage** (Image image, int id, int width, int height)
		public.....................int	**statusAll** (boolean load)
		public.....................int	**statusID** (int id, boolean load)
		public.....................void	**waitForAll** () throws InterruptedException
		public synchronized .. boolean	**waitForAll** (long ms) throws InterruptedException
		public.....................void	**waitForID** (int id) throws InterruptedException
		public synchronized .. boolean	**waitForID** (int id, long ms) throws InterruptedException

---

Member

java.lang.reflect

1.1	*Member* P

▲	public static final.............int	**DECLARED** = 1
	public.................... Class	**getDeclaringClass** ()
	public.....................int	**getModifiers** ()
	public.................... String	**getName** ()
▲	public static final.............int	**PUBLIC** = 0

MemoryImageSource

java.awt.image

Object
└─MemoryImageSource - - - - - - - - - - - - - - - - - - - *ImageProducer* [1]

M

	1	public synchronized ....void	**addConsumer** (*ImageConsumer* ic)
	1	public synchronized .. boolean	**isConsumer** (*ImageConsumer* ic)
*		public...........................	**MemoryImageSource** (int w, int h, int[] pix, int off, int scan)
*		public...........................	**MemoryImageSource** (int w, int h, int[] pix, int off, int scan, java.util.Hashtable props)
*		public...........................	**MemoryImageSource** (int w, int h, ColorModel cm, byte[] pix, int off, int scan)
*		public...........................	**MemoryImageSource** (int w, int h, ColorModel cm, int[] pix, int off, int scan)
*		public...........................	**MemoryImageSource** (int w, int h, ColorModel cm, byte[] pix, int off, int scan, java.util.Hashtable props)
*		public...........................	**MemoryImageSource** (int w, int h, ColorModel cm, int[] pix, int off, int scan, java.util.Hashtable props)
1.1		public.....................void	**newPixels** ()
1.1		public synchronized ......void	**newPixels** (byte[] newpix, ColorModel newmodel, int offset, int scansize)
1.1		public synchronized ......void	**newPixels** (int x, int y, int w, int h)
1.1		public synchronized ......void	**newPixels** (int[] newpix, ColorModel newmodel, int offset, int scansize)
1.1		public synchronized ......void	**newPixels** (int x, int y, int w, int h, boolean framenotify)
	1	public synchronized ......void	**removeConsumer** (*ImageConsumer* ic)
	1	public.....................void	**requestTopDownLeftRightResend** (*ImageConsumer* ic)
1.1		public synchronized ......void	**setAnimated** (boolean animated)
1.1		public synchronized ....void	**setFullBufferUpdates** (boolean fullbuffers)
	1	public.....................void	**startProduction** (*ImageConsumer* ic)

Menu

java.awt

Object
   ○ └─MenuComponent[1] - *java.io.Serializable*
        └─MenuItem[2]
           └─Menu - *MenuContainer* [3]

P[O]

Classes

		public............... MenuItem	**add** (MenuItem mi)
		public.....................void	**add** (String label)
1.1	2	public synchronized ....void	addActionListener (*java.awt.event.ActionListener* l)
	2	public.....................**void**	**addNotify** ()
		public.....................void	**addSeparator** ()
D		public.....................int	**countItems** ()
1.1	2	public.....................void	deleteShortcut ()
1.1 ●	2	protected final..............void	disableEvents (long eventsToDisable)
1.1 ●	1	public final ....void	dispatchEvent (AWTEvent e)
1.1 ●	2	protected final..............void	enableEvents (long eventsToEnable)
1.1	2	public.................... String	getActionCommand ()
	1	public.................... Font	getFont ()
		public............... MenuItem	**getItem** (int index)
1.1		public.....................int	**getItemCount** ()
	2	public.................... String	getLabel ()
1.1	1	public.................... String	getName ()
	1	public.......... *MenuContainer*	getParent ()

Menu

1.1	2	public............MenuShortcut	getShortcut ()	
1.2 ●	1	protected final...........Object	getTreeLock ()	
1.1		public.......................void	**insert** (MenuItem menuitem, int index)	
1.1		public.......................void	**insert** (String label, int index)	
1.1		public.......................void	**insertSeparator** (int index)	
	2	public...............boolean	isEnabled ()	
		public...............boolean	**isTearOff** ()	
1.1 *		public...................	**Menu** ()	
*		public...................	**Menu** (String label)	
*		public...................	**Menu** (String label, boolean tearOff)	
	2	public..............**String**	**paramString** ()	
1.1	2	protected................void	processActionEvent (java.awt.event.ActionEvent e)	
1.1	2	protected................void	processEvent (AWTEvent e)	
		public.......................void	**remove** (int index)	
	3	public.......................void	**remove** (MenuComponent item)	
1.1	2	public synchronized.......void	removeActionListener (*java.awt.event.ActionListener* l)	
1.1		public.......................void	**removeAll** ()	
	1	public..............**void removeNotify** ()		
1.1	2	public.......................void	setActionCommand (String command)	
1.1	2	public synchronized.......void	setEnabled (boolean b)	
	1	public.......................void	setFont (Font f)	
	2	public synchronized.......void	setLabel (String label)	
1.1	1	public.......................void	setName (String name)	
1.1	2	public.......................void	setShortcut (MenuShortcut s)	
	1	public...................String	toString ()	

MenuBar
java.awt
P^O

Object
  └─ MenuComponent [1] - *java.io.Serializable*
       └─ MenuBar - *MenuContainer* [2]

		public....................Menu	**add** (Menu m)	
		public.......................void	**addNotify** ()	
D		public........................int	**countMenus** ()	
1.1		public.......................void	**deleteShortcut** (MenuShortcut s)	
1.1 ●	1	public final.................void	dispatchEvent (AWTEvent e)	
	1	public.....................Font	getFont ()	
		public....................Menu	**getHelpMenu** ()	
		public....................Menu	**getMenu** (int i)	
1.1		public........................int	**getMenuCount** ()	
1.1	1	public...................String	getName ()	
	1	public.........*MenuContainer*	getParent ()	
1.1		public..............MenuItem	**getShortcutMenuItem** (MenuShortcut s)	
1.2 ●	1	protected final...........Object	getTreeLock ()	
*		public...................	**MenuBar** ()	
	1	protected................String	paramString ()	
1.1	1	protected................void	processEvent (AWTEvent e)	
		public.......................void	**remove** (int index)	
	2	public.......................void	**remove** (MenuComponent m)	
	1	public..............**void removeNotify** ()		
	1	public.......................void	setFont (Font f)	
		public.......................void	**setHelpMenu** (Menu m)	
1.1	1	public.......................void	setName (String name)	
1.1		public synchronized..........	**shortcuts** ()	
		..........*java.util.Enumeration*		
	1	public...................String	toString ()	

MenuBarPeer
java.awt.peer

MenuBarPeer ———————————————— *MenuComponentPeer* [1]

- -
	1	*1 inherited members from MenuComponentPeer not shown*	
		public.......................void	**addHelpMenu** (java.awt.Menu)
		public.......................void	**addMenu** (java.awt.Menu)
		public.......................void	**delMenu** (int)
- -

Class   *Interface*   —extends   - - -implements   O abstract   ● final   △ static   ▲ static final   * constructor   x x—inherited   x **x**—declared   **x x**—overridden

MenuBarUI | javax.swing.plaf

```
Object
1.2 ○   └ComponentUI 1
1.2 ○     └MenuBarUI
```

```
      1   11 inherited members from ComponentUI not shown
  *   public.......................... MenuBarUI ()
```

MenuComponent | java.awt

P

```
Object 1
○   └MenuComponent - - - - - - - - - - - - - - - - - - - - - - java.io.Serializable
```

1.1 ●	public final .... void	**dispatchEvent** (AWTEvent e)
	public..................... Font	**getFont** ()
1.1	public..................... String	**getName** ()
	public.......... MenuContainer	**getParent** ()
D	public.................. java.awt↵	**getPeer** ()
	.peer.MenuComponentPeer	
1.2 ●	protected final.......... Object	**getTreeLock** ()
*	public...................	**MenuComponent** ()
	protected .... String	**paramString** ()
D	public.................. boolean	**postEvent** (Event evt)
1.1	protected ....void	**processEvent** (AWTEvent e)
	public.....................void	**removeNotify** ()
	public.....................void	**setFont** (Font f)
1.1	public.....................void	**setName** (String name)
1	public.................... **String**	**toString** ()

MenuComponentPeer | java.awt.peer

```
MenuComponentPeer
```

```
public.......................void dispose ()
```

MenuContainer | java.awt

P

```
MenuContainer
```

	public..................... Font	**getFont** ()
D	public.................. boolean	**postEvent** (Event evt)
	public.....................void	**remove** (MenuComponent comp)

MenuDragMouseEvent | javax.swing.event

```
Object
1.1    └java.util.EventObject 1 - - - - - - - - - - - - - - - - - - - java.io.Serializable
1.1 ○    └java.awt.AWTEvent 2
1.1      └java.awt.event.ComponentEvent 3
1.1 ○      └java.awt.event.InputEvent 4
1.1        └java.awt.event.MouseEvent 5
1.2          └MenuDragMouseEvent
```

4	public.....................void	consume ()
2	protected .... boolean	consumed
2	protected ....void	finalize () throws Throwable
5	public.........................int	getClickCount ()
3	public.... java.awt.Component	getComponent ()
2	public.........................int	getID ()
	public..................javax↵	**getMenuSelectionManager** ()
	.swing.MenuSelectionManager	
4	public.........................int	getModifiers ()
	public..........................	**getPath** ()
	.... javax.swing.MenuElement[]	
5	public........... java.awt.Point	getPoint ()
1	public................... Object	getSource ()
4	public................... long	getWhen ()
5	public.........................int	getX ()
5	public.........................int	getY ()

MenuDragMouseEvent

	2	protected .int	id
	4	public . . . . boolean	isAltDown ()
	4	public . . . . boolean	isAltGraphDown ()
	4	public . . . . boolean	isConsumed ()
	4	public . . . . boolean	isControlDown ()
	4	public . . . . boolean	isMetaDown ()
	5	public . . . . boolean	isPopupTrigger ()
	4	public . . . . boolean	isShiftDown ()
*		public	**MenuDragMouseEvent** (java.awt.Component source, int id, long when, int modifiers, int x, int y, int clickCount, boolean popupTrigger, *javax.swing.MenuElement[]* p, javax.swing.MenuSelectionManager m)
	5	public . . . . String	paramString ()
	1	protected transient . . . . . . Object	source
	2	public . . . . String	toString ()
	5	public synchronized . . . . . . .void	translatePoint (int x, int y)

MenuDragMouseListener

javax.swing.event

1.2	*MenuDragMouseListener* ──────────────── *java.util.EventListener*	
	public .void	**menuDragMouseDragged** (MenuDragMouseEvent e)
	public .void	**menuDragMouseEntered** (MenuDragMouseEvent e)
	public .void	**menuDragMouseExited** (MenuDragMouseEvent e)
	public .void	**menuDragMouseReleased** (MenuDragMouseEvent e)

MenuElement

javax.swing

1.2	*MenuElement*	
	public . . . . java.awt.Component	**getComponent** ()
	public . . . . *MenuElement[]*	**getSubElements** ()
	public .void	**menuSelectionChanged** (boolean isIncluded)
	public .void	**processKeyEvent** (java.awt.event.KeyEvent event, *MenuElement[]* path, MenuSelectionManager manager)
	public .void	**processMouseEvent** (java.awt.event.MouseEvent event, *MenuElement[]* path, MenuSelectionManager manager)

MenuEvent

javax.swing.event

	Object	
1.1	└java.util.EventObject[1] - *java.io.Serializable*	
1.2	└MenuEvent	
1	public . . . . Object	getSource ()
*	public	**MenuEvent** (Object source)
1	protected transient . . . . . . Object	source
1	public . . . . String	toString ()

MenuItem

java.awt
P

		Object	
○		└MenuComponent[1] - *java.io.Serializable*	
		└MenuItem	
1.1		public synchronized . . . . . . .void	**addActionListener** (*java.awt.event.ActionListener* l)
		public .void	**addNotify** ()
1.1		public .void	**deleteShortcut** ()
D		public synchronized . . . . . . .void	**disable** ()
1.1 ●		protected final . . . . .void	**disableEvents** (long eventsToDisable)
1.1 ●	1	public final . . . . .void	dispatchEvent (AWTEvent e)
D		public synchronized . . . . . . .void	**enable** ()
D		public .void	**enable** (boolean b)
1.1 ●		protected final . . . . .void	**enableEvents** (long eventsToEnable)
1.1		public . . . . String	**getActionCommand** ()
	1	public . . . . Font	getFont ()
		public . . . . String	**getLabel** ()
1.1	1	public . . . . String	getName ()
	1	public . . . . *MenuContainer*	getParent ()

Class   *Interface*   ──extends   - - -implements   ○ abstract   ● final   △ static   ▲ static final   ✳ constructor   x x──inherited   x **x**──declared   **x x**──overridden

1.1		public . . . . MenuShortcut	**getShortcut** ()
1.2 ●	1	protected final . . . . Object	getTreeLock ()
		public . . . . boolean	**isEnabled** ()
1.1 ✻		public	**MenuItem** ()
✻		public	**MenuItem** (String label)
1.1 ✻		public	**MenuItem** (String label, MenuShortcut s)
	1	public . . . . **String**	**paramString** ()
1.1		protected . . . . void	**processActionEvent** (java.awt.event.ActionEvent e)
1.1	1	protected . . . . **void**	**processEvent** (AWTEvent e)
1.1		public synchronized . . . . . . void	**removeActionListener** (*java.awt.event.ActionListener* l)
	1	public . . . . void	removeNotify ()
1.1		public . . . . void	**setActionCommand** (String command)
1.1		public synchronized . . . . . . void	**setEnabled** (boolean b)
	1	public . . . . void	setFont (Font f)
		public synchronized . . . . . . void	**setLabel** (String label)
1.1	1	public . . . . void	setName (String name)
1.1		public . . . . void	**setShortcut** (MenuShortcut s)
	1	public . . . . String	toString ()

MenuItemPeer   java.awt.peer

MenuItemPeer————————————————MenuComponentPeer [1]

	1	*1 inherited members from MenuComponentPeer not shown*	
		public . . . . void	**disable** ()
		public . . . . void	**enable** ()
1.1		public . . . . void	**setEnabled** (boolean)
		public . . . . void	**setLabel** (String)

MenuItemUI   javax.swing.plaf

Object
1.2 ○	└ComponentUI [1]
1.2 ○	└ButtonUI
1.2 ○	└MenuItemUI

	1	*11 inherited members from ComponentUI not shown*	
✻		public	**MenuItemUI** ()

MenuKeyEvent   javax.swing.event

Object
1.1	└java.util.EventObject [1] - - - - - - - - - - - - - - - - - - - *java.io.Serializable*
1.1 ○	└java.awt.AWTEvent [2]
1.1	└java.awt.event.ComponentEvent [3]
1.1 ○	└java.awt.event.InputEvent [4]
1.1	└java.awt.event.KeyEvent [5]
1.2	└MenuKeyEvent

	5	*198 inherited members from java.awt.event.KeyEvent not shown*	
	4	public . . . . void	consume ()
	2	protected . . . . boolean	consumed
	2	protected . . . . void	finalize () throws Throwable
	3	public . . . . java.awt.Component	getComponent ()
	2	public . . . . int	getID ()
		public . . . . javax ↩	**getMenuSelectionManager** ()
		.swing.MenuSelectionManager	
	4	public . . . . int	getModifiers ()
		public	**getPath** ()
		. . . . *javax.swing.MenuElement[]*	
	1	public . . . . Object	getSource ()
	4	public . . . . long	getWhen ()
	2	protected . . . . int	id
	4	public . . . . boolean	isAltDown ()
	4	public . . . . boolean	isAltGraphDown ()
	4	public . . . . boolean	isConsumed ()
	4	public . . . . boolean	isControlDown ()
	4	public . . . . boolean	isMetaDown ()
	4	public . . . . boolean	isShiftDown ()

M

Classes

MenuKeyEvent

*	public		**MenuKeyEvent** (java.awt.Component source, int id, long when, int modifiers, int keyCode, char keyChar, *javax.swing.MenuElement[]* p, javax.swing.MenuSelectionManager m)
1	protected transient	Object	source
2	public	String	toString ()

MenuKeyListener javax.swing.event

1.2   *MenuKeyListener*————————————*java.util.EventListener*

	public	void	**menuKeyPressed** (MenuKeyEvent e)
	public	void	**menuKeyReleased** (MenuKeyEvent e)
	public	void	**menuKeyTyped** (MenuKeyEvent e)

MenuListener javax.swing.event

1.2   *MenuListener*————————————*java.util.EventListener*

	public	void	**menuCanceled** (MenuEvent e)
	public	void	**menuDeselected** (MenuEvent e)
	public	void	**menuSelected** (MenuEvent e)

M

MenuPeer java.awt.peer

MenuPeer————————————*MenuItemPeer [1] (MenuComponentPeer [2])*

2	1 inherited members from MenuComponentPeer not shown		
1	4 inherited members from MenuItemPeer not shown		
	public	void	**addItem** (java.awt.MenuItem)
	public	void	**addSeparator** ()
	public	void	**delItem** (int)

MenuSelectionManager javax.swing

Object
1.2   └MenuSelectionManager

	public	void	**addChangeListener** (*javax.swing.event.ChangeListener* l)
	protected transient	javax↵ .swing.event.ChangeEvent	**changeEvent**
	public	void	**clearSelectedPath** ()
	public	java.awt.Component	**componentForPoint** (java.awt.Component source, java.awt.Point sourcePoint)
△	public static	MenuSelectionManager	**defaultManager** ()
	protected	void	**fireStateChanged** ()
	public	*MenuElement[]*	**getSelectedPath** ()
	public	boolean	**isComponentPartOfCurrentMenu** (java.awt.Component c)
	protected	javax↵ .swing.event.EventListenerList	**listenerList**
*	public		**MenuSelectionManager** ()
	public	void	**processKeyEvent** (java.awt.event.KeyEvent e)
	public	void	**processMouseEvent** (java.awt.event.MouseEvent event)
	public	void	**removeChangeListener** (*javax.swing.event.ChangeListener* l)
	public	void	**setSelectedPath** (*MenuElement[]* path)

MenuShortcut java.awt
P^O

Object [1]
1.1   └MenuShortcut ------------------------- *java.io.Serializable*

	public	boolean	**equals** (MenuShortcut s)
1	public	**boolean**	**equals** (Object obj)
	public	int	**getKey** ()
1	public	**int**	**hashCode** ()
*	public		**MenuShortcut** (int key)
*	public		**MenuShortcut** (int key, boolean useShiftModifier)
	protected	String	**paramString** ()
1	public	**String**	**toString** ()

Class   *Interface*   ——extends   - - -implements   ○ abstract   ● final   △ static   ▲ static final   ✳ constructor   x x—inherited   x **x**—declared   **x x**—overridden

public................. boolean **usesShiftModifier** ()

MessageDigest
java.security

Object [1]
1.2 ○ └ MessageDigestSpi [2]
1.1 ○ └ MessageDigest

	2	public....................**Object**	**clone** () throws CloneNotSupportedException
		public....................byte[]	**digest** ()
		public....................byte[]	**digest** (byte[] input)
1.2		public.......................int	**digest** (byte[] buf, int offset, int len) throws DigestException
1.2 ○	2	protected abstract ....byte[]	engineDigest ()
1.2	2	protected ....int	engineDigest (byte[] buf, int offset, int len) throws DigestException
1.2	2	protected ....int	engineGetDigestLength ()
1.2 ○	2	protected abstract ....void	engineReset ()
1.2 ○	2	protected abstract ....void	engineUpdate (byte input)
1.2 ○	2	protected abstract ....void	engineUpdate (byte[] input, int offset, int len)
●		public final ....String	**getAlgorithm** ()
1.2 ●		public final ....int	**getDigestLength** ()
△		public static ... MessageDigest	**getInstance** (String algorithm) throws NoSuchAlgorithmException
△		public static ... MessageDigest	**getInstance** (String algorithm, String provider) throws NoSuchAlgorithmException, NoSuchProviderException
1.2 ●		public final .... Provider	**getProvider** ()
△		public static .... boolean	**isEqual** (byte[] digesta, byte[] digestb)
✳		protected ....**MessageDigest** (String algorithm)
		public....................void	**reset** ()
	1	public....................**String**	**toString** ()
		public....................void	**update** (byte input)
		public....................void	**update** (byte[] input)
		public....................void	**update** (byte[] input, int offset, int len)

MessageDigestSpi
java.security

Object [1]
1.2 ○ └ MessageDigestSpi

	1	public....................**Object**	**clone** () throws CloneNotSupportedException
○		protected abstract ....byte[]	**engineDigest** ()
		protected ....int	**engineDigest** (byte[] buf, int offset, int len) throws DigestException
		protected ....int	**engineGetDigestLength** ()
○		protected abstract ....void	**engineReset** ()
○		protected abstract ....void	**engineUpdate** (byte input)
○		protected abstract ....void	**engineUpdate** (byte[] input, int offset, int len)
✳		public..........................	**MessageDigestSpi** ()

MessageFormat
java.text

Object [1]
1.1 ○ └ Format [2] - java.io.Serializable, Cloneable
1.1 └ MessageFormat

		public....................void	**applyPattern** (String newPattern)
	2	public....................**Object**	**clone** ()
	1	public....................**boolean**	**equals** (Object obj)
●	2	public final ....String	format (Object obj)
△		public static ....String	**format** (String pattern, Object[] arguments)
●	2	public final ....**StringBuffer**	**format** (Object source, StringBuffer result, FieldPosition ignore)
●		public final .... StringBuffer	**format** (Object[] source, StringBuffer result, FieldPosition ignore)
		public................Format[]	**getFormats** ()
		public..........java.util.Locale	**getLocale** ()
	1	public.......................**int**	**hashCode** ()
✳		public..........................	**MessageFormat** (String pattern)
		public................Object[]	**parse** (String source) throws ParseException
		public................Object[]	**parse** (String source, ParsePosition status)
	2	public....................Object	parseObject (String source) throws ParseException
	2	public....................**Object**	**parseObject** (String text, ParsePosition status)
		public....................void	**setFormat** (int variable, Format newFormat)
		public....................void	**setFormats** (Format[] newFormats)
		public....................void	**setLocale** (java.util.Locale theLocale)

MessageFormat

	public	String	**toPattern** ()

Method
java.lang.reflect

P

Object[1]
1.2   └AccessibleObject[2]
1.1 ●   └Method - *Member*[3]

	1	public	**boolean**	**equals** (Object obj)
	3	public	Class	**getDeclaringClass** ()
		public	Class[]	**getExceptionTypes** ()
	3	public	int	**getModifiers** ()
	3	public	String	**getName** ()
		public	Class[]	**getParameterTypes** ()
		public	Class	**getReturnType** ()
	1	public	**int**	**hashCode** ()
		public native	Object	**invoke** (Object obj, Object[] args) throws IllegalAccessException, IllegalArgumentException, InvocationTargetException
1.2	2	public	boolean	isAccessible ()
1.2		public	void	setAccessible (boolean flag) throws SecurityException
1.2 △	2	public static	void	setAccessible (AccessibleObject[] array, boolean flag) throws SecurityException
	1	public	**String**	**toString** ()

M

MethodDescriptor
java.beans

Object
1.1   └FeatureDescriptor[1]
1.1   └MethodDescriptor

	1	public	*java.util.Enumeration*	attributeNames ()
	1	public	String	getDisplayName ()
		public	java.lang.reflect.Method	**getMethod** ()
	1	public	String	getName ()
		public	ParameterDescriptor[]	**getParameterDescriptors** ()
	1	public	String	getShortDescription ()
	1	public	Object	getValue (String attributeName)
	1	public	boolean	isExpert ()
	1	public	boolean	isHidden ()
1.2	1	public	boolean	isPreferred ()
	✳	public		**MethodDescriptor** (java.lang.reflect.Method method)
	✳	public		**MethodDescriptor** (java. lang. reflect. Method method, ParameterDescriptor[] parameterDescriptors)
	1	public	void	setDisplayName (String displayName)
	1	public	void	setExpert (boolean expert)
	1	public	void	setHidden (boolean hidden)
	1	public	void	setName (String name)
1.2	1	public	void	setPreferred (boolean preferred)
	1	public	void	setShortDescription (String text)
	1	public	void	setValue (String attributeName, Object value)

MinimalHTMLWriter
javax.swing.text.html

Object
1.2 ○   └javax.swing.text.AbstractWriter[1]
1.2   └MinimalHTMLWriter

	1	protected	void	decrIndent ()
		protected	void	**endFontTag** () throws java.io.IOException
	1	protected		getDocument ()
			javax.swing.text.Document	
	1	protected	javax↵ .swing.text.ElementIterator	getElementIterator ()
	1	protected	String	getText (*javax. swing. text. Element* elem) throws javax. swing. text↵ .BadLocationException
	1	protected	void	incrIndent ()
	1	protected	void	indent () throws java.io.IOException
		protected	boolean	**inFontTag** ()
	1	protected	boolean	inRange (*javax.swing.text.Element* next)

⌐ Class   *Interface*   —extends   - - -implements   ○ abstract   ● final   △ static   ▲ static final   ✳ constructor   x x—inherited   x **x**—declared   **x x**—overridden

526

	protected .... boolean	**isText** (*javax.swing.text.Element* elem)
*	public...........................	**MinimalHTMLWriter** (java.io.Writer w, *javax.swing.text.StyledDocument* doc)
*	public...........................	**MinimalHTMLWriter** (java.io.Writer w, *javax.swing.text.StyledDocument* doc, int pos, int len)
1	protected ....void	setIndentSpace (int space)
1	protected ....void	setLineLength (int l)
	protected ....void	**startFontTag** (String style) throws java.io.IOException
1	protected .... **void**	**text** (*javax.swing.text.Element* elem) throws java. io. IOException, javax.swing.text.BadLocationException
1	public..................... **void**	**write** () throws java.io.IOException, javax.swing.text.BadLocationException
1	protected ....void	write (char ch) throws java.io.IOException
1	protected ....void	write (String str) throws java.io.IOException
1	protected .... **void**	**writeAttributes** (*javax.swing.text.AttributeSet* attr) throws java.io.IOException
	protected ....void	**writeBody** () throws java.io.IOException, javax.swing.text.BadLocationException
	protected ....void	**writeComponent** (*javax.swing.text.Element* elem) throws java.io.IOException
	protected ....void	**writeContent** (*javax. swing. text. Element* elem, boolean needsIndenting) throws java.io.IOException, javax.swing.text.BadLocationException
	protected ....void	**writeEndParagraph** () throws java.io.IOException
	protected ....void	**writeEndTag** (String endTag) throws java.io.IOException
	protected ....void	**writeHeader** () throws java.io.IOException
	protected ....void	**writeHTMLTags** (*javax.swing.text.AttributeSet* attr) throws java.io.IOException
	protected ....void	**writeImage** (*javax.swing.text.Element* elem) throws java.io.IOException
	protected ....void	**writeLeaf** (*javax.swing.text.Element* elem) throws java.io.IOException
	protected ....void	**writeNonHTMLAttributes** (*javax. swing. text. AttributeSet* attr) throws java.io.IOException
	protected ....void	**writeStartParagraph** (*javax.swing.text.Element* elem) throws java.io.IOException
	protected ....void	**writeStartTag** (String tag) throws java.io.IOException
	protected ....void	**writeStyles** () throws java.io.IOException

MissingResourceException — java.util

P

```
Object
 └Throwable ----------------------------- java.io.Serializable
    └Exception
       └RuntimeException
          └MissingResourceException
```

1.1

	public....................String	**getClassName** ()
	public....................String	**getKey** ()
*	public...........................	**MissingResourceException** (String s, String className, String key)

Modifier — java.lang.reflect

P

```
Object
 └Modifier
```

1.1

▲	public static final ....int	**ABSTRACT** = 1024
▲	public static final ....int	**FINAL** = 16
▲	public static final ....int	**INTERFACE** = 512
△	public static .... boolean	**isAbstract** (int mod)
△	public static .... boolean	**isFinal** (int mod)
△	public static .... boolean	**isInterface** (int mod)
△	public static .... boolean	**isNative** (int mod)
△	public static .... boolean	**isPrivate** (int mod)
△	public static .... boolean	**isProtected** (int mod)
△	public static .... boolean	**isPublic** (int mod)
△	public static .... boolean	**isStatic** (int mod)
1.2 △	public static .... boolean	**isStrict** (int mod)
△	public static .... boolean	**isSynchronized** (int mod)
△	public static .... boolean	**isTransient** (int mod)
△	public static .... boolean	**isVolatile** (int mod)
*	public...........................	**Modifier** ()
▲	public static final ....int	**NATIVE** = 256
▲	public static final ....int	**PRIVATE** = 2
▲	public static final ....int	**PROTECTED** = 4
▲	public static final ....int	**PUBLIC** = 1
▲	public static final ....int	**STATIC** = 8
1.2 ▲	public static final ....int	**STRICT** = 2048
▲	public static final ....int	**SYNCHRONIZED** = 32
△	public static ....String	**toString** (int mod)
▲	public static final ....int	**TRANSIENT** = 128

M

Classes

Modifier

▲   public static final . . . . int **VOLATILE** = 64

MouseAdapter	java.awt.event

P

Object
1.1 ○ └ MouseAdapter - *MouseListener* [1] (*java.util.EventListener*)

❋	public	**MouseAdapter** ()
1	public . . . . void	**mouseClicked** (MouseEvent e)
1	public . . . . void	**mouseEntered** (MouseEvent e)
1	public . . . . void	**mouseExited** (MouseEvent e)
1	public . . . . void	**mousePressed** (MouseEvent e)
1	public . . . . void	**mouseReleased** (MouseEvent e)

MouseDragGestureRecognizer	java.awt.dnd

Object
1.2 ○ └ DragGestureRecognizer [1]
1.2 ○   └ MouseDragGestureRecognizer - - - - - - - - - *java.awt.event.MouseListener* [2] (*java.util.EventListener*),
                                 java.awt.event.MouseMotionListener [3] (*java.util.EventListener*)

M

1	public synchronized . . . . void	addDragGestureListener (*DragGestureListener* dgl)
		throws java.util.TooManyListenersException
1	protected synchronized . . . void	appendEvent (java.awt.event.InputEvent awtie)
1	protected java.awt.Component	component
1	protected *DragGestureListener*	dragGestureListener
1	protected . . . . DragSource	dragSource
1	protected . . . . java.util.ArrayList	events
1	protected synchronized . . . void	fireDragGestureRecognized (int dragAction, java.awt.Point p)
1	public synchronized	getComponent ()
	. . . . java.awt.Component	
1	public . . . . DragSource	getDragSource ()
1	public synchronized . . . . int	getSourceActions ()
1	public	getTriggerEvent ()
	. . . . . . java.awt.event.InputEvent	
2	public . . . . void	**mouseClicked** (java.awt.event.MouseEvent e)
3	public . . . . void	**mouseDragged** (java.awt.event.MouseEvent e)
❋	protected	**MouseDragGestureRecognizer** (DragSource ds)
❋	protected	**MouseDragGestureRecognizer** (DragSource ds, java.awt.Component c)
❋	protected	**MouseDragGestureRecognizer** (DragSource ds, java.awt.Component c, int act)
❋	protected	**MouseDragGestureRecognizer** (DragSource ds, java.awt.Component c, int act,
		DragGestureListener dgl)
2	public . . . . void	**mouseEntered** (java.awt.event.MouseEvent e)
2	public . . . . void	**mouseExited** (java.awt.event.MouseEvent e)
3	public . . . . void	**mouseMoved** (java.awt.event.MouseEvent e)
2	public . . . . void	**mousePressed** (java.awt.event.MouseEvent e)
2	public . . . . void	**mouseReleased** (java.awt.event.MouseEvent e)
1	protected . . . . **void**	**registerListeners** ()
1	public synchronized . . . . void	removeDragGestureListener (*DragGestureListener* dgl)
1	public . . . . void	resetRecognizer ()
1	public synchronized . . . . void	setComponent (java.awt.Component c)
1	public synchronized . . . . void	setSourceActions (int actions)
1	protected . . . . int	sourceActions
1	protected . . . . **void**	**unregisterListeners** ()

MouseEvent	java.awt.event

P

Object
1.1 └ java.util.EventObject [1] - *java.io.Serializable*
1.1 ○   └ java.awt.AWTEvent [2]
1.1   └ ComponentEvent [3]
1.1 ○   └ InputEvent [4]
1.1   └ MouseEvent

4	public . . . . void	consume ()
2	protected . . . . boolean	consumed
2	protected . . . . void	finalize () throws Throwable
	public . . . . int	**getClickCount** ()

Class   *Interface*   —extends   - - -implements   ○ abstract   ● final   △ static   ▲ static final   ❋ constructor   x x—inherited   x **x**—declared   **x x**—overridden

3	public....	java.awt.Component	getComponent ()
2	public.........................	int	getID ()
4	public.........................	int	getModifiers ()
	public.............	java.awt.Point	**getPoint** ()
1	public........................	Object	getSource ()
4	public.....................	long	getWhen ()
	public.....................	int	**getX** ()
	public.....................	int	**getY** ()
2	protected.....................	int	id
4	public.....................	boolean	isAltDown ()
1.2	4 public.....................	boolean	isAltGraphDown ()
4	public.....................	boolean	isConsumed ()
4	public.....................	boolean	isControlDown ()
4	public.....................	boolean	isMetaDown ()
	public.....................	boolean	**isPopupTrigger** ()
4	public.....................	boolean	isShiftDown ()
▲	public static final.............	int	**MOUSE_CLICKED** = 500
▲	public static final.............	int	**MOUSE_DRAGGED** = 506
▲	public static final.............	int	**MOUSE_ENTERED** = 504
▲	public static final.............	int	**MOUSE_EXITED** = 505
▲	public static final.............	int	**MOUSE_FIRST** = 500
▲	public static final.............	int	**MOUSE_LAST** = 506
▲	public static final.............	int	**MOUSE_MOVED** = 503
▲	public static final.............	int	**MOUSE_PRESSED** = 501
▲	public static final.............	int	**MOUSE_RELEASED** = 502
＊	public.........................		**MouseEvent** (java.awt.Component source, int id, long when, int modifiers, int x, int y, int clickCount, boolean popupTrigger)
3	public..................	**String**	**paramString** ()
1	protected transient......	Object	source
2	public..................	String	toString ()
	public synchronized	void	**translatePoint** (int x, int y)

MouseInputAdapter   javax.swing.event

```
Object
 └─MouseInputAdapter - - - - - - - - - - - - - - - - - - - - MouseInputListener (java.awt.event.MouseListener 1
```
1.2 ○

(*java.util.EventListener*), *java.awt.event.MouseMotionListener* [2]
(*java.util.EventListener*))

1	public.....................	void	**mouseClicked** (java.awt.event.MouseEvent e)
2	public.....................	void	**mouseDragged** (java.awt.event.MouseEvent e)
1	public.....................	void	**mouseEntered** (java.awt.event.MouseEvent e)
1	public.....................	void	**mouseExited** (java.awt.event.MouseEvent e)
＊	public.....................		**MouseInputAdapter** ()
2	public.....................	void	**mouseMoved** (java.awt.event.MouseEvent e)
1	public.....................	void	**mousePressed** (java.awt.event.MouseEvent e)
1	public.....................	void	**mouseReleased** (java.awt.event.MouseEvent e)

MouseInputListener   javax.swing.event

1.2   *MouseInputListener*————————————*java.awt.event.MouseListener* [1] (*java.util.EventListener*),
java.awt.event.MouseMotionListener [2] (*java.util.EventListener*)

1	public.....................	void	mouseClicked (java.awt.event.MouseEvent e)
2	public.....................	void	mouseDragged (java.awt.event.MouseEvent e)
1	public.....................	void	mouseEntered (java.awt.event.MouseEvent e)
1	public.....................	void	mouseExited (java.awt.event.MouseEvent e)
2	public.....................	void	mouseMoved (java.awt.event.MouseEvent e)
1	public.....................	void	mousePressed (java.awt.event.MouseEvent e)
1	public.....................	void	mouseReleased (java.awt.event.MouseEvent e)

MouseListener   java.awt.event

1.1   *MouseListener*————————————*java.util.EventListener*   P

	public.....................	void	**mouseClicked** (MouseEvent e)
	public.....................	void	**mouseEntered** (MouseEvent e)
	public.....................	void	**mouseExited** (MouseEvent e)
	public.....................	void	**mousePressed** (MouseEvent e)
	public.....................	void	**mouseReleased** (MouseEvent e)

M

Classes

MouseMotionAdapter

MouseMotionAdapter				java.awt.event

Object
   └─MouseMotionAdapter - - - - - - - - - - - - - - - - - - MouseMotionListener [1] (java.util.EventListener)

1.1 ○

	1	public......................void	**mouseDragged** (MouseEvent e)
✳		public..........................	**MouseMotionAdapter** ()
	1	public......................void	**mouseMoved** (MouseEvent e)

MouseMotionListener				java.awt.event

1.1   *MouseMotionListener*————————————*java.util.EventListener*

public......................void	**mouseDragged** (MouseEvent e)
public......................void	**mouseMoved** (MouseEvent e)

MulticastSocket				java.net

Object
   └─DatagramSocket [1]
      └─MulticastSocket

1.1

M

	1	public......................void	close ()
1.2	1	public......................void	connect (InetAddress address, int port)
1.2	1	public......................void	disconnect ()
1.2	1	public............InetAddress	getInetAddress ()
		public............InetAddress	**getInterface** () throws SocketException
	1	public............InetAddress	getLocalAddress ()
	1	public......................int	getLocalPort ()
1.2	1	public......................int	getPort ()
1.2	1	public synchronized ....int	getReceiveBufferSize () throws SocketException
1.2	1	public synchronized ....int	getSendBufferSize () throws SocketException
	1	public synchronized ....int	getSoTimeout () throws SocketException
1.2		public......................int	**getTimeToLive** () throws java.io.IOException
D		public......................byte	**getTTL** () throws java.io.IOException
		public......................void	**joinGroup** (InetAddress mcastaddr) throws java.io.IOException
		public......................void	**leaveGroup** (InetAddress mcastaddr) throws java.io.IOException
✳		public..........................	**MulticastSocket** () throws java.io.IOException
✳		public..........................	**MulticastSocket** (int port) throws java.io.IOException
	1	public synchronized ......void	receive (DatagramPacket p) throws java.io.IOException
	1	public......................void	send (DatagramPacket p) throws java.io.IOException
		public......................void	**send** (DatagramPacket p, byte ttl) throws java.io.IOException
		public......................void	**setInterface** (InetAddress inf) throws SocketException
1.2	1	public synchronized ......void	setReceiveBufferSize (int size) throws SocketException
1.2	1	public synchronized ......void	setSendBufferSize (int size) throws SocketException
	1	public synchronized ......void	setSoTimeout (int timeout) throws SocketException
1.2		public......................void	**setTimeToLive** (int ttl) throws java.io.IOException
D		public......................void	**setTTL** (byte ttl) throws java.io.IOException

MultiPixelPackedSampleModel				java.awt.image

Object
   └─SampleModel [1]
      └─MultiPixelPackedSampleModel

1.2 ○
1.2

	1	*30 inherited members from SampleModel not shown*	
	1	public............SampleModel	**createCompatibleSampleModel** (int w, int h)
	1	public.............DataBuffer	**createDataBuffer** ()
	1	public............SampleModel	**createSubsetSampleModel** (int[] bands)
		public......................int	**getBitOffset** (int x)
		public......................int	**getDataBitOffset** ()
	1	public..................Object	**getDataElements** (int x, int y, Object obj, DataBuffer data)
	1	public......................int	**getNumDataElements** ()
		public......................int	**getOffset** (int x, int y)
	1	public....................int[]	**getPixel** (int x, int y, int[] iArray, DataBuffer data)
		public......................int	**getPixelBitStride** ()
	1	public......................int	**getSample** (int x, int y, int b, DataBuffer data)
	1	public....................int[]	**getSampleSize** ()
	1	public......................int	**getSampleSize** (int band)

Class   *Interface*   —extends   - - -implements   ○ abstract   ● final   △ static   ▲ static final   ✳ constructor   x x—inherited   x **x**—declared   **x x**—overridden

	public	int	**getScanlineStride** ()
1	public	**int**	**getTransferType** ()
*	public		**MultiPixelPackedSampleModel** (int dataType, int w, int h, int numberOfBits)
*	public		**MultiPixelPackedSampleModel** (int dataType, int w, int h, int numberOfBits, int scanlineStride, int dataBitOffset)
1	public	**void**	**setDataElements** (int x, int y, Object obj, DataBuffer data)
1	public	**void**	**setPixel** (int x, int y, int[] iArray, DataBuffer data)
1	public	**void**	**setSample** (int x, int y, int b, int s, DataBuffer data)

MultipleMaster
java.awt.font

1.2   *MultipleMaster*

	public	java.awt.Font	**deriveMMFont** (float[] axes)
	public	java.awt.Font	**deriveMMFont** (float[] glyphWidths, float avgStemWidth, float typicalCapHeight, float typicalXHeight, float italicAngle)
	public	float[]	**getDesignAxisDefaults** ()
	public	String[]	**getDesignAxisNames** ()
	public	float[]	**getDesignAxisRanges** ()
	public	int	**getNumDesignAxes** ()

MutableAttributeSet
javax.swing.text   **M**

1.2   *MutableAttributeSet*————————— *AttributeSet* [1]

	public	void	**addAttribute** (Object name, Object value)
	public	void	**addAttributes** (*AttributeSet* attributes)
1	public	boolean	containsAttribute (Object name, Object value)
1	public	boolean	containsAttributes (*AttributeSet* attributes)
1	public	*AttributeSet*	copyAttributes ()
1	public	Object	getAttribute (Object key)
1	public	int	getAttributeCount ()
1	public	*java.util.Enumeration*	getAttributeNames ()
1	public	*AttributeSet*	getResolveParent ()
1	public	boolean	isDefined (Object attrName)
1	public	boolean	isEqual (*AttributeSet* attr)
	public	void	**removeAttribute** (Object name)
	public	void	**removeAttributes** (*java.util.Enumeration* names)
	public	void	**removeAttributes** (*AttributeSet* attributes)
	public	void	**setResolveParent** (*AttributeSet* parent)

MutableComboBoxModel
javax.swing

1.2   *MutableComboBoxModel*————————— *ComboBoxModel* [1] (*ListModel* [2])

	public	void	**addElement** (Object obj)
2	public	void	addListDataListener (*javax.swing.event.ListDataListener* l)
2	public	Object	getElementAt (int index)
1	public	Object	getSelectedItem ()
2	public	int	getSize ()
	public	void	**insertElementAt** (Object obj, int index)
	public	void	**removeElement** (Object obj)
	public	void	**removeElementAt** (int index)
2	public	void	removeListDataListener (*javax.swing.event.ListDataListener* l)
1	public	void	setSelectedItem (Object anItem)

MutableTreeNode
javax.swing.tree   **Classes**

1.2   *MutableTreeNode*————————— *TreeNode* [1]

1	public	*java.util.Enumeration*	children ()
1	public	boolean	getAllowsChildren ()
1	public	*TreeNode*	getChildAt (int childIndex)
1	public	int	getChildCount ()
1	public	int	getIndex (*TreeNode* node)
1	public	*TreeNode*	getParent ()
	public	void	**insert** (*MutableTreeNode* child, int index)
1	public	boolean	isLeaf ()
	public	void	**remove** (int index)
	public	void	**remove** (*MutableTreeNode* node)
	public	void	**removeFromParent** ()

MutableTreeNode

public.....................void	**setParent** (*MutableTreeNode* newParent)
public.....................void	**setUserObject** (Object object)

NameComponent
org.omg.CosNaming

Object
1.2 ● └NameComponent - *org.omg.CORBA.portable.IDLEntity (java.io.Serializable)*

	public.....................String	**id**
	public.....................String	**kind**
∗	public.........................	**NameComponent** ()
∗	public.........................	**NameComponent** (String __id, String __kind)

NameComponentHelper
org.omg.CosNaming

Object
1.2 └NameComponentHelper

△	public static . NameComponent	**extract** (org.omg.CORBA.Any a)
△	public static ....String	**id** ()
△	public static ....void	**insert** (org.omg.CORBA.Any a, NameComponent that)
△	public static . NameComponent	**read** (org.omg.CORBA.portable.InputStream in)
△	public static synchronized .... org.omg.CORBA.TypeCode	**type** ()
△	public static ....void	**write** (org.omg.CORBA.portable.OutputStream out, NameComponent that)

NameComponentHolder
org.omg.CosNaming

Object
1.2 ● └NameComponentHolder - - - - - - - - - - - - - - - - - - *org.omg.CORBA.portable.Streamable* [1]

1	public.....................void	**_read** (org.omg.CORBA.portable.InputStream in)
1	public......................... ... org.omg.CORBA.TypeCode	**_type** ()
1	public.....................void	**_write** (org.omg.CORBA.portable.OutputStream out)
∗	public.........................	**NameComponentHolder** ()
∗	public.........................	**NameComponentHolder** (NameComponent __arg)
	public........NameComponent	**value**

NamedValue
org.omg.CORBA

Object
1.2 ○ └NamedValue

○	public abstract ....int	**flags** ()
○	public abstract ....String	**name** ()
∗	public.........................	**NamedValue** ()
○	public abstract .... Any	**value** ()

NameHelper
org.omg.CosNaming

Object
1.2 └NameHelper

△	public static .... NameComponent[]	**extract** (org.omg.CORBA.Any a)
△	public static ....String	**id** ()
△	public static ....void	**insert** (org.omg.CORBA.Any a, NameComponent[] that)
△	public static .... NameComponent[]	**read** (org.omg.CORBA.portable.InputStream in)
△	public static synchronized .... org.omg.CORBA.TypeCode	**type** ()
△	public static ....void	**write** (org.omg.CORBA.portable.OutputStream out, NameComponent[] that)

Class   *Interface*   —extends   - - -implements   ○ abstract   ● final   △ static   ▲ static final   ∗ constructor   x x—inherited   x **x**—declared   **x x**—overridden

NameHolder
`org.omg.CosNaming`

Object
1.2 ● └─NameHolder ------------------------- *org.omg.CORBA.portable.Streamable* [1]

1	public.....................void	**_read** (org.omg.CORBA.portable.InputStream in)
1	public..........................	**_type** ()
	... org.omg.CORBA.TypeCode	
1	public.....................void	**_write** (org.omg.CORBA.portable.OutputStream out)
*	public..........................	**NameHolder** ()
*	public..........................	**NameHolder** (NameComponent[] __arg)
	public...... NameComponent[]	**value**

NameValuePair
`org.omg.CORBA`

Object
1.2 ● └─NameValuePair ------------------------- *org.omg.CORBA.portable.IDLEntity* (*java.io.Serializable*)

	public.....................String	**id**
*	public..........................	**NameValuePair** ()
*	public..........................	**NameValuePair** (String __id, Any __value)
	public.....................Any	**value**

N

Naming
`java.rmi`
P°

Object
1.1 ● └─Naming

△	public static ....void	**bind** (String name, *Remote* obj) throws AlreadyBoundException, java.net.MalformedURLException, RemoteException
△	public static ....String[]	**list** (String name) throws RemoteException, java.net.MalformedURLException
△	public static ....*Remote*	**lookup** (String name) throws NotBoundException, java.net.MalformedURLException, RemoteException
△	public static ....void	**rebind** (String name, *Remote* obj) throws RemoteException, java.net.MalformedURLException
△	public static ....void	**unbind** (String name) throws RemoteException, NotBoundException, java.net.MalformedURLException

NamingContext
`org.omg.CosNaming`

1.2 *NamingContext* ─────────────────── *org.omg.CORBA.Object* [1], *org.omg.CORBA.portable.IDLEntity* (*java.io.Serializable*)

1 13 inherited members from org.omg.CORBA.Object not shown

	public.....................void	**bind** (NameComponent[] n, org. omg. CORBA. Object obj) throws org. omg. CosNaming. NamingContextPackage. NotFound, org. omg. CosNaming. NamingContextPackage. CannotProceed, org. omg. CosNaming. NamingContextPackage. InvalidName, org.omg.CosNaming.NamingContextPackage.AlreadyBound
	public.....................void	**bind_context** (NameComponent[] n, *NamingContext* nc) throws org. omg. CosNaming. NamingContextPackage. NotFound, org. omg. CosNaming. NamingContextPackage. CannotProceed, org. omg. CosNaming. NamingContextPackage. InvalidName, org.omg.CosNaming.NamingContextPackage.AlreadyBound
	public.........*NamingContext*	**bind_new_context** (NameComponent[] n) throws org. omg. CosNaming. NamingContextPackage. NotFound, org. omg. CosNaming. NamingContextPackage. AlreadyBound, org. omg. CosNaming. NamingContextPackage. CannotProceed, org.omg.CosNaming.NamingContextPackage.InvalidName
	public.....................void	**destroy** () throws org.omg.CosNaming.NamingContextPackage.NotEmpty
	public.....................void	**list** (int how_many, BindingListHolder bl, BindingIteratorHolder bi)
	public.........*NamingContext*	**new_context** ()
	public.....................void	**rebind** (NameComponent[] n, org. omg. CORBA. Object obj) throws org. omg. CosNaming. NamingContextPackage. NotFound, org. omg. CosNaming. NamingContextPackage. CannotProceed, org.omg.CosNaming.NamingContextPackage.InvalidName

Classes

NamingContext

public	.....................void	**rebind_context** (NameComponent[] n, *NamingContext* nc)
		throws org. omg. CosNaming. NamingContextPackage. NotFound,
		org. omg. CosNaming. NamingContextPackage. CannotProceed,
		org.omg.CosNaming.NamingContextPackage.InvalidName
public	*org.omg.CORBA.Object*	**resolve** (NameComponent[] n) throws org. omg↵
		. CosNaming. NamingContextPackage. NotFound,
		org. omg. CosNaming. NamingContextPackage. CannotProceed,
		org.omg.CosNaming.NamingContextPackage.InvalidName
public	.....................void	**unbind** (NameComponent[] n) throws org. omg↵
		. CosNaming. NamingContextPackage. NotFound,
		org. omg. CosNaming. NamingContextPackage. CannotProceed,
		org.omg.CosNaming.NamingContextPackage.InvalidName

NamingContextHelper　　　　　　　　　　　　　　　org.omg.CosNaming

Object
1.2　└NamingContextHelper

△　public static ... *NamingContext* **extract** (org.omg.CORBA.Any a)
△　public static ....String **id** ()
△　public static ....void **insert** (org.omg.CORBA.Any a, *NamingContext* that)
△　public static ... *NamingContext* **narrow** (*org.omg.CORBA.Object* that) throws org.omg.CORBA.BAD_PARAM
△　public static ... *NamingContext* **read** (org.omg.CORBA.portable.InputStream in)
△　public static synchronized .... **type** ()
　　... org.omg.CORBA.TypeCode
△　public static ....void **write** (org.omg.CORBA.portable.OutputStream out, *NamingContext* that)

NamingContextHolder　　　　　　　　　　　　　　　org.omg.CosNaming

Object
1.2 ●　└NamingContextHolder - - - - - - - - - - - - - - - - - - *org.omg.CORBA.portable.Streamable* [1]

1　public.....................void **_read** (org.omg.CORBA.portable.InputStream in)
1　public............................ **_type** ()
　　... org.omg.CORBA.TypeCode
1　public.....................void **_write** (org.omg.CORBA.portable.OutputStream out)
＊　public........................ **NamingContextHolder** ()
＊　public.......................... **NamingContextHolder** (*NamingContext* __arg)
　　public.......... *NamingContext* **value**

NegativeArraySizeException　　　　　　　　　　　　　　java.lang
P

Object
└Throwable - *java.io.Serializable*
　└Exception
　　└RuntimeException
　　　└NegativeArraySizeException

＊　public......................... **NegativeArraySizeException** ()
＊　public......................... **NegativeArraySizeException** (String s)

NetPermission　　　　　　　　　　　　　　　　　　　java.net
P

Object
1.2 ○　└java.security.Permission [1] - - - - - - - - - - - - - - - *java.security.Guard*, *java.io.Serializable*
1.2 ○　　└java.security.BasicPermission [2] - - - - - - - - - - *java.io.Serializable*
1.2 ●　　　└NetPermission

1　public.....................void checkGuard (Object object) throws SecurityException
2　public.................. boolean equals (Object obj)
2　public.................. String getActions ()
●　1　public final ....String getName ()
2　public.........................int hashCode ()
2　public.................. boolean implies (java.security.Permission p)
＊　public......................... **NetPermission** (String name)
＊　public......................... **NetPermission** (String name, String actions)

Class　*Interface*　—extends　- - -implements　○ abstract　● final　△ static　▲ static final　＊ constructor　x x—inherited　x **x**—declared　**x x**—overridden

```
    2   public..................... java↵ newPermissionCollection ()
        .security.PermissionCollection
    1   public..................... String toString ()
```

NO_IMPLEMENT   org.omg.CORBA

```
        Object
         └Throwable ------------------------------ java.io.Serializable
           └Exception
             └RuntimeException
1.2 ○         └SystemException 1
1.2 ●           └NO_IMPLEMENT
```

```
    1   public........CompletionStatus completed
    1   public.........................int minor
    *   public...........................  NO_IMPLEMENT ()
    *   public...........................  NO_IMPLEMENT (String s)
    *   public...........................  NO_IMPLEMENT (int minor, CompletionStatus completed)
    *   public...........................  NO_IMPLEMENT (String s, int minor, CompletionStatus completed)
    1   public..................... String toString ()
```

NO_MEMORY   org.omg.CORBA

```
        Object
         └Throwable ------------------------------ java.io.Serializable
           └Exception
             └RuntimeException
1.2 ○         └SystemException 1
1.2 ●           └NO_MEMORY
```

```
    1   public........CompletionStatus completed
    1   public.........................int minor
    *   public...........................  NO_MEMORY ()
    *   public...........................  NO_MEMORY (String s)
    *   public...........................  NO_MEMORY (int minor, CompletionStatus completed)
    *   public...........................  NO_MEMORY (String s, int minor, CompletionStatus completed)
    1   public..................... String toString ()
```

NO_PERMISSION   org.omg.CORBA

```
        Object
         └Throwable ------------------------------ java.io.Serializable
           └Exception
             └RuntimeException
1.2 ○         └SystemException 1
1.2 ●           └NO_PERMISSION
```

```
    1   public........CompletionStatus completed
    1   public.........................int minor
    *   public...........................  NO_PERMISSION ()
    *   public...........................  NO_PERMISSION (String s)
    *   public...........................  NO_PERMISSION (int minor, CompletionStatus completed)
    *   public...........................  NO_PERMISSION (String s, int minor, CompletionStatus completed)
    1   public..................... String toString ()
```

NO_RESOURCES   org.omg.CORBA

```
        Object
         └Throwable ------------------------------ java.io.Serializable
           └Exception
             └RuntimeException
1.2 ○         └SystemException 1
1.2 ●           └NO_RESOURCES
```

```
    1   public........CompletionStatus completed
    1   public.........................int minor
    *   public...........................  NO_RESOURCES ()
    *   public...........................  NO_RESOURCES (String s)
    *   public...........................  NO_RESOURCES (int minor, CompletionStatus completed)
```

N

Classes

NO_RESOURCES

*	public	**NO_RESOURCES** (String s, int minor, CompletionStatus completed)
1	public	String toString ()

NO_RESPONSE
org.omg.CORBA

```
Object
 └Throwable ----------------------------- java.io.Serializable
    └Exception
       └RuntimeException
          └SystemException 1
             └NO_RESPONSE
```
1.2 ○
1.2 ●

1	public	CompletionStatus completed
1	public	int minor
*	public	**NO_RESPONSE** ()
*	public	**NO_RESPONSE** (String s)
*	public	**NO_RESPONSE** (int minor, CompletionStatus completed)
*	public	**NO_RESPONSE** (String s, int minor, CompletionStatus completed)
1	public	String toString ()

NoClassDefFoundError
java.lang
P

```
Object
 └Throwable ----------------------------- java.io.Serializable
    └Error
       └LinkageError
          └NoClassDefFoundError
```

*	public	**NoClassDefFoundError** ()
*	public	**NoClassDefFoundError** (String s)

NoninvertibleTransformException
java.awt.geom

```
Object
 └Throwable ----------------------------- java.io.Serializable
    └Exception
       └NoninvertibleTransformException
```
1.2

*	public	**NoninvertibleTransformException** (String s)

NoRouteToHostException
java.net
P

```
Object
 └Throwable ----------------------------- java.io.Serializable
    └Exception
       └java.io.IOException
          └SocketException
             └NoRouteToHostException
```
1.1

*	public	**NoRouteToHostException** ()
*	public	**NoRouteToHostException** (String msg)

NoSuchAlgorithmException
java.security
P^O

```
Object
 └Throwable ----------------------------- java.io.Serializable
    └Exception
       └GeneralSecurityException
          └NoSuchAlgorithmException
```
1.2
1.1

*	public	**NoSuchAlgorithmException** ()
*	public	**NoSuchAlgorithmException** (String msg)

Class *Interface* —extends - - -implements ○ abstract ● final △ static ▲ static final ✳ constructor x x—inherited x **x**—declared **x x**—overridden

NoSuchElementException
java.util

P

```
Object
└ Throwable ------------------------- java.io.Serializable
  └ Exception
    └ RuntimeException
      └ NoSuchElementException
```

✳	public..........................	**NoSuchElementException** ()
✳	public..........................	**NoSuchElementException** (String s)

NoSuchFieldError
java.lang

P

```
Object
└ Throwable ------------------------- java.io.Serializable
  └ Error
    └ LinkageError
      └ IncompatibleClassChangeError
        └ NoSuchFieldError
```

✳	public..........................	**NoSuchFieldError** ()
✳	public..........................	**NoSuchFieldError** (String s)

NoSuchFieldException
java.lang

P

```
Object
└ Throwable ------------------------- java.io.Serializable
  └ Exception
1.1  └ NoSuchFieldException
```

✳	public..........................	**NoSuchFieldException** ()
✳	public..........................	**NoSuchFieldException** (String s)

NoSuchMethodError
java.lang

P

```
Object
└ Throwable ------------------------- java.io.Serializable
  └ Error
    └ LinkageError
      └ IncompatibleClassChangeError
        └ NoSuchMethodError
```

✳	public..........................	**NoSuchMethodError** ()
✳	public..........................	**NoSuchMethodError** (String s)

NoSuchMethodException
java.lang

P

```
Object
└ Throwable ------------------------- java.io.Serializable
  └ Exception
    └ NoSuchMethodException
```

✳	public..........................	**NoSuchMethodException** ()
✳	public..........................	**NoSuchMethodException** (String s)

NoSuchObjectException
java.rmi

P[O]

```
Object
└ Throwable ------------------------- java.io.Serializable
  └ Exception
    └ java.io.IOException
1.1    └ RemoteException [1]
1.1      └ NoSuchObjectException
```

	1	public...............	Throwable	detail
	1	public...................	String	getMessage ()
✳		public..........................	**NoSuchObjectException** (String s)	
	1	public......................void		printStackTrace ()

N

Classes

537

NoSuchObjectException

1	public....................void	printStackTrace	(java.io.PrintStream ps)
1	public....................void	printStackTrace	(java.io.PrintWriter pw)

NoSuchProviderException java.security

P^O

```
Object
 └Throwable -------------------------- java.io.Serializable
    └Exception
       └GeneralSecurityException
          └NoSuchProviderException
```
1.2 GeneralSecurityException
1.1 NoSuchProviderException

✳	public........................	**NoSuchProviderException** ()
✳	public........................	**NoSuchProviderException** (String msg)

NotActiveException java.io

```
Object
 └Throwable -------------------------- Serializable
    └Exception
       └IOException
          └ObjectStreamException
             └NotActiveException
```
1.1 ○ ObjectStreamException
1.1 NotActiveException

✳	public........................	**NotActiveException** ()
✳	public........................	**NotActiveException** (String reason)

NotBoundException java.rmi

P^O

```
Object
 └Throwable -------------------------- java.io.Serializable
    └Exception
       └NotBoundException
```
1.1 NotBoundException

✳	public........................	**NotBoundException** ()
✳	public........................	**NotBoundException** (String s)

NotEmpty org.omg.CosNaming.NamingContextPackage

```
Object
 └Throwable -------------------------- java.io.Serializable
    └Exception
       └org.omg.CORBA.UserException ------- org.omg.CORBA.portable.IDLEntity (java.io.Serializable)
          └NotEmpty ---------------------- org.omg.CORBA.portable.IDLEntity (java.io.Serializable)
```
1.2 ○ org.omg.CORBA.UserException
1.2 ● NotEmpty

✳	public........................	**NotEmpty** ()

NotEmptyHelper org.omg.CosNaming.NamingContextPackage

```
Object
 └NotEmptyHelper
```
1.2 NotEmptyHelper

△	public static .... NotEmpty	**extract** (org.omg.CORBA.Any a)
△	public static ....String	**id** ()
△	public static ....void	**insert** (org.omg.CORBA.Any a, NotEmpty that)
△	public static .... NotEmpty	**read** (org.omg.CORBA.portable.InputStream in)
△	public static synchronized	**type** ()
	... org.omg.CORBA.TypeCode	
△	public static ....void	**write** (org.omg.CORBA.portable.OutputStream out, NotEmpty that)

NotEmptyHolder org.omg.CosNaming.NamingContextPackage

```
Object
 └NotEmptyHolder ---------------------- org.omg.CORBA.portable.Streamable ¹
```
1.2 ● NotEmptyHolder

Class *Interface* —extends - - -implements ○ abstract ● final △ static ▲ static final ✳ constructor x x—inherited x **x**—declared **x x**—overridden

1	public.....................void	**_read** (org.omg.CORBA.portable.InputStream in)	
1	public...........................	**_type** ()	
	... org.omg.CORBA.TypeCode		
1	public.....................void	**_write** (org.omg.CORBA.portable.OutputStream out)	
*	public...........................	**NotEmptyHolder** ()	
*	public...........................	**NotEmptyHolder** (NotEmpty __arg)	
	public............... NotEmpty	**value**	

NotFound · org.omg.CosNaming.NamingContextPackage

```
Object
 └ Throwable - - - - - - - - - - - - - - - - - - - - - - - - - - java.io.Serializable
    └ Exception
```
| 1.2 ○ | └ org.omg.CORBA.UserException - - - - - - org.omg.CORBA.portable.IDLEntity (java.io.Serializable) |
| 1.2 ● | └ NotFound - - - - - - - - - - - - - - - - - - org.omg.CORBA.portable.IDLEntity (java.io.Serializable) |

*	public...........................	**NotFound** ()
*	public...........................	**NotFound** (NotFoundReason __why, org.omg.CosNaming.NameComponent[] __rest_of_name)
	public. org.omg.CosNaming ↵ .NameComponent[]	**rest_of_name**
	public........ NotFoundReason	**why**

NotFoundHelper · org.omg.CosNaming.NamingContextPackage

```
Object
```
| 1.2 | └ NotFoundHelper |

△	public static .... NotFound	**extract** (org.omg.CORBA.Any a)
△	public static .... String	**id** ()
△	public static ....void	**insert** (org.omg.CORBA.Any a, NotFound that)
△	public static .... NotFound	**read** (org.omg.CORBA.portable.InputStream in)
△	public static synchronized .... org.omg.CORBA.TypeCode	**type** ()
△	public static ....void	**write** (org.omg.CORBA.portable.OutputStream out, NotFound that)

NotFoundHolder · org.omg.CosNaming.NamingContextPackage

```
Object
```
| 1.2 ● | └ NotFoundHolder - org.omg.CORBA.portable.Streamable [1] |

1	public.....................void	**_read** (org.omg.CORBA.portable.InputStream in)
1	public...........................	**_type** ()
	... org.omg.CORBA.TypeCode	
1	public.....................void	**_write** (org.omg.CORBA.portable.OutputStream out)
*	public...........................	**NotFoundHolder** ()
*	public...........................	**NotFoundHolder** (NotFound __arg)
	public............... NotFound	**value**

NotFoundReason · org.omg.CosNaming.NamingContextPackage

```
Object
```
| 1.2 ● | └ NotFoundReason - org.omg.CORBA.portable.IDLEntity (java.io.Serializable) |

▲	public static final.............int	**_missing_node** = 0
▲	public static final.............int	**_not_context** = 1
▲	public static final.............int	**_not_object** = 2
▲	public static final............... .... NotFoundReason	**from_int** (int i) throws org.omg.CORBA.BAD_PARAM
▲	public static final............... .... NotFoundReason	**missing_node**
▲	public static final............... .... NotFoundReason	**not_context**
▲	public static final............... .... NotFoundReason	**not_object**
	public.....................int	**value** ()

	NotFoundReasonHelper	org.omg.CosNaming.NamingContextPackage

	Object	
1.2	└NotFoundReasonHelper	

△	public static . NotFoundReason	**extract** (org.omg.CORBA.Any a)
△	public static .... String	**id** ()
△	public static .... void	**insert** (org.omg.CORBA.Any a, NotFoundReason that)
△	public static . NotFoundReason	**read** (org.omg.CORBA.portable.InputStream in)
△	public static synchronized	**type** ()
	... org.omg.CORBA.TypeCode	
△	public static .... void	**write** (org.omg.CORBA.portable.OutputStream out, NotFoundReason that)

	NotFoundReasonHolder	org.omg.CosNaming.NamingContextPackage

	Object	
1.2 ●	└NotFoundReasonHolder - - - - - - - - - - - - - - - - *org.omg.CORBA.portable.Streamable* [1]	

1	public...................... void	**_read** (org.omg.CORBA.portable.InputStream in)
1	public..........................	**_type** ()
	... org.omg.CORBA.TypeCode	
1	public...................... void	**_write** (org.omg.CORBA.portable.OutputStream out)
*	public...........................	**NotFoundReasonHolder** ()
*	public...........................	**NotFoundReasonHolder** (NotFoundReason __arg)
	public........ NotFoundReason	**value**

	NotOwnerException	java.security.acl
		P[u]

	Object	
	└Throwable - *java.io.Serializable*	
	└Exception	
1.1	└NotOwnerException	

*	public...........................	**NotOwnerException** ()

	NotSerializableException	java.io

	Object	
	└Throwable - *Serializable*	
	└Exception	
	└IOException	
1.1 ○	└ObjectStreamException	
1.1	└NotSerializableException	

*	public...........................	**NotSerializableException** ()
*	public...........................	**NotSerializableException** (String classname)

	NullPointerException	java.lang
		P

	Object	
	└Throwable - *java.io.Serializable*	
	└Exception	
	└RuntimeException	
	└NullPointerException	

*	public...........................	**NullPointerException** ()
*	public...........................	**NullPointerException** (String s)

	Number	java.lang
		P

	Object	
○	└Number - *java.io.Serializable*	

1.1	public...................... byte	**byteValue** ()
○	public abstract ....double	**doubleValue** ()
○	public abstract ....float	**floatValue** ()

Class *Interface* —extends - - -implements ○ abstract ● final △ static ▲ static final ✳ constructor x x—inherited x **x**—declared **x x**—overridden

○	public abstract . . . . int	**intValue** ()	
○	public abstract . . . . long	**longValue** ()	
∗	public	**Number** ()	
1.1	public . . . . short	**shortValue** ()	

NumberFormat java.text

P

Object [1]
└ Format [2] - *java.io.Serializable, Cloneable*
   └ NumberFormat

	2	public . . . . **Object**	**clone** ()	
	1	public . . . . **boolean**	**equals** (Object obj)	
●		public final . . . . String	**format** (double number)	
●	2	public final . . . . String	format (Object obj)	
●		public final . . . . String	**format** (long number)	
○		public abstract . . . . StringBuffer	**format** (double number, StringBuffer toAppendTo, FieldPosition pos)	
●	2	public final . . . . **StringBuffer**	**format** (Object number, StringBuffer toAppendTo, FieldPosition pos)	
○		public abstract . . . . StringBuffer	**format** (long number, StringBuffer toAppendTo, FieldPosition pos)	
▲		public static final . . . . int	**FRACTION_FIELD** = 1	
△		public static . . java.util.Locale[]	**getAvailableLocales** ()	
▲		public static final . . . . NumberFormat	**getCurrencyInstance** ()	
△		public static . . . . NumberFormat	**getCurrencyInstance** (java.util.Locale inLocale)	
▲		public static final . . . . NumberFormat	**getInstance** ()	
△		public static . . . . NumberFormat	**getInstance** (java.util.Locale inLocale)	
		public . . . . int	**getMaximumFractionDigits** ()	
		public . . . . int	**getMaximumIntegerDigits** ()	
		public . . . . int	**getMinimumFractionDigits** ()	
		public . . . . int	**getMinimumIntegerDigits** ()	
▲		public static final . . . . NumberFormat	**getNumberInstance** ()	
△		public static . . . . NumberFormat	**getNumberInstance** (java.util.Locale inLocale)	
▲		public static final . . . . NumberFormat	**getPercentInstance** ()	
△		public static . . . . NumberFormat	**getPercentInstance** (java.util.Locale inLocale)	
	1	public . . . . **int**	**hashCode** ()	
▲		public static final . . . . int	**INTEGER_FIELD** = 0	
		public . . . . boolean	**isGroupingUsed** ()	
		public . . . . boolean	**isParseIntegerOnly** ()	
∗		public	**NumberFormat** ()	
		public . . . . Number	**parse** (String text) throws ParseException	
○		public abstract . . . . Number	**parse** (String text, ParsePosition parsePosition)	
	2	public . . . . Object	parseObject (String source) throws ParseException	
●	2	public final . . . . **Object**	**parseObject** (String source, ParsePosition parsePosition)	
		public . . . . void	**setGroupingUsed** (boolean newValue)	
		public . . . . void	**setMaximumFractionDigits** (int newValue)	
		public . . . . void	**setMaximumIntegerDigits** (int newValue)	
		public . . . . void	**setMinimumFractionDigits** (int newValue)	
		public . . . . void	**setMinimumIntegerDigits** (int newValue)	
		public . . . . void	**setParseIntegerOnly** (boolean value)	

NumberFormatException java.lang

P

Object
└ Throwable - *java.io.Serializable*
  └ Exception
    └ RuntimeException
      └ IllegalArgumentException
        └ NumberFormatException

∗	public	**NumberFormatException** ()	
∗	public	**NumberFormatException** (String s)	

NVList org.omg.CORBA

Object
└ NVList

1.2 ○	

N

Classes

NVList

○	public abstract ... NamedValue	**add** (int flags)	
○	public abstract ... NamedValue	**add_item** (String item_name, int flags)	
○	public abstract ... NamedValue	**add_value** (String item_name, Any val, int flags)	
○	public abstract .... int	**count** ()	
○	public abstract ... NamedValue	**item** (int index) throws Bounds	
✳	public...........................	**NVList** ()	
○	public abstract .... void	**remove** (int index) throws Bounds	

OBJ_ADAPTER — org.omg.CORBA

```
Object
└ Throwable - - - - - - - - - - - - - - - - - - - - - - - - - - - java.io.Serializable
   └ Exception
      └ RuntimeException
         └ SystemException 1
            └ OBJ_ADAPTER
```
1.2 ○ SystemException [1]
1.2 ● OBJ_ADAPTER

1	public........CompletionStatus	completed	
1	public........................int	minor	
✳	public...........................	**OBJ_ADAPTER** ()	
✳	public...........................	**OBJ_ADAPTER** (String s)	
✳	public...........................	**OBJ_ADAPTER** (int minor, CompletionStatus completed)	
✳	public...........................	**OBJ_ADAPTER** (String s, int minor, CompletionStatus completed)	
1	public......................String	toString ()	

Object ❶ — org.omg.CORBA

1.2 *Object*

public................. Request	**_create_request** (Context ctx, String operation, NVList arg_list, NamedValue result)	
public................. Request	**_create_request** (Context ctx, String operation, NVList arg_list, NamedValue result, ExceptionList exclist, ContextList ctxlist)	
public..................... Object	**_duplicate** ()	
public....... DomainManager[]	**_get_domain_managers** ()	
public..................... Object	**_get_interface_def** ()	
public......................Policy	**_get_policy** (int policy_type)	
public.........................int	**_hash** (int maximum)	
public.................. boolean	**_is_a** (String repositoryIdentifier)	
public.................. boolean	**_is_equivalent** (Object other)	
public.................. boolean	**_non_existent** ()	
public......................void	**_release** ()	
public................. Request	**_request** (String operation)	
public..................... Object	**_set_policy_override** (Policy[] policies, SetOverrideType set_add)	

Object ❷ — java.lang

P

Object

	protected native .... Object	**clone** () throws CloneNotSupportedException
	public.................. boolean	**equals** (Object obj)
	protected ....void	**finalize** () throws Throwable
●	public final native .... Class	**getClass** ()
	public native ....int	**hashCode** ()
●	public final native ....void	**notify** ()
●	public final native ....void	**notifyAll** ()
✳	public...........................	**Object** ()
	public.....................String	**toString** ()
●	public final ....void	**wait** () throws InterruptedException
●	public final native ....void	**wait** (long timeout) throws InterruptedException
●	public final ....void	**wait** (long timeout, int nanos) throws InterruptedException

---

Class *Interface* —extends - - -implements ○ abstract ● final △ static ▲ static final ✳ constructor x x—inherited x **x**—declared **x x**—overridden

OBJECT_NOT_EXIST

org.omg.CORBA

```
Object
└ Throwable - - - - - - - - - - - - - - - - - - - - - - - - - - java.io.Serializable
     └ Exception
          └ RuntimeException
1.2 ○            └ SystemException 1
1.2 ●                 └ OBJECT_NOT_EXIST
```

1	public	CompletionStatus	completed
1	public	int	minor
*	public		**OBJECT_NOT_EXIST** ()
*	public		**OBJECT_NOT_EXIST** (String s)
*	public		**OBJECT_NOT_EXIST** (int minor, CompletionStatus completed)
*	public		**OBJECT_NOT_EXIST** (String s, int minor, CompletionStatus completed)
1	public	String	toString ()

ObjectHolder

org.omg.CORBA

```
Object
1.2 ● └ ObjectHolder - - - - - - - - - - - - - - - - - - - - - - - org.omg.CORBA.portable.Streamable 1
```

1	public	void	**_read** (org.omg.CORBA.portable.InputStream input)
1	public	TypeCode	**_type** ()
1	public	void	**_write** (org.omg.CORBA.portable.OutputStream output)
*	public		**ObjectHolder** ()
*	public		**ObjectHolder** (*Object* initial)
	public	*Object*	**value**

O

ObjectImpl

org.omg.CORBA.portable

```
Object 1
1.2 ○ └ ObjectImpl - - - - - - - - - - - - - - - - - - - - - - - - org.omg.CORBA.Object 2
```

2	public ...... org.omg.CORBA.Request		**_create_request** (org.omg. CORBA. Context ctx, String operation, org.omg.CORBA.NVList arg_list, org.omg.CORBA.NamedValue result)
2	public ...... org.omg.CORBA.Request		**_create_request** (org.omg. CORBA. Context ctx, String operation, org.omg.CORBA.NVList arg_list, org.omg.CORBA.NamedValue result, org ↵ .omg.CORBA.ExceptionList exceptions, org.omg.CORBA.ContextList contexts)
2	public org.omg.CORBA.Object		**_duplicate** ()
	public Delegate		**_get_delegate** ()
2	public ...... org.omg ↵ .CORBA.DomainManager[]		**_get_domain_managers** ()
2	public org.omg.CORBA.Object		**_get_interface_def** ()
2	public . org.omg.CORBA.Policy		**_get_policy** (int policy_type)
2	public ...... int		**_hash** (int maximum)
○	public abstract ...... String[]		**_ids** ()
	public ...... InputStream		**_invoke** (OutputStream output) throws ApplicationException, RemarshalException
2	public ...... boolean		**_is_a** (String repository_id)
2	public ...... boolean		**_is_equivalent** (*org.omg.CORBA.Object* that)
	public ...... boolean		**_is_local** ()
2	public ...... boolean		**_non_existent** ()
	public ... org.omg.CORBA.ORB		**_orb** ()
2	public ...... void		**_release** ()
	public ...... void		**_releaseReply** (InputStream input)
2	public ...... org.omg.CORBA.Request		**_request** (String operation)
	public ...... OutputStream		**_request** (String operation, boolean responseExpected)
	public ...... void		**_servant_postinvoke** (ServantObject servant)
	public ...... ServantObject		**_servant_preinvoke** (String operation, Class expectedType)
	public ...... void		**_set_delegate** (Delegate delegate)
2	public org.omg.CORBA.Object		**_set_policy_override** (*org. omg. CORBA. Policy[]* policies, org.omg.CORBA.SetOverrideType set_add)
1	public ...... **boolean**		**equals** (Object obj)
1	public ...... **int**		**hashCode** ()
*	public		**ObjectImpl** ()
1	public ...... **String**		**toString** ()

Classes

ObjectInput — java.io

1.1	*ObjectInput* ——————————————————— *DataInput* [1]

```
     public.....................int  available () throws IOException
     public....................void  close () throws IOException
     public.....................int  read () throws IOException
     public.....................int  read (byte[] b) throws IOException
     public.....................int  read (byte[] b, int off, int len) throws IOException
  1  public.................boolean  readBoolean () throws IOException
  1  public....................byte  readByte () throws IOException
  1  public....................char  readChar () throws IOException
  1  public..................double  readDouble () throws IOException
  1  public...................float  readFloat () throws IOException
  1  public....................void  readFully (byte[] b) throws IOException
  1  public....................void  readFully (byte[] b, int off, int len) throws IOException
  1  public.....................int  readInt () throws IOException
  1  public..................String  readLine () throws IOException
  1  public....................long  readLong () throws IOException
     public..................Object  readObject () throws ClassNotFoundException, IOException
  1  public...................short  readShort () throws IOException
  1  public.....................int  readUnsignedByte () throws IOException
  1  public.....................int  readUnsignedShort () throws IOException
  1  public..................String  readUTF () throws IOException
     public....................long  skip (long n) throws IOException
  1  public.....................int  skipBytes (int n) throws IOException
```

O

ObjectInputStream — java.io

```
       Object
  O    └─InputStream [1]
1.1       └─ObjectInputStream - - - - - - - - - - - - - - - - - - - ObjectInput [2] (DataInput [3]), ObjectStreamConstants
```

```
  1    public.....................int  available () throws IOException
  1    public....................void  close () throws IOException
       public....................void  defaultReadObject () throws IOException, ClassNotFoundException,
                                         NotActiveException
       protected ..............boolean  enableResolveObject (boolean enable) throws SecurityException
  1    public synchronized .......void  mark (int readlimit)
  1    public..................boolean  markSupported ()
1.2 *  protected ....................  ObjectInputStream () throws IOException, SecurityException
    *  public........................  ObjectInputStream (InputStream in) throws IOException,
                                         StreamCorruptedException
  1    public.....................int  read () throws IOException
  1    public.....................int  read (byte[] b) throws IOException
  1    public.....................int  read (byte[] b, int off, int len) throws IOException
  3    public.................boolean  readBoolean () throws IOException
  3    public....................byte  readByte () throws IOException
  3    public....................char  readChar () throws IOException
  3    public..................double  readDouble () throws IOException
1.2    public........................  readFields () throws IOException, ClassNotFoundException, NotActiveException
       ... ObjectInputStream.GetField
  3    public...................float  readFloat () throws IOException
  3    public....................void  readFully (byte[] data) throws IOException
  3    public....................void  readFully (byte[] data, int offset, int size) throws IOException
  3    public.....................int  readInt () throws IOException
D 3    public..................String  readLine () throws IOException
  3    public....................long  readLong () throws IOException
● 2    public final ...........Object  readObject () throws OptionalDataException, ClassNotFoundException,
                                         IOException
1.2    protected ..............Object  readObjectOverride () throws OptionalDataException, ClassNotFoundException,
                                         IOException
  3    public...................short  readShort () throws IOException
       protected ...............void  readStreamHeader () throws IOException, StreamCorruptedException
  3    public.....................int  readUnsignedByte () throws IOException
  3    public.....................int  readUnsignedShort () throws IOException
  3    public..................String  readUTF () throws IOException
       public synchronized ......void  registerValidation (ObjectInputValidation obj, int prio)
                                         throws NotActiveException, InvalidObjectException
  1    public synchronized ......void  reset () throws IOException
       protected ...............Class  resolveClass (ObjectStreamClass v) throws IOException, ClassNotFoundException
```

Class *Interface* —extends - - -implements ○ abstract ● final △ static ▲ static final ✳ constructor x x—inherited x **x**—declared **x x**—overridden

	protected	.... Object	**resolveObject** (Object obj) throws IOException
1	public	.... long	skip (long n) throws IOException
3	public	.... int	**skipBytes** (int len) throws IOException

---

ObjectInputStream.GetField

Object
1.2 ○ └─ObjectInputStream.GetField

○	public abstract	.... boolean	**defaulted** (String name) throws IOException, IllegalArgumentException
○	public abstract	.... long	**get** (String name, long defvalue) throws IOException, IllegalArgumentException
○	public abstract	.... byte	**get** (String name, byte defvalue) throws IOException, IllegalArgumentException
○	public abstract	.... char	**get** (String name, char defvalue) throws IOException, IllegalArgumentException
○	public abstract	........double	**get** (String name, double defvalue) throws IOException, IllegalArgumentException
○	public abstract	........Object	**get** (String name, Object defvalue) throws IOException, IllegalArgumentException
○	public abstract	.............int	**get** (String name, int defvalue) throws IOException, IllegalArgumentException
○	public abstract	...........short	**get** (String name, short defvalue) throws IOException, IllegalArgumentException
○	public abstract	.... boolean	**get** (String name, boolean defvalue) throws IOException, IllegalArgumentException
○	public abstract	...........float	**get** (String name, float defvalue) throws IOException, IllegalArgumentException
*	public	....	**GetField** ()
○	public abstract	....	**getObjectStreamClass** ()
	.... ObjectStreamClass		

ObjectInputValidation

1.1 *ObjectInputValidation*

| | public | ....void | **validateObject** () throws InvalidObjectException |

ObjectOutput

1.1 *ObjectOutput*————————————————— *DataOutput [1]*

	public	....................void	**close** () throws IOException
	public	....................void	**flush** () throws IOException
1	public	....................**void**	**write** (byte[] b) throws IOException
1	public	....................**void**	**write** (int b) throws IOException
1	public	....................**void**	**write** (byte[] b, int off, int len) throws IOException
1	public	....................void	writeBoolean (boolean v) throws IOException
1	public	....................void	writeByte (int v) throws IOException
1	public	....................void	writeBytes (String s) throws IOException
1	public	....................void	writeChar (int v) throws IOException
1	public	....................void	writeChars (String s) throws IOException
1	public	....................void	writeDouble (double v) throws IOException
1	public	....................void	writeFloat (float v) throws IOException
1	public	....................void	writeInt (int v) throws IOException
1	public	....................void	writeLong (long v) throws IOException
	public	....................void	**writeObject** (Object obj) throws IOException
1	public	....................void	writeShort (int v) throws IOException
1	public	....................void	writeUTF (String str) throws IOException

---

ObjectOutputStream

Object
○ └─OutputStream [1]
1.1 └─ObjectOutputStream - - - - - - - - - - - - - - - - - *ObjectOutput [2] (DataOutput [3]), ObjectStreamConstants*

	protected	...................void	**annotateClass** (Class cl) throws IOException
1	public	....................**void**	**close** () throws IOException
	public	....................void	**defaultWriteObject** () throws IOException
	protected	...................void	**drain** () throws IOException
	protected	.... boolean	**enableReplaceObject** (boolean enable) throws SecurityException
1	public	....................**void**	**flush** () throws IOException
1.2 *	protected	....	**ObjectOutputStream** () throws IOException, SecurityException
*	public	....	**ObjectOutputStream** (OutputStream out) throws IOException
1.2	public	....	**putFields** () throws IOException
	..ObjectOutputStream.PutField		
	protected	.... Object	**replaceObject** (Object obj) throws IOException
	public	...................void	**reset** () throws IOException
1.2	public	...................void	**useProtocolVersion** (int version) throws IOException

O

Classes

ObjectOutputStream

	1	public	**void**	**write**	(byte[] b) throws IOException
	1	public	**void**	**write**	(int data) throws IOException
	1	public	**void**	**write**	(byte[] b, int off, int len) throws IOException
	3	public	void	**writeBoolean**	(boolean data) throws IOException
	3	public	void	**writeByte**	(int data) throws IOException
	3	public	void	**writeBytes**	(String data) throws IOException
	3	public	void	**writeChar**	(int data) throws IOException
	3	public	void	**writeChars**	(String data) throws IOException
	3	public	void	**writeDouble**	(double data) throws IOException
1.2		public	void	**writeFields**	() throws IOException
	3	public	void	**writeFloat**	(float data) throws IOException
	3	public	void	**writeInt**	(int data) throws IOException
	3	public	void	**writeLong**	(long data) throws IOException
●	2	public final	void	**writeObject**	(Object obj) throws IOException
1.2		protected	void	**writeObjectOverride**	(Object obj) throws IOException
	3	public	void	**writeShort**	(int data) throws IOException
		protected	void	**writeStreamHeader**	() throws IOException
	3	public	void	**writeUTF**	(String data) throws IOException

ObjectOutputStream.PutField
java.io

Object
   └ObjectOutputStream.PutField   1.2 ○

○	public abstract	void	**put**	(String name, boolean value)
○	public abstract	void	**put**	(String name, byte value)
○	public abstract	void	**put**	(String name, char value)
○	public abstract	void	**put**	(String name, short value)
○	public abstract	void	**put**	(String name, long value)
○	public abstract	void	**put**	(String name, float value)
○	public abstract	void	**put**	(String name, int value)
○	public abstract	void	**put**	(String name, double value)
○	public abstract	void	**put**	(String name, Object value)
✳	public		**PutField**	()
○	public abstract	void	**write**	(*ObjectOutput* out) throws IOException

ObjectStreamClass
java.io

Object [1]
   └ObjectStreamClass ---------------------- *Serializable*   1.1

	public	Class	**forClass**	()
1.2	public	ObjectStreamField	**getField**	(String name)
1.2	public	ObjectStreamField[]	**getFields**	()
	public	String	**getName**	()
	public	long	**getSerialVersionUID**	()
△	public static	ObjectStreamClass	**lookup**	(Class cl)
1.2 ▲	public static final	ObjectStreamField[]	**NO_FIELDS**	
	1 public	String	**toString**	()

ObjectStreamConstants
java.io

ObjectStreamConstants   1.2

▲	public static final	int	**baseWireHandle**	= 8257536
▲	public static final	int	**PROTOCOL_VERSION_1**	= 1
▲	public static final	int	**PROTOCOL_VERSION_2**	= 2
▲	public static final	byte	**SC_BLOCK_DATA**	= 8
▲	public static final	byte	**SC_EXTERNALIZABLE**	= 4
▲	public static final	byte	**SC_SERIALIZABLE**	= 2
▲	public static final	byte	**SC_WRITE_METHOD**	= 1
▲	public static final	short	**STREAM_MAGIC**	= -21267
▲	public static final	short	**STREAM_VERSION**	= 5
▲	public static final SerializablePermission		**SUBCLASS_IMPLEMENTATION_PERMISSION**	
▲	public static final SerializablePermission		**SUBSTITUTION_PERMISSION**	

Class   *Interface*   —extends   - - -implements   ○ abstract   ● final   △ static   ▲ static final   ✳ constructor   x x—inherited   x **x**—declared   **x x**—overridden

▲ public static final .... byte **TC_ARRAY** = 117
▲ public static final .... byte **TC_BASE** = 112
▲ public static final .... byte **TC_BLOCKDATA** = 119
▲ public static final .... byte **TC_BLOCKDATALONG** = 122
▲ public static final .... byte **TC_CLASS** = 118
▲ public static final .... byte **TC_CLASSDESC** = 114
▲ public static final .... byte **TC_ENDBLOCKDATA** = 120
▲ public static final .... byte **TC_EXCEPTION** = 123
▲ public static final .... byte **TC_MAX** = 123
▲ public static final .... byte **TC_NULL** = 112
▲ public static final .... byte **TC_OBJECT** = 115
▲ public static final .... byte **TC_REFERENCE** = 113
▲ public static final .... byte **TC_RESET** = 121
▲ public static final .... byte **TC_STRING** = 116

ObjectStreamException
java.io

Object
└Throwable -------------------------- *Serializable*
　　└Exception
　　　└IOException
1.1 ○　　　└ObjectStreamException

* protected .... **ObjectStreamException** ()
* protected .... **ObjectStreamException** (String classname)

O

ObjectStreamField
java.io

Object[1]
1.2 └ObjectStreamField -------------------- *Comparable*[2]

2 public......................int **compareTo** (Object o)
　public....................String **getName** ()
　public........................int **getOffset** ()
　public.....................Class **getType** ()
　public......................char **getTypeCode** ()
　public....................String **getTypeString** ()
　public...................boolean **isPrimitive** ()
* public......................... **ObjectStreamField** (String n, Class clazz)
　protected..................void **setOffset** (int offset)
1 public..................String **toString** ()

ObjectView
javax.swing.text.html

Object
1.2 ○ └javax.swing.text.View[1] ------------------- *javax.swing.SwingConstants*
1.2 　　└javax.swing.text.ComponentView[2]
1.2 　　　└ObjectView

1 *30 inherited members from javax.swing.text.View not shown*
2 protected .... **createComponent** ()
　　.......... **java.awt.Component**
2 public......................float getAlignment (int axis)
● 2 public final .... getComponent ()
　　.......... java.awt.Component
2 public......................float getMaximumSpan (int axis)
2 public......................float getMinimumSpan (int axis)
2 public......................float getPreferredSpan (int axis)
2 public.......... *java.awt.Shape* modelToView (int pos, *java.awt.Shape* a, javax.swing.text.Position.Bias b)
　　　　　　　　throws javax.swing.text.BadLocationException
* public......................... **ObjectView** (*javax.swing.text.Element* elem)
2 public......................void paint (java.awt.Graphics g, *java.awt.Shape* a)
2 public......................void setParent (javax.swing.text.View p)
2 public......................void setSize (float width, float height)
2 public........................int viewToModel (float x, float y, *java.awt.Shape* a, javax.swing.text.Position.Bias[] bias)

Classes

ObjID · java.rmi.server

P⁰

```
Object¹
  └ObjID - - - - - - - - - - - - - - - - - - - - - - - - - - - - - java.io.Serializable
```

1.1 ●			
1.2 ▲	public static final .... int	**ACTIVATOR_ID** = 1
▲	public static final .... int	**DGC_ID** = 2
1	public .... **boolean**	**equals** (Object obj)
1	public .... **int**	**hashCode** ()
✳	public	**ObjID** ()
✳	public	**ObjID** (int num)
△	public static .... ObjID	**read** (*java.io.ObjectInput* in) throws java.io.IOException
▲	public static final .... int	**REGISTRY_ID** = 0
1	public .... **String**	**toString** ()
	public .... void	**write** (*java.io.ObjectOutput* out) throws java.io.IOException

Observable · java.util

P

```
Object
  └Observable
```

	public synchronized .... void	**addObserver** (*Observer* o)
	protected synchronized ... void	**clearChanged** ()
	public synchronized .... int	**countObservers** ()
	public synchronized .... void	**deleteObserver** (*Observer* o)
	public synchronized .... void	**deleteObservers** ()
	public synchronized .. boolean	**hasChanged** ()
	public .... void	**notifyObservers** ()
	public .... void	**notifyObservers** (Object arg)
✳	public	**Observable** ()
	protected synchronized ... void	**setChanged** ()

Observer · java.util

P

```
Observer
```

public .... void	**update** (Observable o, Object arg)

OpenType · java.awt.font

1.2	*OpenType*	
	public .... byte[]	**getFontTable** (int sfntTag)
	public .... byte[]	**getFontTable** (String strSfntTag)
	public .... byte[]	**getFontTable** (int sfntTag, int offset, int count)
	public .... byte[]	**getFontTable** (String strSfntTag, int offset, int count)
	public .... int	**getFontTableSize** (int sfntTag)
	public .... int	**getFontTableSize** (String strSfntTag)
	public .... int	**getVersion** ()
▲	public static final .... int	**TAG_ACNT** = 1633906292
▲	public static final .... int	**TAG_AVAR** = 1635148146
▲	public static final .... int	**TAG_BASE** = 1111577413
▲	public static final .... int	**TAG_BDAT** = 1650745716
▲	public static final .... int	**TAG_BLOC** = 1651273571
▲	public static final .... int	**TAG_BSLN** = 1651731566
▲	public static final .... int	**TAG_CFF** = 1128678944
▲	public static final .... int	**TAG_CMAP** = 1668112752
▲	public static final .... int	**TAG_CVAR** = 1668702578
▲	public static final .... int	**TAG_CVT** = 1668707360
▲	public static final .... int	**TAG_DSIG** = 1146308935
▲	public static final .... int	**TAG_EBDT** = 1161970772
▲	public static final .... int	**TAG_EBLC** = 1161972803
▲	public static final .... int	**TAG_EBSC** = 1161974595
▲	public static final .... int	**TAG_FDSC** = 1717859171
▲	public static final .... int	**TAG_FEAT** = 1717920116
▲	public static final .... int	**TAG_FMTX** = 1718449272
▲	public static final .... int	**TAG_FPGM** = 1718642541
▲	public static final .... int	**TAG_FVAR** = 1719034226
▲	public static final .... int	**TAG_GASP** = 1734439792

Class   *Interface*   —extends   - - -implements   ○ abstract   ● final   △ static   ▲ static final   ✳ constructor   x x—inherited   x **x**—declared   **x x**—overridden

▲	public static final.............int	**TAG_GDEF**	= 1195656518
▲	public static final.............int	**TAG_GLYF**	= 1735162214
▲	public static final.............int	**TAG_GPOS**	= 1196445523
▲	public static final.............int	**TAG_GSUB**	= 1196643650
▲	public static final.............int	**TAG_GVAR**	= 1735811442
▲	public static final.............int	**TAG_HDMX**	= 1751412088
▲	public static final.............int	**TAG_HEAD**	= 1751474532
▲	public static final.............int	**TAG_HHEA**	= 1751672161
▲	public static final.............int	**TAG_HMTX**	= 1752003704
▲	public static final.............int	**TAG_JSTF**	= 1246975046
▲	public static final.............int	**TAG_JUST**	= 1786082164
▲	public static final.............int	**TAG_KERN**	= 1801810542
▲	public static final.............int	**TAG_LCAR**	= 1818452338
▲	public static final.............int	**TAG_LOCA**	= 1819239265
▲	public static final.............int	**TAG_LTSH**	= 1280594760
▲	public static final.............int	**TAG_MAXP**	= 1835104368
▲	public static final.............int	**TAG_MMFX**	= 1296909912
▲	public static final.............int	**TAG_MMSD**	= 1296913220
▲	public static final.............int	**TAG_MORT**	= 1836020340
▲	public static final.............int	**TAG_NAME**	= 1851878757
▲	public static final.............int	**TAG_OPBD**	= 1836020340
▲	public static final.............int	**TAG_OS2**	= 1330851634
▲	public static final.............int	**TAG_PCLT**	= 1346587732
▲	public static final.............int	**TAG_POST**	= 1886352244
▲	public static final.............int	**TAG_PREP**	= 1886545264
▲	public static final.............int	**TAG_PROP**	= 1886547824
▲	public static final.............int	**TAG_TRAK**	= 1953653099
▲	public static final.............int	**TAG_TYP1**	= 1954115633
▲	public static final.............int	**TAG_VDMX**	= 1447316824
▲	public static final.............int	**TAG_VHEA**	= 1986553185
▲	public static final.............int	**TAG_VMTX**	= 1986884728

O

Operation

java.rmi.server

P^O

Object[1]
1.1 └Operation

D		public....................String	**getOperation** ()
D	∗	public..........................	**Operation** (String op)
D	1	public.................. **String**	**toString** ()

Option

javax.swing.text.html

Object[1]
1.2 └Option

	public...........................	**getAttributes** ()
	...*javax.swing.text.AttributeSet*	
	public....................String	**getLabel** ()
	public....................String	**getValue** ()
	public.................... boolean	**isSelected** ()
∗	public..........................	**Option** (*javax.swing.text.AttributeSet* attr)
	public.....................void	**setLabel** (String label)
	protected...................void	**setSelection** (boolean state)
1	public.................. **String**	**toString** ()

OptionalDataException

java.io

Object
└Throwable - *Serializable*
  └Exception
    └IOException
1.1 ○   └ObjectStreamException
1.1   └OptionalDataException

public................. boolean	**eof**
public.......................int	**length**

Classes

OptionPaneUI

```
        Object
1.2 ○   └ ComponentUI 1
1.2 ○       └ OptionPaneUI
```

	1	*11 inherited members from ComponentUI not shown*	
○	public abstract .... boolean	**containsCustomComponents** (javax.swing.JOptionPane op)
✱	public	**OptionPaneUI** ()
○	public abstract .... void	**selectInitialValue** (javax.swing.JOptionPane op)

```
        Object
1.2 ○   └ ORB
```

	public .... void	**connect** (*Object* obj)
	public .... TypeCode	**create_abstract_interface_tc** (String id, String name)
○	public abstract ...... TypeCode	**create_alias_tc** (String id, String name, TypeCode original_type)
○	public abstract .... Any	**create_any** ()
○	public abstract ...... TypeCode	**create_array_tc** (int length, TypeCode element_type)
	public .... *DynAny*	**create_basic_dyn_any** (TypeCode type) throws org.omg.CORBA.ORBPackage ↵ .InconsistentTypeCode
○	public abstract ..... ContextList	**create_context_list** ()
	public .... *DynAny*	**create_dyn_any** (Any value)
	public .... *DynArray*	**create_dyn_array** (TypeCode type) throws org.omg.CORBA.ORBPackage ↵ .InconsistentTypeCode
	public .... *DynEnum*	**create_dyn_enum** (TypeCode type) throws org.omg.CORBA.ORBPackage ↵ .InconsistentTypeCode
	public .... *DynSequence*	**create_dyn_sequence** (TypeCode type) throws org.omg.CORBA.ORBPackage ↵ .InconsistentTypeCode
	public .... *DynStruct*	**create_dyn_struct** (TypeCode type) throws org.omg.CORBA.ORBPackage ↵ .InconsistentTypeCode
	public .... *DynUnion*	**create_dyn_union** (TypeCode type) throws org.omg.CORBA.ORBPackage ↵ .InconsistentTypeCode
○	public abstract ...... TypeCode	**create_enum_tc** (String id, String name, String[] members)
○	public abstract ... Environment	**create_environment** ()
○	public abstract .. ExceptionList	**create_exception_list** ()
○	public abstract ...... TypeCode	**create_exception_tc** (String id, String name, StructMember[] members)
	public .... TypeCode	**create_fixed_tc** (short digits, short scale)
○	public abstract ...... TypeCode	**create_interface_tc** (String id, String name)
○	public abstract .... NVList	**create_list** (int count)
○	public abstract ... NamedValue	**create_named_value** (String s, Any any, int flags)
	public .... TypeCode	**create_native_tc** (String id, String name)
	public .... NVList	**create_operation_list** (*Object* oper)
○	public abstract .... org.omg.CORBA ↵ .portable.OutputStream	**create_output_stream** ()
	public .... *Policy*	**create_policy** (int type, Any val) throws PolicyError
D ○	public abstract ...... TypeCode	**create_recursive_sequence_tc** (int bound, int offset)
	public .... TypeCode	**create_recursive_tc** (String id)
○	public abstract ...... TypeCode	**create_sequence_tc** (int bound, TypeCode element_type)
○	public abstract ...... TypeCode	**create_string_tc** (int bound)
○	public abstract ...... TypeCode	**create_struct_tc** (String id, String name, StructMember[] members)
○	public abstract ...... TypeCode	**create_union_tc** (String id, String name, TypeCode discriminator_type, UnionMember[] members)
	public .... TypeCode	**create_value_box_tc** (String id, String name, TypeCode boxed_type)
	public .... TypeCode	**create_value_tc** (String id, String name, short type_modifier, TypeCode concrete_base, ValueMember[] members)
○	public abstract ...... TypeCode	**create_wstring_tc** (int bound)
	public .... void	**disconnect** (*Object* obj)
D	public .... *Current*	**get_current** ()
○	public abstract .... Context	**get_default_context** ()
○	public abstract .... Request	**get_next_response** () throws WrongTransaction
○	public abstract ...... TypeCode	**get_primitive_tc** (TCKind tcKind)
	public .... boolean	**get_service_information** (short service_type, ServiceInformationHolder service_info)
△	public static .... ORB	**init** ()
△	public static .... ORB	**init** (java.applet.Applet app, java.util.Properties props)
△	public static .... ORB	**init** (String[] args, java.util.Properties props)

Class *Interface* —extends - - -implements ○ abstract ● final △ static ▲ static final ✱ constructor x x—inherited x **x**—declared **x x**—overridden

O	public abstract	String[]	**list_initial_services** ()
O	public abstract	String	**object_to_string** (*Object* obj)
*	public		**ORB** ()
	public	void	**perform_work** ()
O	public abstract	boolean	**poll_next_response** ()
O	public abstract	*Object*	**resolve_initial_references** (String object_name) throws org.omg.CORBA.ORBPackage.InvalidName
	public	void	**run** ()
O	public abstract	void	**send_multiple_requests_deferred** (Request[] req)
O	public abstract	void	**send_multiple_requests_oneway** (Request[] req)
O	protected abstract	void	**set_parameters** (java.applet.Applet app, java.util.Properties props)
O	protected abstract	void	**set_parameters** (String[] args, java.util.Properties props)
	public	void	**shutdown** (boolean wait_for_completion)
O	public abstract	*Object*	**string_to_object** (String str)
	public	boolean	**work_pending** ()

OutOfMemoryError java.lang

P

```
Object
 └ Throwable --------------------------- java.io.Serializable
    └ Error
       └ VirtualMachineError
          └ OutOfMemoryError
```
O (marker at VirtualMachineError line)

*	public		**OutOfMemoryError** ()
*	public		**OutOfMemoryError** (String s)

O

OutputStream ⓘ org.omg.CORBA.portable

```
Object
 └ java.io.OutputStream ¹
    └ OutputStream
```
1.2 O (markers)

1	public	void	close () throws java.io.IOException
O	public abstract	InputStream	**create_input_stream** ()
1	public	void	flush () throws java.io.IOException
	public	org.omg.CORBA.ORB	**orb** ()
*	public		**OutputStream** ()
1	public	void	write (byte[] b) throws java.io.IOException
1	public	**void**	**write** (int b) throws java.io.IOException
1	public	void	write (byte[] b, int off, int len) throws java.io.IOException
O	public abstract	void	**write_any** (org.omg.CORBA.Any value)
O	public abstract	void	**write_boolean** (boolean value)
O	public abstract	void	**write_boolean_array** (boolean[] value, int offset, int length)
O	public abstract	void	**write_char** (char value)
O	public abstract	void	**write_char_array** (char[] value, int offset, int length)
	public	void	**write_Context** (org.omg.CORBA.Context ctx, org.omg.CORBA.ContextList contexts)
O	public abstract	void	**write_double** (double value)
O	public abstract	void	**write_double_array** (double[] value, int offset, int length)
	public	void	**write_fixed** (java.math.BigDecimal value)
O	public abstract	void	**write_float** (float value)
O	public abstract	void	**write_float_array** (float[] value, int offset, int length)
O	public abstract	void	**write_long** (int value)
O	public abstract	void	**write_long_array** (int[] value, int offset, int length)
O	public abstract	void	**write_longlong** (long value)
O	public abstract	void	**write_longlong_array** (long[] value, int offset, int length)
O	public abstract	void	**write_Object** (*org.omg.CORBA.Object* value)
O	public abstract	void	**write_octet** (byte value)
O	public abstract	void	**write_octet_array** (byte[] value, int offset, int length)
D O	public abstract	void	**write_Principal** (org.omg.CORBA.Principal value)
O	public abstract	void	**write_short** (short value)
O	public abstract	void	**write_short_array** (short[] value, int offset, int length)
O	public abstract	void	**write_string** (String value)
O	public abstract	void	**write_TypeCode** (org.omg.CORBA.TypeCode value)
O	public abstract	void	**write_ulong** (int value)
O	public abstract	void	**write_ulong_array** (int[] value, int offset, int length)
O	public abstract	void	**write_ulonglong** (long value)
O	public abstract	void	**write_ulonglong_array** (long[] value, int offset, int length)
O	public abstract	void	**write_ushort** (short value)
O	public abstract	void	**write_ushort_array** (short[] value, int offset, int length)
O	public abstract	void	**write_wchar** (char value)

Classes

OutputStream ❶

O	public abstract .... void	**write_wchar_array** (char[] value, int offset, int length)	
O	public abstract .... void	**write_wstring** (String value)	

OutputStream ❷ — java.io

Object
└OutputStream

	public....................void	**close** () throws IOException	
	public....................void	**flush** () throws IOException	
✱	public..........................	**OutputStream** ()	
	public....................void	**write** (byte[] b) throws IOException	
O	public abstract ....void	**write** (int b) throws IOException	
	public....................void	**write** (byte[] b, int off, int len) throws IOException	

OutputStreamWriter — java.io

Object
1.1 O └Writer [1]
1.1   └OutputStreamWriter

1	public.................... **void**	**close** () throws IOException	
1	public.................... **void**	**flush** () throws IOException	
	public....................String	**getEncoding** ()	
1	protected ....Object	lock	
✱	public..........................	**OutputStreamWriter** (OutputStream out)	
✱	public..........................	**OutputStreamWriter** (OutputStream out, String enc) throws UnsupportedEncodingException	
1	public....................void	write (char[] cbuf) throws IOException	
1	public.................... **void**	**write** (int c) throws IOException	
1	public....................void	write (String str) throws IOException	
1	public.................... **void**	**write** (char[] cbuf, int off, int len) throws IOException	
1	public.................... **void**	**write** (String str, int off, int len) throws IOException	

OverlayLayout — javax.swing

Object
1.2 └OverlayLayout - *java.awt.LayoutManager2* [1] (*java.awt.LayoutManager* [2]), *java.io.Serializable*

1	public....................void	**addLayoutComponent** (java.awt.Component comp, Object constraints)	
2	public....................void	**addLayoutComponent** (String name, java.awt.Component comp)	
1	public....................float	**getLayoutAlignmentX** (java.awt.Container target)	
1	public....................float	**getLayoutAlignmentY** (java.awt.Container target)	
1	public....................void	**invalidateLayout** (java.awt.Container target)	
2	public....................void	**layoutContainer** (java.awt.Container target)	
1	public......java.awt.Dimension	**maximumLayoutSize** (java.awt.Container target)	
2	public......java.awt.Dimension	**minimumLayoutSize** (java.awt.Container target)	
✱	public..........................	**OverlayLayout** (java.awt.Container target)	
2	public......java.awt.Dimension	**preferredLayoutSize** (java.awt.Container target)	
2	public....................void	**removeLayoutComponent** (java.awt.Component comp)	

Owner — java.security.acl
P[u]

1.1 *Owner*

	public.................boolean	**addOwner** (*java.security.Principal* caller, *java.security.Principal* owner) throws NotOwnerException	
	public.................boolean	**deleteOwner** (*java.security.Principal* caller, *java.security.Principal* owner) throws NotOwnerException, LastOwnerException	
	public.................boolean	**isOwner** (*java.security.Principal* owner)	

Package — java.lang
P

Object [1]
1.2 └Package

Class *Interface* —extends - - -implements O abstract ● final △ static ▲ static final ✱ constructor x x—inherited x **x**—declared **x x**—overridden

552

public	String	**getImplementationTitle** ()
public	String	**getImplementationVendor** ()
public	String	**getImplementationVersion** ()
public	String	**getName** ()
△ public static	Package	**getPackage** (String name)
△ public static	Package[]	**getPackages** ()
public	String	**getSpecificationTitle** ()
public	String	**getSpecificationVendor** ()
public	String	**getSpecificationVersion** ()
1 public	int	**hashCode** ()
public	boolean	**isCompatibleWith** (String desired) throws NumberFormatException
public	boolean	**isSealed** ()
public	boolean	**isSealed** (java.net.URL url)
1 public	String	**toString** ()

PackedColorModel

java.awt.image

Object
└ ColorModel[1] - *java.awt.Transparency*
    └ PackedColorModel

P

1		*34 inherited members from ColorModel not shown*
1 public	**SampleModel**	**createCompatibleSampleModel** (int w, int h)
1 public	**boolean**	**equals** (Object obj)
1 public	**WritableRaster**	**getAlphaRaster** (WritableRaster raster)
● public final	int	**getMask** (int index)
● public final	int[]	**getMasks** ()
1 public	**boolean**	**isCompatibleSampleModel** (SampleModel sm)
✳ public		**PackedColorModel** (java.awt.color.ColorSpace space, int bits, int[] colorMaskArray, int alphaMask, boolean isAlphaPremultiplied, int trans, int transferType)
✳ public		**PackedColorModel** (java.awt.color.ColorSpace space, int bits, int rmask, int gmask, int bmask, int amask, boolean isAlphaPremultiplied, int trans, int transferType)

Pageable

java.awt.print

Pageable

public	int	**getNumberOfPages** ()
public	PageFormat	**getPageFormat** (int pageIndex) throws IndexOutOfBoundsException
public	*Printable*	**getPrintable** (int pageIndex) throws IndexOutOfBoundsException
▲ public static final	int	**UNKNOWN_NUMBER_OF_PAGES** = -1

PageFormat

java.awt.print

Object[1]
└ PageFormat - *Cloneable*

1 public	**Object**	**clone** ()
public	double	**getHeight** ()
public	double	**getImageableHeight** ()
public	double	**getImageableWidth** ()
public	double	**getImageableX** ()
public	double	**getImageableY** ()
public	double[]	**getMatrix** ()
public	int	**getOrientation** ()
public	Paper	**getPaper** ()
public	double	**getWidth** ()
▲ public static final	int	**LANDSCAPE** = 0
✳ public		**PageFormat** ()
▲ public static final	int	**PORTRAIT** = 1
▲ public static final	int	**REVERSE_LANDSCAPE** = 2
public	void	**setOrientation** (int orientation) throws IllegalArgumentException
public	void	**setPaper** (Paper paper)

Classes

Paint

Paint

java.awt

P

1.2   *Paint*————————————————————————— *Transparency* [1]

```
public............ PaintContext createContext (java.awt.image.ColorModel cm, Rectangle deviceBounds,
                                      java.awt.geom.Rectangle2D userBounds, java.awt.geom.AffineTransform xform,
                                      RenderingHints hints)
      1 public.........................int getTransparency ()
```

PaintContext

java.awt

P

1.2   *PaintContext*

```
public.......................void dispose ()
public............................ getColorModel ()
.... java.awt.image.ColorModel
public...java.awt.image.Raster getRaster (int x, int y, int w, int h)
```

PaintEvent

java.awt.event

P

```
Object
1.1    └java.util.EventObject [1] ------------------- java.io.Serializable
1.1 ○    └java.awt.AWTEvent [2]
1.1       └ComponentEvent [3]
1.1         └PaintEvent
```

2	protected	void	consume ()
2	protected	boolean	consumed
2	protected	void	finalize () throws Throwable
3	public....	java.awt.Component	getComponent ()
2	public	int	getID ()
1	public	Object	getSource ()
	public	java.awt.Rectangle	**getUpdateRect** ()
2	protected	int	id
2	protected	boolean	isConsumed ()
▲	public static final	int	**PAINT** = 800
▲	public static final	int	**PAINT_FIRST** = 800
▲	public static final	int	**PAINT_LAST** = 801
*	public		**PaintEvent** (java.awt.Component source, int id, java.awt.Rectangle updateRect)
3	public	**String**	**paramString** ()
	public	void	**setUpdateRect** (java.awt.Rectangle updateRect)
1	protected transient	Object	source
2	public	String	toString ()
▲	public static final	int	**UPDATE** = 801

Panel

java.awt

P

```
       Object
○      └Component [1] -------------------------- java.awt.image.ImageObserver, MenuContainer,
                                                         java.io.Serializable

          └Container [2]
           └Panel
```

```
      1 137 inherited members from Component not shown
      2 50 inherited members from Container not shown
      2 public....................... void addNotify ()
      * public............................ Panel ()
1.1 * public............................ Panel (LayoutManager layout)
```

PanelPeer

java.awt.peer

```
      PanelPeer————————————————————————— ContainerPeer [1] (ComponentPeer [2])
```

```
      2 32 inherited members from ComponentPeer not shown
      1 4 inherited members from ContainerPeer not shown
```

Class   *Interface*   —extends   - - -implements   ○ abstract   ● final   △ static   ▲ static final   * constructor   x x—inherited   x **x**—declared   **x x**—overridden

PanelUI

```
       Object
1.2 ○  └ComponentUI 1
1.2 ○     └PanelUI
```

1	*11 inherited members from ComponentUI not shown*		
*	public...........................	**PanelUI** ()	

Paper

```
       Object 1
1.2    └Paper - - - - - - - - - - - - - - - - - - - - - - - - - - - - - - Cloneable
```

1	public..................**Object**	**clone** ()
	public....................double	**getHeight** ()
	public....................double	**getImageableHeight** ()
	public....................double	**getImageableWidth** ()
	public....................double	**getImageableX** ()
	public....................double	**getImageableY** ()
	public....................double	**getWidth** ()
*	public.............................	**Paper** ()
	public....................void	**setImageableArea** (double x, double y, double width, double height)
	public....................void	**setSize** (double width, double height)

ParagraphView❶

```
       Object
1.2 ○  └View 1 - - - - - - - - - - - - - - - - - - - - - - - - - - - - - javax.swing.SwingConstants
1.2 ○     └CompositeView 2
1.2       └BoxView 3
1.2          └ParagraphView - - - - - - - - - - - - - - - - TabExpander 4
```

	protected....................void	**adjustRow** (javax.swing.text.ParagraphView.Row r, int desiredSpan, int x)
2	public.......................void	append (View v)
3	protected....................void	baselineLayout (int targetSpan, int axis, int[] offsets, int[] spans)
3	protected.......................... .javax.swing.SizeRequirements	baselineRequirements (int axis, javax.swing.SizeRequirements r)
	public.......................View	**breakView** (int axis, float len, *java.awt.Shape* a)
1	public.......................View	breakView (int axis, int offset, float pos, float len)
3	protected.......................... .javax.swing.SizeRequirements	calculateMajorAxisRequirements (int axis, javax.swing.SizeRequirements r)
3	protected..............**javax ↩ .swing.SizeRequirements**	**calculateMinorAxisRequirements** (int axis, javax.swing.SizeRequirements r)
3	public.....................**void**	**changedUpdate** (*javax.swing.event.DocumentEvent* changes, *java.awt.Shape* a, *ViewFactory* f)
3	protected....................void	childAllocation (int index, java.awt.Rectangle alloc)
1	public.......................View	createFragment (int p0, int p1)
	protected.......................int	**findOffsetToCharactersInString** (char[] string, int start)
	protected.......................int	**firstLineIndent**
3	protected........**boolean**	**flipEastAndWestAtEnds** (int position, Position.Bias bias)
3	public...................**float**	**getAlignment** (int axis)
1	public.............*AttributeSet*	getAttributes ()
● 2	protected final............short	getBottomInset ()
	public.......................int	**getBreakWeight** (int axis, float len)
1	public.......................int	getBreakWeight (int axis, float pos, float len)
2	public..........*java.awt.Shape*	getChildAllocation (int index, *java.awt.Shape* a)
	protected.......................int	**getClosestPositionTo** (int pos, Position.Bias b, *java.awt.Shape* a, int direction, Position.Bias[] biasRet, int rowIndex, int x) throws BadLocationException
1	public.......java.awt.Container	getContainer ()
1	public..................*Document*	getDocument ()
1	public....................*Element*	getElement ()
1	public.......................int	getEndOffset ()
● 3	public final ....int	getHeight ()
2	protected .. java.awt.Rectangle	getInsideAllocation (*java.awt.Shape* a)
	protected....................View	**getLayoutView** (int index)
	protected.......................int	**getLayoutViewCount** ()
● 2	protected final............short	getLeftInset ()
3	public....................float	getMaximumSpan (int axis)
3	public....................float	getMinimumSpan (int axis)

P

Classes

ParagraphView ❶

2	protected	int	getNextEastWestVisualPositionFrom (int pos, Position.Bias b, *java.awt.Shape a*, int direction, Position.Bias[] biasRet) throws BadLocationException
2	protected	**int**	**getNextNorthSouthVisualPositionFrom** (int pos, Position.Bias b, *java.awt.Shape a*, int direction, Position.Bias[] biasRet) throws BadLocationException
2	public	int	getNextVisualPositionFrom (int pos, Position.Bias b, *java.awt.Shape a*, int direction, Position.Bias[] biasRet) throws BadLocationException
● 3	protected final	int	getOffset (int axis, int childIndex)
1	public	View	getParent ()
	protected	float	**getPartialSize** (int startOffset, int endOffset)
3	public	float	getPreferredSpan (int axis)
3	public	int	getResizeWeight (int axis)
● 2	protected final	short	getRightInset ()
● 3	protected final	int	getSpan (int axis, int childIndex)
1	public	int	getStartOffset ()
	protected	float	**getTabBase** ()
	protected	TabSet	**getTabSet** ()
● 2	protected final	short	getTopInset ()
2	public	View	getView (int n)
3	protected	View	getViewAtPoint (int x, int y, java.awt.Rectangle alloc)
2	protected	**View**	**getViewAtPosition** (int pos, java.awt.Rectangle a)
2	public	int	getViewCount ()
1	public	*ViewFactory*	getViewFactory ()
2	protected	**int**	**getViewIndexAtPosition** (int pos)
● 3	public final	int	getWidth ()
2	public	void	insert (int offs, View v)
3	public	**void**	**insertUpdate** (*javax.swing.event.DocumentEvent* changes, *java.awt.Shape a*, *ViewFactory* f)
3	protected	boolean	isAfter (int x, int y, java.awt.Rectangle innerAlloc)
3	protected	boolean	isAllocationValid ()
3	protected	boolean	isBefore (int x, int y, java.awt.Rectangle innerAlloc)
1	public	boolean	isVisible ()
3	protected	**void**	**layout** (int width, int height)
3	protected	void	layoutMajorAxis (int targetSpan, int axis, int[] offsets, int[] spans)
3	protected	void	layoutMinorAxis (int targetSpan, int axis, int[] offsets, int[] spans)
2	protected	**void**	**loadChildren** (*ViewFactory* f)
3	public	*java.awt.Shape*	modelToView (int pos, *java.awt. Shape a*, Position. Bias b) throws BadLocationException
2	public	*java.awt.Shape*	modelToView (int p0, Position.Bias b0, int p1, Position.Bias b1, *java.awt.Shape a*) throws BadLocationException
4	public	float	**nextTabStop** (float x, int tabOffset)
3	public	**void**	**paint** (java.awt.Graphics g, *java.awt.Shape a*)
3	protected	void	paintChild (java.awt.Graphics g, java.awt.Rectangle alloc, int index)
＊	public		**ParagraphView** (*Element* elem)
3	public	void	preferenceChanged (View child, boolean width, boolean height)
2	public	void	removeAll ()
3	public	**void**	**removeUpdate** (*javax.swing.event.DocumentEvent* changes, *java.awt.Shape a*, *ViewFactory* f)
3	public	void	replace (int offset, int length, View[] elems)
	protected	void	**setFirstLineIndent** (float fi)
● 2	protected final	void	setInsets (short top, short left, short bottom, short right)
	protected	void	**setJustification** (int j)
	protected	void	**setLineSpacing** (float ls)
● 2	protected final	void	setParagraphInsets (*AttributeSet* attr)
2	public	void	setParent (View parent)
	protected	void	**setPropertiesFromAttributes** ()
	protected	void	setSize (float width, float height)
3	public	int	viewToModel (float x, float y, *java.awt.Shape a*, Position.Bias[] bias)

ParagraphView ❷   javax.swing.text.html

```
      Object
1.2 ○  └ javax.swing.text.View ¹ - - - - - - - - - - - - - - - - - - - javax.swing.SwingConstants
1.2 ○    └ javax.swing.text.CompositeView ²
1.2        └ javax.swing.text.BoxView ³
1.2          └ javax.swing.text.ParagraphView ⁴ - - - - - javax.swing.text.TabExpander
1.2            └ ParagraphView
```

4	*25 inherited members from javax.swing.text.ParagraphView not shown*		
2	public	void	append (javax.swing.text.View v)
3	protected	void	baselineLayout (int targetSpan, int axis, int[] offsets, int[] spans)

Class   *Interface*   —extends   - - -implements   ○ abstract   ● final   △ static   ▲ static final   ＊ constructor   x x—inherited   x **x**—declared   **x x**—overridden

	3	protected .... .javax.swing.SizeRequirements	baselineRequirements (int axis, javax.swing.SizeRequirements r)
	1	public.... javax.swing.text.View	breakView (int axis, int offset, float pos, float len)
	3	protected .... .javax.swing.SizeRequirements	calculateMajorAxisRequirements (int axis, javax.swing.SizeRequirements r)
	4	protected .... **javax ↵** **.swing.SizeRequirements**	**calculateMinorAxisRequirements** (int axis, javax.swing.SizeRequirements r)
	4	public..................... **void**	**changedUpdate** (*javax. swing. event. DocumentEvent* e, *java. awt. Shape* a, *javax.swing.text.ViewFactory* f)
	3	protected ....void	childAllocation (int index, java.awt.Rectangle alloc)
	1	public.... javax.swing.text.View	createFragment (int p0, int p1)
	1	public.............	**getAttributes** ()
		.javax.swing.text.AttributeSet	
●	2	protected final............ short	getBottomInset ()
	1	public........................int	getBreakWeight (int axis, float pos, float len)
	2	public.......... *java.awt.Shape*	getChildAllocation (int index, *java.awt.Shape* a)
	1	public...... java.awt.Container	getContainer ()
	1	public........................	getDocument ()
		.... *javax.swing.text.Document*	
	1	public........................	getElement ()
		.... *javax.swing.text.Element*	
	1	public.......................int	getEndOffset ()
●	3	public final ....int	getHeight ()
	2	protected .. java.awt.Rectangle	getInsideAllocation (*java.awt.Shape* a)
●	2	protected final............ short	getLeftInset ()
●	3	public..................... **float**	**getMaximumSpan** (int axis)
●	3	public..................... **float**	**getMinimumSpan** (int axis)
	2	protected ....int	getNextEastWestVisualPositionFrom (int pos, javax.swing.text.Position.Bias b, *java. awt. Shape* a, int direction, javax.swing.text.Position.Bias[] biasRet) throws javax.swing.text.BadLocationException
	2	public.......................int	getNextVisualPositionFrom (int pos, javax. swing. text. Position. Bias b, *java. awt. Shape* a, int direction, javax.swing.text.Position.Bias[] biasRet) throws javax.swing.text.BadLocationException
●	3	protected final.............int	getOffset (int axis, int childIndex)
	1	public.... javax.swing.text.View	getParent ()
	3	public..................... **float**	**getPreferredSpan** (int axis)
	3	public.......................int	getResizeWeight (int axis)
●	2	protected final............ short	getRightInset ()
●	3	protected final.............int	getSpan (int axis, int childIndex)
	1	public.......................int	getStartOffset ()
		protected ....StyleSheet	**getStyleSheet** ()
●	2	protected final............ short	getTopInset ()
	2	public.... javax.swing.text.View	getView (int n)
	3	protected	getViewAtPoint (int x, int y, java.awt.Rectangle alloc)
		..........javax.swing.text.View	
	2	public.......................int	getViewCount ()
	1	public........................	getViewFactory ()
		.. javax.swing.text.ViewFactory	
●	3	public final ....int	getWidth ()
	2	public.....................void	insert (int offs, javax.swing.text.View v)
	3	protected .... boolean	isAfter (int x, int y, java.awt.Rectangle innerAlloc)
	3	protected .... boolean	isAllocationValid ()
	3	protected .... boolean	isBefore (int x, int y, java.awt.Rectangle innerAlloc)
	1	public.................**boolean**	**isVisible** ()
	3	protected ....void	layoutMajorAxis (int targetSpan, int axis, int[] offsets, int[] spans)
	3	protected ....void	layoutMinorAxis (int targetSpan, int axis, int[] offsets, int[] spans)
	3	public.......... *java.awt.Shape*	modelToView (int pos, *java.awt.Shape* a, javax.swing.text.Position.Bias b) throws javax.swing.text.BadLocationException
	2	public.......... *java.awt.Shape*	modelToView (int p0, javax. swing. text. Position. Bias b0, int p1, javax. swing. text. Position. Bias b1, *java. awt. Shape* a) throws javax.swing.text.BadLocationException
	3	protected ....void	paintChild (java.awt.Graphics g, java.awt.Rectangle alloc, int index)
*		public.............	**ParagraphView** (*javax.swing.text.Element* elem)
	3	public.....................void	preferenceChanged (javax.swing.text.View child, boolean width, boolean height)
	2	public.....................void	removeAll ()
	3	public.....................void	replace (int offset, int length, javax.swing.text.View[] elems)
●	2	protected final...............void	setInsets (short top, short left, short bottom, short right)
●	2	protected final..............void	setParagraphInsets (*javax.swing.text.AttributeSet* attr)
	2	public................... **void**	**setParent** (javax.swing.text.View parent)
	4	protected .... **void**	**setPropertiesFromAttributes** ()
	3	public.....................void	setSize (float width, float height)
	3	public.......................int	viewToModel (float x, float y, *java.awt.Shape* a, javax.swing.text.Position.Bias[] bias)

ParameterBlock

	java.awt.image.renderable
ParameterBlock	

Object [1]
　└ ParameterBlock - *Cloneable, java.io.Serializable* 　(1.2)

```
          public..........ParameterBlock  add (byte b)
          public..........ParameterBlock  add (char c)
          public..........ParameterBlock  add (double d)
          public..........ParameterBlock  add (float f)
          public..........ParameterBlock  add (int i)
          public..........ParameterBlock  add (Object obj)
          public..........ParameterBlock  add (long l)
          public..........ParameterBlock  add (short s)
          public..........ParameterBlock  addSource (Object source)
     1    public..................Object  clone ()
          public....................byte  getByteParameter (int index)
          public....................char  getCharParameter (int index)
          public..................double  getDoubleParameter (int index)
          public...................float  getFloatParameter (int index)
          public.....................int  getIntParameter (int index)
          public....................long  getLongParameter (int index)
          public.....................int  getNumParameters ()
          public.....................int  getNumSources ()
          public..................Object  getObjectParameter (int index)
          public.................Class[]  getParamClasses ()
          public........java.util.Vector  getParameters ()
          public.......RenderableImage    getRenderableSource (int index)
          public...................java↵  getRenderedSource (int index)
          .awt.image.RenderedImage
          public...................short  getShortParameter (int index)
          public..................Object  getSource (int index)
          public........java.util.Vector  getSources ()
  *       public..........................  ParameterBlock ()
  *       public..........................  ParameterBlock (java.util.Vector sources)
  *       public..........................  ParameterBlock (java.util.Vector sources, java.util.Vector parameters)
          protected.......java.util.Vector  parameters
          public....................void  removeParameters ()
          public....................void  removeSources ()
          public..........ParameterBlock  set (byte b, int index)
          public..........ParameterBlock  set (char c, int index)
          public..........ParameterBlock  set (double d, int index)
          public..........ParameterBlock  set (float f, int index)
          public..........ParameterBlock  set (int i, int index)
          public..........ParameterBlock  set (Object obj, int index)
          public..........ParameterBlock  set (long l, int index)
          public..........ParameterBlock  set (short s, int index)
          public....................void  setParameters (java.util.Vector parameters)
          public..........ParameterBlock  setSource (Object source, int index)
          public....................void  setSources (java.util.Vector sources)
          public..................Object  shallowClone ()
          protected.......java.util.Vector  sources
```

	java.beans
ParameterDescriptor	

Object
　└ FeatureDescriptor [1] 　(1.1)
　　└ ParameterDescriptor 　(1.1)

```
     1    public....java.util.Enumeration  attributeNames ()
     1    public....................String  getDisplayName ()
     1    public....................String  getName ()
     1    public....................String  getShortDescription ()
     1    public....................Object  getValue (String attributeName)
     1    public...................boolean  isExpert ()
     1    public...................boolean  isHidden ()
(1.2) 1    public...................boolean  isPreferred ()
  *       public..........................  ParameterDescriptor ()
     1    public......................void  setDisplayName (String displayName)
     1    public......................void  setExpert (boolean expert)
     1    public......................void  setHidden (boolean hidden)
     1    public......................void  setName (String name)
```

Class *Interface* —extends - - -implements ○ abstract ● final △ static ▲ static final ✳ constructor x x—inherited x **x**—declared **x x**—overridden

1.2	1	public......................void	setPreferred (boolean preferred)
	1	public......................void	setShortDescription (String text)
	1	public......................void	setValue (String attributeName, Object value)

ParseException
java.text

```
Object
└─Throwable ---------------------------- java.io.Serializable
   └─Exception
      └─ParseException
```

P

1.1

	public......................int	**getErrorOffset** ()
*	public......................	**ParseException** (String s, int errorOffset)

ParsePosition
java.text

```
Object 1
└─ParsePosition
```

1.1

P

1.2	1	public...............**boolean**	**equals** (Object obj)
		public......................int	**getErrorIndex** ()
		public......................int	**getIndex** ()
	1	public......................**int**	**hashCode** ()
*		public......................	**ParsePosition** (int index)
1.2		public......................void	**setErrorIndex** (int ei)
		public......................void	**setIndex** (int index)
	1	public...............**String**	**toString** ()

P

Parser
javax.swing.text.html.parser

```
Object
1.2 └─Parser ------------------------------- DTDConstants
```

	protected.................DTD	**dtd**
	protected..................void	**endTag** (boolean omitted)
	protected..................void	**error** (String err)
	protected..................void	**error** (String err, String arg1)
	protected..................void	**error** (String err, String arg1, String arg2)
	protected..................void	**error** (String err, String arg1, String arg2, String arg3)
	protected..................void	**flushAttributes** ()
	protected..............javax ↵	**getAttributes** ()
	.swing.text.SimpleAttributeSet	
	protected......................int	**getCurrentLine** ()
	protected......................int	**getCurrentPos** ()
	protected..................void	**handleComment** (char[] text)
	protected..................void	**handleEmptyTag** (TagElement tag) throws javax. swing. text ↵
		.ChangedCharSetException
	protected..................void	**handleEndTag** (TagElement tag)
	protected..................void	**handleEOFInComment** ()
	protected..................void	**handleError** (int ln, String msg)
	protected..................void	**handleStartTag** (TagElement tag)
	protected..................void	**handleText** (char[] text)
	protected..................void	**handleTitle** (char[] text)
	protected.........TagElement	**makeTag** (Element elem)
	protected.........TagElement	**makeTag** (Element elem, boolean fictional)
	protected..................void	**markFirstTime** (Element elem)
	public synchronized.......void	**parse** (java.io.Reader in) throws java.io.IOException
	public......................String	**parseDTDMarkup** () throws java.io.IOException
	protected............boolean	**parseMarkupDeclarations** (StringBuffer strBuff) throws java.io.IOException
*	public......................	**Parser** (DTD dtd)
	protected..................void	**startTag** (TagElement tag) throws javax.swing.text.ChangedCharSetException
	protected............boolean	**strict**

ParserDelegator
javax.swing.text.html.parser

```
Object
1.2 ○ └─javax.swing.text.html.HTMLEditorKit.Parser 1
1.2      └─ParserDelegator
```

ParserDelegator

PasswordAuthentication   java.net

P

Object
└PasswordAuthentication

PasswordView   javax.swing.text

Object
1.2 ○ └View [1] - *javax.swing.SwingConstants*
1.2   └PlainView [2] - *TabExpander*
1.2   └FieldView [3]
1.2   └PasswordView

PathIterator   java.awt.geom

PathIterator

Class *Interface* —extends - - -implements ○ abstract ● final △ static ▲ static final ✳ constructor x x—inherited x **x**—declared **x x**—overridden

Permission ❶			java.security.acl

1.1   *Permission*   P^u

     public . . . . boolean **equals** (Object another)
     public . . . . String **toString** ()

Permission ❷		java.security

     Object [1]
1.2 ◯   └─ Permission - *Guard* [2], *java.io.Serializable*   P^o

     2   public . . . . void **checkGuard** (Object object) throws SecurityException
 ◯ 1   public abstract . . . . **boolean** **equals** (Object obj)
 ◯   public abstract . . . . String **getActions** ()
 ●   public final . . . . String **getName** ()
 ◯ 1   public abstract . . . . **int** **hashCode** ()
 ◯   public abstract . . . . boolean **implies** (Permission permission)
     public . . . . PermissionCollection **newPermissionCollection** ()
 ✶   public . . . . **Permission** (String name)
     1   public . . . . **String** **toString** ()

PermissionCollection		java.security

     Object [1]
1.2 ◯   └─ PermissionCollection - - - - - - - - - - - - - - - - - - - *java.io.Serializable*   P^o

 ◯   public abstract . . . . void **add** (Permission permission)
 ◯   public abstract . . . . **elements** ()
     . . . . *java.util.Enumeration*
 ◯   public abstract . . . . boolean **implies** (Permission permission)
     public . . . . boolean **isReadOnly** ()
 ✶   public . . . . **PermissionCollection** ()
     public . . . . void **setReadOnly** ()
     1   public . . . . **String** **toString** ()

Permissions		java.security

     Object
1.2 ◯   └─ PermissionCollection [1] - - - - - - - - - - - - - - - - - - - *java.io.Serializable*
1.2 ●   └─ Permissions - *java.io.Serializable*   P^o

     1   public . . . . **void** **add** (Permission permission)
     1   public . . *java.util.Enumeration* **elements** ()
     1   public . . . . **boolean** **implies** (Permission permission)
     1   public . . . . boolean isReadOnly ()
 ✶   public . . . . **Permissions** ()
     1   public . . . . void setReadOnly ()
     1   public . . . . String toString ()

PERSIST_STORE		org.omg.CORBA

     Object
     └─ Throwable - *java.io.Serializable*
       └─ Exception
         └─ RuntimeException
1.2 ◯   └─ SystemException [1]
1.2 ●   └─ PERSIST_STORE

     1   public . . . . CompletionStatus completed
     1   public . . . . int minor
 ✶   public . . . . **PERSIST_STORE** ()
 ✶   public . . . . **PERSIST_STORE** (String s)
 ✶   public . . . . **PERSIST_STORE** (int minor, CompletionStatus completed)
 ✶   public . . . . **PERSIST_STORE** (String s, int minor, CompletionStatus completed)
     1   public . . . . String toString ()

P

Classes

PhantomReference

PhantomReference			java.lang.ref

```
         Object
1.2 ○    └─Reference 1
1.2         └─PhantomReference
```

1	public	void	clear ()
1	public	boolean	enqueue ()
1	public	**Object**	**get** ()
1	public	boolean	isEnqueued ()
*	public		**PhantomReference** (Object referent, ReferenceQueue q)

PipedInputStream			java.io

```
         Object
  ○      └─InputStream 1
            └─PipedInputStream
```

1	public synchronized	**int**	**available** () throws IOException
1.1	protected	byte[]	**buffer**
1	public	**void**	**close** () throws IOException
	public	void	**connect** (PipedOutputStream src) throws IOException
1.1	protected	int	**in**
1	public synchronized	void	mark (int readlimit)
1	public	boolean	markSupported ()
1.1	protected	int	**out**
1.1 ▲	protected static final	int	**PIPE_SIZE**
*	public		**PipedInputStream** ()
*	public		**PipedInputStream** (PipedOutputStream src) throws IOException
1	public synchronized	**int**	**read** () throws IOException
1	public	int	read (byte[] b) throws IOException
1	public synchronized	**int**	**read** (byte[] b, int off, int len) throws IOException
1.1	protected synchronized	void	**receive** (int b) throws IOException
1	public synchronized	void	reset () throws IOException
1	public	long	skip (long n) throws IOException

PipedOutputStream			java.io

```
         Object
  ○      └─OutputStream 1
            └─PipedOutputStream
```

1	public	**void**	**close** () throws IOException
	public synchronized	void	**connect** (PipedInputStream snk) throws IOException
1	public synchronized	**void**	**flush** () throws IOException
*	public		**PipedOutputStream** ()
*	public		**PipedOutputStream** (PipedInputStream snk) throws IOException
1	public	void	write (byte[] b) throws IOException
1	public	**void**	**write** (int b) throws IOException
1	public	**void**	**write** (byte[] b, int off, int len) throws IOException

PipedReader			java.io

```
          Object
1.1 ○     └─Reader 1
1.1         └─PipedReader
```

1	public	**void**	**close** () throws IOException
	public	void	**connect** (PipedWriter src) throws IOException
1	protected	Object	lock
1	public	void	mark (int readAheadLimit) throws IOException
1	public	boolean	markSupported ()
*	public		**PipedReader** ()
*	public		**PipedReader** (PipedWriter src) throws IOException
1	public synchronized	**int**	**read** () throws IOException
1	public	int	read (char[] cbuf) throws IOException
1	public synchronized	**int**	**read** (char[] cbuf, int off, int len) throws IOException
1	public synchronized	**boolean**	**ready** () throws IOException

Class *Interface* —extends - - -implements ○ abstract ● final △ static ▲ static final ✳ constructor x x—inherited x **x**—declared **x x**—overridden

```
   1  public.....................void reset () throws IOException
   1  public..................... long skip (long n) throws IOException
```

PipedWriter   java.io

```
        Object
1.1 ○   └Writer 1
1.1          └PipedWriter
```

```
   1  public..................... void close () throws IOException
      public synchronized .......void connect (PipedReader snk) throws IOException
   1  public synchronized ..... void flush () throws IOException
   1  protected ................Object lock
 *    public......................... PipedWriter ()
 *    public......................... PipedWriter (PipedReader snk) throws IOException
   1  public.....................void write (char[] cbuf) throws IOException
   1  public..................... void write (int c) throws IOException
   1  public.....................void write (String str) throws IOException
   1  public..................... void write (char[] cbuf, int off, int len) throws IOException
   1  public.....................void write (String str, int off, int len) throws IOException
```

PixelGrabber   java.awt.image

```
        Object
        └PixelGrabber - - - - - - - - - - - - - - - - - - - - - - - - ImageConsumer 1
```

```
1.1   public synchronized .......void abortGrabbing ()
1.1   public synchronized .......... getColorModel ()
      ..................... ColorModel
1.1   public synchronized .........int getHeight ()
1.1   public synchronized .... Object getPixels ()
1.1   public synchronized .........int getStatus ()
1.1   public synchronized .........int getWidth ()
      public................. boolean grabPixels () throws InterruptedException
      public synchronized .. boolean grabPixels (long ms) throws InterruptedException
1.1 1 public synchronized .......void imageComplete (int status)
1.1 * public.......................... PixelGrabber (java.awt.Image img, int x, int y, int w, int h, boolean forceRGB)
  * public.......................... PixelGrabber (java.awt.Image img, int x, int y, int w, int h, int[] pix, int off, int scansize)
  * public.......................... PixelGrabber (ImageProducer ip, int x, int y, int w, int h, int[] pix, int off, int scansize)
    1 public.....................void setColorModel (ColorModel model)
    1 public.....................void setDimensions (int width, int height)
    1 public.....................void setHints (int hints)
    1 public.....................void setPixels (int srcX, int srcY, int srcW, int srcH, ColorModel model, int[] pixels,
                                   int srcOff, int srcScan)
    1 public.....................void setPixels (int srcX, int srcY, int srcW, int srcH, ColorModel model, byte[] pixels,
                                   int srcOff, int srcScan)
    1 public.....................void setProperties (java.util.Hashtable props)
1.1   public synchronized .......void startGrabbing ()
      public synchronized .......int status ()
```

PixelInterleavedSampleModel   java.awt.image

```
        Object
1.2 ○   └SampleModel 1
1.2        └ComponentSampleModel 2
1.2            └PixelInterleavedSampleModel
```

```
    1 26 inherited members from SampleModel not shown
    2 26 inherited members from ComponentSampleModel not shown
    2 public........... SampleModel createCompatibleSampleModel (int w, int h)
    2 public........... SampleModel createSubsetSampleModel (int[] bands)
  * public.......................... PixelInterleavedSampleModel (int dataType, int w, int h, int pixelStride,
                                   int scanlineStride, int[] bandOffsets)
```

PKCS8EncodedKeySpec

PKCS8EncodedKeySpec	java.security.spec

```
        Object
1.2 ○   └EncodedKeySpec 1 - - - - - - - - - - - - - - - - - - - - - KeySpec
1.2         └PKCS8EncodedKeySpec
```

	1	public.....................**byte[]**	**getEncoded** ()
●	1	public final ....**String**	**getFormat** ()
*		public..........................	**PKCS8EncodedKeySpec** (byte[] encodedKey)

PlainDocument	javax.swing.text

```
        Object
1.2 ○   └AbstractDocument 1 - - - - - - - - - - - - - - - - - - - - Document, java.io.Serializable
1.2         └PlainDocument
```

	1	*43 inherited members from AbstractDocument not shown*	
		protected..........................	**createDefaultRoot** ()
		...........AbstractDocument ↵ .AbstractElement	
	1	public..................***Element***	**getDefaultRootElement** ()
	1	public..................***Element***	**getParagraphElement** (int pos)
	1	protected ....**void**	**insertUpdate** (AbstractDocument.DefaultDocumentEvent chng, *AttributeSet* attr)
▲		public static final.........String	**lineLimitAttribute** = "lineLimit"
*		public..........................	**PlainDocument** ()
*		protected..........................	**PlainDocument** (*AbstractDocument.Content* c)
	1	protected ....**void**	**removeUpdate** (AbstractDocument.DefaultDocumentEvent chng)
▲		public static final.........String	**tabSizeAttribute** = "tabSize"

PlainView	javax.swing.text

```
        Object
1.2 ○   └View 1 - - - - - - - - - - - - - - - - - - - - - - - - - - - - javax.swing.SwingConstants
1.2         └PlainView - - - - - - - - - - - - - - - - - - - - - - - - TabExpander 2
```

	1	*31 inherited members from View not shown*	
	1	public.....................**void**	**changedUpdate** (*javax.swing.event.DocumentEvent* changes, *java.awt.Shape* a, *ViewFactory* f)
		protected ....void	**drawLine** (int lineIndex, java.awt.Graphics g, int x, int y)
		protected ....int	**drawSelectedText** (java. awt. Graphics g, int x, int y, int p0, int p1) throws BadLocationException
		protected ....int	**drawUnselectedText** (java. awt. Graphics g, int x, int y, int p0, int p1) throws BadLocationException
●		protected final........ Segment	**getLineBuffer** ()
	1	public.....................**float**	**getPreferredSpan** (int axis)
		protected ....int	**getTabSize** ()
	1	public.....................**void**	**insertUpdate** (*javax.swing.event.DocumentEvent* changes, *java.awt.Shape* a, *ViewFactory* f)
		protected java.awt.FontMetrics	**metrics**
	1	public..........***java.awt.Shape***	**modelToView** (int pos, *java. awt. Shape* a, Position. Bias b) throws BadLocationException
	2	public.....................float	**nextTabStop** (float x, int tabOffset)
	1	public.....................**void**	**paint** (java.awt.Graphics g, *java.awt.Shape* a)
*		public..........................	**PlainView** (*Element* elem)
	1	public.....................**void**	**preferenceChanged** (View child, boolean width, boolean height)
	1	public.....................**void**	**removeUpdate** (*javax.swing.event.DocumentEvent* changes, *java.awt.Shape* a, *ViewFactory* f)
	1	public.......................**int**	**viewToModel** (float fx, float fy, *java.awt.Shape* a, Position.Bias[] bias)

Point	java.awt
	P

```
        Object 1
1.2 ○   └java.awt.geom.Point2D 2 - - - - - - - - - - - - - - - - Cloneable
            └Point - - - - - - - - - - - - - - - - - - - - - - - - - - - java.io.Serializable
```

	2	public.................Object	clone ()
1.2	2	public...................double	distance (java.awt.geom.Point2D pt)
1.2	2	public...................double	distance (double PX, double PY)

Class   *Interface*   —extends   - - -implements   ○ abstract   ● final   △ static   ▲ static final   * constructor   x x—inherited   x **x**—declared   **x x**—overridden

1.2	△	2	public static ....double	distance (double X1, double Y1, double X2, double Y2)
1.2		2	public....................double	distanceSq (java.awt.geom.Point2D pt)
1.2		2	public....................double	distanceSq (double PX, double PY)
1.2	△	2	public static ....double	distanceSq (double X1, double Y1, double X2, double Y2)
		2	public......................**boolean**	**equals** (Object obj)
1.1			public.......................Point	**getLocation** ()
1.2		2	public....................**double**	**getX** ()
1.2		2	public....................**double**	**getY** ()
		2	public..........................int	hashCode ()
			public.........................void	**move** (int x, int y)
1.1	✳		public............................	**Point** ()
1.1	✳		public............................	**Point** (Point p)
	✳		public............................	**Point** (int x, int y)
1.1			public.........................void	**setLocation** (Point p)
1.2		2	public.........................void	setLocation (java.awt.geom.Point2D p)
1.2		2	public.........................**void**	**setLocation** (double x, double y)
1.1			public.........................void	**setLocation** (int x, int y)
		1	public.......................**String**	**toString** ()
			public.........................void	**translate** (int x, int y)
			public..........................int	**x**
			public..........................int	**y**

Point2D java.awt.geom

Object[1]
└─Point2D - *Cloneable*   (1.2 ○)

	1	public....................**Object**	**clone** ()
		public....................double	**distance** (Point2D pt)
		public....................double	**distance** (double PX, double PY)
△		public static ....double	**distance** (double X1, double Y1, double X2, double Y2)
		public....................double	**distanceSq** (Point2D pt)
		public....................double	**distanceSq** (double PX, double PY)
△		public static ....double	**distanceSq** (double X1, double Y1, double X2, double Y2)
	1	public.................**boolean**	**equals** (Object obj)
○		public abstract ....double	**getX** ()
○		public abstract ....double	**getY** ()
	1	public...........................**int**	**hashCode** ()
✳		protected......................	**Point2D** ()
		public.........................void	**setLocation** (Point2D p)
○		public abstract ....void	**setLocation** (double x, double y)

Point2D.Double java.awt.geom

Object[1]
└─Point2D[2] - *Cloneable*   (1.2 ○)
　└─Point2D.Double   (1.2)

	2	public....................Object	clone ()
	2	public....................double	distance (Point2D pt)
	2	public....................double	distance (double PX, double PY)
△	2	public static ....double	distance (double X1, double Y1, double X2, double Y2)
	2	public....................double	distanceSq (Point2D pt)
	2	public....................double	distanceSq (double PX, double PY)
△	2	public static ....double	distanceSq (double X1, double Y1, double X2, double Y2)
✳		public............................	**Double** ()
✳		public............................	**Double** (double x, double y)
	2	public.................boolean	equals (Object obj)
	2	public....................**double**	**getX** ()
	2	public....................**double**	**getY** ()
	2	public..........................int	hashCode ()
	2	public.........................void	setLocation (Point2D p)
	2	public.........................**void**	**setLocation** (double x, double y)
	1	public.......................**String**	**toString** ()
		public....................double	**x**
		public....................double	**y**

Point2D.Float | java.awt.geom

```
        Object 1
1.2 ○   └ Point2D 2 ----------------------------- Cloneable
1.2         └ Point2D.Float
```

	2	public....................Object	clone ()
	2	public....................double	distance (Point2D pt)
	2	public....................double	distance (double PX, double PY)
△	2	public static ....double	distance (double X1, double Y1, double X2, double Y2)
	2	public....................double	distanceSq (Point2D pt)
	2	public....................double	distanceSq (double PX, double PY)
△	2	public static ....double	distanceSq (double X1, double Y1, double X2, double Y2)
	2	public....................boolean	equals (Object obj)
✳		public......................	**Float** ()
✳		public......................	**Float** (float x, float y)
	2	public......................**double**	**getX** ()
	2	public......................**double**	**getY** ()
	2	public...........................int	hashCode ()
	2	public............................void	setLocation (Point2D p)
	2	public......................**void**	**setLocation** (double x, double y)
		public............................void	**setLocation** (float x, float y)
	1	public......................**String**	**toString** ()
		public.............................float	**x**
		public.............................float	**y**

Policy❶ | java.security
P^O

```
        Object
1.2 ○   └ Policy
```

○	public abstract .... **getPermissions** (CodeSource codesource) .... PermissionCollection	
△	public static ....Policy	**getPolicy** ()
✳	public......................	**Policy** ()
○	public abstract ....void	**refresh** ()
△	public static ....void	**setPolicy** (Policy policy)

Policy❷ | org.omg.CORBA

```
1.2     Policy----------------------------------- Object 1
```

	1	*13 inherited members from Object not shown*
	public....................*Policy*	**copy** ()
	public............................void	**destroy** ()
	public............................int	**policy_type** ()

PolicyError | org.omg.CORBA

```
        Object
        └ Throwable -------------------------- java.io.Serializable
            └ Exception
1.2 ○           └ UserException -------------------- org.omg.CORBA.portable.IDLEntity (java.io.Serializable)
1.2 ●               └ PolicyError
```

✳	public......................	**PolicyError** ()
✳	public......................	**PolicyError** (short __reason)
✳	public......................	**PolicyError** (String reason_string, short __reason)
	public......................short	**reason**

Polygon | java.awt
P

```
        Object
        └ Polygon -------------------------- Shape 1, java.io.Serializable
```

	public............................void	**addPoint** (int x, int y)
1.1	protected ....Rectangle	**bounds**
1.1	public...................boolean	**contains** (Point p)

Class *Interface* —extends - - implements ○ abstract ● final △ static ▲ static final ✳ constructor x x—inherited x **x**—declared **x x**—overridden

1.2	*1*	public	boolean	**contains** (java.awt.geom.Point2D p)
1.2	*1*	public	boolean	**contains** (java.awt.geom.Rectangle2D r)
1.2	*1*	public	boolean	**contains** (double x, double y)
1.1	*1*	public	boolean	**contains** (int x, int y)
1.2	*1*	public	boolean	**contains** (double x, double y, double w, double h)
D		public	Rectangle	**getBoundingBox** ()
1.1	*1*	public	Rectangle	**getBounds** ()
1.2	*1*	public		**getBounds2D** ()
		... java.awt.geom.Rectangle2D		
1.2	*1*	public		**getPathIterator** (java.awt.geom.AffineTransform at)
		.....*java.awt.geom.PathIterator*		
1.2	*1*	public		**getPathIterator** (java.awt.geom.AffineTransform at, double flatness)
		.....*java.awt.geom.PathIterator*		
D		public	boolean	**inside** (int x, int y)
1.2	*1*	public	boolean	**intersects** (java.awt.geom.Rectangle2D r)
1.2	*1*	public	boolean	**intersects** (double x, double y, double w, double h)
		public	int	**npoints**
	*	public		**Polygon** ()
	*	public		**Polygon** (int[] xpoints, int[] ypoints, int npoints)
1.1		public	void	**translate** (int deltaX, int deltaY)
		public	int[]	**xpoints**
		public	int[]	**ypoints**

PopupMenu   java.awt

```
        Object
   ○    └ MenuComponent 1 ----------------------- java.io.Serializable
          └ MenuItem 2
            └ Menu 3 -------------------------- MenuContainer
1.1           └ PopupMenu
```

	3	public	MenuItem	add (MenuItem mi)
	3	public	void	add (String label)
	2	public synchronized	void	addActionListener (*java.awt.event.ActionListener* l)
	3	public	**void**	**addNotify** ()
	3	public	void	addSeparator ()
	2	public	void	deleteShortcut ()
●	2	protected final	void	disableEvents (long eventsToDisable)
●	1	public final	void	dispatchEvent (AWTEvent e)
●	2	protected final	void	enableEvents (long eventsToEnable)
	2	public	String	getActionCommand ()
	1	public	Font	getFont ()
	3	public	MenuItem	getItem (int index)
	3	public	int	getItemCount ()
	2	public	String	getLabel ()
	1	public	String	getName ()
	1	public	*MenuContainer*	getParent ()
	2	public	MenuShortcut	getShortcut ()
1.2 ●	1	protected final	Object	getTreeLock ()
	3	public	void	insert (MenuItem menuitem, int index)
	3	public	void	insert (String label, int index)
	3	public	void	insertSeparator (int index)
	2	public	boolean	isEnabled ()
	3	public	boolean	isTearOff ()
	3	public	String	paramString ()
*		public		**PopupMenu** ()
*		public		**PopupMenu** (String label)
	2	protected	void	processActionEvent (java.awt.event.ActionEvent e)
	2	protected	void	processEvent (AWTEvent e)
	3	public	void	remove (int index)
	3	public	void	remove (MenuComponent item)
	2	public synchronized	void	removeActionListener (*java.awt.event.ActionListener* l)
	3	public	void	removeAll ()
	3	public	void	removeNotify ()
	2	public	void	setActionCommand (String command)
	2	public synchronized	void	setEnabled (boolean b)
	1	public	void	setFont (Font f)
	2	public synchronized	void	setLabel (String label)
	1	public	void	setName (String name)
	2	public	void	setShortcut (MenuShortcut s)
		public	void	**show** (Component origin, int x, int y)
	1	public	String	toString ()

PopupMenuEvent

				javax.swing.event
		PopupMenuEvent		

```
       Object
1.1    └─java.util.EventObject 1 - - - - - - - - - - - - - - - - - - java.io.Serializable
1.2       └─PopupMenuEvent
```

1	public................Object	getSource ()
*	public..........................	**PopupMenuEvent** (Object source)
1	protected transient......Object	source
1	public....................String	toString ()

				javax.swing.event
		PopupMenuListener		

```
1.2    PopupMenuListener─────────────────── java.util.EventListener
```

public.....................void	**popupMenuCanceled** (PopupMenuEvent e)
public.....................void	**popupMenuWillBecomeInvisible** (PopupMenuEvent e)
public.....................void	**popupMenuWillBecomeVisible** (PopupMenuEvent e)

				java.awt.peer
		PopupMenuPeer		

```
1.1    PopupMenuPeer──────────────────── MenuPeer 1 (MenuItemPeer 2 (MenuComponentPeer 3))
```

3	*1 inherited members from MenuComponentPeer not shown*
2	*4 inherited members from MenuItemPeer not shown*
1	*3 inherited members from MenuPeer not shown*
	public......................void **show** (java.awt.Event)

				javax.swing.plaf
		PopupMenuUI		

```
       Object
1.2 ○  └─ComponentUI 1
1.2 ○     └─PopupMenuUI
```

1	*11 inherited members from ComponentUI not shown*	
*	public..........................	**PopupMenuUI** ()

				javax.swing.text
		Position		

```
1.2    Position
```

public..........................int **getOffset** ()

				javax.swing.text
		Position.Bias		

```
       Object 1
1.2 ●  └─Position.Bias
```

▲	public static final . Position.Bias	**Backward**
▲	public static final . Position.Bias	**Forward**
1	public...................... **String**	**toString** ()

				java.sql
		PreparedStatement		P⁰

PreparedStatement in the listing uses italic header

```
1.1    PreparedStatement────────────────── Statement 1
```

1	*28 inherited members from Statement not shown*
1.2	public.......................void **addBatch** () throws SQLException
	public.......................void **clearParameters** () throws SQLException
	public................ boolean **execute** () throws SQLException
	public............... *ResultSet* **executeQuery** () throws SQLException
	public.......................int **executeUpdate** () throws SQLException
1.2	public...... *ResultSetMetaData* **getMetaData** () throws SQLException
1.2	public.......................void **setArray** (int i, *Array* x) throws SQLException
	public.......................void **setAsciiStream** (int parameterIndex, java.io. InputStream x, int length)
	throws SQLException
	public.......................void **setBigDecimal** (int parameterIndex, java.math.BigDecimal x) throws SQLException

---

Class *Interface* —extends - - -implements ○ abstract ● final △ static ▲ static final * constructor x x—inherited x **x**—declared **x x**—overridden

	public......................void	**setBinaryStream** (int parameterIndex, java.io.InputStream x, int length) throws SQLException
1.2	public......................void	**setBlob** (int i, *Blob* x) throws SQLException
	public......................void	**setBoolean** (int parameterIndex, boolean x) throws SQLException
	public......................void	**setByte** (int parameterIndex, byte x) throws SQLException
	public......................void	**setBytes** (int parameterIndex, byte[] x) throws SQLException
1.2	public......................void	**setCharacterStream** (int parameterIndex, java.io.Reader reader, int length) throws SQLException
1.2	public......................void	**setClob** (int i, *Clob* x) throws SQLException
	public......................void	**setDate** (int parameterIndex, Date x) throws SQLException
1.2	public......................void	**setDate** (int parameterIndex, Date x, java.util.Calendar cal) throws SQLException
	public......................void	**setDouble** (int parameterIndex, double x) throws SQLException
	public......................void	**setFloat** (int parameterIndex, float x) throws SQLException
	public......................void	**setInt** (int parameterIndex, int x) throws SQLException
	public......................void	**setLong** (int parameterIndex, long x) throws SQLException
	public......................void	**setNull** (int parameterIndex, int sqlType) throws SQLException
1.2	public......................void	**setNull** (int paramIndex, int sqlType, String typeName) throws SQLException
	public......................void	**setObject** (int parameterIndex, Object x) throws SQLException
	public......................void	**setObject** (int parameterIndex, Object x, int targetSqlType) throws SQLException
	public......................void	**setObject** (int parameterIndex, Object x, int targetSqlType, int scale) throws SQLException
1.2	public......................void	**setRef** (int i, *Ref* x) throws SQLException
	public......................void	**setShort** (int parameterIndex, short x) throws SQLException
	public......................void	**setString** (int parameterIndex, String x) throws SQLException
	public......................void	**setTime** (int parameterIndex, Time x) throws SQLException
1.2	public......................void	**setTime** (int parameterIndex, Time x, java.util.Calendar cal) throws SQLException
	public......................void	**setTimestamp** (int parameterIndex, Timestamp x) throws SQLException
1.2	public......................void	**setTimestamp** (int parameterIndex, Timestamp x, java.util.Calendar cal) throws SQLException
D	public......................void	**setUnicodeStream** (int parameterIndex, java.io.InputStream x, int length) throws SQLException

---

Principal❶   org.omg.CORBA

Object
    └Principal
1.2 ○

D	○	public abstract...........byte[]	**name** ()
D	○	public abstract.............void	**name** (byte[] value)
	✳	public..........................	**Principal** ()

Principal❷   java.security

1.1   *Principal*   P○

	public...................boolean	**equals** (Object another)
	public.....................String	**getName** ()
	public........................int	**hashCode** ()
	public.....................String	**toString** ()

PrincipalHolder   org.omg.CORBA

Object
    └PrincipalHolder ------------------------- *org.omg.CORBA.portable.Streamable* [1]
1.2 ●

	1	public......................void	**_read** (org.omg.CORBA.portable.InputStream input)
	1	public..................TypeCode	**_type** ()
	1	public......................void	**_write** (org.omg.CORBA.portable.OutputStream output)
✳		public..........................	**PrincipalHolder** ()
✳		public..........................	**PrincipalHolder** (Principal initial)
		public..................Principal	**value**

Printable   java.awt.print

1.2   *Printable*

▲	public static final.............int	**NO_SUCH_PAGE** = 1
▲	public static final.............int	**PAGE_EXISTS** = 0
	public........................int	**print** (java.awt.Graphics graphics, PageFormat pageFormat, int pageIndex) throws PrinterException

569

PrinterAbortException

			java.awt.print

```
Object
└Throwable --------------------------- java.io.Serializable
   └Exception
1.2     └PrinterException
1.2        └PrinterAbortException
```

| ✳ | public......................... | **PrinterAbortException** () |
| ✳ | public......................... | **PrinterAbortException** (String msg) |

PrinterException

			java.awt.print

```
Object
└Throwable --------------------------- java.io.Serializable
   └Exception
1.2     └PrinterException
```

| ✳ | public......................... | **PrinterException** () |
| ✳ | public......................... | **PrinterException** (String msg) |

PrinterGraphics

			java.awt.print

```
1.2   PrinterGraphics
```

| | public............... PrinterJob | **getPrinterJob** () |

PrinterIOException

			java.awt.print

```
Object
└Throwable --------------------------- java.io.Serializable
   └Exception
1.2     └PrinterException
1.2        └PrinterIOException
```

| | public...... java.io.IOException | **getIOException** () |
| ✳ | public......................... | **PrinterIOException** (java.io.IOException exception) |

PrinterJob

			java.awt.print

```
Object
1.2 ○ └PrinterJob
```

○	public abstract ....void	**cancel** ()
	public..............PageFormat	**defaultPage** ()
○	public abstract ....PageFormat	**defaultPage** (PageFormat page)
○	public abstract ....int	**getCopies** ()
○	public abstract ....String	**getJobName** ()
△	public static .... PrinterJob	**getPrinterJob** ()
○	public abstract .... String	**getUserName** ()
○	public abstract .... boolean	**isCancelled** ()
○	public abstract ....PageFormat	**pageDialog** (PageFormat page)
○	public abstract ....void	**print** () throws PrinterException
○	public abstract .... boolean	**printDialog** ()
✳	public.........................	**PrinterJob** ()
○	public abstract ....void	**setCopies** (int copies)
○	public abstract ....void	**setJobName** (String jobName)
○	public abstract ....void	**setPageable** (*Pageable* document) throws NullPointerException
○	public abstract ....void	**setPrintable** (*Printable* painter)
○	public abstract ....void	**setPrintable** (*Printable* painter, PageFormat format)
○	public abstract ....PageFormat	**validatePage** (PageFormat page)

Class   *Interface*   —extends   - - -implements   ○ abstract   ● final   △ static   ▲ static final   ✳ constructor   x x—inherited   x **x**—declared   **x x**—overridden

PrintGraphics   java.awt

1.1   *PrintGraphics*   P

    public .... PrintJob **getPrintJob** ()

PrintJob   java.awt

     Object[1]
1.1 ○   └PrintJob   P

○	public abstract .... void	**end** ()
1	public .... **void**	**finalize** ()
○	public abstract .... Graphics	**getGraphics** ()
○	public abstract ...... Dimension	**getPageDimension** ()
○	public abstract .... int	**getPageResolution** ()
○	public abstract .... boolean	**lastPageFirst** ()
*	public	**PrintJob** ()

PrintStream   java.io

     Object
○   └OutputStream
      └FilterOutputStream[1]
       └PrintStream

	public .... boolean	**checkError** ()
1	public .... **void**	**close** ()
1	public: .... **void**	**flush** ()
1	protected .... OutputStream	out
	public .... void	**print** (boolean b)
	public .... void	**print** (char c)
	public .... void	**print** (char[] s)
	public .... void	**print** (double d)
	public .... void	**print** (float f)
	public .... void	**print** (int i)
	public .... void	**print** (Object obj)
	public .... void	**print** (String s)
	public .... void	**print** (long l)
	public .... void	**println** ()
	public .... void	**println** (boolean x)
	public .... void	**println** (char x)
	public .... void	**println** (char[] x)
	public .... void	**println** (double x)
	public .... void	**println** (float x)
	public .... void	**println** (int x)
	public .... void	**println** (Object x)
	public .... void	**println** (String x)
	public .... void	**println** (long x)
*	public	**PrintStream** (OutputStream out)
*	public	**PrintStream** (OutputStream out, boolean autoFlush)
1.1	protected .... void	**setError** ()
1	public .... void	write (byte[] b) throws IOException
1	public .... **void**	**write** (int b)
1	public .... **void**	**write** (byte[] buf, int off, int len)

PrintWriter   java.io

     Object
1.1 ○   └Writer[1]
1.1   └PrintWriter

	public .... boolean	**checkError** ()
1	public .... **void**	**close** ()
1	public .... **void**	**flush** ()
1	protected .... Object	lock
1.2	protected .... Writer	**out**
	public .... void	**print** (boolean b)
	public .... void	**print** (char c)
	public .... void	**print** (char[] s)
	public .... void	**print** (double d)

PrintWriter

	public	void	**print**	(float f)
	public	void	**print**	(int i)
	public	void	**print**	(Object obj)
	public	void	**print**	(String s)
	public	void	**print**	(long l)
	public	void	**println**	()
	public	void	**println**	(boolean x)
	public	void	**println**	(char x)
	public	void	**println**	(char[] x)
	public	void	**println**	(double x)
	public	void	**println**	(float x)
	public	void	**println**	(int x)
	public	void	**println**	(Object x)
	public	void	**println**	(String x)
	public	void	**println**	(long x)
*	public		**PrintWriter**	(OutputStream out)
*	public		**PrintWriter**	(Writer out)
*	public		**PrintWriter**	(OutputStream out, boolean autoFlush)
*	public		**PrintWriter**	(Writer out, boolean autoFlush)
	protected	void	**setError**	()
1	public	**void**	**write**	(char[] buf)
1	public	**void**	**write**	(int c)
1	public	**void**	**write**	(String s)
1	public	**void**	**write**	(char[] buf, int off, int len)
1	public	**void**	**write**	(String s, int off, int len)

P

PRIVATE_MEMBER   org.omg.CORBA

1.2   *PRIVATE_MEMBER*

▲   public static final .... short **value** = 0

PrivateKey   java.security
                                                                              P○

1.1   *PrivateKey* ————————————— *Key [1] (java.io.Serializable)*

1	public	String	getAlgorithm ()
1	public	byte[]	getEncoded ()
1	public	String	getFormat ()
1.2 ▲ 1	public static final	**long**	**serialVersionUID** = 6034044314589513430

PrivilegedAction   java.security
                                                                              P○

1.2   *PrivilegedAction*

public .... Object **run** ()

PrivilegedActionException   java.security
                                                                              P○

Object
└Throwable [1] - *java.io.Serializable*
  └Exception
    └PrivilegedActionException
1.2

	public	Exception	**getException** ()
1	public	**void**	**printStackTrace** ()
1	public	**void**	**printStackTrace** (java.io.PrintStream ps)
1	public	**void**	**printStackTrace** (java.io.PrintWriter pw)
*	public		**PrivilegedActionException** (Exception exception)

PrivilegedExceptionAction   java.security
                                                                              P○

1.2   *PrivilegedExceptionAction*

public .... Object **run** () throws Exception

---

Class   *Interface*   —extends   - - -implements   ○ abstract   ● final   △ static   ▲ static final   * constructor   x x—inherited   x **x**—declared   **x x**—overridden

Process
java.lang

```
Object
└─Process
```
P

○	public abstract .... void	**destroy** ()	
○	public abstract .... int	**exitValue** ()	
○	public abstract	**getErrorStream** ()	
	.... java.io.InputStream		
○	public abstract	**getInputStream** ()	
	.... java.io.InputStream		
○	public abstract	**getOutputStream** ()	
	.... java.io.OutputStream		
*	public	**Process** ()	
○	public abstract .... int	**waitFor** () throws InterruptedException	

ProfileDataException
java.awt.color

```
Object
└─Throwable --------------------------- java.io.Serializable
    └─Exception
        └─RuntimeException
            └─ProfileDataException
```
1.2

*	public	**ProfileDataException** (String s)

ProgressBarUI
javax.swing.plaf

```
Object
1.2 ○  └─ComponentUI [1]
1.2 ○      └─ProgressBarUI
```

[1] *11 inherited members from ComponentUI not shown*

*	public	**ProgressBarUI** ()

ProgressMonitor
javax.swing

```
Object
1.2  └─ProgressMonitor
```

	public .... void	**close** ()	
	public .... int	**getMaximum** ()	
	public .... int	**getMillisToDecideToPopup** ()	
	public .... int	**getMillisToPopup** ()	
	public .... int	**getMinimum** ()	
	public .... String	**getNote** ()	
	public .... boolean	**isCanceled** ()	
*	public	**ProgressMonitor** (java.awt.Component parentComponent, Object message, String note, int min, int max)	
	public .... void	**setMaximum** (int m)	
	public .... void	**setMillisToDecideToPopup** (int millisToDecideToPopup)	
	public .... void	**setMillisToPopup** (int millisToPopup)	
	public .... void	**setMinimum** (int m)	
	public .... void	**setNote** (String note)	
	public .... void	**setProgress** (int nv)	

ProgressMonitorInputStream
javax.swing

```
Object
○  └─java.io.InputStream
      └─java.io.FilterInputStream [1]
1.2       └─ProgressMonitorInputStream
```

1	public .... int	available () throws java.io.IOException	
1	public .... **void**	**close** () throws java.io.IOException	
	public .... ProgressMonitor	**getProgressMonitor** ()	
1	protected .. java.io.InputStream	in	
1	public synchronized .... void	mark (int readlimit)	
1	public .... boolean	markSupported ()	

ProgressMonitorInputStream

*	public		**ProgressMonitorInputStream** (java.awt.Component parentComponent, Object message, java.io.InputStream in)
1	public	**int**	**read** () throws java.io.IOException
1	public	**int**	**read** (byte[] b) throws java.io.IOException
1	public	**int**	**read** (byte[] b, int off, int len) throws java.io.IOException
1	public synchronized	**void**	**reset** () throws java.io.IOException
1	public	**long**	**skip** (long n) throws java.io.IOException

Properties   java.util

P

```
Object
 └ Dictionary
    └ Hashtable 1 - - - - - - - - - - - - - - - - - - - - - - - - Map, Cloneable, java.io.Serializable
       └ Properties
```

	1	public synchronized ....void	clear ()
	1	public synchronized ....Object	clone ()
	1	public synchronized .. boolean	contains (Object value)
	1	public synchronized .. boolean	containsKey (Object key)
1.2	1	public................. boolean	containsValue (Object value)
		protected .... Properties	**defaults**
	1	public synchronized	elements ()
		.... *Enumeration*	
1.2	1	public.......................*Set*	entrySet ()
	1	public synchronized .. boolean	equals (Object o)
	1	public synchronized ....Object	get (Object key)
		public.................... String	**getProperty** (String key)
		public.................... String	**getProperty** (String key, String defaultValue)
	1	public synchronized ....int	hashCode ()
	1	public.................. boolean	isEmpty ()
	1	public synchronized	keys ()
		.... *Enumeration*	
1.2	1	public.......................*Set*	keySet ()
		public....................void	**list** (java.io.PrintStream out)
1.1		public....................void	**list** (java.io.PrintWriter out)
		public synchronized ....void	**load** (java.io.InputStream inStream) throws java.io.IOException
	*	public...........................	**Properties** ()
	*	public...........................	**Properties** (Properties defaults)
		public............. *Enumeration*	**propertyNames** ()
	1	public synchronized .... Object	put (Object key, Object value)
1.2	1	public synchronized ......void	putAll (*Map* t)
	1	protected ....void	rehash ()
	1	public synchronized .... Object	remove (Object key)
D		public synchronized ....void	**save** (java.io.OutputStream out, String header)
1.2		public synchronized ....Object	**setProperty** (String key, String value)
	1	public........................int	size ()
1.2		public synchronized ......void	**store** (java.io.OutputStream out, String header) throws java.io.IOException
	1	public synchronized .....String	toString ()
1.2	1	public............... *Collection*	values ()

PropertyChangeEvent   java.beans

```
Object
 └ java.util.EventObject 1 - - - - - - - - - - - - - - - - - - java.io.Serializable
    └ PropertyChangeEvent
```
(1.1 marks on left for EventObject and PropertyChangeEvent lines)

		public.................... Object	**getNewValue** ()
		public.................... Object	**getOldValue** ()
		public.................... Object	**getPropagationId** ()
		public.................... String	**getPropertyName** ()
	1	public.................... Object	getSource ()
*		public...........................	**PropertyChangeEvent** (Object source, String propertyName, Object oldValue, Object newValue)
		public....................void	**setPropagationId** (Object propagationId)
	1	protected transient...... Object	source
	1	public.................... String	toString ()

Class   *Interface*   —extends   - - -implements   ○ abstract   ● final   △ static   ▲ static final   * constructor   x x—inherited   x **x**—declared   **x x**—overridden

PropertyChangeListener | java.beans

1.1	*PropertyChangeListener*————————————— *java.util.EventListener*	
	public......................void **propertyChange** (PropertyChangeEvent evt)	

PropertyChangeSupport | java.beans

Object
1.1 └PropertyChangeSupport - - - - - - - - - - - - - - - - *java.io.Serializable*

1.1	public synchronized ....void	**addPropertyChangeListener** (*PropertyChangeListener* listener)
1.2	public synchronized ....void	**addPropertyChangeListener** (String propertyName, *PropertyChangeListener* listener)
1.2	public......................void	**firePropertyChange** (PropertyChangeEvent evt)
1.2	public......................void	**firePropertyChange** (String propertyName, int oldValue, int newValue)
1.2	public......................void	**firePropertyChange** (String propertyName, boolean oldValue, boolean newValue)
	public......................void	**firePropertyChange** (String propertyName, Object oldValue, Object newValue)
1.2	public synchronized .. boolean	**hasListeners** (String propertyName)
*	public...........................	**PropertyChangeSupport** (Object sourceBean)
	public synchronized ....void	**removePropertyChangeListener** (*PropertyChangeListener* listener)
1.2	public synchronized ....void	**removePropertyChangeListener** (String propertyName, *PropertyChangeListener* listener)

PropertyDescriptor | java.beans

Object
1.1 └FeatureDescriptor[1]
1.1 └PropertyDescriptor

	1	public.... *java.util.Enumeration*	attributeNames ()
	1	public....................String	getDisplayName ()
	1	public....................String	getName ()
		public......................Class	**getPropertyEditorClass** ()
		public......................Class	**getPropertyType** ()
		public .java.lang.reflect.Method	**getReadMethod** ()
	1	public....................String	getShortDescription ()
	1	public....................Object	getValue (String attributeName)
		public .java.lang.reflect.Method	**getWriteMethod** ()
		public..................boolean	**isBound** ()
		public..................boolean	**isConstrained** ()
	1	public..................boolean	isExpert ()
	1	public..................boolean	isHidden ()
1.2	1	public..................boolean	isPreferred ()
*		public...........................	**PropertyDescriptor** (String propertyName, Class beanClass) throws IntrospectionException
*		public...........................	**PropertyDescriptor** (String propertyName, java.lang.reflect.Method getter, java.lang.reflect.Method setter) throws IntrospectionException
*		public...........................	**PropertyDescriptor** (String propertyName, Class beanClass, String getterName, String setterName) throws IntrospectionException
		public......................void	**setBound** (boolean bound)
		public......................void	**setConstrained** (boolean constrained)
	1	public......................void	setDisplayName (String displayName)
	1	public......................void	setExpert (boolean expert)
	1	public......................void	setHidden (boolean hidden)
	1	public......................void	setName (String name)
1.2	1	public......................void	setPreferred (boolean preferred)
		public......................void	**setPropertyEditorClass** (Class propertyEditorClass)
1.2		public......................void	**setReadMethod** (java.lang.reflect.Method getter) throws IntrospectionException
	1	public......................void	setShortDescription (String text)
	1	public......................void	setValue (String attributeName, Object value)
1.2		public......................void	**setWriteMethod** (java.lang.reflect.Method setter) throws IntrospectionException

PropertyEditor | java.beans

1.1 *PropertyEditor*

public......................void	**addPropertyChangeListener** (*PropertyChangeListener* listener)
public....................String	**getAsText** ()
public.... java.awt.Component	**getCustomEditor** ()
public....................String	**getJavaInitializationString** ()

P

Classes

PropertyEditor

public	String[]	**getTags** ()	
public	Object	**getValue** ()	
public	boolean	**isPaintable** ()	
public	void	**paintValue** (java.awt.Graphics gfx, java.awt.Rectangle box)	
public	void	**removePropertyChangeListener** (*PropertyChangeListener* listener)	
public	void	**setAsText** (String text) throws IllegalArgumentException	
public	void	**setValue** (Object value)	
public	boolean	**supportsCustomEditor** ()	

PropertyEditorManager   java.beans

Object
  └PropertyEditorManager *(1.1)*

△	public static synchronized *PropertyEditor*	**findEditor** (Class targetType)	
△	public static synchronized String[]	**getEditorSearchPath** ()	
✱	public	**PropertyEditorManager** ()	
△	public static void	**registerEditor** (Class targetType, Class editorClass)	
△	public static synchronized void	**setEditorSearchPath** (String[] path)	

PropertyEditorSupport   java.beans

Object
  └PropertyEditorSupport - - - - - - - - - - - - - - - - - - *PropertyEditor* [1] *(1.1)*

1	public synchronized void	**addPropertyChangeListener** (*PropertyChangeListener* listener)	
	public void	**firePropertyChange** ()	
1	public String	**getAsText** ()	
1	public java.awt.Component	**getCustomEditor** ()	
1	public String	**getJavaInitializationString** ()	
1	public String[]	**getTags** ()	
1	public Object	**getValue** ()	
1	public boolean	**isPaintable** ()	
1	public void	**paintValue** (java.awt.Graphics gfx, java.awt.Rectangle box)	
✱	protected	**PropertyEditorSupport** ()	
✱	protected	**PropertyEditorSupport** (Object source)	
1	public synchronized void	**removePropertyChangeListener** (*PropertyChangeListener* listener)	
1	public void	**setAsText** (String text) throws IllegalArgumentException	
1	public void	**setValue** (Object value)	
1	public boolean	**supportsCustomEditor** ()	

PropertyPermission   java.util

P

Object
  └java.security.Permission [1] - - - - - - - - - - - - - - - - *java.security.Guard*, *java.io.Serializable* *(1.2 ○)*
    └java.security.BasicPermission [2] - - - - - - - - - *java.io.Serializable* *(1.2 ○)*
      └PropertyPermission *(1.2 ●)*

1	public void	checkGuard (Object object) throws SecurityException	
2	public boolean	**equals** (Object obj)	
2	public String	**getActions** ()	
● 1	public final String	getName ()	
2	public int	**hashCode** ()	
2	public boolean	**implies** (java.security.Permission p)	
2	public **java.security** ↵ .PermissionCollection	**newPermissionCollection** ()	
✱	public	**PropertyPermission** (String name, String actions)	
1	public String	toString ()	

PropertyResourceBundle   java.util

P

Object
  └ResourceBundle [1] *(1.1 ○)*
    └PropertyResourceBundle *(1.1)*

Class *Interface* ——extends - - -implements ○ abstract ● final △ static ▲ static final ✱ constructor x x—inherited x **x**—declared **x x**—overridden

▲	1	public static final . . . . ResourceBundle	getBundle (String baseName) throws MissingResourceException
▲	1	public static final . . . . ResourceBundle	getBundle (String baseName, Locale locale)
1.2 △	1	public static . . ResourceBundle	getBundle (String baseName, Locale locale, ClassLoader loader) throws MissingResourceException
	1	public . . . . *Enumeration* **getKeys** ()	
1.2	1	public . . . . Locale getLocale ()	
●	1	public final . . . . Object getObject (String key) throws MissingResourceException	
●	1	public final . . . . String getString (String key) throws MissingResourceException	
●	1	public final . . . . String[] getStringArray (String key) throws MissingResourceException	
	1	public . . . . **Object handleGetObject** (String key)	
	1	protected . . . . . ResourceBundle parent	
*		public . . . . **PropertyResourceBundle** (java.io.InputStream stream) throws java.io.IOException	
	1	protected . . . . void setParent (ResourceBundle parent)	

PropertyVetoException | java.beans

```
Object
 └ Throwable ─ ─ ─ ─ ─ ─ ─ ─ ─ ─ ─ ─ ─ ─ ─ ─ ─ ─ java.io.Serializable
    └ Exception
       └ PropertyVetoException
```
1.1

	public . . . PropertyChangeEvent **getPropertyChangeEvent** ()
*	public . . . . **PropertyVetoException** (String mess, PropertyChangeEvent evt)

ProtectionDomain | java.security

P^O
```
Object¹
 └ ProtectionDomain
```
1.2

●	public final . . . . CodeSource **getCodeSource** ()
●	public final . . . . **getPermissions** ()
	. . . . PermissionCollection
	public . . . . boolean **implies** (Permission permission)
*	public . . . . **ProtectionDomain** (CodeSource codesource, PermissionCollection permissions)
	1	public . . . . String **toString** ()

ProtocolException | java.net

P
```
Object
 └ Throwable ─ ─ ─ ─ ─ ─ ─ ─ ─ ─ ─ ─ ─ ─ ─ ─ ─ ─ java.io.Serializable
    └ Exception
       └ java.io.IOException
          └ ProtocolException
```

*	public . . . . **ProtocolException** ()
*	public . . . . **ProtocolException** (String host)

Provider | java.security

P^O
```
Object
 ○ └ java.util.Dictionary
    └ java.util.Hashtable¹ ─ ─ ─ ─ ─ ─ ─ ─ ─ ─ ─ java.util.Map, Cloneable, java.io.Serializable
       └ java.util.Properties²
1.1 ○     └ Provider
```

	1	public synchronized . . . . . . **void clear** ()	
	1	public synchronized . . . . Object clone ()	
	1	public synchronized . . boolean contains (Object value)	
	1	public synchronized . . boolean containsKey (Object key)	
1.2	1	public . . . . boolean containsValue (Object value)	
	2	protected . . . java.util.Properties defaults	
	1	public synchronized . . . . elements ()	
		. . . . java.util.Enumeration	
1.2	1	public . . . . *java.util.Set* **entrySet** ()	
	1	public synchronized . . boolean equals (Object o)	
	1	public synchronized . . . . Object get (Object key)	
		public . . . . String **getInfo** ()	

Provider

		public.....................String	**getName** ()
	2	public.....................String	getProperty (String key)
	2	public.....................String	getProperty (String key, String defaultValue)
		public.....................double	**getVersion** ()
	1	public synchronized ....int	hashCode ()
	1	public.................... boolean	isEmpty ()
	1	public synchronized	keys ()
		.... *java.util.Enumeration*	
1.2	1	public.............. ***java.util.Set***	**keySet** ()
	2	public.......................void	list (java.io.PrintStream out)
	2	public.......................void	list (java.io.PrintWriter out)
	2	public synchronized ...... **void**	**load** (java.io.InputStream inStream) throws java.io.IOException
	2	public... *java.util.Enumeration*	propertyNames ()
*		protected......................	**Provider** (String name, double version, String info)
	1	public synchronized ....**Object**	**put** (Object key, Object value)
1.2	1	public synchronized ...... **void**	**putAll** (*java.util.Map* t)
	1	protected...................void	rehash ()
	1	public synchronized ....**Object**	**remove** (Object key)
1.2	2	public synchronized ....Object	setProperty (String key, String value)
	1	public.........................int	size ()
1.2	2	public synchronized 2 ......void	store (java.io.OutputStream out, String header) throws java.io.IOException
	1	public.................. **String**	**toString** ()
1.2	1	public..... ***java.util.Collection***	**values** ()

ProviderException — java.security
<table>
<tr><td colspan="2">ProviderException</td><td>java.security</td></tr>
<tr><td colspan="3" align="right">P^O</td></tr>
</table>

ProviderException	java.security
	P[O]

```
        Object
         └Throwable - - - - - - - - - - - - - - - - - - - - - - - - - java.io.Serializable
          └Exception
           └RuntimeException
1.1          └ProviderException
```

*		public..................	**ProviderException** ()
*		public..................	**ProviderException** (String s)

PUBLIC_MEMBER	org.omg.CORBA

1.2	*PUBLIC_MEMBER*

▲	public static final ....short	**value** = 1

PublicKey	java.security

1.1	*PublicKey*————————————— Key [1] (*java.io.Serializable*)

(right side: P[O])

	1	public.....................String	getAlgorithm ()
	1	public.....................byte[]	getEncoded ()
	1	public.....................String	getFormat ()
1.2 ▲	1	public static final ....**long**	**serialVersionUID** = 7187392471159151072

PushbackInputStream	java.io

```
        Object
   ○     └InputStream
          └FilterInputStream [1]
           └PushbackInputStream
```

	1	public....................... **int**	**available** () throws IOException
1.1		protected.................byte[]	**buf**
	1	public synchronized ...... **void**	**close** () throws IOException
	1	protected.......... InputStream	**in**
	1	public synchronized ......void	mark (int readlimit)
	1	public.................. **boolean**	**markSupported** ()
1.1		protected.....................int	**pos**
*		public..........................	**PushbackInputStream** (InputStream in)
1.1 *		public..........................	**PushbackInputStream** (InputStream in, int size)
	1	public....................... **int**	**read** () throws IOException
	1	public.......................int	read (byte[] b) throws IOException

---

Class   *Interface*   —extends   - - -implements   ○ abstract   ● final   △ static   ▲ static final   ✳ constructor   x x—inherited   x **x**—declared   **x x**—overridden

1	public	**int**	**read** (byte[] b, int off, int len) throws IOException
1	public synchronized	void	reset () throws IOException
1	public	**long**	**skip** (long n) throws IOException
1.1	public	void	**unread** (byte[] b) throws IOException
	public	void	**unread** (int b) throws IOException
1.1	public	void	**unread** (byte[] b, int off, int len) throws IOException

PushbackReader   java.io

```
     Object
1.1 ○ └─Reader1
1.1 ○    └─FilterReader2
1.1         └─PushbackReader
```

2	public	**void**	**close** () throws IOException
2	protected	Reader	in
1	protected	Object	lock
2	public	**void**	**mark** (int readAheadLimit) throws IOException
2	public	**boolean**	**markSupported** ()
*	public		**PushbackReader** (Reader in)
*	public		**PushbackReader** (Reader in, int size)
2	public	**int**	**read** () throws IOException
1	public	int	read (char[] cbuf) throws IOException
2	public	**int**	**read** (char[] cbuf, int off, int len) throws IOException
2	public	**boolean**	**ready** () throws IOException
2	public	**void**	**reset** () throws IOException
2	public	long	skip (long n) throws IOException
	public	void	**unread** (char[] cbuf) throws IOException
	public	void	**unread** (int c) throws IOException
	public	void	**unread** (char[] cbuf, int off, int len) throws IOException

Q

QuadCurve2D   java.awt.geom

```
     Object1
1.2 ○ └─QuadCurve2D ------------------------- java.awt.Shape2, Cloneable
```

1	public	**Object**	**clone** ()
2	public	boolean	**contains** (Point2D p)
2	public	boolean	**contains** (Rectangle2D r)
2	public	boolean	**contains** (double x, double y)
2	public	boolean	**contains** (double x, double y, double w, double h)
2	public	java.awt.Rectangle	**getBounds** ()
○ 2	public abstract	Rectangle2D	**getBounds2D** ()
○	public abstract	Point2D	**getCtrlPt** ()
○	public abstract	double	**getCtrlX** ()
○	public abstract	double	**getCtrlY** ()
	public	double	**getFlatness** ()
△	public static	double	**getFlatness** (double[] coords, int offset)
△	public static	double	**getFlatness** (double x1, double y1, double ctrlx, double ctrly, double x2, double y2)
	public	double	**getFlatnessSq** ()
△	public static	double	**getFlatnessSq** (double[] coords, int offset)
△	public static	double	**getFlatnessSq** (double x1, double y1, double ctrlx, double ctrly, double x2, double y2)
○	public abstract	Point2D	**getP1** ()
○	public abstract	Point2D	**getP2** ()
2	public	*PathIterator*	**getPathIterator** (AffineTransform at)
2	public	*PathIterator*	**getPathIterator** (AffineTransform at, double flatness)
○	public abstract	double	**getX1** ()
○	public abstract	double	**getX2** ()
○	public abstract	double	**getY1** ()
○	public abstract	double	**getY2** ()
2	public	boolean	**intersects** (Rectangle2D r)
2	public	boolean	**intersects** (double x, double y, double w, double h)
*	protected		**QuadCurve2D** ()
	public	void	**setCurve** (QuadCurve2D c)
	public	void	**setCurve** (double[] coords, int offset)
	public	void	**setCurve** (Point2D[] pts, int offset)
	public	void	**setCurve** (Point2D p1, Point2D cp, Point2D p2)
○	public abstract	void	**setCurve** (double x1, double y1, double ctrlx, double ctrly, double x2, double y2)
△	public static	int	**solveQuadratic** (double[] eqn)
	public	void	**subdivide** (QuadCurve2D left, QuadCurve2D right)

Classes

QuadCurve2D

△	public static	...............void	**subdivide**	(QuadCurve2D src, QuadCurve2D left, QuadCurve2D right)
△	public static	...............void	**subdivide**	(double[] src, int srcoff, double[] left, int leftoff, double[] right, int rightoff)

QuadCurve2D.Double   java.awt.geom

```
        Object
1.2 O   └─QuadCurve2D 1 ------------------------ java.awt.Shape, Cloneable
1.2         └─QuadCurve2D.Double
```

	1	public...................Object	clone	()
	1	public.................. boolean	contains	(Point2D p)
	1	public.................. boolean	contains	(Rectangle2D r)
	1	public.................. boolean	contains	(double x, double y)
	1	public.................. boolean	contains	(double x, double y, double w, double h)
		public....................double	**ctrlx**	
		public....................double	**ctrly**	
✳		public...........................	**Double**	()
✳		public...........................	**Double**	(double x1, double y1, double ctrlx, double ctrly, double x2, double y2)
	1	public...... java.awt.Rectangle	getBounds	()
	1	public........... **Rectangle2D**	**getBounds2D**	()
	1	public..................**Point2D**	**getCtrlPt**	()
	1	public.............. **double**	**getCtrlX**	()
	1	public.............. **double**	**getCtrlY**	()
	1	public....................double	getFlatness	()
△	1	public static ....double	getFlatness	(double[] coords, int offset)
△	1	public static ....double	getFlatness	(double x1, double y1, double ctrlx, double ctrly, double x2, double y2)
	1	public....................double	getFlatnessSq	()
△	1	public static ....double	getFlatnessSq	(double[] coords, int offset)
△	1	public static ....double	getFlatnessSq	(double x1, double y1, double ctrlx, double ctrly, double x2, double y2)
	1	public.............. **Point2D**	**getP1**	()
	1	public.............. **Point2D**	**getP2**	()
	1	public.............. *PathIterator*	getPathIterator	(AffineTransform at)
	1	public.............. *PathIterator*	getPathIterator	(AffineTransform at, double flatness)
	1	public.............. **double**	**getX1**	()
	1	public.............. **double**	**getX2**	()
	1	public.............. **double**	**getY1**	()
	1	public.............. **double**	**getY2**	()
	1	public.................. boolean	intersects	(Rectangle2D r)
	1	public.................. boolean	intersects	(double x, double y, double w, double h)
	1	public....................void	setCurve	(QuadCurve2D c)
	1	public....................void	setCurve	(double[] coords, int offset)
	1	public....................void	setCurve	(Point2D[] pts, int offset)
	1	public....................void	setCurve	(Point2D p1, Point2D cp, Point2D p2)
	1	public............. **void setCurve**		(double x1, double y1, double ctrlx, double ctrly, double x2, double y2)
△	1	public static ....int	solveQuadratic	(double[] eqn)
	1	public....................void	subdivide	(QuadCurve2D left, QuadCurve2D right)
△	1	public static ....void	subdivide	(QuadCurve2D src, QuadCurve2D left, QuadCurve2D right)
△	1	public static ....void	subdivide	(double[] src, int srcoff, double[] left, int leftoff, double[] right, int rightoff)
		public....................double	**x1**	
		public....................double	**x2**	
		public....................double	**y1**	
		public....................double	**y2**	

QuadCurve2D.Float   java.awt.geom

```
        Object
1.2 O   └─QuadCurve2D 1 ------------------------ java.awt.Shape, Cloneable
1.2         └─QuadCurve2D.Float
```

	1	public...................Object	clone	()
	1	public.................. boolean	contains	(Point2D p)
	1	public.................. boolean	contains	(Rectangle2D r)
	1	public.................. boolean	contains	(double x, double y)
	1	public.................. boolean	contains	(double x, double y, double w, double h)
		public....................float	**ctrlx**	
		public....................float	**ctrly**	
✳		public...........................	**Float**	()
✳		public...........................	**Float**	(float x1, float y1, float ctrlx, float ctrly, float x2, float y2)
	1	public...... java.awt.Rectangle	getBounds	()

Class   *Interface*   —extends   - - -implements   O abstract   ● final   △ static   ▲ static final   ✳ constructor   x x—inherited   x **x**—declared   **x x**—overridden

	1	public	**Rectangle2D**	**getBounds2D** ()
	1	public	**Point2D**	**getCtrlPt** ()
	1	public	**double**	**getCtrlX** ()
	1	public	**double**	**getCtrlY** ()
	1	public	double	getFlatness ()
△	1	public static	double	getFlatness (double[] coords, int offset)
△	1	public static	double	getFlatness (double x1, double y1, double ctrlx, double ctrly, double x2, double y2)
	1	public	double	getFlatnessSq ()
△	1	public static	double	getFlatnessSq (double[] coords, int offset)
△	1	public static	double	getFlatnessSq (double x1, double y1, double ctrlx, double ctrly, double x2, double y2)
	1	public	**Point2D**	**getP1** ()
	1	public	**Point2D**	**getP2** ()
	1	public	*PathIterator*	getPathIterator (AffineTransform at)
	1	public	*PathIterator*	getPathIterator (AffineTransform at, double flatness)
	1	public	**double**	**getX1** ()
	1	public	**double**	**getX2** ()
	1	public	**double**	**getY1** ()
	1	public	**double**	**getY2** ()
	1	public	boolean	intersects (Rectangle2D r)
	1	public	boolean	intersects (double x, double y, double w, double h)
	1	public	void	setCurve (QuadCurve2D c)
	1	public	void	setCurve (double[] coords, int offset)
	1	public	void	setCurve (Point2D[] pts, int offset)
	1	public	void	setCurve (Point2D p1, Point2D cp, Point2D p2)
	1	public	**void**	**setCurve** (double x1, double y1, double ctrlx, double ctrly, double x2, double y2)
		public	void	**setCurve** (float x1, float y1, float ctrlx, float ctrly, float x2, float y2)
△	1	public static	int	solveQuadratic (double[] eqn)
	1	public	void	subdivide (QuadCurve2D left, QuadCurve2D right)
△	1	public static	void	subdivide (QuadCurve2D src, QuadCurve2D left, QuadCurve2D right)
△	1	public static	void	subdivide (double[] src, int srcoff, double[] left, int leftoff, double[] right, int rightoff)
		public	float	**x1**
		public	float	**x2**
		public	float	**y1**
		public	float	**y2**

R

Random
java.util

Object
└ Random - *java.io.Serializable*
P

1.1		protected synchronized	int	**next** (int bits)
1.2		public	boolean	**nextBoolean** ()
1.1		public	void	**nextBytes** (byte[] bytes)
		public	double	**nextDouble** ()
		public	float	**nextFloat** ()
		public synchronized	double	**nextGaussian** ()
		public	int	**nextInt** ()
1.2		public	int	**nextInt** (int n)
		public	long	**nextLong** ()
✳		public		**Random** ()
✳		public		**Random** (long seed)
		public synchronized	void	**setSeed** (long seed)

Classes

RandomAccessFile
java.io

Object
└ RandomAccessFile - *DataOutput* [1], *DataInput* [2]
P^O

		public native	void	**close** () throws IOException
●		public final	FileDescriptor	**getFD** () throws IOException
		public native	long	**getFilePointer** () throws IOException
		public native	long	**length** () throws IOException
✳		public		**RandomAccessFile** (File file, String mode) throws IOException
✳		public		**RandomAccessFile** (String name, String mode) throws FileNotFoundException
		public native	int	**read** () throws IOException
		public	int	**read** (byte[] b) throws IOException
		public	int	**read** (byte[] b, int off, int len) throws IOException
●	2	public final	boolean	**readBoolean** () throws IOException
●	2	public final	byte	**readByte** () throws IOException
●	2	public final	char	**readChar** () throws IOException
●	2	public final	double	**readDouble** () throws IOException

RandomAccessFile

●	2	public final	................float	**readFloat**	() throws IOException
●	2	public final	................void	**readFully**	(byte[] b) throws IOException
●	2	public final	................void	**readFully**	(byte[] b, int off, int len) throws IOException
●	2	public final	..................int	**readInt**	() throws IOException
●	2	public final	...............String	**readLine**	() throws IOException
●	2	public final	.... long	**readLong**	() throws IOException
●	2	public final	...............short	**readShort**	() throws IOException
●	2	public final	..................int	**readUnsignedByte**	() throws IOException
●	2	public final	..................int	**readUnsignedShort**	() throws IOException
●	2	public final	...............String	**readUTF**	() throws IOException
		public native	................void	**seek**	(long pos) throws IOException
1.2		public native	................void	**setLength**	(long newLength) throws IOException
	2	public	..................int	**skipBytes**	(int n) throws IOException
	1	public	................void	**write**	(byte[] b) throws IOException
	1	public native	................void	**write**	(int b) throws IOException
	1	public	................void	**write**	(byte[] b, int off, int len) throws IOException
●	1	public final	................void	**writeBoolean**	(boolean v) throws IOException
●	1	public final	................void	**writeByte**	(int v) throws IOException
●	1	public final	................void	**writeBytes**	(String s) throws IOException
●	1	public final	................void	**writeChar**	(int v) throws IOException
●	1	public final	................void	**writeChars**	(String s) throws IOException
●	1	public final	................void	**writeDouble**	(double v) throws IOException
●	1	public final	................void	**writeFloat**	(float v) throws IOException
●	1	public final	................void	**writeInt**	(int v) throws IOException
●	1	public final	................void	**writeLong**	(long v) throws IOException
●	1	public final	................void	**writeShort**	(int v) throws IOException
●	1	public final	................void	**writeUTF**	(String str) throws IOException

Raster

P

```
Object
 └─Raster
```

R 1.2

△	public static .... WritableRaster	**createBandedRaster**	(int dataType, int w, int h, int bands, java.awt.Point location)
△	public static .... WritableRaster	**createBandedRaster**	(int dataType, int w, int h, int scanlineStride, int[] bankIndices, int[] bandOffsets, java.awt.Point location)
△	public static .... WritableRaster	**createBandedRaster**	(DataBuffer dataBuffer, int w, int h, int scanlineStride, int[] bankIndices, int[] bandOffsets, java.awt.Point location)
	public.................... Raster	**createChild**	(int parentX, int parentY, int width, int height, int childMinX, int childMinY, int[] bandList)
	public........... WritableRaster	**createCompatibleWritableRaster**	()
	public........... WritableRaster	**createCompatibleWritableRaster**	(java.awt.Rectangle rect)
	public........... WritableRaster	**createCompatibleWritableRaster**	(int w, int h)
	public........... WritableRaster	**createCompatibleWritableRaster**	(int x, int y, int w, int h)
△	public static .... WritableRaster	**createInterleavedRaster**	(int dataType, int w, int h, int bands, java.awt.Point location)
△	public static .... WritableRaster	**createInterleavedRaster**	(int dataType, int w, int h, int scanlineStride, int pixelStride, int[] bandOffsets, java.awt.Point location)
△	public static .... WritableRaster	**createInterleavedRaster**	(DataBuffer dataBuffer, int w, int h, int scanlineStride, int pixelStride, int[] bandOffsets, java.awt.Point location)
△	public static .... WritableRaster	**createPackedRaster**	(int dataType, int w, int h, int[] bandMasks, java.awt.Point location)
△	public static .... WritableRaster	**createPackedRaster**	(DataBuffer dataBuffer, int w, int h, int bitsPerPixel, java.awt.Point location)
△	public static .... WritableRaster	**createPackedRaster**	(int dataType, int w, int h, int bands, int bitsPerBand, java.awt.Point location)
△	public static .... WritableRaster	**createPackedRaster**	(DataBuffer dataBuffer, int w, int h, int scanlineStride, int[] bandMasks, java.awt.Point location)
△	public static .... Raster	**createRaster**	(SampleModel sm, DataBuffer db, java.awt.Point location)
	public..................... Raster	**createTranslatedChild**	(int childMinX, int childMinY)
△	public static .... WritableRaster	**createWritableRaster**	(SampleModel sm, java.awt.Point location)
△	public static .... WritableRaster	**createWritableRaster**	(SampleModel sm, DataBuffer db, java.awt.Point location)
	protected .... DataBuffer	**dataBuffer** `	
	public...... java.awt.Rectangle	**getBounds**	()
	public.............. DataBuffer	**getDataBuffer**	()
	public..................... Object	**getDataElements**	(int x, int y, Object outData)
	public..................... Object	**getDataElements**	(int x, int y, int w, int h, Object outData)
●	public final ....int	**getHeight**	()
●	public final ....int	**getMinX**	()
●	public final ....int	**getMinY**	()
●	public final ....int	**getNumBands**	()

Class   *Interface*   —extends   - - -implements   ○ abstract   ● final   △ static   ▲ static final   ✳ constructor   x x—inherited   x **x**—declared   **x x**—overridden

●	public final .... int	**getNumDataElements** ()
	public.................... Raster	**getParent** ()
	public..................... float[]	**getPixel** (int x, int y, float[] fArray)
	public......................... int[]	**getPixel** (int x, int y, int[] iArray)
	public................... double[]	**getPixel** (int x, int y, double[] dArray)
	public................... double[]	**getPixels** (int x, int y, int w, int h, double[] dArray)
	public......................... int[]	**getPixels** (int x, int y, int w, int h, int[] iArray)
	public...................... float[]	**getPixels** (int x, int y, int w, int h, float[] fArray)
	public......................... int	**getSample** (int x, int y, int b)
	public..................double	**getSampleDouble** (int x, int y, int b)
	public.........................float	**getSampleFloat** (int x, int y, int b)
	public........... SampleModel	**getSampleModel** ()
●	public final .... int	**getSampleModelTranslateX** ()
●	public final .... int	**getSampleModelTranslateY** ()
	public................... double[]	**getSamples** (int x, int y, int w, int h, int b, double[] dArray)
	public......................... int[]	**getSamples** (int x, int y, int w, int h, int b, int[] iArray)
	public...................... float[]	**getSamples** (int x, int y, int w, int h, int b, float[] fArray)
●	public final .... int	**getTransferType** ()
●	public final .... int	**getWidth** ()
	protected ....int	**height**
	protected.....................int	**minX**
	protected.....................int	**minY**
	protected.....................int	**numBands**
	protected.....................int	**numDataElements**
	protected .... Raster	**parent**
*	protected	**Raster** (SampleModel sampleModel, java.awt.Point origin)
*	protected	**Raster** (SampleModel sampleModel, DataBuffer dataBuffer, java.awt.Point origin)
*	protected	**Raster** (SampleModel sampleModel, DataBuffer dataBuffer, java.awt.Rectangle aRegion, java.awt.Point sampleModelTranslate, Raster parent)
	protected .... SampleModel	**sampleModel**
	protected.....................int	**sampleModelTranslateX**
	protected.....................int	**sampleModelTranslateY**
	protected ....int	**width**

R

RasterFormatException · java.awt.image

```
Object
└ Throwable - - - - - - - - - - - - - - - - - - - - - - - - - - - java.io.Serializable
   └ Exception
      └ RuntimeException
1.2       └ RasterFormatException
```

*	public...........................	**RasterFormatException** (String s)

RasterOp · java.awt.image

1.2 · *RasterOp* · P

	public........... WritableRaster	**createCompatibleDestRaster** (Raster src)
	public........... WritableRaster	**filter** (Raster src, WritableRaster dest)
	public........................... ... java.awt.geom.Rectangle2D	**getBounds2D** (Raster src)
	public.. java.awt.geom.Point2D	**getPoint2D** (java.awt.geom.Point2D srcPt, java.awt.geom.Point2D dstPt)
	public java.awt.RenderingHints	**getRenderingHints** ()

Reader · java.io

```
Object
1.1 ○ └ Reader
```

○	public abstract ....void	**close** () throws IOException
	protected .... Object	**lock**
	public.......................void	**mark** (int readAheadLimit) throws IOException
	public................. boolean	**markSupported** ()
	public.........................int	**read** () throws IOException
	public.........................int	**read** (char[] cbuf) throws IOException
○	public abstract ....int	**read** (char[] cbuf, int off, int len) throws IOException
*	protected	**Reader** ()
*	protected	**Reader** (Object lock)
	public................. boolean	**ready** () throws IOException
	public.......................void	**reset** () throws IOException

Reader

public .... long **skip** (long n) throws IOException

---

Rectangle					java.awt

P

```
         Object 1
1.2 ○    └ java.awt.geom.RectangularShape 2 - - - - - - - -  Shape, Cloneable
1.2 ○       └ java.awt.geom.Rectangle2D 3
               └ Rectangle - - - - - - - - - - - - - - - - - - - - -  Shape, java.io.Serializable
```

		public	void	**add** (Point pt)
		public	void	**add** (Rectangle r)
1.2	3	public	void	add (java.awt.geom.Point2D pt)
1.2	3	public	void	add (java.awt.geom.Rectangle2D r)
1.2	3	public	void	add (double newx, double newy)
		public	void	**add** (int newx, int newy)
	2	public	Object	clone ()
1.1		public	boolean	**contains** (Point p)
1.2		public	boolean	**contains** (Rectangle r)
1.2	2	public	boolean	contains (java.awt.geom.Point2D p)
1.2	2	public	boolean	contains (java.awt.geom.Rectangle2D r)
1.2	3	public	boolean	contains (double x, double y)
1.1		public	boolean	**contains** (int x, int y)
1.2	3	public	boolean	contains (double x, double y, double w, double h)
1.2		public	boolean	**contains** (int X, int Y, int W, int H)
1.2	3	public	..**java.awt.geom.Rectangle2D**	**createIntersection** (java.awt.geom.Rectangle2D r)
1.2	3	public	..**java.awt.geom.Rectangle2D**	**createUnion** (java.awt.geom.Rectangle2D r)
	3	public	**boolean**	equals (Object obj)
1.1	2	public	**Rectangle**	**getBounds** ()
1.2	3	public	..**java.awt.geom.Rectangle2D**	**getBounds2D** ()
1.2	2	public	double	getCenterX ()
1.2	2	public	double	getCenterY ()
1.2	2	public	... java.awt.geom.Rectangle2D	getFrame ()
1.2		public	**double**	**getHeight** ()
1.1		public	Point	**getLocation** ()
1.2	2	public	double	getMaxX ()
1.2	2	public	double	getMaxY ()
1.2	2	public	double	getMinX ()
1.2	2	public	double	getMinY ()
1.2	3	public	.....*java.awt.geom.PathIterator*	getPathIterator (java.awt.geom.AffineTransform at)
1.2	3	public	.....*java.awt.geom.PathIterator*	getPathIterator (java.awt.geom.AffineTransform at, double flatness)
1.1		public	Dimension	**getSize** ()
1.2	2	public	**double**	**getWidth** ()
1.2	2	public	**double**	**getX** ()
1.2	2	public	**double**	**getY** ()
		public	void	**grow** (int h, int v)
	3	public	int	hashCode ()
		public	int	**height**
D		public	boolean	**inside** (int x, int y)
1.2 △	3	public static	void	intersect (java.awt.geom.Rectangle2D src1, java.awt.geom.Rectangle2D src2, java.awt.geom.Rectangle2D dest)
		public	Rectangle	**intersection** (Rectangle r)
		public	boolean	**intersects** (Rectangle r)
1.2	2	public	boolean	intersects (java.awt.geom.Rectangle2D r)
1.2	3	public	boolean	intersects (double x, double y, double w, double h)
1.2	3	public	boolean	intersectsLine (java.awt.geom.Line2D l)
1.2	3	public	boolean	intersectsLine (double x1, double y1, double x2, double y2)
	2	public	**boolean**	**isEmpty** ()
D		public	void	**move** (int x, int y)
1.2	3	public	int	outcode (java.awt.geom.Point2D p)
1.2	3	public	**int**	**outcode** (double x, double y)
*		public		**Rectangle** ()
*		public		**Rectangle** (Dimension d)
*		public		**Rectangle** (Point p)
1.1 *		public		**Rectangle** (Rectangle r)

Class   *Interface*   —extends   - - -implements   ○ abstract   ● final   △ static   ▲ static final   ✳ constructor   x x—inherited   x **x**—declared   **x x**—overridden

∗		public	Rectangle	(int width, int height)
∗		public	Rectangle	(Point p, Dimension d)
∗		public	Rectangle	(int x, int y, int width, int height)
D		public ....void	reshape	(int x, int y, int width, int height)
D		public ....void	resize	(int width, int height)
1.1		public ....void	setBounds	(Rectangle r)
1.1		public ....void	setBounds	(int x, int y, int width, int height)
1.2	2	public ....void	setFrame	(java.awt.geom.Rectangle2D r)
1.2	2	public ....void	setFrame	(java.awt.geom.Point2D loc, java.awt.geom.Dimension2D size)
1.2	3	public ....void	setFrame	(double x, double y, double w, double h)
1.2	2	public ....void	setFrameFromCenter	(java. awt. geom. Point2D center, java.awt.geom.Point2D corner)
1.2	2	public ....void	setFrameFromCenter	(double centerX, double centerY, double cornerX, double cornerY)
1.2	2	public ....void	setFrameFromDiagonal	(java.awt.geom.Point2D p1, java.awt.geom.Point2D p2)
1.2	2	public ....void	setFrameFromDiagonal	(double x1, double y1, double x2, double y2)
1.1		public ....void	setLocation	(Point p)
1.1		public ....void	setLocation	(int x, int y)
1.2	3	public ....void	setRect	(java.awt.geom.Rectangle2D r)
1.2	3	public ....void	setRect	(double x, double y, double width, double height)
1.1		public ....void	setSize	(Dimension d)
1.1		public ....void	setSize	(int width, int height)
	1	public ....String	toString	()
		public ....void	translate	(int x, int y)
		public ....Rectangle	union	(Rectangle r)
1.2 △	3	public static ....void	union	(java.awt.geom.Rectangle2D src1, java.awt.geom.Rectangle2D src2, java.awt.geom.Rectangle2D dest)
		public ....int	width	
		public ....int	x	
		public ....int	y	

Rectangle2D

Object[1]
1.2 ○ └RectangularShape[2] -------------------- *java.awt.Shape, Cloneable*
1.2 ○   └Rectangle2D

		public ....void	add	(Point2D pt)
		public ....void	add	(Rectangle2D r)
		public ....void	add	(double newx, double newy)
	2	public ....Object	clone	()
	2	public ....boolean	contains	(Point2D p)
	2	public ....boolean	contains	(Rectangle2D r)
	2	public ....boolean	contains	(double x, double y)
	2	public ....boolean	contains	(double x, double y, double w, double h)
○		public abstract ...Rectangle2D	createIntersection	(Rectangle2D r)
○		public abstract ...Rectangle2D	createUnion	(Rectangle2D r)
	1	public ....boolean	equals	(Object obj)
	2	public ....java.awt.Rectangle	getBounds	()
	2	public Rectangle2D	getBounds2D	()
	2	public ....double	getCenterX	()
	2	public ....double	getCenterY	()
	2	public Rectangle2D	getFrame	()
○	2	public abstract ....double	getHeight	()
	2	public ....double	getMaxX	()
	2	public ....double	getMaxY	()
	2	public ....double	getMinX	()
	2	public ....double	getMinY	()
	2	public ....*PathIterator*	getPathIterator	(AffineTransform at)
	2	public ....*PathIterator*	getPathIterator	(AffineTransform at, double flatness)
○	2	public abstract ....double	getWidth	()
○	2	public abstract ....double	getX	()
○	2	public abstract ....double	getY	()
	1	public ....int	hashCode	()
△		public static ....void	intersect	(Rectangle2D src1, Rectangle2D src2, Rectangle2D dest)
	2	public ....boolean	intersects	(Rectangle2D r)
	2	public ....boolean	intersects	(double x, double y, double w, double h)
		public ....boolean	intersectsLine	(Line2D l)
		public ....boolean	intersectsLine	(double x1, double y1, double x2, double y2)
○	2	public abstract ....boolean	isEmpty	()
▲		public static final ....int	OUT_BOTTOM	= 8
▲		public static final ....int	OUT_LEFT	= 1
▲		public static final ....int	OUT_RIGHT	= 4

R

Classes

Rectangle2D

▲		public static final ....int	**OUT_TOP** = 2
		public ....int	**outcode** (Point2D p)
○		public abstract ....int	**outcode** (double x, double y)
✳		protected	**Rectangle2D** ()
	2	public ....void	setFrame (Rectangle2D r)
	2	public ....void	setFrame (Point2D loc, Dimension2D size)
	2	public ....**void setFrame**	(double x, double y, double w, double h)
	2	public ....void	setFrameFromCenter (Point2D center, Point2D corner)
	2	public ....void	setFrameFromCenter (double centerX, double centerY, double cornerX, double cornerY)
	2	public ....void	setFrameFromDiagonal (Point2D p1, Point2D p2)
	2	public ....void	setFrameFromDiagonal (double x1, double y1, double x2, double y2)
		public ....void	**setRect** (Rectangle2D r)
○		public abstract ....void	**setRect** (double x, double y, double w, double h)
△		public static ....void	**union** (Rectangle2D src1, Rectangle2D src2, Rectangle2D dest)

Rectangle2D.Double   java.awt.geom

		Object [1]
1.2 ○		└ RectangularShape [2] -------------------- *java.awt.Shape, Cloneable*
1.2 ○		└ Rectangle2D [3]
1.2		└ Rectangle2D.Double

	3	public ....void	add (Point2D pt)
	3	public ....void	add (Rectangle2D r)
	3	public ....void	add (double newx, double newy)
	2	public ....Object	clone ()
	2	public ....boolean	contains (Point2D p)
	2	public ....boolean	contains (Rectangle2D r)
	3	public ....boolean	contains (double x, double y)
	3	public ....boolean	contains (double x, double y, double w, double h)
	3	public ....**Rectangle2D createIntersection**	(Rectangle2D r)
	3	public ....**Rectangle2D createUnion**	(Rectangle2D r)
✳		public	**Double** ()
✳		public	**Double** (double x, double y, double w, double h)
	3	public ....boolean	equals (Object obj)
	2	public .....java.awt.Rectangle	getBounds ()
	3	public **Rectangle2D getBounds2D**	()
	2	public ....double	getCenterX ()
	2	public ....double	getCenterY ()
	2	public Rectangle2D	getFrame ()
	2	public ....**double getHeight**	()
	2	public ....double	getMaxX ()
	2	public ....double	getMaxY ()
	2	public ....double	getMinX ()
	2	public ....double	getMinY ()
	3	public ....*PathIterator*	getPathIterator (AffineTransform at)
	3	public ....*PathIterator*	getPathIterator (AffineTransform at, double flatness)
	2	public ....**double getWidth**	()
	2	public ....**double getX**	()
	2	public ....**double getY**	()
	3	public ....int	hashCode ()
		public ....double	**height**
△	3	public static ....void	intersect (Rectangle2D src1, Rectangle2D src2, Rectangle2D dest)
	2	public ....boolean	intersects (Rectangle2D r)
	3	public ....boolean	intersects (double x, double y, double w, double h)
	3	public ....boolean	intersectsLine (Line2D l)
	3	public ....boolean	intersectsLine (double x1, double y1, double x2, double y2)
	2	public ....**boolean isEmpty**	()
	3	public ....int	outcode (Point2D p)
	3	public ....**int outcode**	(double x, double y)
	2	public ....void	setFrame (Rectangle2D r)
	2	public ....void	setFrame (Point2D loc, Dimension2D size)
	3	public ....void	setFrame (double x, double y, double w, double h)
	2	public ....void	setFrameFromCenter (Point2D center, Point2D corner)
	2	public ....void	setFrameFromCenter (double centerX, double centerY, double cornerX, double cornerY)
	2	public ....void	setFrameFromDiagonal (Point2D p1, Point2D p2)
	2	public ....void	setFrameFromDiagonal (double x1, double y1, double x2, double y2)
	2	public ....**void setRect**	(Rectangle2D r)
	3	public ....**void setRect**	(double x, double y, double w, double`h)

Class *Interface* —extends - - -implements ○ abstract ● final △ static ▲ static final ✳ constructor x x—inherited x **x**—declared **x x**—overridden

	1	public..................... **String**	**toString** ()
△	3	public static ....void	union (Rectangle2D src1, Rectangle2D src2, Rectangle2D dest)
		public...................double	**width**
		public...................double	**x**
		public...................double	**y**

Rectangle2D.Float

```
      Object 1
1.2 ○  └ RectangularShape 2 ------------------- java.awt.Shape, Cloneable
1.2 ○     └ Rectangle2D 3
1.2         └ Rectangle2D.Float
```

	3	public.......................void	add (Point2D pt)
	3	public.......................void	add (Rectangle2D r)
	3	public.......................void	add (double newx, double newy)
	2	public.................∴.Object	clone ()
	2	public.................boolean	contains (Point2D p)
	2	public.................boolean	contains (Rectangle2D r)
	3	public.................boolean	contains (double x, double y)
	3	public.................boolean	contains (double x, double y, double w, double h)
	3	public............ **Rectangle2D**	**createIntersection** (Rectangle2D r)
	3	public............ **Rectangle2D**	**createUnion** (Rectangle2D r)
	3	public:................ boolean	equals (Object obj)
✳		public.........................	**Float** ()
✳		public.........................	**Float** (float x, float y, float w, float h)
	2	public...... java.awt.Rectangle	getBounds ()
	3	public............ **Rectangle2D**	**getBounds2D** ()
	2	public...................double	getCenterX ()
	2	public...................double	getCenterY ()
	2	public............Rectangle2D	getFrame ()
	2	public............ **double**	**getHeight** ()
	2	public...................double	getMaxX ()
	2	public...................double	getMaxY ()
	2	public...................double	getMinX ()
	2	public...................double	getMinY ()
	3	public............ *PathIterator*	getPathIterator (AffineTransform at)
	3	public............ *PathIterator*	getPathIterator (AffineTransform at, double flatness)
	2	public............ **double**	**getWidth** ()
	2	public............ **double**	**getX** ()
	2	public............ **double**	**getY** ()
	3	public......................int	hashCode ()
		public......................float	**height**
△	3	public static ....void	intersect (Rectangle2D src1, Rectangle2D src2, Rectangle2D dest)
	2	public............ boolean	intersects (Rectangle2D r)
	3	public............ boolean	intersects (double x, double y, double w, double h)
	3	public............ boolean	intersectsLine (Line2D l)
	3	public............ boolean	intersectsLine (double x1, double y1, double x2, double y2)
	2	public............ **boolean**	**isEmpty** ()
	3	public......................int	outcode (Point2D p)
	3	public............ **int**	**outcode** (double x, double y)
	2	public...................void	setFrame (Rectangle2D r)
	2	public...................void	setFrame (Point2D loc, Dimension2D size)
	3	public...................void	setFrame (double x, double y, double w, double h)
	2	public...................void	setFrameFromCenter (Point2D center, Point2D corner)
	2	public...................void	setFrameFromCenter (double centerX, double centerY, double cornerX, double cornerY)
	2	public...................void	setFrameFromDiagonal (Point2D p1, Point2D p2)
	2	public...................void	setFrameFromDiagonal (double x1, double y1, double x2, double y2)
	3	public............ **void**	**setRect** (Rectangle2D r)
	3	public............ **void**	**setRect** (double x, double y, double w, double h)
		public...................void	**setRect** (float x, float y, float w, float h)
	1	public............ **String**	**toString** ()
△	3	public static ....void	union (Rectangle2D src1, Rectangle2D src2, Rectangle2D dest)
		public......................float	**width**
		public......................float	**x**
		public......................float	**y**

R

Classes

RectangularShape

RectangularShape					java.awt.geom

```
       Object 1
1.2 ○  └ RectangularShape - - - - - - - - - - - - - - - - - - - -  java.awt.Shape 2, Cloneable
```

	1	public...................**Object**	**clone** ()	
	2	public.................boolean	**contains** (Point2D p)	
	2	public.................boolean	**contains** (Rectangle2D r)	
○	2	public abstract........boolean	**contains** (double, double)	
○	2	public abstract........boolean	**contains** (double, double, double, double)	
	2	public......java.awt.Rectangle	**getBounds** ()	
○	2	public abstract...Rectangle2D	**getBounds2D** ()	
		public...................double	**getCenterX** ()	
		public...................double	**getCenterY** ()	
		public...............Rectangle2D	**getFrame** ()	
○		public abstract.........double	**getHeight** ()	
		public...................double	**getMaxX** ()	
		public...................double	**getMaxY** ()	
		public...................double	**getMinX** ()	
		public...................double	**getMinY** ()	
○	2	public abstract....*PathIterator*	**getPathIterator** (AffineTransform)	
	2	public.............*PathIterator*	**getPathIterator** (AffineTransform at, double flatness)	
○		public abstract.........double	**getWidth** ()	
○		public abstract.........double	**getX** ()	
○		public abstract.........double	**getY** ()	
	2	public.................boolean	**intersects** (Rectangle2D r)	
○	2	public abstract........boolean	**intersects** (double, double, double, double)	
○		public abstract........boolean	**isEmpty** ()	
✳		protected......................	**RectangularShape** ()	
		public......................void	**setFrame** (Rectangle2D r)	
		public......................void	**setFrame** (Point2D loc, Dimension2D size)	
○		public abstract...........void	**setFrame** (double x, double y, double w, double h)	
		public......................void	**setFrameFromCenter** (Point2D center, Point2D corner)	
		public......................void	**setFrameFromCenter** (double centerX, double centerY, double cornerX, double cornerY)	
		public......................void	**setFrameFromDiagonal** (Point2D p1, Point2D p2)	
		public......................void	**setFrameFromDiagonal** (double x1, double y1, double x2, double y2)	

Ref					java.sql

```
                                                                          P O
1.2   Ref
- - - - - - - - - - - - - - - - - - - - - - - - - - - - - - - - - - - - - - - - - - -
      public.....................String  getBaseTypeName () throws SQLException
- - - - - - - - - - - - - - - - - - - - - - - - - - - - - - - - - - - - - - - - - - -
```

Reference					java.lang.ref

```
       Object
1.2 ○  └ Reference

       public......................void  clear ()
       public.................boolean  enqueue ()
       public..................Object  get ()
       public.................boolean  isEnqueued ()
```

ReferenceQueue					java.lang.ref

```
       Object
1.2    └ ReferenceQueue

       public...............Reference  poll ()
  ✳    public...........................  ReferenceQueue ()
       public...............Reference  remove () throws InterruptedException
       public...............Reference  remove (long timeout) throws IllegalArgumentException, InterruptedException
```

Class *Interface* —extends - - -implements ○ abstract ● final △ static ▲ static final ✳ constructor x x—inherited x **x**—declared **x x**—overridden

ReflectPermission				java.lang.reflect
				P

```
       Object
1.2 ○  └java.security.Permission 1 ---------------- java.security.Guard, java.io.Serializable
1.2 ○      └java.security.BasicPermission 2 ---------- java.io.Serializable
1.2 ●          └ReflectPermission
```

	1	public.....................void	checkGuard (Object object) throws SecurityException
	2	public.................. boolean	equals (Object obj)
	2	public..................... String	getActions ()
●	1	public final .... String	getName ()
	2	public.........................int	hashCode ()
	2	public.................. boolean	implies (java.security.Permission p)
	2	public....................... java ↵	newPermissionCollection ()
		.security.PermissionCollection	
*		public..........................	**ReflectPermission** (String name)
*		public..........................	**ReflectPermission** (String name, String actions)
	1	public..................... String	toString ()

Registry		java.rmi.registry
		P⁰

```
1.1    Registry————————————————————java.rmi.Remote
```

	public.....................void	**bind** (String name, *java.rmi.Remote* obj) throws java.rmi.RemoteException,
		java.rmi.AlreadyBoundException, java.rmi.AccessException
	public.................. String[]	**list** () throws java.rmi.RemoteException, java.rmi.AccessException
	public......... *java.rmi.Remote*	**lookup** (String name) throws java. rmi. RemoteException,
		java.rmi.NotBoundException, java.rmi.AccessException
	public.....................void	**rebind** (String name, *java.rmi.Remote* obj) throws java.rmi.RemoteException,
		java.rmi.AccessException
▲	public static final ....int	**REGISTRY_PORT** = 1099
	public.....................void	**unbind** (String name) throws java. rmi. RemoteException,
		java.rmi.NotBoundException, java.rmi.AccessException

RegistryHandler		java.rmi.registry
		P⁰

```
1.1    RegistryHandler
```

D	public.................. *Registry*	**registryImpl** (int port) throws java.rmi.RemoteException
D	public.................. *Registry*	**registryStub** (String host, int port) throws java. rmi. RemoteException,
		java.rmi.UnknownHostException

RemarshalException		org.omg.CORBA.portable

```
       Object
       └Throwable ------------------------- java.io.Serializable
           └Exception
1.2 ●          └RemarshalException
```

*	public..........................	**RemarshalException** ()

Remote		java.rmi
		P⁰

```
1.1    Remote
```

RemoteCall		java.rmi.server
		P⁰

```
1.1    RemoteCall
```

D	public.....................void	**done** () throws java.io.IOException
D	public.....................void	**executeCall** () throws Exception
D	public.... *java.io.ObjectInput*	**getInputStream** () throws java.io.IOException
D	public.... *java.io.ObjectOutput*	**getOutputStream** () throws java.io.IOException
D	public.... *java.io.ObjectOutput*	**getResultStream** (boolean success) throws java. io. IOException,
		java.io.StreamCorruptedException
D	public.....................void	**releaseInputStream** () throws java.io.IOException
D	public.....................void	**releaseOutputStream** () throws java.io.IOException

R

Classes

RemoteException

					java.rmi
			RemoteException		P[O]

```
Object
└Throwable 1 -------------------------- java.io.Serializable
  └Exception
    └java.io.IOException
1.1        └RemoteException
```

	public	Throwable	**detail**	
1	public	**String**	**getMessage** ()	
1	public	**void**	**printStackTrace** ()	
1	public	**void**	**printStackTrace** (java.io.PrintStream ps)	
1	public	**void**	**printStackTrace** (java.io.PrintWriter pw)	
*	public		**RemoteException** ()	
*	public		**RemoteException** (String s)	
*	public		**RemoteException** (String s, Throwable ex)	

RemoteObject

					java.rmi.server
	RemoteObject				P[O]

```
     Object 1
1.1 O └RemoteObject ----------------------- java.rmi.Remote, java.io.Serializable
```

1	public	**boolean**	**equals** (Object obj)	
1.2	public	*RemoteRef*	**getRef** ()	
1	public	**int**	**hashCode** ()	
	protected transient	*RemoteRef*	**ref**	
*	protected		**RemoteObject** ()	
*	protected		**RemoteObject** (*RemoteRef* newref)	
1	public	**String**	**toString** ()	
1.2 △	public static	*java.rmi.Remote*	**toStub** (*java.rmi.Remote* obj) throws java.rmi.NoSuchObjectException	

R

RemoteRef

					java.rmi.server
	RemoteRef				P[O]

```
1.1  RemoteRef————————————————— java.io.Externalizable 1 (java.io.Serializable 2)
```

D	public	void	**done** (*RemoteCall* call) throws java.rmi.RemoteException	
	public	String	**getRefClass** (*java.io.ObjectOutput* out)	
D	public	void	**invoke** (*RemoteCall* call) throws Exception	
1.2	public	Object	**invoke** (*java.rmi.Remote* obj, java.lang.reflect.Method method, Object[] params, long opnum) throws Exception	
D	public	*RemoteCall*	**newCall** (RemoteObject obj, Operation[] op, int opnum, long hash) throws java.rmi.RemoteException	
▲	public static final	String	**packagePrefix** = "sun.rmi.server"	
1	public	void	readExternal (*java.io.ObjectInput* in) throws java.io.IOException, ClassNotFoundException	
	public	boolean	**remoteEquals** (*RemoteRef* obj)	
	public	int	**remoteHashCode** ()	
	public	String	**remoteToString** ()	
1.2 ▲ 2	public static final	**long**	**serialVersionUID** = 3632638527362204081	
1	public	void	writeExternal (*java.io.ObjectOutput* out) throws java.io.IOException	

RemoteServer

					java.rmi.server
	RemoteServer				P[O]

```
      Object
1.1 O └RemoteObject 1 ----------------------- java.rmi.Remote, java.io.Serializable
1.1 O   └RemoteServer
```

1	public	boolean	equals (Object obj)	
△	public static	String	**getClientHost** () throws ServerNotActiveException	
△	public static java.io.PrintStream		**getLog** ()	
1.2 1	public	*RemoteRef*	getRef ()	
1	public	int	hashCode ()	
1	protected transient	*RemoteRef*	ref	
*	protected		**RemoteServer** ()	
*	protected		**RemoteServer** (*RemoteRef* ref)	
△	public static	void	**setLog** (java.io.OutputStream out)	
1	public	String	toString ()	
1.2 △ 1	public static	*java.rmi.Remote*	toStub (*java.rmi.Remote* obj) throws java.rmi.NoSuchObjectException	

Class *Interface* —extends - - -implements ○ abstract ● final △ static ▲ static final ✳ constructor x x—inherited x **x**—declared **x x**—overridden

RemoteStub
java.rmi.server

P°

		Object		
1.1	○	└ RemoteObject[1] -	*java.rmi.Remote, java.io.Serializable*	
1.1	○	└ RemoteStub		

	1	public.................. boolean	equals (Object obj)	
1.2	1	public.............. *RemoteRef*	getRef ()	
	1	public....................int	hashCode ()	
	1	protected transient. *RemoteRef*	ref	
	*	protected......................	**RemoteStub** ()	
	*	protected......................	**RemoteStub** (*RemoteRef* ref)	
D	△	protected static ....void	**setRef** (RemoteStub stub, *RemoteRef* ref)	
	1	public....................String	toString ()	
1.2	△ 1	public static .. *java.rmi.Remote*	toStub (*java.rmi.Remote* obj) throws java.rmi.NoSuchObjectException	

RenderableImage
java.awt.image.renderable

1.2	*RenderableImage*	

	public....................*java*↵ .awt.image.RenderedImage	**createDefaultRendering** ()
	public....................*java*↵ .awt.image.RenderedImage	**createRendering** (RenderContext renderContext)
	public....................*java*↵ .awt.image.RenderedImage	**createScaledRendering** (int w, int h, java.awt.RenderingHints hints)
	public.....................float	**getHeight** ()
	public.....................float	**getMinX** ()
	public.....................float	**getMinY** ()
	public.................... Object	**getProperty** (String name)
	public................... String[]	**getPropertyNames** ()
	public........... java.util.Vector	**getSources** ()
	public.....................float	**getWidth** ()
▲	public static final ....String	**HINTS_OBSERVED** = "HINTS_OBSERVED"
	public.................. boolean	**isDynamic** ()

RenderableImageOp
java.awt.image.renderable

	Object	
1.2	└ RenderableImageOp - *RenderableImage[1]*	

1	public....................*java*↵ .awt.image.RenderedImage	**createDefaultRendering** ()
1	public....................*java*↵ .awt.image.RenderedImage	**createRendering** (RenderContext renderContext)
1	public....................*java*↵ .awt.image.RenderedImage	**createScaledRendering** (int w, int h, java.awt.RenderingHints hints)
1	public.....................float	**getHeight** ()
1	public.....................float	**getMinX** ()
1	public.....................float	**getMinY** ()
	public........... ParameterBlock	**getParameterBlock** ()
1	public.................... Object	**getProperty** (String name)
1	public................... String[]	**getPropertyNames** ()
1	public........... java.util.Vector	**getSources** ()
1	public.....................float	**getWidth** ()
1	public.................. boolean	**isDynamic** ()
*	public......................	**RenderableImageOp** (*ContextualRenderedImageFactory* CRIF, ParameterBlock paramBlock)
	public........... ParameterBlock	**setParameterBlock** (ParameterBlock paramBlock)

RenderableImageProducer
java.awt.image.renderable

	Object	
1.2	└ RenderableImageProducer - - - - - - - - - - - - - - *java.awt.image.ImageProducer[1], Runnable[2]*	

1	public synchronized ....void	**addConsumer** (*java.awt.image.ImageConsumer* ic)
1	public synchronized .. boolean	**isConsumer** (*java.awt.image.ImageConsumer* ic)
1	public synchronized ....void	**removeConsumer** (*java.awt.image.ImageConsumer* ic)
*	public......................	**RenderableImageProducer** (*RenderableImage* rdblImage, RenderContext rc)
1	public....................void	**requestTopDownLeftRightResend** (*java.awt.image.ImageConsumer* ic)

R

Classes

RenderableImageProducer

2	public......................void	**run** ()
	public synchronized ....void	**setRenderContext** (RenderContext rc)
1	public synchronized ....void	**startProduction** (*java.awt.image.ImageConsumer* ic)

RenderContext   java.awt.image.renderable

Object[1]
1.2 └─RenderContext - *Cloneable*

1	public....................**Object**	**clone** ()
	public......................void	**concetenateTransform** (java.awt.geom.AffineTransform modTransform)
	public......... *java.awt.Shape*	**getAreaOfInterest** ()
	public java.awt.RenderingHints	**getRenderingHints** ()
	public............................	**getTransform** ()
	java.awt.geom.AffineTransform	
	public......................void	**preConcetenateTransform** (java.awt.geom.AffineTransform modTransform)
✳	public............................	**RenderContext** (java.awt.geom.AffineTransform usr2dev)
✳	public............................	**RenderContext** (java.awt.geom.AffineTransform usr2dev, *java.awt.Shape* aoi)
✳	public............................	**RenderContext** (java. awt. geom. AffineTransform usr2dev, java.awt.RenderingHints hints)
✳	public............................	**RenderContext** (java.awt.geom.AffineTransform usr2dev, *java.awt.Shape* aoi, java.awt.RenderingHints hints)
	public......................void	**setAreaOfInterest** (*java.awt.Shape* newAoi)
	public......................void	**setRenderingHints** (java.awt.RenderingHints hints)
	public......................void	**setTransform** (java.awt.geom.AffineTransform newTransform)

RenderedImage   java.awt.image

1.2 *RenderedImage*   P

public.......... WritableRaster	**copyData** (WritableRaster raster)
public.............. ColorModel	**getColorModel** ()
public............... Raster	**getData** ()
public............... Raster	**getData** (java.awt.Rectangle rect)
public....................int	**getHeight** ()
public....................int	**getMinTileX** ()
public....................int	**getMinTileY** ()
public....................int	**getMinX** ()
public....................int	**getMinY** ()
public....................int	**getNumXTiles** ()
public....................int	**getNumYTiles** ()
public................. Object	**getProperty** (String name)
public................ String[]	**getPropertyNames** ()
public........... SampleModel	**getSampleModel** ()
public....... java.util.Vector	**getSources** ()
public............... Raster	**getTile** (int tileX, int tileY)
public....................int	**getTileGridXOffset** ()
public....................int	**getTileGridYOffset** ()
public....................int	**getTileHeight** ()
public....................int	**getTileWidth** ()
public....................int	**getWidth** ()

RenderedImageFactory   java.awt.image.renderable

1.2 *RenderedImageFactory*

public...................*java*↵	**create** (ParameterBlock paramBlock, java.awt.RenderingHints hints)
.awt.image.RenderedImage	

Renderer   javax.swing

1.2 *Renderer*

public.... java.awt.Component	**getComponent** ()
public......................void	**setValue** (Object aValue, boolean isSelected)

Class *Interface* —extends - - -implements ○ abstract ● final △ static ▲ static final ✳ constructor x x—inherited x **x**—declared **x x**—overridden

RenderingHints			java.awt
	Object[1]		P
1.2	└ RenderingHints - *java.util.Map*[2], *Cloneable*		

	public.....................void	**add** (RenderingHints hints)
2	public.....................void	**clear** ()
1	public....................**Object**	**clone** ()
2	public................ boolean	**containsKey** (Object key)
2	public................ boolean	**containsValue** (Object value)
2	public..............*java.util.Set*	**entrySet** ()
1	public..................**boolean**	**equals** (Object o)
2	public................Object	**get** (Object key)
1	public...................... **int**	**hashCode** ()
2	public................ boolean	**isEmpty** ()
▲	public static final.............. RenderingHints.Key	**KEY_ALPHA_INTERPOLATION**
▲	public static final.............. RenderingHints.Key	**KEY_ANTIALIASING**
▲	public static final.............. RenderingHints.Key	**KEY_COLOR_RENDERING**
▲	public static final.............. RenderingHints.Key	**KEY_DITHERING**
▲	public static final.............. RenderingHints.Key	**KEY_FRACTIONALMETRICS**
▲	public static final.............. RenderingHints.Key	**KEY_INTERPOLATION**
▲	public static final.............. RenderingHints.Key	**KEY_RENDERING**
▲	public static final.............. RenderingHints.Key	**KEY_TEXT_ANTIALIASING**
2	public..............*java.util.Set*	**keySet** ()
2	public................Object	**put** (Object key, Object value)
2	public.....................void	**putAll** (*java.util.Map* m)
2	public................Object	**remove** (Object key)
*	public..........................	**RenderingHints** (*java.util.Map* init)
*	public..........................	**RenderingHints** (RenderingHints.Key key, Object value)
2	public.....................int	**size** ()
1	public...................**String**	**toString** ()
▲	public static final ....Object	**VALUE_ALPHA_INTERPOLATION_DEFAULT**
▲	public static final ....Object	**VALUE_ALPHA_INTERPOLATION_QUALITY**
▲	public static final ....Object	**VALUE_ALPHA_INTERPOLATION_SPEED**
▲	public static final ....Object	**VALUE_ANTIALIAS_DEFAULT**
▲	public static final ....Object	**VALUE_ANTIALIAS_OFF**
▲	public static final ....Object	**VALUE_ANTIALIAS_ON**
▲	public static final ....Object	**VALUE_COLOR_RENDER_DEFAULT**
▲	public static final ....Object	**VALUE_COLOR_RENDER_QUALITY**
▲	public static final ....Object	**VALUE_COLOR_RENDER_SPEED**
▲	public static final ....Object	**VALUE_DITHER_DEFAULT**
▲	public static final ....Object	**VALUE_DITHER_DISABLE**
▲	public static final ....Object	**VALUE_DITHER_ENABLE**
▲	public static final ....Object	**VALUE_FRACTIONALMETRICS_DEFAULT**
▲	public static final ....Object	**VALUE_FRACTIONALMETRICS_OFF**
▲	public static final ....Object	**VALUE_FRACTIONALMETRICS_ON**
▲	public static final ....Object	**VALUE_INTERPOLATION_BICUBIC**
▲	public static final ....Object	**VALUE_INTERPOLATION_BILINEAR**
▲	public static final ....Object	**VALUE_INTERPOLATION_NEAREST_NEIGHBOR**
▲	public static final ....Object	**VALUE_RENDER_DEFAULT**
▲	public static final ....Object	**VALUE_RENDER_QUALITY**
▲	public static final ....Object	**VALUE_RENDER_SPEED**
▲	public static final ....Object	**VALUE_TEXT_ANTIALIAS_DEFAULT**
▲	public static final ....Object	**VALUE_TEXT_ANTIALIAS_OFF**
▲	public static final ....Object	**VALUE_TEXT_ANTIALIAS_ON**
2	public....... *java.util.Collection*	**values** ()

R

Classes

RenderingHints.Key			java.awt
	Object[1]		P
1.2 ○	└ RenderingHints.Key		

● 1	public final ....**boolean**	**equals** (Object o)
● 1	public final .... **int**	**hashCode** ()

RenderingHints.Key

●	protected final...............int	**intKey** ()
○	public abstract........boolean	**isCompatibleValue** (Object val)
✳	protected.........................	**Key** (int privatekey)

RepaintManager javax.swing

Object [1]
  └ RepaintManager

<small>1.2</small>

	public synchronized.......void	**addDirtyRegion** (JComponent c, int x, int y, int w, int h)
	public synchronized.......void	**addInvalidComponent** (JComponent invalidComponent)
△	public static .. RepaintManager	**currentManager** (java.awt.Component c)
△	public static .. RepaintManager	**currentManager** (JComponent c)
	public...... java.awt.Rectangle	**getDirtyRegion** (JComponent aComponent)
	public......java.awt.Dimension	**getDoubleBufferMaximumSize** ()
	public.......... java.awt.Image	**getOffscreenBuffer** (java. awt. Component c, int proposedWidth, int proposedHeight)
	public................ boolean	**isCompletelyDirty** (JComponent aComponent)
	public................ boolean	**isDoubleBufferingEnabled** ()
	public......................void	**markCompletelyClean** (JComponent aComponent)
	public......................void	**markCompletelyDirty** (JComponent aComponent)
	public......................void	**paintDirtyRegions** ()
	public synchronized.......void	**removeInvalidComponent** (JComponent component)
✳	public.............................	**RepaintManager** ()
△	public static ....void	**setCurrentManager** (RepaintManager aRepaintManager)
	public......................void	**setDoubleBufferingEnabled** (boolean aFlag)
	public......................void	**setDoubleBufferMaximumSize** (java.awt.Dimension d)
1	public synchronized .... **String**	**toString** ()
	public......................void	**validateInvalidComponents** ()

R

ReplicateScaleFilter java.awt.image

P

Object
  └ ImageFilter [1] - *ImageConsumer*, *Cloneable*
    └ ReplicateScaleFilter

<small>1.1</small>

1	public................. Object	clone ()
1	protected..... *ImageConsumer*	consumer
	protected....................int	**destHeight**
	protected....................int	**destWidth**
1	public............... ImageFilter	getFilterInstance (*ImageConsumer* ic)
1	public......................void	imageComplete (int status)
	protected...................Object	**outpixbuf**
✳	public............................	**ReplicateScaleFilter** (int width, int height)
1	public......................void	resendTopDownLeftRight (*ImageProducer* ip)
1	public......................void	setColorModel (ColorModel model)
1	public...................... **void**	**setDimensions** (int w, int h)
1	public......................void	setHints (int hints)
1	public...................... **void**	**setPixels** (int x, int y, int w, int h, ColorModel model, byte[] pixels, int off, int scansize)
1	public...................... **void**	**setPixels** (int x, int y, int w, int h, ColorModel model, int[] pixels, int off, int scansize)
1	public...................... **void**	**setProperties** (java.util.Hashtable props)
	protected...................int[]	**srccols**
	protected....................int	**srcHeight**
	protected...................int[]	**srcrows**
	protected....................int	**srcWidth**

Request org.omg.CORBA

Object
  └ Request

<small>1.2</small> ○

○	public abstract............. Any	**add_in_arg** ()
○	public abstract............. Any	**add_inout_arg** ()
○	public abstract............. Any	**add_named_in_arg** (String name)
○	public abstract............. Any	**add_named_inout_arg** (String name)
○	public abstract............. Any	**add_named_out_arg** (String name)
○	public abstract........... Any	**add_out_arg** ()
○	public abstract.......... NVList	**arguments** ()
○	public abstract..... ContextList	**contexts** ()

Class *Interface* —extends - - -implements ○ abstract ● final △ static ▲ static final ✳ constructor x x—inherited x **x**—declared **x x**—overridden

○	public abstract	........Context	**ctx** ()
○	public abstract	............void	**ctx** (Context c)
○	public abstract	... Environment	**env** ()
○	public abstract	.. ExceptionList	**exceptions** ()
○	public abstract	............void	**get_response** () throws WrongTransaction
○	public abstract	............void	**invoke** ()
○	public abstract	..........String	**operation** ()
○	public abstract	.... boolean	**poll_response** ()
*	public	....	**Request** ()
○	public abstract	... NamedValue	**result** ()
○	public abstract	.... Any	**return_value** ()
○	public abstract	............void	**send_deferred** ()
○	public abstract	............void	**send_oneway** ()
○	public abstract	............void	**set_return_type** (TypeCode tc)
○	public abstract	.... *Object*	**target** ()

RescaleOp   java.awt.image

Object
1.2   └ RescaleOp - *BufferedImageOp* [1], *RasterOp* [2]
P

	1	public ....BufferedImage	**createCompatibleDestImage** (BufferedImage src, ColorModel destCM)
	2	public ....WritableRaster	**createCompatibleDestRaster** (Raster src)
●	1	public final .....BufferedImage	**filter** (BufferedImage src, BufferedImage dst)
●	2	public final ..... WritableRaster	**filter** (Raster src, WritableRaster dst)
●	1	public final java.awt.geom.Rectangle2D	**getBounds2D** (BufferedImage src)
●	2	public final java.awt.geom.Rectangle2D	**getBounds2D** (Raster src)
●		public final ....int	**getNumFactors** ()
●		public final ....float[]	**getOffsets** (float[] offsets)
●	1	public final java.awt.geom.Point2D	**getPoint2D** (java.awt.geom.Point2D srcPt, java.awt.geom.Point2D dstPt)
●	1	public final .... java.awt.RenderingHints	**getRenderingHints** ()
●		public final ....float[]	**getScaleFactors** (float[] scaleFactors)
*		public...........................	**RescaleOp** (float scaleFactor, float offset, java.awt.RenderingHints hints)
*		public...........................	**RescaleOp** (float[] scaleFactors, float[] offsets, java.awt.RenderingHints hints)

R

ResourceBundle   java.util

Object
1.1 ○   └ ResourceBundle
P

▲	public static final............... .... ResourceBundle	**getBundle** (String baseName) throws MissingResourceException
▲	public static final............... .... ResourceBundle	**getBundle** (String baseName, Locale locale)
1.2 △	public static .. ResourceBundle	**getBundle** (String baseName, Locale locale, ClassLoader loader) throws MissingResourceException
○	public abstract ... *Enumeration*	**getKeys** ()
1.2	public.................... Locale	**getLocale** ()
●	public final ....Object	**getObject** (String key) throws MissingResourceException
●	public final ....String	**getString** (String key) throws MissingResourceException
●	public final ....String[]	**getStringArray** (String key) throws MissingResourceException
○	protected abstract ......Object	**handleGetObject** (String key) throws MissingResourceException
	protected ..... ResourceBundle	**parent**
*	public...........................	**ResourceBundle** ()
	protected ....void	**setParent** (ResourceBundle parent)

Classes

ResponseHandler   org.omg.CORBA.portable

1.2   *ResponseHandler*

public............ OutputStream	**createExceptionReply** ()
public............ OutputStream	**createReply** ()

	ResultSet		java.sql
			P⁰
1.1		*ResultSet*	

1.2	public	boolean	**absolute** (int row) throws SQLException
1.2	public	void	**afterLast** () throws SQLException
1.2	public	void	**beforeFirst** () throws SQLException
1.2	public	void	**cancelRowUpdates** () throws SQLException
	public	void	**clearWarnings** () throws SQLException
	public	void	**close** () throws SQLException
1.2 ▲	public static final	int	**CONCUR_READ_ONLY** = 1007
1.2 ▲	public static final	int	**CONCUR_UPDATABLE** = 1008
1.2	public	void	**deleteRow** () throws SQLException
1.2 ▲	public static final	int	**FETCH_FORWARD** = 1000
1.2 ▲	public static final	int	**FETCH_REVERSE** = 1001
1.2 ▲	public static final	int	**FETCH_UNKNOWN** = 1002
	public	int	**findColumn** (String columnName) throws SQLException
1.2	public	boolean	**first** () throws SQLException
1.2	public	*Array*	**getArray** (int i) throws SQLException
1.2	public	*Array*	**getArray** (String colName) throws SQLException
	public	java.io.InputStream	**getAsciiStream** (int columnIndex) throws SQLException
	public	java.io.InputStream	**getAsciiStream** (String columnName) throws SQLException
1.2	public	java.math.BigDecimal	**getBigDecimal** (int columnIndex) throws SQLException
1.2	public	java.math.BigDecimal	**getBigDecimal** (String columnName) throws SQLException
D	public	java.math.BigDecimal	**getBigDecimal** (int columnIndex, int scale) throws SQLException
D	public	java.math.BigDecimal	**getBigDecimal** (String columnName, int scale) throws SQLException
	public	java.io.InputStream	**getBinaryStream** (int columnIndex) throws SQLException
	public	java.io.InputStream	**getBinaryStream** (String columnName) throws SQLException
1.2	public	*Blob*	**getBlob** (int i) throws SQLException
1.2	public	*Blob*	**getBlob** (String colName) throws SQLException
	public	boolean	**getBoolean** (int columnIndex) throws SQLException
	public	boolean	**getBoolean** (String columnName) throws SQLException
	public	byte	**getByte** (int columnIndex) throws SQLException
	public	byte	**getByte** (String columnName) throws SQLException
	public	byte[]	**getBytes** (int columnIndex) throws SQLException
	public	byte[]	**getBytes** (String columnName) throws SQLException
1.2	public	java.io.Reader	**getCharacterStream** (int columnIndex) throws SQLException
1.2	public	java.io.Reader	**getCharacterStream** (String columnName) throws SQLException
1.2	public	*Clob*	**getClob** (int i) throws SQLException
1.2	public	*Clob*	**getClob** (String colName) throws SQLException
1.2	public	int	**getConcurrency** () throws SQLException
	public	String	**getCursorName** () throws SQLException
	public	Date	**getDate** (int columnIndex) throws SQLException
	public	Date	**getDate** (String columnName) throws SQLException
1.2	public	Date	**getDate** (int columnIndex, java.util.Calendar cal) throws SQLException
1.2	public	Date	**getDate** (String columnName, java.util.Calendar cal) throws SQLException
	public	double	**getDouble** (int columnIndex) throws SQLException
	public	double	**getDouble** (String columnName) throws SQLException
1.2	public	int	**getFetchDirection** () throws SQLException
1.2	public	int	**getFetchSize** () throws SQLException
	public	float	**getFloat** (int columnIndex) throws SQLException
	public	float	**getFloat** (String columnName) throws SQLException
	public	int	**getInt** (int columnIndex) throws SQLException
	public	int	**getInt** (String columnName) throws SQLException
	public	long	**getLong** (int columnIndex) throws SQLException
	public	long	**getLong** (String columnName) throws SQLException
	public	*ResultSetMetaData*	**getMetaData** () throws SQLException
	public	Object	**getObject** (int columnIndex) throws SQLException
	public	Object	**getObject** (String columnName) throws SQLException
1.2	public	Object	**getObject** (int i, *java.util.Map* map) throws SQLException
1.2	public	Object	**getObject** (String colName, *java.util.Map* map) throws SQLException
1.2	public	*Ref*	**getRef** (int i) throws SQLException
1.2	public	*Ref*	**getRef** (String colName) throws SQLException
1.2	public	int	**getRow** () throws SQLException
	public	short	**getShort** (int columnIndex) throws SQLException
	public	short	**getShort** (String columnName) throws SQLException
	public	*Statement*	**getStatement** () throws SQLException
	public	String	**getString** (int columnIndex) throws SQLException
	public	String	**getString** (String columnName) throws SQLException
	public	Time	**getTime** (int columnIndex) throws SQLException
	public	Time	**getTime** (String columnName) throws SQLException
1.2	public	Time	**getTime** (int columnIndex, java.util.Calendar cal) throws SQLException

R

Class   *Interface*   —extends   - - -implements   ○ abstract   ● final   △ static   ▲ static final   ✳ constructor   x x—inherited   x **x**—declared   **x x**—overridden

1.2	public	Time	**getTime** (String columnName, java.util.Calendar cal) throws SQLException
	public	Timestamp	**getTimestamp** (int columnIndex) throws SQLException
	public	Timestamp	**getTimestamp** (String columnName) throws SQLException
1.2	public	Timestamp	**getTimestamp** (int columnIndex, java.util.Calendar cal) throws SQLException
1.2	public	Timestamp	**getTimestamp** (String columnName, java.util.Calendar cal) throws SQLException
1.2	public	int	**getType** () throws SQLException
D	public	java.io.InputStream	**getUnicodeStream** (int columnIndex) throws SQLException
D	public	java.io.InputStream	**getUnicodeStream** (String columnName) throws SQLException
	public	SQLWarning	**getWarnings** () throws SQLException
1.2	public	void	**insertRow** () throws SQLException
1.2	public	boolean	**isAfterLast** () throws SQLException
1.2	public	boolean	**isBeforeFirst** () throws SQLException
1.2	public	boolean	**isFirst** () throws SQLException
1.2	public	boolean	**isLast** () throws SQLException
1.2	public	boolean	**last** () throws SQLException
1.2	public	void	**moveToCurrentRow** () throws SQLException
1.2	public	void	**moveToInsertRow** () throws SQLException
	public	boolean	**next** () throws SQLException
1.2	public	boolean	**previous** () throws SQLException
1.2	public	void	**refreshRow** () throws SQLException
1.2	public	boolean	**relative** (int rows) throws SQLException
1.2	public	boolean	**rowDeleted** () throws SQLException
1.2	public	boolean	**rowInserted** () throws SQLException
1.2	public	boolean	**rowUpdated** () throws SQLException
1.2	public	void	**setFetchDirection** (int direction) throws SQLException
1.2	public	void	**setFetchSize** (int rows) throws SQLException
1.2 ▲	public static final	int	**TYPE_FORWARD_ONLY** = 1003
1.2 ▲	public static final	int	**TYPE_SCROLL_INSENSITIVE** = 1004
1.2 ▲	public static final	int	**TYPE_SCROLL_SENSITIVE** = 1005
1.2	public	void	**updateAsciiStream** (int columnIndex, java.io.InputStream x, int length) throws SQLException
1.2	public	void	**updateAsciiStream** (String columnName, java.io.InputStream x, int length) throws SQLException
1.2	public	void	**updateBigDecimal** (int columnIndex, java.math.BigDecimal x) throws SQLException
1.2	public	void	**updateBigDecimal** (String columnName, java.math.BigDecimal x) throws SQLException
1.2	public	void	**updateBinaryStream** (int columnIndex, java.io.InputStream x, int length) throws SQLException
1.2	public	void	**updateBinaryStream** (String columnName, java.io.InputStream x, int length) throws SQLException
1.2	public	void	**updateBoolean** (int columnIndex, boolean x) throws SQLException
1.2	public	void	**updateBoolean** (String columnName, boolean x) throws SQLException
1.2	public	void	**updateByte** (int columnIndex, byte x) throws SQLException
1.2	public	void	**updateByte** (String columnName, byte x) throws SQLException
1.2	public	void	**updateBytes** (int columnIndex, byte[] x) throws SQLException
1.2	public	void	**updateBytes** (String columnName, byte[] x) throws SQLException
1.2	public	void	**updateCharacterStream** (int columnIndex, java.io.Reader x, int length) throws SQLException
1.2	public	void	**updateCharacterStream** (String columnName, java.io.Reader reader, int length) throws SQLException
1.2	public	void	**updateDate** (int columnIndex, Date x) throws SQLException
1.2	public	void	**updateDate** (String columnName, Date x) throws SQLException
1.2	public	void	**updateDouble** (int columnIndex, double x) throws SQLException
1.2	public	void	**updateDouble** (String columnName, double x) throws SQLException
1.2	public	void	**updateFloat** (int columnIndex, float x) throws SQLException
1.2	public	void	**updateFloat** (String columnName, float x) throws SQLException
1.2	public	void	**updateInt** (int columnIndex, int x) throws SQLException
1.2	public	void	**updateInt** (String columnName, int x) throws SQLException
1.2	public	void	**updateLong** (int columnIndex, long x) throws SQLException
1.2	public	void	**updateLong** (String columnName, long x) throws SQLException
1.2	public	void	**updateNull** (int columnIndex) throws SQLException
1.2	public	void	**updateNull** (String columnName) throws SQLException
1.2	public	void	**updateObject** (int columnIndex, Object x) throws SQLException
1.2	public	void	**updateObject** (String columnName, Object x) throws SQLException
1.2	public	void	**updateObject** (int columnIndex, Object x, int scale) throws SQLException
1.2	public	void	**updateObject** (String columnName, Object x, int scale) throws SQLException
1.2	public	void	**updateRow** () throws SQLException
1.2	public	void	**updateShort** (int columnIndex, short x) throws SQLException
1.2	public	void	**updateShort** (String columnName, short x) throws SQLException
1.2	public	void	**updateString** (int columnIndex, String x) throws SQLException
1.2	public	void	**updateString** (String columnName, String x) throws SQLException
1.2	public	void	**updateTime** (int columnIndex, Time x) throws SQLException
1.2	public	void	**updateTime** (String columnName, Time x) throws SQLException

R

Classes

1.2	public	void	**updateTimestamp** (int columnIndex, Timestamp x) throws SQLException
1.2	public	void	**updateTimestamp** (String columnName, Timestamp x) throws SQLException
	public	boolean	**wasNull** () throws SQLException

ResultSetMetaData
java.sql
P○

1.1	*ResultSetMetaData*

▲	public static final	int	**columnNoNulls** = 0
▲	public static final	int	**columnNullable** = 1
▲	public static final	int	**columnNullableUnknown** = 2
	public	String	**getCatalogName** (int column) throws SQLException
1.2	public	String	**getColumnClassName** (int column) throws SQLException
	public	int	**getColumnCount** () throws SQLException
	public	int	**getColumnDisplaySize** (int column) throws SQLException
	public	String	**getColumnLabel** (int column) throws SQLException
	public	String	**getColumnName** (int column) throws SQLException
	public	int	**getColumnType** (int column) throws SQLException
	public	String	**getColumnTypeName** (int column) throws SQLException
	public	int	**getPrecision** (int column) throws SQLException
	public	int	**getScale** (int column) throws SQLException
	public	String	**getSchemaName** (int column) throws SQLException
	public	String	**getTableName** (int column) throws SQLException
	public	boolean	**isAutoIncrement** (int column) throws SQLException
	public	boolean	**isCaseSensitive** (int column) throws SQLException
	public	boolean	**isCurrency** (int column) throws SQLException
	public	boolean	**isDefinitelyWritable** (int column) throws SQLException
	public	int	**isNullable** (int column) throws SQLException
	public	boolean	**isReadOnly** (int column) throws SQLException
	public	boolean	**isSearchable** (int column) throws SQLException
	public	boolean	**isSigned** (int column) throws SQLException
	public	boolean	**isWritable** (int column) throws SQLException

R

RGBImageFilter
java.awt.image
P

```
Object
 └ImageFilter¹ - - - - - - - - - - - - - - - - - - - - - - - - - ImageConsumer, Cloneable
    └RGBImageFilter
```

	protected	boolean	**canFilterIndexColorModel**
1	public	Object	clone ()
1	protected	*ImageConsumer*	consumer
	public	IndexColorModel	**filterIndexColorModel** (IndexColorModel icm)
○	public abstract	int	**filterRGB** (int x, int y, int rgb)
	public	void	**filterRGBPixels** (int x, int y, int w, int h, int[] pixels, int off, int scansize)
1	public	ImageFilter	getFilterInstance (*ImageConsumer* ic)
1	public	void	imageComplete (int status)
	protected	ColorModel	**newmodel**
	protected	ColorModel	**origmodel**
1	public	void	resendTopDownLeftRight (*ImageProducer* ip)
*	public		**RGBImageFilter** ()
1	public	**void**	**setColorModel** (ColorModel model)
1	public	void	setDimensions (int width, int height)
1	public	void	setHints (int hints)
1	public	**void**	**setPixels** (int x, int y, int w, int h, ColorModel model, int[] pixels, int off, int scansize)
1	public	**void**	**setPixels** (int x, int y, int w, int h, ColorModel model, byte[] pixels, int off, int scansize)
1	public	void	setProperties (java.util.Hashtable props)
	public	void	**substituteColorModel** (ColorModel oldcm, ColorModel newcm)

RMIClassLoader
java.rmi.server
P○

```
Object
 └RMIClassLoader
```
1.1	

1.2 △	public static	String	**getClassAnnotation** (Class cl)
D △	public static	Object	**getSecurityContext** (ClassLoader loader)
D △	public static	Class	**loadClass** (String name) throws java.net. MalformedURLException, ClassNotFoundException
1.2 △	public static	Class	**loadClass** (String codebase, String name) throws java.net.MalformedURLException, ClassNotFoundException

---

Class   *Interface*   —extends   - - -implements   ○ abstract   ● final   △ static   ▲ static final   ✱ constructor   x x—inherited   x **x**—declared   **x x**—overridden

△   public static . . . . Class **loadClass** (java. net. URL codebase, String name)
         throws java.net.MalformedURLException, ClassNotFoundException

---

RMIClientSocketFactory	java.rmi.server

1.2   *RMIClientSocketFactory*   P○

    public . . . . java.net.Socket **createSocket** (String host, int port) throws java.io.IOException

---

RMIFailureHandler	java.rmi.server

1.1   *RMIFailureHandler*   P○

    public . . . . boolean **failure** (Exception ex)

RMISecurityException	java.rmi

    Object   P○
    └─Throwable - *java.io.Serializable*
      └─Exception
        └─RuntimeException
          └─SecurityException
1.1   └─RMISecurityException

D ✻   public . . . . **RMISecurityException** (String name)
D ✻   public . . . . **RMISecurityException** (String name, String arg)

RMISecurityManager	java.rmi

    Object   P○
    └─SecurityManager [1]
1.1   └─RMISecurityManager

   1   *41 inherited members from SecurityManager not shown*
   1   public . . . . **void checkPackageAccess** (String pkgname)
  ✻   public . . . . **RMISecurityManager** ()

RMIServerSocketFactory	java.rmi.server

1.2   *RMIServerSocketFactory*   P○

    public . . . java.net.ServerSocket **createServerSocket** (int port) throws java.io.IOException

---

RMISocketFactory	java.rmi.server

    Object   P○
1.1 ○   └─RMISocketFactory - *RMIClientSocketFactory* [1], *RMIServerSocketFactory* [2]

○ 2   public abstract . . . . **createServerSocket** (int port) throws java.io.IOException
        . . . . java.net.ServerSocket
○ 1   public abstract java.net.Socket **createSocket** (String host, int port) throws java.io.IOException
1.2 △   public static synchronized . . . . **getDefaultSocketFactory** ()
        . . . . RMISocketFactory
△   public static synchronized . . . . **getFailureHandler** ()
        . . . . *RMIFailureHandler*
△   public static synchronized . . . . **getSocketFactory** ()
        . . . . RMISocketFactory
✻   public . . . . **RMISocketFactory** ()
△   public static synchronized void **setFailureHandler** (*RMIFailureHandler* fh)
△   public static synchronized void **setSocketFactory** (RMISocketFactory fac) throws java.io.IOException

---

RootPaneContainer	javax.swing

1.2   *RootPaneContainer*

    public . . . . java.awt.Container **getContentPane** ()
    public . . . . java.awt.Component **getGlassPane** ()

R

Classes

public	JLayeredPane	**getLayeredPane** ()	
public	JRootPane	**getRootPane** ()	
public	void	**setContentPane** (java.awt.Container contentPane)	
public	void	**setGlassPane** (java.awt.Component glassPane)	
public	void	**setLayeredPane** (JLayeredPane layeredPane)	

RoundRectangle2D   java.awt.geom

```
     Object
1.2 ○  └ RectangularShape 1 - - - - - - - - - - - - - - - - - - - java.awt.Shape, Cloneable
1.2 ○      └ RoundRectangle2D
```

1	*25 inherited members from RectangularShape not shown*		
1	public	**boolean**	**contains** (double x, double y)
1	public	**boolean**	**contains** (double x, double y, double w, double h)
○	public abstract	double	**getArcHeight** ()
○	public abstract	double	**getArcWidth** ()
1	public	*PathIterator*	**getPathIterator** (AffineTransform at)
1	public	**boolean**	**intersects** (double x, double y, double w, double h)
*	protected		**RoundRectangle2D** ()
1	public	**void**	**setFrame** (double x, double y, double w, double h)
	public	void	**setRoundRect** (RoundRectangle2D rr)
○	public abstract	void	**setRoundRect** (double x, double y, double w, double h, double arcWidth, double arcHeight)

RoundRectangle2D.Double   java.awt.geom

```
      Object
1.2 ○   └ RectangularShape 1 - - - - - - - - - - - - - - - - - - - java.awt.Shape, Cloneable
1.2 ○       └ RoundRectangle2D 2
1.2           └ RoundRectangle2D.Double
```

	public	double	**archeight**
	public	double	**arcwidth**
1	public	Object	clone ()
1	public	boolean	contains (Point2D p)
1	public	boolean	contains (Rectangle2D r)
2	public	boolean	contains (double x, double y)
2	public	boolean	contains (double x, double y, double w, double h)
*	public		**Double** ()
*	public		**Double** (double x, double y, double w, double h, double arcw, double arch)
2	public	**double**	**getArcHeight** ()
2	public	**double**	**getArcWidth** ()
1	public	java.awt.Rectangle	getBounds ()
1	public	**Rectangle2D**	**getBounds2D** ()
1	public	double	getCenterX ()
1	public	double	getCenterY ()
1	public	Rectangle2D	getFrame ()
1	public	**double**	**getHeight** ()
1	public	double	getMaxX ()
1	public	double	getMaxY ()
1	public	double	getMinX ()
1	public	double	getMinY ()
2	public	*PathIterator*	getPathIterator (AffineTransform at)
1	public	*PathIterator*	getPathIterator (AffineTransform at, double flatness)
1	public	**double**	**getWidth** ()
1	public	**double**	**getX** ()
1	public	**double**	**getY** ()
	public	double	**height**
1	public	boolean	intersects (Rectangle2D r)
2	public	boolean	intersects (double x, double y, double w, double h)
1	public	**boolean**	**isEmpty** ()
1	public	void	setFrame (Rectangle2D r)
1	public	void	setFrame (Point2D loc, Dimension2D size)
2	public	void	setFrame (double x, double y, double w, double h)
1	public	void	setFrameFromCenter (Point2D center, Point2D corner)
1	public	void	setFrameFromCenter (double centerX, double centerY, double cornerX, double cornerY)
1	public	void	setFrameFromDiagonal (Point2D p1, Point2D p2)
1	public	void	setFrameFromDiagonal (double x1, double y1, double x2, double y2)

Class   *Interface*   —extends   - - -implements   ○ abstract   ● final   △ static   ▲ static final   ✳ constructor   x x—inherited   x **x**—declared   **x x**—overridden

2	public	void	**setRoundRect** (RoundRectangle2D rr)
2	public	void	**setRoundRect** (double x, double y, double w, double h, double arcw, double arch)
	public	double	**width**
	public	double	**x**
	public	double	**y**

RoundRectangle2D.Float | java.awt.geom

```
       Object
1.2 O  └─RectangularShape 1 -------------------- java.awt.Shape, Cloneable
1.2 O     └─RoundRectangle2D 2
1.2          └─RoundRectangle2D.Float
```

	public	float	**archeight**
	public	float	**arcwidth**
1	public	Object	clone ()
1	public	boolean	contains (Point2D p)
1	public	boolean	contains (Rectangle2D r)
2	public	boolean	contains (double x, double y)
2	public	boolean	contains (double x, double y, double w, double h)
*	public		**Float** ()
*	public		**Float** (float x, float y, float w, float h, float arcw, float arch)
2	public	double	**getArcHeight** ()
2	public	double	**getArcWidth** ()
1	public	java.awt.Rectangle	getBounds ()
1	public	**Rectangle2D**	**getBounds2D** ()
1	public	double	getCenterX ()
1	public	double	getCenterY ()
1	public	Rectangle2D	getFrame ()
1	public	double	**getHeight** ()
1	public	double	getMaxX ()
1	public	double	getMaxY ()
1	public	double	getMinX ()
1	public	double	getMinY ()
2	public	*PathIterator*	getPathIterator (AffineTransform at)
1	public	*PathIterator*	getPathIterator (AffineTransform at, double flatness)
1	public	double	**getWidth** ()
1	public	double	**getX** ()
1	public	double	**getY** ()
	public	float	**height**
1	public	boolean	intersects (Rectangle2D r)
2	public	boolean	intersects (double x, double y, double w, double h)
1	public	**boolean**	**isEmpty** ()
1	public	void	setFrame (Rectangle2D r)
1	public	void	setFrame (Point2D loc, Dimension2D size)
2	public	void	setFrame (double x, double y, double w, double h)
1	public	void	setFrameFromCenter (Point2D center, Point2D corner)
1	public	void	setFrameFromCenter (double centerX, double centerY, double cornerX, double cornerY)
1	public	void	setFrameFromDiagonal (Point2D p1, Point2D p2)
1	public	void	setFrameFromDiagonal (double x1, double y1, double x2, double y2)
2	public	void	**setRoundRect** (RoundRectangle2D rr)
2	public	void	**setRoundRect** (double x, double y, double w, double h, double arcw, double arch)
	public	void	**setRoundRect** (float x, float y, float w, float h, float arcw, float arch)
	public	float	**width**
	public	float	**x**
	public	float	**y**

RowMapper | javax.swing.tree

```
1.2    RowMapper
       public ..................... int[] getRowsForPaths (TreePath[] path)
```

RSAPrivateCrtKey | java.security.interfaces

```
1.2    RSAPrivateCrtKey ─────────── RSAPrivateKey 1 (java.security.PrivateKey (java.security.Key 2 PO
                                     (java.io.Serializable)))
```

2	public	String	getAlgorithm ()
	public	java.math.BigInteger	**getCrtCoefficient** ()

RSAPrivateCrtKey

2	public	byte[]	getEncoded ()
2	public	String	getFormat ()
1	public	java.math.BigInteger	getModulus ()
	public	java.math.BigInteger	**getPrimeExponentP** ()
	public	java.math.BigInteger	**getPrimeExponentQ** ()
	public	java.math.BigInteger	**getPrimeP** ()
	public	java.math.BigInteger	**getPrimeQ** ()
1	public	java.math.BigInteger	getPrivateExponent ()
	public	java.math.BigInteger	**getPublicExponent** ()

RSAPrivateCrtKeySpec   java.security.spec

Object
1.2 └─RSAPrivateKeySpec [1] - - - - - - - - - - - - - - - - - - - *KeySpec*
1.2   └─RSAPrivateCrtKeySpec

	public	java.math.BigInteger	**getCrtCoefficient** ()
1	public	java.math.BigInteger	getModulus ()
	public	java.math.BigInteger	**getPrimeExponentP** ()
	public	java.math.BigInteger	**getPrimeExponentQ** ()
	public	java.math.BigInteger	**getPrimeP** ()
	public	java.math.BigInteger	**getPrimeQ** ()
1	public	java.math.BigInteger	getPrivateExponent ()
	public	java.math.BigInteger	**getPublicExponent** ()
✳	public		**RSAPrivateCrtKeySpec** (java.math.BigInteger modulus, java.math.BigInteger publicExponent, java.math.BigInteger privateExponent, java.math.BigInteger primeP, java.math.BigInteger primeQ, java.math.BigInteger primeExponentP, java.math.BigInteger primeExponentQ, java.math.BigInteger crtCoefficient)

R

RSAPrivateKey   java.security.interfaces

1.2 *RSAPrivateKey*────────────────── *java.security.PrivateKey (java.security.Key [1] (java.io.Serializable))* ᴾᴼ

1	public	String	getAlgorithm ()
1	public	byte[]	getEncoded ()
1	public	String	getFormat ()
	public	java.math.BigInteger	**getModulus** ()
	public	java.math.BigInteger	**getPrivateExponent** ()

RSAPrivateKeySpec   java.security.spec

Object
1.2 └─RSAPrivateKeySpec - - - - - - - - - - - - - - - - - - - *KeySpec*

	public	java.math.BigInteger	**getModulus** ()
	public	java.math.BigInteger	**getPrivateExponent** ()
✳	public		**RSAPrivateKeySpec** (java. math. BigInteger modulus, java.math.BigInteger privateExponent)

RSAPublicKey   java.security.interfaces

1.2 *RSAPublicKey*────────────────── *java.security.PublicKey (java.security.Key [1] (java.io.Serializable))* ᴾᴼ

1	public	String	getAlgorithm ()
1	public	byte[]	getEncoded ()
1	public	String	getFormat ()
	public	java.math.BigInteger	**getModulus** ()
	public	java.math.BigInteger	**getPublicExponent** ()

RSAPublicKeySpec   java.security.spec

Object
1.2 └─RSAPublicKeySpec - - - - - - - - - - - - - - - - - - - *KeySpec*

	public	java.math.BigInteger	**getModulus** ()
	public	java.math.BigInteger	**getPublicExponent** ()

Class *Interface* —extends - - -implements ○ abstract ● final △ static ▲ static final ✳ constructor x x—inherited x **x**—declared **x x**—overridden

*	public..........................	**RSAPublicKeySpec** (java. math. BigInteger modulus, java.math.BigInteger publicExponent)

RTFEditorKit

Object
1.2 ○	└javax.swing.text.EditorKit - - - - - - - - - - - - - - - - - *Cloneable, java.io.Serializable*
1.2	└javax.swing.text.DefaultEditorKit [1]
1.2	└javax.swing.text.StyledEditorKit [2]
1.2	└RTFEditorKit

	1	*48 inherited members from javax.swing.text.DefaultEditorKit not shown*
	2	public.................**Object clone** ()
	2	public.......................... createDefaultDocument ()
		.... *javax.swing.text.Document*
	2	protected ....void createInputAttributes (*javax. swing. text. Element* element, *javax.swing.text.MutableAttributeSet* set)
	2	public......................void deinstall (javax.swing.JEditorPane c)
	2	public..... *javax.swing.Action[]* getActions ()
	2	public.......................... getCharacterAttributeRun ()
		.... *javax.swing.text.Element*
	1	public...................**String getContentType** ()
	2	public.......................*javax↩* getInputAttributes ()
		.swing.text.MutableAttributeSet
	2	public.......................... getViewFactory ()
		.. *javax.swing.text.ViewFactory*
	2	public......................void install (javax.swing.JEditorPane c)
	1	public..................... **void read** (java.io. InputStream in, *javax. swing. text. Document* doc, int pos) throws java.io.IOException, javax.swing.text.BadLocationException
	1	public..................... **void read** (java. io. Reader in, *javax. swing. text. Document* doc, int pos) throws java.io.IOException, javax.swing.text.BadLocationException
*		public.......................... **RTFEditorKit** ()
	1	public..................... **void write** (java.io.OutputStream out, *javax.swing.text.Document* doc, int pos, int len) throws java.io.IOException, javax.swing.text.BadLocationException
	1	public..................... **void write** (java.io.Writer out, *javax. swing. text. Document* doc, int pos, int len) throws java.io.IOException, javax.swing.text.BadLocationException

R

RuleBasedCollator

P

Object
| 1.1 ○ | └Collator [1] - *java.util.Comparator, Cloneable* |
| 1.1 | └RuleBasedCollator |

	1	public...................**Object clone** ()
1.2	1	public......................int compare (Object o1, Object o2)
	1	public...................... **int compare** (String source, String target)
	1	public...............**boolean equals** (Object obj)
	1	public.............. boolean equals (String source, String target)
△	1	public static synchronized .... getAvailableLocales ()
		.... *java.util.Locale[]*
		public. CollationElementIterator **getCollationElementIterator** (String source)
1.2		public. CollationElementIterator **getCollationElementIterator** (*CharacterIterator* source)
	1	public............. **CollationKey getCollationKey** (String source)
	1	public synchronized ....int getDecomposition ()
△	1	public static synchronized .... getInstance ()
		.........................Collator
△	1	public static synchronized .... getInstance (java.util.Locale desiredLocale)
		.........................Collator
		public.......................String **getRules** ()
	1	public synchronized ....int getStrength ()
	1	public........................ **int hashCode** ()
*		public.......................... **RuleBasedCollator** (String rules) throws ParseException
	1	public synchronized ......void setDecomposition (int decompositionMode)
	1	public synchronized ......void setStrength (int newStrength)

Classes

Runnable

Runnable

Runnable   java.lang

         P

      Runnable

      public........................void **run** ()

Runtime   java.lang

         P

      Object
      └Runtime

	public................. Process	**exec** (String command) throws java.io.IOException
	public................. Process	**exec** (String[] cmdarray) throws java.io.IOException
	public................. Process	**exec** (String command, String[] envp) throws java.io.IOException
	public................. Process	**exec** (String[] cmdarray, String[] envp) throws java.io.IOException
	public.....................void	**exit** (int status)
	public native .... long	**freeMemory** ()
	public native ....void	**gc** ()
D	public...... java.io.InputStream	**getLocalizedInputStream** (java.io.InputStream in)
D	public.... java.io.OutputStream	**getLocalizedOutputStream** (java.io.OutputStream out)
△	public static .... Runtime	**getRuntime** ()
	public.....................void	**load** (String filename)
	public.....................void	**loadLibrary** (String libname)
	public.....................void	**runFinalization** ()
D △	public static ....void	**runFinalizersOnExit** (boolean value)
	public native .... long	**totalMemory** ()
	public native ....void	**traceInstructions** (boolean on)
	public native ....void	**traceMethodCalls** (boolean on)

RuntimeException   java.lang

         P

S

      Object
      └Throwable --------------------------- *java.io.Serializable*
         └Exception
            └RuntimeException

✳	public..........................	**RuntimeException** ()
✳	public..........................	**RuntimeException** (String s)

RuntimePermission   java.lang

         P

      Object
1.2 ○ └java.security.Permission[1] ---------------- *java.security.Guard*, *java.io.Serializable*
1.2 ○   └java.security.BasicPermission[2] --------- *java.io.Serializable*
1.2 ●   └RuntimePermission

	1	public.....................void	checkGuard (Object object) throws SecurityException
	2	public................. boolean	equals (Object obj)
	2	public................. String	getActions ()
●	1	public final .... String	getName ()
	2	public........................int	hashCode ()
	2	public................. boolean	implies (java.security.Permission p)
	2	public................... java↵	newPermissionCollection ()
		.security.PermissionCollection	
✳		public..........................	**RuntimePermission** (String name)
✳		public..........................	**RuntimePermission** (String name, String actions)
	1	public................... String	toString ()

SampleModel   java.awt.image

         P

      Object
1.2 ○ └SampleModel

○	public abstract .. SampleModel	**createCompatibleSampleModel** (int w, int h)
○	public abstract ..... DataBuffer	**createDataBuffer** ()
○	public abstract .. SampleModel	**createSubsetSampleModel** (int[] bands)
	protected ....int	**dataType**
○	public abstract .... Object	**getDataElements** (int x, int y, Object obj, DataBuffer data)

Class   *Interface*   —extends   - - -implements   ○ abstract   ● final   △ static   ▲ static final   ✳ constructor   x x—inherited   x **x**—declared   **x x**—overridden

	public	Object	**getDataElements** (int x, int y, int w, int h, Object obj, DataBuffer data)
●	public final	int	**getDataType** ()
●	public final	int	**getHeight** ()
●	public final	int	**getNumBands** ()
○	public abstract	int	**getNumDataElements** ()
	public	float[]	**getPixel** (int x, int y, float[] fArray, DataBuffer data)
	public	double[]	**getPixel** (int x, int y, double[] dArray, DataBuffer data)
	public	int[]	**getPixel** (int x, int y, int[] iArray, DataBuffer data)
	public	float[]	**getPixels** (int x, int y, int w, int h, float[] fArray, DataBuffer data)
	public	int[]	**getPixels** (int x, int y, int w, int h, int[] iArray, DataBuffer data)
	public	double[]	**getPixels** (int x, int y, int w, int h, double[] dArray, DataBuffer data)
○	public abstract	int	**getSample** (int x, int y, int b, DataBuffer data)
	public	double	**getSampleDouble** (int x, int y, int b, DataBuffer data)
	public	float	**getSampleFloat** (int x, int y, int b, DataBuffer data)
	public	int[]	**getSamples** (int x, int y, int w, int h, int b, int[] iArray, DataBuffer data)
	public	float[]	**getSamples** (int x, int y, int w, int h, int b, float[] fArray, DataBuffer data)
	public	double[]	**getSamples** (int x, int y, int w, int h, int b, double[] dArray, DataBuffer data)
○	public abstract	int[]	**getSampleSize** ()
○	public abstract	int	**getSampleSize** (int band)
	public	int	**getTransferType** ()
●	public final	int	**getWidth** ()
	protected	int	**height**
	protected	int	**numBands**
*	public		**SampleModel** (int dataType, int w, int h, int numBands)
○	public abstract	void	**setDataElements** (int x, int y, Object obj, DataBuffer data)
	public	void	**setDataElements** (int x, int y, int w, int h, Object obj, DataBuffer data)
	public	void	**setPixel** (int x, int y, double[] dArray, DataBuffer data)
	public	void	**setPixel** (int x, int y, float[] fArray, DataBuffer data)
	public	void	**setPixel** (int x, int y, int[] iArray, DataBuffer data)
	public	void	**setPixels** (int x, int y, int w, int h, double[] dArray, DataBuffer data)
	public	void	**setPixels** (int x, int y, int w, int h, int[] iArray, DataBuffer data)
	public	void	**setPixels** (int x, int y, int w, int h, float[] fArray, DataBuffer data)
○	public abstract	void	**setSample** (int x, int y, int b, int s, DataBuffer data)
	public	void	**setSample** (int x, int y, int b, float s, DataBuffer data)
	public	void	**setSample** (int x, int y, int b, double s, DataBuffer data)
	public	void	**setSamples** (int x, int y, int w, int h, int b, float[] fArray, DataBuffer data)
	public	void	**setSamples** (int x, int y, int w, int h, int b, int[] iArray, DataBuffer data)
	public	void	**setSamples** (int x, int y, int w, int h, int b, double[] dArray, DataBuffer data)
	protected	int	**width**

Scrollable — javax.swing

1.2 *Scrollable*

	public	java.awt.Dimension	**getPreferredScrollableViewportSize** ()
	public	int	**getScrollableBlockIncrement** (java.awt.Rectangle visibleRect, int orientation, int direction)
	public	boolean	**getScrollableTracksViewportHeight** ()
	public	boolean	**getScrollableTracksViewportWidth** ()
	public	int	**getScrollableUnitIncrement** (java.awt.Rectangle visibleRect, int orientation, int direction)

Scrollbar — java.awt
P[O]

Object
○ └Component[1] ------------------------------ *java.awt.image.ImageObserver*, *MenuContainer*,
java.io.Serializable
      └Scrollbar ------------------------------ *Adjustable*[2]

	1	*159 inherited members from Component not shown*		
1.1	2	public synchronized	void	**addAdjustmentListener** (*java.awt.event.AdjustmentListener* l)
	1	public	**void**	**addNotify** ()
1.1	2	public	int	**getBlockIncrement** ()
D		public	int	**getLineIncrement** ()
	2	public	int	**getMaximum** ()
	2	public	int	**getMinimum** ()
	2	public	int	**getOrientation** ()
D		public	int	**getPageIncrement** ()
1.1	2	public	int	**getUnitIncrement** ()
	2	public	int	**getValue** ()
D		public	int	**getVisible** ()
1.1	2	public	int	**getVisibleAmount** ()

S

Classes

Scrollbar

▲	2	public static final	int	**HORIZONTAL**	= 0
	1	protected	**String**	**paramString** ()	
1.1		protected	void	**processAdjustmentEvent** (java.awt.event.AdjustmentEvent e)	
1.1	1	protected	**void**	**processEvent** (AWTEvent e)	
1.1	2	public synchronized	void	**removeAdjustmentListener** (*java.awt.event.AdjustmentListener* l)	
*		public		**Scrollbar** ()	
*		public		**Scrollbar** (int orientation)	
*		public		**Scrollbar** (int orientation, int value, int visible, int minimum, int maximum)	
1.1	2	public	void	**setBlockIncrement** (int v)	
D		public synchronized	void	**setLineIncrement** (int v)	
1.1	2	public	void	**setMaximum** (int newMaximum)	
1.1	2	public	void	**setMinimum** (int newMinimum)	
1.1		public	void	**setOrientation** (int orientation)	
D		public synchronized	void	**setPageIncrement** (int v)	
1.1	2	public	void	**setUnitIncrement** (int v)	
	2	public	void	**setValue** (int newValue)	
		public synchronized	void	**setValues** (int value, int visible, int minimum, int maximum)	
1.1	2	public	void	**setVisibleAmount** (int newAmount)	
▲	2	public static final	int	**VERTICAL**	= 1

ScrollbarPeer   java.awt.peer

ScrollbarPeer————————————————————*ComponentPeer* [1]

1	*32 inherited members from ComponentPeer not shown*			
	public	void	**setLineIncrement** (int)	
	public	void	**setPageIncrement** (int)	
	public	void	**setValues** (int, int, int, int)	

ScrollBarUI   javax.swing.plaf

Object
  └ ComponentUI [1]   1.2 ○
     └ ScrollBarUI   1.2 ○

1	*11 inherited members from ComponentUI not shown*			
*	public		**ScrollBarUI** ()	

ScrollPane   java.awt
P

Object
  └ Component [1] - *java.awt.image.ImageObserver*, *MenuContainer*,
                                                                   java.io.Serializable
     └ Container [2]
        └ ScrollPane   1.1

	1	*137 inherited members from Component not shown*			
	2	*44 inherited members from Container not shown*			
●	2	protected final	**void**	**addImpl** (Component comp, Object constraints, int index)	
	2	public	**void**	**addNotify** ()	
	2	public	**void**	**doLayout** ()	
		public	*Adjustable*	**getHAdjustable** ()	
		public	int	**getHScrollbarHeight** ()	
		public	int	**getScrollbarDisplayPolicy** ()	
		public	Point	**getScrollPosition** ()	
		public	*Adjustable*	**getVAdjustable** ()	
		public	Dimension	**getViewportSize** ()	
		public	int	**getVScrollbarWidth** ()	
D	2	public	**void**	**layout** ()	
	2	public	**String**	**paramString** ()	
	2	public	**void**	**printComponents** (Graphics g)	
▲		public static final	int	**SCROLLBARS_ALWAYS**	= 1
▲		public static final	int	**SCROLLBARS_AS_NEEDED**	= 0
▲		public static final	int	**SCROLLBARS_NEVER**	= 2
*		public		**ScrollPane** ()	
*		public		**ScrollPane** (int scrollbarDisplayPolicy)	
●	2	public final	**void**	**setLayout** (*LayoutManager* mgr)	
		public	void	**setScrollPosition** (Point p)	

Class *Interface* ——extends - - -implements ○ abstract ● final △ static ▲ static final * constructor x x—inherited x **x**—declared **x x**—overridden

S

public	void	**setScrollPosition** (int x, int y)

---

	javax.swing

1.2   *ScrollPaneConstants*

- ▲ public static final .... String **COLUMN_HEADER** = "COLUMN_HEADER"
- ▲ public static final .... String **HORIZONTAL_SCROLLBAR** = "HORIZONTAL_SCROLLBAR"
- ▲ public static final .... int **HORIZONTAL_SCROLLBAR_ALWAYS** = 32
- ▲ public static final .... int **HORIZONTAL_SCROLLBAR_AS_NEEDED** = 30
- ▲ public static final .... int **HORIZONTAL_SCROLLBAR_NEVER** = 31
- ▲ public static final .... String **HORIZONTAL_SCROLLBAR_POLICY** = "HORIZONTAL_SCROLLBAR_POLICY"
- ▲ public static final .... String **LOWER_LEFT_CORNER** = "LOWER_LEFT_CORNER"
- ▲ public static final .... String **LOWER_RIGHT_CORNER** = "LOWER_RIGHT_CORNER"
- ▲ public static final .... String **ROW_HEADER** = "ROW_HEADER"
- ▲ public static final .... String **UPPER_LEFT_CORNER** = "UPPER_LEFT_CORNER"
- ▲ public static final .... String **UPPER_RIGHT_CORNER** = "UPPER_RIGHT_CORNER"
- ▲ public static final .... String **VERTICAL_SCROLLBAR** = "VERTICAL_SCROLLBAR"
- ▲ public static final .... int **VERTICAL_SCROLLBAR_ALWAYS** = 22
- ▲ public static final .... int **VERTICAL_SCROLLBAR_AS_NEEDED** = 20
- ▲ public static final .... int **VERTICAL_SCROLLBAR_NEVER** = 21
- ▲ public static final .... String **VERTICAL_SCROLLBAR_POLICY** = "VERTICAL_SCROLLBAR_POLICY"
- ▲ public static final .... String **VIEWPORT** = "VIEWPORT"

---

	javax.swing

Object
   └ScrollPaneLayout ---------------------- *java.awt.LayoutManager* [1], *ScrollPaneConstants*,
1.2   *java.io.Serializable*

1	public	void	**addLayoutComponent** (String s, java.awt.Component c)
	protected java.awt.Component		**addSingletonComponent** (java.awt.Component oldC, java.awt.Component newC)
	protected	JViewport	**colHead**
	public	JViewport	**getColumnHeader** ()
	public	java.awt.Component	**getCorner** (String key)
	public	JScrollBar	**getHorizontalScrollBar** ()
	public	int	**getHorizontalScrollBarPolicy** ()
	public	JViewport	**getRowHeader** ()
	public	JScrollBar	**getVerticalScrollBar** ()
	public	int	**getVerticalScrollBarPolicy** ()
	public	JViewport	**getViewport** ()
D	public	java.awt.Rectangle	**getViewportBorderBounds** (JScrollPane scrollpane)
	protected	JScrollBar	**hsb**
	protected	int	**hsbPolicy**
1	public	void	**layoutContainer** (java.awt.Container parent)
	protected java.awt.Component		**lowerLeft**
	protected java.awt.Component		**lowerRight**
1	public	java.awt.Dimension	**minimumLayoutSize** (java.awt.Container parent)
1	public	java.awt.Dimension	**preferredLayoutSize** (java.awt.Container parent)
1	public	void	**removeLayoutComponent** (java.awt.Component c)
	protected	JViewport	**rowHead**
*	public		**ScrollPaneLayout** ()
	public	void	**setHorizontalScrollBarPolicy** (int x)
	public	void	**setVerticalScrollBarPolicy** (int x)
	public	void	**syncWithScrollPane** (JScrollPane sp)
	protected java.awt.Component		**upperLeft**
	protected java.awt.Component		**upperRight**
	protected	JViewport	**viewport**
	protected	JScrollBar	**vsb**
	protected	int	**vsbPolicy**

---

	javax.swing

Object
1.2   └ScrollPaneLayout [1] ------------------------ *java.awt.LayoutManager*, *ScrollPaneConstants*, *java.io.Serializable*
1.2   └ScrollPaneLayout.UIResource ----------- *javax.swing.plaf.UIResource*

1	*29 inherited members from ScrollPaneLayout not shown*		
*	public		**UIResource** ()

S

Classes

ScrollPanePeer | java.awt.peer

| 1.1 | *ScrollPanePeer*———————————— *ContainerPeer* [1] (*ComponentPeer* [2]) |

	2	*32 inherited members from ComponentPeer not shown*
	1	*4 inherited members from ContainerPeer not shown*
		public.........................void	**childResized** (int, int)
		public..........................int	**getHScrollbarHeight** ()
		public..........................int	**getVScrollbarWidth** ()
		public.........................void	**setScrollPosition** (int, int)
		public.........................void	**setUnitIncrement** (*java.awt.Adjustable*, int)
		public.........................void	**setValue** (*java.awt.Adjustable*, int)

ScrollPaneUI | javax.swing.plaf

		Object
1.2	○	└ComponentUI [1]
1.2	○	└ScrollPaneUI

| | 1 | *11 inherited members from ComponentUI not shown* |
| * | | public........................... **ScrollPaneUI** () |

SecureClassLoader | java.security
P[O]

		Object
○		└ClassLoader [1]
1.2		└SecureClassLoader

●	1	protected final............ Class	defineClass (String name, byte[] b, int off, int len) throws ClassFormatError
●	1	protected final............ Class	defineClass (String name, byte[] b, int off, int len, ProtectionDomain protectionDomain) throws ClassFormatError
●		protected final............ Class	**defineClass** (String name, byte[] b, int off, int len, CodeSource cs)
	1	protected .... Package	definePackage (String name, String specTitle, String specVersion, String specVendor, String implTitle, String implVersion, String implVendor, java.net.URL sealBase) throws IllegalArgumentException
	1	protected .... Class	findClass (String name) throws ClassNotFoundException
	1	protected .... String	findLibrary (String libname)
●	1	protected final native .... Class	findLoadedClass (String name)
	1	protected........... java.net.URL	findResource (String name)
	1	protected *java.util.Enumeration*	findResources (String name) throws java.io.IOException
●	1	protected final............ Class	findSystemClass (String name) throws ClassNotFoundException
	1	protected .... Package	getPackage (String name)
	1	protected.........Package[]	getPackages ()
●	1	public final .... ClassLoader	getParent ()
		protected PermissionCollection	**getPermissions** (CodeSource codesource)
	1	public............. java.net.URL	getResource (String name)
	1	public....... java.io.InputStream	getResourceAsStream (String name)
●	1	public final .... *java.util.Enumeration*	getResources (String name) throws java.io.IOException
△	1	public static ...... ClassLoader	getSystemClassLoader ()
△	1	public static ...... java.net.URL	getSystemResource (String name)
△	1	public static .... java.io.InputStream	getSystemResourceAsStream (String name)
△	1	public static .... *java.util.Enumeration*	getSystemResources (String name) throws java.io.IOException
	1	public.....................Class	loadClass (String name) throws ClassNotFoundException
	1	protected synchronized . Class	loadClass (String name, boolean resolve) throws ClassNotFoundException
●	1	protected final..............void	resolveClass (Class c)
*		protected .... **SecureClassLoader** ()
*		protected .... **SecureClassLoader** (ClassLoader parent)
●	1	protected final..............void	setSigners (Class c, Object[] signers)

SecureRandom | java.security
P[O]

		Object
		└java.util.Random [1] - *java.io.Serializable*
1.1		└SecureRandom

Class   *Interface*   —extends   - - -implements   ○ abstract   ● final   △ static   ▲ static final   * constructor   x x—inherited   x **x**—declared   **x x**—overridden

S

1.2		public.....................byte[]	**generateSeed** (int numBytes)
1.2	△	public static ... SecureRandom	**getInstance** (String algorithm) throws NoSuchAlgorithmException
1.2	△	public static ... SecureRandom	**getInstance** (String algorithm, String provider) throws NoSuchAlgorithmException,
			NoSuchProviderException
1.2	●	public final ....Provider	**getProvider** ()
	△	public static ....byte[]	**getSeed** (int numBytes)
	● 1	protected final.............**int**	**next** (int numBits)
1.2	1	public....................boolean	nextBoolean ()
	1	public synchronized ...... **void**	**nextBytes** (byte[] bytes)
	1	public....................double	nextDouble ()
	1	public.......................float	nextFloat ()
	1	public synchronized ....double	nextGaussian ()
	1	public........................int	nextInt ()
1.2	1	public........................int	nextInt (int n)
	1	public........................long	nextLong ()
	✳	public..........................	**SecureRandom** ()
	✳	public..........................	**SecureRandom** (byte[] seed)
1.2	✳	protected.......................	**SecureRandom** (SecureRandomSpi secureRandomSpi, Provider provider)
		public synchronized ....void	**setSeed** (byte[] seed)
	1	public..................... **void**	**setSeed** (long seed)

SecureRandomSpi

java.security

P°

Object
└ SecureRandomSpi - *java.io.Serializable*

1.2 ○

	○	protected abstract ....byte[]	**engineGenerateSeed** (int numBytes)
	○	protected abstract ....void	**engineNextBytes** (byte[] bytes)
	○	protected abstract ....void	**engineSetSeed** (byte[] seed)
	✳	public..........................	**SecureRandomSpi** ()

Security

java.security

P°

Object
└ Security

1.1 ●

	△	public static ....int	**addProvider** (Provider provider)
D	△	public static ....String	**getAlgorithmProperty** (String algName, String propName)
	△	public static ....String	**getProperty** (String key)
	△	public static ....Provider	**getProvider** (String name)
	△	public static ....Provider[]	**getProviders** ()
	△	public static ....int	**insertProviderAt** (Provider provider, int position)
	△	public static ....void	**removeProvider** (String name)
	△	public static ....void	**setProperty** (String key, String datum)

SecurityException

java.lang

P

Object
└ Throwable - *java.io.Serializable*
  └ Exception
    └ RuntimeException
      └ SecurityException

	✳	public..........................	**SecurityException** ()
	✳	public..........................	**SecurityException** (String s)

SecurityManager

java.lang

P

Object
└ SecurityManager

		public.....................void	**checkAccept** (String host, int port)
		public.....................void	**checkAccess** (Thread t)
		public.....................void	**checkAccess** (ThreadGroup g)
1.1		public.....................void	**checkAwtEventQueueAccess** ()
		public.....................void	**checkConnect** (String host, int port)
		public.....................void	**checkConnect** (String host, int port, Object context)
		public.....................void	**checkCreateClassLoader** ()
		public.....................void	**checkDelete** (String file)

S

Classes

SecurityManager

	public	void	**checkExec** (String cmd)
	public	void	**checkExit** (int status)
	public	void	**checkLink** (String lib)
	public	void	**checkListen** (int port)
1.1	public	void	**checkMemberAccess** (Class clazz, int which)
1.1	public	void	**checkMulticast** (java.net.InetAddress maddr)
1.1	public	void	**checkMulticast** (java.net.InetAddress maddr, byte ttl)
	public	void	**checkPackageAccess** (String pkg)
	public	void	**checkPackageDefinition** (String pkg)
1.2	public	void	**checkPermission** (java.security.Permission perm)
1.2	public	void	**checkPermission** (java.security.Permission perm, Object context)
1.1	public	void	**checkPrintJobAccess** ()
	public	void	**checkPropertiesAccess** ()
	public	void	**checkPropertyAccess** (String key)
	public	void	**checkRead** (java.io.FileDescriptor fd)
	public	void	**checkRead** (String file)
	public	void	**checkRead** (String file, Object context)
1.1	public	void	**checkSecurityAccess** (String target)
	public	void	**checkSetFactory** ()
1.1	public	void	**checkSystemClipboardAccess** ()
	public	boolean	**checkTopLevelWindow** (Object window)
	public	void	**checkWrite** (java.io.FileDescriptor fd)
	public	void	**checkWrite** (String file)
D	protected native	int	**classDepth** (String name)
D	protected	int	**classLoaderDepth** ()
D	protected	ClassLoader	**currentClassLoader** ()
D	protected	Class	**currentLoadedClass** ()
	protected native	Class[]	**getClassContext** ()
D	public	boolean	**getInCheck** ()
	public	Object	**getSecurityContext** ()
1.1	public	ThreadGroup	**getThreadGroup** ()
D	protected	boolean	**inCheck**
D	protected	boolean	**inClass** (String name)
D	protected	boolean	**inClassLoader** ()
✳	public		**SecurityManager** ()

S

SecurityPermission — java.security

P^O

Object
  └ Permission [1] - *Guard, java.io.Serializable*
     └ BasicPermission [2] - - - - - - - - - - - - - - - - - - - *java.io.Serializable*
       └ SecurityPermission

(1.2 ○, 1.2 ○, 1.2 ●)

1	public	void	checkGuard (Object object) throws SecurityException
2	public	boolean	equals (Object obj)
2	public	String	getActions ()
● 1	public final	String	getName ()
2	public	int	hashCode ()
2	public	boolean	implies (Permission p)
2	public	PermissionCollection	newPermissionCollection ()
✳	public		**SecurityPermission** (String name)
✳	public		**SecurityPermission** (String name, String actions)
1	public	String	toString ()

Segment — javax.swing.text

Object [1]
  └ Segment

(1.2)

	public	char[]	**array**
	public	int	**count**
	public	int	**offset**
✳	public		**Segment** ()
✳	public		**Segment** (char[] array, int offset, int count)
1	public	String	**toString** ()

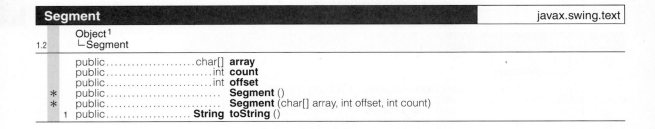

Class *Interface* —extends - - -implements ○ abstract ● final △ static ▲ static final ✳ constructor x x—inherited x **x**—declared **x x**—overridden

610

| **SeparatorUI** | javax.swing.plaf |

```
     Object
1.2 ○  └ ComponentUI 1
1.2 ○    └ SeparatorUI
```

| | 1 | *11 inherited members from ComponentUI not shown* |
| * | | public........................ **SeparatorUI** () |

| **SequenceInputStream** | java.io |

```
     Object
○  └ InputStream 1
     └ SequenceInputStream
```

	1	public..................... **int available** () throws IOException
	1	public..................... **void close** () throws IOException
	1	public synchronized ....void mark (int readlimit)
	1	public.................. boolean markSupported ()
	1	public..................... **int read** () throws IOException
	1	public.....................int read (byte[] b) throws IOException
	1	public..................... **int read** (byte[] b, int off, int len) throws IOException
	1	public synchronized ....void reset () throws IOException
*		public........................ **SequenceInputStream** (*java.util.Enumeration* e)
*		public........................ **SequenceInputStream** (InputStream s1, InputStream s2)
	1	public..................... long skip (long n) throws IOException

---

| *Serializable* | java.io |

| 1.1 | | *Serializable* |
| 1.2 ▲ | | public static final.......... long **serialVersionUID** = 1196656838076753133 |

| **SerializablePermission** | java.io |

```
      Object
1.2 ○  └ java.security.Permission 1 ----------------- java.security.Guard, Serializable
1.2 ○    └ java.security.BasicPermission 2 ---------- Serializable
1.2 ●      └ SerializablePermission
```

	1	public......................void checkGuard (Object object) throws SecurityException
	2	public.................. boolean equals (Object obj)
	2	public.................... String getActions ()
●	1	public final .... String getName ()
	2	public........................int hashCode ()
	2	public.................. boolean implies (java.security.Permission p)
	2	public..................... java↵ newPermissionCollection ()
		.security.PermissionCollection
*		public........................ **SerializablePermission** (String name)
*		public........................ **SerializablePermission** (String name, String actions)
	1	public.................... String toString ()

| **ServantObject** | org.omg.CORBA.portable |

```
     Object
1.2  └ ServantObject
```

| | | public.................... Object **servant** |
| * | | public........................ **ServantObject** () |

| **ServerCloneException** | java.rmi.server |
| | P○ |

```
     Object
     └ Throwable 1 -------------------------- java.io.Serializable
       └ Exception
         └ CloneNotSupportedException
1.1        └ ServerCloneException
```

ServerCloneException

	public	Exception	**detail**
1	public	**String**	**getMessage** ()
1	public	**void**	**printStackTrace** ()
1	public	**void**	**printStackTrace** (java.io.PrintStream ps)
1	public	**void**	**printStackTrace** (java.io.PrintWriter pw)
*	public		**ServerCloneException** (String s)
*	public		**ServerCloneException** (String s, Exception ex)

ServerError   java.rmi

P^O

```
Object
 └Throwable --------------------------- java.io.Serializable
     └Exception
        └java.io.IOException
1.1        └RemoteException 1
1.1           └ServerError
```

1	public	Throwable	detail
1	public	String	getMessage ()
1	public	void	printStackTrace ()
1	public	void	printStackTrace (java.io.PrintStream ps)
1	public	void	printStackTrace (java.io.PrintWriter pw)
*	public		**ServerError** (String s, Error err)

ServerException   java.rmi

P^O

```
Object
 └Throwable --------------------------- java.io.Serializable
     └Exception
        └java.io.IOException
1.1        └RemoteException 1
1.1           └ServerException
```

1	public	Throwable	detail
1	public	String	getMessage ()
1	public	void	printStackTrace ()
1	public	void	printStackTrace (java.io.PrintStream ps)
1	public	void	printStackTrace (java.io.PrintWriter pw)
*	public		**ServerException** (String s)
*	public		**ServerException** (String s, Exception ex)

ServerNotActiveException   java.rmi.server

P^O

```
Object
 └Throwable --------------------------- java.io.Serializable
     └Exception
1.1     └ServerNotActiveException
```

*	public	**ServerNotActiveException** ()
*	public	**ServerNotActiveException** (String s)

ServerRef   java.rmi.server

1.1   *ServerRef*————————————————————— *RemoteRef [1] (java.io.Externalizable [2] (java.io.Serializable))*   P^O

	public	RemoteStub	**exportObject** (*java.rmi.Remote* obj, Object data) throws java.rmi.RemoteException
	public	String	**getClientHost** () throws ServerNotActiveException
1	public	String	getRefClass (*java.io.ObjectOutput* out)
1.2 1	public	Object	invoke (*java.rmi.Remote* obj, java.lang.reflect.Method method, Object[] params, long opnum) throws Exception
2	public	void	readExternal (*java.io.ObjectInput* in) throws java.io.IOException, ClassNotFoundException
1	public	boolean	remoteEquals (*RemoteRef* obj)
1	public	int	remoteHashCode ()
1	public	String	remoteToString ()
1.2 ▲ 1	public static final	**long**	**serialVersionUID** = -4557750989390278438

Class   *Interface*   —extends   - - -implements   ○ abstract   ● final   △ static   ▲ static final   * constructor   x x—inherited   x **x**—declared   **x x**—overridden

```
▆  2  public.....................void  writeExternal (java.io.ObjectOutput out) throws java.io.IOException
```

ServerRequest org.omg.CORBA

		Object	
1.2	○	└ ServerRequest	

	○	public.....................void	**arguments** (NVList args)
	○	public abstract ....Context	**ctx** ()
D		public.....................void	**except** (Any any)
D		public.....................String	**op_name** ()
		public.....................String	**operation** ()
D		public.....................void	**params** (NVList params)
D		public.....................void	**result** (Any any)
	∗	public.....................	**ServerRequest** ()
		public.....................void	**set_exception** (Any any)
		public.....................void	**set_result** (Any any)

ServerRuntimeException java.rmi
P○

```
       Object
        └ Throwable - - - - - - - - - - - - - - - - - - - - - - - - java.io.Serializable
         └ Exception
          └ java.io.IOException
1.1        └ RemoteException 1
1.1         └ ServerRuntimeException
```

1	public.................Throwable	detail
1	public.....................String	getMessage ()
1	public.....................void	printStackTrace ()
1	public.....................void	printStackTrace (java.io.PrintStream ps)
1	public.....................void	printStackTrace (java.io.PrintWriter pw)
D ∗	public.........................	**ServerRuntimeException** (String s, Exception ex)

ServerSocket java.net
P

```
       Object 1
        └ ServerSocket
```

	public.....................Socket	**accept** () throws java.io.IOException
	public.....................void	**close** () throws java.io.IOException
	public..............InetAddress	**getInetAddress** ()
	public.....................int	**getLocalPort** ()
1.1	public synchronized ....int	**getSoTimeout** () throws java.io.IOException
1.1 ●	protected final..............void	**implAccept** (Socket s) throws java.io.IOException
∗	public.........................	**ServerSocket** (int port) throws java.io.IOException
∗	public.........................	**ServerSocket** (int port, int backlog) throws java.io.IOException
1.1 ∗	public.........................	**ServerSocket** (int port, int backlog, InetAddress bindAddr)
		throws java.io.IOException
△	public static synchronized void	**setSocketFactory** (SocketImplFactory fac) throws java.io.IOException
1.1	public synchronized ....void	**setSoTimeout** (int timeout) throws SocketException
1	public.....................String	**toString** ()

ServiceDetail org.omg.CORBA

		Object	
1.2 ●		└ ServiceDetail - org.omg.CORBA.portable.IDLEntity (java.io.Serializable)	

	public.....................byte[]	**service_detail**
	public.....................int	**service_detail_type**
∗	public.........................	**ServiceDetail** ()
∗	public.........................	**ServiceDetail** (int service_detail_type, byte[] service_detail)

ServiceDetailHelper org.omg.CORBA

		Object
1.2		└ ServiceDetailHelper

S

Classes

ServiceDetailHelper

△	public static	ServiceDetail	**extract** (Any a)
△	public static	String	**id** ()
△	public static	void	**insert** (Any a, ServiceDetail that)
△	public static	ServiceDetail	**read** (org.omg.CORBA.portable.InputStream in)
△	public static synchronized TypeCode		**type** ()
△	public static	void	**write** (org.omg.CORBA.portable.OutputStream out, ServiceDetail that)

ServiceInformation org.omg.CORBA

1.2 ● Object
└ServiceInformation - *org.omg.CORBA.portable.IDLEntity* (*java.io.Serializable*)

	public	ServiceDetail[]	**service_details**
	public	int[]	**service_options**
✻	public		**ServiceInformation** ()
✻	public		**ServiceInformation** (int[] __service_options, ServiceDetail[] __service_details)

ServiceInformationHelper org.omg.CORBA

1.2 Object
└ServiceInformationHelper

△	public static ServiceInformation		**extract** (Any a)
△	public static	String	**id** ()
△	public static	void	**insert** (Any a, ServiceInformation that)
△	public static ServiceInformation		**read** (org.omg.CORBA.portable.InputStream in)
△	public static synchronized TypeCode		**type** ()
△	public static	void	**write** (org.omg.CORBA.portable.OutputStream out, ServiceInformation that)

ServiceInformationHolder org.omg.CORBA

1.2 ● Object
└ServiceInformationHolder - - - - - - - - - - - - - - - *org.omg.CORBA.portable.Streamable* [1]

1	public	void	**_read** (org.omg.CORBA.portable.InputStream in)
1	public	TypeCode	**_type** ()
1	public	void	**_write** (org.omg.CORBA.portable.OutputStream out)
✻	public		**ServiceInformationHolder** ()
✻	public		**ServiceInformationHolder** (ServiceInformation arg)
	public	ServiceInformation	**value**

Set java.util

1.2 *Set* ———————————————— *Collection* [1] P

1	public	boolean	**add** (Object o)
1	public	boolean	**addAll** (*Collection* c)
1	public	void	**clear** ()
1	public	boolean	**contains** (Object o)
1	public	boolean	**containsAll** (*Collection* c)
1	public	boolean	**equals** (Object o)
1	public	int	**hashCode** ()
1	public	boolean	**isEmpty** ()
1	public	*Iterator*	**iterator** ()
1	public	boolean	**remove** (Object o)
1	public	boolean	**removeAll** (*Collection* c)
1	public	boolean	**retainAll** (*Collection* c)
1	public	int	**size** ()
1	public	Object[]	**toArray** ()
1	public	Object[]	**toArray** (Object[] a)

Class *Interface* —extends - - -implements ○ abstract ● final △ static ▲ static final ✻ constructor x x—inherited x **x**—declared **x x**—overridden

SetOverrideType | org.omg.CORBA

1.2		Object └SetOverrideType - *org.omg.CORBA.portable.IDLEntity* (*java.io.Serializable*)

▲	public static final . . . . int	**_ADD_OVERRIDE** = 1	
▲	public static final . . . . int	**_SET_OVERRIDE** = 0	
▲	public static final . . . . SetOverrideType	**ADD_OVERRIDE**	
△	public static . . SetOverrideType	**from_int** (int i) throws BAD_PARAM	
▲	public static final . . . . SetOverrideType	**SET_OVERRIDE**	
*	protected	**SetOverrideType** (int _value)	
	public . . . . int	**value** ()	

Shape | java.awt

1.1		*Shape* P

1.2	public . . . . boolean	**contains** (java.awt.geom.Point2D p)	
1.2	public . . . . boolean	**contains** (java.awt.geom.Rectangle2D r)	
1.2	public . . . . boolean	**contains** (double x, double y)	
1.2	public . . . . boolean	**contains** (double x, double y, double w, double h)	
	public . . . . Rectangle	**getBounds** ()	
1.2	public java.awt.geom.Rectangle2D	**getBounds2D** ()	
1.2	public . . . . *java.awt.geom.PathIterator*	**getPathIterator** (java.awt.geom.AffineTransform at)	
1.2	public . . . . *java.awt.geom.PathIterator*	**getPathIterator** (java.awt.geom.AffineTransform at, double flatness)	
1.2	public . . . . boolean	**intersects** (java.awt.geom.Rectangle2D r)	
1.2	public . . . . boolean	**intersects** (double x, double y, double w, double h)	

ShapeGraphicAttribute | java.awt.font

1.2 ○		Object[1] └GraphicAttribute[2]
1.2 ●		└ShapeGraphicAttribute

	2	public . . . . **void**	**draw** (java.awt.Graphics2D graphics, float x, float y)
		public . . . . boolean	**equals** (ShapeGraphicAttribute rhs)
	1	public . . . . **boolean**	**equals** (Object rhs)
▲		public static final . . . . . . boolean	**FILL** = false
	2	public . . . . **float**	**getAdvance** ()
●	2	public final . . . . int	getAlignment ()
	2	public . . . . **float**	**getAscent** ()
	2	public **java.awt.geom.Rectangle2D**	**getBounds** ()
	2	public . . . . **float**	**getDescent** ()
	2	public . . . GlyphJustificationInfo	getJustificationInfo ()
	1	public . . . . **int**	**hashCode** ()
*		public . . . . **ShapeGraphicAttribute** (*java.awt.Shape* shape, int alignment, boolean stroke)	
▲		public static final . . . . . . boolean	**STROKE** = true

Short | java.lang

○		Object[1] └Number[2] - *java.io.Serializable* P
1.1 ●		└Short - *Comparable*[3]

	2	public . . . . **byte**	**byteValue** ()
1.2	3	public . . . . int	**compareTo** (Object o)
1.2		public . . . . int	**compareTo** (Short anotherShort)
△		public static . . . . Short	**decode** (String nm) throws NumberFormatException
	2	public . . . . **double**	**doubleValue** ()
	1	public . . . . **boolean**	**equals** (Object obj)
	2	public . . . . **float**	**floatValue** ()
	1	public . . . . **int**	**hashCode** ()
	2	public . . . . **int**	**intValue** ()
	2	public . . . . **long**	**longValue** ()

S

Classes

Short

▲		public static final	short	**MAX_VALUE** = 32767
▲		public static final	short	**MIN_VALUE** = -32768
△		public static	short	**parseShort** (String s) throws NumberFormatException
△		public static	short	**parseShort** (String s, int radix) throws NumberFormatException
✳		public		**Short** (String s) throws NumberFormatException
✳		public		**Short** (short value)
	2	public	short	**shortValue** ()
	1	public	String	**toString** ()
△		public static	String	**toString** (short s)
▲		public static final	Class	**TYPE**
△		public static	Short	**valueOf** (String s) throws NumberFormatException
△		public static	Short	**valueOf** (String s, int radix) throws NumberFormatException

ShortHolder — org.omg.CORBA

Object
└ShortHolder `1.2 ●` - *org.omg.CORBA.portable.Streamable* [1]

	1	public	void	**_read** (org.omg.CORBA.portable.InputStream input)
	1	public	TypeCode	**_type** ()
	1	public	void	**_write** (org.omg.CORBA.portable.OutputStream output)
✳		public		**ShortHolder** ()
✳		public		**ShortHolder** (short initial)
		public	short	**value**

ShortLookupTable — java.awt.image

P

Object
`1.2` ○ └LookupTable [1]
`1.2` └ShortLookupTable

	1	public	int	**getNumComponents** ()
	1	public	int	**getOffset** ()
●		public final	short[][]	**getTable** ()
	1	public	**int[]**	**lookupPixel** (int[] src, int[] dst)
		public	short[]	**lookupPixel** (short[] src, short[] dst)
✳		public		**ShortLookupTable** (int offset, short[] data)
✳		public		**ShortLookupTable** (int offset, short[][] data)

Signature — java.security

P○

Object [1]
`1.2` ○ └SignatureSpi [2]
`1.1` ○ └Signature

`1.2`		2	protected	SecureRandom	appRandom
		2	public	**Object**	**clone** () throws CloneNotSupportedException
`1.2` ○		2	protected abstract	void	**engineInitSign** (*PrivateKey* privateKey) throws InvalidKeyException
`1.2`		2	protected	void	**engineInitSign** (*PrivateKey* privateKey, SecureRandom random) throws InvalidKeyException
`1.2` ○		2	protected abstract	void	**engineInitVerify** (*PublicKey* publicKey) throws InvalidKeyException
`1.2`		2	protected	void	**engineSetParameter** (*java.security.spec.AlgorithmParameterSpec* params) throws InvalidAlgorithmParameterException
`1.2` ○		2	protected abstract	byte[]	**engineSign** () throws SignatureException
`1.2`		2	protected	int	**engineSign** (byte[] outbuf, int offset, int len) throws SignatureException
`1.2` ○		2	protected abstract	void	**engineUpdate** (byte b) throws SignatureException
`1.2` ○		2	protected abstract	void	**engineUpdate** (byte[] b, int off, int len) throws SignatureException
`1.2` ○		2	protected abstract	boolean	**engineVerify** (byte[] sigBytes) throws SignatureException
●			public final	String	**getAlgorithm** ()
△			public static	Signature	**getInstance** (String algorithm) throws NoSuchAlgorithmException
△			public static	Signature	**getInstance** (String algorithm, String provider) throws NoSuchAlgorithmException, NoSuchProviderException
D ●			public final	Object	**getParameter** (String param) throws InvalidParameterException
`1.2` ●			public final	Provider	**getProvider** ()
●			public final	void	**initSign** (*PrivateKey* privateKey) throws InvalidKeyException
`1.2` ●			public final	void	**initSign** (*PrivateKey* privateKey, SecureRandom random) throws InvalidKeyException
●			public final	void	**initVerify** (*PublicKey* publicKey) throws InvalidKeyException

---

Class · *Interface* · —extends · - - -implements · ○ abstract · ● final · △ static · ▲ static final · ✳ constructor · x x—inherited · x **x**—declared · x **x**—overridden

1.2 ●	public final ....void	**setParameter** (*java.security.spec.AlgorithmParameterSpec* params) throws InvalidAlgorithmParameterException
D ●	public final ....void	**setParameter** (String param, Object value) throws InvalidParameterException
●	public final ....byte[]	**sign** () throws SignatureException
▲	protected static final ....int	**SIGN**
1.2 ●	public final ....int	**sign** (byte[] outbuf, int offset, int len) throws SignatureException
∗	protected	**Signature** (String algorithm)
	protected ....int	**state**
1	public................. **String**	**toString** ()
▲	protected static final ....int	**UNINITIALIZED**
●	public final ....void	**update** (byte b) throws SignatureException
●	public final ....void	**update** (byte[] data) throws SignatureException
●	public final ....void	**update** (byte[] data, int off, int len) throws SignatureException
▲	protected static final ....int	**VERIFY**
●	public final .... boolean	**verify** (byte[] signature) throws SignatureException

SignatureException

java.security
P○

```
Object
 └─Throwable ------------------------- java.io.Serializable
     └─Exception
1.2        └─GeneralSecurityException
1.1            └─SignatureException
```

∗	public.........................	**SignatureException** ()
∗	public.........................	**SignatureException** (String msg)

SignatureSpi

java.security
P○

```
Object 1
 └─SignatureSpi
1.2 ○
```

	protected ...... SecureRandom	**appRandom**
1	public................... **Object**	**clone** () throws CloneNotSupportedException
D ○	protected abstract ...... Object	**engineGetParameter** (String param) throws InvalidParameterException
○	protected abstract ....void	**engineInitSign** (*PrivateKey* privateKey) throws InvalidKeyException
	protected ....void	**engineInitSign** (*PrivateKey* privateKey, SecureRandom random) throws InvalidKeyException
○	protected abstract ....void	**engineInitVerify** (*PublicKey* publicKey) throws InvalidKeyException
	protected ....void	**engineSetParameter** (*java.security.spec.AlgorithmParameterSpec* params) throws InvalidAlgorithmParameterException
D ○	protected abstract ....void	**engineSetParameter** (String param, Object value) throws InvalidParameterException
○	protected abstract .... byte[]	**engineSign** () throws SignatureException
	protected ....int	**engineSign** (byte[] outbuf, int offset, int len) throws SignatureException
○	protected abstract ....void	**engineUpdate** (byte b) throws SignatureException
○	protected abstract ....void	**engineUpdate** (byte[] b, int off, int len) throws SignatureException
○	protected abstract .... boolean	**engineVerify** (byte[] sigBytes) throws SignatureException
∗	public.........................	**SignatureSpi** ()

SignedObject

java.security
P○

```
Object
 └─SignedObject ------------------- java.io.Serializable
1.2 ●
```

	public...................String	**getAlgorithm** ()
	public...................Object	**getObject** () throws java.io.IOException, ClassNotFoundException
	public...................byte[]	**getSignature** ()
∗	public.........................	**SignedObject** (*java.io.Serializable* object, *PrivateKey* signingKey, Signature signingEngine) throws java.io.IOException, InvalidKeyException, SignatureException
	public................ boolean	**verify** (*PublicKey* verificationKey, Signature verificationEngine) throws InvalidKeyException, SignatureException

S

Classes

617

Signer

			Signer	java.security

Object
P^o

1.1 ○ └Identity [1] - *Principal, java.io.Serializable*
1.1 ○   └Signer

	1	public.....................void	addCertificate (*Certificate* certificate) throws KeyManagementException
	1	public.............*Certificate[]*	certificates ()
●	1	public final ....boolean	equals (Object identity)
	1	public....................String	getInfo ()
●	1	public final ....String	getName ()
		public...............*PrivateKey*	**getPrivateKey** ()
	1	public...............*PublicKey*	getPublicKey ()
●	1	public final ......IdentityScope	getScope ()
	1	public.........................int	hashCode ()
	1	protected ....boolean	identityEquals (Identity identity)
	1	public.....................void	removeCertificate (*Certificate* certificate) throws KeyManagementException
	1	public.....................void	setInfo (String info)
●		public final ....void	**setKeyPair** (KeyPair pair) throws InvalidParameterException, KeyException
	1	public.....................void	setPublicKey (*PublicKey* key) throws KeyManagementException
＊		protected	**Signer** ()
＊		public...........................	**Signer** (String name)
＊		public...........................	**Signer** (String name, IdentityScope scope) throws KeyManagementException
	1	public................**String**	**toString** ()
	1	public....................String	toString (boolean detailed)

			SimpleAttributeSet	javax.swing.text

Object [1]

1.2 └SimpleAttributeSet - *MutableAttributeSet* [2] (*AttributeSet* [3]), *java.io.Serializable*,
                                                             Cloneable

	2	public.....................void	**addAttribute** (Object name, Object value)
	2	public.....................void	**addAttributes** (*AttributeSet* attributes)
	1	public................**Object**	**clone** ()
	3	public...............boolean	**containsAttribute** (Object name, Object value)
	3	public...............boolean	**containsAttributes** (*AttributeSet* attributes)
	3	public............*AttributeSet*	**copyAttributes** ()
▲		public static final .. *AttributeSet*	**EMPTY**
	1	public................**boolean**	**equals** (Object obj)
	3	public................Object	**getAttribute** (Object name)
	3	public.........................int	**getAttributeCount** ()
	3	public....*java.util.Enumeration*	**getAttributeNames** ()
	3	public............*AttributeSet*	**getResolveParent** ()
	1	public................**int**	**hashCode** ()
	3	public...............boolean	**isDefined** (Object attrName)
		public...............boolean	**isEmpty** ()
	3	public...............boolean	**isEqual** (*AttributeSet* attr)
	2	public.....................void	**removeAttribute** (Object name)
	2	public.....................void	**removeAttributes** (*java.util.Enumeration* names)
	2	public.....................void	**removeAttributes** (*AttributeSet* attributes)
	2	public.....................void	**setResolveParent** (*AttributeSet* parent)
＊		public...........................	**SimpleAttributeSet** ()
＊		public...........................	**SimpleAttributeSet** (*AttributeSet* source)
	1	public................**String**	**toString** ()

			SimpleBeanInfo	java.beans

Object

1.1 └SimpleBeanInfo - *BeanInfo* [1]

	1	public...............*BeanInfo[]*	**getAdditionalBeanInfo** ()
	1	public...........BeanDescriptor	**getBeanDescriptor** ()
	1	public.........................int	**getDefaultEventIndex** ()
	1	public.........................int	**getDefaultPropertyIndex** ()
	1	public.... EventSetDescriptor[]	**getEventSetDescriptors** ()
	1	public...... java.awt.Image	**getIcon** (int iconKind)
	1	public......MethodDescriptor[]	**getMethodDescriptors** ()
	1	public.....PropertyDescriptor[]	**getPropertyDescriptors** ()

Class   *Interface*   —extends   - - -implements   ○ abstract   ● final   △ static   ▲ static final   ＊ constructor   x x—inherited   x **x**—declared   **x x**—overridden

S

```
         public.......... java.awt.Image  loadImage (String resourceName)
   *     public........................  SimpleBeanInfo ()
```

SimpleDateFormat   java.text

```
         Object                                                                    P
1.1 ○   └Format 1 - - - - - - - - - - - - - - - - - - - - - - - - - - - - - java.io.Serializable, Cloneable
1.1 ○      └DateFormat 2
1.1           └SimpleDateFormat
```

```
     2   48 inherited members from DateFormat not shown
         public.....................void  applyLocalizedPattern (String pattern)
         public.....................void  applyPattern (String pattern)
     2   public..................Object  clone ()
     2   public.................boolean  equals (Object obj)
 ● 1     public final ...............String  format (Object obj)
     2   public............StringBuffer  format (java.util.Date date, StringBuffer toAppendTo, FieldPosition pos)
1.2      public............java.util.Date  get2DigitYearStart ()
         public.....DateFormatSymbols  getDateFormatSymbols ()
     2   public.......................int  hashCode ()
     2   public..........java.util.Date  parse (String text, ParsePosition pos)
     1   public...................Object  parseObject (String source) throws ParseException
1.2      public.....................void  set2DigitYearStart (java.util.Date startDate)
         public.....................void  setDateFormatSymbols (DateFormatSymbols newFormatSymbols)
   *     public........................  SimpleDateFormat ()
   *     public........................  SimpleDateFormat (String pattern)
   *     public........................  SimpleDateFormat (String pattern, java.util.Locale loc)
   *     public........................  SimpleDateFormat (String pattern, DateFormatSymbols formatData)
         public....................String  toLocalizedPattern ()
         public....................String  toPattern ()
```

SimpleTimeZone   java.util

```
         Object 1                                                                  P
1.1 ○   └TimeZone 2 - - - - - - - - - - - - - - - - - - - - - - - - - java.io.Serializable, Cloneable
1.1        └SimpleTimeZone
```

```
     2   public..................Object  clone ()
     1   public.................boolean  equals (Object obj)
 △  2   public static synchronized ....  getAvailableIDs ()
         .........................String[]
 △  2   public static synchronized ....  getAvailableIDs (int rawOffset)
         .........................String[]
 △  2   public static synchronized ....  getDefault ()
         .......................TimeZone
1.2 ● 2  public final ...............String  getDisplayName ()
1.2 ● 2  public final ...............String  getDisplayName (Locale locale)
1.2 ● 2  public final ...............String  getDisplayName (boolean daylight, int style)
1.2   2  public....................String  getDisplayName (boolean daylight, int style, Locale locale)
1.2      public.......................int  getDSTSavings ()
     2   public....................String  getID ()
     2   public.......................int  getOffset (int era, int year, int month, int day, int dayOfWeek, int millis)
     2   public.......................int  getRawOffset ()
 △  2   public static synchronized ....  getTimeZone (String ID)
         .......................TimeZone
     1   public synchronized ........int  hashCode ()
1.2   2  public.................boolean  hasSameRules (TimeZone other)
     2   public.................boolean  inDaylightTime (Date date)
 △  2   public static synchronized void  setDefault (TimeZone zone)
1.2      public.....................void  setDSTSavings (int millisSavedDuringDST)
1.2      public.....................void  setEndRule (int month, int dayOfMonth, int time)
         public.....................void  setEndRule (int month, int dayOfWeekInMonth, int dayOfWeek, int time)
1.2      public.....................void  setEndRule (int month, int dayOfMonth, int dayOfWeek, int time, boolean after)
     2   public.....................void  setID (String ID)
     2   public.....................void  setRawOffset (int offsetMillis)
1.2      public.....................void  setStartRule (int month, int dayOfMonth, int time)
         public.....................void  setStartRule (int month, int dayOfWeekInMonth, int dayOfWeek, int time)
1.2      public.....................void  setStartRule (int month, int dayOfMonth, int dayOfWeek, int time, boolean after)
         public.....................void  setStartYear (int year)
   *     public........................  SimpleTimeZone (int rawOffset, String ID)
```

S

Classes

619

SimpleTimeZone

✳	public........................	**SimpleTimeZone** (int rawOffset, String ID, int startMonth, int startDay, int startDayOfWeek, int startTime, int endMonth, int endDay, int endDayOfWeek, int endTime)
1.2 ✳	public........................	**SimpleTimeZone** (int rawOffset, String ID, int startMonth, int startDay, int startDayOfWeek, int startTime, int endMonth, int endDay, int endDayOfWeek, int endTime, int dstSavings)
1	public................ **String**	**toString** ()
2	public................ **boolean**	**useDaylightTime** ()

SinglePixelPackedSampleModel   java.awt.image

P

```
     Object
1.2 ○  └─ SampleModel¹
1.2        └─ SinglePixelPackedSampleModel
```

1		*27 inherited members from SampleModel not shown*	
1	public.......... **SampleModel**	**createCompatibleSampleModel** (int w, int h)
1	public.............**DataBuffer**	**createDataBuffer** ()
1	public.......... **SampleModel**	**createSubsetSampleModel** (int[] bands)
	public................... int[]	**getBitMasks** ()
	public................... int[]	**getBitOffsets** ()
1	public............**Object**	**getDataElements** (int x, int y, Object obj, DataBuffer data)
1	public..................... **int**	**getNumDataElements** ()
	public......................int	**getOffset** (int x, int y)
1	public................**int[]**	**getPixel** (int x, int y, int[] iArray, DataBuffer data)
1	public................**int[]**	**getPixels** (int x, int y, int w, int h, int[] iArray, DataBuffer data)
1	public................ **int**	**getSample** (int x, int y, int b, DataBuffer data)
1	public................**int[]**	**getSamples** (int x, int y, int w, int h, int b, int[] iArray, DataBuffer data)
1	public................**int[]**	**getSampleSize** ()
1	public................ **int**	**getSampleSize** (int band)
	public......................int	**getScanlineStride** ()
1	public................ **void**	**setDataElements** (int x, int y, Object obj, DataBuffer data)
1	public................ **void**	**setPixel** (int x, int y, int[] iArray, DataBuffer data)
1	public................ **void**	**setPixels** (int x, int y, int w, int h, int[] iArray, DataBuffer data)
1	public................ **void**	**setSample** (int x, int y, int b, int s, DataBuffer data)
1	public................ **void**	**setSamples** (int x, int y, int w, int h, int b, int[] iArray, DataBuffer data)
✳	public........................	**SinglePixelPackedSampleModel** (int dataType, int w, int h, int[] bitMasks)
✳	public........................	**SinglePixelPackedSampleModel** (int dataType, int w, int h, int scanlineStride, int[] bitMasks)

SingleSelectionModel   javax.swing

```
1.2   SingleSelectionModel
```

public................... void	**addChangeListener** (*javax.swing.event.ChangeListener* listener)
public................... void	**clearSelection** ()
public................... int	**getSelectedIndex** ()
public............... boolean	**isSelected** ()
public................... void	**removeChangeListener** (*javax.swing.event.ChangeListener* listener)
public................... void	**setSelectedIndex** (int index)

SizeRequirements   javax.swing

```
     Object¹
1.2   └─ SizeRequirements - - - - - - - - - - - - - - - - - java.io.Serializable
```

△	public static ....int[]	**adjustSizes** (int delta, SizeRequirements[] children)
	public....................float	**alignment**
△	public static ....void	**calculateAlignedPositions** (int allocated, SizeRequirements total, SizeRequirements[] children, int[] offsets, int[] spans)
△	public static ....void	**calculateTiledPositions** (int allocated, SizeRequirements total, SizeRequirements[] children, int[] offsets, int[] spans)
△	public static SizeRequirements	**getAlignedSizeRequirements** (SizeRequirements[] children)
△	public static SizeRequirements	**getTiledSizeRequirements** (SizeRequirements[] children)
	public......................int	**maximum**
	public......................int	**minimum**
	public......................int	**preferred**
✳	public........................	**SizeRequirements** ()
✳	public........................	**SizeRequirements** (int min, int pref, int max, float a)

Class   *Interface*   ──extends   - - -implements   ○ abstract   ● final   △ static   ▲ static final   ✳ constructor   x x─inherited   x **x**─declared   **x x**─overridden

1   public . . . . **String toString** ()

Skeleton — java.rmi.server

1.1	*Skeleton*	P⁰

P⁰

1.1   *Skeleton*

D   public . . . . .void **dispatch** (*java.rmi.Remote* obj, *RemoteCall* theCall, int opnum, long hash)
        throws Exception
D   public . . . . .Operation[] **getOperations** ()

SkeletonMismatchException — java.rmi.server

P⁰

Object
  └Throwable - *java.io.Serializable*
    └Exception
      └java.io.IOException
1.1   └java.rmi.RemoteException ¹
1.1   └SkeletonMismatchException

1   public . . . . Throwable detail
1   public . . . . .String getMessage ()
1   public . . . . .void printStackTrace ()
1   public . . . . .void printStackTrace (java.io.PrintStream ps)
1   public . . . . .void printStackTrace (java.io.PrintWriter pw)
D ✻   public . . . . **SkeletonMismatchException** (String s)

SkeletonNotFoundException — java.rmi.server

P⁰

Object
  └Throwable - *java.io.Serializable*
    └Exception
      └java.io.IOException
1.1   └java.rmi.RemoteException ¹
1.1   └SkeletonNotFoundException

1   public . . . . Throwable detail
1   public . . . . .String getMessage ()
1   public . . . . .void printStackTrace ()
1   public . . . . .void printStackTrace (java.io.PrintStream ps)
1   public . . . . .void printStackTrace (java.io.PrintWriter pw)
✻   public . . . . **SkeletonNotFoundException** (String s)
✻   public . . . . **SkeletonNotFoundException** (String s, Exception ex)

SliderUI — javax.swing.plaf

Object
1.2 ○ └ComponentUI ¹
1.2 ○   └SliderUI

1   *11 inherited members from ComponentUI not shown*
✻   public . . . . **SliderUI** ()

Socket — java.net

P

Object ¹
  └Socket

public synchronized . . . . . . .void **close** () throws java.io.IOException
public . . . . .InetAddress **getInetAddress** ()
public . . . . . . java.io.InputStream **getInputStream** () throws java.io.IOException
1.1   public . . . . .InetAddress **getLocalAddress** ()
public . . . . .int **getLocalPort** ()
public . . . . java.io.OutputStream **getOutputStream** () throws java.io.IOException
public . . . . .int **getPort** ()
1.2   public synchronized . . . . .int **getReceiveBufferSize** () throws SocketException
1.2   public synchronized . . . . .int **getSendBufferSize** () throws SocketException
1.1   public . . . . .int **getSoLinger** () throws SocketException
1.1   public synchronized . . . . .int **getSoTimeout** () throws SocketException

S

Classes

Socket

1.1		public	boolean	**getTcpNoDelay** () throws SocketException	
1.2		public synchronized	void	**setReceiveBufferSize** (int size) throws SocketException	
1.2		public synchronized	void	**setSendBufferSize** (int size) throws SocketException	
	△	public static synchronized	void	**setSocketImplFactory** (*SocketImplFactory* fac) throws java.io.IOException	
1.1		public	void	**setSoLinger** (boolean on, int linger) throws SocketException	
1.1		public synchronized	void	**setSoTimeout** (int timeout) throws SocketException	
1.1		public	void	**setTcpNoDelay** (boolean on) throws SocketException	
1.1	✳	protected		**Socket** ()	
1.1	✳	protected		**Socket** (SocketImpl impl) throws SocketException	
	✳	public		**Socket** (String host, int port) throws UnknownHostException, java.io.IOException	
	✳	public		**Socket** (InetAddress address, int port) throws java.io.IOException	
D	✳	public		**Socket** (String host, int port, boolean stream) throws java.io.IOException	
D	✳	public		**Socket** (InetAddress host, int port, boolean stream) throws java.io.IOException	
1.1	✳	public		**Socket** (String host, int port, InetAddress localAddr, int localPort) throws java.io.IOException	
1.1	✳	public		**Socket** (InetAddress address, int port, InetAddress localAddr, int localPort) throws java.io.IOException	
	1	public	String	**toString** ()	

SocketException   java.net

P

```
Object
└Throwable - - - - - - - - - - - - - - - - - - - - - - - - - - - java.io.Serializable
  └Exception
    └java.io.IOException
      └SocketException
```

✳	public	**SocketException** ()	
✳	public	**SocketException** (String msg)	

S

SocketImpl   java.net

P

```
Object 1
○  └SocketImpl - - - - - - - - - - - - - - - - - - - - - - - - - SocketOptions 2
```

	○	protected abstract	void	**accept** (SocketImpl s) throws java.io.IOException	
		protected	InetAddress	**address**	
	○	protected abstract	int	**available** () throws java.io.IOException	
	○	protected abstract	void	**bind** (InetAddress host, int port) throws java.io.IOException	
	○	protected abstract	void	**close** () throws java.io.IOException	
	○	protected abstract	void	**connect** (String host, int port) throws java.io.IOException	
	○	protected abstract	void	**connect** (InetAddress address, int port) throws java.io.IOException	
	○	protected abstract	void	**create** (boolean stream) throws java.io.IOException	
		protected	java.io.FileDescriptor	**fd**	
		protected	java.io.FileDescriptor	**getFileDescriptor** ()	
		protected	InetAddress	**getInetAddress** ()	
	○	protected abstract	java.io.InputStream	**getInputStream** () throws java.io.IOException	
		protected	int	**getLocalPort** ()	
1.1	○ 2	public abstract	Object	**getOption** (int) throws SocketException	
	○	protected abstract	java.io.OutputStream	**getOutputStream** () throws java.io.IOException	
		protected	int	**getPort** ()	
	○	protected abstract	void	**listen** (int backlog) throws java.io.IOException	
		protected	int	**localport**	
		protected	int	**port**	
1.1	○ 2	public abstract	void	**setOption** (int, Object) throws SocketException	
	✳	public		**SocketImpl** ()	
	1	public	String	**toString** ()	

SocketImplFactory   java.net

P

SocketImplFactory

	public	SocketImpl	**createSocketImpl** ()

Class   *Interface*   —extends   - - -implements   ○ abstract   ● final   △ static   ▲ static final   ✳ constructor   x x—inherited   x **x**—declared   **x x**—overridden

SocketOptions

		java.net
1.2	*SocketOptions*	P

	public..................Object	**getOption** (int optID) throws SocketException
▲	public static final.............int	**IP_MULTICAST_IF** = 16
	public......................void	**setOption** (int optID, Object value) throws SocketException
▲	public static final.............int	**SO_BINDADDR** = 15
▲	public static final.............int	**SO_LINGER** = 128
▲	public static final.............int	**SO_RCVBUF** = 4098
▲	public static final.............int	**SO_REUSEADDR** = 4
▲	public static final.............int	**SO_SNDBUF** = 4097
▲	public static final.............int	**SO_TIMEOUT** = 4102
▲	public static final.............int	**TCP_NODELAY** = 1

SocketPermission

			java.net
	Object		P
1.2 ○	└java.security.Permission [1] ---------------- *java.security.Guard, java.io.Serializable*	
1.2 ●	└SocketPermission -------------------- *java.io.Serializable*	

1	public......................void	checkGuard (Object object) throws SecurityException
1	public.................**boolean**	**equals** (Object obj)
1	public................**String**	**getActions** ()
● 1	public final ....String	getName ()
1	public......................**int**	**hashCode** ()
1	public.................**boolean**	**implies** (java.security.Permission p)
1	public..........**java.security** ↵ .**PermissionCollection**	**newPermissionCollection** ()
*	public..........................	**SocketPermission** (String host, String action)
1	public....................String	toString ()

SocketSecurityException

			java.rmi.server
	Object		P[O]
	└Throwable --------------------------- *java.io.Serializable*	
	└Exception	
	└java.io.IOException	
1.1	└java.rmi.RemoteException [1]	
1.1	└ExportException	
1.1	└SocketSecurityException	

1	public...............Throwable	detail
1	public....................String	getMessage ()
1	public......................void	printStackTrace ()
1	public......................void	printStackTrace (java.io.PrintStream ps)
1	public......................void	printStackTrace (java.io.PrintWriter pw)
*	public..........................	**SocketSecurityException** (String s)
*	public..........................	**SocketSecurityException** (String s, Exception ex)

SoftBevelBorder

			javax.swing.border
	Object		
1.2 ○	└AbstractBorder [1] ---------------------- *Border, java.io.Serializable*	
1.2	└BevelBorder [2]	
1.2	└SoftBevelBorder	

2	protected ....int	bevelType
2	public..........................int	getBevelType ()
2	public..........**java.awt.Insets**	**getBorderInsets** (java.awt.Component c)
2	public...........java.awt.Insets	getBorderInsets (java.awt.Component c, java.awt.Insets insets)
2	public...........java.awt.Color	getHighlightInnerColor (java.awt.Component c)
2	public...........java.awt.Color	getHighlightOuterColor (java.awt.Component c)
1	public...... java.awt.Rectangle	getInteriorRectangle (java.awt.Component c, int x, int y, int width, int height)
△ 1	public static .... java.awt.Rectangle	getInteriorRectangle (java.awt.Component c, *Border* b, int x, int y, int width, int height)
2	public...........java.awt.Color	getShadowInnerColor (java.awt.Component c)
2	public...........java.awt.Color	getShadowOuterColor (java.awt.Component c)
2	protected ....java.awt.Color	highlightInner
2	protected ....java.awt.Color	highlightOuter

S

Classes

SoftBevelBorder

2	public	**boolean**	**isBorderOpaque** ()	
2	public	**void**	**paintBorder** (java.awt.Component c, java.awt.Graphics g, int x, int y, int width, int height)	
2	protected	void	paintLoweredBevel (java.awt.Component c, java.awt.Graphics g, int x, int y, int width, int height)	
2	protected	void	paintRaisedBevel (java.awt.Component c, java.awt.Graphics g, int x, int y, int width, int height)	
2	protected	java.awt.Color	shadowInner	
2	protected	java.awt.Color	shadowOuter	
*	public		**SoftBevelBorder** (int bevelType)	
*	public		**SoftBevelBorder** (int bevelType, java.awt.Color highlight, java.awt.Color shadow)	
*	public		**SoftBevelBorder** (int bevelType, java.awt.Color highlightOuter, java.awt.Color highlightInner, java.awt.Color shadowOuter, java.awt.Color shadowInner)	

SoftReference   java.lang.ref

Object
  └─Reference [1] — 1.2 ○
      └─SoftReference — 1.2

1	public	void	clear ()
1	public	boolean	enqueue ()
1	public	**Object**	**get** ()
1	public	boolean	isEnqueued ()
*	public		**SoftReference** (Object referent)
*	public		**SoftReference** (Object referent, ReferenceQueue q)

SortedMap   java.util

1.2   *SortedMap*——————————————— *Map* [1]   P

1	public	void	clear ()
	public	*Comparator*	**comparator** ()
1	public	boolean	containsKey (Object key)
1	public	boolean	containsValue (Object value)
1	public	*Set*	entrySet ()
1	public	boolean	equals (Object o)
	public	Object	**firstKey** ()
1	public	Object	get (Object key)
1	public	int	hashCode ()
	public	*SortedMap*	**headMap** (Object toKey)
1	public	boolean	isEmpty ()
1	public	*Set*	keySet ()
	public	Object	**lastKey** ()
1	public	Object	put (Object key, Object value)
1	public	void	putAll (*Map* t)
1	public	Object	remove (Object key)
1	public	int	size ()
	public	*SortedMap*	**subMap** (Object fromKey, Object toKey)
	public	*SortedMap*	**tailMap** (Object fromKey)
1	public	*Collection*	values ()

SortedSet   java.util

1.2   *SortedSet*——————————————— *Set* [1] (*Collection*)   P

1	public	boolean	add (Object o)
1	public	boolean	addAll (*Collection* c)
1	public	void	clear ()
	public	*Comparator*	**comparator** ()
1	public	boolean	contains (Object o)
1	public	boolean	containsAll (*Collection* c)
1	public	boolean	equals (Object o)
	public	Object	**first** ()
1	public	int	hashCode ()
	public	*SortedSet*	**headSet** (Object toElement)
1	public	boolean	isEmpty ()
1	public	*Iterator*	iterator ()
	public	Object	**last** ()

Class *Interface* —extends - - -implements ○ abstract ● final △ static ▲ static final ＊ constructor x x—inherited x **x**—declared **x x**—overridden

624

1	public	boolean	remove (Object o)
1	public	boolean	removeAll (*Collection* c)
1	public	boolean	retainAll (*Collection* c)
1	public	int	size ()
	public	*SortedSet*	**subSet** (Object fromElement, Object toElement)
	public	*SortedSet*	**tailSet** (Object fromElement)
1	public	Object[]	toArray ()
1	public	Object[]	toArray (Object[] a)

SplitPaneUI

```
Object
1.2 ○  └─ComponentUI 1
1.2 ○      └─SplitPaneUI
```

1	*11 inherited members from ComponentUI not shown*		
○	public abstract	void	**finishedPaintingChildren** (javax.swing.JSplitPane jc, java.awt.Graphics g)
○	public abstract	int	**getDividerLocation** (javax.swing.JSplitPane jc)
○	public abstract	int	**getMaximumDividerLocation** (javax.swing.JSplitPane jc)
○	public abstract	int	**getMinimumDividerLocation** (javax.swing.JSplitPane jc)
○	public abstract	void	**resetToPreferredSizes** (javax.swing.JSplitPane jc)
○	public abstract	void	**setDividerLocation** (javax.swing.JSplitPane jc, int location)
*	public		**SplitPaneUI** ()

SQLData

1.2   *SQLData*   P○

	public	String	**getSQLTypeName** () throws SQLException
	public	void	**readSQL** (*SQLInput* stream, String typeName) throws SQLException
	public	void	**writeSQL** (*SQLOutput* stream) throws SQLException

---

SQLException

P○

```
Object
 └─Throwable - - - - - - - - - - - - - - - - - - - - - - - *java.io.Serializable*
     └─Exception
1.1      └─SQLException
```

	public	int	**getErrorCode** ()
	public	SQLException	**getNextException** ()
	public	String	**getSQLState** ()
	public synchronized	void	**setNextException** (SQLException ex)
*	public		**SQLException** ()
*	public		**SQLException** (String reason)
*	public		**SQLException** (String reason, String SQLState)
*	public		**SQLException** (String reason, String SQLState, int vendorCode)

SQLInput

1.2   *SQLInput*   P○

	public	*Array*	**readArray** () throws SQLException
	public	java.io.InputStream	**readAsciiStream** () throws SQLException
	public	java.math.BigDecimal	**readBigDecimal** () throws SQLException
	public	java.io.InputStream	**readBinaryStream** () throws SQLException
	public	*Blob*	**readBlob** () throws SQLException
	public	boolean	**readBoolean** () throws SQLException
	public	byte	**readByte** () throws SQLException
	public	byte[]	**readBytes** () throws SQLException
	public	java.io.Reader	**readCharacterStream** () throws SQLException
	public	*Clob*	**readClob** () throws SQLException
	public	Date	**readDate** () throws SQLException
	public	double	**readDouble** () throws SQLException
	public	float	**readFloat** () throws SQLException
	public	int	**readInt** () throws SQLException
	public	long	**readLong** () throws SQLException
	public	Object	**readObject** () throws SQLException
	public	*Ref*	**readRef** () throws SQLException
	public	short	**readShort** () throws SQLException

S

Classes

```
public.....................String readString () throws SQLException
public.....................Time readTime () throws SQLException
public.................Timestamp readTimestamp () throws SQLException
public.................boolean wasNull () throws SQLException
```

SQLOutput   java.sql

1.2 *SQLOutput*   P○

```
public....................void writeArray (Array x) throws SQLException
public....................void writeAsciiStream (java.io.InputStream x) throws SQLException
public....................void writeBigDecimal (java.math.BigDecimal x) throws SQLException
public....................void writeBinaryStream (java.io.InputStream x) throws SQLException
public....................void writeBlob (Blob x) throws SQLException
public....................void writeBoolean (boolean x) throws SQLException
public....................void writeByte (byte x) throws SQLException
public....................void writeBytes (byte[] x) throws SQLException
public....................void writeCharacterStream (java.io.Reader x) throws SQLException
public....................void writeClob (Clob x) throws SQLException
public....................void writeDate (Date x) throws SQLException
public....................void writeDouble (double x) throws SQLException
public....................void writeFloat (float x) throws SQLException
public....................void writeInt (int x) throws SQLException
public....................void writeLong (long x) throws SQLException
public....................void writeObject (SQLData x) throws SQLException
public....................void writeRef (Ref x) throws SQLException
public....................void writeShort (short x) throws SQLException
public....................void writeString (String x) throws SQLException
public....................void writeStruct (Struct x) throws SQLException
public....................void writeTime (Time x) throws SQLException
public....................void writeTimestamp (Timestamp x) throws SQLException
```

S

SQLWarning   java.sql

                                                                        P○
```
Object
└Throwable ---------------------------- java.io.Serializable
  └Exception
1.1  └SQLException 1
1.1    └SQLWarning
```

```
1  public........................int getErrorCode ()
1  public............SQLException getNextException ()
   public.............SQLWarning getNextWarning ()
1  public....................String getSQLState ()
1  public synchronized .......void setNextException (SQLException ex)
   public....................void setNextWarning (SQLWarning w)
*  public........................ SQLWarning ()
*  public........................ SQLWarning (String reason)
*  public........................ SQLWarning (String reason, String SQLstate)
*  public........................ SQLWarning (String reason, String SQLstate, int vendorCode)
```

Stack   java.util

                                                                        P
```
Object
1.2 ○ └AbstractCollection ---------------------- Collection
1.2 ○   └AbstractList 1 ---------------------- List (Collection)
          └Vector 2 ---------------------- List (Collection), Cloneable, java.io.Serializable
            └Stack
```

```
   2  45 inherited members from Vector not shown
      public.................boolean empty ()
1.2  1  public....................Iterator iterator ()
1.2  1  public................ListIterator listIterator ()
1.2  1  public................ListIterator listIterator (int index)
1.2  1  protected transient...........int modCount
      public synchronized ....Object peek ()
      public synchronized ....Object pop ()
      public....................Object push (Object item)
      public synchronized .........int search (Object o)
```

Class *Interface* —extends - - -implements ○ abstract ● final △ static ▲ static final ✻ constructor x x—inherited x **x**—declared **x x**—overridden

*	public........................	**Stack** ()	

StackOverflowError

```
Object
 └Throwable ----------------------------- java.io.Serializable
   └Error
     └VirtualMachineError
       └StackOverflowError
```

P

○

*	public..........................	**StackOverflowError** ()
*	public..........................	**StackOverflowError** (String s)

StateEdit

```
Object
 └AbstractUndoableEdit¹ ------------------- UndoableEdit, java.io.Serializable
   └StateEdit
```

1.2
1.2

1	public................. boolean	addEdit (*UndoableEdit* anEdit)
1	public................. boolean	canRedo ()
1	public................. boolean	canUndo ()
1	public......................void	die ()
	public......................void	**end** ()
1	public.................. **String**	**getPresentationName** ()
1	public................. String	getRedoPresentationName ()
1	public................. String	getUndoPresentationName ()
	protected.................void	**init** (*StateEditable* anObject, String name)
1	public................. boolean	isSignificant ()
	protected........ *StateEditable*	**object**
	protected... java.util.Hashtable	**postState**
	protected... java.util.Hashtable	**preState**
▲	protected static final ..... String	**RCSID**
1	public..................... **void**	**redo** ()
	protected..................void	**removeRedundantState** ()
1	public................. boolean	replaceEdit (*UndoableEdit* anEdit)
*	public..........................	**StateEdit** (*StateEditable* anObject)
*	public..........................	**StateEdit** (*StateEditable* anObject, String name)
1	public.................String	toString ()
1	public..................... **void**	**undo** ()
	protected.................String	**undoRedoName**

StateEditable

1.2 *StateEditable*

▲	public static final .... String	**RCSID** = "$Id: StateEditable.java,v 1.2 1997/09/08 19:39:08 marklin Exp $"
	public.......................void	**restoreState** (java.util.Hashtable state)
	public.......................void	**storeState** (java.util.Hashtable state)

Statement

1.1 *Statement*

P○

1.2	public......................void	**addBatch** (String sql) throws SQLException
	public......................void	**cancel** () throws SQLException
1.2	public......................void	**clearBatch** () throws SQLException
	public......................void	**clearWarnings** () throws SQLException
	public......................void	**close** () throws SQLException
	public................. boolean	**execute** (String sql) throws SQLException
1.2	public...................int[]	**executeBatch** () throws SQLException
	public................*ResultSet*	**executeQuery** (String sql) throws SQLException
	public.......................int	**executeUpdate** (String sql) throws SQLException
1.2	public................*Connection*	**getConnection** () throws SQLException
1.2	public.......................int	**getFetchDirection** () throws SQLException
1.2	public.......................int	**getFetchSize** () throws SQLException
	public.......................int	**getMaxFieldSize** () throws SQLException
	public.......................int	**getMaxRows** () throws SQLException
	public................. boolean	**getMoreResults** () throws SQLException
	public.......................int	**getQueryTimeout** () throws SQLException

S

Classes

627

Statement

	public	.... *ResultSet*	**getResultSet** () throws SQLException
1.2	public	............int	**getResultSetConcurrency** () throws SQLException
1.2	public	............int	**getResultSetType** () throws SQLException
	public	............int	**getUpdateCount** () throws SQLException
	public	SQLWarning	**getWarnings** () throws SQLException
	public	............void	**setCursorName** (String name) throws SQLException
	public	............void	**setEscapeProcessing** (boolean enable) throws SQLException
1.2	public	............void	**setFetchDirection** (int direction) throws SQLException
1.2	public	............void	**setFetchSize** (int rows) throws SQLException
	public	............void	**setMaxFieldSize** (int max) throws SQLException
	public	............void	**setMaxRows** (int max) throws SQLException
	public	............void	**setQueryTimeout** (int seconds) throws SQLException

---

Streamable   org.omg.CORBA.portable

1.2	*Streamable*		
	public	............void	**_read** (InputStream istream)
	public	....	**_type** ()
	... org.omg.CORBA.TypeCode		
	public	............void	**_write** (OutputStream ostream)

StreamCorruptedException   java.io

```
Object
 └Throwable  - - - - - - - - - - - - - - - - - - - - - - - - - - - *Serializable*
   └Exception
     └IOException
       └ObjectStreamException
         └StreamCorruptedException
```
1.1	○			
1.1				
	✳	public	....	**StreamCorruptedException** ()
	✳	public	....	**StreamCorruptedException** (String reason)

StreamTokenizer   java.io

```
Object¹
 └StreamTokenizer
```

		public	............void	**commentChar** (int ch)
		public	............void	**eolIsSignificant** (boolean flag)
		public	............int	**lineno** ()
		public	............void	**lowerCaseMode** (boolean fl)
		public	............int	**nextToken** () throws IOException
		public	............double	**nval**
		public	............void	**ordinaryChar** (int ch)
		public	............void	**ordinaryChars** (int low, int hi)
		public	............void	**parseNumbers** ()
		public	............void	**pushBack** ()
		public	............void	**quoteChar** (int ch)
		public	............void	**resetSyntax** ()
		public	............void	**slashSlashComments** (boolean flag)
		public	............void	**slashStarComments** (boolean flag)
D	✳	public	....	**StreamTokenizer** (InputStream is)
1.1	✳	public	....	**StreamTokenizer** (Reader r)
		public	............String	**sval**
	1	public	............String	**toString** ()
	▲	public static final	............int	**TT_EOF** = -1
	▲	public static final	............int	**TT_EOL** = 10
	▲	public static final	............int	**TT_NUMBER** = -2
	▲	public static final	............int	**TT_WORD** = -3
		public	............int	**ttype**
		public	............void	**whitespaceChars** (int low, int hi)
		public	............void	**wordChars** (int low, int hi)

Class   *Interface*   —extends   - - -implements   ○ abstract   ● final   △ static   ▲ static final   ✳ constructor   x x—inherited   x **x**—declared   **x x**—overridden

S

String

Object [1]
● └ String - *java.io.Serializable*, *Comparable* [2]

1.2	▲		public static final	**CASE_INSENSITIVE_ORDER**
			. . . . *java.util.Comparator*	
			public . . . . char	**charAt** (int index)
1.2		2	public . . . . int	**compareTo** (Object o)
			public . . . . int	**compareTo** (String anotherString)
1.2			public . . . . int	**compareToIgnoreCase** (String str)
			public . . . . String	**concat** (String str)
	△		public static . . . . String	**copyValueOf** (char[] data)
	△		public static . . . . String	**copyValueOf** (char[] data, int offset, int count)
			public . . . . boolean	**endsWith** (String suffix)
		1	public . . . . **boolean**	**equals** (Object anObject)
			public . . . . boolean	**equalsIgnoreCase** (String anotherString)
1.1			public . . . . byte[]	**getBytes** ()
1.1			public . . . . byte[]	**getBytes** (String enc) throws java.io.UnsupportedEncodingException
D			public . . . . void	**getBytes** (int srcBegin, int srcEnd, byte[] dst, int dstBegin)
			public . . . . void	**getChars** (int srcBegin, int srcEnd, char[] dst, int dstBegin)
		1	public . . . . **int**	**hashCode** ()
			public . . . . int	**indexOf** (int ch)
			public . . . . int	**indexOf** (String str)
			public . . . . int	**indexOf** (int ch, int fromIndex)
			public . . . . int	**indexOf** (String str, int fromIndex)
			public native . . . . String	**intern** ()
			public . . . . int	**lastIndexOf** (int ch)
			public . . . . int	**lastIndexOf** (String str)
			public . . . . int	**lastIndexOf** (int ch, int fromIndex)
			public . . . . int	**lastIndexOf** (String str, int fromIndex)
			public . . . . int	**length** ()
			public . . . . boolean	**regionMatches** (int toffset, String other, int ooffset, int len)
			public . . . . boolean	**regionMatches** (boolean ignoreCase, int toffset, String other, int ooffset, int len)
			public . . . . String	**replace** (char oldChar, char newChar)
			public . . . . boolean	**startsWith** (String prefix)
			public . . . . boolean	**startsWith** (String prefix, int toffset)
		✳	public	**String** ()
1.1	✳		public	**String** (byte[] bytes)
	✳		public	**String** (char[] value)
	✳		public	**String** (String value)
	✳		public	**String** (StringBuffer buffer)
1.1	✳		public	**String** (byte[] bytes, String enc) throws java.io.UnsupportedEncodingException
D	✳		public	**String** (byte[] ascii, int hibyte)
1.1	✳		public	**String** (byte[] bytes, int offset, int length)
	✳		public	**String** (char[] value, int offset, int count)
D	✳		public	**String** (byte[] ascii, int hibyte, int offset, int count)
1.1	✳		public	**String** (byte[] bytes, int offset, int length, String enc)
				throws java.io.UnsupportedEncodingException
			public . . . . String	**substring** (int beginIndex)
			public . . . . String	**substring** (int beginIndex, int endIndex)
			public . . . . char[]	**toCharArray** ()
			public . . . . String	**toLowerCase** ()
1.1			public . . . . String	**toLowerCase** (java.util.Locale locale)
		1	public . . . . **String**	**toString** ()
			public . . . . String	**toUpperCase** ()
1.1			public . . . . String	**toUpperCase** (java.util.Locale locale)
			public . . . . String	**trim** ()
	△		public static . . . . String	**valueOf** (boolean b)
	△		public static . . . . String	**valueOf** (char c)
	△		public static . . . . String	**valueOf** (char[] data)
	△		public static . . . . String	**valueOf** (double d)
	△		public static . . . . String	**valueOf** (float f)
	△		public static . . . . String	**valueOf** (int i)
	△		public static . . . . String	**valueOf** (Object obj)
	△		public static . . . . String	**valueOf** (long l)
	△		public static . . . . String	**valueOf** (char[] data, int offset, int count)

S

Classes

StringBuffer

Object [1]
● └ StringBuffer - *java.io.Serializable*

StringBuffer

```
          public .............. StringBuffer  append (boolean b)
          public synchronized ...........    append (char c)
          .................... StringBuffer
          public synchronized ...........    append (char[] str)
          .................... StringBuffer
          public .............. StringBuffer  append (double d)
          public .............. StringBuffer  append (float f)
          public .............. StringBuffer  append (int i)
          public synchronized ...........    append (Object obj)
          .................... StringBuffer
          public synchronized ...........    append (String str)
          .................... StringBuffer
          public .............. StringBuffer  append (long l)
          public synchronized ...........    append (char[] str, int offset, int len)
          .................... StringBuffer
          public....................int       capacity ()
          public synchronized ...... char     charAt (int index)
     1.2  public synchronized ...........    delete (int start, int end)
          .................... StringBuffer
     1.2  public synchronized ...........    deleteCharAt (int index)
          .................... StringBuffer
          public synchronized .......void    ensureCapacity (int minimumCapacity)
          public synchronized .......void    getChars (int srcBegin, int srcEnd, char[] dst, int dstBegin)
          public .............. StringBuffer  insert (int offset, boolean b)
          public .............. StringBuffer  insert (int offset, int i)
          public synchronized ...........    insert (int offset, Object obj)
          .................... StringBuffer
          public .............. StringBuffer  insert (int offset, long l)
          public .............. StringBuffer  insert (int offset, double d)
          public .............. StringBuffer  insert (int offset, float f)
          public synchronized ...........    insert (int offset, char c)
          .................... StringBuffer
          public synchronized ...........    insert (int offset, String str)
          .................... StringBuffer
          public synchronized ...........    insert (int offset, char[] str)
          .................... StringBuffer
     1.2  public synchronized ...........    insert (int index, char[] str, int offset, int len)
          .................... StringBuffer
          public....................int       length ()
     1.2  public synchronized ...........    replace (int start, int end, String str)
          .................... StringBuffer
          public synchronized ...........    reverse ()
          .................... StringBuffer
          public synchronized .......void    setCharAt (int index, char ch)
          public synchronized .......void    setLength (int newLength)
    ✳     public..........................   StringBuffer ()
    ✳     public..........................   StringBuffer (int length)
    ✳     public..........................   StringBuffer (String str)
     1.2  public....................String    substring (int start)
     1.2  public synchronized .....String    substring (int start, int end)
        1 public.................. String     toString ()
```

StringBufferInputStream

```
          Object
     ○    └ InputStream 1
              └ StringBufferInputStream
```

```
        1 public synchronized ........ int   available ()
          protected.................String   buffer
        1 public.....................void    close () throws IOException
          protected....................int   count
        1 public synchronized .......void    mark (int readlimit)
        1 public.................. boolean    markSupported ()
          protected....................int   pos
        1 public synchronized ........ int   read ()
        1 public....................int      read (byte[] b) throws IOException
        1 public synchronized ........ int   read (byte[] b, int off, int len)
        1 public synchronized ...... void    reset ()
        1 public synchronized ...... long    skip (long n)
```

Class *Interface* —extends - - -implements ○ abstract ● final △ static ▲ static final ✳ constructor x x—inherited x **x**—declared **x x**—overridden

*	public...........................	**StringBufferInputStream** (String s)	

StringCharacterIterator
java.text

P

```
      Object 1
1.1 ●  └ StringCharacterIterator ------------------ CharacterIterator 2 (Cloneable)
```

1	public...................**Object**	**clone** ()	
2	public....................... char	**current** ()	
1	public...................**boolean**	**equals** (Object obj)	
2	public....................... char	**first** ()	
2	public.........................int	**getBeginIndex** ()	
2	public.........................int	**getEndIndex** ()	
2	public.........................int	**getIndex** ()	
1	public..................... **int**	**hashCode** ()	
2	public....................... char	**last** ()	
2	public....................... char	**next** ()	
2	public....................... char	**previous** ()	
2	public....................... char	**setIndex** (int p)	
1.2	public......................void	**setText** (String text)	
*	public............................	**StringCharacterIterator** (String text)	
*	public............................	**StringCharacterIterator** (String text, int pos)	
*	public............................	**StringCharacterIterator** (String text, int begin, int end, int pos)	

StringContent
javax.swing.text

```
      Object
1.2 ●  └ StringContent ------------------------- AbstractDocument.Content 1, java.io.Serializable
```

1	public.................*Position*	**createPosition** (int offset) throws BadLocationException	
1	public.......................void	**getChars** (int where, int len, Segment chars) throws BadLocationException	
	protected .... java.util.Vector	**getPositionsInRange** (java.util.Vector v, int offset, int length)	
1	public.....................String	**getString** (int where, int len) throws BadLocationException	
1	public....................*javax↵*	**insertString** (int where, String str) throws BadLocationException	
	.swing.undo.UndoableEdit		
1	public.........................int	**length** ()	
1	public....................*javax↵*	**remove** (int where, int nitems) throws BadLocationException	
	.swing.undo.UndoableEdit		
*	public............................	**StringContent** ()	
*	public............................	**StringContent** (int initialLength)	
	protected ....void	**updateUndoPositions** (java.util.Vector positions)	

StringHolder
org.omg.CORBA

```
      Object
1.2 ●  └ StringHolder ------------------------- org.omg.CORBA.portable.Streamable 1
```

1	public.......................void	**_read** (org.omg.CORBA.portable.InputStream input)	
1	public................TypeCode	**_type** ()	
1	public.......................void	**_write** (org.omg.CORBA.portable.OutputStream output)	
*	public............................	**StringHolder** ()	
*	public............................	**StringHolder** (String initial)	
	public.....................String	**value**	

StringIndexOutOfBoundsException
java.lang

P

```
      Object
       └ Throwable --------------------------- java.io.Serializable
          └ Exception
             └ RuntimeException
                └ IndexOutOfBoundsException
                   └ StringIndexOutOfBoundsException
```

*	public............................	**StringIndexOutOfBoundsException** ()	
*	public............................	**StringIndexOutOfBoundsException** (int index)	
*	public............................	**StringIndexOutOfBoundsException** (String s)	

S

Classes

StringReader

				java.io

```
        Object
1.1 ○   └─Reader 1
1.1         └─StringReader
```

1	public	**void**	**close** ()
1	protected	Object	lock
1	public	**void**	**mark** (int readAheadLimit) throws IOException
1	public	**boolean**	**markSupported** ()
1	public	**int**	**read** () throws IOException
1	public	int	read (char[] cbuf) throws IOException
1	public	**int**	**read** (char[] cbuf, int off, int len) throws IOException
1	public	**boolean**	**ready** () throws IOException
1	public	**void**	**reset** () throws IOException
1	public	**long**	**skip** (long ns) throws IOException
*	public		**StringReader** (String s)

StringSelection

			java.awt.datatransfer
			P

```
        Object
1.1     └─StringSelection - - - - - - - - - - - - - - - - - - - - - - - Transferable 1, ClipboardOwner 2
```

1	public synchronized	Object	**getTransferData** (DataFlavor flavor) throws UnsupportedFlavorException, java.io.IOException
1	public synchronized		**getTransferDataFlavors** ()
		DataFlavor[]	
1	public	boolean	**isDataFlavorSupported** (DataFlavor flavor)
2	public	void	**lostOwnership** (Clipboard clipboard, Transferable contents)
*	public		**StringSelection** (String data)

S

StringTokenizer

			java.util
			P

```
        Object
        └─StringTokenizer - - - - - - - - - - - - - - - - - - - - - - - Enumeration 1
```

	public	int	**countTokens** ()
1	public	boolean	**hasMoreElements** ()
	public	boolean	**hasMoreTokens** ()
1	public	Object	**nextElement** ()
	public	String	**nextToken** ()
	public	String	**nextToken** (String delim)
*	public		**StringTokenizer** (String str)
*	public		**StringTokenizer** (String str, String delim)
*	public		**StringTokenizer** (String str, String delim, boolean returnTokens)

StringWriter

			java.io

```
        Object 1
1.1 ○   └─Writer 2
1.1         └─StringWriter
```

2	public	**void**	**close** () throws IOException
2	public	**void**	**flush** ()
	public	StringBuffer	**getBuffer** ()
2	protected	Object	lock
*	public		**StringWriter** ()
*	public		**StringWriter** (int initialSize)
1	public	**String**	**toString** ()
2	public	void	write (char[] cbuf) throws IOException
2	public	**void**	**write** (int c)
2	public	**void**	**write** (String str)
2	public	**void**	**write** (char[] cbuf, int off, int len)
2	public	**void**	**write** (String str, int off, int len)

Class   *Interface*   —extends   - - -implements   ○ abstract   ● final   △ static   ▲ static final   ✳ constructor   x x—inherited   x **x**—declared   **x x**—overridden

Stroke

		java.awt

1.2 | *Stroke* | P

public................... *Shape* **createStrokedShape** (*Shape* p)

Struct

		java.sql

1.2 | *Struct* | P⁰

public................. Object[] **getAttributes** () throws SQLException
public................. Object[] **getAttributes** (*java.util.Map* map) throws SQLException
public.....................String **getSQLTypeName** () throws SQLException

---

StructMember

		org.omg.CORBA

Object
1.2 ● └StructMember - *org.omg.CORBA.portable.IDLEntity* (*java.io.Serializable*)

*   public...................String **name**
*   public.......................... **StructMember** ()
*   public.......................... **StructMember** (String __name, TypeCode __type, *IDLType* __type_def)
  public.................TypeCode **type**
  public.................*IDLType* **type_def**

StubNotFoundException

		java.rmi

Object
└Throwable - *java.io.Serializable*   P⁰
  └Exception
    └java.io.IOException
1.1   └RemoteException [1]
1.1   └StubNotFoundException

1 public...............Throwable detail
1 public....................String getMessage ()
1 public.......................void printStackTrace ()
1 public.......................void printStackTrace (java.io.PrintStream ps)
1 public.......................void printStackTrace (java.io.PrintWriter pw)
* public.......................... **StubNotFoundException** (String s)
* public.......................... **StubNotFoundException** (String s, Exception ex)

Style

		javax.swing.text

1.2 | *Style*————————————————*MutableAttributeSet* [1] (*AttributeSet* [2]) |

1 public.......................void addAttribute (Object name, Object value)
1 public.......................void addAttributes (*AttributeSet* attributes)
  public.......................void **addChangeListener** (*javax.swing.event.ChangeListener* l)
2 public................. boolean containsAttribute (Object name, Object value)
2 public................. boolean containsAttributes (*AttributeSet* attributes)
2 public.............*AttributeSet* copyAttributes ()
2 public.................Object getAttribute (Object key)
2 public.......................int getAttributeCount ()
2 public....*java.util.Enumeration* getAttributeNames ()
  public....................String **getName** ()
2 public.............*AttributeSet* getResolveParent ()
2 public................. boolean isDefined (Object attrName)
2 public................. boolean isEqual (*AttributeSet* attr)
1 public.......................void removeAttribute (Object name)
1 public.......................void removeAttributes (*java.util.Enumeration* names)
1 public.......................void removeAttributes (*AttributeSet* attributes)
  public.......................void **removeChangeListener** (*javax.swing.event.ChangeListener* l)
1 public.......................void setResolveParent (*AttributeSet* parent)

StyleConstants

		javax.swing.text

Object [1]
1.2 └StyleConstants

S

Classes

StyleConstants

▲	public static final	int	**ALIGN_CENTER** = 1
▲	public static final	int	**ALIGN_JUSTIFIED** = 3
▲	public static final	int	**ALIGN_LEFT** = 0
▲	public static final	int	**ALIGN_RIGHT** = 2
▲	public static final	Object	**Alignment**
▲	public static final	Object	**Background**
▲	public static final	Object	**BidiLevel**
▲	public static final	Object	**Bold**
▲	public static final	Object	**ComponentAttribute**
▲	public static final	String	**ComponentElementName** = "component"
▲	public static final	Object	**ComposedTextAttribute**
▲	public static final	Object	**FirstLineIndent**
▲	public static final	Object	**FontFamily**
▲	public static final	Object	**FontSize**
▲	public static final	Object	**Foreground**
△	public static	int	**getAlignment** (*AttributeSet* a)
△	public static	java.awt.Color	**getBackground** (*AttributeSet* a)
△	public static	int	**getBidiLevel** (*AttributeSet* a)
△	public static	java.awt.Component	**getComponent** (*AttributeSet* a)
△	public static	float	**getFirstLineIndent** (*AttributeSet* a)
△	public static	String	**getFontFamily** (*AttributeSet* a)
△	public static	int	**getFontSize** (*AttributeSet* a)
△	public static	java.awt.Color	**getForeground** (*AttributeSet* a)
△	public static	*javax.swing.Icon*	**getIcon** (*AttributeSet* a)
△	public static	float	**getLeftIndent** (*AttributeSet* a)
△	public static	float	**getLineSpacing** (*AttributeSet* a)
△	public static	float	**getRightIndent** (*AttributeSet* a)
△	public static	float	**getSpaceAbove** (*AttributeSet* a)
△	public static	float	**getSpaceBelow** (*AttributeSet* a)
△	public static	TabSet	**getTabSet** (*AttributeSet* a)
▲	public static final	Object	**IconAttribute**
▲	public static final	String	**IconElementName** = "icon"
△	public static	boolean	**isBold** (*AttributeSet* a)
△	public static	boolean	**isItalic** (*AttributeSet* a)
△	public static	boolean	**isStrikeThrough** (*AttributeSet* a)
△	public static	boolean	**isSubscript** (*AttributeSet* a)
△	public static	boolean	**isSuperscript** (*AttributeSet* a)
△	public static	boolean	**isUnderline** (*AttributeSet* a)
▲	public static final	Object	**Italic**
▲	public static final	Object	**LeftIndent**
▲	public static final	Object	**LineSpacing**
▲	public static final	Object	**ModelAttribute**
▲	public static final	Object	**NameAttribute**
▲	public static final	Object	**Orientation**
▲	public static final	Object	**ResolveAttribute**
▲	public static final	Object	**RightIndent**
△	public static	void	**setAlignment** (*MutableAttributeSet* a, int align)
△	public static	void	**setBackground** (*MutableAttributeSet* a, java.awt.Color fg)
△	public static	void	**setBidiLevel** (*MutableAttributeSet* a, int o)
△	public static	void	**setBold** (*MutableAttributeSet* a, boolean b)
△	public static	void	**setComponent** (*MutableAttributeSet* a, java.awt.Component c)
△	public static	void	**setFirstLineIndent** (*MutableAttributeSet* a, float i)
△	public static	void	**setFontFamily** (*MutableAttributeSet* a, String fam)
△	public static	void	**setFontSize** (*MutableAttributeSet* a, int s)
△	public static	void	**setForeground** (*MutableAttributeSet* a, java.awt.Color fg)
△	public static	void	**setIcon** (*MutableAttributeSet* a, *javax.swing.Icon* c)
△	public static	void	**setItalic** (*MutableAttributeSet* a, boolean b)
△	public static	void	**setLeftIndent** (*MutableAttributeSet* a, float i)
△	public static	void	**setLineSpacing** (*MutableAttributeSet* a, float i)
△	public static	void	**setRightIndent** (*MutableAttributeSet* a, float i)
△	public static	void	**setSpaceAbove** (*MutableAttributeSet* a, float i)
△	public static	void	**setSpaceBelow** (*MutableAttributeSet* a, float i)
△	public static	void	**setStrikeThrough** (*MutableAttributeSet* a, boolean b)
△	public static	void	**setSubscript** (*MutableAttributeSet* a, boolean b)
△	public static	void	**setSuperscript** (*MutableAttributeSet* a, boolean b)
△	public static	void	**setTabSet** (*MutableAttributeSet* a, TabSet tabs)
△	public static	void	**setUnderline** (*MutableAttributeSet* a, boolean b)
▲	public static final	Object	**SpaceAbove**
▲	public static final	Object	**SpaceBelow**
▲	public static final	Object	**StrikeThrough**
▲	public static final	Object	**Subscript**

S

Class   *Interface*   —extends   - - -implements   ○ abstract   ● final   △ static   ▲ static final   ✳ constructor   x x—inherited   x **x**—declared   **x x**—overridden

▲	public static final........Object	**Superscript**
▲	public static final........Object	**TabSet**
1	public................**String**	**toString** ()
▲	public static final........Object	**Underline**

StyleConstants.CharacterConstants

Object
1.2 └StyleConstants [1]
1.2 └StyleConstants.CharacterConstants - - - - - - *AttributeSet.CharacterAttribute*

1 *64 inherited members from StyleConstants not shown*
▲	1	public static final........**Object Background**
▲	1	public static final........**Object BidiLevel**
▲	1	public static final........**Object Bold**
▲	1	public static final........**Object ComponentAttribute**
▲		public static final........Object **Family**
▲	1	public static final........**Object Foreground**
▲	1	public static final........**Object IconAttribute**
▲	1	public static final........**Object Italic**
▲		public static final........Object **Size**
▲	1	public static final........**Object StrikeThrough**
▲	1	public static final........**Object Subscript**
▲	1	public static final........**Object Superscript**
▲	1	public static final........**Object Underline**

StyleConstants.ColorConstants

Object
1.2 └StyleConstants [1]
1.2 └StyleConstants.ColorConstants - - - - - - - - - *AttributeSet.ColorAttribute, AttributeSet.CharacterAttribute*

1 *73 inherited members from StyleConstants not shown*
| ▲ | 1 | public static final........**Object Background** |
| ▲ | 1 | public static final........**Object Foreground** |

StyleConstants.FontConstants

Object
1.2 └StyleConstants [1]
1.2 └StyleConstants.FontConstants - - - - - - - - - *AttributeSet.FontAttribute, AttributeSet.CharacterAttribute*

1 *73 inherited members from StyleConstants not shown*
▲		public static final........**Object Bold**
▲		public static final........Object **Family**
▲		public static final........**Object Italic**
▲		public static final........Object **Size**

StyleConstants.ParagraphConstants

Object
1.2 └StyleConstants [1]
1.2 └StyleConstants.ParagraphConstants - - - - - - *AttributeSet.ParagraphAttribute*

1 *66 inherited members from StyleConstants not shown*
▲	1	public static final........**Object Alignment**
▲	1	public static final........**Object FirstLineIndent**
▲	1	public static final........**Object LeftIndent**
▲	1	public static final........**Object LineSpacing**
▲	1	public static final........**Object Orientation**
▲	1	public static final........**Object RightIndent**
▲	1	public static final........**Object SpaceAbove**
▲	1	public static final........**Object SpaceBelow**
▲	1	public static final........**Object TabSet**

		StyleContext	javax.swing.text

Object [1]
1.2 └ StyleContext - *java.io.Serializable, AbstractDocument.AttributeContext* [2]

	2	public synchronized . . . . *AttributeSet*	**addAttribute** (*AttributeSet* old, Object name, Object value)
	2	public synchronized . . . . *AttributeSet*	**addAttributes** (*AttributeSet* old, *AttributeSet* attr)
		public . . . . void	**addChangeListener** (*javax.swing.event.ChangeListener* l)
		public . . . . *Style*	**addStyle** (String nm, *Style* parent)
		protected . *MutableAttributeSet*	**createLargeAttributeSet** (*AttributeSet* a)
		protected . . . . .StyleContext.SmallAttributeSet	**createSmallAttributeSet** (*AttributeSet* a)
▲		public static final . . . . String	**DEFAULT_STYLE** = "default"
		public . . . . java.awt.Color	**getBackground** (*AttributeSet* attr)
		protected . . . . int	**getCompressionThreshold** ()
▲		public static final . StyleContext	**getDefaultStyleContext** ()
	2	public . . . . *AttributeSet*	**getEmptySet** ()
		public . . . . java.awt.Font	**getFont** (*AttributeSet* attr)
		public . . . . java.awt.Font	**getFont** (String family, int style, int size)
		public . . . . java.awt.FontMetrics	**getFontMetrics** (java.awt.Font f)
		public . . . . java.awt.Color	**getForeground** (*AttributeSet* attr)
△		public static . . . . Object	**getStaticAttribute** (Object key)
△		public static . . . . Object	**getStaticAttributeKey** (Object key)
		public . . . . *Style*	**getStyle** (String nm)
		public . . . . *java.util.Enumeration*	**getStyleNames** ()
		public . . . . void	**readAttributes** (java.io.ObjectInputStream in, *MutableAttributeSet* a) throws ClassNotFoundException, java.io.IOException
△		public static . . . . void	**readAttributeSet** (java.io.ObjectInputStream in, *MutableAttributeSet* a) throws ClassNotFoundException, java.io.IOException
	2	public . . . . void	**reclaim** (*AttributeSet* a)
△		public static . . . . void	**registerStaticAttributeKey** (Object key)
	2	public synchronized . . . . *AttributeSet*	**removeAttribute** (*AttributeSet* old, Object name)
	2	public synchronized . . . . *AttributeSet*	**removeAttributes** (*AttributeSet* old, *AttributeSet* attrs)
	2	public synchronized . . . . *AttributeSet*	**removeAttributes** (*AttributeSet* old, *java.util.Enumeration* names)
		public . . . . void	**removeChangeListener** (*javax.swing.event.ChangeListener* l)
		public . . . . void	**removeStyle** (String nm)
✳		public	**StyleContext** ()
	1	public . . . . String	**toString** ()
		public . . . . void	**writeAttributes** (java.io.ObjectOutputStream out, *AttributeSet* a) throws java.io.IOException
△		public static . . . . void	**writeAttributeSet** (java.io.ObjectOutputStream out, *AttributeSet* a) throws java.io.IOException

		StyleContext.NamedStyle	javax.swing.text

Object [1]
1.2 └ StyleContext.NamedStyle - - - - - - - - - - - - - - - - - *Style* [2] (*MutableAttributeSet* [3] (*AttributeSet* [4])), *java.io.Serializable*

	3	public . . . . void	**addAttribute** (Object name, Object value)
	3	public . . . . void	**addAttributes** (*AttributeSet* attr)
	2	public . . . . void	**addChangeListener** (*javax.swing.event.ChangeListener* l)
		protected transient . . . . . javax↩ .swing.event.ChangeEvent	**changeEvent**
	4	public . . . . boolean	**containsAttribute** (Object name, Object value)
	4	public . . . . boolean	**containsAttributes** (*AttributeSet* attrs)
	4	public . . . . *AttributeSet*	**copyAttributes** ()
		protected . . . . void	**fireStateChanged** ()
	4	public . . . . Object	**getAttribute** (Object attrName)
	4	public . . . . int	**getAttributeCount** ()
	4	public . . . . *java.util.Enumeration*	**getAttributeNames** ()
	2	public . . . . String	**getName** ()
	4	public . . . . *AttributeSet*	**getResolveParent** ()
	4	public . . . . boolean	**isDefined** (Object attrName)
	4	public . . . . boolean	**isEqual** (*AttributeSet* attr)

Class   *Interface*   —extends   - - -implements   ○ abstract   ● final   △ static   ▲ static final   ✳ constructor   x x—inherited   x **x**—declared   **x x**—overridden

636

	protected . . . . javax ↤		**listenerList**
	.swing.event.EventListenerList		
*	public		**NamedStyle** ()
*	public		**NamedStyle** (*Style* parent)
*	public		**NamedStyle** (String name, *Style* parent)
3	public . . . . void		**removeAttribute** (Object name)
3	public . . . . void		**removeAttributes** (*java.util.Enumeration* names)
3	public . . . . void		**removeAttributes** (*AttributeSet* attrs)
2	public . . . . void		**removeChangeListener** (*javax.swing.event.ChangeListener* l)
	public . . . . void		**setName** (String name)
3	public . . . . void		**setResolveParent** (*AttributeSet* parent)
1	public . . . . String		**toString** ()

StyleContext.SmallAttributeSet

javax.swing.text

Object [1]

1.2 └ StyleContext.SmallAttributeSet - - - - - - - - - - - *AttributeSet* [2]

1	public . . . . **Object**		**clone** ()
2	public . . . . boolean		**containsAttribute** (Object name, Object value)
2	public . . . . boolean		**containsAttributes** (*AttributeSet* attrs)
2	public . . . . *AttributeSet*		**copyAttributes** ()
1	public . . . . **boolean**		**equals** (Object obj)
2	public . . . . Object		**getAttribute** (Object key)
2	public . . . . int		**getAttributeCount** ()
2	public . . . . *java.util.Enumeration*		**getAttributeNames** ()
2	public . . . . *AttributeSet*		**getResolveParent** ()
1	public . . . . **int**		**hashCode** ()
2	public . . . . boolean		**isDefined** (Object key)
2	public . . . . boolean		**isEqual** (*AttributeSet* attr)
*	public		**SmallAttributeSet** (Object[] attributes)
*	public		**SmallAttributeSet** (*AttributeSet* attrs)
1	public . . . . String		**toString** ()

S

StyledDocument

javax.swing.text

1.2 *StyledDocument*──────────────── *Document* [1]

1	public . . . . void		addDocumentListener (*javax.swing.event.DocumentListener* listener)
	public . . . . *Style*		**addStyle** (String nm, *Style* parent)
1	public . . . . void		addUndoableEditListener (*javax.swing.event.UndoableEditListener* listener)
1	public . . . . *Position*		createPosition (int offs) throws BadLocationException
	public . . . . java.awt.Color		**getBackground** (*AttributeSet* attr)
	public . . . . *Element*		**getCharacterElement** (int pos)
1	public . . . . *Element*		getDefaultRootElement ()
1	public . . . . *Position*		getEndPosition ()
	public . . . . java.awt.Font		**getFont** (*AttributeSet* attr)
	public . . . . java.awt.Color		**getForeground** (*AttributeSet* attr)
1	public . . . . int		getLength ()
	public . . . . *Style*		**getLogicalStyle** (int p)
	public . . . . *Element*		**getParagraphElement** (int pos)
1	public . . . . Object		getProperty (Object key)
1	public . . . . *Element[]*		getRootElements ()
1	public . . . . *Position*		getStartPosition ()
	public . . . . *Style*		**getStyle** (String nm)
1	public . . . . String		getText (int offset, int length) throws BadLocationException
1	public . . . . void		getText (int offset, int length, Segment txt) throws BadLocationException
1	public . . . . void		insertString (int offset, String str, *AttributeSet* a) throws BadLocationException
1	public . . . . void		putProperty (Object key, Object value)
1	public . . . . void		remove (int offs, int len) throws BadLocationException
1	public . . . . void		removeDocumentListener (*javax.swing.event.DocumentListener* listener)
	public . . . . void		**removeStyle** (String nm)
1	public . . . . void		removeUndoableEditListener (*javax.swing.event.UndoableEditListener* listener)
1	public . . . . void		render (*Runnable* r)
	public . . . . void		**setCharacterAttributes** (int offset, int length, *AttributeSet* s, boolean replace)
	public . . . . void		**setLogicalStyle** (int pos, *Style* s)
	public . . . . void		**setParagraphAttributes** (int offset, int length, *AttributeSet* s, boolean replace)

Classes

StyledEditorKit

StyledEditorKit		javax.swing.text

```
        Object
1.2 ○   └EditorKit¹ - - - - - - - - - - - - - - - - - - - - - - - - - Cloneable, java.io.Serializable
1.2        └DefaultEditorKit²
1.2           └StyledEditorKit
```

2	*53 inherited members from DefaultEditorKit not shown*	
2	public.................**Object**	**clone** ()
2	public.............*Document*	**createDefaultDocument** ()
	protected...................void	**createInputAttributes** (*Element* element, *MutableAttributeSet* set)
1	public.......................**void**	**deinstall** (javax.swing.JEditorPane c)
2	public... *javax.swing.Action[]*	**getActions** ()
	public.....................*Element*	**getCharacterAttributeRun** ()
	public..... *MutableAttributeSet*	**getInputAttributes** ()
2	public.............*ViewFactory*	**getViewFactory** ()
1	public.......................**void**	**install** (javax.swing.JEditorPane c)
✱	public........................	**StyledEditorKit** ()

StyledEditorKit.AlignmentAction		javax.swing.text

```
        Object
1.2 ○   └javax.swing.AbstractAction¹ - - - - - - - - - - - - - - javax.swing.Action (java.awt.event.ActionListener
                                                (java.util.EventListener)), Cloneable, java.io.Serializable
1.2 ○      └TextAction²
1.2 ○         └StyledEditorKit.StyledTextAction³
1.2            └StyledEditorKit.AlignmentAction
```

	1	public.....................**void**	**actionPerformed** (java.awt.event.ActionEvent e)
	1	public synchronized ....void	addPropertyChangeListener (*java.beans.PropertyChangeListener* listener)
✱		public...........................	**AlignmentAction** (String nm, int a)
▲	2	public static final...............	augmentList (*javax.swing.Action[]* list1, *javax.swing.Action[]* list2)
		..........*javax.swing.Action[]*	
	1	protected . javax.swing.event↵	changeSupport
		.SwingPropertyChangeSupport	
	1	protected...............Object	clone () throws CloneNotSupportedException
	1	protected............. boolean	enabled
	1	protected.................void	firePropertyChange (String propertyName, Object oldValue, Object newValue)
●	3	protected final.................	getEditor (java.awt.event.ActionEvent e)
		.... javax.swing.JEditorPane	
●	2	protected final.................	getFocusedComponent ()
		.................JTextComponent	
●	3	protected final *StyledDocument*	getStyledDocument (javax.swing.JEditorPane e)
●	3	protected final.. StyledEditorKit	getStyledEditorKit (javax.swing.JEditorPane e)
●	2	protected final.................	getTextComponent (java.awt.event.ActionEvent e)
		.................JTextComponent	
	1	public...................Object	getValue (String key)
	1	public.................. boolean	isEnabled ()
	1	public synchronized ....void	putValue (String key, Object newValue)
	1	public synchronized ....void	removePropertyChangeListener (*java.beans.PropertyChangeListener* listener)
●	3	protected final..............void	setCharacterAttributes (javax.swing.JEditorPane editor, *AttributeSet* attr,
			boolean replace)
	1	public synchronized ....void	setEnabled (boolean newValue)
●	3	protected final..............void	setParagraphAttributes (javax.swing.JEditorPane editor, *AttributeSet* attr,
			boolean replace)

StyledEditorKit.BoldAction		javax.swing.text

```
        Object
1.2 ○   └javax.swing.AbstractAction¹ - - - - - - - - - - - - - - javax.swing.Action (java.awt.event.ActionListener
                                                (java.util.EventListener)), Cloneable, java.io.Serializable
1.2 ○      └TextAction²
1.2 ○         └StyledEditorKit.StyledTextAction³
1.2            └StyledEditorKit.BoldAction
```

1	public.....................**void**	**actionPerformed** (java.awt.event.ActionEvent e)
1	public synchronized ....void	addPropertyChangeListener (*java.beans.PropertyChangeListener* listener)

Class   *Interface*   —extends   - - -implements   ○ abstract   ● final   △ static   ▲ static final   ✱ constructor   x x—inherited   x **x**—declared   **x x**—overridden

S

▲	2	public static final . . . . *. . . . . javax.swing.Action[]*	augmentList (*javax.swing.Action[]* list1, *javax.swing.Action[]* list2)
*		public.	**BoldAction** ()
	1	protected . javax.swing.event↵ .SwingPropertyChangeSupport	changeSupport
	1	protected . . . . Object	clone () throws CloneNotSupportedException
	1	protected . . . . boolean	enabled
	1	protected . . . . void	firePropertyChange (String propertyName, Object oldValue, Object newValue)
●	3	protected final. . . . . *. . . . . . . javax.swing.JEditorPane*	getEditor (java.awt.event.ActionEvent e)
●	2	protected final. . . . . JTextComponent	getFocusedComponent ()
●	3	protected final *StyledDocument*	getStyledDocument (javax.swing.JEditorPane e)
●	3	protected final . . StyledEditorKit	getStyledEditorKit (javax.swing.JEditorPane e)
●	2	protected final. . . . . JTextComponent	getTextComponent (java.awt.event.ActionEvent e)
	1	public. . . . . Object	getValue (String key)
	1	public. . . . . boolean	isEnabled ()
	1	public synchronized . . . . . . .void	putValue (String key, Object newValue)
	1	public synchronized . . . . . . .void	removePropertyChangeListener (*java.beans.PropertyChangeListener* listener)
●	3	protected final. . . . . .void	setCharacterAttributes (javax.swing.JEditorPane editor, *AttributeSet* attr, boolean replace)
	1	public synchronized . . . . . . .void	setEnabled (boolean newValue)
●	3	protected final. . . . . .void	setParagraphAttributes (javax.swing.JEditorPane editor, *AttributeSet* attr, boolean replace)

StyledEditorKit.FontFamilyAction			javax.swing.text

		Object
1.2 ○		└javax.swing.AbstractAction [1] - - - - - - - - - - - - - - *javax.swing.Action* (*java.awt.event.ActionListener* (*java.util.EventListener*)), *Cloneable, java.io.Serializable*
1.2 ○		└TextAction [2]
1.2 ○		└StyledEditorKit.StyledTextAction [3]
1.2		└StyledEditorKit.FontFamilyAction

	1	public. . . . . **void**	**actionPerformed** (java.awt.event.ActionEvent e)
	1	public synchronized . . . . . . .void	addPropertyChangeListener (*java.beans.PropertyChangeListener* listener)
▲	2	public static final . . . . *. . . . . javax.swing.Action[]*	augmentList (*javax.swing.Action[]* list1, *javax.swing.Action[]* list2)
	1	protected . javax.swing.event↵ .SwingPropertyChangeSupport	changeSupport
	1	protected . . . . Object	clone () throws CloneNotSupportedException
	1	protected . . . . boolean	enabled
	1	protected . . . . void	firePropertyChange (String propertyName, Object oldValue, Object newValue)
*		public.	**FontFamilyAction** (String nm, String family)
●	3	protected final. . . . . *. . . . . . . javax.swing.JEditorPane*	getEditor (java.awt.event.ActionEvent e)
●	2	protected final. . . . . JTextComponent	getFocusedComponent ()
●	3	protected final *StyledDocument*	getStyledDocument (javax.swing.JEditorPane e)
●	3	protected final . . StyledEditorKit	getStyledEditorKit (javax.swing.JEditorPane e)
●	2	protected final. . . . . JTextComponent	getTextComponent (java.awt.event.ActionEvent e)
	1	public. . . . . Object	getValue (String key)
	1	public. . . . . boolean	isEnabled ()
	1	public synchronized . . . . . . .void	putValue (String key, Object newValue)
	1	public synchronized . . . . . . .void	removePropertyChangeListener (*java.beans.PropertyChangeListener* listener)
●	3	protected final. . . . . .void	setCharacterAttributes (javax.swing.JEditorPane editor, *AttributeSet* attr, boolean replace)
	1	public synchronized . . . . . . .void	setEnabled (boolean newValue)
●	3	protected final. . . . . .void	setParagraphAttributes (javax.swing.JEditorPane editor, *AttributeSet* attr, boolean replace)

			StyledEditorKit.FontSizeAction	javax.swing.text

Object
1.2 ○ └ javax.swing.AbstractAction [1] - - - - - - - - - - - - - - *javax.swing.Action (java.awt.event.ActionListener*
(java.util.EventListener)), Cloneable, java.io.Serializable
1.2 ○ └ TextAction [2]
1.2 ○   └ StyledEditorKit.StyledTextAction [3]
1.2   └ StyledEditorKit.FontSizeAction

	1	public..................... **void**	**actionPerformed** (java.awt.event.ActionEvent e)
	1	public synchronized ....void	addPropertyChangeListener (*java.beans.PropertyChangeListener* listener)
▲	2	public static final.............. .... *javax.swing.Action[]*	augmentList (*javax.swing.Action[]* list1, *javax.swing.Action[]* list2)
	1	protected . javax.swing.event ↵ .SwingPropertyChangeSupport	changeSupport
	1	protected................ Object	clone () throws CloneNotSupportedException
	1	protected............. boolean	enabled
	1	protected...................void	firePropertyChange (String propertyName, Object oldValue, Object newValue)
✳		public..........................	**FontSizeAction** (String nm, int size)
●	3	protected final.................. .... javax.swing.JEditorPane	getEditor (java.awt.event.ActionEvent e)
●	2	protected final.................. ....JTextComponent	getFocusedComponent ()
●	3	protected final *StyledDocument*	getStyledDocument (javax.swing.JEditorPane e)
●	3	protected final.. StyledEditorKit	getStyledEditorKit (javax.swing.JEditorPane e)
●	2	protected final.................. ....JTextComponent	getTextComponent (java.awt.event.ActionEvent e)
	1	public................... Object	getValue (String key)
	1	public................. boolean	isEnabled ()
	1	public synchronized ....void	putValue (String key, Object newValue)
	1	public synchronized ....void	removePropertyChangeListener (*java.beans.PropertyChangeListener* listener)
●	3	protected final...............void	setCharacterAttributes (javax.swing.JEditorPane editor, *AttributeSet* attr, boolean replace)
	1	public synchronized ....void	setEnabled (boolean newValue)
●	3	protected final...............void	setParagraphAttributes (javax.swing.JEditorPane editor, *AttributeSet* attr, boolean replace)

			StyledEditorKit.ForegroundAction	javax.swing.text

Object
1.2 ○ └ javax.swing.AbstractAction [1] - - - - - - - - - - - - - - *javax.swing.Action (java.awt.event.ActionListener*
(java.util.EventListener)), Cloneable, java.io.Serializable
1.2 ○ └ TextAction [2]
1.2 ○   └ StyledEditorKit.StyledTextAction [3]
1.2   └ StyledEditorKit.ForegroundAction

	1	public..................... **void**	**actionPerformed** (java.awt.event.ActionEvent e)
	1	public synchronized ....void	addPropertyChangeListener (*java.beans.PropertyChangeListener* listener)
▲	2	public static final.............. .... *javax.swing.Action[]*	augmentList (*javax.swing.Action[]* list1, *javax.swing.Action[]* list2)
	1	protected . javax.swing.event ↵ .SwingPropertyChangeSupport	changeSupport
	1	protected............. Object	clone () throws CloneNotSupportedException
	1	protected............. boolean	enabled
	1	protected...................void	firePropertyChange (String propertyName, Object oldValue, Object newValue)
✳		public..........................	**ForegroundAction** (String nm, java.awt.Color fg)
●	3	protected final.................. .... javax.swing.JEditorPane	getEditor (java.awt.event.ActionEvent e)
●	2	protected final.................. ....JTextComponent	getFocusedComponent ()
●	3	protected final *StyledDocument*	getStyledDocument (javax.swing.JEditorPane e)
●	3	protected final.. StyledEditorKit	getStyledEditorKit (javax.swing.JEditorPane e)
●	2	protected final.................. ....JTextComponent	getTextComponent (java.awt.event.ActionEvent e)
	1	public................... Object	getValue (String key)
	1	public................. boolean	isEnabled ()
	1	public synchronized ....void	putValue (String key, Object newValue)
	1	public synchronized ....void	removePropertyChangeListener (*java.beans.PropertyChangeListener* listener)

Class *Interface* —extends - - -implements ○ abstract ● final △ static ▲ static final ✳ constructor x x—inherited x **x**—declared **x x**—overridden

●	3	protected final..............void	setCharacterAttributes (javax.swing.JEditorPane editor, *AttributeSet* attr, boolean replace)
	1	public synchronized ....void	setEnabled (boolean newValue)
●	3	protected final..............void	setParagraphAttributes (javax.swing.JEditorPane editor, *AttributeSet* attr, boolean replace)

StyledEditorKit.ItalicAction   javax.swing.text

Object
1.2 ○ └javax.swing.AbstractAction [1] - - - - - - - - - - - - - *javax.swing.Action* (*java.awt.event.ActionListener* (*java.util.EventListener*)), *Cloneable*, *java.io.Serializable*
1.2 ○   └TextAction [2]
1.2 ○   └StyledEditorKit.StyledTextAction [3]
1.2   └StyledEditorKit.ItalicAction

	1	public..................... **void**	**actionPerformed** (java.awt.event.ActionEvent e)
	1	public synchronized ....void	addPropertyChangeListener (*java.beans.PropertyChangeListener* listener)
▲	2	public static final............. *javax.swing.Action[]*	augmentList (*javax.swing.Action[]* list1, *javax.swing.Action[]* list2)
	1	protected . javax.swing.event ↵ .SwingPropertyChangeSupport	changeSupport
	1	protected.............. Object	clone () throws CloneNotSupportedException
	1	protected.............. boolean	enabled
	1	protected...................void	firePropertyChange (String propertyName, Object oldValue, Object newValue)
●	3	protected final.................. .... javax.swing.JEditorPane	getEditor (java.awt.event.ActionEvent e)
●	2	protected final.................. ....JTextComponent	getFocusedComponent ()
●	3	protected final *StyledDocument*	getStyledDocument (javax.swing.JEditorPane e)
●	3	protected final.. StyledEditorKit	getStyledEditorKit (javax.swing.JEditorPane e)
●	2	protected final.................. ....JTextComponent	getTextComponent (java.awt.event.ActionEvent e)
	1	public....................Object	getValue (String key)
	1	public.............. boolean	isEnabled ()
*		public............................	**ItalicAction** ()
	1	public synchronized ....void	putValue (String key, Object newValue)
	1	public synchronized ....void	removePropertyChangeListener (*java.beans.PropertyChangeListener* listener)
●	3	protected final..............void	setCharacterAttributes (javax.swing.JEditorPane editor, *AttributeSet* attr, boolean replace)
●	1	public synchronized ....void	setEnabled (boolean newValue)
●	3	protected final..............void	setParagraphAttributes (javax.swing.JEditorPane editor, *AttributeSet* attr, boolean replace)

StyledEditorKit.StyledTextAction   javax.swing.text

Object
1.2 ○ └javax.swing.AbstractAction [1] - - - - - - - - - - - - - *javax.swing.Action* (*java.awt.event.ActionListener* (*java.util.EventListener*)), *Cloneable*, *java.io.Serializable*
1.2 ○   └TextAction [2]
1.2 ○   └StyledEditorKit.StyledTextAction

○	1	public abstract.............void	actionPerformed (java.awt.event.ActionEvent)
	1	public synchronized ....void	addPropertyChangeListener (*java.beans.PropertyChangeListener* listener)
▲	2	public static final............. .... *javax.swing.Action[]*	augmentList (*javax.swing.Action[]* list1, *javax.swing.Action[]* list2)
	1	protected . javax.swing.event ↵ .SwingPropertyChangeSupport	changeSupport
	1	protected................ Object	clone () throws CloneNotSupportedException
	1	protected.............: boolean	enabled
	1	protected...................void	firePropertyChange (String propertyName, Object oldValue, Object newValue)
●		protected final.................. .... javax.swing.JEditorPane	**getEditor** (java.awt.event.ActionEvent e)
●	2	protected final.................. ....JTextComponent	getFocusedComponent ()
●		protected final *StyledDocument*	**getStyledDocument** (javax.swing.JEditorPane e)
●		protected final.. StyledEditorKit	**getStyledEditorKit** (javax.swing.JEditorPane e)
●	2	protected final.................. ....JTextComponent	getTextComponent (java.awt.event.ActionEvent e)
	1	public....................Object	getValue (String key)
	1	public................. boolean	isEnabled ()

StyledEditorKit.StyledTextAction

	1	public synchronized ....void	putValue (String key, Object newValue)
	1	public synchronized ....void	removePropertyChangeListener (*java.beans.PropertyChangeListener* listener)
●		protected final..............void	**setCharacterAttributes** (javax.swing.JEditorPane editor, *AttributeSet* attr, boolean replace)
	1	public synchronized ....void	setEnabled (boolean newValue)
●		protected final..............void	**setParagraphAttributes** (javax.swing.JEditorPane editor, *AttributeSet* attr, boolean replace)
✳		public..........................	**StyledTextAction** (String nm)

StyledEditorKit.UnderlineAction javax.swing.text

Object
1.2 ○ └javax.swing.AbstractAction [1] - - - - - - - - - - - - - *javax.swing.Action* (*java.awt.event.ActionListener* (*java.util.EventListener*)), *Cloneable*, *java.io.Serializable*

1.2 ○   └TextAction [2]
1.2 ○   └StyledEditorKit.StyledTextAction [3]
1.2   └StyledEditorKit.UnderlineAction

	1	public..................... **void**	**actionPerformed** (java.awt.event.ActionEvent e)
	1	public synchronized ....void	addPropertyChangeListener (*java.beans.PropertyChangeListener* listener)
▲	2	public static final............... *javax.swing.Action[]*	augmentList (*javax.swing.Action[]* list1, *javax.swing.Action[]* list2)
	1	protected . javax.swing.event↵ .SwingPropertyChangeSupport	changeSupport
	1	protected...............Object	clone () throws CloneNotSupportedException
	1	protected.............. boolean	enabled
	1	protected..................void	firePropertyChange (String propertyName, Object oldValue, Object newValue)
●	3	protected final................. .... javax.swing.JEditorPane	getEditor (java.awt.event.ActionEvent e)
●	2	protected final................. ....JTextComponent	getFocusedComponent ()
●	3	protected final *StyledDocument*	getStyledDocument (javax.swing.JEditorPane e)
●	3	protected final.. StyledEditorKit	getStyledEditorKit (javax.swing.JEditorPane e)
●	2	protected final................. ....JTextComponent	getTextComponent (java.awt.event.ActionEvent e)
	1	public....................Object	getValue (String key)
	1	public................. boolean	isEnabled ()
	1	public synchronized ....void	putValue (String key, Object newValue)
	1	public synchronized ....void	removePropertyChangeListener (*java.beans.PropertyChangeListener* listener)
●	3	protected final..............void	setCharacterAttributes (javax.swing.JEditorPane editor, *AttributeSet* attr, boolean replace)
	1	public synchronized ....void	setEnabled (boolean newValue)
●	3	protected final..............void	setParagraphAttributes (javax.swing.JEditorPane editor, *AttributeSet* attr, boolean replace)
✳		public..........................	**UnderlineAction** ()

StyleSheet javax.swing.text.html

Object
1.2   └javax.swing.text.StyleContext [1] - - - - - - - - - - - - *java.io.Serializable*, *javax.swing.text.AbstractDocument*↵ .*AttributeContext*

1.2   └StyleSheet

	1	*28 inherited members from javax.swing.text.StyleContext not shown*	
		public.......................void	**addRule** (String rule)
	1	public.......... **java.awt.Color**	**getBackground** (*javax.swing.text.AttributeSet* a)
		public... StyleSheet.BoxPainter	**getBoxPainter** (*javax.swing.text.AttributeSet* a)
		public.......................... ... *javax.swing.text.AttributeSet*	**getDeclaration** (String decl)
	1	public.......... **java.awt.Font**	**getFont** (*javax.swing.text.AttributeSet* a)
	1	public.......... **java.awt.Color**	**getForeground** (*javax.swing.text.AttributeSet* a)
△		public static ....int	**getIndexOfSize** (float pt)
		public... StyleSheet.ListPainter	**getListPainter** (*javax.swing.text.AttributeSet* a)
		public.......................float	**getPointSize** (int index)
		public.......................float	**getPointSize** (String size)
		public.....*javax.swing.text.Style*	**getRule** (String selector)
		public....*javax.swing.text.Style*	**getRule** (HTML.Tag t, *javax.swing.text.Element* e)
		public.......................... ... *javax.swing.text.AttributeSet*	**getViewAttributes** (javax.swing.text.View v)

Class   *Interface*   —extends   - - -implements   ○ abstract   ● final   △ static   ▲ static final   ✳ constructor   x x—inherited   x **x**—declared   **x x**—overridden

public	void	**loadRules** (java.io.Reader in, java.net.URL ref) throws java.io.IOException
public	void	**setBaseFontSize** (int sz)
public	void	**setBaseFontSize** (String size)
public	java.awt.Color	**stringToColor** (String str)
* public		**StyleSheet** ()
public		**translateHTMLToCSS** (*javax.swing.text.AttributeSet* htmlAttrSet)
... *javax.swing.text.AttributeSet*		

StyleSheet.BoxPainter · javax.swing.text.html

Object
1.2 └StyleSheet.BoxPainter - - - - - - - - - - - - - - - - - *java.io.Serializable*

public	float	**getInset** (int side, javax.swing.text.View v)
public	void	**paint** (java.awt.Graphics g, float x, float y, float w, float h, javax.swing.text.View v)

StyleSheet.ListPainter · javax.swing.text.html

Object
1.2 └StyleSheet.ListPainter - - - - - - - - - - - - - - - - - *java.io.Serializable*

public	void	**paint** (java.awt.Graphics g, float x, float y, float w, float h, javax.swing.text.View v, int item)

SwingConstants · javax.swing

1.2 *SwingConstants*

▲ public static final	int	**BOTTOM** = 3
▲ public static final	int	**CENTER** = 0
▲ public static final	int	**EAST** = 3
▲ public static final	int	**HORIZONTAL** = 0
▲ public static final	int	**LEADING** = 10
▲ public static final	int	**LEFT** = 2
▲ public static final	int	**NORTH** = 1
▲ public static final	int	**NORTH_EAST** = 2
▲ public static final	int	**NORTH_WEST** = 8
▲ public static final	int	**RIGHT** = 4
▲ public static final	int	**SOUTH** = 5
▲ public static final	int	**SOUTH_EAST** = 4
▲ public static final	int	**SOUTH_WEST** = 6
▲ public static final	int	**TOP** = 1
▲ public static final	int	**TRAILING** = 11
▲ public static final	int	**VERTICAL** = 1
▲ public static final	int	**WEST** = 7

SwingPropertyChangeSupport · javax.swing.event

Object
1.1 └java.beans.PropertyChangeSupport[1] - - - - - - - *java.io.Serializable*
1.2 ● └SwingPropertyChangeSupport

1	public synchronized	**void**	**addPropertyChangeListener** (*java.beans.PropertyChangeListener* listener)
1	public synchronized	**void**	**addPropertyChangeListener** (String propertyName, *java.beans.PropertyChangeListener* listener)
1	public	**void**	**firePropertyChange** (java.beans.PropertyChangeEvent evt)
1	public	void	firePropertyChange (String propertyName, int oldValue, int newValue)
1	public	void	firePropertyChange (String propertyName, boolean oldValue, boolean newValue)
1	public	**void**	**firePropertyChange** (String propertyName, Object oldValue, Object newValue)
1	public synchronized	**boolean**	**hasListeners** (String propertyName)
1	public synchronized	**void**	**removePropertyChangeListener** (*java.beans.PropertyChangeListener* listener)
1	public synchronized	**void**	**removePropertyChangeListener** (String propertyName, *java.beans.PropertyChangeListener* listener)
*	public		**SwingPropertyChangeSupport** (Object sourceBean)

S

Classes

SwingUtilities

		javax.swing

```
    Object
1.2  └SwingUtilities - - - - - - - - - - - - - - - - - - - - - - - - - SwingConstants
```

△	public static .... java.awt.Rectangle[]	**computeDifference** (java.awt.Rectangle rectA, java.awt.Rectangle rectB)
△	public static .... java.awt.Rectangle	**computeIntersection** (int x, int y, int width, int height, java.awt.Rectangle dest)
△	public static ....int	**computeStringWidth** (java.awt.FontMetrics fm, String str)
△	public static .... java.awt.Rectangle	**computeUnion** (int x, int y, int width, int height, java.awt.Rectangle dest)
△	public static .... java.awt.event.MouseEvent	**convertMouseEvent** (java. awt. Component source, java.awt.event.MouseEvent sourceEvent, java.awt.Component destination)
△	public static ..... java.awt.Point	**convertPoint** (java. awt. Component source, java. awt. Point aPoint, java.awt.Component destination)
△	public static ..... java.awt.Point	**convertPoint** (java. awt. Component source, int x, int y, java.awt.Component destination)
△	public static ....void	**convertPointFromScreen** (java.awt.Point p, java.awt.Component c)
△	public static ....void	**convertPointToScreen** (java.awt.Point p, java.awt.Component c)
△	public static .... java.awt.Rectangle	**convertRectangle** (java.awt.Component source, java.awt.Rectangle aRectangle, java.awt.Component destination)
△	public static .... java.awt.Component	**findFocusOwner** (java.awt.Component c)
△	public static .... javax.accessibility.Accessible	**getAccessibleAt** (java.awt.Component c, java.awt.Point p)
△	public static .... javax.accessibility.Accessible	**getAccessibleChild** (java.awt.Component c, int i)
△	public static ....int	**getAccessibleChildrenCount** (java.awt.Component c)
△	public static ....int	**getAccessibleIndexInParent** (java.awt.Component c)
△	public static .... javax.accessibility↵ .AccessibleStateSet	**getAccessibleStateSet** (java.awt.Component c)
△	public static java.awt.Container	**getAncestorNamed** (String name, java.awt.Component comp)
△	public static java.awt.Container	**getAncestorOfClass** (Class c, java.awt.Component comp)
△	public static .... java.awt.Component	**getDeepestComponentAt** (java.awt.Component parent, int x, int y)
△	public static .... java.awt.Rectangle	**getLocalBounds** (java.awt.Component aComponent)
△	public static .... java.awt.Component	**getRoot** (java.awt.Component c)
△	public static .... JRootPane	**getRootPane** (java.awt.Component c)
△	public static ....void	**invokeAndWait** (*Runnable* doRun) throws InterruptedException, java.lang.reflect.InvocationTargetException
△	public static ....void	**invokeLater** (*Runnable* doRun)
△	public static .... boolean	**isDescendingFrom** (java.awt.Component a, java.awt.Component b)
△	public static .... boolean	**isEventDispatchThread** ()
△	public static .... boolean	**isLeftMouseButton** (java.awt.event.MouseEvent anEvent)
△	public static .... boolean	**isMiddleMouseButton** (java.awt.event.MouseEvent anEvent)
▲	public static final ..... boolean	**isRectangleContainingRectangle** (java.awt.Rectangle a, java.awt.Rectangle b)
△	public static .... boolean	**isRightMouseButton** (java.awt.event.MouseEvent anEvent)
△	public static .... String	**layoutCompoundLabel** (java.awt.FontMetrics fm, String text, *Icon* icon, int verticalAlignment, int horizontalAlignment, int verticalTextPosition, int horizontalTextPosition, java.awt.Rectangle viewR, java.awt.Rectangle iconR, java.awt.Rectangle textR, int textIconGap)
△	public static .... String	**layoutCompoundLabel** (JComponent c, java.awt.FontMetrics fm, String text, *Icon* icon, int verticalAlignment, int horizontalAlignment, int verticalTextPosition, int horizontalTextPosition, java.awt.Rectangle viewR, java.awt.Rectangle iconR, java.awt.Rectangle textR, int textIconGap)
△	public static ....void	**paintComponent** (java. awt. Graphics g, java. awt. Component c, java.awt.Container p, java.awt.Rectangle r)
△	public static ....void	**paintComponent** (java. awt. Graphics g, java. awt. Component c, java.awt.Container p, int x, int y, int w, int h)
△	public static ....void	**updateComponentTreeUI** (java.awt.Component c)
△	public static .. java.awt.Window	**windowForComponent** (java.awt.Component aComponent)

S

Class *Interface* —extends - - -implements ○ abstract ● final △ static ▲ static final ✳ constructor x x—inherited x **x**—declared **x x**—overridden

SyncFailedException
java.io

```
Object
└Throwable ------------------------- Serializable
    └Exception
        └IOException
1.1          └SyncFailedException
```

*	public..........................	**SyncFailedException** (String desc)

System
java.lang

```
Object
●   └System
```
P

△	public static native.........void	**arraycopy** (Object src, int src_position, Object dst, int dst_position, int length)
△	public static native........ long	**currentTimeMillis** ()
▲	public static final..............	**err**
	.............java.io.PrintStream	
△	public static ....void	**exit** (int status)
△	public static ....void	**gc** ()
D △	public static ....String	**getenv** (String name)
△	public static java.util.Properties	**getProperties** ()
△	public static ....String	**getProperty** (String key)
△	public static ....String	**getProperty** (String key, String def)
△	public static . SecurityManager	**getSecurityManager** ()
1.1 △	public static native...........int	**identityHashCode** (Object x)
▲	public static final..............	**in**
	.............java.io.InputStream	
△	public static ....void	**load** (String filename)
△	public static ....void	**loadLibrary** (String libname)
1.2 △	public static native.......String	**mapLibraryName** (String libname)
▲	public static final..............	**out**
	.............java.io.PrintStream	
△	public static ....void	**runFinalization** ()
D △	public static ....void	**runFinalizersOnExit** (boolean value)
1.1 △	public static ....void	**setErr** (java.io.PrintStream err)
1.1 △	public static ....void	**setIn** (java.io.InputStream in)
1.1 △	public static ....void	**setOut** (java.io.PrintStream out)
△	public static ....void	**setProperties** (java.util.Properties props)
1.2 △	public static ....String	**setProperty** (String key, String value)
△	public static synchronized void	**setSecurityManager** (SecurityManager s)

S

SystemColor
java.awt

```
Object
└Color¹ -------------------------- Paint (Transparency), java.io.Serializable
1.1 ●   └SystemColor ----------------------- java.io.Serializable
```
P

	1	*36 inherited members from Color not shown*	
▲	public static final.............int	**ACTIVE_CAPTION** = 1
▲	public static final.............int	**ACTIVE_CAPTION_BORDER** = 3
▲	public static final.............int	**ACTIVE_CAPTION_TEXT** = 2
▲	public static final . SystemColor	**activeCaption**
▲	public static final . SystemColor	**activeCaptionBorder**
▲	public static final . SystemColor	**activeCaptionText**
▲	public static final . SystemColor	**control**
▲	public static final.............int	**CONTROL** = 17
▲	public static final.............int	**CONTROL_DK_SHADOW** = 22
▲	public static final.............int	**CONTROL_HIGHLIGHT** = 19
▲	public static final.............int	**CONTROL_LT_HIGHLIGHT** = 20
▲	public static final.............int	**CONTROL_SHADOW** = 21
▲	public static final.............int	**CONTROL_TEXT** = 18
▲	public static final . SystemColor	**controlDkShadow**
▲	public static final . SystemColor	**controlHighlight**
▲	public static final . SystemColor	**controlLtHighlight**
▲	public static final . SystemColor	**controlShadow**
▲	public static final . SystemColor	**controlText**
1.2 1	public........... *PaintContext*	**createContext** (java.awt.image.ColorModel cm, Rectangle r, java.awt.geom↵ .Rectangle2D r2d, java.awt.geom.AffineTransform xform, RenderingHints hints)
▲	public static final . SystemColor	**desktop**

Classes

SystemColor

▲		public static final............int	**DESKTOP** = 0
	1	public........................ **int**	**getRGB** ()
▲		public static final............int	**INACTIVE_CAPTION** = 4
▲		public static final............int	**INACTIVE_CAPTION_BORDER** = 6
▲		public static final............int	**INACTIVE_CAPTION_TEXT** = 5
▲		public static final . SystemColor	**inactiveCaption**
▲		public static final . SystemColor	**inactiveCaptionBorder**
▲		public static final . SystemColor	**inactiveCaptionText**
▲		public static final . SystemColor	**info**
▲		public static final............int	**INFO** = 24
▲		public static final............int	**INFO_TEXT** = 25
▲		public static final . SystemColor	**infoText**
▲		public static final . SystemColor	**menu**
▲		public static final............int	**MENU** = 10
▲		public static final............int	**MENU_TEXT** = 11
▲		public static final . SystemColor	**menuText**
▲		public static final............int	**NUM_COLORS** = 26
▲		public static final . SystemColor	**scrollbar**
▲		public static final............int	**SCROLLBAR** = 23
▲		public static final . SystemColor	**text**
▲		public static final............int	**TEXT** = 12
▲		public static final............int	**TEXT_HIGHLIGHT** = 14
▲		public static final............int	**TEXT_HIGHLIGHT_TEXT** = 15
▲		public static final............int	**TEXT_INACTIVE_TEXT** = 16
▲		public static final............int	**TEXT_TEXT** = 13
▲		public static final . SystemColor	**textHighlight**
▲		public static final . SystemColor	**textHighlightText**
▲		public static final . SystemColor	**textInactiveText**
▲		public static final . SystemColor	**textText**
	1	public.................... **String**	**toString** ()
▲		public static final . SystemColor	**window**
▲		public static final............int	**WINDOW** = 7
▲		public static final............int	**WINDOW_BORDER** = 8
▲		public static final............int	**WINDOW_TEXT** = 9
▲		public static final . SystemColor	**windowBorder**
▲		public static final . SystemColor	**windowText**

S

SystemException

org.omg.CORBA

```
Object
└Throwable 1 --------------------------- java.io.Serializable
   └Exception
      └RuntimeException
         └SystemException
```
1.2 ○

		public........CompletionStatus	**completed**
		public........................int	**minor**
✳		protected......................	**SystemException** (String reason, int minor, CompletionStatus completed)
	1	public.................. **String**	**toString** ()

SystemFlavorMap

java.awt.datatransfer

```
Object
└SystemFlavorMap ---------------------- FlavorMap 1
```
P

1.2 ●

△		public static .... DataFlavor	**decodeDataFlavor** (String atom) throws ClassNotFoundException
△		public static ....String	**decodeJavaMIMEType** (String atom)
△		public static ....String	**encodeDataFlavor** (DataFlavor df)
△		public static ....String	**encodeJavaMIMEType** (String mimeType)
△		public static ....FlavorMap	**getDefaultFlavorMap** ()
	1	public synchronized .... java.util.Map	**getFlavorsForNatives** (String[] natives)
	1	public synchronized .... java.util.Map	**getNativesForFlavors** (DataFlavor[] flavors)
△		public static .... boolean	**isJavaMIMEType** (String atom)

Class *Interface* —extends - - -implements ○ abstract ● final △ static ▲ static final ✳ constructor x x—inherited x **x**—declared **x x**—overridden

TabableView
javax.swing.text

1.2	*TabableView*	

	public	float	**getPartialSpan** (int p0, int p1)
	public	float	**getTabbedSpan** (float x, *TabExpander* e)

TabbedPaneUI
javax.swing.plaf

Object
	└ ComponentUI [1]
1.2 ○	
1.2 ○	└ TabbedPaneUI

	1	*11 inherited members from ComponentUI not shown*	
○		public abstract	**getTabBounds** (javax.swing.JTabbedPane pane, int index)
		.... java.awt.Rectangle	
○		public abstract .... int	**getTabRunCount** (javax.swing.JTabbedPane pane)
✳		public	**TabbedPaneUI** ()
○		public abstract .... int	**tabForCoordinate** (javax.swing.JTabbedPane pane, int x, int y)

TabExpander
javax.swing.text

1.2	*TabExpander*	

	public	float	**nextTabStop** (float x, int tabOffset)

TableCellEditor
javax.swing.table

1.2	*TableCellEditor*——————————————*javax.swing.CellEditor* [1]	

1	public	void	addCellEditorListener (*javax.swing.event.CellEditorListener* l)
1	public	void	cancelCellEditing ()
1	public	Object	getCellEditorValue ()
	public	java.awt.Component	**getTableCellEditorComponent** (javax.swing.JTable table, Object value, boolean isSelected, int row, int column)
1	public	boolean	isCellEditable (*java.util.EventObject* anEvent)
1	public	void	removeCellEditorListener (*javax.swing.event.CellEditorListener* l)
1	public	boolean	shouldSelectCell (*java.util.EventObject* anEvent)
1	public	boolean	stopCellEditing ()

TableCellRenderer
javax.swing.table

1.2	*TableCellRenderer*	

	public	java.awt.Component	**getTableCellRendererComponent** (javax.swing.JTable table, Object value, boolean isSelected, boolean hasFocus, int row, int column)

TableColumn
javax.swing.table

Object
	└ TableColumn - *java.io.Serializable*
1.2	

	public synchronized	void	**addPropertyChangeListener** (*java.beans.PropertyChangeListener* listener)
▲	public static final	String	**CELL_RENDERER_PROPERTY** = "cellRenderer"
	protected	*TableCellEditor*	**cellEditor**
	protected	*TableCellRenderer*	**cellRenderer**
▲	public static final	String	**COLUMN_WIDTH_PROPERTY** = "columWidth"
	protected	*TableCellRenderer*	**createDefaultHeaderRenderer** ()
	public	void	**disableResizedPosting** ()
	public	void	**enableResizedPosting** ()
	public	*TableCellEditor*	**getCellEditor** ()
	public	*TableCellRenderer*	**getCellRenderer** ()
	public	*TableCellRenderer*	**getHeaderRenderer** ()
	public	Object	**getHeaderValue** ()
	public	Object	**getIdentifier** ()
	public	int	**getMaxWidth** ()
	public	int	**getMinWidth** ()
	public	int	**getModelIndex** ()
	public	int	**getPreferredWidth** ()
	public	boolean	**getResizable** ()

T

Classes

TableColumn

	public....................int	**getWidth** ()
▲	public static final........String	**HEADER_RENDERER_PROPERTY** = "headerRenderer"
▲	public static final........String	**HEADER_VALUE_PROPERTY** = "headerValue"
	protected ... *TableCellRenderer*	**headerRenderer**
	protected................Object	**headerValue**
	protected................Object	**identifier**
	protected..............boolean	**isResizable**
	protected....................int	**maxWidth**
	protected....................int	**minWidth**
	protected....................int	**modelIndex**
	public synchronized ....void	**removePropertyChangeListener** (*java.beans.PropertyChangeListener* listener)
	protected transient...........int	**resizedPostingDisableCount**
	public.....................void	**setCellEditor** (*TableCellEditor* anEditor)
	public.....................void	**setCellRenderer** (*TableCellRenderer* aRenderer)
	public.....................void	**setHeaderRenderer** (*TableCellRenderer* aRenderer)
	public.....................void	**setHeaderValue** (Object aValue)
	public.....................void	**setIdentifier** (Object anIdentifier)
	public.....................void	**setMaxWidth** (int maxWidth)
	public.....................void	**setMinWidth** (int minWidth)
	public.....................void	**setModelIndex** (int anIndex)
	public.....................void	**setPreferredWidth** (int preferredWidth)
	public.....................void	**setResizable** (boolean flag)
	public.....................void	**setWidth** (int width)
	public.....................void	**sizeWidthToFit** ()
✳	public.....................	**TableColumn** ()
✳	public.....................	**TableColumn** (int modelIndex)
✳	public.....................	**TableColumn** (int modelIndex, int width)
✳	public.....................	**TableColumn** (int modelIndex, int width, *TableCellRenderer* cellRenderer, *TableCellEditor* cellEditor)
	protected....................int	**width**

TableColumnModel javax.swing.table

1.2   *TableColumnModel*

	public.....................void	**addColumn** (TableColumn aColumn)
	public.....................void	**addColumnModelListener** (*javax.swing.event.TableColumnModelListener* x)
	public...........TableColumn	**getColumn** (int columnIndex)
	public....................int	**getColumnCount** ()
	public....................int	**getColumnIndex** (Object columnIdentifier)
	public....................int	**getColumnIndexAtX** (int xPosition)
	public....................int	**getColumnMargin** ()
	public.... *java.util.Enumeration*	**getColumns** ()
	public..............boolean	**getColumnSelectionAllowed** ()
	public....................int	**getSelectedColumnCount** ()
	public...................int[]	**getSelectedColumns** ()
	public................... *javax.swing.ListSelectionModel*	**getSelectionModel** ()
	public....................int	**getTotalColumnWidth** ()
	public.....................void	**moveColumn** (int columnIndex, int newIndex)
	public.....................void	**removeColumn** (TableColumn column)
	public.....................void	**removeColumnModelListener** (*javax.swing.event.TableColumnModelListener* x)
	public.....................void	**setColumnMargin** (int newMargin)
	public.....................void	**setColumnSelectionAllowed** (boolean flag)
	public.....................void	**setSelectionModel** (*javax.swing.ListSelectionModel* newModel)

TableColumnModelEvent javax.swing.event

Object
1.1   └java.util.EventObject [1] -------------------- *java.io.Serializable*
1.2   └TableColumnModelEvent

	protected....................int	**fromIndex**
	public....................int	**getFromIndex** ()
1	public...................Object	getSource ()
	public....................int	**getToIndex** ()
1	protected transient......Object	source
✳	public.....................	**TableColumnModelEvent** (*javax.swing.table.TableColumnModel* source, int from, int to)
	protected....................int	**toIndex**

Class   *Interface*   —extends   - - -implements   ○ abstract   ● final   △ static   ▲ static final   ✳ constructor   x x—inherited   x **x**—declared   **x x**—overridden

1	public.....................	String	toString ()

TableColumnModelListener

1.2	*TableColumnModelListener* —————————— *java.util.EventListener*		

	public.......................	void	**columnAdded** (TableColumnModelEvent e)
	public.......................	void	**columnMarginChanged** (ChangeEvent e)
	public.......................	void	**columnMoved** (TableColumnModelEvent e)
	public.......................	void	**columnRemoved** (TableColumnModelEvent e)
	public.......................	void	**columnSelectionChanged** (ListSelectionEvent e)

TableHeaderUI

Object
1.2 ○	└ ComponentUI [1]	
1.2 ○	└ TableHeaderUI	

1	*11 inherited members from ComponentUI not shown*		
＊	public..........................		**TableHeaderUI** ()

TableModel

1.2	*TableModel*

	public.......................	void	**addTableModelListener** (*javax.swing.event.TableModelListener* l)
	public.......................	Class	**getColumnClass** (int columnIndex)
	public.......................	int	**getColumnCount** ()
	public.......................	String	**getColumnName** (int columnIndex)
	public.......................	int	**getRowCount** ()
	public.......................	Object	**getValueAt** (int rowIndex, int columnIndex)
	public.......................	boolean	**isCellEditable** (int rowIndex, int columnIndex)
	public.......................	void	**removeTableModelListener** (*javax.swing.event.TableModelListener* l)
	public.......................	void	**setValueAt** (Object aValue, int rowIndex, int columnIndex)

TableModelEvent

Object
1.1	└ java.util.EventObject [1] - - - - - - - - - - - - - - - - - - *java.io.Serializable*	
1.2	└ TableModelEvent	

▲	public static final.............	int	**ALL_COLUMNS** = -1
	protected......................	int	**column**
▲	public static final.............	int	**DELETE** = -1
	protected......................	int	**firstRow**
	public.......................	int	**getColumn** ()
	public.......................	int	**getFirstRow** ()
	public.......................	int	**getLastRow** ()
1	public.......................	Object	getSource ()
	public.......................	int	**getType** ()
▲	public static final.............	int	**HEADER_ROW** = -1
▲	public static final.............	int	**INSERT** = 1
	protected......................	int	**lastRow**
1	protected transient......	Object	source
＊	public........................		**TableModelEvent** (*javax.swing.table.TableModel* source)
＊	public........................		**TableModelEvent** (*javax.swing.table.TableModel* source, int row)
＊	public........................		**TableModelEvent** (*javax.swing.table.TableModel* source, int firstRow, int lastRow)
＊	public........................		**TableModelEvent** (*javax.swing.table.TableModel* source, int firstRow, int lastRow, int column)
＊	public........................		**TableModelEvent** (*javax.swing.table.TableModel* source, int firstRow, int lastRow, int column, int type)
1	public.......................	String	toString ()
	protected......................	int	**type**
▲	public static final.............	int	**UPDATE** = 0

TableModelListener

		javax.swing.event
1.2	*TableModelListener*————————————*java.util.EventListener*	
	public.....................void **tableChanged** (TableModelEvent e)	

TableUI		javax.swing.plaf
	Object	
1.2 ○	└ ComponentUI [1]	
1.2 ○	└ TableUI	
1	*11 inherited members from ComponentUI not shown*	
✳	public.......................... **TableUI** ()	

TableView		javax.swing.text
	Object	
1.2 ○	└ View [1] - *javax.swing.SwingConstants*	
1.2 ○	└ CompositeView [2]	
1.2	└ BoxView [3]	
1.2 ○	└ TableView	

	3	*30 inherited members from BoxView not shown*	
	2	public.....................void	append (View v)
	1	public..................... View	breakView (int axis, int offset, float pos, float len)
	3	protected .... **javax ↵**	**calculateMinorAxisRequirements** (int axis, javax.swing.SizeRequirements r)
		.swing.SizeRequirements	
	1	public.................... View	createFragment (int p0, int p1)
		protected . TableView.TableCell	**createTableCell** (*Element* elem)
		protected . TableView.TableRow	**createTableRow** (*Element* elem)
	1	public............. *AttributeSet*	getAttributes ()
●	2	protected final............short	getBottomInset ()
	1	public...........................int	getBreakWeight (int axis, float pos, float len)
	2	public......... *java.awt.Shape*	getChildAllocation (int index, *java.awt.Shape* a)
	1	public.......java.awt.Container	getContainer ()
	1	public............... *Document*	getDocument ()
	1	public.................. *Element*	getElement ()
	1	public...........................int	getEndOffset ()
	2	protected .. java.awt.Rectangle	getInsideAllocation (*java.awt.Shape* a)
●	2	protected final............short	getLeftInset ()
	2	protected ....int	getNextEastWestVisualPositionFrom (int pos, Position.Bias b, *java.awt.Shape* a,
			int direction, Position.Bias[] biasRet) throws BadLocationException
	2	protected ....int	getNextNorthSouthVisualPositionFrom (int pos, Position.Bias b, *java.awt.Shape* a,
			int direction, Position.Bias[] biasRet) throws BadLocationException
	2	public...........................int	getNextVisualPositionFrom (int pos, Position.Bias b, *java.awt.Shape* a, int direction,
			Position.Bias[] biasRet) throws BadLocationException
	1	public..................... View	getParent ()
●	2	protected final............short	getRightInset ()
	1	public...........................int	getStartOffset ()
●	2	protected final............short	getTopInset ()
	2	public..................... View	getView (int n)
	2	protected .... **View**	**getViewAtPosition** (int pos, java.awt.Rectangle a)
	2	public...........................int	getViewCount ()
	1	public............. *ViewFactory*	getViewFactory ()
	2	protected ....int	getViewIndexAtPosition (int pos)
	2	public.....................void	insert (int offs, View v)
	1	public.................. boolean	isVisible ()
		protected ....void	**layoutColumns** (int targetSpan, int[] offsets, int[] spans,
			javax.swing.SizeRequirements[] reqs)
	3	protected .... **void**	**layoutMinorAxis** (int targetSpan, int axis, int[] offsets, int[] spans)
	2	protected .... **void**	**loadChildren** (*ViewFactory* f)
	2	public......... *java.awt.Shape*	modelToView (int p0, Position.Bias b0, int p1, Position.Bias b1, *java.awt.Shape* a)
			throws BadLocationException
	2	public.....................void	removeAll ()
●	2	protected final.............void	setInsets (short top, short left, short bottom, short right)
●	2	protected final.............void	setParagraphInsets (*AttributeSet* attr)
	2	public.....................void	setParent (View parent)
✳		public.......................... **TableView** (*Element* elem)

Class *Interface* —extends - - -implements ○ abstract ● final △ static ▲ static final ✳ constructor x x—inherited x **x**—declared **x x**—overridden	

```
        Object
1.2 ○   └View 1 - - - - - - - - - - - - - - - - - - - - - - - - - - - - - javax.swing.SwingConstants
1.2 ○      └CompositeView 2
1.2            └BoxView 3
1.2               └TableView.TableCell - - - - - - - - - - - - - - - javax.swing.text.TableView.GridCell
```

	3	*31 inherited members from BoxView not shown*	
	2	public......................void	append (View v)
	1	public...................... View	breakView (int axis, int offset, float pos, float len)
	1	public...................... View	createFragment (int p0, int p1)
	1	public.............. *AttributeSet*	getAttributes ()
●	2	protected final............short	getBottomInset ()
	1	public........................int	getBreakWeight (int axis, float pos, float len)
	2	public.......... *java.awt.Shape*	getChildAllocation (int index, *java.awt.Shape* a)
		public........................int	**getColumnCount** ()
	1	public....... java.awt.Container	getContainer ()
	1	public................ *Document*	getDocument ()
	1	public................. *Element*	getElement ()
	1	public........................int	getEndOffset ()
		public........................int	**getGridColumn** ()
		public........................int	**getGridRow** ()
	2	protected.. java.awt.Rectangle	getInsideAllocation (*java.awt.Shape* a)
●	2	protected final............short	getLeftInset ()
	2	protected......................int	getNextEastWestVisualPositionFrom (int pos, Position.Bias b, *java.awt.Shape* a, int direction, Position.Bias[] biasRet) throws BadLocationException
	2	protected......................int	getNextNorthSouthVisualPositionFrom (int pos, Position.Bias b, *java.awt.Shape* a, int direction, Position.Bias[] biasRet) throws BadLocationException
	2	public,.......................int	getNextVisualPositionFrom (int pos, Position.Bias b, *java.awt.Shape* a, int direction, Position.Bias[] biasRet) throws BadLocationException
	1	public...................... View	getParent ()
	3	public................... **float getPreferredSpan** (int axis)
●	2	protected final............short	getRightInset ()
		public........................int	**getRowCount** ()
	1	public........................int	getStartOffset ()
●	2	protected final............short	getTopInset ()
	2	public...................... View	getView (int n)
	2	protected.................. View	getViewAtPosition (int pos, java.awt.Rectangle a)
	2	public........................int	getViewCount ()
	1	public.............. *ViewFactory*	getViewFactory ()
	2	protected......................int	getViewIndexAtPosition (int pos)
	2	public......................void	insert (int offs, View v)
	1	public............. boolean	isVisible ()
	2	protected..................void	loadChildren (*ViewFactory* f)
	2	public.......... *java.awt.Shape*	modelToView (int p0, Position.Bias b0, int p1, Position.Bias b1, *java.awt.Shape* a) throws BadLocationException
	2	public......................void	removeAll ()
		public......................void	**setGridLocation** (int row, int col)
●	2	protected final............void	setInsets (short top, short left, short bottom, short right)
●	2	protected final............void	setParagraphInsets (*AttributeSet* attr)
	2	public......................void	setParent (View parent)
✳		public..........................	**TableCell** (*Element* elem)

```
        Object
1.2 ○   └View 1 - - - - - - - - - - - - - - - - - - - - - - - - - - - - - javax.swing.SwingConstants
1.2 ○      └CompositeView 2
1.2            └BoxView 3
1.2               └TableView.TableRow
```

	3	*29 inherited members from BoxView not shown*	
	2	public......................void	append (View v)
	1	public...................... View	breakView (int axis, int offset, float pos, float len)
	1	public...................... View	createFragment (int p0, int p1)
	1	public.............. *AttributeSet*	getAttributes ()
●	2	protected final............short	getBottomInset ()
	1	public........................int	getBreakWeight (int axis, float pos, float len)
	2	public.......... *java.awt.Shape*	getChildAllocation (int index, *java.awt.Shape* a)
	1	public....... java.awt.Container	getContainer ()
	1	public................ *Document*	getDocument ()

TableView.TableRow

	1	public	*Element* **getElement** ()
	1	public	int **getEndOffset** ()
	2	protected .. java.awt.Rectangle	**getInsideAllocation** (*java.awt.Shape* a)
●	2	protected final	short **getLeftInset** ()
	2	protected	int **getNextEastWestVisualPositionFrom** (int pos, Position.Bias b, *java.awt.Shape* a, int direction, Position.Bias[] biasRet) throws BadLocationException
	2	protected	int **getNextNorthSouthVisualPositionFrom** (int pos, Position.Bias b, *java.awt.Shape* a, int direction, Position.Bias[] biasRet) throws BadLocationException
	2	public	int **getNextVisualPositionFrom** (int pos, Position.Bias b, *java.awt.Shape* a, int direction, Position.Bias[] biasRet) throws BadLocationException
	1	public	View **getParent** ()
	3	public	**int getResizeWeight** (int axis)
●	2	protected final	short **getRightInset** ()
	1	public	int **getStartOffset** ()
●	2	protected final	short **getTopInset** ()
	2	public	View **getView** (int n)
	2	protected	**View getViewAtPosition** (int pos, java.awt.Rectangle a)
	2	public	int **getViewCount** ()
	1	public	*ViewFactory* **getViewFactory** ()
	2	protected	int **getViewIndexAtPosition** (int pos)
	2	public	void **insert** (int offs, View v)
	1	public	boolean **isVisible** ()
	3	protected	**void layoutMajorAxis** (int targetSpan, int axis, int[] offsets, int[] spans)
	3	protected	**void layoutMinorAxis** (int targetSpan, int axis, int[] offsets, int[] spans)
	2	protected	**void loadChildren** (*ViewFactory* f)
	2	public	*java.awt.Shape* **modelToView** (int p0, Position.Bias b0, int p1, Position.Bias b1, *java.awt.Shape* a) throws BadLocationException
	2	public	void **removeAll** ()
●	2	protected final	void **setInsets** (short top, short left, short bottom, short right)
●	2	protected final	void **setParagraphInsets** (*AttributeSet* attr)
	2	public	void **setParent** (View parent)
✻		public	**TableRow** (*Element* elem)

TabSet — javax.swing.text

Object [1]
└TabSet - *java.io.Serializable*   1.2

		public	TabStop **getTab** (int index)
		public	TabStop **getTabAfter** (float location)
		public	int **getTabCount** ()
		public	int **getTabIndex** (TabStop tab)
		public	int **getTabIndexAfter** (float location)
✻		public	**TabSet** (TabStop[] tabs)
	1	public	**String toString** ()

TabStop — javax.swing.text

Object [1]
└TabStop - *java.io.Serializable*   1.2

▲		public static final	int **ALIGN_BAR** = 5
▲		public static final	int **ALIGN_CENTER** = 2
▲		public static final	int **ALIGN_DECIMAL** = 4
▲		public static final	int **ALIGN_LEFT** = 0
▲		public static final	int **ALIGN_RIGHT** = 1
	1	public	**boolean equals** (Object other)
		public	int **getAlignment** ()
		public	int **getLeader** ()
		public	float **getPosition** ()
	1	public	**int hashCode** ()
▲		public static final	int **LEAD_DOTS** = 1
▲		public static final	int **LEAD_EQUALS** = 5
▲		public static final	int **LEAD_HYPHENS** = 2
▲		public static final	int **LEAD_NONE** = 0
▲		public static final	int **LEAD_THICKLINE** = 4
▲		public static final	int **LEAD_UNDERLINE** = 3
✻		public	**TabStop** (float pos)
✻		public	**TabStop** (float pos, int align, int leader)

Class   *Interface*   —extends   - - -implements   O abstract   ● final   △ static   ▲ static final   ✻ constructor   x x—inherited   x **x**—declared   **x x**—overridden

1	public	String **toString** ()

TagElement

1.2
```
Object
  └ TagElement
```

	public	boolean	**breaksFlow** ()
	public	boolean	**fictional** ()
	public	Element	**getElement** ()
	public	javax ←	**getHTMLTag** ()
	.swing.text.html.HTML.Tag		
	public	boolean	**isPreformatted** ()
*	public		**TagElement** (Element elem)
*	public		**TagElement** (Element elem, boolean fictional)

TCKind

1.2
```
Object
  └ TCKind
```

▲	public static final	int	**_tk_abstract_interface**	= 32
▲	public static final	int	**_tk_alias**	= 21
▲	public static final	int	**_tk_any**	= 11
▲	public static final	int	**_tk_array**	= 20
▲	public static final	int	**_tk_boolean**	= 8
▲	public static final	int	**_tk_char**	= 9
▲	public static final	int	**_tk_double**	= 7
▲	public static final	int	**_tk_enum**	= 17
▲	public static final	int	**_tk_except**	= 22
▲	public static final	int	**_tk_fixed**	= 28
▲	public static final	int	**_tk_float**	= 6
▲	public static final	int	**_tk_long**	= 3
▲	public static final	int	**_tk_longdouble**	= 25
▲	public static final	int	**_tk_longlong**	= 23
▲	public static final	int	**_tk_native**	= 31
▲	public static final	int	**_tk_null**	= 0
▲	public static final	int	**_tk_objref**	= 14
▲	public static final	int	**_tk_octet**	= 10
▲	public static final	int	**_tk_Principal**	= 13
▲	public static final	int	**_tk_sequence**	= 19
▲	public static final	int	**_tk_short**	= 2
▲	public static final	int	**_tk_string**	= 18
▲	public static final	int	**_tk_struct**	= 15
▲	public static final	int	**_tk_TypeCode**	= 12
▲	public static final	int	**_tk_ulong**	= 5
▲	public static final	int	**_tk_ulonglong**	= 24
▲	public static final	int	**_tk_union**	= 16
▲	public static final	int	**_tk_ushort**	= 4
▲	public static final	int	**_tk_value**	= 29
▲	public static final	int	**_tk_value_box**	= 30
▲	public static final	int	**_tk_void**	= 1
▲	public static final	int	**_tk_wchar**	= 26
▲	public static final	int	**_tk_wstring**	= 27
△	public static	TCKind	**from_int** (int i) throws BAD_PARAM	
*	protected		**TCKind** (int _value)	
▲	public static final	TCKind	**tk_abstract_interface**	
▲	public static final	TCKind	**tk_alias**	
▲	public static final	TCKind	**tk_any**	
▲	public static final	TCKind	**tk_array**	
▲	public static final	TCKind	**tk_boolean**	
▲	public static final	TCKind	**tk_char**	
▲	public static final	TCKind	**tk_double**	
▲	public static final	TCKind	**tk_enum**	
▲	public static final	TCKind	**tk_except**	
▲	public static final	TCKind	**tk_fixed**	
▲	public static final	TCKind	**tk_float**	
▲	public static final	TCKind	**tk_long**	
▲	public static final	TCKind	**tk_longdouble**	
▲	public static final	TCKind	**tk_longlong**	
▲	public static final	TCKind	**tk_native**	
▲	public static final	TCKind	**tk_null**	

T

Classes

TCKind

▲	public static final	TCKind	**tk_objref**
▲	public static final	TCKind	**tk_octet**
▲	public static final	TCKind	**tk_Principal**
▲	public static final	TCKind	**tk_sequence**
▲	public static final	TCKind	**tk_short**
▲	public static final	TCKind	**tk_string**
▲	public static final	TCKind	**tk_struct**
▲	public static final	TCKind	**tk_TypeCode**
▲	public static final	TCKind	**tk_ulong**
▲	public static final	TCKind	**tk_ulonglong**
▲	public static final	TCKind	**tk_union**
▲	public static final	TCKind	**tk_ushort**
▲	public static final	TCKind	**tk_value**
▲	public static final	TCKind	**tk_value_box**
▲	public static final	TCKind	**tk_void**
▲	public static final	TCKind	**tk_wchar**
▲	public static final	TCKind	**tk_wstring**
	public	int	**value** ()

TextAction   javax.swing.text

Object
1.2 ○ └─javax.swing.AbstractAction [1] - - - - - - - - - - - - - *javax.swing.Action* (*java.awt.event.ActionListener*
                                                                (*java.util.EventListener*)), *Cloneable*, *java.io.Serializable*
1.2 ○   └─TextAction

○	1	public abstract .... void	actionPerformed (*java.awt.event.ActionEvent*)
	1	public synchronized .... void	addPropertyChangeListener (*java.beans.PropertyChangeListener* listener)
▲		public static final	**augmentList** (*javax.swing.Action[]* list1, *javax.swing.Action[]* list2)
		.... *javax.swing.Action[]*	
	1	protected . java.swing.event ↩	changeSupport
		.SwingPropertyChangeSupport	
	1	protected .... Object	clone () throws CloneNotSupportedException
	1	protected .... boolean	enabled
	1	protected .... void	firePropertyChange (String propertyName, Object oldValue, Object newValue)
●		protected final	**getFocusedComponent** ()
		.... JTextComponent	
●		protected final	**getTextComponent** (java.awt.event.ActionEvent e)
		.... JTextComponent	
	1	public .... Object	getValue (String key)
	1	public .... boolean	isEnabled ()
	1	public synchronized ...... void	putValue (String key, Object newValue)
	1	public synchronized ...... void	removePropertyChangeListener (*java.beans.PropertyChangeListener* listener)
	1	public synchronized ...... void	setEnabled (boolean newValue)
✳		public	**TextAction** (String name)

TextArea   java.awt
                                                                                          P

Object
○ └─Component [1] - *java.awt.image.ImageObserver*, *MenuContainer*,
                                                                       java.io.Serializable
      └─TextComponent [2]
         └─TextArea

	1	*154 inherited members from Component not shown*	
	1	public .... **void**	**addNotify** ()
1.1	2	public synchronized ...... void	addTextListener (*java.awt.event.TextListener* l)
1.1		public .... void	**append** (String str)
D		public synchronized ...... void	**appendText** (String str)
1.1	2	public synchronized .... int	getCaretPosition ()
		public .... int	**getColumns** ()
1.1	1	public .... **Dimension**	**getMinimumSize** ()
1.1		public .... Dimension	**getMinimumSize** (int rows, int columns)
1.1	1	public .... **Dimension**	**getPreferredSize** ()
1.1		public .... Dimension	**getPreferredSize** (int rows, int columns)
		public .... int	**getRows** ()
1.1		public .... int	**getScrollbarVisibility** ()
	2	public synchronized ..... String	getSelectedText ()
	2	public synchronized .... int	getSelectionEnd ()

Class *Interface* —extends - - -implements ○ abstract ● final △ static ▲ static final ✳ constructor x x—inherited x **x**—declared **x x**—overridden

	2	public synchronized	.........int	getSelectionStart ()
	2	public synchronized	.....String	getText ()
1.1		public	.............void	**insert** (String str, int pos)
D		public synchronized	.......void	**insertText** (String str, int pos)
	2	public	.... boolean	isEditable ()
D	1	public	**Dimension**	**minimumSize** ()
D		public	.Dimension	**minimumSize** (int rows, int columns)
	2	protected	**String**	**paramString** ()
D	1	public	**Dimension**	**preferredSize** ()
D		public	.Dimension	**preferredSize** (int rows, int columns)
1.1	2	protected	.......void	processEvent (AWTEvent e)
1.1	2	protected	.......void	processTextEvent (java.awt.event.TextEvent e)
	2	public	.......void	removeNotify ()
1.1	2	public synchronized	.......void	removeTextListener (*java.awt.event.TextListener* l)
1.1		public	.......void	**replaceRange** (String str, int start, int end)
D		public synchronized	.......void	**replaceText** (String str, int start, int end)
1.1	▲	public static final	............int	**SCROLLBARS_BOTH** = 0
1.1	▲	public static final	............int	**SCROLLBARS_HORIZONTAL_ONLY** = 2
1.1	▲	public static final	............int	**SCROLLBARS_NONE** = 3
1.1	▲	public static final	............int	**SCROLLBARS_VERTICAL_ONLY** = 1
	2	public synchronized	.......void	select (int selectionStart, int selectionEnd)
	2	public synchronized	.......void	selectAll ()
1.1	2	public synchronized	.......void	setCaretPosition (int position)
1.1		public	.......void	**setColumns** (int columns)
	2	public synchronized	.......void	setEditable (boolean b)
1.1		public	.......void	**setRows** (int rows)
1.1	2	public synchronized	.......void	setSelectionEnd (int selectionEnd)
1.1	2	public synchronized	.......void	setSelectionStart (int selectionStart)
	2	public synchronized	.......void	setText (String t)
	*	public	....	**TextArea** ()
	*	public	....	**TextArea** (String text)
	*	public	....	**TextArea** (int rows, int columns)
	*	public	....	**TextArea** (String text, int rows, int columns)
1.1	*	public	....	**TextArea** (String text, int rows, int columns, int scrollbars)
1.1	2	protected transient	....	textListener
		.... *java.awt.event.TextListener*		

TextAreaPeer | java.awt.peer

TextAreaPeer————————————————————TextComponentPeer [1] (ComponentPeer [2])

	2	*32 inherited members from ComponentPeer not shown*		
	1	*8 inherited members from TextComponentPeer not shown*		
1.1		public	java.awt.Dimension	**getMinimumSize** (int, int)
1.1		public	java.awt.Dimension	**getPreferredSize** (int, int)
1.1		public	.......void	**insert** (String, int)
		public	.......void	**insertText** (String, int)
		public	java.awt.Dimension	**minimumSize** (int, int)
		public	java.awt.Dimension	**preferredSize** (int, int)
1.1		public	.......void	**replaceRange** (String, int, int)
		public	.......void	**replaceText** (String, int, int)

TextAttribute | java.awt.font

Object
1.2		└java.text.AttributedCharacterIterator ↩ - - - - - - *java.io.Serializable*
		.Attribute [1]
1.2	●	└TextAttribute

▲		public static final	. TextAttribute	**BACKGROUND**
▲		public static final	. TextAttribute	**BIDI_EMBEDDING**
▲		public static final	. TextAttribute	**CHAR_REPLACEMENT**
●	1	public final	...........boolean	equals (Object obj)
▲		public static final	. TextAttribute	**FAMILY**
▲		public static final	. TextAttribute	**FONT**
▲		public static final	. TextAttribute	**FOREGROUND**
	1	protected	...........String	getName ()
●	1	public final	............int	hashCode ()
▲		public static final	. TextAttribute	**INPUT_METHOD_HIGHLIGHT**
▲		public static final	. TextAttribute	**JUSTIFICATION**
▲		public static final	. Float	**JUSTIFICATION_FULL** = new Float(1.0)
▲		public static final	. Float	**JUSTIFICATION_NONE** = new Float(0.0)

T

TextAttribute

▲	public static final .	TextAttribute	**POSTURE**	
▲	public static final	Float	**POSTURE_OBLIQUE**	= new Float(0.2)
▲	public static final	Float	**POSTURE_REGULAR**	= new Float(0.0)
	1 protected	**Object**	**readResolve** () throws java.io.InvalidObjectException	
▲	public static final .	TextAttribute	**RUN_DIRECTION**	
▲	public static final	Boolean	**RUN_DIRECTION_LTR**	= new Boolean(false)
▲	public static final	Boolean	**RUN_DIRECTION_RTL**	= new Boolean(true)
▲	public static final .	TextAttribute	**SIZE**	
▲	public static final .	TextAttribute	**STRIKETHROUGH**	
▲	public static final	Boolean	**STRIKETHROUGH_ON**	= new Boolean(true)
▲	public static final .	TextAttribute	**SUPERSCRIPT**	
▲	public static final	Integer	**SUPERSCRIPT_SUB**	= new Integer(-1)
▲	public static final	Integer	**SUPERSCRIPT_SUPER**	= new Integer(1)
▲	public static final .	TextAttribute	**SWAP_COLORS**	
▲	public static final	Boolean	**SWAP_COLORS_ON**	= new Boolean(true)
✳	protected		**TextAttribute** (String name)	
	1 public	String	toString ()	
▲	public static final .	TextAttribute	**TRANSFORM**	
▲	public static final .	TextAttribute	**UNDERLINE**	
▲	public static final	Integer	**UNDERLINE_ON**	= new Integer(0)
▲	public static final .	TextAttribute	**WEIGHT**	
▲	public static final	Float	**WEIGHT_BOLD**	= new Float(2.0)
▲	public static final	Float	**WEIGHT_DEMIBOLD**	= new Float(1.75)
▲	public static final	Float	**WEIGHT_DEMILIGHT**	= new Float(0.875)
▲	public static final	Float	**WEIGHT_EXTRA_LIGHT**	= new Float(0.5)
▲	public static final	Float	**WEIGHT_EXTRABOLD**	= new Float(2.5)
▲	public static final	Float	**WEIGHT_HEAVY**	= new Float(2.25)
▲	public static final	Float	**WEIGHT_LIGHT**	= new Float(0.75)
▲	public static final	Float	**WEIGHT_MEDIUM**	= new Float(1.5)
▲	public static final	Float	**WEIGHT_REGULAR**	= new Float(1.0)
▲	public static final	Float	**WEIGHT_SEMIBOLD**	= new Float(1.25)
▲	public static final	Float	**WEIGHT_ULTRABOLD**	= new Float(2.75)
▲	public static final .	TextAttribute	**WIDTH**	
▲	public static final	Float	**WIDTH_CONDENSED**	= new Float(0.75)
▲	public static final	Float	**WIDTH_EXTENDED**	= new Float(1.5)
▲	public static final	Float	**WIDTH_REGULAR**	= new Float(1.0)
▲	public static final	Float	**WIDTH_SEMI_CONDENSED**	= new Float(0.875)
▲	public static final	Float	**WIDTH_SEMI_EXTENDED**	= new Float(1.25)

TextComponent   java.awt

```
    Object
○   └─Component¹ - - - - - - - - - - - - - - - - - - - - - - - - - java.awt.image.ImageObserver, MenuContainer,
                                                                  java.io.Serializable
      └─TextComponent
```

	1	*159 inherited members from Component not shown*	
1.1	public synchronized	void	**addTextListener** (*java.awt.event.TextListener* l)
1.1	public synchronized	int	**getCaretPosition** ()
	public synchronized	String	**getSelectedText** ()
	public synchronized	int	**getSelectionEnd** ()
	public synchronized	int	**getSelectionStart** ()
	public synchronized	String	**getText** ()
	public	boolean	**isEditable** ()
	1 protected	**String**	**paramString** ()
1.1	1 protected	**void**	**processEvent** (AWTEvent e)
1.1	protected	**void**	**processTextEvent** (java.awt.event.TextEvent e)
	1 public	**void**	**removeNotify** ()
1.1	public synchronized	void	**removeTextListener** (*java.awt.event.TextListener* l)
	public synchronized	void	**select** (int selectionStart, int selectionEnd)
	public synchronized	void	**selectAll** ()
1.1	public synchronized	void	**setCaretPosition** (int position)
	public synchronized	void	**setEditable** (boolean b)
1.1	public synchronized	void	**setSelectionEnd** (int selectionEnd)
1.1	public synchronized	void	**setSelectionStart** (int selectionStart)
	public synchronized	void	**setText** (String t)
1.1	protected transient............		**textListener**
	.... *java.awt.event.TextListener*		

Class   *Interface*   —extends   - - -implements   ○ abstract   ● final   △ static   ▲ static final   ✳ constructor   x x—inherited   x **x**—declared   **x x**—overridden

TextComponentPeer

java.awt.peer

TextComponentPeer————————————ComponentPeer[1]

	1	*32 inherited members from ComponentPeer not shown*
1.1	public.........................int	**getCaretPosition** ()
	public.........................int	**getSelectionEnd** ()
	public.........................int	**getSelectionStart** ()
	public.....................String	**getText** ()
	public.......................void	**select** (int, int)
1.1	public.......................void	**setCaretPosition** (int)
	public.......................void	**setEditable** (boolean)
	public.......................void	**setText** (String)

TextEvent

java.awt.event

P

Object
  └java.util.EventObject[1] - - - - - - - - - - - - - - - - - - - *java.io.Serializable*
1.1
1.1 ○   └java.awt.AWTEvent[2]
1.1   └TextEvent

	2	protected...................void consume ()
	2	protected............. boolean consumed
	2	protected...................void finalize () throws Throwable
	2	public.........................int getID ()
	1	public....................Object getSource ()
	2	protected.....................int id
	2	protected............. boolean isConsumed ()
	2	public................. **String paramString** ()
	1	protected transient......Object source
▲		public static final.............int **TEXT_FIRST** = 900
▲		public static final.............int **TEXT_LAST** = 900
▲		public static final.............int **TEXT_VALUE_CHANGED** = 900
＊		public...................... **TextEvent** (Object source, int id)
	2	public....................String toString ()

TextField

java.awt

P

Object
○ └Component[1] - *java.awt.image.ImageObserver*, *MenuContainer*,
                                         java.io.Serializable
    └TextComponent[2]
      └TextField

	1	*154 inherited members from Component not shown*
1.1		public synchronized ....void **addActionListener** (*java.awt.event.ActionListener* l)
	1	public..................... **void addNotify** ()
1.1	2	public synchronized ....void addTextListener (*java.awt.event.TextListener* l)
		public................. boolean **echoCharIsSet** ()
1.1	2	public synchronized ....int getCaretPosition ()
		public.........................int **getColumns** ()
		public..................... char **getEchoChar** ()
1.1	1	public.............. **Dimension getMinimumSize** ()
1.1		public.............Dimension **getMinimumSize** (int columns)
1.1	1	public.............. **Dimension getPreferredSize** ()
1.1		public.............Dimension **getPreferredSize** (int columns)
	2	public synchronized .....String getSelectedText ()
	2	public synchronized ....int getSelectionEnd ()
	2	public synchronized ....int getSelectionStart ()
	2	public synchronized .....String getText ()
	2	public................. boolean isEditable ()
D	1	public.............. **Dimension minimumSize** ()
D		public.............Dimension **minimumSize** (int columns)
	2	protected .... **String paramString** ()
D	1	public.............. **Dimension preferredSize** ()
D		public.............Dimension **preferredSize** (int columns)
1.1		protected ....void **processActionEvent** (java.awt.event.ActionEvent e)
1.1	2	protected .... **void processEvent** (AWTEvent e)
1.1	2	protected ....void processTextEvent (java.awt.event.TextEvent e)
1.1		public synchronized ....void **removeActionListener** (*java.awt.event.ActionListener* l)
	2	public.......................void removeNotify ()
1.1	2	public synchronized ....void removeTextListener (*java.awt.event.TextListener* l)

TextField

	2	public synchronized ....void	**select** (int selectionStart, int selectionEnd)
	2	public synchronized ....void	**selectAll** ()
1.1	2	public synchronized ....void	**setCaretPosition** (int position)
1.1		public synchronized ....void	**setColumns** (int columns)
1.1		public.........................void	**setEchoChar** (char c)
D		public synchronized ....void	**setEchoCharacter** (char c)
	2	public synchronized ....void	**setEditable** (boolean b)
1.1	2	public synchronized ....void	**setSelectionEnd** (int selectionEnd)
1.1	2	public synchronized ....void	**setSelectionStart** (int selectionStart)
	2	public......................**void**	**setText** (String t)
✳		public.........................	**TextField** ()
✳		public.........................	**TextField** (int columns)
✳		public.........................	**TextField** (String text)
✳		public.........................	**TextField** (String text, int columns)
1.1	2	protected transient.............	textListener
		.... *java.awt.event.TextListener*	

TextFieldPeer   java.awt.peer

TextFieldPeer————————————— *TextComponentPeer [1]* (*ComponentPeer [2]*)

	2	*32 inherited members from ComponentPeer not shown*	
	1	*8 inherited members from TextComponentPeer not shown*	
1.1		public......java.awt.Dimension	**getMinimumSize** (int)
1.1		public......java.awt.Dimension	**getPreferredSize** (int)
		public......java.awt.Dimension	**minimumSize** (int)
		public......java.awt.Dimension	**preferredSize** (int)
1.1		public......................void	**setEchoChar** (char)
		public......................void	**setEchoCharacter** (char)

TextHitInfo   java.awt.font

Object [1]
└ TextHitInfo

△		public static ....TextHitInfo	**afterOffset** (int offset)
△		public static ....TextHitInfo	**beforeOffset** (int offset)
		public................... boolean	**equals** (TextHitInfo hitInfo)
	1	public................. **boolean**	**equals** (Object obj)
		public........................int	**getCharIndex** ()
		public........................int	**getInsertionIndex** ()
		public...............TextHitInfo	**getOffsetHit** (int delta)
		public...............TextHitInfo	**getOtherHit** ()
	1	public..................... **int**	**hashCode** ()
		public................... boolean	**isLeadingEdge** ()
△		public static ....TextHitInfo	**leading** (int charIndex)
	1	public................. **String**	**toString** ()
△		public static ....TextHitInfo	**trailing** (int charIndex)

TextLayout   java.awt.font

Object [1]
└ TextLayout - *Cloneable*

▲	1	protected ....**Object**	**clone** ()
		public static final...............	**DEFAULT_CARET_POLICY**
		.... TextLayout.CaretPolicy	
		public......................void	**draw** (java.awt.Graphics2D g2, float x, float y)
		public................. boolean	**equals** (TextLayout rhs)
	1	public................. **boolean**	**equals** (Object obj)
		public.......................float	**getAdvance** ()
		public.......................float	**getAscent** ()
		public....................... byte	**getBaseline** ()
		public.....................float[]	**getBaselineOffsets** ()
		public......... *java.awt.Shape*	**getBlackBoxBounds** (int firstEndpoint, int secondEndpoint)
		public.........................	**getBounds** ()
		... java.awt.geom.Rectangle2D	
		public.....................float[]	**getCaretInfo** (TextHitInfo hit)
		public.....................float[]	**getCaretInfo** (TextHitInfo hit, java.awt.geom.Rectangle2D bounds)

Class   *Interface*   —extends   - - -implements   ○ abstract   ● final   △ static   ▲ static final   ✳ constructor   x x—inherited   x **x**—declared   **x x**—overridden

658

public	java.awt.Shape	**getCaretShape**	(TextHitInfo hit)
public	java.awt.Shape	**getCaretShape**	(TextHitInfo hit, java.awt.geom.Rectangle2D bounds)
public	java.awt.Shape[]	**getCaretShapes**	(int offset)
public	java.awt.Shape[]	**getCaretShapes**	(int offset, java.awt.geom.Rectangle2D bounds)
public	java.awt.Shape[]	**getCaretShapes**	(int offset, java. awt. geom. Rectangle2D bounds, TextLayout.CaretPolicy policy)
public	int	**getCharacterCount**	()
public	byte	**getCharacterLevel**	(int index)
public	float	**getDescent**	()
public	TextLayout	**getJustifiedLayout**	(float justificationWidth)
public	float	**getLeading**	()
public	java.awt.Shape	**getLogicalHighlightShape**	(int firstEndpoint, int secondEndpoint)
public	java.awt.Shape	**getLogicalHighlightShape**	(int firstEndpoint, int secondEndpoint, java.awt.geom.Rectangle2D bounds)
public	int[]	**getLogicalRangesForVisualSelection**	(TextHitInfo firstEndpoint, TextHitInfo secondEndpoint)
public	TextHitInfo	**getNextLeftHit**	(int offset)
public	TextHitInfo	**getNextLeftHit**	(TextHitInfo hit)
public	TextHitInfo	**getNextLeftHit**	(int offset, TextLayout.CaretPolicy policy)
public	TextHitInfo	**getNextRightHit**	(int offset)
public	TextHitInfo	**getNextRightHit**	(TextHitInfo hit)
public	TextHitInfo	**getNextRightHit**	(int offset, TextLayout.CaretPolicy policy)
public	java.awt.Shape	**getOutline**	(java.awt.geom.AffineTransform tx)
public	float	**getVisibleAdvance**	()
public	java.awt.Shape	**getVisualHighlightShape**	(TextHitInfo firstEndpoint, TextHitInfo secondEndpoint)
public	java.awt.Shape	**getVisualHighlightShape**	(TextHitInfo firstEndpoint, TextHitInfo secondEndpoint, java.awt.geom.Rectangle2D bounds)
public	TextHitInfo	**getVisualOtherHit**	(TextHitInfo hit)
protected	void	**handleJustify**	(float justificationWidth)
1 public	int	**hashCode**	()
public	TextHitInfo	**hitTestChar**	(float x, float y)
public	TextHitInfo	**hitTestChar**	(float x, float y, java.awt.geom.Rectangle2D bounds)
public	boolean	**isLeftToRight**	()
public	boolean	**isVertical**	()
* public		**TextLayout**	(java.text.AttributedCharacterIterator text, FontRenderContext frc)
* public		**TextLayout**	(String string, java.awt.Font font, FontRenderContext frc)
* public		**TextLayout**	(String string, java.util.Map attributes, FontRenderContext frc)
1 public	String	**toString**	()

TextLayout.CaretPolicy — java.awt.font

```
    Object
1.2   └ TextLayout.CaretPolicy
```

* public		**CaretPolicy**	()
public	TextHitInfo	**getStrongCaret**	(TextHitInfo hit1, TextHitInfo hit2, TextLayout layout)

TextListener — java.awt.event

1.1 *TextListener* —————————————— *java.util.EventListener* P

public	void	**textValueChanged**	(TextEvent e)

TextUI — javax.swing.plaf

```
    Object
1.2 ○  └ ComponentUI 1
1.2 ○    └ TextUI
```

1 *11 inherited members from ComponentUI not shown*

○ public abstract	void	**damageRange**	(javax.swing.text.JTextComponent t, int p0, int p1)
○ public abstract	void	**damageRange**	(javax.swing.text.JTextComponent t, int p0, int p1, javax.swing↵.text.Position.Bias firstBias, javax.swing.text.Position.Bias secondBias)
○ public abstract	javax.swing.text.EditorKit	**getEditorKit**	(javax.swing.text.JTextComponent t)
○ public abstract	int	**getNextVisualPositionFrom**	(javax.swing.text.JTextComponent t, int pos, javax.swing.text.Position.Bias b, int direction, javax.swing.text.Position.Bias[] biasRet) throws javax.swing.text.BadLocationException
○ public abstract	javax.swing.text.View	**getRootView**	(javax.swing.text.JTextComponent t)

TextUI

○	public abstract . . . . java.awt.Rectangle	**modelToView** (javax. swing. text. JTextComponent t, int pos) throws javax.swing.text.BadLocationException
○	public abstract . . . . java.awt.Rectangle	**modelToView** (javax.swing.text.JTextComponent t, int pos, javax.swing.text↵ .Position.Bias bias) throws javax.swing.text.BadLocationException
∗	public	**TextUI** ()
○	public abstract . . . . int	**viewToModel** (javax.swing.text.JTextComponent t, java.awt.Point pt)
○	public abstract . . . . int	**viewToModel** (javax. swing. text. JTextComponent t, java. awt. Point pt, javax.swing.text.Position.Bias[] biasReturn)

TexturePaint — java.awt

P

Object
 1.2   └ TexturePaint - *Paint* [1] (*Transparency* [2])

1	public . . . . *PaintContext*	**createContext** (java.awt.image.ColorModel cm, Rectangle deviceBounds, java.awt.geom.Rectangle2D userBounds, java.awt.geom.AffineTransform xform, RenderingHints hints)
	public	**getAnchorRect** ()
	. . . java.awt.geom.Rectangle2D	
	public . . . . java.awt.image.BufferedImage	**getImage** ()
2	public . . . . : . . int	**getTransparency** ()
∗	public	**TexturePaint** (java. awt. image. BufferedImage txtr, java.awt.geom.Rectangle2D anchor)

Thread — java.lang

P

Object[1]
 └ Thread - *Runnable* [2]

	△	public static . . . . int	**activeCount** ()
	●	public final . . . . void	**checkAccess** ()
D		public native . . . . int	**countStackFrames** ()
	△	public static native . . . . . Thread	**currentThread** ()
		public . . . . void	**destroy** ()
	△	public static . . . . void	**dumpStack** ()
	△	public static . . . . int	**enumerate** (Thread[] tarray)
1.2		public . . . . ClassLoader	**getContextClassLoader** ()
	●	public final . . . . String	**getName** ()
	●	public final . . . . int	**getPriority** ()
	●	public final . . . . . . ThreadGroup	**getThreadGroup** ()
		public . . . . void	**interrupt** ()
	△	public static . . . . boolean	**interrupted** ()
	●	public final native . . . . . boolean	**isAlive** ()
	●	public final . . . . boolean	**isDaemon** ()
		public . . . . boolean	**isInterrupted** ()
	●	public final . . . . void	**join** () throws InterruptedException
	●	public final synchronized . . void	**join** (long millis) throws InterruptedException
	●	public final synchronized . . void	**join** (long millis, int nanos) throws InterruptedException
	▲	public static final . . . . int	**MAX_PRIORITY** = 10
	▲	public static final . . . . int	**MIN_PRIORITY** = 1
	▲	public static final . . . . int	**NORM_PRIORITY** = 5
D	●	public final . . . . void	**resume** ()
	2	public . . . . void	**run** ()
1.2		public . . . . void	**setContextClassLoader** (ClassLoader cl)
	●	public final . . . . void	**setDaemon** (boolean on)
	●	public final . . . . void	**setName** (String name)
	●	public final . . . . void	**setPriority** (int newPriority)
	△	public static native . . . . void	**sleep** (long millis) throws InterruptedException
	△	public static . . . . void	**sleep** (long millis, int nanos) throws InterruptedException
		public native synchronized void	**start** ()
D	●	public final . . . . void	**stop** ()
D	●	public final synchronized . . void	**stop** (Throwable obj)
D	●	public final . . . . void	**suspend** ()
	∗	public	**Thread** ()
	∗	public	**Thread** (*Runnable* target)
	∗	public	**Thread** (String name)
	∗	public	**Thread** (*Runnable* target, String name)
	∗	public	**Thread** (ThreadGroup group, *Runnable* target)

Class   *Interface*   —extends   - - -implements   ○ abstract   ● final   △ static   ▲ static final   ∗ constructor   x x—inherited   x **x**—declared   **x x**—overridden

*	public	Thread	(ThreadGroup group, String name)
*	public	Thread	(ThreadGroup group, *Runnable* target, String name)
1	public	String toString	()
△	public static native	void yield	()

ThreadDeath java.lang

Object
  └Throwable ------------------------------- *java.io.Serializable*
    └Error
      └ThreadDeath

P

*	public	ThreadDeath	()

ThreadGroup java.lang

Object[1]
  └ThreadGroup

P

		public	int	activeCount ()
		public	int	activeGroupCount ()
D		public	boolean	allowThreadSuspension (boolean b)
	●	public final	void	checkAccess ()
	●	public final	void	destroy ()
		public	int	enumerate (ThreadGroup[] list)
		public	int	enumerate (Thread[] list)
		public	int	enumerate (ThreadGroup[] list, boolean recurse)
		public	int	enumerate (Thread[] list, boolean recurse)
	●	public final	int	getMaxPriority ()
	●	public final	String	getName ()
	●	public final	ThreadGroup	getParent ()
1.2	●	public final	void	interrupt ()
	●	public final	boolean	isDaemon ()
1.1		public synchronized	boolean	isDestroyed ()
		public	void	list ()
	●	public final	boolean	parentOf (ThreadGroup g)
D	●	public final	void	resume ()
	●	public final	void	setDaemon (boolean daemon)
	●	public final	void	setMaxPriority (int pri)
D	●	public final	void	stop ()
D	●	public final	void	suspend ()
	*	public		ThreadGroup (String name)
	*	public		ThreadGroup (ThreadGroup parent, String name)
	1	public	String	toString ()
		public	void	uncaughtException (Thread t, Throwable e)

ThreadLocal java.lang

Object
  └ThreadLocal

1.2

P

	public	Object	get ()
	protected	Object	initialValue ()
	public	void	set (Object value)
*	public		ThreadLocal ()

Throwable java.lang

Object[1]
  └Throwable ------------------------------- *java.io.Serializable*

P

	public native	Throwable	fillInStackTrace ()
1.1	public	String	getLocalizedMessage ()
	public	String	getMessage ()
	public	void	printStackTrace ()
	public	void	printStackTrace (java.io.PrintStream s)
1.1	public	void	printStackTrace (java.io.PrintWriter s)
*	public		Throwable ()
*	public		Throwable (String message)

Throwable

	1	public..................	**String toString** ()	

TileObserver — java.awt.image

1.2	*TileObserver*		
	public.......................void	**tileUpdate** (*WritableRenderedImage* source, int tileX, int tileY, boolean willBeWritable)	

Time — java.sql

java.sql
P^O

```
Object
 └java.util.Date¹ ------------------------- java.io.Serializable, Cloneable, Comparable
    └Time
```

1.1				
	1	public................. boolean	after (java.util.Date when)	
	1	public................. boolean	before (java.util.Date when)	
	1	public................. Object	clone ()	
1.2	1	public.................int	compareTo (Object o)	
1.2	1	public.................int	compareTo (java.util.Date anotherDate)	
	1	public................. boolean	equals (Object obj)	
D	1	public................. **int getDate** ()		
D	1	public................. **int getDay** ()		
D	1	public................. **int getMonth** ()		
	1	public................. long getTime ()		
D	1	public................. **int getYear** ()		
	1	public.................int hashCode ()		
D	1	public................. **void setDate** (int i)		
D	1	public................. **void setMonth** (int i)		
D	1	public................. **void setTime** (long time)		
D	1	public................. **void setYear** (int i)		
	✻	public................. **Time** (long time)		
	✻	public................. **Time** (int hour, int minute, int second)		
	1	public................. **String toString** ()		
△		public static .... Time **valueOf** (String s)		

Timer — javax.swing

javax.swing

```
Object
 └Timer ------------------------------- java.io.Serializable
```

1.2			
	public........................void	**addActionListener** (*java.awt.event.ActionListener* listener)	
	protected ....void	**fireActionPerformed** (java.awt.event.ActionEvent e)	
	public.........................int	**getDelay** ()	
	public.........................int	**getInitialDelay** ()	
△	public static .... boolean	**getLogTimers** ()	
	public................. boolean	**isCoalesce** ()	
	public................. boolean	**isRepeats** ()	
	public................. boolean	**isRunning** ()	
	protected ....javax↵	**listenerList**	
	.swing.event.EventListenerList		
	public........................void	**removeActionListener** (*java.awt.event.ActionListener* listener)	
	public........................void	**restart** ()	
	public........................void	**setCoalesce** (boolean flag)	
	public........................void	**setDelay** (int delay)	
	public........................void	**setInitialDelay** (int initialDelay)	
△	public static ....void	**setLogTimers** (boolean flag)	
	public........................void	**setRepeats** (boolean flag)	
	public........................void	**start** ()	
	public........................void	**stop** ()	
✻	public.........................	**Timer** (int delay, *java.awt.event.ActionListener* listener)	

Timestamp — java.sql

java.sql
P^O

```
Object
 └java.util.Date¹ ------------------------- java.io.Serializable, Cloneable, Comparable
    └Timestamp
```

1.1	

Class *Interface* —extends - - -implements ○ abstract ● final △ static ▲ static final ✻ constructor x x—inherited x **x**—declared **x x**—overridden

T

	1	*26 inherited members from java.util.Date not shown*		
		public.................. boolean	**after** (Timestamp ts)	
		public.................. boolean	**before** (Timestamp ts)	
	1	public................. **boolean**	**equals** (Object ts)	
		public.................. boolean	**equals** (Timestamp ts)	
		public.......................int	**getNanos** ()	
		public.......................void	**setNanos** (int n)	
	✳	public.......................	**Timestamp** (long time)	
D	✳	public.......................	**Timestamp** (int year, int month, int date, int hour, int minute, int second, int nano)	
	1	public................. **String**	**toString** ()	
△		public static .... Timestamp	**valueOf** (String s)	

TimeZone
java.util

Object[1]
  └ TimeZone - *java.io.Serializable, Cloneable*

P

1.1 ○

	1	public.................... **Object**	**clone** ()
△		public static synchronized .... String[]	**getAvailableIDs** ()
△		public static synchronized .... String[]	**getAvailableIDs** (int rawOffset)
△		public static synchronized .... TimeZone	**getDefault** ()
1.2	●	public final .... String	**getDisplayName** ()
1.2	●	public final .... String	**getDisplayName** (Locale locale)
1.2	●	public final .... String	**getDisplayName** (boolean daylight, int style)
1.2		public................. String	**getDisplayName** (boolean daylight, int style, Locale locale)
		public................. String	**getID** ()
○		public abstract ....int	**getOffset** (int era, int year, int month, int day, int dayOfWeek, int milliseconds)
○		public abstract ....int	**getRawOffset** ()
△		public static synchronized .... TimeZone	**getTimeZone** (String ID)
1.2		public................. boolean	**hasSameRules** (TimeZone other)
○		public abstract .... boolean	**inDaylightTime** (Date date)
1.2	▲	public static final ....int	**LONG** = 1
△		public static synchronized void	**setDefault** (TimeZone zone)
		public.......................void	**setID** (String ID)
○		public abstract ....void	**setRawOffset** (int offsetMillis)
1.2	▲	public static final ....int	**SHORT** = 0
	✳	public.......................	**TimeZone** ()
○		public abstract .... boolean	**useDaylightTime** ()

TitledBorder
javax.swing.border

Object
1.2 ○   └ AbstractBorder[1] - *Border, java.io.Serializable*
1.2   └ TitledBorder

▲		public static final ....int	**ABOVE_BOTTOM** = 4
▲		public static final ....int	**ABOVE_TOP** = 1
▲		public static final ....int	**BELOW_BOTTOM** = 6
▲		public static final ....int	**BELOW_TOP** = 3
		protected .... *Border*	**border**
▲		public static final ....int	**BOTTOM** = 5
▲		public static final ....int	**CENTER** = 2
▲		public static final ....int	**DEFAULT_JUSTIFICATION** = 0
▲		public static final ....int	**DEFAULT_POSITION** = 0
▲		protected static final ....int	**EDGE_SPACING**
		public..................... *Border*	**getBorder** ()
	1	public.......... **java.awt.Insets**	**getBorderInsets** (java.awt.Component c)
	1	public.......... **java.awt.Insets**	**getBorderInsets** (java.awt.Component c, java.awt.Insets insets)
		protected ....java.awt.Font	**getFont** (java.awt.Component c)
	1	public...... java.awt.Rectangle	getInteriorRectangle (java.awt.Component c, int x, int y, int width, int height)
△	1	public static .... java.awt.Rectangle	getInteriorRectangle (java.awt.Component c, *Border* b, int x, int y, int width, int height)
		public...... java.awt.Dimension	**getMinimumSize** (java.awt.Component c)
		public.................... String	**getTitle** ()
		public..........java.awt.Color	**getTitleColor** ()
		public...........java.awt.Font	**getTitleFont** ()
		public.......................int	**getTitleJustification** ()

TitledBorder

	public	int	**getTitlePosition** ()	
1	public	**boolean**	**isBorderOpaque** ()	
▲	public static final	int	**LEFT** = 1	
1	public	**void**	**paintBorder** (java.awt.Component c, java.awt.Graphics g, int x, int y, int width, int height)	
▲	public static final	int	**RIGHT** = 3	
	public	void	**setBorder** (*Border* border)	
	public	void	**setTitle** (String title)	
	public	void	**setTitleColor** (java.awt.Color titleColor)	
	public	void	**setTitleFont** (java.awt.Font titleFont)	
	public	void	**setTitleJustification** (int titleJustification)	
	public	void	**setTitlePosition** (int titlePosition)	
▲	protected static final	int	**TEXT_INSET_H**	
▲	protected static final	int	**TEXT_SPACING**	
	protected	String	**title**	
	protected	java.awt.Color	**titleColor**	
*	public		**TitledBorder** (String title)	
*	public		**TitledBorder** (*Border* border)	
*	public		**TitledBorder** (*Border* border, String title)	
*	public		**TitledBorder** (*Border* border, String title, int titleJustification, int titlePosition)	
*	public		**TitledBorder** (*Border* border, String title, int titleJustification, int titlePosition, java.awt.Font titleFont)	
*	public		**TitledBorder** (*Border* border, String title, int titleJustification, int titlePosition, java.awt.Font titleFont, java.awt.Color titleColor)	
	protected	java.awt.Font	**titleFont**	
	protected	int	**titleJustification**	
	protected	int	**titlePosition**	
▲	public static final	int	**TOP** = 2	

ToolBarUI
javax.swing.plaf

```
        Object
1.2 ○   └ComponentUI 1
1.2 ○     └ToolBarUI
```

1			*11 inherited members from ComponentUI not shown*
*	public		**ToolBarUI** ()

Toolkit
java.awt

P○

```
    Object
○   └Toolkit
```

1.2	public	void	**addAWTEventListener** (*java.awt.event.AWTEventListener* listener, long eventMask)
1.2	public synchronized	void	**addPropertyChangeListener** (String name, *java.beans.PropertyChangeListener* pcl)
1.1 ○	public abstract	void	**beep** ()
○	public abstract	int	**checkImage** (Image image, int width, int height, *java.awt.image.ImageObserver* observer)
○	protected abstract ...... java.awt.peer.ButtonPeer		**createButton** (Button target)
○	protected abstract ...... java.awt.peer.CanvasPeer		**createCanvas** (Canvas target)
○	protected abstract .... java.awt.peer.CheckboxPeer		**createCheckbox** (Checkbox target)
○	protected abstract . java.awt↵ .peer.CheckboxMenuItemPeer		**createCheckboxMenuItem** (CheckboxMenuItem target)
○	protected abstract ...... java.awt.peer.ChoicePeer		**createChoice** (Choice target)
1.1	protected .... java.awt.peer.LightweightPeer		**createComponent** (Component target)
1.2	public .... Cursor		**createCustomCursor** (Image cursor, Point hotSpot, String name) throws IndexOutOfBoundsException
○	protected abstract ...... java.awt.peer.DialogPeer		**createDialog** (Dialog target)
1.2	public .... java.awt↵ .dnd.DragGestureRecognizer		**createDragGestureRecognizer** (Class abstractRecognizerClass, java.awt.dnd.DragSource ds, Component c, int srcActions, *java.awt.dnd.DragGestureListener* dgl)

Class *Interface* —extends - - -implements ○ abstract ● final △ static ▲ static final * constructor x x—inherited x **x**—declared **x x**—overridden

1.2	○	public abstract java.awt.dnd ↵ .peer.DragSourceContextPeer	**createDragSourceContextPeer** (java.awt.dnd.DragGestureEvent dge) throws java.awt.dnd.InvalidDnDOperationException
	○	protected abstract ...java.awt.peer.FileDialogPeer	**createFileDialog** (FileDialog target)
	○	protected abstract ....java.awt.peer.FramePeer	**createFrame** (Frame target)
1.1		public.................... Image	**createImage** (byte[] imagedata)
	○	public abstract .... Image	**createImage** (java.awt.image.ImageProducer producer)
1.2	○	public abstract .... Image	**createImage** (String filename)
1.2	○	public abstract .... Image	**createImage** (java.net.URL url)
1.1	○	public abstract .... Image	**createImage** (byte[] imagedata, int imageoffset, int imagelength)
	○	protected abstract .... java.awt.peer.LabelPeer	**createLabel** (Label target)
	○	protected abstract ....java.awt.peer.ListPeer	**createList** (List target)
	○	protected abstract .... java.awt.peer.MenuPeer	**createMenu** (Menu target)
	○	protected abstract .... java.awt.peer.MenuBarPeer	**createMenuBar** (MenuBar target)
	○	protected abstract ....java.awt.peer.MenuItemPeer	**createMenuItem** (MenuItem target)
	○	protected abstract .... java.awt.peer.PanelPeer	**createPanel** (Panel target)
1.1	○	protected abstract .... java.awt.peer.PopupMenuPeer	**createPopupMenu** (PopupMenu target)
	○	protected abstract ....java.awt.peer.ScrollbarPeer	**createScrollbar** (Scrollbar target)
1.1	○	protected abstract ....java.awt.peer.ScrollPanePeer	**createScrollPane** (ScrollPane target)
	○	protected abstract ....java.awt.peer.TextAreaPeer	**createTextArea** (TextArea target)
	○	protected abstract ....java.awt.peer.TextFieldPeer	**createTextField** (TextField target)
	○	protected abstract .... java.awt.peer.WindowPeer	**createWindow** (Window target)
1.2	●	protected final.... java.util.Map	**desktopProperties**
1.2	●	protected final... java.beans ↵ .PropertyChangeSupport	**desktopPropsSupport**
1.2		public................Dimension	**getBestCursorSize** (int preferredWidth, int preferredHeight)
	○	public abstract .... java.awt.image.ColorModel	**getColorModel** ()
	△	public static synchronized .... Toolkit	**getDefaultToolkit** ()
1.2	●	public final synchronized ....Object	**getDesktopProperty** (String propertyName)
D	○	public abstract .... String[]	**getFontList** ()
D	○	public abstract .... FontMetrics	**getFontMetrics** (Font font)
D	○	protected abstract .... java.awt.peer.FontPeer	**getFontPeer** (String name, int style)
	○	public abstract .... Image	**getImage** (String filename)
	○	public abstract .... Image	**getImage** (java.net.URL url)
1.2		public......................int	**getMaximumCursorColors** ()
1.1		public......................int	**getMenuShortcutKeyMask** ()
1.1	△	protected static ..... Container	**getNativeContainer** (Component c)
1.1	○	public abstract .... PrintJob	**getPrintJob** (Frame frame, String jobtitle, java.util.Properties props)
1.1	△	public static ....String	**getProperty** (String key, String defaultValue)
	○	public abstract ....int	**getScreenResolution** ()
	○	public abstract ......Dimension	**getScreenSize** ()
1.1	○	public abstract .... java ↵ .awt.datatransfer.Clipboard	**getSystemClipboard** ()
1.1	●	public final ....EventQueue	**getSystemEventQueue** ()
1.1	○	protected abstract EventQueue	**getSystemEventQueueImpl** ()
1.2		protected ....void	**initializeDesktopProperties** ()
1.2		protected ....Object	**lazilyLoadDesktopProperty** (String name)
1.1		protected ....void	**loadSystemColors** (int[] systemColors)
	○	public abstract .... boolean	**prepareImage** (Image image, int width, int height, java.awt.image.ImageObserver observer)
1.2		public......................void	**removeAWTEventListener** (java.awt.event.AWTEventListener listener)
1.2		public synchronized ....void	**removePropertyChangeListener** (String name, java.beans ↵ .PropertyChangeListener pcl)
1.2	●	protected final synchronized .. ..void	**setDesktopProperty** (String name, Object newValue)
	○	public abstract............void	**sync** ()

Toolkit

✳	public.........................	**Toolkit** ()	

<table>
<tr><td colspan="4">ToolTipManager</td><td align="right">javax.swing</td></tr>
</table>

Object
1.1 ○ └java.awt.event.MouseAdapter [1] ----------- *java.awt.event.MouseListener* (*java.util.EventListener*)
1.2   └ToolTipManager ---------------------- *java.awt.event.MouseMotionListener* [2] (*java.util.EventListener*)

	public......................int	**getDismissDelay** ()	
	public......................int	**getInitialDelay** ()	
	public......................int	**getReshowDelay** ()	
	protected..............boolean	**heavyWeightPopupEnabled**	
	public..................boolean	**isEnabled** ()	
	public..................boolean	**isLightWeightPopupEnabled** ()	
	protected..............boolean	**lightWeightPopupEnabled**	
1	public......................void	mouseClicked (java.awt.event.MouseEvent e)	
2	public......................void	**mouseDragged** (java.awt.event.MouseEvent event)	
1	public...............**void**	**mouseEntered** (java.awt.event.MouseEvent event)	
1	public...............**void**	**mouseExited** (java.awt.event.MouseEvent event)	
2	public......................void	**mouseMoved** (java.awt.event.MouseEvent event)	
1	public...............**void**	**mousePressed** (java.awt.event.MouseEvent event)	
1	public......................void	mouseReleased (java.awt.event.MouseEvent e)	
	public......................void	**registerComponent** (JComponent component)	
	public......................void	**setDismissDelay** (int microSeconds)	
	public......................void	**setEnabled** (boolean flag)	
	public......................void	**setInitialDelay** (int microSeconds)	
D	public......................void	**setLightWeightPopupEnabled** (boolean aFlag)	
	public......................void	**setReshowDelay** (int microSeconds)	
△	public static .. ToolTipManager	**sharedInstance** ()	
	public......................void	**unregisterComponent** (JComponent component)	

<table>
<tr><td colspan="3">ToolTipManager.insideTimerAction</td><td align="center">protected</td><td align="right">javax.swing</td></tr>
</table>

Object
1.2 └ToolTipManager.insideTimerAction -------- *java.awt.event.ActionListener* [1] (*java.util.EventListener*)

1	public......................void	**actionPerformed** (java.awt.event.ActionEvent e)	
✳	protected......................	**insideTimerAction** ()	

<table>
<tr><td colspan="3">ToolTipManager.outsideTimerAction</td><td align="center">protected</td><td align="right">javax.swing</td></tr>
</table>

Object
1.2 └ToolTipManager.outsideTimerAction ------- *java.awt.event.ActionListener* [1] (*java.util.EventListener*)

1	public......................void	**actionPerformed** (java.awt.event.ActionEvent e)	
✳	protected......................	**outsideTimerAction** ()	

<table>
<tr><td colspan="3">ToolTipManager.stillInsideTimerAction</td><td align="center">protected</td><td align="right">javax.swing</td></tr>
</table>

Object
1.2 └ToolTipManager.stillInsideTimerAction ------ *java.awt.event.ActionListener* [1] (*java.util.EventListener*)

1	public......................void	**actionPerformed** (java.awt.event.ActionEvent e)	
✳	protected......................	**stillInsideTimerAction** ()	

<table>
<tr><td colspan="4">ToolTipUI</td><td align="right">javax.swing.plaf</td></tr>
</table>

Object
1.2 ○ └ComponentUI [1]
1.2 ○   └ToolTipUI

1	*11 inherited members from ComponentUI not shown*		
✳	public.........................	**ToolTipUI** ()	

Class *Interface* —extends - - -implements ○ abstract ● final △ static ▲ static final ✳ constructor x x—inherited x **x**—declared **x x**—overridden

TooManyListenersException | java.util

P

```
Object
└Throwable ------------------------------ java.io.Serializable
   └Exception
1.1     └TooManyListenersException
```

*	public	**TooManyListenersException** ()
*	public	**TooManyListenersException** (String s)

TRANSACTION_REQUIRED | org.omg.CORBA

```
Object
└Throwable ------------------------------ java.io.Serializable
   └Exception
      └RuntimeException
1.2 ○     └SystemException 1
1.2 ●        └TRANSACTION_REQUIRED
```

1	public	CompletionStatus	completed
1	public	int	minor
1	public	String	toString ()
*	public		**TRANSACTION_REQUIRED** ()
*	public		**TRANSACTION_REQUIRED** (String s)
*	public		**TRANSACTION_REQUIRED** (int minor, CompletionStatus completed)
*	public		**TRANSACTION_REQUIRED** (String s, int minor, CompletionStatus completed)

TRANSACTION_ROLLEDBACK | org.omg.CORBA

T

```
Object
└Throwable ------------------------------ java.io.Serializable
   └Exception
      └RuntimeException
1.2 ○     └SystemException 1
1.2 ●        └TRANSACTION_ROLLEDBACK
```

1	public	CompletionStatus	completed
1	public	int	minor
1	public	String	toString ()
*	public		**TRANSACTION_ROLLEDBACK** ()
*	public		**TRANSACTION_ROLLEDBACK** (String s)
*	public		**TRANSACTION_ROLLEDBACK** (int minor, CompletionStatus completed)
*	public		**TRANSACTION_ROLLEDBACK** (String s, int minor, CompletionStatus completed)

Transferable | java.awt.datatransfer

Classes

1.1	*Transferable*	P

	public	Object	**getTransferData** (DataFlavor flavor) throws UnsupportedFlavorException, java.io.IOException
	public	DataFlavor[]	**getTransferDataFlavors** ()
	public	boolean	**isDataFlavorSupported** (DataFlavor flavor)

TransformAttribute | java.awt.font

```
Object
1.2 ● └TransformAttribute ---------------------- java.io.Serializable
```

	public		**getTransform** ()
	java.awt.geom.AffineTransform		
*	public		**TransformAttribute** (java.awt.geom.AffineTransform transform)

TRANSIENT | org.omg.CORBA

```
      Object
        └ Throwable - - - - - - - - - - - - - - - - - - - - - - - java.io.Serializable
          └ Exception
            └ RuntimeException
1.2 ○         └ SystemException 1
1.2 ●           └ TRANSIENT
```

	1	public........CompletionStatus	completed
	1	public.........................int	minor
	1	public...................String	toString ()
✴		public.........................	**TRANSIENT** ()
✴		public.........................	**TRANSIENT** (String s)
✴		public.........................	**TRANSIENT** (int minor, CompletionStatus completed)
✴		public.........................	**TRANSIENT** (String s, int minor, CompletionStatus completed)

Transparency | java.awt

P

```
1.2      Transparency
```

▲	public static final.............int	**BITMASK** = 2
	public.........................int	**getTransparency** ()
▲	public static final.............int	**OPAQUE** = 1
▲	public static final.............int	**TRANSLUCENT** = 3

TreeCellEditor | javax.swing.tree

```
1.2      TreeCellEditor───────────────────────javax.swing.CellEditor 1
```

	1	public.....................void	addCellEditorListener (*javax.swing.event.CellEditorListener* l)
	1	public.....................void	cancelCellEditing ()
	1	public...................Object	getCellEditorValue ()
		public.... java.awt.Component	**getTreeCellEditorComponent** (javax.swing. JTree tree, Object value,
			boolean isSelected, boolean expanded, boolean leaf, int row)
	1	public.................. boolean	isCellEditable (java.util.EventObject anEvent)
	1	public.....................void	removeCellEditorListener (*javax.swing.event.CellEditorListener* l)
	1	public.................. boolean	shouldSelectCell (java.util.EventObject anEvent)
	1	public.................. boolean	stopCellEditing ()

TreeCellRenderer | javax.swing.tree

```
1.2      TreeCellRenderer
```

	public.... java.awt.Component	**getTreeCellRendererComponent** (javax.swing. JTree tree, Object value,
		boolean selected, boolean expanded, boolean leaf, int row, boolean hasFocus)

TreeExpansionEvent | javax.swing.event

```
      Object
1.1     └ java.util.EventObject 1 - - - - - - - - - - - - - - - - - - java.io.Serializable
1.2       └ TreeExpansionEvent
```

		public...........................	**getPath** ()
		...... javax.swing.tree.TreePath	
	1	public...................Object	getSource ()
		protected........................	**path**
		...... javax.swing.tree.TreePath	
	1	protected transient......Object	source
	1	public...................String	toString ()
✴		public...........................	**TreeExpansionEvent** (Object source, javax.swing.tree.TreePath path)

Class   *Interface*   —extends   - - -implements   ○ abstract   ● final   △ static   ▲ static final   ✴ constructor   x x—inherited   x **x**—declared   **x x**—overridden

TreeExpansionListener

`javax.swing.event`

1.2   *TreeExpansionListener* ────────────── *java.util.EventListener*

     public.....................void **treeCollapsed** (TreeExpansionEvent event)
     public.....................void **treeExpanded** (TreeExpansionEvent event)

TreeMap

`java.util`

     Object [1]
                                                    P

1.2 ○   └AbstractMap [2] ─────────────────── *Map*
1.2   └TreeMap ───────────────── *SortedMap* [3] (*Map*), *Cloneable, java.io.Serializable*

   2   public.....................**void clear** ()
   1   public.....................**Object clone** ()
   3   public.............*Comparator* **comparator** ()
   2   public.....................**boolean containsKey** (Object key)
   2   public.....................**boolean containsValue** (Object value)
   2   public.....................***Set* entrySet** ()
   2   public.....................boolean equals (Object o)
   3   public.....................Object **firstKey** ()
   2   public.....................**Object get** (Object key)
   2   public.....................int hashCode ()
   3   public.............*SortedMap* **headMap** (Object toKey)
   2   public.....................boolean isEmpty ()
   2   public.....................***Set* keySet** ()
   3   public.....................Object **lastKey** ()
   2   public.....................**Object put** (Object key, Object value)
   2   public.....................**void putAll** (*Map* map)
   2   public.....................**Object remove** (Object key)
   2   public.....................**int size** ()
   3   public.............*SortedMap* **subMap** (Object fromKey, Object toKey)
   3   public.............*SortedMap* **tailMap** (Object fromKey)
   2   public.....................String toString ()
  *   public..................... **TreeMap** ()
  *   public..................... **TreeMap** (*Comparator* c)
  *   public..................... **TreeMap** (*Map* m)
  *   public..................... **TreeMap** (*SortedMap* m)
   2   public.............***Collection* values** ()

TreeModel

`javax.swing.tree`

1.2   *TreeModel*

     public.....................void **addTreeModelListener** (*javax.swing.event.TreeModelListener* l)
     public.....................Object **getChild** (Object parent, int index)
     public.....................int **getChildCount** (Object parent)
     public.....................int **getIndexOfChild** (Object parent, Object child)
     public.....................Object **getRoot** ()
     public.....................boolean **isLeaf** (Object node)
     public.....................void **removeTreeModelListener** (*javax.swing.event.TreeModelListener* l)
     public.....................void **valueForPathChanged** (TreePath path, Object newValue)

TreeModelEvent

`javax.swing.event`

     Object
1.1   └java.util.EventObject [1] ─────────────── *java.io.Serializable*
1.2   └TreeModelEvent

     protected.................int[] **childIndices**
     protected.............Object[] **children**
     public.....................int[] **getChildIndices** ()
     public.................Object[] **getChildren** ()
     public.................Object[] **getPath** ()
   1   public.................Object getSource ()
     public..................... **getTreePath** ()
        ...... javax.swing.tree.TreePath
     protected..................... **path**
        ...... javax.swing.tree.TreePath
   1   protected transient......Object source
   1   public..................... **String toString** ()

T

Classes

TreeModelEvent

✳	public	**TreeModelEvent** (Object source, javax.swing.tree.TreePath path)
✳	public	**TreeModelEvent** (Object source, Object[] path)
✳	public	**TreeModelEvent** (Object source, javax.swing.tree.TreePath path, int[] childIndices, Object[] children)
✳	public	**TreeModelEvent** (Object source, Object[] path, int[] childIndices, Object[] children)

TreeModelListener			javax.swing.event

1.2   *TreeModelListener* ———————————— *java.util.EventListener*

public	void	**treeNodesChanged** (TreeModelEvent e)
public	void	**treeNodesInserted** (TreeModelEvent e)
public	void	**treeNodesRemoved** (TreeModelEvent e)
public	void	**treeStructureChanged** (TreeModelEvent e)

TreeNode			javax.swing.tree

1.2   *TreeNode*

public	*java.util.Enumeration*	**children** ()
public	boolean	**getAllowsChildren** ()
public	*TreeNode*	**getChildAt** (int childIndex)
public	int	**getChildCount** ()
public	int	**getIndex** (*TreeNode* node)
public	*TreeNode*	**getParent** ()
public	boolean	**isLeaf** ()

TreePath			javax.swing.tree

Object [1]
└TreePath - *java.io.Serializable*

1.2

1	public	**boolean**	**equals** (Object o)
	public	Object	**getLastPathComponent** ()
	public	TreePath	**getParentPath** ()
	public	Object[]	**getPath** ()
	public	Object	**getPathComponent** (int element)
	public	int	**getPathCount** ()
1	public	**int**	**hashCode** ()
	public	boolean	**isDescendant** (TreePath aTreePath)
	public	TreePath	**pathByAddingChild** (Object child)
1	public	**String**	**toString** ()
✳	protected		**TreePath** ()
✳	public		**TreePath** (Object singlePath)
✳	public		**TreePath** (Object[] path)
✳	protected		**TreePath** (Object[] path, int length)
✳	protected		**TreePath** (TreePath parent, Object lastElement)

TreeSelectionEvent			javax.swing.event

Object
1.1   └java.util.EventObject [1] - - - - - - - - - - - - - - - - - - *java.io.Serializable*
1.2   └TreeSelectionEvent

	protected	boolean[]	**areNew**
	public	Object	**cloneWithSource** (Object newSource)
	public		**getNewLeadSelectionPath** ()
		...... javax.swing.tree.TreePath	
	public		**getOldLeadSelectionPath** ()
		...... javax.swing.tree.TreePath	
	public		**getPath** ()
		...... javax.swing.tree.TreePath	
	public		**getPaths** ()
		.... javax.swing.tree.TreePath[]	
1	public	Object	getSource ()
	public	boolean	**isAddedPath** ()
	public	boolean	**isAddedPath** (javax.swing.tree.TreePath path)
	protected		**newLeadSelectionPath**
		...... javax.swing.tree.TreePath	

Class   *Interface*   —extends   - - -implements   ○ abstract   ● final   △ static   ▲ static final   ✳ constructor   x x—inherited   x **x**—declared   **x x**—overridden

	protected . . . . javax.swing.tree.TreePath	**oldLeadSelectionPath**	
	protected . . . . javax.swing.tree.TreePath[]	**paths**	
1	protected transient . . . . . . Object	source	
1	public . . . . String	toString ()	
*	public	**TreeSelectionEvent** (Object source, javax.swing.tree.TreePath[] paths, boolean[] areNew, javax.swing.tree.TreePath oldLeadSelectionPath, javax.swing.tree.TreePath newLeadSelectionPath)	
*	public	**TreeSelectionEvent** (Object source, javax.swing.tree.TreePath path, boolean isNew, javax.swing.tree.TreePath oldLeadSelectionPath, javax.swing.tree.TreePath newLeadSelectionPath)	

TreeSelectionListener   javax.swing.event

1.2	*TreeSelectionListener* ———————————— *java.util.EventListener*	
	public . . . . void	**valueChanged** (TreeSelectionEvent e)

TreeSelectionModel   javax.swing.tree

1.2	*TreeSelectionModel*		
	public . . . . void	**addPropertyChangeListener** (*java.beans.PropertyChangeListener* listener)	
	public . . . . void	**addSelectionPath** (TreePath path)	
	public . . . . void	**addSelectionPaths** (TreePath[] paths)	
	public . . . . void	**addTreeSelectionListener** (*javax.swing.event.TreeSelectionListener* x)	
	public . . . . void	**clearSelection** ()	
▲	public static final . . . . int	**CONTIGUOUS_TREE_SELECTION** = 2	
▲	public static final . . . . int	**DISCONTIGUOUS_TREE_SELECTION** = 4	
	public . . . . TreePath	**getLeadSelectionPath** ()	
	public . . . . int	**getLeadSelectionRow** ()	
	public . . . . int	**getMaxSelectionRow** ()	
	public . . . . int	**getMinSelectionRow** ()	
	public . . . . *RowMapper*	**getRowMapper** ()	
	public . . . . int	**getSelectionCount** ()	
	public . . . . int	**getSelectionMode** ()	
	public . . . . TreePath	**getSelectionPath** ()	
	public . . . . TreePath[]	**getSelectionPaths** ()	
	public . . . . int[]	**getSelectionRows** ()	
	public . . . . boolean	**isPathSelected** (TreePath path)	
	public . . . . boolean	**isRowSelected** (int row)	
	public . . . . boolean	**isSelectionEmpty** ()	
	public . . . . void	**removePropertyChangeListener** (*java.beans.PropertyChangeListener* listener)	
	public . . . . void	**removeSelectionPath** (TreePath path)	
	public . . . . void	**removeSelectionPaths** (TreePath[] paths)	
	public . . . . void	**removeTreeSelectionListener** (*javax.swing.event.TreeSelectionListener* x)	
	public . . . . void	**resetRowSelection** ()	
	public . . . . void	**setRowMapper** (*RowMapper* newMapper)	
	public . . . . void	**setSelectionMode** (int mode)	
	public . . . . void	**setSelectionPath** (TreePath path)	
	public . . . . void	**setSelectionPaths** (TreePath[] paths)	
▲	public static final . . . . int	**SINGLE_TREE_SELECTION** = 1	

TreeSet   java.util

P

	Object [1]	
1.2 ○	└AbstractCollection [2] - *Collection*	
1.2 ○	└AbstractSet [3] - *Set* (*Collection*)	
1.2	└TreeSet - *SortedSet* [4] (*Set* (*Collection*)), *Cloneable, java.io.Serializable*	

2	public . . . . **boolean**	**add** (Object o)	
2	public . . . . **boolean**	**addAll** (*Collection* c)	
2	public . . . . **void**	**clear** ()	
1	public . . . . **Object**	**clone** ()	
4	public . . . . *Comparator*	**comparator** ()	
2	public . . . . **boolean**	**contains** (Object o)	
2	public . . . . boolean	**containsAll** (*Collection* c)	
3	public . . . . boolean	equals (Object o)	
4	public . . . . Object	**first** ()	
3	public . . . . int	hashCode ()	

TreeSet

4	public	*SortedSet*	**headSet**	(Object toElement)
2	public	**boolean**	**isEmpty**	()
2	public	*Iterator*	**iterator**	()
4	public	Object	**last**	()
2	public	**boolean**	**remove**	(Object o)
2	public	boolean	removeAll	(*Collection* c)
2	public	boolean	retainAll	(*Collection* c)
2	public	**int**	**size**	()
4	public	*SortedSet*	**subSet**	(Object fromElement, Object toElement)
4	public	*SortedSet*	**tailSet**	(Object fromElement)
2	public	Object[]	toArray	()
2	public	Object[]	toArray	(Object[] a)
2	public	String	toString	()
✳	public		**TreeSet**	()
✳	public		**TreeSet**	(*Collection* c)
✳	public		**TreeSet**	(*Comparator* c)
✳	public		**TreeSet**	(*SortedSet* s)

TreeUI   javax.swing.plaf

Object
 └ ComponentUI [1]
  └ TreeUI

1.2 ○
1.2 ○

1	*11 inherited members from ComponentUI not shown*			
○	public abstract	void	**cancelEditing**	(javax.swing.JTree tree)
○	public abstract	javax.swing.tree.TreePath	**getClosestPathForLocation**	(javax.swing.JTree tree, int x, int y)
○	public abstract	javax.swing.tree.TreePath	**getEditingPath**	(javax.swing.JTree tree)
○	public abstract	java.awt.Rectangle	**getPathBounds**	(javax.swing.JTree tree, javax.swing.tree.TreePath path)
○	public abstract	javax.swing.tree.TreePath	**getPathForRow**	(javax.swing.JTree tree, int row)
○	public abstract	int	**getRowCount**	(javax.swing.JTree tree)
○	public abstract	int	**getRowForPath**	(javax.swing.JTree tree, javax.swing.tree.TreePath path)
○	public abstract	boolean	**isEditing**	(javax.swing.JTree tree)
○	public abstract	void	**startEditingAtPath**	(javax.swing.JTree tree, javax.swing.tree.TreePath path)
○	public abstract	boolean	**stopEditing**	(javax.swing.JTree tree)
✳	public		**TreeUI**	()

TreeWillExpandListener   javax.swing.event

1.2 *TreeWillExpandListener*————————*java.util.EventListener*

public	void	**treeWillCollapse**	(TreeExpansionEvent event) throws javax.swing.tree.ExpandVetoException
public	void	**treeWillExpand**	(TreeExpansionEvent event) throws javax.swing.tree.ExpandVetoException

---

TypeCode   org.omg.CORBA

Object
 └ TypeCode - *org.omg.CORBA.portable.IDLEntity* (*java.io.Serializable*)

1.2 ○

	public	TypeCode	**concrete_base_type**	() throws org.omg.CORBA.TypeCodePackage.BadKind
○	public abstract	TypeCode	**content_type**	() throws org.omg.CORBA.TypeCodePackage.BadKind
○	public abstract	int	**default_index**	() throws org.omg.CORBA.TypeCodePackage.BadKind
○	public abstract	TypeCode	**discriminator_type**	() throws org.omg.CORBA.TypeCodePackage.BadKind
○	public abstract	boolean	**equal**	(TypeCode tc)
	public	boolean	**equivalent**	(TypeCode tc)
	public	short	**fixed_digits**	() throws org.omg.CORBA.TypeCodePackage.BadKind
	public	short	**fixed_scale**	() throws org.omg.CORBA.TypeCodePackage.BadKind
	public	TypeCode	**get_compact_typecode**	()
○	public abstract	String	**id**	() throws org.omg.CORBA.TypeCodePackage.BadKind
○	public abstract	TCKind	**kind**	()
○	public abstract	int	**length**	() throws org.omg.CORBA.TypeCodePackage.BadKind
○	public abstract	int	**member_count**	() throws org.omg.CORBA.TypeCodePackage.BadKind

---

Class *Interface* —extends - - -implements ○ abstract ● final △ static ▲ static final ✳ constructor x x—inherited x **x**—declared **x x**—overridden

○	public abstract . . . . Any	**member_label** (int index) throws org.omg.CORBA.TypeCodePackage.BadKind, org.omg.CORBA.TypeCodePackage.Bounds
○	public abstract . . . . String	**member_name** (int index) throws org.omg.CORBA.TypeCodePackage.BadKind, org.omg.CORBA.TypeCodePackage.Bounds
○	public abstract . . . . . . TypeCode	**member_type** (int index) throws org.omg.CORBA.TypeCodePackage.BadKind, org.omg.CORBA.TypeCodePackage.Bounds
	public . . . . short	**member_visibility** (int index) throws org.omg.CORBA.TypeCodePackage.BadKind, Bounds
○	public abstract . . . . String	**name** () throws org.omg.CORBA.TypeCodePackage.BadKind
	public . . . . short	**type_modifier** () throws org.omg.CORBA.TypeCodePackage.BadKind
✳	public	**TypeCode** ()

TypeCodeHolder
org.omg.CORBA

Object
1.2 ● └TypeCodeHolder - *org.omg.CORBA.portable.Streamable* [1]

1	public . . . . void	**_read** (org.omg.CORBA.portable.InputStream input)
1	public . . . . TypeCode	**_type** ()
1	public . . . . void	**_write** (org.omg.CORBA.portable.OutputStream output)
✳	public	**TypeCodeHolder** ()
✳	public	**TypeCodeHolder** (TypeCode initial)
	public . . . . TypeCode	**value**

TypeMismatch
org.omg.CORBA.DynAnyPackage

Object
└Throwable - *java.io.Serializable*
  └Exception
1.2 ○   └org.omg.CORBA.UserException - - - - - - - *org.omg.CORBA.portable.IDLEntity* (*java.io.Serializable*)
1.2 ●   └TypeMismatch

✳	public	**TypeMismatch** ()
✳	public	**TypeMismatch** (String reason)

Types
java.sql
P○

Object
1.1 └Types

1.2 ▲	public static final . . . . int	**ARRAY** = 2003
▲	public static final . . . . int	**BIGINT** = -5
▲	public static final . . . . int	**BINARY** = -2
▲	public static final . . . . int	**BIT** = -7
1.2 ▲	public static final . . . . int	**BLOB** = 2004
▲	public static final . . . . int	**CHAR** = 1
1.2 ▲	public static final . . . . int	**CLOB** = 2005
▲	public static final . . . . int	**DATE** = 91
▲	public static final . . . . int	**DECIMAL** = 3
1.2 ▲	public static final . . . . int	**DISTINCT** = 2001
▲	public static final . . . . int	**DOUBLE** = 8
▲	public static final . . . . int	**FLOAT** = 6
▲	public static final . . . . int	**INTEGER** = 4
1.2 ▲	public static final . . . . int	**JAVA_OBJECT** = 2000
▲	public static final . . . . int	**LONGVARBINARY** = -4
▲	public static final . . . . int	**LONGVARCHAR** = -1
▲	public static final . . . . int	**NULL** = 0
▲	public static final . . . . int	**NUMERIC** = 2
▲	public static final . . . . int	**OTHER** = 1111
▲	public static final . . . . int	**REAL** = 7
1.2 ▲	public static final . . . . int	**REF** = 2006
▲	public static final . . . . int	**SMALLINT** = 5
1.2 ▲	public static final . . . . int	**STRUCT** = 2002
▲	public static final . . . . int	**TIME** = 92
▲	public static final . . . . int	**TIMESTAMP** = 93
▲	public static final . . . . int	**TINYINT** = -6
▲	public static final . . . . int	**VARBINARY** = -3
▲	public static final . . . . int	**VARCHAR** = 12

T

Classes

UID — java.rmi.server

P⁰ → **PO**

```
        Object¹
1.1 ●    └UID - - - - - - - - - - - - - - - - - - - - - - - - - - - - - - - - - - - java.io.Serializable
```

1	public	**boolean**	**equals** (Object obj)
1	public	**int**	**hashCode** ()
△	public static	UID	**read** (*java.io.DataInput* in) throws java.io.IOException
1	public	**String**	**toString** ()
✳	public		**UID** ()
✳	public		**UID** (short num)
	public	void	**write** (*java.io.DataOutput* out) throws java.io.IOException

UIDefaults — javax.swing

```
        Object
○        └java.util.Dictionary
           └java.util.Hashtable¹ - - - - - - - - - - - - - - - - - - java.util.Map, Cloneable, java.io.Serializable
1.2           └UIDefaults
```

	public synchronized	void	**addPropertyChangeListener** (*java.beans.PropertyChangeListener* listener)
1	public synchronized	void	clear ()
1	public synchronized	Object	clone ()
1	public synchronized	boolean	contains (Object value)
1	public synchronized	boolean	containsKey (Object key)
1	public	boolean	containsValue (Object value)
1	public synchronized	*java.util.Enumeration*	elements ()
1	public	*java.util.Set*	entrySet ()
1	public synchronized	boolean	equals (Object o)
	protected	void	**firePropertyChange** (String propertyName, Object oldValue, Object newValue)
	public	**Object**	**get** (Object key)
	public	*javax.swing.border.Border*	**getBorder** (Object key)
	public	java.awt.Color	**getColor** (Object key)
	public	java.awt.Dimension	**getDimension** (Object key)
	public	java.awt.Font	**getFont** (Object key)
	public	*Icon*	**getIcon** (Object key)
	public	java.awt.Insets	**getInsets** (Object key)
	public	int	**getInt** (Object key)
	public	String	**getString** (Object key)
	public	*javax.swing.plaf.ComponentUI*	**getUI** (JComponent target)
	public	Class	**getUIClass** (String uiClassID)
	public	Class	**getUIClass** (String uiClassID, ClassLoader uiClassLoader)
	protected	void	**getUIError** (String msg)
1	public synchronized	int	hashCode ()
1	public	boolean	isEmpty ()
1	public synchronized	*java.util.Enumeration*	keys ()
1	public	*java.util.Set*	keySet ()
1	public	**Object**	**put** (Object key, Object value)
1	public synchronized	void	putAll (*java.util.Map* t)
	public	void	**putDefaults** (Object[] keyValueList)
	protected	void	rehash ()
1	public synchronized	Object	remove (Object key)
	public synchronized	void	**removePropertyChangeListener** (*java.beans.PropertyChangeListener* listener)
1	public	int	size ()
1	public synchronized	String	toString ()
✳	public		**UIDefaults** ()
✳	public		**UIDefaults** (Object[] keyValueList)
1	public	*java.util.Collection*	values ()

UIDefaults.ActiveValue — javax.swing

```
1.2     UIDefaults.ActiveValue
```

	public	Object	**createValue** (UIDefaults table)

Class *Interface* —extends - - -implements ○ abstract ● final △ static ▲ static final ✳ constructor x x—inherited x **x**—declared **x x**—overridden

UIDefaults.LazyValue

javax.swing

1.2 *UIDefaults.LazyValue*

public.................. Object **createValue** (UIDefaults table)

UIManager

javax.swing

Object
  └UIManager - *java.io.Serializable*

1.2

△	public static ....void	**addAuxiliaryLookAndFeel** (LookAndFeel laf)
△	public static synchronized void	**addPropertyChangeListener** (*java.beans.PropertyChangeListener* listener)
△	public static .... Object	**get** (Object key)
△	public static .... LookAndFeel[]	**getAuxiliaryLookAndFeels** ()
△	public static	**getBorder** (Object key)
	..... *javax.swing.border.Border*	
△	public static .....java.awt.Color	**getColor** (Object key)
△	public static ....String	**getCrossPlatformLookAndFeelClassName** ()
△	public static ....UIDefaults	**getDefaults** ()
△	public static	**getDimension** (Object key)
	............java.awt.Dimension	
△	public static ......java.awt.Font	**getFont** (Object key)
△	public static .... *Icon*	**getIcon** (Object key)
△	public static .... java.awt.Insets	**getInsets** (Object key)
△	public static	**getInstalledLookAndFeels** ()
	. UIManager.LookAndFeelInfo[]	
△	public static ....int	**getInt** (Object key)
△	public static ......LookAndFeel	**getLookAndFeel** ()
△	public static ....UIDefaults	**getLookAndFeelDefaults** ()
△	public static ....String	**getString** (Object key)
△	public static ....String	**getSystemLookAndFeelClassName** ()
△	public static	**getUI** (JComponent target)
	javax.swing.plaf.ComponentUI	
△	public static ....void	**installLookAndFeel** (UIManager.LookAndFeelInfo info)
△	public static ....void	**installLookAndFeel** (String name, String className)
△	public static .... Object	**put** (Object key, Object value)
△	public static .... boolean	**removeAuxiliaryLookAndFeel** (LookAndFeel laf)
△	public static synchronized void	**removePropertyChangeListener** (*java.beans.PropertyChangeListener* listener)
△	public static ....void	**setInstalledLookAndFeels** (UIManager. LookAndFeelInfo[] infos)
		throws SecurityException
△	public static ....void	**setLookAndFeel** (String className) throws ClassNotFoundException,
		InstantiationException, IllegalAccessException, UnsupportedLookAndFeelException
△	public static ....void	**setLookAndFeel** (LookAndFeel newLookAndFeel)
		throws UnsupportedLookAndFeelException
＊	public........................	**UIManager** ()

UIManager.LookAndFeelInfo

javax.swing

Object[1]
  └UIManager.LookAndFeelInfo

1.2

	public....................String	**getClassName** ()
	public....................String	**getName** ()
＊	public........................	**LookAndFeelInfo** (String name, String className)
1	public.................. **String**	**toString** ()

UIResource

javax.swing.plaf

1.2 *UIResource*

UndoableEdit

javax.swing.undo

1.2 *UndoableEdit*

	public................. boolean	**addEdit** (*UndoableEdit* anEdit)
	public................. boolean	**canRedo** ()
	public................. boolean	**canUndo** ()
	public....................void	**die** ()
	public.................String	**getPresentationName** ()

U

Classes

```
          public......................String  getRedoPresentationName ()
          public......................String  getUndoPresentationName ()
          public.................. boolean  isSignificant ()
          public..................void  redo () throws CannotRedoException
          public................. boolean  replaceEdit (UndoableEdit anEdit)
          public...................void  undo () throws CannotUndoException
```

UndoableEditEvent · javax.swing.event

```
          Object
     1.1   └java.util.EventObject¹ - - - - - - - - - - - - - - - - - - - java.io.Serializable
     1.2      └UndoableEditEvent
```

	public...................*javax↩*	getEdit ()
	.swing.undo.UndoableEdit	
1	public....................Object	getSource ()
1	protected transient......Object	source
1	public....................String	toString ()
*	public...........................	**UndoableEditEvent** (Object source, *javax.swing.undo.UndoableEdit* edit)

UndoableEditListener · javax.swing.event

```
     1.2   UndoableEditListener——————————————java.util.EventListener
```

```
          public......................void  undoableEditHappened (UndoableEditEvent e)
```

UndoableEditSupport · javax.swing.undo

```
          Object¹
     1.2   └UndoableEditSupport
```

	protected...................void	**_postEdit** (*UndoableEdit* e)
	public synchronized ....void	**addUndoableEditListener** (*javax.swing.event.UndoableEditListener* l)
	public synchronized ....void	**beginUpdate** ()
	protected.......CompoundEdit	**compoundEdit**
	protected.......CompoundEdit	**createCompoundEdit** ()
	public synchronized ....void	**endUpdate** ()
	public........................int	**getUpdateLevel** ()
	protected....... java.util.Vector	**listeners**
	public synchronized ......void	**postEdit** (*UndoableEdit* e)
	protected ....Object	**realSource**
	public synchronized ......void	**removeUndoableEditListener** (*javax.swing.event.UndoableEditListener* l)
1	public.....................**String**	**toString** ()
*	public...........................	**UndoableEditSupport** ()
*	public...........................	**UndoableEditSupport** (Object r)
	protected...................int	**updateLevel**

UndoManager · javax.swing.undo

```
          Object
     1.2   └AbstractUndoableEdit¹ - - - - - - - - - - - - - - - - - - UndoableEdit, java.io.Serializable
     1.2      └CompoundEdit²
     1.2         └UndoManager - - - - - - - - - - - - - - - javax.swing.event.UndoableEditListener ³ (java.util.EventListener)
```

2	public synchronized .. **boolean**	**addEdit** (*UndoableEdit* anEdit)
2	public synchronized .. **boolean**	**canRedo** ()
2	public synchronized .. **boolean**	**canUndo** ()
	public synchronized .. boolean	**canUndoOrRedo** ()
2	public...................void	die ()
	public synchronized ....void	**discardAllEdits** ()
2	protected .... java.util.Vector	edits
	protected .... *UndoableEdit*	**editToBeRedone** ()
	protected .... *UndoableEdit*	**editToBeUndone** ()
2	public synchronized ...... **void**	**end** ()
	public synchronized ....int	**getLimit** ()
2	public....................String	getPresentationName ()
2	public synchronized .... **String**	**getRedoPresentationName** ()
	public synchronized .....String	**getUndoOrRedoPresentationName** ()

Class · *Interface* · —extends · - - -implements · ○ abstract · ● final · △ static · ▲ static final · ✳ constructor · x x—inherited · x **x**—declared · **x x**—overridden

U

2	public synchronized	**String**	**getUndoPresentationName** ()
2	public..................	boolean	isInProgress ()
2	public..................	boolean	isSignificant ()
2	protected	*UndoableEdit*	lastEdit ()
2	public synchronized	**void**	**redo** () throws CannotRedoException
	protected ....void		**redoTo** (*UndoableEdit* edit) throws CannotRedoException
1	public.................	boolean	replaceEdit (*UndoableEdit* anEdit)
	public synchronized ....void		**setLimit** (int l)
2	public..................	**String**	**toString** ()
	protected ....void		**trimEdits** (int from, int to)
	protected ....void		**trimForLimit** ()
2	public synchronized	**void**	**undo** () throws CannotUndoException
3	public...................void		**undoableEditHappened** (javax.swing.event.UndoableEditEvent e)
*	public......................		**UndoManager** ()
	public synchronized ....void		**undoOrRedo** () throws CannotRedoException, CannotUndoException
	protected ....void		**undoTo** (*UndoableEdit* edit) throws CannotUndoException

UnexpectedException   java.rmi

P O

```
Object
 └Throwable ------------------------- java.io.Serializable
   └Exception
     └java.io.IOException
```
1.1		└RemoteException [1]	
1.1		└UnexpectedException	

1	public..............	Throwable	detail
1	public..................	String	getMessage ()
1	public...................void		printStackTrace ()
1	public...................void		printStackTrace (java.io.PrintStream ps)
1	public...................void		printStackTrace (java.io.PrintWriter pw)
*	public......................		**UnexpectedException** (String s)
*	public......................		**UnexpectedException** (String s, Exception ex)

UnicastRemoteObject   java.rmi.server

P O

	Object [1]	
1.1 O	└RemoteObject [2] ---------------------- *java.rmi.Remote, java.io.Serializable*	
1.1 O	└RemoteServer [3]	
1.1	└UnicastRemoteObject	

	1	public.................	**Object**	**clone** () throws CloneNotSupportedException
	2	public..................	boolean	equals (Object obj)
△		public static	RemoteStub	**exportObject** (*java.rmi.Remote* obj) throws java.rmi.RemoteException
1.2 △		public static ..	*java.rmi.Remote*	**exportObject** (*java.rmi.Remote* obj, int port) throws java.rmi.RemoteException
1.2 △		public static ..	*java.rmi.Remote*	**exportObject** (*java.rmi.Remote* obj, int port, *RMIClientSocketFactory* csf, *RMIServerSocketFactory* ssf) throws java.rmi.RemoteException
△	3	public static	String	**getClientHost** () throws ServerNotActiveException
△	3	public static java.io.PrintStream		**getLog** ()
1.2	2	public..............	*RemoteRef*	**getRef** ()
	2	public.................	int	**hashCode** ()
	2	protected transient.	*RemoteRef*	ref
△	3	public static ....void		**setLog** (java.io.OutputStream out)
	2	public...................	String	**toString** ()
1.2 △	2	public static ..	*java.rmi.Remote*	**toStub** (*java.rmi.Remote* obj) throws java.rmi.NoSuchObjectException
1.2 △	2	public static	boolean	**unexportObject** (*java. rmi. Remote* obj, boolean force) throws java.rmi.NoSuchObjectException
*		protected		**UnicastRemoteObject** () throws java.rmi.RemoteException
1.2 *		protected		**UnicastRemoteObject** (int port) throws java.rmi.RemoteException
1.2 *		protected		**UnicastRemoteObject** (int port, *RMIClientSocketFactory* csf, *RMIServerSocketFactory* ssf) throws java.rmi.RemoteException

UnionMember   org.omg.CORBA

	Object	
1.2 ●	└UnionMember ------------------- *org.omg.CORBA.portable.IDLEntity (java.io.Serializable)*	

public.....................	Any	**label**
public.................	String	**name**
public..............	TypeCode	**type**

U

Classes

UnionMember

	public	*IDLType* **type_def**	
∗	public	**UnionMember** ()	
∗	public	**UnionMember** (String __name, Any __label, TypeCode __type, *IDLType* __type_def)	

UNKNOWN   org.omg.CORBA

```
Object
└Throwable - - - - - - - - - - - - - - - - - - - - - - - - - - java.io.Serializable
  └Exception
    └RuntimeException
      └SystemException 1
        └UNKNOWN
```

1.2 ○ SystemException¹
1.2 ● UNKNOWN

	1	public........CompletionStatus	completed
	1	public.........................int	minor
	1	public.....................String	toString ()
∗		public	**UNKNOWN** ()
∗		public	**UNKNOWN** (String s)
∗		public	**UNKNOWN** (int minor, CompletionStatus completed)
∗		public	**UNKNOWN** (String s, int minor, CompletionStatus completed)

UnknownError   java.lang
P

```
Object
└Throwable - - - - - - - - - - - - - - - - - - - - - - - - - - java.io.Serializable
  └Error
    └VirtualMachineError
      └UnknownError
```

○

∗	public	**UnknownError** ()	
∗	public	**UnknownError** (String s)	

UnknownGroupException   java.rmi.activation

```
Object
└Throwable - - - - - - - - - - - - - - - - - - - - - - - - - - java.io.Serializable
  └Exception
    └ActivationException 1
      └UnknownGroupException
```

1.2
1.2

	1	public................Throwable	detail
	1	public.....................String	getMessage ()
	1	public.........................void	printStackTrace ()
	1	public.........................void	printStackTrace (java.io.PrintStream ps)
	1	public.........................void	printStackTrace (java.io.PrintWriter pw)
∗		public	**UnknownGroupException** (String s)

UnknownHostException❶   java.net
P

```
Object
└Throwable - - - - - - - - - - - - - - - - - - - - - - - - - - java.io.Serializable
  └Exception
    └java.io.IOException
      └UnknownHostException
```

∗	public	**UnknownHostException** ()	
∗	public	**UnknownHostException** (String host)	

Class   *Interface*   —extends   - - -implements   ○ abstract   ● final   △ static   ▲ static final   ∗ constructor   x x—inherited   x **x**—declared   **x x**—overridden

678

U

UnknownHostException⊘ | java.rmi

```
Object
└ Throwable ------------------------- java.io.Serializable
   └ Exception
      └ java.io.IOException
1.1       └ RemoteException 1
1.1          └ UnknownHostException
```
P⁰

	1	public...............Throwable	detail
	1	public....................String	getMessage ()
	1	public.......................void	printStackTrace ()
	1	public.......................void	printStackTrace (java.io.PrintStream ps)
	1	public.......................void	printStackTrace (java.io.PrintWriter pw)
*		public.........................	**UnknownHostException** (String s)
*		public.........................	**UnknownHostException** (String s, Exception ex)

UnknownObjectException | java.rmi.activation

```
Object
└ Throwable ------------------------- java.io.Serializable
   └ Exception
1.2   └ ActivationException 1
1.2      └ UnknownObjectException
```

1	public...............Throwable	detail
1	public....................String	getMessage ()
1	public.......................void	printStackTrace ()
1	public.......................void	printStackTrace (java.io.PrintStream ps)
1	public.......................void	printStackTrace (java.io.PrintWriter pw)
*	public.........................	**UnknownObjectException** (String s)

UnknownServiceException | java.net

```
Object
└ Throwable ------------------------- java.io.Serializable
   └ Exception
      └ java.io.IOException
         └ UnknownServiceException
```
P

*	public.........................	**UnknownServiceException** ()
*	public.........................	**UnknownServiceException** (String msg)

U

UnknownUserException | org.omg.CORBA

```
Object
└ Throwable ------------------------- java.io.Serializable
   └ Exception
1.2 ○   └ UserException -------------------- org.omg.CORBA.portable.IDLEntity (java.io.Serializable)
1.2 ●      └ UnknownUserException
```

	public......................Any	**except**
*	public.........................	**UnknownUserException** ()
*	public.........................	**UnknownUserException** (Any a)

Classes

UnmarshalException | java.rmi

```
Object
└ Throwable ------------------------- java.io.Serializable
   └ Exception
      └ java.io.IOException
1.1       └ RemoteException 1
1.1          └ UnmarshalException
```
P⁰

1	public...............Throwable	detail
1	public....................String	getMessage ()
1	public.......................void	printStackTrace ()
1	public.......................void	printStackTrace (java.io.PrintStream ps)
1	public.......................void	printStackTrace (java.io.PrintWriter pw)

UnmarshalException

✳	public..........................	**UnmarshalException** (String s)	
✳	public..........................	**UnmarshalException** (String s, Exception ex)	

UnrecoverableKeyException · java.security

P^O

```
Object
└─Throwable ---------------------------- java.io.Serializable
   └─Exception
1.2    └─GeneralSecurityException
1.2       └─UnrecoverableKeyException
```

✳	public..........................	**UnrecoverableKeyException** ()	
✳	public..........................	**UnrecoverableKeyException** (String msg)	

Unreferenced · java.rmi.server

P^O

```
1.1   Unreferenced
```

	public.....................void	**unreferenced** ()	

UnresolvedPermission · java.security

P^O

```
       Object
1.2 ○  └─Permission 1 -------------------------- Guard, java.io.Serializable
1.2 ●     └─UnresolvedPermission ----------------- java.io.Serializable
```

	1 public.....................void	checkGuard (Object object) throws SecurityException	
	1 public................**boolean**	**equals** (Object obj)	
	1 public............**String**	**getActions** ()	
●	1 public final ....String	getName ()	
	1 public..................... **int**	**hashCode** ()	
	1 public................**boolean**	**implies** (Permission p)	
	1 public.. **PermissionCollection**	**newPermissionCollection** ()	
	1 public............**String**	**toString** ()	
✳	public..........................	**UnresolvedPermission** (String type, String name, String actions, java.security.cert.Certificate[] certs)	

UnsatisfiedLinkError · java.lang

P

```
Object
└─Throwable ---------------------------- java.io.Serializable
   └─Error
      └─LinkageError
         └─UnsatisfiedLinkError
```

✳	public..........................	**UnsatisfiedLinkError** ()	
✳	public..........................	**UnsatisfiedLinkError** (String s)	

UNSUPPORTED_POLICY · org.omg.CORBA

```
1.2   UNSUPPORTED_POLICY
```

▲	public static final...........short	**value** = 1	

UNSUPPORTED_POLICY_VALUE · org.omg.CORBA

```
1.2   UNSUPPORTED_POLICY_VALUE
```

▲	public static final...........short	**value** = 4	

Class *Interface* ——extends - - -implements ○ abstract ● final △ static ▲ static final ✳ constructor x x—inherited x **x**—declared **x x**—overridden

UnsupportedClassVersionError | java.lang
P

```
Object
 └Throwable --------------------------- java.io.Serializable
    └Error
       └LinkageError
          └ClassFormatError
1.2          └UnsupportedClassVersionError
```

*	public.........................	**UnsupportedClassVersionError** ()
*	public.........................	**UnsupportedClassVersionError** (String s)

UnsupportedEncodingException | java.io

```
Object
 └Throwable --------------------------- Serializable
    └Exception
       └IOException
1.1       └UnsupportedEncodingException
```

*	public.........................	**UnsupportedEncodingException** ()
*	public.........................	**UnsupportedEncodingException** (String s)

UnsupportedFlavorException | java.awt.datatransfer
P

```
Object
 └Throwable --------------------------- java.io.Serializable
    └Exception
1.1    └UnsupportedFlavorException
```

*	public.........................	**UnsupportedFlavorException** (DataFlavor flavor)

UnsupportedLookAndFeelException | javax.swing

U

```
Object
 └Throwable --------------------------- java.io.Serializable
    └Exception
1.2    └UnsupportedLookAndFeelException
```

*	public.........................	**UnsupportedLookAndFeelException** (String s)

UnsupportedOperationException | java.lang
P

```
Object
 └Throwable --------------------------- java.io.Serializable
    └Exception
       └RuntimeException
1.2       └UnsupportedOperationException
```

*	public.........................	**UnsupportedOperationException** ()
*	public.........................	**UnsupportedOperationException** (String message)

URL | java.net
P

```
Object 1
 └URL --------------------------------- java.io.Serializable
```

1	public.................	**boolean**	**equals** (Object obj)
●	public final ....Object		**getContent** () throws java.io.IOException
	public.................	String	**getFile** ()
	public.................	String	**getHost** ()
	public.................	int	**getPort** ()
	public.................	String	**getProtocol** ()
	public.................	String	**getRef** ()
1	public synchronized	**int**	**hashCode** ()
	public..........	URLConnection	**openConnection** () throws java.io.IOException
●	public final java.io.InputStream		**openStream** () throws java.io.IOException
	public.................	boolean	**sameFile** (URL other)

Classes

URL

		protected .... void	**set** (String protocol, String host, int port, String file, String ref)
△		public static synchronized void	**setURLStreamHandlerFactory** (*URLStreamHandlerFactory* fac)
		public ....String	**toExternalForm** ()
	1	public.................... **String**	**toString** ()
✳		public..........................	**URL** (String spec) throws MalformedURLException
✳		public..........................	**URL** (URL context, String spec) throws MalformedURLException
✳		public..........................	**URL** (String protocol, String host, String file) throws MalformedURLException
1.2 ✳		public..........................	**URL** (URL context, String spec, URLStreamHandler handler) throws MalformedURLException
✳		public..........................	**URL** (String protocol, String host, int port, String file) throws MalformedURLException
1.2 ✳		public..........................	**URL** (String protocol, String host, int port, String file, URLStreamHandler handler) throws MalformedURLException

---

URLClassLoader   java.net

P

```
     Object
○    └ClassLoader 1
1.2     └java.security.SecureClassLoader 2
1.2        └URLClassLoader
```

		protected .... void	**addURL** (URL url)
●	1	protected final............ Class	defineClass (String name, byte[] b, int off, int len) throws ClassFormatError
●	2	protected final............ Class	defineClass (String name, byte[] b, int off, int len, java.security.CodeSource cs)
●	1	protected final............ Class	defineClass (String name, byte[] b, int off, int len, java.security.ProtectionDomain protectionDomain) throws ClassFormatError
		protected .... Package	**definePackage** (String name, java. util. jar. Manifest man, URL url) throws IllegalArgumentException
	1	protected .... Package	definePackage (String name, String specTitle, String specVersion, String specVendor, String implTitle, String implVersion, String implVendor, URL sealBase) throws IllegalArgumentException
	1	protected .... **Class**	**findClass** (String name) throws ClassNotFoundException
	1	protected ....String	findLibrary (String libname)
●	1	protected final native .... Class	findLoadedClass (String name)
	1	public..................... **URL**	**findResource** (String name)
	1	public.. *java.util.Enumeration*	**findResources** (String name) throws java.io.IOException
●	1	protected final............ Class	findSystemClass (String name) throws ClassNotFoundException
	1	protected .... Package	getPackage (String name)
	1	protected ....Package[]	getPackages ()
●	1	public final .... ClassLoader	getParent ()
	2	protected ..... **java.security** ↵ **.PermissionCollection**	**getPermissions** (java.security.CodeSource codesource)
	1	public.................. URL	getResource (String name)
	1	public...... java.io.InputStream	getResourceAsStream (String name)
●	1	public final .... *java.util.Enumeration*	getResources (String name) throws java.io.IOException
△	1	public static ...... ClassLoader	getSystemClassLoader ()
△	1	public static .... URL	getSystemResource (String name)
△	1	public static .... java.io.InputStream	getSystemResourceAsStream (String name)
△	1	public static .... *java.util.Enumeration*	getSystemResources (String name) throws java.io.IOException
		public....................URL[]	**getURLs** ()
	1	public..................... Class	loadClass (String name) throws ClassNotFoundException
	1	protected synchronized . Class	loadClass (String name, boolean resolve) throws ClassNotFoundException
△		public static . URLClassLoader	**newInstance** (URL[] urls)
△		public static . URLClassLoader	**newInstance** (URL[] urls, ClassLoader parent)
●	1	protected final..............void	resolveClass (Class c)
●	1	protected final..............void	setSigners (Class c, Object[] signers)
✳		public..........................	**URLClassLoader** (URL[] urls)
✳		public..........................	**URLClassLoader** (URL[] urls, ClassLoader parent)
✳		public..........................	**URLClassLoader** (URL[] urls, ClassLoader parent, *URLStreamHandlerFactory* factory)

URLConnection   java.net

P

```
     Object 1
○    └URLConnection
```

Class   *Interface*   —extends   - - -implements   ○ abstract   ● final   △ static   ▲ static final   ✳ constructor   x x—inherited   x **x**—declared   **x x**—overridden

	protected . . . . boolean	**allowUserInteraction**	
○	public abstract . . . . void	**connect** () throws java.io.IOException	
	protected . . . . boolean	**connected**	
	protected . . . . boolean	**doInput**	
	protected . . . . boolean	**doOutput**	
	public . . . . boolean	**getAllowUserInteraction** ()	
	public . . . . Object	**getContent** () throws java.io.IOException	
	public . . . . String	**getContentEncoding** ()	
	public . . . . int	**getContentLength** ()	
	public . . . . String	**getContentType** ()	
	public . . . . long	**getDate** ()	
△	public static . . . . boolean	**getDefaultAllowUserInteraction** ()	
△	public static . . . . String	**getDefaultRequestProperty** (String key)	
	public . . . . boolean	**getDefaultUseCaches** ()	
	public . . . . boolean	**getDoInput** ()	
	public . . . . boolean	**getDoOutput** ()	
	public . . . . long	**getExpiration** ()	
1.2 △	public static . . . . . *FileNameMap*	**getFileNameMap** ()	
	public . . . . String	**getHeaderField** (int n)	
	public . . . . String	**getHeaderField** (String name)	
	public . . . . long	**getHeaderFieldDate** (String name, long Default)	
	public . . . . int	**getHeaderFieldInt** (String name, int Default)	
	public . . . . String	**getHeaderFieldKey** (int n)	
	public . . . . long	**getIfModifiedSince** ()	
	public . . . . . . java.io.InputStream	**getInputStream** () throws java.io.IOException	
	public . . . . long	**getLastModified** ()	
	public . . . . java.io.OutputStream	**getOutputStream** () throws java.io.IOException	
1.2	public java.security.Permission	**getPermission** () throws java.io.IOException	
	public . . . . String	**getRequestProperty** (String key)	
	public . . . . URL	**getURL** ()	
	public . . . . boolean	**getUseCaches** ()	
△	protected static . . . . String	**guessContentTypeFromName** (String fname)	
△	public static . . . . String	**guessContentTypeFromStream** (java.io.InputStream is) throws java.io.IOException	
	protected . . . . long	**ifModifiedSince**	
	public . . . . void	**setAllowUserInteraction** (boolean allowuserinteraction)	
△	public static synchronized void	**setContentHandlerFactory** (*ContentHandlerFactory* fac)	
△	public static . . . . void	**setDefaultAllowUserInteraction** (boolean defaultallowuserinteraction)	
△	public static . . . . void	**setDefaultRequestProperty** (String key, String value)	
	public . . . . void	**setDefaultUseCaches** (boolean defaultusecaches)	
	public . . . . void	**setDoInput** (boolean doinput)	
	public . . . . void	**setDoOutput** (boolean dooutput)	
1.2 △	public static . . . . void	**setFileNameMap** (*FileNameMap* map)	
	public . . . . void	**setIfModifiedSince** (long ifmodifiedsince)	
	public . . . . void	**setRequestProperty** (String key, String value)	
	public . . . . void	**setUseCaches** (boolean usecaches)	
1	public . . . . **String**	**toString** ()	
	protected . . . . URL	**url**	
＊	protected	**URLConnection** (URL url)	
	protected . . . . boolean	**useCaches**	

URLDecoder
java.net

```
        Object
1.2     └─URLDecoder
```

△	public static . . . . String	**decode** (String s) throws Exception
＊	public	**URLDecoder** ()

URLEncoder
java.net

```
        Object
        └─URLEncoder
```

△	public static . . . . String	**encode** (String s)

URLStreamHandler
java.net

```
        Object
○       └─URLStreamHandler
```

URLStreamHandler

○	protected abstract . . . . URLConnection	**openConnection** (URL u) throws java.io.IOException
	protected . . . . .void	**parseURL** (URL u, String spec, int start, int limit)
	protected . . . . .void	**setURL** (URL u, String protocol, String host, int port, String file, String ref)
	protected . . . . String	**toExternalForm** (URL u)
✱	public.	**URLStreamHandler** ()

URLStreamHandlerFactory   java.net

URLStreamHandlerFactory   P

- -

	public . . . . . . URLStreamHandler	**createURLStreamHandler** (String protocol)

UserException   org.omg.CORBA

Object
└Throwable - *java.io.Serializable*
  └Exception
1.2 ○   └UserException - *org.omg.CORBA.portable.IDLEntity* (*java.io.Serializable*)

✱	protected	**UserException** ()
✱	protected	**UserException** (String reason)

UTFDataFormatException   java.io

Object
└Throwable - *Serializable*
  └Exception
    └IOException
     └UTFDataFormatException

✱	public.	**UTFDataFormatException** ()
✱	public.	**UTFDataFormatException** (String s)

U

Utilities   javax.swing.text

Object
1.2   └Utilities

▲	public static final . . . . .int	**drawTabbedText** (Segment s, int x, int y, java.awt.Graphics g, *TabExpander* e, int startOffset)
▲	public static final . . . . .int	**getBreakLocation** (Segment s, java.awt.FontMetrics metrics, int x0, int x, *TabExpander* e, int startOffset)
▲	public static final . . . . .int	**getNextWord** (JTextComponent c, int offs) throws BadLocationException
▲	public static final . . . . . . *Element*	**getParagraphElement** (JTextComponent c, int offs)
▲	public static final . . . . .int	**getPositionAbove** (JTextComponent c, int offs, int x) throws BadLocationException
▲	public static final . . . . .int	**getPositionBelow** (JTextComponent c, int offs, int x) throws BadLocationException
▲	public static final . . . . .int	**getPreviousWord** (JTextComponent c, int offs) throws BadLocationException
▲	public static final . . . . .int	**getRowEnd** (JTextComponent c, int offs) throws BadLocationException
▲	public static final . . . . .int	**getRowStart** (JTextComponent c, int offs) throws BadLocationException
▲	public static final . . . . .int	**getTabbedTextOffset** (Segment s, java.awt.FontMetrics metrics, int x0, int x, *TabExpander* e, int startOffset)
▲	public static final . . . . .int	**getTabbedTextOffset** (Segment s, java.awt.FontMetrics metrics, int x0, int x, *TabExpander* e, int startOffset, boolean round)
▲	public static final . . . . .int	**getTabbedTextWidth** (Segment s, java.awt.FontMetrics metrics, int x, *TabExpander* e, int startOffset)
▲	public static final . . . . .int	**getWordEnd** (JTextComponent c, int offs) throws BadLocationException
▲	public static final . . . . .int	**getWordStart** (JTextComponent c, int offs) throws BadLocationException
✱	public.	**Utilities** ()

ValueMember   org.omg.CORBA

Object
1.2 ●   └ValueMember - *org.omg.CORBA.portable.IDLEntity* (*java.io.Serializable*)

Class *Interface* —extends - - -implements ○ abstract ● final △ static ▲ static final ✱ constructor x x—inherited x **x**—declared **x x**—overridden

public	short	**access**
public	String	**defined_in**
public	String	**id**
public	String	**name**
public	TypeCode	**type**
public	*IDLType*	**type_def**
* public		**ValueMember** ()
* public		**ValueMember** (String __name, String __id, String __defined_in, String __version, TypeCode __type, *IDLType* __type_def, short __access)
public	String	**version**

VariableHeightLayoutCache   javax.swing.tree

```
      Object
1.2 ○  └─AbstractLayoutCache¹ ------------------- RowMapper
1.2       └─VariableHeightLayoutCache
```

1	public	**java.awt.Rectangle**	**getBounds** (TreePath path, java.awt.Rectangle placeIn)
1	public	**boolean**	**getExpandedState** (TreePath path)
1	public	*TreeModel*	getModel ()
1	public AbstractLayoutCache ↵ .NodeDimensions		getNodeDimensions ()
1	protected	java.awt.Rectangle	getNodeDimensions (Object value, int row, int depth, boolean expanded, java.awt.Rectangle placeIn)
1	public	**TreePath**	**getPathClosestTo** (int x, int y)
1	public	**TreePath**	**getPathForRow** (int row)
1	public	int	getPreferredHeight ()
1	public	**int**	**getPreferredWidth** (java.awt.Rectangle bounds)
1	public	**int**	**getRowCount** ()
1	public	**int**	**getRowForPath** (TreePath path)
1	public	int	getRowHeight ()
1	public	int[]	getRowsForPaths (TreePath[] paths)
1	public	*TreeSelectionModel*	getSelectionModel ()
1	public	**int**	**getVisibleChildCount** (TreePath path)
1	public	**java.util.Enumeration**	**getVisiblePathsFrom** (TreePath path)
1	public	**void**	**invalidatePathBounds** (TreePath path)
1	public	**void**	**invalidateSizes** ()
1	public	**boolean**	**isExpanded** (TreePath path)
1	protected	boolean	isFixedRowHeight ()
1	public	boolean	isRootVisible ()
1	protected		nodeDimensions
	.... AbstractLayoutCache ↵ .NodeDimensions		
1	protected	boolean	rootVisible
1	protected	int	rowHeight
1	public	**void**	**setExpandedState** (TreePath path, boolean isExpanded)
1	public	**void**	**setModel** (*TreeModel* newModel)
1	public	**void**	**setNodeDimensions** (AbstractLayoutCache.NodeDimensions nd)
1	public	**void**	**setRootVisible** (boolean rootVisible)
1	public	**void**	**setRowHeight** (int rowHeight)
1	public	void	setSelectionModel (*TreeSelectionModel* newLSM)
1	protected	*TreeModel*	treeModel
1	public	**void**	**treeNodesChanged** (javax.swing.event.TreeModelEvent e)
1	public	**void**	**treeNodesInserted** (javax.swing.event.TreeModelEvent e)
1	public	**void**	**treeNodesRemoved** (javax.swing.event.TreeModelEvent e)
1	protected	*TreeSelectionModel*	treeSelectionModel
1	public	**void**	**treeStructureChanged** (javax.swing.event.TreeModelEvent e)
*	public		**VariableHeightLayoutCache** ()

Vector   java.util

P

```
      Object¹
1.2 ○  └─AbstractCollection² --------------------- Collection
1.2 ○    └─AbstractList³ ----------------------- List (Collection)
             └─Vector ------------------------- List (Collection), Cloneable, java.io.Serializable
```

1.2	3	public synchronized	**boolean**	**add** (Object o)
1.2	3	public	**void**	**add** (int index, Object element)
1.2	2	public synchronized	**boolean**	**addAll** (*Collection* c)
1.2	3	public synchronized	**boolean**	**addAll** (int index, *Collection* c)
		public synchronized	void	**addElement** (Object obj)

V

Classes

Vector

		public	int	**capacity** ()
		protected	int	**capacityIncrement**
1.2	3	public	**void**	**clear** ()
	1	public synchronized	**Object**	**clone** ()
	2	public	**boolean**	**contains** (Object elem)
1.2	2	public synchronized	**boolean**	**containsAll** (*Collection* c)
		public synchronized	void	**copyInto** (Object[] anArray)
		public synchronized	Object	**elementAt** (int index)
		protected	int	**elementCount**
		protected	Object[]	**elementData**
		public	*Enumeration*	**elements** ()
		public synchronized	void	**ensureCapacity** (int minCapacity)
	3	public synchronized	**boolean**	**equals** (Object o)
		public synchronized	Object	**firstElement** ()
1.2	3	public synchronized	**Object**	**get** (int index)
	3	public synchronized	**int**	**hashCode** ()
	3	public	**int**	**indexOf** (Object elem)
		public synchronized	int	**indexOf** (Object elem, int index)
		public synchronized	void	**insertElementAt** (Object obj, int index)
	2	public	**boolean**	**isEmpty** ()
1.2	3	public	*Iterator*	iterator ()
		public synchronized	Object	**lastElement** ()
	3	public	**int**	**lastIndexOf** (Object elem)
		public synchronized	int	**lastIndexOf** (Object elem, int index)
1.2	3	public	*ListIterator*	listIterator ()
1.2	3	public	*ListIterator*	listIterator (int index)
1.2	3	protected transient	int	modCount
1.2	3	public synchronized	**Object**	**remove** (int index)
1.2	2	public	**boolean**	**remove** (Object o)
1.2	2	public synchronized	**boolean**	**removeAll** (*Collection* c)
		public synchronized	void	**removeAllElements** ()
		public synchronized	boolean	**removeElement** (Object obj)
		public synchronized	void	**removeElementAt** (int index)
1.2	3	protected	**void**	**removeRange** (int fromIndex, int toIndex)
1.2	2	public synchronized	**boolean**	**retainAll** (*Collection* c)
1.2	3	public synchronized	**Object**	**set** (int index, Object element)
		public synchronized	void	**setElementAt** (Object obj, int index)
		public synchronized	void	**setSize** (int newSize)
	2	public	**int**	**size** ()
1.2	3	public	*List*	**subList** (int fromIndex, int toIndex)
1.2	2	public synchronized	**Object[]**	**toArray** ()
1.2	2	public synchronized	**Object[]**	**toArray** (Object[] a)
	2	public synchronized	**String**	**toString** ()
		public synchronized	void	**trimToSize** ()
	*	public		**Vector** ()
	*	public		**Vector** (int initialCapacity)
1.2	*	public		**Vector** (*Collection* c)
	*	public		**Vector** (int initialCapacity, int capacityIncrement)

VerifyError

java.lang

P

```
Object
 └─Throwable ------------------------- java.io.Serializable
    └─Error
       └─LinkageError
          └─VerifyError
```

*	public		**VerifyError** ()
*	public		**VerifyError** (String s)

VetoableChangeListener

java.beans

1.1	*VetoableChangeListener*———————————*java.util.EventListener*		
	public	void	**vetoableChange** (PropertyChangeEvent evt) throws PropertyVetoException

---

Class *Interface* —extends - - -implements ○ abstract ● final △ static ▲ static final ✳ constructor x x—inherited x **x**—declared **x x**—overridden

686

		VetoableChangeSupport	java.beans

1.1		Object	
		└VetoableChangeSupport - - - - - - - - - - - - - - - - - *java.io.Serializable*	

1.2		public synchronized . . . . . . .void	**addVetoableChangeListener** (*VetoableChangeListener* listener)
1.2		public synchronized . . . . . . .void	**addVetoableChangeListener** (String propertyName,
			VetoableChangeListener listener)
1.2		public. . . . . .void	**fireVetoableChange** (PropertyChangeEvent evt) throws PropertyVetoException
1.2		public. . . . . .void	**fireVetoableChange** (String propertyName, int oldValue, int newValue)
			throws PropertyVetoException
		public. . . . . .void	**fireVetoableChange** (String propertyName, Object oldValue, Object newValue)
			throws PropertyVetoException
1.2		public. . . . . .void	**fireVetoableChange** (String propertyName, boolean oldValue, boolean newValue)
			throws PropertyVetoException
1.2		public synchronized . . boolean	**hasListeners** (String propertyName)
		public synchronized . . . . . . .void	**removeVetoableChangeListener** (*VetoableChangeListener* listener)
1.2		public synchronized . . . . . . .void	**removeVetoableChangeListener** (String propertyName,
			VetoableChangeListener listener)
✳		public.	**VetoableChangeSupport** (Object sourceBean)

		View	javax.swing.text

1.2 ○		Object	
		└View - *javax.swing.SwingConstants*	

▲		public static final . . . . .int	**BadBreakWeight** = 0
		public. View	**breakView** (int axis, int offset, float pos, float len)
		public. . . . . .void	**changedUpdate** (*javax.swing.event.DocumentEvent* e, *java.awt.Shape* a,
			ViewFactory f)
		public. View	**createFragment** (int p0, int p1)
▲		public static final . . . . .int	**ExcellentBreakWeight** = 2000
▲		public static final . . . . .int	**ForcedBreakWeight** = 3000
		public. . . . . .float	**getAlignment** (int axis)
		public. . . . . *AttributeSet*	**getAttributes** ()
		public. .int	**getBreakWeight** (int axis, float pos, float len)
		public. . . . . *java.awt.Shape*	**getChildAllocation** (int index, *java.awt.Shape* a)
		public. . . . . . .java.awt.Container	**getContainer** ()
		public. . . . . *Document*	**getDocument** ()
		public. . . . . *Element*	**getElement** ()
		public. .int	**getEndOffset** ()
		public. . . . . .float	**getMaximumSpan** (int axis)
		public. . . . . .float	**getMinimumSpan** (int axis)
		public. .int	**getNextVisualPositionFrom** (int pos, Position.Bias b, *java.awt.Shape* a,
			int direction, Position.Bias[] biasRet) throws BadLocationException
		public. . . . . View	**getParent** ()
○		public abstract . . . . .float	**getPreferredSpan** (int axis)
		public. .int	**getResizeWeight** (int axis)
		public. .int	**getStartOffset** ()
		public. View	**getView** (int n)
		public. .int	**getViewCount** ()
		public. . . . . *ViewFactory*	**getViewFactory** ()
▲		public static final . . . . .int	**GoodBreakWeight** = 1000
		public. . . . . .void	**insertUpdate** (*javax.swing.event.DocumentEvent* e, *java.awt.Shape* a,
			ViewFactory f)
		public. . . . . boolean	**isVisible** ()
D		public. . . . . *java.awt.Shape*	**modelToView** (int pos, *java.awt.Shape* a) throws BadLocationException
○		public abstract *java.awt.Shape*	**modelToView** (int pos, *java.awt.Shape* a, Position.Bias b)
			throws BadLocationException
		public. . . . . *java.awt.Shape*	**modelToView** (int p0, Position.Bias b0, int p1, Position.Bias b1, *java.awt.Shape* a)
			throws BadLocationException
○		public abstract . . . . .void	**paint** (java.awt.Graphics g, *java.awt.Shape* allocation)
		public. . . . . .void	**preferenceChanged** (View child, boolean width, boolean height)
		public. . . . . .void	**removeUpdate** (*javax.swing.event.DocumentEvent* e, *java.awt.Shape* a,
			ViewFactory f)
		public. . . . . .void	**setParent** (View parent)
		public. . . . . .void	**setSize** (float width, float height)
✳		public.	**View** (*Element* elem)
D		public. .int	**viewToModel** (float x, float y, *java.awt.Shape* a)
○		public abstract . . . . .int	**viewToModel** (float x, float y, *java.awt.Shape* a, Position.Bias[] biasReturn)
▲		public static final . . . . .int	**X_AXIS** = 0
▲		public static final . . . . .int	**Y_AXIS** = 1

V

Classes

ViewFactory

		javax.swing.text

1.2	*ViewFactory*	
	public...................... View **create** (*Element* elem)	

ViewportLayout

		javax.swing

	Object	
1.2	└ViewportLayout - *java.awt.LayoutManager* [1], *java.io.Serializable*	

1	public.......................void	**addLayoutComponent** (String name, java.awt.Component c)
1	public.......................void	**layoutContainer** (java.awt.Container parent)
1	public......java.awt.Dimension	**minimumLayoutSize** (java.awt.Container parent)
1	public......java.awt.Dimension	**preferredLayoutSize** (java.awt.Container parent)
1	public.......................void	**removeLayoutComponent** (java.awt.Component c)
✳	public...........................	**ViewportLayout** ()

ViewportUI

		javax.swing.plaf

	Object	
1.2 ○	└ComponentUI [1]	
1.2 ○	└ViewportUI	

1	*11 inherited members from ComponentUI not shown*	
✳	public...........................	**ViewportUI** ()

VirtualMachineError

		java.lang
		P

	Object	
	└Throwable - *java.io.Serializable*	
	└Error	
○	└VirtualMachineError	

✳	public...........................	**VirtualMachineError** ()
✳	public...........................	**VirtualMachineError** (String s)

Visibility

		java.beans

1.1	*Visibility*	
	public.................. boolean	**avoidingGui** ()
	public.......................void	**dontUseGui** ()
	public.................. boolean	**needsGui** ()
	public.......................void	**okToUseGui** ()

VM_ABSTRACT

		org.omg.CORBA

1.2	*VM_ABSTRACT*	
▲	public static final..........short **value** = 2	

VM_CUSTOM

		org.omg.CORBA

1.2	*VM_CUSTOM*	
▲	public static final..........short **value** = 1	

VM_NONE

		org.omg.CORBA

1.2	*VM_NONE*	
▲	public static final..........short **value** = 0	

Class *Interface* —extends - - -implements ○ abstract ● final △ static ▲ static final ✳ constructor x x—inherited x **x**—declared **x x**—overridden

VM_TRUNCATABLE

1.2   *VM_TRUNCATABLE*

▲   public static final .... short **value** = 3

VMID

P⁰

     Object [1]
1.1 ●   └VMID - *java.io.Serializable*

   1   public................... **boolean equals** (Object obj)
   1   public....................... **int hashCode** ()
   △   public static .... boolean **isUnique** ()
   1   public.................... **String toString** ()
   ✳   public........................... **VMID** ()

Void

P

     Object
1.1 ●   └Void

▲   public static final .... Class **TYPE**

WeakHashMap

P

     Object
1.2 ○   └AbstractMap [1] - *Map*
1.2   └WeakHashMap - *Map*

   1   public..................... **void clear** ()
   1   public................. **boolean containsKey** (Object key)
   1   public................. boolean containsValue (Object value)
   1   public...................... ***Set* entrySet** ()
   1   public................. boolean equals (Object o)
   1   public.................... **Object get** (Object key)
   1   public......................int hashCode ()
   1   public................. **boolean isEmpty** ()
   1   public........................*Set* keySet ()
   1   public.................... **Object put** (Object key, Object value)
   1   public....................void putAll (*Map* t)
   1   public.................... **Object remove** (Object key)
   1   public........................ **int size** ()
   1   public................. String toString ()
   1   public................ *Collection* values ()
   ✳   public................. **WeakHashMap** ()
   ✳   public................. **WeakHashMap** (int initialCapacity)
   ✳   public................. **WeakHashMap** (int initialCapacity, float loadFactor)

W

Classes

WeakReference

     Object
1.2 ○   └Reference [1]
1.2   └WeakReference

   1   public......................void clear ()
   1   public................. boolean enqueue ()
   1   public.................... Object get ()
   1   public................. boolean isEnqueued ()
   ✳   public......................... **WeakReference** (Object referent)
   ✳   public......................... **WeakReference** (Object referent, ReferenceQueue q)

Window

Window					java.awt

```
        Object 1
   ○    └ Component 2 ------------------------- java.awt.image.ImageObserver, MenuContainer,
                                                              java.io.Serializable
             └ Container 3
                └ Window
```

	2	*131 inherited members from Component not shown*		
	3	*49 inherited members from Container not shown*		
	3	public..................... **void**	**addNotify** ()	
1.1		public synchronized .... void	**addWindowListener** (*java.awt.event.WindowListener* l)	
1.2		public.........................void	**applyResourceBundle** (String rbName)	
1.2		public.........................void	**applyResourceBundle** (java.util.ResourceBundle rb)	
		public.........................void	**dispose** ()	
	1	protected .... **void**	**finalize** () throws Throwable	
1.1		public............. Component	**getFocusOwner** ()	
1.2	2	public.............................	**getInputContext** ()	
		..... **java.awt.im.InputContext**		
1.1	2	public.......... **java.util.Locale**	**getLocale** ()	
1.2		public...................Window[]	**getOwnedWindows** ()	
1.2		public................... Window	**getOwner** ()	
	2	public................. **Toolkit**	**getToolkit** ()	
●		public final .... String	**getWarningString** ()	
	2	public................. **boolean**	**isShowing** ()	
		public.........................void	**pack** ()	
D	2	public................. **boolean**	**postEvent** (Event e)	
1.1	3	protected .... **void**	**processEvent** (AWTEvent e)	
1.1		protected ....void	**processWindowEvent** (java.awt.event.WindowEvent e)	
1.1		public synchronized .... void	**removeWindowListener** (*java.awt.event.WindowListener* l)	
	2	public................. **void**	**show** ()	
		public.........................void	**toBack** ()	
		public.........................void	**toFront** ()	
✳		public..........................	**Window** (Frame owner)	
1.2	✳	public..........................	**Window** (Window owner)	

WindowAdapter					java.awt.event

```
        Object                                                                                P
1.1 ○   └ WindowAdapter ------------------------- WindowListener 1 (java.util.EventListener)
```

	1	public.........................void	**windowActivated** (WindowEvent e)
✳		public..........................	**WindowAdapter** ()
	1	public.........................void	**windowClosed** (WindowEvent e)
	1	public.........................void	**windowClosing** (WindowEvent e)
	1	public.........................void	**windowDeactivated** (WindowEvent e)
	1	public.........................void	**windowDeiconified** (WindowEvent e)
	1	public.........................void	**windowIconified** (WindowEvent e)
	1	public.........................void	**windowOpened** (WindowEvent e)

WindowConstants					javax.swing

1.2	*WindowConstants*	

▲	public static final.............int	**DISPOSE_ON_CLOSE** = 2	
▲	public static final.............int	**DO_NOTHING_ON_CLOSE** = 0	
▲	public static final.............int	**HIDE_ON_CLOSE** = 1	

WindowEvent					java.awt.event

```
        Object                                                                                P
1.1     └ java.util.EventObject 1 -------------------- java.io.Serializable
1.1 ○     └ java.awt.AWTEvent 2
1.1         └ ComponentEvent 3
1.1           └ WindowEvent
```

	2	protected ....void	consume ()
	2	protected .... boolean	consumed

Class *Interface* —extends - - -implements ○ abstract ● final △ static ▲ static final ✳ constructor x x—inherited x **x**—declared **x x**—overridden

W

2	protected	.................void	finalize () throws Throwable
3	public....	java.awt.Component	getComponent ()
2	public...	.................int	getID ()
1	public..	.................Object	getSource ()
	public..	.......java.awt.Window	**getWindow** ()
2	protected	.................int	id
2	protected	.... boolean	isConsumed ()
3	public.	.................**String**	**paramString** ()
1	protected transient	......Object	source
2	public.	.................String	toString ()
▲	public static final	.............int	**WINDOW_ACTIVATED** = 205
▲	public static final	.............int	**WINDOW_CLOSED** = 202
▲	public static final	.............int	**WINDOW_CLOSING** = 201
▲	public static final	.............int	**WINDOW_DEACTIVATED** = 206
▲	public static final	.............int	**WINDOW_DEICONIFIED** = 204
▲	public static final	.............int	**WINDOW_FIRST** = 200
▲	public static final	.............int	**WINDOW_ICONIFIED** = 203
▲	public static final	.............int	**WINDOW_LAST** = 206
▲	public static final	.............int	**WINDOW_OPENED** = 200
✳	public.	....	**WindowEvent** (java.awt.Window source, int id)

WindowListener · java.awt.event

1.1	*WindowListener*————————*java.util.EventListener*	P

public	...................void	**windowActivated** (WindowEvent e)
public	...................void	**windowClosed** (WindowEvent e)
public	...................void	**windowClosing** (WindowEvent e)
public	...................void	**windowDeactivated** (WindowEvent e)
public	...................void	**windowDeiconified** (WindowEvent e)
public	...................void	**windowIconified** (WindowEvent e)
public	...................void	**windowOpened** (WindowEvent e)

WindowPeer · java.awt.peer

WindowPeer————————————*ContainerPeer [1]* (*ComponentPeer [2]*)

	2	*32 inherited members from ComponentPeer not shown*	
	1	*4 inherited members from ContainerPeer not shown*	
1.2 ▲		public static final ....int	**CONSUME_EVENT** = 1
1.2 ▲		public static final ....int	**FOCUS_NEXT** = 2
1.2 ▲		public static final ....int	**FOCUS_PREVIOUS** = 3
1.2		public.....................int	**handleFocusTraversalEvent** (java.awt.event.KeyEvent)
1.2 ▲		public static final ....int	**IGNORE_EVENT** = 0
		public.....................void	**toBack** ()
		public.....................void	**toFront** ()

WrappedPlainView · javax.swing.text

Object
1.2 ○	└ View [1] - *javax.swing.SwingConstants*
1.2 ○	└ CompositeView [2]
1.2	└ BoxView [3]
1.2	└ WrappedPlainView - - - - - - - - - - - - - - - *TabExpander [4]*

2	public	.....................void	append (View v)
3	protected	.................void	baselineLayout (int targetSpan, int axis, int[] offsets, int[] spans)
3	protected	.javax.swing.SizeRequirements	baselineRequirements (int axis, javax.swing.SizeRequirements r)
1	public	.... View	breakView (int axis, int offset, float pos, float len)
	protected	.................int	**calculateBreakPosition** (int p0, int p1)
3	protected	.javax.swing.SizeRequirements	calculateMajorAxisRequirements (int axis, javax.swing.SizeRequirements r)
3	protected	.javax.swing.SizeRequirements	calculateMinorAxisRequirements (int axis, javax.swing.SizeRequirements r)
3	public	.... **void**	**changedUpdate** (*javax.swing.event.DocumentEvent* e, *java.awt.Shape* a, *ViewFactory* f)
3	protected	.................void	childAllocation (int index, java.awt.Rectangle alloc)
1	public	.... View	createFragment (int p0, int p1)
	protected	.................void	**drawLine** (int p0, int p1, java.awt.Graphics g, int x, int y)

W

Classes

WrappedPlainView

		protected	int	**drawSelectedText** (java.awt.Graphics g, int x, int y, int p0, int p1) throws BadLocationException
		protected	int	**drawUnselectedText** (java.awt.Graphics g, int x, int y, int p0, int p1) throws BadLocationException
	3	protected	boolean	flipEastAndWestAtEnds (int position, Position.Bias bias)
	3	public	float	getAlignment (int axis)
	1	public	*AttributeSet*	getAttributes ()
●	2	protected final	short	getBottomInset ()
	1	public	int	getBreakWeight (int axis, float pos, float len)
	2	public	*java.awt.Shape*	getChildAllocation (int index, *java.awt.Shape* a)
	1	public	java.awt.Container	getContainer ()
	1	public	*Document*	getDocument ()
	1	public	*Element*	getElement ()
	1	public	int	getEndOffset ()
●	3	public final	int	getHeight ()
	2	protected	java.awt.Rectangle	getInsideAllocation (*java.awt.Shape* a)
●	2	protected final	short	getLeftInset ()
●		protected final	Segment	**getLineBuffer** ()
	3	public	**float**	**getMaximumSpan** (int axis)
	3	public	**float**	**getMinimumSpan** (int axis)
	2	protected	int	getNextEastWestVisualPositionFrom (int pos, Position.Bias b, *java.awt.Shape* a, int direction, Position.Bias[] biasRet) throws BadLocationException
	2	protected	int	getNextNorthSouthVisualPositionFrom (int pos, Position.Bias b, *java.awt.Shape* a, int direction, Position.Bias[] biasRet) throws BadLocationException
	2	public	int	getNextVisualPositionFrom (int pos, Position.Bias b, *java.awt.Shape* a, int direction, Position.Bias[] biasRet) throws BadLocationException
●	3	protected final	int	getOffset (int axis, int childIndex)
	1	public	View	getParent ()
	3	public	**float**	**getPreferredSpan** (int axis)
	3	public	int	getResizeWeight (int axis)
●	2	protected final	short	getRightInset ()
●	3	protected final	int	getSpan (int axis, int childIndex)
	1	public	int	getStartOffset ()
		protected	int	**getTabSize** ()
●	2	protected final	short	getTopInset ()
	2	public	View	getView (int n)
	3	protected	View	getViewAtPoint (int x, int y, java.awt.Rectangle alloc)
	2	protected	View	getViewAtPosition (int pos, java.awt.Rectangle a)
	2	public	int	getViewCount ()
	1	public	*ViewFactory*	getViewFactory ()
	2	protected	int	getViewIndexAtPosition (int pos)
●	3	public final	int	getWidth ()
	2	public	void	insert (int offs, View v)
	3	public	**void**	**insertUpdate** (*javax.swing.event.DocumentEvent* e, *java.awt.Shape* a, *ViewFactory* f)
	3	protected	boolean	isAfter (int x, int y, java.awt.Rectangle innerAlloc)
	3	protected	boolean	isAllocationValid ()
	3	protected	boolean	isBefore (int x, int y, java.awt.Rectangle innerAlloc)
	1	public	boolean	isVisible ()
	3	protected	void	layout (int width, int height)
	3	protected	void	layoutMajorAxis (int targetSpan, int axis, int[] offsets, int[] spans)
	3	protected	void	layoutMinorAxis (int targetSpan, int axis, int[] offsets, int[] spans)
	2	protected	**void**	**loadChildren** (*ViewFactory* f)
	3	public	*java.awt.Shape*	modelToView (int pos, *java.awt.Shape* a, Position.Bias b) throws BadLocationException
	2	public	*java.awt.Shape*	modelToView (int p0, Position.Bias b0, int p1, Position.Bias b1, *java.awt.Shape* a) throws BadLocationException
	4	public	float	**nextTabStop** (float x, int tabOffset)
	3	public	**void**	**paint** (java.awt.Graphics g, *java.awt.Shape* a)
	3	protected	void	paintChild (java.awt.Graphics g, java.awt.Rectangle alloc, int index)
	3	public	void	preferenceChanged (View child, boolean width, boolean height)
	2	public	void	removeAll ()
	3	public	**void**	**removeUpdate** (*javax.swing.event.DocumentEvent* e, *java.awt.Shape* a, *ViewFactory* f)
	3	public	void	replace (int offset, int length, View[] elems)
●	2	protected final	void	setInsets (short top, short left, short bottom, short right)
●	2	protected final	void	setParagraphInsets (*AttributeSet* attr)
	2	public	void	setParent (View parent)
	3	public	**void**	**setSize** (float width, float height)
	3	public	int	viewToModel (float x, float y, *java.awt.Shape* a, Position.Bias[] bias)
＊		public		**WrappedPlainView** (*Element* elem)

Class   *Interface*   —extends   - - -implements   ○ abstract   ● final   △ static   ▲ static final   ＊ constructor   x x—inherited   x **x**—declared   **x x**—overridden

*	public	**WrappedPlainView** (*Element* elem, boolean wordWrap)

WritableRaster java.awt.image

Object
1.2 └ Raster[1]
1.2 └ WritableRaster

P

1 *57 inherited members from Raster not shown*

public .... WritableRaster	**createWritableChild** (int parentX, int parentY, int w, int h, int childMinX, int childMinY, int[] bandList)
public .... WritableRaster	**createWritableTranslatedChild** (int childMinX, int childMinY)
public .... WritableRaster	**getWritableParent** ()
public ....void	**setDataElements** (int x, int y, Raster inRaster)
public ....void	**setDataElements** (int x, int y, Object inData)
public ....void	**setDataElements** (int x, int y, int w, int h, Object inData)
public ....void	**setPixel** (int x, int y, float[] fArray)
public ....void	**setPixel** (int x, int y, int[] iArray)
public ....void	**setPixel** (int x, int y, double[] dArray)
public ....void	**setPixels** (int x, int y, int w, int h, double[] dArray)
public ....void	**setPixels** (int x, int y, int w, int h, int[] iArray)
public ....void	**setPixels** (int x, int y, int w, int h, float[] fArray)
public ....void	**setRect** (Raster srcRaster)
public ....void	**setRect** (int dx, int dy, Raster srcRaster)
public ....void	**setSample** (int x, int y, int b, double s)
public ....void	**setSample** (int x, int y, int b, int s)
public ....void	**setSample** (int x, int y, int b, float s)
public ....void	**setSamples** (int x, int y, int w, int h, int b, float[] fArray)
public ....void	**setSamples** (int x, int y, int w, int h, int b, int[] iArray)
public ....void	**setSamples** (int x, int y, int w, int h, int b, double[] dArray)
* protected	**WritableRaster** (SampleModel sampleModel, java.awt.Point origin)
* protected	**WritableRaster** (SampleModel sampleModel, DataBuffer dataBuffer, java.awt.Point origin)
* protected	**WritableRaster** (SampleModel sampleModel, DataBuffer dataBuffer, java.awt↵ .Rectangle aRegion, java.awt.Point sampleModelTranslate, WritableRaster parent)

WritableRenderedImage java.awt.image

1.2 *WritableRenderedImage* ──────────── *RenderedImage*[1]

P

	public ....void	**addTileObserver** (*TileObserver* to)
1	public .... WritableRaster	copyData (WritableRaster raster)
1	public .... ColorModel	getColorModel ()
1	public .... Raster	getData ()
1	public .... Raster	getData (java.awt.Rectangle rect)
1	public ....int	getHeight ()
1	public ....int	getMinTileX ()
1	public ....int	getMinTileY ()
1	public ....int	getMinX ()
1	public ....int	getMinY ()
1	public ....int	getNumXTiles ()
1	public ....int	getNumYTiles ()
1	public .... Object	getProperty (String name)
1	public .... String[]	getPropertyNames ()
1	public .... SampleModel	getSampleModel ()
1	public .... java.util.Vector	getSources ()
1	public .... Raster	getTile (int tileX, int tileY)
1	public ....int	getTileGridXOffset ()
1	public ....int	getTileGridYOffset ()
1	public ....int	getTileHeight ()
1	public ....int	getTileWidth ()
1	public ....int	getWidth ()
	public .... WritableRaster	**getWritableTile** (int tileX, int tileY)
	public .... java.awt.Point[]	**getWritableTileIndices** ()
	public .... boolean	**hasTileWriters** ()
	public .... boolean	**isTileWritable** (int tileX, int tileY)
	public ....void	**releaseWritableTile** (int tileX, int tileY)
	public ....void	**removeTileObserver** (*TileObserver* to)
	public ....void	**setData** (Raster r)

WriteAbortedException · java.io

```
Object
 └ Throwable 1 - - - - - - - - - - - - - - - - - - - - - - - - Serializable
    └ Exception
       └ IOException
1.1 ○      └ ObjectStreamException
1.1         └ WriteAbortedException
```

	public	Exception	**detail**
1	public	**String**	**getMessage** ()
*	public		**WriteAbortedException** (String s, Exception ex)

Writer · java.io

```
     Object
1.1 ○ └ Writer
```

○	public abstract	void	**close** () throws IOException
○	public abstract	void	**flush** () throws IOException
	protected	Object	**lock**
	public	void	**write** (char[] cbuf) throws IOException
	public	void	**write** (int c) throws IOException
	public	void	**write** (String str) throws IOException
○	public abstract	void	**write** (char[] cbuf, int off, int len) throws IOException
	public	void	**write** (String str, int off, int len) throws IOException
*	protected		**Writer** ()
*	protected		**Writer** (Object lock)

WrongTransaction · org.omg.CORBA

```
     Object
     └ Throwable - - - - - - - - - - - - - - - - - - - - - - - - java.io.Serializable
        └ Exception
1.2 ○      └ UserException - - - - - - - - - - - - - - - - - - - - org.omg.CORBA.portable.IDLEntity (java.io.Serializable)
1.2            └ WrongTransaction
```

*	public		**WrongTransaction** ()
*	public		**WrongTransaction** (String reason)

X

X509Certificate · java.security.cert

```
     Object
1.2 ○ └ Certificate 1
1.2 ○    └ X509Certificate - - - - - - - - - - - - - - - - - - - - - X509Extension 2
```

○		public abstract	void	**checkValidity** () throws CertificateExpiredException, CertificateNotYetValidException
○		public abstract	void	**checkValidity** (java.util.Date date) throws CertificateExpiredException, CertificateNotYetValidException
	1	public	boolean	equals (Object other)
○		public abstract	int	**getBasicConstraints** ()
○	2	public abstract	java.util.Set	**getCriticalExtensionOIDs** ()
○	1	public abstract	byte[]	getEncoded () throws CertificateEncodingException
○	2	public abstract	byte[]	**getExtensionValue** (String)
○		public abstract	java.security.Principal	**getIssuerDN** ()
○		public abstract	boolean[]	**getIssuerUniqueID** ()
○		public abstract	boolean[]	**getKeyUsage** ()
○	2	public abstract	java.util.Set	**getNonCriticalExtensionOIDs** ()
○		public abstract	java.util.Date	**getNotAfter** ()
○		public abstract	java.util.Date	**getNotBefore** ()
○	1	public abstract	java.security.PublicKey	getPublicKey ()
○		public abstract	java.math.BigInteger	**getSerialNumber** ()
○		public abstract	String	**getSigAlgName** ()
○		public abstract	String	**getSigAlgOID** ()

Class *Interface* —extends - - -implements ○ abstract ● final △ static ▲ static final ✳ constructor x x—inherited x **x**—declared **x x**—overridden

○		public abstract . . . . byte[]	**getSigAlgParams** ()
○		public abstract . . . . byte[]	**getSignature** ()
○		public abstract	**getSubjectDN** ()
		. . . . *java.security.Principal*	
○		public abstract . . . . boolean[]	**getSubjectUniqueID** ()
○		public abstract . . . . byte[]	**getTBSCertificate** () throws CertificateEncodingException
●	1	public final . . . . String	getType ()
○		public abstract . . . . int	**getVersion** ()
	1	public . . . . int	hashCode ()
○	2	public abstract . . . . boolean	**hasUnsupportedCriticalExtension** ()
○	1	public abstract . . . . String	toString ()
○	1	public abstract . . . . void	verify (*java.security.PublicKey* key) throws CertificateException,
			java.security.NoSuchAlgorithmException, java.security.InvalidKeyException,
			java.security.NoSuchProviderException, java.security.SignatureException
○	1	public abstract . . . . void	verify (*java.security.PublicKey* key, String sigProvider) throws CertificateException,
			java.security.NoSuchAlgorithmException, java.security.InvalidKeyException,
			java.security.NoSuchProviderException, java.security.SignatureException
✳		protected	**X509Certificate** ()

X509CRL   java.security.cert

		Object [1]	
1.2 ○		└CRL [2]	
1.2 ○		└X509CRL - *X509Extension* [3]	
	1	public . . . . **boolean**	**equals** (Object other)
○	3	public abstract . . . . . *java.util.Set*	**getCriticalExtensionOIDs** ()
○		public abstract . . . . byte[]	**getEncoded** () throws CRLException
○	3	public abstract . . . . byte[]	**getExtensionValue** (String)
○		public abstract	**getIssuerDN** ()
		. . . . *java.security.Principal*	
○		public abstract . . . java.util.Date	**getNextUpdate** ()
○	3	public abstract . . . . . *java.util.Set*	**getNonCriticalExtensionOIDs** ()
○		public abstract . X509CRLEntry	**getRevokedCertificate** (java.math.BigInteger serialNumber)
○		public abstract . . . . . *java.util.Set*	**getRevokedCertificates** ()
○		public abstract . . . . String	**getSigAlgName** ()
○		public abstract . . . . String	**getSigAlgOID** ()
○		public abstract . . . . byte[]	**getSigAlgParams** ()
○		public abstract . . . . byte[]	**getSignature** ()
○		public abstract . . . . byte[]	**getTBSCertList** () throws CRLException
○		public abstract . . . java.util.Date	**getThisUpdate** ()
●	2	public final . . . . String	getType ()
○		public abstract . . . . int	**getVersion** ()
	1	public . . . . **int**	**hashCode** ()
○	3	public abstract . . . . boolean	**hasUnsupportedCriticalExtension** ()
○	2	public abstract . . . . boolean	isRevoked (Certificate cert)
○	2	public abstract . . . . String	toString ()
○		public abstract . . . . void	**verify** (*java.security.PublicKey* key) throws CRLException,
			java.security.NoSuchAlgorithmException, java.security.InvalidKeyException,
			java.security.NoSuchProviderException, java.security.SignatureException
○		public abstract . . . . void	**verify** (*java.security.PublicKey* key, String sigProvider) throws CRLException,
			java.security.NoSuchAlgorithmException, java.security.InvalidKeyException,
			java.security.NoSuchProviderException, java.security.SignatureException
✳		protected	**X509CRL** ()

X509CRLEntry   java.security.cert

		Object [1]	
1.2 ○		└X509CRLEntry - *X509Extension* [2]	
	1	public . . . . **boolean**	**equals** (Object other)
○	2	public abstract . . . . . *java.util.Set*	**getCriticalExtensionOIDs** ()
○		public abstract . . . . byte[]	**getEncoded** () throws CRLException
○	2	public abstract . . . . byte[]	**getExtensionValue** (String)
○	2	public abstract . . . . . *java.util.Set*	**getNonCriticalExtensionOIDs** ()
○		public abstract . . . java.util.Date	**getRevocationDate** ()
○		public abstract	**getSerialNumber** ()
		. . . . java.math.BigInteger	
○		public abstract . . . . boolean	**hasExtensions** ()
	1	public . . . . **int**	**hashCode** ()
○	2	public abstract . . . . boolean	**hasUnsupportedCriticalExtension** ()

X

Classes

X509CRLEntry

○	1	public abstract	**String**	**toString** ()
✳		public		**X509CRLEntry** ()

X509EncodedKeySpec
java.security.spec

		Object
1.2 ○		└EncodedKeySpec [1] - *KeySpec*
1.2		└X509EncodedKeySpec

	1	public	**byte[]**	**getEncoded** ()
●	1	public final	**String**	**getFormat** ()
✳		public		**X509EncodedKeySpec** (byte[] encodedKey)

X509Extension
java.security.cert

1.2		*X509Extension*

	public . . . . *java.util.Set*	**getCriticalExtensionOIDs** ()
	public . . . . byte[]	**getExtensionValue** (String oid)
	public . . . . *java.util.Set*	**getNonCriticalExtensionOIDs** ()
	public . . . . boolean	**hasUnsupportedCriticalExtension** ()

ZipEntry
java.util.zip
P

		Object [1]
1.1		└ZipEntry - java.util.zip.ZipConstants, *Cloneable*

	1	public	**Object**	**clone** ()
▲		public static final . . . . int	**DEFLATED**	= 8
		public . . . . String	**getComment** ()
		public . . . . long	**getCompressedSize** ()
		public . . . . long	**getCrc** ()
		public . . . . byte[]	**getExtra** ()
		public . . . . int	**getMethod** ()
		public . . . . String	**getName** ()
		public . . . . long	**getSize** ()
		public . . . . long	**getTime** ()
	1	public . . . . **int**	**hashCode** ()
		public . . . . boolean	**isDirectory** ()
		public . . . . void	**setComment** (String comment)
1.2		public . . . . void	**setCompressedSize** (long csize)
		public . . . . void	**setCrc** (long crc)
		public . . . . void	**setExtra** (byte[] extra)
		public . . . . void	**setMethod** (int method)
		public . . . . void	**setSize** (long size)
		public . . . . void	**setTime** (long time)
▲		public static final . . . . int	**STORED**	= 0
	1	public . . . . **String**	**toString** ()
✳		public	**ZipEntry** (String name)
1.2 ✳		public	**ZipEntry** (ZipEntry e)

ZipException
java.util.zip
P

		Object
		└Throwable - *java.io.Serializable*
		└Exception
		└java.io.IOException
1.1		└ZipException

✳	public	**ZipException** ()
✳	public	**ZipException** (String s)

ZipFile
java.util.zip
P⁰

		Object
1.1		└ZipFile - java.util.zip.ZipConstants

Class   *Interface*   —extends   - - -implements   ○ abstract   ● final   △ static   ▲ static final   ✳ constructor   x x—inherited   x **x**—declared   **x x**—overridden

	public	.....................void	**close** () throws java.io.IOException
	public	.... *java.util.Enumeration*	**entries** ()
	public	.................ZipEntry	**getEntry** (String name)
	public	.......java.io.InputStream	**getInputStream** (ZipEntry entry) throws java.io.IOException
	public	....................String	**getName** ()
1.2	public	.......................int	**size** ()
*	public	....	**ZipFile** (java.io.File file) throws ZipException, java.io.IOException
*	public	....	**ZipFile** (String name) throws java.io.IOException

ZipInputStream   java.util.zip

```
     Object
 ○   └java.io.InputStream
        └java.io.FilterInputStream 1
1.1        └InflaterInputStream 2
1.1           └ZipInputStream - - - - - - - - - - - - - - - - - - java.util.zip.ZipConstants
```
P

2	public	.......................int	**available** () throws java.io.IOException
2	protected	.................byte[]	buf
2	public	.....................void	**close** () throws java.io.IOException
	public	.....................void	**closeEntry** () throws java.io.IOException
1.2	protected	............ZipEntry	**createZipEntry** (String name)
2	protected	.................void	fill () throws java.io.IOException
	public	.................ZipEntry	**getNextEntry** () throws java.io.IOException
1	protected ..	java.io.InputStream	in
2	protected	...............Inflater	inf
2	protected	....................int	len
1	public synchronized	......void	mark (int readlimit)
1	public	.... boolean	markSupported ()
2	public	....................int	read () throws java.io.IOException
1	public	....................int	read (byte[] b) throws java.io.IOException
2	public	.......................int	**read** (byte[] b, int off, int len) throws java.io.IOException
1	public synchronized	......void	reset () throws java.io.IOException
2	public	....................long	**skip** (long n) throws java.io.IOException
*	public	....	**ZipInputStream** (java.io.InputStream in)

ZipOutputStream   java.util.zip

```
     Object
 ○   └java.io.OutputStream
        └java.io.FilterOutputStream 1
1.1        └DeflaterOutputStream 2
1.1           └ZipOutputStream - - - - - - - - - - - - - - - - - - java.util.zip.ZipConstants
```
P○

2	protected	.................byte[]	buf
2	public	.....................void	**close** () throws java.io.IOException
	public	.....................void	**closeEntry** () throws java.io.IOException
2	protected	...............Deflater	def
2	protected	.................void	deflate () throws java.io.IOException
▲	public static final	............int	**DEFLATED** = 8
2	public	.....................void	**finish** () throws java.io.IOException
1	public	.....................void	flush () throws java.io.IOException
1	protected java.io.OutputStream		out
	public	.....................void	**putNextEntry** (ZipEntry e) throws java.io.IOException
	public	.....................void	**setComment** (String comment)
	public	.....................void	**setLevel** (int level)
	public	.....................void	**setMethod** (int method)
▲	public static final	............int	**STORED** = 0
1	public	.....................void	write (byte[] b) throws java.io.IOException
2	public	.....................void	write (int b) throws java.io.IOException
2	public synchronized	...... void	**write** (byte[] b, int off, int len) throws java.io.IOException
*	public	....	**ZipOutputStream** (java.io.OutputStream out)

Z

Classes

Part 3
TOPICS

This part contains quick-reference material on miscellaneous topics. For example, the topic title "Java 1.2" contains a detailed analysis of the API differences between Java 1.1 and Java 1.2. Other useful tables cover documentation comment tags and available system properties, among other topics.

Contents

Statistics

Packages	8	**Members**		2125
		Fields		261
Classes and Interfaces	212	static		3
Classes	172	static final		167
abstract	21	protected		50
final	20	Constructors		319
Interfaces	40	protected		6
		Methods		1545
		abstract		102
		static		149
		final		140
		static final		1
		protected		78

Packages

Package	Classes	Members	Interfaces	Members
java.applet	1	22	3	16
java.awt	44	732	2	8
java.awt.image	9	94	3	30
java.awt.peer	0	0	22	84
java.io	28	310	3	30
java.lang	62	504	2	1
java.net	16	145	3	3
java.util	12	143	2	3

Exceptions and Errors

This is a complete listing of all the exceptions and errors in this version of Java. The "*" indicates a checked exception or error; these must be declared in the throws clause.

java.lang	AbstractMethodError		java.lang	IllegalMonitorStateException
java.lang	ArithmeticException		java.lang	IllegalThreadStateException
java.lang	ArrayIndexOutOfBoundsException		java.lang	IncompatibleClassChangeError
java.lang	ArrayStoreException		java.lang	IndexOutOfBoundsException
java.awt	AWTError		java.lang	InstantiationError
java.awt	*AWTException		java.lang	*InstantiationException
java.lang	ClassCastException		java.lang	InternalError
java.lang	ClassCircularityError		java.lang	*InterruptedException
java.lang	ClassFormatError		java.io	*InterruptedIOException
java.lang	*ClassNotFoundException		java.io	*IOException
java.lang	*CloneNotSupportedException		java.lang	LinkageError
java.util	EmptyStackException		java.net	*MalformedURLException
java.io	*EOFException		java.lang	NegativeArraySizeException
java.lang	Error		java.lang	NoClassDefFoundError
java.lang	*Exception		java.util	NoSuchElementException
java.io	*FileNotFoundException		java.lang	NoSuchFieldError
java.lang	IllegalAccessError		java.lang	NoSuchMethodError
java.lang	*IllegalAccessException		java.lang	*NoSuchMethodException
java.lang	IllegalArgumentException		java.lang	NullPointerException

java.lang	NumberFormatException
java.lang	OutOfMemoryError
java.net	*ProtocolException
java.lang	RuntimeException
java.lang	SecurityException
java.net	*SocketException
java.lang	StackOverflowError
java.lang	StringIndexOutOfBoundsException
java.lang	ThreadDeath

java.lang	*Throwable
java.lang	UnknownError
java.net	*UnknownHostException
java.net	*UnknownServiceException
java.lang	UnsatisfiedLinkError
java.io	*UTFDataFormatException
java.lang	VerifyError
java.lang	VirtualMachineError

Statistics

Packages 23

Classes and Interfaces 504
   Classes 391
      abstract 58
      final 38
   Interfaces 113

Members 5478
   Fields 926
      static 4
      final 2
      static final 764
      protected 111
   Constructors 701
      protected 43
   Methods 3851
      abstract 202
      static 360
      final 207
      static final 24
      protected 191

Packages

New	Package	Classes	Members	Interfaces	Members
	java.applet	1	23	3	16
	java.awt	54	1282	7	35
•	java.awt.datatransfer	4	25	2	4
•	java.awt.event	19	275	11	29
	java.awt.image	11	125	3	30
	java.awt.peer	0	0	27	117
•	java.beans	17	114	6	33
	java.io	61	599	8	46
	java.lang	67	659	2	1
•	java.lang.reflect	6	93	1	5
•	java.math	2	86	0	0
	java.net	22	250	4	4
•	java.rmi	18	68	1	0
•	java.rmi.dgc	2	8	1	2
•	java.rmi.registry	1	5	2	8
•	java.rmi.server	16	71	7	25
•	java.security	21	144	5	14
•	java.security.acl	3	3	5	27
•	java.security.interfaces	0	0	5	8
•	java.sql	9	91	8	332
•	java.text	18	304	1	11
	java.util	23	352	3	3
•	java.util.zip	16	147	1	4

New Classes in Existing Packages

java.awt
Adjustable, AWTEvent, AWTEventMulticaster, Cursor, EventQueue, IllegalComponentStateException, *ItemSelectable*, *LayoutManager2*, MenuShortcut, PopupMenu, *PrintGraphics*, PrintJob, ScrollPane, *Shape*, SystemColor
java.awt.image
AreaAveragingScaleFilter, ReplicateScaleFilter

java.awt.peer
ActiveEvent, *FontPeer*, *LightweightPeer*,
PopupMenuPeer, *ScrollPanePeer*

java.io
BufferedReader, BufferedWriter, CharArrayReader,
CharArrayWriter, CharConversionException,
Externalizable, FileReader, FileWriter, FilterReader,
FilterWriter, InputStreamReader, InvalidClassException,
InvalidObjectException, LineNumberReader,
NotActiveException, NotSerializableException,
ObjectInput, ObjectInputStream, *ObjectInputValidation*,
ObjectOutput, ObjectOutputStream, ObjectStreamClass,
ObjectStreamException, OptionalDataException,
OutputStreamWriter, PipedReader, PipedWriter,
PrintWriter, PushbackReader, Reader, *Serializable*,
StreamCorruptedException, StringReader, StringWriter,

SyncFailedException, UnsupportedEncodingException,
WriteAbortedException, Writer

java.lang
Byte, ExceptionInInitializerError, IllegalStateException,
NoSuchFieldException, Short, Void

java.net
BindException, ConnectException,
DatagramSocketImpl, *FileNameMap*,
HttpURLConnection, MulticastSocket,
NoRouteToHostException

java.util
Calendar, *EventListener*, EventObject,
GregorianCalendar, ListResourceBundle, Locale,
MissingResourceException, PropertyResourceBundle,
ResourceBundle, SimpleTimeZone, TimeZone,
TooManyListenersException

New Members in Existing Classes

java.applet
Applet
getLocale( )

java.awt
BorderLayout
addLayoutComponent( ), CENTER, EAST,
getHgap( ), getLayoutAlignmentX( ),
getLayoutAlignmentY( ), getVgap( ),
invalidateLayout( ), maximumLayoutSize( ), NORTH,
setHgap( ), setVgap( ), SOUTH, WEST

Button
addActionListener( ), getActionCommand( ),
processActionEvent( ), processEvent( ),
removeActionListener( ), setActionCommand( )

CardLayout
addLayoutComponent( ), getHgap( ),
getLayoutAlignmentX( ), getLayoutAlignmentY( ),
getVgap( ), invalidateLayout( ),
maximumLayoutSize( ), setHgap( ), setVgap( )

Checkbox
addItemListener( ), Checkbox( ),
getSelectedObjects( ), processEvent( ),
processItemEvent( ), removeItemListener( )

CheckboxGroup
getSelectedCheckbox( ), setSelectedCheckbox( )

CheckboxMenuItem
addItemListener( ), CheckboxMenuItem( ),
getSelectedObjects( ), processEvent( ),
processItemEvent( ), removeItemListener( )

Choice
add( ), addItemListener( ), getItemCount( ),
getSelectedObjects( ), insert( ), processEvent( ),
processItemEvent( ), remove( ), removeAll( ),
removeItemListener( )

Color
decode( )

Component
add( ), addComponentListener( ),
addFocusListener( ), addKeyListener( ),
addMouseListener( ), addMouseMotionListener( ),
BOTTOM_ALIGNMENT, CENTER_ALIGNMENT,
Component( ), contains( ), disableEvents( ),
dispatchEvent( ), doLayout( ), enableEvents( ),
getAlignmentX( ), getAlignmentY( ), getBounds( ),
getComponentAt( ), getCursor( ), getLocale( ),

getLocation( ), getLocationOnScreen( ),
getMaximumSize( ), getMinimumSize( ), getName( ),
getPreferredSize( ), getSize( ), getTreeLock( ),
isFocusTraversable( ), LEFT_ALIGNMENT, list( ),
processComponentEvent( ), processEvent( ),
processFocusEvent( ), processKeyEvent( ),
processMouseEvent( ), processMouseMotionEvent( ),
remove( ), removeComponentListener( ),
removeFocusListener( ), removeKeyListener( ),
removeMouseListener( ),
removeMouseMotionListener( ),
RIGHT_ALIGNMENT, setBounds( ),
setCursor( ), setEnabled( ), setLocale( ),
setLocation( ), setName( ), setSize( ), setVisible( ),
TOP_ALIGNMENT, transferFocus( )

Container
add( ), addContainerListener( ), addImpl( ),
Container( ), doLayout( ), getAlignmentX( ),
getAlignmentY( ), getComponentAt( ),
getComponentCount( ), getInsets( ),
getMaximumSize( ), getMinimumSize( ),
getPreferredSize( ), invalidate( ),
isAncestorOf( ), list( ), paint( ), print( ),
processContainerEvent( ), processEvent( ),
remove( ), removeContainerListener( ), update( ),
validateTree( )

Dialog
Dialog( ), setModal( ), show( )

Dimension
equals( ), getSize( ), setSize( )

Event
BACK_SPACE, CAPS_LOCK, DELETE, ENTER,
ESCAPE, INSERT, NUM_LOCK, PAUSE,
PRINT_SCREEN, SCROLL_BEGIN, SCROLL_END,
SCROLL_LOCK, TAB

FileDialog
FileDialog( ), setMode( )

FlowLayout
getAlignment( ), getHgap( ), getVgap( ),
setAlignment( ), setHgap( ), setVgap( )

Font
decode( ), getPeer( )

Graphics
drawImage( ), drawPolyline( ), getClip( ),
getClipBounds( ), setClip( )

GridBagLayout
addLayoutComponent( ), getLayoutAlignmentX( ),
getLayoutAlignmentY( ), invalidateLayout( ),
maximumLayoutSize( )
GridLayout
getColumns( ), getHgap( ), getRows( ), getVgap( ),
GridLayout( ), setColumns( ), setHgap( ), setRows( ),
setVgap( )
Image
getScaledInstance( ), SCALE_AREA_AVERAGING,
SCALE_DEFAULT, SCALE_FAST,
SCALE_REPLICATE, SCALE_SMOOTH
Insets
equals( )
List
add( ), addActionListener( ), addItemListener( ),
getItemCount( ), getItems( ), getMinimumSize( ),
getPreferredSize( ), getSelectedObjects( ),
isIndexSelected( ), isMultipleMode( ), List( ),
processActionEvent( ), processEvent( ),
processItemEvent( ), remove( ),
removeActionListener( ), removeAll( ),
removeItemListener( ), setMultipleMode( )
MediaTracker
removeImage( )
Menu
getItemCount( ), insert( ), insertSeparator( ), Menu( ),
paramString( ), removeAll( )
MenuBar
deleteShortcut( ), getMenuCount( ),
getShortcutMenuItem( ), shortcuts( )
MenuComponent
dispatchEvent( ), getName( ), processEvent( ),
setName( )
MenuItem
addActionListener( ), deleteShortcut( ),
disableEvents( ), enableEvents( ),
getActionCommand( ), getShortcut( ), MenuItem( ),
processActionEvent( ), processEvent( ),
removeActionListener( ), setActionCommand( ),
setEnabled( ), setShortcut( )
Panel
Panel( )
Point
getLocation( ), Point( ), setLocation( )
Polygon
bounds, contains( ), getBounds( ), translate( )
Rectangle
contains( ), getBounds( ), getLocation( ), getSize( ),
Rectangle( ), setBounds( ), setLocation( ), setSize( )
Scrollbar
addAdjustmentListener( ), getBlockIncrement( ),
getUnitIncrement( ), getVisibleAmount( ),
processAdjustmentEvent( ), processEvent( ),
removeAdjustmentListener( ), setBlockIncrement( ),
setMaximum( ), setMinimum( ), setOrientation( ),
setUnitIncrement( ), setVisibleAmount( )
TextArea
append( ), getMinimumSize( ), getPreferredSize( ),
getScrollbarVisibility( ), insert( ),
replaceRange( ), SCROLLBARS_BOTH,
SCROLLBARS_HORIZONTAL_ONLY,
SCROLLBARS_NONE,
SCROLLBARS_VERTICAL_ONLY, setColumns( ),
setRows( ), TextArea( )

TextComponent
addTextListener( ), getCaretPosition( ),
processEvent( ), processTextEvent( ),
removeTextListener( ), setCaretPosition( ),
setSelectionEnd( ), setSelectionStart( ), textListener
TextField
addActionListener( ), getMinimumSize( ),
getPreferredSize( ), processActionEvent( ),
processEvent( ), removeActionListener( ),
setColumns( ), setEchoChar( )
Toolkit
beep( ), createComponent( ), createImage( ),
createPopupMenu( ), createScrollPane( ),
getFontPeer( ), getMenuShortcutKeyMask( ),
getNativeContainer( ), getPrintJob( ), getProperty( ),
getSystemClipboard( ), getSystemEventQueue( ),
getSystemEventQueueImpl( ), loadSystemColors( )
Window
addWindowListener( ), getFocusOwner( ),
getLocale( ), isShowing( ), postEvent( ),
processEvent( ), processWindowEvent( ),
removeWindowListener( )

java.awt.image
MemoryImageSource
newPixels( ), setAnimated( ), setFullBufferUpdates( )
PixelGrabber
abortGrabbing( ), getColorModel( ), getHeight( ),
getPixels( ), getStatus( ), getWidth( ), PixelGrabber( ),
startGrabbing( )

java.awt.peer
ChoicePeer
add( ), remove( )
ComponentPeer
getLocationOnScreen( ), getMinimumSize( ),
getPreferredSize( ), handleEvent( ),
isFocusTraversable( ), setBounds( ), setCursor( ),
setEnabled( ), setVisible( )
ContainerPeer
beginValidate( ), endValidate( ), getInsets( )
ListPeer
add( ), getMinimumSize( ), getPreferredSize( ),
removeAll( ), setMultipleMode( )
MenuItemPeer
setEnabled( )
TextAreaPeer
getMinimumSize( ), getPreferredSize( ), insert( ),
replaceRange( )
TextComponentPeer
getCaretPosition( ), setCaretPosition( )
TextFieldPeer
getMinimumSize( ), getPreferredSize( ),
setEchoChar( )

java.io
ByteArrayInputStream
mark, markSupported( )
ByteArrayOutputStream
toString( )
File
getCanonicalPath( )
FileDescriptor
sync( )
FileOutputStream
FileOutputStream( )
PipedInputStream
buffer, in, out, PIPE_SIZE, receive( )
PrintStream
setError( )

Topics

PushbackInputStream
buf, pos, PushbackInputStream( ), unread( )
SequenceInputStream
available( )
StreamTokenizer
StreamTokenizer( )

java.lang
Boolean
TYPE
Character
COMBINING_SPACING_MARK,
CONNECTOR_PUNCTUATION, CONTROL,
CURRENCY_SYMBOL, DASH_PUNCTUATION,
DECIMAL_DIGIT_NUMBER, ENCLOSING_MARK,
END_PUNCTUATION, FORMAT, getNumericValue( ),
getType( ), isIdentifierIgnorable( ), isISOControl( ),
isJavaIdentifierPart( ), isJavaIdentifierStart( ),
isSpaceChar( ), isUnicodeIdentifierPart( ),
isUnicodeIdentifierStart( ), isWhitespace( ),
LETTER_NUMBER, LINE_SEPARATOR,
LOWERCASE_LETTER, MATH_SYMBOL,
MODIFIER_LETTER, MODIFIER_SYMBOL,
NON_SPACING_MARK, OTHER_LETTER,
OTHER_NUMBER, OTHER_PUNCTUATION,
OTHER_SYMBOL, PARAGRAPH_SEPARATOR,
PRIVATE_USE, SPACE_SEPARATOR,
START_PUNCTUATION, SURROGATE,
TITLECASE_LETTER, TYPE, UNASSIGNED,
UPPERCASE_LETTER
Class
getClasses( ), getComponentType( ),
getConstructor( ), getConstructors( ),
getDeclaredClasses( ), getDeclaredConstructor( ),
getDeclaredConstructors( ), getDeclaredField( ),
getDeclaredFields( ), getDeclaredMethod( ),
getDeclaredMethods( ), getDeclaringClass( ),
getField( ), getFields( ), getMethod( ),
getMethods( ), getModifiers( ), getResource( ),
getResourceAsStream( ), getSigners( ), isArray( ),
isAssignableFrom( ), isInstance( ), isPrimitive( )
ClassLoader
defineClass( ), findLoadedClass( ), getResource( ),
getResourceAsStream( ), getSystemResource( ),
getSystemResourceAsStream( ), loadClass( ),
setSigners( )
Double
byteValue( ), shortValue( ), TYPE
Float
byteValue( ), shortValue( ), TYPE

Integer
byteValue( ), decode( ), shortValue( ), TYPE
Long
byteValue( ), shortValue( ), TYPE
Number
byteValue( ), shortValue( )
Runtime
runFinalizersOnExit( )
SecurityManager
checkAwtEventQueueAccess( ),
checkMemberAccess( ), checkMulticast( ),
checkPrintJobAccess( ), checkSecurityAccess( ),
checkSystemClipboardAccess( ),
currentLoadedClass( ), getThreadGroup( )
String
getBytes( ), String( ), `toLowerCase( ), toUpperCase( )
System
identityHashCode( ), runFinalizersOnExit( ), setErr( ),
setIn( ), setOut( )
ThreadGroup
allowThreadSuspension( ), isDestroyed( )
Throwable
getLocalizedMessage( ), printStackTrace( )

java.net
DatagramPacket
setAddress( ), setData( ), setLength( ), setPort( )
DatagramSocket
DatagramSocket( ), getLocalAddress( ),
getSoTimeout( ), setSoTimeout( )
InetAddress
isMulticastAddress( )
ServerSocket
getSoTimeout( ), implAccept( ), ServerSocket( ),
setSoTimeout( )
Socket
getLocalAddress( ), getSoLinger( ), getSoTimeout( ),
getTcpNoDelay( ), setSoLinger( ), setSoTimeout( ),
setTcpNoDelay( ), Socket( )
SocketImpl
getOption( ), setOption( )
URLConnection
fileNameMap

java.util
Properties
list( )
Random
next( ), nextBytes( )

Removed Classes

java.lang
Win32Process

Removed Members

java.awt.peer
    ComponentPeer
      handleEvent( ), nextFocus( )
    FramePeer
      setCursor( )
    ScrollbarPeer
      setValue( )

java.io
    PushbackInputStream
      pushBack
java.lang
    SecurityManager
      checkPropertyAccess( )
java.net
    DatagramSocket
      finalize( )

Modified Classes and Members

These tables show all the classes and members whose signatures were modified from the previous version. "+" indicates an added keyword; "-" indicates a removed keyword.

Class Modifier Changes

java.awt
    Color — - final
java.net
    ServerSocket, Socket — - final

Implements Changes

java.awt
    BorderLayout, CardLayout, GridBagLayout — - java.awt.LayoutManager, + java.awt.LayoutManager2, + java.io.Serializable

    Checkbox, CheckboxMenuItem, Choice, List — + java.awt.ItemSelectable
    CheckboxGroup, Color, Dimension, Event, FlowLayout, Font, FontMetrics, GridBagConstraints, GridLayout, Insets, MediaTracker, MenuComponent, Point — + java.io.Serializable
    Component — + java.awt.MenuContainer, + java.io.Serializable
    Polygon, Rectangle — + java.awt.Shape, + java.io.Serializable
    Scrollbar — + java.awt.Adjustable
java.io
    File — + java.io.Serializable
java.lang
    Boolean, Character, Class, Number, String, StringBuffer, Throwable — + java.io.Serializable
java.net
    InetAddress, URL — + java.io.Serializable
    SocketImpl — + java.net.SocketOptions
java.util
    BitSet, Hashtable, Random, Vector — + java.io.Serializable
    Date — + java.io.Serializable, + java.lang.Cloneable

Member Modifier Changes

java.awt
    Button
      addNotify( ) — - synchronized
      setLabel( ) — + synchronized
    Canvas
      addNotify( ) — - synchronized
    Checkbox
      addNotify( ) — - synchronized
      setLabel( ) — + synchronized

Topics

Java 1.1
Modified Classes and Members

Member Modifier Changes

CheckboxMenuItem
    addNotify( )   - synchronized
    setState( )   + synchronized
Choice
    addNotify( )   - synchronized
    getSelectedItem( ), select( )   + synchronized
Component
    disable( ), enable( ), getColorModel( ), hide( ), inside( ),   - synchronized
        removeNotify( ), reshape( ), setBackground( ), setForeground( ),
        show( )
Container
    add( ), addNotify( ), getComponent( ), getComponents( ), layout( ),   - synchronized
        minimumSize( ), preferredSize( ), remove( ), removeAll( ),
        removeNotify( ), validate( )
Dialog
    addNotify( )   - synchronized
    setResizable( ), setTitle( )   + synchronized
FileDialog
    addNotify( )   - synchronized
    setDirectory( ), setFile( ), setFilenameFilter( )   + synchronized
Frame
    addNotify( )   - synchronized
    setCursor( ), setIconImage( ), setResizable( ), setTitle( )   + synchronized
Graphics
    getClipRect( )   - abstract
Label
    addNotify( )   - synchronized
    setAlignment( ), setText( )   + synchronized
List
    addItem( ), addNotify( ), isSelected( ), removeNotify( ), select( )   - synchronized
    makeVisible( ), setMultipleSelections( )   + synchronized
MediaTracker
    checkAll( ), checkID( )   - synchronized
Menu
    addNotify( ), removeNotify( )   - synchronized
MenuBar
    addNotify( )   - synchronized
MenuItem
    addNotify( )   - synchronized
    disable( ), enable( ), setLabel( )   + synchronized
Panel
    addNotify( )   - synchronized
Scrollbar
    addNotify( )   - synchronized
    setValue( ), setValues( )   + synchronized
TextArea
    addNotify( )   - synchronized
TextComponent
    getSelectedText( ), getSelectionEnd( ), getSelectionStart( ), getText( ),   + synchronized
        select( ), selectAll( ), setEditable( ), setText( )
    removeNotify( )   - synchronized
TextField
    addNotify( )   - synchronized
Window
    addNotify( ), dispose( ), pack( )   - synchronized

java.io
PrintStream
    print( ), println( )   - synchronized

Member Modifier Changes

java.lang
  Double
    toString( ), valueOf( )   - native
  Float
    toString( ), valueOf( )   - native
  String
    intern( )   + native
  System
    err, in, out   + final
  ThreadGroup
    activeCount( ), activeGroupCount( ), destroy( ), list( ), resume( ),   - synchronized
        setMaxPriority( ), stop( ), suspend( )

java.net
  DatagramPacket
    getAddress( ), getData( ), getLength( ), getPort( )   + synchronized
  DatagramSocket
    close( )   - synchronized
  InetAddress
    getAllByName( ), getByName( )   - synchronized
  URLConnection
    guessContentTypeFromStream( )   - protected, + public

java.util
  Date
    toGMTString( ), toLocaleString( ), toString( )   - native
  Observable
    notifyObservers( )   - synchronized
  Stack
    peek( ), pop( ), search( )   + synchronized

Newly Deprecated Classes

java.io
  LineNumberInputStream, StringBufferInputStream

Newly Deprecated Members

java.awt
  BorderLayout
    addLayoutComponent( )
  CardLayout
    addLayoutComponent( )
  CheckboxGroup
    getCurrent( ), setCurrent( )
  Choice
    countItems( )
  Component
    action( ), bounds( ), deliverEvent( ), disable( ),
    enable( ), getPeer( ), gotFocus( ), handleEvent( ),
    hide( ), inside( ), keyDown( ), keyUp( ), layout( ),
    locate( ), location( ), lostFocus( ), minimumSize( ),
    mouseDown( ), mouseDrag( ), mouseEnter( ),
    mouseExit( ), mouseMove( ), mouseUp( ), move( ),
    nextFocus( ), postEvent( ), preferredSize( ),
    reshape( ), resize( ), show( ), size( )
  Container
    countComponents( ), deliverEvent( ), insets( ),
    layout( ), locate( ), minimumSize( ), preferredSize( )

  FontMetrics
    getMaxDecent( )
  Frame
    getCursorType( ), setCursor( )
  Graphics
    getClipRect( )
  List
    allowsMultipleSelections( ), clear( ), countItems( ),
    delItems( ), isSelected( ), minimumSize( ),
    preferredSize( ), setMultipleSelections( )
  Menu
    countItems( )
  MenuBar
    countMenus( )
  MenuComponent
    getPeer( ), postEvent( )
  MenuContainer
    postEvent( )
  MenuItem
    disable( ), enable( )
  Polygon
    getBoundingBox( ), inside( )

Topics

Rectangle
  inside( ), move( ), reshape( ), resize( )
ScrollPane
  layout( )
Scrollbar
  getLineIncrement( ), getPageIncrement( ),
  getVisible( ), setLineIncrement( ),
  setPageIncrement( )
TextArea
  appendText( ), insertText( ), minimumSize( ),
  preferredSize( ), replaceText( )
TextField
  minimumSize( ), preferredSize( ), setEchoCharacter( )
Window
  postEvent( )
java.awt.event
KeyEvent
  setModifiers( )
java.io
ByteArrayOutputStream
  toString( )
DataInputStream
  readLine( )
PrintStream
  PrintStream( )

StreamTokenizer
  StreamTokenizer( )
java.lang
Character
  isJavaLetter( ), isJavaLetterOrDigit( ), isSpace( )
ClassLoader
  defineClass( )
Runtime
  getLocalizedInputStream( ),
  getLocalizedOutputStream( )
String
  getBytes( ), String( )
System
  getenv( )
java.net
Socket
  Socket( )
java.util
Date
  Date( ), getDate( ), getDay( ), getHours( ),
  getMinutes( ), getMonth( ), getSeconds( ),
  getTimezoneOffset( ), getYear( ), parse( ),
  setDate( ), setHours( ), setMinutes( ), setMonth( ),
  setSeconds( ), setYear( ), toGMTString( ),
  toLocaleString( ), UTC( )

Exceptions and Errors

This is a complete listing of all the exceptions and errors in this version of Java. The "*" indicates a checked exception or error; these must be declared in the throws clause.

java.lang	AbstractMethodError		java.lang	IllegalArgumentException
java.rmi	*AccessException		java.awt	IllegalComponentStateException
java.security.acl	*AclNotFoundException		java.lang	IllegalMonitorStateException
java.rmi	*AlreadyBoundException		java.lang	IllegalStateException
java.lang	ArithmeticException		java.lang	IllegalThreadStateException
java.lang	ArrayIndexOutOfBoundsException		java.lang	IncompatibleClassChangeError
java.lang	ArrayStoreException		java.lang	IndexOutOfBoundsException
java.awt	AWTError		java.lang	InstantiationError
java.awt	*AWTException		java.lang	*InstantiationException
java.net	*BindException		java.lang	InternalError
java.io	*CharConversionException		java.lang	*InterruptedException
java.lang	ClassCastException		java.io	*InterruptedIOException
java.lang	ClassCircularityError		java.beans	*IntrospectionException
java.lang	ClassFormatError		java.io	*InvalidClassException
java.lang	*ClassNotFoundException		java.security	*InvalidKeyException
java.lang	*CloneNotSupportedException		java.io	*InvalidObjectException
java.net	*ConnectException		java.security	InvalidParameterException
java.rmi	*ConnectException		java.lang.reflect	*InvocationTargetException
java.rmi	*ConnectIOException		java.io	*IOException
java.util.zip	*DataFormatException		java.security	*KeyException
java.sql	*DataTruncation		java.security	*KeyManagementException
java.security	*DigestException		java.security.acl	*LastOwnerException
java.util	EmptyStackException		java.lang	LinkageError
java.io	*EOFException		java.net	*MalformedURLException
java.lang	Error		java.rmi	*MarshalException
java.lang	*Exception		java.util	MissingResourceException
java.lang	ExceptionInInitializerError		java.lang	NegativeArraySizeException
java.rmi.server	*ExportException		java.lang	NoClassDefFoundError
java.io	*FileNotFoundException		java.net	*NoRouteToHostException
java.lang	IllegalAccessError		java.security	*NoSuchAlgorithmException
java.lang	*IllegalAccessException		java.util	NoSuchElementException

java.lang	NoSuchFieldError	java.rmi.server	*SkeletonMismatchException
java.lang	*NoSuchFieldException	java.rmi.server	*SkeletonNotFoundException
java.lang	NoSuchMethodError	java.net	*SocketException
java.lang	*NoSuchMethodException	java.rmi.server	*SocketSecurityException
java.rmi	*NoSuchObjectException	java.sql	*SQLException
java.security	*NoSuchProviderException	java.sql	*SQLWarning
java.io	*NotActiveException	java.lang	StackOverflowError
java.rmi	*NotBoundException	java.io	*StreamCorruptedException
java.security.acl	*NotOwnerException	java.lang	StringIndexOutOfBoundsException
java.io	*NotSerializableException	java.rmi	*StubNotFoundException
java.lang	NullPointerException	java.io	*SyncFailedException
java.lang	NumberFormatException	java.lang	ThreadDeath
java.io	*ObjectStreamException	java.lang	*Throwable
java.io	*OptionalDataException	java.util	*TooManyListenersException
java.lang	OutOfMemoryError	java.rmi	*UnexpectedException
java.text	*ParseException	java.lang	UnknownError
java.beans	*PropertyVetoException	java.net	*UnknownHostException
java.net	*ProtocolException	java.rmi	*UnknownHostException
java.security	ProviderException	java.net	*UnknownServiceException
java.rmi	*RemoteException	java.rmi	*UnmarshalException
java.rmi	RMISecurityException	java.lang	UnsatisfiedLinkError
java.lang	RuntimeException	java.io	*UnsupportedEncodingException
java.lang	SecurityException	java.awt.datatransfer	*UnsupportedFlavorException
java.rmi.server	*ServerCloneException	java.io	*UTFDataFormatException
java.rmi	*ServerError	java.lang	VerifyError
java.rmi	*ServerException	java.lang	VirtualMachineError
java.rmi.server	*ServerNotActiveException	java.io	*WriteAbortedException
java.rmi	*ServerRuntimeException	java.util.zip	*ZipException
java.security	*SignatureException		

Topics

Statistics

Packages	60	**Members**	20935	

Classes and Interfaces 1781

Classes 1462
    abstract 206
    final 173
    protected 125
    abstract protected 1
Interfaces 319

Members 20935
  Fields 3538
    static 22
    final 31
    static final 2346
    protected 972
  Constructors 2337
    protected 232
  Methods 15060
    abstract 915
    static 1126
    final 417
    static final 55
    protected 1672

Packages

New	Package	Classes	Members	Interfaces	Members
	java.applet	1	24	3	16
	java.awt	67	1666	14	57
•	java.awt.color	7	180	0	0
	java.awt.datatransfer	5	56	3	6
•	java.awt.dnd	17	182	4	13
	java.awt.event	21	376	13	32
•	java.awt.font	14	224	2	64
•	java.awt.geom	32	645	1	12
•	java.awt.im	3	27	1	7
	java.awt.image	40	685	8	70
•	java.awt.image.renderable	4	80	3	19
	java.awt.peer	0	0	26	123
•	java.awt.print	7	57	3	8
	java.beans	17	140	8	38
•	java.beans.beancontext	12	156	11	32
	java.io	66	680	10	73
	java.lang	75	815	3	2
•	java.lang.ref	5	15	0	0
	java.lang.reflect	8	104	1	5
	java.math	2	91	0	0
	java.net	29	320	5	14
	java.rmi	19	46	1	0
•	java.rmi.activation	12	70	4	16
	java.rmi.dgc	2	8	1	2
	java.rmi.registry	1	7	2	8
	java.rmi.server	16	85	9	30
	java.security	54	369	8	20
	java.security.acl	3	3	5	27
•	java.security.cert	13	94	1	4
	java.security.interfaces	0	0	8	20
•	java.security.spec	11	40	2	0
	java.sql	10	107	16	550
	java.text	21	361	2	20

New	Package	Classes	Members	Interfaces	Members
	java.util	39	697	13	103
•	java.util.jar	8	77	0	0
	java.util.zip	16	156	1	4
•	javax.accessibility	7	136	7	59
•	javax.swing	158	3436	23	175
•	javax.swing.border	9	135	1	3
•	javax.swing.colorchooser	3	22	1	4
•	javax.swing.event	23	140	23	60
•	javax.swing.filechooser	3	20	0	0
•	javax.swing.plaf	42	123	1	0
•	javax.swing.plaf.basic	184	1926	1	8
•	javax.swing.plaf.metal	61	531	0	0
•	javax.swing.plaf.multi	29	443	0	0
•	javax.swing.table	9	238	4	30
•	javax.swing.text	75	1036	21	121
•	javax.swing.text.html	41	483	0	0
•	javax.swing.text.html.parser	9	142	1	35
•	javax.swing.text.rtf	1	7	0	0
•	javax.swing.tree	13	319	7	54
•	javax.swing.undo	7	84	2	14
•	org.omg.CORBA	76	607	29	109
•	org.omg.CORBA.DynAnyPackage	4	8	0	0
•	org.omg.CORBA.ORBPackage	2	4	0	0
•	org.omg.CORBA.TypeCodePackage	2	4	0	0
•	org.omg.CORBA.portable	7	129	4	6
•	org.omg.CosNaming	22	142	2	13
•	org.omg.CosNaming.NamingContextPackage	18	91	0	0

New Classes in Existing Packages

java.awt
ActiveEvent, AlphaComposite, AWTPermission, BasicStroke, ComponentOrientation, *Composite*, *CompositeContext*, GradientPaint, Graphics2D, GraphicsConfigTemplate, GraphicsConfiguration, GraphicsDevice, GraphicsEnvironment, *Paint*, *PaintContext*, RenderingHints, RenderingHints.Key, *Stroke*, TexturePaint, *Transparency*

java.awt.datatransfer
FlavorMap, SystemFlavorMap

java.awt.event
AWTEventListener, InputMethodEvent, *InputMethodListener*, InvocationEvent

java.awt.image
AffineTransformOp, BandCombineOp, BandedSampleModel, BufferedImage, BufferedImageFilter, *BufferedImageOp*, ByteLookupTable, ColorConvertOp, ComponentColorModel, ComponentSampleModel, ConvolveOp, DataBuffer, DataBufferByte, DataBufferInt, DataBufferShort, DataBufferUShort, ImagingOpException, Kernel, LookupOp, LookupTable, MultiPixelPackedSampleModel, PackedColorModel, PixelInterleavedSampleModel, Raster, RasterFormatException, *RasterOp*, *RenderedImage*, RescaleOp, SampleModel, ShortLookupTable, SinglePixelPackedSampleModel, *TileObserver*, WritableRaster, *WritableRenderedImage*

java.beans
AppletInitializer, *DesignMode*

java.io
FileFilter, FilePermission, ObjectInputStream.GetField, ObjectOutputStream.PutField, *ObjectStreamConstants*, ObjectStreamField, SerializablePermission

java.lang
Character.Subset, Character.UnicodeBlock, *Comparable*, InheritableThreadLocal, Package, RuntimePermission, ThreadLocal, UnsupportedClassVersionError, UnsupportedOperationException

java.lang.reflect
AccessibleObject, ReflectPermission

java.net
Authenticator, JarURLConnection, NetPermission, PasswordAuthentication, *SocketOptions*, SocketPermission, URLClassLoader, URLDecoder

java.rmi
MarshalledObject

java.rmi.server
RMIClientSocketFactory, *RMIServerSocketFactory*

java.security
AccessControlContext, AccessControlException, AccessController, AlgorithmParameterGenerator, AlgorithmParameterGeneratorSpi, AlgorithmParameters, AlgorithmParametersSpi, AllPermission, BasicPermission, CodeSource, GeneralSecurityException, *Guard*, GuardedObject, InvalidAlgorithmParameterException, KeyFactory, KeyFactorySpi, KeyPairGeneratorSpi, KeyStore, KeyStoreException, KeyStoreSpi, MessageDigestSpi,

Topics

Permission, PermissionCollection, Permissions,
Policy, *PrivilegedAction*, PrivilegedActionException,
PrivilegedExceptionAction, ProtectionDomain,
SecureClassLoader, SecureRandomSpi,
SecurityPermission, SignatureSpi, SignedObject,
UnrecoverableKeyException, UnresolvedPermission
java.security.interfaces
RSAPrivateCrtKey, *RSAPrivateKey*, *RSAPublicKey*
java.sql
Array, BatchUpdateException, *Blob*, *Clob*, *Ref*,
SQLData, *SQLInput*, *SQLOutput*, *Struct*

java.text
Annotation, *AttributedCharacterIterator*,
AttributedCharacterIterator.Attribute, AttributedString
java.util
AbstractCollection, AbstractList, AbstractMap,
AbstractSequentialList, AbstractSet, ArrayList,
Arrays, *Collection*, Collections, *Comparator*,
ConcurrentModificationException, HashMap, HashSet,
Iterator, LinkedList, *List*, *ListIterator*, *Map*, *Map.Entry*,
PropertyPermission, *Set*, *SortedMap*, *SortedSet*,
TreeMap, TreeSet, WeakHashMap

New Members in Existing Classes

java.applet
Applet
    newAudioClip( )
java.awt
AWTEvent
    finalize( ), INPUT_METHOD_EVENT_MASK
AWTEventMulticaster
    add( ), caretPositionChanged( ),
    inputMethodTextChanged( ), remove( )
BorderLayout
    AFTER_LAST_LINE, AFTER_LINE_ENDS,
    BEFORE_FIRST_LINE, BEFORE_LINE_BEGINS
Canvas
    Canvas( )
Color
    Color( ), createContext( ), getAlpha( ),
    getColorComponents( ), getColorSpace( ),
    getComponents( ), getRGBColorComponents( ),
    getRGBComponents( ), getTransparency( )
Component
    addInputMethodListener( ),
    addPropertyChangeListener( ), coalesceEvents( ),
    enableInputMethods( ), firePropertyChange( ),
    getBounds( ), getComponentOrientation( ),
    getDropTarget( ), getHeight( ), getInputContext( ),
    getInputMethodRequests( ), getLocation( ),
    getSize( ), getWidth( ), getX( ), getY( ), hasFocus( ),
    isDisplayable( ), isDoubleBuffered( ), isLightweight( ),
    isOpaque( ), processInputMethodEvent( ),
    removeInputMethodListener( ),
    removePropertyChangeListener( ),
    setComponentOrientation( ), setDropTarget( )
Container
    findComponentAt( ), setFont( )
Cursor
    Cursor( ), CUSTOM_CURSOR, getName( ),
    getSystemCustomCursor( ), name, toString( )
Dialog
    Dialog( )
Dimension
    getHeight( ), getWidth( ), setSize( )
EventQueue
    dispatchEvent( ), invokeAndWait( ), invokeLater( ),
    isDispatchThread( ), pop( ), push( )
FlowLayout
    LEADING, TRAILING
Font
    canDisplay( ), canDisplayUpTo( ),
    CENTER_BASELINE, createGlyphVector( ),
    deriveFont( ), finalize( ), Font( ), getAttributes( ),

getAvailableAttributes( ), getBaselineFor( ),
getFamily( ), getFont( ), getFontName( ),
getItalicAngle( ), getLineMetrics( ),
getMaxCharBounds( ), getMissingGlyphCode( ),
getNumGlyphs( ), getPSName( ), getSize2D( ),
getStringBounds( ), getTransform( ),
HANGING_BASELINE, hasUniformLineMetrics( ),
pointSize, ROMAN_BASELINE
FontMetrics
    getLineMetrics( ), getMaxCharBounds( ),
    getStringBounds( ), hasUniformLineMetrics( )
Frame
    finalize( ), getFrames( ), getState( ), ICONIFIED,
    NORMAL, removeNotify( ), setState( )
Graphics
    drawString( ), getClipBounds( ), hitClip( )
GridBagConstraints
    GridBagConstraints( )
MenuComponent
    getTreeLock( )
MenuShortcut
    equals( ), hashCode( )
Point
    getX( ), getY( ), setLocation( )
Polygon
    contains( ), getBounds2D( ), getPathIterator( ),
    intersects( )
Rectangle
    contains( ), createIntersection( ), createUnion( ),
    getBounds2D( ), getHeight( ), getWidth( ), getX( ),
    getY( ), outcode( ), setRect( )
Shape
    contains( ), getBounds2D( ), getPathIterator( ),
    intersects( )
SystemColor
    createContext( )
TextField
    setText( )
Toolkit
    addAWTEventListener( ),
    addPropertyChangeListener( ),
    createCustomCursor( ),
    createDragGestureRecognizer( ),
    createDragSourceContextPeer( ),
    createImage( ), desktopProperties,
    desktopPropsSupport, getBestCursorSize( ),
    getDesktopProperty( ), getMaximumCursorColors( ),
    initializeDesktopProperties( ),
    lazilyLoadDesktopProperty( ),
    removeAWTEventListener( ),

removePropertyChangeListener( ),
setDesktopProperty( )
Window
applyResourceBundle( ), finalize( ),
getInputContext( ), getOwnedWindows( ),
getOwner( ), Window( )
java.awt.datatransfer
DataFlavor
clone( ), DataFlavor( ), equals( ),
getParameter( ), getPrimaryType( ),
getSubType( ), isFlavorJavaFileListType( ),
isFlavorRemoteObjectType( ),
isFlavorSerializedObjectType( ),
isMimeTypeSerializedObject( ),
isRepresentationClassInputStream( ),
isRepresentationClassRemote( ),
isRepresentationClassSerializable( ),
javaFileListFlavor, javaJVMLocalObjectMimeType,
javaRemoteObjectMimeType,
javaSerializedObjectMimeType, readExternal( ),
tryToLoadClass( ), writeExternal( )
java.awt.event
InputEvent
ALT_GRAPH_MASK, isAltGraphDown( )
KeyEvent
VK_AGAIN, VK_ALL_CANDIDATES,
VK_ALPHANUMERIC, VK_ALT_GRAPH,
VK_AMPERSAND, VK_ASTERISK, VK_AT,
VK_BRACELEFT, VK_BRACERIGHT,
VK_CIRCUMFLEX, VK_CODE_INPUT,
VK_COLON, VK_COMPOSE, VK_COPY, VK_CUT,
VK_DEAD_ABOVEDOT, VK_DEAD_ABOVERING,
VK_DEAD_ACUTE, VK_DEAD_BREVE,
VK_DEAD_CARON, VK_DEAD_CEDILLA,
VK_DEAD_CIRCUMFLEX, VK_DEAD_DIAERESIS,
VK_DEAD_DOUBLEACUTE,
VK_DEAD_GRAVE, VK_DEAD_IOTA,
VK_DEAD_MACRON, VK_DEAD_OGONEK,
VK_DEAD_SEMIVOICED_SOUND,
VK_DEAD_TILDE, VK_DEAD_VOICED_SOUND,
VK_DOLLAR, VK_EURO_SIGN,
VK_EXCLAMATION_MARK, VK_F13, VK_F14,
VK_F15, VK_F16, VK_F17, VK_F18, VK_F19,
VK_F20, VK_F21, VK_F22, VK_F23, VK_F24,
VK_FIND, VK_FULL_WIDTH, VK_GREATER,
VK_HALF_WIDTH, VK_HIRAGANA,
VK_INVERTED_EXCLAMATION_MARK,
VK_JAPANESE_HIRAGANA,
VK_JAPANESE_KATAKANA,
VK_JAPANESE_ROMAN, VK_KATAKANA,
VK_KP_DOWN, VK_KP_LEFT,
VK_KP_RIGHT, VK_KP_UP,
VK_LEFT_PARENTHESIS, VK_LESS, VK_MINUS,
VK_NUMBER_SIGN, VK_PASTE, VK_PLUS,
VK_PREVIOUS_CANDIDATE, VK_PROPS,
VK_QUOTEDBL, VK_RIGHT_PARENTHESIS,
VK_ROMAN_CHARACTERS, VK_STOP,
VK_UNDERSCORE, VK_UNDO
java.awt.image
ColorModel
coerceData( ), ColorModel( ),
createCompatibleSampleModel( ),
createCompatibleWritableRaster( ), equals( ),
getAlpha( ), getAlphaRaster( ), getBlue( ),
getColorSpace( ), getComponents( ),
getComponentSize( ), getDataElement( ),
getDataElements( ), getGreen( ),

getNormalizedComponents( ),
getNumColorComponents( ), getNumComponents( ),
getRed( ), getRGB( ), getTransparency( ),
getUnnormalizedComponents( ), hasAlpha( ),
isAlphaPremultiplied( ), isCompatibleRaster( ),
isCompatibleSampleModel( ), toString( ),
transferType
DirectColorModel
coerceData( ), createCompatibleWritableRaster( ),
DirectColorModel( ), getAlpha( ), getBlue( ),
getComponents( ), getDataElement( ),
getDataElements( ), getGreen( ), getRed( ),
getRGB( ), isCompatibleRaster( ), toString( )
IndexColorModel
convertToIntDiscrete( ),
createCompatibleSampleModel( ),
createCompatibleWritableRaster( ), finalize( ),
getComponents( ), getComponentSize( ),
getDataElement( ), getDataElements( ),
getRGBs( ), getTransparency( ), IndexColorModel( ),
isCompatibleRaster( ), isCompatibleSampleModel( ),
toString( )
java.awt.peer
FramePeer
getState( ), setState( )
WindowPeer
CONSUME_EVENT, FOCUS_NEXT,
FOCUS_PREVIOUS, handleFocusTraversalEvent( ),
IGNORE_EVENT
java.beans
Beans
instantiate( )
FeatureDescriptor
isPreferred( ), setPreferred( )
IndexedPropertyDescriptor
setIndexedReadMethod( ), setIndexedWriteMethod( )
Introspector
flushCaches( ), flushFromCaches( ),
getBeanInfo( ), IGNORE_ALL_BEANINFO,
IGNORE_IMMEDIATE_BEANINFO,
USE_ALL_BEANINFO
PropertyChangeSupport
addPropertyChangeListener( ), firePropertyChange( ),
hasListeners( ), removePropertyChangeListener( )
PropertyDescriptor
setReadMethod( ), setWriteMethod( )
VetoableChangeSupport
addVetoableChangeListener( ),
fireVetoableChange( ), hasListeners( ),
removeVetoableChangeListener( )
java.io
BufferedInputStream
close( )
ByteArrayInputStream
close( )
ByteArrayOutputStream
close( )
File
compareTo( ), createNewFile( ), createTempFile( ),
deleteOnExit( ), getAbsoluteFile( ),
getCanonicalFile( ), getParentFile( ), isHidden( ),
listFiles( ), listRoots( ), setLastModified( ),
setReadOnly( ), toURL( )
ObjectInputStream
ObjectInputStream( ), readFields( ),
readObjectOverride( )

Topics

ObjectOutputStream
  ObjectOutputStream( ), putFields( ),
  useProtocolVersion( ), writeFields( ),
  writeObjectOverride( )
ObjectStreamClass
  getField( ), getFields( ), NO_FIELDS
PipedReader
  read( ), ready( )
PipedWriter
  write( )
PrintWriter
  out
PushbackInputStream
  close( ), skip( )
PushbackReader
  mark( ), reset( )
RandomAccessFile
  setLength( )
Serializable
  serialVersionUID

java.lang

Byte
  compareTo( )
Character
  compareTo( )
Class
  forName( ), getPackage( ), getProtectionDomain( )
ClassLoader
  ClassLoader( ), defineClass( ), definePackage( ),
  findClass( ), findLibrary( ), findResource( ),
  findResources( ), getPackage( ),
  getPackages( ), getParent( ), getResources( ),
  getSystemClassLoader( ), getSystemResources( )
ClassNotFoundException
  ClassNotFoundException( ), getException( ),
  printStackTrace( )
Double
  compareTo( ), parseDouble( )
ExceptionInInitializerError
  printStackTrace( )
Float
  compareTo( ), parseFloat( )
Integer
  compareTo( )
Long
  compareTo( ), decode( )
Math
  toDegrees( ), toRadians( )
SecurityManager
  checkPermission( )
Short
  compareTo( )
String
  CASE_INSENSITIVE_ORDER, compareTo( ),
  compareToIgnoreCase( )
StringBuffer
  delete( ), deleteCharAt( ), insert( ), replace( ),
  substring( )
System
  mapLibraryName( ), setProperty( )
Thread
  getContextClassLoader( ), setContextClassLoader( )
ThreadGroup
  interrupt( )

java.lang.reflect

InvocationTargetException
  printStackTrace( )

Modifier
  isStrict( ), STRICT

java.math

BigDecimal
  compareTo( ), unscaledValue( )
BigInteger
  compareTo( ), ONE, ZERO

java.net

DatagramPacket
  DatagramPacket( ), getOffset( ), setData( )
DatagramSocket
  connect( ), disconnect( ), getInetAddress( ),
  getPort( ), getReceiveBufferSize( ),
  getSendBufferSize( ), setReceiveBufferSize( ),
  setSendBufferSize( )
DatagramSocketImpl
  getTimeToLive( ), setTimeToLive( )
HttpURLConnection
  getErrorStream( ), getPermission( )
MulticastSocket
  getTimeToLive( ), setTimeToLive( )
Socket
  getReceiveBufferSize( ), getSendBufferSize( ),
  setReceiveBufferSize( ), setSendBufferSize( )
URL
  URL( )
URLConnection
  getFileNameMap( ), getPermission( ),
  setFileNameMap( )

java.rmi

RemoteException
  printStackTrace( )

java.rmi.registry

LocateRegistry
  createRegistry( ), getRegistry( )

java.rmi.server

ObjID
  ACTIVATOR_ID
RMIClassLoader
  getClassAnnotation( ), loadClass( )
RMISocketFactory
  getDefaultSocketFactory( )
RemoteObject
  getRef( ), toStub( )
RemoteRef
  invoke( ), serialVersionUID
ServerCloneException
  printStackTrace( )
ServerRef
  serialVersionUID
UnicastRemoteObject
  exportObject( ), unexportObject( ),
  UnicastRemoteObject( )

java.security

Key
  serialVersionUID
KeyPairGenerator
  genKeyPair( ), getProvider( ), initialize( )
MessageDigest
  digest( ), getDigestLength( ), getProvider( )
PrivateKey
  serialVersionUID
Provider
  clear( ), entrySet( ), keySet( ), load( ), put( ), putAll( ),
  remove( ), values( )
PublicKey
  serialVersionUID

SecureRandom
  generateSeed( ), getInstance( ), getProvider( ),
  SecureRandom( )
Signature
  getProvider( ), initSign( ), setParameter( ), sign( )

java.security.interfaces
DSAPrivateKey
  serialVersionUID
DSAPublicKey
  serialVersionUID

java.sql
CallableStatement
  getArray( ), getBigDecimal( ), getBlob( ), getClob( ),
  getDate( ), getObject( ), getRef( ), getTime( ),
  getTimestamp( ), registerOutParameter( )
Connection
  createStatement( ), getTypeMap( ), prepareCall( ),
  prepareStatement( ), setTypeMap( )
DatabaseMetaData
  deletesAreDetected( ), getConnection( ),
  getUDTs( ), insertsAreDetected( ),
  othersDeletesAreVisible( ), othersInsertsAreVisible( ),
  othersUpdatesAreVisible( ),
  ownDeletesAreVisible( ), ownInsertsAreVisible( ),
  ownUpdatesAreVisible( ), supportsBatchUpdates( ),
  supportsResultSetConcurrency( ),
  supportsResultSetType( ), updatesAreDetected( )
DriverManager
  getLogWriter( ), setLogWriter( )
PreparedStatement
  addBatch( ), getMetaData( ), setArray( ), setBlob( ),
  setCharacterStream( ), setClob( ), setDate( ),
  setNull( ), setRef( ), setTime( ), setTimestamp( )
ResultSet
  absolute( ), afterLast( ), beforeFirst( ),
  cancelRowUpdates( ), CONCUR_READ_ONLY,
  CONCUR_UPDATABLE, deleteRow( ),
  FETCH_FORWARD, FETCH_REVERSE,
  FETCH_UNKNOWN, first( ), getArray( ),
  getBigDecimal( ), getBlob( ), getCharacterStream( ),
  getClob( ), getConcurrency( ), getDate( ),
  getFetchDirection( ), getFetchSize( ), getObject( ),
  getRef( ), getRow( ), getStatement( ), getTime( ),
  getTimestamp( ), getType( ), insertRow( ),
  isAfterLast( ), isBeforeFirst( ), isFirst( ), isLast( ),
  last( ), moveToCurrentRow( ), moveToInsertRow( ),
  previous( ), refreshRow( ), relative( ), rowDeleted( ),
  rowInserted( ), rowUpdated( ), setFetchDirection( ),
  setFetchSize( ), TYPE_FORWARD_ONLY,
  TYPE_SCROLL_INSENSITIVE,
  TYPE_SCROLL_SENSITIVE, updateAsciiStream( ),
  updateBigDecimal( ), updateBinaryStream( ),
  updateBoolean( ), updateByte( ), updateBytes( ),
  updateCharacterStream( ), updateDate( ),
  updateDouble( ), updateFloat( ), updateInt( ),
  updateLong( ), updateNull( ), updateObject( ),
  updateRow( ), updateShort( ), updateString( ),
  updateTime( ), updateTimestamp( )
ResultSetMetaData
  getColumnClassName( )
Statement
  addBatch( ), clearBatch( ), executeBatch( ),
  getConnection( ), getFetchDirection( ),
  getFetchSize( ), getResultSetConcurrency( ),
  getResultSetType( ), setFetchDirection( ),
  setFetchSize( )

Timestamp
  equals( )
Types
  ARRAY, BLOB, CLOB, DISTINCT, JAVA_OBJECT,
  REF, STRUCT

java.text
BreakIterator
  isBoundary( ), preceding( )
CollationElementIterator
  getMaxExpansion( ), getOffset( ), previous( ),
  setOffset( ), setText( )
CollationKey
  compareTo( )
Collator
  compare( )
DecimalFormat
  setMaximumFractionDigits( ),
  setMaximumIntegerDigits( ),
  setMinimumFractionDigits( ),
  setMinimumIntegerDigits( )
DecimalFormatSymbols
  getCurrencySymbol( ),
  getInternationalCurrencySymbol( ),
  getMonetaryDecimalSeparator( ),
  setCurrencySymbol( ),
  setInternationalCurrencySymbol( ),
  setMonetaryDecimalSeparator( )
FieldPosition
  equals( ), hashCode( ), setBeginIndex( ),
  setEndIndex( ), toString( )
ParsePosition
  equals( ), getErrorIndex( ), hashCode( ),
  setErrorIndex( ), toString( )
RuleBasedCollator
  getCollationElementIterator( )
SimpleDateFormat
  get2DigitYearStart( ), set2DigitYearStart( )
StringCharacterIterator
  setText( )

java.util
BitSet
  andNot( ), length( )
Calendar
  getActualMaximum( ), getActualMinimum( ),
  hashCode( ), roll( ), toString( )
Date
  clone( ), compareTo( )
GregorianCalendar
  getActualMaximum( ), getActualMinimum( ), roll( )
Hashtable
  containsValue( ), entrySet( ), equals( ), hashCode( ),
  Hashtable( ), keySet( ), putAll( ), values( )
Locale
  getAvailableLocales( ), getISOCountries( ),
  getISOLanguages( )
Properties
  setProperty( ), store( )
Random
  nextBoolean( ), nextInt( )
ResourceBundle
  getBundle( ), getLocale( )
SimpleTimeZone
  getDSTSavings( ), hasSameRules( ),
  setDSTSavings( ), setEndRule( ), setStartRule( ),
  SimpleTimeZone( ), toString( )

Topics

TimeZone
    getDisplayName( ), hasSameRules( ), LONG,
    SHORT
Vector
    add( ), addAll( ), clear( ), containsAll( ), equals( ),
    get( ), hashCode( ), remove( ), removeAll( ),
    removeRange( ), retainAll( ), set( ), subList( ),
    toArray( ), Vector( )

java.util.zip
InflaterInputStream
    available( ), close( )
ZipEntry
    clone( ), hashCode( ), setCompressedSize( ),
    ZipEntry( )
ZipFile
    size( )
ZipInputStream
    available( ), createZipEntry( )

Removed Classes

java.awt.peer
ActiveEvent

Removed Members

java.awt
Frame
    dispose( )
Point
    hashCode( )
Rectangle
    hashCode( )
java.net
URLConnection
    fileNameMap
java.rmi
RMISecurityManager
    checkAccept( ), checkAccess( ),
    checkAwtEventQueueAccess( ), checkConnect( ),
    checkCreateClassLoader( ), checkDelete( ),
    checkExec( ), checkExit( ), checkLink( ),
    checkListen( ), checkMemberAccess( ),
    checkMulticast( ), checkPackageDefinition( ),

    checkPrintJobAccess( ), checkPropertiesAccess( ),
    checkPropertyAccess( ), checkRead( ),
    checkSecurityAccess( ), checkSetFactory( ),
    checkSystemClipboardAccess( ),
    checkTopLevelWindow( ), checkWrite( ),
    getSecurityContext( )
java.security
KeyPairGenerator
    generateKeyPair( )
MessageDigest
    engineDigest( ), engineReset( ), engineUpdate( )
Signature
    engineGetParameter( ), engineInitSign( ),
    engineInitVerify( ), engineSetParameter( ),
    engineSign( ), engineUpdate( ), engineVerify( )
java.util
GregorianCalendar
    after( ), before( )

Modified Classes and Members

These tables show all the classes and members whose signatures were modified from the previous version.
"+" indicates an added keyword; "-" indicates a removed keyword.

Class Modifier Changes

java.awt	
Container	- abstract
java.lang	
SecurityManager	- abstract
java.util	
BitSet	- final

Extends Changes

java.awt	
Dimension	- java.lang.Object, + java.awt.geom.Dimension2D
Point	- java.lang.Object, + java.awt.geom.Point2D
Rectangle	- java.lang.Object, + java.awt.geom.Rectangle2D

Extends Changes

java.awt.image
    DirectColorModel   - java.awt.image.ColorModel,
                                                                + java.awt.image.PackedColorModel

java.lang.reflect
    Constructor, Field, Method   - java.lang.Object,
                                                                  + java.lang.reflect.AccessibleObject

java.security
    DigestException, KeyException, NoSuchAlgorithmException,   - java.lang.Exception,
       NoSuchProviderException, SignatureException   + java.security.GeneralSecurityException
    KeyPairGenerator   - java.lang.Object,
                                                               + java.security.KeyPairGeneratorSpi
    MessageDigest   - java.lang.Object,
                                                               + java.security.MessageDigestSpi
    Signature   - java.lang.Object,
                                                               + java.security.SignatureSpi

java.util
    Vector   - java.lang.Object, + java.util.AbstractList

Implements Changes

java.awt
    AWTEventMulticaster   + java.awt.event.InputMethodListener
    Color   + java.awt.Paint
java.awt.datatransfer
    DataFlavor   + java.io.Externalizable,
                                                                 + java.lang.Cloneable

java.awt.image
    ColorModel   + java.awt.Transparency
java.io
    File   + java.lang.Comparable
java.lang
    Byte, Character, Double, Float, Integer, Long, Short, String   + java.lang.Comparable
java.math
    BigDecimal, BigInteger   + java.lang.Comparable
java.rmi.server
    RMISocketFactory   + java.rmi.server.RMIClientSocketFactory,
                                                               + java.rmi.server.RMIServerSocketFactory

java.security
    KeyPair   + java.io.Serializable
java.text
    BreakIterator   - java.io.Serializable
    CollationKey   + java.lang.Comparable
    Collator   - java.io.Serializable, + java.util.Comparator
java.util
    Date   + java.lang.Comparable
    Hashtable   + java.util.Map
    Vector   + java.util.List
java.util.zip
    ZipEntry   + java.lang.Cloneable

Member Modifier Changes

java.awt
    Button
        setLabel( )   - synchronized
    Checkbox
        setLabel( )   - synchronized
    CheckboxGroup
        setSelectedCheckbox( )   - synchronized
    Choice
        add( ), addItem( ), insert( ), remove( ), removeAll( )   - synchronized

Java 1.2
Modified Classes and Members

Member Modifier Changes

Component
    setFont( )   - synchronized

Container
    Container( )   - protected, + public
    removeContainerListener( )   + synchronized

java.awt.datatransfer

DataFlavor
    plainTextFlavor, stringFlavor   + final

java.awt

Dialog
    setResizable( )   - synchronized

FileDialog
    setDirectory( ), setFile( )   - synchronized

Frame
    remove( ), setMenuBar( ), setResizable( )   - synchronized

Label
    setText( )   - synchronized

List
    add( ), delItem( ), remove( ), removeAll( ), setMultipleMode( )   - synchronized

Menu
    add( ), insert( ), remove( ), removeAll( )   - synchronized

MenuBar
    add( ), remove( ), setHelpMenu( )   - synchronized

PopupMenu
    addNotify( )   - synchronized

Scrollbar
    setBlockIncrement( ), setMaximum( ), setMinimum( ), setOrientation( ),   - synchronized
        setUnitIncrement( ), setValue( ), setVisibleAmount( )
    setLineIncrement( ), setPageIncrement( )   + synchronized

TextArea
    append( ), insert( ), replaceRange( )   - synchronized
    appendText( ), insertText( ), replaceText( )   + synchronized

TextComponent
    getCaretPosition( ), removeTextListener( ), setCaretPosition( )   + synchronized

TextField
    setColumns( ), setEchoCharacter( )   + synchronized

java.beans

Introspector
    getBeanInfoSearchPath( ), setBeanInfoSearchPath( )   + synchronized

PropertyEditorManager
    findEditor( ), getEditorSearchPath( ), setEditorSearchPath( )   + synchronized

java.io

File
    isAbsolute( )   - native

FileDescriptor
    valid( )   - native

ObjectInputStream
    defaultReadObject( ), enableResolveObject( )   - final

ObjectOutputStream
    defaultWriteObject( ), enableReplaceObject( )   - final

PipedOutputStream
    connect( )   + synchronized

PipedReader
    read( )   + synchronized

PipedWriter
    connect( ), flush( )   + synchronized

StringWriter
    StringWriter( )   - protected, + public

Member Modifier Changes

java.lang
  Class
    forName( ), getClassLoader( ), newInstance( )   - native
    getDeclaringClass( )   + native
  ClassLoader
    findLoadedClass( )   + native
    getSystemResource( ), getSystemResourceAsStream( )   - final
    loadClass( )   - abstract, + synchronized

java.lang.reflect
  Constructor
    getModifiers( )   - native
  Field
    getModifiers( )   - native
  Method
    getModifiers( )   - native

java.lang
  Runtime
    load( ), loadLibrary( )   - synchronized
    runFinalization( )   - native
  SecurityManager
    SecurityManager( )   - protected, + public
    classLoaderDepth( ), currentClassLoader( )   - native
  System
    setSecurityManager( )   + synchronized
  Thread
    checkAccess( )   + final

java.net
  InetAddress
    getLocalHost( )   + synchronized
  MulticastSocket
    send( )   - synchronized
  URL
    hashCode( )   + synchronized

java.rmi
  RMISecurityManager
    checkPackageAccess( )   - synchronized

java.rmi.server
  RMISocketFactory
    getFailureHandler( ), getSocketFactory( ), setFailureHandler( ),   + synchronized
      setSocketFactory( )

java.security
  KeyPairGenerator
    initialize( )   - abstract

java.sql
  DriverManager
    deregisterDriver( ), getDriver( ), getDrivers( ), println( ),   + synchronized
      setLogStream( )

java.text
  Collator
    hashCode( )   - synchronized

java.util
  Calendar
    after( ), before( ), equals( )   - abstract
  GregorianCalendar
    hashCode( )   - synchronized
  Locale
    getDefault( )   - synchronized

Topics

Java 1.2

Modified Classes and Members

Member Modifier Changes

Vector
    addElement( ), capacity( ), contains( ), copyInto( ), elementAt( ),   - final
        ensureCapacity( ), firstElement( ), indexOf( ), insertElementAt( ),
        isEmpty( ), lastElement( ), lastIndexOf( ), removeAllElements( ),
        removeElement( ), removeElementAt( ), setElementAt( ), setSize( ),
        size( ), toString( ), trimToSize( )
    elements( )   - final, - synchronized

java.util.zip
  Adler32
    update( )   - native
  CRC32
    update( )   - native
  Deflater
    deflate( ), end( ), getAdler( ), getTotalIn( ), getTotalOut( ), reset( ),   - native
      setDictionary( )
  Inflater
    end( ), getAdler( ), getTotalIn( ), getTotalOut( ), inflate( ), reset( ),   - native
      setDictionary( )

Throws Changes

java.io
  FileOutputStream
    FileOutputStream( )   - java.io.IOException,
               + java.io.FileNotFoundException

  RandomAccessFile
    RandomAccessFile( )   - java.io.IOException,
               + java.io.FileNotFoundException

  StringReader
    ready( )   + java.io.IOException
  StringWriter
    close( )   + java.io.IOException

java.lang
  ClassLoader
    defineClass( )   + java.lang.ClassFormatError

java.math
  BigDecimal
    BigDecimal( ), valueOf( )   - java.lang.NumberFormatException
    divide( ), setScale( )   - java.lang.ArithmeticException,
               - java.lang.IllegalArgumentException

  BigInteger
    BigInteger( )   - java.lang.NumberFormatException
    BigInteger( )   - java.lang.IllegalArgumentException
    add( ), clearBit( ), divide( ), divideAndRemainder( ), flipBit( ),   - java.lang.ArithmeticException
      modInverse( ), pow( ), remainder( ), setBit( ), testBit( )

java.rmi
  Naming
    bind( ), list( ), lookup( ), rebind( ), unbind( )   - java.rmi.UnknownHostException
java.rmi.registry
  LocateRegistry
    getRegistry( )   - java.rmi.UnknownHostException

Newly Deprecated Classes

java.rmi
RMISecurityException, ServerRuntimeException
java.rmi.registry
RegistryHandler
java.rmi.server
LoaderHandler, LogStream, Operation,
RemoteCall, *Skeleton*, SkeletonMismatchException,
SkeletonNotFoundException

java.security
Certificate, Identity, IdentityScope, Signer
javax.swing.text
DefaultTextUI
org.omg.CORBA
Principal, PrincipalHolder

Newly Deprecated Members

java.awt
Font
getPeer( )
Frame
CROSSHAIR_CURSOR, DEFAULT_CURSOR,
E_RESIZE_CURSOR, HAND_CURSOR,
MOVE_CURSOR, N_RESIZE_CURSOR,
NE_RESIZE_CURSOR, NW_RESIZE_CURSOR,
S_RESIZE_CURSOR, SE_RESIZE_CURSOR,
SW_RESIZE_CURSOR, TEXT_CURSOR,
W_RESIZE_CURSOR, WAIT_CURSOR
List
addItem( ), delItem( )
Toolkit
getFontList( ), getFontMetrics( ), getFontPeer( )
java.awt.datatransfer
DataFlavor
normalizeMimeType( ),
normalizeMimeTypeParameter( )
java.io
ObjectInputStream
readLine( )
java.lang
Runtime
runFinalizersOnExit( )
SecurityManager
classDepth( ), classLoaderDepth( ),
currentClassLoader( ), currentLoadedClass( ),
getInCheck( ), inCheck, inClass( ), inClassLoader( )
System
runFinalizersOnExit( )
Thread
countStackFrames( ), resume( ), stop( ), suspend( )
ThreadGroup
allowThreadSuspension( ), resume( ), stop( ),
suspend( )
java.net
DatagramSocketImpl
getTTL( ), setTTL( )
MulticastSocket
getTTL( ), setTTL( )
java.rmi
RMISecurityException
RMISecurityException( )
ServerRuntimeException
ServerRuntimeException( )
java.rmi.registry
RegistryHandler
registryImpl( ), registryStub( )
java.rmi.server
LoaderHandler
getSecurityContext( ), loadClass( )

LogStream
getDefaultStream( ), getOutputStream( ),
log( ), parseLevel( ), setDefaultStream( ),
setOutputStream( ), toString( ), write( )
Operation
getOperation( ), Operation( ), toString( )
RMIClassLoader
getSecurityContext( ), loadClass( )
RemoteCall
done( ), executeCall( ), getInputStream( ),
getOutputStream( ), getResultStream( ),
releaseInputStream( ), releaseOutputStream( )
RemoteRef
done( ), invoke( ), newCall( )
RemoteStub
setRef( )
Skeleton
dispatch( ), getOperations( )
SkeletonMismatchException
SkeletonMismatchException( )
java.security
Security
getAlgorithmProperty( )
Signature
getParameter( ), setParameter( )
SignatureSpi
engineGetParameter( ), engineSetParameter( )
java.sql
CallableStatement
getBigDecimal( )
Date
Date( ), getHours( ), getMinutes( ), getSeconds( ),
setHours( ), setMinutes( ), setSeconds( )
DriverManager
getLogStream( ), setLogStream( )
PreparedStatement
setUnicodeStream( )
ResultSet
getBigDecimal( ), getUnicodeStream( )
Time
getDate( ), getDay( ), getMonth( ), getYear( ),
setDate( ), setMonth( ), setYear( )
Timestamp
Timestamp( )
java.util
Properties
save( )
javax.swing
AbstractButton
getLabel( ), setLabel( )
JInternalFrame
getMenuBar( ), setMenuBar( )
JPasswordField
getText( )

Topics

JRootPane	
getMenuBar( ), setMenuBar( )	
JTable	
createScrollPaneForTable( ), sizeColumnsToFit( )	
KeyStroke	
getKeyStroke( )	
ScrollPaneLayout	
getViewportBorderBounds( )	
ToolTipManager	
setLightWeightPopupEnabled( )	
javax.swing.text	
View	
modelToView( ), viewToModel( )	

org.omg.CORBA
Any
   extract_Principal( ), insert_Principal( )
ORB
   create_recursive_sequence_tc( ), get_current( )
Principal
   name( )
ServerRequest
   except( ), op_name( ), params( ), result( )
org.omg.CORBA.portable
InputStream
   read_Principal( )
OutputStream
   write_Principal( )

Exceptions and Errors

This is a complete listing of all the exceptions and errors in this version of Java. The "*" indicates a checked exception or error; these must be declared in the throws clause.

java.lang	AbstractMethodError
java.security	AccessControlException
java.rmi	*AccessException
java.security.acl	*AclNotFoundException
java.rmi.activation	*ActivateFailedException
java.rmi.activation	*ActivationException
org.omg.CosNaming.NamingContextPackage	*AlreadyBound
java.rmi	*AlreadyBoundException
org.omg.CORBA.portable	*ApplicationException
java.lang	ArithmeticException
java.lang	ArrayIndexOutOfBoundsException
java.lang	ArrayStoreException
java.awt	AWTError
java.awt	*AWTException
org.omg.CORBA	BAD_CONTEXT
org.omg.CORBA	BAD_INV_ORDER
org.omg.CORBA	BAD_OPERATION
org.omg.CORBA	BAD_PARAM
org.omg.CORBA	BAD_TYPECODE
org.omg.CORBA.TypeCodePackage	*BadKind
javax.swing.text	*BadLocationException
java.sql	*BatchUpdateException
java.net	*BindException
org.omg.CORBA	*Bounds
org.omg.CORBA.TypeCodePackage	*Bounds
org.omg.CosNaming.NamingContextPackage	*CannotProceed
javax.swing.undo	CannotRedoException
javax.swing.undo	CannotUndoException
java.security.cert	*CertificateEncodingException
java.security.cert	*CertificateException
java.security.cert	*CertificateExpiredException
java.security.cert	*CertificateNotYetValidException
java.security.cert	*CertificateParsingException
javax.swing.text	*ChangedCharSetException
java.io	*CharConversionException
java.lang	ClassCastException
java.lang	ClassCircularityError
java.lang	ClassFormatError
java.lang	*ClassNotFoundException
java.lang	*CloneNotSupportedException
java.awt.color	CMMException

org.omg.CORBA	COMM_FAILURE
java.util	ConcurrentModificationException
java.net	*ConnectException
java.rmi	*ConnectException
java.rmi	*ConnectIOException
java.security.cert	*CRLException
org.omg.CORBA	DATA_CONVERSION
java.util.zip	*DataFormatException
java.sql	*DataTruncation
java.security	*DigestException
java.util	EmptyStackException
java.io	*EOFException
java.lang	Error
java.lang	*Exception
java.lang	ExceptionInInitializerError
javax.swing.tree	*ExpandVetoException
java.rmi.server	*ExportException
java.io	*FileNotFoundException
org.omg.CORBA	FREE_MEM
java.security	*GeneralSecurityException
java.lang	IllegalAccessError
java.lang	*IllegalAccessException
java.lang	IllegalArgumentException
java.awt	IllegalComponentStateException
java.lang	IllegalMonitorStateException
java.awt.geom	IllegalPathStateException
java.lang	IllegalStateException
java.lang	IllegalThreadStateException
java.awt.image	ImagingOpException
org.omg.CORBA	IMP_LIMIT
java.lang	IncompatibleClassChangeError
org.omg.CORBA.ORBPackage	*InconsistentTypeCode
java.lang	IndexOutOfBoundsException
org.omg.CORBA	INITIALIZE
java.lang	InstantiationError
java.lang	*InstantiationException
org.omg.CORBA	INTERNAL
java.lang	InternalError
java.lang	*InterruptedException
java.io	*InterruptedIOException
org.omg.CORBA	INTF_REPOS
java.beans	*IntrospectionException
org.omg.CORBA	INV_FLAG
org.omg.CORBA	INV_IDENT
org.omg.CORBA	INV_OBJREF
org.omg.CORBA	INV_POLICY
org.omg.CORBA.DynAnyPackage	*Invalid
org.omg.CORBA	INVALID_TRANSACTION
java.security	*InvalidAlgorithmParameterException
java.io	*InvalidClassException
java.awt.dnd	InvalidDnDOperationException
java.security	*InvalidKeyException
java.security.spec	*InvalidKeySpecException
org.omg.CORBA.ORBPackage	*InvalidName
org.omg.CosNaming.NamingContextPackage	*InvalidName
java.io	*InvalidObjectException
java.security	InvalidParameterException
java.security.spec	*InvalidParameterSpecException
org.omg.CORBA.DynAnyPackage	*InvalidSeq
org.omg.CORBA.DynAnyPackage	*InvalidValue
java.lang.reflect	*InvocationTargetException
java.io	*IOException

Topics

725

java.util.jar	*JarException
java.security	*KeyException
java.security	*KeyManagementException
java.security	*KeyStoreException
java.security.acl	*LastOwnerException
java.lang	LinkageError
java.net	*MalformedURLException
org.omg.CORBA	MARSHAL
java.rmi	*MarshalException
java.util	MissingResourceException
java.lang	NegativeArraySizeException
org.omg.CORBA	NO_IMPLEMENT
org.omg.CORBA	NO_MEMORY
org.omg.CORBA	NO_PERMISSION
org.omg.CORBA	NO_RESOURCES
org.omg.CORBA	NO_RESPONSE
java.lang	NoClassDefFoundError
java.awt.geom	*NoninvertibleTransformException
java.net	*NoRouteToHostException
java.security	*NoSuchAlgorithmException
java.util	NoSuchElementException
java.lang	NoSuchFieldError
java.lang	*NoSuchFieldException
java.lang	NoSuchMethodError
java.lang	*NoSuchMethodException
java.rmi	*NoSuchObjectException
java.security	*NoSuchProviderException
java.io	*NotActiveException
java.rmi	*NotBoundException
org.omg.CosNaming.NamingContextPackage	*NotEmpty
org.omg.CosNaming.NamingContextPackage	*NotFound
java.security.acl	*NotOwnerException
java.io	*NotSerializableException
java.lang	NullPointerException
java.lang	NumberFormatException
org.omg.CORBA	OBJ_ADAPTER
org.omg.CORBA	OBJECT_NOT_EXIST
java.io	*ObjectStreamException
java.io	*OptionalDataException
java.lang	OutOfMemoryError
java.text	*ParseException
org.omg.CORBA	PERSIST_STORE
org.omg.CORBA	*PolicyError
java.awt.print	*PrinterAbortException
java.awt.print	*PrinterException
java.awt.print	*PrinterIOException
java.security	*PrivilegedActionException
java.awt.color	ProfileDataException
java.beans	*PropertyVetoException
java.net	*ProtocolException
java.security	ProviderException
java.awt.image	RasterFormatException
org.omg.CORBA.portable	*RemarshalException
java.rmi	*RemoteException
java.rmi	RMISecurityException
java.lang	RuntimeException
java.lang	SecurityException
java.rmi.server	*ServerCloneException
java.rmi	*ServerError
java.rmi	*ServerException
java.rmi.server	*ServerNotActiveException
java.rmi	*ServerRuntimeException

java.security	*SignatureException
java.rmi.server	*SkeletonMismatchException
java.rmi.server	*SkeletonNotFoundException
java.net	*SocketException
java.rmi.server	*SocketSecurityException
java.sql	*SQLException
java.sql	*SQLWarning
java.lang	StackOverflowError
java.io	*StreamCorruptedException
java.lang	StringIndexOutOfBoundsException
java.rmi	*StubNotFoundException
java.io	*SyncFailedException
org.omg.CORBA	SystemException
java.lang	ThreadDeath
java.lang	*Throwable
java.util	*TooManyListenersException
org.omg.CORBA	TRANSACTION_REQUIRED
org.omg.CORBA	TRANSACTION_ROLLEDBACK
org.omg.CORBA	TRANSIENT
org.omg.CORBA.DynAnyPackage	*TypeMismatch
java.rmi	*UnexpectedException
org.omg.CORBA	UNKNOWN
java.lang	UnknownError
java.rmi.activation	*UnknownGroupException
java.rmi	*UnknownHostException
java.net	*UnknownHostException
java.rmi.activation	*UnknownObjectException
java.net	*UnknownServiceException
org.omg.CORBA	*UnknownUserException
java.rmi	*UnmarshalException
java.security	*UnrecoverableKeyException
java.lang	UnsatisfiedLinkError
java.lang	UnsupportedClassVersionError
java.io	*UnsupportedEncodingException
java.awt.datatransfer	*UnsupportedFlavorException
javax.swing	*UnsupportedLookAndFeelException
java.lang	UnsupportedOperationException
org.omg.CORBA	*UserException
java.io	*UTFDataFormatException
java.lang	VerifyError
java.lang	VirtualMachineError
java.io	*WriteAbortedException
org.omg.CORBA	*WrongTransaction
java.util.zip	*ZipException

Topics

Applet

<applet> HTML Tag

Tag	Description
code	Specifies the class name or class filename of the applet. The code tag specifies only the name of the class file and cannot contain any part of the path to the class file. The class file is in the directory specified by the codebase tag or in one of the archive files specified by the archive tag. Either the code attribute or the object attribute must be present. If both attributes are present, the object attribute is ignored.
height	Specifies the initial height in pixels of the applet's display area.

object	Specifies the filename containing the serialized applet. The browser or applet viewer runs the applet by first deserializing it and then invoking the start() method. Note that the init() method will not be invoked on it, so before serializing the applet, you must first call init() on the applet and then call start() and stop() on it. Any attributes or parameters available to the original applet before it was serialized are not available to this applet. This applet has access only to the attributes and parameters available to this instance of the applet.
	    The file is in the directory specified by the codebase tag or in one of the archive files specified by the archive tag.
	    Either the code attribute or the object attribute must be present. If both attributes are present, the object attribute is ignored.

width	Specifies the initial width in pixels of the applet's display area.
align	Specifies the alignment of the applet. Its possible values are left, right, top, texttop, middle, absmiddle, baseline, bottom, and absbottom.
alt	Specifies the text to display if the browser understands the applet tag but for some reason cannot run Java applets.
archive	Specifies a comma-separated list of archive files in JAR format. Each archive file contains classes and other files (such as images and audio files) used by the applet. The archive files are in the directory specified by the codebase attribute.
codebase	Specifies the applet's code base. This base can be either any absolute URL or a URL relative to the document containing the applet. This attribute is optional and defaults to "." (the same directory as the document). Applets that use the same codebase attribute share the same classloader.
hspace	Specifies the horizontal space on the left and right sides of the applet.
name	Specifies the name of the applet. An applet can name itself, thereby allowing other applets to retrieve a reference to it. This attribute is equivalent to specifying a parameter with the name "name". Therefore an applet can retrieve its name by calling getParameter("name"). This attribute is optional and defaults to null.
vspace	Specifies the vertical space on the top and bottom of the applet.

Source: *The Java Class Libraries, Second Edition, Volume 2,* by Patrick Chan and Rosanna Lee.

<param> HTML Tag

Tag	Description
name	Specifies the name of the parameter. The name must be different from the names of other parameters in the same pair of <applet> and </applet> tags. This attribute is mandatory. A special parameter called "name" is automatically supported by all applet contexts and is the name of the applet. There are two ways to name an applet: through the name attribute of the applet tag or by specifying a parameter called "name".
value	Specifies a string that is associated with the parameter name. This attribute is mandatory.

Source: *The Java Class Libraries, Second Edition, Volume 2,* by Patrick Chan and Rosanna Lee.

Java Language

Keywords

abstract	double	int	static
boolean	else	interface	super
break	extends	long	switch
byte	final	native	synchronized
case	finally	new	this
catch	float	null	throw
char	for	package	throws
class	goto*	private	transient
const*	if	protected	try
continue	implements	public	void
default	import	return	volatile
do	instanceof	short	while

Note: Keywords marked with * are reserved but currently unused.
Source: *The Java Programming Language, Second Edition,* by Ken Arnold and James Gosling.

Operator Precedence

Operator Type	Operator	Assoc
Postfix operators	[] . (*params*) *expr*++ *expr*––	R
Unary operators	++*expr* ––*expr* +*expr* –*expr* ˜ !	R
Creation or cast	new (*type*)*expr*	R
Multiplicative	* / %	L
Additive	+ –	L
Shift	<< >> >>>	L
Relational	< > >= <= instanceof	L
Equality	== !=	L
Bitwise AND	&	L
Bitwise exclusive OR	ˆ	L
Bitwise inclusive OR	|	L
Logical AND	&&	L
Logical OR	||	L
Conditional	?:	R
Assignment	= += –= *= /= %= >>= <<= >>>= &= ˆ= |=	R

Source: *The Java Programming Language, Second Edition,* by Ken Arnold and James Gosling.

Special Characters Using '\'

Sequence	Meaning
\n	Newline (\u000A)
\t	Tab (\u0009)
\b	Backspace (\u0008)
\r	Return (\u000D)
\f	Form feed (\u000C)
\\	Backslash itself (\u005C)
\'	Single quote (\u0027)
\"	Double quote (\u0022)
\ddd	An octal char, with each d being an octal digit (0-7)
\udddd	A Unicode char, with each d being a hex digit (0-9, a-f, A-F)

Source: *The Java Programming Language, Second Edition,* by Ken Arnold and James Gosling.

Unicode Digits

Unicode	Description
\u0030 - \u0039	ISO Latin-1 (and ASCII) digits
\u0660 - \u0669	Arabic - Indic digits
\u06f0 - \u06f9	Extended Arabic - Indic digits
\u0966 - \u096f	Devanagari digits
\u09e6 - \u09ef	Bengali digits
\u0a66 - \u0a6f	Gurmukhi digits
\u0ae6 - \u0aef	Gujarati digits
\u0b66 - \u0b6f	Oriya digits
\u0be7 - \u0bef	Tamil digits (only nine-no zero digit)
\u0c66 - \u0c6f	Telugu digits
\u0ce6 - \u0cef	Kannada digits
\u0d66 - \u0d6f	Malayalam digits
\u0e50 - \u0e59	Thai digits
\u0ed0 - \u0ed9	Lao digits
\u0420 - \u0f29	Tibetan digits
\uff10 - \uff19	Fullwidth digits

Source: *The Java Programming Language, Second Edition,* by Ken Arnold and James Gosling.

Unicode Letters and Digits

Unicode	Description
\u0041 - \u005A	ISO Latin-1 (and ASCII) uppercase Latin letters ('A'-'Z')
\u0061 - \u007A	ISO Latin-1 (and ASCII) lowercase Latin letters ('a'-'z')
\u00C0 - \u00D6	ISO Latin-1 supplementary letters
\u00D8 - \u00F6	ISO Latin-1 supplementary letters
\u00F8 - \u00FF	ISO Latin-1 supplementary letters
\u0100 - \u1FFF	Latin extended-A, Latin extended-B, IPA extensions, spacing modifier letters, combining diacritical marks, basic Greek, Greek symbols and Coptic, Cyrillic, Armenian, Hebrew extended-A, Basic Hebrew, Hebrew extended-B, Basic Arabic, Arabic extended, Devanagari, Bengali, Gurmukhi, Gujarati, Oriya, Tamil, Telugu, Kannada, Malayalam, Thai, Lao, Tibetan, Basic Georgian, Georgian extended, Hangul Jamo, Latin extended additional, Greek extended
\u3040 - \u9FFF	Hiragana, Katakana, Bopomofo, Hangul compatibility Jamo, CJK miscellaneous, enclosed CJK characters and months, CJK compatibility, Hangul, Hangul supplementary-A, Hangul supplementary-B, CJK unified ideographs
\uF900 - \uFDFF	CJK compatibility ideographs, alphabetic presentation forms, Arabic presentation forms-A
\uFE70 - \uFEFE	Arabic presentation forms-B
\uFF10 - \uFF19	Fullwidth digits
\uFF21 - \uFF3A	Fullwidth Latin uppercase
\uFF41 - \uFF5A	Fullwidth Latin lowercase
\uFF66 - \uFFDC	Halfwidth Katakana and Hangul

Note: A Unicode character is a letter or digit if it is in one of the above ranges and is also a defined Unicode character. A character is a letter if it is in the table "Unicode Letters and Digits," and not in the table "Unicode Digits."
Source: *The Java Programming Language, Second Edition,* by Ken Arnold and James Gosling.

Documentation Comment Tags

These are the tags that can appear in documentation comments in a Java source file. They are recognized by the javadoc program while it creates documentation files from the Java source files. The tags are listed in the order that should appear in a Java source file.

Tag	Entity	Description
@author *text*	class	Indicates an author of the code. More than one @author tag is allowed. *Example:* @author James Gosling
@version *text*	class	Documents the version of the entity. *text* is a vendor-specific human-readable text representing the version. *Example:* @version 1.2beta3
@param *p text*	method	Documents a parameter of the method. *text* is a description of the parameter named *p*. More than one @param tag is allowed. *Example:* @param index the index of the desired character
@return *text*	method	Documents the return value of the method. *text* is a description of the return value. *Example:* @return a clone of this Vector
@exception *e text*	method	Documents an exception that the method may throw. *text* is a description of the exception named *e*. *Example:* @exception IOException if the file is unreadable
@see *link*	class, field, method	Creates a hyperlink to *link* which can be a URL or the name of a class or member. More than one @see tag is allowed. *Example:* @see java.lang.String *Example:* @see java.awt.Point#move(int, int) *Example:* @see <a href="http://java.sun.com">Home</a>
@since *text*	class, field, method	Documents the version of the system in which the entity first appeared. *text* is a vendor-specific human-readable text representing the version. *Example:* @since JDK1.0
@deprecated *text*	class, field, method	Indicates that the entity has been deprecated. *text* is a comment directing the user to a replacement, if any. *Example:* @deprecated Replaced by setSize(int, int)

Primitive Types, Wrapper Classes, and Class Objects

Primitive Type	Wrapper Class	Class Object
boolean	Boolean	Boolean.TYPE
byte	Byte	Byte.TYPE
char	Character	Character.TYPE
short	Short	Short.TYPE
int	Integer	Integer.TYPE
long	Long	Long.TYPE
float	Float	Float.TYPE
double	Double	Double.TYPE
void	Void	Void.TYPE

Source: *The Java Class Libraries, Second Edition, Volume 1* by Patrick Chan, Rosanna Lee, and Doug Kramer.

Valid Modifiers for Java Entities

Java Entity	Valid Modifiers	Modifier-Retrieval Method
Class	public, abstract, final	java.lang.Class.getModifiers()

Topics

Java Language
Valid Modifiers for Java Entities

Java Entity	Valid Modifiers	Modifier-Retrieval Method
Constructor	public, protected, private	java.lang.reflect.Constructor.reflect.getModifiers()
Field	public, protected, private, static, final, volatile, transient	java.lang.reflect.Field.getModifiers()
Interface	public	java.lang.Class.getModifiers()
Method	public, protected, private, abstract, static, final, synchronized, native	java.lang.reflect.Method.getModifiers()
Inner Class	public, protected, private, abstract, final, static	java.lang.Class.getModifiers()
Inner Interface	public	java.lang.Class.getModifiers()

Source: *The Java Class Libraries, Second Edition, Volume 1* by Patrick Chan, Rosanna Lee, and Doug Kramer.

System Properties

Property Name	Description
appletviewer.security.allowUnsigned	true means unsigned applets can be run
appletviewer.security.mode	specifies network access available to applet ("none", "unrestricted", or "host")
appletviewer.version	version of applet viewer
awt.appletWarning	if set, indicates applet windows contains "Warning: Applet Window" message
awt.font.<font_name>	maps user specified font name to actual font name
awt.image.incrementaldraw	true means Component.imageUpdate() should use awt.image.redrawrate
awt.image.redrawrate	an integer specifying the redraw rate for images
awt.toolkit	the class name of the toolkit to use Toolkit.getDefaultToolkit()
browser	used by JDBC/ODBC driver to determine prefix to use when loading native library
com.sun.CORBA.ORBServerHost	host name of ORB server
com.sun.CORBA.ORBServerPort	port number of ORB server
content.types.temp.file.template	pathname of temporary file template for building MIME table
content.types.user.table	pathname of user-specified default MIME table
doc.url	the base URL for documentation used by HotJava browser
env.class.path	the value of the CLASSPATH environment variable
exec.path	list of paths to use when launching application using MIME entries
file.dir.title	string specifying title for pages returned by the "file" URL stream handler
file.encoding	encoding identifier to use for char-to-byte and byte-to-char conversion (default is "8859_1")
file.encoding.pkg	package prefix for converter class (prefix + .CharToByte + encoding identifier)
file.separator	string used in file pathnames to separate directories
ftp.protocol.user	default password to use when making anonymous FTP connections via the ftp URL stream handler
ftp.proxyHost	host name of FTP proxy to use
ftp.proxyPort	port of FTP proxy to use
ftpProxyHost	host name of FTP proxy to use
ftpProxyPort	port of FTp proxy to use
gopherProxyHost	host name of gopher proxy to use
hotjava.home	directory name of where HotJava browser software has been installed
hotjava.title	name to use for HotJava browser program when posting news articles using the news URL stream handler
http.agent	prefix to use for client's "user agent" in HTTP protocol
http.keepAlive	used to turn off client's use of keep-alive feature of HTTP protocol
http.nonProxyHosts	do not use proxy when accessing to this list of hosts using the HTTP protocol
http.proxyHost	host name of HTTP proxy to use for HotJava browser
http.proxyPort	port number of HTTP proxy to use for HotJava browser
impl.prefix	prefix of implementation class names used in InetAddress and DatagramSocket (e.g. "java.net." + prefix + "DatagramSocketImpl")
java.awt.fonts	name of directory where fonts used by AWT are located (value of JAVA_FONTS environment variable)
java.awt.graphicsenv	class name of the local graphics environment
java.awt.printerjob	class name of java.awt.print.PrinterJob implementation
java.class.path	list of jar files and directories of application class files
java.class.version	Java class library version number
java.compiler	library name of JIT compiler to use instead of default interpreter
java.content.handler.pkgs	list of package prefixes for classes names to use for content handlers (URL.getContent())
java.ext.dirs	directory to find installed Java Standard Extensions
java.home	Directory name of where Java software has been installed
java.iccprofile.path	list of directories to search for files containing ICC profiles
java.io.tmpdir	name of directory for creating temporary files
java.library.path	list of paths to search when loading libraries
java.net.ftp.imagepath.*	used to when setting the image file name in a MIME entry
java.net.ftp.imagepath.directory	used by gopher client to translate gopher document to HTML
java.net.ftp.imagepath.file	used by gopher client to translate gopher document to HTML

Java Runtime
System Properties

Property Name	Description
java.net.ftp.imagepath.gif	used by gopher client to translate gopher document to HTML
java.net.ftp.imagepath.text	used by gopher client to translate gopher document to HTML
java.protocol.handler.pkgs	list of package prefixes for class names to use for URL stream handlers
java.rmi.activation.activator.class	class name of RMI activator to use
java.rmi.activation.port	port number of activation system (rmid)
java.rmi.activation.security.class	class name of RMI security manager to use (defaults to java.rmi.RMISecurityManager)
java.rmi.activation.security.codebase	URL of code base used by RMI class loader
java.rmi.dgc.leaseValue	the maximum lease duration granted for distributed garbage collection (default is 10 minutes)
java.rmi.loader.packagePrefix	package name of class that implements the LoaderHandler interface (defaults to sun.rmi.server)
java.rmi.registry.packagePrefix	package name of class that implements Registry interface (defaults to sun.rmi.registry)
java.rmi.server.codebase	URL of code base used by RMI class loader and when marshalling data
java.rmi.server.disableHttp	boolean property for enabling HTTP tunneling (default is false)
java.rmi.server.hostname	local host name to use in the case of multihomed host or when fully-qualified host name not available
java.rmi.server.logCalls	specifies whether to log RMI calls on server and print to stderr
java.rmi.server.packagePrefix	package name of classes that implements the server reference classes
java.security.debug	used by Java Security for debuggin
java.security.manager	class name of java.lang.SecurityManager implementation to use
java.security.policy	URL of additional or overriding security policy
java.soundpath	pathname of the soundbank
java.vendor	Java vendor-specific information
java.vendor.url	Java vendor's URL
java.vendor.url.bug	URL for filing Java bugs
java.version	Java version number
java.vm.info	used by compiler to record JIT compiler being used
javac.debug	turn on debug mode in javac
javac.dump.modifiers	enables diagnostic dump of class modifier bits
javac.dump.stack	used by javac for debugging to indicate whether to dump stack trace
javac.trace.depend	trace dependencies when running javac
jdbc.drivers	class names of initial JDBC drivers to load
line.separator	string used to separate lines
mail.host	name of host to use for mailhost in SMTP client
nntp.server	name of host to use in news URL stream handler
org.omg.CORBA.ORBClass	class name of an ORB implementation
org.omg.CORBA.ORBInitialHost	host name of ORB's initial services
org.omg.CORBA.ORBInitialPort	port number of ORB's initial services
org.omg.CORBA.ORBInitialServices	URL of ORB's initial services
org.omg.CORBA.ORBPort	ORB's server port number
org.omg.CORBA.ORBSingletonClass	class name of the ORB returned by ORB.init()
os.arch	Machine architecture (e.g. x86, sparc)
os.name	Name of operating system
os.version	
package.restrict.access.<pkg>	specifies whether applet or application is restricted from accessing classes in package with package prefix <pkg>
packages.restrict.definition.<pkg>	specifies whether applet or application is restricted from defining classes in package with package prefix <pkg>
path.separator	String used to separate components in a path variable
policy.provider	class name of security policy provider (default is java.security.PolicyFile)
programname	name of program to use when posting news articles using the news URL stream handler
proxyHost	host name of proxy to use in RMI Socket factory, FTP or HTTP client
proxyPort	port number of proxy to use in RMI Socket factory, FTP or HTTP client
QUERY_STRING	query string for RMI/HTTP tunneling
REQUEST_METHOD	request method for RMI/HTTP tunneling
rmi.home	pathname of directory to find the serialver.properties file
SERVER_NAME	server name for RMI/HTTP tunneling

Property Name	Description
SERVER_PORT	port number for RMI/HTTP tunneling
socksProxyHost	host name of proxy to use for SOCKS protocol
socksProxyPort	port number of proxy to use for SOCKS protocol
sun.boot.class.path	list of jar files and directories for bootstrap class loader
sun.io.unicode.encoding	name of encoding for Unicode character to byte encoding (default is "UnicodeBig")
sun.rmi.dgc.logLevel	an integer indicating the log level for distribute garbage collected used by RMI
sun.rmi.loader.logLevel	an integer indicating the log level to use for RMI loader
sun.rmi.server.logLevel	an integer indicating the log level to use for RMI server
sun.rmi.transport.logLevel	an integer indicating the log level to use for RMI transport
sun.rmi.transport.proxy.logLevel	an integer indicating the log level to use for RMI transport proxy
sun.rmi.transport.tcp.logLevel	an integer indicating the log level to use for RMI over TCP
sun.rmi.transport.tcp.multiplex.logLevel	an integer indicating the log level to use for RMI when multiplexed over single TCP connection
user.dir	pathname of user's current working directory
user.emailname	string to use as the user's email address when posting articles via the news URL stream handler
user.fromaddr	string to use as the "from address" when posting articles via the news URL stream handler
user.home	pathname of user's home directory
user.language	ISO language code for user's preferred language (e.g. "fr")
user.mailcap	pathname of a mailcap format file to include when building MIME table
user.name	user's login/account name
user.region	ISO country code for user's region (e.g. "FR")
user.timezone	timezone of user (default is "GMT")

Topics

735

Java Native Interface (JNI)

The quick reference information contained in this topic is derived from the specification at http://java.sun.com/products/jdk/1.2/docs/guide/jni/jni-12.html.

Primitive Types and JNI Equivalents

Java Type	JNI Type	Bit Size
boolean	jboolean	unsigned 8 bits
byte	jbyte	signed 8 bits
char	jchar	unsigned 16 bits
int	jint	signed 32 bits
long	jlong	signed 64 bits

Java Type	JNI Type	Bit Size
float	jfloat	32 bits
double	jdouble	64 bits
short	jshort	signed 16 bits
void	void	0 bits

Type Signatures

Java Type	Java Signature
boolean	Z
byte	B
char	C
short	S
int	I
long	J

Java Type	Java Signature
float	F
double	D
type []	[type
class or interface	L fully-qualified-name ;
method	(parameter-types) return-type

Constants and Structs

```
#define JNI_FALSE 0
#define JNI_TRUE 1

#define JNI_VERSION_1_1 0x00010001
#define JNI_VERSION_1_2 0x00010002

/* Return values and Error codes */
#define JNI_OK 0 /* success */
#define JNI_ERR (-1) /* unknown error */
#define JNI_EDETACHED (-2) /* thread detached */
#define JNI_EVERSION (-3) /* JNI version error */
#define JNI_ENOMEM (-4) /* not enough memory */
#define JNI_EEXIST (-5) /* VM already created */
#define JNI_EINVAL (-6) /* invalid arguments */

typedef jint jsize;
typedef jobject jclass;
struct _jfieldID;
typedef struct _jfieldID *jfieldID;
struct _jmethodID;
typedef struct _jmethodID *jmethodID;

typedef union jvalue {
    jboolean z;
    jbyte b;
    jchar c;
    jshort s;
    jint i;
    jlong j;
    jfloat f;
```

```
    jdouble d;
    jobject l;
} jvalue;

typedef struct {
    char *name;
    char *signature;
    void *fnPtr;
} JNINativeMethod;

typedef const struct JNINativeInterface *JNIEnv;

typedef struct JavaVMOption {
    char *optionString;
    void *extraInfo;
} JavaVMOption;

typedef struct JavaVMInitArgs {
    jint version;
    jint nOptions;
    JavaVMOption *options;
    jboolean ignoreUnrecognized;
} JavaVMInitArgs;

typedef struct JavaVMAttachArgs {
    jint version;
    char *name;
    jobject group;
} JavaVMAttachArgs;
```

Function Names by Category

Version Operation
GetVersion(), JNI_OnLoad(), JNI_OnUnload

Class Operations
DefineClass(), FindClass(), GetSuperclass(),
IsAssignableFrom()

Exceptions
ExceptionDescribe(), ExceptionCheck(),
ExceptionClear(), ExceptionOccurred(), FatalError(),
Throw(), ThrowNew()

Global and Local References
DeleteGlobalRef(), DeleteLocalRef(),
EnsureLocalCapacity(), NewLocalRef(), NewGlobalRef(),
PopLocalFrame(), PushLocalFrame()

Weak Global References
DeleteWeakGlobalRef(), NewWeakGlobalRef()

Object Operations
AllocObject(), GetObjectClass(), IsInstanceOf(),
IsSameObject(), NewObject(), NewObjectA(),
NewObjectV()

Instance Field Access Operations
GetFieldID(), Get*Type*Field(), Set*Type*Field()

Instance Method Invocation Operations
GetMethodID(), Call*Type*Method(), Call*Type*MethodV(),
Call*Type*MethodA(), CallNonvirtual*Type*Method(),
CallNonvirtual*Type*MethodV(),
CallNonvirtual*Type*MethodA()

Static Field Access Operations
GetStaticFieldID(), GetStatic*Type*Field(),
SetStatic*Type*Field()

Static Method Invocation Operations

GetStaticMethodID(), CallStatic*Type*Method(),
CallStatic*Type*MethodV(), CallStatic*Type*MethodA()

String Operations
GetStringChars(), GetStringCritical(), GetStringLength(),
GetStringRegion(), GetStringUTFChars(),
GetStringUTFLength(), GetStringUTFRegion(),
GetPrimitiveArrayCritical(), NewString(), NewStringUTF(),
ReleasePrimitiveArrayCritical(), ReleaseStringChars(),
ReleaseStringCritical(), ReleaseStringUTFChars()

Array Operations
GetArrayLength(), GetObjectArrayElement(),
NewObjectArray(), SetObjectArrayElement(),
New*Type*Array(), Get*Type*ArrayElements(),
Release*Type*ArrayElements(), Get*Type*ArrayRegion(),
Set*Type*ArrayRegion()

Reflection Operations
FromReflectedField(), FromReflectedMethod(),
ToReflectedField(), ToReflectedMethod()

Native Method Registration Operations
RegisterNatives(), UnregisterNatives()

Monitor Operations
MonitorEnter(), MonitorExit()

Java VM Operation
GetJavaVM()

Invocation API Functions
AttachCurrentThread(), DestroyJavaVM(),
DetachCurrentThread(), GetEnv(),
JNI_GetDefaultJavaVMInitArgs(),
JNI_GetCreatedJavaVMs(), JNI_CreateJavaVM()

Function Prototypes Arranged Alphabetically

jobject	**AllocObject** (JNIEnv *env, jclass clazz)
	throws InstantiationException, OutOfMemoryError
jint	**AttachCurrentThread** (JavaVM *vm, JNIEnv **p_env, void *thr_args)
jboolean	***CallBooleanMethod** (JNIEnv *env, jobject obj, jmethodID methodID, ...)
jboolean	***CallBooleanMethodA** (JNIEnv *env, jobject obj, jmethodID methodID, jvalue * args)
jboolean	***CallBooleanMethodV** (JNIEnv *env, jobject obj, jmethodID methodID, va_list args)
jbyte	***CallByteMethod** (JNIEnv *env, jobject obj, jmethodID methodID, ...)
jbyte	***CallByteMethodA** (JNIEnv *env, jobject obj, jmethodID methodID, jvalue *args)
jbyte	***CallByteMethodV** (JNIEnv *env, jobject obj, jmethodID methodID, va_list args)
jchar	***CallCharMethod** (JNIEnv *env, jobject obj, jmethodID methodID, ...)
jchar	***CallCharMethodA** (JNIEnv *env, jobject obj, jmethodID methodID, jvalue *args)
jchar	***CallCharMethodV** (JNIEnv *env, jobject obj, jmethodID methodID, va_list args)
jdouble	***CallDoubleMethod** (JNIEnv *env, jobject obj, jmethodID methodID, ...)
jdouble	***CallDoubleMethodA** (JNIEnv *env, jobject obj, jmethodID methodID, jvalue *args)
jdouble	***CallDoubleMethodV** (JNIEnv *env, jobject obj, jmethodID methodID, va_list args)
jfloat	***CallFloatMethod** (JNIEnv *env, jobject obj, jmethodID methodID, ...)
jfloat	***CallFloatMethodA** (JNIEnv *env, jobject obj, jmethodID methodID, jvalue *args)
jfloat	***CallFloatMethodV** (JNIEnv *env, jobject obj, jmethodID methodID, va_list args)
jint	***CallIntMethod** (JNIEnv *env, jobject obj, jmethodID methodID, ...)
jint	***CallIntMethodA** (JNIEnv *env, jobject obj, jmethodID methodID, jvalue *args)
jint	***CallIntMethodV** (JNIEnv *env, jobject obj, jmethodID methodID, va_list args)
jlong	***CallLongMethod** (JNIEnv *env, jobject obj, jmethodID methodID, ...)
jlong	***CallLongMethodA** (JNIEnv *env, jobject obj, jmethodID methodID, jvalue *args)

Topics

jlong	***CallLongMethodV** (JNIEnv *env, jobject obj, jmethodID methodID, va_list args)
jboolean	***CallNonvirtualBooleanMethod** (JNIEnv *env, jobject obj, jclass clazz, jmethodID methodID, ...)
jboolean	***CallNonvirtualBooleanMethodA** (JNIEnv *env, jobject obj, jclass clazz, jmethodID methodID, jvalue * args)
jboolean	***CallNonvirtualBooleanMethodV** (JNIEnv *env, jobject obj, jclass clazz, jmethodID methodID, va_list args)
jbyte	***CallNonvirtualByteMethod** (JNIEnv *env, jobject obj, jclass clazz, jmethodID methodID, ...)
jbyte	***CallNonvirtualByteMethodA** (JNIEnv *env, jobject obj, jclass clazz, jmethodID methodID, jvalue *args)
jbyte	***CallNonvirtualByteMethodV** (JNIEnv *env, jobject obj, jclass clazz, jmethodID methodID, va_list args)
jchar	***CallNonvirtualCharMethod** (JNIEnv *env, jobject obj, jclass clazz, jmethodID methodID, ...)
jchar	***CallNonvirtualCharMethodA** (JNIEnv *env, jobject obj, jclass clazz, jmethodID methodID, jvalue *args)
jchar	***CallNonvirtualCharMethodV** (JNIEnv *env, jobject obj, jclass clazz, jmethodID methodID, va_list args)
jdouble	***CallNonvirtualDoubleMethod** (JNIEnv *env, jobject obj, jclass clazz, jmethodID methodID, ...)
jdouble	***CallNonvirtualDoubleMethodA** (JNIEnv *env, jobject obj, jclass clazz, jmethodID methodID, jvalue *args)
jdouble	***CallNonvirtualDoubleMethodV** (JNIEnv *env, jobject obj, jclass clazz, jmethodID methodID, va_list args)
jfloat	***CallNonvirtualFloatMethod** (JNIEnv *env, jobject obj, jclass clazz, jmethodID methodID, ...)
jfloat	***CallNonvirtualFloatMethodA** (JNIEnv *env, jobject obj, jclass clazz, jmethodID methodID, jvalue *args)
jfloat	***CallNonvirtualFloatMethodV** (JNIEnv *env, jobject obj, jclass clazz, jmethodID methodID, va_list args)
jint	***CallNonvirtualIntMethod** (JNIEnv *env, jobject obj, jclass clazz, jmethodID methodID, ...)
jint	***CallNonvirtualIntMethodA** (JNIEnv *env, jobject obj, jclass clazz, jmethodID methodID, jvalue *args)
jint	***CallNonvirtualIntMethodV** (JNIEnv *env, jobject obj, jclass clazz, jmethodID methodID, va_list args)
jlong	***CallNonvirtualLongMethod** (JNIEnv *env, jobject obj, jclass clazz, jmethodID methodID, ...)
jlong	***CallNonvirtualLongMethodA** (JNIEnv *env, jobject obj, jclass clazz, jmethodID methodID, jvalue *args)
jlong	***CallNonvirtualLongMethodV** (JNIEnv *env, jobject obj, jclass clazz, jmethodID methodID, va_list args)
jobject	***CallNonvirtualObjectMethod** (JNIEnv *env, jobject obj, jclass clazz, jmethodID methodID, ...)
jobject	***CallNonvirtualObjectMethodA** (JNIEnv *env, jobject obj, jclass clazz, jmethodID methodID, jvalue * args)
jobject	***CallNonvirtualObjectMethodV** (JNIEnv *env, jobject obj, jclass clazz, jmethodID methodID, va_list args)
jshort	***CallNonvirtualShortMethod** (JNIEnv *env, jobject obj, jclass clazz, jmethodID methodID, ...)
jshort	***CallNonvirtualShortMethodA** (JNIEnv *env, jobject obj, jclass clazz, jmethodID methodID, jvalue *args)
jshort	***CallNonvirtualShortMethodV** (JNIEnv *env, jobject obj, jclass clazz, jmethodID methodID, va_list args)
void	***CallNonvirtualVoidMethod** (JNIEnv *env, jobject obj, jclass clazz, jmethodID methodID, ...)
void	***CallNonvirtualVoidMethodA** (JNIEnv *env, jobject obj, jclass clazz, jmethodID methodID, jvalue * args)
void	***CallNonvirtualVoidMethodV** (JNIEnv *env, jobject obj, jclass clazz, jmethodID methodID, va_list args)
jobject	***CallObjectMethod** (JNIEnv *env, jobject obj, jmethodID methodID, ...)
jobject	***CallObjectMethodA** (JNIEnv *env, jobject obj, jmethodID methodID, jvalue * args)
jobject	***CallObjectMethodV** (JNIEnv *env, jobject obj, jmethodID methodID, va_list args)
jshort	***CallShortMethod** (JNIEnv *env, jobject obj, jmethodID methodID, ...)
jshort	***CallShortMethodA** (JNIEnv *env, jobject obj, jmethodID methodID, jvalue *args)
jshort	***CallShortMethodV** (JNIEnv *env, jobject obj, jmethodID methodID, va_list args)
jboolean	***CallStaticBooleanMethod** (JNIEnv *env, jclass clazz, jmethodID methodID, ...)
jboolean	***CallStaticBooleanMethodA** (JNIEnv *env, jclass clazz, jmethodID methodID, jvalue *args)
jboolean	***CallStaticBooleanMethodV** (JNIEnv *env, jclass clazz, jmethodID methodID, va_list args)
jbyte	***CallStaticByteMethod** (JNIEnv *env, jclass clazz, jmethodID methodID, ...)
jbyte	***CallStaticByteMethodA** (JNIEnv *env, jclass clazz, jmethodID methodID, jvalue *args)
jbyte	***CallStaticByteMethodV** (JNIEnv *env, jclass clazz, jmethodID methodID, va_list args)
jchar	***CallStaticCharMethod** (JNIEnv *env, jclass clazz, jmethodID methodID, ...)
jchar	***CallStaticCharMethodA** (JNIEnv *env, jclass clazz, jmethodID methodID, jvalue *args)
jchar	***CallStaticCharMethodV** (JNIEnv *env, jclass clazz, jmethodID methodID, va_list args)
jdouble	***CallStaticDoubleMethod** (JNIEnv *env, jclass clazz, jmethodID methodID, ...)
jdouble	***CallStaticDoubleMethodA** (JNIEnv *env, jclass clazz, jmethodID methodID, jvalue *args)
jdouble	***CallStaticDoubleMethodV** (JNIEnv *env, jclass clazz, jmethodID methodID, va_list args)
jfloat	***CallStaticFloatMethod** (JNIEnv *env, jclass clazz, jmethodID methodID, ...)
jfloat	***CallStaticFloatMethodA** (JNIEnv *env, jclass clazz, jmethodID methodID, jvalue *args)
jfloat	***CallStaticFloatMethodV** (JNIEnv *env, jclass clazz, jmethodID methodID, va_list args)
jint	***CallStaticIntMethod** (JNIEnv *env, jclass clazz, jmethodID methodID, ...)
jint	***CallStaticIntMethodA** (JNIEnv *env, jclass clazz, jmethodID methodID, jvalue *args)
jint	***CallStaticIntMethodV** (JNIEnv *env, jclass clazz, jmethodID methodID, va_list args)
jlong	***CallStaticLongMethod** (JNIEnv *env, jclass clazz, jmethodID methodID, ...)
jlong	***CallStaticLongMethodA** (JNIEnv *env, jclass clazz, jmethodID methodID, jvalue *args)
jlong	***CallStaticLongMethodV** (JNIEnv *env, jclass clazz, jmethodID methodID, va_list args)
jobject	***CallStaticObjectMethod** (JNIEnv *env, jclass clazz, jmethodID methodID, ...)
jobject	***CallStaticObjectMethodA** (JNIEnv *env, jclass clazz, jmethodID methodID, jvalue *args)
jobject	***CallStaticObjectMethodV** (JNIEnv *env, jclass clazz, jmethodID methodID, va_list args)
jshort	***CallStaticShortMethod** (JNIEnv *env, jclass clazz, jmethodID methodID, ...)

jshort	***CallStaticShortMethodA** (JNIEnv *env, jclass clazz, jmethodID methodID, jvalue *args)
jshort	***CallStaticShortMethodV** (JNIEnv *env, jclass clazz, jmethodID methodID, va_list args)
void	***CallStaticVoidMethod** (JNIEnv *env, jclass cls, jmethodID methodID, ...)
void	***CallStaticVoidMethodA** (JNIEnv *env, jclass cls, jmethodID methodID, jvalue * args)
void	***CallStaticVoidMethodV** (JNIEnv *env, jclass cls, jmethodID methodID, va_list args)
void	***CallVoidMethod** (JNIEnv *env, jobject obj, jmethodID methodID, ...)
void	***CallVoidMethodA** (JNIEnv *env, jobject obj, jmethodID methodID, jvalue * args)
void	***CallVoidMethodV** (JNIEnv *env, jobject obj, jmethodID methodID, va_list args)
jclass	**DefineClass** (JNIEnv *env, jobject loader, const jbyte *buf, jsize bufLen)
	throws ClassFormatError, ClassCircularityError, OutOfMemoryError
void	**DeleteGlobalRef** (JNIEnv *env, jobject globalRef)
void	**DeleteLocalRef** (JNIEnv *env, jobject localRef)
void	**DeleteWeakGlobalRef** (JNIEnv *env, jweak obj)
jint	**DestroyJavaVM** (JavaVM *vm)
jint	**DetachCurrentThread** (JavaVM *vm)
jint	**EnsureLocalCapacity** (JNIEnv *env, jint capacity)
jboolean	**ExceptionCheck** (JNIEnv *env)
void	**ExceptionClear** (JNIEnv *env)
void	**ExceptionDescribe** (JNIEnv *env)
jthrowable	**ExceptionOccurred** (JNIEnv *env)
void	**FatalError** (JNIEnv *env, const char *msg)
jclass	**FindClass** (JNIEnv *env, const char *name)
	throws ClassFormatError, ClassCircularityError, NoClassDefFoundError, OutOfMemoryError
jfieldID	**FromReflectedField** (JNIEnv *env, jobject field)
jmethodID	**FromReflectedMethod** (JNIEnv *env, jobject method)
jsize	**GetArrayLength** (JNIEnv *env, jarray array)
jboolean	****GetBooleanArrayElements** (JNIEnv *env, jbooleanArray array, jboolean *isCopy)
void	***GetBooleanArrayRegion** (JNIEnv *env, jbooleanArray array, jsize start, jsize l, jboolean *buf)
	throws ArrayIndexOutOfBoundsException
jboolean	***GetBooleanField** (JNIEnv *env, jobject obj, jfieldID fieldID)
jbyte	****GetByteArrayElements** (JNIEnv *env, jbyteArray array, jboolean *isCopy)
void	***GetByteArrayRegion** (JNIEnv *env, jbyteArray array, jsize start, jsize len, jbyte *buf)
	throws ArrayIndexOutOfBoundsException
jbyte	***GetByteField** (JNIEnv *env, jobject obj, jfieldID fieldID)
jchar	****GetCharArrayElements** (JNIEnv *env, jcharArray array, jboolean *isCopy)
void	***GetCharArrayRegion** (JNIEnv *env, jcharArray array, jsize start, jsize len, jchar *buf)
	throws ArrayIndexOutOfBoundsException
jchar	***GetCharField** (JNIEnv *env, jobject obj, jfieldID fieldID)
jdouble	****GetDoubleArrayElements** (JNIEnv *env, jdoubleArray array, jboolean *isCopy)
void	***GetDoubleArrayRegion** (JNIEnv *env, jdoubleArray array, jsize start, jsize len, jdouble *buf)
	throws ArrayIndexOutOfBoundsException
jdouble	***GetDoubleField** (JNIEnv *env, jobject obj, jfieldID fieldID)
jint	**GetEnv** (JavaVM *vm, void **env, jint version)
jfieldID	**GetFieldID** (JNIEnv *env, jclass clazz, const char *name, const char *sig)
	throws NoSuchFieldError, ExceptionInInitializerError, OutOfMemoryError
jfloat	****GetFloatArrayElements** (JNIEnv *env, jfloatArray array, jboolean *isCopy)
void	***GetFloatArrayRegion** (JNIEnv *env, jfloatArray array, jsize start, jsize len, jfloat *buf)
	throws ArrayIndexOutOfBoundsException
jfloat	***GetFloatField** (JNIEnv *env, jobject obj, jfieldID fieldID)
jint	****GetIntArrayElements** (JNIEnv *env, jintArray array, jboolean *isCopy)
void	***GetIntArrayRegion** (JNIEnv *env, jintArray array, jsize start, jsize len, jint *buf)
	throws ArrayIndexOutOfBoundsException
jint	***GetIntField** (JNIEnv *env, jobject obj, jfieldID fieldID)
jint	**GetJavaVM** (JNIEnv *env, JavaVM **vm)
jlong	****GetLongArrayElements** (JNIEnv *env, jlongArray array, jboolean *isCopy)
void	***GetLongArrayRegion** (JNIEnv *env, jlongArray array, jsize start, jsize len, jlong *buf)
	throws ArrayIndexOutOfBoundsException
jlong	***GetLongField** (JNIEnv *env, jobject obj, jfieldID fieldID)
jmethodID	**GetMethodID** (JNIEnv *env, jclass clazz, const char *name, const char *sig)
	throws NoSuchMethodError, ExceptionInInitializerError, OutOfMemoryError
jobject	**GetObjectArrayElement** (JNIEnv *env, jobjectArray array, jsize index)
	throws ArrayIndexOutOfBoundsException
jclass	**GetObjectClass** (JNIEnv *env, jobject obj)

Topics

jobject	***GetObjectField** (JNIEnv *env, jobject obj, jfieldID fieldID)
void	***GetPrimitiveArrayCritical** (JNIEnv *env, jarray array, jboolean *isCopy)
jshort	****GetShortArrayElements** (JNIEnv *env, jshortArray array, jboolean *isCopy)
void	***GetShortArrayRegion** (JNIEnv *env, jshortArray array, jsize start, jsize len, jshort *buf)
	throws ArrayIndexOutOfBoundsException
jshort	***GetShortField** (JNIEnv *env, jobject obj, jfieldID fieldID)
jboolean	***GetStaticBooleanField** (JNIEnv *env, jclass clazz, jfieldID fieldID)
jbyte	***GetStaticByteField** (JNIEnv *env, jclass clazz, jfieldID fieldID)
jchar	***GetStaticCharField** (JNIEnv *env, jclass clazz, jfieldID fieldID)
jdouble	***GetStaticDoubleField** (JNIEnv *env, jclass clazz, jfieldID fieldID)
jfieldID	**GetStaticFieldID** (JNIEnv *env, jclass clazz, const char *name, const char *sig)
	throws NoSuchFieldError, ExceptionInInitializerError, OutOfMemoryError
jfloat	***GetStaticFloatField** (JNIEnv *env, jclass clazz, jfieldID fieldID)
jint	***GetStaticIntField** (JNIEnv *env, jclass clazz, jfieldID fieldID)
jlong	***GetStaticLongField** (JNIEnv *env, jclass clazz, jfieldID fieldID)
jmethodID	**GetStaticMethodID** (JNIEnv *env, jclass clazz, const char *name, const char *sig)
	throws NoSuchMethodError, ExceptionInInitializerError, OutOfMemoryError
jobject	***GetStaticObjectField** (JNIEnv *env, jclass clazz, jfieldID fieldID)
jshort	***GetStaticShortField** (JNIEnv *env, jclass clazz, jfieldID fieldID)
const jchar	***GetStringChars** (JNIEnv *env, jstring string, jboolean *isCopy)
const jchar	***GetStringCritical** (JNIEnv *env, jstring string, jboolean *isCopy)
jsize	**GetStringLength** (JNIEnv *env, jstring string)
void	**GetStringRegion** (JNIEnv *env, jstring str, jsize start, jsize len, jchar *buf)
	throws StringIndexOutOfBoundsException
const char	***GetStringUTFChars** (JNIEnv *env, jstring string, jboolean *isCopy)
void	**GetStringUTFRegion** (JNIEnv *env, jstring str, jsize start, jsize len, char *buf)
	throws StringIndexOutOfBoundsException
jsize	**GetStringUTFLength** (JNIEnv *env, jstring string)
jclass	**GetSuperclass** (JNIEnv *env, jclass clazz)
jint	**GetVersion** (JNIEnv *env)
jboolean	**IsAssignableFrom** (JNIEnv *env, jclass clazz1, jclass clazz2)
jboolean	**IsInstanceOf** (JNIEnv *env, jobject obj, jclass clazz)
jboolean	**IsSameObject** (JNIEnv *env, jobject ref1, jobject ref2)
jint	**JNI_CreateJavaVM** (JavaVM **p_vm, JNIEnv **p_env, void *vm_args)
jint	**JNI_GetCreatedJavaVMs** (JavaVM **vmBuf, jsize bufLen, jsize *nVMs)
jint	**JNI_GetDefaultJavaVMInitArgs** (void *vm_args)
jint	**JNI_OnLoad** (JavaVM *vm, void *reserved)
void	**JNI_OnUnload** (JavaVM *vm, void *reserved)
jint	**MonitorEnter** (JNIEnv *env, jobject obj)
jint	**MonitorExit** (JNIEnv *env, jobject obj)
jbooleanArray	***NewBooleanArray** (JNIEnv *env, jsize len)
jbyteArray	***NewByteArray** (JNIEnv *env, jsize len)
jcharArray	***NewCharArray** (JNIEnv *env, jsize len)
jdoubleArray	***NewDoubleArray** (JNIEnv *env, jsize len)
jfloatArray	***NewFloatArray** (JNIEnv *env, jsize len)
jobject	**NewGlobalRef** (JNIEnv *env, jobject obj)
jintArray	***NewIntArray** (JNIEnv *env, jsize len)
jlongArray	***NewLongArray** (JNIEnv *env, jsize len)
jobject	**NewObject** (JNIEnv *env, jclass clazz, jmethodID methodID, ...)
	throws InstantiationException, OutOfMemoryError
jobject	**NewObjectA** (JNIEnv *env, jclass clazz, jmethodID methodID, jvalue *args)
	throws InstantiationException, OutOfMemoryError
jarray	**NewObjectArray** (JNIEnv *env, jsize length, jclass elementClass, jobject initialElement)
	throws OutOfMemoryError
jobject	**NewLocalRef** (JNIEnv *env, jobject ref)
jobject	**NewObjectV** (JNIEnv *env, jclass clazz, jmethodID methodID, va_list args)
	throws InstantiationException, OutOfMemoryError
jshortArray	***NewShortArray** (JNIEnv *env, jsize len)
jstring	**NewString** (JNIEnv *env, const jchar *unicodeChars, jsize len)
	throws OutOfMemoryError
jstring	**NewStringUTF** (JNIEnv *env, const char *bytes)
	throws OutOfMemoryError
jweak	**NewWeakGlobalRef** (JNIEnv *env, jobject obj)

jobject	**PopLocalFrame** (JNIEnv *env, jobject result)
jint	**PushLocalFrame** (JNIEnv *env, jint capacity)
jint	**RegisterNatives** (JNIEnv *env, jclass clazz, const JNINativeMethod *methods, jint nMethods)
	throws NoSuchMethodError
void	***ReleaseBooleanArrayElements** (JNIEnv *env, jbooleanArray array, jboolean *elems, jint mode)
void	***ReleaseByteArrayElements** (JNIEnv *env, jbyteArray array, jbyte *elems, jint mode)
void	***ReleaseCharArrayElements** (JNIEnv *env, jcharArray array, jchar *elems, jint mode)
void	***ReleaseDoubleArrayElements** (JNIEnv *env, jdoubleArray array, jdouble *elems, jint mode)
void	***ReleaseFloatArrayElements** (JNIEnv *env, jfloatArray array, jfloat *elems, jint mode)
void	***ReleaseIntArrayElements** (JNIEnv *env, jintArray array, jint *elems, jint mode)
void	***ReleaseLongArrayElements** (JNIEnv *env, jlongArray array, jlong *elems, jint mode)
void	**ReleasePrimitiveArrayCritical** (JNIEnv *env, jarray array, void *carray, jint mode)
void	***ReleaseShortArrayElements** (JNIEnv *env, jshortArray array, jshort *elems, jint mode)
void	**ReleaseStringChars** (JNIEnv *env, jstring string, const jchar *chars)
void	**ReleaseStringCritical** (JNIEnv *env, jstring string, const jchar *carray)
void	**ReleaseStringUTFChars** (JNIEnv *env, jstring string, const char *utf)
void	***SetBooleanArrayRegion** (JNIEnv *env, jbooleanArray array, jsize start, jsize l, jboolean *buf)
	throws ArrayIndexOutOfBoundsException
void	***SetBooleanField** (JNIEnv *env, jobject obj, jfieldID fieldID, jboolean val)
void	***SetByteArrayRegion** (JNIEnv *env, jbyteArray array, jsize start, jsize len, jbyte *buf)
	throws ArrayIndexOutOfBoundsException
void	***SetByteField** (JNIEnv *env, jobject obj, jfieldID fieldID, jbyte val)
void	***SetCharArrayRegion** (JNIEnv *env, jcharArray array, jsize start, jsize len, jchar *buf)
	throws ArrayIndexOutOfBoundsException
void	***SetCharField** (JNIEnv *env, jobject obj, jfieldID fieldID, jchar val)
void	***SetDoubleArrayRegion** (JNIEnv *env, jdoubleArray array, jsize start, jsize len, jdouble *buf)
	throws ArrayIndexOutOfBoundsException
void	***SetDoubleField** (JNIEnv *env, jobject obj, jfieldID fieldID, jdouble val)
void	***SetFloatArrayRegion** (JNIEnv *env, jfloatArray array, jsize start, jsize len, jfloat *buf)
	throws ArrayIndexOutOfBoundsException
void	***SetFloatField** (JNIEnv *env, jobject obj, jfieldID fieldID, jfloat val)
void	***SetIntArrayRegion** (JNIEnv *env, jintArray array, jsize start, jsize len, jint *buf)
	throws ArrayIndexOutOfBoundsException
void	***SetIntField** (JNIEnv *env, jobject obj, jfieldID fieldID, jint val)
void	***SetLongArrayRegion** (JNIEnv *env, jlongArray array, jsize start, jsize len, jlong *buf)
	throws ArrayIndexOutOfBoundsException
void	***SetLongField** (JNIEnv *env, jobject obj, jfieldID fieldID, jlong val)
void	**SetObjectArrayElement** (JNIEnv *env, jobjectArray array, jsize index, jobject value)
	throws ArrayIndexOutOfBoundsException, ArrayStoreException
void	***SetObjectField** (JNIEnv *env, jobject obj, jfieldID fieldID, jobject val)
void	***SetShortArrayRegion** (JNIEnv *env, jshortArray array, jsize start, jsize len, jshort *buf)
	throws ArrayIndexOutOfBoundsException
void	***SetShortField** (JNIEnv *env, jobject obj, jfieldID fieldID, jshort val)
void	***SetStaticBooleanField** (JNIEnv *env, jclass clazz, jfieldID fieldID, jboolean value)
void	***SetStaticByteField** (JNIEnv *env, jclass clazz, jfieldID fieldID, jbyte value)
void	***SetStaticCharField** (JNIEnv *env, jclass clazz, jfieldID fieldID, jchar value)
void	***SetStaticDoubleField** (JNIEnv *env, jclass clazz, jfieldID fieldID, jdouble value)
void	***SetStaticFloatField** (JNIEnv *env, jclass clazz, jfieldID fieldID, jfloat value)
void	***SetStaticIntField** (JNIEnv *env, jclass clazz, jfieldID fieldID, jint value)
void	***SetStaticLongField** (JNIEnv *env, jclass clazz, jfieldID fieldID, jlong value)
void	***SetStaticObjectField** (JNIEnv *env, jclass clazz, jfieldID fieldID, jobject value)
void	***SetStaticShortField** (JNIEnv *env, jclass clazz, jfieldID fieldID, jshort value)
jint	**Throw** (JNIEnv *env, jthrowable obj)
	throws obj
jint	**ThrowNew** (JNIEnv *env, jclass clazz, const char *message)
	throws the newly constructed object
jobject	**ToReflectedField** (JNIEnv *env, jclass cls, jfieldID fieldID)
	throws OutOfMemoryError
jobject	**ToReflectedMethod** (JNIEnv *env, jclass cls, jmethodID methodID)
	throws OutOfMemoryError
jint	**UnregisterNatives** (JNIEnv *env, jclass clazz)

Topics

PersonalJava Classes

The PersonalJava 1.1 API is a subset of the Java 1.1 API, supplemented by a small number of new classes and interfaces designed to meet the needs of networked embedded applications. These additional API's are described in the next table "Additional Classes and Interfaces." See the PersonalJava 1.0 Specification at http://java.sun.com/products/personaljava for more information.

The legend for this table is as follows: R = required, M = modified, O = optional, U = unsupported.

java.applet	R	FileWriter		O
java.awt	R	FilenameFilter		O
CheckboxMenuItem	O	RandomAccessFile		O
Component	M	**java.lang**		R
Dialog	M	**java.lang.reflect**		R
FileDialog	O	**java.math**		O
Frame	M·	**java.net**		R
Graphics	O	**java.rmi**		O
Menu	O	**java.rmi.dgc**		O
MenuBar	O	**java.rmi.registry**		O
MenuShortcut	O	**java.rmi.server**		O
PopupMenu	M	**java.rmi.security**		O
Scrollbar	O	**java.rmi.security.acl**		U
Toolkit	O	**java.rmi.security.interfaces**		O
Window	M	**java.sql**		O
java.awt.datatransfer	R	**java.text**		R
java.awt.event	R	**java.util**		R
java.awt.image	R	**java.util.zip**		M
java.beans	R	Adler32		O
java.io	R	Deflater		O
File	O	DeflaterOutputStream		O
FileInputStream	O	GZIPOutputStream		O
FileNotFoundException	O	Inflater		M
FileOutputStream	O	ZipFile		O
FileReader	O	ZipOutputStream		O

Protocols

Protocol	Version	Required	Optional	Dependencies
http	1.0	•		
SSL	3.0		•	Requires the SSL Java standard extension.
gopher			•	
ftp			•	
SMTP			•	
file			•	File System.

Source: *The PersonalJava API Specification, Version 1.1* at http://java.sun.com/products/personaljava/spec-1-1/pJavaSpec.html

Image Formats

Image Format	Version	Required	Optional
CompuServe GIF	89a	•	
JPEG (JFIF)		•	
XBM (XBitmap)		•	

Source: *The PersonalJava API Specification, Version 1.1* at http://java.sun.com/products/personaljava/spec-1-1/pJavaSpec.html

Additional Classes and Interfaces

The following classes and interfaces are available in the PersonalJava API but not present in the Java 1.1 API. See the PersonalJava 1.1 Specification at http://java.sun.com/products/personaljava for more information.

java.awt
```
public class Component {
    public boolean isDoubleBuffered()
}
```
com.sun.awt
```
public interface ActionInputPreferred { }
public interface KeyboardInputPreferred { }
public interface NoInputPreferred { }
public interface PositionalInputPreferred { }
```
com.sun.lang
```
public class UnsupportedOperationException extends java.lang.RuntimeException {
    public UnsupportedOperationException();
    public UnsupportedOperationException(String message);
}
```
com.sun.util
```
public abstract class PTimer
    public abstract void deschedule(PTimerSpec t)
    public static PTimer getTimer()
    public abstract void schedule(PTimerSpec t)
}
public class PTimerSpec {
    public void addTimerWentOffListener(PTimerWentOffListener l)
    public long getTime()
    public boolean isAbsolute()
    public boolean isRegular()
    public boolean isRepeat()
    public void notifyListeners(PTimer source)
    public PTimerSpec()
    public void removeTimerWentOffListener(PTimerWentOffListener l)
    public void setAbsolute(boolean absolute)
    public void setAbsoluteTime(long when)
    public void setDelayTime(long delay)
    public void setRegular(boolean regular)
    public void setRepeat(boolean repeat)
    public void setTime(long time)
}
public class PTimerWentOffEvent extends java.util.EventObject {
    public PTimerSpec getTimerSpec()
    public PTimerWentOffEvent(PTimer source, PTimerSpec spec)
}
public interface PTimerWentOffListener {
    void timerWentOff(PTimerWentOffEvent e)
}
```

Topics

Class File Format

The details of the class file structure and bytes codes are documented in Chapter 4 of *The Java Virtual Machine Specification* by Tim Lindholm and Frank Yellin. The following is a quick summary of the structures that comprise a Java class file.

Class File

```
ClassFile {
    u4 magic; // 0xCAFEBABE
    u2 minor_version;
    u2 major_version;
    u2 constant_pool_count;
    cp_info constant_pool[constant_pool_count-1];
    u2 access_flags;
    u2 this_class;
    u2 super_class;
    u2 interfaces_count;
    u2 interfaces[interfaces_count];
    u2 fields_count;
    field_info fields[fields_count];
    u2 methods_count;
    method_info methods[methods_count];
    u2 attributes_count;
    attribute_info attributes[attributes_count];
}
```

Constant Pool

```
cp_info {
    u1 tag;        // See table "Constant Pool Tags"
    u1 info[];
}
CONSTANT_Class_info {
    u1 tag;
    u2 name_index;
}
CONSTANT_Fieldref_info {
    u1 tag;
    u2 class_index;
    u2 name_and_type_index;
}
CONSTANT_Methodref_info {
    u1 tag;
    u2 class_index;
    u2 name_and_type_index;
}
CONSTANT_InterfaceMethodref_info {
    u1 tag;
    u2 class_index;
    u2 name_and_type_index;
}
CONSTANT_String_info {
    u1 tag;
    u2 string_index;
}
CONSTANT_Integer_info {
```

```
    u1 tag;
    u4 bytes;
}
CONSTANT_Float_info {
    u1 tag;
    u4 bytes;
}
CONSTANT_Long_info {
    u1 tag;
    u4 high_bytes;
    u4 low_bytes;
}
CONSTANT_Double_info {
    u1 tag;
    u4 high_bytes;
    u4 low_bytes;
}
CONSTANT_NameAndType_info {
    u1 tag;
    u2 name_index;
    u2 descriptor_index;
}
CONSTANT_Utf8_info {
    u1 tag;
    u2 length;
    u1 bytes[length];
}
```

Fields

```
field_info {
    u2 access_flags;    // See table "Field Access Flags"
    u2 name_index;
    u2 descriptor_index;
    u2 attributes_count;
    attribute_info attributes[attributes_count];
}
```

Methods

```
method_info {
    u2 access_flags;    // See table "Method Access Flags"
    u2 name_index;
    u2 descriptor_index;
    u2 attributes_count;
    attribute_info attributes[attributes_count];
}
```

Attributes

```
attribute_info {
```

```
    u2 attribute_name_index;
    u4 attribute_length;
    u1 info[attribute_length];
}
SourceFile_attribute {
    u2 attribute_name_index;
    u4 attribute_length;
    u2 sourcefile_index;
}
ConstantValue_attribute {
    u2 attribute_name_index;
    u4 attribute_length;
    u2 constantvalue_index;
}
Code_attribute {
    u2 attribute_name_index;
    u4 attribute_length;
    u2 max_stack;
    u2 max_locals;
    u4 code_length;
    u1 code[code_length];
    u2 exception_table_length;
    {
    u2 start_pc;
        u2 end_pc;
        u2 handler_pc;
        u2 catch_type;
    } exception_table[exception_table_length];
    u2 attributes_count;
    attribute_info attributes[attributes_count];
}
Exceptions_attribute {
    u2 attribute_name_index;
    u4 attribute_length;
    u2 number_of_exceptions;
    u2 exception_index_table[number_of_exceptions];
}
```

```
LineNumberTable_attribute {
    u2 attribute_name_index;
    u4 attribute_length;
    u2 line_number_table_length;
    {
        u2 start_pc;
        u2 line_number;
    } line_number_table[line_number_table_length];
}
LocalVariableTable_attribute {
    u2 attribute_name_index;
    u4 attribute_length;
    u2 local_variable_table_length;
    {
        u2 start_pc;
        u2 length;
        u2 name_index;
        u2 descriptor_index;
        u2 index;
    } local_variable_table[local_variable_table_length];
}
InnerClasses_attribute {
    u2 attribute_name_index;
    u4 attribute_length;
    u2 number_of_classes;
    {
        u2 inner_class_info_index;
        u2 outer_class_info_index;
        u2 inner_name_index;
        u2 inner_class_access_flags;
    } classes[number_of_classes];
}
Synthetic_attribute {
    u2 attribute_name_index;
    u4 attribute_length;
}
```

Topics

745

Class File Format Constants

Constant Pool Tags	Value		Field Access Flag Name	Value
CONSTANT_Class	7		ACC_PUBLIC	0x0001
CONSTANT_Fieldref	9		ACC_PRIVATE	0x0002
CONSTANT_Methodref	10		ACC_PROTECTED	0x0004
CONSTANT_InterfaceMethodref	11		ACC_STATIC	0x0008
CONSTANT_String	8		ACC_FINAL	0x0010
CONSTANT_Integer	3		ACC_VOLATILE	0x0040
CONSTANT_Float	4		ACC_TRANSIENT	0x0080
CONSTANT_Long	5			
CONSTANT_Double	6		**Method Access Flag Name**	**Value**
CONSTANT_NameAndType	12			
CONSTANT_Utf8	1		ACC_PUBLIC	0x0001
			ACC_PRIVATE	0x0002
Class Access Flag Name	**Value**		ACC_PROTECTED	0x0004
			ACC_STATIC	0x0008
ACC_PUBLIC	0x0001		ACC_FINAL	0x0010
ACC_FINAL	0x0010		ACC_SYNCHRONIZED	0x0020
ACC_SUPER	0x0020		ACC_NATIVE	0x0100
ACC_INTERFACE	0x0200		ACC_ABSTRACT	0x0400
ACC_ABSTRACT	0x0400			

Inner Class Access Flag Name	Value
ACC_PUBLIC	0x0001
ACC_PRIVATE	0x0002
ACC_PROTECTED	0x0004
ACC_STATIC	0x0008
ACC_FINAL	0x0010
ACC_INTERFACE	0x0200
ACC_ABSTRACT	0x0400

Byte Codes Arranged by Opcode

Opcode	Mnemonic	Opcode	Mnemonic	Opcode	Mnemonic	Opcode	Mnemonic
0	nop	57	dstore	115	drem	173	lreturn
1	aconst_null	58	astore	116	ineg	174	freturn
2	iconst_m1	59	istore_0	117	lneg	175	dreturn
3	iconst_0	60	istore_1	118	fneg	176	areturn
4	iconst_1	61	istore_2	119	dneg	177	return
5	iconst_2	62	istore_3	120	ishl	178	getstatic
6	iconst_3	63	lstore_0	121	lshl	179	putstatic
7	iconst_4	64	lstore_1	122	ishr	180	getfield
8	iconst_5	65	lstore_2	123	lshr	181	putfield
9	lconst_0	66	lstore_3	124	iushr	182	invokevirtual
10	lconst_1	67	fstore_0	125	lushr	183	invokespecial
11	fconst_0	68	fstore_1	126	iand	184	invokestatic
12	fconst_1	69	fstore_2	127	land	185	invokeinterface
13	fconst_2	70	fstore_3	128	ior	186	*unused*
14	dconst_0	71	dstore_0	129	lor	187	new
15	dconst_1	72	dstore_1	130	ixor	188	newarray
16	bipush	73	dstore_2	131	lxor	189	anewarray
17	sipush	74	dstore_3	132	iinc	190	arraylength
18	ldc	75	astore_0	133	i2l	191	athrow
19	ldc_w	76	astore_1	134	i2f	192	checkcast
20	ldc2_w	77	astore_2	135	i2d	193	instanceof
21	iload	78	astore_3	136	l2i	194	monitorenter
22	lload	79	iastore	137	l2f	195	monitorexit
23	fload	80	lastore	138	l2d	196	wide
24	dload	81	fastore	139	f2i	197	multianewarray
25	aload	82	dastore	140	f2l	198	ifnull
26	iload_0	83	aastore	141	f2d	199	ifnonnull
27	iload_1	84	bastore	142	d2i	200	goto_w
28	iload_2	85	castore	143	d2l	201	jsr_w
29	iload_3	86	sastore	144	d2f	202	breakpoint
30	lload_0	87	pop	145	i2b	203	ldc_quick
31	lload_1	88	pop2	146	i2c	204	ldc_w_quick
32	lload_2	89	dup	147	i2s	205	ldc2_w_quick
33	lload_3	90	dup_x1	148	lcmp	206	getfield_quick
34	fload_0	91	dup_x2	149	fcmpl	207	putfield_quick
35	fload_1	92	dup2	150	fcmpg	208	getfield2_quick
36	fload_2	93	dup2_x1	151	dcmpl	209	putfield2_quick
37	fload_3	94	dup2_x2	152	dcmpg	210	getstatic_quick
38	dload_0	95	swap	153	ifeq	211	putstatic_quick
39	dload_1	96	iadd	154	ifne	212	getstatic2_quick
40	dload_2	97	ladd	155	iflt	213	putstatic2_quick
41	dload_3	98	fadd	156	ifge	214	invokevirtual_quick
42	aload_0	99	dadd	157	ifgt	215	invokenonvirtual_quick
43	aload_1	100	isub	158	ifle	216	invokesuper_quick
44	aload_2	101	lsub	159	if_icmpeq	217	invokestatic_quick
45	aload_3	102	fsub	160	if_icmpne	218	invokeinterface_quick
46	iaload	103	dsub	161	if_icmplt	219	invokevirtualobject_quick
47	laload	104	imul	162	if_icmpge	221	new_quick
48	faload	105	lmul	163	if_icmpgt	222	anewarray_quick
49	daload	106	fmul	164	if_icmple	223	multianewarray_quick
50	aaload	107	dmul	165	if_acmpeq	224	checkcast_quick
51	baload	108	idiv	166	if_acmpne	225	instanceof_quick
52	caload	109	ldiv	167	goto	226	invokevirtual_quick_w
53	saload	110	fdiv	168	jsr	227	getfield_quick_w
54	istore	111	ddiv	169	ret	228	putfield_quick_w
55	lstore	112	irem	170	tableswitch	254	impdep1
56	fstore	113	lrem	171	lookupswitch	255	impdep2
		114	frem	172	ireturn		

Topics

Byte Codes Arranged by Mnemonic

Opcode	Mnemonic	Opcode	Mnemonic	Opcode	Mnemonic	Opcode	Mnemonic
aaload	50	dup_x2	91	if_icmpge	162	lcmp	148
aastore	83	f2d	141	if_icmpgt	163	lconst_0	9
aconst_null	1	f2i	139	if_icmple	164	lconst_1	10
aload	25	f2l	140	if_icmplt	161	ldc	18
aload_0	42	fadd	98	if_icmpne	160	ldc2_w	20
aload_1	43	faload	48	ifeq	153	ldc2_w_quick	205
aload_2	44	fastore	81	ifge	156	ldc_quick	203
aload_3	45	fcmpg	150	ifgt	157	ldc_w	19
anewarray	189	fcmpl	149	ifle	158	ldc_w_quick	204
anewarray_quick	222	fconst_0	11	iflt	155	ldiv	109
areturn	176	fconst_1	12	ifne	154	lload	22
arraylength	190	fconst_2	13	ifnonnull	199	lload_0	30
astore	58	fdiv	110	ifnull	198	lload_1	31
astore_0	75	fload	23	iinc	132	lload_2	32
astore_1	76	fload_0	34	iload	21	lload_3	33
astore_2	77	fload_1	35	iload_0	26	lmul	105
astore_3	78	fload_2	36	iload_1	27	lneg	117
athrow	191	fload_3	37	iload_2	28	lookupswitch	171
baload	51	fmul	106	iload_3	29	lor	129
bastore	84	fneg	118	impdep1	254	lrem	113
bipush	16	frem	114	impdep2	255	lreturn	173
breakpoint	202	freturn	174	imul	104	lshl	121
caload	52	fstore	56	ineg	116	lshr	123
castore	85	fstore_0	67	instanceof	193	lstore	55
checkcast	192	fstore_1	68	instanceof_quick	225	lstore_0	63
checkcast_quick	224	fstore_2	69	invokeinterface	185	lstore_1	64
d2f	144	fstore_3	70	invokeinterface_quick	218	lstore_2	65
d2i	142	fsub	102	invokenonvirtual_quick	215	lstore_3	66
d2l	143	getfield	180	invokespecial	183	lsub	101
dadd	99	getfield2_quick	208	invokestatic	184	lushr	125
daload	49	getfield_quick	206	invokestatic_quick	217	lxor	131
dastore	82	getfield_quick_w	227	invokesuper_quick	216	monitorenter	194
dcmpg	152	getstatic	178	invokevirtual	182	monitorexit	195
dcmpl	151	getstatic2_quick	212	invokevirtual_quick	214	multianewarray	197
dconst_0	14	getstatic_quick	210	invokevirtual_quick_w	226	multianewarray_quick	223
dconst_1	15	goto	167	invokevirtualobject_quick	219	new	187
ddiv	111	goto_w	200	ior	128	new_quick	221
dload	24	i2b	145	irem	112	newarray	188
dload_0	38	i2c	146	ireturn	172	nop	0
dload_1	39	i2d	135	ishl	120	pop	87
dload_2	40	i2f	134	ishr	122	pop2	88
dload_3	41	i2l	133	istore	54	putfield	181
dmul	107	i2s	147	istore_0	59	putfield2_quick	209
dneg	119	iadd	96	istore_1	60	putfield_quick	207
drem	115	iaload	46	istore_2	61	putfield_quick_w	228
dreturn	175	iand	126	istore_3	62	putstatic	179
dstore	57	iastore	79	isub	100	putstatic2_quick	213
dstore_0	71	iconst_0	3	iushr	124	putstatic_quick	211
dstore_1	72	iconst_1	4	ixor	130	ret	169
dstore_2	73	iconst_2	5	jsr	168	return	177
dstore_3	74	iconst_3	6	jsr_w	201	saload	53
dsub	103	iconst_4	7	l2d	138	sastore	86
dup	89	iconst_5	8	l2f	137	sipush	17
dup2	92	iconst_m1	2	l2i	136	swap	95
dup2_x1	93	idiv	108	ladd	97	tableswitch	170
dup2_x2	94	if_acmpeq	165	laload	47	wide	196
dup_x1	90	if_acmpne	166	land	127	*unused*	186
		if_icmpeq	159	lastore	80		

Part 4

CROSS-REFERENCE

This part contains a cross-reference of all of the core 1.2 Java classes and interfaces except for the ones in the `javax.swing.plaf.*` packages. To save space, there are no cross-reference entries for primitive types, constructors, `java.lang.Object`, or `java.lang.String`.

The cross-reference consists of entries and subentries. An entry is displayed in bold type and shows a class, interface, or member name. If the entry is a class or interface, the package containing the class or interface is shown on the right. If the entry is a member name, all classes or interfaces that have a member with that name are listed to the right. Member names are shown in a condensed font to conserve space.

A class or interface may be followed by an asterisk (*). This simply indicates that the class or interface has children.

An entry may be followed by subentries that contain more information about that class, interface, or member. For example, the "returned by" subentry for a class lists all members that return an instance of the class. Following is a list of the set of subentries.

It's important to note that this cross-reference does not include any overridden methods. For example, if `C.m()` overrides `A.m()`, the entry "m" shows `A` but not `C`. To discover all classes that implement `m()`, look up the "A" entry and there you will find all the classes that are descendents of `A` and therefore implement `m()`.

Subentry	Description
descendents	Shows the entire list of descendents (except for the ones that already appear in "subclasses") of this class or interface.
extended by	Shows all interfaces that extend this interface.
fields	Shows all fields of this type.
implemented by	Shows all classes that implement this interface.
passed to	Shows each method and constructor whose parameter list includes at least one parameter of this type.
returned by	Shows all methods that return an object of this type.
subclasses	Shows all subclasses of this class.
thrown by	Shows all methods and constructors that throw this exception.

_ADD_OVERRIDE: SetOverrideType
_BindingIteratorImplBase: org.omg.CosNaming
_BindingIteratorStub: org.omg.CosNaming
_COMPLETED_MAYBE: CompletionStatus
_COMPLETED_NO: CompletionStatus
_COMPLETED_YES: CompletionStatus
_create_request(): *org.omg.CORBA.Object** ObjectImpl*
_dk_Alias: DefinitionKind
_dk_all: DefinitionKind
_dk_Array: DefinitionKind
_dk_Attribute: DefinitionKind
_dk_Constant: DefinitionKind
_dk_Enum: DefinitionKind
_dk_Exception: DefinitionKind
_dk_Fixed: DefinitionKind
_dk_Interface: DefinitionKind
_dk_Module: DefinitionKind
_dk_Native: DefinitionKind
_dk_none: DefinitionKind
_dk_Operation: DefinitionKind
_dk_Primitive: DefinitionKind
_dk_Repository: DefinitionKind
_dk_Sequence: DefinitionKind
_dk_String: DefinitionKind
_dk_Struct: DefinitionKind
_dk_Typedef: DefinitionKind
_dk_Union: DefinitionKind
_dk_Value: DefinitionKind
_dk_ValueBox: DefinitionKind
_dk_ValueMember: DefinitionKind
_dk_Wstring: DefinitionKind
_duplicate(): *org.omg.CORBA.Object** ObjectImpl*
_get_delegate(): ObjectImpl*
_get_domain_managers(): *org.omg.CORBA.Object**
  ObjectImpl*
_get_interface_def(): *org.omg.CORBA.Object** ObjectImpl*
_get_policy(): *org.omg.CORBA.Object** ObjectImpl*
_hash(): *org.omg.CORBA.Object** ObjectImpl*
_ids(): ObjectImpl*
_invoke(): *InvokeHandler* ObjectImpl*
_is_a(): *org.omg.CORBA.Object** ObjectImpl*
_is_equivalent(): *org.omg.CORBA.Object** ObjectImpl*
_is_local(): ObjectImpl*
_missing_node: NotFoundReason
_NamingContextImplBase: org.omg.CosNaming
_NamingContextStub: org.omg.CosNaming
_ncontext: BindingType
_nobject: BindingType
_non_existent(): *org.omg.CORBA.Object** ObjectImpl*
_not_context: NotFoundReason
_not_object: NotFoundReason
_orb(): ObjectImpl*
_postEdit(): UndoableEditSupport
_read(): AlreadyBoundHolder AnyHolder BindingHolder
  BindingIteratorHolder BindingListHolder
  BindingTypeHolder BooleanHolder ByteHolder
  CannotProceedHolder CharHolder DoubleHolder
  FixedHolder FloatHolder IntHolder InvalidNameHolder
  LongHolder NameComponentHolder NameHolder
  NamingContextHolder NotEmptyHolder NotFoundHolder
  NotFoundReasonHolder ObjectHolder PrincipalHolder
  ServiceInformationHolder ShortHolder *Streamable*
  StringHolder TypeCodeHolder
_release(): *org.omg.CORBA.Object** ObjectImpl*
_releaseReply(): ObjectImpl*
_request(): *org.omg.CORBA.Object** ObjectImpl*
_servant_postinvoke(): ObjectImpl*
_servant_preinvoke(): ObjectImpl*
_set_delegate(): ObjectImpl*
_SET_OVERRIDE: SetOverrideType
_set_policy_override(): *org.omg.CORBA.Object** ObjectImpl*
_tk_abstract_interface: TCKind

_tk_alias: TCKind
_tk_any: TCKind
_tk_array: TCKind
_tk_boolean: TCKind
_tk_char: TCKind
_tk_double: TCKind
_tk_enum: TCKind
_tk_except: TCKind
_tk_fixed: TCKind
_tk_float: TCKind
_tk_long: TCKind
_tk_longdouble: TCKind
_tk_longlong: TCKind
_tk_native: TCKind
_tk_null: TCKind
_tk_objref: TCKind
_tk_octet: TCKind
_tk_Principal: TCKind
_tk_sequence: TCKind
_tk_short: TCKind
_tk_string: TCKind
_tk_struct: TCKind
_tk_TypeCode: TCKind
_tk_ulong: TCKind
_tk_ulonglong: TCKind
_tk_union: TCKind
_tk_ushort: TCKind
_tk_value: TCKind
_tk_value_box: TCKind
_tk_void: TCKind
_tk_wchar: TCKind
_tk_wstring: TCKind
_type(): AlreadyBoundHolder AnyHolder BindingHolder
  BindingIteratorHolder BindingListHolder
  BindingTypeHolder BooleanHolder ByteHolder
  CannotProceedHolder CharHolder DoubleHolder
  FixedHolder FloatHolder IntHolder InvalidNameHolder
  LongHolder NameComponentHolder NameHolder
  NamingContextHolder NotEmptyHolder NotFoundHolder
  NotFoundReasonHolder ObjectHolder PrincipalHolder
  ServiceInformationHolder ShortHolder *Streamable*
  StringHolder TypeCodeHolder
_write(): AlreadyBoundHolder AnyHolder BindingHolder
  BindingIteratorHolder BindingListHolder
  BindingTypeHolder BooleanHolder ByteHolder
  CannotProceedHolder CharHolder DoubleHolder
  FixedHolder FloatHolder IntHolder InvalidNameHolder
  LongHolder NameComponentHolder NameHolder
  NamingContextHolder NotEmptyHolder NotFoundHolder
  NotFoundReasonHolder ObjectHolder PrincipalHolder
  ServiceInformationHolder ShortHolder *Streamable*
  StringHolder TypeCodeHolder
A: HTML.Tag*
a: AWTEventMulticaster
ABORT: *ImageObserver*
ABORTED: MediaTracker
abortGrabbing(): PixelGrabber
ABOVE_BOTTOM: TitledBorder*
ABOVE_TOP: TitledBorder*
abs(): BigDecimal BigInteger Math
absolute(): *ResultSet*
ABSTRACT: Modifier
AbstractAction*: javax.swing
—subclasses: TextAction*
—descendents: DefaultEditorKit.BeepAction
  DefaultEditorKit.CopyAction DefaultEditorKit.CutAction
  DefaultEditorKit.DefaultKeyTypedAction
  DefaultEditorKit.InsertBreakAction
  DefaultEditorKit.InsertContentAction
  DefaultEditorKit.InsertTabAction DefaultEditorKit.PasteAction
  HTMLEditorKit.HTMLTextAction*
  HTMLEditorKit.InsertHTMLTextAction

StyledEditorKit.AlignmentAction StyledEditorKit.BoldAction
StyledEditorKit.FontFamilyAction
StyledEditorKit.FontSizeAction
StyledEditorKit.ForegroundAction
StyledEditorKit.ItalicAction StyledEditorKit.StyledTextAction*
StyledEditorKit.UnderlineAction

AbstractBorder*: javax.swing.border
—subclasses: BevelBorder* CompoundBorder* EmptyBorder*
EtchedBorder* LineBorder* TitledBorder*
—descendents: BorderUIResource.BevelBorderUIResource
BorderUIResource.CompoundBorderUIResource
BorderUIResource.EmptyBorderUIResource
BorderUIResource.EtchedBorderUIResource
BorderUIResource.LineBorderUIResource
BorderUIResource.MatteBorderUIResource
BorderUIResource.TitledBorderUIResource MatteBorder*
SoftBevelBorder

AbstractButton*: javax.swing
—subclasses: JButton JMenuItem* JToggleButton*
—descendents: JCheckBox JCheckBoxMenuItem JMenu
JRadioButton JRadioButtonMenuItem
—passed to: AbstractButton.AccessibleAbstractButton( )
ButtonGroup.remove( )

AbstractButton.AccessibleAbstractButton*: javax.swing
—subclasses: JButton.AccessibleJButton
JMenuItem.AccessibleJMenuItem*
JToggleButton.AccessibleJToggleButton*
—descendents: JCheckBox.AccessibleJCheckBox
JCheckBoxMenuItem.AccessibleJCheckBoxMenuItem
JMenu.AccessibleJMenu
JRadioButton.AccessibleJRadioButton
JRadioButtonMenuItem.AccessibleJRadioButtonMenuItem

AbstractButton.ButtonChangeListener: javax.swing

AbstractCollection*: java.util
—subclasses: AbstractList* AbstractSet*
—descendents: AbstractSequentialList* ArrayList HashSet
LinkedList Stack TreeSet Vector*

AbstractColorChooserPanel: javax.swing.colorchooser
—passed to: JColorChooser < addChooserPanel( ),
removeChooserPanel( ), setChooserPanels( ) >
—returned
by: ColorChooserComponentFactory.getDefaultChooserPanels( )
JColorChooser.removeChooserPanel( )

AbstractDocument*: javax.swing.text
—subclasses: DefaultStyledDocument* PlainDocument
—descendents: HTMLDocument
—passed to: AbstractDocument.AbstractElement( )
AbstractDocument.DefaultDocumentEvent( )

AbstractDocument.AbstractElement*: javax.swing.text
—subclasses: AbstractDocument.BranchElement*
AbstractDocument.LeafElement*
—descendents: DefaultStyledDocument.SectionElement
HTMLDocument.BlockElement HTMLDocument.RunElement
—returned by: DefaultStyledDocument*.createDefaultRoot( )
PlainDocument.createDefaultRoot( )

AbstractDocument.AttributeContext: javax.swing.text
—passed to: AbstractDocument( )
—returned by: AbstractDocument*.getAttributeContext( )
—implemented by: StyleContext*

AbstractDocument.BranchElement*: javax.swing.text
—subclasses: DefaultStyledDocument.SectionElement
HTMLDocument.BlockElement

AbstractDocument.Content: javax.swing.text
—passed to: AbstractDocument( ) HTMLDocument( )
—returned by: AbstractDocument*.getContent( )
—implemented by: GapContent StringContent

AbstractDocument.DefaultDocumentEvent: javax.swing.text
—passed to: AbstractDocument* < insertUpdate( ),
postRemoveUpdate( ), removeUpdate( ) >
DefaultStyledDocument*.removeUpdate( )
DefaultStyledDocument.ElementBuffer < insert( ), remove( ) >
PlainDocument < insertUpdate( ), removeUpdate( ) >

AbstractDocument.ElementEdit: javax.swing.text
AbstractDocument.LeafElement*: javax.swing.text
—subclasses: HTMLDocument.RunElement
AbstractLayoutCache*: javax.swing.tree
—subclasses: FixedHeightLayoutCache
VariableHeightLayoutCache
AbstractLayoutCache.NodeDimensions: javax.swing.tree
—passed to: AbstractLayoutCache*.setNodeDimensions( )
—returned by: AbstractLayoutCache*.getNodeDimensions( )
—fields: AbstractLayoutCache*.nodeDimensions
AbstractList*: java.util
—subclasses: AbstractSequentialList* ArrayList · Vector*
—descendents: LinkedList Stack
AbstractListModel*: javax.swing
—subclasses: DefaultComboBoxModel DefaultListModel
AbstractMap*: java.util
—subclasses: HashMap TreeMap WeakHashMap
AbstractMethodError: java.lang
AbstractSequentialList*: java.util
—subclasses: LinkedList
AbstractSet*: java.util
—subclasses: HashSet TreeSet
AbstractTableModel*: javax.swing.table
—subclasses: DefaultTableModel
AbstractUndoableEdit*: javax.swing.undo
—subclasses: AbstractDocument.ElementEdit CompoundEdit*
DefaultStyledDocument.AttributeUndoableEdit StateEdit
—descendents: AbstractDocument.DefaultDocumentEvent
UndoManager
AbstractWriter*: javax.swing.text
—subclasses: HTMLWriter MinimalHTMLWriter
accept( ): *java.io.FileFilter* javax.swing.filechooser.FileFilter
FilenameFilter JFileChooser ServerSocket SocketImpl
acceptDrag( ): DropTargetContext DropTargetDragEvent
acceptDrop( ): DropTargetContext DropTargetDropEvent
acceptsURL( ): *Driver*
access: ValueMember
AccessControlContext: java.security
—passed to: AccessController.doPrivileged( )
—returned by: AccessController.getContext( )
AccessControlException: java.security
—thrown by: AccessControlContext.checkPermission( )
AccessController: java.security
AccessException: java.rmi
—thrown by: *Registry* < bind( ), list( ), lookup( ), rebind( ),
unbind( ) >
Accessible: javax.accessibility
—passed to: AccessibleContext*.setAccessibleParent( )
—returned by: *AccessibleComponent*.getAccessibleAt( )
AccessibleContext*.getAccessibleParent( )
Box.AccessibleBox.getAccessibleAt( ) CellRendererPane ↵
.AccessibleCellRendererPane.getAccessibleAt( )
JApplet.AccessibleJApplet.getAccessibleAt( )
JDialog.AccessibleJDialog.getAccessibleAt( )
JList.AccessibleJList.getAccessibleSelection( )
JMenu.AccessibleJMenu.getAccessibleSelection( )
JPopupMenu.WindowPopup ↵
.AccessibleWindowPopup.getAccessibleAt( )
JTable.AccessibleJTable.getAccessibleSelection( )
JTableHeader.AccessibleJTableHeader ↵
.AccessibleJTableHeaderEntry.getAccessibleAt( )
JTree.AccessibleJTree.AccessibleJTreeNode
< getAccessibleSelection( ) > SwingUtilities
< getAccessibleAt( ), getAccessibleChild( ) >
—implemented by: Box Box.Filler CellRendererPane
JApplet JButton JColorChooser JComboBox
JDialog JFileChooser JFrame JInternalFrame
JInternalFrame.JDesktopIcon JLabel JLayeredPane*
JList JList.AccessibleJList.AccessibleJListChild JMenuBar
JMenuItem* JOptionPane JPanel* JPopupMenu
JProgressBar JRootPane JScrollBar* JScrollPane
JSeparator* JSlider JSplitPane JTabbedPane JTable

JTable.AccessibleJTable.AccessibleJTableCell
JTableHeader JTableHeader.AccessibleJTableHeader ↩
.AccessibleJTableHeaderEntry JTextComponent*
JToggleButton* JToolBar JToolTip JTree
JTree.AccessibleJTree.AccessibleJTreeNode JViewport
JWindow
—fields: AccessibleContext*.accessibleParent

ACCESSIBLE_ACTIVE_DESCENDANT_PROPERTY:
   AccessibleContext*
ACCESSIBLE_CARET_PROPERTY: AccessibleContext*
ACCESSIBLE_CHILD_PROPERTY: AccessibleContext*
ACCESSIBLE_DESCRIPTION_PROPERTY:
   AccessibleContext*
ACCESSIBLE_NAME_PROPERTY: AccessibleContext*
ACCESSIBLE_SELECTION_PROPERTY: AccessibleContext*
ACCESSIBLE_STATE_PROPERTY: AccessibleContext*
ACCESSIBLE_TEXT_PROPERTY: AccessibleContext*
ACCESSIBLE_VALUE_PROPERTY: AccessibleContext*
ACCESSIBLE_VISIBLE_DATA_PROPERTY:
   AccessibleContext*

AccessibleAction: javax.accessibility
 —returned by: AccessibleContext*.getAccessibleAction( )
 —implemented by: AbstractButton.AccessibleAbstractButton*
   AccessibleHyperlink* JComboBox.AccessibleJComboBox
   JTree.AccessibleJTree.AccessibleJTreeNode

AccessibleBundle*: javax.accessibility
 —subclasses: AccessibleRole AccessibleState

AccessibleComponent: javax.accessibility
 —returned by: AccessibleContext*.getAccessibleComponent( )
 —implemented by: Box.AccessibleBox
   Box.Filler.AccessibleBoxFiller
   CellRendererPane.AccessibleCellRendererPane
   JApplet.AccessibleJApplet
   JComponent.AccessibleJComponent*
   JDialog.AccessibleJDialog JFrame.AccessibleJFrame
   JList.AccessibleJList.AccessibleJListChild
   JPopupMenu.WindowPopup.AccessibleWindowPopup
   JTable.AccessibleJTable.AccessibleJTableCell
   JTableHeader.AccessibleJTableHeader ↩
   .AccessibleJTableHeaderEntry
   JTree.AccessibleJTree.AccessibleJTreeNode
   JWindow.AccessibleJWindow

accessibleContainerHandler:
   JComponent.AccessibleJComponent*

accessibleContext: Box Box.Filler CellRendererPane
   JApplet JComponent* JDialog JFrame JWindow

AccessibleContext*: javax.accessibility
 —subclasses: Box.AccessibleBox Box.Filler.AccessibleBoxFiller
   CellRendererPane.AccessibleCellRendererPane
   JApplet.AccessibleJApplet
   JComponent.AccessibleJComponent*
   JDialog.AccessibleJDialog JFrame.AccessibleJFrame
   JList.AccessibleJList.AccessibleJListChild
   JPopupMenu.WindowPopup.AccessibleWindowPopup
   JTable.AccessibleJTable.AccessibleJTableCell
   JTableHeader.AccessibleJTableHeader ↩
   .AccessibleJTableHeaderEntry
   JTree.AccessibleJTree.AccessibleJTreeNode
   JWindow.AccessibleJWindow
 —descendents: AbstractButton.AccessibleAbstractButton*
   JButton.AccessibleJButton
   JCheckBox.AccessibleJCheckBox
   JCheckBoxMenuItem.AccessibleJCheckBoxMenuItem
   JColorChooser.AccessibleJColorChooser
   JComboBox.AccessibleJComboBox
   JDesktopPane.AccessibleJDesktopPane
   JEditorPane.AccessibleJEditorPane*
   JEditorPane.AccessibleJEditorPaneHTML
   JEditorPane.JEditorPaneAccessibleHypertextSupport
   JFileChooser.AccessibleJFileChooser
   JInternalFrame.AccessibleJInternalFrame
   JInternalFrame.JDesktopIcon.AccessibleJDesktopIcon

JLabel.AccessibleJLabel
JLayeredPane.AccessibleJLayeredPane
JList.AccessibleJList JMenu.AccessibleJMenu
JMenuBar.AccessibleJMenuBar
JMenuItem.AccessibleJMenuItem*
JOptionPane.AccessibleJOptionPane
JPanel.AccessibleJPanel
JPasswordField.AccessibleJPasswordField
JPopupMenu.AccessibleJPopupMenu
JProgressBar.AccessibleJProgressBar
JRadioButton.AccessibleJRadioButton
JRadioButtonMenuItem.AccessibleJRadioButtonMenuItem
JRootPane.AccessibleJRootPane
JScrollBar.AccessibleJScrollBar
JScrollPane.AccessibleJScrollPane
JSeparator.AccessibleJSeparator
JSlider.AccessibleJSlider JSplitPane.AccessibleJSplitPane
JTabbedPane.AccessibleJTabbedPane
JTable.AccessibleJTable
JTableHeader.AccessibleJTableHeader
JTextArea.AccessibleJTextArea
JTextComponent.AccessibleJTextComponent*
JTextField.AccessibleJTextField*
JToggleButton.AccessibleJToggleButton*
JToolBar.AccessibleJToolBar JToolTip.AccessibleJToolTip
JTree.AccessibleJTree JViewport.AccessibleJViewport
 —returned by: Accessible.getAccessibleContext( )
   Box.Filler.getAccessibleContext( ) JApplet.getAccessibleContext( )
   JDialog.getAccessibleContext( ) JList.AccessibleJList ↩
   .AccessibleJListChild.getAccessibleContext( )
   JTableHeader.AccessibleJTableHeader ↩
   .AccessibleJTableHeaderEntry.getAccessibleContext( )
   JWindow.getAccessibleContext( )
 —fields: Box.accessibleContext
   CellRendererPane.accessibleContext
   JColorChooser.accessibleContext JDialog.accessibleContext
   JFrame.accessibleContext

accessibleDescription: AccessibleContext*
AccessibleHyperlink*: javax.accessibility
 —subclasses: JEditorPane ↩
   .JEditorPaneAccessibleHypertextSupport.HTMLLink
 —returned by: AccessibleHypertext.getLink( )
AccessibleHypertext: javax.accessibility
 —implemented
   by: JEditorPane.JEditorPaneAccessibleHypertextSupport
accessibleName: AccessibleContext*
AccessibleObject*: java.lang.reflect
 —subclasses: Constructor Field Method
 —passed to: AccessibleObject*.setAccessible( )
accessibleParent: AccessibleContext*
AccessibleResourceBundle: javax.accessibility
AccessibleRole: javax.accessibility
 —returned by: AccessibleContext*.getAccessibleRole( )
 —fields: AccessibleRole < ALERT, AWT_COMPONENT,
   CHECK_BOX, COLOR_CHOOSER, COLUMN_HEADER,
   COMBO_BOX, DESKTOP_ICON, DESKTOP_PANE, DIALOG,
   DIRECTORY_PANE, FILE_CHOOSER, FILLER, FRAME,
   GLASS_PANE, INTERNAL_FRAME, LABEL, LAYERED_PANE,
   LIST, MENU, MENU_BAR, MENU_ITEM, OPTION_PANE,
   PAGE_TAB, PAGE_TAB_LIST, PANEL, PASSWORD_TEXT,
   POPUP_MENU, PROGRESS_BAR, PUSH_BUTTON,
   RADIO_BUTTON, ROOT_PANE, ROW_HEADER, SCROLL_BAR,
   SCROLL_PANE, SEPARATOR, SLIDER, SPLIT_PANE,
   SWING_COMPONENT, TABLE, TEXT, TOGGLE_BUTTON,
   TOOL_BAR, TOOL_TIP, TREE, UNKNOWN, VIEWPORT,
   WINDOW >
AccessibleSelection: javax.accessibility
 —returned by: AccessibleContext*.getAccessibleSelection( )
 —implemented by: JList.AccessibleJList
   JMenu.AccessibleJMenu JMenuBar.AccessibleJMenuBar
   JTabbedPane.AccessibleJTabbedPane

JTable.AccessibleJTable JTree.AccessibleJTree
JTree.AccessibleJTreeNode
AccessibleState: javax.accessibility
—passed to: **A**ccessibleStateSet < AccessibleStateSet( ), add( ),
addAll( ), contains( ), remove( ) >
—returned by: **A**ccessibleStateSet.toArray( )
—fields: **A**ccessibleState < ACTIVE, ARMED, BUSY, CHECKED,
COLLAPSED, EDITABLE, ENABLED, EXPANDABLE, EXPANDED,
FOCUSABLE, FOCUSED, HORIZONTAL, ICONIFIED, MODAL,
MULTI_LINE, MULTISELECTABLE, OPAQUE, PRESSED,
RESIZABLE, SELECTABLE, SELECTED, SHOWING, SINGLE_LINE,
TRANSIENT, VERTICAL, VISIBLE >
AccessibleStateSet: javax.accessibility
—returned by: **A**ccessibleContext*.getAccessibleStateSet( )
AccessibleText*: javax.accessibility
—extended by: *AccessibleHypertext*
—returned by: **A**ccessibleContext*.getAccessibleText( )
—implemented by: **J**TextComponent.AccessibleJTextComponent*
AccessibleValue: javax.accessibility
—returned by: **A**ccessibleContext*.getAccessibleValue( )
—implemented by: **A**bstractButton.AccessibleAbstractButton*
JInternalFrame.AccessibleJInternalFrame
JInternalFrame.JDesktopIcon.AccessibleJDesktopIcon
JProgressBar.AccessibleJProgressBar
JScrollBar.AccessibleJScrollBar **J**Slider.AccessibleJSlider
JSplitPane.AccessibleJSplitPane
ACCESSORY_CHANGED_PROPERTY: **J**FileChooser
Acl: java.security.acl
AclEntry: java.security.acl
—passed to: *Acl* < addEntry( ), removeEntry( ) >
AclNotFoundException: java.security.acl
acos( ): **M**ath
ACTION: **H**TML.Attribute
Action: javax.swing
—passed to: **J**Menu < add( ), insert( ) > **J**PopupMenu.insert( )
JToolBar.add( ) *Keymap* < getKeyStrokesForAction( ),
setDefaultAction( ) >
—returned by: **E**ditorKit*.getActions( ) *Keymap* < getAction( ),
getBoundActions( ), getDefaultAction( ) >
—implemented by: **A**bstractAction*
action( ): **C**omponent*
ACTION_COPY: **D**nDConstants
ACTION_COPY_OR_MOVE: **D**nDConstants
ACTION_EVENT: **E**vent
ACTION_EVENT_MASK: **A**WTEvent*
ACTION_FIRST: **A**ctionEvent
ACTION_LAST: **A**ctionEvent
ACTION_LINK: **D**nDConstants
ACTION_MOVE: **D**nDConstants
ACTION_NONE: **D**nDConstants
ACTION_PERFORMED: **A**ctionEvent
ACTION_REFERENCE: **D**nDConstants
actionCommand: **D**efaultButtonModel* **J**ComboBox
ActionEvent: java.awt.event
—passed to: **A**bstractAction*.actionPerformed( )
ActionListener*.actionPerformed( ) **B**utton.processActionEvent( )
DefaultCellEditor.EditorDelegate.actionPerformed( )
DropTarget.DropTargetAutoScroller.actionPerformed( )
java.awt.**L**ist.processActionEvent( )
MenuItem*.processActionEvent( )
TextAction*.getTextComponent( ) **T**imer.fireActionPerformed( )
ToolTipManager.outsideTimerAction.actionPerformed( )
actionListener: **A**bstractButton*
ActionListener*: java.awt.event
—extended by: *Action*
—passed to: **A**bstractButton* < addActionListener( ),
removeActionListener( ) > **A**WTEventMulticaster.remove( )
Button.removeActionListener( )
ButtonModel.removeActionListener( )
ComboBoxEditor.removeActionListener( )
DefaultButtonModel*.removeActionListener( )
java.awt.**L**ist.removeActionListener( ) **J**ComboBox

< addActionListener( ), removeActionListener( ) >
JComponent*.registerKeyboardAction( )
JFileChooser.removeActionListener( )
JTextField*.removeActionListener( )
MenuItem*.removeActionListener( )
TextField.removeActionListener( ) **T**imer
< removeActionListener( ), Timer( ) >
—returned by: **A**bstractButton*.createActionListener( )
AWTEventMulticaster.remove( )
—implemented by: **A**WTEventMulticaster
DefaultCellEditor.EditorDelegate **D**efaultTreeCellEditor
DropTarget.DropTargetAutoScroller **F**ormView
JComboBox **T**oolTipManager.insideTimerAction
ToolTipManager.outsideTimerAction
ToolTipManager.stillInsideTimerAction
—fields: **A**bstractButton*.actionListener
actionName: **J**TextComponent.KeyBinding
actionPerformed( ): **A**bstractAction* *ActionListener**
AWTEventMulticaster **D**efaultCellEditor.EditorDelegate
DefaultTreeCellEditor **D**ropTarget.DropTargetAutoScroller
FormView **J**ComboBox **T**oolTipManager.insideTimerAction
ToolTipManager.outsideTimerAction
ToolTipManager.stillInsideTimerAction
Activatable: java.rmi.activation
activate( ): **A**ctivationID *Activator* *AppletInitializer*
ACTIVATED: **H**yperlinkEvent.EventType
ActivateFailedException: java.rmi.activation
activateFrame( ): **D**efaultDesktopManager *DesktopManager*
activateLink( ): **H**TMLEditorKit.LinkController
ActivationDesc: java.rmi.activation
—passed to: **A**ctivatable.register( )
ActivationGroup_Stub.newInstance( ) *ActivationSystem*
< registerObject( ), setActivationDesc( ) >
—returned by: *ActivationSystem* < getActivationDesc( ),
setActivationDesc( ) >
ActivationException*: java.rmi.activation
—subclasses: **U**nknownGroupException
UnknownObjectException
—thrown by: **A**ctivatable < Activatable( ), exportObject( ),
inactive( ), register( ), unregister( ) > **A**ctivationDesc( )
ActivationGroup < activeObject( ), createGroup( ), getSystem( ),
inactiveObject( ), newInstance( ), setSystem( ) >
ActivationID.activate( ) *ActivationSystem* < activeGroup( ),
getActivationDesc( ), getActivationGroupDesc( ), registerGroup( ),
registerObject( ), setActivationDesc( ), setActivationGroupDesc( ),
unregisterGroup( ), unregisterObject( ) >
ActivationGroup: java.rmi.activation
—returned by: **A**ctivationGroup.createGroup( )
ActivationGroup_Stub: java.rmi.activation
ActivationGroupDesc: java.rmi.activation
—passed to: **A**ctivationGroup.createGroup( )
ActivationSystem.setActivationGroupDesc( )
—returned by: *ActivationSystem* < getActivationGroupDesc( ),
setActivationGroupDesc( ) >
ActivationGroupDesc.CommandEnvironment:
java.rmi.activation
—passed to: **A**ctivationGroupDesc( )
—returned by: **A**ctivationGroupDesc.getCommandEnvironment( )
ActivationGroupID: java.rmi.activation
—passed to: **A**ctivationDesc( ) **A**ctivationGroup.createGroup( )
ActivationSystem < activeGroup( ), getActivationGroupDesc( ),
setActivationGroupDesc( ), unregisterGroup( ) >
—returned by: **A**ctivationDesc.getGroupID( )
ActivationSystem.registerGroup( )
ActivationID: java.rmi.activation
—passed to: **A**ctivatable < Activatable( ),
exportObject( ), inactive( ), unregister( ) >
ActivationGroup < activeObject( ), inactiveObject( ),
newInstance( ) > *ActivationInstantiator*.newInstance( )
ActivationMonitor.inactiveObject( ) *ActivationSystem*
< setActivationDesc( ), unregisterObject( ) >
—returned by: **A**ctivatable < exportObject( ), getID( ) >

A

ActivationInstantiator: java.rmi.activation
— passed to: **A**ctivationSystem.activeGroup( )
— implemented by: **A**ctivationGroup **A**ctivationGroup_Stub
ActivationMonitor: java.rmi.activation
— returned by: **A**ctivationSystem.activeGroup( )
ActivationSystem: java.rmi.activation
— passed to: **A**ctivationGroup.setSystem( )
— returned by: **A**ctivationGroup.getSystem( )
Activator: java.rmi.activation
— passed to: **A**ctivationID( )
ACTIVATOR_ID: **O**bjID
ACTIVE: **A**ccessibleState
ACTIVE_CAPTION: **S**ystemColor
ACTIVE_CAPTION_BORDER: **S**ystemColor
ACTIVE_CAPTION_TEXT: **S**ystemColor
activeCaption: **S**ystemColor
activeCaptionBorder: **S**ystemColor
activeCaptionText: **S**ystemColor
activeCount(): **T**hread **T**hreadGroup
ActiveEvent: java.awt
— implemented by: **I**nvocationEvent
activeGroup(): **A**ctivationSystem
activeGroupCount(): **T**hreadGroup
activeObject(): **A**ctivationGroup **A**ctivationMonitor
AD: **G**regorianCalendar
add(): **A**bstractCollection* **A**ccessibleStateSet **A**rea
AWTEventMulticaster **B**eanContextSupport* **B**igDecimal
BigInteger **B**uttonGroup **C**alendar* *ChoicePeer*
*Collection** **C**omponent **C**ontextList **D**efaultListModel
DefaultMutableTreeNode* **E**ventListenerList **E**xceptionList
ListIterator *ListPeer* **M**enu* **M**enuBar **N**VList
ParameterBlock **P**ermissionCollection* **R**ectangle2D*
RenderingHints
add_in_arg(): **R**equest
add_inout_arg(): **R**equest
add_item(): **N**VList
add_named_in_arg(): **R**equest
add_named_inout_arg(): **R**equest
add_named_out_arg(): **R**equest
add_out_arg(): **R**equest
ADD_OVERRIDE: **S**etOverrideType
add_value(): **N**VList
addAccessibleSelection(): *AccessibleSelection*
JList.AccessibleJList **J**Menu.AccessibleJMenu
JMenuBar.AccessibleJMenuBar
JTabbedPane.AccessibleJTabbedPane
JTable.AccessibleJTable **J**Tree.AccessibleJTree
JTree.AccessibleJTree.AccessibleJTreeNode
addActionForKeyStroke(): *Keymap*
addActionListener(): **A**bstractButton* **B**utton *ButtonModel*
ComboBoxEditor **D**efaultButtonModel* **J**ComboBox
JFileChooser **J**TextField* java.awt.**L**ist **M**enuItem*
TextField **T**imer
addAdjustmentListener(): *Adjustable* **J**ScrollBar* **S**crollbar
addAll(): **A**bstractCollection* **A**ccessibleStateSet
BeanContextSupport* *Collection**
addAncestorListener(): **J**Component*
addAttribute(): **A**bstractDocument.AbstractElement*
AbstractDocument.AttributeContext **A**ttributedString
MutableAttributeSet **S**impleAttributeSet **S**tyleContext*
StyleContext.NamedStyle
addAttributes(): **A**bstractDocument.AbstractElement*
AbstractDocument.AttributeContext **A**ttributedString
MutableAttributeSet **S**impleAttributeSet **S**tyleContext*
StyleContext.NamedStyle
addAuxiliaryLookAndFeel(): **U**IManager
addAWTEventListener(): **T**oolkit
addBatch(): *Statement**
addBeanContextMembershipListener(): *BeanContext**
BeanContextSupport*
addBeanContextServicesListener(): *BeanContextServices*
BeanContextServicesSupport

addCaretListener(): **J**TextComponent*
addCellEditorListener(): *CellEditor** **D**efaultCellEditor
DefaultTreeCellEditor
addCertificate(): **I**dentity*
addChangeListener(): **A**bstractButton* *BoundedRangeModel*
ButtonModel **C**aret *ColorSelectionModel*
DefaultBoundedRangeModel **D**efaultButtonModel*
DefaultCaret **D**efaultColorSelectionModel
DefaultSingleSelectionModel **J**ProgressBar **J**Slider
JTabbedPane **J**Viewport **M**enuSelectionManager
SingleSelectionModel *Style* **S**tyleContext*
StyleContext.NamedStyle
addChoosableFileFilter(): **J**FileChooser
addChooserPanel(): **J**ColorChooser
addColumn(): **D**efaultTableColumnModel **D**efaultTableModel
JTable *TableColumnModel*
addColumnModelListener(): **D**efaultTableColumnModel
TableColumnModel
addColumnSelectionInterval(): **J**Table
addComponentListener(): **C**omponent*
addConsumer(): **F**ilteredImageSource *ImageProducer*
MemoryImageSource **R**enderableImageProducer
addContainerListener(): **C**ontainer*
addContent(): **H**TMLDocument.HTMLReader
addDirtyRegion(): **R**epaintManager
addDocumentListener(): **A**bstractDocument* *Document**
addDragGestureListener(): **D**ragGestureRecognizer*
addDragSourceListener(): **D**ragSourceContext
addDropTargetListener(): **D**ropTarget
addEdit(): **A**bstractUndoableEdit* *UndoableEdit*
addElement(): **D**efaultComboBoxModel **D**efaultListModel
MutableComboBoxModel **V**ector*
addEntry(): *Acl*
addFirst(): **L**inkedList
addFocusListener(): *AccessibleComponent*
Box.AccessibleBox **B**ox.Filler.AccessibleBoxFiller
CellRendererPane.AccessibleCellRendererPane
Component* **J**Applet.AccessibleJApplet
JComponent.AccessibleJComponent
JDialog.AccessibleJDialog **J**Frame.AccessibleJFrame
JList.AccessibleJList.AccessibleJListChild
JPopupMenu.WindowPopup.AccessibleWindowPopup
JTable.AccessibleJTable.AccessibleJTableCell
JTableHeader.AccessibleJTableHeader ↩
.AccessibleJTableHeaderEntry
JTree.AccessibleJTree.AccessibleJTreeNode
JWindow.AccessibleJWindow
addHelpMenu(): *MenuBarPeer*
addHighlight(): *Highlighter* **L**ayeredHighlighter*
addHyperlinkListener(): **J**EditorPane*
addIdentity(): **I**dentityScope
addImage(): **M**ediaTracker
addImpl(): **C**ontainer*
addInputMethodListener(): **C**omponent*
addInternal(): **A**WTEventMulticaster
addInternalFrameListener(): **J**InternalFrame
addInvalidComponent(): **R**epaintManager
addItem(): **C**hoice *ChoicePeer* **J**ComboBox java.awt.**L**ist
ListPeer *MenuPeer*
addItemListener(): **A**bstractButton* **C**heckbox
CheckboxMenuItem **C**hoice **D**efaultButtonModel*
ItemSelectable **J**ComboBox java.awt.**L**ist
AdditionalComments: **H**TMLDocument
addKeyListener(): **C**omponent*
addKeymap(): **J**TextComponent*
addLast(): **L**inkedList
addLayoutComponent(): **B**orderLayout **B**oxLayout
CardLayout **F**lowLayout **G**ridBagLayout **G**ridLayout
JRootPane.RootLayout *LayoutManager** **O**verlayLayout
ScrollPaneLayout* **V**iewportLayout
addListDataListener(): **A**bstractListModel* *ListModel**

A

allocateArray(): GapContent
allowsChildren: DefaultMutableTreeNode*
allowsMultipleSelections(): java.awt.List
allowThreadSuspension(): ThreadGroup
allowUserInteraction: URLConnection*
AllPermission: java.security
allProceduresAreCallable(): *DatabaseMetaData*
allTablesAreSelectable(): *DatabaseMetaData*
ALPHABETIC_PRESENTATION_FORMS:
    Character.UnicodeBlock
AlphaComposite: java.awt
—returned by: AlphaComposite.getInstance()
—fields: AlphaComposite < Clear, DstIn, DstOut, DstOver, Src,
    SrcIn, SrcOut, SrcOver >
AlreadyBound: org.omg.CosNaming.NamingContextPackage
—passed to: AlreadyBoundHelper < insert(), write() >
—returned by: AlreadyBoundHelper < extract(), read() >
—thrown by: _NamingContextImplBase < bind(), bind_context(),
    bind_new_context() > _NamingContextStub < bind_context(),
    bind_new_context() > *NamingContext* < bind_context(),
    bind_new_context() >
—fields: AlreadyBoundHolder.value
AlreadyBoundException: java.rmi
—thrown by: Naming.bind()
AlreadyBoundHelper:
    org.omg.CosNaming.NamingContextPackage
AlreadyBoundHolder:
    org.omg.CosNaming.NamingContextPackage
ALT: HTML.Attribute
ALT_GRAPH_MASK: InputEvent*
ALT_MASK: ActionEvent Event InputEvent*
alternateAddTag: HTMLEditorKit.InsertHTMLTextAction
alternateParentTag: HTMLEditorKit.InsertHTMLTextAction
AM: Calendar*
AM_PM: Calendar*
AM_PM_FIELD: DateFormat*
ANCESTOR_ADDED: AncestorEvent
ANCESTOR_MOVED: AncestorEvent
ANCESTOR_REMOVED: AncestorEvent
ancestorAdded(): *AncestorListener*
AncestorEvent: javax.swing.event
—passed to: *AncestorListener* < ancestorAdded(),
    ancestorMoved(), ancestorRemoved() >
AncestorListener: javax.swing.event
—passed to: JComponent* < addAncestorListener(),
    removeAncestorListener() >
ancestorMoved(): *AncestorListener*
ancestorRemoved(): *AncestorListener*
anchor: GridBagConstraints
and(): BigInteger BitSet
andNot(): BigInteger BitSet
annotateClass(): ObjectOutputStream
Annotation: java.text
ANY: *DTDConstants*
Any: org.omg.CORBA
—passed to: AlreadyBoundHelper < extract(), insert() >
    Any.insert_any() BindingHelper < extract(), insert() >
    BindingIteratorHelper.insert() BindingListHelper.insert()
    BindingTypeHelper.insert() CannotProceedHelper.insert()
    *DynAny** < from_any(), insert_any() >
    DynSequence.set_elements() InvalidNameHelper.insert()
    IstringHelper.insert() NameComponentHelper.insert()
    NameHelper.insert() NamingContextHelper
    < extract(), insert() > NotEmptyHelper.insert()
    NotFoundHelper.insert() NotFoundReasonHelper.insert()
    ORB < create_dyn_any(), create_named_value(),
    create_policy() > ServerRequest < except(), result(),
    set_exception(), set_result() > ServiceDetailHelper.insert()
    ServiceInformationHelper.insert() UnknownUserException()
—returned by: Any.extract_any() *DynAny**.to_any()
    DynSequence.get_elements() ORB.create_any() Request
    < add_in_arg(), add_inout_arg(), add_named_in_arg(),

add_named_inout_arg(), add_named_out_arg(), add_out_arg(),
    return_value() >
—fields: AnyHolder.value UnionMember.label
AnyHolder: org.omg.CORBA
append(): Book CompositeView* GeneralPath JTextArea
    StringBuffer TextArea
appendEvent(): DragGestureRecognizer*
appendText(): TextArea
applet: DTD
APPLET: HTML.Tag*
Applet*: java.applet
—subclasses: JApplet
—passed to: *AppletInitializer* < activate(), initialize() >
    ORB.set_parameters()
—returned by: *AppletContext*.getApplet()
AppletContext: java.applet
—returned by: Applet*.getAppletContext()
AppletInitializer: java.beans
—passed to: Beans.instantiate()
appletResize(): *AppletStub*
AppletStub: java.applet
—passed to: Applet*.setStub()
ApplicationException: org.omg.CORBA.portable
—thrown by: Delegate.invoke()
applyLocalizedPattern(): DecimalFormat SimpleDateFormat
applyPattern(): ChoiceFormat DecimalFormat
    MessageFormat SimpleDateFormat
applyResourceBundle(): Window*
appRandom: SignatureSpi*
APPROVE_BUTTON_MNEMONIC_CHANGED_PROPERTY:
    JFileChooser
APPROVE_BUTTON_TEXT_CHANGED_PROPERTY:
    JFileChooser
APPROVE_BUTTON_TOOL_TIP_TEXT_CHANGED_PROPERTY:
    JFileChooser
APPROVE_OPTION: JFileChooser
APPROVE_SELECTION: JFileChooser
approveSelection(): JFileChooser
APRIL: Calendar*
ARABIC: Character.UnicodeBlock
ARABIC_PRESENTATION_FORMS_A:
    Character.UnicodeBlock
ARABIC_PRESENTATION_FORMS_B:
    Character.UnicodeBlock
Arc2D*: java.awt.geom
—subclasses: Arc2D.Double Arc2D.Float
—passed to: Arc2D*.setArc()
Arc2D.Double: java.awt.geom
Arc2D.Float: java.awt.geom
archeight: RoundRectangle2D.Double
    RoundRectangle2D.Float
ARCHIVE: HTML.Attribute
arcwidth: RoundRectangle2D.Double RoundRectangle2D.Float
AREA: HTML.Tag*
Area: java.awt.geom
—passed to: Area < add(), equals(), exclusiveOr(), intersect(),
    subtract() >
—returned by: Area.createTransformedArea()
AreaAveragingScaleFilter: java.awt.image
areFieldsSet: Calendar*
areNew: TreeSelectionEvent
arePathsContiguous(): DefaultTreeSelectionModel*
arg: Event
ARG_IN: org.omg.CORBA
ARG_INOUT: org.omg.CORBA
ARG_OUT: org.omg.CORBA
arguments(): Request ServerRequest
ArithmeticException: java.lang
ARMED: AccessibleState DefaultButtonModel*
ARMENIAN: Character.UnicodeBlock
ArrangeGrid(): GridBagLayout
array: Segment

C

cancelEditing( ): JTree TreeUI
cancelLatestCommittedText( ): *InputMethodRequests*
cancelRowUpdates( ): *ResultSet*
cancelSelection( ): JFileChooser
canDisplay( ): Font*
canDisplayUpTo( ): Font*
canEdit: DefaultTreeCellEditor
canEditImmediately( ): DefaultTreeCellEditor
canFilterIndexColorModel( ): RGBImageFilter*
CannotProceed: org.omg.CosNaming.NamingContextPackage
—passed to: CannotProceedHelper < insert( ), write( ) >
—returned by: CannotProceedHelper < extract( ), read( ) >
—thrown by: _NamingContextImplBase < bind( ), bind_context( ),
  bind_new_context( ), rebind( ), rebind_context( ), resolve( ),
  unbind( ) > _NamingContextStub < bind_context( ),
  bind_new_context( ), rebind( ), rebind_context( ),
  resolve( ), unbind( ) > *NamingContext* < bind_context( ),
  bind_new_context( ), rebind( ), rebind_context( ), resolve( ),
  unbind( ) >
—fields: CannotProceedHolder.value
CannotProceedHelper:
  org.omg.CosNaming.NamingContextPackage
CannotProceedHolder:
  org.omg.CosNaming.NamingContextPackage
CannotRedoException: javax.swing.undo
—thrown by: AbstractUndoableEdit*.redo( ) UndoManager
  < redoTo( ), undoOrRedo( ) >
CannotUndoException: javax.swing.undo
—thrown by: AbstractUndoableEdit*.undo( ) UndoManager
  < undoOrRedo( ), undoTo( ) >
CANONICAL_DECOMPOSITION: Collator*
canPathsBeAdded( ): DefaultTreeSelectionModel*
canPathsBeRemoved( ): DefaultTreeSelectionModel*
canRead( ): File
canRedo( ): AbstractUndoableEdit* *UndoableEdit*
canUndo( ): AbstractUndoableEdit* *UndoableEdit*
canUndoOrRedo( ): UndoManager
Canvas: java.awt
—passed to: Toolkit.createCanvas( )
CanvasPeer: java.awt.peer
—returned by: Toolkit.createCanvas( )
canWrite( ): File
CAP_BUTT: BasicStroke
CAP_ROUND: BasicStroke
CAP_SQUARE: BasicStroke
capacity( ): DefaultListModel StringBuffer Vector*
capacityIncrement: Vector*
CAPS_LOCK: Event
CAPTION: HTML.Tag*
CardLayout: java.awt
Caret: javax.swing.text
—passed to: JTextComponent*.setCaret( )
—returned by: EditorKit*.createCaret( )
—implemented by: DefaultCaret
CARET_POSITION_CHANGED: InputMethodEvent
CaretEvent: javax.swing.event
—passed to: *CaretListener*.caretUpdate( )
  JTextComponent.AccessibleJTextComponent*.caretUpdate( )
CaretListener: javax.swing.event
—passed to: JTextComponent* < addCaretListener( ),
  removeCaretListener( ) >
—implemented by: JTextComponent.AccessibleJTextComponent*
caretPositionChanged( ): AWTEventMulticaster
  InputMethodListener
caretUpdate( ): *CaretListener*
  JTextComponent.AccessibleJTextComponent*
CASE_INSENSITIVE_ORDER: String
catchExceptions: InvocationEvent
CDATA: *DTDConstants*
ceil( ): Math
CELL_EDITOR_PROPERTY: JTree
CELL_RENDERER_PROPERTY: JTree TableColumn

cellEditor: JTable JTree TableColumn
CellEditor*: javax.swing
—extended by: *TableCellEditor* *TreeCellEditor*
CellEditorListener: javax.swing.event
—passed to: *CellEditor** < addCellEditorListener( ),
  removeCellEditorListener( ) >
  DefaultCellEditor.removeCellEditorListener( )
  DefaultTreeCellEditor.removeCellEditorListener( )
—implemented by: JTable JTable.AccessibleJTable
CELLPADDING: HTML.Attribute
cellRenderer: JTree TableColumn
CellRendererPane: javax.swing
—passed to: CellRendererPane.AccessibleCellRendererPane( )
CellRendererPane.AccessibleCellRendererPane: javax.swing
cellSelectionEnabled: JTable
CELLSPACING: HTML.Attribute
CENTER: BorderLayout FlowLayout GridBagConstraints
  HTML.Tag* Label *SwingConstants* TitledBorder*
CENTER_ALIGNMENT: Component*
CENTER_BASELINE: Font* GraphicAttribute*
Certificate: java.security
—passed to: Identity* < addCertificate( ), removeCertificate( ) >
—returned by: Identity*.certificates( )
Certificate*: java.security.cert
—subclasses: X509Certificate
—passed to: CodeSource( ) KeyStore < getCertificateAlias( ),
  setCertificateEntry( ), setKeyEntry( ) > KeyStoreSpi
  < engineSetCertificateEntry( ), engineSetKeyEntry( ) >
—returned by: CertificateFactory.generateCertificate( )
  CodeSource.getCertificates( )
  JarURLConnection.getCertificates( )
  KeyStore.getCertificateChain( )
  KeyStoreSpi.engineGetCertificateChain( )
CertificateEncodingException: java.security.cert
—thrown by: java.security.cert.Certificate*.getEncoded( )
CertificateException*: java.security.cert
—subclasses: CertificateEncodingException
  CertificateExpiredException CertificateNotYetValidException
  CertificateParsingException
—thrown by: CertificateFactory < generateCertificate( ),
  generateCertificates( ), getInstance( ) >
  CertificateFactorySpi.engineGenerateCertificates( )
  java.security.cert.Certificate*.verify( ) KeyStore.store( )
  KeyStoreSpi.engineStore( )
CertificateExpiredException: java.security.cert
—thrown by: X509Certificate.checkValidity( )
CertificateFactory: java.security.cert
—returned by: CertificateFactory.getInstance( )
CertificateFactorySpi: java.security.cert
—passed to: CertificateFactory( )
CertificateNotYetValidException: java.security.cert
—thrown by: X509Certificate.checkValidity( )
CertificateParsingException: java.security.cert
certificates( ): Identity*
CHANGE: DocumentEvent.EventType
change( ): DefaultStyledDocument.ElementBuffer
CHANGED: DragSourceContext
ChangedCharSetException: javax.swing.text
—thrown by: DocumentParser.handleEmptyTag( )
  Parser*.startTag( )
changedUpdate( ): *DocumentListener*
  JTextComponent.AccessibleJTextComponent* View*
changeEvent: AbstractButton* DefaultBoundedRangeModel
  DefaultButtonModel* DefaultCaret DefaultCellEditor
  DefaultColorSelectionModel DefaultSingleSelectionModel
  DefaultTableColumnModel JProgressBar
  JSlider JTabbedPane MenuSelectionManager
  StyleContext.NamedStyle
ChangeEvent: javax.swing.event
—passed
  to: AbstractButton.ButtonChangeListener.stateChanged( )
  CellEditorListener.editingStopped( )

JMenuItem.AccessibleJMenuItem*.stateChanged( )
JTabbedPane.AccessibleJTabbedPane.stateChanged( )
JTable < columnMarginChanged( ), editingCanceled( ),
editingStopped( ) > JTable.AccessibleJTable
< editingCanceled( ), editingStopped( ) >
TableColumnModelListener.columnMarginChanged( )
—fields: **A**bstractButton*.changeEvent
DefaultButtonModel*.changeEvent
DefaultCellEditor.changeEvent
DefaultSingleSelectionModel.changeEvent
JProgressBar.changeEvent **J**TabbedPane.changeEvent
StyleContext.NamedStyle.changeEvent
changeHighlight( ): *Highlighter* LayeredHighlighter*
changeListener: **A**bstractButton* **J**ProgressBar **J**Slider
JTabbedPane
ChangeListener: javax.swing.event
—passed to: **A**bstractButton*
< addChangeListener( ), removeChangeListener( ) >
BoundedRangeModel.removeChangeListener( )
ButtonModel.removeChangeListener( )
Caret.removeChangeListener( )
ColorSelectionModel.removeChangeListener( )
DefaultBoundedRangeModel.removeChangeListener( )
DefaultButtonModel*.removeChangeListener( )
DefaultCaret.removeChangeListener( )
DefaultColorSelectionModel.removeChangeListener( )
DefaultSingleSelectionModel.removeChangeListener( )
JProgressBar.removeChangeListener( )
JSlider.removeChangeListener( )
JTabbedPane.removeChangeListener( )
JViewport.removeChangeListener( )
MenuSelectionManager.removeChangeListener( )
SingleSelectionModel.removeChangeListener( )
Style.removeChangeListener( )
StyleContext*.removeChangeListener( )
StyleContext.NamedStyle.removeChangeListener( )
—returned by: **A**bstractButton*.createChangeListener( )
JSlider.createChangeListener( )
—implemented by: **A**bstractButton.ButtonChangeListener
JMenuItem.AccessibleJMenuItem*
JScrollPane.AccessibleJScrollPane
JTabbedPane.AccessibleJTabbedPane
JTabbedPane.ModelListener
—fields: **A**bstractButton*.changeListener **J**Slider.changeListener
changeShape( ): **B**ox.Filler
changeSupport: **A**bstractAction* **D**efaultTreeSelectionModel*
changeToParentDirectory( ): **J**FileChooser
changeUpdate( ): **D**efaultStyledDocument.ElementBuffer
CHAR: **T**ypes
CHAR_REPLACEMENT: **T**extAttribute
CHAR_UNDEFINED: **K**eyEvent*
CHARACTER: *AccessibleText*
Character: java.lang
—passed to: **C**haracter.compareTo( )
Character.Subset*: java.lang
—subclasses: **C**haracter.UnicodeBlock **I**nputSubset
—passed to: **I**nputContext.setCharacterSubsets( )
Character.UnicodeBlock: java.lang
—returned by: **C**haracter.UnicodeBlock.of( )
—fields: **C**haracter.UnicodeBlock
< ALPHABETIC_PRESENTATION_FORMS,
ARABIC, ARABIC_PRESENTATION_FORMS_A,
ARABIC_PRESENTATION_FORMS_B, ARMENIAN,
ARROWS, BASIC_LATIN, BENGALI, BLOCK_ELEMENTS,
BOPOMOFO, BOX_DRAWING, CJK_COMPATIBILITY,
CJK_COMPATIBILITY_FORMS, CJK_COMPATIBILITY_IDEOGRAPHS,
CJK_SYMBOLS_AND_PUNCTUATION, CJK_UNIFIED_IDEOGRAPHS,
COMBINING_DIACRITICAL_MARKS, COMBINING_HALF_MARKS,
COMBINING_MARKS_FOR_SYMBOLS, CONTROL_PICTURES,
CURRENCY_SYMBOLS, CYRILLIC, DEVANAGARI,
DINGBATS, ENCLOSED_ALPHANUMERICS,
ENCLOSED_CJK_LETTERS_AND_MONTHS,

GENERAL_PUNCTUATION, GEOMETRIC_SHAPES,
GEORGIAN, GREEK, GREEK_EXTENDED, GUJARATI,
GURMUKHI, HALFWIDTH_AND_FULLWIDTH_FORMS,
HANGUL_COMPATIBILITY_JAMO, HANGUL_JAMO,
HANGUL_SYLLABLES, HEBREW, HIRAGANA, IPA_EXTENSIONS,
KANBUN, KANNADA, KATAKANA, LAO, LATIN_1_SUPPLEMENT,
LATIN_EXTENDED_A, LATIN_EXTENDED_ADDITIONAL,
LATIN_EXTENDED_B, LETTERLIKE_SYMBOLS, MALAYALAM,
MATHEMATICAL_OPERATORS, MISCELLANEOUS_SYMBOLS,
MISCELLANEOUS_TECHNICAL, NUMBER_FORMS,
OPTICAL_CHARACTER_RECOGNITION, ORIYA,
PRIVATE_USE_AREA, SMALL_FORM_VARIANTS,
SPACING_MODIFIER_LETTERS, SPECIALS,
SUPERSCRIPTS_AND_SUBSCRIPTS, SURROGATES_AREA,
TAMIL, TELUGU, THAI, TIBETAN >
CharacterIterator*: java.text
—extended by: *AttributedCharacterIterator*
—passed to: **B**reakIterator.setText( ) **F**ont* < canDisplayUpTo( ),
createGlyphVector( ), getLineMetrics( ), getStringBounds( ) >
FontMetrics.getStringBounds( )
—returned by: **B**reakIterator.getText( )
—implemented by: **S**tringCharacterIterator
CharArrayReader: java.io
CharArrayWriter: java.io
charAt( ): **S**tring **S**tringBuffer
charAttr: **H**TMLDocument.HTMLReader
CharConversionException: java.io
CharHolder: org.omg.CORBA
charsWidth( ): **F**ontMetrics
charValue( ): **C**haracter
charWidth( ): **F**ontMetrics
CHECK_BOX: **A**ccessibleRole
checkAccept( ): **S**ecurityManager*
checkAccess( ): **S**ecurityManager* **T**hread **T**hreadGroup
checkAll( ): **M**ediaTracker
checkAwtEventQueueAccess( ): **S**ecurityManager*
Checkbox: java.awt
—passed to: **C**heckboxGroup < setCurrent( ),
setSelectedCheckbox( ) >
—returned by: **C**heckboxGroup < getCurrent( ),
getSelectedCheckbox( ) >
CheckboxGroup: java.awt
—passed to: **C**heckbox < Checkbox( ), setCheckboxGroup( ) >
—returned by: **C**heckbox.getCheckboxGroup( )
CheckboxMenuItem: java.awt
—passed to: **T**oolkit.createCheckboxMenuItem( )
CheckboxMenuItemPeer: java.awt.peer
—returned by: **T**oolkit.createCheckboxMenuItem( )
CheckboxPeer: java.awt.peer
—returned by: **T**oolkit.createCheckbox( )
checkConnect( ): **S**ecurityManager*
checkCreateClassLoader( ): **S**ecurityManager*
checkDelete( ): **S**ecurityManager*
CHECKED: **A**ccessibleState **H**TML.Attribute
CheckedInputStream: java.util.zip
CheckedOutputStream: java.util.zip
checkError( ): **P**rintStream* **P**rintWriter
checkExec( ): **S**ecurityManager*
checkExit( ): **S**ecurityManager*
checkGuard( ): *Guard* java.security.**P**ermission*
checkHorizontalKey( ): **A**bstractButton* **J**Label*
checkID( ): **M**ediaTracker
checkImage( ): **C**omponent* *ComponentPeer* **T**oolkit
checkLink( ): **S**ecurityManager*
checkListen( ): **S**ecurityManager*
checkMemberAccess( ): **S**ecurityManager*
checkMulticast( ): **S**ecurityManager*
checkPackageAccess( ): **S**ecurityManager*
checkPackageDefinition( ): **S**ecurityManager*
checkPermission( ): **A**ccessControlContext **A**ccessController
Acl *AclEntry* **S**ecurityManager*
checkPrintJobAccess( ): **S**ecurityManager*

C

Collection* DefaultListModel Environment Hashtable*
java.awt.List ListPeer Manifest Map* Reference*
RenderingHints

clearAccessibleSelection( ): AccessibleSelection
JList.AccessibleJList JMenu.AccessibleJMenu
JMenuBar.AccessibleJMenuBar
JTabbedPane.AccessibleJTabbedPane
JTable.AccessibleJTable JTree.AccessibleJTree
JTree.AccessibleJTree.AccessibleJTreeNode

clearAutoscroll( ): DropTarget

clearBatch( ): Statement*   .

clearBit( ): BigInteger

clearChanged( ): Observable

clearParameters( ): PreparedStatement*

clearRect( ): Graphics*

clearSelectedPath( ): MenuSelectionManager

clearSelection( ): DefaultListSelectionModel
DefaultSingleSelectionModel DefaultTreeSelectionModel*
JList JTable JTree ListSelectionModel
SingleSelectionModel TreeSelectionModel

clearToggledPaths( ): JTree

clearWarnings( ): Connection ResultSet Statement*

clickCount: Event

clickCountToStart: DefaultCellEditor

clip( ): Graphics2D

Clipboard: java.awt.datatransfer
—passed to: ClipboardOwner.lostOwnership( )
—returned by: Toolkit.getSystemClipboard( )

ClipboardOwner: java.awt.datatransfer
—passed to: Clipboard.setContents( )
—implemented by: StringSelection
—fields: Clipboard.owner

clipRect( ): Graphics*

CLOB: Types

Clob: java.sql
—passed to: Clob.position( ) SQLOutput.writeClob( )
—returned by: CallableStatement.getClob( ) ResultSet.getClob( )

clone( ): AbstractAction* AclEntry AffineTransform Area
ArrayList Attributes BitSet BreakIterator Calendar*
CharacterIterator* Collator* CubicCurve2D* DataFlavor
java.util.Date* DateFormatSymbols DecimalFormatSymbols
DefaultListSelectionModel DefaultMutableTreeNode*
DefaultStyledDocument.ElementBuffer
DefaultTreeSelectionModel* Dimension2D* EditorKit*
ElementIterator Format* GeneralPath GridBagConstraints
HashMap HashSet Hashtable* ImageFilter* Insets*
Kernel Line2D* LinkedList Locale Manifest
MessageDigestSpi* java.lang.Object PageFormat
Paper ParameterBlock Point2D* QuadCurve2D*
RectangularShape* RenderContext RenderingHints
SignatureSpi* SimpleAttributeSet StringCharacterIterator
StyleContext.SmallAttributeSet TextLayout TimeZone*
TreeMap TreeSet UnicastRemoteObject* Vector*
ZipEntry*

Cloneable*: java.lang
—extended by: AclEntry CharacterIterator*
—descendents: AttributedCharacterIterator
—implemented by: AbstractAction* AffineTransform Area
ArrayList Attributes BitSet BreakIterator Calendar*
Collator* CubicCurve2D* DataFlavor java.util.Date*
DateFormatSymbols DecimalFormatSymbols
DefaultListSelectionModel DefaultMutableTreeNode*
DefaultTreeSelectionModel* Dimension2D* EditorKit*
ElementIterator Format* GeneralPath GlyphVector
GridBagConstraints HashMap HashSet Hashtable*
ImageFilter* Insets* Kernel Line2D* LinkedList Locale
Manifest PageFormat Paper ParameterBlock Point2D*
QuadCurve2D* RectangularShape* RenderContext
RenderingHints SimpleAttributeSet TextLayout TimeZone*
TreeMap TreeSet Vector* ZipEntry*

CloneNotSupportedException*: java.lang
—subclasses: ServerCloneException

—thrown by: AbstractAction*.clone( )
DefaultListSelectionModel.clone( ) java.lang.Object.clone( )
SignatureSpi*.clone( )

cloneWithSource( ): TreeSelectionEvent

closable: JInternalFrame

close( ): Connection DatagramSocket* DatagramSocketImpl
java.io.InputStream* ObjectInput ObjectOutput
java.io.OutputStream* ProgressMonitor RandomAccessFile
Reader* ResultSet ServerSocket Socket SocketImpl
Statement* Writer* ZipFile*

CLOSED_OPTION: JOptionPane

closedIcon: DefaultTreeCellRenderer

closeEntry( ): ZipInputStream* ZipOutputStream*

closeFrame( ): DefaultDesktopManager DesktopManager

closeOutUnwantedEmbeddedTags( ): HTMLWriter

closePath( ): GeneralPath

CMMException: java.awt.color

coalesceEvents( ): Component*

CODE: HTML.Attribute HTML.Tag*

CODEBASE: HTML.Attribute

CodeSource: java.security
—passed to: CodeSource.implies( ) ProtectionDomain( )
SecureClassLoader*.getPermissions( )
—returned by: ProtectionDomain.getCodeSource( )

CODETYPE: HTML.Attribute

coerceData( ): BufferedImage ColorModel*

colHead: ScrollPaneLayout*

COLLAPSED: AccessibleState

collapsePath( ): JTree

collapseRow( ): JTree

CollationElementIterator: java.text
—returned by: RuleBasedCollator.getCollationElementIterator( )

CollationKey: java.text
—passed to: CollationKey.compareTo( )
—returned by: Collator*.getCollationKey( )

Collator*: java.text
—subclasses: RuleBasedCollator
—returned by: Collator*.getInstance( )

Collection*: java.util
—extended by: BeanContext* java.util.List Set*
—descendents: BeanContextServices SortedSet
—passed to: AbstractCollection* < addAll( ), containsAll( ),
removeAll( ), retainAll( ) > ArrayList( ) BeanContextSupport*
< addAll( ), containsAll( ), deserialize( ), removeAll( ),
retainAll( ), serialize( ) > Collection* < containsAll( ),
removeAll( ), retainAll( ) > Collections < max( ), min( ),
synchronizedCollection( ), unmodifiableCollection( ) > java.util.List
< addAll( ), containsAll( ), removeAll( ), retainAll( ) > Set*
< addAll( ), containsAll( ), removeAll( ), retainAll( ) > Vector( )
—returned by: AbstractMap*.values( ) CertificateFactory
< generateCertificates( ), generateCRLs( ) >
CertificateFactorySpi.engineGenerateCRLs( )
Collections.unmodifiableCollection( ) Map*.values( )
—implemented by: AbstractCollection*
—fields: BeanContextMembershipEvent.children

Collections: java.util

COLOR: CSS.Attribute HTML.Attribute

color: MatteBorder*

Color*: java.awt
—subclasses: ColorUIResource SystemColor
—passed to: AccessibleComponent < setBackground( ),
setForeground( ) > BevelBorder( ) BorderFactory
< createBevelBorder( ), createEtchedBorder( ),
createLineBorder( ), createMatteBorder( ), createTitledBorder( ) >
BorderUIResource.BevelBorderUIResource( )
BorderUIResource.EtchedBorderUIResource( )
BorderUIResource.LineBorderUIResource( )
BorderUIResource.TitledBorderUIResource( )
Box.AccessibleBox.setForeground( )
Box.Filler.AccessibleBoxFiller.setForeground( )
CellRendererPane.AccessibleCellRendererPane ↵
.setForeground( ) ColorSelectionModel.setSelectedColor( )

C

C

Component* < setBackground( ), setForeground( ) >
ComponentPeer*.setForeground( ) DefaultColorSelectionModel
< DefaultColorSelectionModel( ), setSelectedColor( ) >
DefaultTreeCellEditor.setBorderSelectionColor( )
DefaultTreeCellRenderer < setBackgroundSelectionColor( ),
setBorderSelectionColor( ), setTextNonSelectionColor( ),
setTextSelectionColor( ) > EtchedBorder( ) GradientPaint( )
Graphics* < drawImage( ), setColor( ), setXORMode( ) >
JApplet.AccessibleJApplet < setBackground( ),
setForeground( ) > JColorChooser < setColor( ), showDialog( ) >
JComponent.AccessibleJComponent*.setForeground( )
JDialog.AccessibleJDialog.setForeground( )
JFrame.AccessibleJFrame.setForeground( )
JList.setSelectionForeground( )
JList.AccessibleJList.AccessibleJListChild.setForeground( )
JPopupMenu.WindowPopup.AccessibleWindowPopup ↵
.setForeground( ) JTabbedPane.setForegroundAt( )
JTable < setSelectionBackground( ),
setSelectionForeground( ) > JTable.AccessibleJTable ↵
.AccessibleJTableCell.setForeground( )
JTableHeader.AccessibleJTableHeader ↵
.AccessibleJTableHeaderEntry.setForeground( )
JTextComponent* < setDisabledTextColor( ),
setSelectedTextColor( ), setSelectionColor( ) >
JTree.AccessibleJTree.AccessibleJTreeNode.setForeground( )
JWindow.AccessibleJWindow.setForeground( ) LineBorder( )
SoftBevelBorder( ) StyleConstants*.setForeground( )
TitledBorder* < setTitleColor( ), TitledBorder( ) >
— returned by: AbstractColorChooserPanel.setColorFromModel( )
AccessibleComponent.getForeground( ) BevelBorder*
< getHighlightOuterColor( ), getShadowInnerColor( ),
getShadowOuterColor( ) > Box.AccessibleBox.getForeground( )
Box.Filler.AccessibleBoxFiller.getForeground( )
CellRendererPane.AccessibleCellRendererPane ↵
.getForeground( ) Color* < darker( ), decode( ),
getColor( ), getHSBColor( ) > Component*
< getBackground( ), getForeground( ) >
DefaultColorSelectionModel.getSelectedColor( )
DefaultStyledDocument* < getBackground( ), getForeground( ) >
DefaultTreeCellRenderer < getBackgroundNonSelectionColor( ),
getBackgroundSelectionColor( ), getBorderSelectionColor( ),
getTextNonSelectionColor( ), getTextSelectionColor( ) >
EtchedBorder*.getShadowColor( )
GradientPaint.getColor2( ) Graphics2D.getBackground( )
JApplet.AccessibleJApplet.getForeground( )
JColorChooser.showDialog( )
JComponent.AccessibleJComponent*.getForeground( )
JDialog.AccessibleJDialog.getForeground( )
JFrame.AccessibleJFrame.getForeground( )
JList.getSelectionForeground( )
JList.AccessibleJList.AccessibleJListChild.getForeground( )
JPopupMenu.WindowPopup.AccessibleWindowPopup ↵
.getForeground( ) JTabbedPane.getForegroundAt( )
JTable < getSelectionBackground( ),
getSelectionForeground( ) > JTable.AccessibleJTable ↵
.AccessibleJTableCell.getForeground( )
JTableHeader.AccessibleJTableHeader ↵
.AccessibleJTableHeaderEntry.getForeground( )
JTextComponent* < getDisabledTextColor( ),
getSelectedTextColor( ), getSelectionColor( ) >
JTree.AccessibleJTree.AccessibleJTreeNode.getForeground( )
JWindow.AccessibleJWindow.getForeground( )
StyleConstants* < getBackground( ),
getForeground( ) > StyleContext*.getForeground( )
StyledDocument.getForeground( ) TitledBorder*.getTitleColor( )
UIManager.getColor( )
— fields: BevelBorder* < highlightInner, highlightOuter,
shadowInner, shadowOuter > Color* < blue, cyan,
darkGray, gray, green, lightGray, magenta, orange,
pink, red, white, yellow > DefaultTreeCellRenderer
< backgroundNonSelectionColor, backgroundSelectionColor,
borderSelectionColor, textNonSelectionColor, textSelectionColor >

EtchedBorder*.shadow JTable < selectionBackground,
selectionForeground > MatteBorder*.color
COLOR_ACTION: HTMLEditorKit
COLOR_CHOOSER: AccessibleRole
ColorChooserComponentFactory: javax.swing.colorchooser
ColorChooserUI: javax.swing.plaf
— passed to: JColorChooser.setUI( )
— returned by: JColorChooser.getUI( )
ColorConvertOp: java.awt.image
ColorModel*: java.awt.image
— subclasses: ComponentColorModel IndexColorModel
PackedColorModel*
— descendents: DirectColorModel
— passed to: AffineTransformOp.createCompatibleDestImage( )
BufferedImage( ) Color*.createContext( )
Composite.createContext( ) GradientPaint.createContext( )
ImageConsumer.setPixels( ) ImageFilter*.setPixels( )
MemoryImageSource < MemoryImageSource( ), newPixels( ) >
PixelGrabber < setColorModel( ), setPixels( ) >
RGBImageFilter*.substituteColorModel( )
— returned by: BufferedImage.getColorModel( )
ColorModel*.getRGBdefault( ) ComponentPeer*.getColorModel( )
GraphicsConfiguration.getColorModel( )
PixelGrabber.getColorModel( ) Toolkit.getColorModel( )
— fields: RGBImageFilter* < newmodel, origmodel >
ColorSelectionModel: javax.swing.colorchooser
— passed to: JColorChooser < JColorChooser( ),
setSelectionModel( ) >
— returned
by: AbstractColorChooserPanel.getColorSelectionModel( )
— implemented by: DefaultColorSelectionModel
ColorSpace*: java.awt.color
— subclasses: ICC_ColorSpace
— passed to: Color* < Color( ), getColorComponents( ),
getComponents( ) > ColorConvertOp( )
ComponentColorModel( ) PackedColorModel( )
— returned by: Color*.getColorSpace( ) ColorSpace*.getInstance( )
ColorUIResource: javax.swing.plaf
COLS: HTML.Attribute
COLSPAN: HTML.Attribute
column: TableModelEvent
COLUMN_HEADER: AccessibleRole ScrollPaneConstants
COLUMN_WIDTH_PROPERTY: TableColumn
columnAdded( ): JTable JTable.AccessibleJTable
JTableHeader TableColumnModelListener
columnAtPoint( ): JTable JTableHeader
columnHeader: JScrollPane
columnIdentifiers: DefaultTableModel
columnMargin: DefaultTableColumnModel
columnMarginChanged( ): JTable JTable.AccessibleJTable
JTableHeader TableColumnModelListener
columnModel: JTable JTableHeader
columnMoved( ): JTable JTable.AccessibleJTable
JTableHeader TableColumnModelListener
columnNoNulls: DatabaseMetaData ResultSetMetaData
columnNullable: DatabaseMetaData ResultSetMetaData
columnNullableUnknown: DatabaseMetaData
ResultSetMetaData
columnRemoved( ): JTable JTable.AccessibleJTable
JTableHeader TableColumnModelListener
columnSelectionAllowed: DefaultTableColumnModel
columnSelectionChanged( ): JTable JTable.AccessibleJTable
JTableHeader TableColumnModelListener
columnWeights: GridBagLayout
columnWidths: GridBagLayout
COMBINING: GlyphMetrics
COMBINING_DIACRITICAL_MARKS: Character.UnicodeBlock
COMBINING_HALF_MARKS: Character.UnicodeBlock
COMBINING_MARKS_FOR_SYMBOLS:
Character.UnicodeBlock
COMBINING_SPACING_MARK: Character
COMBO_BOX: AccessibleRole

Component* / CompositeView*

TableView.TableCell TableView.TableRow
WrappedPlainView
CompoundBorder*: javax.swing.border
—subclasses: **B**orderUIResource.CompoundBorderUIResource
—returned by: **B**orderFactory.createCompoundBorder()
compoundEdit: **U**ndoableEditSupport
CompoundEdit*: javax.swing.undo
—subclasses: **A**bstractDocument.DefaultDocumentEvent
UndoManager
—returned by: **U**ndoableEditSupport.createCompoundEdit()
—fields: **U**ndoableEditSupport.compoundEdit
comptable: **G**ridBagLayout
computeBlit(): **J**Viewport
computeDifference(): **S**wingUtilities
computeFields(): **C**alendar*
computeIntersection(): **S**wingUtilities
computeStringWidth(): **S**wingUtilities
computeTime(): **C**alendar*
computeUnion(): **S**wingUtilities
computeVisibleRect(): **J**Component*
concat(): **S**tring
concatenate(): **A**ffineTransform
concetenateTransform(): **R**enderContext
concrete_base_type(): **T**ypeCode
CONCUR_READ_ONLY: *ResultSet*
CONCUR_UPDATABLE: *ResultSet*
ConcurrentModificationException: java.util
configureEditor(): **J**ComboBox
configureEnclosingScrollPane(): **J**Table
connect(): **D**atagramSocket* *Driver* **O**RB **P**ipedInputStream
PipedOutputStream **P**ipedReader **P**ipedWriter **S**ocketImpl
URLConnection*
connected: **U**RLConnection*
ConnectException: java.net
ConnectException: java.rmi
ConnectIOException: java.rmi
Connection: java.sql
—returned by: *DatabaseMetaData*.getConnection()
DriverManager.getConnection()
CONNECTOR_PUNCTUATION: **C**haracter
CONREF: *DTDConstants*
Constructor: java.lang.reflect
—returned by: **C**lass < getConstructor(), getConstructors(),
getDeclaredConstructor(), getDeclaredConstructors() >
consume(): **A**WTEvent*
CONSUME_EVENT: *WindowPeer**
consumed: **A**WTEvent*
consumer: **I**mageFilter*
Container*: java.awt
—subclasses: **B**ox **C**ellRendererPane
DefaultTreeCellEditor.EditorContainer **J**Component* **P**anel*
ScrollPane **W**indow*
—descendents: **A**bstractButton* **A**bstractColorChooserPanel
Applet* **D**efaultListCellRenderer*
DefaultListCellRenderer.UIResource
DefaultTableCellRenderer*
DefaultTableCellRenderer.UIResource
DefaultTreeCellEditor.DefaultTextField
DefaultTreeCellRenderer **D**ialog* **F**ileDialog **F**rame*
JApplet **J**Button **J**CheckBox **J**CheckBoxMenuItem
JColorChooser **J**ComboBox **J**DesktopPane
JDialog **J**EditorPane* **J**FileChooser **J**Frame
JInternalFrame **J**InternalFrame.JDesktopIcon **J**Label*
JLayeredPane* **J**List **J**Menu **J**MenuBar **J**MenuItem*
JOptionPane **J**Panel* **J**PasswordField **J**PopupMenu
JPopupMenu.Separator **J**ProgressBar **J**RadioButton
JRadioButtonMenuItem **J**RootPane **J**ScrollBar*
JScrollPane **J**ScrollPane.ScrollBar **J**Separator* **J**Slider
JSplitPane **J**TabbedPane **J**Table **J**TableHeader
JTextArea **J**TextComponent* **J**TextField* **J**TextPane
JToggleButton* **J**ToolBar **J**ToolBar.Separator **J**ToolTip
JTree **J**Viewport **J**Window

—passed to: **A**ncestorEvent() **B**orderLayout
< getLayoutAlignmentY(), invalidateLayout(), layoutContainer(),
maximumLayoutSize(), minimumLayoutSize(),
preferredLayoutSize() > **B**oxLayout < getLayoutAlignmentX(),
getLayoutAlignmentY(), invalidateLayout(), layoutContainer(),
maximumLayoutSize(), minimumLayoutSize(),
preferredLayoutSize() > **C**ardLayout < getLayoutAlignmentX(),
getLayoutAlignmentY(), invalidateLayout(), last(),
layoutContainer(), maximumLayoutSize(), minimumLayoutSize(),
next(), preferredLayoutSize(), previous(), show() >
CellRendererPane.paintComponent() **D**efaultFocusManager
< getComponentBefore(), getFirstComponent(),
getLastComponent() > **F**lowLayout < minimumLayoutSize(),
preferredLayoutSize() > **G**ridBagLayout < getLayoutAlignmentX(),
getLayoutAlignmentY(), GetLayoutInfo(), GetMinSize(),
invalidateLayout(), layoutContainer(), maximumLayoutSize(),
minimumLayoutSize(), preferredLayoutSize() > **G**ridLayout
< minimumLayoutSize(), preferredLayoutSize() >
JDialog.setContentPane() **J**InternalFrame.setContentPane()
JRootPane.RootLayout < getLayoutAlignmentX(),
getLayoutAlignmentY(), invalidateLayout(), layoutContainer(),
maximumLayoutSize(), minimumLayoutSize(),
preferredLayoutSize() > *LayoutManager** < layoutContainer(),
minimumLayoutSize(), preferredLayoutSize() >
LayoutManager2 < getLayoutAlignmentY(),
invalidateLayout(), maximumLayoutSize() > **O**verlayLayout
< getLayoutAlignmentY(), invalidateLayout(), layoutContainer(),
maximumLayoutSize(), minimumLayoutSize(), OverlayLayout(),
preferredLayoutSize() > **S**crollPaneLayout* < layoutContainer(),
minimumLayoutSize(), preferredLayoutSize() >
SwingUtilities.paintComponent() **V**iewportLayout
< minimumLayoutSize(), preferredLayoutSize() >
—returned by: **A**ncestorEvent < getAncestor(),
getAncestorParent() > **C**omponent*.getParent()
DefaultTreeCellEditor.createContainer()
JComponent*.getTopLevelAncestor() **J**Frame.getContentPane()
JRootPane < createContentPane(), getContentPane() >
RootPaneContainer.getContentPane()
SwingUtilities.getAncestorOfClass() *View**.getContainer()
—fields: **D**efaultTreeCellEditor.editingContainer
CONTAINER_EVENT_MASK: **A**WTEvent*
CONTAINER_FIRST: **C**ontainerEvent
CONTAINER_LAST: **C**ontainerEvent
ContainerAdapter: java.awt.event
ContainerEvent: java.awt.event
—passed to: **A**WTEventMulticaster < componentAdded(),
componentRemoved() > **C**ontainerAdapter
< componentAdded(), componentRemoved() >
ContainerListener.componentRemoved()
JComponent.AccessibleJComponent↵
.AccessibleContainerHandler.componentRemoved()
ContainerListener: java.awt.event
—passed to: **A**WTEventMulticaster < add(), remove() >
Container*.removeContainerListener()
—returned by: **A**WTEventMulticaster < add(), remove() >
—implemented by: **A**WTEventMulticaster **C**ontainerAdapter
JComponent.AccessibleJComponent↵
.AccessibleContainerHandler
—fields: **J**Component.AccessibleJComponent* ↵
.accessibleContainerHandler
ContainerPeer*: java.awt.peer
—extended by: *PanelPeer ScrollPanePeer WindowPeer**
—descendents: *DialogPeer* FileDialogPeer FramePeer*
contains(): **A**bstractCollection*
AccessibleComponent **A**ccessibleStateSet **A**rea
BeanContextMembershipEvent **B**eanContextSupport*
Box.AccessibleBox **B**ox.Filler.AccessibleBoxFiller
CellRendererPane.AccessibleCellRendererPane
Collection* **C**omponent* **C**omponentUI*
CubicCurve2D* **D**efaultListModel **G**eneralPath
Hashtable* **J**Applet.AccessibleJApplet
JComponent.AccessibleJComponent*

JDialog.AccessibleJDialog JFrame.AccessibleJFrame
JList.AccessibleJList.AccessibleJListChild
JPopupMenu.WindowPopup.AccessibleWindowPopup
JTable.AccessibleJTable.AccessibleJTableCell
JTableHeader.AccessibleJTableHeader ↵
.AccessibleJTableHeaderEntry
JTree.AccessibleJTree.AccessibleJTreeNode
JWindow.AccessibleJWindow Line2D* Polygon
QuadCurve2D* RectangularShape* *Shape*
containsAlias(): KeyStore
containsAll(): AbstractCollection* BeanContextSupport*
*Collection**
containsAngle(): Arc2D*
containsAttribute(): AbstractDocument.AbstractElement*
*AttributeSet** SimpleAttributeSet StyleContext.NamedStyle
StyleContext.SmallAttributeSet
containsAttributes(): AbstractDocument.AbstractElement*
*AttributeSet** SimpleAttributeSet StyleContext.NamedStyle
StyleContext.SmallAttributeSet
containsCustomComponents(): OptionPaneUI
containsKey(): AbstractMap* Attributes
BeanContextSupport* Hashtable* *Map** RenderingHints
containsValue(): AbstractMap* Attributes Hashtable* *Map**
RenderingHints
content: ContentModel javax.swing.text.html.parser.Element
CONTENT: HTML.Attribute HTML.Tag*
CONTENT_AREA_FILLED_CHANGED_PROPERTY:
AbstractButton*
CONTENT_PANE_PROPERTY: JInternalFrame
CONTENT_TYPE: Attributes.Name
content_type(): TypeCode
ContentElementName: AbstractDocument*
ContentHandler: java.net
— returned by: *ContentHandlerFactory*.createContentHandler()
ContentHandlerFactory: java.net
— passed to: URLConnection*.setContentHandlerFactory()
ContentModel: javax.swing.text.html.parser
— passed to: ContentModel() DTD < defElement(),
defineElement() >
— returned by: DTD.defContentModel()
— fields: ContentModel.next
contentPane: JRootPane
contents: Clipboard
CONTENTS_CHANGED: ListDataEvent
contentsChanged(): JComboBox JList.AccessibleJList
ListDataListener
ContentType: DefaultStyledDocument.ElementSpec
context: DropTargetEvent*
Context: org.omg.CORBA
— passed to: Delegate.create_request()
ObjectImpl*._create_request()
*org.omg.CORBA.Object**._create_request() Request.ctx()
— returned by: Context < create_child(), parent() >
org.omg.CORBA.portable.InputStream.read_Context()
ServerRequest.ctx()
context_name(): Context
ContextList: org.omg.CORBA
— passed to: Delegate.create_request()
*org.omg.CORBA.Object**._create_request()
— returned by: ORB.create_context_list()
contexts(): Request
ContextualRenderedImageFactory: java.awt.image.renderable
— passed to: RenderableImageOp()
CONTIGUOUS_TREE_SELECTION: *TreeSelectionModel*
CONTINUOUS_LAYOUT_PROPERTY: JSplitPane
continuousLayout: JSplitPane
CONTROL: Character SystemColor
control: SystemColor
CONTROL_DK_SHADOW: SystemColor
CONTROL_HIGHLIGHT: SystemColor
CONTROL_LT_HIGHLIGHT: SystemColor
CONTROL_PICTURES: Character.UnicodeBlock

CONTROL_SHADOW: SystemColor
CONTROL_TEXT: SystemColor
controlDkShadow: SystemColor
controlDown(): Event
controlHighlight: SystemColor
controlLtHighlight: SystemColor
controlShadow: SystemColor
controlText: SystemColor
convertColumnIndexToModel(): JTable
convertColumnIndexToView(): JTable
CONVERTED_TEXT: InputMethodHighlight
convertMouseEvent(): SwingUtilities
convertPoint(): SwingUtilities
convertPointFromScreen(): SwingUtilities
convertPointToScreen(): SwingUtilities
convertRectangle(): SwingUtilities
convertToIntDiscrete(): IndexColorModel
convertToVector(): DefaultTableModel
convertValueToText(): JTree
ConvolveOp: java.awt.image
COORDS: HTML.Attribute
copy: DefaultStyledDocument.AttributeUndoableEdit
copy(): Collections *DynAny** JTextComponent*
org.omg.CORBA.Policy
copyAction: DefaultEditorKit*
copyArea(): Graphics*
copyAttributes(): AbstractDocument.AbstractElement*
*AttributeSet** SimpleAttributeSet StyleContext.NamedStyle
StyleContext.SmallAttributeSet
copyChildren(): BeanContextSupport*
copyData(): BufferedImage *RenderedImage**
copyInto(): DefaultListModel Vector*
copyValueOf(): String
cos(): Math
count: BufferedInputStream BufferedOutputStream
ByteArrayInputStream ByteArrayOutputStream
CharArrayReader CharArrayWriter Segment
StringBufferInputStream
count(): ContextList ExceptionList NVList
countComponents(): Container*
countItems(): Choice java.awt.List Menu*
countMenus(): MenuBar
countObservers(): Observable
countStackFrames(): Thread
countTokens(): StringTokenizer
crc: GZIPInputStream GZIPOutputStream
CRC32: java.util.zip
— fields: GZIPInputStream.crc
create(): DatagramSocketImpl DefaultStyledDocument*
Graphics* HTMLEditorKit.HTMLFactory
RenderedImageFactory SocketImpl *ViewFactory*
create_abstract_interface_tc(): ORB
create_alias_tc(): ORB
create_any(): ORB
create_array_tc(): ORB
create_basic_dyn_any(): ORB
create_child(): Context
create_context_list(): ORB
create_dyn_any(): ORB
create_dyn_array(): ORB
create_dyn_enum(): ORB
create_dyn_sequence(): ORB
create_dyn_struct(): ORB
create_dyn_union(): ORB
create_enum_tc(): ORB
create_environment(): ORB
create_exception_list(): ORB
create_exception_tc(): ORB
create_fixed_tc(): ORB
create_input_stream(): Any
org.omg.CORBA.portable.OutputStream
create_interface_tc(): ORB

DataBuffer*: java.awt.image
—subclasses: **D**ataBufferByte **D**ataBufferInt **D**ataBufferShort **D**ataBufferUShort
—passed to: **R**aster* < createBandedRaster( ), createInterleavedRaster( ), createPackedRaster( ), createRaster( ), createWritableRaster( ), Raster( ) > **S**ampleModel* < getDataElements( ), getPixel( ), getPixels( ), getSample( ), getSampleDouble( ), getSampleFloat( ), getSamples( ), setDataElements( ), setPixel( ), setPixels( ), setSample( ), setSamples( ) > **W**ritableRaster( )
—returned by: **R**aster*.getDataBuffer( )
—fields: **R**aster*.dataBuffer
DataBufferByte: java.awt.image
DataBufferInt: java.awt.image
DataBufferShort: java.awt.image
DataBufferUShort: java.awt.image
dataDefinitionCausesTransactionCommit( ): *DatabaseMetaData*
dataDefinitionIgnoredInTransactions( ): *DatabaseMetaData*
DataFlavor: java.awt.datatransfer
—passed to: **D**ataFlavor < equals( ), isMimeTypeEqual( ) > **D**ropTargetContext.TransferableProxy < getTransferData( ), isDataFlavorSupported( ) > **D**ropTargetDropEvent.isDataFlavorSupported( ) **S**tringSelection < getTransferData( ), isDataFlavorSupported( ) > **S**ystemFlavorMap.getNativesForFlavors( ) *Transferable*.isDataFlavorSupported( )
—returned by: **D**ropTargetContext.getCurrentDataFlavors( ) **D**ropTargetDragEvent.getCurrentDataFlavors( ) **S**tringSelection.getTransferDataFlavors( ) *Transferable*.getTransferDataFlavors( )
—fields: **D**ataFlavor < javaFileListFlavor, plainTextFlavor, stringFlavor >
DataFormatException: java.util.zip
—thrown by: **I**nflater.inflate( )
DatagramPacket: java.net
—passed to: **D**atagramSocket* < receive( ), send( ) > **D**atagramSocketImpl.send( )
DatagramSocket*: java.net
—subclasses: **M**ulticastSocket
DatagramSocketImpl: java.net
DataInput*: java.io
—extended by: *ObjectInput*
—passed to: **D**ataInputStream.readUTF( )
—implemented by: **D**ataInputStream **R**andomAccessFile
DataInputStream: java.io
—passed to: **D**TD.read( )
dataModel: **J**ComboBox **J**Table
DataOutput*: java.io
—extended by: *ObjectOutput*
—passed to: **U**ID.write( )
—implemented by: **D**ataOutputStream **R**andomAccessFile
DataOutputStream: java.io
DataTruncation: java.sql
dataType: **D**ataBuffer* **S**ampleModel*
dataVector: **D**efaultTableModel
DATE: **C**alendar* **T**ypes
Date: java.sql
—passed to: *PreparedStatement**.setDate( ) *ResultSet*.updateDate( )
—returned by: *CallableStatement*.getDate( ) *ResultSet*.getDate( )
Date*: java.util
—subclasses: java.sql.**D**ate **T**ime **T**imestamp
—passed to: **C**alendar*.setTime( ) **D**ateFormat*.format( ) java.util.**D**ate* < after( ), before( ), compareTo( ) > **T**imeZone*.inDaylightTime( )
—returned by: **C**alendar*.getTime( ) **D**ateFormat*.parse( ) **K**eyStore.getCreationDate( ) **S**impleDateFormat.get2DigitYearStart( ) **X**509Certificate.getNotBefore( ) **X**509CRL.getThisUpdate( )
DATE_FIELD: **D**ateFormat*
DateFormat*: java.text

—subclasses: **S**impleDateFormat
—returned by: **D**ateFormat* < getDateInstance( ), getDateTimeInstance( ), getInstance( ), getTimeInstance( ) >
DateFormatSymbols: java.text
—passed to: **S**impleDateFormat < setDateFormatSymbols( ), SimpleDateFormat( ) >
—returned by: **S**impleDateFormat.getDateFormatSymbols( )
DAY_OF_MONTH: **C**alendar*
DAY_OF_WEEK: **C**alendar*
DAY_OF_WEEK_FIELD: **D**ateFormat*
DAY_OF_WEEK_IN_MONTH: **C**alendar*
DAY_OF_WEEK_IN_MONTH_FIELD: **D**ateFormat*
DAY_OF_YEAR: **C**alendar*
DAY_OF_YEAR_FIELD: **D**ateFormat*
DD: **H**TML.Tag*
deactivateFrame( ): **D**efaultDesktopManager *DesktopManager*
DebugGraphics: javax.swing
decapitalize( ): **I**ntrospector
DECEMBER: **C**alendar*
DECIMAL: **T**ypes
DECIMAL_DIGIT_NUMBER: **C**haracter
DecimalFormat: java.text
DecimalFormatSymbols: java.text
—passed to: **D**ecimalFormat < DecimalFormat( ), setDecimalFormatSymbols( ) >
—returned by: **D**ecimalFormat.getDecimalFormatSymbols( )
DECLARE: **H**TML.Attribute
DECLARED: *Member*
decode( ): **B**yte *java.security.Certificate* **C**olor* **F**ont* **I**nteger **L**ong **S**hort **U**RLDecoder
decodeDataFlavor( ): **S**ystemFlavorMap
decodeJavaMIMEType( ): **S**ystemFlavorMap
decrIndent( ): **A**bstractWriter*
def: **D**eflaterOutputStream*
def_kind( ): *IRObject**
defAttributeList( ): **D**TD
DEFAULT: *Action* **D**ateFormat* **D**ragSourceContext *DTDConstants*
DEFAULT_CARET_POLICY: **T**extLayout
DEFAULT_COMPRESSION: **D**eflater
DEFAULT_CSS: **H**TMLEditorKit
DEFAULT_CURSOR: **C**ursor **F**rame*
default_index( ): **T**ypeCode
DEFAULT_JUSTIFICATION: **T**itledBorder*
DEFAULT_KEYMAP: **J**TextComponent*
DEFAULT_LAYER: **J**LayeredPane*
DEFAULT_OPTION: **J**OptionPane
DEFAULT_POSITION: **T**itledBorder*
DEFAULT_STRATEGY: **D**eflater
DEFAULT_STYLE: **S**tyleContext*
DefaultBoundedRangeModel: javax.swing
defaultButton: **J**RootPane
DefaultButtonModel*: javax.swing
—subclasses: **J**ToggleButton.ToggleButtonModel
DefaultCaret: javax.swing.text
DefaultCellEditor: javax.swing
—passed to: **D**efaultCellEditor.EditorDelegate( )
DefaultCellEditor.EditorDelegate: javax.swing
—fields: **D**efaultCellEditor.delegate
DefaultColorSelectionModel: javax.swing.colorchooser
DefaultComboBoxModel: javax.swing
defaultConstraints: **G**ridBagLayout
DefaultCopyDrop: **D**ragSource
DefaultCopyNoDrop: **D**ragSource
DefaultDesktopManager: javax.swing
defaulted( ): **O**bjectInputStream.GetField
DefaultEditorKit*: javax.swing.text
—subclasses: **S**tyledEditorKit*
—descendents: **H**TMLEditorKit **R**TFEditorKit
DefaultEditorKit.BeepAction: javax.swing.text
DefaultEditorKit.CopyAction: javax.swing.text
DefaultEditorKit.CutAction: javax.swing.text

D

D

—returned by: **J**DesktopPane.getUI( )
desktopProperties: **T**oolkit
desktopPropsSupport: **T**oolkit
destHeight: **R**eplicateScaleFilter*
destroy( ): _BindingIteratorImplBase _BindingIteratorStub
  _NamingContextImplBase _NamingContextStub **A**pplet*
  BindingIterator *DynAny** *IRObject** *NamingContext*
  org.omg.CORBA.Policy **P**rocess **T**hread **T**hreadGroup
destWidth: **R**eplicateScaleFilter*
detail: **A**ctivationException* **R**emoteException*
  ServerCloneException **W**riteAbortedException
determineOffset( ): **D**efaultTreeCellEditor
DEVANAGARI: **C**haracter.UnicodeBlock
DFN: **H**TML.Tag*
DGC: java.rmi.dgc
DGC_ID: **O**bjID
DIALOG: **A**ccessibleRole
Dialog*: java.awt
  —subclasses: **F**ileDialog **J**Dialog
  —passed to: **D**ialog( ) **J**Dialog( )
DIALOG_TITLE_CHANGED_PROPERTY: **J**FileChooser
DIALOG_TYPE_CHANGED_PROPERTY: **J**FileChooser
dialogInit( ): **J**Dialog
*DialogPeer**: java.awt.peer
  —extended by: *FileDialogPeer*
  —returned by: **T**oolkit.createDialog( )
Dictionary*: java.util
  —subclasses: **H**ashtable*
  —descendents: **P**roperties* **P**rovider **U**IDefaults
  —passed to: **A**bstractDocument*.setDocumentProperties( )
  —returned by: **A**bstractDocument*.getDocumentProperties( )
die( ): **A**bstractUndoableEdit* *UndoableEdit*
digest: **D**igestInputStream **D**igestOutputStream
digest( ): **M**essageDigest
DigestException: java.security
  —thrown by: **M**essageDigest.digest( )
DigestInputStream: java.security
DigestOutputStream: java.security
digit( ): **C**haracter
Dimension*: java.awt
  —subclasses: **D**imensionUIResource
  —passed to: *AccessibleComponent*.setSize( )
  Box.AccessibleBox.setSize( ) **B**ox.Filler( )
  CellRendererPane.AccessibleCellRendererPane.setSize( )
  Component* < resize( ), setSize( ) > **D**imension*.setSize( )
  JComponent* < setMaximumSize( ), setMinimumSize( ),
  setPreferredSize( ) > **J**Dialog.AccessibleJDialog.setSize( )
  JList.AccessibleJList.AccessibleJListChild.setSize( )
  JPopupMenu.WindowPopup.AccessibleWindowPopup ↵
  .setSize( ) **J**Table.setPreferredScrollableViewportSize( )
  JTableHeader.AccessibleJTableHeader ↵
  .AccessibleJTableHeaderEntry.setSize( ) **J**ToolBar.Separator
  < Separator( ), setSeparatorSize( ) > **J**Viewport < computeBlit( ),
  setExtentSize( ), setViewSize( ), toViewCoordinates( ) >
  Rectangle* < AccessibleRole, setLine( ) >
  —returned by: *AccessibleComponent*.getSize( ) **B**orderLayout
  < minimumLayoutSize( ), preferredLayoutSize( ) >
  Box.Filler.AccessibleBoxFiller.getSize( ) **B**oxLayout
  < minimumLayoutSize( ), preferredLayoutSize( ) > **C**ardLayout
  < minimumLayoutSize( ), preferredLayoutSize( ) > **C**omponent*
  < getMaximumSize( ), getMinimumSize( ), getPreferredSize( ),
  getSize( ), minimumSize( ), preferredSize( ), size( ) >
  *ComponentPeer** < getPreferredSize( ), minimumSize( ),
  preferredSize( ) > **C**omponentUI* < getMinimumSize( ),
  getPreferredSize( ) > **F**lowLayout < minimumLayoutSize( ),
  preferredLayoutSize( ) > **G**ridBagLayout < maximumLayoutSize( ),
  minimumLayoutSize( ), preferredLayoutSize( ) >
  GridLayout.preferredLayoutSize( ) java.awt.**L**ist
  < getMinimumSize( ), getPreferredSize( ), minimumSize( ),
  preferredSize( ) > **J**Dialog.AccessibleJDialog.getSize( )
  JList.getPreferredScrollableViewportSize( )
  JPopupMenu.WindowPopup.AccessibleWindowPopup ↵

.getSize( ) **J**RootPane.RootLayout
  < minimumLayoutSize( ), preferredLayoutSize( ) >
  JTable.getPreferredScrollableViewportSize( )
  JTableHeader.AccessibleJTableHeader ↵
  .AccessibleJTableHeaderEntry.getSize( )
  JToolBar.Separator.getSeparatorSize( )
  JTree.AccessibleJTree.AccessibleJTreeNode.getSize( )
  JViewport < getViewSize( ), toViewCoordinates( ) >
  *LayoutManager** < minimumLayoutSize( ),
  preferredLayoutSize( ) > *ListPeer* < getMinimumSize( ),
  getPreferredSize( ), minimumSize( ), preferredSize( ) >
  OverlayLayout < minimumLayoutSize( ),
  preferredLayoutSize( ) > **R**ectangle*.getSize( )
  Scrollable.getPreferredScrollableViewportSize( )
  ScrollPaneLayout* < minimumLayoutSize( ),
  preferredLayoutSize( ) > **T**extArea < getPreferredSize( ),
  minimumSize( ), preferredSize( ) > *TextAreaPeer*
  < getPreferredSize( ), minimumSize( ), preferredSize( ) >
  TextField < getPreferredSize( ), minimumSize( ),
  preferredSize( ) > *TextFieldPeer* < getPreferredSize( ),
  minimumSize( ), preferredSize( ) > **T**oolkit < getBestCursorSize( ),
  getScreenSize( ) > **U**IManager.getDimension( )
  ViewportLayout.preferredLayoutSize( )
  —fields: **J**Table.preferredViewportSize
Dimension2D*: java.awt.geom
  —subclasses: **D**imension*
  —descendents: **D**imensionUIResource
  —passed to: **A**rc2D*.setArc( ) **R**ectangularShape*.setFrame( )
DimensionUIResource: javax.swing.plaf
DINGBATS: **C**haracter.UnicodeBlock
DIR: **H**TML.Attribute **H**TML.Tag*
DirectColorModel: java.awt.image
DIRECTORIES_ONLY: **J**FileChooser
DIRECTORY_CHANGED_PROPERTY: **J**FileChooser
DIRECTORY_PANE: **A**ccessibleRole
dirty( ): *DGC*
disable( ): **C**ompiler **C**omponent* *ComponentPeer**
  MenuItem* *MenuItemPeer**
DISABLED_ICON_CHANGED_PROPERTY: **A**bstractButton*
DISABLED_SELECTED_ICON_CHANGED_PROPERTY:
  AbstractButton*
disableEvents( ): **C**omponent* **M**enuItem*
disableResizedPosting( ): **T**ableColumn
disableSwingFocusManager( ): **F**ocusManager*
discardAllEdits( ): **U**ndoManager
disconnect( ): **D**atagramSocket* **H**ttpURLConnection **O**RB
DISCONTIGUOUS_TREE_SELECTION: *TreeSelectionModel*
discriminator( ): *DynUnion*
discriminator_kind( ): *DynUnion*
discriminator_type( ): **T**ypeCode
dispatch( ): *ActiveEvent* **I**nvocationEvent *Skeleton*
dispatchEvent( ): **C**omponent* **E**ventQueue **I**nputContext
  MenuComponent*
DISPLAY: **C**SS.Attribute
dispose( ): *ComponentPeer** **C**ompositeContext **G**raphics*
  InputContext **J**InternalFrame *MenuComponentPeer**
  PaintContext **W**indow*
DISPOSE_ON_CLOSE: *WindowConstants*
distance( ): **P**oint2D*
distanceSq( ): **P**oint2D*
DISTINCT: **T**ypes
DIV: **H**TML.Tag*
divide( ): **B**igDecimal **B**igInteger
divideAndRemainder( ): **B**igInteger
DIVIDER: **J**SplitPane
DIVIDER_SIZE_PROPERTY: **J**SplitPane
dividerSize: **J**SplitPane
dk_Alias: **D**efinitionKind
dk_all: **D**efinitionKind
dk_Array: **D**efinitionKind
dk_Attribute: **D**efinitionKind
dk_Constant: **D**efinitionKind

drawImage( ): **G**raphics*
drawLine( ): **G**raphics* **P**lainView* **W**rappedPlainView
drawOval( ): **G**raphics*
drawPolygon( ): **G**raphics*
drawPolyline( ): **G**raphics*
drawRect( ): **G**raphics*
drawRenderableImage( ): **G**raphics2D
drawRenderedImage( ): **G**raphics2D
drawRoundRect( ): **G**raphics*
drawSelectedText( ): **P**lainView* **W**rappedPlainView
drawString( ): **G**raphics*
drawTabbedText( ): **U**tilities
drawUnselectedText( ): **P**lainView* **W**rappedPlainView
Driver: java.sql
— passed to: **D**riverManager < deregisterDriver( ), registerDriver( ) >
— returned by: **D**riverManager.getDriver( )
DriverManager: java.sql
DriverPropertyInfo: java.sql
— returned by: *Driver*.getPropertyInfo( )
drop( ): **D**ropTarget *DropTargetListener*
dropActionChanged( ): **D**ragSourceContext
    DragSourceListener **D**ropTarget *DropTargetListener*
dropComplete( ): **D**ropTargetContext *DropTargetDropEvent*
DropTarget: java.awt.dnd
— passed to: **C**omponent*.setDropTarget( )
— returned by: **C**omponent*.getDropTarget( )
DropTarget.DropTargetAutoScroller: java.awt.dnd
— returned by: **D**ropTarget.createDropTargetAutoScroller( )
DropTargetContext*: java.awt.dnd
— passed to: **D**ropTargetDragEvent( ) **D**ropTargetDropEvent( )
— returned by: **D**ropTarget < createDropTargetContext( ),
    getDropTargetContext( ) >
— fields: **D**ropTargetEvent*.context
DropTargetContext.TransferableProxy: java.awt.dnd
— passed to: **D**ropTargetContext.addNotify( )
DropTargetDragEvent: java.awt.dnd
— passed to: **D**ropTarget < dragEnter( ), dragOver( ),
    dropActionChanged( ) > *DropTargetListener* < dragOver( ),
    dropActionChanged( ) >
DropTargetDropEvent: java.awt.dnd
— passed to: **D**ropTarget.drop( )
DropTargetEvent*: java.awt.dnd
— subclasses: **D**ropTargetDragEvent **D**ropTargetDropEvent
— passed to: **D**ropTarget.dragExit( )
DropTargetListener: java.awt.dnd
— passed to: **D**ropTarget < addDropTargetListener( ), DropTarget( ),
    removeDropTargetListener( ) >
— implemented by: **D**ropTarget
*DSAKey**: java.security.interfaces
— extended by: *DSAPrivateKey* *DSAPublicKey*
DSAKeyPairGenerator: java.security.interfaces
DSAParameterSpec: java.security.spec
DSAParams: java.security.interfaces
— passed to: *DSAKeyPairGenerator*.initialize( )
— returned by: *DSAKey**.getParams( )
— implemented by: **D**SAParameterSpec
DSAPrivateKey: java.security.interfaces
DSAPrivateKeySpec: java.security.spec
DSAPublicKey: java.security.interfaces
DSAPublicKeySpec: java.security.spec
DST_IN: **A**lphaComposite
DST_OFFSET: **C**alendar*
DST_OUT: **A**lphaComposite
DST_OVER: **A**lphaComposite
DstIn: **A**lphaComposite
DstOut: **A**lphaComposite
DstOver: **A**lphaComposite
DT: **H**TML.Tag*
dtd: **P**arser*
DTD: javax.swing.text.html.parser
— passed to: **D**ocumentParser( ) **P**arser( )
— returned by: **D**TD.getDTD( )

— fields: **P**arser*.dtd
DTDConstants: javax.swing.text.html.parser
— implemented by: **A**ttributeList **D**TD
    javax.swing.text.html.parser.**E**lement **E**ntity **P**arser*
DUMMY: **H**TML.Attribute
dump( ): **A**bstractDocument*
    AbstractDocument.AbstractElement*
dumpStack( ): **T**hread
duplicate( ): **D**elegate
*DynamicImplementation**: org.omg.CORBA
— subclasses: _BindingIteratorImplBase
    _NamingContextImplBase
*DynAny**: org.omg.CORBA
— extended by: *DynArray* *DynEnum* *DynFixed* *DynSequence*
    DynStruct *DynUnion* *DynValue*
— passed to: *DynAny**.assign( )
— returned by: *DynAny** < copy( ), current_component( ) >
    DynUnion.member( ) **O**RB.create_dyn_any( )
DynArray: org.omg.CORBA
— returned by: **O**RB.create_dyn_array( )
DynEnum: org.omg.CORBA
— returned by: **O**RB.create_dyn_enum( )
DynFixed: org.omg.CORBA
DynSequence: org.omg.CORBA
— returned by: **O**RB.create_dyn_sequence( )
DynStruct: org.omg.CORBA
— returned by: **O**RB.create_dyn_struct( )
DynUnion: org.omg.CORBA
— returned by: **O**RB.create_dyn_union( )
DynValue: org.omg.CORBA
E: **M**ath
E_RESIZE_CURSOR: **C**ursor **F**rame*
EAST: **B**orderLayout **G**ridBagConstraints *SwingConstants*
echoCharIsSet( ): **J**PasswordField **T**extField
EDGE_NO_OP: **C**onvolveOp
EDGE_SPACING: **T**itledBorder*
EDGE_ZERO_FILL: **C**onvolveOp
EDITABLE: **A**ccessibleState
editable: **J**Tree
EDITABLE_PROPERTY: **J**Tree
editCellAt( ): **J**Table
editingCanceled( ): *CellEditorListener* **J**Table
    JTable.AccessibleJTable
editingColumn: **J**Table
editingComponent: **D**efaultTreeCellEditor
editingContainer: **D**efaultTreeCellEditor
editingIcon: **D**efaultTreeCellEditor
editingRow: **J**Table
editingStopped( ): *CellEditorListener* **J**Table
    JTable.AccessibleJTable
editor: **J**ComboBox
editorComp: **J**Table
editorComponent: **D**efaultCellEditor
EditorContainer( ): **D**efaultTreeCellEditor.EditorContainer
EditorKit: javax.swing.text
— subclasses: **D**efaultEditorKit*
— descendents: **H**TMLEditorKit **R**TFEditorKit **S**tyledEditorKit*
— passed to: **J**EditorPane* < setEditorKit( ),
    setEditorKitForContentType( ) >
— returned by: **J**EditorPane* < createDefaultEditorKit( ),
    createEditorKitForContentType( ), getEditorKit( ),
    getEditorKitForContentType( ) > **T**extUI.getEditorKit( )
edits: **C**ompoundEdit*
editToBeRedone( ): **U**ndoManager
editToBeUndone( ): **U**ndoManager
element: **D**efaultStyledDocument.AttributeUndoableEdit
Element: javax.swing.text
— passed to: **A**bstractDocument* < createBranchElement( ),
    createLeafElement( ) > **A**bstractDocument.BranchElement*
    < BranchElement( ), replace( ) >
    AbstractDocument.ElementEdit( ) **A**bstractWriter*
    < AbstractWriter( ), getText( ), inRange( ), text( ) > **B**oxView( )

E

E

engineSetSeed( ): SecureRandomSpi
engineSign( ): SignatureSpi*
engineSize( ): KeyStoreSpi
engineStore( ): KeyStoreSpi
engineToString( ): AlgorithmParametersSpi
engineTranslateKey( ): KeyFactorySpi
engineUpdate( ): MessageDigestSpi* SignatureSpi*
engineVerify( ): SignatureSpi*
ENGLISH: Locale
enqueue( ): Reference*
ensureCapacity( ): ArrayList DefaultListModel StringBuffer
  Vector*
ensureFileIsVisible( ): FileChooserUI JFileChooser
ensureIndexIsVisible( ): JList
ENTER: DragSourceContext Event
ENTERED: HyperlinkEvent.EventType
ENTITIES: *DTDConstants*
ENTITY: *DTDConstants*
Entity: javax.swing.text.html.parser
—returned by: **D**TD < defEntity( ), defineEntity( ), getEntity( ) >
entityHash: DTD
entries( ): *Acl* ZipFile*
entrySet( ): AbstractMap* Attributes Hashtable* *Map**
  RenderingHints
enumerate( ): Thread ThreadGroup
Enumeration: java.util
—passed
  to: **A**bstractDocument.AbstractElement*.removeAttributes( )
  JTree.removeDescendantToggledPaths( )
  SequenceInputStream( ) StyleContext*.removeAttributes( )
—returned by: **A**bstractDocument.AbstractElement* < children( ),
  getAttributeNames( ) > *Acl* < entries( ), getPermissions( ) >
  AppletContext.getApplets( ) *AttributeSet*.getAttributeNames( )
  ClassLoader* < findResources( ), getResources( ),
  getSystemResources( ) > DefaultListModel.elements( )
  DefaultMutableTreeNode* < children( ),
  depthFirstEnumeration( ), pathFromAncestorEnumeration( ),
  postorderEnumeration( ), preorderEnumeration( ) >
  DefaultTableColumnModel.getColumns( )
  Dictionary*.keys( ) FeatureDescriptor*.attributeNames( )
  IdentityScope.identities( ) JTree.getExpandedDescendants( )
  KeyStoreSpi.engineAliases( ) PermissionCollection*.elements( )
  ResourceBundle*.getKeys( ) StyleContext*.getStyleNames( )
  StyleContext.SmallAttributeSet.getAttributeNames( )
  *TreeNode**.children( ) Vector*.elements( )
—implemented by: **S**tringTokenizer
—fields: **D**efaultMutableTreeNode*.EMPTY_ENUMERATION
enumeration( ): Collections
env( ): Request
Environment: org.omg.CORBA
—returned by: **O**RB.create_environment( )
eof: OptionalDataException
EOFException: java.io
eolIsSignificant( ): StreamTokenizer
eos: GZIPInputStream
equal( ): *Any* TypeCode
equals( ): Area Arrays Collator* *Collection** Comparator
  DataFlavor Delegate GlyphVector ImageGraphicAttribute
  *Map** Map.Entry MenuShortcut java.lang.Object
  *java.security.acl.Permission java.security.Principal**
  ShapeGraphicAttribute TextHitInfo TextLayout Timestamp
equalsIgnoreCase( ): String
equivalent( ): TypeCode
ERA: Calendar*
ERA_FIELD: DateFormat*
err: FileDescriptor System
ERROR: *ImageObserver*
Error*: java.lang
—subclasses: **A**WTError LinkageError* ThreadDeath
  VirtualMachineError*
—descendents: **A**bstractMethodError ClassCircularityError
  ClassFormatError* ExceptionInInitializerError

IllegalAccessError IncompatibleClassChangeError*
InstantiationError InternalError NoClassDefFoundError
NoSuchFieldError NoSuchMethodError OutOfMemoryError
StackOverflowError UnknownError UnsatisfiedLinkError
UnsupportedClassVersionError VerifyError
—passed to: **S**erverError( )
error( ): Parser*
ERROR_MESSAGE: JOptionPane
ERROR_OPTION: JFileChooser
ERRORED: MediaTracker
ESCAPE: Event
EtchedBorder*: javax.swing.border
—subclasses: **B**orderUIResource.EtchedBorderUIResource
etchType: EtchedBorder*
event: ExpandVetoException
Event: java.awt
—passed to: **A**WTEvent( ) Component* < deliverEvent( ),
  gotFocus( ), handleEvent( ), keyDown( ), keyUp( ),
  lostFocus( ), mouseDown( ), mouseDrag( ), mouseEnter( ),
  mouseExit( ), mouseMove( ), mouseUp( ), postEvent( ) >
  MenuContainer.postEvent( )
—fields: **E**vent.evt
eventDispatched( ): *A*WTEventListener
*EventListener**: java.util
—extended by: *A*ctionListener* AdjustmentListener
  AncestorListener *A*WTEventListener
  BeanContextMembershipListener
  *BeanContextServiceRevokedListener** CaretListener
  CellEditorListener ChangeListener ComponentListener
  ContainerListener DocumentListener
  DragGestureListener DragSourceListener
  DropTargetListener FocusListener HyperlinkListener
  InputMethodListener InternalFrameListener ItemListener
  KeyListener ListDataListener ListSelectionListener
  MenuDragMouseListener MenuKeyListener MenuListener
  MouseListener* MouseMotionListener* PopupMenuListener
  PropertyChangeListener TableColumnModelListener
  TableModelListener TextListener TreeExpansionListener
  TreeModelListener TreeSelectionListener
  TreeWillExpandListener UndoableEditListener
  VetoableChangeListener WindowListener
—descendents: *A*ction BeanContextServices
  BeanContextServicesListener MouseInputListener
—passed to: *A*WTEventMulticaster < addInternal( ),
  AWTEventMulticaster( ), remove( ), removeInternal( ), save( ) >
  EventListenerList.remove( )
—returned by: *A*WTEventMulticaster < addInternal( ), remove( ),
  removeInternal( ) >
—fields: *A*WTEventMulticaster < a, b >
EventListenerList: javax.swing.event
—fields: **A**bstractDocument*.listenerList
  AbstractTableModel*.listenerList
  DefaultButtonModel*.listenerList DefaultCellEditor.listenerList
  DefaultListSelectionModel.listenerList
  DefaultTableColumnModel.listenerList
  DefaultTreeSelectionModel*.listenerList
  MenuSelectionManager.listenerList Timer.listenerList
EventObject*: java.util
—subclasses: **A**WTEvent* BeanContextEvent* CaretEvent
  ChangeEvent DragGestureEvent DragSourceEvent*
  DropTargetEvent* HyperlinkEvent* ListDataEvent
  ListSelectionEvent MenuEvent PopupMenuEvent
  PropertyChangeEvent TableColumnModelEvent
  TableModelEvent TreeExpansionEvent TreeModelEvent
  TreeSelectionEvent UndoableEditEvent
—descendents: **A**ctionEvent AdjustmentEvent
  AncestorEvent BeanContextMembershipEvent
  BeanContextServiceAvailableEvent
  BeanContextServiceRevokedEvent ComponentEvent*
  ContainerEvent DragSourceDragEvent
  DragSourceDropEvent DropTargetDragEvent
  DropTargetDropEvent FocusEvent

E

E

HTMLFrameHyperlinkEvent InputEvent* InputMethodEvent
InternalFrameEvent InvocationEvent ItemEvent KeyEvent*
MenuDragMouseEvent MenuKeyEvent MouseEvent*
PaintEvent TextEvent WindowEvent
—passed to: *CellEditor* < isCellEditable( ),
shouldSelectCell( ) > DefaultCellEditor.shouldSelectCell( )
DefaultCellEditor.EditorDelegate.startCellEditing( )
DefaultTreeCellEditor < isCellEditable( ), shouldSelectCell( ),
shouldStartEditingTimer( ) >

EventQueue: java.awt
—passed to: EventQueue.push( )
—returned by: Toolkit < getSystemEventQueue( ),
getSystemEventQueueImpl( ) >

events: DragGestureRecognizer*
EventSetDescriptor: java.beans
—returned by: *BeanInfo*.getEventSetDescriptors( )

evt: Event
ExcellentBreakWeight: View*
except: UnknownUserException
except(): ServerRequest
Exception*: java.lang
—subclasses: AclNotFoundException ActivationException*
AlreadyBoundException ApplicationException
AWTException BadLocationException
ClassNotFoundException CloneNotSupportedException*
DataFormatException ExpandVetoException
GeneralSecurityException IllegalAccessException
InstantiationException InterruptedException
IntrospectionException InvocationTargetException
IOException* LastOwnerException
NoninvertibleTransformException NoSuchFieldException
NoSuchMethodException NotBoundException
NotOwnerException ParseException PrinterException*
PrivilegedActionException PropertyVetoException
RemarshalException RuntimeException*
ServerNotActiveException SQLException*
TooManyListenersException UnsupportedFlavorException
UnsupportedLookAndFeelException UserException*
—descendents: AccessControlException AccessException
ActivateFailedException AlreadyBound
ArithmeticException ArrayIndexOutOfBoundsException
ArrayStoreException BAD_CONTEXT
BAD_INV_ORDER BAD_OPERATION BAD_PARAM
BAD_TYPECODE BadKind BatchUpdateException
BindException org.omg.CORBA.Bounds
org.omg.CORBA.TypeCodePackage.Bounds
CannotProceed CannotRedoException
CannotUndoException CertificateEncodingException
CertificateException* CertificateExpiredException
CertificateNotYetValidException CertificateParsingException
ChangedCharSetException CharConversionException
ClassCastException CMMException COMM_FAILURE
ConcurrentModificationException java.net.ConnectException
java.rmi.ConnectException ConnectIOException
CRLException DATA_CONVERSION DataTruncation
DigestException EmptyStackException EOFException
ExportException* FileNotFoundException FREE_MEM
IllegalArgumentException* IllegalComponentStateException
IllegalMonitorStateException IllegalPathStateException
IllegalStateException* IllegalThreadStateException
ImagingOpException IMP_LIMIT InconsistentTypeCode
IndexOutOfBoundsException* INITIALIZE
INTERNAL InterruptedIOException INTF_REPOS
INV_FLAG INV_IDENT INV_OBJREF
INV_POLICY Invalid INVALID_TRANSACTION
InvalidAlgorithmParameterException
InvalidClassException InvalidDnDOperationException
InvalidKeyException InvalidKeySpecException
org.omg.CORBA.ORBPackage.InvalidName
org.omg.CosNaming.NamingContextPackage.InvalidName
InvalidObjectException InvalidParameterException
InvalidParameterSpecException InvalidSeq InvalidValue

JarException KeyException* KeyManagementException
KeyStoreException MalformedURLException MARSHAL
MarshalException MissingResourceException
NegativeArraySizeException NO_IMPLEMENT
NO_MEMORY NO_PERMISSION NO_RESOURCES
NO_RESPONSE NoRouteToHostException
NoSuchAlgorithmException NoSuchElementException
NoSuchObjectException NoSuchProviderException
NotActiveException NotEmpty NotFound
NotSerializableException NullPointerException
NumberFormatException OBJ_ADAPTER
OBJECT_NOT_EXIST ObjectStreamException*
OptionalDataException PERSIST_STORE PolicyError
PrinterAbortException PrinterIOException
ProfileDataException ProtocolException ProviderException
RasterFormatException RemoteException*
RMISecurityException SecurityException*
ServerCloneException ServerError ServerException
ServerRuntimeException SignatureException
SkeletonMismatchException SkeletonNotFoundException
SocketException* SocketSecurityException
SQLWarning* StreamCorruptedException
StringIndexOutOfBoundsException
StubNotFoundException SyncFailedException
SystemException* TRANSACTION_REQUIRED
TRANSACTION_ROLLEDBACK TRANSIENT
TypeMismatch UnexpectedException UNKNOWN
UnknownGroupException java.net.UnknownHostException
java.rmi.UnknownHostException UnknownObjectException
UnknownServiceException UnknownUserException
UnmarshalException UnrecoverableKeyException
UnsupportedEncodingException
UnsupportedOperationException UTFDataFormatException
WriteAbortedException WrongTransaction ZipException*
—passed to: AccessException( ) ConnectIOException( )
ExportException( ) java.rmi.UnknownHostException( )
PrivilegedActionException( ) ServerCloneException( )
ServerRuntimeException( ) SocketSecurityException( )
UnexpectedException( ) WriteAbortedException( )
—returned by: Environment.exception( )
PrivilegedActionException.getException( )
—thrown by: *PrivilegedExceptionAction*.run( )
RemoteRef.invoke( ) URLDecoder.decode( )
—fields: ServerCloneException.detail

exception(): Environment
ExceptionInInitializerError: java.lang
ExceptionList: org.omg.CORBA
—passed to: Delegate.create_request( )
org.omg.CORBA.Object._create_request( )
—returned by: ORB.create_exception_list( )

exceptions(): Request
exclusions: javax.swing.text.html.parser.Element
exclusiveOr(): Area
exec(): Runtime
execute(): *Statement*
executeBatch(): *Statement*
executeCall(): *RemoteCall*
executeQuery(): *Statement*
executeUpdate(): *Statement*
exists(): File
exit(): Runtime System
EXITED: HyperlinkEvent.EventType
exitValue(): Process
exp(): Math
EXPANDABLE: AccessibleState
EXPANDED: AccessibleState
expandPath(): JTree
expandRow(): JTree
ExpandVetoException: javax.swing.tree
—thrown by: JTree < fireTreeWillCollapse( ), fireTreeWillExpand( ) >
TreeWillExpandListener.treeWillExpand( )

ExportException*: java.rmi.server

F

—subclasses: **S**ocketSecurityException
exportObject(): **A**ctivatable *ServerRef* **U**nicastRemoteObject*
extent: **A**rc2D.Double **A**rc2D.Float
Externalizable*: java.io
—extended by: *RemoteRef**
—descendents: *ServerRef*
—implemented by: **D**ataFlavor
extract(): **A**lreadyBoundHelper **B**indingHelper
   BindingIteratorHelper **B**indingListHelper
   BindingTypeHelper **C**annotProceedHelper
   InvalidNameHelper **I**stringHelper **N**ameComponentHelper
   NameHelper **N**amingContextHelper **N**otEmptyHelper
   NotFoundHelper **N**otFoundReasonHelper
   ServiceDetailHelper **S**erviceInformationHelper
extract_any(): **A**ny
extract_boolean(): **A**ny
extract_char(): **A**ny
extract_double(): **A**ny
extract_fixed(): **A**ny
extract_float(): **A**ny
extract_long(): **A**ny
extract_longlong(): **A**ny
extract_Object(): **A**ny
extract_octet(): **A**ny
extract_Principal(): **A**ny
extract_short(): **A**ny
extract_string(): **A**ny
extract_TypeCode(): **A**ny
extract_ulong(): **A**ny
extract_ulonglong(): **A**ny
extract_ushort(): **A**ny
extract_Value(): **A**ny
extract_wchar(): **A**ny
extract_wstring(): **A**ny
F1: **E**vent
F10: **E**vent
F11: **E**vent
F12: **E**vent
F2: **E**vent
F3: **E**vent
F4: **E**vent
F5: **E**vent
F6: **E**vent
F7: **E**vent
F8: **E**vent
F9: **E**vent
FACE: **H**TML.Attribute
failure(): *RMIFailureHandler*
FALSE: **B**oolean
Family: **S**tyleConstants.CharacterConstants
   StyleConstants.FontConstants
FAMILY: **T**extAttribute
fd: **D**atagramSocketImpl **S**ocketImpl
FeatureDescriptor*: java.beans
—subclasses: **B**eanDescriptor **E**ventSetDescriptor
   MethodDescriptor **P**arameterDescriptor
   PropertyDescriptor*
—descendents: **I**ndexedPropertyDescriptor
FEBRUARY: **C**alendar*
FETCH_FORWARD: *ResultSet*
FETCH_REVERSE: *ResultSet*
FETCH_UNKNOWN: *ResultSet*
fictional(): **T**agElement
Field: java.lang.reflect
—returned by: **C**lass < getDeclaredField( ), getDeclaredFields( ),
   getField( ), getFields( ) >
FIELD_COUNT: **C**alendar*
FieldPosition: java.text
—passed to: **D**ateFormat*.format( ) **M**essageFormat.format( )
   NumberFormat*.format( )
fields: **C**alendar*
FieldView*: javax.swing.text

—subclasses: **P**asswordView
File: java.io
—passed to: **F**ile < compareTo( ), createTempFile( ), File( ),
   renameTo( ) > **F**ileInputStream( ) **F**ileOutputStream( )
   FileSystemView < createFileObject( ), createNewFolder( ),
   getFiles( ), getParentDirectory( ), isHiddenFile( ),
   isRoot( ) > **F**ileView < getIcon( ), getName( ),
   getTypeDescription( ), isTraversable( ) > **J**arFile( )
   javax.swing.filechooser.FileFilter.accept( ) **J**FileChooser
   < ensureFileIsVisible( ), getDescription( ), getIcon( ), getName( ),
   getTypeDescription( ), isTraversable( ), JFileChooser( ),
   setCurrentDirectory( ), setSelectedFile( ), setSelectedFiles( ) >
   ZipFile( )
—returned by: **F**ile < createTempFile( ), getAbsoluteFile( ),
   getCanonicalFile( ), getParentFile( ), listFiles( ), listRoots( ) >
   FileSystemView < createFileObject( ), createNewFolder( ),
   getFiles( ), getHomeDirectory( ), getParentDirectory( ),
   getRoots( ) > **J**FileChooser < getSelectedFile( ),
   getSelectedFiles( ) >
FILE_CHOOSER: **A**ccessibleRole
FILE_FILTER_CHANGED_PROPERTY: **J**FileChooser
FILE_HIDING_CHANGED_PROPERTY: **J**FileChooser
FILE_SELECTION_MODE_CHANGED_PROPERTY:
   JFileChooser
FILE_SYSTEM_VIEW_CHANGED_PROPERTY: **J**FileChooser
FILE_VERSION: **D**TD
FILE_VIEW_CHANGED_PROPERTY: **J**FileChooser
FileChooserUI: javax.swing.plaf
—returned by: **J**FileChooser.getUI( )
FileDescriptor: java.io
—passed to: **F**ileInputStream( ) **F**ileReader( ) **S**ecurityManager*
   < checkRead( ), checkWrite( ) >
—returned by: **D**atagramSocketImpl.getFileDescriptor( )
   FileOutputStream.getFD( ) **S**ocketImpl.getFileDescriptor( )
—fields: **D**atagramSocketImpl.fd **F**ileDescriptor < in, out >
FileDialog: java.awt
—passed to: **T**oolkit.createFileDialog( )
FileDialogPeer: java.awt.peer
—returned by: **T**oolkit.createFileDialog( )
FileFilter: java.io
—passed to: **F**ile.listFiles( )
FileFilter: javax.swing.filechooser
—passed to: **J**FileChooser < addChoosableFileFilter( ),
   removeChoosableFileFilter( ), setFileFilter( ) >
—returned by: **F**ileChooserUI.getAcceptAllFileFilter( ) **J**FileChooser
   < getChoosableFileFilters( ), getFileFilter( ) >
FileInputStream: java.io
FilenameFilter: java.io
—passed to: **F**ile < list( ), listFiles( ) >
   FileDialogPeer.setFilenameFilter( )
—returned by: **F**ileDialog.getFilenameFilter( )
FileNameMap: java.net
—passed to: **U**RLConnection*.setFileNameMap( )
—returned by: **U**RLConnection*.getFileNameMap( )
FileNotFoundException: java.io
—thrown by: **F**ileInputStream( ) **F**ileOutputStream( )
   FileReader( )
FileOutputStream: java.io
FilePermission: java.io
FileReader: java.io
FILES_AND_DIRECTORIES: **J**FileChooser
FILES_ONLY: **J**FileChooser
FileSystemView: javax.swing.filechooser
—passed to: **J**FileChooser < JFileChooser( ), setFileSystemView( ),
   setup( ) >
—returned by: **F**ileSystemView.getFileSystemView( )
FileView: javax.swing.filechooser
—passed to: **J**FileChooser.setFileView( )
—returned by: **F**ileChooserUI.getFileView( )
FileWriter: java.io
fill: **G**ridBagConstraints
FILL: **S**hapeGraphicAttribute

F

FlavorMap: java.awt.datatransfer
—passed to: **D**ragSource.startDrag( ) **D**ropTarget.setFlavorMap( )
—returned by: **D**ragSource.getFlavorMap( )
SystemFlavorMap.getDefaultFlavorMap( )
—implemented by: **S**ystemFlavorMap
flipBit( ): **B**igInteger
flipEastAndWestAtEnds( ): **C**ompositeView*
FLOAT: **C**SS.Attribute **T**ypes
Float: java.lang
—passed to: **F**loat.compareTo( )
—returned by: **F**loat.valueOf( )
—fields: **T**extAttribute < JUSTIFICATION_FULL,
JUSTIFICATION_NONE, POSTURE_OBLIQUE, POSTURE_REGULAR,
WEIGHT_BOLD, WEIGHT_DEMIBOLD, WEIGHT_DEMILIGHT,
WEIGHT_EXTRA_LIGHT, WEIGHT_EXTRABOLD,
WEIGHT_HEAVY, WEIGHT_LIGHT, WEIGHT_MEDIUM,
WEIGHT_REGULAR, WEIGHT_SEMIBOLD, WEIGHT_ULTRABOLD,
WIDTH_CONDENSED, WIDTH_EXTENDED, WIDTH_REGULAR,
WIDTH_SEMI_CONDENSED, WIDTH_SEMI_EXTENDED >
FloatHolder: org.omg.CORBA
floatToIntBits( ): **F**loat
floatValue( ): **N**umber*
floor( ): **M**ath
FlowLayout: java.awt
flush( ): **H**TMLEditorKit.ParserCallback* **I**mage* *ObjectOutput*
java.io.**O**utputStream* **W**riter*
flushAttributes( ): **P**arser
flushCaches( ): **I**ntrospector
flushFromCaches( ): **I**ntrospector
FOCUS_ACCELERATOR_KEY: **J**TextComponent*
FOCUS_EVENT_MASK: **A**WTEvent*
FOCUS_FIRST: **F**ocusEvent
FOCUS_GAINED: **F**ocusEvent
FOCUS_LAST: **F**ocusEvent
FOCUS_LOST: **F**ocusEvent
FOCUS_MANAGER_CLASS_PROPERTY: **F**ocusManager*
FOCUS_NEXT: *WindowPeer*
FOCUS_PAINTED_CHANGED_PROPERTY: **A**bstractButton*
FOCUS_PREVIOUS: *WindowPeer*
FOCUSABLE: **A**ccessibleState
FocusAdapter: java.awt.event
FOCUSED: **A**ccessibleState
FocusEvent: java.awt.event
—passed to: **A**WTEventMulticaster < focusGained( ),
focusLost( ) > **D**efaultCaret < focusGained( ), focusLost( ) >
FocusAdapter.focusLost( ) *FocusListener*.focusLost( )
focusGained( ): **A**WTEventMulticaster **D**efaultCaret
FocusAdapter *FocusListener*
FocusListener: java.awt.event
—passed to: *AccessibleComponent* < addFocusListener( ),
removeFocusListener( ) > **A**WTEventMulticaster.remove( )
Box.AccessibleBox.removeFocusListener( )
Box.Filler.AccessibleBoxFiller.removeFocusListener( )
CellRendererPane.AccessibleCellRendererPane ↵
.removeFocusListener( ) **C**omponent*.removeFocusListener( )
JApplet.AccessibleJApplet.removeFocusListener( )
JComponent.AccessibleJComponent*.removeFocusListener( )
JDialog.AccessibleJDialog.removeFocusListener( )
JFrame.AccessibleJFrame.removeFocusListener( ) **J**List ↵
.AccessibleJList.AccessibleJListChild.removeFocusListener( )
JPopupMenu.WindowPopup ↵
.AccessibleWindowPopup.removeFocusListener( )
JTable.AccessibleJTable ↵
.AccessibleJTableCell.removeFocusListener( )
JTableHeader.AccessibleJTableHeader ↵
.AccessibleJTableHeaderEntry.removeFocusListener( )
JTree.AccessibleJTree ↵
.AccessibleJTreeNode.removeFocusListener( )
JWindow.AccessibleJWindow.removeFocusListener( )
—returned by: **A**WTEventMulticaster < add( ), remove( ) >
—implemented by: **A**WTEventMulticaster **D**efaultCaret
FocusAdapter

focusLost( ): **A**WTEventMulticaster **D**efaultCaret
FocusAdapter *FocusListener*
FocusManager*: javax.swing
—subclasses: **D**efaultFocusManager
—passed to: **F**ocusManager*.setCurrentManager( )
—returned by: **F**ocusManager*.getCurrentManager( )
focusNextComponent( ): **F**ocusManager*
focusPreviousComponent( ): **F**ocusManager*
following( ): **B**reakIterator
FONT: **C**SS.Attribute **H**TML.Tag* **T**extAttribute
font: **D**efaultTreeCellEditor **F**ontMetrics
Font*: java.awt
—subclasses: **F**ontUIResource
—passed to: *AccessibleComponent* < getFontMetrics( ),
setFont( ) > **B**orderFactory.createTitledBorder( )
BorderUIResource.TitledBorderUIResource( )
Box.AccessibleBox.setFont( )
Box.Filler.AccessibleBoxFiller.setFont( )
CellRendererPane.AccessibleCellRendererPane.setFont( )
Component*.setFont( ) *ComponentPeer*.setFont( )
Font*.getFont( ) **F**ontUIResource( ) **G**raphics*.setFont( )
JApplet.AccessibleJApplet.setFont( )
JComponent.AccessibleJComponent*.setFont( )
JDialog.AccessibleJDialog.setFont( )
JFrame.AccessibleJFrame.setFont( )
JList.AccessibleJList.AccessibleJListChild.setFont( )
JPopupMenu.WindowPopup ↵
.AccessibleWindowPopup.setFont( )
JTable.AccessibleJTable.AccessibleJTableCell.setFont( )
JTableHeader.AccessibleJTableHeader ↵
.AccessibleJTableHeaderEntry.setFont( )
JTree.AccessibleJTree.AccessibleJTreeNode.setFont( )
JWindow.AccessibleJWindow.setFont( )
StyleContext*.getFontMetrics( ) **T**itledBorder* < setTitleFont( ),
TitledBorder* >
—returned by: *AccessibleComponent*.getFont( )
Box.Filler.AccessibleBoxFiller.getFont( )
Component*.getFont( ) **D**efaultTreeCellEditor.getFont( )
Font* < deriveFont( ), getFont( ) > **G**lyphVector.getFont( )
GraphicsEnvironment.getAllFonts( )
JComponent.AccessibleJComponent*.getFont( )
JFrame.AccessibleJFrame.getFont( ) **J**PopupMenu ↵
.WindowPopup.AccessibleWindowPopup.getFont( )
JTableHeader.AccessibleJTableHeader ↵
.AccessibleJTableHeaderEntry.getFont( )
JWindow.AccessibleJWindow.getFont( )
MenuComponent*.getFont( ) *MultipleMaster*.deriveMMFont( )
StyleContext*.getFont( ) **T**itledBorder* < getFont( ),
getTitleFont( ) > **U**IManager.getFont( )
—fields: **D**efaultTreeCellEditor.font **T**itledBorder*.titleFont
FONT_CHANGE_BIGGER: **H**TMLEditorKit
FONT_CHANGE_SMALLER: **H**TMLEditorKit
FONT_FAMILY: **C**SS.Attribute
FONT_SIZE: **C**SS.Attribute
FONT_STYLE: **C**SS.Attribute
FONT_VARIANT: **C**SS.Attribute
FONT_WEIGHT: **C**SS.Attribute
FontFamily: **S**tyleConstants*
FontMetrics: java.awt
—passed to: **S**wingUtilities < computeStringWidth( ),
layoutCompoundLabel( ) > **U**tilities < getTabbedTextOffset( ),
getTabbedTextWidth( ) >
—returned by: *AccessibleComponent*.getFontMetrics( )
Box.Filler.AccessibleBoxFiller.getFontMetrics( )
Component*.getFontMetrics( )
FieldView*.getFontMetrics( ) **G**raphics*.getFontMetrics( )
JComponent.AccessibleJComponent*.getFontMetrics( )
JFrame.AccessibleJFrame.getFontMetrics( ) **J**PopupMenu ↵
.WindowPopup.AccessibleWindowPopup.getFontMetrics( )
JTableHeader.AccessibleJTableHeader ↵
.AccessibleJTableHeaderEntry.getFontMetrics( )

G

getAuxiliaryLookAndFeels(): UIManager
getAvailableAttributes(): Font*
getAvailableFontFamilyNames(): GraphicsEnvironment
getAvailableIDs(): TimeZone*
getAvailableLocales(): BreakIterator Calendar* Collator*
    DateFormat* Locale NumberFormat*
getBackground(): *AccessibleComponent*
    Box.AccessibleBox Box.Filler.AccessibleBoxFiller
    CellRendererPane.AccessibleCellRendererPane
    Component* DefaultStyledDocument*
    Graphics2D JApplet.AccessibleJApplet
    JComponent.AccessibleJComponent*
    JDialog.AccessibleJDialog JFrame.AccessibleJFrame
    JList.AccessibleJList.AccessibleJListChild
    JPopupMenu.WindowPopup.AccessibleWindowPopup
    JTable.AccessibleJTable.AccessibleJTableCell
    JTableHeader.AccessibleJTableHeader ↵
    .AccessibleJTableHeaderEntry
    JTree.AccessibleJTree.AccessibleJTreeNode
    JWindow.AccessibleJWindow StyleConstants*
    StyleContext* *StyledDocument*
getBackgroundAt(): JTabbedPane
getBackgroundNonSelectionColor(): DefaultTreeCellRenderer
getBackgroundSelectionColor(): DefaultTreeCellRenderer
getBandOffsets(): ComponentSampleModel*
getBankData(): DataBufferByte DataBufferInt DataBufferShort
    DataBufferUShort
getBankIndices(): ComponentSampleModel*
getBase(): HTMLDocument
getBaseline(): TextLayout
getBaselineFor(): Font*
getBaselineIndex(): LineMetrics
getBaselineOffsets(): LineMetrics TextLayout
getBaseType(): *java.sql.Array*
getBaseTypeName(): *java.sql.Array Ref*
getBasicConstraints(): X509Certificate
getBeanClass(): BeanDescriptor
getBeanContext(): *BeanContextChild*
    BeanContextChildSupport* BeanContextEvent*
getBeanContextChildPeer(): BeanContextChildSupport*
getBeanContextPeer(): BeanContextSupport*
getBeanContextProxy(): *BeanContextProxy*
getBeanContextServicesPeer(): BeanContextServicesSupport
getBeanDescriptor(): *BeanInfo* SimpleBeanInfo
getBeanInfo(): Introspector
getBeanInfoSearchPath(): Introspector
getBeforeIndex(): *AccessibleText*
    JTextComponent.AccessibleJTextComponent*
getBeginIndex(): *CharacterIterator* FieldPosition
    StringCharacterIterator
getBestConfiguration(): GraphicsConfigTemplate
    GraphicsDevice
getBestCursorSize(): Toolkit
getBestRowIdentifier(): *DatabaseMetaData*
getBevelType(): BevelBorder*
getBidiLevel(): StyleConstants*
getBidiRootElement(): AbstractDocument*
getBigDecimal(): *CallableStatement ResultSet*
getBinaryStream(): *Blob ResultSet*
getBitMasks(): SinglePixelPackedSampleModel
getBitOffset(): MultiPixelPackedSampleModel
getBitOffsets(): SinglePixelPackedSampleModel
getBlackBoxBounds(): TextLayout
getBlackLineBorderUIResource(): BorderUIResource
getBlinkRate(): *Caret* DefaultCaret
getBlob(): *CallableStatement ResultSet*
getBlockIncrement(): *Adjustable* JScrollBar* Scrollbar
getBlue(): Color* ColorModel*
getBlueMask(): DirectColorModel
getBlues(): IndexColorModel
getBoolean(): java.lang.reflect.Array Boolean
    CallableStatement Field *ResultSet*

getBorder(): JComponent* TitledBorder* UIDefaults
    UIManager
getBorderInsets(): AbstractBorder* *Border*
    BorderUIResource
getBorderSelectionColor(): DefaultTreeCellEditor
    DefaultTreeCellRenderer
getBorderTitle(): JComponent.AccessibleJComponent*
getBottomComponent(): JSplitPane
getBottomInset(): CompositeView*
getBoundActions(): *Keymap*
getBoundingBox(): Polygon
getBoundKeyStrokes(): *Keymap*
getBounds(): AbstractLayoutCache* *AccessibleComponent*
    Area Box.AccessibleBox Box.Filler.AccessibleBoxFiller
    CellRendererPane.AccessibleCellRendererPane
    Component* CubicCurve2D* GeneralPath
    GraphicAttribute* JApplet.AccessibleJApplet
    JComponent.AccessibleJComponent*
    JDialog.AccessibleJDialog JFrame.AccessibleJFrame
    JList.AccessibleJList.AccessibleJListChild
    JPopupMenu.WindowPopup.AccessibleWindowPopup
    JTable.AccessibleJTable.AccessibleJTableCell
    JTableHeader.AccessibleJTableHeader ↵
    .AccessibleJTableHeaderEntry
    JTree.AccessibleJTree.AccessibleJTreeNode
    JWindow.AccessibleJWindow Line2D* Polygon
    QuadCurve2D* Raster* RectangularShape* *Shape*
    TextLayout
getBounds2D(): AffineTransformOp Area
    BandCombineOp *BufferedImageOp* ColorConvertOp
    ContextualRenderedImageFactory ConvolveOp
    CubicCurve2D* GeneralPath GlyphMetrics Line2D*
    LookupOp Polygon QuadCurve2D* *RasterOp*
    RectangularShape* RescaleOp *Shape*
getBoundsAt(): JTabbedPane
getBoundsForIconOf(): DefaultDesktopManager
getBoxPainter(): StyleSheet
getBreakLocation(): Utilities
getBreakWeight(): View*
getBuffer(): StringWriter
getBufferedImageOp(): BufferedImageFilter
getBundle(): ResourceBundle*
getByName(): InetAddress
getByte(): java.lang.reflect.Array *CallableStatement* Field
    ResultSet
getByteParameter(): ParameterBlock
getBytes(): *Blob CallableStatement ResultSet* String
getCalendar(): DateFormat*
getCanonicalFile(): File
getCanonicalPath(): File
getCaret(): InputMethodEvent JTextComponent*
getCaretColor(): JTextComponent*
getCaretInfo(): TextLayout
getCaretPosition(): *AccessibleText* JTextComponent*
    JTextComponent.AccessibleJTextComponent*
    TextComponent* *TextComponentPeer*
getCaretShape(): TextLayout
getCaretShapes(): TextLayout
getCatalog(): *Connection*
getCatalogName(): *ResultSetMetaData*
getCatalogs(): *DatabaseMetaData*
getCatalogSeparator(): *DatabaseMetaData*
getCatalogTerm(): *DatabaseMetaData*
getCellBounds(): JList ListUI
getCellEditor(): JTable JTree TableColumn
getCellEditorValue(): *CellEditor* DefaultCellEditor
    DefaultCellEditor.EditorDelegate DefaultTreeCellEditor
getCellRect(): JTable
getCellRenderer(): JList JTable JTree TableColumn
getCellSelectionEnabled(): JTable
getCenterX(): RectangularShape*
getCenterY(): RectangularShape*

getCertificate( ): **K**eyStore
getCertificateAlias( ): **K**eyStore
getCertificateChain( ): **K**eyStore
getCertificates( ): **C**odeSource **J**arEntry **J**arURLConnection
getChange( ): **A**bstractDocument.DefaultDocumentEvent
  DocumentEvent
getChar( ): java.lang.reflect.**A**rray **F**ield
getCharacterAttribute( ): *AccessibleText**
  JTextComponent.AccessibleJTextComponent*
getCharacterAttributeRun( ): **S**tyledEditorKit*
getCharacterAttributes( ): **J**TextPane
getCharacterBounds( ): *AccessibleText**
  JTextComponent.AccessibleJTextComponent*
getCharacterCount( ): **T**extLayout
getCharacterElement( ): **D**efaultStyledDocument*
  StyledDocument
getCharacterInstance( ): **B**reakIterator
getCharacterLevel( ): **T**extLayout
getCharacterStream( ): *Clob* **R**esultSet
getCharCount( ): *AccessibleText**
  JTextComponent.AccessibleJTextComponent*
getCharIndex( ): **T**extHitInfo
getCharParameter( ): **P**arameterBlock
getChars( ): *AbstractDocument.Content* **G**apContent **S**tring
  StringBuffer **S**tringContent
getCharSetSpec( ): **C**hangedCharSetException
getCheckboxGroup( ): **C**heckbox
getChecksum( ): **C**heckedInputStream **C**heckedOutputStream
getChild( ): **C**ontainerEvent **D**efaultTreeModel *TreeModel*
getChildAfter( ): **D**efaultMutableTreeNode*
getChildAllocation( ): **V**iew*
getChildAt( ): **A**bstractDocument.AbstractElement*
  DefaultMutableTreeNode* *TreeNode**
getChildBeanContextChild( ): **B**eanContextSupport*
getChildBeanContextMembershipListener( ):
  BeanContextSupport*
getChildBeanContextServicesListener( ):
  BeanContextServicesSupport
getChildBefore( ): **D**efaultMutableTreeNode*
getChildCount( ): **A**bstractDocument.AbstractElement*
  DefaultMutableTreeNode* **D**efaultTreeModel *TreeModel*
  *TreeNode**
getChildIndices( ): **T**reeModelEvent
getChildPropertyChangeListener( ): **B**eanContextSupport*
getChildren( ): **T**reeModelEvent
getChildrenAdded( ): **A**bstractDocument.ElementEdit
  DocumentEvent.ElementChange
getChildrenRemoved( ): **A**bstractDocument.ElementEdit
  DocumentEvent.ElementChange
getChildSerializable( ): **B**eanContextSupport*
getChildVetoableChangeListener( ): **B**eanContextSupport*
getChildVisibility( ): **B**eanContextSupport*
getChoosableFileFilters( ): **J**FileChooser
getChooserPanels( ): **J**ColorChooser
getClass( ): java.lang.**O**bject
getClassAnnotation( ): **R**MIClassLoader
getClassContext( ): **S**ecurityManager*
getClasses( ): **C**lass
getClassLoader( ): **C**lass
getClassName( ): **A**ctivationDesc **A**ctivationGroupDesc
  MissingResourceException **U**IManager.LookAndFeelInfo
getClickCount( ): **M**ouseEvent*
getClickCountToStart( ): **D**efaultCellEditor
getClientHost( ): **R**emoteServer* *ServerRef*
getClientProperty( ): **J**Component*
getClip( ): **G**raphics*
getClipBounds( ): **G**raphics*
getClipRect( ): **G**raphics*
getClob( ): *CallableStatement* **R**esultSet
getClosedIcon( ): **D**efaultTreeCellRenderer
getClosestPathForLocation( ): **J**Tree **T**reeUI
getClosestPositionTo( ): javax.swing.text.**P**aragraphView*

getClosestRowForLocation( ): **J**Tree
getCodeBase( ): **A**pplet* *AppletStub*
getCodeSource( ): **P**rotectionDomain
getCollationElementIterator( ): **R**uleBasedCollator
getCollationKey( ): **C**ollator*
getColor( ): **C**olor* **D**efaultHighlighter.DefaultHighlightPainter
  Graphics* **J**ColorChooser **U**IDefaults **U**IManager
getColor1( ): **G**radientPaint
getColor2( ): **G**radientPaint
getColorComponents( ): **C**olor*
getColorFromModel( ): **A**bstractColorChooserPanel
getColorModel( ): **B**ufferedImage **C**omponent*
  *ComponentPeer** **G**raphicsConfiguration *PaintContext*
  PixelGrabber *RenderedImage** **T**oolkit
getColorSelectionModel( ): **A**bstractColorChooserPanel
getColorSpace( ): **C**olor* **C**olorModel*
getColorSpaceType( ): **I**CC_Profile*
getColumn( ): **D**efaultTableColumnModel **J**Table
  TableColumnModel **T**ableModelEvent
getColumnClass( ): **A**bstractTableModel* **J**Table *TableModel*
getColumnClassName( ): *ResultSetMetaData*
getColumnCount( ): **A**bstractTableModel*
  DefaultTableColumnModel **J**Table *ResultSetMetaData*
  TableColumnModel **T**ableModel **T**ableView.TableCell
getColumnDisplaySize( ): *ResultSetMetaData*
getColumnHeader( ): **J**ScrollPane **S**crollPaneLayout*
getColumnIndex( ): **D**efaultTableColumnModel
  TableColumnModel
getColumnIndexAtX( ): **D**efaultTableColumnModel
  TableColumnModel
getColumnLabel( ): *ResultSetMetaData*
getColumnMargin( ): **D**efaultTableColumnModel
  TableColumnModel
getColumnModel( ): **J**Table **J**TableHeader
getColumnName( ): **A**bstractTableModel* **J**Table
  ResultSetMetaData *TableModel*
getColumnPrivileges( ): *DatabaseMetaData*
getColumns( ): *DatabaseMetaData* **D**efaultTableColumnModel
  GridLayout **J**TextArea **J**TextField* *TableColumnModel*
  TextArea **T**extField
getColumnSelectionAllowed( ): **D**efaultTableColumnModel
  JTable *TableColumnModel*
getColumnType( ): *ResultSetMetaData*
getColumnTypeName( ): *ResultSetMetaData*
getColumnWidth( ): **J**TextArea **J**TextField*
getCommandEnvironment( ): **A**ctivationGroupDesc
getCommandOptions( ):
  ActivationGroupDesc.CommandEnvironment
getCommandPath( ):
  ActivationGroupDesc.CommandEnvironment
getComment( ): **Z**ipEntry*
getCommittedCharacterCount( ): **I**nputMethodEvent
getCommittedText( ): *InputMethodRequests*
getCommittedTextLength( ): *InputMethodRequests*
getComponent( ): **A**ncestorEvent
  BeanContextChildComponentProxy **C**omponentEvent*
  ComponentView* **C**ontainer* **D**efaultCaret **D**efaultCellEditor
  DragGestureEvent **D**ragGestureRecognizer*
  DragSourceContext **D**ropTarget **D**ropTargetContext
  MenuElement **R**enderer *StyleConstants**
getComponentAfter( ): **D**efaultFocusManager
getComponentAt( ): **C**omponent*
getComponentAtIndex( ): **J**MenuBar **J**PopupMenu **J**ToolBar
getComponentBefore( ): **D**efaultFocusManager
getComponentCount( ): **C**ontainer*
getComponentCountInLayer( ): **J**LayeredPane*
getComponentGraphics( ): **J**Component*
getComponentIndex( ): **J**MenuBar **J**PopupMenu **J**ToolBar
getComponentOrientation( ): **C**omponent*
getComponents( ): **C**olor* **C**olorModel* **C**ontainer*
getComponentsInLayer( ): **J**LayeredPane*
getComponentSize( ): **C**olorModel*

G

getComponentToLayer(): **J**LayeredPane*
getComponentType(): **C**lass
getComposite(): **G**raphics2D
getCompressedSize(): **Z**ipEntry*
getCompressionThreshold(): **S**tyleContext*
getConcurrency(): *ResultSet*
getConditionForKeyStroke(): **J**Component*
getConfigurations(): **G**raphicsDevice
getConnection(): *DatabaseMetaData* **D**riverManager
   *Statement**
getConstraints(): **G**ridBagLayout
getConstructor(): **C**lass
getConstructors(): **C**lass
getContainer(): *BeanContextContainerProxy* **C**ontainerEvent
   View*
getContent(): **A**bstractDocument* **C**ontentHandler
   javax.swing.text.html.parser.**E**lement **U**RL **U**RLConnection*
getContentEncoding(): **U**RLConnection*
getContentLength(): **U**RLConnection*
getContentPane(): **J**Applet **J**Dialog **J**Frame **J**InternalFrame
   JRootPane **J**Window *RootPaneContainer*
getContents(): **C**lipboard **L**istResourceBundle*
getContentType(): **E**ditorKit* **J**EditorPane* **U**RLConnection*
getContentTypeFor(): *FileNameMap*
getContext(): **A**ccessController
getContextClassLoader(): **T**hread
getCopies(): **P**rinterJob
getCorner(): **J**ScrollPane **S**crollPaneLayout*
getCountry(): **L**ocale
getCrc(): **Z**ipEntry*
getCreationDate(): **K**eyStore
getCriticalExtensionOIDs(): **X**509Certificate **X**509CRL
   X509CRLEntry *X509Extension*
getCrossPlatformLookAndFeelClassName(): **U**IManager
getCrossReference(): *DatabaseMetaData*
getCrtCoefficient(): *RSAPrivateCrtKey* **R**SAPrivateCrtKeySpec
getCtrlP1(): **C**ubicCurve2D*
getCtrlP2(): **C**ubicCurve2D*
getCtrlPt(): **Q**uadCurve2D*
getCtrlX(): **Q**uadCurve2D*
getCtrlX1(): **C**ubicCurve2D*
getCtrlX2(): **C**ubicCurve2D*
getCtrlY(): **Q**uadCurve2D*
getCtrlY1(): **C**ubicCurve2D*
getCtrlY2(): **C**ubicCurve2D*
getCurrencyInstance(): **N**umberFormat*
getCurrencySymbol(): **D**ecimalFormatSymbols
getCurrent(): **C**heckboxGroup
getCurrentAccessibleValue():
   AbstractButton.AccessibleAbstractButton*
   AccessibleValue **J**InternalFrame.AccessibleJInternalFrame
   JInternalFrame.JDesktopIcon.AccessibleJDesktopIcon
   JProgressBar.AccessibleJProgressBar
   JScrollBar.AccessibleJScrollBar **J**Slider.AccessibleJSlider
   JSplitPane.AccessibleJSplitPane
getCurrentDataFlavors(): **D**ropTargetContext
   DropTargetDragEvent **D**ropTargetDropEvent
getCurrentDataFlavorsAsList(): **D**ropTargetContext
   DropTargetDragEvent **D**ropTargetDropEvent
getCurrentDirectory(): **J**FileChooser
getCurrentLine(): **P**arser*
getCurrentManager(): **F**ocusManager*
getCurrentPoint(): **G**eneralPath
getCurrentPos(): **P**arser*
getCurrentServiceClasses(): *BeanContextServices*
   BeanContextServicesSupport
getCurrentServiceSelectors():
   BeanContextServiceAvailableEvent
   BeanContextServiceProvider *BeanContextServices*
   BeanContextServicesSupport
   BeanContextServicesSupport.BCSSProxyServiceProvider
getCurrentWriter(): **A**bstractDocument*

getCursor(): *AccessibleComponent*
   Box.AccessibleBox **B**ox.Filler.AccessibleBoxFiller
   CellRendererPane.AccessibleCellRendererPane
   Component* **D**ragSourceContext
   JApplet.AccessibleJApplet
   JComponent.AccessibleJComponent*
   JDialog.AccessibleJDialog **J**Frame.AccessibleJFrame
   JList.AccessibleJList.AccessibleJListChild
   JPopupMenu.WindowPopup.AccessibleWindowPopup
   JTable.AccessibleJTable.AccessibleJTableCell
   JTableHeader.AccessibleJTableHeader↵
   .AccessibleJTableHeaderEntry
   JTree.AccessibleJTree.AccessibleJTreeNode
   JWindow.AccessibleJWindow
getCursorName(): *ResultSet*
getCursorType(): **F**rame*
getCustomEditor(): *PropertyEditor* **P**ropertyEditorSupport
getCustomizerClass(): **B**eanDescriptor
getDashArray(): **B**asicStroke
getDashPhase(): **B**asicStroke
getData(): **A**ctivationDesc **A**ctivationGroupDesc
   BufferedImage **D**ataBufferByte **D**ataBufferInt
   DataBufferShort **D**ataBufferUShort **D**atagramPacket **E**ntity
   ICC_Profile* *RenderedImage**
getDatabaseProductName(): *DatabaseMetaData*
getDatabaseProductVersion(): *DatabaseMetaData*
getDataBitOffset(): **M**ultiPixelPackedSampleModel
getDataBuffer(): **R**aster*
getDataElement(): **C**olorModel*
getDataElements(): **C**olorModel* **R**aster* **S**ampleModel*
getDataSize(): **D**ataTruncation
getDataType(): **D**ataBuffer* **S**ampleModel*
getDataTypeSize(): **D**ataBuffer*
getDataVector(): **D**efaultTableModel
getDate(): *CallableStatement* java.util.**D**ate* *ResultSet*
   URLConnection*
getDateFormatSymbols(): **S**impleDateFormat
getDateInstance(): **D**ateFormat*
getDateTimeInstance(): **D**ateFormat*
getDay(): java.util.**D**ate*
getDebugGraphicsOptions(): **J**Component*
getDebugOptions(): **D**ebugGraphics
getDecimalFormatSymbols(): **D**ecimalFormat
getDecimalSeparator(): **D**ecimalFormatSymbols
getDeclaration(): **S**tyleSheet
getDeclaredClasses(): **C**lass
getDeclaredConstructor(): **C**lass
getDeclaredConstructors(): **C**lass
getDeclaredField(): **C**lass
getDeclaredFields(): **C**lass
getDeclaredMethod(): **C**lass
getDeclaredMethods(): **C**lass
getDeclaringClass(): **C**lass **C**onstructor **F**ield *Member*
   Method
getDecomposition(): **C**ollator*
getDeepestComponentAt(): **S**wingUtilities
getDefault(): **L**ocale **T**imeZone*
getDefaultAction(): *Keymap*
getDefaultActions(): **D**ropTarget
getDefaultAllowUserInteraction(): **U**RLConnection*
getDefaultButton(): **J**RootPane
getDefaultChooserPanels(): **C**olorChooserComponentFactory
getDefaultClosedIcon(): **D**efaultTreeCellRenderer
getDefaultCloseOperation(): **J**Dialog **J**Frame **J**InternalFrame
getDefaultConfiguration(): **G**raphicsDevice
getDefaultCursor(): **C**ursor
getDefaultDragSource(): **D**ragSource
getDefaultEditor(): **J**Table
getDefaultEventIndex(): *BeanInfo** **S**impleBeanInfo
getDefaultFlavorMap(): **S**ystemFlavorMap
getDefaultLeafIcon(): **D**efaultTreeCellRenderer
getDefaultLightWeightPopupEnabled(): **J**PopupMenu

getDefaultOpenIcon(): DefaultTreeCellRenderer
getDefaultPropertyIndex(): *BeanInfo* SimpleBeanInfo
getDefaultRenderer(): JTable
getDefaultRequestProperty(): URLConnection*
getDefaultRootElement(): AbstractDocument* *Document*
getDefaults(): LookAndFeel UIManager
getDefaultScreenDevice(): GraphicsEnvironment
getDefaultSocketFactory(): RMISocketFactory
getDefaultStream(): LogStream
getDefaultStyleContext(): StyleContext*
getDefaultToolkit(): Toolkit
getDefaultTransactionIsolation(): *DatabaseMetaData*
getDefaultTransform(): GraphicsConfiguration
getDefaultTreeModel(): JTree
getDefaultType(): KeyStore
getDefaultUseCaches(): URLConnection*
getDefaultValue(): CSS.Attribute
getDelay(): JMenu Timer
getDepth(): DefaultMutableTreeNode*
getDescendantToggledPaths(): JTree
getDescent(): FontMetrics GraphicAttribute* LineMetrics
    TextLayout
getDescription(): javax.swing.filechooser.FileFilter FileView
    HyperlinkEvent* ImageIcon JFileChooser LookAndFeel
getDesignAxisDefaults(): *MultipleMaster*
getDesignAxisNames(): *MultipleMaster*
getDesignAxisRanges(): *MultipleMaster*
getDesktopIcon(): JInternalFrame
getDesktopManager(): JDesktopPane
getDesktopPane(): JInternalFrame
    JInternalFrame.JDesktopIcon
getDesktopPaneForComponent(): JOptionPane
getDesktopProperty(): Toolkit
getDeterminant(): AffineTransform
getDevice(): GraphicsConfiguration
getDeviceConfiguration(): Graphics2D
getDialogTitle(): FileChooserUI JFileChooser
getDialogType(): JFileChooser
getDigestLength(): MessageDigest
getDigit(): DecimalFormatSymbols
getDimension(): UIDefaults UIManager
getDirection(): DefaultStyledDocument.ElementSpec
getDirectory(): FileDialog
getDirtyRegion(): RepaintManager
getDisabledIcon(): AbstractButton* JLabel*
getDisabledIconAt(): JTabbedPane
getDisabledSelectedIcon(): AbstractButton*
getDisabledTextColor(): JTextComponent*
getDismissDelay(): ToolTipManager
getDisplayCountry(): Locale
getDisplayedMnemonic(): JLabel*
getDisplayLanguage(): Locale
getDisplayName(): AbstractColorChooserPanel
    FeatureDescriptor* Locale TimeZone*
getDisplayVariant(): Locale
getDividerLocation(): JSplitPane SplitPaneUI
getDividerSize(): JSplitPane
getDocument(): AbstractDocument.AbstractElement*
    AbstractDocument.DefaultDocumentEvent AbstractWriter*
    DocumentEvent javax.swing.text.*Element* JTextComponent*
    View*
getDocumentBase(): Applet* *AppletStub*
getDocumentProperties(): AbstractDocument*
getDoInput(): URLConnection*
getDoOutput(): URLConnection*
getDot(): *Caret* CaretEvent DefaultCaret
getDouble(): java.lang.reflect.Array *CallableStatement* Field
    ResultSet
getDoubleBufferMaximumSize(): RepaintManager
getDoubleParameter(): ParameterBlock
getDragAction(): DragGestureEvent
getDraggedColumn(): JTableHeader

getDraggedDistance(): JTableHeader
getDragOrigin(): DragGestureEvent
getDragSource(): DragGestureEvent DragGestureRecognizer*
    DragSourceContext
getDragSourceContext(): DragSourceEvent*
getDrawsLayeredHighlights(): DefaultHighlighter
getDriver(): DriverManager
getDriverMajorVersion(): *DatabaseMetaData*
getDriverMinorVersion(): *DatabaseMetaData*
getDriverName(): *DatabaseMetaData*
getDrivers(): DriverManager
getDriverVersion(): *DatabaseMetaData*
getDropAction(): DragSourceDragEvent
    DragSourceDropEvent DropTargetDragEvent
    DropTargetDropEvent
getDropSuccess(): DragSourceDropEvent
getDropTarget(): Component* DropTargetContext
getDropTargetContext(): DropTarget DropTargetEvent*
getDSTSavings(): SimpleTimeZone
getDTD(): DTD
getEchoChar(): JPasswordField TextField
getEdgeCondition(): ConvolveOp
getEdit(): UndoableEditEvent
getEditingColumn(): JTable
getEditingPath(): JTree TreeUI
getEditingRow(): JTable
getEditor(): JComboBox StyledEditorKit.StyledTextAction*
getEditorComponent(): *ComboBoxEditor* JTable
getEditorKit(): JEditorPane* TextUI
getEditorKitForContentType(): JEditorPane*
getEditorSearchPath(): PropertyEditorManager
getElem(): DataBuffer*
getElemDouble(): DataBuffer*
getElement(): AbstractDocument.AbstractElement*
    AbstractDocument.ElementEdit
    DocumentEvent.ElementChange DTD
    javax.swing.text.*Element* TagElement View*
getElementAt(): AbstractListModel* *ListModel*
getElementCount(): AbstractDocument.AbstractElement*
    javax.swing.text.*Element*
getElementIndex(): AbstractDocument.AbstractElement*
    javax.swing.text.*Element*
getElementIterator(): AbstractWriter*
getElements(): ButtonGroup ContentModel
getElementsAt(): HTMLEditorKit.HTMLTextAction*
getElemFloat(): DataBuffer*
getEmptySet(): *AbstractDocument.AttributeContext*
    StyleContext*
getEncoded(): AlgorithmParameters
    java.security.cert.Certificate* EncodedKeySpec* *Key*
    X509CRL X509CRLEntry
getEncoding(): InputStreamReader* OutputStreamWriter*
getEndCap(): BasicStroke
getEndIndex(): AccessibleHyperlink* *CharacterIterator*
    FieldPosition StringCharacterIterator
getEndOffset(): AbstractDocument.AbstractElement*
    javax.swing.text.*Element* Highlighter.Highlight
    HTMLDocument.Iterator View*
getEndPoint(): Arc2D*
getEndPosition(): AbstractDocument* *Document*
getEntity(): DTD
getEntries(): Manifest
getEntry(): ZipFile*
getEntryName(): JarURLConnection
getenv(): System
getEras(): DateFormatSymbols
getErrorCode(): SQLException*
getErrorIndex(): ParsePosition
getErrorOffset(): ParseException
getErrorsAny(): MediaTracker
getErrorsID(): MediaTracker
getErrorStream(): HttpURLConnection Process

G

getEtchedBorderUIResource( ): BorderUIResource
getEtchType( ): EtchedBorder*
getEventSetDescriptors( ): *BeanInfo* SimpleBeanInfo
getEventType( ): HyperlinkEvent*
getException( ): ClassNotFoundException
    ExceptionInInitializerError InvocationEvent
    PrivilegedActionException
getExceptionTypes( ): Constructor Method
getExpandedDescendants( ): JTree
getExpandedState( ): AbstractLayoutCache*
getExpiration( ): URLConnection*
getExportedKeys( ): *DatabaseMetaData*
getExtensionValue( ): X509Certificate X509CRL
    X509CRLEntry *X509Extension*
getExtent( ): *BoundedRangeModel*
    DefaultBoundedRangeModel JSlider
getExtentSize( ): JViewport
getExtra( ): ZipEntry*
getExtraNameCharacters( ): *DatabaseMetaData*
getFailureHandler( ): RMISocketFactory
getFamily( ): Font*
getFD( ): FileInputStream FileOutputStream
    RandomAccessFile
getFetchDirection( ): *ResultSet Statement*
getFetchSize( ): *ResultSet Statement*
getField( ): Class FieldPosition ObjectStreamClass
getFields( ): Class ObjectStreamClass
getFile( ): FileDialog URL
getFileDescriptor( ): DatagramSocketImpl SocketImpl
getFileFilter( ): JFileChooser
getFilenameFilter( ): FileDialog
getFileNameMap( ): URLConnection*
getFilePointer( ): RandomAccessFile
getFiles( ): FileSystemView
getFileSelectionMode( ): JFileChooser
getFileSystemView( ): FileSystemView JFileChooser
getFileView( ): FileChooserUI JFileChooser
getFilterInstance( ): ImageFilter*
getFirst( ): LinkedList
getFirstChild( ): DefaultMutableTreeNode*
getFirstComponent( ): DefaultFocusManager
getFirstDayOfWeek( ): Calendar*
getFirstIndex( ): ListSelectionEvent
getFirstLeaf( ): DefaultMutableTreeNode*
getFirstLineIndent( ): StyleConstants*
getFirstRow( ): TableModelEvent
getFirstVisibleIndex( ): JList
getFixedCellHeight( ): JList
getFixedCellWidth( ): JList
getFlatness( ): CubicCurve2D* FlatteningPathIterator
    QuadCurve2D*
getFlatnessSq( ): CubicCurve2D* QuadCurve2D*
getFlavorMap( ): DragSource DropTarget
getFlavorsForNatives( ): *FlavorMap* SystemFlavorMap
getFloat( ): java.lang.reflect.Array *CallableStatement* Field
    ResultSet
getFloatParameter( ): ParameterBlock
getFocusAccelerator( ): JTextComponent*
getFocusedComponent( ): TextAction*
getFocusOwner( ): Window*
getFollowRedirects( ): HttpURLConnection
getFont( ): *AccessibleComponent*
    Box.AccessibleBox Box.Filler.AccessibleBoxFiller
    CellRendererPane.AccessibleCellRendererPane
    Component* DefaultStyledDocument*
    DefaultTreeCellEditor Font* FontMetrics
    GlyphVector Graphics* JApplet.AccessibleJApplet
    JComponent.AccessibleJComponent*
    JDialog.AccessibleJDialog JFrame.AccessibleJFrame
    JList.AccessibleJList.AccessibleJListChild
    JPopupMenu.WindowPopup.AccessibleWindowPopup
    JTable.AccessibleJTable.AccessibleJTableCell

JTableHeader.AccessibleJTableHeader ↵
    .AccessibleJTableHeaderEntry
    JTree.AccessibleJTree.AccessibleJTreeNode
    JWindow.AccessibleJWindow LabelView*
    MenuComponent* *MenuContainer* StyleContext*
    StyledDocument TitledBorder* UIDefaults UIManager
getFontFamily( ): StyleConstants*
getFontList( ): Toolkit
getFontMetrics( ): *AccessibleComponent*
    Box.AccessibleBox Box.Filler.AccessibleBoxFiller
    CellRendererPane.AccessibleCellRendererPane
    Component* *ComponentPeer* FieldView*
    Graphics* JApplet.AccessibleJApplet
    JComponent.AccessibleJComponent*
    JDialog.AccessibleJDialog JFrame.AccessibleJFrame
    JList.AccessibleJList.AccessibleJListChild
    JPopupMenu.WindowPopup.AccessibleWindowPopup
    JTable.AccessibleJTable.AccessibleJTableCell
    JTableHeader.AccessibleJTableHeader ↵
    .AccessibleJTableHeaderEntry
    JTree.AccessibleJTree.AccessibleJTreeNode
    JWindow.AccessibleJWindow LabelView* StyleContext*
    Toolkit
getFontName( ): Font*
getFontPeer( ): Toolkit
getFontRenderContext( ): GlyphVector Graphics2D
getFontSize( ): StyleConstants*
getFontTable( ): *OpenType*
getFontTableSize( ): *OpenType*
getForeground( ): *AccessibleComponent*
    Box.AccessibleBox Box.Filler.AccessibleBoxFiller
    CellRendererPane.AccessibleCellRendererPane
    Component* DefaultStyledDocument*
    JApplet.AccessibleJApplet
    JComponent.AccessibleJComponent*
    JDialog.AccessibleJDialog JFrame.AccessibleJFrame
    JList.AccessibleJList.AccessibleJListChild
    JPopupMenu.WindowPopup.AccessibleWindowPopup
    JTable.AccessibleJTable.AccessibleJTableCell
    JTableHeader.AccessibleJTableHeader ↵
    .AccessibleJTableHeaderEntry
    JTree.AccessibleJTree.AccessibleJTreeNode
    JWindow.AccessibleJWindow StyleConstants*
    StyleContext* *StyledDocument*
getForegroundAt( ): JTabbedPane
getFormat( ): *java.security.Certificate* EncodedKeySpec* *Key**
getFormats( ): ChoiceFormat MessageFormat
getFrame( ): RectangularShape*
getFrameForComponent( ): JOptionPane
getFrameIcon( ): JInternalFrame
getFrames( ): Frame*
getFromIndex( ): TableColumnModelEvent
getG( ): DSAParameterSpec *DSAParams* DSAPrivateKeySpec
    DSAPublicKeySpec
getGamma( ): ICC_ProfileGray ICC_ProfileRGB
getGestureModifiers( ): DragSourceDragEvent
getGlassPane( ): JApplet JDialog JFrame JInternalFrame
    JRootPane JWindow *RootPaneContainer*
getGlyphCode( ): GlyphVector
getGlyphCodes( ): GlyphVector
getGlyphJustificationInfo( ): GlyphVector
getGlyphLogicalBounds( ): GlyphVector
getGlyphMetrics( ): GlyphVector
getGlyphOutline( ): GlyphVector
getGlyphPosition( ): GlyphVector
getGlyphPositions( ): GlyphVector
getGlyphTransform( ): GlyphVector
getGlyphVisualBounds( ): GlyphVector
getGraphics( ): Component* *ComponentPeer* Image*
    PrintJob
getGreatestMinimum( ): Calendar*
getGreen( ): Color* ColorModel*

getGreenMask( ): **D**irectColorModel
getGreens( ): **I**ndexColorModel
getGregorianChange( ): **G**regorianCalendar
getGridColor( ): **J**Table
getGridColumn( ): **T**ableView.TableCell
getGridRow( ): **T**ableView.TableCell
getGroupID( ): **A**ctivationDesc
getGroupingSeparator( ): **D**ecimalFormatSymbols
getGroupingSize( ): **D**ecimalFormat
getGuarantor( ): *java.security.***C**ertificate
getHAdjustable( ): **S**crollPane
getHeaderField( ): **U**RLConnection*
getHeaderFieldDate( ): **U**RLConnection*
getHeaderFieldInt( ): **U**RLConnection*
getHeaderFieldKey( ): **U**RLConnection*
getHeaderRect( ): **J**TableHeader
getHeaderRenderer( ): **T**ableColumn
getHeaderValue( ): **T**ableColumn
getHeight( ): **B**oxView* **C**omponent* **D**imension2D*
    FontMetrics **I**mage* **K**ernel **L**ineMetrics **P**ageFormat
    Paper **P**ixelGrabber **R**aster* **R**ectangularShape*
    RenderableImage **R**enderableImageOp *RenderedImage**
    SampleModel*
getHelpMenu( ): **J**MenuBar **M**enuBar
getHgap( ): **B**orderLayout **C**ardLayout **F**lowLayout **G**ridLayout
getHighlightColor( ): **E**tchedBorder*
getHighlighter( ): **J**TextComponent*
getHighlightInnerColor( ): **B**evelBorder*
getHighlightOuterColor( ): **B**evelBorder*
getHighlights( ): *Highlighter* **L**ayeredHighlighter*
getHomeDirectory( ): **F**ileSystemView
getHorizontalAlignment( ): **A**bstractButton* **J**Label*
    JTextField*
getHorizontalScrollBar( ): **J**ScrollPane **S**crollPaneLayout*
getHorizontalScrollBarPolicy( ): **J**ScrollPane
    ScrollPaneLayout*
getHorizontalTextPosition( ): **A**bstractButton* **J**Label*
getHorizontalVisibility( ): **J**TextField*
getHost( ): **U**RL
getHostAddress( ): **I**netAddress
getHostName( ): **I**netAddress
getHours( ): **j**ava.util.Date*
getHSBColor( ): **C**olor*
getHScrollbarHeight( ): **S**crollPane *ScrollPanePeer*
getHTMLDocument( ): **H**TMLEditorKit.HTMLTextAction*
getHTMLEditorKit( ): **H**TMLEditorKit.HTMLTextAction*
getHTMLTag( ): **T**agElement
getHumanPresentableName( ): **D**ataFlavor
getICC_Profiles( ): **C**olorConvertOp
getIcon( ): **A**bstractButton* *BeanInfo** **F**ileView **J**FileChooser
    JLabel* **J**OptionPane **S**impleBeanInfo **S**tyleConstants*
    UIDefaults **U**IManager
getIconAt( ): **J**TabbedPane
getIconHeight( ): *Icon* **I**conUIResource **I**mageIcon
getIconImage( ): **F**rame*
getIconTextGap( ): **J**Label*
getIconWidth( ): *Icon* **I**conUIResource **I**mageIcon
getID( ): **A**ctivatable **A**WTEvent* **L**ookAndFeel **T**imeZone*
getId( ): **A**pplicationException
getIdentifier( ): **T**ableColumn
getIdentifierQuoteString( ): *DatabaseMetaData*
getIdentity( ): **I**dentityScope
getIDstring( ): **G**raphicsDevice
getIfModifiedSince( ): **U**RLConnection*
getImage( ): **A**pplet* *AppletContext* **I**mageIcon **T**exturePaint
    Toolkit
getImageableHeight( ): **P**ageFormat **P**aper
getImageableWidth( ): **P**ageFormat **P**aper
getImageableX( ): **P**ageFormat **P**aper
getImageableY( ): **P**ageFormat **P**aper
getImageLoadStatus( ): **I**mageIcon
getImageObserver( ): **I**mageIcon

getImplementationTitle( ): **P**ackage
getImplementationVendor( ): **P**ackage
getImplementationVersion( ): **P**ackage
getImportedKeys( ): *DatabaseMetaData*
getInCheck( ): **S**ecurityManager*
getIndex( ): **A**bstractDocument.AbstractElement*
    AbstractDocument.ElementEdit *CharacterIterator**
    DataTruncation **D**efaultMutableTreeNode*
    DocumentEvent.ElementChange
    javax.swing.text.html.parser.**E**lement **P**arsePosition
    StringCharacterIterator *TreeNode**
getIndex0( ): **L**istDataEvent
getIndex1( ): **L**istDataEvent
getIndexAtPoint( ): *AccessibleText**
    JTextComponent.AccessibleJTextComponent*
getIndexedPropertyType( ): **I**ndexedPropertyDescriptor
getIndexedReadMethod( ): **I**ndexedPropertyDescriptor
getIndexedWriteMethod( ): **I**ndexedPropertyDescriptor
getIndexInfo( ): *DatabaseMetaData*
getIndexOf( ): **D**efaultComboBoxModel **J**LayeredPane*
getIndexOfChild( ): **D**efaultTreeModel *TreeModel*
getIndexOfSize( ): **S**tyleSheet
getInetAddress( ): **D**atagramSocket* **S**erverSocket **S**ocket
    SocketImpl
getInfinity( ): **D**ecimalFormatSymbols
getInfo( ): **I**dentity* **P**rovider
getInitialDelay( ): **T**imer **T**oolTipManager
getInitialSelectionValue( ): **J**OptionPane
getInitialValue( ): **J**OptionPane
getInputAttributes( ): **J**TextPane **S**tyledEditorKit*
getInputContext( ): **C**omponent*
getInputMethodControlObject( ): **I**nputContext
getInputMethodRequests( ): **C**omponent*
getInputStream( ): **A**pplicationException **P**rocess *RemoteCall*
    Socket **S**ocketImpl **U**RLConnection* **Z**ipFile*
getInputValue( ): **J**OptionPane
getInsertionIndex( ): **T**extHitInfo
getInsertPositionOffset( ): *InputMethodRequests*
getInset( ): **S**tyleSheet.BoxPainter
getInsets( ): **C**ontainer* *ContainerPeer* **U**IDefaults
    UIManager
getInsideAllocation( ): **C**ompositeView*
getInsideBorder( ): **C**ompoundBorder*
getInstalledLookAndFeels( ): **U**IManager
getInstance( ): **A**lgorithmParameterGenerator
    AlgorithmParameters **A**lphaComposite **C**alendar*
    CertificateFactory **C**ollator* **C**olorSpace* **D**ateFormat*
    ICC_Profile* **I**nputContext **K**eyFactory **K**eyPairGenerator
    KeyStore **M**essageDigest **N**umberFormat* **S**ecureRandom
    Signature
getInstanceOf( ): **B**eans
getInt( ): **j**ava.lang.reflect.Array *CallableStatement* **F**ield
    ResultSet **U**IDefaults **U**IManager
getInteger( ): **I**nteger
getIntegerAttributeValue( ): **H**TML
getIntercellSpacing( ): **J**Table
getInterface( ): **M**ulticastSocket
getInterfaces( ): **C**lass
getInteriorRectangle( ): **A**bstractBorder*
getInternalFrame( ): **J**InternalFrame.JDesktopIcon
getInternationalCurrencySymbol( ): **D**ecimalFormatSymbols
getInterpolationType( ): **A**ffineTransformOp
getIntParameter( ): **P**arameterBlock
getInverted( ): **J**Slider
getInvoker( ): **J**PopupMenu
getInvokesStopCellEditing( ): **J**Tree
getIOException( ): **P**rinterIOException
getISO3Country( ): **L**ocale
getISO3Language( ): **L**ocale
getISOCountries( ): **L**ocale
getISOLanguages( ): **L**ocale
getIssuerDN( ): **X**509Certificate **X**509CRL

G

getIssuerUniqueID(): X509Certificate
getItalicAngle(): Font*
getItem(): Choice *ComboBoxEditor* ItemEvent JMenu
  java.awt.List Menu*
getItemAt(): JComboBox
getItemCount(): Choice JComboBox JMenu java.awt.List
  Menu*
getItems(): java.awt.List
getItemSelectable(): ItemEvent
getIterator(): AttributedString HTMLDocument
getJarEntry(): JarFile JarURLConnection
getJarFile(): JarURLConnection
getJarFileURL(): JarURLConnection
getJavaInitializationString(): *PropertyEditor*
  PropertyEditorSupport
getJMenuBar(): JApplet JDialog JFrame JInternalFrame
  JRootPane
getJobName(): PrinterJob
getJustificationInfo(): GraphicAttribute*
getJustifiedLayout(): TextLayout
getKernel(): ConvolveOp
getKernelData(): Kernel
getKey(): KeyStore *Map.Entry* MenuShortcut
  MissingResourceException
getKeyChar(): KeyEvent* KeyStroke
getKeyCode(): KeyEvent* KeyStroke
getKeymap(): JTextComponent*
getKeyModifiersText(): KeyEvent*
getKeys(): ResourceBundle*
getKeySelectionManager(): JComboBox
getKeySpec(): KeyFactory
getKeyStroke(): KeyStroke
getKeyStrokeForEvent(): KeyStroke
getKeyStrokesForAction(): *Keymap*
getKeyText(): KeyEvent*
getKeyUsage(): X509Certificate
getLabel(): AbstractButton* Button Checkbox JPopupMenu
  MenuItem* Option
getLabelFor(): JLabel*
getLabelTable(): JSlider
getLanguage(): Locale
getLargeDisplayIcon(): AbstractColorChooserPanel
getLast(): LinkedList
getLastChild(): DefaultMutableTreeNode*
getLastComponent(): DefaultFocusManager
getLastDividerLocation(): JSplitPane
getLastIndex(): ListSelectionEvent
getLastLeaf(): DefaultMutableTreeNode*
getLastModified(): URLConnection*
getLastPathComponent(): TreePath
getLastRow(): TableModelEvent
getLastSelectedPathComponent(): JTree
getLastVisibleIndex(): JList
getLayer(): JInternalFrame JLayeredPane*
getLayeredPane(): JApplet JDialog JFrame JInternalFrame
  JRootPane JWindow *RootPaneContainer*
getLayeredPaneAbove(): JLayeredPane*
getLayout(): Container*
getLayoutAlignmentX(): BorderLayout BoxLayout
  CardLayout GridBagLayout JRootPane.RootLayout
  LayoutManager2 OverlayLayout
getLayoutAlignmentY(): BorderLayout BoxLayout
  CardLayout GridBagLayout JRootPane.RootLayout
  LayoutManager2 OverlayLayout
getLayoutDimensions(): GridBagLayout
GetLayoutInfo(): GridBagLayout
getLayoutOrigin(): GridBagLayout
getLayoutView(): javax.swing.text.ParagraphView*
getLayoutViewCount(): javax.swing.text.ParagraphView*
getLayoutWeights(): GridBagLayout
getLeader(): TabStop
getLeading(): FontMetrics LineMetrics TextLayout

getLeadSelectionIndex(): DefaultListSelectionModel JList
  ListSelectionModel
getLeadSelectionPath(): DefaultTreeSelectionModel* JTree
  TreeSelectionModel
getLeadSelectionRow(): DefaultTreeSelectionModel* JTree
  TreeSelectionModel
getLeafCount(): DefaultMutableTreeNode*
getLeafIcon(): DefaultTreeCellRenderer
getLeastMaximum(): Calendar*
getLeftComponent(): JSplitPane
getLeftIndent(): StyleConstants*
getLeftInset(): CompositeView*
getLength(): AbstractDocument*
  AbstractDocument.DefaultDocumentEvent
  java.lang.reflect.Array DatagramPacket
  DefaultStyledDocument.ElementSpec *Document*
  DocumentEvent
getLevel(): DefaultMutableTreeNode*
getLimit(): UndoManager
getLimits(): ChoiceFormat
getLineBuffer(): PlainView* WrappedPlainView
getLineColor(): LineBorder*
getLineCount(): JTextArea
getLineEndOffset(): JTextArea
getLineIncrement(): Scrollbar
getLineInstance(): BreakIterator
getLineJoin(): BasicStroke
getLineMetrics(): Font* FontMetrics
getLineNumber(): LineNumberInputStream
  LineNumberReader
getLineOfOffset(): JTextArea
getLineSpacing(): StyleConstants*
getLineStartOffset(): JTextArea
getLineWidth(): BasicStroke
getLineWrap(): JTextArea
getLink(): *AccessibleHypertext*
  JEditorPane.JEditorPaneAccessibleHypertextSupport
getLinkCount(): *AccessibleHypertext*
  JEditorPane.JEditorPaneAccessibleHypertextSupport
getLinkIndex(): *AccessibleHypertext*
  JEditorPane.JEditorPaneAccessibleHypertextSupport
getLinkText():
  JEditorPane.JEditorPaneAccessibleHypertextSupport
getListCellRendererComponent(): DefaultListCellRenderer*
  ListCellRenderer
getListenerCount(): EventListenerList
getListenerList(): EventListenerList
getListenerMethodDescriptors(): EventSetDescriptor
getListenerMethods(): EventSetDescriptor
getListenerType(): EventSetDescriptor
getListPainter(): StyleSheet
getLocalAddress(): DatagramSocket* Socket
getLocalBounds(): SwingUtilities
getLocale(): AccessibleContext* BeanContextSupport*
  Component* MessageFormat ResourceBundle*
getLocalGraphicsEnvironment(): GraphicsEnvironment
getLocalHost(): InetAddress
getLocalizedInputStream(): Runtime
getLocalizedMessage(): Throwable*
getLocalizedOutputStream(): Runtime
getLocalPatternChars(): DateFormatSymbols
getLocalPort(): DatagramSocket* DatagramSocketImpl
  ServerSocket Socket SocketImpl
getLocation(): *AccessibleComponent*
  ActivationDesc ActivationGroupDesc
  Box.AccessibleBox Box.Filler.AccessibleBoxFiller
  CellRendererPane.AccessibleCellRendererPane
  CodeSource Component* DropTargetDragEvent
  DropTargetDropEvent JApplet.AccessibleJApplet
  JComponent.AccessibleJComponent*
  JDialog.AccessibleJDialog JFrame.AccessibleJFrame
  JList.AccessibleJList.AccessibleJListChild

G

getMinorTickSpacing(): JSlider
getMinorVersion(): *Driver* ICC_Profile*
getMinSelectionIndex(): DefaultListSelectionModel JList
   ListSelectionModel
getMinSelectionRow(): DefaultTreeSelectionModel* JTree
   TreeSelectionModel
GetMinSize(): GridBagLayout
getMinTileX(): BufferedImage *RenderedImage**
getMinTileY(): BufferedImage *RenderedImage**
getMinusSign(): DecimalFormatSymbols
getMinutes(): java.util.Date*
getMinWidth(): TableColumn
getMinX(): BufferedImage Raster* RectangularShape*
   RenderableImage RenderableImageOp *RenderedImage**
getMinY(): BufferedImage Raster* RectangularShape*
   RenderableImage RenderableImageOp *RenderedImage**
getMissingGlyphCode(): Font*
getMiterLimit(): BasicStroke
getMnemonic(): AbstractButton* *ButtonModel*
   DefaultButtonModel*
getMode(): FileDialog
getModel(): AbstractButton* AbstractLayoutCache*
   JComboBox JList JProgressBar JScrollBar* JSlider
   JTabbedPane JTable JTree
getModelIndex(): TableColumn
getModifier(): AttributeList
getModifiers(): ActionEvent Class Constructor Field
   InputEvent* KeyStroke *Member* Method
getModulus(): *RSAPrivateKey** RSAPrivateKeySpec*
   RSAPublicKey RSAPublicKeySpec
getMonetaryDecimalSeparator(): DecimalFormatSymbols
getMonth(): java.util.Date*
getMonths(): DateFormatSymbols
getMoreResults(): *Statement**
getMultiplier(): DecimalFormat
getName(): AbstractDocument.AbstractElement* *Acl*
   AttributedCharacterIterator.Attribute* AttributeList
   Class Clipboard ColorSpace* Component*
   Constructor Cursor DTD *javax.swing.text.Element*
   javax.swing.text.html.parser.Element Entity
   FeatureDescriptor* Field File FileView Font* Identity*
   Keymap LookAndFeel *Member* MenuComponent*
   Method ObjectStreamClass ObjectStreamField Package
   java.security.Permission* *java.security.Principal** Provider
   Style StyleContext.NamedStyle Thread ThreadGroup
   UIManager.LookAndFeelInfo ZipEntry* ZipFile*
getNaN(): DecimalFormatSymbols
getNanos(): Timestamp
getNativeContainer(): Toolkit
getNativesForFlavors(): *FlavorMap* SystemFlavorMap
getNegativePrefix(): DecimalFormat
getNegativeSuffix(): DecimalFormat
getNewLeadSelectionPath(): TreeSelectionEvent
getNewValue(): PropertyChangeEvent
getNext(): AttributeList
getNextEastWestVisualPositionFrom(): CompositeView*
getNextEntry(): ZipInputStream*
getNextEvent(): EventQueue
getNextException(): SQLException*
getNextFocusableComponent(): JComponent*
getNextJarEntry(): JarInputStream
getNextLeaf(): DefaultMutableTreeNode*
getNextLeftHit(): TextLayout
getNextNode(): DefaultMutableTreeNode*
getNextNorthSouthVisualPositionFrom(): CompositeView*
getNextRightHit(): TextLayout
getNextSibling(): DefaultMutableTreeNode*
getNextUpdate(): X509CRL
getNextVisualPositionFrom(): TextUI View*
getNextWarning(): SQLWarning*
getNextWord(): Utilities

getNodeDimensions(): AbstractLayoutCache*
   AbstractLayoutCache.NodeDimensions
getNonCriticalExtensionOIDs(): X509Certificate X509CRL
   X509CRLEntry *X509Extension*
getNormalizedComponents(): ColorModel*
getNormalizingTransform(): GraphicsConfiguration
getNotAfter(): X509Certificate
getNotBefore(): X509Certificate
getNote(): ProgressMonitor
getNumBands(): Raster* SampleModel*
getNumBanks(): DataBuffer*
getNumberFormat(): DateFormat*
getNumberInstance(): NumberFormat*
getNumberOfPages(): Book *Pageable*
getNumChars(): LineMetrics
getNumColorComponents(): ColorModel*
getNumComponents(): ColorModel* ColorSpace*
   ICC_Profile* LookupTable*
getNumDataElements(): Raster* SampleModel*
getNumDesignAxes(): *MultipleMaster*
getNumericFunctions(): *DatabaseMetaData*
getNumericValue(): Character
getNumFactors(): RescaleOp
getNumGlyphs(): Font* GlyphVector
getNumParameters(): ParameterBlock
getNumSources(): ParameterBlock
getNumXTiles(): BufferedImage *RenderedImage**
getNumYTiles(): BufferedImage *RenderedImage**
getObject(): *CallableStatement* GuardedObject
   ResourceBundle* *ResultSet* SignedObject
getObjectForLayer(): JLayeredPane
getObjectParameter(): ParameterBlock
getObjectStreamClass(): ObjectInputStream.GetField
getOffscreenBuffer(): RepaintManager
getOffset(): AbstractDocument.DefaultDocumentEvent
   BoxView* CollationElementIterator
   ComponentSampleModel* DataBuffer*
   DatagramPacket DefaultStyledDocument.ElementSpec
   DocumentEvent LookupTable*
   MultiPixelPackedSampleModel ObjectStreamField *Position*
   SinglePixelPackedSampleModel TimeZone*
getOffsetHit(): TextHitInfo
getOffsets(): DataBuffer* RescaleOp
getOldLeadSelectionPath(): TreeSelectionEvent
getOldValue(): PropertyChangeEvent
getOpenIcon(): DefaultTreeCellRenderer
getOperation(): Operation
getOperations(): *Skeleton*
getOption(): DatagramSocketImpl SocketImpl *SocketOptions*
getOptions(): JOptionPane
getOptionType(): JOptionPane
getOrientation(): *Adjustable* ComponentOrientation
   JProgressBar JScrollBar* JSeparator* JSlider JSplitPane
   JToolBar PageFormat Scrollbar
getOtherHit(): TextHitInfo
getOutline(): GlyphVector TextLayout
getOutputStream(): LogStream Process *RemoteCall* Socket
   SocketImpl URLConnection*
getOutsideBorder(): CompoundBorder
getOwnedWindows(): Window*
getOwner(): Window*
getP(): DSAParameterSpec *DSAParams* DSAPrivateKeySpec
   DSAPublicKeySpec
getP1(): CubicCurve2D* Line2D* QuadCurve2D*
getP2(): CubicCurve2D* Line2D* QuadCurve2D*
getPackage(): Class ClassLoader* Package
getPackages(): ClassLoader* Package
getPage(): JEditorPane
getPageDimension(): PrintJob
getPageFormat(): Book *Pageable*
getPageIncrement(): Scrollbar
getPageResolution(): PrintJob

G

KeyPairGenerator KeyStore MessageDigest
SecureRandom Security Signature
getProviders(): Security
getPSName(): Font*
getPublic(): KeyPair
getPublicExponent(): *RSAPrivateCrtKey*
*R*SAPrivateCrtKeySpec *RSAPublicKey* RSAPublicKeySpec
getPublicKey(): *java.security.*Certificate
java.security.cert.Certificate* Identity*
getQ(): DSAParameterSpec *DSAParams* DSAPrivateKeySpec
DSAPublicKeySpec
getQueryTimeout(): *Statement*
getRaisedBevelBorderUIResource(): BorderUIResource
getRaster(): BufferedImage *PaintContext*
getRawOffset(): TimeZone*
getRead(): DataTruncation
getReader(): HTMLDocument
getReadMethod(): PropertyDescriptor*
getReceiveBufferSize(): DatagramSocket* Socket
getRecursionLimit(): FlatteningPathIterator
getRed(): Color* ColorModel*
getRedMask(): DirectColorModel
getRedoPresentationName(): AbstractUndoableEdit*
*U*ndoableEdit
getReds(): IndexColorModel
getRef(): *CallableStatement* RemoteObject* *ResultSet* URL
getRefClass(): *RemoteRef*
getRegisteredKeyStrokes(): JComponent*
getRegistry(): LocateRegistry
getRemaining(): Inflater
getRemoveListenerMethod(): EventSetDescriptor
getRenderableSource(): ParameterBlock
getRenderedSource(): ParameterBlock
getRenderer(): JComboBox
getRenderingHint(): Graphics2D
getRenderingHints(): AffineTransformOp BandCombineOp
BufferedImageOp ColorConvertOp ConvolveOp
Graphics2D LookupOp *RasterOp* RenderContext
RescaleOp
getReorderingAllowed(): JTableHeader
getRepresentationClass(): DataFlavor
getRequestingPort(): Authenticator
getRequestingPrompt(): Authenticator
getRequestingProtocol(): Authenticator
getRequestingScheme(): Authenticator
getRequestingSite(): Authenticator
getRequestMethod(): HttpURLConnection
getRequestProperty(): URLConnection*
getReshowDelay(): ToolTipManager
getResizable(): TableColumn
getResizeWeight(): View*
getResizingAllowed(): JTableHeader
getResizingColumn(): JTableHeader
getResolveParent(): AbstractDocument.AbstractElement*
*A*ttributeSet* *Keymap* SimpleAttributeSet
StyleContext.NamedStyle StyleContext.SmallAttributeSet
getResource(): *BeanContext* BeanContextSupport* Class
ClassLoader*
getResourceAsStream(): *BeanContext* BeanContextSupport*
Class ClassLoader*
getResources(): ClassLoader*
getResponseCode(): HttpURLConnection
getResponseMessage(): HttpURLConnection
getRestartMode(): ActivationDesc
getResultSet(): *java.sql.*Array *Statement*
getResultSetConcurrency(): *Statement*
getResultSetType(): *Statement*
getResultStream(): *RemoteCall*
getReturnType(): Method
getRevocationDate(): X509CRLEntry
getRevokedCertificate(): X509CRL
getRevokedCertificates(): X509CRL

getRGB(): BufferedImage Color* ColorModel*
getRGBColorComponents(): Color*
getRGBComponents(): Color*
getRGBdefault(): ColorModel*
getRGBs(): IndexColorModel
getRightComponent(): JSplitPane
getRightIndent(): StyleConstants*
getRightInset(): CompositeView*
getRolloverIcon(): AbstractButton*
getRolloverSelectedIcon(): AbstractButton*
getRoot(): DefaultMutableTreeNode* DefaultTreeModel
SwingUtilities *TreeModel*
getRootElement(): DefaultStyledDocument.ElementBuffer
getRootElements(): AbstractDocument* *Document*
getRootFrame(): JOptionPane
getRootPane(): JApplet JComponent* JDialog JFrame
JWindow *RootPaneContainer* SwingUtilities
getRoots(): FileSystemView
getRootView(): TextUI
getRotateInstance(): AffineTransform
getRow(): *ResultSet*
getRowBounds(): JTree
getRowCount(): AbstractLayoutCache* AbstractTableModel*
JTable JTree *TableModel* TableView.TableCell TreeUI
getRowEnd(): Utilities
getRowForLocation(): JTree
getRowForPath(): AbstractLayoutCache* JTree TreeUI
getRowHeader(): JScrollPane ScrollPaneLayout*
getRowHeight(): AbstractLayoutCache* JTable JTextArea
JTree
getRowMapper(): DefaultTreeSelectionModel*
*T*reeSelectionModel
getRowMargin(): JTable
getRows(): GridLayout JTextArea java.awt.List TextArea
getRowSelectionAllowed(): JTable
getRowsForPaths(): AbstractLayoutCache* *RowMapper*
getRowStart(): Utilities
getRSB(): GlyphMetrics
getRule(): AlphaComposite StyleSheet
getRules(): RuleBasedCollator
getRunLimit(): *AttributedCharacterIterator*
getRunStart(): *AttributedCharacterIterator*
getRuntime(): Runtime
getSample(): Raster* SampleModel*
getSampleDouble(): Raster* SampleModel*
getSampleFloat(): Raster* SampleModel*
getSampleModel(): BufferedImage Raster* *RenderedImage*
getSampleModelTranslateX(): Raster*
getSampleModelTranslateY(): Raster*
getSamples(): Raster* SampleModel*
getSampleSize(): SampleModel*
getScale(): *ResultSetMetaData*
getScaledInstance(): Image*
getScaleFactors(): RescaleOp
getScaleInstance(): AffineTransform
getScaleX(): AffineTransform
getScaleY(): AffineTransform
getScanlineStride(): ComponentSampleModel*
MultiPixelPackedSampleModel
SinglePixelPackedSampleModel
getSchemaName(): *ResultSetMetaData*
getSchemas(): *DatabaseMetaData*
getSchemaTerm(): *DatabaseMetaData*
getScope(): Identity*
getScreenDevices(): GraphicsEnvironment
getScreenResolution(): Toolkit
getScreenSize(): Toolkit
getScrollableBlockIncrement(): JList JTable
JTextComponent* JTree *Scrollable*
getScrollableTracksViewportHeight(): JList JTable
JTextComponent* JTree *Scrollable*

G

getScrollableTracksViewportWidth( ): JList JTable
JTextComponent* JTree *Scrollable*

getScrollableUnitIncrement( ): JList JTable JTextComponent*
JTree *Scrollable*

getScrollbarDisplayPolicy( ): ScrollPane

getScrollbarVisibility( ): TextArea

getScrollOffset( ): JTextField*

getScrollPosition( ): ScrollPane

getScrollsOnExpand( ): JTree

getSearchStringEscape( ): *DatabaseMetaData*

getSeconds( ): java.util.Date*

getSecurityContext( ): *LoaderHandler* RMIClassLoader
SecurityManager*

getSecurityManager( ): System

getSeed( ): SecureRandom

getSelectedCheckbox( ): CheckboxGroup

getSelectedColor( ): *ColorSelectionModel*
DefaultColorSelectionModel

getSelectedColumn( ): JTable

getSelectedColumnCount( ): DefaultTableColumnModel
JTable *TableColumnModel*

getSelectedColumns( ): DefaultTableColumnModel JTable
TableColumnModel

getSelectedComponent( ): JTabbedPane

getSelectedFile( ): JFileChooser

getSelectedFiles( ): JFileChooser

getSelectedIcon( ): AbstractButton*

getSelectedIndex( ): Choice DefaultSingleSelectionModel
JComboBox JList JTabbedPane java.awt.List
SingleSelectionModel

getSelectedIndexes( ): java.awt.List *ListPeer*

getSelectedIndices( ): JList

getSelectedItem( ): Choice *ComboBoxModel*
DefaultComboBoxModel JComboBox java.awt.List

getSelectedItems( ): java.awt.List

getSelectedObjects( ): AbstractButton* Checkbox
CheckboxMenuItem Choice DefaultButtonModel*
ItemSelectable JComboBox java.awt.List

getSelectedPath( ): MenuSelectionManager

getSelectedRow( ): JTable

getSelectedRowCount( ): JTable

getSelectedRows( ): JTable

getSelectedText( ): *AccessibleText*
InputMethodRequests JTextComponent*
JTextComponent.AccessibleJTextComponent*
TextComponent*

getSelectedTextColor( ): JTextComponent*

getSelectedValue( ): JList

getSelectedValues( ): JList

getSelection( ): ButtonGroup

getSelectionBackground( ): JList JTable

getSelectionColor( ): JTextComponent*

getSelectionCount( ): DefaultTreeSelectionModel* JTree
TreeSelectionModel

getSelectionEnd( ): *AccessibleText* JTextComponent*
JTextComponent.AccessibleJTextComponent*
TextComponent* *TextComponentPeer*

getSelectionForeground( ): JList JTable

getSelectionMode( ): DefaultListSelectionModel
DefaultTreeSelectionModel* JList *ListSelectionModel*
TreeSelectionModel

getSelectionModel( ): AbstractLayoutCache*
DefaultTableColumnModel JColorChooser JList JMenuBar
JPopupMenu JTable JTree *TableColumnModel*

getSelectionPainter( ): DefaultCaret

getSelectionPath( ): DefaultTreeSelectionModel* JTree
TreeSelectionModel

getSelectionPaths( ): DefaultTreeSelectionModel* JTree
TreeSelectionModel

getSelectionRows( ): DefaultTreeSelectionModel* JTree
TreeSelectionModel

getSelectionStart( ): *AccessibleText* JTextComponent*
JTextComponent.AccessibleJTextComponent*
TextComponent* *TextComponentPeer*

getSelectionValues( ): JOptionPane

getSendBufferSize( ): DatagramSocket* Socket

getSentenceInstance( ): BreakIterator

getSeparatorSize( ): JToolBar.Separator

getSerialNumber( ): X509Certificate X509CRLEntry

getSerialVersionUID( ): ObjectStreamClass

getService( ): *BeanContextServiceProvider*
BeanContextServices BeanContextServicesSupport
BeanContextServicesSupport.BCSSProxyServiceProvider

getServiceClass( ): BeanContextServiceAvailableEvent
BeanContextServiceRevokedEvent

getServiceProvider( ):
BeanContextServicesSupport.BCSSServiceProvider

getServicesBeanInfo( ): *BeanContextServiceProviderBeanInfo*

getShadowColor( ): EtchedBorder*

getShadowInnerColor( ): BevelBorder*

getShadowOuterColor( ): BevelBorder*

getSharedAncestor( ): DefaultMutableTreeNode*

getShearInstance( ): AffineTransform

getShearX( ): AffineTransform

getShearY( ): AffineTransform

getShort( ): java.lang.reflect.Array *CallableStatement* Field
ResultSet

getShortcut( ): MenuItem*

getShortcutMenuItem( ): MenuBar

getShortDescription( ): FeatureDescriptor*

getShortMonths( ): DateFormatSymbols

getShortParameter( ): ParameterBlock

getShortWeekdays( ): DateFormatSymbols

getShowHorizontalLines( ): JTable

getShowsRootHandles( ): JTree

getShowVerticalLines( ): JTable

getSiblingCount( ): DefaultMutableTreeNode*

getSigAlgName( ): X509Certificate X509CRL

getSigAlgOID( ): X509Certificate X509CRL

getSigAlgParams( ): X509Certificate X509CRL

getSignature( ): SignedObject X509Certificate X509CRL

getSigners( ): Class

getSize( ): AbstractListModel* *AccessibleComponent*
Box.AccessibleBox Box.Filler.AccessibleBoxFiller
CellRendererPane.AccessibleCellRendererPane
Component* DataBuffer* Dimension*
Font* JApplet.AccessibleJApplet
JComponent.AccessibleJComponent*
JDialog.AccessibleJDialog JFrame.AccessibleJFrame
JList.AccessibleJList.AccessibleJListChild
JPopupMenu.WindowPopup.AccessibleWindowPopup
JTable.AccessibleJTable.AccessibleJTableCell
JTableHeader.AccessibleJTableHeader ↵
.AccessibleJTableHeaderEntry
JTree.AccessibleJTree.AccessibleJTreeNode
JWindow.AccessibleJWindow *ListModel* Rectangle*
ZipEntry*

getSize2D( ): Font*

getSmallDisplayIcon( ): AbstractColorChooserPanel

getSnapToTicks( ): JSlider

getSocketFactory( ): RMISocketFactory

getSoLinger( ): Socket

getSoTimeout( ): DatagramSocket* ServerSocket Socket

getSource( ): EventObject* Image* ParameterBlock

getSourceActions( ): DragGestureRecognizer*
DragSourceContext DropTargetDragEvent
DropTargetDropEvent

getSourceAsBeanContextServices( ):
BeanContextServiceAvailableEvent
BeanContextServiceRevokedEvent

getSourceAsDragGestureRecognizer( ): DragGestureEvent

getSourceElement( ): HTMLFrameHyperlinkEvent

getSources( ): BufferedImage ParameterBlock
  RenderableImage RenderableImageOp *RenderedImage**
getSourceString( ): CollationKey
getSpaceAbove( ): StyleConstants*
getSpaceBelow( ): StyleConstants*
getSpan( ): BoxView*
getSpecificationTitle( ): Package
getSpecificationVendor( ): Package
getSpecificationVersion( ): Package
getSQLKeywords( ): *DatabaseMetaData*
getSQLState( ): SQLException*
getSQLTypeName( ): *SQLData* *Struct*
getStartIndex( ): AccessibleHyperlink*
getStartOffset( ): AbstractDocument.AbstractElement*
  javax.swing.text.Element Highlighter.Highlight
  HTMLDocument.Iterator View*
getStartPoint( ): Arc2D*
getStartPosition( ): AbstractDocument* *Document*
getState( ): Checkbox CheckboxMenuItem Frame*
  FramePeer InputMethodHighlight JCheckBoxMenuItem
getStateChange( ): ItemEvent
getStatement( ): ResultSet
getStaticAttribute( ): StyleContext*
getStaticAttributeKey( ): StyleContext*
getStatus( ): PixelGrabber
getStream( ): JEditorPane
getStrength( ): Collator*
getStrikethroughOffset( ): LineMetrics
getStrikethroughThickness( ): LineMetrics
getString( ): *AbstractDocument.Content* CallableStatement
  Entity GapContent JProgressBar ResourceBundle*
  ResultSet StringContent UIDefaults UIManager
getStringArray( ): ResourceBundle*
getStringBounds( ): Font* FontMetrics
getStringFunctions( ): *DatabaseMetaData*
getStroke( ): Graphics2D
getStrongCaret( ): TextLayout.CaretPolicy
getStyle( ): DefaultStyledDocument* Font* JTextPane
  StyleContext* *StyledDocument*
getStyledDocument( ): JTextPane
  StyledEditorKit.StyledTextAction*
getStyledEditorKit( ): JTextPane
  StyledEditorKit.StyledTextAction*
getStyleNames( ): DefaultStyledDocument* StyleContext*
getStyleSheet( ): BlockView* HTMLDocument* HTMLEditorKit
  InlineView javax.swing.text.html.ParagraphView
getSubElements( ): JMenuBar JMenuItem* JPopupMenu
  MenuElement
getSubimage( ): BufferedImage
getSubjectDN( ): X509Certificate
getSubjectUniqueID( ): X509Certificate
getSubString( ): *Clob*
getSubType( ): DataFlavor
getSuperclass( ): Class
getSystem( ): ActivationGroup ActivationGroupID
getSystemClassLoader( ): ClassLoader*
getSystemClipboard( ): Toolkit
getSystemCustomCursor( ): Cursor
getSystemEventQueue( ): Toolkit
getSystemEventQueueImpl( ): Toolkit
getSystemFunctions( ): *DatabaseMetaData*
getSystemLookAndFeelClassName( ): UIManager
getSystemResource( ): ClassLoader*
getSystemResourceAsStream( ): ClassLoader*
getSystemResources( ): ClassLoader*
getSystemScope( ): IdentityScope
getTab( ): TabSet
getTabAfter( ): TabSet
getTabBase( ): javax.swing.text.ParagraphView*
getTabbedSpan( ): *TabableView*
getTabbedTextOffset( ): Utilities
getTabbedTextWidth( ): Utilities

getTabBounds( ): TabbedPaneUI
getTabCount( ): JTabbedPane TabSet
getTabIndex( ): TabSet
getTabIndexAfter( ): TabSet
getTable( ): ByteLookupTable JTableHeader LookupOp
  ShortLookupTable
getTableCellEditorComponent( ): DefaultCellEditor
  TableCellEditor
getTableCellRendererComponent( ):
  DefaultTableCellRenderer* *TableCellRenderer*
getTableHeader( ): JTable
getTableName( ): *ResultSetMetaData*
getTablePrivileges( ): *DatabaseMetaData*
getTables( ): *DatabaseMetaData*
getTableTypes( ): *DatabaseMetaData*
getTabPlacement( ): JTabbedPane
getTabRunCount( ): JTabbedPane TabbedPaneUI
getTabSet( ): javax.swing.text.ParagraphView* StyleConstants*
getTabSize( ): JTextArea PlainView* WrappedPlainView
getTag( ): HTML HTMLDocument.Iterator
getTags( ): *PropertyEditor* PropertyEditorSupport
getTarget( ): HTMLFrameHyperlinkEvent
getTargetActions( ): DragSourceDragEvent DropTargetContext
getTargetException( ): InvocationTargetException
getTBSCertificate( ): X509Certificate
getTBSCertList( ): X509CRL
getTcpNoDelay( ): Socket
getText( ): AbstractButton* AbstractDocument*
  AbstractWriter* BreakIterator *Document*
  InputMethodEvent JLabel* JTextComponent* Label
  TextComponent* *TextComponentPeer**
getTextComponent( ): TextAction*
getTextLocation( ): *InputMethodRequests*
getTextNonSelectionColor( ): DefaultTreeCellRenderer
getTextSelectionColor( ): DefaultTreeCellRenderer
getThickness( ): LineBorder*
getThisUpdate( ): X509CRL
getThreadGroup( ): SecurityManager* Thread
getTile( ): BufferedImage *RenderedImage**
getTiledSizeRequirements( ): SizeRequirements
getTileGridXOffset( ): BufferedImage *RenderedImage**
getTileGridYOffset( ): BufferedImage *RenderedImage**
getTileHeight( ): BufferedImage *RenderedImage**
getTileWidth( ): BufferedImage *RenderedImage**
getTime( ): Calendar* *CallableStatement* java.util.Date*
  ResultSet ZipEntry*
getTimeDateFunctions( ): *DatabaseMetaData*
getTimeInMillis( ): Calendar*
getTimeInstance( ): DateFormat*
getTimestamp( ): *CallableStatement* ResultSet
getTimeToLive( ): DatagramSocketImpl MulticastSocket
getTimeZone( ): Calendar* DateFormat* TimeZone*
getTimezoneOffset( ): java.util.Date*
getTipText( ): JToolTip
getTitle( ): Dialog* Frame* JInternalFrame TitledBorder*
getTitleAt( ): JTabbedPane
getTitleColor( ): TitledBorder*
getTitleFont( ): TitledBorder*
getTitleJustification( ): TitledBorder*
getTitlePosition( ): TitledBorder*
getToIndex( ): TableColumnModelEvent
getTokenThreshold( ): HTMLDocument
getToolkit( ): Component* *ComponentPeer**
getToolTipLocation( ): JComponent*
getToolTipText( ): JComponent*
getTopComponent( ): JSplitPane
getTopInset( ): CompositeView*
getTopLevelAncestor( ): JComponent*
getTotalColumnWidth( ): DefaultTableColumnModel
  TableColumnModel
getTotalIn( ): Deflater Inflater
getTotalOut( ): Deflater Inflater

getTransactionIsolation( ): *Connection*

getTransferable( ): DragSourceContext DropTargetContext
    DropTargetDropEvent

getTransferData( ): DropTargetContext.TransferableProxy
    StringSelection *Transferable*

getTransferDataFlavors( ):
    DropTargetContext.TransferableProxy StringSelection
    Transferable

getTransferSize( ): DataTruncation

getTransferType( ): Raster* SampleModel*

getTransform( ): AffineTransformOp Font* FontRenderContext
    Graphics2D RenderContext TransformAttribute

getTranslateInstance( ): AffineTransform

getTranslateX( ): AffineTransform

getTranslateY( ): AffineTransform

getTransparency( ): Color* ColorModel* GradientPaint
    TexturePaint *Transparency**

getTransparentPixel( ): IndexColorModel

getTRC( ): ICC_ProfileGray ICC_ProfileRGB

getTreeCellEditorComponent( ): DefaultCellEditor
    DefaultTreeCellEditor *TreeCellEditor*

getTreeCellRendererComponent( ): DefaultTreeCellRenderer
    TreeCellRenderer

getTreeLock( ): Component* MenuComponent*

getTreePath( ): TreeModelEvent

getTrigger( ): DragSourceContext

getTriggerEvent( ): DragGestureEvent
    DragGestureRecognizer*

getTTL( ): DatagramSocketImpl MulticastSocket

getType( ): AbstractDocument.DefaultDocumentEvent
    AffineTransform AttributeList BufferedImage
    java.security.cert.Certificate* CertificateFactory
    Character ColorSpace* CRL* Cursor
    DefaultStyledDocument.ElementSpec *DocumentEvent*
    javax.swing.text.html.parser.Element Entity Field
    GlyphMetrics GraphicsDevice KeyStore ListDataEvent
    ObjectStreamField *ResultSet* TableModelEvent

getTypeCode( ): ObjectStreamField

getTypeDescription( ): FileView JFileChooser

getTypeInfo( ): *DatabaseMetaData*

getTypeMap( ): *Connection*

getTypeString( ): ObjectStreamField

getUDTs( ): *DatabaseMetaData*

getUI( ): AbstractButton* JColorChooser JComboBox
    JDesktopPane JFileChooser JInternalFrame
    JInternalFrame.JDesktopIcon JLabel* JList JMenuBar
    JOptionPane JPopupMenu JProgressBar JScrollBar*
    JScrollPane JSeparator* JSlider JSplitPane
    JTabbedPane JTable JTableHeader JTextComponent*
    JToolBar JToolTip JTree UIDefaults UIManager

getUIClass( ): UIDefaults

getUIClassID( ): JComponent*

getUIError( ): UIDefaults

getUnderlineOffset( ): LineMetrics

getUnderlineThickness( ): LineMetrics

getUndoOrRedoPresentationName( ): UndoManager

getUndoPresentationName( ): AbstractUndoableEdit*
    UndoableEdit

getUnicodeStream( ): *ResultSet*

getUnitIncrement( ): *Adjustable* JScrollBar* Scrollbar

getUnnormalizedComponents( ): ColorModel*

getUpdateCount( ): *Statement**

getUpdateCounts( ): BatchUpdateException

getUpdateLevel( ): UndoableEditSupport

getUpdateRect( ): PaintEvent

getUpdateTableInRealTime( ): JTableHeader

getURL( ): *DatabaseMetaData* HyperlinkEvent*
    URLConnection*

getURLs( ): URLClassLoader

getUseCaches( ): URLConnection*

getUserAction( ): DragSourceDragEvent

getUserName( ): *DatabaseMetaData* PasswordAuthentication
    PrinterJob

getUserObject( ): DefaultMutableTreeNode*

getUserObjectPath( ): DefaultMutableTreeNode*

getVAdjustable( ): ScrollPane

getValue( ): AbstractAction* *Action* *Adjustable*
    AdjustmentEvent Adler32 Annotation AttributeList
    Attributes *BoundedRangeModel* *Checksum* CRC32
    DefaultBoundedRangeModel FeatureDescriptor*
    JOptionPane JProgressBar JScrollBar* JSlider Lease
    Map.Entry Option *PropertyEditor* PropertyEditorSupport
    Scrollbar

getValueAt( ): AbstractTableModel* JTable *TableModel*

getValueIsAdjusting( ): *BoundedRangeModel*
    DefaultBoundedRangeModel DefaultListSelectionModel
    JList JScrollBar* JSlider ListSelectionEvent
    ListSelectionModel

getValues( ): AttributeList

getVariant( ): Locale

getVariation( ): InputMethodHighlight

getVersion( ): *OpenType* Provider X509Certificate X509CRL

getVersionColumns( ): *DatabaseMetaData*

getVerticalAlignment( ): AbstractButton* JLabel*

getVerticalScrollBar( ): JScrollPane ScrollPaneLayout*

getVerticalScrollBarPolicy( ): JScrollPane ScrollPaneLayout*

getVerticalTextPosition( ): AbstractButton* JLabel*

getVgap( ): BorderLayout CardLayout FlowLayout GridLayout

getView( ): JViewport View*

getViewAtPoint( ): CompositeView*

getViewAtPosition( ): CompositeView*

getViewAttributes( ): StyleSheet

getViewCount( ): View*

getViewFactory( ): EditorKit* View*

getViewIndexAtPosition( ): CompositeView*

getViewport( ): JScrollPane ScrollPaneLayout*

getViewportBorder( ): JScrollPane

getViewportBorderBounds( ): JScrollPane ScrollPaneLayout*

getViewportSize( ): ScrollPane

getViewPosition( ): JViewport

getViewRect( ): JViewport

getViewSize( ): JViewport

getVisible( ): Scrollbar

getVisibleAdvance( ): TextLayout

getVisibleAmount( ): *Adjustable* JScrollBar* Scrollbar

getVisibleChildCount( ): AbstractLayoutCache*

getVisibleIndex( ): java.awt.List

getVisiblePathsFrom( ): AbstractLayoutCache*

getVisiblePosition( ): InputMethodEvent

getVisibleRect( ): JComponent*

getVisibleRowCount( ): JList JTree

getVisualBounds( ): GlyphVector

getVisualHighlightShape( ): TextLayout

getVisualOtherHit( ): TextLayout

getVMID( ): Lease

getVScrollbarWidth( ): ScrollPane *ScrollPanePeer*

getWantsInput( ): JOptionPane

getWarnings( ): *Connection* *ResultSet* *Statement**

getWarningString( ): JInternalFrame Window*

getWeekdays( ): DateFormatSymbols

getWhen( ): InputEvent*

getWidth( ): BoxView* Component* Dimension2D*
    Image* Kernel PageFormat Paper PixelGrabber
    Raster* RectangularShape* *RenderableImage*
    RenderableImageOp *RenderedImage** SampleModel*
    TableColumn

getWidths( ): FontMetrics

getWindingRule( ): FlatteningPathIterator GeneralPath
    PathIterator

getWindow( ): WindowEvent

getWordEnd( ): Utilities

getWordInstance( ): BreakIterator

getWordStart( ): Utilities

G

G

handleText( ): HTMLEditorKit.ParserCallback* **P**arser*
handleTitle( ): **P**arser*
HANGING_BASELINE: **F**ont* **G**raphicAttribute*
HANGUL_COMPATIBILITY_JAMO: **C**haracter.UnicodeBlock
HANGUL_JAMO: **C**haracter.UnicodeBlock
HANGUL_SYLLABLES: **C**haracter.UnicodeBlock
HANJA: **I**nputSubset
hasAlpha( ): **C**olorModel*
hasBeenExpanded( ): **J**Tree
hasChanged( ): **O**bservable
hasChildren: **J**Tree.DynamicUtilTreeNode
hasExtensions( ): **X**509CRLEntry
hasFocus( ): **C**omponent*
hash( ): **D**elegate
hashCode( ): *Collection* **D**elegate *Map* *Map.Entry*
    java.lang.**O**bject *java.security.***P**rincipal*
HashMap: java.util
   —fields: **B**eanContextServicesSupport.services
HashSet: java.util
Hashtable*: java.util
   —subclasses: **P**roperties* **U**IDefaults
   —descendents: **P**rovider
   —passed to: **B**ufferedImage( ) **I**mageFilter*.setProperties( )
    MemoryImageSource( ) *StateEditable* < restoreState( ),
    storeState( ) >
   —returned by: **J**LayeredPane*.getComponentToLayer( )
    JSlider.createStandardLabels( )
   —fields: **D**TD < elementHash, entityHash > **J**Table
    < defaultEditorsByColumnClass, defaultRenderersByColumnClass >
    StateEdit.preState
hasListeners( ): **P**ropertyChangeSupport*
    VetoableChangeSupport
hasMoreElements( ): *Enumeration* **S**tringTokenizer
hasMoreTokens( ): **S**tringTokenizer
hasNext( ): **B**eanContextSupport.BCSIterator *Iterator**
hasPrevious( ): *ListIterator*
hasSameRules( ): **T**imeZone*
hasService( ): *BeanContextServices*
    BeanContextServicesSupport
hasTileWriters( ): **B**ufferedImage *WritableRenderedImage*
hasUniformLineMetrics( ): **F**ont* **F**ontMetrics
hasUnsupportedCriticalExtension( ): **X**509Certificate
    X509CRL **X**509CRLEntry *X509Extension*
head: **D**TD
HEAD: **H**TML.Tag*
HEADER_RENDERER_PROPERTY: **T**ableColumn
HEADER_ROW: **T**ableModelEvent
HEADER_VALUE_PROPERTY: **T**ableColumn
headerRenderer: **T**ableColumn
headerValue: **T**ableColumn
headMap( ): *SortedMap* **T**reeMap
headSet( ): *SortedSet* **T**reeSet
heavyWeightPopupEnabled: **T**oolTipManager
HEBREW: **C**haracter.UnicodeBlock
HEIGHT: **C**SS.Attribute **H**TML.Attribute *ImageObserver*
height: **A**rc2D.Double **A**rc2D.Float **D**imension*
    Ellipse2D.Double **E**llipse2D.Float **R**aster*
    Rectangle* **R**ectangle2D.Double **R**ectangle2D.Float
    RoundRectangle2D.Double **R**oundRectangle2D.Float
    SampleModel*
hide( ): **C**omponent* *ComponentPeer**
HIDE_ON_CLOSE: *WindowConstants*
hidePopup( ): **J**ComboBox
highestLayer( ): **J**LayeredPane*
highlight: **E**tchedBorder*
Highlighter: javax.swing.text
   —passed to: **J**TextComponent*.setHighlighter( )
   —returned by: **J**TextComponent*.getHighlighter( )
   —implemented by: **L**ayeredHighlighter*
Highlighter.Highlight: javax.swing.text
   —returned by: *Highlighter*.getHighlights( )
Highlighter.HighlightPainter: javax.swing.text

   —passed to: *Highlighter*.addHighlight( )
   —returned by: **D**efaultCaret.getSelectionPainter( )
   —implemented by: **L**ayeredHighlighter.LayerPainter*
highlightInner: **B**evelBorder*
highlightOuter: **B**evelBorder*
HINTS_OBSERVED: *RenderableImage*
HIRAGANA: **C**haracter.UnicodeBlock
hit( ): **G**raphics2D
hitClip( ): **G**raphics*
hitTestChar( ): **T**extLayout
HOME: **E**vent
HORIZONTAL: **A**ccessibleState *Adjustable*
    GridBagConstraints **S**crollbar *SwingConstants*
HORIZONTAL_ALIGNMENT_CHANGED_PROPERTY:
    AbstractButton*
HORIZONTAL_SCROLLBAR: *ScrollPaneConstants*
HORIZONTAL_SCROLLBAR_ALWAYS: *ScrollPaneConstants*
HORIZONTAL_SCROLLBAR_AS_NEEDED:
    ScrollPaneConstants
HORIZONTAL_SCROLLBAR_NEVER: *ScrollPaneConstants*
HORIZONTAL_SCROLLBAR_POLICY: *ScrollPaneConstants*
HORIZONTAL_SPLIT: **J**SplitPane
HORIZONTAL_TEXT_POSITION_CHANGED_PROPERTY:
    AbstractButton*
horizontalScrollBar: **J**ScrollPane
horizontalScrollBarPolicy: **J**ScrollPane
HOUR: **C**alendar*
HOUR0_FIELD: **D**ateFormat*
HOUR1_FIELD: **D**ateFormat*
HOUR_OF_DAY: **C**alendar*
HOUR_OF_DAY0_FIELD: **D**ateFormat*
HOUR_OF_DAY1_FIELD: **D**ateFormat*
HR: **H**TML.Tag*
HREF: **H**TML.Attribute
hsb: **S**crollPaneLayout*
hsbPolicy: **S**crollPaneLayout*
HSBtoRGB( ): **C**olor*
HSPACE: **H**TML.Attribute
html: **D**TD **H**TMLEditorKit.InsertHTMLTextAction
HTML: **H**TML.Tag*
HTML: javax.swing.text.html
HTML.Attribute: javax.swing.text.html
   —passed to: **H**TML.getIntegerAttributeValue( )
   —returned by: **H**TML < getAllAttributeKeys( ), getAttributeKey( ) >
   —fields: **H**TML.Attribute < ACTION, ALIGN, ALINK, ALT,
    ARCHIVE, BACKGROUND, BGCOLOR, BORDER, CELLPADDING,
    CELLSPACING, CHECKED, CLASS, CLASSID, CLEAR, CODE,
    CODEBASE, CODETYPE, COLOR, COLS, COLSPAN, COMMENT,
    COMPACT, CONTENT, COORDS, DATA, DECLARE, DIR,
    DUMMY, ENCTYPE, ENDTAG, FACE, FRAMEBORDER, HALIGN,
    HEIGHT, HREF, HSPACE, HTTPEQUIV, ID, ISMAP, LANG,
    LANGUAGE, LINK, LOWSRC, MARGINHEIGHT, MARGINWIDTH,
    MAXLENGTH, METHOD, MULTIPLE, N, NAME, NOHREF,
    NORESIZE, NOSHADE, NOWRAP, PROMPT, REL, REV,
    ROWS, ROWSPAN, SCROLLING, SELECTED, SHAPE, SHAPES,
    SIZE, SRC, STANDBY, START, STYLE, TARGET, TEXT, TITLE,
    TYPE, USEMAP, VALIGN, VALUE, VALUETYPE, VERSION,
    VLINK, VSPACE, WIDTH >
HTML.Tag*: javax.swing.text.html
   —subclasses: **H**TML.UnknownTag
   —passed to: **H**TMLDocument < getIterator( ), getReader( ) >
    HTMLDocument.HTMLReader < blockClose( ),
    blockOpen( ), **H**TMLReader( ), registerTag( ) >
    HTMLDocument.HTMLReader.TagAction*.start( )
    HTMLEditorKit.HTMLTextAction*
    < elementCountToTag( ), findElementMatchingTag( ) >
    HTMLEditorKit.InsertHTMLTextAction < insertHTML( ),
    InsertHTMLTextAction( ) > **H**TMLEditorKit.ParserCallback*
    < handleSimpleTag( ), handleStartTag( ) > **S**tyleSheet.getRule( )
   —returned by: **H**TML < getAllTags( ), getTag( ) >
    TagElement.getHTMLTag( )

H

—fields: **H**TML.Tag* < A, ADDRESS, APPLET, AREA, B, BASE, BASEFONT, BIG, BLOCKQUOTE, BODY, BR, CAPTION, CENTER, CITE, CODE, COMMENT, CONTENT, DD, DFN, DIR, DIV, DL, DT, EM, FONT, FORM, FRAME, FRAMESET, H1, H2, H3, H4, H5, H6, HEAD, HR, HTML, I, IMG, IMPLIED, INPUT, ISINDEX, KBD, LI, LINK, MAP, MENU, META, NOFRAMES, OBJECT, OL, OPTION, P, PARAM, PRE, S, SAMP, SCRIPT, SELECT, SMALL, STRIKE, STRONG, STYLE, SUB, SUP, TABLE, TD, TEXTAREA, TH, TITLE, TR, TT, U, UL, VAR > **H**TMLEditorKit.InsertHTMLTextAction < alternateAddTag, alternateParentTag, parentTag >

HTML.UnknownTag: javax.swing.text.html
HTMLDocument: javax.swing.text.html
—passed to: **H**TMLDocument.BlockElement( )
 HTMLDocument.HTMLReader( ) **H**TMLEditorKit.insertHTML( )
 HTMLEditorKit.HTMLTextAction*
 < findElementMatchingTag( ), getElementsAt( ) >
 HTMLEditorKit.InsertHTMLTextAction.insertHTML( )
 HTMLWriter( )
—returned
 by: **H**TMLEditorKit.HTMLTextAction*.getHTMLDocument( )
HTMLDocument.BlockElement: javax.swing.text.html
HTMLDocument.HTMLReader: javax.swing.text.html
—passed to: **H**TMLDocument.HTMLReader.BlockAction( )
 HTMLDocument.HTMLReader.FormAction( )
 HTMLDocument.HTMLReader.IsindexAction( )
 HTMLDocument.HTMLReader.PreAction( )
 HTMLDocument.HTMLReader.TagAction( )
HTMLDocument.HTMLReader.BlockAction*:
 javax.swing.text.html
—subclasses: **H**TMLDocument.HTMLReader.ParagraphAction
 HTMLDocument.HTMLReader.PreAction
HTMLDocument.HTMLReader.CharacterAction:
 javax.swing.text.html
HTMLDocument.HTMLReader.FormAction:
 javax.swing.text.html
HTMLDocument.HTMLReader.HiddenAction:
 javax.swing.text.html
HTMLDocument.HTMLReader.IsindexAction:
 javax.swing.text.html
HTMLDocument.HTMLReader.ParagraphAction:
 javax.swing.text.html
HTMLDocument.HTMLReader.PreAction:
 javax.swing.text.html
HTMLDocument.HTMLReader.SpecialAction*:
 javax.swing.text.html
—subclasses: **H**TMLDocument.HTMLReader.FormAction
HTMLDocument.HTMLReader.TagAction*:
 javax.swing.text.html
—subclasses: **H**TMLDocument.HTMLReader.BlockAction*
 HTMLDocument.HTMLReader.CharacterAction
 HTMLDocument.HTMLReader.HiddenAction
 HTMLDocument.HTMLReader.IsindexAction
 HTMLDocument.HTMLReader.SpecialAction*
—descendents: **H**TMLDocument.HTMLReader.FormAction
 HTMLDocument.HTMLReader.ParagraphAction
 HTMLDocument.HTMLReader.PreAction
—passed to: **H**TMLDocument.HTMLReader.registerTag( )
HTMLDocument.Iterator: javax.swing.text.html
—returned by: **H**TMLDocument.getIterator( )
HTMLDocument.RunElement: javax.swing.text.html
HTMLEditorKit: javax.swing.text.html
—returned by: **H**TMLEditorKit.HTMLTextAction*.getHTMLEditorKit( )
HTMLEditorKit.HTMLFactory: javax.swing.text.html
HTMLEditorKit.HTMLTextAction*: javax.swing.text.html
—subclasses: **H**TMLEditorKit.InsertHTMLTextAction
HTMLEditorKit.InsertHTMLTextAction: javax.swing.text.html
HTMLEditorKit.LinkController: javax.swing.text.html
HTMLEditorKit.Parser*: javax.swing.text.html
—subclasses: **P**arserDelegator
—returned by: **H**TMLEditorKit.getParser( )
HTMLEditorKit.ParserCallback*: javax.swing.text.html

—subclasses: **H**TMLDocument.HTMLReader
—passed to: **D**ocumentParser.parse( )
—returned by: **H**TMLDocument.getReader( )
HTMLFrameHyperlinkEvent: javax.swing.text.html
—passed to: **H**TMLDocument.processHTMLFrameHyperlinkEvent( )
HTMLWriter: javax.swing.text.html
HTTP_ACCEPTED: **H**ttpURLConnection
HTTP_BAD_GATEWAY: **H**ttpURLConnection
HTTP_BAD_METHOD: **H**ttpURLConnection
HTTP_BAD_REQUEST: **H**ttpURLConnection
HTTP_CLIENT_TIMEOUT: **H**ttpURLConnection
HTTP_CONFLICT: **H**ttpURLConnection
HTTP_CREATED: **H**ttpURLConnection
HTTP_ENTITY_TOO_LARGE: **H**ttpURLConnection
HTTP_FORBIDDEN: **H**ttpURLConnection
HTTP_GATEWAY_TIMEOUT: **H**ttpURLConnection
HTTP_GONE: **H**ttpURLConnection
HTTP_INTERNAL_ERROR: **H**ttpURLConnection
HTTP_LENGTH_REQUIRED: **H**ttpURLConnection
HTTP_MOVED_PERM: **H**ttpURLConnection
HTTP_MOVED_TEMP: **H**ttpURLConnection
HTTP_MULT_CHOICE: **H**ttpURLConnection
HTTP_NO_CONTENT: **H**ttpURLConnection
HTTP_NOT_ACCEPTABLE: **H**ttpURLConnection
HTTP_NOT_AUTHORITATIVE: **H**ttpURLConnection
HTTP_NOT_FOUND: **H**ttpURLConnection
HTTP_NOT_MODIFIED: **H**ttpURLConnection
HTTP_OK: **H**ttpURLConnection
HTTP_PARTIAL: **H**ttpURLConnection
HTTP_PAYMENT_REQUIRED: **H**ttpURLConnection
HTTP_PRECON_FAILED: **H**ttpURLConnection
HTTP_PROXY_AUTH: **H**ttpURLConnection
HTTP_REQ_TOO_LONG: **H**ttpURLConnection
HTTP_RESET: **H**ttpURLConnection
HTTP_SEE_OTHER: **H**ttpURLConnection
HTTP_SERVER_ERROR: **H**ttpURLConnection
HTTP_UNAUTHORIZED: **H**ttpURLConnection
HTTP_UNAVAILABLE: **H**ttpURLConnection
HTTP_UNSUPPORTED_TYPE: **H**ttpURLConnection
HTTP_USE_PROXY: **H**ttpURLConnection
HTTP_VERSION: **H**ttpURLConnection
HTTPEQUIV: **H**TML.Attribute
HttpURLConnection: java.net
HUFFMAN_ONLY: **D**eflater
HyperlinkEvent*: javax.swing.event
—subclasses: **H**TMLFrameHyperlinkEvent
—passed to: *HyperlinkListener*.hyperlinkUpdate( )
HyperlinkEvent.EventType: javax.swing.event
—passed to: **H**TMLFrameHyperlinkEvent( ) **H**yperlinkEvent( )
—returned by: **H**yperlinkEvent*.getEventType( )
—fields: **H**yperlinkEvent.EventType < ACTIVATED, ENTERED, EXITED >
HyperlinkListener: javax.swing.event
—passed to: **J**EditorPane* < addHyperlinkListener( ), removeHyperlinkListener( ) >
hyperlinkUpdate( ): *HyperlinkListener*
I: **H**TML.Tag*
icAbsoluteColorimetric: **I**CC_Profile*
ICC_ColorSpace: java.awt.color
ICC_Profile*: java.awt.color
—subclasses: **I**CC_ProfileGray **I**CC_ProfileRGB
—passed to: **C**olorConvertOp( )
—returned by: **C**olorConvertOp.getICC_Profiles( )
 ICC_Profile*.getInstance( )
ICC_ProfileGray: java.awt.color
ICC_ProfileRGB: java.awt.color
icCurveCount: **I**CC_Profile*
icCurveData: **I**CC_Profile*
icHdrAttributes: **I**CC_Profile*
icHdrCmmId: **I**CC_Profile*
icHdrColorSpace: **I**CC_Profile*
icHdrCreator: **I**CC_Profile*

H

I

NameHelper NamingContextHelper NotEmptyHelper
NotFoundHelper NotFoundReasonHelper
ServiceDetailHelper ServiceInformationHelper TypeCode
IDENTICAL: **C**ollator*
identifier: **T**ableColumn
identities(): **I**dentityScope
Identity*: java.security
—subclasses: **I**dentityScope **S**igner
—passed to: **I**dentity*.identityEquals()
  IdentityScope.removeIdentity()
—returned by: **I**dentityScope.getIdentity()
identityEquals(): **I**dentity*
identityHashCode(): **S**ystem
IdentityScope: java.security
—passed to: **I**dentity() **I**dentityScope.setSystemScope()
—returned by: **I**dentity*.getScope()
*IDLEntity**: org.omg.CORBA.portable
—extended by: *BindingIterator* *IRObject** *NamingContext*
—implemented by: **A**ny **B**inding **B**indingType
  CompletionStatus **D**efinitionKind **N**ameComponent
  NameValuePair **N**otFoundReason **S**erviceDetail
  ServiceInformation **S**etOverrideType **S**tructMember
  TypeCode **U**nionMember **U**serException* **V**alueMember
IDLType: org.omg.CORBA
—passed to: **S**tructMember() **V**alueMember()
—fields: **S**tructMember.type_def **V**alueMember.type_def
IDREF: *DTDConstants*
IDREFS: *DTDConstants*
IEEEremainder(): **M**ath
ifModifiedSince: **U**RLConnection*
IGNORE_ALL_BEANINFO: **I**ntrospector
IGNORE_EVENT: *WindowPeer**
IGNORE_IMMEDIATE_BEANINFO: **I**ntrospector
IllegalAccessError: java.lang
IllegalAccessException: java.lang
—thrown by: **C**lass.newInstance() **F**ield < get(), getBoolean(),
  getByte(), getChar(), getDouble(), getFloat(), getInt(),
  getLong(), getShort(), set(), setBoolean(), setByte(),
  setChar(), setDouble(), setFloat(), setInt(), setLong(),
  setShort() > **U**IManager.setLookAndFeel()
IllegalArgumentException*: java.lang
—subclasses: **I**llegalThreadStateException
  InvalidParameterException **N**umberFormatException
—thrown by: *BeanContext** < getResource(),
  getResourceAsStream() > **C**onstructor.newInstance() **F**ield
  < getBoolean(), getByte(), getChar(), getDouble(), getFloat(),
  getInt(), getLong(), getShort(), set(), setBoolean(), setByte(),
  setChar(), setDouble(), setFloat(), setInt(), setLong(),
  setShort() > java.lang.reflect.**A**rray < getBoolean(), getByte(),
  getChar(), getDouble(), getFloat(), getInt(), getLength(),
  getLong(), getShort(), newInstance(), set(), setBoolean(),
  setByte(), setChar(), setDouble(), setFloat(), setInt(),
  setLong(), setShort() > **O**bjectInputStream.GetField
  < defaulted(), get() > *PropertyEditor*.setAsText()
  ReferenceQueue.remove()
IllegalComponentStateException: java.awt
—thrown by: **A**ccessibleContext*.getLocale()
IllegalMonitorStateException: java.lang
IllegalPathStateException: java.awt.geom
IllegalStateException*: java.lang
—subclasses: **I**llegalComponentStateException
  InvalidDnDOperationException
IllegalThreadStateException: java.lang
Image*: java.awt
—subclasses: **B**ufferedImage
—passed to: **C**omponent* < checkImage(), imageUpdate(),
  prepareImage() > *ComponentPeer*.prepareImage()
  DragSource < createDragSourceContext(), startDrag() >
  Frame*.setIconImage() **G**raphics*.drawImage()
  GrayFilter.createDisabledImage() ImageGraphicAttribute()
  ImageIcon < ImageIcon(), loadImage(), setImage() >

MediaTracker < addImage(), removeImage() > **P**ixelGrabber()
  Toolkit < createCustomCursor(), prepareImage() >
—returned by: **A**pplet*.getImage() *BeanInfo*.getIcon()
  Component*.createImage() *ComponentPeer*.createImage()
  GrayFilter.createDisabledImage() ImageIcon.getImage()
  SimpleBeanInfo < getIcon(), loadImage() > **T**oolkit
  < createImage(), getImage() >
—fields: **J**Viewport.backingStoreImage
IMAGEABORTED: *ImageConsumer*
imageComplete(): *ImageConsumer* ImageFilter*
  PixelGrabber
ImageConsumer: java.awt.image
—passed to: **F**ilteredImageSource < addConsumer(),
  isConsumer(), removeConsumer(),
  requestTopDownLeftRightResend(), startProduction() >
  ImageProducer < addConsumer(), isConsumer(),
  removeConsumer(), requestTopDownLeftRightResend(),
  startProduction() > **M**emoryImageSource < isConsumer(),
  removeConsumer(), requestTopDownLeftRightResend(),
  startProduction() > **R**enderableImageProducer < isConsumer(),
  removeConsumer(), requestTopDownLeftRightResend(),
  startProduction() >
—implemented by: **I**mageFilter* **P**ixelGrabber
—fields: **I**mageFilter*.consumer
IMAGEERROR: *ImageConsumer*
ImageFilter*: java.awt.image
—subclasses: **B**ufferedImageFilter **C**ropImageFilter
  ReplicateScaleFilter* **R**GBImageFilter*
—descendents: **A**reaAveragingScaleFilter **G**rayFilter
—passed to: **F**ilteredImageSource()
—returned by: **I**mageFilter*.getFilterInstance()
ImageGraphicAttribute: java.awt.font
—passed to: **I**mageGraphicAttribute.equals()
ImageIcon: javax.swing
ImageObserver: java.awt.image
—passed to: **C**omponent* < checkImage(), prepareImage() >
  ComponentPeer.prepareImage() **G**raphics*.drawImage()
  Image* < getHeight(), getProperty(), getWidth() > **T**oolkit
  < checkImage(), prepareImage() >
—returned by: **I**mageIcon.getImageObserver()
—implemented by: **C**omponent*
ImageProducer: java.awt.image
—passed to: **C**omponent*.createImage() **F**ilteredImageSource()
  PixelGrabber()
—returned by: **I**mage*.getSource()
—implemented by: **F**ilteredImageSource **M**emoryImageSource
  RenderableImageProducer
imageSubmit(): **F**ormView
imageUpdate(): **C**omponent* *ImageObserver*
ImagingOpException: java.awt.image
IMG: **H**TML.Tag*
IMG_ALIGN_BOTTOM: **H**TMLEditorKit
IMG_ALIGN_MIDDLE: **H**TMLEditorKit
IMG_ALIGN_TOP: **H**TMLEditorKit
IMG_BORDER: **H**TMLEditorKit
IMP_LIMIT: org.omg.CORBA
implAccept(): **S**erverSocket
IMPLEMENTATION_TITLE: **A**ttributes.Name
IMPLEMENTATION_VENDOR: **A**ttributes.Name
IMPLEMENTATION_VERSION: **A**ttributes.Name
IMPLIED: *DTDConstants* **H**TML.Tag*
implies(): **C**odeSource java.security.**P**ermission*
  PermissionCollection* **P**rotectionDomain
importedKeyCascade: *DatabaseMetaData*
importedKeyInitiallyDeferred: *DatabaseMetaData*
importedKeyInitiallyImmediate: *DatabaseMetaData*
importedKeyNoAction: *DatabaseMetaData*
importedKeyNotDeferrable: *DatabaseMetaData*
importedKeyRestrict: *DatabaseMetaData*
importedKeySetDefault: *DatabaseMetaData*
importedKeySetNull: *DatabaseMetaData*

—returned by: *BeanContext**.getResourceAsStream( )
Blob.getBinaryStream( ) ClassLoader*
< getResourceAsStream( ), getSystemResourceAsStream( ) >
HttpURLConnection.getErrorStream( ) Process
< getErrorStream( ), getInputStream( ) > *ResultSet*
< getAsciiStream( ), getBinaryStream( ), getUnicodeStream( ) >
Socket.getInputStream( ) *SQLInput* < readAsciiStream( ),
readBinaryStream( ) > URLConnection*.getInputStream( )
—fields: FilterInputStream*.in

InputStream: org.omg.CORBA.portable
—passed to: AlreadyBoundHelper.read( ) Any.read_value( )
ApplicationException( ) BindingHolder._read( )
BindingIteratorHolder._read( ) BindingListHolder._read( )
BindingTypeHolder._read( ) ByteHolder._read( )
CannotProceedHolder._read( ) Delegate.releaseReply( )
FixedHolder._read( ) IntHolder._read( )
InvalidNameHolder._read( ) IstringHelper.read( )
NameComponentHelper.read( ) NameHelper.read( )
NamingContextHelper.read( ) NotEmptyHelper.read( )
NotFoundHelper.read( ) NotFoundReasonHelper.read( )
ObjectHolder._read( ) PrincipalHolder._read( )
ServiceInformationHelper.read( ) ShortHolder._read( )
StringHolder._read( )
—returned by: Any.create_input_stream( ) Delegate.invoke( )
org.omg.CORBA.portable.OutputStream.create_input_stream( )

InputStreamReader*: java.io
—subclasses: FileReader

InputSubset: java.awt.im
—fields: InputSubset < HALFWIDTH_KATAKANA, HANJA,
KANJI, LATIN, LATIN_DIGITS, SIMPLIFIED_HANZI,
TRADITIONAL_HANZI >

inputValue: JOptionPane
inRange(): AbstractWriter*
INSERT: DocumentEvent.EventType Event TableModelEvent
insert(): AlreadyBoundHelper
BindingHelper BindingIteratorHelper
BindingListHelper BindingTypeHelper
CannotProceedHelper Choice CompositeView*
DefaultMutableTreeNode* DefaultStyledDocument*
DefaultStyledDocument.ElementBuffer InvalidNameHelper
IstringHelper JMenu JPopupMenu JTextArea Menu*
MutableTreeNode NameComponentHelper NameHelper
NamingContextHelper NotEmptyHelper NotFoundHelper
NotFoundReasonHelper ServiceDetailHelper
ServiceInformationHelper StringBuffer TextArea
TextAreaPeer

insert_any(): Any *DynAny**
insert_boolean(): Any *DynAny**
insert_char(): Any *DynAny**
insert_double(): Any *DynAny**
insert_fixed(): Any
insert_float(): Any *DynAny**
insert_long(): Any *DynAny**
insert_longlong(): Any *DynAny**
insert_Object(): Any
insert_octet(): Any *DynAny**
insert_Principal(): Any
insert_reference(): *DynAny**
insert_short(): Any *DynAny**
insert_Streamable(): Any
insert_string(): Any *DynAny**
insert_typecode(): *DynAny**
insert_TypeCode(): Any
insert_ulong(): Any *DynAny**
insert_ulonglong(): Any *DynAny**
insert_ushort(): Any *DynAny**
insert_val(): *DynAny**
insert_Value(): Any
insert_wchar(): Any *DynAny**
insert_wstring(): Any *DynAny**
insertAtBoundry(): HTMLEditorKit.InsertHTMLTextAction
insertBreakAction: DefaultEditorKit*

insertChar(): LineBreakMeasurer
insertComponent(): JTextPane
insertContentAction: DefaultEditorKit*
insertElementAt(): DefaultComboBoxModel DefaultListModel
MutableComboBoxModel Vector*
insertHTML(): HTMLEditorKit
HTMLEditorKit.InsertHTMLTextAction
insertIcon(): JTextPane
insertIndexForLayer(): JLayeredPane*
insertIndexInterval(): DefaultListSelectionModel
ListSelectionModel
insertItemAt(): JComboBox
insertNodeInto(): DefaultTreeModel
insertProviderAt(): Security
insertRow(): DefaultTableModel *ResultSet*
insertsAreDetected(): DatabaseMetaData
insertSeparator(): JMenu Menu*
insertString(): AbstractDocument* *AbstractDocument.Content*
*Document** GapContent StringContent
insertTab(): JTabbedPane
insertTabAction: DefaultEditorKit*
insertText(): TextArea *TextAreaPeer*
insertUpdate(): AbstractDocument*
DefaultStyledDocument.ElementBuffer *DocumentListener*
JTextComponent.AccessibleJTextComponent* View*
insets: GridBagConstraints
Insets*: java.awt
—subclasses: InsetsUIResource
—passed to: AbstractBorder*.getBorderInsets( )
BorderUIResource.EmptyBorderUIResource( )
GridBagConstraints( ) JMenuBar.setMargin( )
JToolBar.setMargin( )
—returned by: AbstractBorder*.getBorderInsets( )
Autoscroll.getAutoscrollInsets( )
BorderUIResource.getBorderInsets( ) Container*.insets( )
ContainerPeer.insets( ) JMenuBar.getMargin( )
JTextComponent*.getMargin( ) UIDefaults.getInsets( )
—fields: GridBagConstraints.insets
insets(): Container* *ContainerPeer**
InsetsUIResource: javax.swing.plaf
inside(): Component* Polygon Rectangle*
insideBorder: CompoundBorder*
install(): *Caret* DefaultCaret EditorKit* *Highlighter*
LayeredHighlighter*
installAncestorListener(): JComboBox
installBorder(): LookAndFeel
installChooserPanel(): AbstractColorChooserPanel
installColors(): LookAndFeel
installColorsAndFont(): LookAndFeel
installLookAndFeel(): UIManager
installUI(): ComponentUI*
instantiate(): Beans
instantiateChild(): *BeanContext** BeanContextSupport*
InstantiationError: java.lang
InstantiationException: java.lang
—thrown by: Class.newInstance( ) UIManager.setLookAndFeel( )
insureRowContinuity(): DefaultTreeSelectionModel*
insureUniqueness(): DefaultTreeSelectionModel*
intBitsToFloat(): Float
INTEGER: Types
Integer: java.lang
—passed to: Integer < compareTo( ), getInteger( ) >
—returned by: Integer < decode( ), getInteger( ), valueOf( ) >
—fields: JLayeredPane* < DEFAULT_LAYER, DRAG_LAYER,
FRAME_CONTENT_LAYER, MODAL_LAYER, PALETTE_LAYER,
POPUP_LAYER > TextAttribute < SUPERSCRIPT_SUPER,
UNDERLINE_ON >
INTEGER_FIELD: NumberFormat*
INTERFACE: Modifier
intern(): String
INTERNAL: org.omg.CORBA
INTERNAL_FRAME: AccessibleRole

INTERNAL_FRAME_ACTIVATED: InternalFrameEvent
INTERNAL_FRAME_CLOSED: InternalFrameEvent
INTERNAL_FRAME_CLOSING: InternalFrameEvent
INTERNAL_FRAME_DEACTIVATED: InternalFrameEvent
INTERNAL_FRAME_DEICONIFIED: InternalFrameEvent
INTERNAL_FRAME_FIRST: InternalFrameEvent
INTERNAL_FRAME_ICONIFIED: InternalFrameEvent
INTERNAL_FRAME_LAST: InternalFrameEvent
INTERNAL_FRAME_OPENED: InternalFrameEvent
InternalError: java.lang
internalFrameActivated(): InternalFrameAdapter
InternalFrameListener
InternalFrameAdapter: javax.swing.event
internalFrameClosed(): InternalFrameAdapter
InternalFrameListener
internalFrameClosing(): InternalFrameAdapter
InternalFrameListener
internalFrameDeactivated(): InternalFrameAdapter
InternalFrameListener
internalFrameDeiconified(): InternalFrameAdapter
InternalFrameListener
InternalFrameEvent: javax.swing.event
—passed to: InternalFrameAdapter < internalFrameActivated( ),
internalFrameClosed( ), internalFrameClosing( ),
internalFrameDeactivated( ), internalFrameDeiconified( ),
internalFrameIconified( ), internalFrameOpened( ) >
InternalFrameListener < internalFrameClosed( ),
internalFrameClosing( ), internalFrameDeactivated( ),
internalFrameDeiconified( ), internalFrameIconified( ),
internalFrameOpened( ) >
internalFrameIconified(): InternalFrameAdapter
InternalFrameListener
InternalFrameListener: javax.swing.event
—passed to: JInternalFrame < addInternalFrameListener( ),
removeInternalFrameListener( ) >
—implemented by: InternalFrameAdapter
internalFrameOpened(): InternalFrameAdapter
InternalFrameListener
InternalFrameUI: javax.swing.plaf
—passed to: JInternalFrame.setUI( )
—returned by: JInternalFrame.getUI( )
internalGet(): Calendar*
interrupt(): Thread ThreadGroup
interrupted(): Thread
InterruptedException: java.lang
—thrown by: EventQueue < getNextEvent( ), invokeAndWait( ) >
java.lang.Object.wait( ) MediaTracker < waitForAll( ),
waitForID( ) > PixelGrabber.grabPixels( )
ReferenceQueue.remove( ) Thread < join( ), sleep( ) >
InterruptedIOException: java.io
intersect(): Area Rectangle2D*
intersection(): Rectangle*
intersects(): Area CubicCurve2D* GeneralPath Line2D*
Polygon QuadCurve2D* RectangularShape* *Shape*
intersectsLine(): Line2D* Rectangle2D*
INTERVAL_ADDED: ListDataEvent
INTERVAL_REMOVED: ListDataEvent
intervalAdded(): JComboBox JList.AccessibleJList
ListDataListener
intervalRemoved(): JComboBox JList.AccessibleJList
ListDataListener
INTF_REPOS: org.omg.CORBA
IntHolder: org.omg.CORBA
intKey(): RenderingHints.Key
IntrospectionException: java.beans
—thrown by: EventSetDescriptor( ) IndexedPropertyDescriptor
< IndexedPropertyDescriptor( ), setIndexedReadMethod( ),
setIndexedWriteMethod( ) > Introspector.getBeanInfo( )
PropertyDescriptor* < PropertyDescriptor( ), setReadMethod( ),
setWriteMethod( ) >
Introspector: java.beans
intValue(): Number*

INV_FLAG: org.omg.CORBA
INV_IDENT: org.omg.CORBA
INV_OBJREF: org.omg.CORBA
INV_POLICY: org.omg.CORBA
Invalid: org.omg.CORBA.DynAnyPackage
—thrown by: *DynAny** < assign( ), from_any( ), to_any( ) >
INVALID_TRANSACTION: org.omg.CORBA
InvalidAlgorithmParameterException: java.security
—thrown by: AlgorithmParameterGenerator.init( )
KeyPairGenerator.initialize( ) Signature.setParameter( )
invalidate(): Component*
invalidateLayout(): BorderLayout BoxLayout CardLayout
GridBagLayout JRootPane.RootLayout *LayoutManager2*
OverlayLayout
invalidatePathBounds(): AbstractLayoutCache*
invalidateSizes(): AbstractLayoutCache*
InvalidClassException: java.io
InvalidDnDOperationException: java.awt.dnd
—thrown by: DragGestureEvent.startDrag( )
DragSource.startDrag( ) DropTargetContext.getTransferable( )
InvalidKeyException: java.security
—thrown by: java.security.cert.Certificate*.verify( )
KeyFactorySpi.engineTranslateKey( ) Signature < initSign( ),
initVerify( ) > SignatureSpi* < engineInitSign( ),
engineInitVerify( ) > SignedObject.verify( ) X509CRL.verify( )
InvalidKeySpecException: java.security.spec
—thrown by: KeyFactory < generatePrivate( ), generatePublic( ),
getKeySpec( ) > KeyFactorySpi < engineGeneratePublic( ),
engineGetKeySpec( ) >
InvalidName: org.omg.CORBA.ORBPackage
—thrown by: ORB.resolve_initial_references( )
InvalidName: org.omg.CosNaming.NamingContextPackage
—passed to: InvalidNameHelper < insert( ), write( ) >
—returned by: InvalidNameHelper < extract( ), read( ) >
—thrown by: _NamingContextImplBase < bind( ), bind_context( ),
bind_new_context( ), rebind( ), rebind_context( ), resolve( ),
unbind( ) > _NamingContextStub < bind_context( ),
bind_new_context( ), rebind( ), rebind_context( ),
resolve( ), unbind( ) > *NamingContext* < bind_context( ),
bind_new_context( ), rebind( ), rebind_context( ), resolve( ),
unbind( ) >
—fields: InvalidNameHolder.value
InvalidNameHelper:
org.omg.CosNaming.NamingContextPackage
InvalidNameHolder:
org.omg.CosNaming.NamingContextPackage
InvalidObjectException: java.io
—thrown by: AttributedCharacterIterator.Attribute*.readResolve( )
ObjectInputValidation.validateObject( )
InvalidParameterException: java.security
—thrown by: *DSAKeyPairGenerator*.initialize( )
Signature.setParameter( ) SignatureSpi*.engineSetParameter( )
InvalidParameterSpecException: java.security.spec
—thrown by: AlgorithmParameters < getParameterSpec( ), init( ) >
AlgorithmParametersSpi.engineInit( )
InvalidSeq: org.omg.CORBA.DynAnyPackage
—thrown by: *DynArray*.set_elements( ) *DynStruct*.set_members( )
InvalidValue: org.omg.CORBA.DynAnyPackage
—thrown by: *DynAny** < insert_any( ), insert_boolean( ),
insert_char( ), insert_double( ), insert_float( ), insert_long( ),
insert_longlong( ), insert_octet( ), insert_reference( ),
insert_short( ), insert_string( ), insert_typecode( ), insert_ulong( ),
insert_ulonglong( ), insert_ushort( ), insert_val( ), insert_wchar( ),
insert_wstring( ) >
inverseTransform(): AffineTransform
INVOCATION_DEFAULT: InvocationEvent
INVOCATION_FIRST: InvocationEvent
INVOCATION_LAST: InvocationEvent
InvocationEvent: java.awt.event
InvocationTargetException: java.lang.reflect
—thrown by: Constructor.newInstance( ) Method.invoke( )

I

invoke(): **D**elegate **D**ynamicImplementation* **M**ethod
  RemoteRef* **R**equest
invokeAndWait(): **E**ventQueue **S**wingUtilities
InvokeHandler: org.omg.CORBA.portable
invokeLater(): **E**ventQueue **S**wingUtilities
INVOKES_STOP_CELL_EDITING_PROPERTY: **J**Tree
invokesStopCellEditing: **J**Tree
IOException*: java.io
—subclasses: **C**hangedCharSetException
  CharConversionException **E**OFException
  FileNotFoundException **I**nterruptedIOException
  MalformedURLException **O**bjectStreamException*
  ProtocolException **R**emoteException* **S**ocketException*
  SyncFailedException java.net.**U**nknownHostException
  UnknownServiceException **U**nsupportedEncodingException
  UTFDataFormatException **Z**ipException*
—descendents: **A**ccessException **A**ctivateFailedException
  BindException java.net.**C**onnectException
  java.rmi.**C**onnectException **C**onnectIOException
  ExportException* **I**nvalidClassException
  InvalidObjectException **J**arException **M**arshalException
  NoRouteToHostException **N**oSuchObjectException
  NotActiveException **N**otSerializableException
  OptionalDataException **S**erverError **S**erverException
  ServerRuntimeException **S**keletonMismatchException
  SkeletonNotFoundException **S**ocketSecurityException
  StreamCorruptedException **S**tubNotFoundException
  UnexpectedException java.rmi.**U**nknownHostException
  UnmarshalException **W**riteAbortedException
—passed to: **P**rinterIOException
—returned by: **P**rinterIOException.getIOException()
—thrown by: **A**bstractWriter* < indent(), text(), write(),
  writeAttributes() > **A**lgorithmParameters < getEncoded(),
  init() > **A**lgorithmParametersSpi < engineGetEncoded(),
  engineInit() > **A**WTEventMulticaster.saveInternal()
  BeanContextServicesSupport < bcsPreDeserializationHook(),
  bcsPreSerializationHook() > **B**eanContextSupport*
  < bcsPreSerializationHook(), deserialize(), instantiateChild(),
  readChildren(), serialize(), writeChildren() > **B**eans.instantiate()
  BufferedWriter.newLine() **C**harArrayWriter.writeTo()
  ClassLoader* < getResources(), getSystemResources() >
  DataFlavor < readExternal(), writeExternal() >
  DatagramSocket*.send() **D**atagramSocketImpl < getTTL(),
  join(), leave(), peek(), receive(), send(), setTimeToLive(),
  setTTL() > *DataInput** < readByte(), readChar(), readDouble(),
  readFloat(), readFully(), readInt(), readLine(), readLong(),
  readShort(), readUnsignedByte(), readUnsignedShort(),
  readUTF(), skipBytes() > **D**ataInputStream < readByte(),
  readChar(), readDouble(), readFloat(), readFully(), readInt(),
  readLine(), readLong(), readShort(), readUnsignedByte(),
  readUnsignedShort(), readUTF(), skipBytes() > *DataOutput**
  < write(), writeBoolean(), writeByte(), writeBytes(), writeChar(),
  writeChars(), writeDouble(), writeFloat(), writeInt(),
  writeLong(), writeShort(), writeUTF() > **D**ataOutputStream
  < writeByte(), writeBytes(), writeChar(), writeChars(),
  writeDouble(), writeFloat(), writeInt(), writeLong(),
  writeShort(), writeUTF() > **D**eflaterOutputStream*.finish()
  DropTargetContext.TransferableProxy.getTransferData()
  DTD.read() **E**ditorKit* < read(), write() >
  Externalizable*.writeExternal() **F**ile < createTempFile(),
  getCanonicalFile(), getCanonicalPath() >
  FileInputStream.getFD() **F**ileOutputStream < finalize(),
  getFD() > **F**ileWriter() **G**ZIPInputStream()
  GZIPOutputStream() **H**TMLEditorKit.Parser*.parse()
  HTMLWriter < comment(), emptyTag(), endTag(),
  selectContent(), startTag(), text(), textAreaContent(), write(),
  writeAttributes(), writeEmbeddedTags(), writeOption() >
  HttpURLConnection.getResponseMessage() **I**CC_Profile*
  < getInstance(), write() > **J**arEntry.getAttributes()
  JarFile() **J**arInputStream() **J**arOutputStream()
  JarURLConnection < getCertificates(), getJarEntry(),
  getJarFile(), getMainAttributes(), getManifest() >

java.io.**I**nputStream* < close(), read(), reset(),
  skip() > java.io.**O**utputStream* < flush(), write() >
  *java.security.**C**ertificate*.encode() **J**EditorPane*
  < JEditorPane(), read(), setPage() > **J**TextComponent*.write()
  KeyStore.store() **K**eyStoreSpi.engineStore() **M**anifest
  < read(), write() > **M**arshalledObject() **M**inimalHTMLWriter
  < startFontTag(), text(), write(), writeAttributes(), writeBody(),
  writeComponent(), writeContent(), writeEndParagraph(),
  writeEndTag(), writeHeader(), writeHTMLTags(),
  writeImage(), writeLeaf(), writeNonHTMLAttributes(),
  writeStartParagraph(), writeStartTag(), writeStyles() >
  MulticastSocket < getTTL(), joinGroup(), leaveGroup(),
  MulticastSocket(), send(), setTimeToLive(), setTTL() >
  ObjectInput* < close(), read(), readObject(), skip() >
  ObjectInputStream < ObjectInputStream(), readBoolean(),
  readByte(), readChar(), readDouble(), readFields(),
  readFloat(), readFully(), readInt(), readLine(), readLong(),
  readObject(), readObjectOverride(), readShort(),
  readStreamHeader(), readUnsignedByte(), readUnsignedShort(),
  readUTF(), resolveClass(), resolveObject(), skipBytes() >
  ObjectInputStream.GetField.get() *ObjectOutput* < flush(),
  write(), writeObject() > **O**bjectOutputStream
  < defaultWriteObject(), drain(), ObjectOutputStream(),
  putFields(), replaceObject(), reset(), useProtocolVersion(),
  writeBoolean(), writeByte(), writeBytes(), writeChar(),
  writeChars(), writeDouble(), writeFields(), writeFloat(),
  writeInt(), writeLong(), writeObject(), writeObjectOverride(),
  writeShort(), writeStreamHeader(), writeUTF() > **O**bjID
  < read(), write() > **P**arser* < parseDTDMarkup(),
  parseMarkupDeclarations() > **P**ipedInputStream
  < PipedInputStream(), receive() > **P**ipedOutputStream()
  PipedReader() **P**ipedWriter() **P**roperties*.store()
  PushbackInputStream.unread() **P**ushbackReader.unread()
  RandomAccessFile < getFD(), getFilePointer(), length(),
  RandomAccessFile(), read(), readBoolean(), readByte(),
  readChar(), readDouble(), readFloat(), readFully(), readInt(),
  readLine(), readLong(), readShort(), readUnsignedByte(),
  readUnsignedShort(), readUTF(), seek(), setLength(),
  skipBytes(), write(), writeBoolean(), writeByte(), writeBytes(),
  writeChar(), writeChars(), writeDouble(), writeFloat(),
  writeInt(), writeLong(), writeShort(), writeUTF() > **R**eader*
  < mark(), read(), ready(), reset(), skip() > *RemoteCall*
  < getInputStream(), getOutputStream(), getResultStream(),
  releaseInputStream(), releaseOutputStream() >
  RMIServerSocketFactory.createServerSocket()
  RMISocketFactory < createSocket(), setSocketFactory() >
  Runtime.exec() **S**erverSocket < close(), getSoTimeout(),
  implAccept(), ServerSocket(), setSocketFactory() >
  SignedObject() **S**ocket < getInputStream(), getOutputStream(),
  setSocketImplFactory(), Socket() > **S**ocketImpl < available(),
  bind(), close(), connect(), create(), getInputStream(),
  getOutputStream(), listen() > **S**tringSelection.getTransferData()
  StyleContext* < readAttributeSet(), writeAttributes(),
  writeAttributeSet() > *Transferable*.getTransferData() **U**ID.write()
  URL < openConnection(), openStream() > **U**RLConnection*
  < connect(), getContent(), getInputStream(), getOutputStream(),
  getPermission(), guessContentTypeFromStream() >
  Writer* < close(), flush(), write() > **Z**ipFile*
  < getInputStream(), ZipFile() > **Z**ipInputStream*.getNextEntry()
  ZipOutputStream*.putNextEntry()
IP_MULTICAST_IF: *SocketOptions*
IPA_EXTENSIONS: **C**haracter.UnicodeBlock
ipadx: **G**ridBagConstraints
ipady: **G**ridBagConstraints
IRObject*: org.omg.CORBA
—extended by: *IDLType*
is_a(): **D**elegate
IS_CLOSED_PROPERTY: **J**InternalFrame
is_equivalent(): **D**elegate
IS_ICON_PROPERTY: **J**InternalFrame
is_local(): **D**elegate
IS_MAXIMUM_PROPERTY: **J**InternalFrame

IS_SELECTED_PROPERTY: JInternalFrame
isAbsolute(): File
isAbstract(): Modifier
isAccessible(): AccessibleObject*
isAccessibleChildSelected(): AccessibleSelection
    JList.AccessibleJList JMenu.AccessibleJMenu
    JMenuBar.AccessibleJMenuBar
    JTabbedPane.AccessibleJTabbedPane
    JTable.AccessibleJTable JTree.AccessibleJTree
    JTree.AccessibleJTree.AccessibleJTreeNode
isActionKey(): KeyEvent*
isActive(): Applet* AppletStub DropTarget
isAddedPath(): TreeSelectionEvent
isAfter(): CompositeView*
isAfterLast(): ResultSet
isAlive(): Thread
isAllocationValid(): BoxView*
isAlphaPremultiplied(): BufferedImage ColorModel*
isAltDown(): InputEvent*
isAltGraphDown(): InputEvent*
isAncestorOf(): Container*
isAntiAliased(): FontRenderContext
isArmed(): ButtonModel DefaultButtonModel* JMenuItem*
isArray(): Class
isAssignableFrom(): Class
isAutoIncrement(): ResultSetMetaData
isBackingStoreEnabled(): JViewport
isBefore(): CompositeView*
isBeforeFirst(): ResultSet
isBlock(): HTML.Tag*
isBlockTag(): HTMLWriter
isBold(): Font* StyleConstants*
isBorderOpaque(): AbstractBorder* Border
    BorderUIResource
isBorderPainted(): AbstractButton* JMenuBar JPopupMenu
    JProgressBar JToolBar
isBound(): PropertyDescriptor*
isBoundary(): BreakIterator
isCanceled(): ProgressMonitor
isCancelled(): PrinterJob
isCaseSensitive(): ResultSetMetaData
isCatalogAtStart(): DatabaseMetaData
isCellEditable(): AbstractTableModel* CellEditor*
    DefaultCellEditor DefaultCellEditor.EditorDelegate
    DefaultTreeCellEditor JTable TableModel
isCellSelected(): JTable
isCertificateEntry(): KeyStore
isClosable(): JInternalFrame
isClosed(): JInternalFrame
isClosed(): Connection JInternalFrame
isCoalesce(): Timer
isCollapsed(): JTree
isColumnSelected(): JTable
isCombining(): GlyphMetrics
isCompatibleRaster(): ColorModel*
isCompatibleSampleModel(): ColorModel*
isCompatibleValue(): RenderingHints.Key
isCompatibleWith(): Package
isCompletelyDirty(): RepaintManager
isComponent(): GlyphMetrics
isComponentPartOfCurrentMenu(): MenuSelectionManager
isConstrained(): PropertyDescriptor*
isConsumed(): AWTEvent*
isConsumer(): FilteredImageSource ImageProducer
    MemoryImageSource RenderableImageProducer
isContentAreaFilled(): AbstractButton*
isContinuousLayout(): JSplitPane
isControlDown(): InputEvent*
isCS_sRGB(): ColorSpace*
isCurrency(): ResultSetMetaData
isCurrentServiceInvalidNow():
    BeanContextServiceRevokedEvent

isCyclic(): GradientPaint
isDaemon(): Thread ThreadGroup
isDataFlavorSupported(): DropTargetContext
    DropTargetContext.TransferableProxy DropTargetDragEvent
    DropTargetDropEvent StringSelection Transferable
isDecimalSeparatorAlwaysShown(): DecimalFormat
isDefaultButton(): JButton
isDefaultCapable(): JButton
isDefined(): AbstractDocument.AbstractElement* AttributeSet*
    Character SimpleAttributeSet StyleContext.NamedStyle
    StyleContext.SmallAttributeSet
isDefinitelyWritable(): ResultSetMetaData
isDelegated(): BeanContextChildSupport*
isDescendant(): TreePath
isDescendingFrom(): SwingUtilities
isDesignTime(): BeanContextSupport* Beans DesignMode*
isDestroyed(): ThreadGroup
isDigit(): Character
isDirectory(): File ZipEntry*
isDirectorySelectionEnabled(): JFileChooser
isDispatchThread(): EventQueue
isDisplayable(): Component*
isDone(): FlatteningPathIterator PathIterator
isDoubleBuffered(): Component*
isDoubleBufferingEnabled(): RepaintManager
isDragImageSupported(): DragSource
isDrawingBuffer(): DebugGraphics
isDynamic(): ContextualRenderedImageFactory
    RenderableImage RenderableImageOp
isEditable(): JComboBox
isEditable(): JComboBox JTextComponent* JTree
    TextComponent*
isEditing(): JTable JTree TreeUI
isEmpty(): AbstractCollection* AbstractMap* Area Attributes
    BeanContextSupport* Collection* DefaultListModel
    Dictionary* javax.swing.text.html.parser.Element Map*
    RectangularShape* RenderingHints SimpleAttributeSet
isEnabled(): AbstractAction* AccessibleComponent
    Action Box.AccessibleBox
    Box.Filler.AccessibleBoxFiller ButtonModel
    CellRendererPane.AccessibleCellRendererPane
    Component* DefaultButtonModel*
    JApplet.AccessibleJApplet
    JComponent.AccessibleJComponent*
    JDialog.AccessibleJDialog JFrame.AccessibleJFrame
    JList.AccessibleJList.AccessibleJListChild
    JPopupMenu.WindowPopup.AccessibleWindowPopup
    JTable.AccessibleJTable.AccessibleJTableCell
    JTableHeader.AccessibleJTableHeader ↩
    .AccessibleJTableHeaderEntry
    JTree.AccessibleJTree.AccessibleJTreeNode
    JWindow.AccessibleJWindow MenuItem* ToolTipManager
isEnabledAt(): JTabbedPane
isEnqueued(): Reference*
isEqual(): AbstractDocument.AbstractElement*
    AttributeSet* MessageDigest SimpleAttributeSet
    StyleContext.NamedStyle StyleContext.SmallAttributeSet
isErrorAny(): MediaTracker
isErrorID(): MediaTracker
isEventDispatchThread(): SwingUtilities
isExpanded(): AbstractLayoutCache* JTree
isExpert(): FeatureDescriptor*
isFile(): File
isFileHidingEnabled(): JFileChooser
isFileSelectionEnabled(): JFileChooser
isFinal(): Modifier
isFirst(): ResultSet
isFixedRowHeight(): AbstractLayoutCache* JTree
isFlavorJavaFileListType(): DataFlavor
isFlavorRemoteObjectType(): DataFlavor
isFlavorSerializedObjectType(): DataFlavor
isFloatable(): JToolBar

isFocusCycleRoot(): JComponent*
isFocusManagerEnabled(): FocusManager*
isFocusPainted(): AbstractButton*
isFocusTraversable(): *AccessibleComponent*
    Box.AccessibleBox   Box.Filler.AccessibleBoxFiller
    CellRendererPane.AccessibleCellRendererPane
    ComboBoxUI Component*
    ComponentPeer JApplet.AccessibleJApplet
    JComponent.AccessibleJComponent*
    JDialog.AccessibleJDialog JFrame.AccessibleJFrame
    JList.AccessibleJList.AccessibleJListChild
    JPopupMenu.WindowPopup.AccessibleWindowPopup
    JTable.AccessibleJTable.AccessibleJTableCell
    JTableHeader.AccessibleJTableHeader ↩
    .AccessibleJTableHeaderEntry
    JTree.AccessibleJTree.AccessibleJTreeNode
    JWindow.AccessibleJWindow
isGeneral(): Entity
isGraphicsConfigSupported(): GraphicsConfigTemplate
isGroupingUsed(): NumberFormat*
isGuiAvailable(): Beans
isHidden(): FeatureDescriptor* File
isHiddenFile(): FileSystemView
isHorizontal(): ComponentOrientation
isIcon: JInternalFrame
isIcon(): JInternalFrame
isIconifiable(): JInternalFrame
isIdentifierIgnorable(): Character
isIdentity(): AffineTransform
isInDefaultEventSet(): EventSetDescriptor
isindex: DTD
ISINDEX: HTML.Tag*
isIndexSelected(): java.awt.List
isInfinite(): Double Float
isInherited(): CSS.Attribute
isInProgress(): CompoundEdit*
isInstance(): Class
isInstanceOf(): Beans
isInterface(): Class Modifier
isInterrupted(): Thread
isISOControl(): Character
isItalic(): Font* StyleConstants*
isJavaIdentifierPart(): Character
isJavaIdentifierStart(): Character
isJavaLetter(): Character
isJavaLetterOrDigit(): Character
isJavaMIMEType(): SystemFlavorMap
isKeyEntry(): KeyStore
isLargeModel(): JTree
isLast(): *ResultSet*
isLeadAnchorNotificationEnabled():
    DefaultListSelectionModel
isLeadingEdge(): TextHitInfo
isLeaf(): AbstractDocument.AbstractElement*
    DefaultMutableTreeNode* DefaultTreeModel
    javax.swing.text.Element *TreeModel* *TreeNode*
isLeapYear(): GregorianCalendar
isLeftMouseButton(): SwingUtilities
isLeftToRight(): ComponentOrientation TextLayout
isLenient(): Calendar* DateFormat*
isLetter(): Character
isLetterOrDigit(): Character
isLigature(): GlyphMetrics
isLightweight(): Component
isLightweightComponent(): JComponent*
isLightWeightPopupEnabled(): JComboBox JPopupMenu
    ToolTipManager
isLocal: DropTargetContext.TransferableProxy
isLocallyDefined(): *Keymap*
isLocalTransfer(): DropTargetDropEvent
isLowerCase(): Character
isManagingFocus(): JComponent*

ISMAP: HTML.Attribute
isMaximizable(): JInternalFrame
isMaximum: JInternalFrame
isMaximum(): JInternalFrame
isMember(): *Group*
isMenuComponent(): JMenu
isMetaDown(): InputEvent*
isMiddleMouseButton(): SwingUtilities
isMimeTypeEqual(): DataFlavor
isMimeTypeSerializedObject(): DataFlavor
isModal(): Dialog*
isMulticastAddress(): InetAddress
isMultipleMode(): java.awt.List
isMultiSelectionEnabled(): JFileChooser
isNaN(): Double Float
isNative(): Modifier
isNativeLookAndFeel(): LookAndFeel
isNegative(): *AclEntry*
isNodeAncestor(): DefaultMutableTreeNode*
isNodeChild(): DefaultMutableTreeNode*
isNodeDescendant(): DefaultMutableTreeNode*
isNodeRelated(): DefaultMutableTreeNode*
isNodeSibling(): DefaultMutableTreeNode*
isNullable(): *ResultSetMetaData*
isOneTouchExpandable(): JSplitPane
isOnKeyRelease(): KeyStroke
isOpaque(): Component
isOptimizedDrawingEnabled(): JComponent*
isOwner(): *Owner*
isPaintable(): *PropertyEditor* PropertyEditorSupport
isPaintingTile(): JComponent*
isParameter(): Entity
isParseIntegerOnly(): NumberFormat*
isPathEditable(): JTree
isPathSelected(): DefaultTreeSelectionModel* JTree
    TreeSelectionModel
isPlain(): Font*
isPolygonal(): Area
isPopupMenuVisible(): JMenu
isPopupTrigger(): MouseEvent*
isPopupVisible(): ComboBoxUI JComboBox
isPreferred(): FeatureDescriptor*
isPreformatted(): HTML.Tag* TagElement
isPressed(): *ButtonModel* DefaultButtonModel*
isPrimitive(): Class ObjectStreamField
isPrivate(): Modifier
isProbablePrime(): BigInteger
isPropagated(): BeanContextEvent*
isProtected(): Modifier
isPublic(): Modifier
isReadOnly(): *Connection* *DatabaseMetaData*
    PermissionCollection* *ResultSetMetaData*
isRectangleContainingRectangle(): SwingUtilities
isRectangular(): Area
isRepeats(): Timer
isReplacing(): DefaultStyledDocument.AttributeUndoableEdit
isRepresentationClassInputStream(): DataFlavor
isRepresentationClassRemote(): DataFlavor
isRepresentationClassSerializable(): DataFlavor
isRequestFocusEnabled(): JComponent*
isResizable: TableColumn
isResizable(): Dialog* Frame* JInternalFrame
isRevoked(): CRL*
isRightMouseButton(): SwingUtilities
isRollover(): *ButtonModel* DefaultButtonModel*
isRolloverEnabled(): AbstractButton*
isRoot(): DefaultMutableTreeNode* FileSystemView
isRootPaneCheckingEnabled(): JApplet JDialog JFrame
    JInternalFrame JWindow
isRootVisible(): AbstractLayoutCache* JTree
isRowSelected(): DefaultTreeSelectionModel* JTable JTree
    TreeSelectionModel

J

JarEntry: java.util.jar
— passed to: JarEntry( )
— returned by: JarFile.getJarEntry( )
JarURLConnection.getJarEntry( )
JarException: java.util.jar
JarFile: java.util.jar
— returned by: JarURLConnection.getJarFile( )
jarFileURLConnection: JarURLConnection
JarInputStream: java.util.jar
JarOutputStream: java.util.jar
JarURLConnection: java.net
JAVA_OBJECT: Types
javaFileListFlavor: DataFlavor
javaJVMLocalObjectMimeType: DataFlavor
javaRemoteObjectMimeType: DataFlavor
javaSerializedObjectMimeType: DataFlavor
JButton: javax.swing
— passed to: JButton.AccessibleJButton( )
JToolBar.createActionChangeListener( )
— returned by: JRootPane.getDefaultButton( )
— fields: JRootPane.defaultButton
JButton.AccessibleJButton: javax.swing
JCheckBox: javax.swing
— passed to: DefaultCellEditor( )
JCheckBox.AccessibleJCheckBox: javax.swing
JCheckBoxMenuItem: javax.swing
— passed
to: JCheckBoxMenuItem.AccessibleJCheckBoxMenuItem( )
JCheckBoxMenuItem.AccessibleJCheckBoxMenuItem:
javax.swing
JColorChooser: javax.swing
— passed to: AbstractColorChooserPanel
< installChooserPanel( ), uninstallChooserPanel( ) >
JColorChooser.AccessibleJColorChooser( )
JColorChooser.AccessibleJColorChooser: javax.swing
JComboBox: javax.swing
— passed to: ComboBoxUI < isFocusTraversable( ), isPopupVisible( ),
setPopupVisible( ) > JComboBox.AccessibleJComboBox( )
JComboBox.AccessibleJComboBox: javax.swing
JComboBox.KeySelectionManager: javax.swing
— passed to: JComboBox.setKeySelectionManager( )
— returned by: JComboBox < createDefaultKeySelectionManager( ),
getKeySelectionManager( ) >
— fields: JComboBox.keySelectionManager
JComponent*: javax.swing
— subclasses: AbstractButton* JColorChooser JComboBox
JFileChooser JInternalFrame JInternalFrame.JDesktopIcon
JLabel* JLayeredPane* JList JMenuBar JOptionPane
JPanel* JPopupMenu JProgressBar JRootPane
JScrollBar* JScrollPane JSeparator* JSlider JSplitPane
JTabbedPane JTable JTableHeader JTextComponent*
JToolBar JToolTip JTree JViewport
— descendents: AbstractColorChooserPanel
DefaultListCellRenderer*
DefaultListCellRenderer.UIResource
DefaultTableCellRenderer*
DefaultTableCellRenderer.UIResource
DefaultTreeCellEditor.DefaultTextField
DefaultTreeCellRenderer JButton JCheckBox
JCheckBoxMenuItem JDesktopPane JEditorPane* JMenu
JMenuItem* JPasswordField JPopupMenu.Separator
JRadioButton JRadioButtonMenuItem JScrollPane.ScrollBar
JTextArea JTextField* JTextPane JToggleButton*
JToolBar.Separator
— passed to: AncestorEvent( ) ComponentUI* < createUI( ),
getAccessibleChild( ), getAccessibleChildrenCount( ),
getMaximumSize( ), getMinimumSize( ),
getPreferredSize( ), installUI( ), paint( ),
uninstallUI( ), update( ) > DefaultDesktopManager
< beginDraggingFrame( ), beginResizingFrame( ),
dragFrame( ), endDraggingFrame( ), endResizingFrame( ),
resizeFrame( ), setBoundsForFrame( ) > *DesktopManager*

< beginResizingFrame( ), dragFrame( ), endDraggingFrame( ),
endResizingFrame( ), resizeFrame( ), setBoundsForFrame( ) >
JComponent.AccessibleJComponent( ) JLayeredPane*
< getLayer( ), putLayer( ) > LookAndFeel < installBorder( ),
installColors( ), installColorsAndFont( ), uninstallBorder( ) >
RepaintManager < addInvalidComponent( ), currentManager( ),
getDirtyRegion( ), isCompletelyDirty( ), markCompletelyClean( ),
markCompletelyDirty( ), removeInvalidComponent( ) >
ToolTipManager < registerComponent( ),
unregisterComponent( ) > UIManager.getUI( )
— returned by: AncestorEvent.getComponent( )
JColorChooser.getPreviewPanel( ) JToolTip.getComponent( )
— fields: DefaultCellEditor.editorComponent
JComponent.AccessibleJComponent*: javax.swing
— subclasses: AbstractButton.AccessibleAbstractButton*
JColorChooser.AccessibleJColorChooser
JComboBox.AccessibleJComboBox
JDesktopPane.AccessibleJDesktopPane
JFileChooser.AccessibleJFileChooser
JInternalFrame.AccessibleJInternalFrame
JInternalFrame.JDesktopIcon.AccessibleJDesktopIcon
JLabel.AccessibleJLabel
JLayeredPane.AccessibleJLayeredPane
JList.AccessibleJList JMenuBar.AccessibleJMenuBar
JOptionPane.AccessibleJOptionPane
JPanel.AccessibleJPanel
JPopupMenu.AccessibleJPopupMenu
JProgressBar.AccessibleJProgressBar
JRootPane.AccessibleJRootPane
JScrollBar.AccessibleJScrollBar
JScrollPane.AccessibleJScrollPane
JSeparator.AccessibleJSeparator
JSlider.AccessibleJSlider JSplitPane.AccessibleJSplitPane
JTabbedPane.AccessibleJTabbedPane
JTable.AccessibleJTable
JTableHeader.AccessibleJTableHeader
JTextComponent.AccessibleJTextComponent*
JToolBar.AccessibleJToolBar JToolTip.AccessibleJToolTip
JTree.AccessibleJTree JViewport.AccessibleJViewport
— descendents: JButton.AccessibleJButton
JCheckBox.AccessibleJCheckBox
JCheckBoxMenuItem.AccessibleJCheckBoxMenuItem
JEditorPane.AccessibleJEditorPane*
JEditorPane.AccessibleJEditorPaneHTML
JEditorPane.JEditorPaneAccessibleHypertextSupport
JMenu.AccessibleJMenu JMenuItem.AccessibleJMenuItem*
JPasswordField.AccessibleJPasswordField
JRadioButton.AccessibleJRadioButton
JRadioButtonMenuItem.AccessibleJRadioButtonMenuItem
JTextArea.AccessibleJTextArea
JTextField.AccessibleJTextField*
JToggleButton.AccessibleJToggleButton*
— passed to: JComponent.AccessibleJComponent ↵
.AccessibleContainerHandler( )
**JComponent.AccessibleJComponent ↵
.AccessibleContainerHandler**:
javax.swing
jdbcCompliant( ): *Driver*
JDesktopPane: javax.swing
— passed to: JDesktopPane.AccessibleJDesktopPane( )
— returned by: JInternalFrame.getDesktopPane( )
JOptionPane.getDesktopPaneForComponent( )
JDesktopPane.AccessibleJDesktopPane: javax.swing
JDialog: javax.swing
— passed to: JDialog.AccessibleJDialog( )
— returned by: JColorChooser.createDialog( )
JDialog.AccessibleJDialog: javax.swing
JEditorPane*: javax.swing
— subclasses: JTextPane
— passed to: EditorKit* < deinstall( ), install( ) >
HTMLEditorKit.HTMLTextAction*.getHTMLEditorKit( )
HTMLEditorKit.InsertHTMLTextAction.insertHTML( )

L

LANGUAGE: AttributedCharacterIterator.Attribute*
    HTML.Attribute
LAO: Character.UnicodeBlock
LARGE_MODEL_PROPERTY: JTree
largeModel: JTree
last(): BreakIterator CardLayout *CharacterIterator* *ResultSet*
    SortedSet StringCharacterIterator TreeSet
LAST_DIVIDER_LOCATION_PROPERTY: JSplitPane
lastDividerLocation: JSplitPane
lastEdit(): CompoundEdit*
lastElement(): DefaultListModel Vector*
lastIndexOf(): AbstractList* DefaultListModel *java.util.List*
    String
lastKey(): *SortedMap* TreeMap
lastModified(): File
LastOwnerException: java.security.acl
  —thrown by: *Owner*.deleteOwner( )
lastPageFirst(): PrintJob
lastPaintPosition: JViewport
lastPath: DefaultTreeCellEditor
lastRow: DefaultTreeCellEditor TableModelEvent
LATIN: InputSubset
LATIN_1_SUPPLEMENT: Character.UnicodeBlock
LATIN_DIGITS: InputSubset
LATIN_EXTENDED_A: Character.UnicodeBlock
LATIN_EXTENDED_ADDITIONAL: Character.UnicodeBlock
LATIN_EXTENDED_B: Character.UnicodeBlock
LAYER_PROPERTY: JLayeredPane*
LAYERED_PANE: AccessibleRole
LAYERED_PANE_PROPERTY: JInternalFrame
LayeredHighlighter*: javax.swing.text
  —subclasses: DefaultHighlighter
LayeredHighlighter.LayerPainter*: javax.swing.text
  —subclasses: DefaultHighlighter.DefaultHighlightPainter
  —fields: DefaultHighlighter.DefaultPainter
layeredPane: JRootPane
layout(): BoxView* Component*
layoutColumns(): TableView
layoutCompoundLabel(): SwingUtilities
layoutContainer(): BorderLayout BoxLayout CardLayout
    FlowLayout GridBagLayout GridLayout
    JRootPane.RootLayout *LayoutManager** OverlayLayout
    ScrollPaneLayout* ViewportLayout
layoutInfo: GridBagLayout
layoutMajorAxis(): BoxView*
LayoutManager*: java.awt
  —extended by: *LayoutManager2*
  —passed to: Container*.setLayout( ) JPanel( )
  —returned by: Container*.getLayout( )
    JViewport.createLayoutManager( )
  —implemented by: FlowLayout GridLayout ScrollPaneLayout*
    ViewportLayout
LayoutManager2: java.awt
  —implemented by: BorderLayout BoxLayout CardLayout
    GridBagLayout JRootPane.RootLayout OverlayLayout
layoutMinorAxis(): BoxView*
lazilyLoadDesktopProperty(): Toolkit
LEAD_DOTS: TabStop
LEAD_EQUALS: TabStop
LEAD_HYPHENS: TabStop
LEAD_NONE: TabStop
LEAD_THICKLINE: TabStop
LEAD_UNDERLINE: TabStop
leadAnchorNotificationEnabled: DefaultListSelectionModel
leadIndex: DefaultTreeSelectionModel*
LEADING: FlowLayout *SwingConstants*
leading(): TextHitInfo
leadPath: DefaultTreeSelectionModel*
leadRow: DefaultTreeSelectionModel*
leafIcon: DefaultTreeCellRenderer
Lease: java.rmi.dgc
  —passed to: *DGC*.dirty( )

  —returned by: *DGC*.dirty( )
leave(): DatagramSocketImpl
leaveGroup(): MulticastSocket
left: EmptyBorder* Insets*
LEFT: Event FlowLayout JSplitPane Label *SwingConstants*
    TitledBorder*
LEFT_ALIGNMENT: Component*
LEFT_TO_RIGHT: ComponentOrientation
leftComponent: JSplitPane
LeftIndent: StyleConstants*
len: InflaterInputStream*
length: OptionalDataException
length(): *AbstractDocument.Content* BitSet *Blob* *Clob*
    DynSequence File GapContent RandomAccessFile
    String StringBuffer StringContent TypeCode
LETTER_NUMBER: Character
LETTER_SPACING: CSS.Attribute
LETTERLIKE_SYMBOLS: Character.UnicodeBlock
LI: HTML.Tag*
LIGATURE: GlyphMetrics
lightGray: Color*
LightweightPeer*: java.awt.peer
  —returned by: Toolkit.createComponent( )
lightWeightPopupEnabled: JComboBox ToolTipManager
Line2D*: java.awt.geom
  —subclasses: Line2D.Double Line2D.Float
  —passed to: Line2D* < intersectsLine( ), setLine( ) >
Line2D.Double: java.awt.geom
Line2D.Float: java.awt.geom
LINE_HEIGHT: CSS.Attribute
LINE_SEPARATOR: Character
LineBorder*: javax.swing.border
  —subclasses: BorderUIResource.LineBorderUIResource
LineBreakMeasurer: java.awt.font
lineColor: LineBorder*
lineLimitAttribute: PlainDocument
LineMetrics: java.awt.font
  —returned by: Font*.getLineMetrics( ) FontMetrics.getLineMetrics( )
lineno(): StreamTokenizer
LineNumberInputStream: java.io
LineNumberReader: java.io
linesIntersect(): Line2D*
LineSpacing: StyleConstants*
lineTo(): GeneralPath
LINK: HTML.Attribute HTML.Tag*
LinkageError*: java.lang
  —subclasses: ClassCircularityError ClassFormatError*
    ExceptionInInitializerError IncompatibleClassChangeError*
    NoClassDefFoundError UnsatisfiedLinkError VerifyError
  —descendents: AbstractMethodError IllegalAccessError
    InstantiationError NoSuchFieldError NoSuchMethodError
    UnsupportedClassVersionError
LinkedList: java.util
LIST: AccessibleRole
List: java.awt
  —passed to: Toolkit.createList( )
List: java.util
  —passed to: Collections < binarySearch( ), copy( ), fill( ),
    reverse( ), shuffle( ), sort( ), synchronizedList( ),
    unmodifiableList( ) >
  —returned by: AbstractList*.subList( ) Collections
    < nCopies( ), synchronizedList( ), unmodifiableList( ) >
    DropTargetDragEvent.getCurrentDataFlavorsAsList( )
    java.util.List.subList( )
  —implemented by: AbstractList*
  —fields: Collections.EMPTY_LIST
list(): _NamingContextImplBase _NamingContextStub
    Component* File Naming *NamingContext* Properties*
    Registry ThreadGroup
LIST_DESELECT: Event
list_initial_services(): ORB
LIST_SELECT: Event

L

LIST_STYLE: **C**SS.Attribute
LIST_STYLE_IMAGE: **C**SS.Attribute
LIST_STYLE_POSITION: **C**SS.Attribute
LIST_STYLE_TYPE: **C**SS.Attribute
ListCellRenderer: javax.swing
— passed to: **J**ComboBox.setRenderer( )
— returned by: **J**ComboBox.getRenderer( )
— implemented by: **D**efaultListCellRenderer*
— fields: **J**ComboBox.renderer
ListDataEvent: javax.swing.event
— passed to: **J**ComboBox < contentsChanged( ), intervalAdded( ),
intervalRemoved( ) > **J**List.AccessibleJList < intervalAdded( ),
intervalRemoved( ) > *ListDataListener* < intervalAdded( ),
intervalRemoved( ) >
ListDataListener: javax.swing.event
— passed to: **A**bstractListModel* < addListDataListener( ),
removeListDataListener( ) > *ListModel**.removeListDataListener( )
— implemented by: **J**ComboBox **J**List.AccessibleJList
listen( ): **S**ocketImpl
listenerList: **A**bstractDocument* **A**bstractListModel*
AbstractTableModel* **D**efaultBoundedRangeModel
DefaultButtonModel* **D**efaultCaret **D**efaultCellEditor
DefaultColorSelectionModel **D**efaultListSelectionModel
DefaultSingleSelectionModel **D**efaultTableColumnModel
DefaultTreeModel **D**efaultTreeSelectionModel*
EventListenerList **J**Component* **M**enuSelectionManager
StyleContext.NamedStyle **T**imer
listeners: **U**ndoableEditSupport
listFiles( ): **F**ile
ListIterator: java.util
— returned by: **A**bstractList*.listIterator( ) *java.util.List*.listIterator( )
listIterator( ): **A**bstractList* *java.util.List*
*ListModel**: javax.swing
— extended by: *ComboBoxModel**
— descendents: *MutableComboBoxModel**
— passed to: **J**List < JList( ), setModel( ) >
— returned by: **J**List.getModel( )
— implemented by: **A**bstractListModel*
ListPeer: java.awt.peer
— returned by: **T**oolkit.createList( )
ListResourceBundle*: java.util
— subclasses: **A**ccessibleResourceBundle
listRoots( ): **F**ile
ListSelectionEvent: javax.swing.event
— passed to: **D**efaultTableColumnModel
< fireColumnSelectionChanged( ), valueChanged( ) > **J**Table
< columnSelectionChanged( ), valueChanged( ) >
JTable.AccessibleJTable.valueChanged( )
ListSelectionListener.valueChanged( )
ListSelectionListener: javax.swing.event
— passed to: **D**efaultListSelectionModel
< addListSelectionListener( ), removeListSelectionListener( ) >
JList.removeListSelectionListener( )
ListSelectionModel.removeListSelectionListener( )
— implemented by: **D**efaultTableColumnModel
JList.AccessibleJList **J**Table **J**Table.AccessibleJTable
listSelectionModel: **D**efaultTreeSelectionModel*
ListSelectionModel: javax.swing
— passed to: **D**efaultTableColumnModel.setSelectionModel( )
JTable < JTable( ), setSelectionModel( ) >
— returned by: **D**efaultTableColumnModel < createSelectionModel( ),
getSelectionModel( ) > **J**List.getSelectionModel( )
JTable.getSelectionModel( )
— implemented by: **D**efaultListSelectionModel
— fields: **D**efaultTableColumnModel.selectionModel
ListUI: javax.swing.plaf
— passed to: **J**List.setUI( )
— returned by: **J**List.getUI( )
ListView: javax.swing.text.html
LOAD: **F**ileDialog
load( ): **K**eyStore **P**roperties* **R**untime **S**ystem
LOAD_FILE: **E**vent

loadChildren( ): **C**ompositeView* **J**Tree.DynamicUtilTreeNode
loadClass( ): **C**lassLoader* *LoaderHandler* **R**MIClassLoader
loadedChildren( ): **J**Tree.DynamicUtilTreeNode
LoaderHandler: java.rmi.server
loadImage( ): **I**mageIcon **S**impleBeanInfo
LOADING: **M**ediaTracker
loadKeymap( ): **J**TextComponent*
loadLibrary( ): **R**untime **S**ystem
loadRules( ): **S**tyleSheet
loadSystemColors( ): **T**oolkit
locale: **B**eanContextSupport*
Locale: java.util
— passed to: **A**ccessibleBundle*.toDisplayString( )
BeanContextServicesSupport* **B**eanContextSupport*
< BeanContextSupport( ), setLocale( ) > **B**reakIterator
< getLineInstance( ), getSentenceInstance( ), getWordInstance( ) >
Calendar*.getInstance( ) **C**omponent*.setLocale( )
DateFormat* < getDateInstance( ), getDateTimeInstance( ),
getTimeInstance( ) > **D**ecimalFormatSymbols( )
Font*.getFontName( ) **G**regorianCalendar( ) **L**ocale
< getDisplayCountry( ), getDisplayLanguage( ), getDisplayName( ),
getDisplayVariant( ), setDefault( ) > **N**umberFormat*
< getCurrencyInstance( ), getInstance( ), getNumberInstance( ),
getPercentInstance( ) > **R**esourceBundle*.getBundle( ) **S**tring
< toLowerCase( ), toUpperCase( ) > **T**imeZone*.getDisplayName( )
— returned by: **A**ccessibleContext*.getLocale( )
BreakIterator.getAvailableLocales( )
Collator*.getAvailableLocales( )
DateFormat*.getAvailableLocales( ) **L**ocale.getDefault( )
NumberFormat*.getAvailableLocales( )
— fields: **B**eanContextSupport*.locale **L**ocale < CANADA_FRENCH,
CHINA, CHINESE, ENGLISH, FRANCE, FRENCH, GERMAN,
GERMANY, ITALIAN, ITALY, JAPAN, JAPANESE, KOREA,
KOREAN, PRC, SIMPLIFIED_CHINESE, TAIWAN,
TRADITIONAL_CHINESE, UK, US >
localport: **S**ocketImpl
localPort: **D**atagramSocketImpl
locate( ): **C**omponent*
LocateRegistry: java.rmi.registry
location( ): **C**omponent* **G**ridBagLayout
locationToIndex( ): **J**List **L**istUI
lock: **R**eader* **W**riter*
log( ): **L**ogStream **M**ath
LOG_OPTION: **D**ebugGraphics
LOGICAL_STYLE_ACTION: **H**TMLEditorKit
LogStream: java.rmi.server
— returned by: **L**ogStream.log( )
logStream( ): **D**ebugGraphics
LONG: **D**ateFormat* **T**imeZone*
Long: java.lang
— passed to: **L**ong < compareTo( ), getLong( ) >
— returned by: **L**ong < decode( ), getLong( ), valueOf( ) >
LONG_DESCRIPTION: *Action*
longBitsToDouble( ): **D**ouble
LongHolder: org.omg.CORBA
longValue( ): **N**umber*
LONGVARBINARY: **T**ypes
LONGVARCHAR: **T**ypes
LookAndFeel: javax.swing
— passed to: **U**IManager < addAuxiliaryLookAndFeel( ),
removeAuxiliaryLookAndFeel( ), setLookAndFeel( ) >
— returned by: **U**IManager < getAuxiliaryLookAndFeels( ),
getLookAndFeel( ) >
lookup( ): **N**aming **O**bjectStreamClass *Registry*
lookupConstraints( ): **G**ridBagLayout
LookupOp: java.awt.image
lookupPixel( ): **L**ookupTable*
LookupTable*: java.awt.image
— subclasses: **B**yteLookupTable **S**hortLookupTable
— passed to: **L**ookupOp( )
— returned by: **L**ookupOp.getTable( )
loop( ): *AudioClip*

MenuComponentPeer*: java.awt.peer
—extended by: *MenuBarPeer* *MenuItemPeer**
—descendents: **C**heckboxMenuItemPeer *MenuPeer**
  PopupMenuPeer
—returned by: **M**enuComponent*.getPeer( )
MenuContainer: java.awt
—returned by: **M**enuComponent*.getParent( )
—implemented by: **C**omponent* **M**enu* **M**enuBar
menuDeselected( ): *MenuListener*
menuDragMouseDragged( ): *MenuDragMouseListener*
menuDragMouseEntered( ): *MenuDragMouseListener*
MenuDragMouseEvent: javax.swing.event
—passed to: **J**MenuItem* < fireMenuDragMouseDragged( ),
fireMenuDragMouseEntered( ), fireMenuDragMouseExited( ),
fireMenuDragMouseReleased( ), processMenuDragMouseEvent( ) >
  MenuDragMouseListener < menuDragMouseEntered( ),
  menuDragMouseExited( ), menuDragMouseReleased( ) >
menuDragMouseExited( ): *MenuDragMouseListener*
MenuDragMouseListener: javax.swing.event
—passed to: **J**MenuItem* < addMenuDragMouseListener( ),
removeMenuDragMouseListener( ) >
menuDragMouseReleased( ): *MenuDragMouseListener*
MenuElement: javax.swing
—passed to: **J**MenuBar < processKeyEvent( ),
processMouseEvent( ) > **J**MenuItem*.processMouseEvent( )
JPopupMenu.processMouseEvent( ) *MenuElement*
< processKeyEvent( ), processMouseEvent( ) >
  MenuSelectionManager.setSelectedPath( )
—returned by: **J**MenuBar.getSubElements( )
JPopupMenu.getSubElements( )
MenuElement.getSubElements( )
  MenuSelectionManager.getSelectedPath( )
—implemented by: **J**MenuBar **J**MenuItem* **J**PopupMenu
MenuEvent: javax.swing.event
—passed to: *MenuListener* < menuCanceled( ), menuDeselected( ),
menuSelected( ) >
MenuItem*: java.awt
—subclasses: **C**heckboxMenuItem **M**enu*
—descendents: **P**opupMenu
—passed to: **M**enu* < add( ), insert( ) > **T**oolkit.createMenuItem( )
—returned by: **M**enu* < add( ), getItem( ) >
MenuItemPeer*: java.awt.peer
—extended by: *CheckboxMenuItemPeer* *MenuPeer**
—descendents: **P**opupMenuPeer
—returned by: **T**oolkit.createMenuItem( )
MenuItemUI: javax.swing.plaf
—passed to: **J**MenuItem*.setUI( )
MenuKeyEvent: javax.swing.event
—passed to: **J**MenuItem* < fireMenuKeyPressed( ),
fireMenuKeyReleased( ), fireMenuKeyTyped( ),
processMenuKeyEvent( ) > *MenuKeyListener*
< menuKeyReleased( ), menuKeyTyped( ) >
MenuKeyListener: javax.swing.event
—passed to: **J**MenuItem* < addMenuKeyListener( ),
removeMenuKeyListener( ) >
menuKeyPressed( ): *MenuKeyListener*
menuKeyReleased( ): *MenuKeyListener*
menuKeyTyped( ): *MenuKeyListener*
MenuListener: javax.swing.event
—passed to: **J**Menu < addMenuListener( ), removeMenuListener( ) >
MenuPeer*: java.awt.peer
—extended by: *PopupMenuPeer*
—returned by: **T**oolkit.createMenu( )
menuSelected( ): *MenuListener*
menuSelectionChanged( ): **J**MenuBar **J**MenuItem*
JPopupMenu *MenuElement*
MenuSelectionManager: javax.swing
—passed to: **J**MenuBar < processKeyEvent( ),
processMouseEvent( ) > **J**MenuItem*.processMouseEvent( )
JPopupMenu.processMouseEvent( ) *MenuElement*
< processKeyEvent( ), processMouseEvent( ) >

—returned by: **M**enuDragMouseEvent.getMenuSelectionManager( )
  MenuSelectionManager.defaultManager( )
MenuShortcut: java.awt
—passed to: **M**enuBar < deleteShortcut( ), getShortcutMenuItem( ) >
  MenuItem*.setShortcut( )
—returned by: **M**enuItem*.getShortcut( )
menuText: **S**ystemColor
message: **J**OptionPane
MESSAGE_PROPERTY: **J**OptionPane
MESSAGE_TYPE_PROPERTY: **J**OptionPane
MessageDigest: java.security
—passed to: **D**igestInputStream < DigestInputStream( ),
setMessageDigest( ) > **D**igestOutputStream.setMessageDigest( )
—returned by: **D**igestInputStream.getMessageDigest( )
  MessageDigest.getInstance( )
—fields: **D**igestInputStream.digest
MessageDigestSpi*: java.security
—subclasses: **M**essageDigest
MessageFormat: java.text
messageType: **J**OptionPane
meta: **D**TD
META: **H**TML.Tag*
META_MASK: **A**ctionEvent **E**vent **I**nputEvent*
metaDown( ): **E**vent
method: **H**ttpURLConnection
METHOD: **H**TML.Attribute
Method: java.lang.reflect
—passed to: **E**ventSetDescriptor( ) **I**ndexedPropertyDescriptor
< setIndexedReadMethod( ), setIndexedWriteMethod( ) >
  MethodDescriptor( ) **P**ropertyDescriptor* < setReadMethod( ),
setWriteMethod( ) >
—returned by: **C**lass < getDeclaredMethod( ), getDeclaredMethods( ),
getMethod( ), getMethods( ) > **E**ventSetDescriptor
< getListenerMethods( ), getRemoveListenerMethod( ) >
  IndexedPropertyDescriptor.getIndexedWriteMethod( )
  PropertyDescriptor* < getReadMethod( ), getWriteMethod( ) >
MethodDescriptor: java.beans
—passed to: **E**ventSetDescriptor( )
—returned by: *BeanInfo**.getMethodDescriptors( )
  SimpleBeanInfo.getMethodDescriptors( )
metrics: **P**lainView*
MILLISECOND: **C**alendar*
MILLISECOND_FIELD: **D**ateFormat*
min( ): **B**igDecimal **B**igInteger **C**ollections **M**ath
MIN_PRIORITY: **T**hread
MIN_RADIX: **C**haracter
MIN_VALUE: **B**yte **C**haracter **D**ouble **F**loat **I**nteger **L**ong
  Short
MinimalHTMLWriter: javax.swing.text.html
minimizeFrame( ): **D**efaultDesktopManager *DesktopManager*
minimum: **S**izeRequirements
minimumLayoutSize( ): **B**orderLayout **B**oxLayout
  CardLayout **F**lowLayout **G**ridBagLayout **G**ridLayout
  JRootPane.RootLayout *LayoutManager** **O**verlayLayout
  ScrollPaneLayout **V**iewportLayout
minimumSize( ): **C**omponent* *ComponentPeer**
minor: **S**ystemException*
minorTickSpacing: **J**Slider
MINSIZE: **G**ridBagLayout
MINUTE: **C**alendar*
MINUTE_FIELD: **D**ateFormat*
minWidth: **T**ableColumn
minX: **R**aster*
minY: **R**aster*
MISCELLANEOUS_SYMBOLS: **C**haracter.UnicodeBlock
MISCELLANEOUS_TECHNICAL: **C**haracter.UnicodeBlock
missing_node: **N**otFoundReason
MissingResourceException: java.util
—thrown by: **L**ocale < getISO3Country( ), getISO3Language( ) >
  ResourceBundle* < getBundle( ), getObject( ), getString( ),
getStringArray( ), handleGetObject( ) >
mkdir( ): **F**ile

M

MutableAttributeSet*: javax.swing.text
—extended by: *Style*
—passed to: **H**TMLDocument.HTMLReader < addSpecialElement( ),
blockOpen( ) > **H**TMLEditorKit.createInputAttributes( )
HTMLEditorKit.ParserCallback*.handleStartTag( )
StyleConstants* < setBackground( ), setBidiLevel( ), setBold( ),
setComponent( ), setFirstLineIndent( ), setFontFamily( ),
setFontSize( ), setForeground( ), setIcon( ), setItalic( ),
setLeftIndent( ), setLineSpacing( ), setRightIndent( ),
setSpaceAbove( ), setSpaceBelow( ), setStrikeThrough( ),
setSubscript( ), setSuperscript( ), setTabSet( ), setUnderline( ) >
StyleContext*.readAttributeSet( )
—returned by: **J**TextPane.getInputAttributes( )
StyledEditorKit*.getInputAttributes( )
—implemented by: **A**bstractDocument.AbstractElement*
SimpleAttributeSet
—fields: **H**TMLDocument.HTMLReader.charAttr
MutableComboBoxModel: javax.swing
—implemented by: **D**efaultComboBoxModel
MutableTreeNode: javax.swing.tree
—passed to: **D**efaultMutableTreeNode*
< add( ), insert( ), remove( ), setParent( ) >
DefaultTreeModel.removeNodeFromParent( ) *MutableTreeNode*
< remove( ), setParent( ) >
—implemented by: **D**efaultMutableTreeNode*
—fields: **D**efaultMutableTreeNode*.parent
N: **H**TML.Attribute
N_RESIZE_CURSOR: **C**ursor **F**rame*
name: **A**ttributeList **C**ursor **D**riverPropertyInfo **D**TD
javax.swing.text.html.parser.**E**lement **F**ont*
StructMember **U**nionMember **V**alueMember
NAME: *Action* *DTDConstants* **H**TML.Attribute
name( ): **N**amedValue org.omg.CORBA.**P**rincipal **T**ypeCode
name2type( ): **A**ttributeList
javax.swing.text.html.parser.**E**lement **E**ntity
NameAttribute: *AttributeSet** **S**tyleConstants*
NameComponent: org.omg.CosNaming
—passed to: _NamingContextImplBase < bind( ), bind_context( ),
bind_new_context( ), rebind( ), rebind_context( ), resolve( ),
unbind( ) > _NamingContextStub < bind_context( ),
bind_new_context( ), rebind( ), rebind_context( ), resolve( ),
unbind( ) > **C**annotProceed( ) **N**ameComponentHelper.write( )
NameHelper < insert( ), write( ) > *NamingContext* < bind( ),
bind_context( ), bind_new_context( ), rebind( ), rebind_context( ),
resolve( ), unbind( ) >
—returned by: **N**ameComponentHelper < extract( ), read( ) >
NameHelper.read( )
—fields: **B**inding.binding_name **N**ameComponentHolder.value
NotFound.rest_of_name
NameComponentHelper: org.omg.CosNaming
NameComponentHolder: org.omg.CosNaming
NamedValue: org.omg.CORBA
—passed to: **D**elegate.create_request( )
ObjectImpl*._create_request( )
org.omg.CORBA.Object*._create_request( )
—returned by: **N**VList < add( ), add_item( ), add_value( ), item( ) >
Request.result( )
NameHelper: org.omg.CosNaming
NameHolder: org.omg.CosNaming
NAMES: *DTDConstants*
NameValuePair: org.omg.CORBA
—passed to: *DynStruct*.set_members( )
—returned by: *DynStruct*.get_members( )
Naming: java.rmi
NamingContext: org.omg.CosNaming
—passed to: _NamingContextImplBase < bind_context( ),
rebind_context( ) > _NamingContextStub.rebind_context( )
NamingContext < bind_context( ), rebind_context( ) >
NamingContextHelper.write( )
—returned by: _NamingContextImplBase < bind_new_context( ),
new_context( ) > _NamingContextStub.new_context( )

NamingContext.new_context( ) **N**amingContextHelper
< narrow( ), read( ) >
—implemented by: _NamingContextImplBase
_NamingContextStub
—fields: **C**annotProceed.cxt
NamingContextHelper: org.omg.CosNaming
NamingContextHolder: org.omg.CosNaming
NaN: **D**ouble **F**loat
narrow( ): **B**indingIteratorHelper **N**amingContextHelper
NATIVE: **M**odifier
nativeSQL( ): *Connection*
ncontext: **B**indingType
nCopies( ): **C**ollections
NE_RESIZE_CURSOR: **C**ursor **F**rame*
needsDictionary( ): **I**nflater
needsGui( ): **B**eanContextSupport* *Visibility**
needsInput( ): **D**eflater **I**nflater
negate( ): **B**igDecimal **B**igInteger
NEGATIVE_INFINITY: **D**ouble **F**loat
NegativeArraySizeException: java.lang
—thrown by: java.lang.reflect.**A**rray.newInstance( )
NetPermission: java.net
new_context( ): _NamingContextImplBase
_NamingContextStub *NamingContext*
newAttributes: **D**efaultStyledDocument.AttributeUndoableEdit
newAudioClip( ): **A**pplet*
newCall( ): *RemoteRef**
newDataAvailable( ): **D**efaultTableModel
newInstance( ): **A**ctivationGroup **A**ctivationGroup_Stub
ActivationInstantiator java.lang.reflect.**A**rray **C**lass
Constructor **U**RLClassLoader
newLeadSelectionPath: **T**reeSelectionEvent
NEWLINE: **A**bstractWriter*
newLine( ): **B**ufferedWriter
newmodel: **R**GBImageFilter*
newPermissionCollection( ): java.security.**P**ermission*
newPixels( ): **M**emoryImageSource
newRowsAdded( ): **D**efaultTableModel
next: **A**ttributeList **C**ontentModel
next( ): **B**eanContextSupport.BCSIterator **B**reakIterator
CardLayout *CharacterIterator** **C**ollationElementIterator
DynAny* **E**lementIterator **F**latteningPathIterator
HTMLDocument.Iterator *Iterator** *PathIterator** **R**andom*
ResultSet **S**tringCharacterIterator
next_n( ): _BindingIteratorImplBase _BindingIteratorStub
BindingIterator
next_one( ): _BindingIteratorImplBase _BindingIteratorStub
BindingIterator
nextBoolean( ): **R**andom*
nextBytes( ): **R**andom*
nextDouble( ): **C**hoiceFormat **R**andom*
nextElement( ): *Enumeration* **S**tringTokenizer
nextFloat( ): **R**andom*
nextFocus( ): **C**omponent*
nextGaussian( ): **R**andom*
nextIndex( ): *ListIterator*
nextInt( ): **R**andom*
nextLayout( ): **L**ineBreakMeasurer
nextLong( ): **R**andom*
nextOffset( ): **L**ineBreakMeasurer
nextTabStop( ): javax.swing.text.**P**aragraphView* **P**lainView*
TabExpander **W**rappedPlainView
nextToken( ): **S**treamTokenizer **S**tringTokenizer
nextWordAction: **D**efaultEditorKit*
NMTOKEN: *DTDConstants*
NMTOKENS: *DTDConstants*
NO_COMPRESSION: **D**eflater
NO_DECOMPOSITION: **C**ollator*
NO_FIELDS: **O**bjectStreamClass
NO_IMPLEMENT: org.omg.CORBA
NO_MEMORY: org.omg.CORBA
NO_OPTION: **J**OptionPane

NO_PERMISSION: org.omg.CORBA
NO_RESOURCES: org.omg.CORBA
NO_RESPONSE: org.omg.CORBA
NO_SUCH_PAGE: *Printable*
nobject: **B**indingType
NoClassDefFoundError: java.lang
nodeChanged(): **D**efaultTreeModel
nodeDimensions: **A**bstractLayoutCache*
nodesChanged(): **D**efaultTreeModel
nodeStructureChanged(): **D**efaultTreeModel
nodesWereInserted(): **D**efaultTreeModel
nodesWereRemoved(): **D**efaultTreeModel
noFocusBorder: **D**efaultListCellRenderer*
    DefaultTableCellRenderer*
NOFRAMES: **H**TML.Tag*
NOHREF: **H**TML.Attribute
non_existent(): **D**elegate
NON_SPACING_MARK: **C**haracter
NONE: **G**ridBagConstraints
NONE_OPTION: **D**ebugGraphics
NoninvertibleTransformException: java.awt.geom
    —thrown by: **A**ffineTransform < createInverse( ),
    inverseTransform( ) >
NORESIZE: **H**TML.Attribute
NORM_PRIORITY: **T**hread
NORMAL: **F**rame*
normalizeMimeType(): **D**ataFlavor
normalizeMimeTypeParameter(): **D**ataFlavor
NoRouteToHostException: java.net
NORTH: **B**orderLayout **G**ridBagConstraints *SwingConstants*
NORTH_EAST: *SwingConstants*
NORTH_WEST: *SwingConstants*
NORTHEAST: **G**ridBagConstraints
NORTHWEST: **G**ridBagConstraints
NOSHADE: **H**TML.Attribute
NoSuchAlgorithmException: java.security
    —thrown by: **A**lgorithmParameterGenerator.getInstance( )
    AlgorithmParameters.getInstance( )
    java.security.cert.**C**ertificate*.verify( ) **K**eyFactory.getInstance( )
    KeyPairGenerator.getInstance( ) **K**eyStore < load( ),
    store( ) > **K**eyStoreSpi < engineLoad( ), engineStore( ) >
    MessageDigest.getInstance( ) **S**ecureRandom.getInstance( )
    Signature.getInstance( ) **X**509CRL.verify( )
NoSuchElementException: java.util
NoSuchFieldError: java.lang
NoSuchFieldException: java.lang
    —thrown by: **C**lass < getDeclaredField( ), getField( ) >
NoSuchMethodError: java.lang
NoSuchMethodException: java.lang
    —thrown by: **C**lass < getConstructor( ), getDeclaredConstructor( ),
    getDeclaredMethod( ), getMethod( ) >
NoSuchObjectException: java.rmi
    —thrown by: **A**ctivatable.unexportObject( )
    UnicastRemoteObject*.unexportObject( )
NoSuchProviderException: java.security
    —thrown by: **A**lgorithmParameterGenerator.getInstance( )
    CertificateFactory.getInstance( )
    java.security.cert.**C**ertificate*.verify( )
    KeyPairGenerator.getInstance( ) **M**essageDigest.getInstance( )
    Signature.getInstance( ) **X**509CRL.verify( )
not(): **B**igInteger
not_context: **N**otFoundReason
not_object: **N**otFoundReason
NotActiveException: java.io
    —thrown by: **O**bjectInputStream < defaultReadObject( ),
    readFields( ), registerValidation( ) >
NOTATION: *DTDConstants*
NotBoundException: java.rmi
    —thrown by: **N**aming < lookup( ), unbind( ) > *Registry*.unbind( )
NotEmpty: org.omg.CosNaming.NamingContextPackage
    —passed to: **N**otEmptyHelper < insert( ), write( ) >
    —returned by: **N**otEmptyHelper < extract( ), read( ) >

—thrown by: _NamingContextImplBase.destroy( )
    NamingContext.destroy( )
    —fields: **N**otEmptyHolder.value
NotEmptyHelper: org.omg.CosNaming.NamingContextPackage
NotEmptyHolder:
    org.omg.CosNaming.NamingContextPackage
NotFound: org.omg.CosNaming.NamingContextPackage
    —passed to: **N**otFoundHelper < insert( ), write( ) >
    —returned by: **N**otFoundHelper < extract( ), read( ) >
    —thrown by: _NamingContextImplBase < bind( ), bind_context( ),
    bind_new_context( ), rebind( ), rebind_context( ), resolve( ),
    unbind( ) > _NamingContextStub < bind_context( ),
    bind_new_context( ), rebind( ), rebind_context( ),
    resolve( ), unbind( ) > *NamingContext* < bind_context( ),
    bind_new_context( ), rebind( ), rebind_context( ), resolve( ),
    unbind( ) >
    —fields: **N**otFoundHolder.value
NotFoundHelper: org.omg.CosNaming.NamingContextPackage
NotFoundHolder:
    org.omg.CosNaming.NamingContextPackage
NotFoundReason:
    org.omg.CosNaming.NamingContextPackage
    —passed to: **N**otFound( ) **N**otFoundReasonHelper.write( )
    —returned by: **N**otFoundReason.from_int( )
    NotFoundReasonHelper.read( )
    —fields: **N**otFound.why **N**otFoundReason < not_context,
    not_object >
NotFoundReasonHelper:
    org.omg.CosNaming.NamingContextPackage
NotFoundReasonHolder:
    org.omg.CosNaming.NamingContextPackage
notifier: **I**nvocationEvent
notify(): java.lang.**O**bject
notifyAction: **J**TextField*
notifyAll(): java.lang.**O**bject
notifyObservers(): **O**bservable
notifyPathChange(): **D**efaultTreeSelectionModel*
NotOwnerException: java.security.acl
    —thrown by: **A**cl < addEntry( ), removeEntry( ), setName( ) >
    Owner.deleteOwner( )
NotSerializableException: java.io
NOVEMBER: **C**alendar*
NOWRAP: **H**TML.Attribute
npoints: **P**olygon
NULL: **T**ypes
NULL_ATTRIBUTE_VALUE: **H**TML
NULLORDER: **C**ollationElementIterator
nullPlusNonNullIsNull(): *DatabaseMetaData*
NullPointerException: java.lang
    —thrown by: **P**rinterJob.setPageable( )
nullsAreSortedAtEnd(): *DatabaseMetaData*
nullsAreSortedAtStart(): *DatabaseMetaData*
nullsAreSortedHigh(): *DatabaseMetaData*
nullsAreSortedLow(): *DatabaseMetaData*
NUM_COLORS: **S**ystemColor
NUM_LOCK: **E**vent
numBands: **R**aster* **S**ampleModel*
numBanks: **C**omponentSampleModel*
NUMBER: *DTDConstants*
Number*: java.lang
    —subclasses: **B**igDecimal **B**igInteger **B**yte **D**ouble **F**loat
    Integer **L**ong **S**hort
    —passed to: **A**bstractButton↵
    .AccessibleAbstractButton*.setCurrentAccessibleValue( )
    JInternalFrame.AccessibleJInternalFrame↵
    .setCurrentAccessibleValue( )
    JProgressBar.AccessibleJProgressBar↵
    .setCurrentAccessibleValue( )
    JSlider.AccessibleJSlider.setCurrentAccessibleValue( )
    —returned by: **A**bstractButton.AccessibleAbstractButton*
    < getCurrentAccessibleValue( ), getMaximumAccessibleValue( ),
    getMinimumAccessibleValue( ) > *AccessibleValue*

< getMaximumAccessibleValue( ), getMinimumAccessibleValue( ) >
JInternalFrame.AccessibleJInternalFrame
< getMaximumAccessibleValue( ), getMinimumAccessibleValue( ) >
JInternalFrame.JDesktopIcon.AccessibleJDesktopIcon
< getMaximumAccessibleValue( ), getMinimumAccessibleValue( ) >
JProgressBar.AccessibleJProgressBar
< getMaximumAccessibleValue( ), getMinimumAccessibleValue( ) >
JScrollBar.AccessibleJScrollBar
< getMaximumAccessibleValue( ),
getMinimumAccessibleValue( ) > **J**Slider.AccessibleJSlider
< getMaximumAccessibleValue( ), getMinimumAccessibleValue( ) >
JSplitPane.AccessibleJSplitPane
< getMaximumAccessibleValue( ), getMinimumAccessibleValue( ) >
NumberFormat*.parse( )
NUMBER_FORMS: **C**haracter.UnicodeBlock
numberFormat: **D**ateFormat*
NumberFormat*: java.text
—subclasses: **C**hoiceFormat **D**ecimalFormat
—passed to: **D**ateFormat*.setNumberFormat( )
—returned by: **D**ateFormat*.getNumberFormat( ) **N**umberFormat*
< getCurrencyInstance( ), getInstance( ), getNumberInstance( ),
getPercentInstance( ) >
—fields: **D**ateFormat*.numberFormat
NumberFormatException: java.lang
—thrown by: **B**yte < Byte( ), decode( ), parseByte( ), valueOf( ) >
Double < Double( ), parseDouble( ), valueOf( ) > **F**loat
< parseFloat( ), valueOf( ) > **I**nteger < Integer( ), parseInt( ),
valueOf( ) > **L**ong < Long( ), parseLong( ), valueOf( ) > **S**hort
< decode( ), parseShort( ), Short( ), valueOf( ) >
NUMBERS: **D**TDConstants
numDataElements: **R**aster*
NUMERIC: **T**ypes
NUTOKEN: **D**TDConstants
NUTOKENS: **D**TDConstants
nval: **S**treamTokenizer
NVList: org.omg.CORBA
—passed to: **C**ontext.set_values( )
Delegate.create_request( ) **O**bjectImpl*._create_request( )
org.omg.CORBA.**O**bject*._create_request( )
ServerRequest.params( )
—returned by: **C**ontext.get_values( ) **O**RB.create_operation_list( )
NW_RESIZE_CURSOR: **C**ursor **F**rame*
OBJ_ADAPTER: org.omg.CORBA
OBJECT: **H**TML.Tag*
object: **S**tateEdit
Object*: org.omg.CORBA
—extended by: **B**indingIterator **C**urrent **D**omainManager
DynAny* **I**RObject* **N**amingContext
org.omg.CORBA.**P**olicy
—passed to: _NamingContextImplBase < bind( ), rebind( ) >
_NamingContextStub.rebind( ) **A**ny.insert_Object( )
Delegate < create_request( ), duplicate( ), equals( ),
get_domain_managers( ), get_interface_def( ), get_policy( ),
hash( ), hashCode( ), invoke( ), is_a( ), is_equivalent( ),
is_local( ), non_existent( ), orb( ), release( ), releaseReply( ),
request( ), servant_postinvoke( ), servant_preinvoke( ),
set_policy_override( ), toString( ) > **N**amingContext
< bind( ), rebind( ) > **O**bjectHolder( ) **O**RB < connect( ),
create_operation_list( ), disconnect( ), object_to_string( ) >
org.omg.CORBA.portable.**O**utputStream.write_Object( )
—returned by: _NamingContextImplBase.resolve( )
Any.extract_Object( ) **D**elegate < get_interface_def( ),
set_policy_override( ) > **N**amingContext.resolve( ) **O**bjectImpl*
< _get_interface_def( ), _set_policy_override( ) >
ORB.string_to_object( ) org.omg.CORBA.**O**bject*
< _get_interface_def( ), _set_policy_override( ) >
org.omg.CORBA.portable.**I**nputStream.read_Object( )
—implemented by: **O**bjectImpl*
—fields: **O**bjectHolder.value
OBJECT_NOT_EXIST: org.omg.CORBA
object_to_string( ): **O**RB
ObjectHolder: org.omg.CORBA

ObjectImpl*: org.omg.CORBA.portable
—subclasses: _BindingIteratorStub _NamingContextStub
DynamicImplementation*
—descendents: _BindingIteratorImplBase
_NamingContextImplBase
ObjectInput: java.io
—passed to: **D**ataFlavor.readExternal( ) **O**bjID.read( )
—returned by: **R**emoteCall.getInputStream( )
—implemented by: **O**bjectInputStream
ObjectInputStream: java.io
—passed
to: **B**eanContextServicesSupport.bcsPreDeserializationHook( )
BeanContextSupport* < deserialize( ), readChildren( ) >
StyleContext*.readAttributeSet( )
ObjectInputStream.GetField: java.io
—returned by: **O**bjectInputStream.readFields( )
ObjectInputValidation: java.io
—passed to: **O**bjectInputStream.registerValidation( )
ObjectOutput: java.io
—passed to: **D**ataFlavor.writeExternal( )
ObjectOutputStream.PutField.write( )
RemoteRef*.writeRefClass( )
—returned by: **R**emoteCall < getOutputStream( ),
getResultStream( ) >
—implemented by: **O**bjectOutputStream
ObjectOutputStream: java.io
—passed to: **A**WTEventMulticaster < save( ), saveInternal( ) >
BeanContextSupport* < bcsPreSerializationHook( ), serialize( ),
writeChildren( ) > **S**tyleContext*.writeAttributeSet( )
ObjectOutputStream.PutField: java.io
—returned by: **O**bjectOutputStream.putFields( )
ObjectStreamClass: java.io
—passed to: **O**bjectInputStream.resolveClass( )
—returned by: **O**bjectInputStream.GetField.getObjectStreamClass( )
ObjectStreamConstants: java.io
—implemented by: **O**bjectInputStream **O**bjectOutputStream
ObjectStreamException*: java.io
—subclasses: **I**nvalidClassException **I**nvalidObjectException
NotActiveException **N**otSerializableException
OptionalDataException **S**treamCorruptedException
WriteAbortedException
ObjectStreamField: java.io
—returned by: **O**bjectStreamClass < getField( ), getFields( ) >
—fields: **O**bjectStreamClass.NO_FIELDS
ObjectView: javax.swing.text.html
ObjID: java.rmi.server
—passed to: **D**GC < clean( ), dirty( ) >
—returned by: **O**bjID.read( )
Observable: java.util
—passed to: **O**bserver.update( )
Observer: java.util
—passed to: **O**bservable < addObserver( ), deleteObserver( ) >
OCTOBER: **C**alendar*
oEnd: javax.swing.text.html.parser.**E**lement
of( ): **C**haracter.UnicodeBlock
offset: **D**ataBuffer* **D**efaultTreeCellEditor **S**egment
offsetRequested( ): **B**adLocationException
offsets: **D**ataBuffer*
OK_CANCEL_OPTION: **J**OptionPane
OK_OPTION: **J**OptionPane
okToUseGui: **B**eanContextSupport*
okToUseGui( ): **B**eanContextSupport* **V**isibility*
OL: **H**TML.Tag*
oldLeadSelectionPath: **T**reeSelectionEvent
omitEnd( ): javax.swing.text.html.parser.**E**lement
omitStart( ): javax.swing.text.html.parser.**E**lement
on( ): **D**igestInputStream **D**igestOutputStream
ONE: **B**igInteger
ONE_TOUCH_EXPANDABLE_PROPERTY: **J**SplitPane
oneTouchExpandable: **J**SplitPane
op_name( ): **S**erverRequest
OPAQUE: **A**ccessibleState **T**ransparency*

O

OPEN: **A**rc2D*
OPEN_DIALOG: **J**FileChooser
openConnection( ): **U**RL **U**RLStreamHandler
openFrame( ): **D**efaultDesktopManager *DesktopManager*
openIcon: **D**efaultTreeCellRenderer
openStream( ): **U**RL
OpenType: java.awt.font
Operation: java.rmi.server
—passed to: *RemoteRef*.newCall( )
—returned by: *Skeleton*.getOperations( )
operation( ): **R**equest **S**erverRequest
OPTICAL_CHARACTER_RECOGNITION:
   Character.UnicodeBlock
OPTION: **H**TML.Tag*
Option: javax.swing.text.html
—passed to: **H**TMLWriter.writeOption( )
OPTION_PANE: **A**ccessibleRole
OPTION_TYPE_PROPERTY: **J**OptionPane
OptionalDataException: java.io
—thrown by: **O**bjectInputStream < readObject( ),
   readObjectOverride( ) >
OptionPaneUI: javax.swing.plaf
—passed to: **J**OptionPane.setUI( )
—returned by: **J**OptionPane.getUI( )
options: **J**OptionPane
OPTIONS_PROPERTY: **J**OptionPane
optionType: **J**OptionPane
or( ): **B**igInteger **B**itSet
orange: **C**olor*
ORB: org.omg.CORBA
—returned by: **D**elegate.orb( ) **O**RB.init( )
   org.omg.CORBA.portable.**O**utputStream.orb( )
orb( ): **D**elegate org.omg.CORBA.portable.**I**nputStream
   org.omg.CORBA.portable.**O**utputStream
ordinaryChar( ): **S**treamTokenizer
ordinaryChars( ): **S**treamTokenizer
Orientation: **S**tyleConstants*
orientation: **J**ProgressBar **J**ScrollBar* **J**Slider **J**SplitPane
ORIENTATION_PROPERTY: **J**SplitPane
OriginateDirection: **D**efaultStyledDocument.ElementSpec
origmodel: **R**GBImageFilter*
ORIYA: **C**haracter.UnicodeBlock
oStart: javax.swing.text.html.parser.**E**lement
OTHER: **T**ypes
OTHER_LETTER: **C**haracter
OTHER_NUMBER: **C**haracter
OTHER_PUNCTUATION: **C**haracter
OTHER_SYMBOL: **C**haracter
othersDeletesAreVisible( ): *DatabaseMetaData*
othersInsertsAreVisible( ): *DatabaseMetaData*
othersUpdatesAreVisible( ): *DatabaseMetaData*
out: **F**ileDescriptor **F**ilterOutputStream* **F**ilterWriter
   PipedInputStream **P**rintWriter **S**ystem
OUT_BOTTOM: **R**ectangle2D*
OUT_LEFT: **R**ectangle2D*
OUT_RIGHT: **R**ectangle2D*
OUT_TOP: **R**ectangle2D*
outcode( ): **R**ectangle2D*
OutOfMemoryError: java.lang
outpixbuf: **R**eplicateScaleFilter*
OutputStream*: java.io
—subclasses: **B**yteArrayOutputStream **F**ileOutputStream
   FilterOutputStream* **O**bjectOutputStream
   org.omg.CORBA.portable.**O**utputStream
   PipedOutputStream
—descendents: **B**ufferedOutputStream **C**heckedOutputStream
   DataOutputStream **D**eflaterOutputStream*
   DigestOutputStream **G**ZIPOutputStream **J**arOutputStream
   LogStream **P**rintStream* **Z**ipOutputStream*
—passed to: **B**ufferedOutputStream( ) **C**heckedOutputStream( )
   DeflaterOutputStream( ) **E**ditorKit*.write( )
   GZIPOutputStream( ) **J**arOutputStream( ) **K**eyStore.store( )

LogStream.setOutputStream( ) **O**bjectOutputStream( )
   OutputStreamWriter( ) **P**rintStream( ) **P**rintWriter( )
   Properties*.store( ) **R**untime.getLocalizedOutputStream( )
—returned by: **L**ogStream.getOutputStream( )
   Runtime.getLocalizedOutputStream( )
   SocketImpl.getOutputStream( )
—fields: **F**ilterOutputStream*.out
OutputStream: org.omg.CORBA.portable
—passed to: **A**lreadyBoundHelper.write( ) **A**ny.write_value( )
   BindingHelper.write( ) **B**indingIteratorHelper.write( )
   BindingListHelper.write( ) **B**indingTypeHelper.write( )
   BooleanHolder._write( ) **C**annotProceedHelper.write( )
   CharHolder._write( ) **D**oubleHolder._write( )
   FloatHolder._write( ) **I**nvalidNameHelper.write( )
   IstringHelper.write( ) **N**ameComponentHelper.write( )
   NameHelper.write( ) **N**amingContextHelper.write( )
   NotEmptyHelper.write( ) **N**otFoundHelper.write( )
   NotFoundReasonHelper.write( ) **O**bjectHolder._write( )
   PrincipalHolder._write( ) **S**erviceInformationHelper.write( )
   ShortHolder._write( ) **S**tringHolder._write( )
—returned by: **A**ny.create_output_stream( )
   InvokeHandler._invoke( ) **O**RB.create_output_stream( )
   ResponseHandler.createReply( )
OutputStreamWriter*: java.io
—subclasses: **F**ileWriter
outsideBorder: **C**ompoundBorder*
OVER: **D**ragSourceContext
OverlayLayout: javax.swing
ownDeletesAreVisible( ): *DatabaseMetaData*
owner: **C**lipboard
*Owner**: java.security.acl
—extended by: *Acl*
ownInsertsAreVisible( ): *DatabaseMetaData*
ownUpdatesAreVisible( ): *DatabaseMetaData*
P: **H**TML.Tag*
p: **D**TD
pack( ): **J**InternalFrame **J**PopupMenu **W**indow*
Package: java.lang
—returned by: **C**lass.getPackage( ) **C**lassLoader* < getPackage( ),
   getPackages( ) > **P**ackage.getPackages( )
packagePrefix: *LoaderHandler* *RemoteRef**
PackedColorModel*: java.awt.image
—subclasses: **D**irectColorModel
PADDING: **C**SS.Attribute
PADDING_BOTTOM: **C**SS.Attribute
PADDING_LEFT: **C**SS.Attribute
PADDING_RIGHT: **C**SS.Attribute
PADDING_TOP: **C**SS.Attribute
PAGE_EXISTS: *Printable*
PAGE_TAB: **A**ccessibleRole
PAGE_TAB_LIST: **A**ccessibleRole
Pageable: java.awt.print
—passed to: **P**rinterJob.setPageable( )
—implemented by: **B**ook
pageDialog( ): **P**rinterJob
pageDownAction: **D**efaultEditorKit*
PageFormat: java.awt.print
—passed to: **B**ook < append( ), setPage( ) > **P**rinterJob
   < defaultPage( ), pageDialog( ), setPrintable( ), validatePage( ) >
—returned by: **B**ook.getPageFormat( ) **P**rinterJob < defaultPage( ),
   pageDialog( ), validatePage( ) >
pageUpAction: **D**efaultEditorKit*
PAINT: **P**aintEvent
Paint: java.awt
—passed to: **G**raphics2D.setPaint( )
—returned by: **G**raphics2D.getPaint( )
—implemented by: **C**olor* **G**radientPaint **T**exturePaint
paint( ): *Caret* **C**omponent* **C**omponentPeer* **C**omponentUI*
   DefaultCaret *Highlighter* *Highlighter.HighlightPainter*
   LayeredHighlighter* **L**ayeredHighlighter.LayerPainter*
   StyleSheet.BoxPainter **S**tyleSheet.ListPainter **V**iew*
PAINT_FIRST: **P**aintEvent

O

PAINT_LAST: PaintEvent
paintAll(): Component*
paintBorder: JProgressBar
paintBorder(): AbstractBorder* *Border* BorderUIResource
  JComponent*
paintChild(): BoxView*
paintChildren(): JComponent*
paintComponent(): CellRendererPane JComponent*
  SwingUtilities
paintComponents(): Container*
PaintContext: java.awt
  —returned by: Color*.createContext() *Paint*.createContext()
paintDirtyRegions(): RepaintManager
PaintEvent: java.awt.event
paintIcon(): *Icon* IconUIResource ImageIcon
paintImmediately(): JComponent*
paintLayer(): LayeredHighlighter.LayerPainter*
paintLayeredHighlights(): LayeredHighlighter*
paintLoweredBevel(): BevelBorder*
paintRaisedBevel(): BevelBorder*
paintString: JProgressBar
paintValue(): *PropertyEditor* PropertyEditorSupport
PALETTE_LAYER: JLayeredPane*
PANEL: AccessibleRole
Panel*: java.awt
  —subclasses: Applet*
  —descendents: JApplet
  —passed to: Toolkit.createPanel()
PanelPeer: java.awt.peer
  —returned by: Toolkit.createPanel()
PanelUI: javax.swing.plaf
Paper: java.awt.print
  —passed to: PageFormat.setPaper()
  —returned by: PageFormat.getPaper()
PARA_INDENT_LEFT: HTMLEditorKit
PARA_INDENT_RIGHT: HTMLEditorKit
PARAGRAPH_SEPARATOR: Character
ParagraphElementName: AbstractDocument*
ParagraphView*: javax.swing.text
  —subclasses: javax.swing.text.html.ParagraphView
ParagraphView: javax.swing.text.html
  —passed to: javax.swing.text.ParagraphView*.adjustRow()
PARAM: HTML.Tag*
param: DTD
PARAMETER: *DTDConstants*
ParameterBlock: java.awt.image.renderable
  —passed to: *ContextualRenderedImageFactory* < create(),
    getBounds2D(), getProperty(), mapRenderContext() >
    RenderableImageOp.setParameterBlock()
  —returned by: ParameterBlock < add(), addSource(), set(),
    setSource() > RenderableImageOp.setParameterBlock()
ParameterDescriptor: java.beans
  —passed to: MethodDescriptor()
  —returned by: MethodDescriptor.getParameterDescriptors()
parameters: ParameterBlock
params(): ServerRequest
paramString(): AWTEvent* Component* Event
  MenuComponent* MenuShortcut
parent: DefaultMutableTreeNode* Raster* ResourceBundle*
parent(): Context
parentOf(): ThreadGroup
parentTag: HTMLEditorKit.InsertHTMLTextAction
parse(): java.util.Date* DateFormat* HTMLEditorKit.Parser*
  MessageFormat NumberFormat* Parser*
parseBuffer: HTMLDocument.HTMLReader
parseByte(): Byte
parseDouble(): Double
parseDTDMarkup(): Parser*
ParseException: java.text
  —thrown by: DateFormat*.parse() MessageFormat.parse()
    RuleBasedCollator()
parseFloat(): Float

parseInt(): Integer
parseLevel(): LogStream
parseLong(): Long
parseMarkupDeclarations(): Parser*
parseNumbers(): StreamTokenizer
parseObject(): Format*
ParsePosition: java.text
  —passed to: DateFormat*.parse() MessageFormat.parse()
Parser*: javax.swing.text.html.parser
  —subclasses: DocumentParser
ParserDelegator: javax.swing.text.html.parser
parseShort(): Short
parseURL(): URLStreamHandler
PASSWORD_TEXT: AccessibleRole
PasswordAuthentication: java.net
  —returned by: Authenticator < getPasswordAuthentication(),
    requestPasswordAuthentication() >
PasswordView: javax.swing.text
paste(): JTextComponent*
pasteAction: DefaultEditorKit*
path: TreeExpansionEvent TreeModelEvent
pathByAddingChild(): TreePath
pathFromAncestorEnumeration(): DefaultMutableTreeNode*
PathIterator: java.awt.geom
  —passed to: FlatteningPathIterator()
  —returned by: Area.getPathIterator()
    CubicCurve2D*.getPathIterator()
    GeneralPath.getPathIterator() Line2D*.getPathIterator()
    Polygon.getPathIterator() QuadCurve2D*.getPathIterator()
    RectangularShape*.getPathIterator() *Shape*.getPathIterator()
  —implemented by: FlatteningPathIterator
paths: TreeSelectionEvent
pathSeparator: File
pathSeparatorChar: File
PAUSE: Event
pcdata: DTD
pcSupport: BeanContextChildSupport*
peek(): DatagramSocketImpl Stack
peekEvent(): EventQueue
perform_work(): ORB
performDefaultLayout(): GlyphVector
Permission*: java.security
  —subclasses: AllPermission BasicPermission* FilePermission
    SocketPermission UnresolvedPermission
  —descendents: AWTPermission NetPermission
    PropertyPermission ReflectPermission RuntimePermission
    SecurityPermission SerializablePermission
  —passed to: AccessControlContext.checkPermission()
    AccessController.checkPermission() PermissionCollection*
    < add(), implies() > SecurityManager*.checkPermission()
  —returned by: AccessControlException.getPermission()
Permission: java.security.acl
  —passed to: Acl.checkPermission() AclEntry < checkPermission(),
    removePermission() >
PermissionCollection*: java.security
  —subclasses: Permissions
  —passed to: ProtectionDomain()
  —returned by: java.security.Permission*.newPermissionCollection()
    ProtectionDomain.getPermissions()
    URLClassLoader.getPermissions()
Permissions: java.security
permissions(): AclEntry
PERSIST_STORE: org.omg.CORBA
PGDN: Event
PGUP: Event
PhantomReference: java.lang.ref
PI: *DTDConstants* Math
PIE: Arc2D*
pink: Color*
PIPE_SIZE: PipedInputStream
PipedInputStream: java.io

—passed to: **P**ipedOutputStream < connect( ),
PipedOutputStream( ) >
PipedOutputStream: java.io
—passed to: **P**ipedInputStream < connect( ), PipedInputStream( ) >
PipedReader: java.io
—passed to: **P**ipedWriter < connect( ), PipedWriter( ) >
PipedWriter: java.io
—passed to: **P**ipedReader < connect( ), PipedReader( ) >
pixel_bits: **C**olorModel*
PixelGrabber: java.awt.image
PixelInterleavedSampleModel: java.awt.image
pixelStride: **C**omponentSampleModel*
PKCS8EncodedKeySpec: java.security.spec
PLAIN: **F**ont*
PLAIN_MESSAGE: **J**OptionPane
PlainDocument: javax.swing.text
plainTextFlavor: **D**ataFlavor
PlainView*: javax.swing.text
—subclasses: **F**ieldView*
—descendents: **P**asswordView
play( ): **A**pplet* **A**udioClip
PM: **C**alendar*
Point: java.awt
—passed to: **A**ccessibleComponent < contains( ),
getAccessibleAt( ), setLocation( ) > **A**utoscroll.autoscroll( )
Box.AccessibleBox < getAccessibleAt( ),
setLocation( ) > **B**ox.Filler.AccessibleBoxFiller
< getAccessibleAt( ), setLocation( ) >
CellRendererPane.AccessibleCellRendererPane
< contains( ), getAccessibleAt( ), setLocation( ) >
Component* < getComponentAt( ), getLocation( ),
setLocation( ) > **D**efaultCaret.setMagicCaretPosition( )
DragGestureEvent.startDrag( ) **D**ragSource
< createDragSourceContext( ), startDrag( ) >
DropTarget < createDropTargetAutoScroller( ),
initializeAutoscrolling( ), updateAutoscroll( ) >
DropTarget.DropTargetAutoScroller.updateLocation( )
DropTargetDropEvent( ) **J**Applet.AccessibleJApplet
< getAccessibleAt( ), setLocation( ) >
JComponent.AccessibleJComponent* < getAccessibleAt( ),
setLocation( ) > **J**Dialog.AccessibleJDialog < getAccessibleAt( ),
setLocation( ) > **J**Frame.AccessibleJFrame < getAccessibleAt( ),
setLocation( ) > **J**List.AccessibleJList.AccessibleJListChild
< contains( ), getAccessibleAt( ), setLocation( ) >
JPopupMenu.WindowPopup.AccessibleWindowPopup
< getAccessibleAt( ), setLocation( ) > **J**Table.rowAtPoint( )
JTable.AccessibleJTable.AccessibleJTableCell
< getAccessibleAt( ), setLocation( ) >
JTableHeader.AccessibleJTableHeader ↵
.AccessibleJTableHeaderEntry < contains( ),
getAccessibleAt( ), setLocation( ) > **J**TextComponent ↵
.AccessibleJTextComponent*.getIndexAtPoint( )
JTree.AccessibleJTree.AccessibleJTreeNode
< getAccessibleAt( ), setLocation( ) > **J**Viewport
< setViewPosition( ), toViewCoordinates( ) >
JWindow.AccessibleJWindow < getAccessibleAt( ),
setLocation( ) > **M**enuSelectionManager.componentForPoint( )
Point.setLocation( ) **R**aster* < createBandedRaster( ),
createInterleavedRaster( ), createPackedRaster( ), createRaster( ),
createWritableRaster( ), Raster( ) > **R**ectangle* < contains( ),
Rectangle( ), setLocation( ) > **S**wingUtilities < convertPoint( ),
convertPointFromScreen( ), convertPointToScreen( ),
getAccessibleAt( ) > **T**extUI.viewToModel( ) **W**ritableRaster*
—returned by: **A**ccessibleComponent
< getLocation( ), getLocationOnScreen( ) >
Box.AccessibleBox.getLocationOnScreen( )
Box.Filler.AccessibleBoxFiller.getLocationOnScreen( )
Caret.getMagicCaretPosition( ) **C**ellRendererPane ↵
.AccessibleCellRendererPane.getLocationOnScreen( )
Component* < getLocation( ), getLocationOnScreen( ),
location( ) > **D**efaultCaret.getMagicCaretPosition( )
DropTargetDragEvent.getLocation( )

GridBagLayout < getLayoutOrigin( ), location( ) >
JApplet.AccessibleJApplet.getLocationOnScreen( )
JComponent.AccessibleJComponent*
< getLocation( ), getLocationOnScreen( ) >
JDialog.AccessibleJDialog.getLocationOnScreen( )
JFrame.AccessibleJFrame.getLocationOnScreen( )
JList.AccessibleJList.AccessibleJListChild < getLocation( ),
getLocationOnScreen( ) > **J**PopupMenu.WindowPopup ↵
.AccessibleWindowPopup.getLocationOnScreen( )
JTable.AccessibleJTable ↵
.AccessibleJTableCell.getLocationOnScreen( )
JTableHeader.AccessibleJTableHeader ↵
.AccessibleJTableHeaderEntry.getLocationOnScreen( )
JTree.AccessibleJTree.AccessibleJTreeNode
< getLocationInJTree( ), getLocationOnScreen( ) >
JViewport.toViewCoordinates( )
JWindow.AccessibleJWindow.getLocationOnScreen( )
MouseEvent*.getPoint( ) **R**ectangle*.getLocation( )
SwingUtilities.convertPoint( )
—fields: **J**Viewport.lastPaintPosition
Point2D*: java.awt.geom
—subclasses: **P**oint **P**oint2D.Double **P**oint2D.Float
—passed to: **A**ffineTransform < deltaTransform( ),
inverseTransform( ), transform( ) > **A**rc2D* < setAngles( ),
setAngleStart( ), setArc( ), setArcByTangent( ) >
BandCombineOp.getPoint2D( ) **C**olorConvertOp.getPoint2D( )
CubicCurve2D* < contains( ), setCurve( ) >
GlyphVector.setGlyphPosition( ) **G**radientPaint( ) **L**ine2D*
< ptLineDist( ), ptLineDistSq( ), ptSegDist( ), ptSegDistSq( ),
relativeCCW( ), setLine( ) > **L**ine2D.Float( ) **P**oint2D*
< distance( ), distanceSq( ), setLocation( ) > **Q**uadCurve2D*
< contains( ), setCurve( ) > **R**ectangle2D* < add( ), outcode( ) >
RectangularShape* < setFrame( ), setFrameFromCenter( ),
setFrameFromDiagonal( ) > **S**hape.contains( )
—returned by: **A**ffineTransform < deltaTransform( ),
inverseTransform( ), transform( ) > **A**rc2D* < getEndPoint( ),
getStartPoint( ) > **B**ufferedImageOp.getPoint2D( )
ConvolveOp.getPoint2D( ) **C**ubicCurve2D* < getCtrlP2( ),
getP1( ), getP2( ) > **G**lyphVector.getGlyphPosition( )
GradientPaint.getPoint2( ) **L**ine2D*.getP2( ) **Q**uadCurve2D*
< getCtrlPt( ), getP1( ), getP2( ) > **R**escaleOp.getPoint2D( )
Point2D.Double: java.awt.geom
Point2D.Float: java.awt.geom
pointSize: **F**ont*
Policy: java.security
—passed to: java.security.**P**olicy.setPolicy( )
—returned by: java.security.**P**olicy.getPolicy( )
Policy: org.omg.CORBA
—passed to: **D**elegate.set_policy_override( )
org.omg.CORBA.**O**bject*._set_policy_override( )
—returned by: **D**elegate.get_policy( ) **O**bjectImpl*._get_policy( )
org.omg.CORBA.**O**bject*._get_policy( )
policy_type( ): org.omg.CORBA.**P**olicy
PolicyError: org.omg.CORBA
—thrown by: **O**RB.create_policy( )
poll( ): **R**eferenceQueue
poll_next_response( ): **O**RB
poll_response( ): **R**equest
Polygon: java.awt
—passed to: **G**raphics* < drawPolygon( ), fillPolygon( ) >
pop( ): **E**ventQueue **S**tack
popCharacterStyle( ): **H**TMLDocument.HTMLReader
POPUP_LAYER: **J**LayeredPane*
POPUP_MENU: **A**ccessibleRole
popupListener: **J**Menu
PopupMenu: java.awt
—passed to: **C**omponent*.add( )
popupMenuCanceled( ): **P**opupMenuListener
PopupMenuEvent: javax.swing.event
—passed to: **P**opupMenuListener < popupMenuCanceled( ),
popupMenuWillBecomeInvisible( ),
popupMenuWillBecomeVisible( ) >

PopupMenuListener: javax.swing.event
—passed to: **J**PopupMenu < addPopupMenuListener( ), removePopupMenuListener( ) >
PopupMenuPeer: java.awt.peer
—returned by: **T**oolkit.createPopupMenu( )
PopupMenuUI: javax.swing.plaf
—passed to: **J**PopupMenu.setUI( )
—returned by: **J**PopupMenu.getUI( )
popupMenuWillBecomeInvisible( ): *PopupMenuListener*
popupMenuWillBecomeVisible( ): *PopupMenuListener*
port: **S**ocketImpl
PORTRAIT: **P**ageFormat
pos: **B**ufferedInputStream **B**yteArrayInputStream **C**harArrayReader **P**ushbackInputStream **S**tringBufferInputStream
Position: javax.swing.text
—returned by: **A**bstractDocument* < createPosition( ), getEndPosition( ), getStartPosition( ) > *Document**
< createPosition( ), getEndPosition( ), getStartPosition( ) > **S**tringContent.createPosition( )
position( ): *Blob Clob*
Position.Bias: javax.swing.text
—passed to: **B**oxView*.flipEastAndWestAtEnds( ) **C**ompositeView* < getNextEastWestVisualPositionFrom( ), getNextNorthSouthVisualPositionFrom( ) >
javax.swing.text.**P**aragraphView* < getClosestPositionTo( ), getNextNorthSouthVisualPositionFrom( ) > **T**extUI
< getNextVisualPositionFrom( ), modelToView( ), viewToModel( ) >
View* < modelToView( ), viewToModel( ) >
—fields: **P**osition.Bias < **B**ackward, **F**orward >
positionCaret( ): **D**efaultCaret
positionToElement( ): **A**bstractDocument.BranchElement*
POSITIVE_INFINITY: **D**ouble **F**loat
postActionEvent( ): **J**TextField*
postEdit( ): **U**ndoableEditSupport
postEvent( ): **C**omponent* **E**ventQueue **M**enuComponent* *MenuContainer*
postorderEnumeration( ): **D**efaultMutableTreeNode*
postRemoveUpdate( ): **A**bstractDocument*
postState: **S**tateEdit
POSTURE: **T**extAttribute
POSTURE_OBLIQUE: **T**extAttribute
POSTURE_REGULAR: **T**extAttribute
pow( ): **B**igInteger **M**ath
PRC: **L**ocale
PRE: **H**TML.Tag*
preceding( ): **B**reakIterator
preConcatenate( ): **A**ffineTransform
preConcetenateTransform( ): **R**enderContext
preContent( ): **H**TMLDocument.HTMLReader
predefined: **C**ursor
preferenceChanged( ): **V**iew*
preferred: **S**izeRequirements
PREFERRED: **G**raphicsConfigTemplate
preferredLayoutSize( ): **B**orderLayout **B**oxLayout **C**ardLayout **F**lowLayout **G**ridBagLayout **G**ridLayout **J**RootPane.RootLayout *LayoutManager** **O**verlayLayout **S**crollPaneLayout* **V**iewportLayout
PREFERREDSIZE: **G**ridBagLayout
preferredSize( ): **C**omponent* *ComponentPeer**
preferredViewportSize: **J**Table
preorderEnumeration( ): **D**efaultMutableTreeNode*
prepareCall( ): *Connection*
PreparedStatement*: java.sql
—extended by: *CallableStatement*
—returned by: *Connection*.prepareStatement( )
prepareEditor( ): **J**Table
prepareForEditing( ): **D**efaultTreeCellEditor
prepareImage( ): **C**omponent* *ComponentPeer** **T**oolkit
prepareRenderer( ): **J**Table
prepareStatement( ): *Connection*
PRESSED: **A**ccessibleState **D**efaultButtonModel*

PRESSED_ICON_CHANGED_PROPERTY: **A**bstractButton*
preState: **S**tateEdit
PREVIEW_PANEL_PROPERTY: **J**ColorChooser
previous( ): **B**reakIterator **C**ardLayout *CharacterIterator** **C**ollationElementIterator **E**lementIterator *ListIterator* *ResultSet* **S**tringCharacterIterator
previousDouble( ): **C**hoiceFormat
previousIndex( ): *ListIterator*
previousWordAction: **D**efaultEditorKit*
PRIMARY: **C**ollator*
primaryOrder( ): **C**ollationElementIterator
Principal*: java.security
—extended by: **G**roup
—passed to: *Acl* < addEntry( ), checkPermission( ), getPermissions( ), removeEntry( ), setName( ) > *Group*
< addMember( ), isMember( ), removeMember( ) > *Owner**
< addOwner( ), deleteOwner( ), isOwner( ) >
—returned by: *AclEntry*.getPrincipal( )
java.security.*Certificate*.getPrincipal( )
X509Certificate.getSubjectDN( )
—implemented by: **I**dentity*
Principal: org.omg.CORBA
—passed to: **A**ny.insert_Principal( ) **P**rincipalHolder( )
—returned by: **A**ny.extract_Principal( )
—fields: **P**rincipalHolder.value
PrincipalHolder: org.omg.CORBA
print( ): **C**omponent* *ComponentPeer** *Printable* **P**rinterJob **P**rintStream* **P**rintWriter
PRINT_SCREEN: **E**vent
Printable: java.awt.print
—passed to: **B**ook < append( ), setPage( ) > **P**rinterJob.setPrintable( )
—returned by: **B**ook.getPrintable( )
printAll( ): **C**omponent*
printComponents( ): **C**ontainer*
printDialog( ): **P**rinterJob
PrinterAbortException: java.awt.print
PrinterException*: java.awt.print
—subclasses: **P**rinterAbortException **P**rinterIOException
—thrown by: *Printable*.print( )
PrinterGraphics: java.awt.print
PrinterIOException: java.awt.print
PrinterJob: java.awt.print
—returned by: *PrinterGraphics*.getPrinterJob( )
PrintGraphics: java.awt
PrintJob: java.awt
—returned by: *PrintGraphics*.getPrintJob( )
println( ): **D**riverManager **P**rintStream* **P**rintWriter
printStackTrace( ): **T**hrowable*
PrintStream*: java.io
—subclasses: **L**ogStream
—passed to: **A**bstractDocument*.dump( ) **C**omponent*.list( ) **D**riverManager.setLogStream( ) **P**roperties*.list( ) **S**ystem.setOut( )
—returned by: **D**ebugGraphics.logStream( ) **L**ogStream.getDefaultStream( )
—fields: **S**ystem < err, out >
PrintWriter: java.io
—passed to: **C**omponent*.list( ) **P**roperties*.list( )
—returned by: **D**riverManager.getLogWriter( )
PRIORITY_INTERCHAR: **G**lyphJustificationInfo
PRIORITY_KASHIDA: **G**lyphJustificationInfo
PRIORITY_NONE: **G**lyphJustificationInfo
PRIORITY_WHITESPACE: **G**lyphJustificationInfo
PRIVATE: **M**odifier
PRIVATE_MEMBER: org.omg.CORBA
PRIVATE_USE: **C**haracter
PRIVATE_USE_AREA: **C**haracter.UnicodeBlock
PrivateKey*: java.security
—extended by: *DSAPrivateKey* *RSAPrivateKey**
—descendents: *RSAPrivateCrtKey*

P

R

ReferenceQueue: java.lang.ref
—passed to: **P**hantomReference( ) **W**eakReference( )
ReflectPermission: java.lang.reflect
refresh( ): java.security.**P**olicy
refreshRow( ): *ResultSet*
regionMatches( ): **S**tring
register( ): **A**ctivatable
registerComponent( ): **T**oolTipManager
registerDriver( ): **D**riverManager
registerEditor( ): **P**ropertyEditorManager
registerEditorKitForContentType( ): **J**EditorPane*
registerGroup( ): *ActivationSystem*
registerKeyboardAction( ): **J**Component*
registerListeners( ): **D**ragGestureRecognizer*
registerObject( ): *ActivationSystem*
registerOutParameter( ): *CallableStatement*
registerStaticAttributeKey( ): **S**tyleContext*
registerTag( ): **H**TMLDocument.HTMLReader
registerValidation( ): **O**bjectInputStream
Registry: java.rmi.registry
—returned by: **L**ocateRegistry < createRegistry( ), getRegistry( ) >
  RegistryHandler.registryStub( )
REGISTRY_ID: **O**bjID
REGISTRY_PORT: *Registry*
RegistryHandler: java.rmi.registry
registryImpl( ): *RegistryHandler*
registryStub( ): *RegistryHandler*
rehash( ): **H**ashtable*
rejectDrag( ): **D**ropTargetContext **D**ropTargetDragEvent
rejectDrop( ): **D**ropTargetContext **D**ropTargetDropEvent
rejectedSetBCOnce( ): **B**eanContextChildSupport*
REL: **H**TML.Attribute
RELATIVE: **G**ridBagConstraints
relative( ): *ResultSet*
relativeCCW( ): **L**ine2D*
release( ): **D**elegate
releaseBeanContextResources( ): **B**eanContextChildSupport*
releaseInputStream( ): *RemoteCall*
releaseOutputStream( ): *RemoteCall*
releaseReply( ): **D**elegate
releaseService( ): *BeanContextServiceProvider*
  BeanContextServices **B**eanContextServicesSupport
  BeanContextServicesSupport.BCSSProxyServiceProvider
releaseWritableTile( ): **B**ufferedImage *WritableRenderedImage*
reload( ): **D**efaultTreeModel
REMAINDER: **G**ridBagConstraints
remainder( ): **B**igInteger
RemarshalException: org.omg.CORBA.portable
—thrown by: **D**elegate.invoke( )
Remote*: java.rmi
—extended by: *ActivationInstantiator* *ActivationMonitor*
  ActivationSystem *Activator* *DGC* *Registry*
—passed to: **A**ctivatable < exportObject( ), unexportObject( ) >
  Naming < bind( ), rebind( ) > *Registry*.rebind( )
  RemoteRef.invoke( ) *Skeleton*.dispatch( )
  UnicastRemoteObject* < exportObject( ), unexportObject( ) >
—returned by: **A**ctivatable < exportObject( ), register( ) >
  Naming.lookup( ) **R**emoteObject*.toStub( )
  UnicastRemoteObject*.exportObject( )
—implemented by: **R**emoteObject*
RemoteCall: java.rmi.server
—passed to: *RemoteRef* < done( ), invoke( ) >
—returned by: *RemoteRef*.newCall( )
remoteEquals( ): *RemoteRef*
RemoteException*: java.rmi
—subclasses: **A**ccessException **A**ctivateFailedException
  java.rmi.**C**onnectException **C**onnectIOException
  ExportException* **M**arshalException
  NoSuchObjectException **S**erverError **S**erverException
  ServerRuntimeException **S**keletonMismatchException
  SkeletonNotFoundException **S**tubNotFoundException

UnexpectedException java.rmi.**U**nknownHostException
UnmarshalException
—descendents: **S**ocketSecurityException
—thrown by: **A**ctivatable < Activatable( ), exportObject( ), inactive( ),
  register( ), unregister( ) > **A**ctivationGroup < activeObject( ),
  inactiveGroup( ), inactiveObject( ), newInstance( ) >
  ActivationID.activate( ) *ActivationMonitor* < activeObject( ),
  inactiveGroup( ), inactiveObject( ) > *ActivationSystem*
  < getActivationDesc( ), getActivationGroupDesc( ),
  registerGroup( ), registerObject( ), setActivationDesc( ),
  setActivationGroupDesc( ), shutdown( ), unregisterGroup( ),
  unregisterObject( ) > *DGC* < clean( ), dirty( ) > **L**ocateRegistry
  < createRegistry( ), getRegistry( ) > **N**aming < list( ),
  lookup( ), rebind( ), unbind( ) > *Registry* < list( ), lookup( ),
  rebind( ), unbind( ) > *RegistryHandler*.registryStub( )
  RemoteRef.newCall( ) **U**nicastRemoteObject*
  < exportObject( ), UnicastRemoteObject( ) >
remoteHashCode( ): *RemoteRef*
RemoteObject*: java.rmi.server
—subclasses: **R**emoteServer* **R**emoteStub*
—descendents: **A**ctivatable **A**ctivationGroup
  ActivationGroup_Stub **U**nicastRemoteObject*
—passed to: *RemoteRef*.newCall( )
RemoteRef*: java.rmi.server
—extended by: *ServerRef*
—passed to: **A**ctivationGroup_Stub( ) *RemoteRef*.remoteEquals( )
  RemoteStub* < RemoteStub( ), setRef( ) >
—returned by: **R**emoteObject*.getRef( )
—fields: **R**emoteObject*.ref
RemoteServer*: java.rmi.server
—subclasses: **A**ctivatable **U**nicastRemoteObject*
—descendents: **A**ctivationGroup
RemoteStub*: java.rmi.server
—subclasses: **A**ctivationGroup_Stub
—passed to: **R**emoteStub*.setRef( )
—returned by: *ServerRef*.exportObject( )
remoteToString( ): *RemoteRef*
REMOVE: **D**ocumentEvent.EventType
remove( ): **A**bstractCollection* **A**bstractDocument*
  AbstractDocument.Content **A**bstractMap*
  AccessibleStateSet **A**ttributes **A**WTEventMulticaster
  BeanContextSupport* **B**eanContextSupport.BCSIterator
  ButtonGroup *ChoicePeer Collection** **C**omponent*
  ContextList **D**efaultListModel **D**efaultMutableTreeNode*
  DefaultStyledDocument.ElementBuffer **D**ictionary*
  *Document** **E**ventListenerList **E**xceptionList **G**apContent
  Iterator *Map** **M**enu* **M**enuBar *MenuContainer*
  MutableTreeNode **N**VList **R**eferenceQueue
  RenderingHints **S**tringContent
removeAccessibleSelection( ): *AccessibleSelection*
  JList.AccessibleJList **J**Menu.AccessibleJMenu
  JMenuBar.AccessibleJMenuBar
  JTabbedPane.AccessibleJTabbedPane
  JTable.AccessibleJTable **J**Tree.AccessibleJTree
  JTree.AccessibleJTree.AccessibleJTreeNode
removeActionListener( ): **A**bstractButton* **B**utton
  ButtonModel ComboBoxEditor **D**efaultButtonModel*
  JComboBox **J**FileChooser **J**TextField* java.awt.**L**ist
  MenuItem* **T**extField **T**imer
removeAdjustmentListener( ): *Adjustable* **J**ScrollBar*
  Scrollbar
removeAll( ): **A**bstractCollection* **B**eanContextSupport*
  Choice *Collection** **C**ompositeView* **C**ontainer*
  java.awt.**L**ist *ListPeer* **M**enu*
removeAllChildren( ): **D**efaultMutableTreeNode*
removeAllElements( ): **D**efaultComboBoxModel
  DefaultListModel **V**ector*
removeAllHighlights( ): *Highlighter* **L**ayeredHighlighter*
removeAllItems( ): **J**ComboBox
removeAncestorListener( ): **J**Component*

R

renameTo( ): File
render( ): AbstractDocument* *Document**
RenderableImage: java.awt.image.renderable
—passed
  to: *ContextualRenderedImageFactory*.mapRenderContext( )
  RenderableImageProducer( )
—returned by: ParameterBlock.getRenderableSource( )
—implemented by: RenderableImageOp
RenderableImageOp: java.awt.image.renderable
RenderableImageProducer: java.awt.image.renderable
RenderContext: java.awt.image.renderable
—passed to: *ContextualRenderedImageFactory* < create( ),
  mapRenderContext( ) > RenderableImageOp.createRendering( )
  RenderableImageProducer.setRenderContext( )
—returned
  by: *ContextualRenderedImageFactory*.mapRenderContext( )
RenderedImage*: java.awt.image
—extended by: *WritableRenderedImage*
—passed to: Graphics2D.drawRenderedImage( )
—returned by: *ContextualRenderedImageFactory*.create( )
  RenderableImage < createDefaultRendering( ),
  createRendering( ), createScaledRendering( ) >
  RenderableImageOp < createRendering( ),
  createScaledRendering( ) >
RenderedImageFactory*: java.awt.image.renderable
—extended by: *ContextualRenderedImageFactory*
renderer: DefaultTreeCellEditor JComboBox
Renderer: javax.swing
RenderingHints: java.awt
—passed to: AffineTransformOp( ) BandCombineOp( )
  ColorConvertOp( ) ConvolveOp( ) LookupOp( )
  RenderableImage.createScaledRendering( ) RenderContext
  < RenderContext( ), setRenderingHints( ) > RenderingHints.add( )
  RescaleOp( )
—returned by: AffineTransformOp.getRenderingHints( )
  BufferedImageOp.getRenderingHints( )
  ConvolveOp.getRenderingHints( )
  LookupOp.getRenderingHints( )
  RenderContext.getRenderingHints( )
RenderingHints.Key: java.awt
—passed to: Graphics2D < getRenderingHint( ),
  setRenderingHint( ) >
—fields: RenderingHints < KEY_ALPHA_INTERPOLATION,
  KEY_ANTIALIASING, KEY_COLOR_RENDERING, KEY_DITHERING,
  KEY_FRACTIONALMETRICS, KEY_INTERPOLATION,
  KEY_RENDERING, KEY_TEXT_ANTIALIASING >
reorderingAllowed: JTableHeader
repaint( ): Component* ComponentPeer* DefaultCaret
RepaintManager: javax.swing
—passed to: RepaintManager.setCurrentManager( )
—returned by: RepaintManager.currentManager( )
replace( ): AbstractDocument.BranchElement* CompositeView*
  String StringBuffer
replaceEdit( ): AbstractUndoableEdit* *UndoableEdit*
replaceItem( ): java.awt.List
replaceObject( ): ObjectOutputStream
replaceRange( ): JTextArea TextArea *TextAreaPeer*
replaceSelection( ): JTextComponent*
replaceText( ): TextArea *TextAreaPeer*
ReplicateScaleFilter*: java.awt.image
—subclasses: AreaAveragingScaleFilter
Request: org.omg.CORBA
—passed to: ORB < send_multiple_requests_deferred( ),
  send_multiple_requests_oneway( ) >
—returned by: Delegate < create_request( ), request( ) >
  ObjectImpl* < _create_request( ), _request( ) >
  org.omg.CORBA.Object < _create_request( ), _request( ) >
request( ): Delegate
requestDefaultFocus( ): JComponent*
requestFocus( ): *AccessibleComponent*
  Box.AccessibleBox Box.Filler.AccessibleBoxFiller
  CellRendererPane.AccessibleCellRendererPane

Component* *ComponentPeer* JApplet.AccessibleJApplet
JComponent.AccessibleJComponent*
JDialog.AccessibleJDialog JFrame.AccessibleJFrame
JList.AccessibleJList.AccessibleJListChild
JPopupMenu.WindowPopup.AccessibleWindowPopup
JTable.AccessibleJTable.AccessibleJTableCell
JTableHeader.AccessibleJTableHeader ↵
.AccessibleJTableHeaderEntry
JTree.AccessibleJTree.AccessibleJTreeNode
JWindow.AccessibleJWindow
requestPasswordAuthentication( ): Authenticator
requestTopDownLeftRightResend( ): FilteredImageSource
  ImageProducer MemoryImageSource
  RenderableImageProducer
REQUIRED: *DTDConstants* GraphicsConfigTemplate
required: DriverPropertyInfo
RescaleOp: java.awt.image
rescanCurrentDirectory( ): FileChooserUI JFileChooser
resendTopDownLeftRight( ): ImageFilter*
RESERVED_ID_MAX: AWTEvent*
RESET: FormView
reset( ): Adler32 Area ByteArrayOutputStream
  CharArrayWriter *Checksum* CollationElementIterator
  CRC32 Deflater GeneralPath Inflater java.io.InputStream*
  MessageDigest ObjectOutputStream Reader*
resetChoosableFileFilters( ): JFileChooser
resetKeyboardActions( ): JComponent*
resetMarksAtZero( ): GapContent
resetRecognizer( ): DragGestureRecognizer*
resetRowSelection( ): DefaultTreeSelectionModel*
  TreeSelectionModel
resetSyntax( ): StreamTokenizer
resetToPreferredSizes( ): JSplitPane SplitPaneUI
resetViewPort( ): JScrollPane.AccessibleJScrollPane
reshape( ): Component* ComponentPeer* Rectangle*
RESIZABLE: AccessibleState
resizable: JInternalFrame
resize( ): Component* Rectangle*
resizeAndRepaint( ): JTable JTableHeader
resizedPostingDisableCount: TableColumn
resizeFrame( ): DefaultDesktopManager *DesktopManager*
resizingAllowed: JTableHeader
resizingColumn: JTableHeader
resolve( ): _NamingContextImplBase _NamingContextStub
  NamingContext
resolve_initial_references( ): ORB
ResolveAttribute: *AttributeSet* StyleConstants*
resolveClass( ): ClassLoader* ObjectInputStream
resolveObject( ): ObjectInputStream
ResourceBundle*: java.util
—subclasses: ListResourceBundle* PropertyResourceBundle
—descendents: AccessibleResourceBundle
—passed to: ComponentOrientation.getOrientation( )
  Window*.applyResourceBundle( )
—returned by: ResourceBundle*.getBundle( )
—fields: ResourceBundle*.parent
responseCode: HttpURLConnection
ResponseHandler: org.omg.CORBA.portable
—passed to: *InvokeHandler*._invoke( )
responseMessage: HttpURLConnection
rest_of_name: CannotProceed NotFound
restart( ): Timer
restoreState( ): *StateEditable*
result( ): Request ServerRequest
ResultSet: java.sql
—returned by: *DatabaseMetaData* < getBestRowIdentifier( ),
  getCatalogs( ), getColumnPrivileges( ), getColumns( ),
  getCrossReference( ), getExportedKeys( ), getImportedKeys( ),
  getIndexInfo( ), getPrimaryKeys( ), getProcedureColumns( ),
  getProcedures( ), getSchemas( ), getTablePrivileges( ),
  getTables( ), getTableTypes( ), getTypeInfo( ), getUDTs( ),

R

Cross-Ref

R

—descendents: **A**ccessControlException
ArrayIndexOutOfBoundsException **B**AD_CONTEXT
BAD_INV_ORDER **B**AD_OPERATION **B**AD_PARAM
BAD_TYPECODE **C**OMM_FAILURE **D**ATA_CONVERSION
FREE_MEM **I**llegalComponentStateException
IllegalThreadStateException **I**MP_LIMIT **I**NITIALIZE
INTERNAL **I**NTF_REPOS **I**NV_FLAG **I**NV_IDENT
INV_OBJREF **I**NV_POLICY **I**NVALID_TRANSACTION
InvalidDnDOperationException **I**nvalidParameterException
MARSHAL **N**O_IMPLEMENT **N**O_MEMORY
NO_PERMISSION **N**O_RESOURCES **N**O_RESPONSE
NumberFormatException **O**BJ_ADAPTER
OBJECT_NOT_EXIST **P**ERSIST_STORE
RMISecurityException **S**tringIndexOutOfBoundsException
TRANSACTION_REQUIRED **T**RANSACTION_ROLLEDBACK
TRANSIENT **U**NKNOWN
RuntimePermission: java.lang
S: HTML.Tag*
S_RESIZE_CURSOR: **C**ursor **F**rame*
sameFile( ): **U**RL
SAMP: HTML.Tag*
sampleModel: **R**aster*
SampleModel*: java.awt.image
—subclasses: **C**omponentSampleModel*
MultiPixelPackedSampleModel
SinglePixelPackedSampleModel
—descendents: **B**andedSampleModel
PixelInterleavedSampleModel
—passed to: **C**olorModel*.isCompatibleSampleModel( ) **R**aster*
< createWritableRaster( ), Raster* > **W**ritableRaster( )
—returned by: **B**ufferedImage.getSampleModel( )
Raster*.getSampleModel( ) **S**ampleModel*
< createCompatibleSampleModel( ), createSubsetSampleModel( ) >
—fields: **R**aster*.sampleModel
sampleModelTranslateX: **R**aster*
sampleModelTranslateY: **R**aster*
SATURDAY: **C**alendar*
SAVE: **F**ileDialog
save( ): **A**WTEventMulticaster **P**roperties*
SAVE_DIALOG: **J**FileChooser
SAVE_FILE: **E**vent
saveInternal( ): **A**WTEventMulticaster
SC_BLOCK_DATA: *O*bjectStreamConstants
SC_EXTERNALIZABLE: *O*bjectStreamConstants
SC_SERIALIZABLE: *O*bjectStreamConstants
SC_WRITE_METHOD: *O*bjectStreamConstants
scale( ): **A**ffineTransform **B**igDecimal **G**raphics2D
SCALE_AREA_AVERAGING: **I**mage*
SCALE_DEFAULT: **I**mage*
SCALE_FAST: **I**mage*
SCALE_REPLICATE: **I**mage*
SCALE_SMOOTH: **I**mage*
scanlineStride: **C**omponentSampleModel*
SCRIPT: HTML.Tag*
SCROLL_ABSOLUTE: **E**vent
SCROLL_BAR: **A**ccessibleRole
SCROLL_BEGIN: **E**vent
SCROLL_END: **E**vent
SCROLL_LINE_DOWN: **E**vent
SCROLL_LINE_UP: **E**vent
SCROLL_LOCK: **E**vent
SCROLL_PAGE_DOWN: **E**vent
SCROLL_PAGE_UP: **E**vent
SCROLL_PANE: **A**ccessibleRole
Scrollable: javax.swing
—implemented by: **J**List **J**Table **J**TextComponent* **J**Tree
scrollbar: **S**ystemColor
SCROLLBAR: **S**ystemColor
Scrollbar: java.awt
—passed to: **T**oolkit.createScrollbar( )
ScrollbarPeer: java.awt.peer
—returned by: **T**oolkit.createScrollbar( )

SCROLLBARS_ALWAYS: **S**crollPane
SCROLLBARS_AS_NEEDED: **S**crollPane
SCROLLBARS_BOTH: **T**extArea
SCROLLBARS_HORIZONTAL_ONLY: **T**extArea
SCROLLBARS_NEVER: **S**crollPane
SCROLLBARS_NONE: **T**extArea
SCROLLBARS_VERTICAL_ONLY: **T**extArea
ScrollBarUI: javax.swing.plaf
—returned by: **J**ScrollBar*.getUI( )
SCROLLING: **H**TML.Attribute
ScrollPane: java.awt
—passed to: **T**oolkit.createScrollPane( )
ScrollPaneConstants: javax.swing
—implemented by: **J**ScrollPane **S**crollPaneLayout*
ScrollPaneLayout*: javax.swing
—subclasses: **S**crollPaneLayout.UIResource
ScrollPaneLayout.UIResource: javax.swing
ScrollPanePeer: java.awt.peer
—returned by: **T**oolkit.createScrollPane( )
ScrollPaneUI: javax.swing.plaf
—passed to: **J**ScrollPane.setUI( )
—returned by: **J**ScrollPane.getUI( )
scrollPathToVisible( ): **J**Tree
scrollRectToVisible( ): **J**Component*
scrollRowToVisible( ): **J**Tree
SCROLLS_ON_EXPAND_PROPERTY: **J**Tree
scrollsOnExpand: **J**Tree
scrollToReference( ): **J**EditorPane*
scrollUnderway: **J**Viewport
SDATA: *D*TDConstants
SE_RESIZE_CURSOR: **C**ursor **F**rame*
SEALED: **A**ttributes.Name
search( ): **S**tack
SECOND: **C**alendar*
SECOND_FIELD: **D**ateFormat*
SECONDARY: **C**ollator*
secondaryOrder( ): **C**ollationElementIterator
SectionElementName: **A**bstractDocument*
SecureClassLoader*: java.security
—subclasses: **U**RLClassLoader
SecureRandom: java.security
—passed to: **A**lgorithmParameterGenerator.init( )
AlgorithmParameterGeneratorSpi.engineInit( )
*D*SAKeyPairGenerator.initialize( )
KeyPairGeneratorSpi*.initialize( )
SignatureSpi*.engineInitSign( )
—returned by: **S**ecureRandom.getInstance( )
—fields: **S**ignatureSpi*.appRandom
SecureRandomSpi: java.security
—passed to: **S**ecureRandom( )
Security: java.security
SecurityException*: java.lang
—subclasses: **A**ccessControlException **R**MISecurityException
—thrown by: **A**ccessibleObject*.setAccessible( )
Beans.setGuiAvailable( ) **C**lass < getConstructors( ),
getDeclaredClasses( ), getDeclaredConstructor( ),
getDeclaredConstructors( ), getDeclaredField( ),
getDeclaredFields( ), getDeclaredMethod( ), getDeclaredMethods( ),
getField( ), getFields( ), getMethod( ), getMethods( ) >
GuardedObject.getObject( ) **O**bjectInputStream
< enableResolveObject( ), ObjectInputStream( ) >
ObjectOutputStream( )
SecurityManager*: java.lang
—subclasses: **R**MISecurityManager
—passed to: **S**ystem.setSecurityManager( )
—returned by: **S**ystem.getSecurityManager( )
SecurityPermission: java.security
seek( ): *D*ynAny* **R**andomAccessFile
SEG_CLOSE: *P*athIterator
SEG_CUBICTO: *P*athIterator
SEG_LINETO: *P*athIterator
SEG_MOVETO: *P*athIterator

S

serialVersionUID: *Serializable**
servant: ServantObject
servant_postinvoke(): **D**elegate
servant_preinvoke(): **D**elegate
ServantObject: org.omg.CORBA.portable
—passed to: **D**elegate.servant_postinvoke( )
—returned by: **D**elegate.servant_preinvoke( )
ServerCloneException: java.rmi.server
ServerError: java.rmi
ServerException: java.rmi
ServerNotActiveException: java.rmi.server
—thrown by: **R**emoteServer*.getClientHost( )
ServerRef: java.rmi.server
ServerRequest: org.omg.CORBA
—passed to: **D**ynamicImplementation*.invoke( )
ServerRuntimeException: java.rmi
ServerSocket: java.net
—returned by: *RMIServerSocketFactory*.createServerSocket( )
service_detail: ServiceDetail
service_detail_type: ServiceDetail
service_details: ServiceInformation
service_options: ServiceInformation
serviceAvailable(): BeanContextChildSupport*
BeanContextServicesListener*
serviceClass: BeanContextServiceAvailableEvent
BeanContextServiceRevokedEvent
ServiceDetail: org.omg.CORBA
—passed to: **S**erviceDetailHelper < insert( ), write( ) >
—returned by: **S**erviceDetailHelper < extract( ), read( ) >
—fields: **S**erviceInformation.service_details
ServiceDetailHelper: org.omg.CORBA
ServiceInformation: org.omg.CORBA
—passed to: **S**erviceInformationHelper < insert( ), write( ) >
—returned by: **S**erviceInformationHelper < extract( ), read( ) >
—fields: **S**erviceInformationHolder.value
ServiceInformationHelper: org.omg.CORBA
ServiceInformationHolder: org.omg.CORBA
—passed to: **O**RB.get_service_information( )
serviceProvider:
BeanContextServicesSupport.BCSSServiceProvider
serviceRevoked(): BeanContextChildSupport*
BeanContextServiceRevokedListener*
BeanContextServicesSupport.BCSSProxyServiceProvider
services: BeanContextServicesSupport
Set*: java.util
—extended by: *SortedSet*
—passed to: *AttributedCharacterIterator* < getRunLimit( ),
getRunStart( ) > **C**ollections.unmodifiableSet( )
—returned by: **A**bstractMap* < entrySet( ), keySet( ) >
Attributes < entrySet( ), keySet( ) > **C**ollections
< synchronizedSet( ), unmodifiableSet( ) > **H**ashtable*.keySet( )
Map*.keySet( ) **R**enderingHints.keySet( )
X509Certificate.getNonCriticalExtensionOIDs( ) **X**509CRL
< getNonCriticalExtensionOIDs( ), getRevokedCertificates( ) >
X509CRLEntry.getNonCriticalExtensionOIDs( )
X509Extension.getNonCriticalExtensionOIDs( )
—implemented by: **A**bstractSet*
—fields: **C**ollections.EMPTY_SET
set(): **A**bstractList* java.lang.reflect.**A**rray **B**itSet **C**alendar*
DefaultListModel **F**ield *java.util.*List ListIterator
ParameterBlock **T**hreadLocal* **U**RL
set2DigitYearStart(): **S**impleDateFormat
set_as_default(): *DynUnion*
set_elements(): *DynArray DynSequence*
set_exception(): ServerRequest
set_members(): *DynStruct DynValue*
set_one_value(): Context
SET_OVERRIDE: SetOverrideType
set_parameters(): ORB
set_policy_override(): **D**elegate
set_result(): ServerRequest
set_return_type(): Request

set_value(): *DynFixed*
set_values(): Context
setAccelerator(): JMenuItem*
setAccessible(): **A**ccessibleObject*
setAccessibleDescription(): **A**ccessibleContext*
setAccessibleName(): **A**ccessibleContext*
setAccessibleParent(): **A**ccessibleContext*
setAccessory(): JFileChooser
setActionCommand(): **A**bstractButton* Button *ButtonModel*
DefaultButtonModel* JComboBox JTextField* MenuItem*
setActivationDesc(): *ActivationSystem*
setActivationGroupDesc(): *ActivationSystem*
setActive(): **D**ropTarget
setAddress(): **D**atagramPacket
setAlignment(): **F**lowLayout **L**abel *LabelPeer*
StyleConstants*
setAlignmentX(): JComponent*
setAlignmentY(): JComponent*
setAllowsChildren(): **D**efaultMutableTreeNode*
setAllowUserInteraction(): **U**RLConnection*
setAmPmStrings(): **D**ateFormatSymbols
setAnchorSelectionIndex(): **D**efaultListSelectionModel
ListSelectionModel
setAngleExtent(): **A**rc2D*
setAngles(): **A**rc2D*
setAngleStart(): **A**rc2D*
setAnimated(): **M**emoryImageSource
setApproveButtonMnemonic(): JFileChooser
setApproveButtonText(): JFileChooser
setApproveButtonToolTipText(): JFileChooser
setArc(): **A**rc2D*
setArcByCenter(): **A**rc2D*
setArcByTangent(): **A**rc2D*
setArcType(): **A**rc2D*
setAreaOfInterest(): **R**enderContext
setArmed(): *ButtonModel* **D**efaultButtonModel* JMenuItem*
setArray(): *PreparedStatement**
setAsciiStream(): *PreparedStatement**
setAsksAllowsChildren(): **D**efaultTreeModel
setAsText(): *PropertyEditor* **P**ropertyEditorSupport
setAsynchronousLoadPriority(): **A**bstractDocument*
setAutoCommit(): *Connection*
setAutoCreateColumnsFromModel(): JTable
setAutoResizeMode(): JTable
setAutoscrolls(): JComponent*
setBackground(): **A**ccessibleComponent
Box.AccessibleBox **B**ox.Filler.AccessibleBoxFiller
CellRendererPane.AccessibleCellRendererPane
Component* *ComponentPeer**
Graphics2D **J**Applet.AccessibleJApplet
JComponent.AccessibleJComponent*
JDialog.AccessibleJDialog **J**Frame.AccessibleJFrame
JList.AccessibleJList.AccessibleJListChild
JPopupMenu.WindowPopup.AccessibleWindowPopup
JTable.AccessibleJTable.AccessibleJTableCell
JTableHeader.AccessibleJTableHeader ↵
.AccessibleJTableHeaderEntry
JTree.AccessibleJTree.AccessibleJTreeNode
JWindow.AccessibleJWindow **S**tyleConstants*
setBackgroundAt(): JTabbedPane
setBackgroundNonSelectionColor(): **D**efaultTreeCellRenderer
setBackgroundSelectionColor(): **D**efaultTreeCellRenderer
setBackingStoreEnabled(): JViewport
setBase(): **H**TMLDocument
setBaseFontSize(): **S**tyleSheet
setBeanContext(): *BeanContextChild**
BeanContextChildSupport*
setBeanInfoSearchPath(): **I**ntrospector
setBeginIndex(): **F**ieldPosition
setBidiLevel(): **S**tyleConstants*
setBigDecimal(): *PreparedStatement**
setBinaryStream(): *PreparedStatement**

S

setBit(): BigInteger
setBlinkRate(): *Caret* DefaultCaret
setBlob(): *PreparedStatement**
setBlockIncrement(): *Adjustable* JScrollBar* Scrollbar
setBold(): StyleConstants*
setBoolean(): java.lang.reflect.**A**rray Field
    PreparedStatement*
setBorder(): JComponent* TitledBorder*
setBorderPainted(): AbstractButton* JMenuBar JPopupMenu
    JProgressBar JToolBar
setBorderSelectionColor(): DefaultTreeCellEditor
    DefaultTreeCellRenderer
setBottomComponent(): JSplitPane
setBound(): PropertyDescriptor*
setBounds(): *AccessibleComponent*
    Box.AccessibleBox   Box.Filler.AccessibleBoxFiller
    CellRendererPane.AccessibleCellRendererPane
    Component* *ComponentPeer** JApplet.AccessibleJApplet
    JComponent.AccessibleJComponent*
    JDialog.AccessibleJDialog   JFrame.AccessibleJFrame
    JList.AccessibleJList.AccessibleJListChild
    JPopupMenu.WindowPopup.AccessibleWindowPopup
    JTable.AccessibleJTable.AccessibleJTableCell
    JTableHeader.AccessibleJTableHeader ↵
    .AccessibleJTableHeaderEntry
    JTree.AccessibleJTree.AccessibleJTreeNode
    JWindow.AccessibleJWindow   Rectangle*
setBoundsForFrame(): DefaultDesktopManager
    DesktopManager
setByte(): java.lang.reflect.**A**rray Field *PreparedStatement**
setBytes(): *PreparedStatement**
setCalendar(): DateFormat*
setCaret(): JTextComponent*
setCaretColor(): JTextComponent*
setCaretPosition(): JTextComponent* TextComponent*
    TextComponentPeer*
setCatalog(): *Connection*
setCellEditor(): JTable JTree TableColumn
setCellRenderer(): JList JTree TableColumn
setCellSelectionEnabled(): JTable
setCertificateEntry(): KeyStore
setChanged(): Observable
setChar(): java.lang.reflect.**A**rray Field
setCharacterAttributes(): DefaultStyledDocument* JTextPane
    StyledDocument StyledEditorKit.StyledTextAction*
setCharacterStream(): *PreparedStatement**
setCharacterSubsets(): InputContext
setCharAt(): StringBuffer
setCheckboxGroup(): Checkbox *CheckboxPeer*
setChoices(): ChoiceFormat
setChooserPanels(): JColorChooser
setClickCountToStart(): DefaultCellEditor
setClip(): Graphics*
setClob(): *PreparedStatement**
setClosable(): JInternalFrame
setClosed(): JInternalFrame
setClosedIcon(): DefaultTreeCellRenderer
setCoalesce(): Timer
setColor(): Graphics* JColorChooser
setColorModel(): *ImageConsumer* ImageFilter* PixelGrabber
setColumnHeader(): JScrollPane
setColumnHeaderView(): JScrollPane
setColumnIdentifiers(): DefaultTableModel
setColumnMargin(): DefaultTableColumnModel
    TableColumnModel
setColumnModel(): JTable JTableHeader
setColumns(): GridLayout JTextArea JTextField* TextArea
    TextField
setColumnSelectionAllowed(): DefaultTableColumnModel
    JTable *TableColumnModel*
setColumnSelectionInterval(): JTable
setComment(): ZipEntry* ZipOutputStream*

setComponent(): DragGestureRecognizer* DropTarget
    JToolTip StyleConstants*
setComponentAt(): JTabbedPane
setComponentOrientation(): Component*
setComposite(): Graphics2D
setCompressedSize(): ZipEntry*
setConstrained(): PropertyDescriptor*
setConstraints(): GridBagLayout
setContentAreaFilled(): AbstractButton*
setContentHandlerFactory(): URLConnection*
setContentPane(): JApplet JDialog JFrame JInternalFrame
    JRootPane JWindow *RootPaneContainer*
setContents(): Clipboard
setContentType(): JEditorPane*
setContextClassLoader(): Thread
setContinuousLayout(): JSplitPane
setCopies(): PrinterJob
setCorner(): JScrollPane
setCrc(): ZipEntry*
setCurrencySymbol(): DecimalFormatSymbols
setCurrent(): CheckboxGroup
setCurrentAccessibleValue():
    AbstractButton.AccessibleAbstractButton*
    AccessibleValue JInternalFrame.AccessibleJInternalFrame
    JInternalFrame.JDesktopIcon.AccessibleJDesktopIcon
    JProgressBar.AccessibleJProgressBar
    JScrollBar.AccessibleJScrollBar   JSlider.AccessibleJSlider
    JSplitPane.AccessibleJSplitPane
setCurrentDirectory(): JFileChooser
setCurrentManager(): FocusManager* RepaintManager
setCursor(): *AccessibleComponent*
    Box.AccessibleBox   Box.Filler.AccessibleBoxFiller
    CellRendererPane.AccessibleCellRendererPane
    Component* *ComponentPeer**
    DragSourceContext   JApplet.AccessibleJApplet
    JComponent.AccessibleJComponent*
    JDialog.AccessibleJDialog   JFrame.AccessibleJFrame
    JList.AccessibleJList.AccessibleJListChild
    JPopupMenu.WindowPopup.AccessibleWindowPopup
    JTable.AccessibleJTable.AccessibleJTableCell
    JTableHeader.AccessibleJTableHeader ↵
    .AccessibleJTableHeaderEntry
    JTree.AccessibleJTree.AccessibleJTreeNode
    JWindow.AccessibleJWindow
setCursorName(): *Statement**
setCurve(): CubicCurve2D* QuadCurve2D*
setDaemon(): Thread ThreadGroup
setData(): BufferedImage DatagramPacket ICC_Profile*
    WritableRenderedImage
setDataElements(): SampleModel* WritableRaster
setDataVector(): DefaultTableModel
setDate(): java.util.**D**ate* *PreparedStatement**
setDateFormatSymbols(): SimpleDateFormat
setDebugGraphicsOptions(): JComponent*
setDebugOptions(): DebugGraphics
setDecimalFormatSymbols(): DecimalFormat
setDecimalSeparator(): DecimalFormatSymbols
setDecimalSeparatorAlwaysShown(): DecimalFormat
setDecomposition(): Collator
setDefault(): Authenticator Locale TimeZone*
setDefaultAction(): *Keymap*
setDefaultActions(): DropTarget
setDefaultAllowUserInteraction(): URLConnection*
setDefaultButton(): JRootPane
setDefaultCapable(): JButton
setDefaultCloseOperation(): JDialog JFrame JInternalFrame
setDefaultDTD(): ParserDelegator
setDefaultEditor(): JTable
setDefaultLightWeightPopupEnabled(): JPopupMenu
setDefaultRenderer(): JTable
setDefaultRequestProperty(): URLConnection*
setDefaultStream(): LogStream

S

S

setGlassPane(): JApplet JDialog JFrame JInternalFrame JRootPane JWindow. *RootPaneContainer*
setGlyphPosition(): GlyphVector
setGlyphTransform(): GlyphVector
setGregorianChange(): GregorianCalendar
setGridColor(): JTable
setGridLocation(): TableView.TableCell
setGroup(): *ButtonModel* DefaultButtonModel*
setGroupingSeparator(): DecimalFormatSymbols
setGroupingSize(): DecimalFormat
setGroupingUsed(): NumberFormat*
setGuiAvailable(): Beans
setHeaderRenderer(): TableColumn
setHeaderValue(): TableColumn
setHelpMenu(): JMenuBar MenuBar
setHgap(): BorderLayout CardLayout FlowLayout GridLayout
setHidden(): FeatureDescriptor*
setHighlighter(): JTextComponent*
setHints(): *ImageConsumer* ImageFilter* PixelGrabber
setHorizontalAlignment(): AbstractButton* JLabel* JTextField*
setHorizontalScrollBar(): JScrollPane
setHorizontalScrollBarPolicy(): JScrollPane ScrollPaneLayout*
setHorizontalTextPosition(): AbstractButton* JLabel*
setHours(): java.util.Date*
setHumanPresentableName(): DataFlavor
setIcon(): AbstractButton* JInternalFrame JLabel* JOptionPane StyleConstants*
setIconAt(): JTabbedPane
setIconifiable(): JInternalFrame
setIconImage(): Frame* *FramePeer*
setIconTextGap(): JLabel*
setID(): TimeZone*
setIdentifier(): TableColumn
setIfModifiedSince(): URLConnection*
setImage(): ImageIcon
setImageableArea(): Paper
setImageObserver(): ImageIcon
setIn(): System
setInDefaultEventSet(): EventSetDescriptor
setIndentSpace(): AbstractWriter*
setIndex(): *CharacterIterator* ParsePosition StringCharacterIterator
setIndexedReadMethod(): IndexedPropertyDescriptor
setIndexedWriteMethod(): IndexedPropertyDescriptor
setInfinity(): DecimalFormatSymbols
setInfo(): Identity*
setInitialDelay(): Timer ToolTipManager
setInitialSelectionValue(): JOptionPane
setInitialValue(): JOptionPane
setInput(): Deflater Inflater
setInputValue(): JOptionPane
setInsets(): CompositeView*
setInstalledLookAndFeels(): UIManager
setInt(): java.lang.reflect.Array Field *PreparedStatement*
setIntercellSpacing(): JTable
setInterface(): MulticastSocket
setInternalFrame(): JInternalFrame.JDesktopIcon
setInternationalCurrencySymbol(): DecimalFormatSymbols
setInverted(): JSlider
setInvoker(): JPopupMenu
setInvokesStopCellEditing(): JTree
setItalic(): StyleConstants*
setItem(): *ComboBoxEditor*
setJMenuBar(): JApplet JDialog JFrame JInternalFrame JRootPane
setJobName(): PrinterJob
setJustification(): javax.swing.text.ParagraphView*
setKeyChar(): KeyEvent*
setKeyCode(): KeyEvent*
setKeyEntry(): KeyStore

setKeymap(): JTextComponent*
setKeyPair(): Signer
setKeySelectionManager(): JComboBox
setLabel(): AbstractButton* Button *ButtonPeer* Checkbox *CheckboxPeer* JPopupMenu MenuItem* *MenuItemPeer* Option
setLabelFor(): JLabel*
setLabelTable(): JSlider
setLargeModel(): JTree
setLastDividerLocation(): JSplitPane
setLastModified(): File
setLayer(): JInternalFrame JLayeredPane*
setLayeredPane(): JApplet JDialog JFrame JInternalFrame JRootPane JWindow *RootPaneContainer*
setLayout(): Container*
setLeadAnchorNotificationEnabled(): DefaultListSelectionModel
setLeadSelectionIndex(): DefaultListSelectionModel *ListSelectionModel*
setLeafIcon(): DefaultTreeCellRenderer
setLeftComponent(): JSplitPane
setLeftIndent(): StyleConstants*
setLength(): DatagramPacket RandomAccessFile StringBuffer
setLenient(): Calendar* DateFormat*
setLevel(): Deflater ZipOutputStream*
setLightWeightPopupEnabled(): JComboBox JPopupMenu ToolTipManager
setLimit(): UndoManager
setLine(): Line2D*
setLineIncrement(): Scrollbar *ScrollbarPeer*
setLineLength(): AbstractWriter*
setLineNumber(): LineNumberInputStream LineNumberReader
setLineSpacing(): javax.swing.text.ParagraphView* StyleConstants*
setLineWrap(): JTextArea
setListData(): JList
setLocale(): BeanContextSupport* Component* MessageFormat
setLocalPatternChars(): DateFormatSymbols
setLocation(): *AccessibleComponent* Box.AccessibleBox Box.Filler.AccessibleBoxFiller CellRendererPane.AccessibleCellRendererPane Component* JApplet.AccessibleJApplet JComponent.AccessibleJComponent* JDialog.AccessibleJDialog JFrame.AccessibleJFrame JList.AccessibleJList.AccessibleJListChild JPopupMenu.WindowPopup.AccessibleWindowPopup JTable.AccessibleJTable.AccessibleJTableCell JTableHeader.AccessibleJTableHeader↵ .AccessibleJTableHeaderEntry JTree.AccessibleJTree.AccessibleJTreeNode JWindow.AccessibleJWindow Point2D* Rectangle*
setLocationRelativeTo(): JDialog
setLog(): RemoteServer*
setLogicalStyle(): DefaultStyledDocument* JTextPane *StyledDocument*
setLoginTimeout(): DriverManager
setLogStream(): DebugGraphics DriverManager
setLogTimers(): Timer
setLogWriter(): DriverManager
setLong(): java.lang.reflect.Array Field *PreparedStatement*
setLookAndFeel(): UIManager
setMagicCaretPosition(): *Caret* DefaultCaret
setMajorTickSpacing(): JSlider
setMargin(): AbstractButton* JMenuBar JTextComponent* JToolBar
setMaxFieldSize(): *Statement*
setMaximizable(): JInternalFrame

setMaximum( ): *A*djustable *B*oundedRangeModel
*D*efaultBoundedRangeModel *J*InternalFrame *J*ProgressBar
*J*ScrollBar* *J*Slider *P*rogressMonitor *S*crollbar
setMaximumFractionDigits( ): *N*umberFormat*
setMaximumIntegerDigits( ): *N*umberFormat*
setMaximumRowCount( ): *J*ComboBox
setMaximumSize( ): *J*Component*
setMaxPriority( ): *T*hreadGroup
setMaxRows( ): *S*tatement*
setMaxWidth( ): *T*ableColumn
setMenuBar( ): *F*rame* *FramePeer* *J*InternalFrame
*J*RootPane
setMenuLocation( ): *J*Menu
setMessage( ): *J*OptionPane
setMessageDigest( ): *D*igestInputStream *D*igestOutputStream
setMessageType( ): *J*OptionPane
setMethod( ): *Z*ipEntry* *Z*ipOutputStream*
setMillisToDecideToPopup( ): *P*rogressMonitor
setMillisToPopup( ): *P*rogressMonitor
setMinimalDaysInFirstWeek( ): *C*alendar*
setMinimum( ): *A*djustable *B*oundedRangeModel
*D*efaultBoundedRangeModel *J*ProgressBar *J*ScrollBar*
*J*Slider *P*rogressMonitor *S*crollbar
setMinimumFractionDigits( ): *N*umberFormat*
setMinimumIntegerDigits( ): *N*umberFormat*
setMinimumSize( ): *J*Component*
setMinorTickSpacing( ): *J*Slider
setMinusSign( ): *D*ecimalFormatSymbols
setMinutes( ): java.util.*D*ate*
setMinWidth( ): *T*ableColumn
setMnemonic( ): *A*bstractButton* *ButtonModel*
*D*efaultButtonModel*
setModal( ): *D*ialog*
setMode( ): *F*ileDialog
setModel( ): *A*bstractButton* *A*bstractLayoutCache*
*J*ComboBox *J*List *J*ProgressBar *J*ScrollBar* *J*Slider
*J*TabbedPane *J*Table *J*Tree
setModelIndex( ): *T*ableColumn
setModifiers( ): *K*eyEvent*
setMonetaryDecimalSeparator( ): *D*ecimalFormatSymbols
setMonth( ): java.util.*D*ate*
setMonths( ): *D*ateFormatSymbols
setMultipleMode( ): java.awt.*L*ist *ListPeer*
setMultipleSelections( ): java.awt.*L*ist *ListPeer*
setMultiplier( ): *D*ecimalFormat
setMultiSelectionEnabled( ): *J*FileChooser
setName( ): *A*cl *C*omponent* *F*eatureDescriptor*
*M*enuComponent* *S*tyleContext.NamedStyle *T*hread
setNaN( ): *D*ecimalFormatSymbols
setNanos( ): *T*imestamp
setNegativePermissions( ): *A*clEntry
setNegativePrefix( ): *D*ecimalFormat
setNegativeSuffix( ): *D*ecimalFormat
setNextException( ): *S*QLException*
setNextFocusableComponent( ): *J*Component*
setNextWarning( ): *S*QLWarning*
setNodeDimensions( ): *A*bstractLayoutCache*
setNote( ): *P*rogressMonitor
setNull( ): *P*reparedStatement*
setNumberFormat( ): *D*ateFormat*
setNumRows( ): *D*efaultTableModel
setObject( ): *C*ustomizer *P*reparedStatement*
setOffset( ): *C*ollationElementIterator *O*bjectStreamField
setOneTouchExpandable( ): *J*SplitPane
setOpaque( ): *J*Component*
setOpenIcon( ): *D*efaultTreeCellRenderer
setOption( ): *D*atagramSocketImpl *S*ocketImpl *SocketOptions*
setOptions( ): *J*OptionPane
setOptionType( ): *J*OptionPane
setOrientation( ): *J*ProgressBar *J*ScrollBar* *J*Separator*
*J*Slider *J*SplitPane *J*ToolBar *P*ageFormat *S*crollbar
setOut( ): *S*ystem

setOutputStream( ): *L*ogStream
SetOverrideType: org.omg.CORBA
—passed to: *D*elegate.set_policy_override( )
org.omg.CORBA.Object.*_set_policy_override( )
—returned by: *S*etOverrideType.from_int( )
—fields: *S*etOverrideType < ADD_OVERRIDE, SET_OVERRIDE >
setPage( ): *B*ook *J*EditorPane*
setPageable( ): *P*rinterJob
setPageIncrement( ): *S*crollbar *ScrollbarPeer*
setPaint( ): *G*raphics2D
setPaintLabels( ): *J*Slider
setPaintMode( ): *G*raphics*
setPaintTicks( ): *J*Slider
setPaintTrack( ): *J*Slider
setPaper( ): *P*ageFormat
setParagraphAttributes( ): *D*efaultStyledDocument* *J*TextPane
StyledDocument *S*tyledEditorKit.StyledTextAction*
setParagraphInsets( ): *C*ompositeView*
setParameter( ): *S*ignature
setParameterBlock( ): *R*enderableImageOp
setParameters( ): *P*arameterBlock
setParent( ): *D*efaultMutableTreeNode* *MutableTreeNode*
*R*esourceBundle* *V*iew*
setParseIntegerOnly( ): *N*umberFormat*
setPatternSeparator( ): *D*ecimalFormatSymbols
setPercent( ): *D*ecimalFormatSymbols
setPerMill( ): *D*ecimalFormatSymbols
setPixel( ): *S*ampleModel* *W*ritableRaster
setPixels( ): *ImageConsumer* *I*mageFilter* *P*ixelGrabber
*S*ampleModel* *W*ritableRaster
setPolicy( ): java.security.*P*olicy
setPopupMenuVisible( ): *J*Menu
setPopupSize( ): *J*PopupMenu
setPopupVisible( ): *C*omboBoxUI *J*ComboBox
setPort( ): *D*atagramPacket
setPosition( ): *J*LayeredPane* *L*ineBreakMeasurer
setPositivePrefix( ): *D*ecimalFormat
setPositiveSuffix( ): *D*ecimalFormat
setPreferred( ): *F*eatureDescriptor*
setPreferredScrollableViewportSize( ): *J*Table
setPreferredSize( ): *J*Component*
setPreferredWidth( ): *T*ableColumn
setPreservesUnknownTags( ): *H*TMLDocument
setPressed( ): *ButtonModel* *D*efaultButtonModel*
setPressedIcon( ): *A*bstractButton*
setPreviewPanel( ): *J*ColorChooser
setPreviousBounds( ): *D*efaultDesktopManager
setPrincipal( ): *A*clEntry
setPrintable( ): *P*rinterJob
setPriority( ): *T*hread
setProgress( ): *P*rogressMonitor
setPropagatedFrom( ): *B*eanContextEvent*
setPropagationId( ): *P*ropertyChangeEvent
setProperties( ): *ImageConsumer* *I*mageFilter* *P*ixelGrabber
*S*ystem
setPropertiesFromAttributes( ): *B*lockView* *L*abelView*
javax.swing.text.*P*aragraphView*
setProperty( ): *P*roperties* *S*ecurity *S*ystem
setPropertyEditorClass( ): *P*ropertyDescriptor*
setPrototypeCellValue( ): *J*List
setPublicKey( ): *I*dentity*
setQueryTimeout( ): *S*tatement*
setRangeProperties( ): *B*oundedRangeModel
*D*efaultBoundedRangeModel
setRawOffset( ): *T*imeZone*
setReadMethod( ): *P*ropertyDescriptor*
setReadOnly( ): *C*onnection *F*ile *P*ermissionCollection*
setReceiveBufferSize( ): *D*atagramSocket* *S*ocket
setRect( ): *R*ectangle2D* *W*ritableRaster
setRef( ): *PreparedStatement* *R*emoteStub*
setRenderContext( ): *R*enderableImageProducer
setRenderer( ): *J*ComboBox

S

setRenderingHint(): Graphics2D
setRenderingHints(): Graphics2D RenderContext
setReorderingAllowed(): JTableHeader
setRepeats(): Timer
setRequestFocusEnabled(): JComponent*
setRequestMethod(): HttpURLConnection
setRequestProperty(): URLConnection*
setReshowDelay(): ToolTipManager
setResizable(): Dialog* *DialogPeer** Frame* *FramePeer*
 JInternalFrame TableColumn
setResizingAllowed(): JTableHeader
setResizingColumn(): JTableHeader
setResolveParent(): AbstractDocument.AbstractElement*
 Keymap MutableAttributeSet* SimpleAttributeSet
 StyleContext.NamedStyle
setRGB(): BufferedImage
setRightComponent(): JSplitPane
setRightIndent(): StyleConstants*
setRollover(): *ButtonModel* DefaultButtonModel*
setRolloverEnabled(): AbstractButton*
setRolloverIcon(): AbstractButton*
setRolloverSelectedIcon(): AbstractButton*
setRoot(): DefaultTreeModel
setRootFrame(): JOptionPane
setRootPane(): JApplet JDialog JFrame JInternalFrame
 JWindow
setRootPaneCheckingEnabled(): JApplet JDialog JFrame
 JInternalFrame JWindow
setRootVisible(): AbstractLayoutCache* JTree
setRoundRect(): RoundRectangle2D*
setRowHeader(): JScrollPane
setRowHeaderView(): JScrollPane
setRowHeight(): AbstractLayoutCache* JTable JTree
setRowMapper(): DefaultTreeSelectionModel*
 TreeSelectionModel
setRowMargin(): JTable
setRows(): GridLayout JTextArea TextArea
setRowSelectionAllowed(): JTable
setRowSelectionInterval(): JTable
setSample(): SampleModel* WritableRaster
setSamples(): SampleModel* WritableRaster
setScale(): BigDecimal
setScrollOffset(): JTextField*
setScrollPosition(): ScrollPane *ScrollPanePeer*
setScrollsOnExpand(): JTree
setSeconds(): java.util.Date*
setSecurityManager(): System
setSeed(): Random*
setSelected(): AbstractButton* ButtonGroup *ButtonModel*
 DefaultButtonModel* JInternalFrame JMenuBar
 JPopupMenu
setSelectedCheckbox(): CheckboxGroup
setSelectedColor(): *ColorSelectionModel*
 DefaultColorSelectionModel
setSelectedComponent(): JTabbedPane
setSelectedFile(): JFileChooser
setSelectedFiles(): JFileChooser
setSelectedIcon(): AbstractButton*
setSelectedIndex(): DefaultSingleSelectionModel JComboBox
 JList JTabbedPane *SingleSelectionModel*
setSelectedIndices(): JList
setSelectedItem(): *ComboBoxModel** DefaultComboBoxModel
 JComboBox
setSelectedPath(): MenuSelectionManager
setSelectedTextColor(): JTextComponent*
setSelectedValue(): JList
setSelection(): Option
setSelectionBackground(): JList JTable
setSelectionColor(): JTextComponent*
setSelectionEnd(): JTextComponent* TextComponent*
setSelectionForeground(): JList JTable

setSelectionInterval(): DefaultListSelectionModel JList JTree
 ListSelectionModel
setSelectionMode(): DefaultListSelectionModel
 DefaultTreeSelectionModel* JList JTable
 ListSelectionModel *TreeSelectionModel*
setSelectionModel(): AbstractLayoutCache*
 DefaultTableColumnModel JColorChooser JList JMenuBar
 JPopupMenu JTable JTree *TableColumnModel*
setSelectionPath(): DefaultTreeSelectionModel* JTree
 TreeSelectionModel
setSelectionPaths(): DefaultTreeSelectionModel* JTree
 TreeSelectionModel
setSelectionRow(): JTree
setSelectionRows(): JTree
setSelectionStart(): JTextComponent* TextComponent*
setSelectionValues(): JOptionPane
setSelectionVisible(): *Caret* DefaultCaret
setSendBufferSize(): DatagramSocket* Socket
setSeparatorSize(): JToolBar.Separator
setShort(): java.lang.reflect.Array Field *PreparedStatement**
setShortcut(): MenuItem*
setShortDescription(): FeatureDescriptor*
setShortMonths(): DateFormatSymbols
setShortWeekdays(): DateFormatSymbols
setShowGrid(): JTable
setShowHorizontalLines(): JTable
setShowsRootHandles(): JTree
setShowVerticalLines(): JTable
setSigners(): ClassLoader*
setSize(): *AccessibleComponent*
 Box.AccessibleBox Box.Filler.AccessibleBoxFiller
 CellRendererPane.AccessibleCellRendererPane
 Component* DefaultListModel
 Dimension2D* JApplet.AccessibleJApplet
 JComponent.AccessibleJComponent*
 JDialog.AccessibleJDialog JFrame.AccessibleJFrame
 JList.AccessibleJList.AccessibleJListChild
 JPopupMenu.WindowPopup.AccessibleWindowPopup
 JTable.AccessibleJTable.AccessibleJTableCell
 JTableHeader.AccessibleJTableHeader↵
 .AccessibleJTableHeaderEntry
 JTree.AccessibleJTree.AccessibleJTreeNode
 JWindow.AccessibleJWindow Paper Rectangle* Vector*
 View* ZipEntry*
setSnapToTicks(): JSlider
setSocketFactory(): RMISocketFactory ServerSocket
setSocketImplFactory(): Socket
setSoLinger(): Socket
setSoTimeout(): DatagramSocket* ServerSocket Socket
setSource(): ParameterBlock
setSourceActions(): DragGestureRecognizer*
setSources(): ParameterBlock
setSpaceAbove(): StyleConstants*
setSpaceBelow(): StyleConstants*
setStartRule(): SimpleTimeZone
setStartYear(): SimpleTimeZone
setState(): Checkbox CheckboxMenuItem
 CheckboxMenuItemPeer *CheckboxPeer* Frame*
 FramePeer JCheckBoxMenuItem
setStrategy(): Deflater
setStrength(): Collator*
setStrikeThrough(): LabelView* StyleConstants*
setString(): JProgressBar *PreparedStatement**
setStringPainted(): JProgressBar
setStroke(): Graphics2D
setStub(): Applet*
setStyledDocument(): JTextPane
setStyleSheet(): HTMLEditorKit
setSubscript(): LabelView* StyleConstants*
setSuperscript(): LabelView* StyleConstants*
setSystem(): ActivationGroup
setSystemScope(): IdentityScope

S

shiftLeft( ): **B**igInteger
shiftRight( ): **B**igInteger
SHORT: **D**ateFormat* **T**imeZone*
Short: java.lang
—passed to: **S**hort.compareTo( )
—returned by: **S**hort < decode( ), valueOf( ) >
SHORT_DESCRIPTION: **A**ction
shortcuts( ): **M**enuBar
ShortHolder: org.omg.CORBA
ShortLookupTable: java.awt.image
shortValue( ): **N**umber*
shouldSelectCell( ): *CellEditor** **D**efaultCellEditor
DefaultTreeCellEditor
shouldStartEditingTimer( ): **D**efaultTreeCellEditor
show( ): **C**ardLayout **C**omponent* *ComponentPeer**
PopupMenu *PopupMenuPeer*
showConfirmDialog( ): **J**OptionPane
showDialog( ): **J**ColorChooser **J**FileChooser
showDocument( ): *AppletContext*
showHorizontalLines: **J**Table
SHOWING: **A**ccessibleState
showInputDialog( ): **J**OptionPane
showInternalConfirmDialog( ): **J**OptionPane
showInternalInputDialog( ): **J**OptionPane
showInternalMessageDialog( ): **J**OptionPane
showInternalOptionDialog( ): **J**OptionPane
showMessageDialog( ): **J**OptionPane
showOpenDialog( ): **J**FileChooser
showOptionDialog( ): **J**OptionPane
showPopup( ): **J**ComboBox
SHOWS_ROOT_HANDLES_PROPERTY: **J**Tree
showSaveDialog( ): **J**FileChooser
showsRootHandles: **J**Tree
showStatus( ): **A**pplet* *AppletContext*
showVerticalLines: **J**Table
shrinkAbsorb: **G**lyphJustificationInfo
shrinkLeftLimit: **G**lyphJustificationInfo
shrinkPriority: **G**lyphJustificationInfo
shrinkRightLimit: **G**lyphJustificationInfo
shuffle( ): **C**ollections
shutdown( ): **A**ctivationSystem **O**RB
SIGN: **S**ignature
sign( ): **S**ignature
Signature: java.security
—passed to: **S**ignedObject < SignedObject( ), verify( ) >
—returned by: **S**ignature.getInstance( )
SIGNATURE_VERSION: **A**ttributes.Name
SignatureException: java.security
—thrown by: java.security.cert.**C**ertificate*.verify( ) **S**ignature
< sign( ), update( ), verify( ) > **S**ignatureSpi* < engineSign( ),
engineUpdate( ), engineVerify( ) > **S**ignedObject.verify( )
X509CRL.verify( )
SignatureSpi*: java.security
—subclasses: **S**ignature
SignedObject: java.security
Signer: java.security
signum( ): **B**igDecimal **B**igInteger
SILENT: **L**ogStream
SimpleAttributeSet: javax.swing.text
—returned by: **P**arser*.getAttributes( )
SimpleBeanInfo: java.beans
SimpleDateFormat: java.text
SimpleTimeZone: java.util
SIMPLIFIED_CHINESE: **L**ocale
SIMPLIFIED_HANZI: **I**nputSubset
sin( ): **M**ath
SINGLE_INTERVAL_SELECTION: *ListSelectionModel*
SINGLE_LINE: **A**ccessibleState
SINGLE_SELECTION: *ListSelectionModel*
SINGLE_TREE_SELECTION: *TreeSelectionModel*
SINGLEFRAME: *ImageConsumer*
SINGLEFRAMEDONE: *ImageConsumer*

SINGLEPASS: *ImageConsumer*
SinglePixelPackedSampleModel: java.awt.image
SingleSelectionModel: javax.swing
—passed to: **J**MenuBar.setSelectionModel( )
JTabbedPane.setModel( )
—returned by: **J**MenuBar.getSelectionModel( )
JTabbedPane.getModel( )
—implemented by: **D**efaultSingleSelectionModel
—fields: **J**TabbedPane.model
singleton( ): **C**ollections
Size: **S**tyleConstants.CharacterConstants
StyleConstants.FontConstants
size: **D**ataBuffer* **F**ont*
SIZE: **H**TML.Attribute **T**extAttribute
size( ): **A**bstractCollection* **A**bstractMap* **A**ttributes
BeanContextMembershipEvent **B**eanContextSupport*
BitSet **B**yteArrayOutputStream **C**harArrayWriter **C**ollection*
Component* **D**ataOutputStream **D**efaultListModel
Dictionary* **I**dentityScope **K**eyStore *Map** **R**enderingHints
ZipFile*
sizeColumnsToFit( ): **J**Table
SizeRequirements: javax.swing
—passed to: **B**oxView* < baselineRequirements( ),
calculateMajorAxisRequirements( ),
calculateMinorAxisRequirements( ) > javax.swing.text↩
.**P**aragraphView*.calculateMinorAxisRequirements( )
SizeRequirements < calculateAlignedPositions( ),
calculateTiledPositions( ), getAlignedSizeRequirements( ),
getTiledSizeRequirements( ) > **T**ableView.layoutColumns( )
—returned by: **B**oxView* < baselineRequirements( ),
calculateMajorAxisRequirements( ),
calculateMinorAxisRequirements( ) > javax.swing.text↩
.**P**aragraphView*.calculateMinorAxisRequirements( )
SizeRequirements.getTiledSizeRequirements( )
sizeWidthToFit( ): **T**ableColumn
Skeleton: java.rmi.server
SkeletonMismatchException: java.rmi.server
SkeletonNotFoundException: java.rmi.server
skip( ): java.io.**I**nputStream* *ObjectInput* **R**eader*
skipBytes( ): *DataInput** **D**ataInputStream **O**bjectInputStream
RandomAccessFile
slashSlashComments( ): **S**treamTokenizer
slashStarComments( ): **S**treamTokenizer
sleep( ): **T**hread
SLIDER: **A**ccessibleRole
sliderModel: **J**Slider
SliderUI: javax.swing.plaf
—passed to: **J**Slider.setUI( )
—returned by: **J**Slider.getUI( )
SMALL: **H**TML.Tag*
SMALL_FORM_VARIANTS: **C**haracter.UnicodeBlock
SMALL_ICON: **A**ction
SMALLINT: **T**ypes
snapToTicks: **J**Slider
SO_BINDADDR: *SocketOptions*
SO_LINGER: *SocketOptions*
SO_RCVBUF: *SocketOptions*
SO_REUSEADDR: *SocketOptions*
SO_SNDBUF: *SocketOptions*
SO_TIMEOUT: *SocketOptions*
Socket: java.net
—passed to: **S**erverSocket.implAccept( )
—returned by: *RMIClientSocketFactory*.createSocket( )
ServerSocket.accept( )
SocketException*: java.net
—subclasses: **B**indException java.net.**C**onnectException
NoRouteToHostException
—thrown by: **D**atagramSocket* < DatagramSocket( ),
getReceiveBufferSize( ), getSendBufferSize( ), getSoTimeout( ),
setReceiveBufferSize( ), setSendBufferSize( ), setSoTimeout( ) >
DatagramSocketImpl < create( ), getOption( ), setOption( ) >
MulticastSocket.setInterface( ) **S**ocket < getReceiveBufferSize( ),

getSendBufferSize( ), getSoLinger( ), getSoTimeout( ),
getTcpNoDelay( ), setReceiveBufferSize( ), setSendBufferSize( ),
setSoLinger( ), setSoTimeout( ), setTcpNoDelay( ), Socket( ) >
SocketImpl.setOption( ) *SocketOptions*.setOption( )

SocketImpl: java.net
— passed to: **S**ocket( )
— returned by: *SocketImplFactory*.createSocketImpl( )
SocketImplFactory: java.net
— passed to: **S**erverSocket.setSocketFactory( )
SocketOptions: java.net
— implemented by: **D**atagramSocketImpl **S**ocketImpl
SocketPermission: java.net
SocketSecurityException: java.rmi.server
SoftBevelBorder: javax.swing.border
SoftReference: java.lang.ref
solveCubic( ): **C**ubicCurve2D*
solveQuadratic( ): **Q**uadCurve2D*
SOMEBITS: *ImageObserver*
sort( ): **A**rrays **C**ollections
SortedMap: java.util
— passed to: **C**ollections < synchronizedSortedMap( ),
unmodifiableSortedMap( ) >
— returned by: **C**ollections < synchronizedSortedMap( ),
unmodifiableSortedMap( ) > *SortedMap* < subMap( ), tailMap( ) >
TreeMap < subMap( ), tailMap( ) >
— implemented by: **T**reeMap
SortedSet: java.util
— passed to: **C**ollections < synchronizedSortedSet( ),
unmodifiableSortedSet( ) >
— returned by: **C**ollections < synchronizedSortedSet( ),
unmodifiableSortedSet( ) > *SortedSet* < subSet( ), tailSet( ) >
TreeSet < subSet( ), tailSet( ) >
— implemented by: **T**reeSet
source: **E**ventObject*
sourceActions: **D**ragGestureRecognizer*
sources: **P**arameterBlock
SOUTH: **B**orderLayout **G**ridBagConstraints *SwingConstants*
SOUTH_EAST: *SwingConstants*
SOUTH_WEST: *SwingConstants*
SOUTHEAST: **G**ridBagConstraints
SOUTHWEST: **G**ridBagConstraints
SPACE_SEPARATOR: **C**haracter
SpaceAbove: **S**tyleConstants*
SpaceBelow: **S**tyleConstants*
SPACING_MODIFIER_LETTERS: **C**haracter.UnicodeBlock
SPECIALS: **C**haracter.UnicodeBlock
SPECIFICATION_TITLE: **A**ttributes.Name
SPECIFICATION_VENDOR: **A**ttributes.Name
SPECIFICATION_VERSION: **A**ttributes.Name
SPLIT_PANE: **A**ccessibleRole
SplitPaneUI: javax.swing.plaf
— passed to: **J**SplitPane.setUI( )
— returned by: **J**SplitPane.getUI( )
SQLData: java.sql
— passed to: *SQLOutput*.writeObject( )
SQLException*: java.sql
— subclasses: **B**atchUpdateException **S**QLWarning*
— descendents: **D**ataTruncation
— passed to: **S**QLException*.setNextException( )
— returned by: **S**QLException*.getNextException( )
— thrown by: *Blob* < getBinaryStream( ), getBytes( ), length( ),
position( ) > *CallableStatement* < getBigDecimal( ), getBlob( ),
getBoolean( ), getByte( ), getBytes( ), getClob( ),
getDate( ), getDouble( ), getFloat( ), getInt( ), getLong( ),
getObject( ), getRef( ), getShort( ), getString( ), getTime( ),
getTimestamp( ), registerOutParameter( ), wasNull( ) > *Clob*
< getCharacterStream( ), getSubString( ), length( ), position( ) >
Connection < close( ), commit( ), createStatement( ),
getAutoCommit( ), getCatalog( ), getMetaData( ),
getTransactionIsolation( ), getTypeMap( ), getWarnings( ),
isClosed( ), isReadOnly( ), nativeSQL( ), prepareCall( ),
prepareStatement( ), rollback( ), setAutoCommit( ),

setCatalog( ), setReadOnly( ), setTransactionIsolation( ),
setTypeMap( ) > *DatabaseMetaData* < allTablesAreSelectable( ),
dataDefinitionCausesTransactionCommit( ),
dataDefinitionIgnoredInTransactions( ), deletesAreDetected( ),
doesMaxRowSizeIncludeBlobs( ), getBestRowIdentifier( ),
getCatalogs( ), getCatalogSeparator( ), getCatalogTerm( ),
getColumnPrivileges( ), getColumns( ), getConnection( ),
getCrossReference( ), getDatabaseProductName( ),
getDatabaseProductVersion( ), getDefaultTransactionIsolation( ),
getDriverName( ), getDriverVersion( ), getExportedKeys( ),
getExtraNameCharacters( ), getIdentifierQuoteString( ),
getImportedKeys( ), getIndexInfo( ), getMaxBinaryLiteralLength( ),
getMaxCatalogNameLength( ), getMaxCharLiteralLength( ),
getMaxColumnNameLength( ), getMaxColumnsInGroupBy( ),
getMaxColumnsInIndex( ), getMaxColumnsInOrderBy( ),
getMaxColumnsInSelect( ), getMaxColumnsInTable( ),
getMaxConnections( ), getMaxCursorNameLength( ),
getMaxIndexLength( ), getMaxProcedureNameLength( ),
getMaxRowSize( ), getMaxSchemaNameLength( ),
getMaxStatementLength( ), getMaxStatements( ),
getMaxTableNameLength( ), getMaxTablesInSelect( ),
getMaxUserNameLength( ), getNumericFunctions( ),
getPrimaryKeys( ), getProcedureColumns( ), getProcedures( ),
getProcedureTerm( ), getSchemas( ), getSchemaTerm( ),
getSearchStringEscape( ), getSQLKeywords( ),
getStringFunctions( ), getSystemFunctions( ), getTablePrivileges( ),
getTables( ), getTableTypes( ), getTimeDateFunctions( ),
getTypeInfo( ), getUDTs( ), getURL( ), getUserName( ),
getVersionColumns( ), insertsAreDetected( ),
isCatalogAtStart( ), isReadOnly( ), nullPlusNonNullIsNull( ),
nullsAreSortedAtEnd( ), nullsAreSortedAtStart( ),
nullsAreSortedHigh( ), nullsAreSortedLow( ),
othersDeletesAreVisible( ), othersInsertsAreVisible( ),
othersUpdatesAreVisible( ), ownDeletesAreVisible( ),
ownInsertsAreVisible( ), ownUpdatesAreVisible( ),
storesLowerCaseIdentifiers( ), storesLowerCaseQuotedIdentifiers( ),
storesMixedCaseIdentifiers( ), storesMixedCaseQuotedIdentifiers( ),
storesUpperCaseIdentifiers( ), storesUpperCaseQuotedIdentifiers( ),
supportsAlterTableWithAddColumn( ),
supportsAlterTableWithDropColumn( ),
supportsANSI92EntryLevelSQL( ), supportsANSI92FullSQL( ),
supportsANSI92IntermediateSQL( ), supportsBatchUpdates( ),
supportsCatalogsInDataManipulation( ),
supportsCatalogsInIndexDefinitions( ),
supportsCatalogsInPrivilegeDefinitions( ),
supportsCatalogsInProcedureCalls( ),
supportsCatalogsInTableDefinitions( ),
supportsColumnAliasing( ), supportsConvert( ),
supportsCoreSQLGrammar( ), supportsCorrelatedSubqueries( ),
supportsDataDefinitionAndDataManipulationTransactions( ),
supportsDataManipulationTransactionsOnly( ),
supportsDifferentTableCorrelationNames( ),
supportsExpressionsInOrderBy( ), supportsExtendedSQLGrammar( ),
supportsFullOuterJoins( ), supportsGroupBy( ),
supportsGroupByBeyondSelect( ), supportsGroupByUnrelated( ),
supportsIntegrityEnhancementFacility( ),
supportsLikeEscapeClause( ), supportsLimitedOuterJoins( ),
supportsMinimumSQLGrammar( ), supportsMixedCaseIdentifiers( ),
supportsMixedCaseQuotedIdentifiers( ),
supportsMultipleResultSets( ), supportsMultipleTransactions( ),
supportsNonNullableColumns( ),
supportsOpenCursorsAcrossCommit( ),
supportsOpenCursorsAcrossRollback( ),
supportsOpenStatementsAcrossCommit( ),
supportsOpenStatementsAcrossRollback( ),
supportsOrderByUnrelated( ), supportsOuterJoins( ),
supportsPositionedDelete( ), supportsPositionedUpdate( ),
supportsResultSetConcurrency( ), supportsResultSetType( ),
supportsSchemasInDataManipulation( ),
supportsSchemasInIndexDefinitions( ),
supportsSchemasInPrivilegeDefinitions( ),

S

S

storesUpperCaseQuotedIdentifiers( ): *DatabaseMetaData*
STREAM_MAGIC: *ObjectStreamConstants*
STREAM_VERSION: *ObjectStreamConstants*
Streamable: org.omg.CORBA.portable
—passed to: **A**ny.insert_Streamable( )
—implemented by: **A**lreadyBoundHolder **A**nyHolder
  BindingHolder **B**indingIteratorHolder **B**indingListHolder
  BindingTypeHolder **B**ooleanHolder **B**yteHolder
  CannotProceedHolder **C**harHolder **D**oubleHolder
  FixedHolder **F**loatHolder **I**ntHolder **I**nvalidNameHolder
  LongHolder **N**ameComponentHolder **N**ameHolder
  NamingContextHolder **N**otEmptyHolder **N**otFoundHolder
  NotFoundReasonHolder **O**bjectHolder **P**rincipalHolder
  ServiceInformationHolder **S**hortHolder **S**tringHolder
  TypeCodeHolder
StreamCorruptedException: java.io
—thrown by: **O**bjectInputStream < ObjectInputStream( ),
  readStreamHeader( ) >
StreamDescriptionProperty: *Document**
StreamTokenizer: java.io
strict: **P**arser*
STRICT: **M**odifier
STRIKE: **H**TML.Tag*
STRIKETHROUGH: **T**extAttribute
StrikeThrough: **S**tyleConstants*
STRIKETHROUGH_ON: **T**extAttribute
String: java.lang
string_to_object( ): **O**RB
StringBuffer: java.lang
—passed to: **D**ateFormat*.format( ) **M**essageFormat.format( )
  NumberFormat*.format( ) **S**tring( )
—returned by: **D**ateFormat*.format( ) **M**essageFormat.format( )
  NumberFormat*.format( ) **S**tringBuffer < append( ), delete( ),
  deleteCharAt( ), insert( ), replace( ), reverse( ) >
StringBufferInputStream: java.io
StringCharacterIterator: java.text
StringContent: javax.swing.text
stringFlavor: **D**ataFlavor
StringHolder: org.omg.CORBA
StringIndexOutOfBoundsException: java.lang
StringReader: java.io
StringSelection: java.awt.datatransfer
stringToColor( ): **S**tyleSheet
StringTokenizer: java.util
stringWidth( ): **F**ontMetrics
StringWriter: java.io
STROKE: **S**hapeGraphicAttribute
Stroke: java.awt
—passed to: **G**raphics2D.setStroke( )
—returned by: **G**raphics2D.getStroke( )
—implemented by: **B**asicStroke
STRONG: **H**TML.Tag*
STRUCT: **T**ypes
Struct: java.sql
—passed to: **S**QLOutput.writeStruct( )
StructMember: org.omg.CORBA
—passed to: **O**RB < create_exception_tc( ), create_struct_tc( ) >
StubNotFoundException: java.rmi
STYLE: **H**TML.Attribute **H**TML.Tag*
style: **F**ont*
Style: javax.swing.text
—passed to: **D**efaultStyledDocument* < addStyle( ),
  setLogicalStyle( ), styleChanged( ) > **J**TextPane.setLogicalStyle( )
  StyleContext.NamedStyle( ) *StyledDocument*.setLogicalStyle( )
—returned by: **D**efaultStyledDocument* < addStyle( ),
  getLogicalStyle( ), getStyle( ) > **J**TextPane < getLogicalStyle( ),
  getStyle( ) > **S**tyleContext*.getStyle( ) *StyledDocument*
  < getLogicalStyle( ), getStyle( ) > **S**tyleSheet.getRule( ) >
—implemented by: **S**tyleContext.NamedStyle
styleChanged( ): **D**efaultStyledDocument*
StyleConstants*: javax.swing.text

—subclasses: **S**tyleConstants.CharacterConstants
  StyleConstants.ColorConstants
  StyleConstants.FontConstants
  StyleConstants.ParagraphConstants
StyleConstants.CharacterConstants: javax.swing.text
StyleConstants.ColorConstants: javax.swing.text
StyleConstants.FontConstants: javax.swing.text
StyleConstants.ParagraphConstants: javax.swing.text
StyleContext*: javax.swing.text
—subclasses: **S**tyleSheet
—passed to: **D**efaultStyledDocument( )
  StyleContext.NamedStyle( ) **S**tyleContext.SmallAttributeSet( )
—returned by: **S**tyleContext*.getDefaultStyleContext( )
StyleContext.NamedStyle: javax.swing.text
StyleContext.SmallAttributeSet: javax.swing.text
—returned by: **S**tyleContext*.createSmallAttributeSet( )
StyledDocument: javax.swing.text
—passed to: **J**TextPane < JTextPane( ), setStyledDocument( ) >
  MinimalHTMLWriter( )
—returned by: **J**TextPane.getStyledDocument( )
—implemented by: **D**efaultStyledDocument*
StyledEditorKit*: javax.swing.text
—subclasses: **H**TMLEditorKit **R**TFEditorKit
—returned by: **J**TextPane.getStyledEditorKit( )
StyledEditorKit.AlignmentAction: javax.swing.text
StyledEditorKit.BoldAction: javax.swing.text
StyledEditorKit.FontFamilyAction: javax.swing.text
StyledEditorKit.FontSizeAction: javax.swing.text
StyledEditorKit.ForegroundAction: javax.swing.text
StyledEditorKit.ItalicAction: javax.swing.text
StyledEditorKit.StyledTextAction*: javax.swing.text
—subclasses: **H**TMLEditorKit.HTMLTextAction*
  StyledEditorKit.AlignmentAction **S**tyledEditorKit.BoldAction
  StyledEditorKit.FontFamilyAction
  StyledEditorKit.FontSizeAction
  StyledEditorKit.ForegroundAction **S**tyledEditorKit.ItalicAction
  StyledEditorKit.UnderlineAction
—descendents: **H**TMLEditorKit.InsertHTMLTextAction
StyledEditorKit.UnderlineAction: javax.swing.text
StyleSheet: javax.swing.text.html
—passed to: **H**TMLDocument( )
—returned by: **B**lockView*.getStyleSheet( )
  HTMLEditorKit.getStyleSheet( )
  javax.swing.text.html.**P**aragraphView.getStyleSheet( )
StyleSheet.BoxPainter: javax.swing.text.html
—returned by: **S**tyleSheet.getBoxPainter( )
StyleSheet.ListPainter: javax.swing.text.html
—returned by: **S**tyleSheet.getListPainter( )
SUB: **H**TML.Tag*
SUBCLASS_IMPLEMENTATION_PERMISSION:
  ObjectStreamConstants
subdivide( ): **C**ubicCurve2D* **Q**uadCurve2D*
subList( ): **A**bstractList* *java.util.List*
subMap( ): *SortedMap* **T**reeMap
SUBMIT: **F**ormView
submitData( ): **F**ormView
Subscript: **S**tyleConstants*
subSet( ): *SortedSet* **T**reeSet
substituteColorModel( ): **R**GBImageFilter*
SUBSTITUTION_PERMISSION: *ObjectStreamConstants*
substring( ): **S**tring **S**tringBuffer
subtract( ): **A**rea **B**igDecimal **B**igInteger
SUNDAY: **C**alendar*
SUP: **H**TML.Tag*
Superscript: **S**tyleConstants*
SUPERSCRIPT: **T**extAttribute
SUPERSCRIPT_SUB: **T**extAttribute
SUPERSCRIPT_SUPER: **T**extAttribute
SUPERSCRIPTS_AND_SUBSCRIPTS:
  Character.UnicodeBlock
supportsAlterTableWithAddColumn( ): *DatabaseMetaData*
supportsAlterTableWithDropColumn( ): *DatabaseMetaData*

S

supportsANSI92EntryLevelSQL(): *DatabaseMetaData*
supportsANSI92FullSQL(): *DatabaseMetaData*
supportsANSI92IntermediateSQL(): *DatabaseMetaData*
supportsBatchUpdates(): *DatabaseMetaData*
supportsCatalogsInDataManipulation(): *DatabaseMetaData*
supportsCatalogsInIndexDefinitions(): *DatabaseMetaData*
supportsCatalogsInPrivilegeDefinitions(): *DatabaseMetaData*
supportsCatalogsInProcedureCalls(): *DatabaseMetaData*
supportsCatalogsInTableDefinitions(): *DatabaseMetaData*
supportsColumnAliasing(): *DatabaseMetaData*
supportsConvert(): *DatabaseMetaData*
supportsCoreSQLGrammar(): *DatabaseMetaData*
supportsCorrelatedSubqueries(): *DatabaseMetaData*
supportsCustomEditor(): *PropertyEditor*
  PropertyEditorSupport
supportsDataDefinitionAndDataManipulationTransactions():
  DatabaseMetaData
supportsDataManipulationTransactionsOnly():
  DatabaseMetaData
supportsDifferentTableCorrelationNames():
  DatabaseMetaData
supportsExpressionsInOrderBy(): *DatabaseMetaData*
supportsExtendedSQLGrammar(): *DatabaseMetaData*
supportsFullOuterJoins(): *DatabaseMetaData*
supportsGroupBy(): *DatabaseMetaData*   .
supportsGroupByBeyondSelect(): *DatabaseMetaData*
supportsGroupByUnrelated(): *DatabaseMetaData*
supportsIntegrityEnhancementFacility(): *DatabaseMetaData*
supportsLikeEscapeClause(): *DatabaseMetaData*
supportsLimitedOuterJoins(): *DatabaseMetaData*
supportsMinimumSQLGrammar(): *DatabaseMetaData*
supportsMixedCaseIdentifiers(): *DatabaseMetaData*
supportsMixedCaseQuotedIdentifiers(): *DatabaseMetaData*
supportsMultipleResultSets(): *DatabaseMetaData*
supportsMultipleTransactions(): *DatabaseMetaData*
supportsNonNullableColumns(): *DatabaseMetaData*
supportsOpenCursorsAcrossCommit(): *DatabaseMetaData*
supportsOpenCursorsAcrossRollback(): *DatabaseMetaData*
supportsOpenStatementsAcrossCommit():
  DatabaseMetaData
supportsOpenStatementsAcrossRollback():
  DatabaseMetaData
supportsOrderByUnrelated(): *DatabaseMetaData*
supportsOuterJoins(): *DatabaseMetaData*
supportsPositionedDelete(): *DatabaseMetaData*
supportsPositionedUpdate(): *DatabaseMetaData*
supportsResultSetConcurrency(): *DatabaseMetaData*
supportsResultSetType(): *DatabaseMetaData*
supportsSchemasInDataManipulation(): *DatabaseMetaData*
supportsSchemasInIndexDefinitions(): *DatabaseMetaData*
supportsSchemasInPrivilegeDefinitions():
  DatabaseMetaData
supportsSchemasInProcedureCalls(): *DatabaseMetaData*
supportsSchemasInTableDefinitions(): *DatabaseMetaData*
supportsSelectForUpdate(): *DatabaseMetaData*
supportsStoredProcedures(): *DatabaseMetaData*
supportsSubqueriesInComparisons(): *DatabaseMetaData*
supportsSubqueriesInExists(): *DatabaseMetaData*
supportsSubqueriesInIns(): *DatabaseMetaData*
supportsSubqueriesInQuantifieds(): *DatabaseMetaData*
supportsTableCorrelationNames(): *DatabaseMetaData*
supportsTransactionIsolationLevel(): *DatabaseMetaData*
supportsTransactions(): *DatabaseMetaData*
supportsUnion(): *DatabaseMetaData*
supportsUnionAll(): *DatabaseMetaData*
SURROGATE: **C**haracter
SURROGATES_AREA: **C**haracter.UnicodeBlock
suspend(): **T**hread **T**hreadGroup
sval: **S**treamTokenizer
SW_RESIZE_CURSOR: **C**ursor **F**rame*
SWAP_COLORS: **T**extAttribute
SWAP_COLORS_ON: **T**extAttribute

SWING_COMPONENT: **A**ccessibleRole
SwingConstants: javax.swing
—implemented by: **A**bstractButton* **J**Label* **J**ProgressBar
  JSeparator* **J**Slider **J**TabbedPane **J**TextField* **J**ToolBar
  SwingUtilities **V**iew*
SwingPropertyChangeSupport: javax.swing.event
—fields: **A**bstractAction*.changeSupport
SwingUtilities: javax.swing
sync(): **F**ileDescriptor **T**oolkit
SyncFailedException: java.io
—thrown by: **F**ileDescriptor.sync()
SYNCHRONIZED: **M**odifier
synchronizedCollection(): **C**ollections
synchronizedList(): **C**ollections
synchronizedMap(): **C**ollections
synchronizedSet(): **C**ollections
synchronizedSortedMap(): **C**ollections
synchronizedSortedSet(): **C**ollections
syncWithScrollPane(): **S**crollPaneLayout*
synthesizedElement(): **H**TMLWriter
SYSTEM: *DTDConstants*
System: java.lang
SYSTEM_PORT: *ActivationSystem*
SystemColor: java.awt
—fields: **S**ystemColor < activeCaption, activeCaptionBorder,
  activeCaptionText, control, controlDkShadow, controlHighlight,
  controlLtHighlight, controlShadow, controlText, desktop,
  inactiveCaption, inactiveCaptionBorder, inactiveCaptionText, info,
  infoText, menu, menuText, scrollbar, text, textHighlight,
  textHighlightText, textInactiveText, textText, window,
  windowBorder, windowText >
SystemException*: org.omg.CORBA
—subclasses: **B**AD_CONTEXT **B**AD_INV_ORDER
  BAD_OPERATION **B**AD_PARAM **B**AD_TYPECODE
  COMM_FAILURE **D**ATA_CONVERSION **F**REE_MEM
  IMP_LIMIT **I**NITIALIZE **I**NTERNAL **I**NTF_REPOS
  INV_FLAG **I**NV_IDENT **I**NV_OBJREF **I**NV_POLICY
  INVALID_TRANSACTION **M**ARSHAL **N**O_IMPLEMENT
  NO_MEMORY **N**O_PERMISSION **N**O_RESOURCES
  NO_RESPONSE **O**BJ_ADAPTER **O**BJECT_NOT_EXIST
  PERSIST_STORE **T**RANSACTION_REQUIRED
  TRANSACTION_ROLLEDBACK **T**RANSIENT **U**NKNOWN
—thrown by: *InvokeHandler*._invoke()
SystemFlavorMap: java.awt.datatransfer
TAB: **E**vent
TabableView: javax.swing.text
TabbedPaneUI: javax.swing.plaf
—passed to: **J**TabbedPane.setUI()
—returned by: **J**TabbedPane.getUI()
TabExpander: javax.swing.text
—passed to: *TabableView*.getTabbedSpan() **U**tilities
  < getBreakLocation(), getTabbedTextOffset(),
  getTabbedTextWidth() >
—implemented by: javax.swing.text.**P**aragraphView* **P**lainView*
  WrappedPlainView
tabForCoordinate(): **T**abbedPaneUI
table: **J**TableHeader
TABLE: **A**ccessibleRole **H**TML.Tag*
TableCellEditor: javax.swing.table
—passed to: **J**Table < prepareEditor(), setCellEditor(),
  setDefaultEditor() > **T**ableColumn()
—returned by: **J**Table < getCellEditor(), getDefaultEditor() >
—implemented by: **D**efaultCellEditor
—fields: **J**Table.cellEditor
TableCellRenderer: javax.swing.table
—passed to: **J**Table < prepareRenderer(), setDefaultRenderer() >
  TableColumn < setHeaderRenderer(), TableColumn() >
—returned by: **J**Table < getCellRenderer(), getDefaultRenderer() >
  TableColumn < getCellRenderer(), getHeaderRenderer() >
—implemented by: **D**efaultTableCellRenderer*
—fields: **T**ableColumn < cellRenderer, headerRenderer >

S

tableChanged(): JTable   JTable.AccessibleJTable
  TableModelListener
TableColumn: javax.swing.table
  —passed to: **D**efaultTableColumnModel < addColumn( ),
  removeColumn( ) >   **J**Table.removeColumn( )
  JTableHeader.setResizingColumn( )
  TableColumnModel.removeColumn( )
  —returned by: **D**efaultTableColumnModel.getColumn( )
  JTableHeader < getDraggedColumn( ), getResizingColumn( ) >
  —fields: **J**TableHeader < draggedColumn, resizingColumn >
TableColumnModel: javax.swing.table
  —passed to: **J**Table < JTable( ), setColumnModel( ) >
  JTableHeader.setColumnModel( )
  —returned by: **J**Table < createDefaultColumnModel( ),
  getColumnModel( ) >   **J**TableHeader.getColumnModel( )
  —implemented by: **D**efaultTableColumnModel
  —fields: **J**Table.columnModel
TableColumnModelEvent: javax.swing.event
  —passed to: **D**efaultTableColumnModel < fireColumnAdded( ),
  fireColumnMoved( ), fireColumnRemoved( ) >
  JTable < columnMoved( ), columnRemoved( ) >
  JTable.AccessibleJTable < columnMoved( ),
  columnRemoved( ) >   **J**TableHeader < columnMoved( ),
  columnRemoved( ) >   *TableColumnModelListener*
  < columnMoved( ), columnRemoved( ) >
TableColumnModelListener: javax.swing.event
  —passed to: **D**efaultTableColumnModel
  < addColumnModelListener( ), removeColumnModelListener( ) >
  TableColumnModel.removeColumnModelListener( )
  —implemented by: **J**Table   JTable.AccessibleJTable
  JTableHeader
tableColumns: **D**efaultTableColumnModel
tableHeader: **J**Table
TableHeaderUI: javax.swing.plaf
  —passed to: **J**TableHeader.setUI( )
  —returned by: **J**TableHeader.getUI( )
tableIndexClustered: *DatabaseMetaData*
tableIndexHashed: *DatabaseMetaData*
tableIndexOther: *DatabaseMetaData*
tableIndexStatistic: *DatabaseMetaData*
TableModel: javax.swing.table
  —passed to: **J**Table < JTable( ), setModel( ) >   **T**ableModelEvent( )
  —returned by: **J**Table < createDefaultDataModel( ), getModel( ) >
  —implemented by: **A**bstractTableModel*
  —fields: **J**Table.dataModel
TableModelEvent: javax.swing.event
  —passed to: **A**bstractTableModel*.fireTableChanged( )
  DefaultTableModel < newRowsAdded( ), rowsRemoved( ) >
  JTable.AccessibleJTable < tableChanged( ), tableRowsDeleted( ),
  tableRowsInserted( ) >
TableModelListener: javax.swing.event
  —passed to: **A**bstractTableModel*
  < addTableModelListener( ), removeTableModelListener( ) >
  TableModel.removeTableModelListener( )
  —implemented by: **J**Table   JTable.AccessibleJTable
tableRowsDeleted(): JTable.AccessibleJTable
tableRowsInserted(): JTable.AccessibleJTable
TableUI: javax.swing.plaf
  —passed to: **J**Table.setUI( )
  —returned by: **J**Table.getUI( )
TableView: javax.swing.text
  —passed to: **T**ableView.TableCell( )
  —implemented by: **T**ableView.TableCell
TableView.TableCell: javax.swing.text
  —returned by: **T**ableView.createTableCell( )
TableView.TableRow: javax.swing.text
  —returned by: **T**ableView.createTableRow( )
tabPlacement: **J**TabbedPane
TabSet: **S**tyleConstants*
TabSet: javax.swing.text
  —passed to: **S**tyleConstants*.setTabSet( )
  —returned by: javax.swing.text.**P**aragraphView*.getTabSet( )

tabSizeAttribute: **P**lainDocument
TabStop: javax.swing.text
  —passed to: **T**abSet < getTabIndex( ), TabSet( ) >
  —returned by: **T**abSet < getTab( ), getTabAfter( ) >
TAG_ACNT: *OpenType*
TAG_AVAR: *OpenType*
TAG_BASE: *OpenType*
TAG_BDAT: *OpenType*
TAG_BLOC: *OpenType*
TAG_BSLN: *OpenType*
TAG_CFF: *OpenType*
TAG_CMAP: *OpenType*
TAG_CVAR: *OpenType*
TAG_CVT: *OpenType*
TAG_DSIG: *OpenType*
TAG_EBDT: *OpenType*
TAG_EBLC: *OpenType*
TAG_EBSC: *OpenType*
TAG_FDSC: *OpenType*
TAG_FEAT: *OpenType*
TAG_FMTX: *OpenType*
TAG_FPGM: *OpenType*
TAG_FVAR: *OpenType*
TAG_GASP: *OpenType*
TAG_GDEF: *OpenType*
TAG_GLYF: *OpenType*
TAG_GPOS: *OpenType*
TAG_GSUB: *OpenType*
TAG_GVAR: *OpenType*
TAG_HDMX: *OpenType*
TAG_HEAD: *OpenType*
TAG_HHEA: *OpenType*
TAG_HMTX: *OpenType*
TAG_JSTF: *OpenType*
TAG_JUST: *OpenType*
TAG_KERN: *OpenType*
TAG_LCAR: *OpenType*
TAG_LOCA: *OpenType*
TAG_LTSH: *OpenType*
TAG_MAXP: *OpenType*
TAG_MMFX: *OpenType*
TAG_MMSD: *OpenType*
TAG_MORT: *OpenType*
TAG_NAME: *OpenType*
TAG_OPBD: *OpenType*
TAG_OS2: *OpenType*
TAG_PCLT: *OpenType*
TAG_POST: *OpenType*
TAG_PREP: *OpenType*
TAG_PROP: *OpenType*
TAG_TRAK: *OpenType*
TAG_TYP1: *OpenType*
TAG_VDMX: *OpenType*
TAG_VHEA: *OpenType*
TAG_VMTX: *OpenType*
TagElement: javax.swing.text.html.parser
  —passed to: **D**ocumentParser < handleEmptyTag( ),
  handleEndTag( ), handleStartTag( ) >   **P**arser* < handleEndTag( ),
  handleStartTag( ), startTag( ) >
  —returned by: **P**arser*.makeTag( )
tailMap(): *SortedMap*   **T**reeMap
tailSet(): *SortedSet*   **T**reeSet
TAIWAN: **L**ocale
TAMIL: **C**haracter.UnicodeBlock
tan(): **M**ath
TARGET: **H**TML.Attribute
target: **E**vent
target(): **R**equest
TC_ARRAY: *ObjectStreamConstants*
TC_BASE: *ObjectStreamConstants*
TC_BLOCKDATA: *ObjectStreamConstants*
TC_BLOCKDATALONG: *ObjectStreamConstants*

T

THURSDAY: Calendar*
TIBETAN: Character.UnicodeBlock
tileIcon: MatteBorder*
TileObserver: java.awt.image
—passed to: BufferedImage
< addTileObserver(),   removeTileObserver() >
WritableRenderedImage.removeTileObserver()
tileUpdate(): *TileObserver*
TIME: Types
time: Calendar*
Time: java.sql
—passed to: *PreparedStatement**.setTime()
ResultSet.updateTime()
—returned by: *CallableStatement*.getTime() *ResultSet*.getTime()
Time.valueOf()
timer: DefaultTreeCellEditor
Timer: javax.swing
—fields: DefaultTreeCellEditor.timer
TIMESTAMP: Types
Timestamp: java.sql
—passed to: *PreparedStatement**.setTimestamp()
ResultSet.updateTimestamp() Timestamp < after(), before(),
equals() >
—returned by: *CallableStatement*.getTimestamp()
ResultSet.getTimestamp() Timestamp.valueOf()
TimeZone*: java.util
—subclasses: SimpleTimeZone
—passed to: Calendar* < Calendar(), getInstance(),
setTimeZone() > GregorianCalendar() TimeZone*.setDefault()
—returned by: Calendar*.getTimeZone() TimeZone*
< getDefault(), getTimeZone() >
TIMEZONE_FIELD: DateFormat*
TINYINT: Types
title: DTD JInternalFrame TitledBorder*
TITLE: HTML.Attribute HTML.Tag*
TITLE_PROPERTY: JInternalFrame
TITLECASE_LETTER: Character
titleColor: TitledBorder*
TitledBorder*: javax.swing.border
—subclasses: BorderUIResource.TitledBorderUIResource
—returned by: BorderFactory.createTitledBorder()
titleFont: TitledBorder*
titleJustification: TitledBorder*
titlePosition: TitledBorder*
TitleProperty: *Document**
tk_abstract_interface: TCKind
tk_alias: TCKind
tk_any: TCKind

T

Cross-Ref

tk_array: TCKind
tk_boolean: TCKind
tk_char: TCKind
tk_double: TCKind
tk_enum: TCKind
tk_except: TCKind
tk_fixed: TCKind
tk_float: TCKind
tk_long: TCKind
tk_longdouble: TCKind
tk_longlong: TCKind
tk_native: TCKind
tk_null: TCKind
tk_objref: TCKind
tk_octet: TCKind
tk_Principal: TCKind
tk_sequence: TCKind
tk_short: TCKind
tk_string: TCKind
tk_struct: TCKind
tk_TypeCode: TCKind
tk_ulong: TCKind
tk_ulonglong: TCKind
tk_union: TCKind
tk_ushort: TCKind
tk_value: TCKind
tk_value_box: TCKind
tk_void: TCKind
tk_wchar: TCKind
tk_wstring: TCKind
to_any(): *DynAny**
toArray(): **A**bstractCollection* **A**ccessibleStateSet
    BeanContextMembershipEvent **B**eanContextSupport*
    Collection* **D**efaultListModel **D**ragGestureEvent
toBack(): **J**InternalFrame **W**indow* *WindowPeer**
toBigInteger(): BigDecimal
toBinaryString(): **I**nteger **L**ong
toByteArray(): **B**igInteger **B**yteArrayOutputStream
    CollationKey
toCharArray(): **C**harArrayWriter **S**tring
toCIEXYZ(): **C**olorSpace*
toDegrees(): Math
toDisplayString(): **A**ccessibleBundle*
toExternalForm(): URL URLStreamHandler
toFront(): **J**InternalFrame **W**indow* *WindowPeer**
TOGGLE_BUTTON: AccessibleRole
toggleClickCount: JTree
toGMTString(): java.util.**D**ate*
toHexString(): **I**nteger **L**ong
toIndex: TableColumnModelEvent
toLocaleString(): java.util.**D**ate*
toLocalizedPattern(): **D**ecimalFormat **S**impleDateFormat
toLowerCase(): **C**haracter **S**tring
toOctalString(): **I**nteger **L**ong
TOOL_BAR: AccessibleRole
TOOL_TIP: AccessibleRole
TOOL_TIP_TEXT_KEY: JComponent*
ToolBarUI: javax.swing.plaf
  —passed to: JToolBar.setUI( )
  —returned by: **J**ToolBar.getUI( )
Toolkit: java.awt
  —returned by: **C**omponent*.getToolkit( ) **T**oolkit.getDefaultToolkit( )
ToolTipManager: javax.swing
  —passed to: ToolTipManager.insideTimerAction( )
    ToolTipManager.stillInsideTimerAction( )
  —returned by: ToolTipManager.sharedInstance( )
ToolTipManager.insideTimerAction: javax.swing
ToolTipManager.outsideTimerAction: javax.swing
ToolTipManager.stillInsideTimerAction: javax.swing
ToolTipUI: javax.swing.plaf
  —returned by: **J**ToolTip.getUI( )
TooManyListenersException: java.util

—thrown by: *B*eanContextServices.getService( )
    DragGestureRecognizer*.addDragGestureListener( )
    DropTarget.addDropTargetListener( )
top: EmptyBorder* **I**nsets*
TOP: JSplitPane *SwingConstants* **T**itledBorder*
TOP_ALIGNMENT: **C**omponent* **G**raphicAttribute*
toPattern(): **C**hoiceFormat **D**ecimalFormat **M**essageFormat
    SimpleDateFormat
TOPDOWNLEFTRIGHT: *ImageConsumer*
toRadians(): Math
toRGB(): ColorSpace*
toString(): *Acl* **A**clEntry BigInteger Byte
    ByteArrayOutputStream *java.security.**C**ertificate* **D**elegate
    Double **F**loat **I**dentity* **I**nteger **L**ong **M**odifier
    java.lang.**O**bject *java.security.acl.**P**ermission*
    *java.security.**P**rincipal** **S**hort
toStub(): RemoteObject*
totalColumnWidth: DefaultTableColumnModel
totalMemory(): Runtime
toTitleCase(): Character
toUpperCase(): **C**haracter **S**tring
toURL(): File
toViewCoordinates(): JViewport
TR: HTML.Tag*
traceInstructions(): Runtime
traceMethodCalls(): Runtime
TRACK: AdjustmentEvent
tracker: ImageIcon
TRADITIONAL_CHINESE: Locale
TRADITIONAL_HANZI: InputSubset
TRAILING: FlowLayout *SwingConstants*
trailing(): TextHitInfo
TRANSACTION_NONE: *Connection*
TRANSACTION_READ_COMMITTED: *Connection*
TRANSACTION_READ_UNCOMMITTED: *Connection*
TRANSACTION_REPEATABLE_READ: *Connection*
TRANSACTION_REQUIRED: org.omg.CORBA
TRANSACTION_ROLLEDBACK: org.omg.CORBA
TRANSACTION_SERIALIZABLE: *Connection*
transferable: DropTargetContext.TransferableProxy
Transferable: java.awt.datatransfer
  —passed to: **C**lipboard.setContents( )
    DragGestureEvent.startDrag( ) **D**ragSource.startDrag( )
    DropTargetContext.createTransferableProxy( )
  —returned by: **C**lipboard.getContents( ) **D**ropTargetContext
    < createTransferableProxy( ), getTransferable( ) >
  —implemented by: **D**ropTargetContext.TransferableProxy
    StringSelection
  —fields: Clipboard.contents
transferablesFlavorsChanged(): DragSourceContext
transferFocus(): Component*
transferType: ColorModel*
TRANSFORM: TextAttribute
transform(): **A**ffineTransform **A**rea **G**eneralPath **G**raphics2D
TransformAttribute: java.awt.font
TRANSIENT: **A**ccessibleState **M**odifier
TRANSIENT: org.omg.CORBA
translate(): **A**ffineTransform **E**vent **G**raphics* **P**oint **P**olygon
    Rectangle*
translateHTMLToCSS(): StyleSheet
translateKey(): KeyFactory
translatePoint(): MouseEvent*
TRANSLUCENT: *Transparency**
Transparency*: java.awt
  —extended by: *Paint*
  —implemented by: ColorModel*
tree: DefaultTreeCellEditor
TREE: AccessibleRole
TREE_MODEL_PROPERTY: JTree
TreeCellEditor: javax.swing.tree
  —passed to: **D**efaultTreeCellEditor( )
  —returned by: **D**efaultTreeCellEditor.createTreeCellEditor( )

—implemented by: **D**efaultCellEditor   **D**efaultTreeCellEditor
—fields: **D**efaultTreeCellEditor.realEditor
TreeCellRenderer: javax.swing.tree
—passed to: **J**Tree.setCellRenderer( )
—returned by: **J**Tree.getCellRenderer( )
—implemented by: **D**efaultTreeCellRenderer
—fields: **J**Tree.cellRenderer
treeCollapsed( ): **J**Tree.AccessibleJTree
   TreeExpansionListener
treeDidChange( ): **J**Tree
treeExpanded( ): **J**Tree.AccessibleJTree
   TreeExpansionListener
TreeExpansionEvent: javax.swing.event
—passed to: **E**xpandVetoException( )
   JTree.AccessibleJTree.treeExpanded( )
   TreeExpansionListener.treeExpanded( )
   TreeWillExpandListener.treeWillExpand( )
—fields: **E**xpandVetoException.event
TreeExpansionListener: javax.swing.event
—passed to: **J**Tree < addTreeExpansionListener( ),
   removeTreeExpansionListener( ) >
—implemented by: **J**Tree.AccessibleJTree
TreeMap: java.util
treeModel: **A**bstractLayoutCache*   **J**Tree
TreeModel: javax.swing.tree
—passed to: **A**bstractLayoutCache*.setModel( )   **J**Tree.setModel( )
—returned by: **A**bstractLayoutCache*.getModel( )   **J**Tree
   < getDefaultTreeModel( ), getModel( ) >
—implemented by: **D**efaultTreeModel
—fields: **A**bstractLayoutCache*.treeModel
TreeModelEvent: javax.swing.event
—passed to: **A**bstractLayoutCache* < treeNodesChanged( ),
   treeNodesInserted( ),   treeNodesRemoved( ),
   treeStructureChanged( ) >   **J**Tree.AccessibleJTree
   < treeNodesInserted( ),   treeNodesRemoved( ),
   treeStructureChanged( ) >   **J**Tree.TreeModelHandler
   < treeNodesInserted( ),   treeNodesRemoved( ),
   treeStructureChanged( ) >   *TreeModelListener*
   < treeNodesInserted( ),   treeNodesRemoved( ),
   treeStructureChanged( ) >
treeModelListener: **J**Tree
TreeModelListener: javax.swing.event
—passed to: **D**efaultTreeModel
   < addTreeModelListener( ),   removeTreeModelListener( ) >
   TreeModel.removeTreeModelListener( )
—returned by: **J**Tree.createTreeModelListener( )
—implemented by: **J**Tree.AccessibleJTree
   JTree.TreeModelHandler
—fields: **J**Tree.treeModelListener
TreeNode*: javax.swing.tree
—extended by: *MutableTreeNode*
—passed to: **A**bstractDocument.AbstractElement*.getIndex( )
   DefaultMutableTreeNode* < getChildBefore( ),   getIndex( ),
   getPathToRoot( ),   isNodeAncestor( ),   isNodeChild( ),
   isNodeSibling( ),   pathFromAncestorEnumeration( ) >
   DefaultTreeModel < DefaultTreeModel( ),   getPathToRoot( ),
   nodeChanged( ),   nodesChanged( ),   nodeStructureChanged( ),
   nodesWereInserted( ),   nodesWereRemoved( ),   reload( ),
   setRoot( ) >   **J**Tree( )
—returned by: **A**bstractDocument.AbstractElement*
   < getChildAt( ),   getParent( ) >   **D**efaultMutableTreeNode*
   < getChildAt( ),   getChildBefore( ),   getFirstChild( ),   getLastChild( ),
   getParent( ),   getPath( ),   getPathToRoot( ),   getRoot( ),
   getSharedAncestor( ) >   **D**efaultTreeModel.getPathToRoot( )
   TreeNode.getParent( )
—implemented by: **A**bstractDocument.AbstractElement*
—fields: **D**efaultTreeModel.root
treeNodesChanged( ): **A**bstractLayoutCache*
   JTree.AccessibleJTree   **J**Tree.TreeModelHandler
   TreeModelListener

treeNodesInserted( ): **A**bstractLayoutCache*
   JTree.AccessibleJTree   **J**Tree.TreeModelHandler
   TreeModelListener
treeNodesRemoved( ): **A**bstractLayoutCache*
   JTree.AccessibleJTree   **J**Tree.TreeModelHandler
   TreeModelListener
TreePath: javax.swing.tree
—passed to: **A**bstractLayoutCache* < getBounds( ),
   getExpandedState( ),   getRowForPath( ),   getRowsForPaths( ),
   getVisibleChildCount( ),   getVisiblePathsFrom( ),
   invalidatePathBounds( ),   isExpanded( ),   setExpandedState( ) >
   DefaultTreeSelectionModel* < addSelectionPath( ),
   addSelectionPaths( ),   arePathsContiguous( ),   canPathsBeAdded( ),
   canPathsBeRemoved( ),   isPathSelected( ),   notifyPathChange( ),
   removeSelectionPath( ),   removeSelectionPaths( ),
   setSelectionPath( ),   setSelectionPaths( ) >   **J**Tree
   < addSelectionPaths( ),   collapsePath( ),   expandPath( ),
   fireTreeCollapsed( ),   fireTreeExpanded( ),   fireTreeWillCollapse( ),
   fireTreeWillExpand( ),   getDescendantToggledPaths( ),
   getExpandedDescendants( ),   getPathBounds( ),
   getRowForPath( ),   hasBeenExpanded( ),   isCollapsed( ),
   isExpanded( ),   isPathEditable( ),   isPathSelected( ),
   isVisible( ),   makeVisible( ),   removeSelectionPath( ),
   removeSelectionPaths( ),   scrollPathToVisible( ),
   setExpandedState( ),   setSelectionPath( ),   setSelectionPaths( ),
   startEditingAtPath( ) >   *RowMapper*.getRowsForPaths( )
   TreeModel.valueForPathChanged( )   **T**reeModelEvent( )
   TreePath( )   **T**reeSelectionEvent( )   *TreeSelectionModel*
   < addSelectionPaths( ),   isPathSelected( ),   removeSelectionPath( ),
   removeSelectionPaths( ),   setSelectionPath( ),   setSelectionPaths( ) >
   TreeUI < getRowForPath( ),   startEditingAtPath( ) >
—returned by: **A**bstractLayoutCache* < getPathClosestTo( ),
   getPathForRow( ) >   **D**efaultTreeSelectionModel*
   < getSelectionPath( ),   getSelectionPaths( ) >   **J**Tree
   < getEditingPath( ),   getLeadSelectionPath( ),
   getPathBetweenRows( ),   getPathForLocation( ),
   getPathForRow( ),   getSelectionPath( ),   getSelectionPaths( ) >
   TreeModelEvent.getTreePath( )   **T**reePath.pathByAddingChild( )
   TreeSelectionEvent < getOldLeadSelectionPath( ),   getPath( ),
   getPaths( ) >   *TreeSelectionModel* < getSelectionPath( ),
   getSelectionPaths( ) >   **T**reeUI < getEditingPath( ),
   getPathForRow( ) >
—fields: **D**efaultTreeCellEditor.lastPath
   DefaultTreeSelectionModel*.selection   **T**reeModelEvent.path
   TreeSelectionEvent < oldLeadSelectionPath,   paths >
TreeSelectionEvent: javax.swing.event
—passed to: **D**efaultTreeCellEditor.valueChanged( )
   JTree.fireValueChanged( )
   JTree.TreeSelectionRedirector.valueChanged( )
TreeSelectionListener: javax.swing.event
—passed to: **D**efaultTreeSelectionModel*
   < addTreeSelectionListener( ),   removeTreeSelectionListener( ) >
   JTree.removeTreeSelectionListener( )
   TreeSelectionModel.removeTreeSelectionListener( )
—implemented by: **D**efaultTreeCellEditor   **J**Tree.AccessibleJTree
   JTree.TreeSelectionRedirector
treeSelectionModel: **A**bstractLayoutCache*
TreeSelectionModel: javax.swing.tree
—passed to: **A**bstractLayoutCache*.setSelectionModel( )
—returned by: **A**bstractLayoutCache*.getSelectionModel( )
—implemented by: **D**efaultTreeSelectionModel*
—fields: **A**bstractLayoutCache*.treeSelectionModel
TreeSet: java.util
treeStructureChanged( ): **A**bstractLayoutCache*
   JTree.AccessibleJTree   **J**Tree.TreeModelHandler
   TreeModelListener
TreeUI: javax.swing.plaf
—passed to: **J**Tree.setUI( )
—returned by: **J**Tree.getUI( )
treeWillCollapse( ): *TreeWillExpandListener*
treeWillExpand( ): *TreeWillExpandListener*
TreeWillExpandListener: javax.swing.event

T

U

VALUE_INTERPOLATION_NEAREST_NEIGHBOR:
RenderingHints
VALUE_PROPERTY: JOptionPane
VALUE_RENDER_DEFAULT: RenderingHints
VALUE_RENDER_QUALITY: RenderingHints
VALUE_RENDER_SPEED: RenderingHints
VALUE_TEXT_ANTIALIAS_DEFAULT: RenderingHints
VALUE_TEXT_ANTIALIAS_OFF: RenderingHints
VALUE_TEXT_ANTIALIAS_ON: RenderingHints
valueChanged(): DefaultTableColumnModel
DefaultTreeCellEditor JList.AccessibleJList JTable
JTable.AccessibleJTable JTree.AccessibleJTree
JTree.TreeSelectionRedirector *ListSelectionListener*
TreeSelectionListener
valueForPathChanged(): DefaultTreeModel *TreeModel*
ValueMember: org.omg.CORBA
—passed to: ORB.create_value_tc()
valueOf(): BigDecimal BigInteger Boolean Byte
java.sql.Date Double Float Integer Long Short String
Time Timestamp
values: AttributeList
values(): AbstractMap* Attributes Hashtable* *Map*
RenderingHints
VALUETYPE: HTML.Attribute
VAR: HTML.Tag*
VARBINARY: Types
VARCHAR: Types
VariableHeightLayoutCache: javax.swing.tree
vcSupport: BeanContextChildSupport*
Vector*: java.util
—subclasses: Stack
—passed to: AttributeList() DefaultComboBoxModel()
DefaultTableModel < addRow(), DefaultTableModel(),
insertRow(), setColumnIdentifiers(), setDataVector() >
GapContent < getPositionsInRange(), updateUndoPositions() >
JList < JList(), setListData() > JTree() ParameterBlock
< ParameterBlock(), setParameters(), setSources() >
StringContent.updateUndoPositions()
—returned by: BufferedImage.getSources()
DefaultTableModel < convertToVector(),
getDataVector() > ParameterBlock < getParameters(),
getSources() > RenderableImageOp.getSources()
StringContent.getPositionsInRange()
—fields: AccessibleStateSet.states ButtonGroup.buttons
DefaultMutableTreeNode*.children
DefaultTableModel < columnIdentifiers, dataVector >
HTMLDocument.HTMLReader.parseBuffer
ParameterBlock.sources
VERBOSE: LogStream
VERIFY: Signature
verify(): java.security.cert.Certificate* Signature SignedObject
X509CRL
VerifyError: java.lang
VERSION: HTML.Attribute
version: ValueMember
versionColumnNotPseudo: *DatabaseMetaData*
versionColumnPseudo: *DatabaseMetaData*
versionColumnUnknown: *DatabaseMetaData*
VERTICAL: AccessibleState *Adjustable* GridBagConstraints
Scrollbar *SwingConstants*
VERTICAL_ALIGN: CSS.Attribute
VERTICAL_ALIGNMENT_CHANGED_PROPERTY:
AbstractButton*
VERTICAL_SCROLLBAR: *ScrollPaneConstants*
VERTICAL_SCROLLBAR_ALWAYS: *ScrollPaneConstants*
VERTICAL_SCROLLBAR_AS_NEEDED: *ScrollPaneConstants*
VERTICAL_SCROLLBAR_NEVER: *ScrollPaneConstants*
VERTICAL_SCROLLBAR_POLICY: *ScrollPaneConstants*
VERTICAL_SPLIT: JSplitPane
VERTICAL_TEXT_POSITION_CHANGED_PROPERTY:
AbstractButton*
verticalScrollBar: JScrollPane

verticalScrollBarPolicy: JScrollPane
vetoableChange(): BeanContextSupport*
VetoableChangeListener
VetoableChangeListener: java.beans
—passed to: *BeanContextChild** < addVetoableChangeListener(),
removeVetoableChangeListener() >
BeanContextChildSupport*.removeVetoableChangeListener()
JComponent*.removeVetoableChangeListener()
VetoableChangeSupport < addVetoableChangeListener(),
removeVetoableChangeListener() >
—returned
by: BeanContextSupport*.getChildVetoableChangeListener()
—implemented by: BeanContextSupport*
VetoableChangeSupport: java.beans
—fields: BeanContextChildSupport*.vcSupport
View*: javax.swing.text
—subclasses: ComponentView* CompositeView* IconView
LabelView* PlainView*
—descendents: BlockView* BoxView*
FieldView* FormView InlineView ListView
ObjectView javax.swing.text.ParagraphView*
javax.swing.text.html.ParagraphView PasswordView
TableView TableView.TableCell TableView.TableRow
WrappedPlainView
—passed to: CompositeView* < append(), insert(),
replace() > LayeredHighlighter.LayerPainter*.paintLayer()
StyleSheet.BoxPainter < getInset(), paint() > View*
< preferenceChanged(), setParent() >
—returned by: BoxView*.getViewAtPoint()
CompositeView*.getViewAtPosition()
javax.swing.text.ParagraphView* < breakView(),
getLayoutView(), getViewAtPosition() >
TableView.TableRow.getViewAtPosition() View* < breakView(),
createFragment(), getParent(), getView() >
ViewFactory: javax.swing.text
—passed to: CompositeView*.loadChildren()
TableView.loadChildren() View* < changedUpdate(),
insertUpdate(), removeUpdate() >
—returned by: EditorKit*.getViewFactory()
—implemented by: HTMLEditorKit.HTMLFactory
VIEWPORT: AccessibleRole *ScrollPaneConstants*
viewPort: JScrollPane.AccessibleJScrollPane
viewport: JScrollPane *ScrollPaneLayout*
ViewportLayout: javax.swing
ViewportUI: javax.swing.plaf
viewToModel(): JTextComponent* TextUI View*
VirtualMachineError*: java.lang
—subclasses: InternalError OutOfMemoryError
StackOverflowError UnknownError
Visibility: java.beans
—extended by: *BeanContext**
—descendents: *BeanContextServices*
—returned by: BeanContextSupport*.getChildVisibility()
VISIBLE: AccessibleState
VISIBLE_ROW_COUNT_PROPERTY: JTree
visibleRowCount: JTree
VK_0: KeyEvent*
VK_1: KeyEvent*
VK_2: KeyEvent*
VK_3: KeyEvent*
VK_4: KeyEvent*
VK_5: KeyEvent*
VK_6: KeyEvent*
VK_7: KeyEvent*
VK_8: KeyEvent*
VK_9: KeyEvent*
VK_A: KeyEvent*
VK_ACCEPT: KeyEvent*
VK_ADD: KeyEvent*
VK_AGAIN: KeyEvent*
VK_ALL_CANDIDATES: KeyEvent*
VK_ALPHANUMERIC: KeyEvent*

V

VK_ALT: KeyEvent*
VK_ALT_GRAPH: KeyEvent*
VK_AMPERSAND: KeyEvent*
VK_ASTERISK: KeyEvent*
VK_AT: KeyEvent*
VK_B: KeyEvent*
VK_BACK_QUOTE: KeyEvent*
VK_BACK_SLASH: KeyEvent*
VK_BACK_SPACE: KeyEvent*
VK_BRACELEFT: KeyEvent*
VK_BRACERIGHT: KeyEvent*
VK_C: KeyEvent*
VK_CANCEL: KeyEvent*
VK_CAPS_LOCK: KeyEvent*
VK_CIRCUMFLEX: KeyEvent*
VK_CLEAR: KeyEvent*
VK_CLOSE_BRACKET: KeyEvent*
VK_CODE_INPUT: KeyEvent*
VK_COLON: KeyEvent*
VK_COMMA: KeyEvent*
VK_COMPOSE: KeyEvent*
VK_CONTROL: KeyEvent*
VK_CONVERT: KeyEvent*
VK_COPY: KeyEvent*
VK_CUT: KeyEvent*
VK_D: KeyEvent*
VK_DEAD_ABOVEDOT: KeyEvent*
VK_DEAD_ABOVERING: KeyEvent*
VK_DEAD_ACUTE: KeyEvent*
VK_DEAD_BREVE: KeyEvent*
VK_DEAD_CARON: KeyEvent*
VK_DEAD_CEDILLA: KeyEvent*
VK_DEAD_CIRCUMFLEX: KeyEvent*
VK_DEAD_DIAERESIS: KeyEvent*
VK_DEAD_DOUBLEACUTE: KeyEvent*
VK_DEAD_GRAVE: KeyEvent*
VK_DEAD_IOTA: KeyEvent*
VK_DEAD_MACRON: KeyEvent*
VK_DEAD_OGONEK: KeyEvent*
VK_DEAD_SEMIVOICED_SOUND: KeyEvent*
VK_DEAD_TILDE: KeyEvent*
VK_DEAD_VOICED_SOUND: KeyEvent*
VK_DECIMAL: KeyEvent*
VK_DELETE: KeyEvent*
VK_DIVIDE: KeyEvent*
VK_DOLLAR: KeyEvent*
VK_DOWN: KeyEvent*
VK_E: KeyEvent*
VK_END: KeyEvent*
VK_ENTER: KeyEvent*
VK_EQUALS: KeyEvent*
VK_ESCAPE: KeyEvent*
VK_EURO_SIGN: KeyEvent*
VK_EXCLAMATION_MARK: KeyEvent*
VK_F: KeyEvent*
VK_F1: KeyEvent*
VK_F10: KeyEvent*
VK_F11: KeyEvent*
VK_F12: KeyEvent*
VK_F13: KeyEvent*
VK_F14: KeyEvent*
VK_F15: KeyEvent*
VK_F16: KeyEvent*
VK_F17: KeyEvent*
VK_F18: KeyEvent*
VK_F19: KeyEvent*
VK_F2: KeyEvent*
VK_F20: KeyEvent*
VK_F21: KeyEvent*
VK_F22: KeyEvent*
VK_F23: KeyEvent*
VK_F24: KeyEvent*

VK_F3: KeyEvent*
VK_F4: KeyEvent*
VK_F5: KeyEvent*
VK_F6: KeyEvent*
VK_F7: KeyEvent*
VK_F8: KeyEvent*
VK_F9: KeyEvent*
VK_FINAL: KeyEvent*
VK_FIND: KeyEvent*
VK_FULL_WIDTH: KeyEvent*
VK_G: KeyEvent*
VK_GREATER: KeyEvent*
VK_H: KeyEvent*
VK_HALF_WIDTH: KeyEvent*
VK_HELP: KeyEvent*
VK_HIRAGANA: KeyEvent*
VK_HOME: KeyEvent*
VK_I: KeyEvent*
VK_INSERT: KeyEvent*
VK_INVERTED_EXCLAMATION_MARK: KeyEvent*
VK_J: KeyEvent*
VK_JAPANESE_HIRAGANA: KeyEvent*
VK_JAPANESE_KATAKANA: KeyEvent*
VK_JAPANESE_ROMAN: KeyEvent*
VK_K: KeyEvent*
VK_KANA: KeyEvent*
VK_KANJI: KeyEvent*
VK_KATAKANA: KeyEvent*
VK_KP_DOWN: KeyEvent*
VK_KP_LEFT: KeyEvent*
VK_KP_RIGHT: KeyEvent*
VK_KP_UP: KeyEvent*
VK_L: KeyEvent*
VK_LEFT: KeyEvent*
VK_LEFT_PARENTHESIS: KeyEvent*
VK_LESS: KeyEvent*
VK_M: KeyEvent*
VK_META: KeyEvent*
VK_MINUS: KeyEvent*
VK_MODECHANGE: KeyEvent*
VK_MULTIPLY: KeyEvent*
VK_N: KeyEvent*
VK_NONCONVERT: KeyEvent*
VK_NUM_LOCK: KeyEvent*
VK_NUMBER_SIGN: KeyEvent*
VK_NUMPAD0: KeyEvent*
VK_NUMPAD1: KeyEvent*
VK_NUMPAD2: KeyEvent*
VK_NUMPAD3: KeyEvent*
VK_NUMPAD4: KeyEvent*
VK_NUMPAD5: KeyEvent*
VK_NUMPAD6: KeyEvent*
VK_NUMPAD7: KeyEvent*
VK_NUMPAD8: KeyEvent*
VK_NUMPAD9: KeyEvent*
VK_O: KeyEvent*
VK_OPEN_BRACKET: KeyEvent*
VK_P: KeyEvent*
VK_PAGE_DOWN: KeyEvent*
VK_PAGE_UP: KeyEvent*
VK_PASTE: KeyEvent*
VK_PAUSE: KeyEvent*
VK_PERIOD: KeyEvent*
VK_PLUS: KeyEvent*
VK_PREVIOUS_CANDIDATE: KeyEvent*
VK_PRINTSCREEN: KeyEvent*
VK_PROPS: KeyEvent*
VK_Q: KeyEvent*
VK_QUOTE: KeyEvent*
VK_QUOTEDBL: KeyEvent*
VK_R: KeyEvent*
VK_RIGHT: KeyEvent*

V

W

windowClosing( ), windowDeactivated( ), windowDeiconified( ), windowIconified( ), windowOpened( ) >
windowForComponent( ): **S**wingUtilities
windowIconified( ): **A**WTEventMulticaster **W**indowAdapter* *W*indowListener
windowInit( ): **J**Window
WindowListener: java.awt.event
—passed to: **A**WTEventMulticaster < add( ), remove( ) > **W**indow*.removeWindowListener( )
—returned by: **A**WTEventMulticaster < add( ), remove( ) >
—implemented by: **A**WTEventMulticaster **W**indowAdapter*
windowOpened( ): **A**WTEventMulticaster **W**indowAdapter* *W*indowListener
*WindowPeer**: java.awt.peer
—extended by: *DialogPeer** *FramePeer*
—descendents: *FileDialogPeer*
—returned by: **T**oolkit.createWindow( )
windowText: **S**ystemColor
WORD: *AccessibleText**
WORD_SPACING: **C**SS.Attribute
wordChars( ): **S**treamTokenizer
work_pending( ): **O**RB
WrappedPlainView: javax.swing.text
writableAction: **D**efaultEditorKit*
WritableRaster: java.awt.image
—passed to: **A**ffineTransformOp.filter( ) **B**ufferedImage < BufferedImage( ), copyData( ) > **C**olorModel* < coerceData( ), getAlphaRaster( ) > **C**onvolveOp.filter( ) *RasterOp*.filter( ) **R**escaleOp.filter( )
—returned by: **A**ffineTransformOp < createCompatibleDestRaster( ), filter( ) > **B**andCombineOp.filter( ) **B**ufferedImage < getAlphaRaster( ), getRaster( ), getWritableTile( ) > **C**olorConvertOp.filter( ) **C**olorModel*.getAlphaRaster( ) **C**onvolveOp.filter( ) **L**ookupOp.filter( ) **R**aster* < createBandedRaster( ), createCompatibleWritableRaster( ), createInterleavedRaster( ), createPackedRaster( ), createWritableRaster( ) > *RasterOp*.filter( ) **R**escaleOp < createCompatibleDestRaster( ), filter( ) > **W**ritableRaster < createWritableTranslatedChild( ), getWritableParent( ) >
WritableRenderedImage: java.awt.image
—passed to: *TileObserver*.tileUpdate( )
—implemented by: **B**ufferedImage
write( ): **A**bstractWriter* **A**lreadyBoundHelper **B**indingHelper **B**indingIteratorHelper **B**indingListHelper **B**indingTypeHelper **C**annotProceedHelper *DataOutput** **E**ditorKit* **I**CC_Profile* **I**nvalidNameHelper **I**stringHelper **J**TextComponent* **M**anifest **N**ameComponentHelper **N**ameHelper **N**amingContextHelper **N**otEmptyHelper **N**otFoundHelper **N**otFoundReasonHelper **O**bjectOutputStream.PutField **O**bjID java.io.**O**utputStream* **R**andomAccessFile **S**erviceDetailHelper **S**erviceInformationHelper **U**ID **W**riter*
write_any( ): org.omg.CORBA.portable.**O**utputStream
write_boolean( ): org.omg.CORBA.portable.**O**utputStream
write_boolean_array( ): org.omg.CORBA.portable.**O**utputStream
write_char( ): org.omg.CORBA.portable.**O**utputStream
write_char_array( ): org.omg.CORBA.portable.**O**utputStream
write_Context( ): org.omg.CORBA.portable.**O**utputStream
write_double( ): org.omg.CORBA.portable.**O**utputStream
write_double_array( ): org.omg.CORBA.portable.**O**utputStream
write_fixed( ): org.omg.CORBA.portable.**O**utputStream
write_float( ): org.omg.CORBA.portable.**O**utputStream
write_float_array( ): org.omg.CORBA.portable.**O**utputStream
write_long( ): org.omg.CORBA.portable.**O**utputStream
write_long_array( ): org.omg.CORBA.portable.**O**utputStream
write_longlong( ): org.omg.CORBA.portable.**O**utputStream
write_longlong_array( ): org.omg.CORBA.portable.**O**utputStream
write_Object( ): org.omg.CORBA.portable.**O**utputStream
write_octet( ): org.omg.CORBA.portable.**O**utputStream
write_octet_array( ): org.omg.CORBA.portable.**O**utputStream

write_Principal( ): org.omg.CORBA.portable.**O**utputStream
write_short( ): org.omg.CORBA.portable.**O**utputStream
write_short_array( ): org.omg.CORBA.portable.**O**utputStream
write_string( ): org.omg.CORBA.portable.**O**utputStream
write_TypeCode( ): org.omg.CORBA.portable.**O**utputStream
write_ulong( ): org.omg.CORBA.portable.**O**utputStream
write_ulong_array( ): org.omg.CORBA.portable.**O**utputStream
write_ulonglong( ): org.omg.CORBA.portable.**O**utputStream
write_ulonglong_array( ): org.omg.CORBA.portable.**O**utputStream
write_ushort( ): org.omg.CORBA.portable.**O**utputStream
write_ushort_array( ): org.omg.CORBA.portable.**O**utputStream
write_value( ): **A**ny
write_wchar( ): org.omg.CORBA.portable.**O**utputStream
write_wchar_array( ): org.omg.CORBA.portable.**O**utputStream
write_wstring( ): org.omg.CORBA.portable.**O**utputStream
WriteAbortedException: java.io
writeArray( ): *SQLOutput*
writeAsciiStream( ): *SQLOutput*
writeAttributes( ): **A**bstractWriter* **S**tyleContext*
writeAttributeSet( ): **S**tyleContext*
writeBigDecimal( ): *SQLOutput*
writeBinaryStream( ): *SQLOutput*
writeBlob( ): *SQLOutput*
writeBody( ): **M**inimalHTMLWriter
writeBoolean( ): *DataOutput** **D**ataOutputStream **O**bjectOutputStream **R**andomAccessFile *SQLOutput*
writeByte( ): *DataOutput** **D**ataOutputStream **O**bjectOutputStream **R**andomAccessFile *SQLOutput*
writeBytes( ): *DataOutput** **D**ataOutputStream **O**bjectOutputStream **R**andomAccessFile *SQLOutput*
writeChar( ): *DataOutput** **D**ataOutputStream **O**bjectOutputStream **R**andomAccessFile
writeCharacterStream( ): *SQLOutput*
writeChars( ): *DataOutput** **D**ataOutputStream **O**bjectOutputStream **R**andomAccessFile
writeChildren( ): **B**eanContextSupport*
writeClob( ): *SQLOutput*
writeComponent( ): **M**inimalHTMLWriter
writeContent( ): **M**inimalHTMLWriter
writeDate( ): *SQLOutput*
writeDouble( ): *DataOutput** **D**ataOutputStream **O**bjectOutputStream **R**andomAccessFile *SQLOutput*
writeEmbeddedTags( ): **H**TMLWriter
writeEndParagraph( ): **M**inimalHTMLWriter
writeEndTag( ): **M**inimalHTMLWriter
writeExternal( ): **D**ataFlavor *Externalizable**
writeFields( ): **O**bjectOutputStream
writeFloat( ): *DataOutput** **D**ataOutputStream **O**bjectOutputStream **R**andomAccessFile *SQLOutput*
writeHeader( ): **M**inimalHTMLWriter
writeHTMLTags( ): **M**inimalHTMLWriter
writeImage( ): **M**inimalHTMLWriter
writeInt( ): *DataOutput** **D**ataOutputStream **O**bjectOutputStream **R**andomAccessFile *SQLOutput*
writeLeaf( ): **M**inimalHTMLWriter
writeLock( ): **A**bstractDocument*
writeLong( ): *DataOutput** **D**ataOutputStream **O**bjectOutputStream **R**andomAccessFile *SQLOutput*
writeNonHTMLAttributes( ): **M**inimalHTMLWriter
writeObject( ): *ObjectOutput* **O**bjectOutputStream *SQLOutput*
writeObjectOverride( ): **O**bjectOutputStream
writeOption( ): **H**TMLWriter
Writer*: java.io
—subclasses: **B**ufferedWriter **C**harArrayWriter **F**ilterWriter **O**utputStreamWriter* **P**ipedWriter **P**rintWriter **S**tringWriter
—descendents: **F**ileWriter
—passed to: **A**bstractWriter( ) **B**ufferedWriter( ) **E**ditorKit*.write( ) **H**TMLWriter( ) **M**inimalHTMLWriter( ) **P**rintWriter( )
—fields: **F**ilterWriter.out
writeRef( ): *SQLOutput*

W

writeShort(): *DataOutput** **D**ataOutputStream
  ObjectOutputStream **R**andomAccessFile *SQLOutput*
writeSQL(): *SQLData*
writeStartParagraph(): **M**inimalHTMLWriter
writeStartTag(): **M**inimalHTMLWriter
writeStreamHeader(): **O**bjectOutputStream
writeString(): *SQLOutput*
writeStruct(): *SQLOutput*
writeStyles(): **M**inimalHTMLWriter
writeTime(): *SQLOutput*
writeTimestamp(): *SQLOutput*
writeTo(): **B**yteArrayOutputStream **C**harArrayWriter
writeUnlock(): **A**bstractDocument*
writeUTF(): *DataOutput** **D**ataOutputStream
  ObjectOutputStream **R**andomAccessFile
written: **D**ataOutputStream
WrongTransaction: org.omg.CORBA
  —thrown by: **O**RB.get_next_response( )
x: **A**rc2D.Double **A**rc2D.Float **E**llipse2D.Double
  Ellipse2D.Float **E**vent **P**oint **P**oint2D.Double **P**oint2D.Float
  Rectangle* **R**ectangle2D.Double **R**ectangle2D.Float
  RoundRectangle2D.Double **R**oundRectangle2D.Float
x1: **C**ubicCurve2D.Double **C**ubicCurve2D.Float
  Line2D.Double **L**ine2D.Float **Q**uadCurve2D.Double
  QuadCurve2D.Float
x2: **C**ubicCurve2D.Double **C**ubicCurve2D.Float
  Line2D.Double **L**ine2D.Float **Q**uadCurve2D.Double
  QuadCurve2D.Float
X509Certificate: java.security.cert
X509CRL: java.security.cert
X509CRLEntry: java.security.cert
  —returned by: **X**509CRL.getRevokedCertificate( )
X509EncodedKeySpec: java.security.spec
X509Extension: java.security.cert
  —implemented by: **X**509Certificate **X**509CRL **X**509CRLEntry
X_AXIS: **B**oxLayout **V**iew*
xor(): **B**igInteger **B**itSet
xpoints: **P**olygon

y: **A**rc2D.Double **A**rc2D.Float **E**llipse2D.Double
  Ellipse2D.Float **E**vent **P**oint **P**oint2D.Double **P**oint2D.Float
  Rectangle* **R**ectangle2D.Double **R**ectangle2D.Float
  RoundRectangle2D.Double **R**oundRectangle2D.Float
y1: **C**ubicCurve2D.Double **C**ubicCurve2D.Float
  Line2D.Double **L**ine2D.Float **Q**uadCurve2D.Double
  QuadCurve2D.Float
y2: **C**ubicCurve2D.Double **C**ubicCurve2D.Float
  Line2D.Double **L**ine2D.Float **Q**uadCurve2D.Double
  QuadCurve2D.Float
Y_AXIS: **B**oxLayout **V**iew*
YEAR: **C**alendar*
YEAR_FIELD: **D**ateFormat*
yellow: **C**olor*
YES_NO_CANCEL_OPTION: **J**OptionPane
YES_NO_OPTION: **J**OptionPane
YES_OPTION: **J**OptionPane
yield(): **T**hread
ypoints: **P**olygon
ZERO: **B**igInteger
  —implemented by: **Z**ipEntry* **Z**ipFile* **Z**ipInputStream*
  ZipOutputStream*
ZipEntry*: java.util.zip
  —subclasses: **J**arEntry
  —passed to: **J**arEntry( ) **Z**ipFile*.getInputStream( )
  —returned by: **J**arInputStream.createZipEntry( ) **Z**ipInputStream*
  < createZipEntry( ), getNextEntry( ) >
ZipException*: java.util.zip
  —subclasses: **J**arException
  —thrown by: **Z**ipFile( )
ZipFile*: java.util.zip
  —subclasses: **J**arFile
ZipInputStream*: java.util.zip
  —subclasses: **J**arInputStream
ZipOutputStream*: java.util.zip
  —subclasses: **J**arOutputStream
ZONE_OFFSET: **C**alendar*

Z

Addison-Wesley Computer and Engineering Publishing Group

How to Register Your Book

1. Register this Book

Visit: **http://www.awl.com/cseng/register**

Enter this unique code: **aiin-ipbb-lyfs-gdcq**

Then you will receive:

- More than 200 examplets™
- Online updates about new versions of *The Java Developers Almanac 1999*
- Exclusive offers on other Addison-Wesley Java Series books
- More supplemental packages

You can also tell us what we can do to make future editions even more useful!

2. Visit our Web site

http://www.awl.com/cseng

When you think you've read enough, there's always more content for you at Addison-Wesley's web site. Our web site contains a directory of complete product information including:

- Chapters
- Exclusive author interviews
- Links to authors' pages
- Tables of contents
- Source code

You can also discover what tradeshows and conferences Addison-Wesley will be attending, read what others are saying about our titles, and find out where and when you can meet our authors and have them sign your book.

We encourage you to patronize the many fine retailers who stock Addison-Wesley titles. Visit our online directory to find stores near you or visit our online store: **http://store.awl.com/** or call **800-824-7799**.

3. Contact Us via Email

cepubprof@awl.com

Ask general questions about our books.
Sign up for our electronic mailing lists.
Submit corrections for our web site.

bexpress@awl.com

Request an Addison-Wesley catalog.
Get answers to questions regarding
your order or our products.

innovations@awl.com

Request a current Innovations Newsletter.

webmaster@awl.com

Send comments about our web site.

mikeh@awl.com

Submit a book proposal.
Send errata for an Addison-Wesley book.

cepubpublicity@awl.com

Request a review copy for a member of the media
interested in reviewing new Addison-Wesley titles.

Addison Wesley Longman
Computer and Engineering Publishing Group
One Jacob Way, Reading, Massachusetts 01867 USA
TEL 781-944-3700 • FAX 781-942-3076

The Addison-Wesley Java™ Series

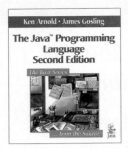

Ken Arnold · James Gosling

The Java™ Programming Language Second Edition

ISBN 0-201-31006-6

Mary Campione · Kathy Walrath

The Java™ Tutorial Second Edition

Object-Oriented Programming for the Internet

ISBN 0-201-31007-4

Campione · Walrath · Huml · Tutorial Team

The Java™ Tutorial Continued

The Rest of the JDK™

ISBN 0-201-48558-3

Patrick Chan

The Java™ Developers ALMANAC 1999

ISBN 0-201-43298-6

Patrick Chan · Rosanna Lee

The Java™ Class Libraries Second Edition, Volume 2

java.applet java.awt java.beans

ISBN 0-201-31003-1

Patrick Chan · Rosanna Lee · Douglas Kramer

The Java™ Class Libraries Second Edition, Volume 1

java.io java.lang java.math java.net java.text java.util

ISBN 0-201-31002-3

Patrick Chan · Rosanna Lee · Douglas Kramer

The Java™ Class Libraries Second Edition, Volume 1

1.2 Supplement

ISBN 0-201-48552-4

James Gosling · Bill Joy · Guy Steele

The Java™ Language Specification

ISBN 0-201-63451-1

James Gosling · Frank Yellin · The Java Team

The Java™ Application Programming Interface, Volume 1

Core Packages

ISBN 0-201-63453-8

James Gosling · Frank Yellin · The Java Team

The Java™ Application Programming Interface, Volume 2

Window Toolkit and Applets

ISBN 0-201-63459-7

Graham Hamilton · Rick Cattell · Maydene Fisher

JDBC™ Database Access with Java™

A Tutorial and Annotated Reference

ISBN 0-201-30995-5

Jonni Kanerva

The Java™ FAQ

ISBN 0-201-63456-2

Doug Lea

Concurrent Programming in Java™

Design Principles and Patterns

ISBN 0-201-69581-2

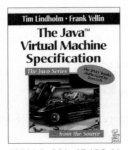

Tim Lindholm · Frank Yellin

The Java™ Virtual Machine Specification

ISBN 0-201-63452-X

Henry Sowizral · Kevin Rushforth · Michael Deering

The Java™ 3D API Specification

ISBN 0-201-32576-4

Please see our web site (http://www.awl.com/cseng/javaseries) for more information on these titles.